INTRODUCTION TO MANAGEMENT SCIENCE

THE IRWIN/MCGRAW-HILL SERIES
Operations and Decision Sciences

OPERATIONS MANAGEMENT

Bowersox and Closs
Logistical Management: *The Integrated Supply Chain Process*
First Edition

Chase, Aquilano, and Jacobs
Production and Operations Management
Eighth Edition

Chu, Hottenstein, and Greenlaw
PROSIM for Windows
Third Edition

Cohen and Apte
Manufacturing Automation
First Edition

Davis, Aquilano, and Chase
Fundamentals of Operations Management
Third Edition

Dobler and Burt
Purchasing and Supply Management
Sixth Edition

Flaherty
Global Operations Management
First Edition

Fitzsimmons and Fitzsimmons
Service Management: *Operations, Strategy, Information Technology*
Second Edition

Gray and Larson
Project Management: *The Managerial Process*
First Edition

Hill
Manufacturing Strategy: *Text & Cases*
Third Edition

Hopp and Spearman
Factory Physics
Second Edition

Lambert and Stock
Strategic Logistics Management
Third Edition

Leenders and Fearon
Purchasing and Supply Chain Management
Eleventh Edition

Melnyk and Denzler
Operations Management
First Edition

Moses, Seshadri, and Yakir
HOM Operations Management Software for Windows
First Edition

Nahmias
Production and Operations Analysis
Third Edition

Nicholas
Competitive Manufacturing Management
First Edition

Pinedo and Chao
Operations Scheduling
First Edition

Sanderson and Uzumeri
Managing Product Families
First Edition

Schroeder
Operations Management: *Contemporary Concepts and Cases*
First Edition

Schonberger and Knod
Operations Management: *Customer-Focused Principles*
Sixth Edition

Simchi-Levi, Kaminsky, and Simchi-Levi
Designing and Managing the Supply Chain: *Concepts, Strategies, and Case Studies*
First Edition

Sterman
Business Dynamics: *Systems Thinking and Modeling for a Complex World*
First Edition

Stevenson
Production/Operations Management
Sixth Edition

Vollmann, Berry, and Whybark
Manufacturing Planning & Control Systems
Fourth Edition

Zipkin
Foundations of Inventory Management
First Edition

BUSINESS STATISTICS

Alwan
Statistical Process Analysis
First Edition

Aczel
Complete Business Statistics
Fourth Edition

Bowerman and O'Connell
Applied Statistics: *Improving Business Processes*
First Edition

Bryant and Smith
Practical Data Analysis: *Case Studies in Business Statistics, Volumes I and II*
Second Edition;
Volume III
First Edition

Butler
Business Research Sources
First Edition

Cooper and Schindler
Business Research Methods
Sixth Edition

Delurgio
Forecasting Principles and Applications
First Edition

Doane, Mathieson, and Tracy
Visual Statistics
First Edition

Gitlow, Oppenheim, and Oppenheim
Quality Management: *Tools and Methods for Improvement*
Second Edition

Hall
Computerized Business Statistics
Fifth Edition

Lind, Mason, and Marchal
Basic Statistics for Business and Economics
Third Edition

Mason, Lind, and Marchal
Statistical Techniques in Business and Economics
Tenth Edition

Merchant, Goffinet, Koehler
Basic Statistics Using Excel
First Edition

Merchant, Goffinet, Koehler
Basic Statistics Using Excel for Office 97
First Edition

Neter, Kutner, Nachtsheim, and Wasserman
Applied Linear Statistical Models
Fourth Edition

Neter, Kutner, Nachtsheim, and Wasserman
Applied Linear Regression Models
Third Edition

Siegel
Practical Business Statistics
Fourth Edition

Simchi-Levi, Kaminsky, Simchi-Levi
Designing and Managing the Supply Chain
First Edition

Webster
Applied Statistics for Business and Economics: An Essentials Version
Third Edition

Wilson and Keating
Business Forecasting
Third Edition

QUANTITATIVE METHODS AND MANAGEMENT SCIENCE

Bodily, Carraway, Frey, Pfeifer
Quantitative Business Analysis: *Casebook*
First Edition

Bodily, Carraway, Frey, Pfeifer
Quantitative Business Analysis: *Text and Cases*
First Edition

Bonini, Hausman, and Bierman
Quantitative Analysis for Business Decisions
Ninth Edition

Hesse
Managerial Spreadsheet Modeling and Analysis
First Edition

Hillier, Hillier, Lieberman
Introduction to Management Science: *A Modeling and Case Studies Approach with Spreadsheets*
First Edition

INTRODUCTION TO MANAGEMENT SCIENCE
A Modeling and Case Studies Approach with Spreadsheets

Frederick S. Hillier
Stanford University

Mark S. Hillier
University of Washington

Gerald J. Lieberman
Late of Stanford University

Cases developed by

Karl Schmedders
Northwestern University

Molly Stephens

Boston • Burr Ridge, IL • Dubuque, IA • Madison, WI •
New York • San Francisco • St. Louis • Bangkok • Bogotá • Caracas •
Lisbon • London • Madrid • Mexico City • Milan • New Delhi • Seoul •
Singapore • Sydney • Taipei • Toronto

McGraw-Hill Higher Education

*A Division of The **McGraw-Hill** Companies*

1 2 3 4 5 6 7 8 9 0 KGP/KGP 9 0 9 8 7 6 5 4 3 2 1 0 9

ISBN 0–07–037816–9

Vice president/Editor-in-Chief: *Michael W. Junior*
Publisher: *Jeffrey J. Shelstad*
Senior sponsoring editor: *Scott Isenberg*
Developmental editor: *Wanda J. Zeman*
Senior marketing manager: *Colleen J. Suljic*
Project manager: *Jim Labeots*
Senior production supervisor: *Lori Koetters*
Freelance design coordinator: *Laurie J. Entringer*
Supplement coordinator: *Carol Loreth*
Typeface: *10/12 Times Roman*
Compositor: *Carlisle Communications, Ltd.*
Printer: *Quebecor Printing Book Group/Kingsport*
Cover image: *Lois & Bob Schlowsky ©1999 Tony Stone Images*

Library of Congress Cataloging-in-Publication Data

Hillier, Frederick S.
    Introduction to management science: a modeling and case studies
  approach with spreadsheets / Frederick S. Hillier, Mark S. Hillier,
  Gerald J. Lieberman; with cases developed by Karl Schmedders, Molly Stephens
      p. cm.—(The Irwin/McGraw-Hill series in operations and
  decision sciences)
    Includes index.
    ISBN 0–07-037816–9
    1. Management science. 2. Operations research. I. Hillier, Mark
S. II. Lieberman, Gerald J. III. Title. IV. Series.
T56.H55   2000
658.5—dc21   99–27654

To our wives—Ann, Christine, and Helen—for their steadfast support

and

To the memory of one of the true giants
of our field, Jerry Lieberman, who got to see
the completion of this book but not its publication

ABOUT THE AUTHORS

Frederick S. Hillier is professor emeritus of operations research at Stanford University. Dr. Hillier is especially known for his classic, award winning text, *Introduction to Operations Research,* co-authored with Gerald J. Lieberman, which has been translated into well over a dozen languages and is currently going into its 7th edition. His other books include *The Evaluation of Risky Interrelated Investments, Queueing Tables and Graphs, Introduction to Stochastic Models in Operations Research,* and *Introduction to Mathematical Programming.* He received his BS in industrial engineering and doctorate specializing in operations research and management science from Stanford University. The winner of many awards in high school and college for writing, mathematics, debate and music, he ranked first in his undergraduate engineering class and was awarded three national fellowships (National Science Foundation, Tau Beta Pi, and Danforth) for graduate study. Dr. Hillier's research has extended into a variety of areas, including integer programming, queueing theory and its application, statistical quality control, and production and operations management. He also has won a major prize for research in capital budgeting. Twice elected a national officer of professional societies, he has served in many important professional and editorial capacities. He has had visiting appointments at Cornell University, the Graduate School of Industrial Administration of Carnegie-Mellon University, the Technical University of Denmark, the University of Canterbury (New Zealand) and the Judge Institute of Management Studies (as an Arthur Andersen Visiting Fellow) at the University of Cambridge (England).

Mark S. Hillier, son of Fred Hillier, is assistant professor of management science at the School of Business Administration at the University of Washington. Dr. Hillier received his BS in engineering (plus a concentration in computer science) from Swarthmore College, MS with distinction in operations research and PhD in industrial engineering and engineering management from Stanford University. As an undergraduate, he won the McCabe Award for ranking first in his engineering class, won election to Phi Beta Kappa based on his work in mathematics, set school records on the men's swim team,

and was awarded two national fellowships (National Science Foundation and Tau Beta Pi) for graduate study. As a graduate student, he taught a PhD-level seminar in operations management at Stanford and won a national prize for his PhD dissertation. At the University of Washington, he teaches courses in logistics, management science, and spreadsheet modeling. He also won a university wide teaching award for his work in teaching undergraduate classes in operations management. He has developed a software tutorial package, *OR Courseware,* which is packaged with several texts written by the other co-authors. His research interests include mathematical programming applications, issues in component commonality, inventory, manufacturing, and the design of production systems.

The late **Gerald J. Lieberman** sadly passed away shortly after the completion of this book. He had been professor emeritus of operations research and statistics at Stanford University, where he was the founding chair of the Department of Operations Research. He also served as the university's provost or acting provost under three different Stanford presidents. Dr. Lieberman was the co-author of *Introduction to Operations Research* with Fred Hillier. His other books are *Introduction to Mathematical Programming, Introduction to Stochastic Models in Operations Research, Handbook of Industrial Statistics, Tables of the Non-Central t-Distribution, Tables of the Hypergeometric Probability Distribution,* and *Engineering Statistics.* His research was in the stochastic areas of management science, often at the interface of applied probability and statistics, in such areas as reliability and quality control. Highly respected as a senior statesman of the field, he served in numerous leadership roles, including as the elected president of The Institute of Management Sciences. Dr. Lieberman received many honors and awards including the prestigious Kimball Medal by INFORMS for his exceptional contributions to the field of operations research and management science. He received his undergraduate degree in mechanical engineering from Cooper Union, a graduate degree in mathematical statistics from Columbia University, and a doctorate in statistics from Stanford University.

ABOUT THE CASE WRITERS

Karl Schmedders is assistant professor in the Department of Managerial Economics and Decision Sciences at the Kellogg Graduate School of Management at Northwestern University, where he teaches quantitative methods for managerial decision making. His research interests include applications of management science in economic theory, general equilibrium theory with incomplete markets, asset pricing, and computational economics. Dr. Schmedders received his doctorate in operations research from Stanford University, where he taught both undergraduate and graduate classes in management science. Among the classes taught was a case studies course in management science and he subsequently was invited to speak at a conference sponsored by the Institute of Operations Research and Management Sciences (INFORMS) about his successful experience with this course. He received several teaching awards at Stanford, including the university's prestigious Walter J. Gores Teaching Award.

Molly Stephens is currently pursuing a J.D. degree with a concentration in technology and law. She graduated from Stanford with a BS in industrial engineering and an MS in operations research. A champion debater in both high school and college, and president of the Stanford Debating Society, Ms. Stephens taught public speaking in Stanford's School of Engineering and served as a teaching assistant for a case studies course in management science. As a teaching assistant, she analyzed management science problems encountered in the real world and transformed these into classroom case studies. Her research was rewarded when she won an undergraduate research grant from Stanford to continue her work and was invited to speak at INFORMS to present her conclusions regarding successful classroom case studies. Following graduation, Ms. Stephens worked at Andersen Consulting as a systems integrator, experiencing real cases from the inside, before resuming her graduate studies.

PREFACE

We are excited about this book. Although any birth of a new book is exciting, this one has been special for us. It represents the culmination of many years of careful planning and meticulous development. As we prepare to enter the 21st century, we have particularly enjoyed the challenge of writing a book that befits the new century. Our goal has been to develop a book that breaks out of old molds and presents innovative new ways of teaching management science more effectively.

The Motivation for This Book

We previously have had the privilege of introducing several hundred thousand students (including many current instructors of management science courses) to this field through our *Introduction to Operations Research* textbook (co-authored by two of us with software developed by the third). First published in 1967 and now about to enter its 7th edition, a recent award citation (Lanchester Prize) credited Introduction to Operations Research with having had "an enormous cumulative impact . . . on the development of our field." Award citations tend to exaggerate, but Introduction to Operations Research did take the lead in establishing the curriculum for introductory courses in our field. Introduction to Operations Research is aimed mainly at engineering and mathematical sciences students, so it gives considerable emphasis to the mathematical theory and algorithms of the field.

As gratified as we have been by the response to this previous book, we have been bothered by one unfortunate side effect. In the years following its initial publication, introductory management science textbooks began to appear that were aimed directly at business students. A few of these were very well done and have continued to be standard textbooks in the field. However, the unfortunate aspect is that these books tended to mirror the orientation of Introduction to Operations Research far too closely, albeit at a more elementary level. Rather than focusing on the aspects of management science that are particularly relevant to business students, much of the quantitative content of Introduction to Operations Research was still there, including a full smorgasbord of algorithms. An algebraic curtain descended on the teaching of management science in business schools. The introductory course was universally required back then, so a captive audience had to face the rigors of this mathematical course that stood apart from most of the business curriculum. In many cases, the course acquired the reputation of being a bear that had to be endured even though it didn't seem to have much relevance for the future careers of the students.

How unfortunate. This perception of the irrelevance of management science could not be further from the truth, as this book will demonstrate.

We have long been concerned that traditional management science textbooks have taken the wrong approach in introducing business students to this exciting field. The mathematics and algorithms of the field are easy to teach, but difficult to learn. Worse, they are indeed largely irrelevant to business students aspiring to become managers. Computers compute. Managers make decisions. There is no good reason why managers should know the details of algorithms executed by computers. Within the time constraints of a one-term management science course, there are far more important lessons to be learned by a future manager. Our motivation for writing this book has been to focus on what we believe are these far more important lessons.

Recent events have added urgency to this task. The decision in 1991 by the AACSB to drop management science from its core body of knowledge meant that management science courses had to begin competing in the open market. The introductory management science course will continue to be required only as long as it is proving its worth. At those schools where it is now an elective, its survival depends on its ability to continue to attract students. In some cases, it will be a module within a larger course. Proving its usefulness in functional areas and its relevance to the future careers of the students have become essential.

This should be easy with the right kind of course and textbook. However, we believe that traditional management science textbooks now are an endangered species. Anecdotal evidence consistently indicates that the traditional algebra-heavy courses are the ones in trouble while the thriving courses are those that have broken away from the old molds.

The following extract from the 1996 report of the Operating Subcommittee of the INFORMS Business School Education Task Force directly speaks to this point. "There is clear evidence that there must be a major change in the character of the [introductory management science] course in this environment. There is little patience with courses centered on algorithms. Instead, the demand is for courses that focus on business situations, include prominent nonmathematical issues, use spreadsheets, and involve model formulation and assessment more than model structuring. Such a course requires new teaching materials." This book is designed to provide the teaching materials for such a course.

In line with the recommendations of this task force, we believe that a modern introductory management science textbook should have three key elements. As summarized in the subtitle of this book, these elements are a *modeling* and *case studies* approach with *spreadsheets*.

Spreadsheets

The new wave in the teaching of management science clearly is to use spreadsheets as a primary medium of instruction. Both business students and managers now live with spreadsheets, so they provide a comfortable and enjoyable learning environment. Modern spreadsheet software, including Microsoft Excel used in this book, now can be used to do real management science. For student-scale models (which include many practical real-world models), spreadsheets are a much better way of implementing management science models than traditional algebraic solvers. This means that the algebraic curtain that was so prevalent in traditional management science courses and textbooks can now be lifted.

However, with the new enthusiasm for spreadsheets, there is a danger in going overboard. Spreadsheets are not the only useful tool for performing management science analyses. Occasional modest use of algebraic and graphical analyses still have their place and we would be doing a disservice to the students by not developing their skills in these areas when appropriate. Furthermore, the book should not be mainly a spreadsheet cookbook that focuses largely on spreadsheet mechanics. Spreadsheets are a means to an end, not an end in themselves.

A Modeling Approach

This brings us to the second key feature of the book, a *modeling approach.* Model formulation lies at the heart of

management science methodology. Therefore, we heavily emphasize the art of model formulation, the role of a model, and the analysis of model results. We primarily (but not exclusively) use a spreadsheet format rather than algebra for formulating and presenting a model. However, formulating a spreadsheet model of a real problem typically involves much more than designing the spreadsheet and entering the data. Therefore, we work through the process step by step: understand the unstructured problem, verbally develop some structure for the problem, gather the data, express the relationships in quantitative terms, and then lay out the spreadsheet model. The structured approach highlights the typical components of the model (the data, the decisions to be made, the constraints, and the measure of performance) and the different types of spreadsheet cells used for each. Consequently, the emphasis is on the modeling rather than spreadsheet mechanics.

A Case Studies Approach

However, all this still would be quite sterile if we simply presented a long series of brief examples with their spreadsheet formulations. This leads to the third key feature of this book—a *case studies* approach. In addition to examples, nearly every chapter includes one or two case studies patterned after actual applications (but reduced to textbook size) to convey the whole process of applying management science. In a few instances, the entire chapter revolves around a case study. By drawing the student into the story, we have designed each case study to bring that chapter's technique to life in a context that vividly illustrates the relevance of the technique for aiding managerial decision making. This storytelling, case-centered approach should make the material more enjoyable and stimulating while also conveying the practical considerations that are key factors in applying management science. Except for Chapter 1, every chapter also contains full-fledged cases following the problem material at the end of the chapter. These cases continue to employ a stimulating storytelling approach, so they can be assigned as interesting and challenging projects. Most of these end-of-chapter cases were developed jointly by two talented case writers, Karl Schmedders (a faculty member at the Kellogg Graduate School of Management at Northwestern University) and Molly Stephens (recently a management science consultant with Andersen Consulting). In addition, two of the cases are INFORMS teaching cases and several others have been adapted from cases in the 6th edition of *Introduction to Operations Research*.

Since students are less likely to read a preface than the instructor, we have elaborated on these three key features of the book (and a few other special features as well) in Section 1.3.

We are, of course, not the first to incorporate any of these key features into a management science textbook. However, we believe that the book currently is unique in the way that it fully incorporates all three key features together.

Other Special Features

We also should mention some additional special features of the book.

- Diverse examples, problems, and cases convey the pervasive relevance of management science.
- An integration of numerous management science success stories into the text (not separate boxes).
- Further descriptions of what is happening in practice.
- A strong managerial perspective.
- Review questions at the end of each section.
- A glossary at the end of each chapter.
- Partial answers to selected problems in the back of the book.
- Supplementary text material on the CD-ROM (as identified in the table of contents).
- An Excel-based software package (MS Courseware) on the CD-ROM that includes many add-ins, templates, and files (described below).
- Other helpful supplements are described below.

Although the orientation of this book is drastically different from our *Introduction to Operations Research* textbook, we also believe that we have managed to maintain, and perhaps even surpass, the high level of clarity and expositional excellence that has often been credited to this previous textbook.

Software

The *MS Courseware* package on the CD-ROM provides a separate Excel file for each chapter in the book that includes spreadsheets for the various examples and case studies. In addition to further investigating the examples and case studies, these spreadsheets can be used by either the student or instructor as templates to formulate and solve similar problems. The package also includes dozens of Excel templates for solving various models in the book.

Another key resource is a collection of Excel add-ins that are integrated into the corresponding chapters. The collection includes Premium Solver, TreePlan, SensIt, and RiskSim (all on the CD-ROM) as well as PrecisionTree and @RISK that can be downloaded from a web site. Microsoft Project and other software are included as well.

Other Supplements

The instructor's manual includes complete solutions to all problems and cases, as well as additional guidance. Another supplement is a test bank with computest that includes many hundred multiple-choice questions and true-false questions. Extensive presentation materials on PowerPoint slides also are available on the book's CD-ROM for use by the instructor (and for viewing by students). These slides include both lecture materials for nearly every chapter and all the figures (including spreadsheets) in the book.

To assist students, the CD-ROM also includes a tutorial with sample test questions (different from those in the instructor's test bank) for self-testing quizzes on the various chapters.

A Web page will provide updates about the book, including an errata. To access this site, visit www.mhhe.com/hilliermgtsci. In addition, the publisher's operations management supersite at www.mhhe.com/pom/ links to many resources on the internet that you might find pertinent to this book.

We welcome your comments, suggestions and errata. We hope that you enjoy the book.

Frederick S. Hillier,
Stanford University (fhillier@leland.stanford.edu)
Mark S. Hillier,
University of Washington (mhillier@u.washington.edu)
Gerald J. Lieberman,
Stanford University

March 1999

ACKNOWLEDGMENTS

This book has benefited greatly from the sage advice of numerous individuals. To begin, we would like to express our deep appreciation to the following individuals who provided formal reviews of the manuscript at various stages:

Shad Dowlatshahi
University of Texas at El Paso

Bruce Faaland
University of Washington

Frank Forst
Loyola University

Ken Gordon
University of Colorado at Boulder

Jeffery Guyse
Univerity of California at Irvine

Fred Hughes
Faulkner University

Vaidyanathan Jayaraman
University of Southern Mississippi

L. Robin Keller
University of California at Irvine

Larry LeBlanc
Vanderbilt University

Cynthia S. McCahon
Kansas State University

Barbara J. Mardis
University of Northern Iowa

Jerrold H. May
University of Pittsburgh

David L. Olson
Texas A&M

Ceyhun Ozgur
Valparaiso University

John R. Pickett
Georgia Southern University

Stephan K. Pollard
California State University at Los Angeles

Stephen G. Powell
Dartmouth College

Cindy H. Randall
Georgia Southern University

Robert M. Saltzman
San Francisco State University

Bala Shetty
Texas A&M

Willbann D. Terpening
Gonzaga University

Don Waters
University of Calgary

Others who provided helpful advice on the manuscript or on case development included Philip Davies, Jo Ford, and John Tuttle.

A major portion of the developmental work on this book occurred while the first co-author was on sabbatical leave in England as an Arthur Andersen Visiting Fellow at the Judge Institute of Management Studies of the University of Cambridge. In recognition of this important support, we are pleased to donate a copy of this book to the Judge Institute library.

This book was a team effort involving far more than the three co-authors. Our case writers, Karl Schmedders and Molly Stephens, were invaluable members of the team. Ann Hillier devoted numerous long days and nights to sitting with a Macintosh, doing word processing and constructing many figures and tables. While caring for two young children, Christine Hillier also managed to devote an enormous number of hours to doing a critique of the manuscript, developing solutions for the problems, and preparing the test bank. Helen Lieberman carried a heavy burden as well in providing support for the third co-author. They all were vital members of the team.

This book is a much better product because of the guidance and hard work of the editorial and production staff, including Scott Isenberg (Senior Sponsoring Editor), Wanda Zeman (Developmental Editor), Michael Elia (a previous Developmental Editor), and James Labeots (Project Manager). It has been a real pleasure working with such a thoroughly professional staff.

BRIEF CONTENTS

Contents on the CD-ROM

CONTENTS

Supplements on the CD-ROM

INTRODUCTION TO MANAGEMENT SCIENCE

INTRODUCTION

Welcome to the field of *management science!* We think that it is a particularly exciting and interesting field. Exciting because management science is having a dramatic impact on the profitability of numerous business firms around the world. Interesting because the methods used to do this are so ingenious. We are looking forward to giving you a guided tour to introduce you to the special features of the field.

Many students approach a course (and textbook) about management science with considerable anxiety and skepticism. The main source of the anxiety is the reputation of the field as being highly mathematical. This reputation then generates skepticism that such a theoretical approach can have much relevance for dealing with practical managerial problems. Most traditional courses (and textbooks) about management science have only reinforced these perceptions by emphasizing the mathematics of the field rather than its practical application.

Rest easy. This is not a traditional management science textbook. We realize that most readers of this book are aspiring to become managers, not mathematicians. Therefore, the emphasis throughout is on conveying what a future manager needs to know about management science. Yes, this means including a little mathematics here and there, because it is a major language of the field. The mathematics you do see will be at the level of high school algebra plus (in the later chapters) basic concepts of elementary probability theory. We think you will be pleasantly surprised by the new appreciation you gain for how useful and intuitive mathematics at this level can be. However, managers do not need to know any of the heavy mathematical theory that underlies the various techniques of management science. Therefore, the use of mathematics plays only a strictly secondary role in the book.

One reason we can deemphasize mathematics is that powerful *spreadsheet packages* now are available for applying management science. Spreadsheets provide a comfortable and familiar environment for formulating and analyzing managerial problems. The spreadsheet package takes care of applying the necessary mathematics automatically in the background with only a minimum of guidance by the user. This has begun to revolutionize the use of management science. In the past, technically trained management scientists were needed to carry out significant management science studies for management. Now spreadsheets are bringing many of the tools and concepts of management science within the reach of managers for conducting their own analyses. Although busy managers will continue to call upon management science teams to conduct major studies for them, they are increasingly becoming direct users themselves through the medium of spreadsheet packages. Therefore, since this book is aimed at future managers (and management consultants), we will emphasize the use of spreadsheets for applying management science.

What does an enlightened future manager need to learn from a management science course?

1. Gain an appreciation for the relevance and power of management science.
   (Therefore, we will give many examples of *actual applications* of management science and the *impact* they had on the organizations involved.)

2. Learn to recognize when management science can (and cannot) be fruitfully applied. (Therefore, we will emphasize the *kinds of problems* to which the various management science techniques can be applied.)

3. Learn how to apply the major techniques of management science to analyze a variety of managerial problems. (Therefore, we will focus largely on how spreadsheets enable many such applications with no more background in management science than provided by this book.)

4. Develop an understanding of how to interpret the results of a management science study. (Therefore, we will present many *case studies* that illustrate management science studies and how their results depend on the assumptions and data that were used.)

These are the key teaching goals of this book.

We begin this process in the next two sections by introducing the nature of management science and the impact that it is having on many organizations. (These themes will continue throughout the remaining chapters as well.) The concluding section then points out some of the special features of this book that you can look forward to seeing in the subsequent chapters.

1.1 The Nature of Management Science

What is the name *management science* (sometimes abbreviated MS) supposed to convey? It does involve *management* and *science* or, more precisely, *the science of management,* but this still is too vague. Here is a more suggestive definition.

> **Management science** is a *discipline* that attempts to *aid managerial decision making* by applying a *scientific approach* to managerial problems that involve *quantitative factors.*

Now let us see how elaborating upon each of the italicized terms in this definition conveys much more about the nature of management science.

Management Science Is a Discipline

As a discipline, management science is a whole body of knowledge and techniques that are based on a scientific foundation. For example, it is analogous in some ways to the *medical field.* A medical doctor has been trained in a whole body of knowledge and techniques that are based on the scientific foundations of the medical field. After receiving this training and entering practice, the doctor must diagnose a patient's illness and then choose the appropriate medical procedures to apply to the illness. The patient then makes the final decision on which medical procedures to accept. For less serious cases, the patient may choose not to consult a doctor and instead use his own basic knowledge of medical principles to treat himself. Similarly, a management scientist must receive substantial training (albeit considerably less than for a medical doctor). This training also is in a whole body of knowledge and techniques that are based on the scientific foundations of the discipline. After entering practice, the management scientist must diagnose a managerial problem and then choose the appropriate management science techniques to apply in analyzing the problem. The cognizant manager then makes the final decision as to which conclusions from this analysis to accept. For less extensive managerial problems where management science can be helpful, the manager may choose not to consult a management scientist and instead use his or her own basic knowledge of management science principles to analyze the problem.

Although it has considerably longer roots, the rapid development of the discipline began in the 1940s and 1950s. The initial impetus came early in World War II, when large numbers of scientists were called upon to apply a scientific approach to the management of the war effort for the allies. Another landmark event was the discovery in 1947 by George Dantzig of the *simplex method* for solving linear programming problems. (Linear programming is the subject of the next several chapters.) Another factor that gave great impetus to the growth of the discipline was the onslaught of the *computer revolution.*

The traditional name given to the discipline (and the one that still is widely used today outside of business schools) is **operations research.** This name was applied because the teams of scientists in World War II were doing *research* on how to manage military *opera-*

tions. The abbreviation OR also is widely used. This abbreviation often is combined with the one for management science (MS), thereby referring to the discipline as OR/MS.

One major international professional society for the discipline is the *Institute for Operations Research and the Management Sciences* (INFORMS). Headquartered in the United States, with about 12,000 members, this society holds major conferences in the United States each year plus occasional conferences elsewhere. It also publishes several prominent journals, including *Management Science, Operations Research,* and *Interfaces.* (Articles describing actual applications of management science are featured in *Interfaces,* so you will see many references to this journal throughout the book.)

In addition, there now are a few dozen member countries in the *International Federation of Operational Research Societies* (IFORS), with each member country having a national operations research society. Both Europe and Asia also have federations of operations research societies to coordinate holding international conferences and publishing international journals in those continents.

Thus, operations research/management science (OR/MS) is a truly international discipline. (We hereafter will just use the name *management science.*)

Management Science Aids Managerial Decision Making

The key word here is that management science *aids* managerial decision making. Management scientists don't make managerial decisions. Managers do. A management science study only provides an analysis and recommendations, based on the quantitative factors involved in the problem, as input to the cognizant managers. Managers must also take into account various intangible considerations that are outside the realm of management science and then use their best judgment to make the decision. Sometimes managers find that qualitative factors are as important as quantitative factors in making a decision.

A small informal management science study might be conducted by just a single individual, who may be the cognizant manager. However, management science *teams* normally are used for larger studies. (We will use the term *team* to cover both cases throughout the book.) Such a team often includes some members who are not management scientists but who provide other types of expertise needed for the study. Although a management science team often is entirely *in-house* (employees of the company), part or all of the team may instead be *consultants* who have been hired for just the one study. Consulting firms that partially or entirely specialize in management science currently are a growing industry.

Management Science Uses a Scientific Approach

Management science is based strongly on some scientific fields, including mathematics and computer science. It also draws on the social sciences, especially economics. Since it is concerned with the practical management of organizations, a management scientist should have solid training in business administration, including its various functional areas, as well.

To a considerable extent, a management science team will attempt to use the *scientific method* in conducting its study. This means that the team will emphasize conducting a *systematic investigation* that includes careful data gathering, developing and testing hypotheses about the problem (typically in the form of a mathematical model), and then applying sound logic in the subsequent analysis.

When conducting this systematic investigation, the management science team typically will follow the (overlapping) steps outlined and described below.

Step 1: Define the Problem and Gather Data. In this step, the team will consult with management to clearly identify the problem of concern and ascertain the appropriate objectives for the study. The team then typically spends a surprisingly large amount of time gathering relevant data about the problem with the assistance of other key individuals in the organization. A common frustration is that some key data are either very rough or completely unavailable. This may necessitate installing a new computer-based management information system. After doing what it can to improve the precision and availability of the needed data, the team will make do with what can be obtained.

Step 2: Formulate a Model (Typically a Mathematical Model) to Represent the Problem. **Models,** or idealized representations, are an integral part of everyday life. Common examples include model airplanes, portraits, globes, and so on. Similarly, models play an important role in science and business, as illustrated by models of the atom, models of genetic structure, mathematical equations describing physical laws of motion or chemical reactions, graphs, organization charts, and industrial accounting systems. Such models are invaluable for abstracting the essence of the subject of inquiry, showing interrelationships, and facilitating analysis.

Mathematical models are also idealized representations, but they are expressed in terms of mathematical symbols and expressions. Such laws of physics as $F = ma$ and $E = mc^2$ are familiar examples. Similarly, the mathematical model of a business problem is the system of equations and related mathematical expressions that describes the essence of the problem.

With the emergence of powerful spreadsheet technology, **spreadsheet models** now are widely used to analyze managerial problems. A spreadsheet model lays out the relevant data, measures of performance, interrelationships, and so forth, on a spreadsheet in an organized way that facilitates fruitful analysis of the problem. It also frequently incorporates an underlying mathematical model to assist in the analysis, but the mathematics is kept in the background so the user can concentrate on the analysis.

The *modeling process* is a creative one. When dealing with real managerial problems (as opposed to some cut-and-dried textbook problems), there normally is no single "correct" model but rather a number of alternative ways to approach the problem. The modeling process also is typically an evolutionary process that begins with a simple "verbal model" to define the essence of the problem, and then gradually evolves into increasingly more complete mathematical models (perhaps in a spreadsheet format).

We further describe and illustrate such mathematical models later in this section.

Step 3: Develop a Computer-Based Procedure for Deriving Solutions to the Problem from the Model.   The beauty of a well-designed mathematical model is that it enables using mathematical procedures run on a computer to find good solutions to the problem. In some cases, the management science team will need to develop the procedure. In others, a standard software package already will be available for solving the model. When the mathematical model is incorporated into a spreadsheet, the spreadsheet package normally includes a Solver that usually will solve the model.

Step 4: Test the Model and Refine It as Needed.   Now that the model can be solved, the team needs to thoroughly check and test the model to make sure that it provides a sufficiently accurate representation of the real problem. A number of questions should be addressed, perhaps with the help of others who are particularly familiar with the problem. Have all the relevant factors and interrelationships in the problem been accurately incorporated into the model? Does the model seem to provide reasonable solutions? When it is applied to a past situation, does the solution improve upon what was actually done? When assumptions about costs and revenues are changed, do the solutions change in a plausible manner?

Step 5: Apply the Model to Analyze the Problem and Develop Recommendations for Management.   The management science team now is ready to solve the model, perhaps under a variety of assumptions, in order to analyze the problem. The resulting recommendations then are presented to the managers who must make the decisions about how to deal with the problem.

If the model is to be applied repeatedly to help guide decisions on an ongoing basis, the team might also develop a **decision support system.** This is an interactive computer-based system that aids managerial decision making. The system draws current data from *databases* or *management information systems* and then solves the various versions of the model specified by the manager.

Step 6: Help to Implement the Team's Recommendations That Are Adopted by Management.   Once management makes its decisions, the management science team normally is asked to help oversee the implementation of the new procedures. This includes providing some information to the operating management and personnel involved on the rationale for the changes that are being made. The team also makes sure that the new operating system is consistent with its recommendations as they have been modified and approved by management. If successful, the new system may be used for years to come. With this in mind, the team monitors the initial experience with the system and seeks to identify any modifications that should be made in the future.

Management Science Considers Quantitative Factors

Many managerial problems revolve around such quantitative factors as production quantities, revenues, costs, the amounts available of needed resources, and so on. By incorporating these quantitative factors into a *mathematical model* and then applying mathematical procedures to solve the model, management science provides a uniquely powerful way of analyzing such managerial problems. Although management science is concerned with the practical management of organizations, including taking into account relevant qualitative factors, its special contribution lies in this unique ability to deal with the quantitative factors.

Let us look at a small example of a mathematical model.

An Example: A Mathematical Model for Break-Even Analysis

The Special Products Company produces expensive and unusual gifts to be sold in stores that cater to affluent customers who already have everything. The latest new-product proposal to management from the company's Research Department is a *limited edition grandfather clock*. Management now needs to decide whether to introduce this new product and, if so, how many units to produce for sale.

To address this problem, we introduce the algebraic variable

x = number of grandfather clocks to produce for sale

where x is referred to as a **decision variable** for the model. Choosing a value of 0 for this variable would correspond to deciding not to introduce the product. Since the number of clocks produced cannot be less than 0,

$$x \geq 0$$

is one of the **constraints** for the mathematical model. Another restriction on the value of x is that it should not exceed the number of clocks that can be sold. A sales forecast has not yet been obtained, so let the symbol s represent this currently unknown value.

s = forecast (not yet available) of the number of grandfather clocks that can be sold

Consequently,

$$x \leq s$$

is another constraint, where s is a **parameter** of the model whose value has not yet been chosen.

If the company goes ahead with this product, a cost of $50,000 would be incurred for setting up the production facilities. In addition, there would be a production cost of $400 for each unit produced, so producing x units would cost $400 *times x*. Therefore, the total cost would be

$$\text{Cost} = \begin{cases} 0 & \text{if } x = 0 \\ \$50,000 + \$400x & \text{if } x > 0 \end{cases}$$

Thus, producing any units would result in a *fixed cost* (independent of production volume) of $50,000 and a *variable cost* (dependent on production volume) of $400x$, so the *marginal cost* (the cost for each additional unit) is $400.

Each grandfather clock sold would generate a revenue of $900 for the company. Therefore, the total revenue from selling x units would be

$$\text{Revenue} = \$900x$$

Consequently, the profit from producing and selling x units would be

$$\text{Profit} = \text{Revenue} - \text{Cost}$$

$$= \begin{cases} 0 & \text{if } x = 0 \\ \$900x - (\$50,000 + \$400x) & \text{if } x > 0 \end{cases}$$

Thus, since $\$900x - \$400x = \$500x$,

$$\text{Profit} = -\$50,000 + \$500x \qquad \text{if } x > 0$$

This last equation shows that the attractiveness of the proposed new product depends greatly on the value of x, that is, on the number of grandfather clocks that can be produced and sold. A small value of x means a loss (negative profit) for the company, whereas a sufficiently large value would generate a positive profit for the company. For example, look at the difference between $x = 20$ and $x = 200$.

$$\text{Profit} = -\$50,000 + \$500(20) = -\$40,000 \qquad \text{if } x = 20$$

$$\text{Profit} = -\$50,000 + \$500(200) = \$50,000 \qquad \text{if } x = 200$$

Figure 1.1 plots both the company's total cost and total revenue for the various values of x. Note that the cost line and the revenue line intersect at $x = 100$. For any value of $x < 100$, cost exceeds revenue, so the gap between the two lines represents the *loss* to the company. For any $x > 100$, revenue exceeds cost, so the gap between the two lines now shows positive profit. At $x = 100$, the profit is 0. Since 100 units is the production and sales volume at which the company would break even on the proposed new product, this volume is referred to as the **break-even point.** This is the point that must be exceeded to make it worthwhile to introduce the product.

Figure 1.1 illustrates the *graphical procedure* for finding the break-even point. Another alternative is to use an *algebraic procedure* to solve for the point. Because the profit is 0 at this point, the procedure consists of solving the following equation for the unknown x.

$$\text{Profit} = -\$50,000 + \$500x = 0$$

Thus,

$$\$500x = \$50,000$$

$$x = \frac{\$50,000}{\$500}$$

$$x = 100$$

FIGURE 1.1

Break-even analysis for the Special Products Company shows that the cost line and revenue line intersect at x = 100 units, so this is the break-even point for the proposed new product.

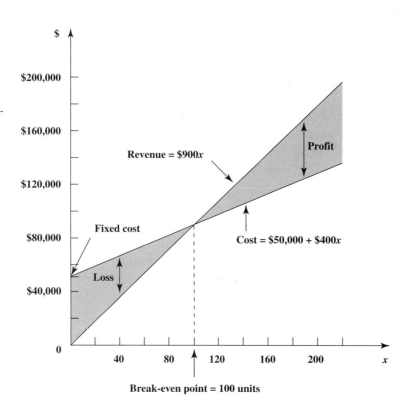

Break-even point = 100 units

Recall that the issue facing management is whether to introduce this new product and, if so, how many units to produce for sale. The overall mathematical model for this problem is to find the value of the decision variable x so as to

$$\text{Maximize} \quad \text{Profit} = \begin{cases} 0 & \text{if } x = 0 \\ -\$50,000 + \$500x & \text{if } x > 0 \end{cases}$$

subject to

$$x \leq s$$

$$x \geq 0$$

where the algebraic expression given for Profit is called the **objective function** for the model. The value of x that solves this model depends on the value that will be assigned to the parameter s (the future forecast of the number of units that can be sold). Because the break-even point is 100, here is how the solution for x depends on s.

SOLUTION FOR MATHEMATICAL MODEL

$$\text{Break-even point} = \frac{\$50,000}{\$900 - \$400} = 100$$

If $s \leq 100$, then set $x = 0$.
If $s > 100$, then set $x = s$.

Therefore, the company should introduce the product and produce the number of units that can be sold *only* if this production and sales volume exceeds the break-even point.

Figure 1.2 shows the initial steps in incorporating this mathematical model into an Excel spreadsheet. The data for the problem (including a sales forecast that 300 grandfather clocks can be sold) have been entered into cells C4 to C7. Cell C9 is used to record a trial value for the decision on how many units to produce for sale. As one of many possibilities that might eventually be tried, Figure 1.2 shows the specific trial value of 200. Cells F4 to F7 then give the resulting revenue, costs, and profit by using the Excel equations shown under the spreadsheet.

Note that the equation for cell F4 uses the MIN(a, b) function, which gives the minimum of a and b. In this case, the estimated number of grandfather clocks that will be sold is the minimum of the sales forecast and the production quantity, so

F4 = C4*MIN(C7, C9)

enters the minimum of C4*C7 (the total revenue if the number of grandfather clocks sold equals the sales forecast) and C4*C9 (the total revenue if the number sold equals the production quantity) into cell F4.

FIGURE 1.2

A spreadsheet formulation of the Special Products Company problem.

	A	B	C	D	E	F
1		Special Products Co. Break–Even Analysis				
2						
3		Data			Results	
4		Unit Revenue =	$900		Total Revenue =	$180,000
5		Fixed Cost =	$50,000		Total Fixed Cost =	$50,000
6		Marginal Cost =	$400		Total Variable Cost =	$80,000
7		Sales Forecast =	300		Profit (Loss) =	$50,000
8						
9		Production Quantity =	200			

	F
4	=C4*MIN(C7,C9)
5	=IF(C9>0,C5,0)
6	=C6*C9
7	=F4−(F5+F6)

FIGURE 1.3

An expansion of the spreadsheet in Figure 1.2 that uses the solution for the mathematical model to calculate the break-even point.

	A	B	C	D	E	F
1		**Special Products Co. Break–Even Analysis**				
2						
3		**Data**			**Results**	
4		Unit Revenue =	$900		Total Revenue =	$270,000
5		Fixed Cost =	$50,000		Total Fixed Cost =	$50,000
6		Marginal Cost =	$400		Total Variable Cost =	$120,000
7		Sales Forecast =	300		Profit (Loss) =	$100,000
8						
9		**Production Quantity =**	300		**Break-Even Point =**	100

	F
4	=C4*MIN(C7,C9)
5	=IF(C9>0,C5,0)
6	=C6*C9
7	=F4–(F5+F6)
8	
9	=C5/(C4–C6)

Also note that the equation for cell F5 uses the IF(*a, b, c*) function, which does the following: if statement *a* is true, it uses *b;* otherwise, it uses *c.* Therefore,

$$F5 = IF(C9>0, C5, 0)$$

says to enter C5 (the fixed cost) into cell F5 if C9 > 0 (production is initiated), but otherwise enter 0 (the fixed cost is avoided if production is not initiated).

Although the spreadsheet in Figure 1.2 enables trying a variety of trial values for the production quantity, it does not directly indicate what the production quantity should be. Figure 1.3 shows how this spreadsheet can be expanded to provide this additional guidance. As indicated by its equation at the bottom of the figure, cell F9 calculates the break-even point by dividing the fixed cost ($50,000) by the net profit per grandfather clock sold ($500), where this net profit is the unit revenue ($900) *minus* the marginal cost ($400). Since the sales forecast of 300 exceeds the break-even point of 100, this forecast has been entered into cell C9.

If desired, the mathematical model for break-even analysis can be *fully* incorporated into the spreadsheet by requiring that the model solution for the production quantity be entered into cell C9. This would be done by using the equation

$$C9 = IF(C7 > F9, C7, 0).$$

However, the disadvantage of introducing this equation is that it would eliminate the possibility of trying other production quantities that might still be of interest. For example, if management does not have much confidence in the sales forecast and wants to minimize the danger of producing more grandfather clocks than can be sold, consideration would be given to production quantities smaller than the forecast. For example, the trial value shown in cell C9 of Figure 1.2 might be chosen instead. As in any application of management science, a mathematical model can provide useful guidance but management needs to make the final decision after considering factors that may not be included in the model.

When a mathematical model is incorporated into a spreadsheet as illustrated here, it commonly is referred to as a *spreadsheet model.* You will see numerous examples of spreadsheet models throughout the book.

Review Questions

1. When did the rapid development of the management science discipline begin?
2. What is the traditional name given to this discipline that still is widely used outside of business schools?

3. What does a management science study provide to managers to aid their decision making?
4. Upon which scientific fields and social sciences is management science especially based?
5. What is a decision support system?
6. What are some common quantitative factors around which many managerial problems revolve?
7. How do the production and sales volume of a new product need to compare to its break-even point to make it worthwhile to introduce the product?

1.2 The Impact of Management Science

Management science has had an impressive impact on improving the efficiency of numerous organizations around the world. In the process, it has made a significant contribution to increasing the productivity of the economies of various countries.

The best way to convey the impact that management science is having is to describe some *actual* applications and the benefits they have provided. Therefore, you will see many examples of actual applications throughout the book (especially in the later chapters). (These applications are highlighted by giving the names of the organizations involved in **boldface.**) Some illustrate how a wide variety of organizations are using management science. Others are especially noteworthy applications that have won major awards.

TABLE 1.1 SOME CLASSIC AWARD WINNING APPLICATIONS OF MANAGEMENT SCIENCE

Organization	Nature of Application	Issue of Interfaces	Chapter Where Discussed	Annual Savings
United Airlines	Schedule shift work at reservations offices and airports to meet customer needs with minimum cost	Jan.–Feb. 1986	2, 3, 13, 14	$6 million
Citgo Petroleum Corp.	Optimize refinery operations and the supply, distribution, and marketing of products	Jan.–Feb. 1987	2, 3, 6	$70 million
San Francisco Police Department	Optimally schedule and deploy police patrol officers with a computerized system	Jan.–Feb. 1989	8	$11 million
Homart Development Co.	Optimally schedule the sale of shopping malls and office buildings	Jan.–Feb. 1987	9	$40 million
AT&T	Optimize the selection of sites for telemarketing centers for AT&T business customers	Jan.–Feb. 1990	9	$406 million more sales
Amoco Oil Co.	Define and evaluate new strategies for merchandising the company's products	Dec. 1982	10	$10 million
U.S. Postal Service	Perform technical and economic analyses of options for postal automation	March–April 1987 Jan.–Feb. 1992	10, 15	$200 million
Standard Brands, Inc.	Control finished-goods inventory (safety stocks, reorder points, and order quantities) of 100 items	Dec. 1981	11	$3.8 million
IBM	Integrate a national network of spare-parts inventories to improve service support	Jan.–Feb. 1990	12	$20 million + $250 million less inventory
Hydroeléctrica Español	Apply statistical forecasting to manage a system of reservoirs used to generate hydroelectric power	Jan.–Feb. 1990	13	$2 million
Xerox Corp.	Modify the strategy for repairing customer machines to reduce response time and improve repairer productivity	Nov. 1975, Part 2	14	50% better productivity

TABLE 1.2   SOME AWARD-WINNING APPLICATIONS OF MANAGEMENT SCIENCE FROM THE 1990S

Organization	Nature of Application	Issue of Interfaces	Chapter Where Discussed	Annual Savings
Procter & Gamble	Redesign the North American production and distribution system to reduce costs and improve speed to market	Jan.–Feb. 1997	5	$200 million
South African National Defense Force	Optimally redesign the size and shape of the defense force and its weapons systems	Jan.–Feb. 1997	9	$1.1 billion
Digital Equipment Corp.	Restructure the global supply chain of suppliers, plants, distribution centers, potential sites, and market areas	Jan.–Feb. 1995	9	$800 million
Reynolds Metals Co.	Automate a dispatching system for freight shipments from over 200 plants, warehouses, and suppliers	Jan.–Feb. 1991	9, 15	$7 million
China	Optimally select and schedule massive projects for meeting the country's future energy needs	Jan.–Feb. 1995	9	$425 million
Delta Airlines	Maximize the profit from assigning airplane types to over $2,500 domestic flights	Jan.–Feb. 1994	9	$100 million
American Airlines	Optimally assign sequences of flight legs to crews of pilots and flight attendants	Jan.–Feb. 1991	9	$20 million
Merit Brass Co.	Install statistical sales forecasting and finished-goods inventory management to improve customer service	Jan.–Feb. 1993	13	Much better service
American Airlines	Design a system of fare structures, overbooking, and coordinating flights to increase revenue	Jan.–Feb. 1992	12, 13	$500 million more revenue
L.L. Bean, Inc.	Optimally allocate telephone trunk lines, hold positions, and telephone agents to a large call center	Jan.–Feb. 1991	14	$9.5 million
New York City	Overhaul the process from when individuals are arrested until they are arraigned to reduce waiting times	Jan.–Feb. 1993	14, 15	$9.5 million
AT&T	Develop a PC-based system to guide business customers in designing their call centers	Jan.–Feb. 1993	14, 15	$750 million

The most prestigious prize that a practitioner of management science can win is one of the annual Franz Edelman Awards for Management Science Achievement. These awards are given for the year's best applications of management science anywhere throughout the world. The competition is sponsored jointly by the international Institute for Operations Research and the Management Sciences (INFORMS) and its College for the Practice of the Management Sciences.

Each year, several dozen entries are submitted to this competition. After an arduous review process, about six finalists are selected for awards, with approximately $10,000 going to the first-prize winner and smaller amounts to the other finalists. More important than the money is the prestige of being an award winner. An entire issue of *Interfaces* (currently the first issue of the following year) is devoted to articles describing the award-winning applications in detail.

Tables 1.1 and 1.2 provide a preview of those award-winning applications that will be discussed in subsequent chapters. The first table lists *classic* applications (conducted before 1990) that still provide valuable lessons today. The second table focuses on management science studies conducted during the 1990s. The third column of each table indicates the issue of *Interfaces* in which each study is fully described. The fourth column shows the chapter (or chapters) of this book in which the study will be discussed because it illustrates the application of that chapter's technique(s). The rightmost column indicates that these studies typically resulted in *annual savings* in the millions (often *many* millions) of dollars. Furthermore, additional benefits not recorded in the table (e.g., improved service to customers and better managerial control) sometimes were considered to be even more important than these financial benefits.

The subsequent chapters also discuss many other actual applications of management science that did not win awards. These more routine applications often provide considerably more modest benefits than the award-winning applications. However, the figures in the rightmost column of the tables do accurately reflect the dramatic impact that large, well-designed management science studies occasionally can have.

Review Question

1. What is the order of magnitude of the annual savings that typically result from award-winning applications of management science?

1.3 Some Special Features of This Book

The focus of this book is on teaching what an enlightened future manager needs to learn from a management science course. It is not on trying to train technical analysts. This focus has led us to include a number of special features that we hope you enjoy.

One special feature is that the entire book revolves around *modeling* as an aid to managerial decision making. This is what is particularly relevant to a manager. Although they may not use this term, all managers often engage in at least informal modeling (abstracting the essence of a problem to better analyze it), so learning more about the art of modeling is important. Since managers instigate larger management science studies done by others, they also need to be able to recognize the kinds of managerial problems where such a study might be helpful. Thus, a future manager should acquire the ability both to recognize when a management science model might be applicable and to properly interpret the results from analyzing the model. Therefore, rather than spending substantial time in this book on mathematical theory, the mechanics of solution procedures, or the manipulation of spreadsheets, the focus is on the art of model formulation, the role of a model, and the analysis of model results. A wide range of model types are considered.

Another special feature is a heavy emphasis on *case studies* to better convey these ideas in an interesting way in the context of applications. Almost every chapter includes at least one case study that introduces and illustrates the application of that chapter's techniques in a realistic setting. In a few instances, the entire chapter revolves around a case study. Although considerably smaller and simpler than most real studies (to maintain clarity), these case studies are patterned after actual applications requiring a major management science study. Consequently, they convey the whole process of such a study, some of the pitfalls involved, and the complementary roles of the management science team and the manager responsible for the decisions to be made.

To complement these case studies, almost every chapter also includes approximately two major cases at the end. These realistic cases can be used for individual assignments, team projects, or case studies in class.

The book also places heavy emphasis on conveying the diversity of application areas for the various models and techniques of management science. These application areas cut across the spectrum of the functional areas of business for a wide variety of organizations.

In addition, we try to provide you with a broad perspective about the nature of the real world of management science in practice. It is easy to lose sight of this world when cranking through textbook exercises to master the mechanics of a series of techniques. Therefore, we shift some emphasis from mastering these mechanics to seeing the big picture. The case studies, cases, and descriptions of actual applications are part of this effort. We also give further descriptions of what is happening in practice. We provide some perspectives about solving management science models, including the size of problems being solved in practice, but we try not to bother you with details that you will never need to know. We indicate how widely the various models and techniques are being used. We also point out the shortcomings of some techniques and what new developments are beginning to address these shortcomings.

The last, but certainly not the least, of the special features of this book is the accompanying software. We will describe and illustrate how to use today's premier spreadsheet package, Microsoft Excel, to formulate many management science models in a spreadsheet format. The Excel Solver then provides the solution to the models. Spreadsheets have many advantages over other software options, both for helping you formulate your models in a comfortable environment and for nicely displaying your solutions.

Given this choice of software, we should point out that Excel and its Solver are not designed for dealing with the really large management science models that occasionally arise in practice. More powerful software packages that are not based on spreadsheets, such as CPLEX or IBM's OSL, generally are used to solve such models instead. However, management science teams, not managers, primarily use these sophisticated packages (including using *modeling languages* to help input the large models). Since this book is aimed mainly at future managers rather than future management scientists, we will not have you use these packages.

The Excel Solver can readily solve all the models of the size considered in this book (and considerably larger ones as well). Furthermore, more powerful Solver packages (such as Premium Solver and Premium Solver Plus) are available that are used exactly like the basic Solver that comes with Excel. Therefore, learning how to use Excel and the Solver for formulating and solving management science models provides a manager with the main computer tool needed for personally applying management science.

Shrink-wrapped in the back of the book is a software package called **MS Courseware.** This package includes a separate Excel file for every chapter in this book. Each file typically includes several spreadsheets that will help you formulate and solve the various kinds of models described in the chapter. Two types of spreadsheets are included. First, each time an example is presented that can be solved using Excel, the complete spreadsheet formulation and solution are given in that chapter's Excel file. This provides a convenient reference, or even useful templates, when you set up spreadsheets to solve similar problems. Second, for many of the models in the book, template files are provided that already include all the equations necessary to solve the model. You simply enter the data for the model and the solution is immediately calculated.

MS Courseware also includes several Excel add-ins to help you do your computer work for several of the chapters more efficiently. One of these add-ins is Premium Solver for Excel. The other add-ins will be introduced later as they become relevant.

To alert you to relevant material in MS Courseware, the end of each chapter has a list entitled "Learning Aids for This Chapter in Your MS Courseware."

1.4 Summary

Management science is a discipline area that attempts to aid managerial decision making by applying a scientific approach to managerial problems that involve quantitative factors. The rapid development of this discipline began in the 1940s and 1950s. The onslaught of the computer revolution has since continued to give great impetus to its growth. Further impetus now is being provided by the widespread use of spreadsheet packages, which greatly facilitate the application of management science by managers and others.

A major management science study involves conducting a systematic investigation that includes careful data gathering, developing and testing hypotheses about the problem (typically in the form of a mathematical model), and applying sound logic in the subsequent analysis. The management science team then presents its recommendations to the managers who must make the decisions about how to resolve the problem.

A major part of a typical management science study involves incorporating the quantitative factors into a mathematical model (perhaps incorporated into a spreadsheet) and then applying mathematical procedures to solve the model. Such a model uses *decision variables* to represent the quantifiable decisions to be made. An *objective function* expresses the appropriate measure of performance in terms of these decision variables. The *constraints* of the model express the restrictions on the values that can be assigned to the decision variables. The *parameters* of the model are the constants that appear in the objective function and the constraints. An example involving *break-even analysis* was used to illustrate a mathematical model.

Management science has had an impressive impact on improving the efficiency of numerous organizations around the world. In fact, many award-winning applications have resulted in annual savings in the millions, tens of millions, or even hundreds of millions of dollars.

The focus of this book is on emphasizing what an enlightened future manager needs to learn from a management science course. Therefore, the book revolves around modeling as an aid to managerial decision making. Many case studies (within the chapters) and cases (at the end of chapters) are used to better convey these ideas.

Glossary

Break-even point   The production and sales volume for a product that must be exceeded to achieve a profit. (Section 1.1)   8

Constraint   An inequality or equation in a mathematical model that expresses some restrictions on the values that can be assigned to the decision variables. (Section 1.1)   7

Decision support system   An interactive computer-based system that aids managerial decision making. (Section 1.1)   6

Decision variable   An algebraic variable that represents a quantifiable decision to be made. (Section 1.1)   7

Mathematical model   An idealized representation of, for example, a business problem that is expressed in terms of mathematical symbols and expressions. (Section 1.1)   6

Model   An idealized representation of something. (Section 1.1)   5

MS Courseware   The name of the software package that is shrink-wrapped with the book. (Section 1.3)   14

Objective function   A mathematical expression in a model that gives the measure of performance for a problem in terms of the decision variables. (Section 1.1)   9

Operations research   The traditional name for management science that still is widely used outside of business schools. (Section 1.1)   4

Parameter   One of the constants in a mathematical model. (Section 1.1)   7

Spreadsheet model   An idealized representation of, for example, a business problem that is laid out on a spreadsheet in a way that facilitates analysis of the problem. (Section 1.1)   6

Learning Aid for This Chapter in Your MS Courseware

"Ch. 1—Introduction" Excel File:

Special Products Co. Example

Problems

1.1. Select one of the applications listed in Table 1.1. Read the article describing the application in the indicated issue of *Interfaces*. Write a one-page description of the benefits (including nonfinancial benefits) that resulted from this application of management science.

1.2. Follow the instructions of Problem 1.1 for one of the applications listed in Table 1.2.

1.3. Reconsider the problem facing the management of the Special Products Company that was presented at the end of Section 1.1.

A more detailed investigation now has provided better estimates of the data for the problem. The fixed cost of initiating production of the limited edition grandfather clocks still is estimated to be $50,000, but the new estimate of the marginal cost is $500. The revenue from each grandfather sold now is estimated to be $700.

a. Use a graphical procedure to find the new break-even point.

b. Use an algebraic procedure to find the new break-even point.

c. State the mathematical model for this problem with the new data.

d. Incorporate this mathematical model into a spreadsheet with a sales forecast of 300. Use this spreadsheet model to find the new break-even point, and then determine the production quantity and the estimated total profit indicated by the model.

e. Suppose that management fears that the sales forecast may be overly optimistic and so does not want to consider producing more than 200 grandfather clocks. Use the spreadsheet from part *d* to determine what the production quantity should be and the estimated total profit that would result.

1.4. Reconsider the Special Products Company problem presented at the end of Section 1.1.

    Although the company is well-qualified to do most of the work in producing the limited edition grandfather clocks, it currently lacks expertise in one key area, namely, constructing the time-keeping mechanism for the clocks. Therefore, management now is considering contracting out this part of the job to another company that has this expertise and already has some of its production facilities set up to do this kind of work. If this were done, the Special Products Company would not incur any fixed cost for initiating production of the clocks but would incur a marginal cost of $650 (including its payment to the other company) while still obtaining revenue of $900 for each clock produced and sold. However, if the company does all the production itself, all the data presented in Section 1.1 still applies. After obtaining an analysis of the sales potential, management believes that 300 grandfather clocks can be sold.

    Management now wants to determine whether the *make option* (do all the production internally) or the *buy option* (contract out the production of the time-keeping mechanism) is better.

a. Use a spreadsheet to display and analyze the buy option. Show the relevant data and financial output, including the total profit that would be obtained by producing and selling 300 grandfather clocks.

b. Figure 1.3 shows the analysis for the make option. Compare these results with those from part *a* to determine which option (make or buy) appears to be better.

c. Another way to compare these two options is to find a *break-even point* for the production and sales volume, below which the buy option is better and above which the make option is better. Begin this process by developing an expression for the *difference* in profit between the make and buy options in terms of the number of grandfather clocks to produce for sale. Thus, this expression should give the *incremental profit* from choosing the make option rather than the buy option, where this incremental profit is 0 if 0 grandfather clocks are produced but otherwise is negative below the break-even point and positive above the break-even point. Using this expression as the objective function, state the overall mathematical model (including constraints) for the problem of determining whether to choose the make option and, if so, how many units of the time-keeping mechanism (one per clock) to produce.

d. Use a graphical procedure to find the break-even point described in part *c.*

e. Use an algebraic procedure to find the break-even point described in part *c.*

f. Use a spreadsheet model to find the break-even point described in part *c.* What is the conclusion about what the company should do?

LINEAR PROGRAMMING: BASIC CONCEPTS

The management of any organization regularly must make decisions about how to allocate its resources to various activities to best meet organizational objectives. Linear programming is a powerful problem-solving tool that aids management in making such decisions. It is applicable to both profit-making and not-for-profit organizations, as well as governmental agencies. The resources being allocated to activities can be, for example, money, different kinds of personnel, and different kinds of machinery and equipment. In many cases, a wide variety of resources must be allocated simultaneously. The activities needing these resources might be various production activities (e.g., producing different products), marketing activities (e.g., advertising in different media), financial activities (e.g., making capital investments), or some other activity. Some problems might even involve activities of *all* these types (and perhaps others), because they are competing for the same resources.

You will see as we progress that even this description of the scope of linear programming is not sufficiently broad. Some of its applications go beyond the allocation of resources. However, activities always are involved. Thus, a recurring theme in linear programming is the need to find the *best mix* of activities—which ones to pursue and at what levels.

Like the other management science techniques, linear programming uses a *mathematical model* to represent the problem being studied. The word *linear* in the name refers to the form of the mathematical expressions in this model. *Programming* does not refer to computer programming; rather, it is essentially a synonym for planning. Thus, linear programming means the *planning of activities* represented by a *linear* mathematical model.

Because it comprises a major part of management science, linear programming takes up several chapters of this book. Furthermore, many of the lessons learned about how to apply linear programming also will carry over to the application of other management science techniques.

This chapter focuses on the basic concepts of linear programming.

2.1 Three Classic Applications of Linear Programming

To give you a perspective about the role linear programming can play in managerial decision making, we will briefly describe how it was used in three *real* situations. Each of these is a *classic* application, initiated some years ago, that has come to be regarded as a standard of excellence for future applications of linear programming. After you develop your facility with linear programming, we will refer back to each of these applications in Section 3.8, fleshing them out in more detail.

Choosing the Product Mix at Ponderosa Industrial[1]

Until its sale in 1988, **Ponderosa Industrial** was a Mexican company that produced 25 percent of the country's plywood. Like any plywood manufacturer, Ponderosa's many plywood products were differentiated by thickness and by the quality of the wood used. Because they

---

[1] Asim Roy, Emma E. DeFalomir, and Leon Lasdon, "An Optimization-Based Decision Support System for a Product Mix Problem," *Interfaces* 12, no. 2 (April 1982), pp. 26–33.

were sold in a competitive environment, the market established the prices of the products, so the prices fluctuated considerably from month to month. As a result, each product's contribution to Ponderosa's overall profit also fluctuated widely. Thus, if one product was considerably more profitable than another in one month, the reverse could well be true the following month. Therefore, a critical issue facing management each month was the choice of *product mix*—how much to produce of each product—to generate as much profit as possible. This choice was very complex, since it needed to take into account the current amounts available of various resources needed to produce the products. The six most important resources were (1) four types of logs (based on the quality of their wood) and (2) production capacities for each of the two key operations in producing plywood (the pressing operation and the polishing operation).

Starting in 1980, Ponderosa management used linear programming on a monthly basis to guide the product-mix decision for the upcoming month. The mathematical model for linear programming considered all relevant restrictions on this decision, including the limited amounts available of the resources required to make the products. The model was then solved to find the product mix that was feasible and yielded the *largest possible profit.*

This maximum profit would occur as long as the data incorporated into the model, including the estimated product prices for the upcoming month, turned out to be accurate. However, management knew that forecasting product prices even one month ahead was a risky business, so it was important to check on how the product-mix decision should change (if at all) under other plausible forecasts for these prices. Fortunately, the linear programming computer system was interactive, which enabled management to quickly solve the model again under different scenarios for where the market was headed. This ability to investigate various scenarios of interest proved to be invaluable in fine-tuning the product-mix decision.

Linear programming provided Ponderosa's management with other valuable information as well, including the effect on profit of changing a decision on how much of any particular resource to make available for current production. For example, suppose that the company had only a small supply of a certain type of log needed for producing a particularly profitable product. Linear programming indicates how much profit would change if a quick purchase were to be made of additional logs of this type in time to change the product-mix decision.

The impact of linear programming at Ponderosa was reported to be "tremendous." It led to a dramatic shift in the types of plywood products emphasized by the company. The improved product-mix decisions were credited with increasing the overall profitability of the company by 20 percent. Other contributions of linear programming included better utilization of raw material, capital equipment, and personnel.

Personnel Scheduling at United Airlines[2]

Despite unprecedented industry competition in 1983 and 1984, **United Airlines** managed to achieve substantial growth with service to 48 new airports. In 1984, it became the only airline with service to cities in all 50 U.S. states. United's 1984 revenues reached $6.2 billion, a 6 percent increase over 1983, while costs grew less than 2 percent, thereby boosting operating profit to $564 million.

Cost control is essential for survival in the airline industry. In 1982, upper management of United Airlines initiated a cost-control project as part of its ensuing expansion. The goal was to improve the utilization of personnel at the airline's reservations offices and airports by matching work schedules to customer needs more closely.

At the time, United Airlines employed over 4,000 reservations sales representatives and support personnel at its 11 reservations offices and about 1,000 customer service agents at its 10 largest airports. Some were part-time, working shifts from two to eight hours; most were full-time, working 8- or 10-hour shifts. Shifts started at several different times. Each reservations office was open (by telephone) 24 hours a day, as was each of the major airports. However, the number of employees needed at each location to provide the required level of service varied greatly during the 24-hour day, and might fluctuate considerably from one half-hour to the next.

---

[2]Thomas J. Holloran and Judson E. Bryn, "United Airlines Station Manpower Planning System," *Interfaces* 16, no. 1 (January–February 1986), pp. 39–50.

Trying to design the work schedules for all the employees at a given location to meet these service requirements most efficiently is a nightmare of combinatorial considerations. Once an employee arrives, he or she will be there continuously for the entire shift (2 to 10 hours, depending on the employee), *except* for either a meal break or short rest breaks every 2 hours. Given the *minimum* number of employees needed on duty for *each* half-hour interval over a 24-hour day (this minimum changes from day to day over a seven-day week), *how many* employees of *each shift length* should begin work at *what start time* over *each* 24-hour day of a seven-day week? Fortunately, linear programming thrives on such combinatorial nightmares.

Actually, several management science techniques described in this book were used in the planning system developed to attack this problem. *Forecasting* (Chapter 13) and *queueing models* (Chapter 14) were both used to determine the minimum number of employees needed on duty for each half-hour interval. *Integer programming* (Chapter 9) was used to determine when shifts would start. However, the core of the planning system was *linear programming,* which did all the actual scheduling to provide the needed service at the smallest possible labor cost. A new work schedule was developed each month to reflect changing conditions.

This application of linear programming was reported to have had "an overwhelming impact not only on United's management and members of the project team, but also for many who had never before heard of management science or mathematical modeling." It earned rave reviews from upper management, operating managers, and affected employees alike. For example, one manager described the scheduling system as "magical, . . . just as the (customer) lines begin to build, someone shows up for work; and just as you begin to think you're overstaffed, people start going home."

In tangible terms, this computerized planning system based on linear programming was credited with saving United Airlines more than $6 million *annually* in just direct salary and benefit costs. Other benefits included improved customer service and reduced workloads for support staff. After some updating in the early 1990s, the system is providing similar benefits today.

Planning Supply, Distribution, and Marketing at Citgo Petroleum Corporation[3]

Citgo Petroleum Corporation specializes in refining and marketing petroleum. In the mid-1980s, it had annual sales of several billion dollars, ranking it among the 150 largest industrial companies in the United States.

After several years of financial losses, Citgo was acquired in 1983 by Southland Corporation, the owner of the 7-Eleven convenience store chain (whose sales include two billion gallons of quality motor fuels annually). To turn Citgo's financial losses around, Southland created a task force composed of Southland personnel, Citgo personnel, and outside consultants. A management science consultant was appointed director of the task force and reported directly to both the president of Citgo and the chairman of the board of Southland.

During 1984 and 1985, this task force applied various management science techniques to analyze Citgo's activities in such diverse areas as refining, supply and distribution, market planning, accounts payable and receivable, inventory control, and acquisitions. It was reported that these management science applications "have changed the way Citgo does business and resulted in approximately $70 million per year profit improvement."

The bulk of this profit improvement resulted from two *linear programming systems* developed by the task force. One, called the *refinery LP system* (LP is a common abbreviation for linear programming), led to improvements in refinery yield, substantial reductions in the cost of labor, and other cost savings. The refinery LP system enabled management to operate Citgo's refinery (a major player in the profit-and-loss picture) so much more efficiently that it contributed $50 million of the $70 million profit improvement in 1985.

The other linear programming system was the Supply, Distribution, and Marketing modeling system (or simply the SDM system). Now, many years after its introduction,

[3]Darwin Klingman, Nancy Phillips, David Steiger, Ross Wirth, and Warren Young, "The Challenges and Success Factors in Implementing an Integrated Products Planning System for Citgo," *Interfaces* 16, no. 3 (May–June 1986), pp. 1–19. Also see Darwin Klingman, Nancy Phillips, David Steiger, and Warren Young, "The Successful Deployment of Management Science throughout Citgo Petroleum Corporation," *Interfaces* 17, no. 1 (January–February 1987), pp. 4–25.

Citgo continues to use and benefit from this system. It is based on a special kind of linear programming model that uses a network to describe the system being studied. The model in this case provides a representation of Citgo's entire marketing and distribution network. Because it introduces some new features of linear programming, we shall return to the SDM system again in Chapters 3 and 6 after providing some more background here.

At the time this system was introduced, Citgo owned or leased 36 product storage terminals that were supplied through five distribution center terminals via a distribution network of pipelines, tankers, and barges. In addition, Citgo sold product from over 350 storage terminals that were shared with other petroleum marketers. To supply its customers, product might be acquired by Citgo from its refinery in Lake Charles, Louisiana; from bulk purchases in five major markets; or from product trades with other industry refiners. Many acquisition decisions and shipping decisions were made every day. It could take as long as 11 weeks after an acquisition decision until the product reached Citgo's customers. Therefore, the linear programming model used an 11-week planning horizon.

The SDM system is used to coordinate the supply, distribution, and marketing of each of Citgo's major products throughout the United States. Management uses the system to make decisions such as where to sell, what price to charge, where to buy or trade, how much to buy or trade, how much to hold in inventory, and how much to ship by each mode of transportation. Linear programming guides these decisions and when to implement them so as to minimize the total cost (or maximize the total profit) for Citgo. The SDM system also is used in "what-if" sessions, where management explores *what* would happen to the solution *if* a scenario evolves that is not assumed by the model.

The SDM system has greatly improved the efficiency of Citgo's supply, distribution, and marketing operations, enabling a huge reduction in product inventory with no drop in service levels. Soon after its introduction, the value of petroleum products being held in inventory was reduced by $116.5 million. This huge reduction in capital tied up in carrying inventory resulted in saving about $14 million annually in interest expenses for borrowed capital, adding $14 million to Citgo's annual profits. Improvements in coordination, pricing, and purchasing decisions have been estimated to add at least another $2.5 million to annual profits.

Review Questions

1. Linear programming guided managerial decision making at Ponderosa Industrial on which critical issue facing management each month?
2. What was the impact of this application of linear programming at Ponderosa?
3. What was the goal of the described application of linear programming at United Airlines?
4. What was the impact of this application at United Airlines?
5. The SDM linear programming system at Citgo Petroleum Corp. was used to coordinate what?
6. What was the impact of this application of linear programming at Citgo?

2.2 A Case Study: The Wyndor Glass Co. Product-Mix Problem

Jim Baker is excited. The group he heads has really hit the jackpot this time. They have had some notable successes in the past, but he feels that this one will be really special. He can hardly wait for the reaction after his memorandum reaches top management.

Jim has had an excellent track record during his seven years as Manager of New Product Development for the Wyndor Glass Company. Although the company is a small one, it has been experiencing considerable growth largely because of the innovative new products developed by Jim's group. Wyndor's president, John Hill, has often acknowledged publicly the key role that Jim has played in the recent success of the company.

Therefore, John felt considerable confidence six months ago in asking Jim's group to develop the following new products:

- An 8-foot glass door with aluminum framing.
- A 4-foot × 6-foot double-hung, wood-framed window.

Although several other companies already had products meeting these specifications, John felt that Jim would be able to work his usual magic in introducing exciting new features that would establish new industry standards.

Now, Jim can't remove the smile from his face. They have done it.

Background

The Wyndor Glass Co. produces high-quality glass products, including windows and glass doors that feature handcrafting and the finest workmanship. Although the products are expensive, they fill a market niche by providing the highest quality available in the industry for the most discriminating buyers. The company has three plants.

Plant 1 produces aluminum frames and hardware.

Plant 2 produces wood frames.

Plant 3 produces the glass and assembles the windows and doors.

Because of declining sales for certain products, top management has decided to revamp the company's product line. Unprofitable products are being discontinued, releasing production capacity to launch the two new products developed by Jim Baker's group if management approves their release.

The 8-foot glass door requires some of the production capacity in Plants 1 and 3, but not Plant 2. The 4-foot × 6-foot double-hung window needs only Plants 2 and 3.

Management now needs to address two issues:

1. Should the company go ahead with launching these two new products?
2. If so, what should be the *product mix*—the number of units of each produced per week—for the two new products?

Management's Discussion of the Issues

Having received Jim Baker's memorandum describing the two new products, John Hill now has called a meeting to discuss the current issues. In addition to John and Jim, the meeting includes Bill Tasto, Vice President for Manufacturing, and Ann Lester, Vice President for Marketing.

Let's eavesdrop on the meeting.

John Hill (president): Jim, Bill, Ann, thanks for coming. Jim, thanks for your good memorandum, which we all have received. These two proposed new products certainly sound promising. Tell us more about their special features. What will stand out to make customers willing to pay more for these products, given the similar products already available from other companies. Let's start with the glass door.

Jim Baker (Manager of New Product Development): Well, I hardly know where to begin. This glass door is loaded with special features. But there are three in particular that I think will really make the customer sit up and notice. One is that this door will have a substantially higher insulating value than any door currently on the market.

John: How is that achieved?

Jim: In three ways. First, we use dual-pane glazing. Second, we insert a new inert gas, even better than argon, between the two panes of glass. It works great. Third, we also use some special coatings and tints for solar and energy control.

John: Wonderful. The insulating value is very important to a lot of customers. Now, what are the other two features you wanted to highlight?

Jim: One is that the glass we are using provides much better protection against ultraviolet light than usual. The other is that the glass is virtually unbreakable. You would have to take a sledgehammer to the glass, and even then you would have trouble breaking it. Somebody walking into the glass, or a bird flying into it, isn't going to faze it.

John: Those are good selling points. Now, tell us about the features that would sell your new double-hung window.

Jim: Well, that's easy. First of all, this window would have all three of the special features that I have just described for the glass door. In addition, the wood finish is extremely long-lasting, and the window has a special mechanism that makes it much easier to slide than usual.

John: Wow, those are great features. But aren't we pricing ourselves out of the market by loading on all those features?

Jim: That's the best part. We've worked hard on designing these products so that they can be produced for only about a thousand dollars more than the run-of-the-mill versions of these products that other companies are putting out.

John: Terrific. Ann, how is all this going to play out in the marketplace? Are these the kinds of special features that affluent customers want?

Ann Lester (Vice President for Marketing): Well, we just updated our market research on this question a few months ago. In fact, we fed Jim all our key findings. He has managed to hit all the special features for which these customers are asking. Given the kind of pricing that Jim is indicating, there is no doubt that these products would sell well. Extremely well.

John: Great. Well, Jim, it looks like you've outdone yourself this time. These should be outstanding products for the company. Congratulations!

Jim: Thank you. My group worked especially hard on this project.

John: Bill, we will want to rev up to start production of these products as soon as we can. About how much production output do you think we can achieve?

Bill Tasto (Vice President for Manufacturing): We do have a little available production capacity, because of the products we are discontinuing, but not a lot. We should be able to achieve a production rate of a few units per week for each of these two products.

John: Is that all?

Bill: Yes. These are complicated products requiring careful crafting. And, as I said, we don't have much production capacity available.

John: Ann, will we be able to sell several of each per week?

Ann: Easily.

John: OK, good. I would like to set the launch date for these products in six weeks. Bill and Ann, is that feasible?

Bill: Yes.

Ann: We'll have to scramble to give these products a proper marketing launch that soon. But we can do it.

John: Good. Now there's one more issue to resolve. With this limited production capacity, we need to decide how to split it between the two products. Do we want to produce the same number of both products? Or mostly one of them? Or even just produce as much as we can of one and postpone launching the other one for a little while?

Jim: It would be dangerous to hold one of the products back and give our competition a chance to scoop us.

Ann: I agree. Furthermore, launching them together has some advantages from a marketing standpoint. Since they share a lot of the same special features, we can combine the advertising for the two products. This is going to make a big splash.

John: OK. But which mixture of the two products is going to be most profitable for the company?

Bill: I have a suggestion.

John: What's that?

Bill: A couple times in the past, our Management Science Group has helped us with these same kinds of product-mix decisions, and they've done a good job. They ferret out all the relevant data and then dig into some detailed analysis of the issue. I've found their input very helpful. And this is right down their alley.

John: Yes, you're right. That's a good idea. Let's get our Management Science Group working on this issue. Bill, will you coordinate with them?

Bill: Sure.

John: And tell them that we want them to report their findings back to us within a month.

Bill: Will do.

The meeting ends.

The Management Science Group Begins Its Work

At the outset, the Management Science Group spends considerable time with Bill Tasto to clarify the general problem and specific issues that management wants addressed. A particular concern is to ascertain the appropriate objective for the problem from management's viewpoint. Bill points out that John Hill posed the issue as determining which mixture of the two products is going to be most profitable for the company.

Therefore, with Bill's concurrence, the group defines the key issue to be addressed as follows.

> **Question:** Which combination of *production rates* (the number of units produced per week) for the two new products would *maximize the total profit* from both of them?

The group also concludes that it should consider *all* possible combinations of production rates of both new products permitted by the available production capacities in the three plants. For example, one alternative (despite Jim Baker's and Ann Lester's objections) is to forgo producing one of the products for now (thereby setting its production rate equal to zero) in order to produce as much as possible of the other product. (We must not neglect the possibility that maximum profit from both products might be attained by producing none of one and as much as possible of the other.)

The Management Science Group next identifies the information they need to gather to conduct this study:

1. Available production capacity in each of the plants.
2. How much of the production capacity in each plant would be needed by each product.
3. Profitability of each product.

Concrete data are not available for any of these quantities, so estimates have to be made. Estimating these quantities requires enlisting the help of key personnel in other units of the company.

Bill Tasto's staff develop the estimates that involve production capacities. Specifically, the staff estimates that the production facilities in Plant 1 needed for the new kind of doors will be available approximately 4 hours per week. (The rest of the time Plant 1 will continue with current products.) The production facilities in Plant 2 will be available for the new kind of windows about 12 hours per week. The facilities needed for both products in Plant 3 will be available approximately 18 hours per week.

The amount of each plant's production capacity actually used by each product depends on its production rate. It is estimated that each door will require one hour of production time in Plant 1 and three hours in Plant 3. For each window, about two hours will be needed in Plant 2 and two hours in Plant 3.

By analyzing the cost data and the pricing decision, the Accounting Department estimates the profit from the two products. The projection is that the profit per unit will be $300 for the doors and $500 for the windows.

Table 2.1 summarizes the data now gathered.

The Management Science Group recognizes this as being a classic **product-mix problem** (just like the one at Ponderosa Industrial described earlier). Therefore, the next step is to develop a *mathematical model*—that is, a *linear programming model*—to represent the

TABLE 2.1 Data for the Wyndor Glass Co. Product-Mix Problem

Plant	Production Time Used for Each Unit Produced		*Production Time Available per Week*
	Doors	*Windows*	
1	1 hour	0	4 hours
2	0	2 hours	12 hours
3	3 hours	2 hours	18 hours
Unit profit	$300	$500	

problem so that it can be solved mathematically. The next four sections focus on how to develop this model and then how to solve it to find the most profitable mix between the two products, assuming the estimates in Table 2.1 are accurate.

Review Questions

1. What is the market niche being filled by the Wyndor Glass Co.?
2. What were the two issues addressed by management?
3. The Management Science Group was asked to help analyze which of these issues?
4. How did this group define the key issue to be addressed?
5. What information did the group need to gather to conduct their study?

2.3 Formulating the Wyndor Problem on a Spreadsheet

Spreadsheets provide a powerful and intuitive tool for displaying and analyzing many management problems. We now will focus on how to do this for the Wyndor problem with the popular spreadsheet package Microsoft Excel.[4]

Formulating a Spreadsheet Model for the Wyndor Problem

Figure 2.1 displays the Wyndor problem by transferring the data in Table 2.1 onto a spreadsheet. (Columns E and F are being reserved for later entries described below.) We will refer to the cells showing the data as **data cells.**

Three questions need to be answered to begin the process of using the spreadsheet to formulate a mathematical model (in this case, a **linear programming model**) for the problem.

1. What are the *decisions* to be made?
2. What are the *constraints* on these decisions?
3. What is the overall *measure of performance* for these decisions?

The preceding section described how Wyndor's Management Science Group spent considerable time with Bill Tasto, Vice President for Manufacturing, to clarify management's view of their problem. These discussions provided the following answers to these questions.

1. The decisions to be made are the *production rates* for the two new products.
2. The constraints on these decisions are that the number of hours of production time used per week by the two products in the respective plants cannot exceed the number of hours available.
3. The overall measure of performance for these decisions is the *total profit* from the two products.

FIGURE 2.1

The initial spreadsheet for the Wyndor problem after transferring the data in Table 2.1 into data cells.

	A	B	C	D	E	F	G
1		Wyndor Glass Co. Product–Mix Problem					
2							
3			Hours Used per Unit Produced				Hours
4			Doors	Windows			Available
5		Plant 1	1	0			4
6		Plant 2	0	2			12
7		Plant 3	3	2			18
8		Unit Profit	$300	$500			

---

[4]Other spreadsheet packages with similar capabilities also are available, and the basic ideas presented here are still applicable.

Figure 2.2 shows how these answers can be incorporated into the spreadsheet. Based on the first answer, the *production rates* (number of units produced per week) of the two products are placed in cells C9 and D9 to locate them in the columns for these products just under the data cells. Since we don't know yet what these production rates should be, they are just entered as zeroes in Figure 2.2. (Actually, any trial solution can be entered, although *negative* production rates should be excluded since they are impossible.) Later, these numbers will be changed while seeking the best mix of production rates. Therefore, these cells containing the decisions to be made are called **changing cells** (or *adjustable cells*).

Using the second answer, the total number of hours of production time used per week by the two products in the respective plants is entered in cells E5, E6, and E7, just to the right of the corresponding data cells. The total number of production hours depends on the production rates of the two products, so this total is zero when the production rates are zero. With positive production rates, the total number of production hours used per week in a plant is the sum of the production hours used per week by the respective products. The production hours used by a product is the number of hours needed for *each* unit of the product *times* the number of units being produced. Therefore, when positive numbers are entered in cells C9 and D9 for the number of doors and windows to produce per week, the data in cells C5:D7 are used to calculate the total production hours per week as follows:

$$\text{Production hours in Plant 1} = 1(\# \text{ of doors}) + 0(\# \text{ of windows})$$

$$\text{Production hours in Plant 2} = 0(\# \text{ of doors}) + 2(\# \text{ of windows})$$

$$\text{Production hours in Plant 3} = 3(\# \text{ of doors}) + 2(\# \text{ of windows})$$

(The colon in C5:D7 is Excel shorthand for *the range from* C5 *to* D7.) Consequently, the Excel equations for the first three cells in column E are

$$E5 = C5 * C9 + D5 * D9$$

$$E6 = C6 * C9 + D6 * D9$$

$$E7 = C7 * C9 + D7 * D9$$

where each asterisk denotes multiplication. Since each of these cells provides output that depends on the changing cells (C9 and D9), they are called **output cells.**

Notice that each of the equations for the output cells involves the sum of two products. There is a function in Excel called SUMPRODUCT that will sum up the product of each of the individual terms in two different ranges of cells when the two ranges have the same number of rows and the same number of columns. Each product being summed is the product of a term in the first range and the term in the corresponding location in the second range. For example, consider the two ranges, C5:D5 and C9:D9, so that each range has one row and two columns. In this case, SUMPRODUCT (C5:D5, C9:D9) takes each of the individual terms in the range C5:D5, multiplies them by the corresponding term in the range C9:D9, and then sums up these individual products, just as shown in the first equation above. Although optional with such short equations, this function is especially handy as a shortcut for entering longer equations.

Next, ≤ signs are entered in cells F5, F6, and F7 to indicate that each total value to their left cannot be allowed to exceed the corresponding number in column G. The spreadsheet still will allow you to enter trial solutions that violate the ≤ signs. However, these ≤

FIGURE 2.2

The complete spreadsheet for the Wyndor problem with an initial trial solution (both production rates equal to zero) entered into the changing cells (C9 and D9).

	A	B	C	D	E	F	G
1		Wyndor Glass Co. Product–Mix Problem					
2							
3			Hours Used per Unit Produced				Hours
4			Doors	Windows	Totals		Available
5		Plant 1	1	0	0	≤	4
6		Plant 2	0	2	0	≤	12
7		Plant 3	3	2	0	≤	18
8		Unit Profit	$300	$500	$0		
9		Solution	0	0			

signs serve as a reminder that such trial solutions need to be rejected if no changes are made in the numbers in column G.

Finally, since the answer to the third question is that the overall measure of performance is the total profit from the two products, this profit (per week) is entered in cell E8, just to the right of the data cells that are used to help calculate total profit. Much like the other numbers in column E, it is the sum of products. Since cells C8 and D8 give the profit from *each* door and window produced, the total profit per week from these products is

$$\text{Profit} = \$300(\text{\# of doors}) + \$500(\text{\# of windows})$$

Hence, the equation for cell E8 is

$$\text{E8} = \text{SUMPRODUCT(C8:D8, C9:D9)}$$

Cell E8 is a special kind of output cell. It is the particular cell that is being targeted to be made as large as possible when making the decisions on the production rates. Therefore, cell E8 is referred to as the **target cell** (or *objective cell*).

Figure 2.3 summarizes all the above formulas that need to be entered in the Totals column (column E) for the Wyndor problem. This completes the formulation of the spreadsheet model for the Wyndor problem.

With this formulation, it becomes easy to analyze any trial solution for the production rates. Each time production rates are entered in cells C9 and D9, Excel immediately calculates the values in the Totals column. For example, Figure 2.4 shows the spreadsheet when the production rates are set at four doors per week and three windows per week. Cell E8 shows that this yields a total profit of $2,700 per week. Also note that E5 = G5, E6 < G6, and E7 = G7, so the ≤ signs in column F are all satisfied. Thus, this trial solution is *feasible*. However, it would *not* be feasible to further increase both production rates, since this would cause E5 > G5 and E7 > G7.

FIGURE 2.3

The spreadsheet model for the Wyndor problem, including the formulas for the output cells in column D, where the objective is to maximize the target cell (E8).

	A	B	C	D	E	F	G
1		Wyndor Glass Co. Product–Mix Problem					
2							
3			Hours Used per Unit Produced				Hours
4			Doors	Windows	Totals		Available
5		Plant 1	1	0	0	≤	4
6		Plant 2	0	2	0	≤	12
7		Plant 3	3	2	0	≤	18
8		Unit Profit	$300	$500	$0		
9		Solution	0	0			

	E
5	=SUMPRODUCT(C5:D5,C9:D9)
6	=SUMPRODUCT(C6:D6,C9:D9)
7	=SUMPRODUCT(C7:D7,C9:D9)
8	=SUMPRODUCT(C8:D8,C9:D9)

FIGURE 2.4

The spreadsheet for the Wyndor problem with a new trial solution entered into the changing cells (C9 and D9).

	A	B	C	D	E	F	G
1		Wyndor Glass Co. Product–Mix Problem					
2							
3			Hours Used per Unit Produced				Hours
4			Doors	Windows	Totals		Available
5		Plant 1	1	0	4	≤	4
6		Plant 2	0	2	6	≤	12
7		Plant 3	3	2	18	≤	18
8		Unit Profit	$300	$500	$2,700		
9		Solution	4	3			

Does this trial solution provide the best mix of production rates? Not necessarily. It might be possible to further increase the total profit by simultaneously increasing one production rate and decreasing the other. However, it is not necessary to continue using trial and error to explore such possibilities. We shall describe in Section 2.6 how the Excel Solver can be used to quickly find the best (optimal) solution.

This Spreadsheet Model Is a Linear Programming Model

The spreadsheet model displayed in Figure 2.3 is an example of a *linear programming* model. The reason is that it possesses all the following characteristics.

Characteristics of a Linear Programming Model on a Spreadsheet
1. Decisions need to be made on the levels of a number of activities, so *changing cells* are used to display these levels.
2. These activity levels can have any value (including fractional values) that satisfy a number of constraints.
3. Each **constraint** (that is, each restriction on the feasible values of the decisions on activity levels) has either an output cell or a changing cell on the left, a mathematical sign in the middle, and a data cell on the right. The three options for the mathematical sign to choose are $\leq$, $\geq$, and $=$.
4. The decisions on activity levels are to be based on an overall measure of performance, which is entered in the *target cell*. The objective is to either *maximize* the target cell or *minimize* the target cell, depending on the nature of the measure of performance.
5. The Excel equation for each *output cell* (including the target cell) can be expressed as a SUMPRODUCT function,[5] where each term in the sum is the product of a *data cell* and a *changing cell*.

Characteristics 2 and 5 are key ones for differentiating a linear programming model from other kinds of mathematical models that can be formulated on a spreadsheet.

Characteristic 2 rules out situations where the activity levels need to have *integer* values. For example, such a situation would arise in the Wyndor problem if the decisions to be made were the *total* numbers of doors and windows to produce (which must be integers) rather than the numbers per week (which can have fractional values since a door or window can be started in one week and completed in the next week).

Characteristic 5 prohibits those cases where the Excel equation for an output cell cannot be expressed as a SUMPRODUCT function. To illustrate such a case, suppose that the weekly profit from producing Wyndor's new windows can be *more* than doubled by doubling the production rate because of economies in marketing larger amounts. This would mean that the Excel equation for the target cell would need to be more complicated than a SUMPRODUCT function.

We will defer to Chapter 8 consideration of how to formulate models for these more complicated kinds of situations.

Summary of the Formulation Procedure

The procedure used to formulate a linear programming model on a spreadsheet for the Wyndor problem can be adapted to many other problems as well. Here is a summary of the steps involved in the procedure.

1. Gather the data for the problem (such as summarized in Table 2.1 for the Wyndor problem).
2. Enter the data into *data cells* on a spreadsheet.
3. Identify the decisions to be made on the levels of activities and designate *changing cells* for displaying these decisions.
4. Identify the constraints on these decisions and introduce *output cells* as needed to specify these constraints.
5. Choose the overall measure of performance to be entered into the *target cell*.
6. Use a SUMPRODUCT function to enter the appropriate value into each output cell (including the target cell).

---

[5]There also are some special situations where a SUM function can be used instead because all the numbers that would have gone into the corresponding data cells are 1's. Chapter 5 will show some examples.

This procedure does not spell out the details of how to set up the spreadsheet. There generally are alternative ways of doing this rather than a single "right" way. One of the great strengths of spreadsheets is their flexibility for dealing with a wide variety of problems.

Review Questions

1. What are the three questions that need to be answered to begin the process of formulating a linear programming model on a spreadsheet?
2. What are the roles for the data cells, the changing cells, the output cells, and the target cell when formulating such a model?
3. What is the form of the Excel equation for each output cell (including the target cell) when formulating such a model.

2.4 The Mathematical Model in the Spreadsheet

There are two widely used methods for formulating a linear programming model. One is to formulate it directly on a spreadsheet, as described in the preceding section. The other is to use algebra to present the model. The two versions of the model are equivalent. The only difference is whether the language of spreadsheets or the language of algebra is used to describe the model. Both versions have their advantages, and it can be helpful to be bilingual. For example, the two versions lead to different, but complementary, ways of analyzing problems like the Wyndor problem (as discussed in the next two sections). Since this book emphasizes the spreadsheet approach, we will only briefly describe the algebraic approach.

Formulating the Wyndor Model Algebraically

The reasoning for the algebraic approach is similar to that for the spreadsheet approach. In fact, except for making entries on a spreadsheet, the initial steps are just as described in the preceding section for the Wyndor problem.

1. Gather the relevant data (Table 2.1 in Section 2.2).
2. Identify the decisions to be made (the production rates for the two new products).
3. Identify the constraints on these decisions (the production time used in the respective plants cannot exceed the amount available).
4. Identify the overall measure of performance for these decisions (the total profit from the two products).
5. Convert the verbal description of the constraints and measure of performance into quantitative expressions in terms of the data and decisions (see below).

Table 2.1 indicates that the number of hours of production time available per week for the two new products in the respective plants are 4, 12, and 18. Using the data in this table for the number of hours used per door or window produced then leads to the following quantitative expressions for the constraints:

$$\text{Plant 1:} \quad (\text{\# of doors}) \leq 4$$

$$\text{Plant 2:} \quad 2(\text{\# of windows}) \leq 12$$

$$\text{Plant 3:} \quad 3(\text{\# of doors}) + 2(\text{\# of windows}) \leq 18$$

In addition, negative production rates are impossible, so two other constraints on the decisions are

$$(\text{\# of doors}) \geq 0 \qquad (\text{\# of windows}) \geq 0$$

The overall measure of performance has been identified as the total profit from the two products. Since Table 2.1 gives the unit profits for doors and windows as $300 and $500, respectively, the expression obtained in the preceding section for the total profit per week from these products is

$$\text{Profit} = \$300(\text{\# of doors}) + \$500(\text{\# of windows})$$

The objective is to make the decisions (number of doors and number of windows) so as to maximize this profit, subject to satisfying all the constraints identified above.

To state this objective in a compact algebraic model, we introduce algebraic symbols to represent the measure of performance and the decisions. Let

P = Profit (total profit per week from the two products, in dollars)
D = # of doors (number of the special new doors to be produced per week)
W = # of windows (number of the special new windows to be produced per week).

Substituting these symbols into the above expressions for the constraints and the measure of performance (and dropping the dollar signs in the latter expression), the linear programming model for the Wyndor problem now can be written in algebraic form as shown below.

ALGEBRAIC MODEL

Choose the values of D and W so as to maximize

$$P = 300D + 500W$$

subject to satisfying all the following constraints:

$$D \leq 4$$
$$2W \leq 12$$
$$3D + 2W \leq 18$$

and

$$D \geq 0 \qquad W \geq 0$$

Some Terminology for Linear Programming Models

Much of the terminology of algebraic models also is sometimes used with spreadsheet models. Here are the key terms in the context of the Wyndor problem.

1. D and W (or C9 and D9 in Figure 2.3) are the **decision variables.**
2. $300D + 500W$ (or C8 * C9 + D8 * D9) is the **objective function.**
3. P (or E8) is the *value of the objective function* (or *objective value* for short).
4. $D \geq 0$ and $W \geq 0$ (or C9 $\geq$ 0 and D9 $\geq$ 0) are called the **nonnegativity constraints** (or *nonnegativity conditions*).
5. The other constraints are referred to as **functional constraints** (or *structural constraints*).
6. The **parameters** of the model are the constants in the algebraic model (the numbers in the data cells).
7. *Any* choice of values for the decision variables (regardless of how desirable or undesirable the choice) is called a **solution** for the model.
8. A **feasible solution** is one that satisfies all the constraints, whereas an **infeasible solution** violates at least one constraint.
9. The *best* feasible solution, the one that maximizes P (or E8), is called the **optimal solution.**

Comparisons

So what are the relative advantages of algebraic models and spreadsheet models? An algebraic model provides a very concise and explicit statement of the problem. Sophisticated software packages that can solve huge problems generally are based on algebraic models because of both their compactness and their ease of use in rescaling the size of a problem. Management science practitioners with an extensive mathematical background find algebraic models very useful. For others, however, spreadsheet models are far more intuitive. Many very intelligent people (including many managers and business students) find algebraic models overly abstract. Spreadsheets lift this "algebraic curtain." Both managers and business students training to be managers generally live with spreadsheets, not algebraic models. Therefore, the emphasis throughout this book is on spreadsheet models.

Review Questions

1. When formulating a linear programming model, what are the initial steps that are the same with either a spreadsheet formulation or an algebraic formulation?
2. When formulating a linear programming model algebraically, algebraic symbols need to be introduced to represent which kinds of quantities in the model?
3. What are decision variables for a linear programming model? The objective function? Nonnegativity constraints? Functional constraints?
4. What is meant by a feasible solution for the model? An optimal solution?

2.5 The Graphical Method for Solving Two-Variable Problems

Linear programming problems having only two decision variables, like the Wyndor problem, can be solved by a **graphical method.**

Although this method cannot be used to solve problems with more than two decision variables (and most linear programming problems have far more than two), it still is well worth learning. The procedure provides geometric intuition about linear programming and what it is trying to achieve. This intuition is helpful in analyzing larger problems that cannot be solved directly by the graphical method.

It is more convenient to apply the graphical method to the *algebraic version* of the linear programming model rather than the spreadsheet version. We shall illustrate the method by using the algebraic model obtained for the Wyndor problem in the preceding section. For this purpose, keep in mind that

D = production rate for the special new doors (the number in changing cell C9 of the spreadsheet)

W = production rate for the special new windows (the number in changing cell D9 of the spreadsheet)

Displaying Solutions as Points on a Graph

The key to the graphical method is the fact that possible solutions can be displayed as points on a two-dimensional graph that has a horizontal axis giving the value of D and a vertical axis giving the value of W. Figure 2.5 shows some sample points.

> *Notation*: Either $(D, W) = (2, 3)$ or just $(2, 3)$ refers to both the solution and the point in the graph where $D = 2$ and $W = 3$. Similarly, $(D, W) = (4, 6)$ means $D = 4$ and $W = 6$, whereas the origin $(0, 0)$ means $D = 0$ and $W = 0$.

To find the optimal solution (the best feasible solution), we first need to display graphically where the feasible solutions are. To do this, we must consider each constraint, identify the solutions graphically that are permitted by that constraint, and then combine this information to identify the solutions permitted by all the constraints.

To begin, the constraint $D \geq 0$ implies that consideration must be limited to points that lie on or to the right of the W axis in Figure 2.5. Similarly, the constraint $W \geq 0$ restricts consideration to the points on or above the D axis. Combining these two facts, the region of interest at this juncture is the one shaded in on Figure 2.6. (This region also includes *larger* values of D and W than can be shown shaded in the available space.)

Graphing Nonnegative Solutions Permitted by Each Functional Constraint

We now will look individually at the nonnegative solutions that are permitted by each functional constraint. Later, we will combine all these constraints.

Let us begin with the first functional constraint, $D \leq 4$, which limits the usage of Plant 1 for producing the special new doors to a maximum of four hours per week. The solutions permitted by this constraint are those that lie on, or to the left of, the vertical line that intercepts the D axis at $D = 4$ (so $D = 4$ is the equation for the line). Combining this permissible region with the one given in Figure 2.6 yields the shaded region shown in Figure 2.7.

The second functional constraint, $2W \leq 12$, has a similar effect, except now the boundary of its permissible region is given by a *horizontal* line with the equation, $2W = 12$ (or $W = 6$), as shown in Figure 2.8. The line forming the boundary of what is permitted by a

FIGURE 2.5

Graph showing the points (D, W) = (2, 3) and (D, W) = (4, 6) for the Wyndor Glass Co. product-mix problem.

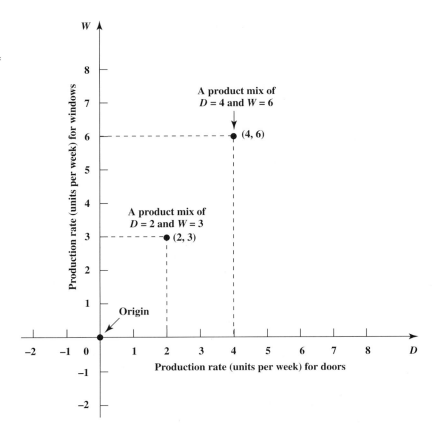

FIGURE 2.6

Graph showing that the constraints D ≥ 0 and W ≥ 0 rule out solutions for the Wyndor Glass Co. product-mix problem that are to the left of the vertical axis or under the horizontal axis.

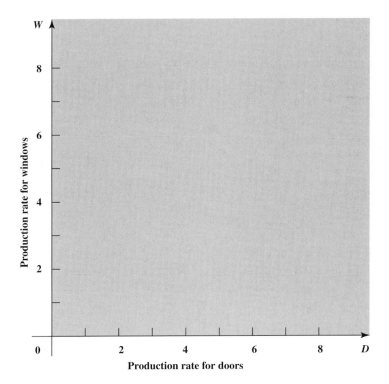

constraint is sometimes referred to as a **constraint boundary line,** and its equation may be called a **constraint boundary equation.** Frequently, a *constraint boundary line* is identified by its equation.

For each of the first two functional constraints, $D \leq 4$ and $2W \leq 12$, note that the equation for the constraint boundary line ($D = 4$ and $2W = 12$, respectively) is obtained

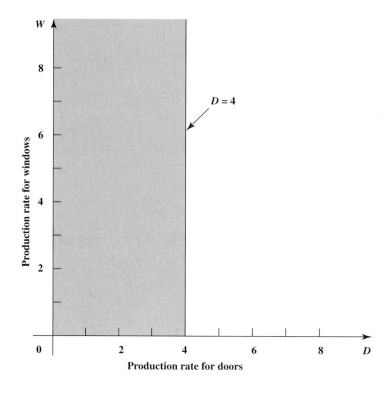

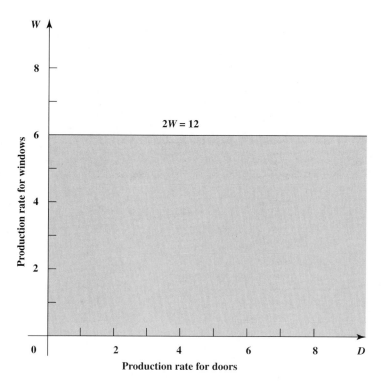

by replacing the inequality sign with an equality sign. For *any* constraint with an inequality sign (whether a functional constraint or a nonnegativity constraint), the general rule for obtaining its constraint boundary equation is to substitute an equality sign for the inequality sign.

We now need to consider one more functional constraint, $3D + 2W \leq 18$. Its constraint boundary equation

$$3D + 2W = 18$$

FIGURE 2.9

Graph showing that the boundary line for the constraint 3D + 2W ≤ 18 intercepts the horizontal axis at D = 6 and intercepts the vertical axis at W = 9.

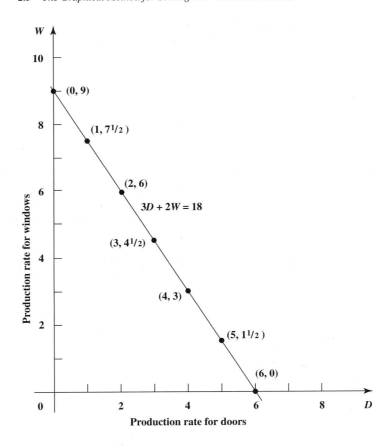

includes both variables, so the boundary line it represents is neither a vertical line nor a horizontal line. Therefore, the boundary line must intercept (cross through) both axes somewhere. But where?

When a constraint boundary line is neither a vertical line nor a horizontal line, the line *intercepts* the D axis at the point on the line where $W = 0$. Similarly, the line *intercepts* the W axis at the point on the line where $D = 0$.

Hence, the constraint boundary line $3D + 2W = 18$ intercepts the D axis at the point where $W = 0$.

When $W = 0$, $3D + 2W = 18$ becomes $3D = 18$
so the intercept with the D axis is at $D = 6$

Similarly, the line intercepts the W axis where $D = 0$.

When $D = 0$, $3D + 2W = 18$ becomes $2W = 18$
so the intercept with the D axis is at $W = 9$

Consequently, the constraint boundary line is the line that passes through these two intercept points, as shown in Figure 2.9.

Another way to find this constraint boundary line is to change the form of the constraint boundary equation so that it expresses W in terms of D.

$$3D + 2W = 18 \quad \text{implies} \quad 2W = -3D + 18$$

so

$$W = -\frac{3}{2}D + 9$$

This form, $W = -\frac{3}{2}D + 9$, is called the **slope-intercept form** of the constraint boundary equation.

The constant term, 9, automatically is the intercept of the line with the W axis (since $W = 9$ when $D = 0$). The coefficient of D, $-\tfrac{3}{2}$, is the *slope* of the line.

The **slope of a line** is the change in W when D is increased by 1.

For example, consider the series of points shown on the constraint boundary line in Figure 2.9 when moving from $(0,9)$ toward $(6,0)$. Note how W changes by the fixed amount $-\tfrac{3}{2}$ each time D is increased by 1.

This derivation of the *slope-intercept form* demonstrates that the *only* numbers in the equation $3D + 2W = 18$ that determine the slope of the line are 3 and 2, the coefficients of D and W. Therefore, if the equation $3D + 2W = 18$ were to be changed *only* by changing the right-hand side (18), the slope of the new line still would be $-\tfrac{3}{2}$. In other words, the new line would be *parallel* to the original line. To illustrate, suppose that the new equation is $3D + 2W = 12$. Since the original line had an intercept with the W axis of $\tfrac{18}{2} = 9$, the new parallel line has an intercept of $\tfrac{12}{2} = 6$, so the new line is closer to the origin, as shown in Figure 2.10. This figure also shows the parallel line for the equation, $3D + 2W = 24$, which has an intercept with the W axis of $\tfrac{24}{2} = 12$, and so is further from the origin than the original line.

This analysis also shows that the solutions permitted by the constraint $3D + 2W \leq 18$ are those that lie on the *origin* side of the constraint boundary line $3D + 2W = 18$. The easiest way to verify this is to check whether the origin itself, $(D, W) = (0,0)$, satisfies the constraint.[6] If it does, then the permissible region lies on the side of the constraint boundary line where the origin is. Otherwise, it lies on the other side. In this case,

FIGURE 2.10

Graph showing that changing only the right-hand side of a constraint (such as $3D + 2W \leq 18$) creates parallel constraint boundary lines.

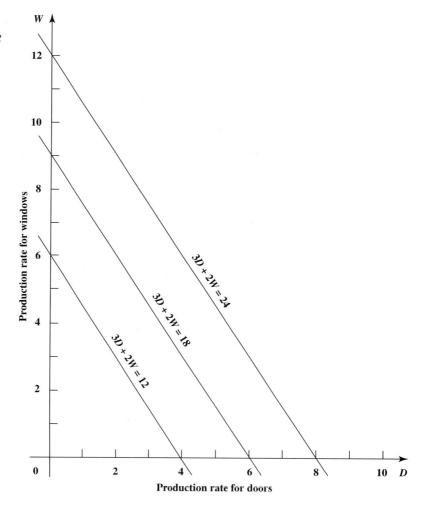

---

[6]The one case where using the origin to help determine the permissible region does *not* work is if the constraint boundary line passes through the origin. In this case, any other point *not* lying on this line can be used just like the origin.

$$3(0) + 2(0) = 0$$

so $(D, W) = (0, 0)$ satisfies

$$3D + 2W \leq 18$$

(In fact, the origin satisfies *any* constraint with a $\leq$ sign and a positive right-hand side.) Therefore, the region permitted by this constraint is the one shown in Figure 2.11.

Graphing the Feasible Region

We now have graphed the region where solutions are permitted by the *individual* constraints in Figures 2.6, 2.7, 2.8, and 2.11. However, a feasible solution for a linear programming problem must satisfy *all* the constraints *simultaneously.* To find where these feasible solutions are located, we need to combine all the constraints in one graph and identify the points representing the solutions that are in *every* constraint's permissible region.

Figure 2.12 shows the constraint boundary line for each of the three functional constraints. We also have added arrows to each line to show which side of the line is permitted by the corresponding constraint (as identified in the preceding figures). Note that the nonnegative solutions permitted by each of these constraints lie on the side of the constraint boundary line where the origin is (or on the line itself). Therefore, the *feasible solutions* are those that lie nearer to the origin than *all three* constraint boundary lines (or on the line nearest the origin). The resulting region of feasible solutions, called the **feasible region,** is the shaded portion of Figure 2.12.

Graphing the Objective Function

Having identified the feasible region, the final step is to find which of these feasible solutions is the best one—the *optimal solution.* For the Wyndor problem, the objective happens to be to *maximize* the total profit per week from the two products (denoted by P). Therefore, we want to find the feasible solution (D, W) that makes the value of the objective function

$$P = 300D + 500W$$

as large as possible.

To accomplish this, we need to be able to locate all the points (D, W) on the graph that give a specified value of the objective function. For example, consider a value of $P = 1,500$ for the objective function. Which points (D, W) give $300D + 500W = 1,500$?

FIGURE 2.11

Graph showing that nonnegative solutions permitted by the constraint 3D + 2W ≤ 18 lie within the triangle formed by the two axes and this constraint's boundary line, 3D + 2W = 18.

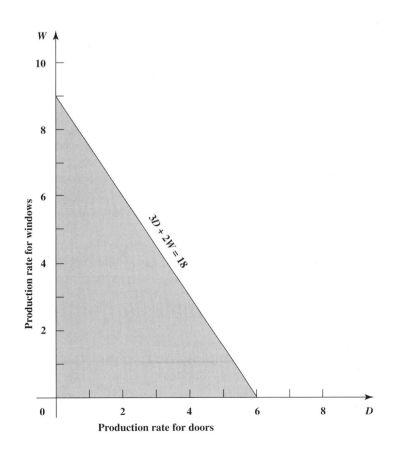

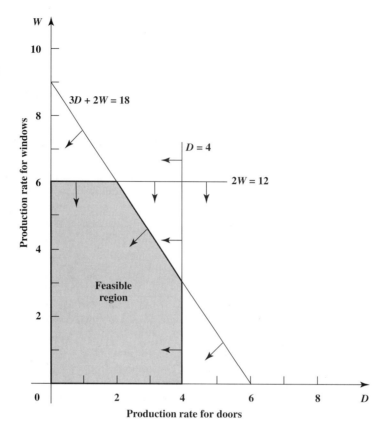

This equation is the equation of a *line*. Just as when plotting constraint boundary lines, the location of this line is found by identifying its intercepts with the two axes. When $W = 0$, this equation yields $D = 5$, and similarly, $W = 3$ when $D = 0$, so these are the two intercepts, as shown in Figure 2.13.

$P = 1,500$ is just one sample value of the objective function. For any other specified value of P, the points (D, W) that give this value of P also lie on a line called an *objective function line*.

An **objective function line** is a line whose points all have the same value of the objective function.

For the objective function line in Figure 2.13, the points on this line that lie in the feasible region provide alternate ways of achieving an objective function value of $P = 1,500$. Can we do better? Let us try doubling the value of P to $P = 3,000$. The corresponding objective function line

$$300D + 500W = 3,000$$

is shown as the middle line in Figure 2.14. (Ignore the top line for the moment.) Once again, this line includes points in the feasible region, so $P = 3,000$ is achievable.

Let us pause to note two interesting features of these objective function lines for $P = 1,500$ and $P = 3,000$. First, these lines are *parallel*. Second, *doubling* the value of P from 1,500 to 3,000 also *doubles* the value of W at which the line intercepts the W axis from $W = 3$ to $W = 6$. These features are no coincidence, as indicated by the following properties.

Key Properties of Objective Function Lines: All objective function lines for the same problem are *parallel*. Furthermore, the value of W at which an objective function line intercepts the W axis is *proportional* to the value of P.

To see why these properties hold, look at the *slope-intercept form* of an objective function line for the Wyndor problem:

$$W = -\frac{300}{500}D + \frac{1}{500}P$$

FIGURE 2.13

Graph showing the line containing all the points (D, W) that give a value of P = 1,500 for the objective function.

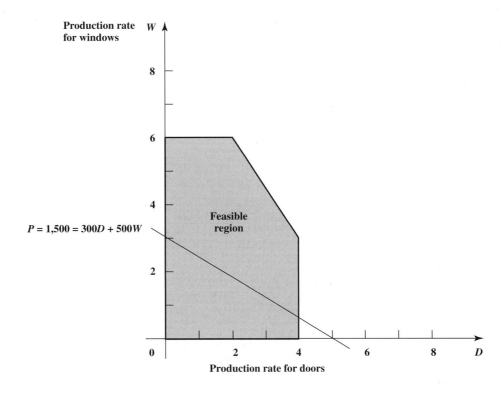

FIGURE 2.14

Graph showing the three objective function lines for the Wyndor Glass Co. product-mix problem, where the top one passes through the optimal solution.

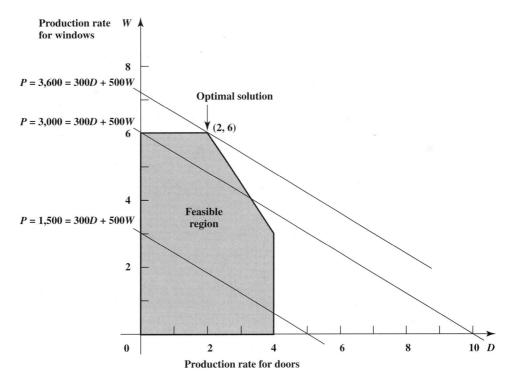

which reduces to

$$W = -\frac{3}{5}D + \frac{1}{500}P$$

This slope-intercept form indicates that the *slope* of the lines for various values of *P* always is the *same*, $-\frac{3}{5}$, so these lines are parallel. Furthermore, this form indicates that the value of *W* at which a line intercepts the *W* axis is $\frac{1}{500}P$, so this value of *W* is *proportional* to *P*.

These key properties of objective function lines suggest the strategy to follow to find the optimal solution. We already have tried $P = 1,500$ and $P = 3,000$ in Figure 2.14 and found that their objective function lines include points in the feasible region. Increasing P again will generate another parallel objective function line farther from the origin. The objective function line of special interest is the one farthest from the origin that still includes a point in the feasible region. This is the third objective function line in Figure 2.14. The point on this line that is in the feasible region, $(D, W) = (2, 6)$, is the optimal solution since no other feasible solution has a larger value of P.

OPTIMAL SOLUTION

$D = 2$ (Produce 2 special new doors per week)

$W = 6$ (Produce 6 special new windows per week)

These values of D and W can be substituted into the objective function to find the value of P.

$$P = 300D + 500W = 300(2) + 500(6) = 3,600$$

You can graphically implement this strategy for finding the optimal solution by using any straight edge, such as a ruler. Rotate the straight edge in the feasible region until it has the slope of the objective function lines. (You can use any objective function line, such as the $P = 1,500$ line in Figure 2.13, to obtain this slope.) Then push the straight edge with this fixed slope through the feasible region in the direction that increases P. Stop moving the straight edge at the last instant that it still passes through a point in the feasible region. This point is the optimal solution.

In addition to finding the optimal solution, another important use of the graphical method is to perform *what-if analysis* to determine what would happen to the optimal solution if any of the numbers (parameters) in the model change. The graphical approach provides key insights for answering a variety of what-if questions. We will pursue this topic further in Chapter 4.

Summary of the Graphical Method

The graphical method can be used to solve any linear programming problem having only two decision variables. The method uses the following steps:

1. Draw the constraint boundary line for each functional constraint. Use the origin (or any point not on the line) to determine which side of the line is permitted by the constraint.
2. Find the feasible region by determining where all constraints are satisfied simultaneously.
3. Determine the slope of one objective function line. All other objective function lines will have the same slope.
4. Move a straight edge with this slope through the feasible region in the direction of improving values of the objective function. Stop at the last instant that the straight edge still passes through a point in the feasible region. This line given by the straight edge is the optimal objective function line.
5. A feasible point on the optimal objective function line is an optimal solution.

Review Questions

1. The graphical method can be used to solve linear programming problems with how many decision variables?
2. What do the axes represent when applying the graphical method to the Wyndor problem?
3. What is a constraint boundary line? A constraint boundary equation?
4. In the slope-intercept form of a constraint boundary equation, which part of the equation gives the *slope* of the constraint boundary line? Which part gives the point on the vertical axis where the line intercepts this axis?
5. What is the easiest way of determining which side of a constraint boundary line is permitted by the constraint?

2.6 Using Excel to Solve Linear Programming Problems

The graphical method is very useful for gaining geometric intuition about linear programming, but its practical use is severely limited by only being able to solve tiny problems with two decision variables. Another procedure that will solve linear programming problems of any reasonable size is needed. Fortunately, Excel includes a tool called **Solver** that will do this once the spreadsheet model has been formulated as described in Section 2.3. (A more powerful version of Solver, called *Premium Solver,* also is available in your MS Courseware.)

Figure 2.3 in Section 2.3 shows the spreadsheet model for the Wyndor problem, where the key cells (C9, D9, and E8) have been highlighted. The values of the decision variables (the production rates for the two products) are in the *changing cells,* C9 and D9, and the value of the objective function (the total profit per week from the two products) is in the *target cell,* E8. To get started, an arbitrary trial solution has been entered by placing zeroes in the changing cells. The Solver will then change these to the optimal values after solving the problem.

This procedure is started by choosing Solver in the Tools menu. The Solver dialogue box is shown in Figure 2.15.

Before the Solver can start its work, it needs to know exactly where each component of the model is located on the spreadsheet. You can either type in the cell addresses or click on them. The addresses are entered as E8 for the target cell and the range C9:D9 for the changing cells. Excel then automatically enters the dollar signs shown in Figure 2.15 to fix these addresses. Since the goal is to maximize the target cell, Max also has been selected.

Next, the cells containing the functional constraints need to be specified. This is done by clicking on the Add button on the Solver dialogue box. This brings up the Add Constraint dialogue box shown in Figure 2.16. The ≤ signs in cells F5, F6, and F7 of Figure 2.3 are a reminder that the cells E5 through E7 all need to be less than or equal to the corresponding cells in G5 through G7. These constraints are specified for the Solver by entering the range E5:E7 on the left-hand side of the Add Constraint dialogue box and the range G5:G7 on the right-hand side. For the sign between these two sides, there is a menu to choose between <=, =, or >=, so <= has been chosen. This choice is needed even though ≤ signs were previously entered in column F of the spreadsheet because the Solver only uses the constraints that are specified with the Add Constraint dialogue box.

If there were more functional constraints to add, you would click on Add to bring up a new Add Constraint dialogue box. However, since there are no more in this example, the next step is to click on OK to go back to the Solver dialogue box.

FIGURE 2.15

The Solver dialogue box after specifying which cells in Figure 2.3 are the target cell and the changing cells, plus indicating that the target cell is to be maximized.

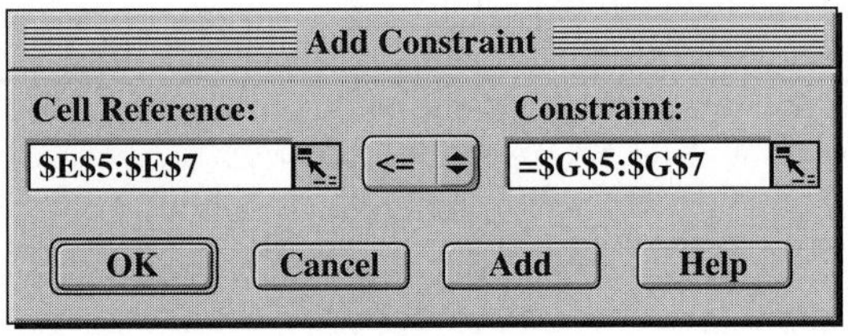

FIGURE 2.16

The Add Constraint dialogue box after specifying that cells E5, E6, and E7 in Figure 2.3 are required to be less than or equal to cells G5, G6, and G7, respectively.

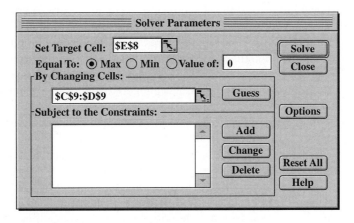

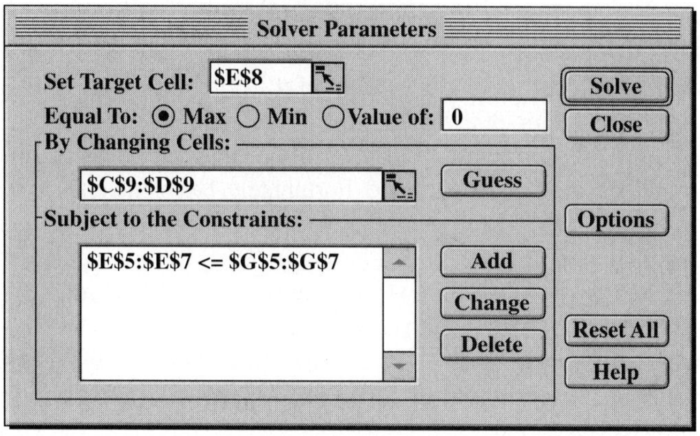

FIGURE 2.17

The Solver dialogue box after specifying the entire model in terms of the spreadsheet.

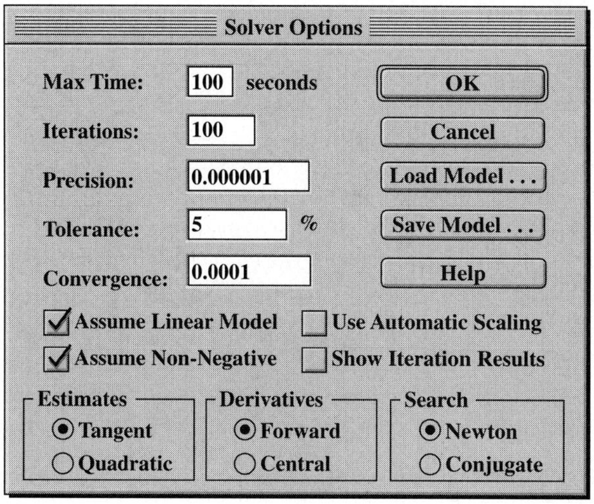

FIGURE 2.18

The Solver Options dialogue box after checking the Assume Linear Model and Assume Non-Negative options to indicate that we wish to solve a linear programming model that has nonnegativity constraints.

The Solver dialogue box now summarizes the complete model (see Figure 2.17) in terms of the spreadsheet in Figure 2.3. However, before asking Solver to solve the model, one more step should be taken. Clicking on the Options button brings up the dialogue box shown in Figure 2.18. This box allows you to specify a number of options about how the problem will be solved. The most important of these are the Assume Linear Model option and the Assume Non-Negative option. Be sure that both options are checked as shown in the figure. This tells Solver that the problem is a *linear* programming problem and that non-negativity constraints are needed for the changing cells to reject negative production rates.[7] Regarding the other options, accepting the default values shown in the figure usually is fine for small problems. Clicking on the OK button then returns you to the Solver dialogue box.

Now you are ready to click on Solve in the Solver dialogue box, which will start the solving of the problem in the background. After a few seconds (for a small problem), Solver will then indicate the results. Typically, it will indicate that it has found an optimal solution, as specified in the Solver Results dialogue box shown in Figure 2.19. If the model has no feasible solutions or no optimal solution, the dialogue box will indicate that instead by stating that "Solver could not find a feasible solution" or that "The Set Cell values do not converge." (Section 16.1 will describe how these possibilities can occur.) The dialogue box also presents the option of generating various reports. One of these (the Sensitivity Report) will be discussed in detail in Chapter 4.

After solving the model, the Solver replaces the original numbers in the changing cells with the optimal numbers, as shown in Figure 2.20. Thus, the optimal solution is to produce

---

[7]In older versions of Excel prior to Excel 97, the Assume Non-Negative option is not available, so nonnegativity constraints have to be added with the Add Constraint dialogue box. Not every linear programming model has nonnegativity constraints, but nearly all do.

FIGURE 2.19

The Solver Results dialogue box that indicates that an optimal solution has been found.

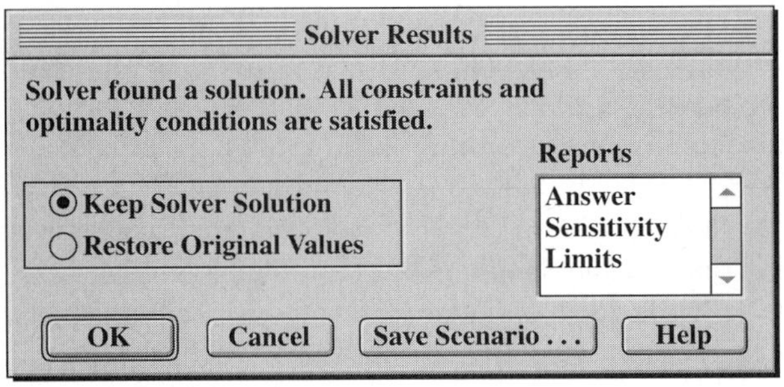

FIGURE 2.20

The spreadsheet obtained after solving the Wyndor problem.

	A	B	C	D	E	F	G
1		Wyndor Glass Co. Product–Mix Problem					
2							
3			Hours Used per Unit Produced				Hours
4			Doors	Windows	Totals		Available
5		Plant 1	1	0	2	≤	4
6		Plant 2	0	2	12	≤	12
7		Plant 3	3	2	18	≤	18
8		Unit Profit	$300	$500	$3,600		
9		Solution	2	6			

two doors per week and six windows per week, just as was found by the graphical method in the preceding section. The spreadsheet also indicates the corresponding number in the target cell (a total profit of $3,600 per week), as well as the numbers in the other output cells in column E.

At this point, you might want to check what would happen to the optimal solution if any of the numbers in the data cells were to be changed to other possible values. This is easy to do because Solver saves all the addresses for the target cell, changing cells, constraints, and so on when you save the file. All you need to do is make the changes you want in the data cells and then click on Solve in the Solver dialogue box again. (Chapter 4 will focus on this kind of *what-if analysis,* including how to use the Solver's Sensitivity Report to expedite the analysis.)

To assist you with experimenting with these kinds of changes, your MS Courseware includes an Excel file for this chapter (as for others) that provides a complete formulation and solution of the examples here (the Wyndor problem and the one in the next section) in a spreadsheet format. We encourage you to "play" with these examples to see what happens with different data, with different solutions, and so forth. You might also find these spreadsheets useful as templates for homework problems.

Review Questions

1. Which dialogue box is used to enter the addresses for the target cell and the changing cells?
2. Which dialogue box is used to specify the functional constraints for the model?
3. With the Solver Options dialogue box, which options normally need to be chosen to solve a linear programming model?

2.7 A Minimization Example—The Profit & Gambit Co. Advertising-Mix Problem

The analysis of the Wyndor Glass Co. case study in Sections 2.3 and 2.6 illustrated how to formulate and solve one type of linear programming model on a spreadsheet. The same general approach can be applied to many other problems as well. The great flexibility of linear programming and spreadsheets provides a variety of options for how to adapt the formulation of the spreadsheet model to fit each new problem. Our next example illustrates some options not used for the Wyndor problem.

Planning an Advertising Campaign

The Profit & Gambit Co. produces cleaning products for home use. This is a highly competitive market, and the company continually struggles to increase its market share. Management has decided to undertake a major new advertising campaign that will focus on the following three key products:

- A spray prewash stain remover.
- A new liquid laundry detergent.
- A well-established powder laundry detergent.

This campaign will use both television and the print media. A commercial has been developed to run on national television that will feature the liquid detergent to help establish this new product. The advertisement for the print media will promote all three products and will include cents-off coupons that consumers can use to purchase the products at reduced prices. Management has set minimum goals for the campaign: (1) The stain remover should capture an additional 3 percent of its market; (2) the new liquid detergent should gain 18 percent of the laundry detergent market; and (3) a 4 percent increase of this same market should be captured by the powder detergent. Table 2.2 shows the estimated increase in these market shares for each *unit* of advertising in the respective outlets. (A *unit* is a standard block of advertising that Profit & Gambit commonly purchases, but other amounts also are allowed.) The reason for −1 percent for the powder detergent in the Television column is that the TV commercial featuring the new liquid detergent will take away some sales from the powder detergent. The bottom row of the table shows the cost per unit of advertising for each of the two outlets.

Management's objective is to determine how much to advertise in each medium to meet the market share goals at a minimum total cost.

Formulating a Spreadsheet Model for This Problem

The procedure summarized at the end of Section 2.3 can be used to formulate the spreadsheet model for this problem. Each step of the procedure is repeated below, followed by a description of how it is performed here.

1. Gather the data for the problem. This has been done as presented in Table 2.2.
2. Enter the data into *data cells* on a spreadsheet. The top half of Figure 2.21 shows this spreadsheet. The data cells are in columns C and D (rows 6 to 9), as well as in column G. Note how this particular formatting of the spreadsheet has facilitated a direct transfer of the data from Table 2.2.
3. Identify the decisions to be made on the levels of activities and designate *changing cells* for making these decisions. In this case, the activities of concern are *advertising on television* and *advertising in the print media*. Therefore, the decisions to be made are

Decision 1: TV = number of units of advertising on television,

Decision 2: PM = number of units of advertising in the print media.

TABLE 2.2   Data for the Profit & Gambit Co. Advertising-Mix Problem

Product	Increase in Market Share per Unit of Advertising		Minimum Required Increase
	Television	*Print Media*	
Stain remover	0%	1%	3%
Liquid detergent	3%	2%	18%
Powder detergent	−1%	4%	4%
Unit cost	$1 million	$2 million	

Two of the shaded cells in Figure 2.21— C10 and D10 —have been designated as the changing cells to hold these numbers:

$$TV \rightarrow cell \; C10 \qquad PM \rightarrow cell \; D10$$

These are natural locations for the changing cells, since each one is in the column for the corresponding advertising medium and directly under its unit cost. To get started, an arbitrary trial solution (such as all zeroes) is entered into these cells. (Figure 2.21 shows the optimal solution after having already applied the Solver.)

4. Identify the constraints on these decisions and introduce *output cells* as needed to specify these constraints. The three constraints imposed by management are the minimum goals for the increased market share for the respective products, as shown in the rightmost column of Table 2.2. These constraints are

Stain remover: Total increase in market share $\geq$ 3%
Liquid detergent: Total increase in market share $\geq$ 18%
Powder detergent: Total increase in market share $\geq$ 4%

The second and third columns of Table 2.2 indicate that the *total* increases in market share from both forms of advertising are

$$\text{Total for stain remover} \quad = 1\% \text{ of PM}$$

$$\text{Total for liquid detergent} \; = 3\% \text{ of TV} + 2\% \text{ of PM}$$

$$\text{Total for powder detergent} = -1\% \text{ of TV} + 4\% \text{ of PM}$$

Consequently, since rows 6, 7, and 8 in the spreadsheet are being used to provide information about the three products, cells E6, E7, and E8 are introduced as output cells to show the total increase in market share for the respective products. In addition, $\geq$ signs have been entered in column F to remind us that the increased market shares need to be at least as large as the numbers in column G. (The use of $\geq$ signs here rather than $\leq$ signs is one key difference from the spreadsheet model for the Wyndor problem in Figure 2.3.)

5. Choose the overall measure of performance to be entered into the *target cell*. Management's stated objective is to determine how much to advertise in each medium to meet the market share goals at a *minimum total cost*. Therefore, the *total cost* of the advertising is entered in the target cell. The natural location for this cell is in the Cost row and Totals

FIGURE 2.21

The spreadsheet model for the Profit & Gambit problem, including the formulas for the output cells in column E and the specifications needed to set up the Solver. The changing cells (C10 and D10) show the optimal solution obtained by the Solver.

	A	B	C	D	E	F	G
1		Profit & Gambit Co. Advertising–Mix Problem					
2							
3		Increase in Market Share per Unit of Advertising					Minimum
4							Required
5			Television	Print Media	Totals		Increase
6		Stain Remover	0%	1%	3%	$\geq$	3%
7		Liquid Detergent	3%	2%	18%	$\geq$	18%
8		Powder Detergent	–1%	4%	8%	$\geq$	4%
9		Unit Cost ($millions)	1	2	10		
10		Solution	4	3			

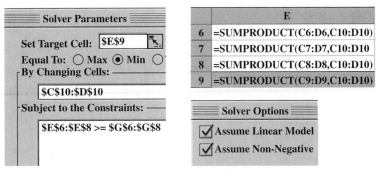

	E
6	=SUMPRODUCT(C6:D6,C10:D10)
7	=SUMPRODUCT(C7:D7,C10:D10
8	=SUMPRODUCT(C8:D8,C10:D10)
9	=SUMPRODUCT(C9:D9,C10:D10)

Solver Parameters

Set Target Cell: $E$9

Equal To: ○ Max ● Min ○
By Changing Cells:
$C$10:$D$10

Subject to the Constraints:
$E$6:$E$8 >= $G$6:$G$8

Solver Options

☑ Assume Linear Model
☑ Assume Non-Negative

column, so its address is E9. The bottom row of Table 2.2 indicates that the number going into this cell is

$$\text{Cost} = (\$1 \text{ million}) \text{ TV} + (\$2 \text{ million}) \text{ PM} \rightarrow \text{cell E9}$$

6. Use a SUMPRODUCT function to enter the appropriate value into each output cell (including the target cell). Based on the above expressions for cost and total increases in market share, the SUMPRODUCT functions needed here for the output cells are those shown directly under column E of the spreadsheet in Figure 2.21. Note that each of these functions involves the data cells in the same row and the changing cells, so that

$$E6 = C6 * C10 + D6 * D10$$

$$E7 = C7 * C10 + D7 * D10$$

$$E8 = C8 * C10 + D8 * D10$$

$$E9 = C9 * C10 + D9 * D10$$

which gives the desired totals.

This spreadsheet model is a linear programming model, since it possesses all the characteristics of such models enumerated in Section 2.3.

Applying the Solver to This Model

The procedure for using the Excel Solver to obtain an optimal solution for this model is basically the same as described in Section 2.6. The key part of the Solver dialogue box is shown in the lower left-hand corner of Figure 2.21. In addition to giving the addresses for the target cell and changing cells, the constraints that E6 ≥ G6, E7 ≥ G7, and E8 ≥ G8 have been specified in this box by using the Add Constraint dialogue box. Since the objective is to *minimize* total cost, Min also has been selected. (This is in contrast to the choice of Max for the Wyndor problem.)

The lower right-hand side of Figure 2.21 shows the options selected after clicking on the Options button in the Solver dialogue box. The Assume Linear Model option specifies that the model is a linear programming model. The Assume Non-Negative option specifies that the changing cells need nonnegativity constraints because negative values of advertising levels are not possible alternatives.

After clicking on Solve in the Solver dialogue box, the optimal solution shown in the changing cells of the spreadsheet in Figure 2.21 is obtained.

OPTIMAL SOLUTION

C10 = 4   (Undertake 4 units of advertising on television)

D10 = 3   (Undertake 3 units of advertising in the print media)

The target cell indicates that the total cost of this advertising plan would be $10 million.

The Mathematical Model in the Spreadsheet

When performing step 5 of the procedure for formulating a spreadsheet model, the total cost of advertising was determined to be

$$\text{Cost} = \text{TV} + 2\text{ PM}   \text{(in millions of dollars)}$$

where the objective is to choose the values of TV (number of units of advertising on television) and PM (number of units of advertising in the print media) so as to minimize this cost. Step 4 identified three functional constraints:

Stain remover: 1% of PM ≥ 3%
Liquid detergent: 3% of TV + 2% of PM ≥ 18%
Powder detergent: −1% of TV + 4% of PM ≥ 4%

Choosing the Assume Non-Negative option with the Solver recognized that TV and PM cannot be negative. Therefore, after dropping the percentage signs from the functional constraints, the complete mathematical model in the spreadsheet can be stated in the following succinct form.

Minimize   Cost = TV + 2 PM   (in millions of dollars)

subject to

Stain remover increased market share: PM $\geq$ 3
Liquid detergent increased market share: 3 TV + 2 PM $\geq$ 18
Powder detergent increased market share: $-$TV + 4 PM $\geq$ 4

and

$$TV \geq 0 \qquad PM \geq 0$$

Implicit in this statement is "Choose the values of TV and PM so as to . . . ." The term "subject to" is short hand for "Choose these values *subject to* the requirement that the values satisfy all the following constraints."

This model is the *algebraic* version of the *linear programming* model in the spreadsheet. Note how the parameters (constants) of this algebraic model come directly from the numbers in Table 2.2. In fact, the entire model could have been formulated directly from this table.

The differences between this algebraic model and the one obtained for the Wyndor problem in Section 2.4 lead to some interesting changes in how the graphical method is applied to solve the model. To further expand your geometric intuition about linear programming, we briefly describe this application of the graphical method next.

Applying the Graphical Method

Since this linear programming model has only two decision variables, it can be solved by the graphical method described in Section 2.5. The interesting new features here are how this method adapts to *minimization* and to functional constraints with a $\geq$ sign.

Figure 2.22 shows the feasible region for this model. The three constraint boundary lines are obtained in the manner described in Section 2.5. However, the arrows indicating which side of each line satisfies that constraint now all point away from the origin. The reason is that the origin does not satisfy any functional constraint with a $\geq$ sign and a positive right-hand side.

FIGURE 2.22

Graph showing the feasible region for the Profit & Gambit Co. advertising-mix problem, where the $\geq$ functional constraints have moved this region up and away from the origin.

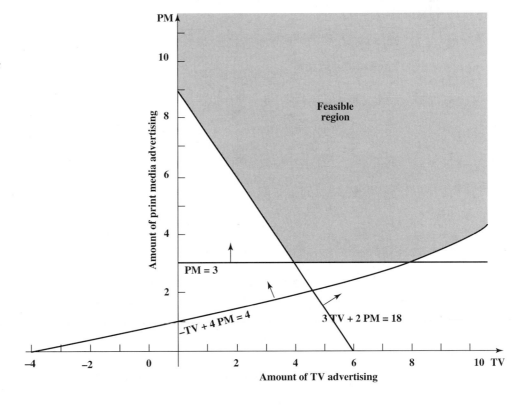

FIGURE 2.23

Graph showing two objective function lines for the Profit & Gambit Co. advertising-mix problem, where the bottom one passes through the optimal solution.

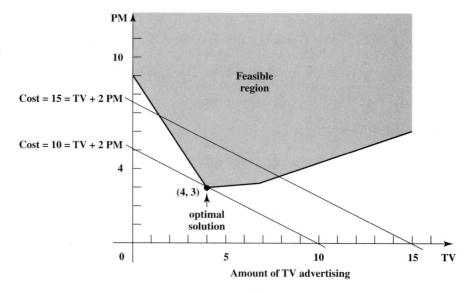

To find the *best* solution in this feasible region (one that minimizes Cost = TV + 2 PM), we first construct a sample objective function line for one specific value of the objective function that appears to be attainable, say, Cost = 15. Figure 2.23 shows that a large segment of this line passes through the feasible region. Since this is a *minimization* problem, we're looking for the *smallest* value of Cost that provides an objective function line that still passes through a point in the feasible region. The origin automatically has an objective function value of Cost = 0, so objective function lines with a positive value of Cost less than 15 will be closer to the origin than the Cost = 15 line. Therefore, we want to move from the Cost =15 line to objective function lines closer to the origin. Figure 2.23 shows the objective function line with the smallest value of Cost (10) that still passes through a point in the feasible region. This point, (TV, PM) = (4, 3), is the optimal solution.

Review Questions

1. What kind of product is produced by the Profit & Gambit Co.?
2. Which advertising media are being considered for the three products under consideration?
3. What is management's objective for the problem being addressed?
4. What was the rationale for the placement of the target cell and the changing cells in the spreadsheet model.
5. The algebraic form of the linear programming model for this problem differs from that for the Wyndor Glass Co. problem in which two major ways?
6. Does the solution $(x_1, x_2) = (0, 0)$ satisfy a $\geq$ functional constraint with a positive right-hand side?
7. For this minimization problem, should objective function lines passing through the feasible region be moved closer to the origin or further from the origin to reach the optimal solution?

2.8 Linear Programming from a Managerial Perspective

Linear programming is an invaluable aid to managerial decision making in all kinds of companies throughout the world. The emergence of powerful spreadsheet packages has helped to further spread the use of this technique. The ease of formulating and solving small linear programming models on a spreadsheet now enables some managers with a very modest background in management science to do this themselves on their own desktop. Many linear programming studies are major projects involving decisions on the levels of many hundreds or thousands of activities. Sophisticated software packages that go beyond spreadsheets generally are used for both the formulation and solution processes. Such studies normally are conducted by technically trained teams of management scientists, sometimes called operations research analysts, at the instigation of management. Management needs to keep in touch with the management science team to ensure that the study reflects management's objectives and needs. However, management generally does not get involved with the technical details of the study.

Consequently, there is little reason for a manager to know the details of how linear programming models are solved beyond the rudiments of using the Excel Solver. (Even most management science teams will use commercial software packages for solving their models on a computer rather than developing their own software.) Similarly, a manager does not need to know the technical details of how to formulate complex models, how to validate such a model, how to interact with the computer when formulating and solving a large model, how to efficiently perform what-if analysis with such a model, and so forth. Therefore, these technical details are de-emphasized in this book. A student who becomes interested in conducting technical analyses as part of a management science team should plan to take additional, more technically oriented courses in management science.

So what does an enlightened manager need to know about linear programming? A manager needs to have a good intuitive feeling for what linear programming is. One objective of this chapter is to begin to develop that intuition. That's the purpose of studying the graphical method for solving two-variable problems. It is rare to have a *real* linear programming problem with as few as two decision variables. Therefore, the graphical method has essentially no practical value for solving real problems. However, it has great value for conveying the basic notion that linear programming involves pushing up against constraint boundaries and moving objective function values in a favorable direction as far as possible. You also will see in Chapter 16 that this approach provides considerable geometric insight into how to analyze larger models by other methods.

A manager must also have an appreciation for the relevance and power of linear programming to encourage its use where appropriate. For *future* managers using this book, this appreciation is being promoted by describing *real* applications of linear programming and the resulting impact, as well as by including (in miniature form) various realistic examples and case studies that illustrate what can be done.

Certainly a manager must be able to recognize situations where linear programming is applicable. We focus on developing this skill in the next chapter, where you will learn how to recognize the *identifying features* for each of the three major types of linear programming problems (and their mixtures).

In addition, a manager should recognize situations where linear programming should *not* be applied. Chapter 8 will help to develop this skill by examining the underlying assumptions of linear programming and the circumstances that violate these assumptions. Chapter 8 also describes other approaches that *can* be applied where linear programming should not.

A manager needs to be able to distinguish between competent and shoddy studies using linear programming (or any other management science technique). Therefore, another goal of the upcoming chapters is to demystify the overall process involved in conducting a management science study, all the way from first studying a problem to final implementation of the managerial decisions based on the study. This is one purpose of the case studies throughout the book.

Finally, a manager must understand how to interpret the results of a linear programming study. He or she especially needs to understand what kinds of information can be obtained through *what-if analysis*, as well as the implications of such information for managerial decision making. Chapter 4 focuses on these issues.

Review Questions

1. Does management generally get heavily involved with the technical details of a linear programming study?

2. What is the purpose of studying the graphical method for solving problems with two decision variables when essentially all real linear programming problems have more than two?

3. List the things that an enlightened manager should know about linear programming?

2.9 Summary

Linear programming is a powerful technique for aiding managerial decision making for certain kinds of problems. The basic approach is to formulate a mathematical model called a linear programming model to represent the problem and then to analyze this model. Any linear programming model includes decision variables to represent the decisions to be made, constraints to represent the restrictions on the feasible values of these decision variables, and an objective function that expresses the overall measure of performance for the problem.

Spreadsheets provide a flexible and intuitive way of formulating and solving a linear programming model. The data are entered into data cells. Changing cells display the values of the decision variables, and a target cell shows the value of the objective function. Output cells are used to help specify the constraints. After formulating the model on the spreadsheet and specifying it further with the Solver dialogue box, the Solver is used to quickly find an optimal solution.

The graphical method can be used to solve a linear programming model having just two decision variables. This method provides considerable insight into the nature of linear programming models and optimal solutions.

Glossary

Changing cells   The cells in the spreadsheet that show the values of the decision variables. (Section 2.3)   27

Constraint   A restriction on the feasible values of the decision variables. (Sections 2.3 and 2.4)   29

Constraint boundary equation   The equation for the constraint boundary line. (Section 2.5)   33

Constraint boundary line   For linear programming problems with two decision variables, the line forming the boundary of the solutions that are permitted by the constraint. (Section 2.5)   33

Data cells   The cells in the spreadsheet that show the data of the problem. (Section 2.3)   26

Decision variable   An algebraic variable that represents a decision regarding the level of a particular activity. The value of the decision variable appears in a changing cell on the spreadsheet. (Section 2.4)   31

Feasible region   The geometric region that consists of all the feasible solutions. (Section 2.5)   37

Feasible solution   A solution that simultaneously satisfies all the constraints in the linear programming model. (Section 2.4)   31

Functional constraint   A constraint with a function of the decision variables on the left-hand side. All constraints in a linear programming model that are not nonnegativity constraints are called functional constraints. (Section 2.4)   31

Graphical method   A method for solving linear programming problems with two decision variables on a two-dimensional graph. (Sections 2.5 and 2.7)   32

Infeasible solution   A solution that violates at least one of the constraints in the linear programming model. (Section 2.4)   31

Linear programming model   The mathematical model that represents a linear programming problem. (Sections 2.3 and 2.4)   26

Nonnegativity constraint   A constraint that expresses the restriction that a particular decision variable must be nonnegative (greater than or equal to zero). (Sections 2.3 and 2.4)   31

Objective function   The part of a linear programming model that expresses what needs to be either maximized or minimized, depending on the objective for the problem. The value of the objective function appears in the target cell on the spreadsheet. (Section 2.4)   31

Objective function line   For a linear programming problem with two decision variables, a line whose points all have the same value of the objective function. (Section 2.5)   38

Optimal solution   The best feasible solution according to the objective function. (Section 2.4)   31

Output cells   The cells in the spreadsheet that provide output that depends on the changing cells. These cells frequently are used to help specify constraints. (Section 2.3)   27

Parameter   The parameters of a linear programming model are the constants (coefficients or right-hand sides) in the functional constraints and the objective function. Each parameter represents a quantity (e.g., the amount available of a resource) that is of importance for the analysis of the problem (Section 2.4)   31

Product-mix problem   A type of linear programming problem where the objective is to find the most profitable mix of production levels for the products under consideration. (Section 2.2)   25

Slope-intercept form   For linear programming problems with two decision variables, the slope-intercept form of a constraint boundary equation displays both the slope of the constraint boundary line and the intercept of this line with the vertical axis. (Section 2.5)   35

Slope of a line   For a graph where the horizontal axis represents the variable x and the vertical axis represents y, the slope of a line is the change in y when x is increased by 1. (Section 2.5)   36

Solution   Any single assignment of values to the decision variables, regardless of whether the assignment is a good one or even a feasible one. (Section 2.4)   31

Solver   The spreadsheet tool that is used to specify the model in the spreadsheet and then to obtain an optimal solution for this model. (Section 2.6)   41

Target cell   The cell in the spreadsheet that shows the overall measure of performance of the decisions. (Section 2.3)   28

Learning Aids for This Chapter in Your MS Courseware

"Ch. 2—LP Basic Concepts" Excel File:

Wyndor Example
Profit & Gambit Example

An Excel Add-in:

Premium Solver

Problems

We have inserted the symbol E* (for Excel) to the left of each problem or part where Excel should be used. An asterisk on the problem number indicates that at least a partial answer is given in the back of the book.

2.1. Read the article footnoted in Section 2.1 that describes the first case study presented in that section: "Choosing the Product Mix at Ponderosa Industrial."

   a. Describe the two factors that, according to the article, often hinder the use of optimization models by managers.

   b. Section 2.1 indicates without elaboration that using linear programming at Ponderosa "led to a dramatic shift in the types of plywood products emphasized by the company." Identify this shift.

   c. With the success of this application, management then was eager to use optimization for other problems as well. Identify these other problems.

2.2. Read the article footnoted in Section 2.1 that describes the second case study presented in that section: "Personnel Scheduling at United Airlines."

   a. Describe how United Airlines prepared shift schedules at airports and reservations offices prior to this management science study.

   b. When this study began, the *problem definition* phase defined five specific project requirements. Identify these project requirements.

   c. Describe the flexibility built into the scheduling system to satisfy the group culture at each office. Why was this flexibility needed?

   d. Briefly describe the tangible and intangible benefits that resulted from the study.

2.3. Read the 1986 article footnoted in Section 2.1 that describes the third case study presented in that section: "Planning Supply, Distribution, and Marketing at Citgo Petroleum Corporation."

   a. What happened during the years preceding this management science study that made it vastly more important to control the amount of capital tied up in inventory.

   b. What geographical area is spanned by Citgo's distribution network of pipelines, tankers, and barges? Where do they market their products?

   c. What time periods are included in the model?

   d. Which computer did Citgo use to solve the model? What were typical run times?

   e. Who are the four types of model users? How does each one use the model?

   f. List the major types of reports generated by the SDM system.

   g. What were the major implementation challenges for this study?

   h. List the direct and indirect benefits that were realized from this study.

2.4. Reconsider the Wyndor Glass Co. case study introduced in Section 2.2. Suppose that the estimates of the unit profits for the two new products now have been revised to $600 for the doors and $300 for the windows.

E*   a. Formulate the revised linear programming model for this problem on a spreadsheet.

E*   b. Use the Excel Solver to solve this revised model.

   c. Formulate this same model algebraically.

   d. Use the graphical method to solve this revised model.

2.5. Reconsider the Wyndor Glass Co. case study introduced in Section 2.2. Suppose that Bill Tasto (Wyndor's Vice President for Manufacturing) now has found a way to provide a little additional production time in Plant 2 to the new products.

   a. Use the graphical method to find the new optimal solution and the resulting total profit if *one* additional hour per week is provided.

   b. Repeat part a if *two* additional hours per week are provided instead.

   c. Repeat part a if *three* additional hours per week are provided instead.

   d. Use these results to determine how much each additional hour per week would be worth in terms of increasing the total profit from the two new products.

E*2.6. Use the Excel Solver to do Problem 2.5.

2.7. The following table summarizes the key facts about two products, A and B, and the resources, Q, R and S, required to produce them.

	Resource Usage per Unit Produced		
Resource	Product A	Product B	Amount of Resource Available
Q	2	1	2
R	1	2	2
S	3	3	4
Profit/unit	$3,000	$2,000	

All the assumptions of linear programming hold.

E*   *a.* Formulate a linear programming model for this problem on a spreadsheet.

E*   *b.* Use the Excel Solver to solve this model.

     c. Formulate this same model algebraically.

     d. Use the graphical method to solve this model.

2.8.* This is your lucky day. You have just won a $10,000 prize. You are setting aside $4,000 for taxes and partying expenses, but you have decided to invest the other $6,000. Upon hearing this news, two different friends have offered you an opportunity to become a partner in two different entrepreneurial ventures, one planned by each friend. In both cases, this investment would involve expending some of your time next summer as well as putting up cash. Becoming a *full* partner in the first friend's venture would require an investment of $5,000 and 400 hours, and your estimated profit (ignoring the value of your time) would be $4,500. The corresponding figures for the second friend's venture are $4,000 and 500 hours, with an estimated profit to you of $4,500. However, both friends are flexible and would allow you to come in at any *fraction* of a full partnership you would like. If you choose a fraction of a full partnership, all the above figures given for a full partnership (money investment, time investment, and your profit) would be multiplied by this same fraction.

     Because you were looking for an interesting summer job anyway (maximum of 600 hours), you have decided to participate in one or both friends' ventures in whichever combination would maximize your total estimated profit. You now need to solve the problem of finding the best combination.

     a. Describe the analogy between this problem and the Wyndor Glass Co. problem discussed in Section 2.2. Then construct and fill in a table like Table 2.1 for this problem, identifying both the activities and the resources.

     b. Identify verbally the decisions to be made, the constraints on these decisions, and the overall measure of performance for the decisions.

     c. Convert these verbal descriptions of the constraints and the measure of performance into quantitative expressions in terms of the data and decisions.

E*   *d.* Formulate a spreadsheet model for this problem. Identify the data cells, the changing cells, and the target cell. Also show the Excel equation for each output cell expressed as a SUMPRODUCT function.

E*   *e.* Use the Excel Solver to solve this model.

f. Indicate why this spreadsheet model is a linear programming model.

g. Formulate this same model algebraically.

h. Identify the decision variables, objective function, nonnegativity constraints, functional constraints, and parameters in both the algebraic version and spreadsheet version of the model.

i. Use the graphical method to solve this model. What is your total estimated profit?

2.9. You are given the following linear programming model in algebraic form, where x_1 and x_2 are the decision variables and Z is the value of the overall measure of performance.

$$\text{Maximize} \quad Z = x_1 + 2x_2$$

subject to

Constraint on resource 1:	$x_1 + x_2 \le 5$	(amount available)
Constraint on resource 2:	$x_1 + 3x_2 \le 9$	(amount available)

and

$$x_1 \ge 0 \qquad x_2 \ge 0$$

     a. Identify the objective function, the functional constraints, and the nonnegativity constraints in this model.

E*   *b.* Incorporate this model into a spreadsheet.

     c. Is $(x_1, x_2) = (3, 1)$ a feasible solution?

     d. Is $(x_1, x_2) = (1, 3)$ a feasible solution?

E*   *e.* Use the Excel Solver to solve this model.

     f. Use the graphical method to solve this model.

2.10. You are given the following linear programming model in algebraic form, where x_1 and x_2 are the decision variables and Z is the value of the overall measure of performance.

$$\text{Maximize} \quad Z = 3x_1 + 2x_2$$

subject to

Constraint on resource 1:	$3x_1 + x_2 \le 9$	(amount available)
Constraint on resource 2:	$x_1 + 2x_2 \le 8$	(amount available)

and

$$x_1 \ge 0 \qquad x_2 \ge 0$$

     a. Identify the objective function, the functional constraints, and the nonnegativity constraints in this model.

E*   *b.* Incorporate this model into a spreadsheet.

     c. Is $(x_1, x_2) = (2, 1)$ a feasible solution?

     d. Is $(x_1, x_2) = (2, 3)$ a feasible solution?

     e. Is $(x_1, x_2) = (0, 5)$ a feasible solution?

E*   *f.* Use the Excel Solver to solve this model.

     g. Use the graphical method to solve this model.

2.11. The Whitt Window Company is a company with only three employees that makes two different kinds of handcrafted windows: a wood-framed and an aluminum-framed window. They earn $60 profit for each wood-framed window and $30 profit for each aluminum framed window. Doug makes the wood frames and can make 6 per day. Linda makes the aluminum frames and can make

4 per day. Bob forms and cuts the glass and can make 48 square feet of glass per day. Each wood-framed window uses 6 square feet of glass and each aluminum framed window uses 8 square feet of glass.

The company wishes to determine how many windows of each type to produce per day to maximize total profit.

 a. Describe the analogy between this problem and the Wyndor Glass Co. problem discussed in Section 2.2. Then construct and fill in a table like Table 2.1 for this problem, identifying both the activities and the resources.

 b. Identify verbally the decisions to be made, the constraints on these decisions, and the overall measure of performance for the decisions.

 c. Convert these verbal descriptions of the constraints and the measure of performance into quantitative expressions in terms of the data and decisions.

E* *d.* Formulate a spreadsheet model for this problem. Identify the data cells, the changing cells, and the target cell. Also show the Excel equation for each output cell expressed as a SUMPRODUCT function.

E* *e.* Use the Excel Solver to solve this model.

 f. Indicate why this spreadsheet model is a linear programming model.

 g. Formulate this same model algebraically.

 h. Identify the decision variables, objective function, nonnegativity constraints, functional constraints, and parameters in both the algebraic version and spreadsheet version of the model.

 i. Use the graphical method to solve this model.

 j. A new competitor in town has started making wood-framed windows as well. This may force the company to lower the price it charges and so lower the profit made for each wood-framed window. How would the optimal solution change (if at all) if the profit per wood-framed window decreases from $60 to $40? From $60 to $20?

 k. Doug is considering lowering his working hours, which would decrease the number of wood frames he makes per day. How would the optimal solution change if he only makes 5 wood frames per day?

2.12. The Apex Television Company has to decide on the number of 27″ and 20″ sets to be produced at one of its factories. Market research indicates that at most 40 of the 27″ sets and 10 of the 20″ sets can be sold per month. The maximum number of work-hours available is 500 per month. A 27″ set requires 20 work-hours and a 20″ set requires 10 work-hours. Each 27″ set sold produces a profit of $120 and each 20″ set produces a profit of $80. A wholesaler has agreed to purchase all the television sets produced if the numbers do not exceed the maxima indicated by the market research.

E* *a.* Formulate and solve a linear programming model for this problem on a spreadsheet.

 b. Formulate this same model algebraically.

 c. Use the graphical method to solve this model.

2.13.* You are given the following equation for a line:

$$2x_1 + x_2 = 4$$

 a. Identify the value of x_1 when $x_2 = 0$. Do the same for x_2 when $x_1 = 0$.

 b. Construct a two-dimensional graph with x_1 on the horizontal axis and x_2 on the vertical axis. Then use the information from part *a* to draw the line.

 c. Determine the numerical value of the slope of this line.

 d. Find the slope-intercept form of this equation. Then use this form to identify both the slope of the line and the intercept of the line with the vertical axis.

2.14. Follow the instructions of Problem 2.13 for the following equation of a line.

$$2x_1 + 5x_2 = 10$$

2.15. Follow the instructions of Problem 2.13 for the following equation of a line.

$$2x_1 - 3x_2 = 12$$

2.16.* For each of the following constraints on the decision variables, x_1 and x_2, draw a separate graph to show the nonnegative solutions that satisfy this constraint.

 a. $x_1 + 3x_2 \leq 6$

 b. $4x_1 + 3x_2 \leq 12$

 c. $4x_1 + x_2 \leq 8$

 d. Now combine these constraints into a single graph to show the feasible region for the entire set of functional constraints plus nonnegativity constraints.

2.17. For each of the following constraints on the decision variables, x_1 and x_2, draw a separate graph to show the nonnegative solutions that satisfy this constraint.

 a. $10x_1 + 20x_2 \leq 40$

 b. $5x_1 + 3x_2 \geq 15$

 c. $5x_1 - x_2 \leq 15$

 d. Now combine these constraints into a single graph to show the feasible region for the entire set of functional constraints plus nonnegativity constraints.

2.18. For each of the following constraints on the decision variables, x_1 and x_2, draw a separate graph to show the nonnegative solutions that satisfy this constraint.

 a. $x_1 - x_2 \leq 2$

 b. $-3x_1 + 6x_2 \geq 3$

 c. $4x_1 - 3x_2 \geq 1$

 d. Now combine these constraints into a single graph to show the feasible region for the entire set of functional constraints plus nonnegativity constraints.

2.19. The WorldLight Company produces two light fixtures (products 1 and 2) that require both metal frame parts and electrical components. Management wants to determine how many units of each product to produce so as to maximize profit. For each unit of product 1, 1 unit of frame parts and 2 units of electrical components are required. For each unit of product 2, 3 units of frame parts and 2 units of electrical components are required. The company has 200 units of frame parts and 300 units of electrical components. Each unit of product 1 gives a profit of $1, and each unit of product 2, up to 60 units, gives a profit of $2. Any excess over 60 units of product 2 brings no profit, so such an excess has been ruled out.

 a. Identify verbally the decisions to be made, the constraints on these decisions, and the overall measure of performance for the decisions.

 b. Convert these verbal descriptions of the constraints and the measure of performance into quantitative expressions in terms of the data and decisions.

E*   c.   Formulate and solve a linear programming model for this problem on a spreadsheet.

d.   Formulate this same model algebraically.

e.   Use the graphical method to solve this model. What is the resulting total profit?

2.20.   The Primo Insurance Company is introducing two new product lines: special risk insurance and mortgages. The expected profit is $5 per unit on special risk insurance and $2 per unit on mortgages.

Management wishes to establish sales quotas for the new product lines to maximize total expected profit. The work requirements are as follows:

Department	Work-Hours per Unit		Work-Hours Available
	Special Risk	Mortgage	
Underwriting	3	2	2,400
Administration	0	1	800
Claims	2	0	1,200

a.   Identify verbally the decisions to be made, the constraints on these decisions, and the overall measure of performance for the decisions.

b.   Convert these verbal descriptions of the constraints and the measure of performance into quantitative expressions in terms of the data and decisions.

E*   c.   Formulate and solve a linear programming model for this problem on a spreadsheet.

d.   Formulate this same model algebraically.

e.   Use the graphical method to solve this model.

2.21.*   Consider the following objective function for a linear programming model with decision variables, x_1 and x_2:

$$\text{Maximize}\quad \text{Profit} = 2x_1 + 3x_2$$

a.   Draw a graph that shows the corresponding objective function lines for Profit = 6, Profit = 12, and Profit = 18.

b.   Find the slope-intercept form of the equation for each of these three objective function lines. Compare the slope for these three lines. Also compare the intercept with the x_2 axis.

2.22.   Using the symbol P to represent total profit, you are given the following objective function for a linear programming model with decision variables x_1 and x_2:

$$\text{Maximize}\quad P = 25x_1 + 10x_2$$

a.   Draw a graph that shows the corresponding objective function lines for $P = 100$, $P = 200$, and $P = 300$.

b.   Find the slope-intercept form of the equation for each of these three objective function lines. Compare the slope for these three lines. Also compare the intercept with the x_2 axis.

2.23.   Consider the following objective function for a linear programming model with decision variables x_1 and x_2:

$$\text{Minimize}\quad \text{Cost} = 5x_1 - x_2$$

a.   Draw a graph that shows the corresponding objective function lines for Cost = 300, Cost = 200, and Cost = 100.

b.   Find the slope-intercept form of the equation for each of these three objective function lines. Compare the slope for these three lines. Also compare the intercept with the x_2 axis.

2.24.   Consider the following equation of a line:

$$20x_1 + 40x_2 = 400$$

a.   Find the slope-intercept form of this equation.

b.   Use this form to identify the slope and the intercept with the x_2 axis for this line.

c.   Use the information from part b to draw a graph of this line.

2.25.*   Find the slope-intercept form of the following equation of a line:

$$8x_1 + 5x_2 = 40$$

2.26.   Find the slope-intercept form of the following equations of lines:

a. $10x_1 + 5x_2 = 20$

b. $-2x_1 + 3x_2 = 6$

c. $5x_1 - 2x_2 = 10$

2.27.   Consider the following constraint on the decision variables x_1 and x_2:

$$x_1 - 2x_2 \leq 0$$

a.   Write the constraint boundary equation for this constraint.

b.   Find the slope-intercept form of this equation.

c.   Use this form to identify the slope and the intercept with the x_2 axis for the constraint boundary line.

d.   Use the information from part c to draw a graph of the constraint boundary line.

e.   Identify which side of this line is permitted by the constraint.

2.28.   You are given the following linear programming model in algebraic form, where x_1 and x_2 are the decision variables and Z is the value of the overall measure of performance.

$$\text{Maximize}\quad Z = 20x_1 + 10x_2$$

subject to

$$x_1 - x_2 \leq 1$$
$$3x_1 + x_2 \leq 7$$

and

$$x_1 \geq 0 \qquad x_2 \geq 0$$

a.   Use the graphical method to solve this model.

E*   b.   Incorporate this model into a spreadsheet.

E*   c.   Use the Excel Solver to solve this model.

2.29.*   You are given the following linear programming model in algebraic form, with x_1 and x_2 as the decision variables and constraints on the usage of four resources:

$$\text{Maximize}\quad \text{Profit} = 2x_1 + x_2$$

subject to

$$x_2 \le 10 \qquad \text{(resource 1)}$$

$$2x_1 + 5x_2 \le 60 \qquad \text{(resource 2)}$$

$$x_1 + x_2 \le 18 \qquad \text{(resource 3)}$$

$$3x_1 + x_2 \le 44 \qquad \text{(resource 4)}$$

and

$$x_1 \ge 0 \qquad x_2 \ge 0$$

    a. Use the graphical method to solve this model.

E*   *b.* Incorporate this model into a spreadsheet.

E*   *c.* Use the Excel Solver to solve this model.

2.30. Because of your knowledge of management science, your boss has asked you to analyze a product-mix problem involving two products and two resources. The model is shown below in algebraic form, where x_1 and x_2 are the production rates for the two products and P is the total profit.

$$\text{Maximize} \qquad P = 3x_1 + 2x_2$$

subject to

$$x_1 + x_2 \le 8 \qquad \text{(resource 1)}$$

$$2x_1 + x_2 \le 10 \qquad \text{(resource 2)}$$

and

$$x_1 \ge 0 \qquad x_2 \ge 0$$

    a. Use the graphical method to solve this model.

E*   *b.* Incorporate this model into a spreadsheet.

E*   *c.* Use the Excel Solver to solve this model.

2.31. You are given the linear programming model in algebraic form shown below, where the objective is to choose the levels of two activities (x_1 and x_2) so as to maximize their total profit, subject to constraints on the amounts of three resources available.

$$\text{Maximize} \qquad \text{Profit} = 10x_1 + 20x_2$$

subject to

$$-x_1 + 2x_2 \le 15 \qquad \text{(resource 1)}$$

$$x_1 + x_2 \le 12 \qquad \text{(resource 2)}$$

$$5x_1 + 3x_2 \le 45 \qquad \text{(resource 3)}$$

and

$$x_1 \ge 0 \qquad x_2 \ge 0$$

    a. Use the graphical method to solve this model.

E*   *b.* Incorporate this model into a spreadsheet.

E*   *c.* Use the Excel Solver to solve this model.

2.32. Consider the algebraic form of a linear programming model shown below, where x_1 and x_2 are the decision variables. Use the graphical method to solve this model.

$$\text{Maximize} \qquad \text{Profit} = 400x_1 + 500x_2$$

subject to

$$20x_1 + 10x_2 \le 100$$

$$5x_1 + 10x_2 \le 50$$

$$3x_1 - x_2 \le 10$$

$$-x_1 + 4x_2 \le 15$$

and

$$x_1 \ge 0 \qquad x_2 \ge 0$$

2.33. Weenies and Buns is a food processing plant that manufactures hot dogs and hot dog buns. They grind their own flour for the hot dog buns at a maximum rate of 200 pounds per week. Each hot dog bun requires 0.1 pound of flour. They currently have a contract with Pigland, Inc., which specifies that a delivery of 800 pounds of pork product is delivered every Monday. Each hot dog requires ¼ pound of pork product. All the other ingredients in the hot dogs and hot dog buns are in plentiful supply. Finally, the labor force at Weenies and Buns consists of 5 employees working full time (40 hours per week each). Each hot dog requires 3 minutes of labor, and each hot dog bun requires 2 minutes of labor. Each hot dog yields a profit of $0.20, and each bun yields a profit of $0.10.

    Weenies and Buns would like to know how many hot dogs and how many hot dog buns they should produce each week so as to achieve the highest possible profit.

    a. Identify verbally the decisions to be made, the constraints on these decisions, and the overall measure of performance for the decisions.

    b. Convert these verbal descriptions of the constraints and the measure of performance into quantitative expressions in terms of the data and decisions.

E*   *c.* Formulate and solve a linear programming model for this problem on a spreadsheet.

    d. Formulate this same model algebraically.

    e. Use the graphical method to solve this model.

2.34. The Oak Works is a family-owned business that makes handcrafted dining room tables and chairs. They obtain the oak from a local tree farm, which ships them 2,500 pounds of oak each month. Each table uses 50 pounds of oak while each chair uses 25 pounds of oak. The family builds all the furniture itself and has 480 hours of labor available each month. Each table or chair requires 6 hours of labor. Each table nets Oak Works $400 in profit, while each chair nets $100 in profit. Since chairs are often sold with the tables, they want to produce *at least* twice as many chairs as tables.

    The Oak Works would like to decide how many tables and chairs to produce so as to maximize profit.

E*   *a.* Formulate and solve a linear programming model for this problem on a spreadsheet.

    b. Formulate this same model algebraically.

    c. Use the graphical method to solve this model.

2.35. Nutri-Jenny is a weight-management center. It produces a wide variety of frozen entrees for consumption by its clients. The entrees are strictly monitored for nutritional content to ensure that the clients are eating a balanced diet. One new entree will be a "beef sirloin tips dinner." It will consist of beef tips and gravy, plus some combination of peas, carrots, and a dinner roll. Nutri-Jenny would like to determine what quantity of each item to include in the entree to meet the nutritional requirements, while costing as little as possible. The nutritional information for each item and its cost are given in the following table.

Item	Calories (per oz.)	Calories from Fat (per oz.)	Vitamin A (IU per oz.)	Vitamin C (mg per oz.)	Protein (gr. per oz.)	Cost (per oz.)
Beef tips	54	19	0	0	8	40¢
Gravy	20	15	0	1	0	35¢
Peas	15	0	15	3	1	15¢
Carrots	8	0	350	1	1	18¢
Dinner roll	40	10	0	0	1	10¢

The nutritional requirements for the entree are as follows: (1) it must have between 280 and 320 calories, (2) calories from fat should be no more than 30 percent of the total number of calories, and (3) it must have at least 600 IUs of vitamin A, 10 milligrams of vitamin C, and 30 grams of protein. Furthermore, for practical reasons, it must include at least 2 ounces of beef, and it must have at least half an ounce of gravy per ounce of beef.

E* *a.* Formulate and solve a linear programming model for this problem on a spreadsheet.

   b. Formulate this same model algebraically.

2.36. Consider the following algebraic form of a linear programming model, where the value of c_1 has not yet been ascertained.

$$\text{Maximize} \quad Z = c_1 x_1 + x_2$$

subject to

$$x_1 + x_2 \leq 6$$
$$x_1 + 2x_2 \leq 10$$

and

$$x_1 \geq 0 \qquad x_2 \geq 0$$

Use graphical analysis to determine the optimal solution(s) for (x_1, x_2) for the various possible values of c_1 (both positive and negative).

2.37. Consider the following algebraic form of a linear programming model, where the value of c_1 has not yet been ascertained.

$$\text{Maximize} \quad Z = c_1 x_1 + 2x_2$$

subject to

$$4x_1 + x_2 \leq 12$$
$$x_1 - x_2 \geq 2$$

and

$$x_1 \geq 0 \qquad x_2 \geq 0$$

Use graphical analysis to determine the optimal solution(s) for (x_1, x_2) for the various possible values of c_1 (both positive and negative).

2.38. Consider the following algebraic form of a linear programming model, where the value of k has not yet been ascertained.

$$\text{Maximize} \quad Z = x_1 + 2x_2$$

subject to

$$-x_1 + x_2 \leq 2$$
$$x_2 \leq 3$$
$$kx_1 + x_2 \leq 2k + 3 \qquad \text{where } k \geq 0$$

and

$$x_1 \geq 0 \qquad x_2 \geq 0$$

The solution currently being used is $(x_1, x_2) = (2, 3)$. Use graphical analysis to determine the values of k such that this solution actually is optimal.

2.39. Ralph Edmund loves steaks and potatoes. Therefore, he has decided to go on a steady diet of only these two foods (plus some liquids and vitamin supplements) for all his meals. Ralph realizes that this isn't the healthiest diet, so he wants to make sure that he eats the right quantities of the two foods to satisfy some key nutritional requirements. He has obtained the following nutritional and cost information:

Ingredient	Grams of Ingredient per Serving		Daily Requirement (grams)
	Steak	Potatoes	
Carbohydrates	5	15	≥ 50
Protein	20	5	≥ 40
Fat	15	2	≤ 60
Cost per serving	$4	$2	

Ralph wishes to determine the number of daily servings (may be fractional) of steak and potatoes that will meet these requirements at a minimum cost.

   a. Identify verbally the decisions to be made, the constraints on these decisions, and the overall measure of performance for the decisions.

   b. Convert these verbal descriptions of the constraints and the measure of performance into quantitative expressions in terms of the data and decisions.

E* *c.* Formulate and solve a linear programming model for this problem.

   d. Formulate this same model algebraically.

   e. Use the graphical method to solve this model.

2.40.* Your boss has asked you to use your background in management science to determine what the levels of two activities (x_1 and x_2) should be to minimize their total cost while satisfying some constraints. The algebraic form of the model is shown below.

$$\text{Minimize} \quad \text{Cost} = 15x_1 + 20x_2$$

subject to

Constraint 1: $x_1 + 2x_2 \geq 10$
Constraint 2: $2x_1 - 3x_2 \leq 6$
Constraint 3: $x_1 + x_2 \geq 6$

and

$$x_1 \geq 0 \qquad x_2 \geq 0$$

    a. Use the graphical method to solve this model.
E*   *b.* Incorporate this model into a spreadsheet.
E*   *c.* Use the Excel Solver to solve this model.

2.41. Dwight is an elementary school teacher who also raises pigs for supplemental income. He is trying to decide what to feed his pigs. He is considering using a combination of pig feeds available from local suppliers. He would like to feed the pigs at minimum cost while also making sure each pig receives an adequate supply of calories and vitamins. The cost, calorie content, and vitamin content of each feed is given in the table below.

Contents	Feed Type A	Feed Type B
Calories (per pound)	800	1,000
Vitamins (per pound)	140 units	70 units
Cost (per pound)	$0.40	$0.80

Each pig requires at least 8,000 calories per day and at least 700 units of vitamins. A further constraint is that no more than 1/3 of the diet (by weight) can consist of Feed Type A, since it contains an ingredient that is toxic if consumed in too large a quantity.

    a. Identify verbally the decisions to be made, the constraints on these decisions, and the overall measure of performance for the decisions.
    b. Convert these verbal descriptions of the constraints and the measure of performance into quantitative expressions in terms of the data and decisions.
E*   *c.* Formulate and solve a linear programming model for this problem on a spreadsheet.
    d. Formulate this same model algebraically.
    e. Use the graphical method to solve this model. What is the resulting daily cost per pig?

2.42. Reconsider the Profit & Gambit Co. problem described in Section 2.7. Suppose that the estimated data given in Table 2.2 now have been changed as shown above.

E*   *a.* Formulate a linear programming model on a spreadsheet for this revised version of the problem.
E*   *b.* Use the Excel Solver to solve this model.
    c. Formulate this same model algebraically.
    d. Use the graphical method to solve this model.
    e. What were the key changes in the data that caused your answer for the optimal solution to change from

Increase in Market Share per Unit of Advertising

Product	Television	Print Media	Minimum Required Increase
Stain remover	0	1.5%	3%
Liquid detergent	3%	4%	18%
Powder detergent	-1%	2%	4%
Unit cost	$1 million	$2 million	

the one given in Figures 2.21 and 2.23 for the original version of the problem?

    f. Write a paragraph to the management of the Profit & Gambit Co. presenting your conclusions from the above parts. Include the potential effect of further refining the key data in the above table. Also point out the leverage that your results might provide to management in negotiating a decrease in the unit cost for either of the advertising media.

2.43. You are given the following linear programming model in algebraic form, with x_1 and x_2 as the decision variables:

$$\text{Minimize} \quad \text{Cost} = 40x_1 + 50x_2$$

subject to

Constraint 1: $2x_1 + 3x_2 \geq 30$
Constraint 2: $x_1 + x_2 \geq 12$
Constraint 3: $2x_1 + x_2 \geq 20$

and

$$x_1 \geq 0 \qquad x_2 \geq 0$$

    a. Use the graphical method to solve this model.
    b. How does the optimal solution change if the objective function is changed to Cost = $40x_1 + 70x_2$?
    c. How does the optimal solution change if the third functional constraint is changed to $2x_1 + x_2 \geq 15$?
E*   *d.* Now incorporate the original model into a spreadsheet.
E*   *e.* Use the Excel Solver to solve this model.
E*   *f.* Use Excel to do parts *b* and *c*.

2.44. For the following algebraic form of a linear programming model, the objective is to choose the levels of two activities (x_1 and x_2) so as to minimize their total cost while satisfying some constraints.

$$\text{Minimize} \quad \text{Cost} = 3x_1 + 2x_2$$

subject to

Constraint 1: $x_1 + 2x_2 \leq 12$
Constraint 2: $2x_1 + 3x_2 = 12$
Constraint 3: $2x_1 + x_2 \geq 8$

and

$$x_1 \geq 0 \qquad x_2 \geq 0$$

    a. Use the graphical method to solve this model.
E*   *b.* Incorporate this model into a spreadsheet.
E*   *c.* Use the Excel Solver to solve this model.

2.45. The Learning Center runs a day camp for 6–10-year-olds during the summer. Its manager, Elizabeth Reed, is trying to reduce the center's operating costs to avoid having to raise the tuition fee. Elizabeth is currently planning what to feed the children for lunch. She would like to keep costs to a minimum, but also wants to make sure she is meeting the nutritional requirements of the children. She has already decided to go with peanut butter and jelly sandwiches, and some combination of apples, milk, and/or cranberry juice. The nutritional content of each food choice and its cost are given in the table below.

Food Item	Calories from Fat	Total Calories	Vitamin C (mg)	Fiber (g)	Cost (¢)
Bread (1 slice)	15	80	0	4	6
Peanut butter (1 tbsp)	80	100	0	0	5
Jelly (1 tbsp)	0	70	4	3	8
Apple	0	90	6	10	35
Milk (1 cup)	60	120	2	0	20
Cranberry juice (1 cup)	0	110	80	1	40

The nutritional requirements are as follows. Each child should receive between 300 and 500 calories, but no more than 30 percent of these calories should come from fat. Each child should receive at least 60 milligrams (mg) of vitamin C and at least 10 grams (g) of fiber.

To ensure tasty sandwiches, Elizabeth wants each child to have a minimum of 2 slices of bread, 1 tablespoon (tbsp) of peanut butter, and 1 tbsp of jelly, along with at least 1 cup of liquid (milk and/or cranberry juice).

Elizabeth would like to select the food choices that would minimize cost while meeting all these requirements.

E* *a.* Formulate and solve a linear programming model for this problem on a spreadsheet.

b. Formulate this same model algebraically.

CASE 2.1
AUTO ASSEMBLY

Automobile Alliance, a large automobile manufacturing company, organizes the vehicles it manufactures into three families: a family of trucks, a family of small cars, and a family of mid-sized and luxury cars. One plant outside Detroit, Michigan, assembles two models from the family of mid-sized and luxury cars. The first model, the Family Thrillseeker, is a four-door sedan with vinyl seats, plastic interior, standard features, and excellent gas mileage. It is marketed as a smart buy for middle-class families with tight budgets, and each Family Thrillseeker sold generates a modest profit of $3,600 for the company. The second model, the Classy Cruiser, is a two-door luxury sedan with leather seats, wooden interior, custom features, and navigational capabilities. It is marketed as a privilege of affluence for upper-middle-class families, and each Classy Cruiser sold generates a healthy profit of $5,400 for the company.

Rachel Rosencrantz, the manager of the assembly plant, is currently deciding the production schedule for the next month. Specifically, she must decide how many Family Thrillseekers and how many Classy Cruisers to assemble in the plant to maximize profit for the company. She knows that the plant possesses a capacity of 48,000 labor-hours during the month. She also knows that it takes six labor-hours to assemble one Family Thrillseeker and 10.5 labor-hours to assemble one Classy Cruiser.

Because the plant is simply an assembly plant, the parts required to assemble the two models are not produced at the plant. Instead, they are shipped from other plants around the Michigan area to the assembly plant. For example, tires, steering wheels, windows, seats, and doors all arrive from various supplier plants. For the next month, Rachel knows that she will only be able to obtain 20,000 doors from the door supplier. A recent labor strike forced the shutdown of that particular supplier plant for several days, and that plant will not be able to meet its production schedule for the next month. Both the Family Thrillseeker and the Classy Cruiser use the same door part.

In addition, a recent company forecast of the monthly demands for different automobile models suggests that the demand for the Classy Cruiser is limited to 3,500 cars. There is no limit on the demand for the Family Thrillseeker within the capacity limits of the assembly plant.

a. Formulate and solve a linear programming model to determine the number of Family Thrillseekers and the number of Classy Cruisers that should be assembled.

Before she makes her final production decisions, Rachel plans to explore the following questions independently, except where otherwise indicated.

b. The marketing department knows that it can pursue a targeted $500,000 advertising campaign that will raise the demand for the Classy Cruiser next month by 20 percent. Should the campaign be undertaken?

c. Rachel knows that she can increase next month's plant capacity by using overtime labor. She can increase the plant's labor-hour capacity by 25 percent. With the new assembly plant capacity, how many Family Thrillseekers and how many Classy Cruisers should be assembled?

d. Rachel knows that overtime labor does not come without an extra cost. What is the maximum amount she should be willing to pay for all overtime labor beyond the cost of this labor at regular-time rates? Express your answer as a lump sum.

e. Rachel explores the option of using both the targeted advertising campaign and the overtime labor hours. The advertising campaign raises the demand for the Classy Cruiser by 20 percent, and the overtime labor increases the plant's labor-hour capacity by 25 percent. How many Family Thrillseekers and how many Classy Cruisers should be assembled using the advertising campaign and overtime labor-hours if the profit from each Classy Cruiser sold continues to be 50 percent more than for each Family Thrillseeker sold?

f. Knowing that the advertising campaign costs $500,000 and the maximum usage of overtime labor hours costs $1,600,000 beyond regular time rates, is the solution found in part *e* a wise decision compared to the solution found in part *a*?

g. Automobile Alliance has determined that dealerships are actually heavily discounting the price of the Family Thrillseekers to move them off the lot. Because of a profit-sharing agreement with its dealers, the company is not making a profit of $3,600 on the Family Thrillseeker but instead is making a profit of $2,800. Determine the number of Family Thrillseekers and the number of Classy Cruisers that should be assembled given this new discounted profit.

h. The company has discovered quality problems with the Family Thrillseeker by randomly testing Thrillseekers at the end of the assembly line. Inspectors have discovered that in over 60 percent of the cases, two of the four doors on a Thrillseeker do not seal properly. Because the percentage of defective Thrillseekers determined by the random testing is so high, the floor foreman has decided to perform quality control tests on every Thrillseeker at the end of the line. Because of the added tests, the time it takes to assemble one Family Thrillseeker has increased from 6 hours to 7.5 hours. Determine the number of units of each model that should be assembled given the new assembly time for the Family Thrillseeker.

i. The board of directors of Automobile Alliance wishes to capture a larger share of the luxury sedan market and therefore would like to meet the full demand for Classy Cruisers. They ask Rachel to determine by how much the profit of her assembly plant would decrease as compared to the profit found in part *a*. They then ask her to meet the full demand for Classy Cruiser if the decrease in profit is not more than $2,000,000.

j. Rachel now makes her final decision by combining all the new considerations described in parts *f, g,* and *h*. What are her final decisions on whether to undertake the advertising campaign, whether to use overtime labor, the number of Family Thrillseekers to assemble, and the number of Classy Cruisers to assemble?

CASE 2.2
CUTTING CAFETERIA COSTS

A cafeteria at All-State University has one special dish it serves like clockwork every Thursday at noon. This supposedly tasty dish is a casserole that contains sautéed onions, boiled sliced potatoes, green beans, and cream of mushroom soup. Unfortunately, students fail to see the special quality of this dish, and they loathingly refer to it as the Killer Casserole. The students reluctantly eat the casserole, however, because the cafeteria provides only a limited selection of dishes for Thursday's lunch (namely, the casserole).

Maria Gonzalez, the cafeteria manager, is looking to cut costs for the coming year, and she believes that one sure way to cut costs is to buy less expensive and perhaps lower quality ingredients. Because the casserole is a weekly staple of the cafeteria menu, she concludes that if she can cut costs on the ingredients purchased for the casserole, she can significantly reduce overall cafeteria operating costs. She therefore decides to invest time in determining how to minimize the costs of the casserole while maintaining nutritional and taste requirements.

Maria focuses on reducing the costs of the two main ingredients in the casserole, the potatoes and green beans. These two ingredients are responsible for the greatest costs, nutritional content, and taste of the dish.

Maria buys the potatoes and green beans from a wholesaler each week. Potatoes cost $0.40 per pound (lb), and green beans cost $1.00 per lb.

All-State University has established nutritional requirements that each main dish of the cafeteria must meet. Specifically, the dish must contain 180 grams (g) of protein, 80 milligrams (mg) of iron, and 1,050 mg of vitamin C. (There are 454 g in one lb and 1,000 mg in one g.) For simplicity when planning, Maria assumes that only the potatoes and green beans contribute to the nutritional content of the casserole.

Because Maria works at a cutting-edge technological university, she has been exposed to the numerous resources on the World Wide Web. She decides to surf the Web to find the nutritional content of potatoes and green beans. Her research yields the following nutritional information about the two ingredients:

	Potatoes	Green Beans
Protein	1.5 g per 100 g	6.22 g per 10 ounces
Iron	0.3 mg per 100 g	3.732 mg per 10 ounces
Vitamin C	12 mg per 100 g	31.1 mg per 10 ounces

(There are 31.1 g in one ounce.)

Edson Branner, the cafeteria cook who is surprisingly concerned about taste, informs Maria that an edible casserole must contain at least a six-to-five ratio in the weight of potatoes to green beans.

Given the number of students who eat in the cafeteria, Maria knows that she must purchase enough potatoes and green beans to prepare a minimum of 10 kilograms (kg) of casserole each week. (There are 1,000 g in one kg.) Again, for simplicity in planning, she assumes that only the potatoes and green beans determine the amount of casserole that can be prepared. Maria does not establish an upper limit on the amount of casserole to prepare since she knows all leftovers can be served for many days thereafter or can be used creatively in preparing other dishes.

  a. Determine the amount of potatoes and green beans Maria should purchase each week for the casserole to minimize the ingredient costs while meeting nutritional, taste, and demand requirements.

Before she makes her final decision, Maria plans to explore the following questions independently, except where otherwise indicated.

  b. Maria is not very concerned about the taste of the casserole; she is only concerned about meeting nutritional requirements and cutting costs. She therefore forces Edson to change the recipe to allow only for at least a one-to-two ratio in the weight of potatoes to green beans. Given the new recipe, determine the amount of potatoes and green beans Maria should purchase each week.

  c. Maria decides to lower the iron requirement to 65 mg since she determines that the other ingredients, such as the onions and cream of mushroom soup, also provide iron. Determine the amount of potatoes and green beans Maria should purchase each week given this new iron requirement.

  d. Maria learns that the wholesaler has a surplus of green beans and is therefore selling the green beans for a lower price of \$0.50 per lb. Using the same iron requirement from part c and the new price of green beans, determine the amount of potatoes and green beans Maria should purchase each week.

  e. Maria decides that she wants to purchase lima beans instead of green beans since lima beans are less expensive and provide a greater amount of protein and iron than green beans. Maria again wields her absolute power and forces Edson to change the recipe to include lima beans instead of green beans. Maria knows she can purchase lima beans for \$0.60 per lb from the wholesaler. She also knows that lima beans contain 24.88 g of protein and 7.464 mg of iron per 10 ounces of lima beans and no vitamin C. Using the new cost and nutritional content of lima beans, determine the amount of potatoes and lima beans Maria should purchase each week to minimize the ingredient costs while meeting nutritional, taste, and demand requirements. The nutritional requirements include the reduced iron requirement from part c.

  f. Will Edson be happy with the solution in part e? Why or why not?

  g. An All-State student task force meets during Body Awareness Week and determines that All-State University's nutritional requirements for iron are too lax and that those for vitamin C are too stringent. The task force urges the university to adopt a policy that requires each serving of an entrée to contain at least 120 mg of iron and at least 500 mg of vitamin C. Using potatoes and lima beans as the ingredients for the dish and using the new nutritional requirements, determine the amount of potatoes and lima beans Maria should purchase each week.

CASE 2.3
STAFFING A CALL CENTER

California Children's Hospital has been receiving numerous customer complaints because of its confusing, decentralized appointment and registration process. When customers want to make appointments or register child patients, they must contact the clinic or department they plan to visit. Several problems exist with this current strategy. Parents do not always know the most appropriate clinic or department they must visit to address their children's ailments. They therefore spend a significant amount of time on the phone being transferred from clinic to clinic until they reach the most appropriate clinic for their needs. The hospital also does not publish the phone numbers of all clinics and departments, and parents must therefore invest a large amount of time in detective work to track down the correct phone number. Finally, the various clinics and departments do not communicate with each other. For example, when a doctor schedules a referral with a colleague located in another department or clinic, that department or clinic almost never receives word of the referral. The parent must contact the correct department or clinic and provide the needed referral information.

In efforts to reengineer and improve its appointment and registration process, the children's hospital has decided to centralize the process by establishing one call center devoted exclusively to appointments and registration. The hospital is currently in the middle of the planning stages for the call center. Lenny Davis, the hospital manager, plans to operate the call center from 7 AM to 9 PM during the weekdays.

Several months ago, the hospital hired an ambitious management consulting firm, Creative Chaos Consultants, to forecast the number of calls the call center would receive each hour of the day. Since all appointment and registration-related calls would be received by the call center, the consultants decided that they could forecast the calls at the call center by totaling the number of appointment and registration-related calls received by all clinics and departments. The team members visited all the clinics and departments, where they diligently recorded every call relating to appointments and registration. They then totaled these calls and altered the totals to account for calls missed during data collection. They also altered totals to account for repeat calls that occurred when the same parent called the hospital many times because of the confusion surrounding the decentralized process. Creative Chaos Consultants determined the average number of calls the call center should expect during each hour of a weekday. The following table provides the forecasts.

Source: This case is based on an actual project completed by a team of master's students in the Department of Engineering Economic Systems and Operations Research at Stanford University.

Work Shift	Average Number of Calls
7 AM to 9 AM	40 calls per hour
9 AM to 11 AM	85 calls per hour
11 AM to 1 PM	70 calls per hour
1 PM to 3 PM	95 calls per hour
3 PM to 5 PM	80 calls per hour
5 PM to 7 PM	35 calls per hour
7 PM to 9 PM	10 calls per hour

After the consultants submitted these forecasts, Lenny became interested in the percentage of calls from Spanish speakers since the hospital services many Spanish patients. Lenny knows that he has to hire some operators who speak Spanish to handle these calls. The consultants performed further data collection and determined that, on average, 20 percent of the calls were from Spanish speakers.

Given these call forecasts, Lenny must now decide how to staff the call center during each two-hour shift of a weekday. During the forecasting project, Creative Chaos Consultants closely observed the operators working at the individual clinics and departments and determined the number of calls operators process per hour. The consultants informed Lenny that an operator is able to process an average of six calls per hour. Lenny also knows that he has both full-time and part-time workers available to staff the call center. A full-time employee works eight hours per day, but because of paperwork that must also be completed, the employee spends only four hours per day on the phone. To balance the schedule, the employee alternates the two-hour shifts between answering phones and completing paperwork. Full-time employees can start their day either by answering phones or by completing paperwork on the first shift. The full-time employees speak either Spanish or English, but none of them are bilingual. Both Spanish-speaking and English-speaking employees are paid $10 per hour for work before 5 PM and $12 per hour for work after 5 PM. The full-time employees can begin work at the beginning of the 7 AM to 9 AM shift, 9 AM to 11 AM shift, 11 AM to 1 PM shift, or 1 PM to 3 PM shift. The part-time employees work for four hours, only answer calls, and only speak English. They can start work at the beginning of the 3 PM to 5 PM shift or the 5 PM to 7 PM shift, and,

like the full-time employees, they are paid $10 per hour for work before 5 PM and $12 per hour for work after 5 PM.

For the following analysis, consider only the labor cost for the time employees spend answering phones. The cost for paperwork time is charged to other cost centers.

a. How many Spanish-speaking operators and how many English-speaking operators does the hospital need to staff the call center during each two-hour shift of the day in order to answer all calls? Please provide an integer number since half a human operator makes no sense.

b. Lenny needs to determine how many full-time employees who speak Spanish, full-time employees who speak English, and part-time employees he should hire to begin on each shift. Creative Chaos Consultants advises him that linear programming can be used to do this in such a way as to minimize operating costs while answering all calls. Formulate a linear programming model of this problem.

c. Obtain an optimal solution for the linear programming model formulated in part *b* to guide Lenny's decision.

d. Because many full-time workers do not want to work late into the evening, Lenny can find only one qualified English-speaking operator willing to begin work at 1 PM. Given this new constraint, how many full-time English-speaking operators, full-time Spanish-speaking operators, and part-time operators should Lenny hire for each shift to minimize operating costs while answering all calls?

e. Lenny now has decided to investigate the option of hiring bilingual operators instead of monolingual operators. If all the operators are bilingual, how many operators should be working during each two-hour shift to answer all phone calls? As in part *a*, please provide an integer answer.

f. If all employees are bilingual, how many full-time and part-time employees should Lenny hire to begin on each shift to minimize operating costs while answering all calls? As in part *b*, formulate a linear programming model to guide Lenny's decision.

g. What is the maximum percentage increase in the hourly wage rate that Lenny can pay bilingual employees over monolingual employees without increasing the total operating costs?

h. What other features of the call center should Lenny explore to improve service or minimize operating costs?

3

LINEAR PROGRAMMING: FORMULATION AND APPLICATIONS

Linear programming problems come in many guises. And their models take various forms. This diversity can be confusing to both students and managers, making it difficult to recognize when linear programming can be applied to address a managerial problem. Since managers instigate management science studies, the ability to recognize the applicability of linear programming is an important managerial skill. This chapter focuses largely on developing this skill.

The usual textbook approach to trying to teach this skill is to present a series of *diverse* examples of linear programming applications. The weakness of this approach is that it emphasizes *differences* rather than the *common threads* between these applications. Our approach will be to emphasize these common threads—the **identifying features**—that tie together linear programming problems even when they arise in very different contexts. We will describe some broad categories of linear programming problems and the *identifying features* that characterize them. Then we will use *diverse* examples, but with the purpose of illustrating and emphasizing the *common threads* among them.

We will focus on three key categories of linear programming problems: *resource-allocation* problems, *cost–benefit–trade-off* problems, and *distribution-network* problems. In each case, an important identifying feature is the nature of the *restrictions* on what decisions can be made, and thus the nature of the resulting *functional constraints* in the linear programming model. In particular, the functional constraints for each category of problems are *resource* constraints, *benefit* constraints, and (primarily) *fixed-requirement* constraints, respectively. For each category, you will see how the basic data for a problem lead directly to a linear programming model with a certain distinctive form. Thus, *model formulation* becomes a by-product of proper *problem formulation.*

Although many linear programming problems fall completely into one of these categories, and so have only the corresponding kind of functional constraint, many others do not because they have at least a few functional constraints of one or both of the other kinds. Problems with a mixture of constraint types fall into a fourth category of linear programming problems—*mixed problems.*

The chapter begins with a case study that initially involves a *resource-allocation* problem. We then return to the case study in Section 3.5, where additional managerial considerations turn the problem into a *mixed* problem.

Sections 3.2, 3.3, 3.4, and 3.6 focus on the four categories of linear programming problems in turn. Section 3.7 then will take a broader look at the formulation of linear programming models from a managerial perspective. This section (along with Section 3.5) will highlight the importance of having the model accurately reflect the managerial view of the problem. These (and other) sections also will describe the flexibility available to managers for having the model structured to best fit their view of the important considerations.

Finally, Section 3.8 will revisit the three case studies of classic applications of linear programming presented in Section 2.1. This revisit will include a discussion of some of the factors that made these applications so successful.

As you read on, keep in mind the following five teaching goals for this chapter:

1. To become familiar with the different categories of linear programming problems.
2. To understand the basic formulation procedure for linear programming problems.
3. To gain insight into how such problems can arise in different contexts.
4. To learn how to recognize managerial problems that can be formulated and analyzed as linear programming problems.
5. To understand the flexibility that managers have in prescribing key considerations that can then be incorporated into the linear programming model.

3.1 A Case Study: The Super Grain Corp. Advertising-Mix Problem

Claire Syverson, Vice President for Marketing of the Super Grain Corporation, is facing a daunting challenge: how to break into an already overly crowded breakfast cereal market in a big way. Fortunately, the company's new breakfast cereal—Crunchy Start—has a lot going for it: Great taste. Nutritious. Crunchy from start to finish. She can recite the litany in her sleep now. It has the makings of a winning promotional campaign.

However, Claire knows that she has to avoid the mistakes she made in her last campaign for a breakfast cereal. That had been her first big assignment since she won this promotion, and what a disaster! She thought she had developed a really good campaign. But somehow it had failed to connect with the most crucial segments of the market—young children and parents of young children. She also has concluded that it was a mistake not to include cents-off coupons in the magazine and newspaper advertising. Oh well. Live and learn.

But she had better get it right this time, especially after the big stumble last time. The company's president, David Sloan, already has impressed on her how important the success of Crunchy Start is to the future of the company. She remembers exactly how David concluded the conversation. "The company's shareholders are not happy. We need to get those earnings headed in the right direction again." Claire had heard this tune before, but she saw in David's eyes how deadly serious he is this time.

David also is very helpful. He said he is assigning a top-notch management science team to work with her to help optimize the promotional campaign. That is good news. Not having had the management science people involved with the last campaign was another mistake she has since regretted.

Now it is time to sit down with the management science team and take a hard look together at the problem.

The Problem

Claire already has employed a leading advertising firm, Giacomi & Jackowitz, to help design a nationwide promotional campaign that will achieve the largest possible exposure for Crunchy Start. Super Grain will pay this firm a fee based on services performed (not to exceed $1 million) and has allocated an additional $4 million for advertising expenses.

Giacomi & Jackowitz has identified the three most effective advertising media for this product:

Medium 1: Television commercials on Saturday morning programs for children.
Medium 2: Advertisements in food and family-oriented magazines.
Medium 3: Advertisements in Sunday supplements of major newspapers.

The problem now is to determine which *levels* should be chosen for these *advertising activities* to obtain the most effective *advertising mix.*

To determine the *best mix of activity levels* for this particular advertising problem, it is necessary (as always) to identify the *overall measure of performance* for the problem and then the contribution of each activity toward this measure. An ultimate goal for Super Grain is to maximize its profits, but it is difficult to make a direct connection between advertising exposure and profits. Therefore, as a surrogate for profit, Claire and the management science team agree to use *expected exposure* as the overall measure of performance. Each *unit*

TABLE 3.1   Data for the Super Grain Corp. Advertising-Mix Problem

Resource	Resource Usage per Unit of Each Activity			Amount of Resource Available
	TV Commercials	Magazine Ads	Sunday Ads	
1. Ad budget	$300,000	$150,000	$100,000	$4 million
2. Planning budget	$90,000	$30,000	$40,000	$1 million
3. TV spots	1	0	0	5
Contribution per unit	130	60	50	

Contribution per unit = number of expected exposure units per advertisement

of expected exposure represents a certain amount of positive impact from an advertisement, based on the number of people reached, the audience profile, and the likelihood that seeing it will induce a purchase.

Giacomi & Jackowitz has made preliminary plans for advertisements in the three media. The firm also has estimated the number of expected exposure units for each advertisement[1] in each medium, as given in the bottom row of Table 3.1.

The number of advertisements that can be run in the different media are restricted by both the advertising budget (a limit of $4 million) and the planning budget (a limit of $1 million for the fee to Giacomi & Jackowitz). Another restriction: Because few spots for commercials on children's television programs Saturday morning (medium 1) still are available for purchase during the time of the promotional campaign, only five different commercials could be run for the desired length of time. (The other two media have an ample number of spots available.)

Consequently, the three *limited resources* for this problem are

Resource 1: Advertising budget ($4 million).
Resource 2: Planning budget ($1 million).
Resource 3: Commercial spots available (5).

The amounts available of these resources are shown in the last column of Table 3.1. An estimate of the amount of each resource that would be used by each advertisement in the respective media is then shown in the main body of this table.

- The first row gives the cost per advertisement in each medium.
- The second row shows Giacomi & Jackowitz's estimates of its total cost (including overhead and profit) for designing and developing each advertisement for the respective media.[2] (This cost represents the billable fee from Super Grain.)
- The third row indicates that each advertisement (commercial) run on television uses up one of the five commercial spots that are available for purchase.
- The last row then gives the expected number of exposure units per advertisement.

Analysis of the Problem by the Management Science Team

The management science team decides to formulate and solve a linear programming model for this problem on a spreadsheet. The formulation procedure summarized at the end of Section 2.3 guides this process. Like any linear programming model, this model will have four components:

---

[1]The simplifying assumption is being made that each additional advertisement in a medium provides the same number of expected exposure units as the first advertisement in that medium.

[2]When presenting its estimates in this form, the firm is making two simplifying assumptions. One is that its cost for designing and developing each additional advertisement in a medium is roughly the same as for the first advertisement in that medium. The second is that its cost when working with one medium is unaffected by how much work it is doing (if any) with the other media.

1. The data
2. The decisions
3. The constraints
4. The measure of performance

The spreadsheet needs to be formatted to provide the following kinds of cells for these components:

Data → data cells

Decisions → changing cells

Constraints → output cells

Measure of performance → target cell

Figure 3.1 shows the spreadsheet model formulated by the team. Let us see how the team did this by considering each of the components of the model individually.

The Data.   Table 3.1 provides the key data for the problem. Using units of *thousands of dollars,* these data have been transferred directly into data cells in rows 6–9 (columns C, D, E, and H) in the spreadsheet.

The Decisions.   The problem has been defined as determining the most effective advertising mix among the three media selected by Giacomi & Jackowitz. Therefore, there are three decisions:

Decision 1:   TV = number of commercials on television.

Decision 2:   *M* = number of advertisements in magazines.

Decision 3:   SS = number of advertisements in Sunday supplements.

The changing cells to hold these numbers have been placed just under the data (row 10) in the columns for these media:

TV → cell C10   *M* → cell D10   SS → cell E10

The Constraints.   These changing cells need to be nonnegative. In addition, there are three limited resources listed in cells B6, B7, and B8, where the amounts available are shown in

FIGURE 3.1

The spreadsheet model for the Super Grain problem (Section 3.1), including the formulas for the output cells in column F and the specifications needed to set up the Solver. The changing cells (C10:E10) show the optimal solution obtained by the Solver.

	A	B	C	D	E	F	G	H
1		Super Grain Corp. Advertising – Mix Problem						
2								
3			Resource Usage per Unit of Each Activity					
4								Resource
5		Resource	TV Commercials	Magazine Ads	SS Ads	Totals		Available
6		Ad Budget	300	150	100	4000	≤	4000
7		Planning Budget	90	30	40	1000	≤	1000
8		TV Spots	1	0	0	0	≤	5
9		Unit Exposure	130	60	50	1700		
10		Solution	0	20	10			

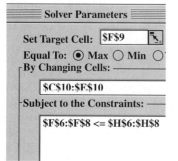

Solver Parameters

Set Target Cell: $F$9

Equal To: ⦿ Max ◯ Min ◯

By Changing Cells:

$C$10:$F$10

Subject to the Constraints:

$F$6:$F$8 <= $H$6:$H$8

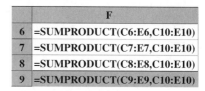

	F
6	=SUMPRODUCT(C6:E6,C10:E10)
7	=SUMPRODUCT(C7:E7,C10:E10)
8	=SUMPRODUCT(C8:E8,C10:E10)
9	=SUMPRODUCT(C9:E9,C10:E10)

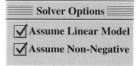

Solver Options

☑ Assume Linear Model

☑ Assume Non-Negative

column H. As suggested by the $\leq$ signs entered into column G, the corresponding constraints are

Total spending on advertising $\leq$ 4,000	(Ad budget in $1,000s)
Total cost of planning $\leq$ 1,000	(Planning budget in $1,000s)
Total number of television spots $\leq$ 5	(Number available for purchase)

Using the data in columns C, D, and E for the resources, these totals are

$$\text{Total spending on advertising} = 300TV + 150M + 100SS$$

$$\text{Total cost of planning} = 90TV + 30M + 40SS$$

$$\text{Total number of television spots} = TV$$

These sums of products on the right-hand side are entered into output cells F6, F7, and F8 by using the SUMPRODUCT functions shown in the lower right-hand side of Figure 3.1. Although the $\leq$ signs entered to the right of these output cells are only cosmetic (trial solutions still can be entered in the changing cells that violate these inequalities), they will serve as a reminder later to use these same $\leq$ signs when entering the constraints in the Solver dialogue box.

The Measure of Performance.   Claire Syverson and the management science team have agreed to use *expected exposure* as the overall measure of performance. Since cells C10, D10, and E10 give the number of expected exposure units per advertisement in the respective media, the total expected exposure from all the advertising is

$$\text{Exposure} = 130TV + 60M + 50SS$$

$$= \text{SUMPRODUCT (C9:E9, C10:E10)}$$

which needs to be entered into the target cell. Cell F9 is chosen as the target cell because it lies in the Exposure row and Totals column.

Summary of the Formulation.   The above analysis of the four components of the model has formulated the following linear programming model (in algebraic form) on the spreadsheet:

$$\text{Maximize} \quad \text{Exposure} = 130TV + 60M + 50SS$$

subject to

Ad spending:	$300TV + 150M + 100SS$	$\leq 4{,}000$
Planning costs:	$90TV + 30M + 40SS$	$\leq 1{,}000$
Number of television spots:	TV	≤ 5

and

$$TV \geq 0 \qquad M \geq 0 \qquad SS \geq 0$$

The difficult work of defining the problem and gathering all the relevant data in Table 3.1 leads directly to this formulation.

Solving the Model.   To solve the spreadsheet model formulated above, some key information needs to be entered into the Solver dialogue box. The lower left-hand side of Figure 3.1 shows the needed entries: the addresses of the target cell and the changing cells, the objective of maximizing the target cell, and the constraints that F6 $\leq$ H6, F7 $\leq$ H7, and F8 $\leq$ H8. In addition, the lower right-hand corner of the figure shows that two Solver options need to be selected: Assume Linear Model (because the model is a linear programming model) and Assume Non-Negative (because negative levels of advertising are impossible). Clicking on the Solve button then tells the Solver to find an optimal solution for the model and display it in the changing cells.

The optimal solution given in row 10 of the spreadsheet provides the following plan for the promotional campaign:

Do not run any television commercials.

Run 20 advertisements in magazines.

Run 10 advertisements in Sunday supplements.

Since the "profit" in this case is measured in expected exposure units, cell F9 indicates this plan would provide 1,700 expected exposure units.

Evaluation of the Adequacy of the Model.   When it chose to use a linear programming model to represent this advertising-mix problem, the management science team recognized that this kind of model does not provide a perfect match to this problem. However, a mathematical model is intended to be only an idealized representation of the real problem. Approximations and simplifying assumptions generally are required to have a workable model. All that is really needed is that there be a reasonably high correlation between the prediction of the model and what would actually happen in the real problem. The team now needs to check whether this criterion is satisfied.

One assumption of linear programming is that *fractional* solutions are allowed. For the current problem, this means that a fractional number (e.g., 3½) of television commercials (or of ads in magazines or Sunday supplements) should be allowed. This is technically true, since a commercial can be aired for less than a normal run, or an ad can be run in just a fraction of the usual magazines or Sunday supplements. However, one defect of the model is that it assumes that Giacomi & Jackowitz's cost for planning and developing a commercial or ad that receives only a fraction of its usual run is only that fraction of its usual cost, even though the actual cost would be the same as for a full run. Fortunately, the optimal solution obtained above was an *integer* solution (0 television commercials, 20 ads in magazines, and 10 ads in Sunday supplements), so the assumption that fractional solutions are allowed was not even needed.

Another key assumption of linear programming is that the equation for each of the output cells, including the target cell, can be expressed as a SUMPRODUCT function. For the target cell in Figure 3.1, this implies that the number of expected exposure units to be obtained from each advertising medium is *proportional* to the number of advertisements in that medium. Actually, this proportionality is only an approximation in this case because running too many advertisements in a medium reaches a saturation level where the impact of one more advertisement is substantially less than for the first advertisement in that medium. Another implication of using a SUMPRODUCT function is that the number of expected exposure units to be obtained from an advertising medium is unaffected by the number of advertisements in the other media. Again, this is not strictly true, especially when the total level of advertising reaches a saturation level.

To check how reasonable it is to use a SUMPRODUCT function for the target cell, the team meets with Sid Jackowitz, one of the senior partners of Giacomi & Jackowitz. Sid indicates that the contemplated promotional campaign (20 advertisements in magazines and 10 in Sunday supplements) is a relatively modest one well below saturation levels. Most readers will only notice these ads once or twice, and a second notice is very helpful for reinforcing the first one. Furthermore, the readership of magazines and Sunday supplements is sufficiently different that the interaction of the advertising impact in these two media should be small. Consequently, the management science team concludes that the SUMPRODUCT function for the target cell in Figure 3.1 provides a reasonable approximation.

Next, the team quizzes Sid about his firm's costs for planning and developing advertisements in these media. Is it reasonable to assume that the cost in a given medium is proportional to the number of advertisements in that medium? Is it reasonable to assume that the cost of developing advertisements in one medium would not be substantially reduced if the firm had just finished developing advertisements in another medium that might have similar themes? Sid acknowledges that there is some carryover in ad planning from one medium to another, especially if both are print media (e.g., magazines and Sunday supplements), but that the carryover is quite limited because of the distinct differences in these media. Furthermore, he feels that the proportionality assumption is quite reasonable for any given medium since the amount of work involved in planning and developing each additional advertisement in the medium is nearly the same as for the first one in the medium. The total fee that Super Grain will pay Giacomi & Jackowitz will eventually be based on a detailed accounting of the amount of work done by the firm. Nevertheless, Sid feels that the cost estimates previously provided by the firm (as entered in cells C7, D7, and E7 in units of thousands of dollars) give a reasonable basis for roughly projecting what the fee will be for any given plan (the entries in the changing cells) for the promotional campaign.

Based on this information, the management science team concludes that using a SUMPRODUCT function for cell F7 provides a reasonable approximation. Doing the same for cells F6 and F8 is clearly justified. Given its earlier conclusions as well, the team decides that the linear programming model incorporated into Figure 3.1 is a sufficiently accurate representation of the real advertising-mix problem. It will not be necessary to refine the results from this model by turning next to a more complicated kind of mathematical model (such as those to be described in Chapter 8).

Therefore, the team proceeds to develop a report of its study that includes a recommendation for the promotional campaign that corresponds to the optimal solution from the linear programming model (no TV commercials, 20 ads in magazines, and 10 ads in Sunday supplements). The team then submits this report to Claire and other members of management for their consideration.

Management's Reaction

Soon thereafter, Claire Syverson and David Sloan meet to discuss the report from the management science team.

> *David Sloan (president):* Thanks for passing on a copy of the management science team's report, Claire. It looks like they have developed a good proposal, although I was surprised to see that they're not making any use of TV commercials. What is your reaction, Claire?
>
> *Claire Syverson (Vice President for Marketing):* Yes, I think the team did a good job. But I am very concerned about the idea of not using TV commercials. Having commercials on the Saturday morning programs for children is our primary method of reaching young children. You know how important it will be to get young children to ask their parents for Crunchy Start. That is our best way of generating first-time sales. Those commercials also get seen by a lot of parents who are watching the programs with their kids. What we need is a commercial that is appealing to both parents and kids, and that gets the kids immediately bugging their parents to go buy Crunchy Start. I think that is a real key to a successful campaign.
>
> *David:* Yes, I agree with you, Claire. It looks like we should ask the management science team to go back and redo their study after taking this factor into account.
>
> *Claire:* Yes, I guess so. But they are using some technique called linear programming. I'm not very familiar with it. I don't know if it can handle this kind of consideration.
>
> *David:* Yes, it can. All you need to do is spell out to the team what your goals are regarding the number of young children and the number of parents of young children that need to be reached by this promotional campaign.
>
> *Claire:* That's easy. I already have those goals in mind.
>
> *David:* Good. Are there any other factors that the management science study has overlooked so far?
>
> *Claire:* Well, yes, one. The proposed plan doesn't take into account my budget for cents-off coupons in magazines and newspapers.
>
> *David:* Yes. Well, I'm sure the management science team will be able to handle that as well.
>
> *Claire:* Great. I'll get back to them right away. Thanks for all your help, David.
>
> *David:* You're welcome. Tell the team to keep up their good work and that I'll look forward to seeing their next report.
>
> *Claire:* Will do.

We will pick up this story again in Section 3.5.

Review Questions

1. What is the problem being addressed in this case study?
2. What overall measure of performance is being used?
3. Why is Claire Syverson concerned about the plan proposed by the management science team?
4. What are the assumptions of linear programming that the management science team needs to check to evaluate the adequacy of using a linear programming model to represent the problem under consideration.

3.2 Resource-Allocation Problems

In the opening paragraph of Chapter 2, we described managerial problems involving the allocation of limited resources to an organization's various productive activities. Those were *resource-allocation* problems.

Resource-allocation problems are linear programming problems involving the allocation of limited resources to activities. The *identifying feature* for any such problem is that each functional constraint in the linear programming model is a **resource constraint,** which has the form,

Amount of resource used $\leq$ Amount of resource available

for one of the limited resources.

The management science team studying a resource-allocation problem needs to gather (with considerable help) three kinds of data:

1. The *amount available* of each limited resource for the collective use of all the activities being considered in the study.
2. The amount of each resource needed by each activity. Specifically, for each combination of resource and activity, the *amount of resource used per unit of activity* must be estimated.
3. The *contribution per unit of each activity* to the overall measure of performance. (This measure of performance commonly is the *total profit* from the activities.)

These data can be gathered together into a single table having the format shown in Table 3.2, just as was done in Table 3.1 for the Super Grain case study. The data then can be entered on a spreadsheet with a similar format to begin the process of formulating a spreadsheet model, as illustrated in Figure 3.1 for the case study. (In fact, these two steps can be combined into one by gathering the data directly into a spreadsheet, but we will first show this kind of table throughout the chapter to clarify the problem being addressed before beginning the formulation of the spreadsheet model.)

TABLE 3.2   Format of a Parameter Table for a Resource-Allocation Problem

	Resource Usage per Unit of Each Activity				Amount of Resource Available
Resource	*1*	*2*	*3*	*. . .*	
1					
2					
.					
.					
.					
Contribution per unit					

There generally is considerable work involved in actually developing the data for a table like Table 3.2. A substantial amount of digging and consultation is needed to obtain the best estimates available in a timely fashion. This step is critical: Well-informed estimates of parameters are needed to obtain a valid linear programming model for guiding managerial decisions. The dangers involved in inaccurate estimates are one reason why *what-if analysis* (Chapter 4) is such an important part of most linear programming studies.

Once you fill in a table or spreadsheet like Table 3.2 with all the required data, you are well under way in formulating the linear programming model. In fact, Table 3.2 is called the **parameter table** because the data in the table are the parameters for the model.

Beginning with the case study and then the familiar Wyndor Glass Co. product-mix problem, we will take a brief look at three resource-allocation problems. These examples illustrate the formulation process for this type of problem and demonstrate how it can arise in a variety of contexts.

The Super Grain Corp. Advertising-Mix Problem

The linear programming model formulated in Section 3.1 for the Super Grain case study is one example of a resource-allocation problem. The three *activities* under consideration are the advertising in the three types of media chosen by Giacomi & Jackowitz. The limited *resources* to be allocated to these activities are

> Resource 1: Advertising budget ($4 million).
> Resource 2: Planning budget ($1 million).
> Resource 3: Commercial spots available (5).

Thus, each of the functional constraints in the model is a *resource constraint* for one of these resources. The preceding section describes how the numbers in the model come directly from Table 3.1, which is the parameter table for this problem.

The Wyndor Glass Co. Product-Mix Problem

The product-mix problem facing the management of the Wyndor Glass Co. in Section 2.2 is to determine the most profitable mix of production rates for the two new products, considering the limited availability of spare production capacity in the company's three plants. This is a resource-allocation problem. The *activities* under consideration are

> Activity 1: Produce the special new doors.
> Activity 2: Produce the special new windows.

The limited *resources* to be allocated to these activities are

> Resource 1: Production capacity in Plant 1.
> Resource 2: Production capacity in Plant 2.
> Resource 3: Production capacity in Plant 3.

Each of the three functional constraints in the linear programming model formulated in Section 2.3 is a *resource constraint* for one of these three resources.

Table 2.1 in Section 2.2 provides the data for this problem. This table is one example of Table 3.2 as applied to a specific problem. You already have seen how the numbers in Table 2.1 become the parameters in the linear programming model in either its spreadsheet formulation (Section 2.3) or its algebraic form (Section 2.4).

Capital Budgeting

Financial planning is one of the most important areas of application for resource-allocation problems. The limited resources being allocated in this area are quite different from those for applications in the *production planning* area (such as the Wyndor Glass Co. product-mix problem), where the resources tend to be *production facilities* of various kinds. For financial planning, the resources tend to be *financial assets* such as cash, securities, accounts receivable, lines of credit, and so forth. Our specific example involves *capital budgeting,* where the limited resources are amounts of investment capital available at different points in time.

The Problem. The Think-Big Development Co. is a major investor in commercial real-estate development projects. It currently has the opportunity to share in three large construction projects:

Project 1: A high-rise office building.

Project 2: A hotel.

Project 3: A shopping center.

Each project requires each partner to make investments at four different points in time: a down payment now, and additional capital after one, two, and three years. Table 3.3 shows for each project the *total* amount of investment capital required from all the partners at these four points in time. Thus, a partner taking a certain percentage share of a project is obligated to invest that percentage of each of the amounts shown in the table for the project.

All three projects are expected to be very profitable in the long run. So the management of Think-Big wants to invest as much as possible in some or all of them. Management is willing to commit all the company's investment capital currently available, as well as all additional investment capital expected to become available over the next three years. The objective is to determine the *investment mix* that will be most profitable, based on current estimates of profitability.

Since it will be several years before each project begins to generate income, which will continue for many years thereafter, we need to take into account the *time value of money* in evaluating how profitable it might be. This is done by *discounting* future cash outflows (capital invested) and cash inflows (income), and then adding discounted net cash flows, to calculate a project's *net present value*.

Based on current estimates of future cash flows (not included here except for outflows), the estimated net present value for each project is shown in the bottom row of Table 3.3. All the investors, including Think-Big, then will split this net present value in proportion to their share of the total investment.

For each project, 100 1 percent *shares* (or fractions thereof) are being sold to major investors, such as Think-Big, who become the partners for the project by investing their proportional shares at the four specified points in time. For example, if Think-Big takes 10 shares of Project 1, it will need to provide $4 million now, and then $6 million, $9 million, and $1 million in 1 year, 2 years, and 3 years, respectively.

The company currently has $25 million available for capital investment. Projections are that another $20 million will become available after one year, $20 million more after two years, and another $15 million after three years. How many shares should Think-Big take in the respective projects to maximize the total net present value of these investments?

Formulation. This is a *resource-allocation problem*. The activities under consideration are

Activity 1: Invest in Project 1.

Activity 2: Invest in Project 2.

Activity 3: Invest in Project 3.

The limited resources to be allocated to these activities are the funds available at the four investment points. Funds not used at one point are available at the next point. (For simplicity, we will ignore any interest earned on these funds.) Therefore, the *resource constraint* for each point must reflect the cumulative funds to that point.

TABLE 3.3 Financial Data for the Projects Being Considered for Partial Investment by the Think-Big Development Co.

| Year | Investment Capital Requirements | | |
	Project 1	Project 2	Project 3
0	$40 million	$80 million	$90 million
1	$60 million	$80 million	$60 million
2	$90 million	$80 million	$20 million
3	$10 million	$70 million	$60 million
Net present value	$45 million	$70 million	$50 million

Resource 1: Total investment capital available now.
Resource 2: Cumulative investment capital available by the end of one year.
Resource 3: Cumulative investment capital available by the end of two years.
Resource 4: Cumulative investment capital available by the end of three years.

By using cumulative amounts for the resources, and by using units of 1 percent shares for the projects, Table 3.2 can be filled in for this problem as shown in Table 3.4. Note that the numbers in Table 3.3 have been multiplied here by 1 percent, because each unit of an activity (investment in a project) is 1 percent of the total investment. To illustrate the effect of using cumulative amounts for the resources, consider the numbers in the Project 1 column of Table 3.4. These numbers are obtained from the corresponding column in Table 3.3 as follows:

Calculations for the Project 1 Column of Table 3.4
Row 1:   0.01 ($40 million) = $0.40 million
Row 2:   0.01 [$ (40 + 60) million] = $1.0 million
Row 3:   0.01 [$ (40 + 60 + 90) million] = $1.9 million
Row 4:   0.01 [$ (40 + 60 + 90 + 10) million] = $2.0 million
Bottom: 0.01 ($45 million) = $0.45 million

As outlined below, this table leads directly to the spreadsheet model in Figure 3.2.

The Data.   After developing Table 3.4, the first step in formulating the spreadsheet model is to enter the data in the table into data cells in rows 7–11 (columns C, D, E, and H). To save space on the spreadsheet, these numbers are entered in units of millions of dollars.

The Decisions.   With three activities under consideration, there are three decisions to be made:

Decision 1: P_1 = number of shares in Project 1 (an office building)
Decision 2: P_2 = number of shares in Project 2 (a hotel)
Decision 3: P_3 = number of shares in Project 3 (a shopping center)

These numbers are placed in changing cells just under the data cells (row 12) in the columns for the three projects, so

$$P_1 \rightarrow \text{cell C12} \qquad P_2 \rightarrow \text{cell D12} \qquad P_3 \rightarrow \text{cell E12}$$

The Constraints.   The numbers in these changing cells make sense only if they are nonnegative, so nonnegativity constraints are needed. In addition, the four resources require resource constraints:

Total invested now $\leq$ 25   (millions of dollars available)
Total invested within 1 year $\leq$ 45   (millions of dollars available)
Total invested within 2 years $\leq$ 65   (millions of dollars available)
Total invested within 3 years $\leq$ 80   (millions of dollars available)

TABLE 3.4   **Parameter Table for the Think-Big Development Co. Investment-Mix Problem**

| | Resource Usage per Unit of Each Activity (cumulative investment per 1% share) | | | |
Resource	Project 1	Project 2	Project 3	Amount of Resource Available
1	$0.40 million	$0.80 million	$0.90 million	$25 million
2	$1.00 million	$1.60 million	$1.40 million	$45 million
3	$1.90 million	$2.40 million	$1.60 million	$65 million
4	$2.00 million	$3.10 million	$2.20 million	$80 million
Contribution per unit	$0.45 million	$0.70 million	$0.50 million	

Contribution per unit = net present value of each 1 percent share in this project.

FIGURE 3.2

The spreadsheet model for the Think-Big problem, including the formulas for the output cells in column F and the specifications needed to set up the Solver. The changing cells (C12:E12) show the optimal solution obtained by the Solver.

	A	B	C	D	E	F	G	H
1		**Think–Big Development Co. Capital Budgeting Problem**						
2								
3			**Resource Usage per Unit of Each Activity**					
4			**(cumulative investment per 1% share)**					
5								**Resource**
6		**Resource**	**Project 1**	**Project 2**	**Project 3**	**Totals**		**Available**
7		**Capital Now**	0.4	0.8	0.9	25	≤	25
8		**Capital End Year 1**	1	1.6	1.4	44.76	≤	45
9		**Capital End Year 2**	1.9	2.4	1.6	60.58	≤	65
10		**Capital End Year 3**	2	3.1	2.2	80	≤	80
11		**Unit Profit ($millions)**	0.45	0.7	0.5	**18.11**		
12		**Solution**	0	16.505	13.107			

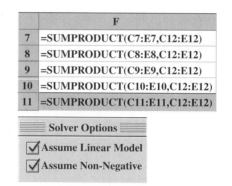

The data in columns C, D, and E indicate that (in millions of dollars)

$$\text{Total invested now} \qquad = 0.4\,P_1 + 0.8P_2 + 0.9P_3$$

$$\text{Total invested within 1 year} \; = \quad P_1 + 1.6\,P_2 + 1.4\,P_3$$

$$\text{Total invested within 2 years} = 1.9\,P_1 + 2.4\,P_2 + 1.6\,P_3$$

$$\text{Total invested within 3 years} = \quad 2\,P_1 + 3.1\,P_2 + 2.2\,P_3$$

The lower right-hand side of Figure 3.2 shows the SUMPRODUCT functions used to enter these totals into output cells in column F. Finally, ≤ signs are entered into column G to indicate the resource constraints that will need to be entered in the Solver dialogue box.

The Measure of Performance.   The objective is to

$$\text{Maximize} \qquad \text{NPV} = \text{total } \textit{net present value} \text{ of the investments}$$

Row 11 shows the net present value of each share of the respective investments, so the total net present value of all the shares purchased in all three projects is (in millions of dollars)

$$\text{NPV} = 0.45\,P_1 + 0.7\,P_2 + 0.5\,P_3$$

$$= \text{SUMPRODUCT (C11:E11, C12:E12)}$$

$$\rightarrow \text{cell F11}$$

where F11 is chosen as the address for the target cell because it is in the NPV row and Totals column.

Summary of the Formulation.   This completes the formulation of the linear programming model on the spreadsheet, as summarized below (in algebraic form).

$$\text{Maximize} \qquad \text{NPV} = 0.45P_1 + 0.7P_2 + 0.5P_3$$

subject to

Total invested now: $\qquad 0.4P_1 + 0.8P_2 + 0.9P_3 \leq 25$
Total invested within 1 year: $\qquad P_1 + 1.6P_2 + 1.4P_3 \leq 45$
Total invested within 2 years: $1.9P_1 + 2.4P_2 + 1.6 P_3 \leq 65$
Total invested within 3 years: $\qquad 2P_1 + 3.1P_2 + 2.2 P_3 \leq 80$

and

$$P_1 \geq 0 \qquad P_2 \geq 0 \qquad P_3 \geq 0$$

where all these numbers from Table 3.4 are in units of millions of dollars.

Note that this model possesses the key *identifying feature* for resource-allocation problems, namely, each functional constraint is a *resource constraint* that has the form

Amount of resource used $\leq$ Amount of resource available

Solving the Model. The lower left-hand side of Figure 3.2 shows the entries needed in the Solver dialogue box to specify the model, along with the selection of the usual two options shown in the bottom on the right-hand side. The spreadsheet shows the resulting optimal solution in row 12, namely,

Invest nothing in Project 1.
Invest in 16.505 shares of Project 2.
Invest in 13.107 shares of Project 3.

Cell F11 indicates that this investment program would provide a total net present value of $18.11 million.

Another Look at Resource Constraints

These examples of resource-allocation problems illustrated a variety of resources: financial allocations for advertising and planning purposes, TV commercial spots available for purchase, available production capacities of different plants, and cumulative investment capital available by certain times. However, these illustrations only scratch the surface of the realm of possible *limited resources* that need to be allocated to activities in resource-allocation problems. In fact, by interpreting *resource* sufficiently broadly, *any* restriction on the decisions to be made that has the form

Amount used $\leq$ Amount available

can be thought of as a *resource constraint,* where the thing whose amount is being measured is the corresponding "resource." Since *any* functional constraint with a $\leq$ sign in a linear programming model can be verbalized in this form, any such constraint can be thought of as a resource constraint.

> Hereafter, we will use **resource constraint** to refer to *any* functional constraint with a $\leq$ sign in a linear programming model. The constant on the right-hand side represents the *amount available* of a resource. Therefore, the left-hand side represents the *amount used* of this resource. In the algebraic form of the constraint, the coefficient (positive or negative) of each decision variable is the *resource usage per unit* of the corresponding activity.

Summary of the Formulation Procedure for Resource-Allocation Problems

The three examples illustrate that the following steps are used for any resource-allocation problem to define the specific problem, gather the relevant data, and then formulate the linear programming model.

1. Since any linear programming problem involves finding the *best mix* of levels of various activities, identify these *activities* for the problem at hand. The decisions to be made are the levels of these activities.
2. From the viewpoint of management, identify an appropriate *overall measure of performance* (commonly *profit,* or a surrogate for profit) for solutions of the problem.

3. For each activity, estimate the *contribution per unit of the activity* to this overall measure of performance. Insert these contributions in the bottom row of a *parameter table* like Table 3.2.

4. Identify the *limited resources* that must be allocated to the activities.

5. For each resource, identify the *amount available* and then the *amount used per unit of each activity.* Insert these quantities for each resource into the corresponding row of a *parameter table* like Table 3.2.

6. Enter the data gathered in steps 3 and 5 into *data cells* in a spreadsheet. A convenient format is the one used in a parameter table (see Table 3.2) except for leaving two blank columns between the *activity* columns and the *amount of resource available* column.

7. Designate *changing cells* for displaying the decisions on activity levels. A convenient location for these changing cells is in the activity columns just under the rows for the data cells.

8. For the two blank columns created in step 6, use the left one as a *Totals* column for *output cells* and enter ≤ signs into the right one for all the resources. In the row for each resource, use the SUMPRODUCT function to enter the *total amount used* in the Totals column.

9. Designate a *target cell* for displaying the overall measure of performance. A convenient location is in the row giving the data for this measure and in the Totals column. Use a SUMPRODUCT function to enter this measure of performance.

All the functional constraints in this linear programming model in a spreadsheet are *resource constraints,* that is, constraints with a ≤ sign. This is the *identifying feature* that classifies the problem as being a resource-allocation problem.

Review Questions

1. What is the identifying feature for a resource-allocation problem?

2. What is the form of a resource constraint?

3. What are the three kinds of data that need to be gathered for a resource-allocation problem?

4. What is the relationship between the parameter table for a resource-allocation problem and the corresponding linear programming model in a spreadsheet?

5. Compare the types of activities for the three examples of resource-allocation problems.

6. Compare the types of resources for the three examples of resource-allocation problems.

3.3 Cost–Benefit–Trade-off Problems

Cost–benefit–trade-off problems have a form that is very different from resource-allocation problems. The difference arises from *managerial objectives* that are very different for the two kinds of problems.

For resource-allocation problems, limits are set on the use of various resources (including financial resources), and then the objective is to make the most effective use (according to some overall measure of performance) of these given resources.

For cost–benefit–trade-off problems, management takes a more aggressive stance, prescribing what *benefits* must be achieved by the activities under consideration (regardless of the resulting resource usage), and then the objective is to achieve all these benefits with *minimum cost.* By prescribing a *minimum acceptable level* for each kind of benefit, and then minimizing the cost needed to achieve these levels, management hopes to obtain an appropriate *trade-off* between cost and benefits. (You will see in Chapter 4 that *what-if analysis* plays a key role in providing the additional information needed for management to choose the best trade-off between cost and benefits.)

TABLE 3.5 **Format of a Parameter Table for a Cost–Benefit–Trade-off Problem**

Benefit	Benefit Contribution per Unit of Each Activity				Minimum Acceptable Level
	1	*2*	*3*	*. . .*	
1					
2					
.					
.					
.					
Unit cost					

Cost–benefit–trade-off problems are linear programming problems where the mix of levels of various activities is chosen to achieve minimum acceptable levels for various benefits at a minimum cost. The *identifying feature* is that each functional constraint is a **benefit constraint,** which has the form

Level achieved ≥ Minimum acceptable level

for one of the benefits.

Interpreting *benefit* broadly, we can think of *any* functional constraint with a ≥ sign as a *benefit constraint.* In most cases, the *minimum acceptable level* will be prescribed by management as a policy decision, but occasionally this number will be dictated by other circumstances.

For any cost–benefit–trade-off problem, a major part of the study involves identifying all the activities and benefits that should be considered and then gathering the data relevant to these activities and benefits. Table 3.5 summarizes the kinds of data needed. For each benefit, you need to estimate how much each activity contributes to that benefit (per unit of the activity) and then prescribe the minimum acceptable level. You must also estimate the cost per unit of each activity. The resulting *parameter table* provides all the parameters needed for a linear programming model.

Let's examine three examples of cost–benefit–trade-off problems.

The Profit & Gambit Co. Advertising-Mix Problem

As described in Section 2.7, the Profit & Gambit Co. will be undertaking a major new advertising campaign focusing on three cleaning products. The two kinds of advertising to be used are television and the print media. Management has established minimum goals—the minimum acceptable increase in market share for each product—to be gained by the campaign.

The problem is to determine how much to advertise in each medium to meet all the market-share goals at a minimum total cost.

The activities in this cost–benefit–trade-off problem are

Activity 1:   Advertise on television.
Activity 2:   Advertise in the print media.

The benefits being sought from these activities are

Benefit 1: Increased market share for a spray prewash stain remover.
Benefit 2: Increased market share for a new liquid laundry detergent.
Benefit 3: Increased market share for a well-established powder laundry detergent.

As shown in Section 2.7, each benefit leads to a *benefit constraint* that incorporates the managerial goal for the *minimum acceptable level* of increase in the market share for the corresponding product.

The data for this problem are given in Table 2.2 (Section 2.7), which is a *parameter table* for a cost–benefit–trade-off problem, just like Table 3.5 but with more specific column headings to fit this particular problem. Section 2.7 describes how the linear programming model is formulated directly from the numbers in this table.

This example provides an interesting contrast with the Super Grain Corp. case study in Section 3.1, which led to a formulation as a resource-allocation problem. Both are advertising-mix problems, yet they lead to entirely different linear programming models. They differ because of the differences in the managerial view of the key issues in each case:

- As the Vice President for Marketing of Super Grain, Claire Syverson focused first on how much to spend on the advertising campaign and then set limits (an advertising budget of $4 million and a planning budget of $1 million) that led to resource constraints.
- The management of Profit & Gambit instead focused on what it wanted the advertising campaign to accomplish and then set goals (minimum required increases in market share) that led to benefit constraints.

From this comparison, we see that it is not the nature of the *application* that determines the classification of the resulting linear programming formulation. Rather, it is the nature of the *restrictions* imposed on the decisions regarding the mix of activity levels. If the restrictions involve *limits* on the usage of resources, that identifies a resource-allocation problem. If the restrictions involve *goals* on the levels of benefits, that characterizes a cost–benefit–trade-off problem. Frequently, the nature of the restrictions arise from the way management frames the problem.

However, we don't want you to get the idea that every linear programming problem falls entirely and neatly into either one type or the other. In the preceding section and this one, we are looking at *pure* resource-allocation problems and *pure* cost–benefit–trade-off problems. Although many *real* problems tend to be either one type or the other, it is fairly common to have *both* resource constraints and benefit constraints, even though one may predominate. Furthermore, we still need to consider one more category of linear programming problems (distribution-network problems) in the next section. This category will feature a third distinctive kind of constraint that sometimes arises in other problems as well. Mixed problems that combine features from these three categories are discussed and illustrated in Section 3.6.

Now, another example of a pure cost–benefit–trade-off problem.

Personnel Scheduling

One of the *real* applications of linear programming described in Section 2.1 involved a massive personnel scheduling problem at United Airlines. The resulting improvements saved the company more than $6 million annually. Part of that application concerned developing the *weekly* work schedules for customer service agents at major airports, where variations in the number of flights during different hours of the day can cause great fluctuations in the number of agents needed from one half-hour to the next.

We now will present a *greatly* simplified "textbook example" of this same kind of application. Among our simplifications, we will only consider a *daily* work schedule comprising intervals of two hours or longer. Nevertheless, the example will give you some feeling for how United Airlines approached its problem. It also will demonstrate the key role *benefit constraints* play in this kind of application.

The Problem.   Union Airways is adding more flights to and from its hub airport, and so needs to hire additional customer service agents. However, it is not clear just how many more should be hired. Management recognizes the need for cost control while also consistently providing a satisfactory level of service to the company's customers, so a desirable trade-off between these two factors is being sought. Therefore, a management science team is studying how to schedule the agents to provide satisfactory service with the smallest personnel cost.

Based on the new schedule of flights, an analysis has been made of the *minimum* number of customer service agents that need to be on duty at different times of the day to provide a satisfactory level of service. These numbers are shown in the last column of Table 3.6 for the time periods given in the first column. The other entries in this table reflect one

TABLE 3.6 Data for the Union Airways Personnel Scheduling Problem

	Time Periods Covered by Shift					Minimum Number of Agents Needed
Time Period	*1*	*2*	*3*	*4*	*5*	
6:00 AM to 8:00 AM	✓					48
8:00 AM to 10:00 AM	✓	✓				79
10:00 AM to noon	✓	✓				65
Noon to 2:00 PM	✓	✓	✓			87
2:00 PM to 4:00 PM		✓	✓			64
4:00 PM to 6:00 PM			✓	✓		73
6:00 PM to 8:00 PM			✓	✓		82
8:00 PM to 10:00 PM				✓		43
10:00 PM to midnight				✓	✓	52
Midnight to 6:00 AM					✓	15
Daily cost per agent	$170	$160	$175	$180	$195	

of the provisions in the company's current contract with the union that represents the customer service agents. The provision is that each agent works an eight-hour shift and the authorized shifts are

Shift 1: 6:00 AM to 2:00 PM.
Shift 2: 8:00 AM to 4:00 PM.
Shift 3: Noon to 8:00 PM.
Shift 4: 4:00 PM to midnight.
Shift 5: 10:00 PM to 6:00 AM.

Check marks in the main body of Table 3.6 show the time periods covered by the respective shifts. Because some shifts are less desirable than others, the wages specified in the contract differ by shift. For each shift, the daily compensation (including benefits) for each agent is shown in the bottom row. The problem is to determine how many agents should be assigned to the respective shifts each day to minimize the *total* personnel cost for agents, based on this bottom row, while meeting (or surpassing) the service requirements given in the last column.

Formulation. This problem is, in fact, a pure cost–benefit–trade-off problem. To formulate the problem, we need to identify the *activities* and *benefits* involved.

Activities correspond to shifts.
The *level* of each activity is the number of agents assigned to that shift.
A *unit* of each activity is one agent assigned to that shift.

Thus, the general description of a linear programming problem as finding the *best mix of activity levels* can be expressed for this specific application as finding the *best mix of shift sizes.*

Benefits correspond to time periods.
For each time period, the *benefit* provided by the activities is the service that agents provide customers during that period.
The *level* of a benefit is measured by the number of agents on duty during that time period.

With these interpretations, the data in Table 3.6 can be converted directly into a *parameter table for a cost–benefit–trade-off problem* (like Table 3.5), as shown in Table 3.7. For each benefit, note that the *benefit contribution per unit of each activity* is just the number of additional agents on duty in that time period because of assigning one more

TABLE 3.7   Parameter Table for the Union Airways Personnel Scheduling Problem

	Benefit Contribution per Unit of Each Activity					
Benefit	*6 AM Shift*	*8 AM Shift*	*Noon Shift*	*4 PM Shift*	*10 PM Shift*	*Minimum Acceptable Level*
Serve 6–8 AM	1	0	0	0	0	48
Serve 8–10 AM	1	1	0	0	0	79
Serve 10–noon	1	1	0	0	0	65
Serve noon–2 PM	1	1	1	0	0	87
Serve 2–4 PM	0	1	1	0	0	64
Serve 4–6 PM	0	0	1	1	0	73
Serve 6–8 PM	0	0	1	1	0	82
Serve 8–10 PM	0	0	0	1	0	43
Serve 10–midnight	0	0	0	1	1	52
Serve midnight–6 AM	0	0	0	0	1	15
Unit cost	$170	$160	$175	$180	$195	

agent to that shift. Assigning one more agent to a shift will add either 1 or 0 agents to a time period, depending on whether the shift covers the time period or not. Therefore, the benefit contribution per unit of an activity is either 1 or 0.

Once again, a careful formulation of the problem, including gathering all the relevant data in a parameter table, leads rather directly to a spreadsheet model. This model is shown in Figure 3.3, and we outline its formulation below.

The Data.   As indicated in this figure, all the data in Table 3.7 have been entered directly into the data cells in rows 6–16 in columns C to G and column J. (In fact, once you get the hang of it, you probably will want to construct a parameter table directly on a spreadsheet in this way from the outset.)

The Decisions.   Since the activities in this case correspond to the five shifts, the decisions to be made are

S_1 = number of agents to assign to Shift 1 (starts at 6 AM)
S_2 = number of agents to assign to Shift 2 (starts at 8 AM)
S_3 = number of agents to assign to Shift 3 (starts at noon)
S_4 = number of agents to assign to Shift 4 (starts at 4 PM)
S_5 = number of agents to assign to Shift 5 (starts at 10 PM)

The changing cells to hold these numbers have been placed in the activity columns in row 17, just under the rows for the data cells, so

$$S_1 \rightarrow \text{cell C17} \qquad S_2 \rightarrow \text{cell D17} \qquad \ldots \qquad S_5 \rightarrow \text{cell G17}$$

The Constraints.   These changing cells need to be nonnegative. In addition, we need 10 *benefit constraints,* where each one specifies that the *total* number of agents serving in the corresponding time period listed in column B must be no less than the minimum acceptable number given in column J. Thus, these constraints are

Total number of agents serving 6–8 AM ≥ 48 (min. acceptable)

Total number of agents serving 8–10 AM ≥ 79 (min. acceptable)

.

.

.

Total number of agents serving midnight–6 AM ≥ 15 (min. acceptable).

FIGURE 3.3

The spreadsheet model for the Union Airways problem, including the formulas for the output cells in column H and the specifications needed to set up the Solver. The changing cells (C17:G17) show the optimal solution obtained by the Solver.

	A	B	C	D	E	F	G	H	I	J
1		Union Airways Personnel Scheduling Problem								
2										
3			Benefit Contribution per Unit of Each Activity							Minimum
4										Acceptable
5		Benefit	6am Shift	8am Shift	Noon Shift	4pm Shift	10pm Shift	Totals		Level
6		Serve 6–8am	1	0	0	0	0	48	≥	48
7		Serve 8–10am	1	1	0	0	0	79	≥	79
8		Serve 10–12m	1	1	0	0	0	79	≥	65
9		Serve 12–2pm	1	1	1	0	0	118	≥	87
10		Serve 2–4pm	0	1	1	0	0	70	≥	64
11		Serve 4–6pm	0	0	1	1	0	82	≥	73
12		Serve 6–8pm	0	0	1	1	0	82	≥	82
13		Serve 8–10pm	0	0	0	1	0	43	≥	43
14		Serve 10–12m	0	0	0	1	1	58	≥	52
15		Serve 12–6am	0	0	0	0	1	15	≥	15
16		Unit Cost	$170	$160	$175	$180	$195	$30,610		
17		Solution	48	31	39	43	15			

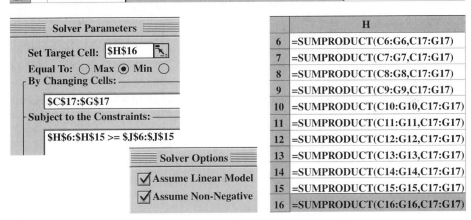

	Solver Parameters
	Set Target Cell: $H$16
	Equal To: ○ Max ◉ Min ○
	By Changing Cells:
	$C$17:$G$17
	Subject to the Constraints:
	$H$6:$H$15 >= $J$6:$J$15

	Solver Options
	☑ Assume Linear Model
	☑ Assume Non-Negative

	H
6	=SUMPRODUCT(C6:G6,C17:G17)
7	=SUMPRODUCT(C7:G7,C17:G17)
8	=SUMPRODUCT(C8:G8,C17:G17)
9	=SUMPRODUCT(C9:G9,C17:G17)
10	=SUMPRODUCT(C10:G10,C17:G17)
11	=SUMPRODUCT(C11:G11,C17:G17)
12	=SUMPRODUCT(C12:G12,C17:G17)
13	=SUMPRODUCT(C13:G13,C17:G17)
14	=SUMPRODUCT(C14:G14,C17:G17)
15	=SUMPRODUCT(C15:G15,C17:G17)
16	=SUMPRODUCT(C16:G16,C17:G17)

Since columns C to G indicate which of the shifts serve each of the time periods, these totals are

Total number of agents serving 6–8 AM $= S_1$

Total number of agents serving 8–10 AM $= S_1 + S_2$

.

.

.

Total number of agents serving midnight–6 AM $= S_5$

These totals are entered into the output cells in column H by using the SUMPRODUCT functions shown in the lower right-hand corner of Figure 3.3.

The Measure of Performance. The objective is to

Minimize Cost = total daily personnel cost for all agents

Since row 16 (columns C to G) gives the daily cost per agent on each shift,

Cost $= 170S_1 + 160S_2 + 175S_3 + 180S_4 + 195S_5$ (in dollars)

$=$ SUMPRODUCT (C16:G16, C17:G17)

→ cell H16

This target cell is placed in H16 because it is in both the Cost row and the Totals column.

Summary of the Formulation.   The above steps provide the complete formulation of the linear programming model on a spreadsheet, as summarized below (in algebraic form).

$$\text{Minimize} \quad \text{Cost} = 170S_1 + 160S_2 + 175S_3 + 180S_4 + 195S_5 \quad \text{(in dollars)}$$

subject to

Total agents 6–8 AM:	S_1	≥ 48
Total agents 8–10 AM:	$S_1 + S_2$	≥ 79

$$\cdot$$
$$\cdot$$
$$\cdot$$

$$\text{Total agents midnight–6 AM:} \qquad S_5 \geq 15$$

and

$$S_1 \geq 0 \qquad S_2 \geq 0 \qquad S_3 \geq 0 \qquad S_4 \geq 0 \qquad S_5 \geq 0$$

Solving the Model.   The Solver now can be applied to this model by making the entries in the Solver dialogue box shown in the lower left-hand corner of Figure 3.3, along with selecting the usual two Solver options indicated in the figure. Row 17 in the spreadsheet shows the resulting optimal solution for the number of agents that should be assigned to each shift. Cell H16 indicates that this plan would cost $30,610 per day.

Controlling Air Pollution

Our next example is a preview of Case 4.1 at the end of the next chapter. Rather than giving a full description of the problem and its data now, we will give a synopsis and then focus on our current theme—illustrating how *benefits* and *benefit constraints* arise to yield a *cost–benefit–trade-off problem.*

The Nori & Leets Co. is a major producer of steel in its part of the world. However, uncontrolled air pollution from the company's furnaces is endangering the health of nearby residents. The company and governmental officials together have developed stringent air quality standards for the region's airshed. These standards will require the company to reduce its annual emission rate for three main pollutants—particulate matter, sulfur oxides, and hydrocarbons—by 60 million pounds, 150 million pounds, and 125 million pounds, respectively. The company's engineers have analyzed various pollution abatement methods. On a per-unit basis, they have estimated for each method how much it would cost and how much it would reduce the emission rate for each of the three pollutants. It is clear that some mix of the pollution abatement methods will be needed to do the job. Consequently, a management science team is studying the problem of determining the *best mix* of pollution abatement methods to minimize the cost of meeting (or surpassing) the required reduction in the annual emission rates for the three pollutants.

This is a cost–benefit–trade-off problem.

The *activities* are the pollution abatement methods.

The *benefits* provided by these activities are the reductions in the emission of each of the three pollutants.

The *level* of a benefit is measured by the reduction in the annual emission rate (in units of millions of pounds) for the corresponding pollutant.

This problem has three *benefit constraints* (one for each pollutant), stated in the following form.

Particulate matter:	Reduction ≥ 60
Sulfur oxides:	Reduction ≥ 150
Hydrocarbons:	Reduction ≥ 125

You will have an opportunity to formulate these constraints and the remainder of the linear programming model as part of Case 4.1.

It is typical in cost–benefit–trade-off problems that the prescribed minimum acceptable levels for the benefits before formulating the linear programming model are very tentative. What management really wants is the *best trade-off* between cost and benefits. But that cannot be determined until after exploring the cost consequences of a variety of benefit levels.

Therefore, after obtaining an optimal solution (and its corresponding total cost) for the initial model, *what-if analysis* is used to explore how the total cost changes as changes are made in the minimum acceptable levels of the benefits. If the *marginal cost* (i.e., the rate of change in total cost) is small when benefit levels are increased, then a better trade-off would be achieved by increasing these levels. Conversely, if the marginal cost is large, then perhaps the minimum acceptable levels of benefits should be adjusted downward. Ultimately, choosing the best trade-off between cost and benefits is a *managerial judgment decision* that is guided by the information provided by *what-if analysis.*

This process of seeking the best trade-off between cost and benefits for the Nori & Leets problem is the focus of Case 4.1.

Summary of the Formulation Procedure for Cost–Benefit–Trade-off Problems

The nine steps in formulating any cost–benefit–trade-off problem follow the same pattern as presented at the end of the preceding section for resource-allocation problems, so we will not repeat them here. The main differences are that the overall measure of performance now is the total cost of the activities (or some surrogate of total cost chosen by management) in steps 2 and 3, benefits now replace resources in steps 4 and 5, and $\geq$ signs now are entered to the right of the output cells for benefits in step 8.

All the functional constraints in the resulting model are *benefit constraints,* that is, constraints with a $\geq$ sign. This is the *identifying feature* of a pure cost–benefit–trade-off problem.

Review Questions

1. What is the difference in managerial objectives between resource-allocation problems and cost–benefit–trade-off problems?
2. What is the identifying feature for a cost–benefit–trade-off problem?
3. What is the form of a benefit constraint?
4. What are the three kinds of data that need to be gathered for a cost–benefit–trade-off problem?
5. What is the relationship between the parameter table for a cost–benefit–trade-off problem and the corresponding linear programming model in a spreadsheet?
6. Compare the types of activities for the three examples of cost–benefit–trade-off problems.
7. Compare the types of benefits for the three examples of cost–benefit–trade-off problems.

3.4 Distribution-Network Problems

We now come to a third category of linear programming problems—**distribution-network problems**—so called because they deal with the *distribution* of goods through a *distribution network* at minimum cost. One example described in Section 2.1 is the Supply, Distribution, and Marketing (SDM) modeling system used by Citgo Petroleum Corporation to achieve savings of $16.5 million annually.

We will focus on distribution-network problems in Chapters 5 and 6. However, we include a small example here to complete your perspective on major categories of linear programming problems.

In this example, you'll see a new type of constraint—*fixed-requirement constraints.* These constraints are an *identifying feature* of distribution-network problems. Thus, fixed-requirement constraints play the same role for distribution-network problems as do *resource constraints* for resource-allocation problems and *benefit constraints* for cost–benefit–trade-off problems. Therefore, rather than identify resources or benefits, for distribution-network problems we need to identify *requirements* and their corresponding fixed-requirement constraints.

Fixed-requirement constraints also arise in *other* linear programming problems, as you will see in the next two sections.

TABLE 3.8 Some Data for the Distribution Unlimited Co. Distribution-Network Problem

| | Unit Shipping Cost | | | |
From \ To	Distribution Center	Warehouse 1	Warehouse 2	Output
Factory 1	$300	$700	—	80 units
Factory 2	$400	—	$900	70 units
Distribution Center	—	$200	$400	—
Allocation	—	60 units	90 units	

Distributing Goods through a Distribution Network

The Problem. The Distribution Unlimited Co. will be producing the same new product at two different factories, and then the product must be shipped to two warehouses. Factory 1 can send an unlimited amount by rail to Warehouse 1 only, whereas Factory 2 can send an unlimited amount by rail to Warehouse 2 only. Independent truckers can be used to ship up to 50 units from each factory to a distribution center, from which up to 50 units can be shipped to each warehouse. The shipping cost per unit for each alternative is shown in Table 3.8, along with the amounts to be produced at the factories and the amounts needed at the warehouses. The objective is to determine how to ship the needed units at a minimum total cost.

Figure 3.4 displays the distribution network for this problem. Each arrow shows one of the feasible *shipping lanes;* the corresponding unit shipping cost is given along the middle of the arrow. Also shown is the capacity limit (if any) for how much can be shipped through each shipping lane.

Formulation of the Problem in Linear Programming Terms. We need to identify the *activities* and *requirements* of this distribution-network problem to formulate it as a linear programming problem. In this case, two kinds of activities have been mentioned—the *production* of the new product at the two factories and the *shipping* of the product along the various shipping lanes. However, we know the specific amounts to be produced at each factory, so no decisions need to be made about the production activities. The decisions to be made concern the levels of the *shipping activities*—how much to ship through each shipping lane. Therefore, we need to focus on the shipping activities for the linear programming formulation.

The *activities* correspond to shipping lanes, depicted by arrows in Figure 3.4.

The *level* of each activity is the number of units shipped through the corresponding shipping lane.

Just as any linear programming problem can be described as finding the best mix of activity levels, this one involves finding the *best mix of shipping amounts* for the various shipping lanes. The decisions to be made are

$S_{F1\text{-}DC}$ = number of units shipped from Factory 1 to the Distribution Center (50 maximum)

$S_{F2\text{-}DC}$ = number of units shipped from Factory 2 to the Distribution Center (50 maximum)

$S_{F1\text{-}W1}$ = number of units shipped from Factory 1 to Warehouse 1

$S_{F2\text{-}W2}$ = number of units shipped from Factory 2 to Warehouse 2

$S_{DC\text{-}W1}$ = number of units shipped from the Distribution Center to Warehouse 1 (50 maximum)

$S_{DC\text{-}W2}$ = number of units shipped from the Distribution Center to Warehouse 2 (50 maximum)

so six changing cells will be needed in the spreadsheet. In addition to needing to be nonnegative, note that four of the changing cells will have a constraint that they cannot exceed 50.

FIGURE 3.4

The distribution network for the Distribution Unlimited Co. problem.

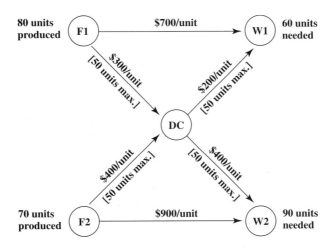

The objective is to

Minimize   Cost = total cost for shipping the needed units

Using the unit shipping costs given in Table 3.8,

$$\text{Cost} = 300S_{\text{F1-DC}} + 400S_{\text{F2-DC}} + 700S_{\text{F1-W1}} + 900S_{\text{F2-W2}} + 200S_{\text{DC-W1}} + 400\,S_{\text{DC-W2}}$$

is the quantity in dollars to be entered into the target cell. (We will use a SUMPRODUCT function to do this a little later.)

The spreadsheet model also will need some constraints involving *fixed requirements*. Both Table 3.8 and Figure 3.4 show four of these requirements for the problem.

Requirement 1: The total amount shipped from Factory 1 must be 80 units.
Requirement 2: The total amount shipped from Factory 2 must be 70 units.
Requirement 3: The total amount shipped to Warehouse 1 must be 60 units.
Requirement 4: The total amount shipped to Warehouse 2 must be 90 units.

Yet, there is one other requirement that is not so apparent! The units are all ultimately needed at the warehouses. So any units shipped from the factories to the distribution center should be forwarded to the warehouses. Therefore, the total amount shipped from the distribution center to the warehouses should *equal* the total amount shipped from the factories to the distribution center. In other words, the *difference* of these two shipping amounts should be *zero*.

Requirement 5: For the Distribution Center, the amount shipped out *minus* amount shipped in = 0.

With this subtle but significant point, you should now be able to see that there is a specific requirement associated with each of the five locations in the distribution network shown in Figure 3.4. Having one requirement for each location is a characteristic common to all distribution-network problems.

All five of these requirements can be expressed in constraint form as

Amount Provided = Required Amount

For example, Requirement 1 can be expressed algebraically as

$$S_{\text{F1-DC}} + S_{\text{F1-W1}} = 80$$

where the left-hand side gives the total amount shipped from Factory 1, and 80 is the required amount to be shipped from Factory 1. Therefore, this constraint restricts $S_{\text{F1-DC}}$ and $S_{\text{F1-W1}}$ to values that sum to the required amount of 80. In contrast to the ≤ form for resource constraints and the ≥ form for benefit constraints, the constraints express *fixed requirements* that must hold with equality.

TABLE 3.9 Parameter Table for the Distribution Unlimited Co. Distribution-Network Problem

| Requirement | Contribution Toward Required Amount per Unit Shipped Using Shipping Lane | | | | | | Required Amount |
	F1-DC	F2-DC	F1-W1	F2-W2	DC-W1	DC-W2	
1. F1 amount	1	0	1	0	0	0	80
2. F2 amount	0	1	0	1	0	0	70
3. W1 amount	0	0	1	0	1	0	60
4. W2 amount	0	0	0	1	0	1	90
5. DC amount	−1	−1	0	0	1	1	0
Capacity	50	50	Unlim.	Unlim.	50	50	
Unit cost	$300	$400	$700	$900	$200	$400	

Fixed-requirement constraints in a linear programming model are functional constraints that use an = sign. Each such constraint can be interpreted as expressing a fixed requirement that, for some type of quantity,

$$\text{Amount provided} = \text{Required amount}$$

One *identifying feature* of pure distribution-network problems is that the main functional constraints in the final form of their model are fixed-requirement constraints. However, *other* linear programming problems sometimes include fixed-requirement constraints as well.

Just as we developed a *parameter table* for resource-allocation problems (Table 3.2) and cost–benefit–trade-off problems (Table 3.5) preparatory to formulating the linear programming model in a spreadsheet, we can prepare a similar table for distribution-network problems, as demonstrated in Table 3.9 for the current example. The first column lists the types of quantities that have a fixed requirement and the last column gives the required amount for each of these quantities. Each entry in the main body of the table shows how much one unit shipped through that shipping lane would contribute toward fulfilling the required amount in the last column. The Capacity row shows the maximum number of units that can be shipped through each shipping lane (unlimited for the lanes in the two middle columns).

Formulation of the Spreadsheet Model. This completes the formulation of the problem, including identifying the decisions to be made, the constraints on these decisions, and the overall measure of performance, as well as gathering all the important data displayed in Table 3.9. Since careful *problem* formulation needs to precede *model* formulation, we now are able to formulate the spreadsheet model shown in Figure 3.5. The data cells in rows 6–12 (columns C to H and column K) hold all the data from Table 3.9. The changing cells in row 13 give the decisions on the amounts to be shipped through the respective shipping lanes. Column I is used for the output cells, where the SUMPRODUCT functions entered into these cells are shown in the lower right-hand side of the figure. Thus,

I6 = total amount shipped from Factory 1
I7 = total amount shipped from Factory 2
I8 = total amount shipped to Warehouse 1
I9 = total amount shipped to Warehouse 2
I10 = amount shipped out *minus* amount shipped in for the Distribution Center

where = signs have been entered into column J to remind us that these amounts are required to equal the respective amounts in column K. Since the Solver does not consider such mathematical symbols in the spreadsheet, these same constraints also have been entered into the bottom of the Solver dialogue box in the figure. Cell I12 is the target cell, where its SUMPRODUCT function gives the total shipping cost. The Solver dialogue box specifies that the objective

FIGURE 3.5

The spreadsheet model for the Distribution Unlimited problem, including the formulas for the output cells in column I and the specifications needed to set up the Solver. The changing cells (C13:H13) show the optimal solution obtained by the Solver.

	A	B	C	D	E	F	G	H	I	J	K
1	Distribution Unlimited Co. Distribution Problem										
2											
3			Contribution Toward Required Amount per Unit Shipped								
4			Using Shipping Lane								Required
5		Requirement	F1–DC	F2–DC	F1–W1	F2–W2	DC–W1	DC–W2	Totals		Amount
6		F1 Amount	1	0	1	0	0	0	80	=	80
7		F2 Amount	0	1	0	1	0	0	70	=	70
8		W1 Amount	0	0	1	0	1	0	60	=	60
9		W2 Amount	0	0	0	1	0	1	90	=	90
10		DC Amount	–1	–1	0	0	1	1	0	=	0
11		Capacity	50	50	–	–	50	50			
12		Unit Cost	$300	$400	$700	$900	$200	$400	$110,000		
13		Solution	50	30	30	40	30	50			

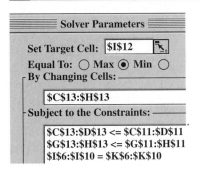

Solver Parameters

Set Target Cell: $I$12

Equal To: ◯ Max ⦿ Min ◯
By Changing Cells:

$C$13:$H$13

Subject to the Constraints:

$C$13:$D$13 <= $C$11:$D$11
$G$13:$H$13 <= $G$11:$H$11
$I$6:$I$10 = $K$6:$K$10

	I
6	=SUMPRODUCT(C6:H6,C13:H13)
7	=SUMPRODUCT(C7:H7,C13:H13)
8	=SUMPRODUCT(C8:H8,C13:H13)
9	=SUMPRODUCT(C9:H9,C13:H13)
10	=SUMPRODUCT(C10:H10,C13:H13)
12	=SUMPRODUCT(C12:H12,C13:H13)

Solver Options

☑ Assume Linear Model
☑ Assume Non-Negative

is to minimize this cost. The box also specifies that the shipping amounts in four of the changing cells cannot exceed the shipping capacities given in row 11. (The fact that cells E13 and F13 have unlimited shipping capacities has been indicated by inserting dashes into cells E11 and F11.) Finally, the figure indicates that the usual two Solver options have been selected to specify that the model is a linear programming model that has nonnegativity constraints.

Row 13 of the spreadsheet in Figure 3.5 shows the result of applying the Solver to obtain an optimal solution for the number of units to ship through each shipping lane. Cell I12 indicates that the total shipping cost for this shipping plan is $110,000.

To summarize, here is the algebraic form of the linear programming model that has been formulated in the spreadsheet.

Minimize $\text{Cost} = 300S_{\text{F1-DC}} + 400S_{\text{F2-DC}} + 700S_{\text{F1-W1}} + 900S_{\text{F2-W2}} + 200S_{\text{DC-W1}} + 400S_{\text{DC-W2}}$

subject to the following constraints:

1. *Fixed-requirement constraints:*

$$S_{\text{F1-DC}} \quad\; + S_{\text{F1-W1}} \qquad\qquad\qquad\qquad\qquad = 80 \qquad \text{(Factory 1)}$$

$$S_{\text{F2-DC}} \quad\; + S_{\text{F2-W2}} \qquad\qquad\qquad\qquad = 70 \qquad \text{(Factory 2)}$$

$$S_{\text{F1-W1}} \qquad\; + S_{\text{DC-W1}} \qquad\qquad = 60 \qquad \text{(Warehouse 1)}$$

$$S_{\text{F2-W2}} \qquad\qquad + S_{\text{DC-W2}} = 90 \qquad \text{(Warehouse 2)}$$

$$- S_{\text{F1-DC}} - S_{\text{F2-DC}} \qquad\qquad + S_{\text{DC-W1}} + S_{\text{DC-W2}} = 0 \qquad \text{(Distribution Center)}$$

2. *Upper-bound constraints:*

$$S_{\text{F1-DC}} \leq 50 \qquad S_{\text{F2-DC}} \leq 50 \qquad S_{\text{DC-W1}} \leq 50 \qquad S_{\text{DC-W2}} \leq 50$$

3. *Nonnegativity constraints:*

$$S_{\text{F1-DC}} \geq 0 \qquad S_{\text{F2-DC}} \geq 0 \qquad S_{\text{F1-W1}} \geq 0 \qquad S_{\text{F2-W2}} \geq 0 \qquad S_{\text{DC-W1}} \geq 0 \qquad S_{\text{DC-W2}} \geq 0$$

Review Questions

1. Why are distribution-network problems given this name?
2. What is an identifying feature of distribution-network problems?
3. How does the form of a fixed-requirement constraint differ from those for resource constraints and benefit constraints?
4. What are the quantities with fixed requirements in the Distribution Unlimited Co. problem?

3.5 Continuing the Super Grain Case Study

We now pick up the story of the Super Grain case study introduced in Section 3.1. As we left matters before, the management science team has just submitted a report to management recommending a plan for the promotional campaign for Crunchy Start. The team has based this recommendation on both the planning done by the advertising firm, Giacomi & Jackowitz, and the information provided by Super Grain's Vice President for Marketing, Claire Syverson, about management's objectives and constraints for the campaign. However, after seeing that the team has not recommended any television advertising, Claire now realizes that she has failed to provide some vital information about the target audiences for the campaign.

Incorporating Additional Managerial Considerations

Therefore, Claire and David Sloan (Super Grain's president) have concluded that the management science study needs to be expanded to incorporate some additional considerations. In particular, since the promotional campaign is for a breakfast cereal that should have special appeal to young children, they feel that two audiences should be targeted—*young children* and *parents of young children*. (This is why one of the three advertising media recommended by Giacomi & Jackowitz is commercials on children's television programs Saturday morning.) Consequently, Claire now has set two new goals for the campaign.

Goal 1: The advertising should be seen by at least five million young children.
Goal 2: The advertising should be seen by at least five million parents of young children.

In effect, these two goals are *minimum acceptable levels* for two special *benefits* to be achieved by the advertising activities.

Benefit 1: Promoting the new breakfast cereal to young children.
Benefit 2: Promoting the new breakfast cereal to parents of young children.

Because of the way the goals have been articulated, the *level* of each of these benefits is measured by the *number of people* in the specified category that are reached by the advertising.

To enable constructing the corresponding *benefit constraints* (as described in Section 3.3), the management science team asks Giacomi & Jackowitz to estimate how much each unit of each type of advertising activity will contribute to each benefit, as measured by the number of people reached in the specified category. These estimates are given in Table 3.10.

It is interesting to observe that management wants special consideration given to these two kinds of benefits even though the original spreadsheet model (Figure 3.1) already takes

---

TABLE 3.10   Parameter Table for the Benefit Constraints for the Revised Super Grain Corp. Advertising-Mix Problem

	Benefit Contribution per Unit of Each Activity			
Benefit	*TV Commercials*	*Magazine Ads*	*Sunday Ads*	*Minimum Acceptable Level*
Young children	1.2 million	0.1 million	0	5 million
Parents of young children	0.5 million	0.2 million	0.2 million	5 million

them into account to some extent. As described in Section 3.1, the *number of expected exposure units* is the overall measure of performance to be maximized. This measure considers various factors such as the number of people reached, the audience profile, and so on. However, maximizing this *general* measure of performance does *not* ensure that the two *specific* goals prescribed by management (Claire Syverson) will be achieved. Claire feels that achieving these goals is essential to a successful promotional campaign. Therefore, she complements the general objective with specific benefit constraints that *do* ensure that the goals will be achieved. Having benefit constraints added to incorporate managerial goals into the model is a prerogative of management.

Claire has one more consideration she wants incorporated into the model. She is a strong believer in the promotional value of *cents-off coupons* (coupons that shoppers can clip from printed advertisements to obtain a refund of a designated amount when purchasing the advertised item). Consequently, she always earmarks a major portion of her annual marketing budget for the redemption of these coupons. She still has $1,490,000 left from this year's allotment for coupon redemptions. Because of the importance of Crunchy Start to the company, she has decided to use this entire remaining allotment in the campaign promoting this cereal.

This *fixed amount* for coupon redemptions is a *fixed requirement* that needs to be expressed as a *fixed-requirement constraint*. As described in Section 3.4, the form of a fixed-requirement constraint is that, for some type of quantity,

$$\text{Amount provided} = \text{Required amount}$$

In this case, the quantity involved is the amount of money provided for the redemption of cents-off coupons. To specify this constraint in the spreadsheet, we need to estimate how much each unit of each type of advertising activity will contribute toward fulfilling the required amount for the quantity. Both medium 2 (advertisements in food and family-oriented magazines) and medium 3 (advertisements in Sunday supplements of major newspapers) will feature cents-off coupons. The estimates of the amount of coupon redemption per unit use of each of these media is given in Table 3.11.

Formulation of the Revised Spreadsheet Model

Figure 3.6 shows one way of formatting the spreadsheet to expand the original spreadsheet model in Figure 3.1 to incorporate the additional managerial considerations. We outline the four components of the revised model below.

The Data. Additional data cells in rows 13, 14, and 19 (columns C, D, E, and H) give the data in Tables 3.10 and 3.11, and the Unit Exposure data have been moved down from row 9 to row 21.

The Decisions. Recall that, as before, the decisions to be made are

TV	= number of commercials on television
M	= number of advertisements in magazines
SS	= number of advertisements in Sunday supplements

The changing cells to hold these numbers still are in the respective activity columns just under the last data row, so

$$\text{TV} \rightarrow \text{cell C22} \qquad M \rightarrow \text{cell D22} \qquad \text{SS} \rightarrow \text{cell E22}$$

TABLE 3.11 **Parameter Table for the Fixed-Requirement Constraint for the Revised Super Grain Corp. Advertising-Mix Problem**

	Contribution Toward Required Amount per Unit of Each Activity			
Requirement	TV Commercials	Magazine Ads	Sunday Ads	Required Amount
Coupon redemption	0	$40,000	$120,000	$1,490,000

FIGURE 3.6

The spreadsheet model for the revised Super Grain problem (Section 3.5), including the formulas for the output cells in column F and the specifications needed to set up the Solver. The changing cells (C22:E22) show the optimal solution obtained by the Solver.

	A	B	C	D	E	F	G	H
1		Super Grain Corp. Advertising – Mix Problem						
2								
3			Resource Usage per Unit of Each Activity					
4								Resource
5		Resource	TV Commercials	Magazine Ads	SS Ads	Totals		Available
6		Ad Budget	300	150	100	3775	≤	4000
7		Planning Budget	90	30	40	1000	≤	1000
8		TV Spots	1	0	0	3	≤	5
9								
10		Benefit Contribution per Unit of Each Activity						Minimum
11								Acceptable
12		Benefit	TV Commercials	Magazine Ads	SS Ads	Totals		Level
13		Young Children	1.2	0.1	0	5	≥	5
14		Parents of Young Children	0.5	0.2	0.2	5.85	≥	5
15								
16		Contribution Toward Required Amount per Unit of Each Activity						
17								Required
18		Requirement	TV Commercials	Magazine Ads	SS Ads	Totals		Amount
19		Coupon Redemption	0	40	120	1490	=	1490
20								
21		Unit Exposure	130	60	50	1617.5		
22		Solution	3	14	7.75			

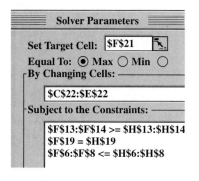

Solver Parameters
Set Target Cell: $F$21
Equal To: ● Max ○ Min ○
By Changing Cells:
$C$22:$E$22
Subject to the Constraints:
$F$13:$F$14 >= $H$13:$H$14
$F$19 = $H$19
$F$6:$F$8 <= $H$6:$H$8

	F
6	=SUMPRODUCT(C6:E6,C22:E22)
7	=SUMPRODUCT(C7:E7,C22:E22)
8	=SUMPRODUCT(C8:E8,C22:E22)
13	=SUMPRODUCT(C13:E13,C22:E22)
14	=SUMPRODUCT(C14:E14,C22:E22)
19	=SUMPRODUCT(C19:E19,C22:E22)
21	=SUMPRODUCT(C21:E21,C22:E22)

Solver Options
☑ Assume Linear Model
☑ Assume Non-Negative

The Constraints. In addition to the original constraints, we now have two benefit constraints and one fixed-requirement constraint. As specified for us (but not for the Solver) in rows 13 and 14, columns F to H, the benefit constraints are

Total number of young children reached ≥ 5 (goal 1 in millions)

Total number of their parents reached ≥ 5 (goal 2 in millions)

Using the data in columns C to E of these rows,

Total number of young children reached $= 1.2TV + 0.1M + 0SS$

$$= \text{SUMPRODUCT(C13:E13,C22:E22)}$$

$$\rightarrow \text{cell F13}$$

Total number of their parents reached $= 0.5TV + 0.2M + 0.2SS$

$$= \text{SUMPRODUCT(C14:E14,C22:E22)}$$

$$\rightarrow \text{cell F14}$$

Thus, column F is continuing to be used for output cells.

The fixed-requirement constraint indicated in row 19 is that

$$\text{Total coupon redemption} = 1{,}490 \qquad \text{(allotment in \$1{,}000s)}$$

where

$$\text{Total coupon redemption} = 0TV + 40M + 120SS$$

$$= \text{SUMPRODUCT(C19:E19,C22:E22)}$$

$$\rightarrow \text{cell F19}$$

These same constraints are specified for the Solver in the Solver dialogue box, along with the original constraints, in Figure 3.6.

The Measure of Performance.   Except for shifting rows 9 and 10 in Figure 3.1 down to rows 21 and 22 in Figure 3.6, the measure of performance continues to be

$$\text{Exposure} = 130TV + 60M + 50SS$$

$$= \text{SUMPRODUCT(C21:E21,C22:E22)}$$

$$\rightarrow \text{cell F21}$$

so F21 is the new address for the target cell.

Summary of the Formulation.   The above steps have resulted in formulating the following linear programming model (in algebraic form) on a spreadsheet.

$$\text{Maximize} \qquad \text{Exposure} = 130TV + 60M + 50SS$$

subject to the following constraints:

  1. *Resource constraints:*

$$300TV + 150M + 100SS \leq 4{,}000 \qquad \text{(ad budget in \$1{,}000s)}$$

$$90TV + \;\; 30M + \;\; 40SS \leq 1{,}000 \qquad \text{(planning budget in \$1{,}000s)}$$

$$TV \qquad\qquad\qquad\quad \leq \quad 5 \qquad \text{(television spots available)}$$

  2. *Benefit constraints:*

$$1.2TV + 0.1M \qquad\qquad \geq \quad 5 \qquad \text{(millions of young children)}$$

$$0.5TV + 0.2M + 0.2SS \geq \quad 5 \qquad \text{(millions of their parents)}$$

  3. *Fixed-requirement constraint:*

$$40M + 120SS = 1{,}490 \qquad \text{(coupon budget in \$1{,}000s)}$$

  4. *Nonnegativity constraints:*

$$TV \geq 0 \qquad M \geq 0 \qquad SS \geq 0$$

Solving the Model.   After making all the entries in the Solver dialogue box shown in Figure 3.6, plus selecting the usual two Solver options, the Solver finds the optimal solution given in row 22. This optimal solution provides the following plan for the promotional campaign:

  Run 3 television commercials.

  Run 14 advertisements in magazines.

  Run 7.75 advertisements in Sunday supplements (so the eighth advertisement would appear in only 75 percent of the newspapers).

Although the expected exposure with this plan is only 1,617.5, versus the 1,700 with the first plan shown in Figure 3.1, both Claire Syverson and David Sloan feel that the new plan does a much better job of meeting all of management's goals for this campaign. They decide to adopt the new plan.

This case study illustrates a common theme in real applications of linear programming—the continuing evolution of the linear programming model. It is common to make later adjustments in the initial version of the model, perhaps even many times, as experience is gained in using the model. Frequently, these adjustments are made to more adequately reflect some important managerial considerations.

Review Questions

1. What managerial goals needed to be incorporated into the expanded management science study for the Super Grain Corp.?
2. Which categories of functional constraints are included in the new linear programming model?
3. Why did management adopt the new plan even though it provides less expected exposure than the original plan recommended by the management science team?

3.6 Mixed Problems

Sections 3.2, 3.3, and 3.4 each described a broad category of linear programming problem—resource-allocation, cost–benefit–trade-off, and distribution-network problems. As summarized in Table 3.12, each features one of the three types of functional constraints. In fact, the *identifying feature* of a *pure* resource-allocation problem is that *all* its functional constraints are *resource constraints*. The *identifying feature* of a *pure* cost–benefit–trade-off problem is that *all* its functional constraints are *benefit constraints*. The main functional constraints in a distribution-network problem are *fixed-requirement constraints* of a certain kind (although the problem may have some simple resource constraints where each left-hand side is a single decision variable).

However, as illustrated by the Super Grain case study in Section 3.5, many linear programming problems do not fall into one of these three categories. Some *almost* fit one of the categories because they have functional constraints that mostly correspond to the type indicated in Table 3.12. Others do not come close to any category because no single type of functional constraint dominates. In either case, we will refer to them as *mixed problems*.

> The fourth (and final) category of linear programming problems is **mixed problems.** This category includes any problem that does not fit into one of the first three categories.

Some mixed problems have only two of the three types of functional constraints. Others have all three. For example, the formulation of the Super Grain Corp. problem in Section 3.5 includes two benefit constraints and one fixed-requirement constraint, in addition to the three resource constraints in the original problem.

We next give one new example of a different kind of application that further illustrates how all three types of functional constraints can arise in the same problem. This example also will illustrate a different kind of spreadsheet formulation for a linear programming model.

TABLE 3.12   Types of Functional Constraints

Type	Form*	Typical Interpretation	Main Usage
Resource constraint	LHS ≤ RHS	For some resource, Amount used ≤ Amount available	Resource-allocation problems and mixed problems
Benefit constraint	LHS ≥ RHS	For some benefit, Level achieved ≥ Minimum acceptable level	Cost–benefit–trade-off problems and mixed problems
Fixed-requirement constraint	LHS = RHS	For some quantity, Amount provided = Required amount	Distribution-network problems and mixed problems

*LHS = Left-hand side (a SUMPRODUCT function).
RHS = Right-hand side (a constant).

*Reclaiming Solid
Wastes*

The Problem.   The Save-It Company operates a reclamation center that collects four types of solid waste materials and then treats them so that they can be amalgamated (treating and amalgamating are separate processes) into a salable product. Three different grades of this product can be made, depending on the mix of the materials used. (See Table 3.13.) Although there is some flexibility in the mix for each grade, quality standards specify the minimum or maximum amount of the materials allowed in that product grade. (This minimum or maximum amount is the weight of the material expressed as a percentage of the total weight for that product grade.) For each of the two higher grades, a fixed percentage is specified for one of the materials. These specifications are given in Table 3.13 along with the cost of amalgamation and the selling price for each grade.

The reclamation center collects its solid waste materials from some regular sources and so is normally able to maintain a steady rate for treating them. Table 3.14 gives the quantities available for collection and treatment each week, as well as the cost of treatment, for each type of material.

The Save-It Co. is solely owned by Green Earth, an organization that is devoted to dealing with environmental issues; Save-It's profits are all used to help support Green Earth's activities. Green Earth has raised contributions and grants, amounting to $30,000 per week, to be used exclusively to cover the entire treatment cost for the solid waste materials. The board of directors of Green Earth has instructed the management of Save-It to divide this money among the materials in such a way that *at least half* of the amount available of each material is actually collected and treated. These additional restrictions are listed in Table 3.14.

Within the restrictions specified in Tables 3.13 and 3.14, management wants to allocate the materials to product grades so as to maximize the total weekly profit (total sales income *minus* total amalgamation cost).

Formulation of the Problem in Linear Programming Terms.   This is a *mixed* linear programming problem. To formulate it, we need to identify all the *activities, resources, benefits,* and *fixed requirements* lurking within it. The key to identifying the activities lies in management's goal to find the *best allocation of materials to product grades.* Each combination of a material and a product grade requires a decision: how much of that material should go into that product grade? This amount becomes the *level* of an *activity.*

> Each *activity* corresponds to the treatment of one solid waste material preparing it for amalgamation into one product grade.
>
> The *level* of this activity is the *amount* of the material treated preparatory to amalgamation into the product grade.

TABLE 3.13   Product Data for the Save-It Company

Grade	Specification	Amalgamation Cost per Pound	Selling Price per Pound
A	Material 1: Not more than 30% of the total Material 2: Not less than 40% of the total Material 3: Not more than 50% of the total Material 4: Exactly 20% of the total	$3.00	$8.50
B	Material 1: Not more than 50% of the total Material 2: Not less than 10% of the total Material 4: Exactly 10% of the total	$2.50	$7.00
C	Material 1: Not more than 70% of the total	$2.00	$5.50

TABLE 3.14   Solid Waste Materials Data for the Save-It Company

Material	Pounds/Week Available	Treatment Cost per Pound	Additional Restrictions
1	3,000	$3.00	1. For each material, at least half of the pounds/week available should be collected and treated.
2	2,000	$6.00	
3	4,000	$4.00	
4	1,000	$5.00	2. $30,000 per week should be used to treat these materials.

Thus, the decisions to be made are the number of pounds of each type of material to allocate to each product grade per week.

There are many constraints on these decisions because of limited resources, prescribed benefits, and fixed requirements, as summarized below.

> *Limited Resources:* The four solid waste materials, where the amounts available are given in the second column of Table 3.14. In addition, the limited usages of materials 1 and 3 specified in the second column of Table 3.13 are interpreted as limited resources that lead to resource constraints.
>
> *Prescribed Benefits:* The collection and treatment of each solid waste material is a benefit, where the minimum acceptable level (half of what is available) is prescribed on the right side of Table 3.14. In addition, the second column of Table 3.13 specifies minimum acceptable usages of material 2, so these are interpreted as prescribed benefits.
>
> *Fixed Requirements:*
> 1. The fixed usages of material 4 specified in the second column of Table 3.13.
> 2. The fixed amount of money to be used for treating the solid waste materials, as specified on the right side of Table 3.14.

Management's objective is to maximize the *total weekly profit* from all three product grades, so this is the overall measure of performance for the problem. It is calculated by subtracting the total amalgamation cost from the total sales income. The contributions and grants of $30,000 per week specifically for treating the solid waste materials completely cover the treatment costs, so these costs are not included in calculating profit. The only cost considered, therefore, is the amalgamation cost. Thus, for each product grade, the profit per pound is obtained by subtracting the amalgamation cost given in the third column of Table 3.13 from the selling price in the fourth column.

Formulation of the Spreadsheet Model.   As always, there is no single "right" way to format the spreadsheet for the formulation of the model for this problem. Since this problem is larger and more complicated than the previous examples, there are even more reasonable possibilities than usual in this case. For example, one possibility is to adopt the approach shown in Figure 3.6 of having separate rows of the spreadsheet used for the resource constraints, the benefit constraints, and the fixed-requirement constraints. However, we feel that the formulation shown in Figure 3.7 is preferable in this case because it is more compact and intuitive. We outline this formulation below.

The Data.   Tables 3.13 and 3.14 provide all the data for this problem. The numbers in the second and third columns of Table 3.14 have been entered into data cells in columns H and K (rows 6–9) of the spreadsheet. The minimum treatment quantities for the first additional restriction in this table are in column J (rows 6–9) and the $30,000 for the second additional restriction is in cell K12. The data in the last two columns of Table 3.13 have been entered in rows 12 and 13 (columns C to E). The percentages for the specifications in the second column are listed in rows 18–25 and column F.

FIGURE 3.7

The spreadsheet model for the Save-It problem, including the formulas for the output cells and the specifications needed to set up the Solver. The changing cells (C6:E9) show the optimal solution obtained by the Solver.

	A	B	C	D	E	F	G	H	I	J	K
1		Save-it Company Reclamation Problem									
2											
3			**Material Allocation**								Unit
4			(pounds of material used for each product grade)					Amount		Minimum	Treatment
5			Grade A	Grade B	Grade C	Total		Available		to Treat	Cost
6		Material 1	412.28	2587.7	0	3000	≤	3000	≥	1500	$3
7		Material 2	859.65	517.54	0	1377.19	≤	2000	≥	1000	$6
8		Material 3	447.37	1552.6	0	2000	≤	4000	≥	2000	$4
9		Material 4	429.82	517.54	0	947.37	≤	1000	≥	500	$5
10		Total	2149.1	5175.4	0	7324.56		Total Treatment Cost =			$30,000
11											=
12		Unit Amalg. Cost	$3	$2.50	$2	Total	Treatment Funds Available =				$30,000
13		Unit Selling Price	$8.50	$7	$5.50	Profit					
14		Unit Profit	$5.50	$4.50	$3.50	$35,109.65					
15											
16											
17		**Mixture Specifications**									
18		Grade A, Material 1	412.28	≤	644.74	30% Grade A					
19		Grade A, Material 2	859.65	≥	859.65	40% Grade A					
20		Grade A, Material 3	447.37	≤	1074.6	50% Grade A					
21		Grade A, Material 4	429.82	=	429.82	20% Grade A					
22		Grade B, Material 1	2587.7	≤	2587.7	50% Grade B					
23		Grade B, Material 2	517.54	≥	517.54	10% Grade B					
24		Grade B, Material 4	517.54	=	517.54	10% Grade B					
25		Grade C, Material 1	0	≤	0	70% Grade C					

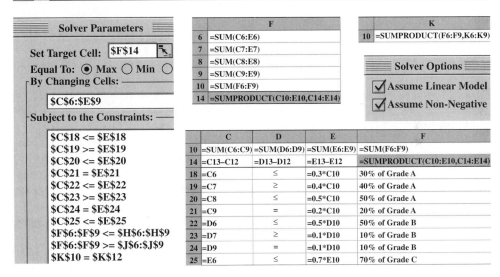

Solver Parameters

Set Target Cell: $F$14

Equal To: ⦿ Max ○ Min ○

By Changing Cells:

$C$6:$E$9

Subject to the Constraints:

$C$18 <= $E$18
$C$19 >= $E$19
$C$20 <= $E$20
$C$21 = $E$21
$C$22 <= $E$22
$C$23 >= $E$23
$C$24 = $E$24
$C$25 <= $E$25
$F$6:$F$9 <= $H$6:$H$9
$F$6:$F$9 >= $J$6:$J$9
$K$10 = $K$12

	F
6	=SUM(C6:E6)
7	=SUM(C7:E7)
8	=SUM(C8:E8)
9	=SUM(C9:E9)
10	=SUM(F6:F9)
14	=SUMPRODUCT(C10:E10,C14:E14)

	K
10	=SUMPRODUCT(F6:F9,K6:K9)

Solver Options

☑ Assume Linear Model
☑ Assume Non-Negative

	C	D	E	F
10	=SUM(C6:C9)	=SUM(D6:D9)	=SUM(E6:E9)	=SUM(F6:F9)
14	=C13–C12	=D13–D12	=E13–E12	=SUMPRODUCT(C10:E10,C14:E14)
18	=C6	≤	=0.3*C10	30% of Grade A
19	=C7	≥	=0.4*C10	40% of Grade A
20	=C8	≤	=0.5*C10	50% of Grade A
21	=C9	=	=0.2*C10	20% of Grade A
22	=D6	≤	=0.5*D10	50% of Grade B
23	=D7	≥	=0.1*D10	10% of Grade B
24	=D9	=	=0.1*D10	10% of Grade B
25	=E6	≤	=0.7*E10	70% of Grade C

The Decisions. The 12 decisions to be made are

x_{A1} = number of pounds of material 1 allocated to product grade A per week

x_{A2} = number of pounds of material 2 allocated to product grade A per week

.

.

.

x_{C4} = number of pounds of material 4 allocated to product grade C per week

The 12 changing cells to hold these numbers have been placed in rows 6–9 and columns C to E.

The Constraints. In addition to the nonnegativity constraints, there are 17 functional constraints that need to be specified in both the spreadsheet and the Solver dialogue box. Eight of these use output cells in column F (rows 6–9) that calculate the total number of pounds of the respective materials collected and treated for amalgamation per week. These calculations are

$$\text{Total (material 1)} = x_{A1} + x_{B1} + x_{C1} = \text{SUM(C6:E6)} \rightarrow \text{cell F6}$$

$$\text{Total (material 2)} = x_{A2} + x_{B2} + x_{C2} = \text{SUM(C7:E7)} \rightarrow \text{cell F7}$$

$$\text{Total (material 3)} = x_{A3} + x_{B3} + x_{C3} = \text{SUM(C8:E8)} \rightarrow \text{cell F8}$$

$$\text{Total (material 4)} = x_{A4} + x_{B4} + x_{C4} = \text{SUM(C9:E9)} \rightarrow \text{cell F9}$$

The eight constraints then are F6:F9 $\leq$ H6:H9 (resource constraints based on the second column of Table 3.14) and F6:F9 $\geq$ J6:J9 (benefit constraints based on the first additional restriction in this same table).

The second additional restriction in Table 3.14 also uses these output cells in column F (rows 6–9) to form the following fixed-requirement constraint:

$$\text{K10} = \text{K12} \qquad \text{where} \qquad \text{K10} = \text{SUMPRODUCT(F6:F9, K6:K9)}$$

so K10 is an output cell that is based on four other output cells.

Finally, the eight constraints specified in the second column of Table 3.13 need to be incorporated into the spreadsheet model. This is done by using the box in rows 18–25. The numbers in column C are entered directly from the corresponding changing cells, so C18 = C6, C19 = C7, . . . , C25 = E6. Each number in column E is the percentage indicated in column F of the total for that grade given in cell C10, D10, or E10. For example, the constraint for row 18 needs to specify that

$$x_{A1} \leq 0.3 \, (\text{Total for Grade A})$$

where

$$\text{Total for Grade A} = x_{A1} + x_{A2} + x_{A3} + x_{A4}$$

which is done by requiring that

$$\text{C18} \leq \text{E18}$$

where

$$\text{E18} = 0.3*\text{C10}$$

$$\text{C10} = \text{SUM(C6:C9)}$$

(The entries for columns C, D, and E shown on the bottom of Figure 3.7 spell out all the details for these eight constraints.)

The Measure of Performance.   The unit profit for each product grade is given in row 14, where C14 = C13 − C12, D14 = D13 − D12, and E14 = E13 − E12. Therefore, since the overall measure of performance is the *total weekly profit* from all three product grades, the equation for the target cell F14 is

$$\text{F14} = \text{SUMPRODUCT(C10:E10, C14:E14)}$$

Summary of the Formulation.   The complete formulation developed above for the linear programming model in the spreadsheet can now be summarized (in algebraic form) as follows:

Maximize $\text{Profit} = 5.5 \, (x_{A1} + x_{A2} + x_{A3} + x_{A4}) + 4.5(x_{B1} + x_{B2} + x_{B3} + x_{B4})$
$+ 3.5(x_{C1} + x_{C2} + x_{C3} + x_{C4})$

subject to the following constraints:

1. *Mixture specifications* (second column of Table 3.13):

$$x_{A1} \leq 0.3(x_{A1} + x_{A2} + x_{A3} + x_{A4}) \qquad \text{(grade A, material 1)}$$

$$x_{A2} \geq 0.4(x_{A1} + x_{A2} + x_{A3} + x_{A4}) \qquad \text{(grade A, material 2)}$$

$$x_{A3} \le 0.5(x_{A1} + x_{A2} + x_{A3} + x_{A4}) \qquad \text{(grade A, material 3)}$$

$$x_{A4} = 0.2(x_{A1} + x_{A2} + x_{A3} + x_{A4}) \qquad \text{(grade A, material 4)}$$

$$x_{B1} \le 0.5(x_{B1} + x_{B2} + x_{B3} + x_{B4}) \qquad \text{(grade B, material 1)}$$

$$x_{B2} \ge 0.1(x_{B1} + x_{B2} + x_{B3} + x_{B4}) \qquad \text{(grade B, material 2)}$$

$$x_{B4} = 0.1(x_{B1} + x_{B2} + x_{B3} + x_{B4}) \qquad \text{(grade B, material 4)}$$

$$x_{C1} \le 0.7(x_{C1} + x_{C2} + x_{C3} + x_{C4}) \qquad \text{(grade C, material 1)}$$

2. *Availability of materials* (second column of Table 3.14):

$$x_{A1} + x_{B1} + x_{C1} \le 3{,}000 \qquad \text{(material 1)}$$

$$x_{A2} + x_{B2} + x_{C2} \le 2{,}000 \qquad \text{(material 2)}$$

$$x_{A3} + x_{B3} + x_{C3} \le 4{,}000 \qquad \text{(material 3)}$$

$$x_{A4} + x_{B4} + x_{C4} \le 1{,}000 \qquad \text{(material 4)}$$

3. *Restriction on amounts treated* (right side of Table 3.14):

$$x_{A1} + x_{B1} + x_{C1} \ge 1{,}500 \qquad \text{(material 1)}$$

$$x_{A2} + x_{B2} + x_{C2} \ge 1{,}000 \qquad \text{(material 2)}$$

$$x_{A3} + x_{B3} + x_{C3} \ge 2{,}000 \qquad \text{(material 3)}$$

$$x_{A4} + x_{B4} + x_{C4} \ge 500 \qquad \text{(material 4)}$$

4. *Restriction on treatment cost* (right side of Table 3.14):

$$3(x_{A1} + x_{B1} + x_{C1}) + 6(x_{A2} + x_{B2} + x_{C2})$$
$$+ 4(x_{A3} + x_{B3} + x_{C3}) + 5(x_{A4} + x_{B4} + x_{C4}) = 30{,}000$$

5. *Nonnegativity constraints:*

$$x_{A1} \ge 0 \qquad x_{A2} \ge 0 \qquad \dots \qquad x_{C4} \ge 0$$

Solving the Model.   Applying the Solver to the spreadsheet model formulated in Figure 3.7 gives the optimal solution shown in the changing cells (C6:E9) for the number of pounds of each type of material allocated to each product grade per week. The resulting total weekly profit is given in the target cell F14 as $35,109.65.

Some Observations about This Example

In comparison with other linear programming examples in this book, the above model is a rather large one. It has 12 decision variables and 17 functional constraints, including 8 resource constraints, 6 benefit constraints, and 3 fixed-requirement constraints. Nevertheless, most real linear programming problems are much larger.

When dealing with large linear programming models of the size commonly found in practice, practitioners usually do not attempt to enter the model one number at a time on a spreadsheet. Instead, a *mathematical programming modeling language* commonly is used to efficiently generate the model from existing databases.

The Save-It Co. problem is an example of a **blending problem.** Blending problems are a special type of *mixed* linear programming problem where the objective is to find the best blend of ingredients into final products to meet certain specifications. Some of the earliest applications of linear programming were for *gasoline blending,* where various petroleum ingredients were blended to obtain various grades of gasoline. Other blending problems involve such final products as steel, fertilizer, animal feed, and so on.

However, *mixed* linear programming problems arise in many other contexts as well.

Summary of the Formulation Procedure for Mixed Linear Programming Problems

The procedure for formulating *mixed* problems is similar to those for the other three categories of linear programming problems. However, each of these other categories features just one of the three types of functional constraints (resource constraints, benefit constraints, and fixed-requirement constraints), whereas mixed problems can include all three types. The following summary for mixed problems includes separate steps for dealing with these different types of functional constraints.

1. Since any linear programming problem involves finding the *best mix* of levels of various activities, identify these *activities* for the problem at hand. The decisions to be made are the levels of these activities.

2. From the viewpoint of management, identify an appropriate *overall measure of performance* for solutions of the problem.

3. For each activity, estimate the *contribution per unit* of the activity to this overall measure of performance.

4. Identify any *limited resources* that must be allocated to the activities (as described in Section 3.2). For each one, identify the *amount available* and then the *amount used per unit of each activity.*

5. Identify any *benefits* to be obtained from the activities (as described in Section 3.3). For each one, identify the *minimum acceptable level* prescribed by management and then the *benefit contribution per unit of each activity.*

6. Identify any *fixed requirements* that, for some type of quantity, the amount provided must equal a required amount (as described in Section 3.4). For each fixed requirement, identify the *required amount* and then the *contribution toward this required amount per unit of each activity.*

7. Enter the data gathered in steps 3–6 into *data cells* in a spreadsheet.

8. Designate *changing cells* for displaying the decisions on activity levels.

9. Use *output cells* to specify the constraints on resources, benefits, and fixed requirements.

10. Designate a *target cell* for displaying the overall measure of performance.

Review Questions

1. What types of functional constraints can appear in a mixed linear programming problem?

2. The Save-It Co. problem is an example of what special type of mixed linear programming problem?

3.7 Model Formulation from a Managerial Perspective

Formulating and analyzing a linear programming model provides information to help managers make their decisions. That means the model must accurately reflect the managerial view of the problem:

- The overall *measure of performance* must capture what management wants accomplished.

- When management limits the amounts of resources that will be made available to the activities under consideration, these limitations should be expressed as *resource constraints.*

- When management establishes minimum acceptable levels for benefits to be gained from the activities, these managerial goals should be incorporated into the model as *benefit constraints.*

- If management has fixed requirements for certain quantities, then *fixed-requirement constraints* are needed.

With the help of spreadsheets, some managers now are able to formulate and solve small linear programming models themselves. However, larger linear programming models generally are formulated by *management science teams,* not managers. When this is done, the management science team must thoroughly understand the managerial view of the problem. This requires clear communication with management from the very beginning of the study and maintaining effective communication as new issues requiring managerial guidance are identified. Management needs to clearly convey its view of the problem and the important issues involved. (Recall that Claire Syverson initially failed to do this in the Super Grain case study.) A manager cannot expect to obtain a helpful linear programming study without making clear just what help is wanted.

You will gain a greater appreciation for the importance of clear communication between the management science team and management when you become involved with real applications of linear programming. As is necessary in any textbook, the examples in this chapter are far smaller, simpler, and more clearly spelled out than is typical of real applications. Many real studies require formulating complicated linear programming models involving hundreds or thousands of decisions and constraints. In these cases, there usually are many ambiguities about just what should be incorporated into the model. Strong managerial input and support are vital to the success of a linear programming study for such complex problems.

When dealing with huge real problems, there is no such thing as "the" correct linear programming model for the problem. The model continually evolves throughout the course of the study. Early in the study, a variety of techniques are used to test initial versions of the model to identify the errors and omissions that inevitably occur when constructing such a large model. This testing process is referred to as **model validation.**

Once the basic formulation has been validated, there are many reasonable variations of the model that could be used. Which variation to use depends on such factors as the assumptions about the problem that seem most reasonable, the estimates of the parameters of the model that seem most reliable, and the degree of detail desired in the model.

In large linear programming studies, a good approach is to begin with a relatively simple version of the model and then use the experience gained with this model to evolve toward more elaborate models that more nearly reflect the complexity of the real problem. This process of **model enrichment** continues only as long as the model remains reasonably easy to solve. It must be curtailed when the study's results are needed by management. Managers often need to curb the natural instinct of management science teams to continue adding "bells and whistles" to the model rather than winding up the study in a timely fashion with a less elegant but adequate model.

When managers study the output of the current model, they often detect some undesirable characteristics that point toward needed model enrichments. These enrichments frequently take the form of new *benefit constraints* to satisfy some managerial goals not previously articulated.

Even though many reasonable variations of the model could be used, an *optimal solution* can be solved for only with respect to one specific version of the model at a time. This is the reason that *what-if analysis* is such an important part of a linear programming study. After obtaining an optimal solution with respect to one specific model, management will have many what-if questions:

- What if the estimates of the parameters in the model are incorrect?
- How do the conclusions change if different plausible assumptions are made about the problem?
- What happens when certain managerial options are pursued that are not incorporated into the current model?

The next chapter is devoted primarily to describing how *what-if analysis* addresses these and related issues, as well as how managers use this information.

Because managers *instigate* management science studies, they need to know enough about linear programming models and their formulation to be able to recognize managerial problems to which linear programming can be applied. Furthermore, since managerial input is so important for linear programming studies, managers need to understand the kinds of managerial concerns that can be incorporated into the model. Developing these two skills have been the most important goals of this chapter.

Review Questions

1. A linear programming model needs to reflect accurately whose view of the problem?
2. Who generally formulates large linear programming models?
3. What line of communication is vital in a linear programming study?
4. What is meant by *model validation?*
5. What is meant by the process of *model enrichment?*
6. Why is what-if analysis an important part of a linear programming study?

3.8 Classic Applications of Linear Programming, Revisited

In Section 2.1, we described three representative *real* applications of linear programming and the resulting impact on the companies involved. Now that you have progressed through Chapters 2 and 3, we can tell you more about these applications. For each, we now will discuss the following features:

1. The type of linear programming problem considered (relative to the categories described in this chapter).
2. The size of the problem.
3. Some factors that helped make this application so successful.

You may find it helpful to review each of these case studies in Section 2.1 before picking up the continuing story below.

Choosing the Product Mix at Ponderosa Industrial

Recall the critical issue facing the management of Ponderosa Industrial: choosing the most profitable mix of lumber to produce on a monthly basis. The volatility of the market prices for these products made this an especially difficult problem with a great impact on profitability.

This problem is similar to the Wyndor Glass Co. problem described in Sections 2.2 and 3.2. Both are *product-mix problems.* Both have *limited resources* that must be allocated to the production of various products. In both cases, these limited resources include certain kinds of *limited production capacities.* And in both cases, these limited resources lead to *resource constraints* in the linear programming model.

However, as is the case when comparing real applications to textbook examples, the Ponderosa problem is far more complicated than the Wyndor problem. Instead of the two decision variables and three functional constraints for Wyndor, the Ponderosa linear programming model has 90 decisions to be made and 45 functional constraints. Furthermore, whereas the Wyndor problem is a *resource-allocation problem,* the Ponderosa problem does not fit purely into this category. The Ponderosa model includes a considerable number of *fixed-requirement constraints* that express fixed relationships between the components of the products. And its model also includes some *benefit constraints* that ensure that the production and sale of certain products will not fall below minimum acceptable levels needed to satisfy the company's customers. Therefore, the Ponderosa problem falls into the *mixed* category described in Section 3.6.

Two factors helped make the Ponderosa application successful. One is that they implemented a financial planning system with a *natural-language* user interface, with the optimization codes operating in the background. Using natural language rather than mathematical symbols to display the components of the linear programming model and its output made the process understandable to the managers making the product-mix decisions. You have already seen examples of the natural-language approach in this chapter when using Excel to formulate linear programming models in a spreadsheet format with names for the activities, resources, benefits, and fixed requirements of a problem. Reporting to management in the language of managers is a key ingredient for the successful application of linear programming.

The other success factor was that the optimization system used was *interactive.* After obtaining an optimal solution for one version of the model, this feature enabled managers to ask a variety of what-if questions and receive immediate responses. Better decisions can result from exploring other plausible scenarios—a process that gave managers more confidence that their decision would perform well under most foreseeable circumstances.

In any application, this ability to respond quickly to management's needs and queries through what-if analysis (whether interactive or not) is a vital part of a linear programming study.

Personnel Scheduling at United Airlines

As described in Section 2.1, linear programming has been used by United Airlines to design the weekly work schedule for all the employees (dozens or hundreds of them) at each of its regional reservations offices and at each of its major airports. The objective is to minimize the labor cost while meeting the service requirements for each half-hour time period in each 24-hour day of the week.

Although the details about the linear programming model have not been published, it is clear that the basic approach used is the one illustrated by the Union Airways example in Section 3.3. The main functional constraints are *benefit constraints* that ensure that the number of employees on duty during each time period will not fall below minimum acceptable levels. Therefore, the model is basically a *cost–benefit–trade-off problem.*

However, the Union Airways example only has five decisions to be made. By contrast, the United Airlines model for some of the locations scheduled involves over 20,000 decisions! The difference is that a real application must consider a myriad of important details that can be ignored in a textbook example. For example, the United Airlines model takes into account such things as the meal and break assignment times for each employee scheduled, differences in shift lengths for different employees, and days off over a weekly schedule, among other scheduling details.

The most important success factor in this application was "the support of operational managers and their staffs." Since these are the people who implement scheduling procedures, nothing much could be accomplished to improve these procedures without gaining their cooperation and support. This was a lesson learned by experience, because the management science team initially failed to establish a good line of communication with the operating managers, who then resisted the team's initial recommendations. The team leaders described their mistake as follows: "The cardinal rule for earning the trust and respect of operating managers and support staffs—'getting them involved in the development process'—had been violated." The team then worked much more closely with the operating managers—with outstanding results.

Planning Supply, Distribution, and Marketing at Citgo Petroleum Corporation

Section 2.1 describes how the application of management science techniques, including especially linear programming, literally turned around the fortunes of Citgo Petroleum Corporation during the mid-1980s. For example, one linear programming system (the Supply, Distribution, and Marketing modeling system) coordinated the supply, distribution, and marketing of each major product through Citgo's vast marketing and distribution network.

This linear programming model is of the same type as the model for the Distribution Unlimited Co. problem in Section 3.4. Both are *distribution-network problems.* In fact, Chapter 6 will describe how both are the same specific type of distribution-network problem (a *minimum-cost flow problem*).

However, the Distribution Unlimited model involves just six decisions to be made and five fixed-requirement constraints. By contrast, the Citgo model for each major product involves about 15,000 decisions and 3,000 fixed-requirement constraints!

When dealing with such huge models, it is inevitable that many errors will creep into the initial model. Therefore, it is extremely important to conduct a thorough process of *model validation* to test and correct the model. Citgo's management science team reported that when they checked their initial model for data errors and inconsistencies, the paper log of error messages generated was about an inch thick! After thorough model validation was completed, each new application of the working model typically would generate fewer than 10 error and warning messages about bad or questionable numbers that needed checking.

Some of the factors that contributed to the success of this application of linear programming were the same as for the two preceding companies discussed. Like Ponderosa Industrial, one factor was developing output reports in the language of managers to really meet their needs. These output reports are designed to be easy for managers to understand

and use, and they address the issues that are important to management. Also like Ponderosa, another factor was enabling management to respond quickly to the dynamics of the industry by using the linear programming system extensively in what-if sessions. As in so many applications of linear programming, what-if analysis proved more important than the initial optimal solution obtained for one version of the model.

Much like the United Airlines application, another success factor was the enthusiastic support of operational managers during the development and implementation of this linear programming system.

However, the most important success factor was the unlimited support provided the management science task force by top management, ranging right up to the chief executive officer and the chairman of the board of Citgo's parent company, Southland Corporation. (We mentioned in Section 2.1 that the director of the task force, an eminent management science consultant, reported directly to both the president of Citgo and the chairman of the board of Southland.) This backing by top management included strong financial and organizational support.

When discussing both this linear programming system and other applications of management science implemented by the task force, team members described the financial support of top management as follows:

> The total cost of the systems implemented, $20–$30 million, was the greatest obstacle to this project. However, because of the information explosion in the petroleum industry, top management realized that numerous information systems were essential to gather, store, and analyze data. The incremental cost of adding management science technologies to these computers and systems was small, in fact very small in light of the enormous benefits they provided.

The organizational support provided by top management took a variety of forms. One example was the creation and staffing of the position of Senior Vice President of Operations Coordination to evaluate and coordinate recommendations based on the model which spanned organizational boundaries.

Review Questions

1. Compare these three applications of linear programming regarding which category (resource-allocation, cost–benefit–trade-off, distribution-network, or mixed problem) each fits.
2. Compare these applications regarding the number of decisions to be made.
3. What were the factors that helped make the Ponderosa application successful?
4. What were the factors that helped make the United Airlines application successful?
5. What were the factors that helped make the Citgo application successful?

3.9 Summary

Functional constraints with a $\leq$ sign are called *resource constraints,* because they require that the *amount used* of some resource must be *less than or equal to* the *amount available* of that resource. The identifying feature of *resource-allocation problems* is that all their functional constraints are resource constraints.

Functional constraints with a $\geq$ sign are called *benefit constraints,* since their form is that the *level achieved* for some benefit must be *greater than or equal to* the *minimum acceptable level* for that benefit. Frequently, benefit constraints express goals prescribed by management. If every functional constraint is a benefit constraint, then the problem is a *cost–benefit–trade-off problem.*

Functional constraints with an $=$ sign are called *fixed-requirement constraints,* because they express the fixed requirement that, for some quantity, the *amount provided* must be *equal to* the *required amount.* One identifying feature of *distribution-network problems* is that their main functional constraints are fixed-requirement constraints with a certain form.

Linear programming problems that do not fit into any of these three categories are called *mixed problems*.

In many real applications, management science teams formulate and analyze large linear programming models to help guide managerial decision making. Such teams need strong managerial input and support to help ensure that their work really meets management's needs.

Glossary

Benefit constraint A functional constraint with a $\geq$ sign. The left-hand side is interpreted as the level of some benefit that is achieved by the activities under consideration, and the right-hand side is the minimum acceptable level for that benefit. (Section 3.3) 77

Blending problem A type of mixed linear programming problem where the objective is to find the best way of blending ingredients into final products to meet certain specifications. (Section 3.6) 97

Cost–benefit–trade-off problem A type of linear programming problem involving the tradeoff between the total cost of the activities under consideration and the benefits to be achieved by these activities. Its identifying feature is that each functional constraint in the linear programming model is a benefit constraint. (Section 3.3) 77

Distribution-network problem A type of linear programming problem concerned with the optimal distribution of goods through a distribution network. Its main functional constraints are fixed-requirement constraints. (Section 3.4) 83

Fixed-requirement constraint A functional constraint with an = sign. The left-hand side represents the amount provided of some type of quantity, and the right-hand side represents the required amount for that quantity. (Section 3.4) 86

Identifying feature A feature of a model that identifies the category of linear programming problem it represents. (Chapter introduction) 63

Mixed problem Any linear programming problem that does not fit into any of the other three categories (resource-allocation problems, cost–benefit–trade-off problems, and distribution-network problems). (Section 3.6) 92

Model enrichment The process of using experience with a model to identify and add important details that will provide a better representation of the real problem. (Section 3.7) 99

Model validation The process of checking and testing a model to develop a valid model. (Section 3.7) 99

Parameter table A table giving the values of some or all of the parameters of a linear programming model. (Sections 3.2–3.4) 71

Resource-allocation problem A type of linear programming problem concerned with allocating resources to activities. Its identifying feature is that each functional constraint in its model is a resource constraint. (Section 3.2) 70

Resource constraint A functional constraint with a $\leq$ sign. The left-hand side represents the amount of some resource that is used by the activities under consideration, and the right-hand side represents the amount available of that resource. (Section 3.2) 70, 75

Learning Aids for This Chapter in Your MS Courseware

"Ch. 3—LP Formulations" Excel File:

Super Grain Example
Think-Big Example
Union Airways Example
Distribution Unlimited Example

Revised Super Grain Example
Save-It Example

An Excel Add-in:
Premium Solver

Problems

We have inserted the symbol E* to the left of each problem (or its parts) where Excel should be used (unless your instructor gives you contrary instructions). An asterisk on the problem number indicates that at least a partial answer is given in the back of the book.

3.1 Reconsider the Super Grain Corp. case study as presented in Section 3.1. The advertising firm, Giacomi & Jackowitz, now has suggested a fourth promising advertising medium—radio commercials—to promote the company's new breakfast cereal, Crunchy Start. Young children are potentially major consumers of this cereal, but parents of young children (the major potential purchasers) often are

too busy to do much reading (so may miss the company's advertisements in magazines and Sunday supplements) or even to watch the Saturday morning programs for children where the company's television commercials are aired. However, these parents do tend to listen to the radio during the commute to and from work. Therefore, to better reach these parents, Giacomi & Jackowitz suggests giving consideration to running commercials for Crunchy Start on nationally syndicated radio programs that appeal to young adults during typical commuting hours.

Giacomi & Jackowitz estimates that the cost of developing each new radio commercial would be $50,000, and that the number of expected exposure units per commercial would be 90. The firm has determined that 10 spots are available for different radio commercials, and each one would cost $200,000 for a normal run.

E* a. Formulate a spreadsheet model for the revised advertising-mix problem that includes this fourth advertising medium. Identify the data cells, the changing cells, and the target. Also show the Excel equation for each output cell expressed as a SUMPRODUCT function.

E* b. Use the Excel Solver to solve this model.
  c. Indicate why this spreadsheet model is a linear programming model.
  d. Express this model in algebraic form.

3.2.* Consider a resource-allocation problem having the following parameter table:

| Resource | Resource Usage per Unit of Each Activity | | Amount of Resource Available |
	1	2	
1	2	1	10
2	3	3	20
3	2	4	20
Contribution per unit	$20	$30	

Contribution per unit = profit per unit of the activity.

E* a. Formulate a linear programming model for this problem on a spreadsheet.

E* b. Use the spreadsheet to check the following solutions: $(x_1, x_2) = (2, 2), (3, 3), (2, 4), (4, 2), (3, 4), (4, 3)$. Which of these solutions are feasible? Which of these feasible solutions has the best value of the objective function?
  c. Use the Solver to find an optimal solution.
  d. Express this model in algebraic form.
  e. Use the graphical method to solve this model.

3.3. Consider a resource-allocation problem having the following parameter table:

| Resource | Resource Usage per Unit of Each Activity | | | Amount of Resource Available |
	1	2	3	
A	30	20	0	500
B	0	10	40	600
C	20	20	30	1,000
Contribution per unit	$50	$40	$70	

Contribution per unit = profit per unit of the activity.

E* a. Formulate and solve a linear programming model for this problem on a spreadsheet.
  b. Express this model in algebraic form.

E*3.4. Consider a resource-allocation problem having the following parameter table:

| Resource | Resource Usage per Unit of Each Activity | | | | Amount of Resource Available |
	1	2	3	4	
P	3	5	−2	4	400
Q	4	−1	3	2	300
R	6	3	2	−1	400
S	−2	2	5	3	300
Contribution per unit	$11	$9	$8	$9	

Contribution per unit = profit per unit of the activity.

a. Formulate a linear programming model for this problem on a spreadsheet.
b. Make five guesses of your own choosing for the optimal solution. Use the spreadsheet to check each one for feasibility and, if feasible, for the value of the objective function. Which feasible guess has the best objective function value?
c. Use the Solver to find an optimal solution.

3.5.* The Omega Manufacturing Company has discontinued the production of a certain unprofitable product line. This act created considerable excess production capacity. Management is considering devoting this excess capacity to one or more of three products, products 1, 2, and 3. The available capacity of the machines that might limit output is summarized in the following table:

Machine Type	Available Time (in Machine-Hours per Week)
Milling machine	500
Lathe	350
Grinder	150

The number of machine hours required for each unit of the respective products is as follows:

Productivity Coefficient (in Machine-Hours per Unit)

Machine Type	Product 1	Product 2	Product 3
Milling machine	9	3	5
Lathe	5	4	0
Grinder	3	0	2

The Sales Department indicates that the sales potential for products 1 and 2 exceeds the maximum production rate and that the sales potential for product 3 is 20 units per week. The unit profit would be $50, $20, and $25, respectively, for products 1, 2, and 3. The objective is to determine how much of each product Omega should produce to maximize profit.

a. Indicate why this is a resource-allocation problem by identifying both the activities and the limited resources to be allocated to these activities.

b. Construct the parameter table for this resource-allocation problem.

c. Identify verbally the decisions to be made, the constraints on these decisions, and the overall measure of performance for the decisions.

d. Convert these verbal descriptions of the constraints and the measure of performance into quantitative expressions in terms of the data and decisions.

E* e. Formulate a spreadsheet model for this problem. Identify the data cells, the changing cells, the target cell, and the other output cells. Also show the Excel equation for each output cell expressed as a SUMPRODUCT function.

E* f. Use the Excel Solver to solve the model.

g. Summarize the model in algebraic form.

3.6. Ed Butler is the production manager for the Bilco Corporation, which produces three types of spare parts for automobiles. The manufacture of each part requires processing on each of two machines, with the following processing times (in hours):

	Part		
Machine	A	B	C
1	0.02	0.03	0.05
2	0.05	0.02	0.04

Each machine is available 40 hours per month. Each part manufactured will yield a unit profit as follows:

	Part		
	A	B	C
Profit	$50	$40	$30

Ed wants to determine the mix of spare parts to produce to maximize total profit.

a. Construct the parameter table for this resource-allocation problem. Identify both the activities and the resources.

E* b. Formulate a linear programming model for this problem on a spreadsheet.

E* c. Make three guesses of your own choosing for the optimal solution. Use the spreadsheet to check each one for feasibility and, if feasible, for the value of the objective function. Which feasible guess has the best objective function value?

E* d. Use the Solver to find an optimal solution.

e. Express the model in algebraic form.

3.7. Consider the following algebraic formulation of a resource-allocation problem with three resources, where the decisions to be made are the levels of three activities (A_1, A_2, and A_3).

Maximize   Profit $= 20A_1 + 40A_2 + 30A_3$

subject to

Resource 1: $3A_1 + 5A_2 + 4A_3 \le 400$ (amount available)

Resource 2: $A_1 + A_2 + A_3 \le 100$ (amount available)

Resource 3: $A_1 + 3A_2 + 2A_3 \le 200$ (amount available)

and

$$A_1 \ge 0 \qquad A_2 \ge 0 \qquad A_3 \ge 0$$

a. Construct the parameter table for this problem.

E* b. Formulate and solve the spreadsheet model for this problem.

3.8. Consider a cost–benefit–trade-off problem having the following parameter table:

	Benefit Contribution per Unit of Each Activity		
Benefit	1	2	Minimum Acceptable Level
1	5	3	60
2	2	2	30
3	7	9	126
Unit cost	$60	$50	

E* a. Formulate a linear programming model for this problem on a spreadsheet.

E* b. Use the spreadsheet to check the following solutions: $(x_1, x_2) = (7, 7), (7, 8), (8, 7), (8, 8), (8, 9), (9, 8)$. Which of these solutions are feasible? Which of these feasible solutions has the best value of the objective function?

E* c. Use the Solver to find an optimal solution.

d. Express the model in algebraic form.

e. Use the graphical method to solve this model.

E*3.9. Consider a cost–benefit–trade-off problem having the following parameter table:

	Benefit Contribution per Unit of Each Activity				
Benefit	1	2	3	4	Minimum Acceptable Level
P	2	-1	4	3	80
Q	1	4	-1	2	60
R	3	5	4	-1	110
Unit cost	$400	$600	$500	$300	

a. Formulate a linear programming model for this problem on a spreadsheet.

b. Make five guesses of your own choosing for the optimal solution. Use the spreadsheet to check each one for feasibility and, if feasible, for the value of the objective function. Which feasible guess has the best objective function value?

c. Use the Solver to find an optimal solution.

3.10.* Fred Jonasson manages a family-owned farm. To supplement several food products grown on the farm, Fred also raises pigs for market. He now wishes to determine the quantities of the available types of feed (corn, tankage, and alfalfa) that should be given to each pig. Since pigs will eat any mix of these feed types, the objective is to determine which mix will meet certain nutritional requirements at a *minimum cost*. The number of units of each type of basic nutritional ingredient contained within a kilogram of each feed type is given in the following table, along with the daily nutritional requirements and feed costs:

Nutritional Ingredient	Kilogram of Corn	Kilogram of Tankage	Kilogram of Alfalfa	Minimum Daily Requirement
Carbohydrates	90	20	40	200
Protein	30	80	60	180
Vitamins	10	20	60	150
Cost (¢)	84	72	60	

a. Construct the parameter table for this cost–benefit–trade-off problem.

E* b. Formulate a linear programming model for this problem on a spreadsheet.

E* c. Use the spreadsheet to check if $(x_1, x_2, x_3) = (1, 2, 2)$ is a feasible solution and, if so, what the daily cost would be for this diet. How many units of each nutritional ingredient would this diet provide daily?

E* d. Take a few minutes to use a trial-and-error approach with the spreadsheet to develop your best guess for the optimal solution. What is the daily cost for your solution?

E* e. Use the Solver to find an optimal solution.

f. Express the model in algebraic form.

3.11. Maureen Laird is the chief financial officer for the Alva Electric Co., a major public utility in the Midwest. The company has scheduled the construction of new hydroelectric plants 5, 10, and 20 years from now to meet the needs of the growing population in the region served by the company. To cover the construction costs, Maureen needs to invest some of the company's money now to meet these future cash-flow needs. Maureen may purchase only three kinds of financial assets, each of which costs $1 million per unit. Fractional units may be purchased. The assets produce income 5, 10, and 20 years from now, and that income is needed to cover minimum cash-flow requirements in those years, as shown in the following table.

Income per Unit of Asset

Year	Asset 1	Asset 2	Asset 3	Minimum Cash Flow Required
5	$2 million	$1 million	$0.5 million	$400 million
10	$0.5 million	$0.5 million	$1 million	$100 million
20	0	$1.5 million	$2 million	$300 million

Maureen wishes to determine the mix of investments in these assets that will cover the cash-flow requirements while minimizing the total amount invested.

a. Construct the parameter table for this cost–benefit–trade-off problem.

E* b. Formulate a linear programming model for this problem on a spreadsheet.

E* c. Use the spreadsheet to check the possibility of purchasing 100 units of asset 1, 100 units of asset 2, and 200 units of asset 3. How much cash flow would this mix of investments generate 5, 10, and 20 years from now? What would be the total amount invested?

E* d. Take a few minutes to use a trial-and-error approach with the spreadsheet to develop your best guess for the optimal solution. What is the total amount invested for your solution?

E* e. Use the Solver to find an optimal solution.

f. Summarize the model in algebraic form.

3.12. Web Mercantile sells many household products through an on-line catalog. The company needs substantial warehouse space for storing its goods. Plans now are being made for leasing warehouse storage space over the next five months. Just how much space will be required in each of these months is known. However, since these space requirements are quite different, it may be most economical to lease only the amount needed each month on a month-by-month basis. On the other hand, the additional cost for leasing space for additional months is much less than for the first month, so it may be less expensive to lease the maximum amount needed for the entire five months. Another option is the intermediate approach of changing the total amount of space leased (by adding a new lease and/or having an old lease expire) at least once but not every month.

The space requirement and the leasing costs for the various leasing periods are as follows:

Month	Required Space	Leasing Period (Months)	Cost per Sq. Ft. Leased
1	30,000 sq. ft.	1	$ 65
2	20,000 sq. ft.	2	$100
3	40,000 sq. ft.	3	$135
4	10,000 sq. ft.	4	$160
5	50,000 sq. ft.	5	$190

The objective is to minimize the total leasing cost for meeting the space requirements.

a. Indicate why this is a cost–benefit–trade-off problem by identifying both the activities and the benefits being sought from these activities.

b. Construct the parameter table for this cost–benefit–trade-off problem.

c. Identify verbally the decisions to be made, the constraints on these decisions, and the overall measure of performance for the decisions.

d. Convert these verbal descriptions of the constraints and the measure of performance into quantitative expressions in terms of the data and decisions.

E* e. Formulate a spreadsheet model for this problem. Identify the data cells, the changing cells, the target cell, and the other output cells. Also show the Excel equation for each output cell expressed as a SUMPRODUCT function.

E* f. Use the Excel Solver to solve the model.

g. Summarize the model in algebraic form.

3.13. Consider the following algebraic formulation of a cost–benefit–trade-off problem involving three benefits, where the decisions to be made are the levels of four activities ($A_1, A_2, A_3,$ and A_4)

$$\text{Minimize} \quad \text{Cost} = 2A_1 + A_2 - A_3 + 3A_4$$

subject to

$$\text{Benefit 1:} \quad 3A_1 + 2A_2 - 2A_3 + 5A_4 \geq 80$$
(minimum acceptable level)
$$\text{Benefit 2:} \quad A_1 - A_2 \quad + A_4 \geq 10$$
(minimum acceptable level)
$$\text{Benefit 3:} \quad A_1 + A_2 - A_3 + 2A_4 \geq 30$$
(minimum acceptable level)

and

$$A_1 \geq 0 \qquad A_2 \geq 0 \qquad A_3 \geq 0 \qquad A_4 \geq 0$$

a. Construct the parameter table for this problem.

E* b. Formulate and solve the spreadsheet model for this problem.

3.14. Larry Edison is the Director of the Computer Center for Buckly College. He now needs to schedule the staffing of the center. It is open from 8 AM until midnight. Larry has monitored the usage of the center at various times of the day and determined that the following number of computer consultants are required:

Time of Day	Minimum Number of Consultants Required to be on Duty
8 AM–noon	4
Noon–4 PM	8
4 PM–8 PM	10
8 PM–midnight	6

Two types of computer consultants can be hired: full-time and part-time. The full-time consultants work for eight consecutive hours in any of the following shifts: morning (8 AM–4 PM), afternoon (noon–8 PM), and evening (4 PM–midnight). Full-time consultants are paid $14 per hour.

Part-time consultants can be hired to work any of the four shifts listed in the table. Part-time consultants are paid $12 per hour.

An additional requirement is that during every time period, there must be at least two full-time consultants on duty for every part-time consultant on duty.

Larry would like to determine how many full-time and part-time consultants should work each shift to meet the above requirements at the minimum possible cost.

a. Which category of linear programming problem does this problem fit? Why?

b. Construct the appropriate parameter table for this problem.

E* c. Formulate a linear programming model for this problem on a spreadsheet.

E* d. Use the Solver to solve this model.

e. Summarize the model in algebraic form.

3.15.* The Medequip Company produces precision medical diagnostic equipment at two factories. Three medical centers have placed orders for this month's production output. The following table shows what the cost would be for shipping each unit from each factory to each of these customers. Also shown are the number of units that will be produced at each factory and the number of units ordered by each customer.

	Unit Shipping Cost			
To From	Customer 1	Customer 2	Customer 3	Output
Factory 1	$600	$800	$700	400 units
Factory 2	$400	$900	$600	500 units
Order size	300 units	200 units	400 units	

A decision now needs to be made about the shipping plan for how many units to ship from each factory to each customer.

a. Which category of linear programming problem does this problem fit? Why?

b. Construct the appropriate parameter table for this problem.

E* c. Formulate and solve a linear programming model for this problem on a spreadsheet.

d. Summarize this formulation in algebraic form.

3.16. The Fagersta Steelworks currently is working two mines to obtain its iron ore. This iron ore is shipped to either of two storage facilities. When needed, it then is shipped on to the company's steel plant. The diagram below depicts this distribution network, where M1 and M2 are the two mines, S1 and S2 are the two storage facilities, and P is the steel plant. The diagram also shows the monthly amounts produced at the mines and needed at the plant, as well as the shipping cost and the maximum amount that can be shipped per month through each shipping lane.

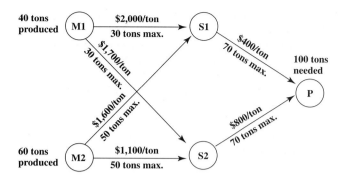

Management now wants to determine the most economical plan for shipping the iron ore from the mines through the distribution network to the steel plant.

a. Identify all the requirements that will need to be expressed in fixed-requirement constraints.

b. Construct the appropriate parameter table for this problem.

E*   c. Formulate and solve a linear programming model for this problem on a spreadsheet.

d. Express this model in algebraic form.

3.17.* Al Ferris has $60,000 that he wishes to invest now in order to use the accumulation for purchasing a retirement annuity in five years. After consulting with his financial advisor, he has been offered four types of fixed-income investments, which we will label as investments A, B, C, and D.

Investments A and B are available at the beginning of each of the next five years (call them years 1 to 5). Each dollar invested in A at the beginning of a year returns $1.40 (a profit of $0.40) two years later (in time for immediate reinvestment). Each dollar invested in B at the beginning of a year returns $1.70 three years later.

Investments C and D will each be available at one time in the future. Each dollar invested in C at the beginning of year 2 returns $1.90 at the end of year 5. Each dollar invested in D at the beginning of year 5 returns $1.30 at the end of year 5.

Al wishes to know which investment plan maximizes the amount of money that can be accumulated by the beginning of year 6.

a. Although this is not a distribution-network problem, all its functional constraints can be expressed as fixed-requirement constraints. To do this, let A_t, Bt, C_t, and D_t be the amount invested in investments A, B, C and D, respectively, at the beginning of year t for each t where the investment is available and will mature by the end of year 5. Also let R_t be the number of available dollars *not* invested at the beginning of year t (and so available for investment in a later year). Thus, the amount invested at the beginning of year t *plus* R_t must equal the number of dollars available for investment at that time. Write such an equation in terms of the relevant variables above for the beginning of each of the five years to obtain the five fixed requirement constraints for this problem.

b. Formulate a complete linear programming model for this problem in algebraic form.

E*   c. Formulate this model on a spreadsheet.

E*   d. Use the Solver to solve this model.

3.18. The Metalco Company desires to blend a new alloy of 40 percent tin, 35 percent zinc, and 25 percent lead from several available alloys having the following properties:

	Alloy				
Property	*1*	*2*	*3*	*4*	*5*
Percentage of tin	60	25	45	20	50
Percentage of zinc	10	15	45	50	40
Percentage of lead	30	60	10	30	10
Cost ($/lb)	22	20	25	24	27

The objective is to determine the proportions of these alloys that should be blended to produce the new alloy at a minimum cost.

a. Identify all the requirements that will need to be expressed in fixed-requirement constraints.

b. Construct the appropriate parameter table for this problem.

E*   c. Formulate and solve a linear programming model for this problem on a spreadsheet.

d. Express this model in algebraic form.

3.19. The Weigelt Corporation has three branch plants with excess production capacity. Fortunately, the corporation has a new product ready to begin production, and all three plants have this capability, so some of the excess capacity can be used in this way. This product can be made in three sizes—large, medium, and small—that yield a net unit profit of $420, $360, and $300, respectively. Plants 1, 2, and 3 have the excess capacity to produce 750, 900, and 450 units per day of this product, respectively, regardless of the size or combination of sizes involved.

The amount of available in-process storage space also imposes a limitation on the production rates of the new product. Plants 1, 2, and 3 have 13,000, 12,000, and 5,000 square feet, respectively, of in-process storage space available for a day's production of this product. Each unit of the large, medium, and small sizes produced per day requires 20, 15, and 12 square feet, respectively.

Sales forecasts indicate that if available, 900, 1,200, and 750 units of the large, medium, and small sizes, respectively, would be sold per day.

At each plant, some employees will need to be laid off unless most of the plant's excess production capacity can be used to produce the new product. To avoid layoffs if possible, management has decided that the plants should use the same percentage of their excess capacity to produce the new product.

Management wishes to know how much of each of the sizes should be produced by each of the plants to maximize profit.

a. This is a mixed problem that is mostly a resource-allocation problem but also includes a small number of fixed-requirement constraints. Construct a parameter table that includes everything but the fixed-requirement constraints. Then construct a separate parameter table for just the fixed-requirement constraints.

E* b. Formulate a linear programming model for this problem on a spreadsheet.

E* c. Use the Solver to solve this model.

d. Express the model in algebraic form.

3.20.* A cargo plane has three compartments for storing cargo: front, center, and back. These compartments have capacity limits on both *weight* and *space,* as summarized below:

Compartment	Weight Capacity (Tons)	Space Capacity (Cubic Feet)
Front	12	7,000
Center	18	9,000
Back	10	5,000

Furthermore, the weight of the cargo in the respective compartments must be the same proportion of that compartment's weight capacity to maintain the balance of the airplane.

The following four cargoes have been offered for shipment on an upcoming flight as space is available:

Cargo	Weight (Tons)	Volume (Cubic Feet/Ton)	Profit ($/Ton)
1	20	500	320
2	16	700	400
3	25	600	360
4	13	400	290

Any portion of these cargoes can be accepted. The objective is to determine how much (if any) of each cargo should be accepted and how to distribute each among the compartments to maximize the total profit for the flight.

a. This is a mixed problem that is mostly a resource-allocation problem but also includes a small number of fixed-requirement constraints. Construct a parameter table that includes everything but the fixed-requirement constraints. Then construct a separate parameter table for just the fixed-requirement constraints.

E* b. Formulate and solve a linear programming model for this problem on a spreadsheet.

c. Express the model in algebraic form.

3.21. Comfortable Hands is a company that features a product line of winter gloves for the entire family—men, women, and children. They are trying to decide what mix of these three types of gloves to produce.

Comfortable Hands' manufacturing labor force is unionized. Each full-time employee works a 40-hour week. In addition, by union contract, the number of full-time employees can never drop below 20. Nonunion, part-time workers can also be hired with the following union-imposed restrictions: (1) each part-time worker works 20 hours per week and (2) there must be at least 2 full-time employees for each part-time employee.

All three types of gloves are made out of the same 100 percent genuine cowhide leather. Comfortable Hands has a long-term contract with a supplier of the leather and receives a 5,000-square-foot shipment of the material each week. The material requirements and labor requirements, along with the *gross profit* per glove sold (not considering labor costs), are given in the following table.

Glove	Material Required (Square Feet)	Labor Required (Minutes)	Gross Profit (per Pair)
Men's	2	30	$ 8
Women's	1.5	45	$10
Children's	1	40	$ 6

Each full-time employee earns $13 per hour, while each part-time employee earns $10 per hour. Management wishes to know what mix of each of the three types of gloves to produce per week, as well as how many full-time and part-time workers to employ. They would like to maximize their *net profit*—their gross profit from sales minus their labor costs.

E* a. Formulate and solve a linear programming model for this problem on a spreadsheet.

b. Summarize this formulation in algebraic form.

E* 3.22. Oxbridge University maintains a powerful mainframe computer for research use by its faculty, Ph.D. students, and research associates. During all working hours, an operator must be available to operate and maintain the computer, as well as to perform some programming services. Beryl Ingram, the director of the computer facility, oversees the operation.

It is now the beginning of the fall semester and Beryl is confronted with the problem of assigning different working hours to her operators. Because all the operators are currently enrolled in the university, they are available to work only a limited number of hours each day.

There are six operators (four undergraduate students and two graduate students). They all have different wage rates because of differences in their experience with computers and in their programming ability. The following table shows their wage rates, along with the maximum number of hours that each can work each day.

Maximum Hours of Availability

Operators	Wage Rate	Mon.	Tue.	Wed.	Thurs.	Fri.
K. C.	$10.00/hour	6	0	6	0	6
D. H.	$10.10/hour	0	6	0	6	0
H. B.	$9.90/hour	4	8	4	0	4
S. C.	$9.80/hour	5	5	5	0	5
K. S.	$10.80/hour	3	0	3	8	0
N. K	$11.30/hour	0	0	0	6	2

Each operator is guaranteed a certain minimum number of hours per week that will maintain an adequate knowledge of the operation. This level is set arbitrarily at 8 hours per week for the undergraduate students (K.C., D.H., H.B., and S.C.) and 7 hours per week for the graduate students (K. S. and N. K.).

The computer facility is to be open for operation from 8 AM to 10 PM Monday through Friday with exactly one operator on duty during these hours. On Saturdays and Sundays, the computer is to be operated by other staff.

Because of a tight budget, Beryl has to minimize cost. She wishes to determine the number of hours she should assign to each operator on each day. Formulate and solve a spreadsheet model for this problem.

3.23. Slim-Down Manufacturing makes a line of nutritionally complete, weight-reduction beverages. One of their products is a strawberry shake that is designed to be a complete meal. The strawberry shake consists of several ingredients. Some information about each of these ingredients is given below.

Ingredient	Calories from Fat (per tbsp.)	Total Calories (per tbsp.)	Vitamin Content (mg/tbsp.)	Thickeners (mg/tbsp.)	Cost (¢/tbsp.)
Strawberry flavoring	1	50	20	3	10
Cream	75	100	0	8	8
Vitamin supplement	0	0	50	1	25
Artificial sweetener	0	120	0	2	15
Thickening agent	30	80	2	25	6

The nutritional requirements are as follows. The beverage must total between 380 and 420 calories (inclusive). No more than 20 percent of the total calories should come from fat. There must be at least 50 milligrams (mg) of vitamin content. For taste reasons, there must be at least two tablespoons (tbsp.) of strawberry flavoring for each tbsp. of artificial sweetener. Finally, to maintain proper thickness, there must be exactly 15 mg of thickeners in the beverage.

Management would like to select the quantity of each ingredient for the beverage that would minimize cost while meeting the above requirements.

a. Identify the requirements that lead to resource constraints, to benefit constraints, and to fixed-requirement constraints.

E*   b. Formulate and solve a linear programming model for this problem on a spreadsheet.

c. Summarize this formulation in algebraic form.

3.24. Joyce and Marvin run a day care for preschoolers. They are trying to decide what to feed the children for lunches. They would like to keep their costs down, but they also need to meet the nutritional requirements of the children. They have already decided to go with peanut butter and jelly sandwiches, and some combination of graham crackers, milk, and orange juice. The nutritional content of each food choice and its cost are given in the table below.

Food Item	Calories from Fat	Total Calories	Vitamin C (mg)	Protein (g)	Cost (¢)
Bread (1 slice)	10	70	0	3	5
Peanut butter (1 tbsp.)	75	100	0	4	4
Strawberry jelly (1 tbsp.)	0	50	3	0	7
Graham cracker (1 cracker)	20	60	0	1	8
Milk (1 cup)	70	150	2	8	15
Juice (1 cup)	0	100	120	1	35

The nutritional requirements are as follows. Each child should receive between 400 and 600 calories. No more than 30 percent of the total calories should come from fat. Each child should consume at least 60 milligrams (mg) of vitamin C and 12 grams (g) of protein. Furthermore, for practical reasons, each child needs exactly 2 slices of bread (to make the sandwich), at least twice as much peanut butter as jelly, and at least 1 cup of liquid (milk and/or juice).

Joyce and Marvin would like to select the food choices for each child that minimize cost while meeting the above requirements.

a. Identify the requirements that lead to resource constraints, to benefit constraints, and to fixed-requirement constraints.

E* b. Formulate a linear programming model for this problem on a spreadsheet.

E* c. Use the Solver to solve this model.

d. Express the model in algebraic form.

CASE 3.1
FABRICS AND FALL FASHIONS

From the 10th floor of her office building, Katherine Rally watches the swarms of New Yorkers fight their way through the streets infested with yellow cabs and the sidewalks littered with hot dog stands. On this sweltering July day, she pays particular attention to the fashions worn by the various women and wonders what they will choose to wear in the fall. Her thoughts are not simply random musings; they are critical to her work since she owns and manages TrendLines, an elite women's clothing company.

Today is an especially important day because she must meet with Ted Lawson, the production manager, to decide upon next month's production plan for the fall line. Specifically, she must determine the quantity of each clothing item she should produce given the plant's production capacity, limited resources, and demand forecasts. Accurate planning for next month's production is critical to fall sales since the items produced next month will appear in stores during September and women generally buy the majority of the fall fashions when they first appear in September.

She turns back to her sprawling glass desk and looks at the numerous papers covering it. Her eyes roam across the clothing patterns designed almost six months ago, the lists of material requirements for each pattern, and the lists of demand forecasts for each pattern determined by customer surveys at fashion shows. She remembers the hectic and sometimes nightmarish days of designing the fall line and presenting it at fashion shows in New York, Milan, and Paris. Ultimately, she paid her team of six designers a total of $860,000 for their work on her fall line. With the cost of hiring runway models, hair stylists, and make-up artists; sewing and fitting clothes; building the set; choreographing and rehearsing the show; and renting the conference hall, each of the three fashion shows cost her an additional $2,700,000.

She studies the clothing patterns and material requirements. Her fall line consists of both professional and casual fashions. She determined the prices for each clothing item by taking into account the quality and cost of material, the cost of labor and machining, the demand for the item, and the prestige of the TrendLines brand name.

The fall professional fashions include

Clothing Item	Material Requirements	Price	Labor and Machine Cost
Tailored wool slacks	3 yards of wool 2 yards of acetate for lining	$300	$160
Cashmere sweater	1.5 yards of cashmere	$450	$150
Silk blouse	1.5 yards of silk	$180	$100
Silk camisole	0.5 yard of silk	$120	$ 60
Tailored skirt	2 yards of rayon 1.5 yards of acetate for lining	$270	$120
Wool blazer	2.5 yards of wool 1.5 yards of acetate for lining	$320	$140

The fall casual fashions include

Clothing Item	Materials Requirements	Price	Labor and Machine Cost
Velvet pants	3 yards of velvet 2 yards of acetate for lining	$350	$175
Cotton sweater	1.5 yards of cotton	$130	$ 60
Cotton mini-skirt	0.5 yard of cotton	$ 75	$ 40
Velvet shirt	1.5 yards of velvet	$200	$160
Button-down blouse	1.5 yards of rayon	$120	$ 90

She knows that for the next month, she has ordered 45,000 yards of wool, 28,000 yards of acetate, 9,000 yards of cashmere, 18,000 yards of silk, 30,000 yards of rayon, 20,000 yards of velvet and 30,000 yards of cotton for production. The prices of the materials are listed below.

Material	Price per Yard
Wool	$ 9.00
Acetate	$ 1.50
Cashmere	$60.00
Silk	$13.00
Rayon	$ 2.25
Velvet	$12.00
Cotton	$ 2.50

Any material that is not used in production can be sent back to the textile wholesaler for a full refund, although scrap material cannot be sent back to the wholesaler.

She knows that the production of both the silk blouse and cotton sweater leaves leftover scraps of material. Specifically, for the production of one silk blouse or one cotton sweater, 2 yards of silk and cotton, respectively, are needed. From these 2 yards, 1.5 yards are used for the silk blouse or the cotton sweater and 0.5 yard is left as scrap material. She does not want to waste the material, so she plans to use the rectangular scrap of silk or cotton to produce a silk camisole or cotton mini-skirt, respectively. Therefore, whenever a silk blouse is produced, a silk camisole is also produced. Likewise, whenever a cotton sweater is produced, a cotton mini-skirt is also produced. Note that it is possible to produce a silk camisole without producing a silk blouse and a cotton mini-skirt without producing a cotton sweater.

The demand forecasts indicate that some items have limited demand. Specifically, because the velvet pants and velvet shirts are fashion fads, TrendLines has forecasted that it can sell only 5,500 pairs of velvet pants and 6,000 velvet shirts. TrendLines does not want to produce more than the forecasted demand because once the pants and shirts go out of style, the company cannot sell them. TrendLines can produce less than the forecasted demand, however, since the company is not required to meet the demand. The cashmere sweater also has limited demand because it is quite expensive, and TrendLines knows it can sell at most 4,000 cashmere sweaters. The silk blouses and camisoles have limited demand because many women think silk is too hard to care for, and TrendLines projects that it can sell at most 12,000 silk blouses and 15,000 silk camisoles.

The demand forecasts also indicate that the wool slacks, tailored skirts, and wool blazers have a great demand because they are basic items needed in every professional wardrobe. Specifically, the demand is 7,000 pairs of wool slacks and 5,000 wool blazers. Katherine wants to meet at least 60 percent of the demand for these two items to maintain her loyal customer base and not lose business in the future. Although the demand for tailored skirts could not be estimated, Katherine feels she should make at least 2,800 of them.

a. Ted is trying to convince Katherine not to produce any velvet shirts since the demand for this fashion fad is quite low. He argues that this fashion fad alone accounts for $500,000 of the fixed design and other costs. The net contribution (price of clothing item − materials cost − labor cost) from selling the fashion fad should cover these fixed costs. Each velvet shirt generates a net contribution of $22. He argues that given the net contribution, even satisfying the maximum demand will not yield a profit. What do you think of Ted's argument?

b. Formulate and solve a linear programming problem to maximize profit given the production, resource, and demand constraints.

Before she makes her final decision, Katherine plans to explore the following questions independently, except where otherwise indicated.

c. The textile wholesaler informs Katherine that the velvet cannot be sent back because the demand forecasts show that the demand for velvet will decrease in the future. Katherine can therefore get no refund for the velvet. How does this fact change the production plan?

d. What is an intuitive economic explanation for the difference between the solutions found in parts b and c?

e. The sewing staff encounters difficulties sewing the arms and lining into the wool blazer since the blazer pattern has an awkward shape and the heavy wool material is difficult to cut and sew. The increased labor time to sew a wool blazer increases the labor and machine cost for each blazer by $80. Given this new cost, how many of each clothing item should TrendLines produce to maximize profit?

f. The textile wholesaler informs Katherine that since another textile customer canceled his order, she can obtain an extra 10,000 yards of acetate. How many of each clothing item should TrendLines now produce to maximize profit?

g. TrendLines assumes that it can sell every item that was not sold during September and October in a big sale in November at 60 percent of the original price. Therefore, it can sell all items in unlimited quantity during the November sale. (The previously mentioned upper limits on demand only concern the sales during September and October.) What should the new production plan be to maximize profit?

CASE 3.2
NEW FRONTIERS

Rob Richman, president of AmeriBank, takes off his glasses, rubs his eyes in exhaustion, and squints at the clock in his study. It reads 3 AM. For the last several hours, Rob has been poring over AmeriBank's financial statements from the last three quarters of operation. AmeriBank, a medium-sized bank with branches throughout the United States, is headed for dire economic straits. The bank, which provides transaction, savings, investment, and loan services, has been experiencing a steady decline in its net income over the past year, and trends show that the decline will continue. The bank is simply losing customers to nonbank and foreign bank competitors.

AmeriBank is not alone in its struggle to stay out of the red. From his daily industry readings, Rob knows that many American banks have been suffering significant losses because of increasing competition from nonbank and foreign bank competitors offering services typically in the domain of American banks. Because the nonbank and foreign bank competitors specialize in particular services, they are able to better capture the market for those services by offering less expensive, more efficient, more convenient services. For example, large corporations now turn to foreign banks and commercial paper offerings for loans, and affluent Americans now turn to money-market funds for investment. Banks face the daunting challenge of distinguishing themselves from nonbank and foreign bank competitors.

Rob has concluded that one strategy for distinguishing AmeriBank from its competitors is to improve services that nonbank and foreign bank competitors do not readily provide: transaction services. He has decided that a more convenient transaction method must logically succeed the automatic teller machine, and he believes that electronic banking over the Internet allows this convenient transaction method. Over the Internet, customers are able to perform transactions on their desktop computers either at home or work. The explosion of the Internet means that many potential customers understand and use the World Wide Web. He therefore feels that if AmeriBank offers Web banking (as the practice of Internet banking is commonly called), the bank will attract many new customers.

Before Rob undertakes the project to make Web banking possible, however, he needs to understand the market for Web banking and the services AmeriBank should provide over the Internet. For example, should the bank only allow customers to access account balances and historical transaction information over the Internet, or should the bank develop a strategy to allow customers to make deposits and withdrawals over the Internet? Should the bank try to recapture a portion of the investment market by continuously running stock prices and allowing customers to make stock transactions over the Internet for a minimal fee?

Because AmeriBank is not in the business of performing surveys, Rob has decided to outsource the survey project to a professional survey company. He has opened the project up for bidding by several survey companies and will award the project to the company that is willing to perform the survey for the least cost. Rob provided each survey company with a list of survey requirements to ensure that AmeriBank receives the needed information for planning the Web banking project.

Because different age groups require different services, AmeriBank is interested in surveying four different age groups. The first group encompasses customers who are 18 to 25 years

old. The bank assumes that this age group has limited yearly income and performs minimal transactions. The second group encompasses customers who are 26 to 40 years old. This age group has significant sources of income, performs many transactions, requires numerous loans for new houses and cars, and invests in various securities. The third group encompasses customers who are 41 to 50 years old. These customers typically have the same level of income and perform the same number of transactions as the second age group, but the bank assumes that these customers are less likely to use Web banking since they have not become as comfortable with the explosion of computers or the Internet. Finally, the fourth group encompasses customers who are 51 years of age and over. These customers commonly crave security and require continuous information on retirement funds. The bank believes that it is highly unlikely that customers in this age group will use Web banking, but the bank desires to learn the needs of this age group for the future. AmeriBank wants to interview 2,000 customers with at least 20 percent from the first age group, at least 27.5 percent from the second age group, at least 15 percent from the third age group, and at least 15 percent from the fourth age group.

Rob understands that the Internet is a recent phenomenon and that some customers may not have heard of the World Wide Web. He therefore wants to ensure that the survey includes a mix of customers who know the Internet well and those that have less exposure to the Internet. To ensure that AmeriBank obtains the correct mix, he wants to interview at least 15 percent of customers from the Silicon Valley where Internet use is high, at least 35 percent of customers from big cities where Internet use is medium, and at least 20 percent of customers from small towns where Internet use is low.

Sophisticated Surveys is one of three survey companies competing for the project. It has performed an initial analysis of these survey requirements to determine the cost of surveying different populations. The costs per person surveyed are listed in the following table:

| | Age Group | | | |
Region	18 to 25	26 to 40	41 to 50	51 and over
Silicon Valley	$4.75	$6.50	$6.50	$5.00
Big cities	$5.25	$5.75	$6.25	$6.25
Small towns	$6.50	$7.50	$7.50	$7.25

Sophisticated Surveys explores the following options cumulatively.

a. Formulate a linear programming model to minimize costs while meeting all survey constraints imposed by AmeriBank.

b. If the profit margin for Sophisticated Surveys is 15 percent of cost, what bid will they submit?

c. After submitting its bid, Sophisticated Surveys is informed that it has the lowest cost but that AmeriBank does not like the solution. Specifically, Rob feels that the selected survey population is not representative enough of the banking customer population. Rob wants at least 50 people of each age group surveyed in each region. What is the new bid made by Sophisticated Surveys?

d. Rob feels that Sophisticated Surveys oversampled the 18-to-25-year-old population and the Silicon Valley population. He imposes a new constraint that no more than 600 individuals can be surveyed from the 18-to-25-year-old population and no more than 650 individuals can be surveyed from the Silicon Valley population. What is the new bid?

e. When Sophisticated Surveys calculated the cost of reaching and surveying particular individuals, the company thought that reaching individuals in young populations would be easiest. In a recently completed survey, however, Sophisticated Surveys learned that this assumption was wrong. The new costs for surveying the 18 to 25 year-old population are listed below:

Region	Cost per Person
Silicon Valley	$6.50
Big cities	$6.75
Small towns	$7.00

Given the new costs, what is the new bid?

f. To ensure the desired sampling of individuals, Rob imposes even stricter requirements. He fixes the exact percentage of people that should be surveyed from each population. The requirements are listed below:

Population	Percentage of People Surveyed
18 to 25	25%
26 to 40	35%
41 to 50	20%
51 and over	20%
Silicon Valley	20%
Big cities	50%
Small towns	30%

By how much would these new requirements increase the cost of surveying for Sophisticated Surveys? Given the 15 percent profit margin, what would Sophisticated Surveys bid?

CASE 3.3
ASSIGNING STUDENTS TO SCHOOLS

The Springfield School Board has made the decision to close one of its middle schools (sixth, seventh, and eighth grades) at the end of this school year and reassign all of next year's middle school students to the three remaining middle schools. The school district provides bussing for all middle school students who must travel more than approximately a mile, so the school board wants a plan for reassigning the students that will minimize the total bussing cost. The annual cost per student for bussing from each of the six residential areas of the city to each of the schools is shown in the following table (along with other basic data for next year), where 0 indicates that bussing is not needed and a dash indicates an infeasible assignment.

Area	Number of Students	Percentage in 6th Grade	Percentage in 7th Grade	Percentage in 8th Grade	Bussing Cost per Student		
					School 1	School 2	School 3
1	450	32	38	30	$300	0	$700
2	600	37	28	35	—	$400	$500
3	550	30	32	38	$600	$300	$200
4	350	28	40	32	$200	$500	—
5	500	39	34	27	0	—	$400
6	450	34	28	38	$500	$300	0
				School capacity:	900	1,100	1,000

The school board also has imposed the restriction that each grade must constitute between 30 and 36 percent of each school's population. The above table shows the percentage of each area's middle school population for next year that falls into each of the three grades. The school attendance zone boundaries can be drawn so as to split any given area among more than one school, but assume that the percentages shown in the table will continue to hold for any partial assignment of an area to a school.

You have been hired as a management science consultant to assist the school board in determining how many students in each area should be assigned to each school.

a. Formulate a linear programming model for this problem.

b. Solve the model.

c. What is your resulting recommendation to the school board?

After seeing your recommendation, the school board expresses concern about all the splitting of residential areas among multiple schools. They indicate that they "would like to keep each neighborhood together."

d. Adjust your recommendation as well as you can to enable each area to be assigned to just one school. (Adding this restriction may force you to fudge on some other constraints.) How much does this increase the total bussing cost? (This line of analysis will be pursued more rigorously in Case 9.3.)

The school board is considering eliminating some bussing to reduce costs. Option 1 is to only eliminate bussing for students traveling 1 to 1.5 miles, where the cost per student is given in the table as $200. Option 2 is to also eliminate bussing for students traveling 1.5 to 2 miles, where the estimated cost per student is $300.

e. Revise the model from part *a* to fit Option 1, and solve. Compare these results with those from part *c,* including the reduction in total bussing cost.

f. Repeat part *e* for Option 2.

The school board now needs to choose among the three alternative bussing plans (the current one or Option 1 or Option 2). One important factor is bussing costs. However, the school board also wants to place equal weight on a second factor: the inconvenience and safety problems caused by forcing students to travel by foot or bicycle a substantial distance (more than a mile, and especially more than 1.5 miles). Therefore, they want to choose a plan that provides the best trade-off between these two factors.

g. Use your results from parts *c, e,* and *f* to summarize the key information related to these two factors that the school board needs to make this decision.

h. Which decision do you think should be made? Why?

Note: This case will be continued in later chapters (Cases 4.3 and 9.3), so we suggest that you save your analysis, including your basic spreadsheet model.

CASE 3.4
KUWAIT'S AL-MANAKH STOCK MARKET

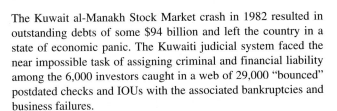

The Kuwait al-Manakh Stock Market crash in 1982 resulted in outstanding debts of some $94 billion and left the country in a state of economic panic. The Kuwaiti judicial system faced the near impossible task of assigning criminal and financial liability among the 6,000 investors caught in a web of 29,000 "bounced" postdated checks and IOUs with the associated bankruptcies and business failures.

Postdated checks and IOUs, written on behalf of speculative Kuwaiti investors and traders, funded the market's boom and led to its dramatic crash. Developing a method to disentangle the web of outstanding debt could save many years, and nearly $10 billion in court and attorney fees. In addition, the disentanglement would "net out" offsetting debts and reduce the magnitude of the total outstanding debt resulting from the crash, thereby reducing the negative impact of the market crash on the economy.

The government of Kuwait recognized that this complex web had to be disentangled quickly, fairly, and in a way most beneficial to the economy. His Excellency Shaikh Ali Al-Khalifa Al-Sabah, Minister of Finance and Oil of Kuwait, turned to the Kuwait Institute for Scientific Research for help.

Events Leading up to the Creation of the al-Manakh Stock Exchange

The al-Manakh Stock Market was established in 1979 by Kuwaiti trading companies and speculative investors to take the place of the very tightly controlled official stock market of Kuwait (KSE). After the KSE had undergone a major crash in 1977, permanent gov-

ernment controls were put in place to control Kuwait's highly speculative investors, who were motivated by high liquidity coupled with poor returns on Kuwaiti investments abroad as a result of volatile exchange rates. Oil-rich Kuwaitis had few places to invest their money other than in the country's stock market, but as the KSE began to boom, speculative traders entered the market, and the rapid speculative growth eventually caused the KSE to crash. Speculators writing postdated checks for investments that they could not afford meant that the market's boom was supported by funds that did not exist. Once out of control, when one investor defaulted, a chain reaction of bankruptcies was inevitable since investors could not honor their checks and IOUs because their accounts receivable and expected market returns were needed to fund these debts.

After the crash, the complicated puzzle of unpayable debts led to the bottom falling out of the KSE and produced a widespread panic in the Kuwaiti economy. As a result, the government bailed out creditors at a cost of $525 million. Tight government controls, including new laws severely restricting the use of postdated checks on the KSE, were established following this crash to curb further speculative trading.

Events Leading up to the al-Manakh Crash

The Kuwaiti government owned nearly half of the country's share-holding companies, and with very few investment opportunities other than oil, wealthy Kuwaitis had few investment alternatives at home. After a third major oil hike in 1979, wealthy Kuwaitis enjoyed a time of prosperity. Public spending and the demand for places to invest money rose. This increase in liquidity combined with few investment alternatives led to another speculative bubble. Since returns on foreign investments were poor, investors looked at the al-Manakh Stock Exchange as a place where they could carry out the speculative trading that had occurred on the KSE prior to the 1977 crash.

Source: This is one of the INFORMS Teaching Cases that have been prepared to provide material for class discussion. This particular case was prepared by Sam Ridesec under the supervision of Professor Peter Bell, Richard Ivey School of Business, the University of Western Ontario, Canada. Copyright 1998, by The Institute for Operations Research and the Management Sciences. In press. Reproduced by permission of INFORMS, the copyright owner.

The al-Manakh exchange was unregulated, and in the absence of government regulation or supervision, the use of postdated checks soared along with stock prices. Traders created numerous Gulf companies in neighboring Arab states solely for speculative purposes to avoid domestic regulations governing new companies. Investors poured money anywhere they could. At the peak of the stock market's explosion, 3.5 billion shares were traded, or more than four times the 837 million of the KSE. A 100 percent increase in stock value within a few weeks was not surprising to the 6,000 individuals and corporations feverishly trading in the al-Manakh market.

By 1982, the al-Manakh exchange was out of control. Untrained and uncertified brokers were trading worthless securities at astronomical P/E ratios. With a complicated mesh of postdated checks being traded to fund the explosion, traders used crude and often illegal methods of settlement. The inevitable crash left traders in a complicated puzzle of postdated checks and IOUs, making it difficult to determine who was responsible for each trade. Traders faced the disastrous implications of having written postdated checks against funds that they expected to receive in the future, from the sale of stocks at a profit before the postdated checks came due.

The Crash

In August 1982, the bubble burst when one of the largest of the 18 major trading companies defaulted on its debts. During the month, traded shares fell from 602 to 72 million as securities traded in the market lost 60 to 98 percent of their value.

The crash was a huge shock to the Kuwaiti economy. Initially, neither the central bank nor the government knew the magnitude of the crash and the resulting outstanding debt. Traders were left with worthless stocks in defunct Gulf companies as well as a web of two-way IOU notes and postdated checks.

First calculations of the resulting outstanding debt after the crash produced a figure of $94 billion, or 4.3 times the Kuwaiti gross domestic product. The majority of this figure was the sum of the face value of nearly 29,000 postdated checks. In addition, 95 percent of the total outstanding debt involved only 18 traders who were caught in a mesh of entangled debt responsibilities.

Attempts to Rectify the Situation

In late 1982, the government took some steps to attempt to contain the damage. It established a clearinghouse with the purpose of collecting, matching, verifying, and systematizing the financial accounts of individuals and brokers, and set aside a $1.7 billion trust fund to compensate small investors (losses less than $1.7 million). Finally, an arbitration panel was established to effect settlements, and to sanction and finalize settlements reached voluntarily between traders.

Unfortunately, the government's initial strategy of forcing traders to pay their debts as part of the solution did not work. Many traders had become insolvent and few were willing to meet their accounts payable before collecting their receivables, especially when their accounts receivable were needed to pay off their debts. This problem, and the fact that a resolution did not seem to be arising in the near future, led the Kuwait government to form the Corporation for the Settlement of Company Forward Share Transactions. This company established a special task force made up of A. A. Eliman (San Francisco State University), M. Girgis (LTC Techno-Economics Research Group, Inc.), and S. Kotob (Kuwait Institute for Scientific Research). Under the supervision

of the Kuwaiti minister of Oil and Finance, the task force began the high priority task of untangling traders and settling debts.

Appreciating the Traders' Entanglement

Figure 1 illustrates the example of four entangled traders. Each trader had some assets, (potentially) an uncollected receivable from each other trader, and (potentially) an unpaid payable to each other trader.

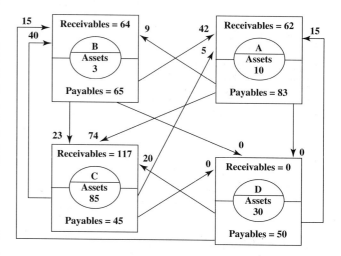

Each trader's assets were further broken down into four asset classes. These were, in order of decreasing risk, cash and KSE shares, real estate, receivables from other entangled traders, and shares of Gulf companies. For the example, consider the four traders' assets to be as follows:

	Trader			
	A	B	C	D
Cash and KSE shares	1	0.6	15	5
Real estate	4	1.2	24	7
Receivables from solvents	3	0.2	27	3
Shares of Gulf companies	2	1	19	15
Total Assets	10	3	85	30

In this situation, three of the traders (A, B, and D) could not determine how much of their debt they could pay before knowing what portion of their receivables they would collect from the other entangled traders. Therefore, one can appreciate how the situation could not be resolved without outside intervention to decide who could and should pay what and to whom. In addition, there was the issue of how the different asset types were to be treated and in what proportion they were to be paid.

The task force first defined the debt settlement ratio (DSR):

$$DSR = Minimum \left[\frac{Assets + Actual\ Receivables}{Payables}, 1 \right]$$

In order to determine the portion of debt that could be honored by each trader, the task force set out a series of equations to determine each trader's DSR that was dependent on actual receivables: computing each trader's DSR would essentially require first determining the payments that each trader would make. A further problem with this method was the necessity to restrict the payments from solvent traders to the amount they actually owed. The task force, however, was able to use DSRs as a method of trader classification without knowing what portion of actual receivables would be collected (Figure 2).

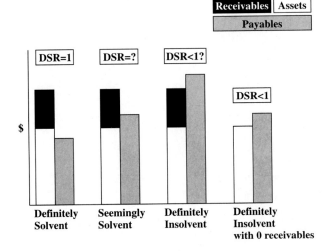

A Method for Disentangling the Traders

After considering the dilemma faced in determining the traders' DSRs, the task force realized that determining DSRs would actually disentangle the traders, since each inter-trader payment would have to be calculated to determine traders' actual receivables. However, the rationale behind these payments needed to be decided. What should these payments accomplish? What possible settlement options were the fairest and/or the most beneficial to the economy?

Possible payment disentanglement rationales considered included attempting to:

- Limit the number of bankruptcies.
- Pay off as many solvent creditors as possible.
- Achieve the largest possible total payments to all creditors.
- Maximize the sum of insolvents' DSRs.
- Minimize insolvents' deficits (assets + receivables − payables).
- Determine DSRs that were least susceptible to further deterioration in asset value.
- Determine DSRs while keeping the DSRs of the largest 18 insolvent traders equal.

The task force also needed to consider the following factors:

- All traders had to be treated equally and in accordance with the strengths and weaknesses of their financial portfolios, al-Manakh stock trading, and their choice of trade cohorts.
- Maximizing the ability for traders to pay their debts in full would minimize the negative effect of the crash on the economy.
- A trader's DSR could not be higher than one, since that would imply that the trader would be paying out more than the amount owed.
- By Kuwaiti law, debts to multiple creditors had to be paid in equal proportion of the amount owed to each creditor.
- All solvent traders should honor their payables in cash (even if this required them to liquidate other assets).
- The disentanglement solution must prevent traders who actually owed money from making net gains.

The task force had many decisions to make to arrive at an equitable solution that would disentangle the web of debts and "net out" the actual loss to the economy. If a credible solution could not be found, each of the 29,000 postdated checks and IOUs would require three court cases to settle: a criminal case, a commercial case, and a bankruptcy case. The outcome of this legal process would send many Kuwaiti entrepreneurs to jail, including many with strong political and social ties; would cost the government some $380 million; and would require the judicial system to increase capacity 18-fold for five years. Most importantly, the Kuwaiti economy's state of panic and recession would not improve until the situation was resolved. Time was of the essence.

a. Address the following issues:
  1. Determine a method of allocating payments between traders using the example given in the case, while ignoring the asset breakdown.
  2. How should the total payments be allocated among asset classes?

b. Discuss the following questions:
  1. What management science tools can be used to help resolve this problem?
  2. What is the advantage of a model-based approach over a legal or political procedure?
  3. What is the most appropriate and fair rationale (or objective) to guide disentangling payments?
  4. What constraints must be taken into account?
  5. How should different assets be treated?

WHAT-IF ANALYSIS FOR LINEAR PROGRAMMING

The preceding two chapters have described and illustrated how to formulate a linear programming model on a spreadsheet to represent a variety of managerial problems, and then how to use the Solver to find an optimal solution for this model. You might think that this would finish our story about linear programming: once the manager learns the optimal solution, she would immediately implement this solution and then turn her attention to other matters. However, this is not the case. The enlightened manager demands much more from linear programming, and linear programming has much more to offer her—as you will discover in this chapter.

An optimal solution is only optimal with respect to a particular mathematical model that provides only a rough representation of the real problem. A manager is interested in much more than just finding such a solution. The purpose of a linear programming study is to help guide management's final decision by providing insights into the likely consequences of pursuing various managerial options under a variety of assumptions about future conditions. Most of the important insights are gained while conducting analysis *after* finding an optimal solution for the original version of the basic model. This analysis is commonly referred to as **what-if analysis** because it involves addressing some questions about *what* would happen to the optimal solution *if* different assumptions are made about future conditions. Spreadsheets play a central role in addressing these *what-if questions*.

This chapter focuses on the types of information provided by what-if analysis and why it is valuable to managers. The first section provides an overview. Section 4.2 returns to the Wyndor Glass Co. product-mix case study (Section 2.2) to describe the what-if analysis that is needed in this situation. The subsequent sections then flesh out the picture in the context of this case study.

4.1 The Importance of What-If Analysis to Managers

The examples and problems in the preceding chapters on linear programming have provided the data needed to determine precisely all the numbers that should go into the data cells for the spreadsheet formulation of the linear programming model. (Recall that these numbers are referred to as the **parameters of the model.**) Real applications seldom are this straightforward. Substantial time and effort often are needed to track down the needed data. Even then, it may only be possible to develop rough estimates of the parameters of the model.

For example, in the Wyndor case study, two key parameters of the model are the coefficients in the objective function that represent the unit profits of the two new products. These parameters were estimated to be $300 for the doors and $500 for the windows. However, what these unit profits actually will turn out to be depends on many factors—the costs of raw materials, production, shipping, advertising, and so on, as well as such things as the market reception to the new products and the amount of competition encountered. Some of these factors cannot be estimated with real accuracy until long after the linear programming study has been completed and the new products have been on the market for some time.

Therefore, before Wyndor's management makes a decision on the product mix, it will want to know what the effect would be if the unit profits turn out to differ significantly from the estimates. For example, would the optimal solution change if the unit profit for the doors turns out to be $200 instead of the estimate of $300? How inaccurate can the estimate be in either direction before the optimal solution would change?

Such questions are addressed in Section 4.3 when only one estimate is inaccurate. Section 4.4 will address similar questions when all the estimates are inaccurate.

If the optimal solution will remain the same over a wide range of values for a particular coefficient in the objective function, then management will be content with a fairly rough estimate for this coefficient. On the other hand, if even a small error in the estimate would change the optimal solution, then management will want to take special care to refine this estimate. Management sometimes will get involved directly in adjusting such estimates to its satisfaction.

Here then is a summary of the first benefit of what-if analysis.

1. Typically, many of the parameters of a linear programming model are only *estimates* of quantities (e.g., unit profits) that cannot be determined precisely at this time. What-if analysis reveals how close each of these estimates needs to be to avoid obtaining an erroneous optimal solution, and therefore pinpoints the **sensitive parameters** where extra care is needed to refine their estimates.

Several sections describe how what-if analysis provides this benefit for the most important parameters. Sections 4.3 and 4.4 do this for the coefficients in the objective function (these numbers appear in the spreadsheet in the row for the unit contribution of each activity toward the overall measure of performance). Sections 4.6 and 4.7 do the same for the *right-hand sides of the functional constraints* (these are the numbers that typically are in the right-hand column of the spreadsheet just to the right of the ≤, ≥, or = signs).

Businesses operate in a dynamic environment. Even when management becomes satisfied with the current estimates and implements the corresponding optimal solution, conditions may change later. For example, suppose that Wyndor's management is satisfied with $300 as the estimate of the unit profit for the doors, but increased competition later forces a price reduction that reduces this unit profit. Does this change the optimal product mix? The what-if analysis shown in Section 4.3 immediately indicates in advance which new unit profits would leave the optimal product mix unchanged, which can help guide management in its new pricing decision. Furthermore, if the optimal product mix is unchanged, then there is no need to solve the model again with the new coefficient. Avoiding solving the model again is no big deal for the tiny two-variable Wyndor problem, but it is extremely welcome for real applications that may have hundreds or thousands of constraints and variables.

Thus, here is the second benefit of what-if analysis.

2. If conditions change after the study has been completed (a common occurrence), what-if analysis leaves signposts that indicate (without solving the model again) whether a resulting change in a parameter of the model changes the optimal solution.

Again, several subsequent sections describe how what-if analysis does this.

These sections focus on studying how changes in the parameters of a linear programming model affect the optimal solution. This type of what-if analysis commonly is referred to as **sensitivity analysis,** because it involves checking how *sensitive* the optimal solution is to the value of each parameter. Sensitivity analysis is a vital part of what-if analysis.

However, rather than being content with the passive sensitivity analysis approach of checking the effect of parameter estimates being inaccurate, what-if analysis often goes further to take a proactive approach. An analysis may be made of various possible managerial actions that would result in changes to the model.

A prime example of this proactive approach arises when certain parameters of the model represent *managerial policy decisions* rather than quantities that are largely outside the control of management. For example, consider the Profit & Gambit Co. advertising-mix problem presented in Section 2.7. The algebraic form of the linear programming model formulated there is

$$\text{Minimize} \quad \text{Cost} = TV + 2PM \quad \text{(in millions of dollars)}$$

subject to

Stain remover increased market share:	$PM \geq 3$
Liquid detergent increased market share:	$3TV + 2PM \geq 18$
Powder detergent increased market share:	$-TV + 4PM \geq 4$

and

$$TV \geq 0 \qquad PM \geq 0$$

(See Figure 2.21 for the corresponding spreadsheet formulation.) For the advertising campaign being planned for the three products, the right-hand sides of the three functional constraints (3, 18, 4) represent managerial policy decisions on the minimum required increase in the company's percentage share of the market for the respective products. The optimal solution is $TV = 4$ (4 units of television advertising) and $PM = 3$ (3 units of print media advertising), with a total advertising cost of $10 million. Once this optimal solution has been obtained, management will want to know how much the total advertising cost would change if it changed any or all of its policy decisions about increases in market share. For example, how much more would it cost to require that the stain remover increase its market share by at least 4 percent instead of 3 percent? If the answer is not much, then management probably will want to boost its market share requirement for this product. Conversely, management may want to reduce this requirement if it would save a lot of money.

The *shadow price analysis* presented in Section 4.5 provides a very convenient way of addressing these kinds of questions. We will return to this same example there.

You may recognize this example as being a *cost–benefit–trade-off problem,* as described in Section 3.3. Shadow price analysis is widely used to help management find the best trade-off between costs and benefits for such problems.

This same kind of what-if analysis also is widely used for those *resource-allocation problems* (Section 3.2) where management controls the amounts of the resources being made available to the activities under consideration. For example, for the Wyndor product-mix problem, the right-hand sides of the three functional constraints (4, 12, 18) represent the number of hours of production time in the three respective plants being made available per week for the production of the two new products. Management can change these three resource amounts by altering the production levels for the old products in these plants. Therefore, after learning the optimal solution, management will want to know the impact on the profit from the new products if these resource amounts are changed in certain ways. Shadow price analysis quickly answers these questions, as you will see in Section 4.5.

We now can summarize the third benefit of what-if analysis.

3. When certain parameters of the model represent managerial policy decisions, what-if analysis provides valuable guidance to management about what the impact would be of altering these policy decisions.

What-if analysis sometimes goes even further in providing helpful guidance to management, such as when analyzing alternate scenarios for how business conditions might evolve. However, this chapter will focus on the three benefits summarized above.

Review Questions

1. What are the *parameters* of a linear programming model?
2. How can inaccuracies arise in the parameters of a model?
3. What does what-if analysis reveal about the parameters of a model that are only estimates?
4. Is it always inappropriate to make only a fairly rough estimate for a parameter of a model? Why?

5. How is it possible for the parameters of a model to be accurate initially and then become inaccurate at a later date?
6. How does what-if analysis help management prepare for changing conditions?
7. What is meant by *sensitivity analysis?*
8. For what kinds of managerial policy decisions does what-if analysis provide guidance?

4.2 Continuing the Wyndor Case Study

We now return to the case study introduced in Section 2.2 involving the Wyndor Glass Co. product-mix problem.

To review briefly, recall that the company is preparing to introduce two exciting new products:

- An 8-foot glass door with aluminum framing.
- A 4-foot × 6-foot double-hung wood-framed window.

To analyze which mix of the two products would be most profitable, the company's Management Science Group introduced two decision variables:

D = production rate of this new kind of door
W = production rate of this new kind of window

where this rate measures the number of units produced per week. Three plants will be involved in the production of these products. Based on managerial decisions regarding how much these plants will continue to be used to produce current products, the number of hours of production time per week being made available in plants 1, 2, and 3 for the new products is 4, 12, and 18, respectively. After obtaining rough estimates that the profit per unit will be $300 for the doors and $500 for the windows, the Management Science Group then formulated the linear programming model shown in Figure 4.1, where the objective is to choose the values of D and W in the changing cells (C9 and D9) so as to maximize the total profit (per week) given in the target cell (E8). Applying the Solver to this model yielded the optimal solution shown on this spreadsheet and summarized as follows.

FIGURE 4.1

The spreadsheet model and its optimal solution for the original Wyndor problem before beginning what-if analysis.

	A	B	C	D	E	F	G
1		Wyndor Glass Co. Product–Mix Problem					
2							
3			Hours Used per Unit Produced				Hours
4			Doors	Windows	Totals		Available
5		Plant 1	1	0	2	≤	4
6		Plant 2	0	2	12	≤	12
7		Plant 3	3	2	18	≤	18
8		Unit Profit	$300	$500	$3,600		
9		Solution	2	6			

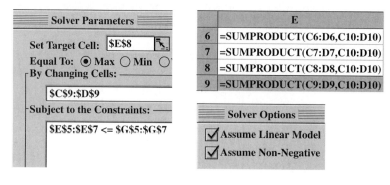

Solver Parameters
Set Target Cell: $E$8
Equal To: ● Max ○ Min ○
By Changing Cells:
$C$9:$D$9
Subject to the Constraints:
$E$5:$E$7 <= $G$5:$G$7

	E
6	=SUMPRODUCT(C6:D6,C10:D10)
7	=SUMPRODUCT(C7:D7,C10:D10)
8	=SUMPRODUCT(C8:D8,C10:D10)
9	=SUMPRODUCT(C9:D9,C10:D10)

Solver Options
✓ Assume Linear Model
✓ Assume Non-Negative

OPTIMAL SOLUTION

$D = 2$ (Produce 2 doors per week.)

$W = 6$ (Produce 6 windows per week.)

Profit $= 3,600$ (The estimated total weekly profit is \$3,600.)

However, this optimal solution assumes that all the estimates that provide the parameters of the model (as shown in the data cells over the ranges C5:D8 and G5:G7) are accurate.

The head of the Management Science Group, Lisa Taylor, now is ready to meet with management to discuss the group's recommendation that the above product mix be used.

Management's Discussion of the Recommended Product Mix

John Hill (president): Thanks for your preliminary report, Lisa. It appears that your group has done a fine study as usual.

Lisa Taylor (head of Management Science Group): Thank you. All the members of the group made important contributions. However, we're not done yet. I asked for this meeting so we could explore what questions you and Bill would like us to pursue further. In particular, I am especially concerned that we weren't able to better pin down just what the numbers should be to go into our model. If any of these estimates are very far off, it could change what the product mix should be.

John: That concerns me also. Bill, you've been coordinating with Lisa's group. Which estimates do you think are the shakiest?

Bill Tasto (Vice President for Manufacturing): Without question, the estimates of the unit profits for the two products. The other numbers are pretty solid. We have a good handle on how many hours of production time will be needed in each plant to produce a unit of either product. Also, we already have made our preliminary decisions on how many hours of production time per week will be made available in each plant for these new products.

John: How were the estimates of the unit profits obtained?

Lisa: We got a tentative pricing decision on the new products from Ann Lester. Then we asked the Accounting Department, with some help from Bill's and Ann's staffs, to analyze the cost data for producing and marketing these products. However, since the products haven't gone into production yet, all they could do is analyze the data from similar current products and then try to project what the changes would be for these new products. They gave us some numbers, but said they were pretty rough. They would need to do a lot more work to pin down the numbers better.

John: We may need to ask them to do that. To determine whether we have to do that, we first have to find out if a correction in the estimate of the unit profit for either product is likely to change what the product mix should be. Do you have a way of checking how far off one of these estimates can be without changing the optimal product mix?

Lisa: Yes, we do. We can quickly find what we call the *range of optimality* for each unit profit. As long as the true value of the unit profit is within this range of optimality, and the other unit profit is correct, the optimal product mix will not change. If this range is pretty wide, you don't need to worry about refining the estimate of the unit profit. However, if the range is quite narrow, then it is important to pin down the estimate more closely.

John: OK. Clearly we want you to get this range of optimality for each unit profit for us. But we also want to know what happens if both estimates are off.

Lisa: Yes, we can provide a way of checking whether the optimal product mix might change for any new combination of unit profits you think might be the true one.

John: Great. That's what we need. There's also one more thing.

Lisa: What's that?

John: Bill gave you the numbers for how many hours of production time we're making available per week in the three plants for these new products. I noticed you used these numbers on your spreadsheet.

Lisa: Yes. They're the right-hand sides of our constraints. Is something wrong with these numbers?

John: No, not at all. I just wanted to let you know that we haven't made a final decision on whether these are the numbers we want to use. We would like your group to provide us with some analysis of what the effect would be if we change any of those numbers. How much more profit could we get from the new products for each additional hour of production time per week we provide in one of the plants? That sort of thing. Then, to decide what to do, we would compare this additional profit with the profit we would lose by cutting back on the production of current products.
Lisa: Yes, we can get that analysis to you right away also.
John: We might also be interested in making simultaneous changes in the available production hours for two or three of the plants.
Lisa: No problem. We'll give you information about that as well.
John: Wonderful. We'll look forward to getting your final report. Thank you, Lisa. And thank your group for the great work all of you are doing.
Lisa: You're welcome. It is an excellent group and they'll be pleased to hear about your commendation.

Summary of Management's What-If Questions

Here is a summary of John Hill's what-if questions that Lisa and her group will be addressing in the coming sections.

1. What happens if the estimate of the unit profit of one of Wyndor's new products is inaccurate? (Section 4.3)
2. What happens if the estimates of the unit profits of both of Wyndor's new products are inaccurate? (Section 4.4)
3. What happens if a change is made in the number of hours of production time per week being made available to Wyndor's new products in one of the plants? (Sections 4.5 and 4.6)
4. What happens if simultaneous changes are made in the number of hours of production time per week being made available to Wyndor's new products in all the plants? (Section 4.7)

Review Questions

1. Which estimates of the parameters in the linear programming model for the Wyndor problem are most questionable?
2. Which numbers in this model represent tentative managerial decisions that management might want to change after receiving analysis from the Management Science Group?

4.3 Range-of-Optimality Sensitivity Analysis

Section 4.1 began by discussing the fact that many of the parameters of a linear programming model typically are only *estimates* of quantities that cannot be determined precisely at the time. What-if analysis (or *sensitivity analysis* in particular) reveals how close each of these estimates needs to be to avoid obtaining an erroneous optimal solution.

We focus in this section on how sensitivity analysis does this when the parameters involved are *coefficients in the objective function.* (Recall that each of these coefficients gives the *unit contribution* of one of the activities toward the overall measure of performance.) In the process, we will address the first of the what-if questions posed by Wyndor management in the preceding section.

Question 1: What happens if the estimate of the unit profit of one of Wyndor's new products is inaccurate?

To start this process, first consider the question of what happens if the estimate of $300 for the unit profit for Wyndor's new kind of door is inaccurate. To address this question, let

P_D = unit profit for the new kind of door
   = cell C8 in the spreadsheet

Although $P_D = \$300$ in the current version of Wyndor's linear programming model, we now want to explore how much larger or how much smaller P_D can be and still have $(D, W) = (2, 6)$ as the optimal solution. In other words, how much can the estimate of $300 for the unit profit for these doors be off before the model will give an erroneous optimal solution?

Using the Spreadsheet to Do Sensitivity Analysis

One of the great strengths of a spreadsheet is the ease with which it can be used interactively to perform various kinds of what-if analysis, including the sensitivity analysis being considered in this section. Once the Solver has been set up to obtain an optimal solution, you can immediately find out what would happen if one of the parameters of the model were to be changed to some other value. All you have to do is make this change on the spreadsheet and then click on the Solve button again.

To illustrate, Figure 4.2 shows what would happen if the unit profit for doors were to be decreased from $P_D = \$300$ to $P_D = \$200$. Comparing with Figure 4.1, there is no change at all in the optimal solution. In fact, the *only* changes in the new spreadsheet are the new value of P_D in cell C8 and a decrease of $200 in the total profit shown in cell E8 (because each of the two doors produced per week provides $100 less profit). Because the optimal solution does not change, we now know that the original estimate of $P_D = \$300$ can be considerably *too high* without invalidating the model's optimal solution.

But what happens if this estimate is *too low* instead. Figure 4.3 shows what would happen if P_D were to be increased to $P_D = \$500$. Again, there is no change in the optimal solution.

Because the original value of $P_D = \$300$ can be changed considerably in either direction without changing the optimal solution, P_D is said to be *not a sensitive parameter*. It is not necessary to pin down this estimate with great accuracy to have confidence that the model is providing the correct optimal solution.

This may be all the information that is needed about P_D. However, if there is a good possibility that the true value of P_D will turn out to be outside this broad range from $200 to $500, further investigation would be desirable. How much higher or lower can P_D be before the optimal solution would change?

Figure 4.4 demonstrates that the optimal solution would indeed change if P_D is increased all the way up to $P_D = \$1,000$. Thus, we now know that this change occurs somewhere between $500 and $1,000 during the process of increasing P_D.

FIGURE 4.2

The revised Wyndor problem where the estimate of the unit profit for doors has been decreased from $P_D = \$300$ to $P_D = \$200$, but no change occurs in the optimal solution.

	A	B	C	D	E	F	G
1		Wyndor Glass Co. Product–Mix Problem					
2							
3			Hours Used per Unit Produced				Hours
4			Doors	Windows	Totals		Available
5		Plant 1	1	0	2	≤	4
6		Plant 2	0	2	12	≤	12
7		Plant 3	3	2	18	≤	18
8		Unit Profit	$200	$500	$3,400		
9		Solution	2	6			

FIGURE 4.3

The revised Wyndor problem where the estimate of the unit profit for doors has been increased from $P_D = \$300$ to $P_D = \$500$, but no change occurs in the optimal solution.

	A	B	C	D	E	F	G
1		Wyndor Glass Co. Product–Mix Problem					
2							
3			Hours Used per Unit Produced				Hours
4			Doors	Windows	Totals		Available
5		Plant 1	1	0	2	≤	4
6		Plant 2	0	2	12	≤	12
7		Plant 3	3	2	18	≤	18
8		Unit Profit	$500	$500	$4,000		
9		Solution	2	6			

FIGURE 4.4

The revised Wyndor problem where the estimate of the unit profit for doors has been increased from $P_D = \$300$ to $P_D = \$1000$, which results in a change in the optimal solution.

	A	B	C	D	E	F	G
1		Wyndor Glass Co. Product–Mix Problem					
2							
3			Hours Used per Unit Produced				Hours
4			Doors	Windows	Totals		Available
5		Plant 1	1	0	4	≤	4
6		Plant 2	0	2	6	≤	12
7		Plant 3	3	2	18	≤	18
8		Unit Profit	$1,000	$500	$5,500		
9		Solution	4	3			

FIGURE 4.5

A data table that shows the effect of systematically varying the estimate of the unit profit for doors in the Wyndor problem.

	A	B	C	D	E
1		Wyndor Glass Co. Data Table (Unit Profit for Doors)			
2					
3		Unit Profit	Optimal Production Rates		Total
4		for Doors	Doors	Windows	Profit
5		$100	2	6	$3,200
6		$200	2	6	$3,400
7		$300	2	6	$3,600
8		$400	2	6	$3,800
9		$500	2	6	$4,000
10		$600	2	6	$4,200
11		$700	2	6	$4,400
12		$800	4	3	$4,700
13		$900	4	3	$5,100
14		$1,000	4	3	$5,500

To pin down just where this change occurs, we could continue selecting new values of P_D at random. However, a better approach is to systematically consider a uniform range of values of P_D, such as shown in Figure 4.5. This *data table* reveals that the optimal solution remains the same all the way from $P_D = \$100$ (and perhaps lower) to $P_D = \$700$, but that a change occurs somewhere between $800 and $800.

We next could systematically consider values of P_D between $700 and $800 to determine more closely where the optimal solution changes. However, here is a shortcut. The range of values of P_D over which $(D, W) = (2, 6)$ remains as the optimal solution is referred to as the **allowable range to stay optimal** for P_D, or just its **range of optimality** for short. Upon request, the Excel Solver will provide a report called the *sensitivity report* that, after a couple of simple calculations, reveals exactly what this range of optimality is.

Using the Sensitivity Report to Find the Range of Optimality

As was shown in Figure 2.19, when the Solver gives the message that it has found a solution, it also gives on the right a list of three reports that can be provided. By selecting the second one (labeled Sensitivity), you will obtain the sensitivity report.

Figure 4.6 shows the relevant part of this report for the Wyndor problem. The Final Value column indicates the optimal solution. The next column gives the *reduced costs*. (We will not discuss these reduced costs because the information they provide can also be gleaned from the range of optimality.) The next three columns provide the information needed to identify the *range of optimality* for each coefficient in the objective function. The Objective Coefficient column gives the current value of each coefficient, and then the next two columns give the *allowable increase* and the *allowable decrease* from this value to remain within the range of optimality.

For example, consider P_D, the coefficient of D in the objective function. Since D is the production rate for these special doors, the Doors row in the table provides the following information (without the dollar sign) about P_D:

FIGURE 4.6

Part of the sensitivity report generated by the Excel Solver for the original Wyndor problem (Figure 4.1), where the last three columns enable identifying the ranges of optimality for the unit profits for doors and windows.

Adjustable Cells

Cell	Name	Final Value	Reduced Cost	Objective Coefficient	Allowable Increase	Allowable Decrease
$C$9	Solution Doors	2	0	300	450	300
$D$9	Solution Windows	6	0	500	1E+30	300

FIGURE 4.7

The two dashed lines that pass through solid constraint boundary lines are the objective function lines when P_D (the unit profit for doors) is at an endpoint of its range of optimality, $0 \leq P_D \leq 750$, since either line or any objective function line in between still yields $(D, W) = (2, 6)$ as an optimal solution for the Wyndor problem.

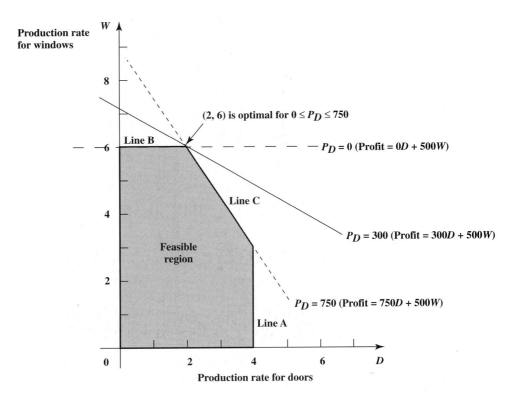

Current value of P_D: 300	
Allowable increase in P_D: 450.	So $P_D \leq 300 + 450 = 750$
Allowable decrease in P_D: 300.	So $P_D \geq 300 - 300 = 0$
Range of optimality for P_D: $0 \leq P_D \leq 750$	

Therefore, if P_D is changed from its current value (without making any other change in the model), the current solution $(D, W) = (2, 6)$ will remain optimal so long as the new value of P_D is within this range of optimality.

Figure 4.7 provides graphical insight into this range of optimality. For the original value of $P_D = 300$, the solid line in the figure shows the slope of the objective function line passing through $(2, 6)$. At the lower end of the range of optimality, when $P_D = 0$, the objective function line that passes through $(2, 6)$ now is line B in the figure, so every point on the line segment between $(0, 6)$ and $(2, 6)$ is an optimal solution. For any value of $P_D < 0$, the objective function line will have rotated even further so that $(0, 6)$ becomes the only optimal solution. At the upper end of the range of optimality, when $P_D = 750$, the objective function line that passes through $(2, 6)$ becomes line C, so every point on the line segment between $(2, 6)$ and $(4, 3)$ becomes an optimal solution. For any value of $P_D > 750$, the objective function line is even steeper than line C, so $(4, 3)$ becomes the only optimal solution.

Conclusion: The range of optimality for P_D is $0 \leq P_D \leq 750$, because $(D, W) = (2, 6)$ remains optimal over this range but not beyond. (When $P_D = 0$ or $P_D = 750$, there are multiple optimal solutions, but $(D, W) = (2, 6)$ still is one of them.) With the range this wide around the original estimate of \$300 ($P_D = 300$) for the unit profit for doors, we can be quite confident of obtaining the correct optimal solution for the true unit profit even though the discussion in Section 4.2 indicates that this estimate is fairly rough.

This same approach can be used to find the range of optimality for the unit profit for Wyndor's other new product. In particular, let

P_W = unit profit for Wyndor's new kind of window
    = cell D8 in the spreadsheet

Referring to the Windows row of the sensitivity report (Figure 4.6), this row indicates that the allowable decrease in P_W is 300 (so $P_W \geq 500 - 300 = 200$) and the allowable increase is 1E+30. What is meant by 1E+30? This is shorthand in Excel for 10^{30} (1 with 30 zeroes after it). This tremendously huge number is used by Excel to represent *infinity*. Therefore, the range of optimality of P_W is obtained from the sensitivity report as follows:

Current value of P_W: 500
Allowable increase in P_W: unlimited.   So P_W has no upper limit.
Allowable decrease in P_W: 300.   So $P_W \geq 500 - 300 = 200$
Range of optimality: $P_W \geq 200$

The range of optimality is quite wide for both objective function coefficients. Thus, even though $P_D = \$300$ and $P_W = \$500$ were only rough estimates of the true unit profit for the doors and windows, respectively, we can still be confident that we have obtained the correct optimal solution.

We are not always so lucky. For some linear programming problems, even a small change in the value of certain coefficients in the objective function can change the optimal solution. Such coefficients are referred to as *sensitive parameters*. The sensitivity report will immediately indicate which of the objective function coefficients (if any) are sensitive parameters. These are parameters that have a small allowable increase and/or a small allowable decrease. Hence, extra care should be taken to refine these estimates.

Once this has been done and the final version of the model has been solved, the ranges of optimality continue to serve an important purpose. As indicated in Section 4.1, the second benefit of what-if analysis is that if conditions change after the study has been completed (a common occurrence), what-if analysis leaves signposts that indicate (without solving the model again) whether a resulting change in a parameter of the model changes the optimal solution. Thus, if weeks, months, or even years later, the unit profit for one of Wyndor's new products changes substantially, its range of optimality indicates immediately whether the old optimal product mix still is the appropriate one to use. Being able to draw an affirmative conclusion without reconstructing and solving the revised model is extremely helpful for any linear programming problem, but especially so when the model is a large one.

Review Questions

1. What is meant by the *range of optimality* for a coefficient in the objective function?
2. What is the significance if the true value for a coefficient in the objective function turns out to be so different from its estimate that it lies outside its range of optimality?
3. In Excel's sensitivity report, what is the interpretation of the Objective Coefficient column? The Allowable Increase column? The Allowable Decrease column?

4.4 Simultaneous Changes in Objective Function Coefficients

The coefficients in the objective function typically represent quantities (e.g., unit profits) that can only be estimated because of considerable uncertainty about what their true values will turn out to be. The ranges of optimality described in the preceding section deal with this uncertainty by focusing on just one coefficient at a time. In effect, the range of optimality for a particular coefficient assumes that the original estimates for all the other coefficients are completely accurate so that this coefficient is the only one whose true value may differ from its original estimate.

In actuality, the estimates for *all* the coefficients (or at least more than one of them) may be inaccurate simultaneously. The crucial question is whether this is likely to result in obtaining the wrong optimal solution. If so, greater care should be taken to refine these estimates as much as possible, at least for the more crucial coefficients. On the other hand, if what-if analysis reveals that the anticipated errors in estimating the coefficients are unlikely to affect the optimal solution, then management can be reassured that the current linear programming model and its results are providing appropriate guidance.

This section focuses on how to determine, without solving the problem again, whether the optimal solution might change if certain changes occur simultaneously in the coefficients of the objective function (due to their true values differing from their estimates). In the process, we will address the second of Wyndor management's what-if questions.

> **Question 2:** What happens if the estimates of the unit profits of both of Wyndor's new products are inaccurate?

Using Spreadsheets for This Analysis

Once again, the quickest and easiest way to address this kind of question is to simply try out different estimates on the spreadsheet formulation of the model and see what happens each time when clicking on the Solve button.

In this case, the optimal product mix indicated by the model is heavily weighted toward producing the windows (6 per week) rather than the doors (only 2 per week). Since there is equal enthusiasm for both new products, management is concerned about this imbalance. Therefore, Ann Lester (Vice President for Marketing) has raised a what-if question. What would happen if the estimate of the unit profit for the doors ($300) is too low and the corresponding estimate for the windows ($500) is too high. The estimates could easily be off in these directions (as could be checked with considerable additional investigation). If this were the case, would this lead to a more balanced product mix being the most profitable one?

This question can be answered in a matter of seconds simply by substituting new estimates of the unit profits in the original spreadsheet in Figure 4.1 and clicking on the Solve button. Figure 4.8 shows that new estimates of $450 for doors and $400 for windows causes no change at all in the solution for the optimal product mix. (The total profit does change, but this occurs only because of the changes in the unit profits.) Would even larger changes in the estimates of unit profits finally lead to a change in the optimal product mix? Figure 4.9 shows that this does happen, yielding a relatively balanced product mix of $(D, W) = (4, 3)$, when estimates of $600 for doors and $300 for windows are used.

To gain additional insight into how much the estimates of unit profits need to change before the optimal product mix will change, a *data table* can be generated by systematically changing the unit profits in Figure 4.1. Figure 4.10 shows one way of systematically enumerating possible unit profits to generate such a data table. This table indicates that the original estimates would need to be very inaccurate indeed before the optimal product mix would change. Although the estimates are fairly rough, management is confident that they are not that inaccurate. Therefore, there is no need to expend the considerable effort that would be needed to refine the estimates.

FIGURE 4.8

The revised Wyndor problem where the estimates of the unit profits for doors and windows have been changed to $P_D = \$450$ and $P_W = \$400$, respectively, but no change occurs in the optimal solution.

	A	B	C	D	E	F	G
1		Wyndor Glass Co. Product–Mix Problem					
2							
3			Hours Used per Unit Produced				Hours
4			Doors	Windows	Totals		Available
5		Plant 1	1	0	2	≤	4
6		Plant 2	0	2	12	≤	12
7		Plant 3	3	2	18	≤	18
8		Unit Profit	$450	$400	$3,300		
9		Solution	2	6			

FIGURE 4.9

The revised Wyndor problem where the estimates of the unit profits for doors and windows have been changed to $600 and $300, respectively, which results in a change in the optimal solution.

	A	B	C	D	E	F	G
1		Wyndor Glass Co. Product–Mix Problem					
2							
3			Hours Used per Unit Produced				Hours
4			Doors	Windows	Totals		Available
5		Plant 1	1	0	4	≤	4
6		Plant 2	0	2	6	≤	12
7		Plant 3	3	2	18	≤	18
8		Unit Profit	$600	$300	$3,300		
9		Solution	4	3			

FIGURE 4.10

A data table that shows the effect of systematically varying the estimates of the unit profits for both doors and windows in the Wyndor problem.

	A	B	C	D	E	F
1		Wyndor Glass Co. Data Table (Unit Profit for Doors and Windows)				
2						
3		Unit Profit	Unit Profit	Optimal Production Rates		Total
4		for Doors	for Windows	Doors	Windows	Profit
5		$300	$500	2	6	$3,600
6		$300	$300	2	6	$2,400
7		$300	$100	4	3	$1,500
8		$400	$500	2	6	$3,800
9		$400	$300	2	6	$2,600
10		$400	$100	4	3	$1,900
11		$500	$500	2	6	$4,000
12		$500	$300	4	3	$2,900
13		$500	$100	4	3	$2,300
14		$600	$500	2	6	$4,200
15		$600	$300	4	3	$3,300
16		$600	$100	4	3	$2,700

At this point, it continues to appear that $(D, W) = (2, 6)$ is the best product mix for initiating the production of the two new products (although additional what-if questions remain to be addressed in subsequent sections). However, we also now know from Figure 4.10 that as conditions change in the future, if the unit profits for both products change enough, it may be advisable to change the product mix later. We still need to leave clear signposts behind to signal when a future change in the product mix should be considered, as described next.

Gleaning Additional Information from the Sensitivity Report

The preceding section described how the data in the sensitivity report enable finding the range of optimality for an individual coefficient in the objective function when that coefficient is the only one that changes from its original value. These same data (the allowable increase and allowable decrease in each coefficient) also can be used to analyze the effect of *simultaneous* changes in these coefficients. Here is how.

The 100 Percent Rule for Simultaneous Changes in Objective Function Coefficients: If simultaneous changes are made in the coefficients of the objective function, calculate for each change the percentage of the allowable change (increase or decrease) for that coefficient to remain within its range of optimality. If the *sum* of the percentage changes does *not* exceed 100 percent, the original optimal solution definitely will still be optimal. (If the sum *does* exceed 100 percent, then we cannot be sure.)

This rule does not spell out what happens if the sum of the percentage changes *does* exceed 100 percent. The consequence depends on the directions of the changes in the coefficients. Exceeding 100 percent may or may not change the optimal solution, but so long as 100 percent is not exceeded, the original optimal solution *definitely will* still be optimal.

Keep in mind that we can safely use the entire allowable increase or decrease in a single objective function coefficient only if none of the other coefficients have changed at all.

With simultaneous changes in the coefficients, we focus on the *percentage* of the allowable increase or decrease that is being used for each coefficient.

To illustrate, consider the Wyndor problem again, along with the information provided by the sensitivity report in Figure 4.6. Suppose conditions have changed after the initial study, and the unit profit for doors (P_D) has increased from $300 to $450 while the unit profit for windows (P_W) has decreased from $500 to $400. The calculations for the 100 percent rule then are

P_D: $300 → $450

$$\text{Percentage of allowable increase} = 100\left(\frac{450-300}{450}\right)\% = 33\tfrac{1}{3}\%$$

P_W: $ 500 → $400

$$\text{Percentage of allowable decrease} = 100\left(\frac{500-400}{300}\right)\% = 33\tfrac{1}{3}\%$$

$$\text{Sum} = 66\tfrac{2}{3}\%$$

Since the sum of the percentages does not exceed 100 percent, the original optimal solution $(D, W) = (2, 6)$ definitely is still optimal, just as we found earlier in Figure 4.8.

Now suppose conditions have changed even further, so P_D has increased from $300 to $600 while P_W has decreased from $500 to $300. The calculations for the 100 percent rule now are

P_D: $300 → $600

$$\text{Percentage of allowable increase} = 100\left(\frac{600-300}{450}\right)\% = 66\tfrac{2}{3}\%$$

P_W: $500 → $300

$$\text{Percentage of allowable decrease} = 100\left(\frac{500-300}{300}\right)\% = 66\tfrac{2}{3}\%$$

$$\text{Sum} = 133\tfrac{1}{3}\%$$

Since the sum of the percentages now exceeds 100 percent, the 100 percent rule says that we can no longer guarantee that $(D, W) = (2, 6)$ is still optimal. In fact, we found earlier in Figure 4.9 that the optimal solution has changed to $(D, W) = (4, 3)$.

These results suggest how to find just where the optimal solution changes while P_D is being increased and P_W is being decreased in this way. Since 100 percent is midway between 66⅔ percent and 133⅓ percent, the sum of the percentage changes will equal 100 percent when the values of P_D and P_W are midway between their values in the above cases. In particular, $P_D = $525 is midway between $450 and $600 and $P_W = $350 is midway between $400 and $300. The corresponding calculations for the 100 percent rule are

P_D: $300 → $525

$$\text{Percentage of allowable increase} = 100\left(\frac{525-300}{450}\right)\% = 50\%$$

P_W: $500 → $350

$$\text{Percentage of allowable decrease} = 100\left(\frac{500-350}{300}\right)\% = 50\%$$

$$\text{Sum} = 100\%$$

Although the sum of the percentages equals 100 percent, the fact that it does not *exceed* 100 percent guarantees that $(D, W) = (2, 6)$ is still optimal. Figure 4.11 shows graphically that *both* (2, 6) and (4, 3) are now optimal, as well as all the points on the line segment connecting these two points. However, if P_D and P_W were to be changed any further from their original values (so that the sum of the percentages exceeds 100 percent), the objective function line would be rotated so far toward the vertical that $(D, W) = (4, 3)$ would become the only optimal solution.

FIGURE 4.11

When the estimates of the unit profits for doors and windows change to $P_D = 525 and $P_W = 350, which lies at the edge of what is allowed by the 100 percent rule, the graphical method shows that $(D, W) = (2, 6)$ still is an optimal solution, but now every other point on the line segment between this solution and $(4, 3)$ also is optimal.

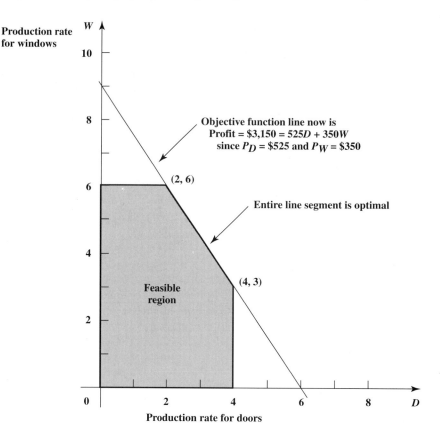

At the same time, keep in mind that having the sum of the percentages of allowable changes exceed 100 percent does not automatically mean that the optimal solution will change. For example, suppose that the estimates of both unit profits are halved. The resulting calculations for the 100 percent rule are

P_D: \$300 → \$150

$$\text{Percentage of allowable decrease} = 100\left(\frac{300 - 150}{300}\right)\% = 50\%$$

P_W: \$500 → \$250

$$\text{Percentage of allowable decrease} = 100\left(\frac{500 - 250}{300}\right)\% = 83\%$$

$$\text{Sum} = 133\%$$

Even though this sum exceeds 100 percent, Figure 4.12 shows that the original optimal solution is still optimal. In fact, the objective function line has the same slope as the original objective function line (the solid line in Figure 4.7). This happens whenever *proportional changes* are made to all the unit profits, which will automatically lead to the same optimal solution.

Comparisons

You now have seen two approaches to investigating what happens if simultaneous changes occur in the coefficients of the objective function: (1) try out changes directly on a spreadsheet and (2) apply the 100 percent rule.

The spreadsheet approach is a good place to start, especially for less experienced modelers, because it is simple and quick. If you are only interested in checking one specific set of changes in the coefficients, you can immediately see what happens after making the changes in the spreadsheet. More often, there will be numerous possibilities for what the true values of the coefficients will turn out to be, because of uncertainty in the original estimates of these coefficients. Trying out representative possibilities on the spreadsheet may provide all the insight that is needed. Perhaps the optimal solution for the original model will remain optimal over nearly all these possibilities, so this solution can be confidently

FIGURE 4.12

When the estimates of the unit profits for doors and windows change to $P_D = \$150$ and $P_W = \$250$ (half their original values), the graphical method shows that the optimal solution still is $(D, W) = (2, 6)$, even though the 100 percent rule says that the optimal solution might change.

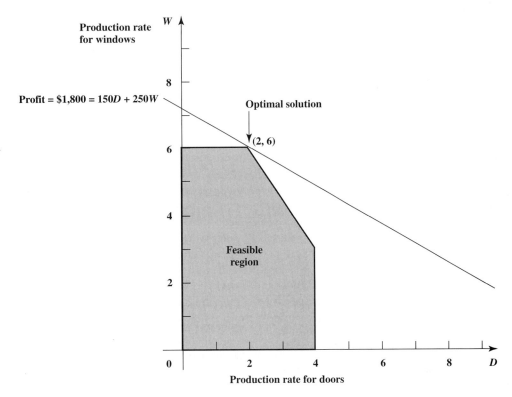

used. Or perhaps it will become clear that the original estimates need to be refined before selecting a solution.

When the spreadsheet approach does not provide a clear conclusion, the 100 percent rule can usefully complement this approach in the following ways:

- The 100 percent rule can be used to determine just how large the changes in the objective function coefficients need to be before the original optimal solution may no longer be optimal.
- When the model has a large number of decision variables (as is common for real problems), it may become impractical to use the spreadsheet approach to systematically try out a variety of simultaneous changes in many or all of the coefficients in the objective function because of the huge number of representative possibilities. However, by dividing each coefficient's allowable increase or allowable decrease by the number of decision variables, the 100 percent rule immediately indicates how much each coefficient can be safely changed without invalidating the current optimal solution.
- After completing the study, if conditions change in the future that cause some or all of the coefficients in the objective function to change, the 100 percent rule quickly indicates whether the original optimal solution must remain optimal. If the answer is affirmative, there is no need to take all the time that may be required to reconstruct the (revised) spreadsheet model. The time saved can be very substantial for large models.

Review Questions

1. In the 100 percent rule for simultaneous changes in objective function coefficients, what are the percentage changes that are being considered?
2. In this 100 percent rule, if the sum of the percentage changes do not exceed 100 percent, what does this say about the original optimal solution?
3. In this 100 percent rule, if the sum of the percentage changes exceeds 100 percent, does this mean that the original optimal solution will no longer be optimal?

4.5 Shadow Price Analysis for Right-Hand Sides

We now turn our focus from the coefficients in the objective function to the effect of changing the constants on the right-hand sides of the functional constraints.

We might be interested in the effect of changes in the right-hand sides for the same reason as for objective function coefficients, namely, that these parameters of the model are only *estimates* of quantities that cannot be determined precisely at this time so we want to determine the effect if these estimates are inaccurate.

However, a more common reason for this interest is the one discussed at the end of Section 4.1, namely, that the right-hand sides may well represent *managerial policy decisions* rather than quantities that are largely outside the control of management. Therefore, after the model has been solved, management will want to analyze the effect of altering these policy decisions in a variety of ways to see if these decisions can be improved. What *shadow price analysis* does is provide valuable guidance to management about what the effect would be of altering these policy decisions. (Recall that this was cited as the third benefit of what-if analysis in Section 4.1.) Thus, shadow price analysis is an important part of what-if analysis.

This analysis is done for each *functional constraint,* one at a time, to determine what the effect would be on the optimal value of the objective function if a small change were to be made in the right-hand side of the constraint. This involves finding the constraint's *shadow price,* described below.

> Given an optimal solution and the corresponding value of the objective function for a linear programming model, the **shadow price** for a functional constraint is the *rate* at which the value of the objective function can be increased by increasing the right-hand side of the constraint by a small amount.[1]

Generally, an easy way to find this shadow price with a spreadsheet is to simply increase the right-hand side by one and click on the Solve button again to see how much the value of the objective function (as given by the target cell) increases. Alternatively, the Solver's sensitivity report also provides the shadow price for each of the functional constraints.

A constraint's shadow price enables one to immediately check what the effect would be of altering a managerial policy decision that changes that constraint's right-hand side. As long as the change is not too large (as discussed in the next section), the resulting change in the optimal value of the objective function will just be this change in the right-hand side (positive or negative) *times* the shadow price.

Section 4.1 illustrated the concept of shadow price analysis by referring back to the Profit & Gambit Co. advertising-mix problem presented in Section 2.7. We now return to this example.

Shadow Price Analysis for the Profit & Gambit Problem

Review of the Problem.   As formulated in Section 2.7, the spreadsheet giving the original linear programming model for this problem is shown again in Figure 4.13 (without some of the details given in Figure 2.21). The three right-hand sides (3, 18, and 4) in column G represent the *minimum required increase in the percentage of market share* for the three products in the advertising campaign. Thus, these three numbers actually result from *managerial policy decisions* on what should be achieved by the advertising campaign.

The changing cells (C10 and D10) indicate that an optimal solution is to use 4 units of advertising on television and 3 units of advertising in the print media. The target cell (E9) shows that the total cost for this advertising campaign would be $10 million.

After receiving this information, Profit & Gambit management now wants to analyze the trade-off between the total advertising cost and the resulting benefits achieved by increasing the market share of the three products. Examining this trade-off may well result in management altering its policy decisions on market share increases. To analyze this trade-off, management needs to know the effect on cost per unit increase in the market share requirement for each product, that is, what are the *shadow prices* for the three functional constraints. Beginning with the first product listed in column B of the spreadsheet—the stain remover—Figure 4.14 shows the effect of changing the minimum required increase in the

---

[1]The next section will discuss how large this "small amount" can be. Meanwhile, we will assume that it can be at least one.

FIGURE 4.13

The spreadsheet model and its optimal solution for the original Profit & Gambit problem before beginning what-if analysis regarding the goals for increased market shares.

	A	B	C	D	E	F	G
1		Profit & Gambit Advertising–Mix Problem					
2							
3			Increase in Market Share per Unit of Advertising				Minimum
4							Required
5			Television	Print Media	Totals		Increase
6		Stain Remover	0%	1%	3%	≥	3%
7		Liquid Detergent	3%	2%	18%	≥	18%
8		Powder Detergent	–1%	4%	8%	≥	4%
9		Unit Cost ($millions)	1	2	10		
10		Solution	4	3			

FIGURE 4.14

The revised Profit & Gambit problem where the minimum required increase in the market share for the stain remover has been changed from 3 percent to 4 percent, which results in an increase of $1⅓ million in the total cost.

	A	B	C	D	E	F	G
1		Profit & Gambit Advertising–Mix Problem					
2							
3			Increase in Market Share per Unit of Advertising				Minimum
4							Required
5			Television	Print Media	Totals		Increase
6		Stain Remover	0%	1%	4%	≥	4%
7		Liquid Detergent	3%	2%	18%	≥	18%
8		Powder Detergent	–1%	4%	13%	≥	4%
9		Unit Cost ($millions)	1	2	11.33		
10		Solution	3.333	4			

FIGURE 4.15

The revised Profit & Gambit problem where the minimum required increase in the market share for the stain remover has been changed again from 4 percent to 5 percent, which results in an additional increase of $1⅓ million in the total cost.

	A	B	C	D	E	F	G
1		Profit & Gambit Advertising–Mix Problem					
2							
3			Increase in Market Share per Unit of Advertising				Minimum
4							Required
5			Television	Print Media	Totals		Increase
6		Stain Remover	0%	1%	5%	≥	5%
7		Liquid Detergent	3%	2%	18%	≥	18%
8		Powder Detergent	–1%	4%	17%	≥	4%
9		Unit Cost ($millions)	1	2	12.67		
10		Solution	2.667	5			

market share for this product from 3 percent to 4 percent. Comparing the target cell in this spreadsheet to the one in Figure 4.13, the resulting increase in the total advertising cost is

$$\text{Change in cost} = \$11.33 \text{ million} - \$10 \text{ million}$$

$$= \$1⅓ \text{ million}$$

This calculation reveals that·

Shadow price for stain remover constraint = $1⅓ million (per 1% market share)

This shadow price indicates that an additional small increase in the market share goal should cost $1 1/3 million per 1 percent increase in market share. Figure 4.15 demonstrates this by further increasing the minimum required increase in market share from 4 percent to 5 percent. Comparing the target cells in Figures 4.15 and 4.14,

$$\text{Change in cost} = \$12.67 \text{ million} - \$11.33 \text{ million}$$

$$= \$1⅓ \text{ million}$$

just as predicted by the shadow price.

FIGURE 4.16

The part of the sensitivity report generated by the Excel Solver for the Profit & Gambit problem that deals with the functional constraints, where the fourth column provides the shadow prices.

Constraints

Cell	Name	Final Value	Shadow Price	Constraint R.H. Side	Allowable Increase	Allowable Decrease
$D$4	**Stain Remover Totals**	3%	133.33	0.03	0.06	0.00857
$D$5	**Liquid Detergent Totals**	18%	33.333	0.18	0.12	0.12
$D$6	**Powder Detergent Totals**	8%	0	0.04	0.04	1E+30

Although calculating a shadow price as illustrated above is straightforward, the shadow prices for all the functional constraints also can be obtained from the Solver's sensitivity report. Figure 4.16 shows the part of the sensitivity report that deals with the functional constraints, where the shadow prices are given in the fourth column. Since Excel treats 100 percent as a single unit, this column shows the rate of increase in the total cost (in millions of dollars) per increase of 100 percent in each right-hand side individually (column G) in Figure 4.13. In this case, market shares over 100 percent are not meaningful, so let's change the units by dividing the numbers in the shadow price column by 100. This yields

Shadow price for stain remover constraint = $1.33 million

Shadow price for liquid detergent constraint = $0.33 million

Shadow price for powder detergent constraint = $0

where these are the costs per increase of 1 percent (rather than 100 percent) in the required market share.

Why is the shadow price $0 for the powder detergent constraint? You can see why by comparing cells E8 and G8 in Figure 4.13. The optimal solution already is providing an increase of 8 percent in the market share for the powder detergent, so boosting the minimum required increase from 4 percent to 5 percent does not necessitate any change in this solution or in the total cost.

Now that we have obtained all the shadow prices, let us explore further how this information should be interpreted by management.

The Message to Management.   The term *shadow price* has been defined in terms of the increase in the value of the objective function of the linear programming model when the right-hand side of a functional constraint is increased. However, most managers do not want to get into discussions of such technical matters. If a management science team is conducting the study for members of management, those managers should insist that the team interpret the shadow prices (and all other technical results) in the language of management.

For the Profit & Gambit problem, recall that the value of the objective function is expressed in units of *millions of dollars* of advertising cost. The right-hand side of a functional constraint represents the managerial policy decision on the *minimum required increase* in the percentage of market share for the corresponding product. These terms, *advertising cost* and *market share*, not *value of the objective function* and *right-hand side of a functional constraint*, are the language of management.

See the box for the memorandum that the management science team sent to management to convey the message of the shadow prices in the language of management.

Memorandum

To: Profit & Gambit management
From: The management science team
Subject: The trade-off between advertising expenditures and market shares

   As instructed, we have been continuing our analysis of the plans for the major new advertising campaign that will focus on our spray prewash stain remover, our new liquid formulation laundry detergent, and our powder laundry detergent.

concluded

Our recent report presented our preliminary conclusions on how much advertising to do in the different media to meet the market share goals at a minimum total cost:

Allocate $4 million to advertising on television.

Allocate $6 million to advertising in the print media.

Total advertising cost: $10 million.

We estimate that the resulting increases in market share will be

Stain remover: 3 percent increase in market share

Liquid detergent: 18 percent increase in market share

Powder detergent: 8 percent increase in market share.

You had specified that these increases should be at least 3 percent, 18 percent, and 4 percent, respectively, so we have met the minimum levels for the first two products and substantially exceeded it for the third.

However, you also indicated that your decisions on these minimum required increases in market share (3 percent, 18 percent, and 4 percent) had been tentative ones. Now that we have more specific information on what the advertising costs and the resulting increases in market shares will be, you plan to reevaluate these decisions to see if small changes might improve the trade-off between advertising cost and increased market share.

To assist you in reevaluating your decision, we now have analyzed this trade-off for each of the three products. Our best estimate is that each additional 1 percent boost in your original minimum goal for increased market share would require the following increase in total advertising cost:

Stain remover: $1.33 million per 1 percent increase in the minimum goal for market share.

Liquid detergent: $0.33 million per 1 percent increase in the minimum goal for market share.

Powder detergent: No cost for a small increase in the minimum goal for market share.

For example, increasing the minimum goal for increased market share from 3 percent to 4 percent for the stain remover would cost about $1.33 million (above the current total advertising cost of $10 million). Increasing the minimum goal from 18 percent to 20 percent for the liquid detergent would cost about $0.67 million. Doing both simultaneously would cost roughly $2 million, thereby increasing the total advertising cost from $10 million to $12 million. A small increase in the minimum goal of 4 percent for the powder detergent would not cost anything since we already are achieving 8 percent with the preliminary proposal for advertising expenditures.

If you decide that you might want to *decrease* any of these minimum goals instead to reduce the total advertising cost, these same dollar figures show what the savings would be. That is, each 1 percent *decrease* in the minimum goal for market share would save about $1.33 million for the stain remover, about $0.33 million for the liquid detergent, and nothing for the powder detergent.

You also can use these dollar amounts to check on the effect of simultaneously *increasing* some minimum goals and *decreasing* others. For example, increasing the minimum goal for the stain remover from 18 percent to 19 percent would cost about $0.33 million and simultaneously decreasing the minimum goal for the liquid detergent from 3 percent to 2 percent would save about $1.33 million, so the net saving would be about $1 million.

We also should caution you that these dollar amounts only apply for relatively small changes (a few percent of market share) in the minimum goals. If you decide that you want to consider larger changes, we will be happy to develop better estimates of the required changes in the total advertising cost.

Meanwhile, we are about to undertake the task of determining just how much each minimum goal can be changed before the corresponding dollar amount given above would no longer apply. We will report our findings shortly.

The last paragraph of the memorandum refers (in different language) to determining how much the right-hand side of a functional constraint can be changed before the corresponding shadow price is no longer valid for indicating the resulting change in the optimal value of the objective function. Section 4.6 describes how to make this determination.

Note in the memorandum that the management science team does not make any decisions about changing the minimum goals for market share increases. It is the prerogative of management to make these decisions, using its best judgment to determine an appropriate trade-off between advertising costs and the benefits (both tangible and intangible) of increasing the market share for each of its products. As with any management science study, the responsibility of the management science team is to provide information that will aid management in making its decisions. In this case, the shadow prices (expressed in the language of management) provide the information that management needs.

Application to the Wyndor Problem

Now we return to the Wyndor case study to address the third of the what-if questions posed by Wyndor management in Section 4.2.

> **Question 3:** What happens if a change is made in the number of hours of production time per week being made available to Wyndor's new products in one of the plants?

In comparing the analysis here to the preceding example, note that the Wyndor problem is a maximization problem whereas the Profit & Gambit problem is a minimization problem.

The Wyndor Sensitivity Report.   Figure 4.17 shows the full sensitivity report provided by the Solver for the original Wyndor problem after obtaining the optimal solution given in Figure 4.1. The top half is the part already shown in Figure 4.6 for finding ranges of optimality. The bottom half focuses on the functional constraints, including providing the shadow prices for these constraints in the fourth column. The first three columns remind us that (1) the output cells for these constraints in Figure 4.1 are cells E5 to E7, (2) these cells give the totals (on the number of production hours used per week) for the three plants, and (3) the final values in these cells are 2, 12, and 18 (as shown in column E of Figure 4.1). The fifth column repeats the current numbers on the right-hand side of the constraints, as given in column G of Figure 4.1. The last two columns of the sensitivity report on constraints will be discussed in the next section.

The shadow price given in the fourth column for each constraint tells us how much the value of the objective function (target cell E8 in Figure 4.1) would increase if the right-hand side of that constraint (cell G5, G6, or G7) were to be increased by 1. The shadow price for the plant 1 constraint is 0, because this plant already is using less hours (2) than are available (4) so there would be no benefit to making an additional hour available. However, plants 2 and 3 are using all the hours available to them for the two new products (with the product mix given by the changing cells). Thus, it is not surprising that the shadow prices indicate that the target cell would increase if the hours available in either plant 2 or plant 3 were to be increased.

The Message to Management.   The value of the objective function for this problem (target cell E8 in Figure 4.1) represents the *total profit* in dollars per week from the two new

FIGURE 4.17

The complete sensitivity report generated by the Excel Solver for the original Wyndor problem as formulated in Figure 4.1.

Adjustable Cells

Cell	Name	Final Value	Reduced Cost	Objective Coefficient	Allowable Increase	Allowable Decrease
$C$9	Solution Doors	2	0	300	450	300
$D$9	Solution Windows	6	0	500	1E+30	300

Constraints

Cell	Name	Final Value	Shadow Price	Constraint R.H. Side	Allowable Increase	Allowable Decrease
$E$5	Plant 1 Totals	2	0	4	1E+30	2
$E$6	Plant 2 Totals	12	150	12	6	6
$E$7	Plant 3 Totals	18	100	18	6	6

products under consideration. The right-hand side of each functional constraint represents the number of hours of production time being made available per week for these products in the plant that corresponds to this constraint. Therefore, the shadow price for a functional constraint informs management about how much the total profit from the two new products could be increased for each additional hour of production time made available to these products per week in the corresponding plant. This will apply as long as the number of hours of additional production time is not very large.

The production time made available for these two new products can be increased only if it is decreased for other products. Therefore, management will need to assess the disadvantages of decreasing the production time for any other products (including both lost profit and less tangible disadvantages) before deciding whether to increase the production time for the new products. This analysis might also lead to *decreasing* the production time made available to the two new products in one or more of the plants.

Review Questions

1. Why might it be possible to alter the right-hand side of a functional constraint?
2. What is meant by a *shadow price*?
3. Why are shadow prices of interest to managers?
4. Can shadow prices be used to determine the effect of *decreasing* rather than increasing the right-hand side of a functional constraint?
5. What does a shadow price of 0 tell a manager?

4.6 Range-of-Feasibility Sensitivity Analysis

The shadow price for a functional constraint provides valuable information because it indicates how much the optimal value of the objective function will increase per unit *increase* in the right-hand side of the constraint. Conversely, the negative of the shadow price gives the change in the optimal objective function value per unit *decrease* in the right-hand side.

However, this information is only valid for fairly small changes in the right-hand side. We now will focus in this section on determining just how large these changes can be before the shadow price is no longer applicable.

Continuing with the Wyndor problem, let us begin by considering the functional constraint with the largest shadow price. As indicated by Figure 4.17, this is the plant 2 constraint with a shadow price of 150. Its current right-hand side is

$$RHS = 12$$

that is, 12 hours of production time currently are being made available per week for the two new products. Therefore, this shadow price tells us that the total profit will increase by \$150 per increase of 1 in RHS (or decrease by \$150 per decrease of 1 in RHS), provided the change in RHS is not too large. We want to determine how large this change in RHS can be.

One way to investigate this is to start with a small value (say, 0) of RHS in its spot (cell G6) on the spreadsheet in Figure 4.1 and then repeatedly increase the value by 1 and see how the total profit (cell E8) changes each time. Figure 4.18 shows the data table generated in this way. The key column is column F, which shows the increase in total profit (column E) for each increase of 1 in RHS (column B). This incremental profit first becomes \$150 when RHS is increased from 6 to 7, and it remains \$150 all the way up to RHS = 18. Therefore, the shadow price of 150 is valid for

$$6 \leq RHS \leq 18$$

Figure 4.19 provides graphical insight into why this is the range of validity for the shadow price. The optimal solution for the original problem, $(D, W) = (2, 6)$, lies at the intersection of line B and line C. The equation for line B is $2W = 12$ because this is the constraint boundary line for the plant 2 constraint ($2W \leq 12$). However, if the value of this right-hand-side (RHS = 12) is changed, line B will either shift upward (for a larger value

FIGURE 4.18

A data table that shows the effect of varying the number of hours of production time being made available per week in plant 2 for Wyndor's two new products.

	A	B	C	D	E	F
1		**Wyndor Glass Co. Data Table (Time Available in Plant 2)**				
2						
3		**Time Available**	**Optimal Production Rates**		**Total**	**Incremental**
4		**in Plant 2**	**Doors**	**Windows**	**Profit**	**Profit**
5		0	4	0	$1,200	—
6		1 hour	4	0.5	$1,450	$250
7		2 hours	4	1	$1,700	$250
8		3 hours	4	1.5	$1,950	$250
9		4 hours	4	2	$2,200	$250
10		5 hours	4	2.5	$2,450	$250
11		6 hours	4	3	$2,700	$250
12		7 hours	3.667	3.5	$2,850	$150
13		8 hours	3.333	4	$3,000	$150
14		9 hours	3	4.5	$3,150	$150
15		10 hours	2.667	5	$3,300	$150
16		11 hours	2.333	5.5	$3,450	$150
17		12 hours	2	6	$3,600	$150
18		13 hours	1.667	6.5	$3,750	$150
19		14 hours	1.333	7	$3,900	$150
20		15 hours	1	7.5	$4,050	$150
21		16 hours	0.667	8	$4,200	$150
22		17 hours	0.333	8.5	$4,350	$150
23		18 hours	0	9	$4,500	$150
24		19 hours	0	9	$4,500	$0
25		20 hours	0	9	$4,500	$0

of RHS) or downward (for a smaller value of RHS). As line B shifts, the boundary of the feasible region shifts accordingly and the optimal solution continues to lie at the intersection of the shifted line B and line C—provided the shift in line B is not so large that this intersection is no longer feasible. Figure 4.19 indicates that this intersection remains feasible (and so optimal) as RHS increases from 12 to 18, because the feasible region expands upward as line B shifts upward. However, for values of RHS larger than 18, this intersection is no longer feasible because it gives a negative value of D (the production rate for doors). Similarly, as RHS decreases from 12 to 6, this intersection remains feasible (and so optimal) as line B shifts down accordingly. However, for values of RHS less than 6, this intersection is no longer feasible because it violates the plant 1 constraint ($D \leq 4$) whose boundary line is line A. Consequently, the **allowable range to stay feasible** (or **range of feasibility** for short) for RHS is

$$6 \leq RHS \leq 18$$

Thus, the range of feasibility gives the range over which the shadow price is valid.

The Solver's sensitivity report actually provides all the data needed to identify the range of feasibility for each functional constraint. Refer back to the bottom of this report given in Figure 4.17. The final three columns enable calculating this range. The "Constraint R.H. Side" column indicates the original value of the right-hand side before any change is made. Adding the number in the "Allowable increase" column to this original value then gives the upper endpoint of the range of feasibility. Similarly, subtracting the number in the "Allowable decrease" column from this original value gives the lower endpoint. Using the fact that 1E + 30 represents infinity (∞), these calculations of the ranges of feasibility are shown below, where a subscript has been added to each RHS to identify the constraint involved.

Plant 1 constraint: $4 - 2 \leq RHS_1 \leq 4 + \infty$,   so $2 \leq RHS_1$ (no upper limit)

Plant 2 constraint: $12 - 6 \leq RHS_2 \leq 12 + 6$,   so $6 \leq RHS_2 \leq 18$

Plant 3 constraint: $18 - 6 \leq RHS_3 \leq 18 + 6$,   so $12 \leq RHS_3 \leq 24$

FIGURE 4.19

A graphical interpretation of the range of feasibility, 6 ≤ RHS ≤ 18, for the right-hand side of Wyndor's plant 2 constraint.

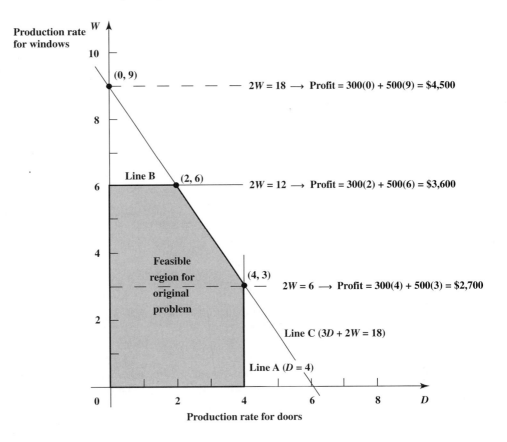

Recall again that each right-hand side here represents the number of hours of production time per week in the corresponding plant that is being made available to the two new products. Therefore, each shadow price can be applied by management to evaluate a change in its original decision on the number of hours as long as the new number is within the corresponding range of feasibility.

Review Questions

1. Which columns of the Solver's sensitivity report are used to find the range of feasibility for the right-hand side of a functional constraint.
2. Why are ranges of feasibility of interest to managers?

4.7 Simultaneous Changes in Right-Hand Sides

The range of feasibility for the right-hand side of a functional constraint identifies the range of values over which the shadow price for this constraint can be applied to evaluate the effect of changes in this right-hand side. This is very helpful when management is considering changing a policy decision that would change this right-hand side. However, the range of feasibility is completely valid only if this right-hand side is the only one that may be changed. Managerial decisions regarding right-hand sides are interrelated and so frequently are considered simultaneously. What happens when management wants to evaluate possible *simultaneous* changes in right-hand sides?

In addressing this general question, we also will deal with the last of Wyndor management's what-if questions.

Question 4: What happens if simultaneous changes are made in the number of hours of production time per week being made available to Wyndor's new products in all the plants?

In particular, after seeing that the plant 2 constraint has the largest shadow price (150), versus a shadow price of 100 for the plant 3 constraint, management now is interested in exploring a specific type of simultaneous change in these production hours. By shifting the production of one of the company's current products from plant 2 to plant 3, it is possible to increase the number of production hours available to the new products in plant 2 by decreasing the number available in plant 3 by the same amount. Management wonders what would happen if these simultaneous changes in production hours were made.

According to the shadow prices, the effect of shifting one hour of production time per week from plant 3 to plant 2 would be the following.

$$\text{RHS}_2:\ 12 \to 13 \quad \text{Change in total profit} = \text{shadow price} = \$150$$

$$\text{RHS}_3:\ 18 \to 17 \quad \text{Change in total profit} = -\text{shadow price} = -100$$

$$\text{Net increase in total profit} = \$50$$

However, we don't know if these shadow prices remain valid if *both* right-hand sides are changed by this much.

A quick way to check this is to substitute the new right-hand sides into the original spreadsheet in Figure 4.1 and click on the Solve button again. The resulting spreadsheet in Figure 4.20 shows that the net increase in total profit (from $3,600 to $3,650) is indeed $50, so the shadow prices are valid for these particular simultaneous changes in right-hand sides.

How much further will these shadow prices remain valid if we continue shifting production hours from plant 3 to plant 2? Figure 4.21 shows the data table obtained by repeatedly re-solving the spreadsheet model with larger and larger shifts in the production hours. The key column is column G, which indicates that the incremental profit of $50 per hour shifted remains valid up to the point where three hours have been shifted from plant 3 to plant 2, but not thereafter.

It can become tedious, or even impractical, to use the spreadsheet and a data table to systematically investigate a large number of simultaneous changes in right-hand sides, especially when more than two right-hand sides are being changed. Fortunately, there is a *100 percent rule* (analogous to the one presented in Section 4.4) that can greatly expedite larger investigations of this kind.

FIGURE 4.20

The revised Wyndor problem where column G in Figure 4.1 has been changed by shifting one of the hours available in plant 3 to plant 2, and then re-solving.

	A	B	C	D	E	F	G
1		Wyndor Glass Co. Product–Mix Problem					
2							
3			Hours Used per Unit Produced				Hours
4			Doors	Windows	Totals		Available
5		Plant 1	1	0	1.333	≤	4
6		Plant 2	0	2	13	≤	13
7		Plant 3	3	2	17	≤	17
8		Unit Profit	$300	$500	$3,650		
9		Solution	1.333	6.5			

FIGURE 4.21

A data table that shows the effect of shifting more and more of the hours available from plant 3 to plant 2.

	A	B	C	D	E	F	G
1		Wyndor Glass Co. Data Table (Time Available in Plants 2 and 3)					
2							
3		Time Available	Time Available	Optimal Production Rates		Total	Incremental
4		in Plant 2	in Plant 3	Doors	Windows	Profit	Profit
5		12 hours	18 hours	2	6	$3,600	—
6		13 hours	17 hours	1.333	6.5	$3,650	$50
7		14 hours	16 hours	0.667	7	$3,700	$50
8		15 hours	15 hours	0	7.5	$3,750	$50
9		16 hours	14 hours	0	7	$3,500	–$250
10		17 hours	13 hours	0	6.5	$3,250	–$250
11		18 hours	12 hours	0	6	$3,000	–$250

Another 100 Percent Rule

Recall that the 100 percent rule described in Section 4.4 is used to investigate simultaneous changes in *objective function coefficients*. The new 100 percent rule presented below investigates simultaneous changes in *right-hand sides* in a similar way.

The data needed to apply the new 100 percent rule for the Wyndor problem are given by the last three columns in the bottom part of the sensitivity report in Figure 4.17. Keep in mind that we can safely use the entire allowable decrease or increase from the current value of a right-hand side only if none of the other right-hand sides are changed at all. With simultaneous changes in the right-hand sides, we focus for each change on the *percentage* of the allowable decrease or increase that is being used. As detailed below, the 100 percent rule basically says that we can safely make the simultaneous changes only if the *sum* of these percentages does not exceed 100 percent.

> *The 100 Percent Rule for Simultaneous Changes in Right-Hand Sides:* The shadow prices remain valid for predicting the effect of simultaneously changing the right-hand sides of some of the functional constraints as long as the changes are not too large. To check whether the changes are small enough, calculate for each change the percentage of the allowable change (decrease or increase) for that right-hand side to remain within its range of feasibility. If the *sum* of the percentage changes does *not* exceed 100 percent, the shadow prices definitely will still be valid. (If the sum *does* exceed 100 percent, then we cannot be sure.)

To illustrate this rule, consider again the simultaneous changes (shifting one hour of production time per week from plant 3 to plant 2) that led to Figure 4.20. The calculations for the 100 percent rule in this case are

RHS_2: $12 \rightarrow 13$

Percentage of allowable increase $= 100\left(\dfrac{13 - 12}{6}\right) = 16\tfrac{2}{3}\%$

RHS_3: $18 \rightarrow 17$

Percentage of allowable decrease $= 100\left(\dfrac{18 - 17}{6}\right) = 16\tfrac{2}{3}\%$

$$\text{Sum} = 33\tfrac{1}{3}\%$$

Since the sum of $33\tfrac{1}{3}$ percent is less than 100 percent, the shadow prices definitely are valid for predicting the effect of these changes, as was illustrated with Figure 4.20.

The fact that $33\tfrac{1}{3}$ percent is one-third of 100 percent suggests that the changes can be three times as large as above without invalidating the shadow prices. To check this, let us apply the 100 percent rule with these larger changes.

RHS_2: $12 \rightarrow 15$

Percentage of allowable increase $= \left(\dfrac{15 - 12}{6}\right)\% = 50\%$

RHS_3: $18 \rightarrow 15$

Percentage of allowable decrease $= \left(\dfrac{18 - 15}{6}\right)\% = 50\%$

$$\text{Sum} = 100\%$$

Because the sum does *not exceed* 100 percent, the shadow prices are still valid, but these are the largest changes in the right-hand sides that can provide this guarantee. In fact, Figure 4.21 demonstrated that the shadow prices become invalid for larger changes.

Review Questions

1. Why might a manager be interested in considering simultaneous changes in right-hand sides?
2. What are the data needed to apply the 100 percent rule for simultaneous changes in right-hand sides?

3. What is guaranteed if the sum of the percentages of allowable changes in the right-hand sides does not exceed 100 percent?

4. What is the conclusion if the sum of the percentages of allowable changes in the right-hand sides does exceed 100 percent?

4.8 Summary

What-if analysis is analysis done *after* finding an optimal solution for the original version of the basic model. This analysis provides important insights to help guide managerial decision making. This chapter describes how this is done when the basic model is a linear programming model. Both the spreadsheet for the model and the Solver's sensitivity report play a central role in this process.

The coefficients in the objective function typically represent quantities that can only be roughly estimated when the model is formulated. Will the optimal solution obtained from the model be the correct one if the true value of one of these coefficients is significantly different from its estimate used in the model? The spreadsheet can be used to quickly check specific changes in the coefficient. For a broader investigation, *the range of optimality* for each coefficient identifies the interval within which the true value must lie for this solution to still be the correct optimal solution. These ranges are easily calculated from the data in the sensitivity report provided by the Excel Solver.

What happens if there are significant inaccuracies in the estimates of two or more coefficients in the objective function? Specific simultaneous changes can be checked with the spreadsheet. To go further, the *100 percent rule for simultaneous changes in objective function coefficients* provides a convenient way of checking whole ranges of simultaneous changes, again by using the data in the Solver's sensitivity report.

The right-hand sides of the functional constraints frequently represent managerial policy decisions. If so, *shadow price analysis* provides valuable guidance to management about what the effect would be of altering these policy decisions.

Shadow price analysis can be validly applied to investigate possible changes in right-hand sides as long as these changes are not too large. The *range of feasibility* for each right-hand side indicates just how far it can be changed, assuming no other changes are made. If, in fact, other changes are made as well, the *100 percent rule for simultaneous changes in right-hand sides* enables checking whether the changes definitely are not too large. The Solver's sensitivity report provides the key information needed to find each range of feasibility or to apply this 100 percent rule.

Glossary

Allowable range to stay feasible   The longer name for *range of feasibility*, defined below. (Section 4.6)   140

Allowable range to stay optimal   The longer name for *range of optimality*, defined below. (Section 4.3)   126

Parameters of the model   The parameters of a linear programming model are the constants (coefficients or right-hand sides) in the functional constraints and the objective function. (Section 4.1)   119

Range of feasibility   The range of values for the right-hand side of a functional constraint over which this constraint's shadow price remains valid. (Section 4.6)   140

Range of optimality   The range of values for a particular coefficient in the objective function over which the optimal solution for the original model remains optimal. (Section 4.3)   126

Sensitive parameter   A parameter is considered sensitive if even a small change in its value can change the optimal solution. (Section 4.1)   120

Sensitivity analysis   The part of what-if analysis that focuses on individual parameters of the model. It involves checking how sensitive the optimal solution is to the value of each parameter. (Section 4.1)   120

Shadow price   The shadow price for a functional constraint is the rate at which the optimal value of the objective function can be increased by increasing the right-hand side of the constraint by a small amount. (Section 4.5)   134

What-if analysis   Analysis that addresses questions about what would happen to the optimal solution if different assumptions are made about future conditions. (Chapter introduction)   119

Learning Aids for This Chapter in Your MS Courseware

"Ch. 4—What-If Analysis for LP" Excel File:

Wyndor Example
Wyndor Sensitivity Report
Profit & Gambit Example
Profit & Gambit Sensitivity Report

Homework Spreadsheet
Homework Sensitivity Report

An Excel Add-in:
Premium Solver

Problems

We have inserted the symbol E* to the left of each problem (or its parts) where Excel should be used (unless your instructor gives you contrary instructions). An asterisk on the problem number indicates that at least a partial answer is given in the back of the book.

E* 4.1.* One of the products of the G.A. Tanner Company is a special kind of toy that provides an estimated unit profit of $3. Because of a large demand for this toy, management would like to increase its production rate from the current level of 1,000 per day. However, a limited supply of two subassemblies (A and B) from vendors makes this difficult. Each toy requires two subassemblies of type A, but the vendor providing these subassemblies would only be able to increase its supply rate from the current 2,000 per day to a maximum of 3,000 per day. Each toy requires only one subassembly of type B, but the vendor providing these subassemblies would be unable to increase its supply rate above the current level of 1,000 per day.

Because no other vendors currently are available to provide these subassemblies, management is considering initiating a new production process internally that would simultaneously produce an equal number of subassemblies of the two types to supplement the supply from the two vendors. It is estimated that the company's cost for producing one subassembly of each type would be $2.50 more than the cost of purchasing these subassemblies from the two vendors. Management wants to determine both the production rate of the toy and the production rate of each pair of subassemblies (one A and one B) that would maximize the total profit.

Viewing this problem as a resource-allocation problem, one of the company's managers has constructed its parameter table as follows:

| | **Resource Usage per Unit of Each Activity** | | **Amount of** |
Resource	Produce Toys	Produce Subassemblies	Resource Available
Subassembly A	2	−1	3,000
Subassembly B	1	−1	1,000
Unit profit	$3	−$2.50	

a. Formulate and solve a spreadsheet model for this problem.

b. Since the stated unit profits for the two activities are only estimates, management wants to know how much each of these estimates can be off before the optimal

solution would change. Begin exploring this question for the first activity (producing toys) by using the spreadsheet and Solver to generate a data table that gives the optimal solution and total profit as the unit profit for this activity increases in 50¢ increments from $2.00 to $4.00. What conclusion can be drawn about how much the estimate of this unit profit can differ in each direction from its original value of $3.00 before the optimal solution would change?

c. Repeat part b for the second activity (producing subassemblies) by generating a data table as the unit profit for this activity increases in 50¢ increments from −$3.50 to −$1.50 (with the unit profit for the first activity fixed at $3).

d. Use the Excel Solver to obtain the range of optimality for each unit profit.

4.2. Consider a resource-allocation problem having the following parameter table:

| | **Resource Usage per Unit of Each Activity** | | |
Resource	1	2	Amount of Resource Available
1	1	2	10
2	1	3	12
Unit profit	$2	$5	

The objective is to determine the number of units of each activity to undertake so as to maximize the total profit.

While doing what-if analysis, you learn that the estimates of the unit profits are accurate only to within ± 50 percent. In other words, the ranges of *likely values* for these unit profits are $1 to $3 for activity 1 and $2.50 to $7.50 for activity 2.

E* a. Formulate a spreadsheet model for this problem based on the original estimates of the unit profits. Then use the Solver to find an optimal solution and to generate the sensitivity report.

E* b. Use the spreadsheet and Solver to check whether this optimal solution remains optimal if the unit profit for activity 1 changes from $2 to $1. From $2 to $3.

E* c. Also check whether the optimal solution remains optimal if the unit profit for activity 1 still is $2 but the unit profit for activity 2 changes from $5 to $2.50. From $5 to $7.50.

E* d. Use the sensitivity report to find the range of optimality for each of the unit profits. Then use these ranges to check your answers in parts b and c.

e. Use graphical analysis to interpret your answers in parts *b, c,* and *d* graphically.

E* 4.3. Consider the Distribution Unlimited Co. problem presented in Section 3.4, including the spreadsheet in Figure 3.5 showing its formulation and optimal solution.

There is some uncertainty about what the unit costs will be for shipping through the various shipping lanes. Therefore, before adopting the optimal solution in Figure 3.5, management wants additional information about the effect of inaccuracies in estimating these unit costs.

Use the Excel Solver to generate the sensitivity report preparatory to addressing the following questions.

a. Which of the unit shipping costs given in Table 3.8 has the smallest margin for error without invalidating the optimal solution given in Figure 3.5? Where should the greatest effort be placed in estimating the unit shipping costs?

b. What is the range of optimality for each of the unit shipping costs?

c. How should the range of optimality be interpreted to management?

d. If the estimates change for more than one of the unit shipping costs, how can you use the sensitivity report to determine whether the optimal solution might change?

E*4.4.* Consider the Union Airways problem presented in Section 3.3, including the spreadsheet in Figure 3.3 showing its formulation and optimal solution.

Management is about to begin negotiations on a new contract with the union that represents the company's customer service agents. This might result in some small changes in the daily costs per agent given in Table 3.6 for the various shifts. Several possible changes listed below are being considered separately. In each case, management would like to know whether the change might result in the solution in Figure 3.3 no longer being optimal. Answer this question in parts *a* to *e* by using the spreadsheet and Solver directly. If the optimal solution changes, record the new solution.

a. The daily cost per agent for shift 2 changes from $160 to $165.

b. The daily cost per agent for shift 4 changes from $180 to $170.

c. The changes in parts *a* and *b* both occur.

d. The daily cost per agent increases by $4 for shifts 2, 4, and 5, but decreases by $4 for shifts 1 and 3.

e. The daily cost per agent increases by 2 percent for each shift.

f. Use the Solver to generate the sensitivity report for this problem. Suppose that the above changes are being considered later without having the spreadsheet model immediately available on a computer. Show in each case how the sensitivity report can be used to check whether the original optimal solution must still be optimal.

E* 4.5. Consider the Think-Big Development Co. problem presented in Section 3.2, including the spreadsheet in Figure 3.2 showing its formulation and optimal solution. Use the spreadsheet and Solver to check whether the optimal solution would change and, if so, what the new optimal solution would be, if the estimates in Table 3.3 of the net present values of the projects were to be changed in each of the following ways. (Consider each part by itself.)

a. The net present value of project 1 increases by $200,000.

b. The net present value of project 2 increases by $200,000.

c. The net present value of project 1 decreases by $5 million.

d. The net present value of project 3 decreases by $200,000.

e. All three changes in parts *b, c,* and *d* occur simultaneously.

f. The net present values of projects 1, 2, and 3 change to $46 million, $69 million, and $49 million, respectively.

g. The net present values of projects 1, 2, and 3 change to $54 million, $84 million, and $60 million, respectively.

h. Use the Solver to generate the sensitivity report for this problem. For each of the above parts, suppose that the change occurs later without having the spreadsheet model immediately available on a computer. Show in each case how the sensitivity report can be used to check whether the original optimal solution must still be optimal.

4.6. Ken and Larry, Inc., supplies its ice cream parlors with three flavors of ice cream: chocolate, vanilla, and banana. Due to extremely hot weather and a high demand for its products, the company has run short of its supply of ingredients: milk, sugar, and cream. Hence, they will not be able to fill all the orders received from their retail outlets, the ice cream parlors. Due to these circumstances, the company has decided to choose the amount of each flavor to produce that will maximize total profit, given the constraints on supply of the basic ingredients.

The chocolate, vanilla, and banana flavors generate, respectively, $1.00, $0.90, and $0.95 of profit per gallon sold. The company has only 200 gallons of milk, 150 pounds of sugar, and 60 gallons of cream left in its inventory. The linear programming formulation for this problem is shown below in algebraic form.

Let C = gallons of chocolate ice cream produced
 V = gallons of vanilla ice cream produced
 B = gallons of banana ice cream produced

Maximize   Profit $= 1.00C + 0.90V + 0.95B$

subject to

Milk: $0.45C + 0.50V + 0.40B \le 200$ gallons

Sugar: $0.50C + 0.40V + 0.40B \le 150$ pounds

Cream: $0.10C + 0.15V + 0.20B \le 60$ gallons

and
$$C \ge 0 \qquad V \ge 0 \qquad B \ge 0$$

This problem was solved using the Excel Solver. The spreadsheet (already solved) and the sensitivity report are shown below. [Note: The numbers in the sensitivity report for the milk constraint are missing on purpose, since you will be asked to fill in these numbers in part *f.*]

	A	B	C	D	E	F	G
1							
2		Resource Usage per Unit of Each Activity					Resource
3	Resource	Chocolate	Vanilla	Banana	Totals		Available
4	Milk	0.45	0.5	0.4	180	≤	200
5	Sugar	0.5	0.4	0.4	150	≤	150
6	Cream	0.1	0.15	0.2	60	≤	60
7	Unit Profit	1	0.9	0.95	$341.25		
8	Solution	0	300	75			

Changing Cells

Cell	Name	Final Value	Reduced Cost	Objective Coefficient	Allowable Increase	Allowable Decrease
$B$8	Solution Chocolate	0	–0.0375	1	0.0375	1E+30
$C$8	Solution Vanilla	300	0	0.9	0.05	0.0125
$D$8	Solution Banana	75	0	0.95	0.021428571	0.05

Constraints

Cell	Name	Final Value	Shadow Price	Constraint R.H. Side	Allowable Increase	Allowable Decrease
$E$4	Milk Totals					
$E$5	Sugar Totals	150	1.875	150	10	30
$E$6	Cream Totals	60	1	60	15	3.75

For each of the following parts, answer the question as specifically and completely as is possible without solving the problem again with the Excel Solver. Note: Each part is independent (i.e., any change made to the model in one part does not apply to any other parts).

a. What is the optimal solution and total profit?

b. Suppose the profit per gallon of banana changes to $1.00. Will the optimal solution change and what can be said about the effect on total profit?

c. Suppose the profit per gallon of banana changes to 92¢. Will the optimal solution change and what can be said about the effect on total profit?

d. Suppose the company discovers that three gallons of cream have gone sour and so must be thrown out. Will the optimal solution change and what can be said about the effect on total profit?

e. Suppose the company has the opportunity to buy an additional 15 pounds of sugar at a total cost of $15. Should they? Explain.

f. Fill in all the sensitivity report information for the milk constraint, given just the optimal solution for the problem. Explain how you were able to deduce each number.

4.7. David, LaDeana, and Lydia are the sole partners and workers in a company that produces fine clocks. David and LaDeana are each available to work a maximum of 40 hours per week at the company, while Lydia is available to work a maximum of 20 hours per week.

The company makes two different types of clocks: a grandfather clock and a wall clock. To make a clock, David (a mechanical engineer) assembles the inside mechanical parts of the clock while LaDeana (a woodworker) produces the hand-carved wood casings. Lydia is responsible for taking orders and shipping the clocks. The amount of time required for each of these tasks is shown next.

	Time Required	
Task	Grandfather Clock	Wall Clock
Assemble clock mechanism	6 hours	4 hours
Carve wood casing	8 hours	4 hours
Shipping	3 hours	3 hours

Each grandfather clock built and shipped yields a profit of $300, while each wall clock yields a profit of $200.

The three partners now want to determine how many clocks of each type should be produced per week to maximize the total profit.

a. Formulate a linear programming model for this problem.

b. Use the graphical method to solve the model.

E* c. Display the model on a spreadsheet.

E* d. Use the Excel Solver to obtain an optimal solution and generate the sensitivity report.

e. Use the sensitivity report to determine whether this optimal solution must remain optimal if the estimate of the unit profit for grandfather clocks is changed from $300 to $375 (with no other changes in the model).

f. Repeat part e if, in addition to this change in the unit profit for grandfather clocks, the estimated unit profit for wall clocks also changes from $200 to $175.

g. Use graphical analysis to verify your answers in parts e and f.

h. To increase the total profit, the three partners have agreed that one of them will slightly increase the maximum number of hours available to work per week. The choice of which one will be based on which one would increase the total profit the most. Use the sensitivity report to make this choice. (Assume no change in the original estimates of the unit profits.)

i. Explain why one of the shadow prices is equal to zero.

j. Can the shadow prices in the sensitivity report be validly used to determine the effect if Lydia were to change her maximum number of hours available to work per week from 20 to 25? If so, what would be the increase in the total profit?

k. Repeat part *j* if, in addition to the change for Lydia, David also were to change his maximum number of hours available to work per week from 40 to 35.

l. Use graphical analysis to verify your answer in part *k*.

4.8. Reconsider the Profit & Gambit Co. problem described in Section 2.7. The optimal solution of (TV, PM) = (4, 3) given in Figures 2.21 and 2.23 results in a total cost of $10 million for the advertising campaign. Management now is wondering how much it would cost to increase the minimum goal (currently 18 percent) for the market share that its new liquid laundry detergent would capture in the laundry detergent market.

E* *a.* Use the spreadsheet (Figure 2.21) and Solver to generate a data table that gives the optimal solution and its total cost as the minimum goal for market share is increased in 3 percent increments from 18 percent to 36 percent.

b. Use these results to determine (1) the cost per 1 percent increase of market share for small increases from 18 percent and (2) how much the market share can be increased before the cost per 1 percent goes up.

E* *c.* Use the Solver to generate the sensitivity report. Describe how this report provides the information requested in part *b*.

d. Use graphical analysis to interpret this information graphically.

E* 4.9.* Reconsider Problem 4.1. After further negotiations with each vendor, management of the G.A. Tanner Company has learned that either of them would be willing to consider increasing their supply of their respective subassemblies over the previously stated maxima (3,000 subassemblies of type A per day and 1,000 of type B per day) if the company would pay a small premium over the regular price for the extra subassemblies. The size of the premium for each type of subassembly remains to be negotiated. The demand for the toy being produced is sufficiently high that 2,500 per day could be sold if the supply of subassemblies could be increased enough to support this production rate. Assume that the original estimates of unit profits given in Problem 4.1 are accurate.

a. Formulate and solve a spreadsheet model for this problem with the original maximum supply levels and the additional constraint that no more than 2,500 toys should be produced per day.

b. Without considering the premium, use the spreadsheet and Solver to determine the shadow price for the subassembly A constraint by solving the model again after increasing the maximum supply by one. Use this shadow price to determine the maximum premium that the company should be willing to pay for each subassembly of this type.

c. Repeat part *b* for the subassembly B constraint.

d. Estimate how much the maximum supply of subassemblies of type A could be increased before the shadow price (and the corresponding premium) found in part *b* would no longer be valid by generating a data table that gives the optimal

solution and total profit (excluding the premium) as the maximum supply increases in increments of 100 from 3,000 to 4,000.

e. Repeat part *d* for subassemblies of type B by generating a data table as the maximum supply increases in increments of 100 from 1,000 to 2,000.

f. Use the Solver's sensitivity report to determine the shadow price for each of the subassembly constraints and the range of feasibility for the right-hand side of each of these constraints.

E* 4.10. Reconsider the model given in Problem 4.2. While doing what-if analysis, you learn that the estimates of the right-hand sides of the two functional constraints are accurate only to within ± 50 percent. In other words, the ranges of *likely values* for these parameters are 5 to 15 for the first right-hand side and 6 to 18 for the second right-hand side.

a. After solving the original spreadsheet model, determine the shadow price for the first functional constraint by increasing its right-hand side by one and solving again.

b. Generate a data table that gives the optimal solution and total profit as the right-hand side of the first functional constraint is incremented by one from 5 to 15. Use this data table to estimate the range of feasibility for this right-hand side, that is, the range over which the shadow price obtained in part *a* is valid.

c. Repeat part *a* for the second functional constraint.

d. Repeat part *b* for the second functional constraint where its right-hand side is incremented by one from 6 to 18.

e. Use the Solver's sensitivity report to determine the shadow price for each functional constraint and the range of feasibility for the right-hand side of each of these constraints.

4.11. Consider a resource-allocation problem having the following parameter table:

| | Resource Usage per Unit of Each Activity | | |
Resource	1	2	Amount of Resource Available
1	1	3	8
2	1	1	4
Unit profit	$1	$2	

The objective is to determine the number of units of each activity to undertake so as to maximize the total profit.

a. Use the graphical method to solve this model.

b. Use graphical analysis to determine the shadow price for each of these resources by solving again after increasing the amount of the resource available by one.

E* *c.* Use the spreadsheet model and the Solver instead to do parts *a* and *b*.

E* *d.* Use the Solver's sensitivity report to obtain the shadow prices.

e. Describe why these shadow prices are useful when management has the flexibility to change the amounts of the resources being made available.

4.12. Follow the instructions of Problem 4.11 for a resource-allocation problem that again has the objective of maximizing total profit and that has the following parameter table:

	Resource Usage per Unit of Each Activity		Amount of Resource Available
Resource	*1*	*2*	
1	1	0	4
2	1	3	15
3	2	1	10
Unit profit	$3	$2	

E* 4.13.* Consider the Super Grain Corp. case study as presented in Section 3.1, including the spreadsheet in Figure 3.1 showing its formulation and optimal solution. Use the Excel Solver to generate the sensitivity report. Then use this report to independently address each of the following questions.

a. How much could the total number of expected exposure units be increased for each additional $1,000 added to the advertising budget?

b. Your answer in part *a* would remain valid for how large of an increase in the advertising budget?

c. How much could the total number of expected exposure units be increased for each additional $1,000 added to the planning budget?

d. Your answer in part *c* would remain valid for how large of an increase in the planning budget?

e. Would your answers in parts *a* and *c* definitely remain valid if *both* the advertising budget and planning budget were increased by $100,000 each?

f. If only $100,000 can be added to *either* the advertising budget or the planning budget, where should it be added to do the most good?

g. If $100,000 must be *removed* from either the advertising budget or the planning budget, from which budget should it be removed to do the least harm?

E* 4.14. Follow the instructions of Problem 4.13 for the continuation of the Super Grain Corp. case study as presented in Section 3.5 including the spreadsheet in Figure 3.6 showing its formulation and optimal solution.

E* 4.15. Consider the Union Airways problem presented in Section 3.3, including the spreadsheet in Figure 3.3 showing its formulation and optimal solution.

Management now is considering increasing the level of service provided to customers by increasing one or more of the numbers in the rightmost column of Table 3.6 for the minimum number of agents needed in the various time periods. To guide them in making this decision, they would like to know what impact this change would have on total cost.

Use the Excel Solver to generate the sensitivity report in preparation for addressing the following questions.

a. Which of the numbers in the rightmost column of Table 3.6 can be increased without increasing total cost? In each case, indicate how much it can be increased (if it is the only one being changed) without increasing total cost.

b. For each of the other numbers, how much would the total cost increase per increase of one in the number? For each answer, indicate how much the number can be increased (if it is the only one being changed) before the answer is no longer valid.

c. Do your answers in part *b* definitely remain valid if all the numbers considered in part *b* are simultaneously increased by one?

d. Do your answers in part *b* definitely remain valid if all 10 numbers are simultaneously increased by one?

e. How far can all 10 numbers be simultaneously increased by the same amount before your answers in part *b* may no longer be valid?

CASE 4.1
CONTROLLING AIR POLLUTION

As introduced in Section 3.3, the Nori & Leets Co. is one of the major producers of steel in its part of the world. It is located in the city of Steeltown and is the only large employer there. Steeltown has grown and prospered along with the company, which now employs nearly 50,000 residents. Therefore, the attitude of the townspeople always has been "What's good for Nori & Leets is good for the town." However, this attitude is now changing; uncontrolled air pollution from the company's furnaces is ruining the appearance of the city and endangering the health of its residents.

A recent stockholders' revolt resulted in the election of a new enlightened board of directors for the company. These directors are determined to follow socially responsible policies, and they have been discussing with Steeltown city officials and citizens' groups what to do about the air pollution problem. Together they have worked out stringent air quality standards for the Steeltown airshed.

The three main types of pollutants in this airshed are particulate matter, sulfur oxides, and hydrocarbons. The new standards require that the company reduce its annual emission of these pollutants by the amounts shown in the following table.

Pollutant	Required Reduction in Annual Emission Rate (Million Pounds)
Particulates	60
Sulfur oxides	150
Hydrocarbons	125

The board of directors has instructed management to have the engineering staff determine how to achieve these reductions in the most economical way.

The steelworks have two primary sources of pollution, namely, the blast furnaces for making pig iron and the open-hearth furnaces for changing iron into steel. In both cases, the engineers have decided that the most effective abatement methods are (1) increasing the height of the smokestacks,[2] (2) using filter devices (including gas traps) in the smokestacks, and (3) including cleaner, high-grade materials among the fuels for the furnaces. Each of these methods has a technological limit on how heavily it can be used (e.g., a maximum feasible increase in the height of the smokestacks), but there also is considerable flexibility for using the method at a fraction of its technological limit.

The next table shows how much emissions (in millions of pounds per year) can be eliminated from each type of furnace by fully using any abatement method to its technological limit.

Reduction in Emission Rate from the Maximum Feasible Use of an Abatement Method

	Taller Smokestacks		Filters		Better Fuels	
Pollutant	Blast Furnaces	Open-Hearth Furnaces	Blast Furnaces	Open-Hearth Furnaces	Blast Furnaces	Open-Hearth Furnaces
Particulates	12	9	25	20	17	13
Sulfur oxides	35	42	18	31	56	49
Hydrocarbons	37	53	28	24	29	20

For purposes of analysis, it is assumed that each method also can be less fully used to achieve any fraction of the abatement capacities shown in this table. Furthermore, the fractions can be different for blast furnaces and open-hearth furnaces. For either type of furnace, the emission reduction achieved by each method is not substantially affected by whether or not the other methods also are used.

After these data were developed, it became clear that no single method by itself could achieve all the required reductions. On the other hand, combining all three methods at full capacity on both types of furnaces (which would be prohibitively expensive if the company's products are to remain competitively priced) is much more than adequate. Therefore, the engineers concluded that they would have to use some combination of the methods, perhaps with fractional capacities, based on their relative costs. Furthermore, because of the differences between the blast and the open-hearth furnaces, the two types probably should not use the same combination.

An analysis was conducted to estimate the total annual cost that would be incurred by each abatement method. A method's annual cost includes increased operating and maintenance expenses, as well as reduced revenue due to any loss in the efficiency of the production process caused by using the method. The other major cost is the start-up cost (the initial capital outlay) required to install the method. To make this one-time cost commensurable with the ongoing annual costs, the time value of money was used to calculate the annual expenditure that would be equivalent in value to this start-up cost.

This analysis led to the total annual cost estimates given in the following table for using the methods at their full abatement capacities.

Total Annual Cost from the Maximum Feasible Use of an Abatement Method

Abatement Method	Blast Furnaces	Open-Hearth Furnaces
Taller smokestacks	$8 million	$10 million
Filters	7 million	6 million
Better fuels	11 million	9 million

It also was determined that the cost of a method being used at a lower level is roughly proportional to the fraction of the abatement capacity given in the preceding table that is achieved. Thus, for any given fraction achieved, the total annual cost would be roughly that fraction of the corresponding quantity in the cost table.

The stage now is set to develop the general framework of the company's plan for pollution abatement. This plan needs to specify which types of abatement methods will be used and at what fractions of their abatement capacities for (1) the blast furnaces and (2) the open-hearth furnaces.

You have been asked to head a management science team to analyze this problem. Management wants you to begin by determining which plan would minimize the total annual cost of achieving the required reductions in annual emission rates for the three pollutants.

a. Identify verbally the components of a linear programming model for this problem.

b. Display the model on a spreadsheet.

c. Obtain an optimal solution and generate the sensitivity report.

---

[2]Subsequent to this study, this particular abatement method has become a controversial one. Because its effect is to reduce ground-level pollution by spreading emissions over a greater distance, environmental groups contend that this creates more acid rain by keeping sulfur oxides in the air longer. Consequently, the U.S. Environmental Protection Agency adopted new rules to remove incentives for using tall smokestacks.

Management now wants to conduct some what-if analysis with your help. Since the company does not have much prior experience with the pollution abatement methods under consideration, the cost estimates given in the third table are fairly rough, and each one could easily be off by as much as 10 percent in either direction. There also is some uncertainty about the values given in the second table, but less so than for the third table. By contrast, the values in the first table are policy standards and so are prescribed constants.

However, there still is considerable debate about where to set these policy standards on the required reductions in the emission rates of the various pollutants. The numbers in the first table actually are preliminary values tentatively agreed upon before learning what the total cost would be to meet these standards. Both the city and company officials agree that the final decision on these policy standards should be based on the *trade-off* between costs and benefits. With this in mind, the city has concluded that each 10 percent increase in the policy standards over the current values (all the numbers in the first table) would be worth $3.5 million to the city. Therefore, the city has agreed to reduce the company's tax payments to the city by $3.5 million for *each* 10 percent increase in the policy standards (up to 50 percent) that is accepted by the company.

Finally, there has been some debate about the *relative* values of the policy standards for the three pollutants. As indicated in the first table, the required reduction for particulates now is less than half of that for either sulfur oxides or hydrocarbons. Some have argued for decreasing this disparity. Others contend that an even greater disparity is justified because sulfur oxides and hydrocarbons cause considerably more damage than particulates. Agreement has been reached that this issue will be reexamined after information is obtained about which trade-offs in policy standards (increasing one while decreasing another) are available without increasing the total cost.

d. Identify the parameters of the linear programming model that should be classified as *sensitive parameters*. Make a resulting recommendation about which parameters should be estimated more closely, if possible.

e. Analyze the effect of an inaccuracy in estimating each cost parameter given in the third table. If the true value is 10 percent *less* than the estimated value, would this change the optimal solution? Would it change if the true value is 10 percent *more* than the estimated value? Make a resulting recommendation about where to focus further work in estimating the cost parameters more closely.

f. For each pollutant, specify the rate at which the total cost of an optimal solution would change with any small change in the required reduction in the annual emission rate of the pollutant. Also specify how much this required reduction can be changed (up or down) without affecting the rate of change in the total cost.

g. For each unit change in the policy standard for particulates given in the first table, determine the change in the opposite direction for sulfur oxides that would keep the total cost of an optimal solution unchanged. Repeat this for hydrocarbons instead of sulfur oxides. Then do it for a simultaneous and equal change for both sulfur oxides and hydrocarbons in the opposite direction from particulates.

h. Letting θ denote the percentage increase in all the policy standards given in the first table, find an optimal solution for the revised linear programming problem for each $\theta = 10, 20, 30, 40, 50$. Considering the tax incentive offered by the city, use these results to determine which value of θ (including the option of $\theta = 0$) should be chosen by the company to minimize their total cost of both pollution abatement and taxes.

i. For the value of θ chosen in part *h*, generate the sensitivity report and repeat parts *f* and *g* so that the decision makers can make a final decision on the *relative* values of the policy standards for the three pollutants.

CASE 4.2
FARM MANAGEMENT

The Ploughman family owns and operates a 640-acre farm that has been in the family for several generations. The Ploughmans always have had to work hard to make a decent living from the farm and have had to endure some occasional difficult years. Stories about earlier generations overcoming hardships due to droughts, floods, and so forth, are an important part of the family history. However, the Ploughmans enjoy their self-reliant lifestyle and gain considerable satisfaction from continuing the family tradition of successfully living off the land during an era when many family farms are being abandoned or taken over by large agricultural corporations.

John Ploughman is the current manager of the farm, while his wife Eunice runs the house and manages the farm's finances. John's father, Grandpa Ploughman, lives with them and still puts in many hours working on the farm. John and Eunice's older children, Frank, Phyllis, and Carl, also are given heavy chores before and after school.

The entire family can produce a total of 4,000 person-hours' worth of labor during the winter and spring months and 4,500 per-

son-hours during the summer and fall. If any of these person-hours are not needed, Frank, Phyllis, and Carl will use them to work on a neighboring farm for $5/hour during the winter and spring months and $5.50/hour during the summer and fall.

The farm supports two types of livestock, dairy cows and laying hens, as well as three crops: soybeans, corn, and wheat. (All three are cash crops, but the corn also is a feed crop for the cows and the wheat also is used for chicken feed.) The crops are harvested during the late summer and fall. During the winter months, John, Eunice, and Grandpa make a decision about the mix of livestock and crops for the coming year.

Currently, the family has just completed a particularly successful harvest that has provided an investment fund of $20,000 that can be used to purchase more livestock. (Other money is available for ongoing expenses, including the next planting of crops.) The family currently has 30 cows valued at $35,000 and 2,000 hens valued at $5,000. They wish to keep all this livestock and perhaps purchase more. Each new cow would cost $1,500, and each new hen would cost $3.

Over a year's time, the value of a herd of cows will decrease by about 10 percent and the value of a flock of hens will decrease by about 25 percent due to aging.

Each cow will require 2 acres of land for grazing and 10 person-hours of work per month, while producing a net annual cash income of $850 for the family. The corresponding figures for each hen are no significant acreage, 0.05 person-hour per month, and an annual net cash income of $4.25. The chicken house can accommodate a maximum of 5,000 hens, and the size of the barn limits the herd to a maximum of 42 cows.

For each acre planted in each of the three crops, the following table gives the number of person-hours of work that will be required during the first and second halves of the year, as well as a rough estimate of the crop's net value (in either income or savings in purchasing feed for the livestock).

Data per Acre Planted

	Soybeans	Corn	Wheat
Winter and spring, person-hours	1.0	0.9	0.6
Summer and fall, person-hours	1.4	1.2	0.7
Net value	$70	$60	$40

To provide much of the feed for the livestock, John wants to plant at least 1 acre of corn for each cow in the coming year's herd and at least 0.05 acre of wheat for each hen in the coming year's flock.

John, Eunice, and Grandpa now are discussing how much acreage should be planted in each of the crops and how many cows and hens to have for the coming year. Their objective is to maximize the family's monetary worth at the end of the coming year (the *sum* of the net income from the livestock for the coming year *plus* the net value of the crops for the coming year *plus* what remains from the investment fund *plus* the value of the livestock at the end of the coming year *minus* living expenses of $40,000 for the year).

a. Identify verbally the components of a linear programming model for this problem.
b. Display the model on a spreadsheet.
c. Obtain an optimal solution and generate the sensitivity report. What does the model predict regarding the family's monetary worth at the end of the coming year?
d. Find the range of optimality for the net value per acre planted for each of the three crops.

The above estimates of the net value per acre planted in each of the three crops assumes good weather conditions. Adverse weather conditions would harm the crops and greatly reduce the resulting value. The scenarios particularly feared by the family are a drought, a flood, an early frost, *both* a drought and an early frost, and *both* a flood and an early frost. The estimated net values for the year under these scenarios are shown next.

Net Value per Acre Planted

Scenario	Soybeans	Corn	Wheat
Drought	−$10	−$15	0
Flood	15	20	$10
Early frost	50	40	30
Drought and early frost	−15	−20	−10
Flood and early frost	10	10	5

e. Find an optimal solution under each scenario after making the necessary adjustments to the linear programming model formulated in part *b*. In each case, what is the prediction regarding the family's monetary worth at the end of the year?
f. For the optimal solution obtained under each of the six scenarios (including the good weather scenario considered in parts *a*–*d*), calculate what the family's monetary worth would be at the end of the year if each of the other five scenarios occurs instead. In your judgment, which solution provides the best balance between yielding a large monetary worth under good weather conditions and avoiding an overly small monetary worth under adverse weather conditions.

Grandpa has researched what the weather conditions were in past years as far back as weather records have been kept and obtained the following data.

Scenario	Frequency
Good weather	40%
Drought	20
Flood	10
Early frost	15
Drought and early frost	10
Flood and early frost	5

With these data, the family has decided to use the following approach to making its planting and livestock decisions. Rather than the optimistic approach of assuming that good weather conditions will prevail (as done in parts *a*–*d*), the *average* net value under all weather conditions will be used for each crop (weighting the net values under the various scenarios by the frequencies in the above table).

g. Modify the linear programming model formulated in part *b* to fit this new approach.
h. Repeat part *c* for this modified model.
i. Use a shadow price obtained in part *h* to analyze whether it would be worthwhile for the family to obtain a bank loan with a 10 percent interest rate to purchase more livestock

now beyond what can be obtained with the $20,000 from the investment fund.

j. For each of the three crops, use the sensitivity report obtained in part h to identify how much latitude for error is available in estimating the net value per acre planted for that crop without changing the optimal solution. Which two net values need to be estimated most carefully? If both estimates are incorrect simultaneously, how close do the estimates need to be to guarantee that the optimal solution will not change?

This problem illustrates a kind of situation that is frequently faced by various kinds of organizations. To describe the situation in general terms, an organization faces an uncertain future where any one of a number of scenarios may unfold. Which one will occur depends on conditions that are outside the control of the organization. The organization needs to choose the levels of various activities, but the unit contribution of each activity to the overall measure of performance is greatly affected by which scenario unfolds. Under these circumstances, what is the best mix of activities?

k. Think about specific situations outside of farm management that fit this description. Describe one.

CASE 4.3
ASSIGNING STUDENTS TO SCHOOLS (REVISITED)

Reconsider Case 3.3. The Springfield School Board still has the policy of providing bussing for all middle school students who must travel more than approximately a mile. Another current policy is to allow splitting residential areas among multiple schools if this will reduce the total bussing cost. (This latter policy will be reversed in Case 9.3.) However, before adopting a bussing plan based on parts *a* and *b* of Case 3.3, the school board now wants to conduct some what-if analysis.

a. If you have not already done so for parts *a* and *b* of Case 3.3, formulate and solve a linear programming model for this problem on a spreadsheet.

b. Use the Solver to generate the sensitivity report.

One concern of the school board is the ongoing road construction in area 6. These construction projects have been delaying traffic considerably and are likely to affect the cost of bussing students from area 6, perhaps increasing them as much as 10 percent.

c. Use the sensitivity report to check how much the bussing cost from area 6 to school 1 can increase (assuming no change in the costs for the other schools) before the current optimal solution would no longer be optimal. If the allowable increase is less than 10 percent, use the Solver to find the new optimal solution with a 10 percent increase.

d. Repeat part *c* for school 2 (assuming no change in the costs for the other schools).

e. Now assume that the bussing cost from area 6 would increase by the same percentage for all the schools. Use the sensitivity report to determine how large this percentage can be before the current optimal solution might no longer be optimal. If the allowable increase is less than 10 percent, use the Solver to find the new optimal solution with a 10 percent increase.

The school board has the option of adding portable classrooms to increase the capacity of one or more of the middle schools for a few years. However, this is a costly move that the board would only consider if it would significantly decrease bussing costs. Each portable classroom holds 20 students and has a leasing cost of $2,500 per year. To analyze this option, the school board decides to assume that the road construction in area 6 will wind down without significantly increasing the bussing costs from that area.

f. For each school, use the corresponding shadow price from the sensitivity report to determine whether it would be worthwhile to add any portable classrooms.

g. For each school where it is worthwhile to add any portable classrooms, use the sensitivity report to determine how many could be added before the shadow price would no longer be valid (assuming this is the only school receiving portable classrooms).

h. If it would be worthwhile to add portable classrooms to more than one school, use the sensitivity report to determine the combinations of the number to add for which the shadow prices definitely would still be valid. Then use the shadow prices to determine which of these combinations is best in terms of minimizing the total cost of bussing students and leasing portable classrooms. Use the Solver for finding the corresponding optimal solution for assigning students to schools.

i. If part *h* was applicable, modify the best combination of portable classrooms found there by adding one more to the school with the most favorable shadow price. Use the Solver to find the corresponding optimal solution for assigning students to schools and to generate the corresponding sensitivity report. Use this information to assess whether the plan developed in part *h* is the best one available for minimizing the total cost of bussing students and leasing portables. If not, find the best plan.

5

TRANSPORTATION AND ASSIGNMENT PROBLEMS

You have seen in the preceding chapters just how useful linear programming can be to an enlightened manager in dealing with a wide variety of problems. You will continue to broaden your horizons in this chapter about the breadth of applicability of linear programming. The focus will be on two related special types of linear programming problems that are so important that they have been given their own names, namely, *transportation problems* and *assignment problems*. Both fall into the third category of linear programming problems introduced in Chapter 3—distribution-network problems.

Transportation problems received this name because many of their applications involve determining how to transport goods optimally. However, you will see that some of their important applications have nothing to do with transportation.

Assignment problems are best known for applications involving assigning people to tasks. However, they have a variety of other applications as well.

The overriding goal of the chapter is to enable you to recognize when a problem you might face as a future manager can be formulated and analyzed as a transportation or assignment problem. To address this overriding goal, the chapter has three specific learning goals:

1. To understand the characteristics of transportation and assignment problems, as well as variants of these problems.

2. To learn when a problem can be formulated to fit one of these problem types.

3. To survey the variety of applications of each problem type.

The following sections parallel these learning goals for, first, transportation problems and then assignment problems.

5.1 A Case Study: The P & T Company Distribution Problem

Douglas Whitson is concerned. Costs have been escalating and revenues have not been keeping pace. If this trend continues, shareholders are going to be very unhappy with the next earnings report. As CEO of the P & T Company, he knows that the buck stops with him. He's got to find a way to bring costs under control.

Douglas suddenly picks up the telephone and places a call to his distribution manager, Richard Powers.

Douglas (CEO): Richard. Douglas Whitson here.
Richard (distribution manager): Hello, Douglas.
Douglas: Say, Richard. I've just been looking over some cost data and one number jumped out at me.
Richard: Oh? What's that?
Douglas: The shipping costs for our peas. $178,000 last season! I remember it running under $100,000 just a few years ago. What's going on here?

Richard: Yes, you're right. Those costs have really been going up. One factor is that our shipping volume is up a little. However, the main thing is that the fees charged by the truckers we've been using have really shot up. We complained. They said something about their new contract with the union representing their drivers pushed their costs up substantially. And their insurance costs are up.

Douglas: Have you looked into changing truckers?

Richard: Yes. In fact, we've already selected new truckers for the upcoming growing season.

Douglas: Good. So your shipping costs should come down quite a bit next season?

Richard: Well, my projection is that they should run about $165,000.

Douglas: Ouch. That's still too high.

Richard: That seems to be the best we can do.

Douglas: Well, let's approach this from another angle. You're shipping the peas from our three canneries to all four of our warehouses?

Richard: That's right.

Douglas: How do you decide how much each cannery will ship to each warehouse?

Richard: We have a standard strategy that we've been using for many years.

Douglas: Does this strategy minimize your total shipping cost?

Richard: I think it does a pretty good job of that.

Douglas: But does it use an algorithm to generate a shipping plan that is guaranteed to minimize the total shipping cost?

Richard: No, I can't say it does that. Is there a way of doing that?

Douglas: Yes. I understand there are management science techniques for doing that. I think we should have our Management Science Group look at your shipping plan and see if they can improve upon it.

Richard: Sounds reasonable.

Douglas: OK, good. I would like you to coordinate with the Management Science Group and report back to me soon.

Richard: Will do.

The conversation ends quickly.

Background

The P & T Company is a small family-owned business. It receives raw vegetables, processes and cans them at its canneries, and then distributes the canned goods for eventual sale.

One of the company's main products is canned peas. The peas are prepared at three canneries (near Bellingham, Washington; Eugene, Oregon; and Albert Lea, Minnesota) and then shipped by truck to four distributing warehouses in the western United States (Sacramento, California; Salt Lake City, Utah; Rapid City, South Dakota; and Albuquerque, New Mexico), as shown in Figure 5.1.

The Company's Current Approach

For many years, the company has used the following strategy for determining how much of each warehouse's needs to ship from each of the canneries.

Current Shipping Strategy

1. Since the cannery in Bellingham is furthest from the warehouses, ship its output to its nearest warehouse, namely, the one in Sacramento, with any surplus going to the warehouse in Salt Lake City.

2. Since the warehouse in Albuquerque is furthest from the canneries, have its nearest cannery (the one in Albert Lea) ship its output to Albuquerque, with any surplus going to the warehouse in Rapid City.

3. Use the cannery in Eugene to supply the remaining needs of the warehouses.

For the upcoming harvest season, an estimate has been made of the output from each cannery, and each warehouse has been allocated a certain amount from the total supply of peas. This information is given in Table 5.1.

Applying the current shipping strategy to the data in Table 5.1 gives the shipping plan shown in Table 5.2. The shipping costs per truckload for the upcoming season are shown in Table 5.3.

FIGURE 5.1

Location of the canneries and warehouses for the P & T Co. problem.

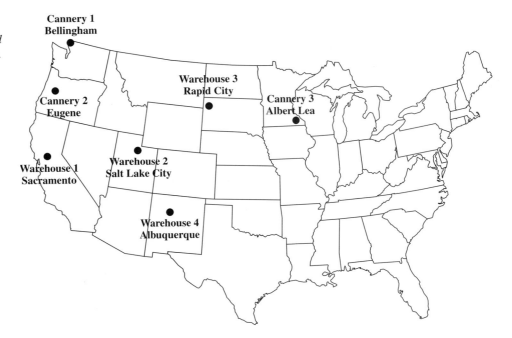

TABLE 5.1   Shipping Data for the P & T Co.

Cannery	Output		Warehouse	Allocation
Bellingham	75 truckloads		Sacramento	80 truckloads
Eugene	125 truckloads		Salt Lake City	65 truckloads
Albert Lea	100 truckloads		Rapid City	70 truckloads
			Albuquerque	85 truckloads
Total	300 truckloads		Total	300 truckloads

TABLE 5.2   Current Shipping Plan for the P & T Co.

To / From	Warehouse			
	Sacramento	Salt Lake City	Rapid City	Albuquerque
Cannery				
Bellingham	75	0	0	0
Eugene	5	65	55	0
Albert Lea	0	0	15	85

TABLE 5.3   Shipping Costs per Truckload for the P & T Co.

To / From	Warehouse			
	Sacramento	Salt Lake City	Rapid City	Albuquerque
Cannery				
Bellingham	$464	$513	$654	$867
Eugene	352	416	690	791
Albert Lea	995	682	388	685

Combining the data in Tables 5.2 and 5.3 yields the total shipping cost under the current plan for the upcoming season:

Total shipping cost = 75($464) + 5($352) + 65($416) + 55($690) + 15($388) + 85($685)
= $165,595

The Management Science Group now is reexamining the current shipping strategy to see if they can develop a new shipping plan that would reduce the total shipping cost to an absolute minimum.

The Management Science Approach

The Management Science Group immediately recognizes that this problem is just a classic example of a *transportation problem*. Formulating the problem in this way is straightforward. Furthermore, software is readily available for quickly finding an optimal solution on a desktop computer. This enables the Management Science Group to return to management the next day with a new shipping plan that would reduce the total shipping cost by over $13,000.

This story will unfold in the next section after we provide more background about transportation problems.

Review Questions

1. What is the specific concern being raised by the CEO of the P & T Co. in this case study?
2. What is the Management Science Group being asked to do?

5.2 Characteristics of Transportation Problems

The Model for Transportation Problems

To describe the model for transportation problems, we need to use terms that are considerably less specific than for the P & T Co. problem. Transportation problems in general are concerned (literally or figuratively) with distributing *any* commodity from *any* group of supply centers, called **sources,** to *any* group of receiving centers, called **destinations,** in such a way as to minimize the total distribution cost. The correspondence in terminology between the specific application to the P & T Co. problem and the general model for any transportation problem is summarized in Table 5.4.

As indicated by the fourth and fifth rows of the table, each source has a certain **supply** of units to distribute to the destinations, and each destination has a certain **demand** for units to be received from the sources. The model for a transportation problem makes the following assumption about these supplies and demands.

> **The Requirements Assumption:** Each source has a fixed *supply* of units, where this entire supply must be distributed to the destinations. Similarly, each destination has a fixed *demand* for units, where this entire demand must be received from the sources.

TABLE 5.4   Terminology for a Transportation Problem

P & T Co. Problem	*General Model*
Truckloads of canned peas	Units of a commodity
Canneries	Sources
Warehouses	Destinations
Output from a cannery	Supply from a source
Allocation to a warehouse	Demand at a destination
Shipping cost per truckload from a cannery to a warehouse	Cost per unit distributed from a source to a destination

This assumption that there is no leeway in the amounts to be sent or received means that there needs to be a balance between the total supply from all sources and the total demand at all destinations.

> **The Feasible Solutions Property:** A transportation problem will have feasible solutions if and only if the *sum* of its supplies *equals* the *sum* of its demands.

Fortunately, these sums are equal for the P & T Co. since Table 5.1 indicates that the supplies (outputs) sum to 300 truckloads and so do the demands (allocations).

In some real problems, the supplies actually represent *maximum* amounts (rather than fixed amounts) to be distributed. Similarly, in other cases, the demands represent maximum amounts (rather than fixed amounts) to be received. Such problems do not fit the model for a transportation problem because they violate the *requirements assumption,* so they are *variants* of a transportation problem. Fortunately, it is relatively straightforward to formulate a spreadsheet model for such variants that the Excel Solver can still solve, as will be illustrated in Section 5.3.

The last row of Table 5.4 refers to a cost per unit distributed. This reference to a *unit cost* implies the following basic assumption for any transportation problem.

> **The Cost Assumption:** The cost of distributing units from any particular source to any particular destination is *directly proportional* to the number of units distributed. Therefore, this cost is just the *unit cost* of distribution *times* the *number of units distributed.*

The only data needed for a transportation problem model are the supplies, demands, and unit costs. These are the *parameters of the model.* All these parameters can be summarized conveniently in a single **parameter table.** The parameter table for the P & T Co. problem is shown in Table 5.5. This table (including the description implied by its column and row headings) summarizes the model for the problem.

> **The Model:** Any problem (whether involving transportation or not) fits the model for a transportation problem if it can be described completely in terms of a *parameter table* like Table 5.5 and it satisfies both the *requirements assumption* and the *cost assumption.* The objective is to minimize the total cost of distributing the units. All the parameters of the model are included in this parameter table.

Therefore, formulating a problem as a transportation problem only requires filling out a parameter table in the format of Table 5.5. It is not necessary to write out a formal mathematical model (even though we will do this for demonstration purposes later).

Using Excel to Formulate and Solve Transportation Problems

To formulate and solve a transportation problem using Excel, two separate tables need to be entered on a spreadsheet. The first one is the parameter table, presenting all the data for the problem. The second is a solution table, containing the quantities to ship from each source to each destination. Figure 5.2 shows these two tables, along with the additional needed formulation, for the P & T problem.

The two types of functional constraints need to be included in the spreadsheet. For the supply constraints, the total amount shipped from each source is calculated in column H of

TABLE 5.5 **The Parameter Table for the P & T Co. Problem**

	Unit Cost				
Destination (Warehouse):	*Sacramento*	*Salt Lake City*	*Rapid City*	*Albuquerque*	*Supply*
Source (Cannery)					
Bellingham	$464	$513	$654	$867	75
Eugene	$352	$416	$690	$791	125
Albert Lea	$995	$682	$388	$685	100
Demand	80	65	70	85	

FIGURE 5.2

A spreadsheet formulation of the P & T Co. problem as a transportation problem, where rows 3–9 show the parameter table and rows 12–20 display the solution table after using the Excel Solver to obtain an optimal distribution plan. Both the formulas for the output cells and the specifications needed to set up the Solver are given at the bottom.

	A	B	C	D	E	F	G	H	I	J
1		P&T Co. Distribution Problem								
2										
3					Unit Cost					
4					Destination (Warehouse)					
5				Sacramento	Salt Lake City	Rapid City	Albuquerque	Supply		
6		Source	Bellingham	$464	$513	$654	$867	75		
7		(Cannery)	Eugene	$352	$416	$690	$791	125		
8			Albert Lea	$995	$682	$388	$685	100		
9		Demand		80	65	70	85			
10										
11										
12					Shipment Quantities (Truckloads)					
13					Destination (Warehouse)					
14				Sacramento	Salt Lake City	Rapid City	Albuquerque	Totals		Supply
15		Source	Bellingham	0	20	0	55	75	=	75
16		(Cannery)	Eugene	80	45	0	0	125	=	125
17			Albert Lea	0	0	70	30	100	=	100
18		Totals		80	65	70	85	$152,535	=	Total Cost
19				=	=	=	=			
20		Demand		80	65	70	85			

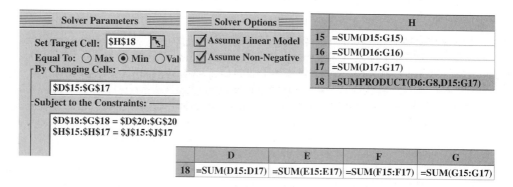

Solver Parameters

Set Target Cell: $H$18

Equal To: ○ Max ● Min ○ Val

By Changing Cells:

$D$15:$G$17

Subject to the Constraints:

$D$18:$G$18 = $D$20:$G$20
$H$15:$H$17 = $J$15:$J$17

Solver Options

☑ Assume Linear Model
☑ Assume Non-Negative

	H
15	=SUM(D15:G15)
16	=SUM(D16:G16)
17	=SUM(D17:G17)
18	=SUMPRODUCT(D6:G8,D15:G17)

	D	E	F	G
18	=SUM(D15:D17)	=SUM(E15:E17)	=SUM(F15:F17)	=SUM(G15:G17)

the solution table in Figure 5.2. It is the sum of all the decision variable cells in the corresponding row. For example, the equation in cell H15 is "=D15+E15+F15+G15" or "=SUM(D15:G15)". The supply at each source is included in column J. Hence, the cells in column H must equal the corresponding cells in column J.

For the demand constraints, the total amount shipped to each destination is calculated in row 18 of the spreadsheet. For example, the equation in cell D18 is "=SUM(D15:D17)". The demand at each destination is then included in row 20.

The total cost is calculated in cell H18. This cost is the sum of the products of the corresponding cells in the main bodies of the parameter table and the solution table. Hence, the equation contained in cell H18 is "=SUMPRODUCT(D6:G8, D15:G17)".

Now let us look at the entries in the Solver dialogue box shown at the bottom of Figure 5.2. These entries indicate that we are minimizing the total cost (calculated in cell H18) by changing the shipment quantities (in cells D15 through G17), subject to the constraints that the total amount shipped to each destination equals its demand (D18:G18 = D20:G20) and that the total amount shipped from each source equals its supply (H15:H17 = J15:J17). One of the selected Solver options (Assume Non-Negative) specifies that all shipment quantities must be nonnegative. The other one (Assume Linear Model) indicates that this transportation problem is also a linear programming problem (as described later in this section).

The values of the decision variables (the shipment quantities) are contained in the changing cells (D15:G17). To begin, any value (such as 0) can be entered in each of these cells. After clicking on the Solve button, the Solver will use the simplex method to solve the transportation problem and determine the best value for each of the decision variables. This optimal solution is shown in Figure 5.2, along with the resulting total cost.

FIGURE 5.3

The network representation of the P & T Co. transportation problem shows all the data in Table 5.5 graphically.

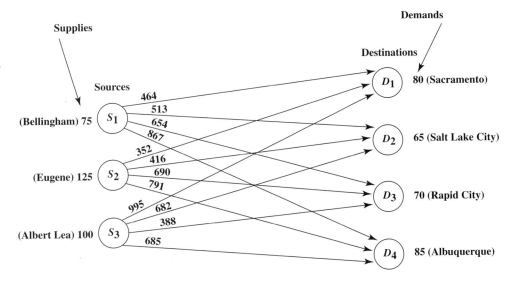

The Network Representation of a Transportation Problem

A nice way to visualize a transportation problem graphically is to use its *network representation*. This representation ignores the geographical layout of the sources and destinations. Instead, it simply lines up all the sources in one column on the left (where S_1 is the symbol for Source 1, etc.) and all the destinations in one column on the right (where D_1 is the symbol for Destination 1, etc.). Figure 5.3 shows the network representation for the P & T Co. problem, where the numbering of the sources (canneries) and destinations (warehouses) is that given in Figure 5.1. The arrows show the possible routes for the truckloads of canned peas, where the number next to each arrow is the shipping cost (in dollars) per truckload for that route. Since the figure also includes the supplies and demands, it includes all the data provided by the parameter table (Table 5.5). Therefore, this network representation provides an alternative way of summarizing the model for a transportation problem model.

For larger problems, it is not very convenient to draw the entire network and display all the data. Consequently, the network representation is mainly a visualization device.

Recall that Section 3.4 describes distribution-network problems as a major category of linear programming problems that involve the distribution of goods through a distribution network. The network in Figure 5.3 is a simple type of distribution network where every shipping lane goes directly from a source to a destination. Consequently, transportation problems are a special type of distribution-network problem.

In the next chapter, you will see many more network representations of other distribution-network problems.

The Transportation Problem Is a Linear Programming Problem

To demonstrate that the P & T Co. problem (or any other transportation problem) is, in fact, a linear programming problem, let us formulate its mathematical model in algebraic form.

Using the numbering of canneries and warehouses given in Figure 5.1, let x_{ij} be the number of truckloads to be shipped from Cannery i to Warehouse j for each $i = 1, 2, 3$ and $j = 1, 2, 3, 4$. The objective is to choose the values of these 12 decision variables (the x_{ij}) so as to

Minimize $\text{Cost} = 464x_{11} + 513x_{12} + 654x_{13} + 867x_{14} + 352x_{21} + 416x_{22} + 690x_{23}$
$\qquad\qquad\qquad + 791x_{24} + 995x_{31} + 682x_{32} + 388x_{33} + 685x_{34}$

subject to the constraints

$$x_{11} + x_{12} + x_{13} + x_{14} \qquad\qquad\qquad\qquad\qquad\qquad\qquad\qquad\quad = 75$$

$$x_{21} + x_{22} + x_{23} + x_{24} \qquad\qquad\qquad\qquad\quad = 125$$

$$x_{31} + x_{32} + x_{33} + x_{34} = 100$$

$$x_{11} \qquad\qquad\qquad\qquad + x_{21} \qquad\qquad\qquad\quad + x_{31} \qquad\qquad\qquad\quad = 80$$

$$x_{12} \qquad\qquad +x_{22} \qquad\qquad +x_{32} \qquad\qquad = \quad 65$$
$$x_{13} \qquad\qquad +x_{23} \qquad\qquad +x_{33} \qquad\qquad = \quad 70$$
$$x_{14} \qquad\qquad +x_{24} \qquad\qquad +x_{34} \quad = \quad 85$$

and

$$x_{ij} \geq 0 \qquad (i = 1, 2, 3; \; j = 1, 2, 3, 4)$$

This is indeed a linear programming problem.

The P & T Co. always ships *full* truckloads of canned peas since anything less would be uneconomical. This implies that each x_{ij} should have an *integer* value (0, 1, 2, . . .). To avoid obtaining an optimal solution for our model that has *fractional* values for any of the decision variables, we could add another set of constraints specifying that each x_{ij} must have an integer value. This would convert our linear programming problem into an *integer programming* problem, which is more difficult to solve. (We will discuss integer programming problems in Section 8.1.) Fortunately, this conversion is not necessary because of the following property of transportation problems.

> **Integer Solutions Property:** As long as all its supplies and demands have integer values, any transportation problem with feasible solutions is guaranteed to have an optimal solution with integer values for all its decision variables. Therefore, it is not necessary to add constraints to the model that restrict these variables to only have integer values.

When dealing with transportation problems, practitioners typically do not bother to write out the complete linear programming model in algebraic form since all the essential information can be presented much more compactly in a parameter table or in the corresponding spreadsheet model.

Before leaving this linear programming model though, take a good look at the left-hand side of the functional constraints. Note that every coefficient is either 0 (so the variable is deleted) or 1. Also note the distinctive pattern for the locations of the coefficients of 1, including the fact that each variable has a coefficient of 1 in exactly two constraints. These distinctive features of the coefficients play a key role in being able to solve transportation problems extremely efficiently.

Solving Transportation Problems

Because transportation problems are a special type of linear programming problem, it can be solved by the *simplex method* (the procedure used by the Excel Solver to solve linear programming problems). However, because of the very distinctive pattern of coefficients in its functional constraints noted above, it is possible to greatly *streamline* the simplex method to solve transportation problems far more quickly. This streamlined version of the simplex method is called the **transportation simplex method.** It sometimes can solve large transportation problems more than 100 times faster than the regular simplex method. However, it is only applicable to transportation problems.

Just like a transportation problem, other *distribution-network problems* also have a similar distinctive pattern of coefficients in their functional constraints. Therefore, the simplex method can be greatly streamlined in much the same way as for the transportation simplex method to solve *any* distribution-network problem (including any transportation problem) very quickly. This streamlined method is called the **network simplex method.**

Linear programming software often includes the network simplex method, and may include the transportation simplex method as well. When only the network-simplex method is available, it provides an excellent alternative way of solving transportation problems. In fact, the network simplex method has become quite competitive with the transportation simplex method in recent years.

After obtaining an optimal solution, *what-if analysis* generally is done for transportation problems in much the same way as described in Chapter 4 for other linear programming problems. Either the transportation or network simplex method can readily obtain the range of optimality for each coefficient in the objective function. Dealing with changes in right-hand sides (supplies and demands) is more complicated now because of the requirement that the sum of the supplies must equal the sum of the demands. Thus, each change in a supply must be accompanied by a corresponding change in a demand (or demands), and vice versa.

Because the Excel Solver is not intended to solve the really large linear programming problems that often arise in practice, it simply uses the simplex method to solve transportation problems as well as other distribution-network problems encountered in this book (and considerably larger ones as well), so we will continue to use the Solver and thereby forgo any use of the transportation simplex method or network simplex method.

Completing the P & T Co. Case Study

We now can summarize the end of the story of how the P & T Co. Management Science Group was able to substantially improve on the current shipping plan shown in Table 5.2, which has a total shipping cost of $165,595.

You already have seen how the Management Science Group was able to formulate this problem as a *transportation problem* simply by filling out the parameter table shown in Table 5.5. The corresponding formulation on a spreadsheet was shown in Figure 5.2. Applying the Solver then gave the optimal solution shown in cells D15:G17.

Note that this optimal solution is not an intuitive one. Of the 75 truckloads being supplied by Bellingham, 55 of them are being sent to Albuquerque, even though this is far more expensive ($867 per truckload) than to any other warehouse. However, this sacrifice for Cannery 1 enables low-cost shipments for both Canneries 2 and 3. Although it would have been difficult to find this optimal solution manually, the simplex method in the Excel Solver finds it readily.

As given in the target cell (H18), the total shipping cost for this optimal shipping plan is

$$\text{Total shipping cost} = 20 \ (\$513) + 55 \ (\$867) + 80 \ (\$352) + 45 \ (\$416) + 70 \ (\$388)$$
$$+ \ 30 \ (\$685)$$
$$= \$152,535$$

a reduction of $13,060 from the current shipping plan. Richard Powers is pleased to report this reduction to his CEO, Douglas Whitson, who congratulates him and the Management Science Group for achieving this significant savings.

An Award-Winning Application of a Transportation Problem

Except for its small size, the P & T Co. problem is typical of the problems faced by many corporations that must ship goods from its manufacturing plants to its customers.

For example, consider an award-winning management science study conducted at **Procter & Gamble** (as described in the January–February 1997 issue of *Interfaces*). Prior to the study, the company's supply chain consisted of hundreds of suppliers, over 50 product categories, over 60 plants, 15 distribution centers, and over 1,000 customer zones. However, as the company moved toward global brands, management realized that it needed to consolidate plants to reduce manufacturing expenses, improve speed to market, and reduce capital investment. Therefore, the study focused on redesigning the company's production and distribution system for its North American operations. The result was a reduction in the number of North American plants by almost 20 percent, saving over $200 million in pretax costs per year.

A major part of the study revolved around formulating and solving transportation problems for individual product categories. For each option regarding the plants to keep open, and so forth, solving the corresponding transportation problem for a product category shows what the distribution cost would be for shipping the product category from those plants to the distribution centers and customer zones. Numerous such transportation problems were solved in the process of identifying the best new production and distribution system.

Review Questions

1. Give a one-sentence description of transportation problems.
2. What are the data needed for the model of a transportation problem?
3. What needs to be done to formulate a problem as a transportation problem?
4. What is required for a transportation problem to have feasible solutions?
5. Under what circumstances will a transportation problem automatically have an optimal solution with integer values for all its decision variables?
6. Name two algorithms that can solve transportation problems much faster than the general simplex method.

5.3 Modeling Variants of Transportation Problems

The P & T Co. problem is an example of a transportation problem where everything fits immediately. Real life is seldom this easy. Linear programming problems frequently arise that are *almost* transportation problems, but one or more features do not quite fit. Here are the features that we will consider in this section.

1. The sum of the supplies *exceeds* the sum of the demands, so each supply represents a *maximum* amount (not a *fixed* amount) to be distributed from that source.
2. The sum of the supplies is *less* than the sum of the demands, so each demand represents a *maximum* amount (not a *fixed* amount) to be received at that destination.
3. A destination has both a *minimum* demand and a *maximum* demand, so any amount between these two values can be received.
4. Certain source–destination combinations cannot be used for distributing units.
5. The objective is to maximize the total profit associated with distributing units rather than to minimize the total cost.

For each of these features, it is possible to reformulate the problem in a clever way to make it fit the format for transportation problems. When this is done with a really big problem (say, one with many hundreds or thousands of sources and destinations), it is extremely helpful because either the transportation simplex method or network simplex method can solve the problem in this format *much* faster (perhaps more than 100 times faster) than the simplex method can solve the general linear programming formulation.

However, when the problem is *not* really big, the simplex method still is capable of solving the general linear programming formulation in a reasonable period of time. Therefore, a basic software package (such as the Excel Solver) that includes the simplex method but not the transportation simplex method or network simplex method can be applied to such problems without trying to force them into the format for a transportation problem. This is the approach we will use. In particular, this section illustrates the formulation of spreadsheet models for *variants* of transportation problems that have some of the features listed above.

Our first example focuses on features 1 and 4. A second example will illustrate the other features.

Example 1: Assigning Plants to Products

The Better Products Company has decided to initiate the production of four new products, using three plants that currently have excess production capacity. The products require a comparable production effort per unit, so the available production capacity of the plants is measured by the number of units of any product that can be produced per day, as given in the rightmost column of Table 5.6. The bottom row gives the required production rate (number of units produced per day) to meet projected sales. Each plant can produce any of these products, *except* that Plant 2 *cannot* produce Product 3. However, the variable costs per unit of each product differ from plant to plant, as shown in the main body of the table.

TABLE 5.6   **Data for the Better Products Co. Problem**

		Unit Cost				
	Product:	*1*	*2*	*3*	*4*	*Capacity Available*
Plant						
1		$41	$27	$28	$24	75
2		40	29	—	23	75
3		37	30	27	21	45
Required production		20	30	30	40	

Management now needs to make a decision about which plants should produce which products. *Product splitting,* where the same product is produced in more than one plant, is permitted. (We shall return to this same example in Section 5.7 to consider the option where product splitting is prohibited, which requires a different kind of formulation.)

Formulation of a Spreadsheet Model. This problem is almost a transportation problem. In fact, after substituting conventional terminology (supply, demand, etc.) for the column and row headings in Table 5.6, this table is basically a *parameter table,* as shown in Table 5.7. But there are two ways in which this problem deviates from a transportation problem.

One (minor) deviation is that a transportation problem requires a unit cost for *every* source–destination combination, but plant 2 cannot produce product 3, so no unit cost is available for this particular combination. The other deviation is that the sum of the supplies (75 + 75 + 45 = 195) *exceeds* the sum of the demands (20 + 30 + 30 + 40 = 120) in Table 5.7. Thus, as the *feasible solutions property* (Section 5.2) indicates, the transportation problem represented by this parameter table would have no feasible solutions. The *requirements assumption* (Section 5.2) specifies that the entire supply from each source must be used.

In reality, these supplies in Table 5.7 represent production capacities that will not need to be fully used to meet the sales demand for the products. Thus, these supplies are *upper bounds* on the amounts to be used.

The spreadsheet model for this problem, shown in Figure 5.4, has the same format as the one in Figure 5.2 for the P & T Co. transportation problem with two key differences. First, because plant 2 cannot produce product 3, a dash is inserted into cell F7 and the constraint that F16 = 0 is included in the Solver dialogue box. Second, because the supplies are upper bounds, cells I15:I17 have ≤ signs instead of = signs and the corresponding constraints in the Solver dialogue box are H15:H17 ≤ J15:J17.

Using the Excel Solver then gives the optimal solution shown in the changing cells (D15:G17) for the production rate of each product at each plant. This solution minimizes the cost of distributing 120 units of production from the total supply of 195 to meet the total demand of 120 at the four destinations (products). The total cost given in cell H18 is $3,260 per day.

Example 2: Choosing Customers

The Nifty Company specializes in the production of a single product, which it produces in three plants. The product is doing very well, so the company currently is receiving more purchase requests than it can fill. Plans have been made to open an additional plant, but it will not be ready until next year.

For the coming month, four potential customers (wholesalers) in different parts of the country would like to make major purchases. Customer 1 is the company's best customer, so his full order will be met. Customers 2 and 3 also are valued customers, so the marketing manager has decided that, at a minimum, at least a third of their order quantities should be met. However, she does not feel that customer 4 warrants special consideration, and so is unwilling to guarantee any minimum amount for this customer. There will be enough units produced to go somewhat above these minimum amounts.

Due largely to substantial variations in shipping costs, the net profit that would be earned on each unit sold varies greatly depending on which plant is supplying which customer.

TABLE 5.7 **Parameter Table for the Better Products Co. Problem**

Destination (Product):	1	Unit Cost 2	3	4	Supply
Source (Plant)					
1	$41	$27	$28	$24	75
2	40	29	—	23	75
3	37	30	27	21	45
Demand	20	30	30	40	

FIGURE 5.4

A spreadsheet formulation of the Better Products Co. problem as a variant of a transportation problem, where rows 3–9 display the parameter table and the changing cells (D15:G17) show the optimal production plan obtained by the Solver.

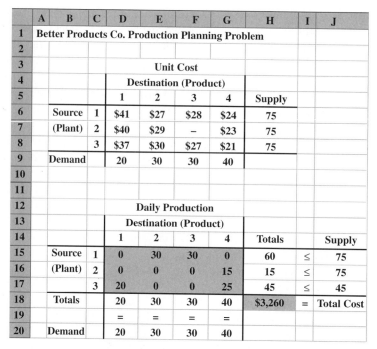

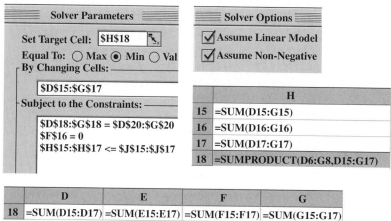

TABLE 5.8   Data for the Nifty Co. Problem

		Unit Profit				Production Quantity
	Customer:	1	2	3	4	
Plant						
1		$55	$42	$46	$53	8,000
2		37	18	32	48	5,000
3		29	59	51	35	7,000
Minimum purchase		7,000	3,000	2,000	0	
Requested purchase		7,000	9,000	6,000	8,000	

Therefore, the final decision on how much to send to each customer (above the minimum amounts established by the marketing manager) will be based on maximizing profit.

The unit profit for each combination of a plant supplying a customer is shown in Table 5.8. The rightmost column gives the number of units that each plant will produce for the coming month (a total of 20,000). The bottom row shows the order quantities that have been requested by the customers (a total of 30,000). The next-to-last row gives the minimum

FIGURE 5.5

A spreadsheet formulation of the Nifty Co. problem as a variant of a transportation problem, where rows 3–10 show the parameter table and the changing cells (D16:G18) display the optimal product-distribution plan obtained by the Solver.

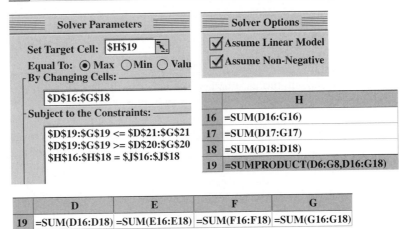

	A	B	C	D	E	F	G	H	I	J
1	Nifty Co. Product–Distribution Problem									
2										
3					Unit Cost					
4				Destination (Customer)						
5				1	2	3	4	Supply		
6		Source	1	$55	$42	$46	$53	8000		
7		(Plant)	2	$37	$18	$32	$48	5000		
8			3	$29	$59	$51	$35	7000		
9		Minimum		7000	3000	2000	0			
10		Maximum		7000	9000	6000	8000			
11										
12										
13					Shipments					
14				Destination (Customer)						
15				1	2	3	4	Totals		Supply
16		Source	1	7000	0	1000	0	8000	=	8000
17		(Plant)	2	0	0	0	5000	5000	=	5000
18			3	0	6000	1000	0	7000	=	7000
19		Totals		7000	6000	2000	5000	$1,076,000	=	Total Profit
20		Minimum		7000	3000	2000	0			
21		Maximum		7000	9000	6000	8000			

Solver Parameters

Set Target Cell: $H$19

Equal To: ● Max ○ Min ○ Valu

By Changing Cells:

$D$16:$G$18

Subject to the Constraints:

$D$19:$G$19 <= $D$21:$G$21
$D$19:$G$19 >= $D$20:$G$20
$H$16:$H$18 = $J$16:$J$18

Solver Options

☑ Assume Linear Model
☑ Assume Non-Negative

	H
16	=SUM(D16:G16)
17	=SUM(D17:G17)
18	=SUM(D18:D18)
19	=SUMPRODUCT(D6:G8,D16:G18)

	D	E	F	G
19	=SUM(D16:D18)	=SUM(E16:E18)	=SUM(F16:F18)	=SUM(G16:G18)

amounts that will be provided (a total of 12,000), based on the marketing manager's decisions described above.

The marketing manager needs to determine how many units to sell to each customer (observing these minimum amounts) and how many units to ship from each plant to each customer to maximize profit.

Formulation of a Spreadsheet Model. This problem is almost a transportation problem, since the plants can be viewed as *sources* and the customers as *destinations,* where the production quantities are the *supplies* from the sources.

If this were fully a transportation problem, the purchase quantities would be the *demands* for the destinations. However, this does not work here because the *requirements assumption* (Section 5.2) says that the demand must be a *fixed* quantity to be received from the sources. Except for customer 1, all we have here are *ranges* for the purchase quantities between the minimum and the maximum given in the last two rows of Table 5.8. In fact, one objective is to solve for the most desirable values of these purchase quantities.

Figure 5.5 shows the spreadsheet model for this variant of a transportation problem. Instead of a demand row at the bottom of the parameter table and the solution table, we instead have both a minimum row and a maximum row. The corresponding constraints in the Solver dialogue box are D19:G19 ≥ D20:G20 and D19:G19 ≤ D21:G21, along with the usual supply constraints. Since the objective is to maximize the total profit rather than minimize the total cost, the Solver dialogue box specifies that the target cell (H19) is to be maximized.

After clicking on the Solve button, the optimal solution shown in Figure 5.5 is obtained. Cells D19:G19 indicate how many units to sell to the respective customers. The changing cells (D16:G18) show how many units to ship from each plant to each customer. The resulting total profit of $1.076 million is given in cell H19.

Review Questions

1. What needs to be done to formulate the spreadsheet model for a variant of a transportation problem where each supply from a source represents a maximum amount rather than a fixed amount to be distributed from that source?
2. What needs to be done to formulate the spreadsheet model for a variant of a transportation problem where the demand for a destination can be anything between a specified minimum amount and a specified maximum amount?

5.4 Some Other Applications of Variants of Transportation Problems

You now have seen examples illustrating three areas of application of transportation problems and their variants:

1. Shipping goods (the P & T Co. problem).
2. Assigning plants to products (the Better Products Co. problem).
3. Choosing customers (the Nifty Co. problem).

You will further broaden your horizons in this section by seeing examples illustrating some (but far from all) other areas of application.

Distributing Natural Resources

Metro Water District is an agency that administers water distribution in a large geographic region. The region is fairly arid, so the district must purchase and bring in water from outside the region. The sources of this imported water are the Colombo, Sacron, and Calorie rivers. The district then resells the water to users in its region. Its main customers are the water departments of the cities of Berdoo, Los Devils, San Go, and Hollyglass.

It is possible to supply any of these cities with water brought in from any of the three rivers, with the exception that no provision has been made to supply Hollyglass with Calorie River water. However, because of the geographic layouts of the aqueducts and the cities in the region, the cost to the district of supplying water depends upon both the source of the water and the city being supplied. The variable cost per acre foot of water for each combination of river and city is given in Table 5.9.

Using units of 1 million acre feet, the bottom row of the table shows the amount of water needed by each city in the coming year (a total of 12.5). The rightmost column shows the amount available from each river (a total of 16).

TABLE 5.9 Water Resources Data for Metro Water District

	Berdoo	Los Devils	San Go	Hollyglass	Available
			Cost per Acre Foot		
Colombo River	$160	$130	$220	$170	5
Sacron River	140	130	190	150	6
Calorie River	190	200	230		5
Needed	2	5	4	1.5	(million acre feet)

FIGURE 5.6

A spreadsheet formulation of the Metro Water District problem as a variant of a transportation problem, where rows 3–9 display the parameter table and the changing cells (D15:G17) give the optimal water distribution plan obtained by the Solver.

	A	B	C	D	E	F	G	H	I	J
1		Metro Water District Distribution Problem								
2										
3				Unit Cost (Millions of Dollars)						
4				Destination (City)						
5				Berdoo	Los Devils	San Go	Hollyglass	Supply		
6		Source	Colombo	160	130	220	170	5		
7		(River)	Sacron	140	130	190	150	6		
8			Calorie	190	200	230	–	5		
9		Demand		2	5	4	1.5			
10										
11										
12				Water Distribution (Millions of Acre–Feet)						
13				Destination (City)						
14				Berdoo	Los Devils	San Go	Hollyglass	Totals		Supply
15		Source	Colombo	0	5	0	0	5	≤	5
16		(River)	Sacron	2	0	2.5	1.5	6	≤	6
17			Calorie	0	0	1.5	0	1.5	≤	5
18		Totals		2	5	4	1.5	$1,975,000,000	=	Total Cost
19				=	=	=	=			
20		Demand		2	5	4	1.5			

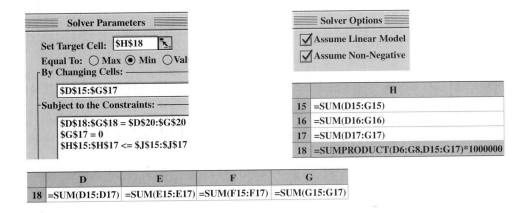

Solver Parameters

Set Target Cell: $H$18

Equal To: ○ Max ⦿ Min ○ Val

By Changing Cells:

$D$15:$G$17

Subject to the Constraints:

$D$18:$G$18 = $D$20:$G$20
$G$17 = 0
$H$15:$H$17 <= $J$15:$J$17

Solver Options

☑ Assume Linear Model
☑ Assume Non-Negative

	H
15	=SUM(D15:G15)
16	=SUM(D16:G16)
17	=SUM(D17:G17)
18	=SUMPRODUCT(D6:G8,D15:G17)*1000000

	D	E	F	G
18	=SUM(D15:D17)	=SUM(E15:E17)	=SUM(F15:F17)	=SUM(G15:G17)

Since the total amount available exceeds the total amount needed, management wants to determine how much water to take from each river, and then how much to send from each river to each city. The objective is to minimize the total cost of meeting the needs of the four cities.

Formulation and Solution. Figure 5.6 shows a spreadsheet model for this variant of a transportation problem. Because Hollyglass cannot be supplied with Calorie River water, the Solver dialogue box includes the constraint that $G17 = 0$. The supplies in column J represent maximum amounts rather than fixed amounts, so $\leq$ signs are used for the corresponding constraints, $H15{:}H17 \leq J15{:}J17$.

The Excel Solver then gives the optimal solution shown in the solution table. Cells H15:H17 indicate that the entire available supply from the Colombo and Sacron Rivers should be used whereas only 1.5 million acre feet of the 5 million acre feet available from the Calorie River should be used. The changing cells (D15:G17) provide the plan for how much to send from each river to each city. The total cost is given in cell H18 as $1.975 billion.

Production Scheduling

The Northern Airplane Company builds commercial airplanes for various airline companies around the world. The last stage in the production process is to produce the jet engines and then to install them (a very fast operation) in the completed airplane frame. The company has been working under some contracts to deliver a considerable number of airplanes in the near future, and the production of the jet engines for these planes must now be scheduled for the next four months.

TABLE 5.10   Production Scheduling Data for the Northern Airplane Company Problem

Month	Scheduled Installations	Maximum Production		Unit Cost of Production		Unit Cost of Storage
		Regular Time	Overtime	Regular Time	Overtime	
1	10	20	10	$1.08 million	$1.10 million	$15,000
2	15	30	15	$1.11 million	$1.12 million	$15,000
3	25	25	10	$1.10 million	$1.11 million	$15,000
4	20	5	10	$1.13 million	$1.15 million	

To meet the contracted dates for delivery, the company must supply engines for installation in the quantities indicated in the second column of Table 5.10. Thus, the cumulative number of engines produced by the end of months 1, 2, 3, and 4 must be at least 10, 25, 50, and 70, respectively.

The facilities that will be available for producing the engines vary according to other production, maintenance, and renovation work scheduled during this period. The resulting monthly differences in the maximum number that can be produced during *regular time* hours (no overtime) are shown in the third column of Table 5.10, and the additional numbers that can be produced during *overtime* hours are shown in the fourth column. The cost of producing each one on either regular time or overtime is given in the fifth and sixth columns.

Because of the variations in production costs, it may well be worthwhile to produce some of the engines a month or more before they are scheduled for installation, and this possibility is being considered. The drawback is that such engines must be stored until the scheduled installation (the airplane frames will not be ready early) at a storage cost of $15,000 per month (including interest on expended capital) for each engine,[1] as shown in the rightmost column of Table 5.10.

The production manager wants a schedule developed for the number of engines to be produced in each of the four months so that the total of the production and storage costs will be minimized.

Formulation and Solution.   Figure 5.7 shows the formulation of this problem as a variant of a transportation problem. The *sources* of the jet engines are their production on *regular time* (RT) and on *overtime* (OT) in each of the four months. Their *supplies* are obtained from the third and fourth columns of Table 5.10. The *destinations* for these engines are their installation in each of the four months, so their *demands* are given in the second column of Table 5.10.

It is not possible to install an engine in some month prior to its production, so the Solver dialogue box includes constraints that the number installed must be zero in each of these cases. Similarly, dashes are inserted into the parameter table for these cases. Otherwise, the unit costs given in the parameter table (in units of $1 million) are obtained by combining the unit cost of production from the fifth or sixth column of Table 5.10 with any storage costs ($0.015 million per unit per month stored). Since the supplies in column J of the solution table represent the maximum amounts that can be produced, they are preceded by $\leq$ signs in column I. The corresponding supply constraints, H20:H27 $\leq$ J20:J27, are included in the Solver dialogue box along with the usual demand constraints.

The changing cells (D20:G27) show an optimal solution for this problem. Table 5.11 summarizes the key features of this solution. Overtime is used only once (in month 3). Despite the hefty costs incurred by storing engines, extra engines are produced in the first and third months to be stored for installation later. Even month 2 produces enough engines that five will remain in storage for installation in month 3, despite the fact that production costs

---

[1]For modeling purposes, it is being assumed that this storage cost is incurred at the end of the month for just those engines that are being held over into the next month. Thus, engines that are produced in a given month for installation in the same month are assumed to incur no storage cost.

FIGURE 5.7 *A spreadsheet formulation of the Northern Airplane Co. problem as a variant of a transportation problem, where rows 3–14 show the parameter table and the changing cells (D20:G27) display the optimal production schedule obtained by the Solver.*

	A	B	C	D	E	F	G	H	I	J
1	Northern Airplane Co. Production–Scheduling Problem									
2										
3				Unit Cost (Millions of Dollars)						
4				Destination (Month Installed)						
5				1	2	3	4	Supply		
6			1 (RT)	1.08	1.095	1.11	1.125	20		
7			1 (OT)	1.1	1.115	1.13	1.145	10		
8		Source	2 (RT)	–	1.11	1.125	1.14	30		
9		(Month	2 (OT)	–	1.12	1.135	1.15	15		
10		Produced)	3 (RT)	–	–	1.1	1.115	25		
11			3 (OT)	–	–	1.11	1.125	10		
12			4 (RT)	–	–	–	1.13	5		
13			4 (OT)	–	–	–	1.15	10		
14		Demand		10	15	25	20			
15										
16										
17				Units Produced						
18				Destination (Month Installed)						
19				1	2	3	4	Totals		Supply
20			1 (RT)	10	5	5	0	20	≤	20
21			1 (OT)	0	0	0	0	0	≤	10
22		Source	2 (RT)	0	10	0	0	10	≤	30
23		(Month	2 (OT)	0	0	0	0	0	≤	15
24		Produced)	3 (RT)	0	0	20	5	25	≤	25
25			3 (OT)	0	0	0	10	10	≤	10
26			4 (RT)	0	0	0	5	5	≤	5
27			4 (OT)	0	0	0	0	0	≤	10
28		Totals		10	15	25	20	$77,400,000	=	Total Cost
29				=	=	=	=			
30		Demand		10	15	25	20			

Solver Parameters
Set Target Cell: $H$28
Equal To: ○ Max ● Min ○ Val
By Changing Cells:
$D$20:$G$27
Subject to the Constraints:
$D$22:$D$27 = 0
$D$28:$G$28 = $D$30:$G$30
$E$24:$E$27 = 0
$F$26:$F$27 = 0
$H$20:$H$27 <= $J$20:$J$27

	H
20	=SUM(D20:G20)
21	=SUM(D21:G21)
22	=SUM(D22:G22)
23	=SUM(D23:G23)
24	=SUM(D24:G24)
25	=SUM(D25:G25)
26	=SUM(D26:G26)
27	=SUM(D27:G27)
28	=SUMPRODUCT(D6:G13,D20:G27)*1000000

Solver Options
☑ Assume Linear Model
☑ Assume Non-Negative

	D	E	F	G
28	=SUM(D20:D27)	=SUM(E20:E27)	=SUM(F20:F27)	=SUM(G20:G27)

are higher in month 2 than in month 3. Thus, a human scheduler would have difficulty in finding this schedule. However, the Excel Solver has no difficulty in balancing all the factors involved to reduce the total cost to an absolute minimum, which turns out to be $77.4 million (as shown in cell H28) in this case.

Designing School Attendance Zones

The Middletown School District is opening a third high school and thus needs to redraw the boundaries for the areas of the city that will be assigned to the respective schools.

For preliminary planning, the city has been divided into nine tracts with approximately equal populations. (Subsequent detailed planning will divide the city further into over 100 smaller tracts.) The main body of Table 5.12 shows the approximate distance between each tract and school. The rightmost column gives the number of high school students in each tract next year. (These numbers are expected to slowly grow over the next several years.) The last two rows show the minimum and maximum number of students each school should be assigned.

TABLE 5.11 Optimal Production Schedule for the Northern Airplane Co.

Month	Production	Installations	Stored
1 (RT)	20	10	10
2 (RT)	10	15	5
3 (RT)	25	25	5
3 (OT)	10	0	10
4 (RT)	5	20	0

TABLE 5.12 Data for the Middletown School District Problem

| | Distance (Miles) to School | | | |
	1	*2*	*3*	*Number of High School Students*
Tract				
1	2.2	1.9	2.5	500
2	1.4	1.3	1.7	400
3	0.5	1.8	1.1	450
4	1.2	0.3	2.0	400
5	0.9	0.7	1.0	500
6	1.1	1.6	0.6	450
7	2.7	0.7	1.5	450
8	1.8	1.2	0.8	400
9	1.5	1.7	0.7	500
Minimum enrollment	1,200	1,100	1,000	
Maximum enrollment	1,800	1,700	1,500	

The school district management has decided that the appropriate objective in setting school attendance zone boundaries is to minimize the *average distance* that students must travel to school. At this preliminary stage, they want to determine how many students from each tract should be assigned to each school to achieve this objective.

Formulation and Solution. *Minimizing the average distance* that students must travel is equivalent to *minimizing the sum of the distances* that individual students must travel. Therefore, adopting the latter objective, this is just a variant of a transportation problem where the unit costs are distances.

Because each school has both a minimum and maximum enrollment, we proceed just as in the Nifty Co. example (Section 5.3) to provide a minimum row and a maximum row at the bottom of both the parameter table and the solution table in the spreadsheet model shown in Figure 5.8. The corresponding constraints are included in the Solver dialogue box along with the usual supply constraints. Clicking on the Solve button then gives the optimal solution shown in the changing cells (D22:F30).

This optimal solution gives the following plan:

Assign tracts 2 and 3 to school 1.

Assign tracts 1, 4, and 7 to school 2.

Assign tracts 6, 8, and 9 to school 3.

Split tract 5, with 350 students assigned to school 1 and 150 students assigned to school 2.

As indicated in cell G31, the total distance traveled to school by all the students is 3,530 miles (an average of 0.872 mile per student).

FIGURE 5.8

A spreadsheet formulation of the Middletown School District problem as a variant of a transportation problem, where rows 3–16 display the parameter table and the changing cells (D22:F30) show the optimal zoning plan obtained by the Solver.

	A	B	C	D	E	F	G	H	I
1		Middletown School District Zoning Problem							
2									
3					Unit Cost (Miles)				
4					Destination (School)				
5				1	2	3	Supply		
6			1	2.2	1.9	2.5	500		
7			2	1.4	1.3	1.7	400		
8			3	0.5	1.8	1.1	450		
9		Source	4	1.2	0.3	2	400		
10		(Tract)	5	0.9	0.7	1	500		
11			6	1.1	1.6	0.6	450		
12			7	2.7	0.7	1.5	450		
13			8	1.8	1.2	0.8	400		
14			9	1.5	1.7	0.7	500		
15		Minimum		1200	1100	500			
16		Maximum		1800	1700	1500			
17									
18									
19					Number of Students				
20					Destination (School)				
21				1	2	3	Totals		Supply
22			1	0	500	0	500	=	500
23			2	400	0	0	400	=	400
24			3	450	0	0	450	=	450
25		Source	4	0	400	0	400	=	400
26		(Tract)	5	350	150	0	500	=	500
27			6	0	0	450	450	=	450
28			7	0	450	0	450	=	450
29			8	0	0	400	400	=	400
30			9	0	0	500	500	=	500
31		Totals		1200	1500	1350	3530	=	Total Miles
32		Minimum		1200	1100	500			
33		Maximum		1800	1700	1500			

Solver Parameters
Set Target Cell: $G$31
Equal To: ○ Max ◉ Min ○ Val
By Changing Cells:
$D$22:$F$30
Subject to the Constraints:
$D$31:$F$31 <= $D$33:$F$33
$D$31:$F$31 >= $D$32:$F$32
$G$22:$G$30 = $I$22:$I$30

Solver Options
☑ Assume Linear Model
☑ Assume Non-Negative

	G
22	=SUM(D22:F22)
23	=SUM(D23:F23)
24	=SUM(D24:F24)
25	=SUM(D25:F25)
26	=SUM(D26:F26)
27	=SUM(D27:F27)
28	=SUM(D28:F28)
29	=SUM(D29:F29)
30	=SUM(D30:F30)
31	=SUMPRODUCT(D6:F14,D22:F30)

	D	E	F
31	=SUM(D22:D30)	=SUM(E22:E30)	=SUM(F22:F30)

Meeting Energy Needs Economically

The Energetic Company needs to make plans for the *energy systems* for a new building.

The *energy needs* in the building fall into three categories: (1) electricity, (2) heating water, and (3) heating space in the building. The daily requirements for these three categories (all measured in the same units) are 20 units, 10 units, and 30 units, respectively.

The three possible *sources of energy* to meet these needs are electricity, natural gas, and a solar heating unit that can be installed on the roof. The size of the roof limits the largest possible solar heater to providing 30 units per day. However, there is no limit to the amount of electricity and natural gas available.

Electricity needs can be met only by purchasing electricity. Both other energy needs (water heating and space heating) can be met by any of the three sources of energy or a combination thereof.

The unit costs for meeting these energy needs from these sources of energy are shown in Table 5.13. The objective of management is to minimize the total cost of meeting all the energy needs.

Formulation and Solution.   Figure 5.9 shows the formulation of this problem as a variant of a transportation problem. The changing cells (D16:F18) show the resulting optimal solution for how many units of each energy source should be used to meet each energy need. The target cell (G19) gives the total cost as $24,000 per day.

Choosing a New Site Location

One of the most important decisions that the management of many companies must face is where to locate a major new facility. The facility might be a new factory, a new distribution center, a new administrative center, or some other building. The new facility might be needed because of expansion. In other cases, the company may be abandoning an unsatisfactory location.

There generally are several attractive potential sites from which to choose. Increasingly, in today's global economy, the potential sites may extend across national borders.

TABLE 5.13   Cost Data for the Energetic Co. Problem

	Unit Cost		
Energy Need:	*Electricity*	*Water Heating*	*Space Heating*
Source of Energy			
Electricity	$400	$500	$600
Natural gas	—	600	500
Solar heater	—	300	400

FIGURE 5.9

A spreadsheet formulation of the Energetic Co. problem as a variant of a transportation problem, where rows 3–9 show the parameter table and the changing cells (D16:F18) give the optimal energy-sourcing plan obtained by the Solver.

	A	B	C	D	E	F	G	H	I
1	Energetic Co. Energy–Sourcing Problem								
2									
3					Unit Cost ($/day)				
4					Destination (Energy Need)				
5				Electricity	Water Heating	Space Heating	Supply		
6			Electricity	$400	$500	$600	unlimited		
7		Source	Natural gas	–	$600	$500	unlimited		
8			Solar heater	–	$300	$400	30		
9		Demand		20	10	30			
10									
11									
12									
13					Daily Energy Use				
14					Destination (Energy Need)				
15				Electricity	Water Heating	Space Heating	Totals		Supply
16			Electricity	20	0	0	20		unlimited
17		Source	Natural gas	0	0	10	10		unlimited
18			Solar heater	0	10	20	30	≤	30
19		Totals		20	10	30	$24,000	=	Total Cost
20				=	=	=			
21		Demand		20	10	30			

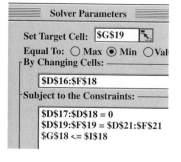

Solver Parameters
Set Target Cell: $G$19
Equal To: ○ Max ● Min ○ Val
By Changing Cells:
$D$16:$F$18
Subject to the Constraints:
$D$17:$D$18 = 0
$D$19:$F$19 = $D$21:$F$21
$G$18 <= $I$18

Solver Options
☑ Assume Linear Model
☑ Assume Non-Negative

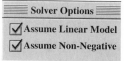

	G
16	=SUM(D16:F16)
17	=SUM(D17:F17)
18	=SUM(D18:F18)
19	=SUMPRODUCT(D6:F8,D16:F18)

	D	E	F
19	=SUM(D16:D18)	=SUM(E16:E18)	=SUM(F16:F18)

There are a number of important factors that go into management's decision. One of these is *shipping costs*. For example, when evaluating a potential site for a new factory, management needs to consider the impact of choosing this site on the cost of shipping goods from *all* the factories (including the new factory at this site) to the distribution centers. By locating the new factory near some distribution centers that are far from all the current factories, the company can obtain low shipping costs for the new factory and, at the same time, substantially reduce the shipping costs from the current factories as well. Management needs to know what the *total* shipping cost would be, following an optimal shipping plan, for each potential site for the new factory.

A similar question may arise regarding the total cost of shipping some raw material from its various sources to all the factories (including the new one) for each potential site for the new factory.

A transportation problem (or a variant) often provides the appropriate way of formulating such questions. Solving this formulation for each potential site then provides key input to management, who must evaluate both this information and other relevant considerations in making its final selection of the site.

The case study presented in the next section illustrates this kind of application.

Review Questions

1. What are the areas of application illustrated in this section for variants of transportation problems?
2. What is the objective of management for the Metro Water District problem?
3. What are the sources and destinations in the formulation of the Northern Airplane Co. production scheduling problem?
4. What plays the role of unit costs in the Middletown School District problem?
5. What is the objective of management for the Energetic Co. problem?

5.5 A Case Study: The Texago Corp. Site Selection Problem

The Texago Corporation is a large, fully integrated petroleum company based in the United States. The company produces most of its oil in its own oil fields and then imports the rest of what it needs from the Middle East. An extensive distribution network is used to transport the oil to the company's refineries and then to transport the petroleum products from the refineries to Texago's distribution centers. The locations of these various facilities are given in Table 5.14.

Texago is continuing to increase its market share for several of its major products. Therefore, management has made the decision to expand its output by building an additional

TABLE 5.14   Location of Texago's Current Facilities

Type of Facility	Locations
Oil fields	1. Several in Texas 2. Several in California 3. Several in Alaska
Refineries	1. Near New Orleans, Louisiana 2. Near Charleston, South Carolina 3. Near Seattle, Washington
Distribution centers	1. Pittsburgh, Pennsylvania 2. Atlanta, Georgia 3. Kansas City, Missouri 4. San Francisco, California

refinery and increasing its imports of crude oil from the Middle East. The crucial remaining decision is where to locate the new refinery.

The addition of the new refinery will have a great impact on the operation of the entire distribution system, including decisions on how much crude oil to transport from each of its sources to each refinery (including the new one) and how much finished product to ship from each refinery to each distribution center. Therefore, the three key factors for management's decision on the location of the new refinery are

1. The cost of transporting the oil from its sources to all the refineries, including the new one.
2. The cost of transporting finished product from all the refineries, including the new one, to the distribution centers.
3. Operating costs for the new refinery, including labor costs, taxes, the cost of needed supplies (other than crude oil), energy costs, the cost of insurance, and so on. (Capitol costs are not a factor since they would be essentially the same at any of the potential sites.)

Management has set up a task force to study the issue of where to locate the new refinery. After considerable investigation, the task force has determined that there are three attractive potential sites. These sites and the main advantages of each are spelled out in Table 5.15.

Gathering the Necessary Data

The task force needs to gather a large amount of data, some of which requires considerable digging, in order to perform the analysis requested by management.

Management wants all the refineries, including the new one, to operate at full capacity. Therefore, the task force begins by determining how much crude oil each refinery would need brought in annually under these conditions. Using units of 1 million barrels, these needed amounts are shown on the left side of Table 5.16. The right side of the table shows the current annual output of crude oil from the various oil fields. These quantities are expected to remain stable for some years to come. Since the refineries need a total of 360

TABLE 5.15   Potential Sites for Texago's New Refineries and Their Main Advantages

Potential Site	Main Advantages
Near Los Angeles, California	1. Near California oil fields. 2. Ready access from Alaska oil fields. 3. Fairly near San Francisco distribution center.
Near Galveston, Texas	1. Near Texas oil fields. 2. Ready access from Middle East imports. 3. Near corporate headquarters.
Near St. Louis, Missouri	1. Low operating costs. 2. Centrally located for distribution centers. 3. Ready access to crude oil via the Mississippi River.

TABLE 5.16   Production Data for Texago Corp.

Refinery	Crude Oil Needed Annually (Million Barrels)	Oil Fields	Crude Oil Produced Annually (Million Barrels)
New Orleans	100	Texas	80
Charleston	60	California	60
Seattle	80	Alaska	100
New one	120		
		Total	240
Total	360	Needed imports = 360 − 240 = 120	

million barrels of crude oil, and the oil fields will produce a total of 240 million barrels, the difference of 120 million barrels will need to be imported from the Middle East.

Since the amounts of crude oil produced or purchased will be the same regardless of which location is chosen for the new refinery, the task force concludes that the associated production or purchase costs (exclusive of shipping costs) are not relevant to the site selection decision. On the other hand, the costs for transporting the crude oil from its source to a refinery are very relevant. These costs are shown in Table 5.17 for both the three current refineries and the three potential sites for the new refinery.

Also very relevant are the costs of shipping the finished product from a refinery to a distribution center. Letting one unit of finished product correspond to a refinery's production from one million barrels of crude oil, these costs are given in Table 5.18. The bottom row of the table shows the number of units of finished product needed by each distribution center.

The final key body of data involves the *operating costs* for a refinery at each potential site. Estimating these costs requires site visits by several members of the task force to collect detailed information about local labor costs, taxes, and so forth. Comparisons then are made with the operating costs of the current refineries to help refine these data. In addition, the task force gathers information on one-time site costs for land, construction, and other expenses and amortizes these costs on an equivalent uniform annual cost basis. This process leads to the estimates shown in Table 5.19.

Analysis (Six Applications of the Transportation Problem)

Armed with these data, the task force now needs to develop the following key financial information for management:

1. Total shipping cost for crude oil with each potential choice of a site for the new refinery.
2. Total shipping cost for finished product with each potential choice of a site for the new refinery.

TABLE 5.17 Cost Data for Shipping Crude Oil to a Texago Refinery

	Cost per Unit Shipped to Refinery or Potential Refinery (Millions of Dollars per Million Barrels)					
	New Orleans	Charleston	Seattle	Los Angeles	Galveston	St. Louis
Source						
Texas	2	4	5	3	1	3
California	4	5	2	1	3	4
Alaska	5	7	3	4	5	6
Middle East	2	2	5	4	3	4

TABLE 5.18 Cost Data for Shipping Finished Product to a Distribution Center

	Cost per Unit Shipped to Distribution Center (Millions of Dollars)			
	Pittsburgh	Atlanta	Kansas City	San Francisco
Refinery				
New Orleans	5	2	6	8
Charleston	6	4	3	5
Seattle	7	8	4	3
Potential Refinery				
Los Angeles	8	6	3	2
Galveston	5	4	3	6
St. Louis	4	3	1	5
Number of units needed	100	80	80	100

TABLE 5.19   Estimated Operating Costs for a Texago Refinery at Each Potential Site

Site	Annual Operating Cost (Millions of Dollars)
Los Angeles	620
Galveston	570
St. Louis	530

FIGURE 5.10

The basic spreadsheet formulation for the Texago transportation problem for shipping crude oil from the oil fields to the refineries, including the new refinery at a site still to be selected.

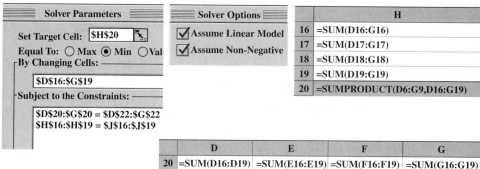

	A	B	C	D	E	F	G	H	I	J
1	Texago Corp. Site–Selection Problem (Shipping to Refineries)									
2										
3				Unit Cost (Millions of Dollars)						
4				Destination (Refinery)						
5				New Orleans	Charleston	Seattle	New Site	Supply		
6			Texas	2	4	5		80		
7		Source	California	4	5	2		60		
8		(Oil Fields)	Alaska	5	7	3		100		
9			Middle East	2	2	5		120		
10		Demand		100	60	80	120			
11										
12										
13				Shipment Quantities (Millions of Barrels)						
14				Destination (Refinery)						
15				New Orleans	Charleston	Seattle	New Site	Totals		Supply
16			Texas	0	0	0	0	0	=	80
17		Source	California	0	0	0	0	0	=	60
18		(Oil Fields)	Alaska	0	0	0	0	0	=	100
19			Middle East	0	0	0	0	0	=	120
20		Totals		0	0	0	0	0	=	Total Cost
21				=	=	=	=			($millions)
22		Demand		100	60	80	120			

Solver Parameters

Set Target Cell: $H$20

Equal To: ○ Max ● Min ○ Val

By Changing Cells:

$D$16:$G$19

Subject to the Constraints:

$D$20:$G$20 = $D$22:$G$22
$H$16:$H$19 = $J$16:$J$19

Solver Options

☑ Assume Linear Model
☑ Assume Non-Negative

	H
16	=SUM(D16:G16)
17	=SUM(D17:G17)
18	=SUM(D18:G18)
19	=SUM(D19:G19)
20	=SUMPRODUCT(D6:G9,D16:G19)

	D	E	F	G
20	=SUM(D16:D19)	=SUM(E16:E19)	=SUM(F16:F19)	=SUM(G16:G19)

For both types of costs, once a site is selected, an optimal shipping plan will be determined and then followed. Therefore, to find either type of cost with a *potential* choice of a site, it is necessary to solve for the optimal shipping plan given that choice and then calculate the corresponding cost.

The task force recognizes that the problem of finding an optimal shipping plan for a given choice of a site is just a transportation problem. In particular, for shipping crude oil, Figure 5.10 shows the spreadsheet model for this transportation problem, where the entries in the parameter table (rows 6–9) come directly from Tables 5.16 and 5.17. The entries for the *New Site* column (cells G6:G9) will come from one of the last three columns of Table 5.17, depending on which potential site currently is being evaluated. At this point, before entering this column and clicking on the Solve button, a trial solution of 0 for each of the shipment quantities has been entered into the changing cells (D16:G19).

FIGURE 5.11

The changing cells (D16:G19) give Texago management an optimal plan for shipping crude oil if Los Angeles is selected as the new site for a refinery in column G of Figure 5.10.

	A	B	C	D	E	F	G	H	I	J
1		Texago Corp. Site–Selection Problem (Shipping to Refineries, Including Los Angeles Site)								
2										
3				Unit Cost (Millions of Dollars)						
4				Destination (Refinery)						
5				New Orleans	Charleston	Seattle	Los Angeles	Supply		
6			Texas	2	4	5	3	80		
7		Source	California	4	5	2	1	60		
8		(Oil Fields)	Alaska	5	7	3	4	100		
9			Middle East	2	2	5	4	120		
10		Demand		100	60	80	120			
11										
12										
13				Shipment Quantities (Millions of Barrels)						
14				Destination (Refinery)						
15				New Orleans	Charleston	Seattle	Los Angeles	Totals		Supply
16			Texas	40	0	0	40	80	=	80
17		Source	California	0	0	0	60	60	=	60
18		(Oil Fields)	Alaska	0	0	80	20	100	=	100
19			Middle East	60	60	0	0	120	=	120
20		Totals		100	60	80	120	820	=	Total Cost
21				=	=	=	=			($millions)
22		Demand		100	60	80	120			

FIGURE 5.12

The changing cells (D16:G19) give Texago management an optimal plan for shipping crude oil if Galveston is selected as the new site for a refinery in column G of Figure 5.10.

	A	B	C	D	E	F	G	H	I	J
1		Texago Corp. Site–Selection Problem (Shipping to Refineries, Including Galveston Site)								
2										
3				Unit Cost (Millions of Dollars)						
4				Destination (Refinery)						
5				New Orleans	Charleston	Seattle	Galveston	Supply		
6			Texas	2	4	5	1	80		
7		Source	California	4	5	2	3	60		
8		(Oil Fields)	Alaska	5	7	3	5	100		
9			Middle East	2	2	5	3	120		
10		Demand		100	60	80	120			
11										
12										
13				Shipment Quantities (Millions of Barrels)						
14				Destination (Refinery)						
15				New Orleans	Charleston	Seattle	Galveston	Totals		Supply
16			Texas	0	0	0	80	80	=	80
17		Source	California	0	0	20	40	60	=	60
18		(Oil Fields)	Alaska	40	0	60	0	100	=	100
19			Middle East	60	60	0	0	120	=	120
20		Totals		100	60	80	120	860	=	Total Cost
21				=	=	=	=			($millions)
22		Demand		100	60	80	120			

These same changing cells in Figures 5.11, 5.12, and 5.13 show the optimal shipping plan for each of the three possible choices of a site. The target cell (H20) gives the resulting total annual shipping cost in millions of dollars. In particular, if Los Angeles were to be chosen as the site for the new refinery (Figure 5.11), the total annual cost of shipping crude oil in the optimal manner would be $820 million. If Galveston were chosen instead (Figure 5.12), this cost would be $860 million, whereas it would be $1.04 billion if St. Louis were chosen (Figure 5.13).

The analysis of the cost of shipping finished product is similar. Figure 5.14 shows the spreadsheet model for this transportation problem, where rows 6–8 come directly from the first three rows of Table 5.18. The *New Site* row would be filled in from one of the next three rows of Table 5.18, depending on which potential site for the new refinery is currently

FIGURE 5.13

The changing cells (D16:G19) give Texago management an optimal plan for shipping crude oil if St. Louis is selected as the new site for a refinery in column G of Figure 5.10.

	A	B	C	D	E	F	G	H	I	J
1		Texago Corp. Site–Selection Problem (Shipping to Refineries, Including St. Louis Site)								
2										
3					Unit Cost (Millions of Dollars)					
4					Destination (Refinery)					
5				New Orleans	Charleston	Seattle	St. Louis	Supply		
6			Texas	2	4	5	3	80		
7		Source	California	4	5	2	4	60		
8		(Oil Fields)	Alaska	5	7	3	6	100		
9			Middle East	2	2	5	4	120		
10		Demand		100	60	80	120			
11										
12										
13					Shipment Quantities (Millions of Barrels)					
14					Destination (Refinery)					
15				New Orleans	Charleston	Seattle	St. Louis	Totals		Supply
16			Texas	40	0	0	40	80	=	80
17		Source	California	0	0	0	60	60	=	60
18		(Oil Fields)	Alaska	0	0	80	20	100	=	100
19			Middle East	60	60	0	0	120	=	120
20		Totals		100	60	80	120	1,040	=	Total Cost
21				=	=	=	=			($millions)
22		Demand		100	60	80	120			

FIGURE 5.14

The basic spreadsheet formulation for the Texago transportation problem for shipping finished product from the refineries (including the new one at a site still to be selected) to the distribution centers.

	A	B	C	D	E	F	G	H	I	J
1		Texago Corp. Site–Selection Problem (Shipping to D.C's)								
2										
3					Unit Cost (Millions of Dollars)					
4					Destination (Distribution Center)					
5				Pittsburgh	Atlanta	Kansas City	San Francisco	Supply		
6			New Orleans	5	2	6	8	100		
7		Source	Charleston	6	4	3	5	60		
8		(Refinery)	Seattle	7	8	4	3	80		
9			New Site					120		
10		Demand		100	80	80	100			
11										
12										
13					Shipment Quantities (Million Barrel Equivalents)					
14					Destination (Distribution Center)					
15				Pittsburgh	Atlanta	Kansas City	San Francisco	Totals		Supply
16			New Orleans	0	0	0	0	0	=	100
17		Source	Charleston	0	0	0	0	0	=	60
18		(Refinery)	Seattle	0	0	0	0	0	=	80
19			New Site	0	0	0	0	0	=	120
20		Totals		0	0	0	0	0	=	Total Cost
21				=	=	=	=			($millions)
22		Demand		100	80	80	100			

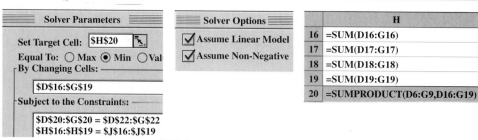

Solver Parameters
Set Target Cell: $H$20
Equal To: ○ Max ● Min ○ Val
By Changing Cells:
$D$16:$G$19
Subject to the Constraints:
$D$20:$G$20 = $D$22:$G$22
$H$16:$H$19 = $J$16:$J$19

Solver Options
☑ Assume Linear Model
☑ Assume Non-Negative

	H
16	=SUM(D16:G16)
17	=SUM(D17:G17)
18	=SUM(D18:G18)
19	=SUM(D19:G19)
20	=SUMPRODUCT(D6:G9,D16:G19)

	D	E	F	G
20	=SUM(D16:D19)	=SUM(E16:E19)	=SUM(F16:F19)	=SUM(G16:G19)

FIGURE 5.15

*The changing cells
(D16:G19) give Texago
management an optimal plan
for shipping finished product
if Los Angeles is selected as
the new site for a refinery in
rows 9 and 19 of Figure 5.14.*

	A	B	C	D	E	F	G	H	I	J
1		Texago Corp. Site–Selection Problem (Shipping to D.C's When Choose Los Angeles Site)								
2										
3				Unit Cost (Millions of Dollars)						
4				Destination (Distribution Center)						
5				Pittsburgh	Atlanta	Kansas City	San Francisco	Supply		
6			New Orleans	5	2	6	8	100		
7		Source	Charleston	6	4	3	5	60		
8		(Refinery)	Seattle	7	8	4	3	80		
9			Los Angeles	8	6	3	2	120		
10		Demand		100	80	80	100			
11										
12										
13				Shipment Quantities (Million Barrel Equivalents)						
14				Destination (Distribution Center)						
15				Pittsburgh	Atlanta	Kansas City	San Francisco	Totals		Supply
16			New Orleans	20	80	0	0	100	=	100
17		Source	Charleston	60	0	0	0	60	=	60
18		(Refinery)	Seattle	20	0	0	60	80	=	80
19			Los Angeles	0	0	80	40	120	=	120
20		Totals		100	80	80	100	1,260	=	Total Cost
21				=	=	=	=			($millions)
22		Demand		100	80	80	100			

FIGURE 5.16

*The changing cells
(D16:G19) give Texago
management an optimal plan
for shipping finished product
if Galveston is selected as the
new site for a refinery in rows
9 and 19 of Figure 5.14.*

	A	B	C	D	E	F	G	H	I	J
1		Texago Corp. Site–Selection Problem (Shipping to D.C's When Choose Galveston Site)								
2										
3				Unit Cost (Millions of Dollars)						
4				Destination (Distribution Center)						
5				Pittsburgh	Atlanta	Kansas City	San Francisco	Supply		
6			New Orleans	5	2	6	8	100		
7		Source	Charleston	6	4	3	5	60		
8		(Refinery)	Seattle	7	8	4	3	80		
9			Galveston	5	4	3	6	120		
10		Demand		100	80	80	100			
11										
12										
13				Shipment Quantities (Million Barrel Equivalents)						
14				Destination (Distribution Center)						
15				Pittsburgh	Atlanta	Kansas City	San Francisco	Totals		Supply
16			New Orleans	20	80	0	0	100	=	100
17		Source	Charleston	0	0	40	20	60	=	60
18		(Refinery)	Seattle	0	0	0	80	80	=	80
19			Galveston	80	0	40	0	120	=	120
20		Totals		100	80	80	100	1,240	=	Total Cost
21				=	=	=	=			($millions)
22		Demand		100	80	80	100			

under evaluation. Since the units for finished product leaving a refinery are equivalent to the units for crude oil coming in, the supplies in cells H6:H9 and J16:J19 come from the left side of Table 5.16.

The changing cells (D16:G19) in Figures 5.15, 5.16, and 5.17 show the optimal plan for shipping finished product for each of the sites being considered for the new refinery. The target cell (H20) in Figure 5.15 indicates that the resulting total annual cost for shipping finished product if the new refinery were in Los Angeles is $1.26 billion. Similarly, this total cost would be $1.24 billion if Galveston were the chosen site (Figure 5.16) and $1.08 billion if St. Louis were chosen (Figure 5.17).

The Message to Management

The task force now has completed its financial analysis of the three alternative sites for the new refinery. Table 5.20 shows all the major *variable* costs (costs that vary with the decision) on an annual basis that would result from each of the three possible choices of the site. The second column summarizes what the total annual cost of shipping crude oil to all refineries (including the new one) would be for each alternative (as already given in Figures 5.11, 5.12, and 5.13). The third column repeats the data in Figures 5.15, 5.16, and 5.17 on the total annual cost of shipping finished product from the refineries to the distribution centers. The fourth column shows the estimated operating costs for a refinery at each potential site, as first given in Table 5.19.

Adding across these three columns gives the total variable cost for each alternative.

Conclusion: From a purely financial viewpoint, St. Louis is the best site for the new refinery. This site would save the company about $20 million annually as compared to the Galveston alternative and about $50 million as compared to the Los Angeles alternative.

However, as with any site selection decision, management must consider a wide variety of factors, including some nonfinancial ones. (For example, remember that one important advantage of the Galveston site is that it is close to corporate headquarters.) Furthermore, if ways can be found to reduce some of the costs in Table 5.20 for either the Los Angeles or Galveston sites, this might change the financial evaluation substantially. Management also must consider whether there are any cost trends or trends in the marketplace that might alter the picture in the future.

After careful consideration, Texago management chooses the St. Louis site.

FIGURE 5.17

The changing cells (D16:G19) give Texago management an optimal plan for shipping finished product if St. Louis is selected as the new site for a refinery in rows 9 and 19 of Figure 5.14.

	A	B	C	D	E	F	G	H	I	J
1		Texago Corp. Site–Selection Problem (Shipping to D.C's When Choose St. Louis Site)								
2										
3				Unit Cost (Millions of Dollars)						
4				Destination (Distribution Center)						
5				Pittsburgh	Atlanta	Kansas City	San Francisco	Supply		
6			New Orleans	5	2	6	8	100		
7		Source	Charleston	6	4	3	5	60		
8		(Refinery)	Seattle	7	8	4	3	80		
9			St. Louis	4	3	1	5	120		
10		Demand		100	80	80	100			
11										
12										
13				Shipment Quantities (Million Barrel Equivalents)						
14				Destination (Distribution Center)						
15				Pittsburgh	Atlanta	Kansas City	San Francisco	Totals		Supply
16			New Orleans	20	80	0	0	100	=	100
17		Source	Charleston	40	0	0	20	60	=	60
18		(Refinery)	Seattle	0	0	0	80	80	=	80
19			St. Louis	40	0	80	0	120	=	120
20		Totals		100	80	80	100	1,080	=	Total Cost
21				=	=	=	=			($millions)
22		Demand		100	80	80	100			

TABLE 5.20 **Annual Variable Costs Resulting from the Choice of Each Site for the New Texago Refinery**

Site	Total Cost of Shipping Crude Oil	Total Cost of Shipping Finished Product	Operating Cost for New Refinery	Total Variable Cost
Los Angeles	$820 million	$1.26 billion	$620 million	$2.7 billion
Galveston	860 million	1.24 billion	570 million	2.67 billion
St. Louis	1.04 billion	1.08 billion	530 million	2.65 billion

Review Questions

1. What are the three key factors for management's decision on the location of the new refinery?
2. Why do shipping costs to and from the *current* refineries need to be considered along with those for the new refinery?
3. Why did the Texago task force find it necessary to solve six transportation problems instead of just one?
4. What else must Texago management consider in addition to the financial analysis based on solving six transportation problems?

5.6 Characteristics of Assignment Problems

We now turn to another special type of linear programming problem called *assignment problems*. As the name suggests, this kind of problem involves making *assignments*. Frequently, these are assignments of people to jobs. Thus, many applications of the assignment problem involve aiding managers in matching up their personnel with tasks to be performed. Other applications might instead involve assigning machines, vehicles, or plants to tasks.

We begin with an example.

An Example: The Sellmore Company Problem

The marketing manager of the Sellmore Company will be holding the company's annual *sales conference* soon for sales regional managers and personnel. To assist in the administration of the conference, he is hiring four temporary employees (Ann, Ian, Joan, and Sean), where each will handle one of the following four tasks:

1. Word processing of written presentations.
2. Computer graphics for both oral and written presentations.
3. Preparation of conference packets, including copying and organizing of written materials.
4. Handling of advance and on-site registrations for the conference.

He now needs to decide which person to assign to each task.

Although each temporary employee has at least the minimal background necessary to perform any of the four tasks, they differ considerably in how efficiently they can handle the different types of work. Table 5.21 shows how many hours each would need for each task. The rightmost column gives the hourly wage based on background for each.

Formulation of a Spreadsheet Model. Figure 5.18 shows a spreadsheet model for this problem. Table 5.21 is entered at the top. Combining these required times and wages (see the equations for cells D15:G18 at the bottom), rows 15–18 give the cost for each possible assignment of a temporary employee to a task. This *cost table* is just the way that any assignment problem is displayed. The objective is to determine which assignments should be made to minimize the sum of the associated costs.

TABLE 5.21 **Data for the Sellmore Co. Problem**

Temporary Employee	Required Time per Task (Hours)				Hourly Wage
	Word Processing	Graphics	Packets	Registrations	
Ann	35	41	27	40	$14
Ian	47	45	32	51	$12
Joan	39	56	36	43	$13
Sean	32	51	25	46	$15

FIGURE 5.18

A spreadsheet formulation of the Sellmore Co. problem as an assignment problem, where rows 12–19 show the cost table and rows 22–31 display the solution table after using the Excel Solver to obtain an optimal plan for assigning the people to the tasks. Both the formulas for the output cells and the specifications needed to set up the Solver are given at the bottom.

	A	B	C	D	E	F	G	H	I	J
1	Sellmore Co. Assignment Problem									
2										
3					Required Time (Hours)					
4					Task			Hourly		
5				Word Processing	Graphics	Packets	Registrations	Wage		
6			Ann	35	41	27	40	$14		
7		Assignee	Ian	47	45	32	51	$12		
8			Joan	39	56	36	43	$13		
9			Sean	32	51	25	46	$15		
10										
11										
12					Cost					
13					Task					
14				Word Processing	Graphics	Packets	Registrations	Supply		
15			Ann	$490	$574	$378	$560	1		
16		Assignee	Ian	$564	$540	$384	$612	1		
17			Joan	$507	$728	$468	$559	1		
18			Sean	$480	$765	$375	$690	1		
19		Demand		1	1	1	1			
20										
21										
22					Assignments					
23					Task					
24				Word Processing	Graphics	Packets	Registrations	Totals		Supply
25			Ann	0	0	1	0	1	=	1
26		Assignee	Ian	0	1	0	0	1	=	1
27			Joan	0	0	0	1	1	=	1
28			Sean	1	0	0	0	1	=	1
29		Totals		1	1	1	1	$1,957	=	Total Cost
30				=	=	=	=			
31		Demand		1	1	1	1			

Solver Parameters

Set Target Cell: $H$29

Equal To: ○ Max ◉ Min ○ Val

By Changing Cells:

$D$25:$G$28

Subject to the Constraints:

$D$29:$G$29 = $D$31:$G$31
$H$25:$H$28 = $J$25:$J$28

Solver Options

☑ Assume Linear Model
☑ Assume Non-Negative

	H
25	=SUM(D25:G25)
26	=SUM(D26:G26)
27	=SUM(D27:G27)
28	=SUM(D28:G28)
29	=SUMPRODUCT(D15:G18,D25:G28)

	D	E	F	G
15	=D6*$H6	=E6*$H6	=F6*$H6	=G6*$H6
16	=D7*$H7	=E7*$H7	=F7*$H7	=G7*$H7
17	=D8*$H8	=E8*$H8	=F8*$H8	=G8*$H8
18	=D9*$H9	=E9*$H9	=F9*$H9	=G9*$H9
29	=SUM(D25:D28)	=SUM(E25:E28)	=SUM(F25:F28)	=SUM(G25:G28)

The supplies of 1 in cells H15:H18 and J25:J28 indicate that each person (assignee) listed in column C must perform exactly one task. The demands of 1 in rows 19 and 31 indicate that each task must be performed by exactly one person. These requirements then are specified in the constraints given in the Solver dialogue box.

Each of the changing cells (D25:G28) is given a value of 1 when the corresponding assignment is being made, and a value of 0 otherwise. Therefore, the Excel equation for the target cell, H29 = SUMPRODUCT (D15:G18, D25:G28), gives the total cost for the assignments being made. The Solver dialogue box specifies that the objective is to minimize this target cell.

The changing cells in Figure 5.18 show the optimal solution obtained after clicking on the Solve button. This solution is

Assign Ann to prepare conference packets.

Assign Ian to do the computer graphics.

Assign Joan to handle registrations.

Assign Sean to do the word processing.

The total cost given in cell H29 is $1,957.

The Model for Assignment Problems

Any assignment problem can be described in the following general terms. Given a set of **tasks** to be performed and a set of **assignees** who are available to perform these tasks, the problem is to determine which assignee should be assigned to each task.

To fit the model for an assignment problem, the following assumptions need to be satisfied:

1. The number of assignees and the number of tasks are the same.
2. Each assignee is to be assigned to exactly *one* task.
3. Each task is to be performed by exactly *one* assignee.
4. There is a cost associated with each combination of an assignee performing a task.
5. The objective is to determine how all the assignments should be made to minimize the total cost.

The first three assumptions are fairly restrictive. Many potential applications do not quite fit these assumptions. However, these *variants* of assignment problems still can be solved by the Excel Solver, as we will describe in Section 5.7.

When the assumptions are satisfied, all that needs to be done to formulate a problem as an assignment problem is to (1) identify the assignees and tasks and (2) construct a **cost table** that gives the cost associated with each combination of an assignee performing a task. After displaying this formulation on a spreadsheet, as illustrated in Figure 5.18, it can be solved by the Excel Solver.

The Network Representation of an Assignment Problem

In addition to a cost table, the *network representation* provides an alternative way of displaying an assignment problem. Figure 5.19 shows the network representation of the Sellmore Co. assignment problem, where all the assignees are lined up in order on the left and all the tasks are lined up in order on the right. The arrows show the possible assignments, where exactly four arrows are to be chosen, with one from each assignee and with one into each task. The number next to each arrow gives the cost if that particular assignment is chosen.

This network representation provides a way of visualizing an assignment problem graphically. You also will see in the next chapter that this representation shows the relationship between assignment problems and other linear programming problems of the *distribution-network type*.

The Assignment Problem Is a Special Type of Transportation Problem

Did you happen to notice that the network representation in Figure 5.19 is strikingly similar to the network representation for a transportation problem shown in Figure 5.3? Look and see.

This similarity is no coincidence. The assignment problem is, in fact, just a special type of transportation problem where the *sources* now are *assignees* and the *destinations* now are *tasks*. Furthermore, as illustrated by the Sellmore Co. assignment problem in Figure 5.18, every source has a supply of 1 (since each assignee is to be assigned to exactly one task) and every destination has a demand of 1 (since each task is to be performed by exactly one assignee).

Therefore, all the characteristics of transportation problems described in Section 5.2 also apply to assignment problems.

Solving Assignment Problems

The Excel Solver uses the simplex method to solve any kind of linear programming problem, including both transportation problems and assignment problems and their variants. This works fine for problems of the size considered in this book (or even considerably larger).

However, as discussed in Section 5.2, either the *transportation simplex method* or the *network simplex method* provides a far more efficient way of solving big transportation problems. Consequently, since the assignment problem is a special type of transportation problem, these same algorithms can be used to solve big assignment problems quickly.

FIGURE 5.19

The network representation of the Sellmore Co. assignment problem shows all the possible assignments and their costs graphically.

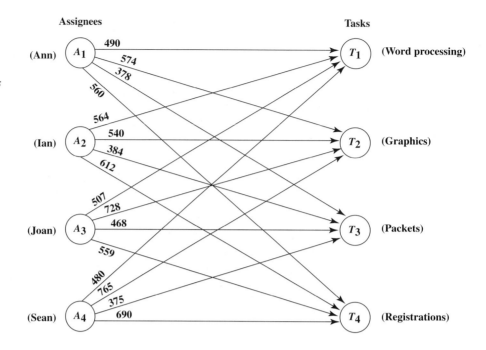

Nevertheless, even these special algorithms do not provide the fastest way of solving assignment problems. There are much faster algorithms available that have been designed specifically to solve assignment problems. The most famous of these is called the **Hungarian method.** In practice, one of these special algorithms normally would be used to solve large assignment problems. Although the Excel Solver does not have *special-purpose algorithms* such as the Hungarian method for efficiently solving special types of linear programming problems, other linear programming software packages are available that do.

Review Questions

1. Give a one-sentence description of assignment problems.
2. What assumptions about *assignees* and *tasks* need to hold to be an assignment problem?
3. What needs to be done to formulate a problem as an assignment problem?
4. What are the sources, destinations, supplies, and demands when an assignment problem is described as a special kind of transportation problem?
5. Name an algorithm that has been designed specifically just to solve assignment problems very quickly.

5.7 Modeling Variants of Assignment Problems

Variants of assignments problems frequently arise because they have one or more features that do not quite fit all the assumptions enumerated in the preceding section for the model of an assignment problem. The features we will consider are the following:

1. Certain assignees are unable to perform certain tasks.
2. Although each assignee will perform exactly one task, there are more tasks than assignees, so some tasks will not be done.
3. Although each task will be performed by exactly one assignee, there are more assignees than tasks, so some assignees will not perform any task.
4. Each assignee can be assigned to perform more than one task simultaneously.
5. Each task can be performed jointly by more than one assignee.

TABLE 5.22   **Materials-Handling Cost Data for the Job Shop Co. Problem**

		Cost per Hour				
Location:		*1*	*2*	*3*	*4*	*5*
Machine						
	1	$13	$16	$12	$14	$15
	2	15	—	13	20	16
	3	4	7	10	6	7

For each of these features, there is a clever way of reformulating the problem to make it fit the format for an assignment problem, which then enables using an extremely efficient special-purpose algorithm (such as the *Hungarian method*). However, this isn't necessary except on problems that are much larger than any considered in this book. Therefore, we instead will formulate a spreadsheet model in the most straightforward way and solve it with the Excel Solver.

Three examples are presented below to illustrate the above features. The first example focuses on features 1 and 2. The second combines feature 4 with a variation of feature 3. The third deals with feature 5.

To illuminate the close relationships between transportation problems and assignment problems, the second and third examples are based on earlier examples of variants of transportation problems.

Example 1: Assigning Machines to Locations

The Job Shop Company has purchased three new machines of different types. There are five available locations in the shop where a machine could be installed. Some of these locations are more desirable than others for particular machines because of their proximity to work centers that will have a heavy work flow to and from these machines. (There will be no work flow *between* the new machines.) Therefore, the objective is to assign the new machines to the available locations to minimize the total cost of materials handling. The estimated cost per hour of materials handling involving each of the machines is given in Table 5.22 for the respective locations. Location 2 is not considered suitable for machine 2, so no cost is given for this case.

Formulation of a Spreadsheet Model.   As it stands, this is almost an assignment problem, since the machines can be viewed as *assignees* to be assigned to locations as the *tasks*. However, it does not quite qualify because assumption 1 for the assignment problem model is violated (we have two more locations than machines), as are assumption 3 (two locations will not be filled by a machine) and assumption 4 (we do not have a cost associated with assigning machine 2 to location 2).

Figure 5.20 shows a spreadsheet model for this variant of an assignment problem, where the cost table is at the top and the solution table is below. Because location 2 cannot be used for machine 2, the Solver dialogue box includes the constraint that E17 = 0. The usual supply constraints, I16:I18 = K16:K18, ensure that each machine will be assigned to exactly one location. The fact that two locations will not be used is taken into account by using a ≤ sign in the demand constraints, D19:H19 ≤ D21:H21.

The changing cells (D16:H18) with a value of 1 show the assignments being made in the optimal solution after clicking on the Solve button. Since none of these cells for locations 2 and 5 have a value of 1, a machine will not be placed in either of these locations. The target cell (I19) indicates that the total cost for this optimal solution is $31 per hour.

Example 2: Assigning Plants to Products

Reconsider Example 1 in Section 5.3, where the Better Products Co. needs to assign three plants to produce four new products. The relevant data are given in Table 5.6.

As described in Section 5.3, management had permitted *product splitting* (where the same product is produced in more than one plant). However, there are some *hidden costs* associated with product splitting that are not reflected in Table 5.6, including extra setup,

FIGURE 5.20

A spreadsheet formulation of the Job Shop Co. problem as a variant of an assignment problem, where rows 3–9 display the cost table and the changing cells (D16:H18) show the optimal plan obtained by the Solver for assigning the machines to the locations.

	A	B	C	D	E	F	G	H	I	J	K
1	Job Shop Co. Machine–Location Problem										
2											
3						Cost ($/hour)					
4						Task (Location)					
5				1	2	3	4	5	Supply		
6		Assignee	1	$13	$16	$12	$14	$15	1		
7		(Machine)	2	$15	–	$13	$20	$16	1		
8			3	$4	$7	$10	$6	$7	1		
9		Demand		1	1	1	1	1			
10											
11											
12											
13						Assignments					
14						Task (Location)					
15				1	2	3	4	5	Totals		Supply
16		Assignee	1	0	0	0	1	0	1	=	1
17		(Machine)	2	0	0	1	0	0	1	=	1
18			3	1	0	0	0	0	1	=	1
19		Totals		1	0	1	1	0	$31	=	Total Cost
20				≤	≤	≤	≤	≤			
21		Demand		1	1	1	1	1			

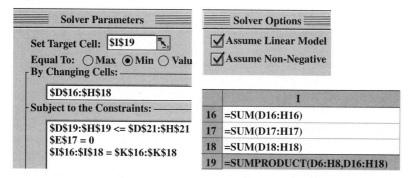

Solver Parameters
Set Target Cell: $I$19
Equal To: ○ Max ● Min ○ Valu
By Changing Cells:
$D$16:$H$18
Subject to the Constraints:
$D$19:$H$19 <= $D$21:$H$21
$E$17 = 0
$I$16:$I$18 = $K$16:$K$18

Solver Options
☑ Assume Linear Model
☑ Assume Non-Negative

	I
16	=SUM(D16:H16)
17	=SUM(D17:H17)
18	=SUM(D18:H18)
19	=SUMPRODUCT(D6:H8,D16:H18)

	D	E	F	G	H
19	=SUM(D16:D18)	=SUM(E16:E18)	=SUM(F16:F18)	=SUM(G16:G18)	=SUM(H16:H18)

distribution, and administration costs. Therefore, management now has decided to have the problem analyzed again under the additional restriction that *product splitting is prohibited.*

> *New Problem Statement:* Given the data in Table 5.6, minimize the total cost of assigning each plant to at least one new product where each product is to be produced in only one plant (no product splitting). Since there are three plants and four new products, two plants will produce one new product and a third plant will produce two. Only plants 1 and 2 have the capacity to produce two.

Formulation of a Spreadsheet Model.   Since we want to assign plants to products, the plants can be viewed as *assignees* and the products as the *tasks* to be performed for this variant of an assignment problem. Figure 5.21 shows the resulting spreadsheet model.

The data from Table 5.6 are given at the top. However, the unit costs given in cells D6:G8 are not the appropriate costs for the cost table for a variant of an assignment problem. To construct the appropriate cost table, we must determine each cost associated with assigning a plant to *all* the required production of a product. The corresponding unit cost shown in rows 6–8 is only the cost of producing one unit rather than the entire required (daily) production given in row 9. Therefore, we must multiply this unit cost by the required (daily) production to obtain the total (daily) cost of the assignment. For example, consider the assignment of plant 1 to product 1.

FIGURE 5.21

A spreadsheet formulation of the Better Products Co. problem as a variant of an assignment problem, where rows 12–18 show the cost table and the changing cells (D24:G26) display the optimal production plan obtained by the Solver.

Better Products Co. Production–Planning Problem (Revised)

Unit Cost

			Product			
		1	2	3	4	
	1	$41	$27	$28	$24	
Plant	2	$40	$29	–	$23	
	3	$37	$30	$27	$21	
Required Production		20	30	30	40	

Cost ($/day)

		Task (Product)				
		1	2	3	4	Supply
Assignee	1	$820	$810	$840	$960	2
(Plant)	2	$800	$870	–	$920	2
	3	$740	$900	$810	$840	1
Demand		1	1	1	1	

Assignments

		Task (Product)						
		1	2	3	4	Totals		Supply
Assignee	1	0	1	1	0	2	≤	2
(Plant)	2	1	0	0	0	1	≤	2
	3	0	0	0	1	1	=	1
Totals		1	1	1	1	$3,290	=	Total Cost
		=	=	=	=			
Demand		1	1	1	1			

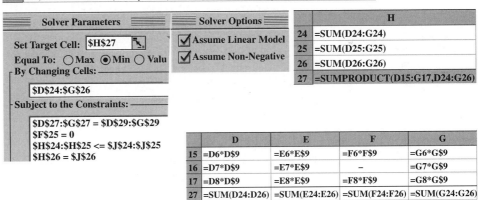

Solver Parameters

Set Target Cell: $H$27

Equal To: ○ Max ● Min ○ Valu

By Changing Cells:

$D$24:$G$26

Subject to the Constraints:

$D$27:$G$27 = $D$29:$G$29
$F$25 = 0
$H$24:$H$25 <= $J$24:$J$25
$H$26 = $J$26

Solver Options

☑ Assume Linear Model
☑ Assume Non-Negative

	H
24	=SUM(D24:G24)
25	=SUM(D25:G25)
26	=SUM(D26:G26)
27	=SUMPRODUCT(D15:G17,D24:G26)

	D	E	F	G
15	=D6*D$9	=E6*E$9	=F6*F$9	=G6*G$9
16	=D7*D$9	=E7*E$9	–	=G7*G$9
17	=D8*D$9	=E8*E$9	=F8*F$9	=G8*G$9
27	=SUM(D24:D26)	=SUM(E24:E26)	=SUM(F24:F26)	=SUM(G24:G26)

Cost of plant 1 producing one unit of product 1   = $41

Required (daily) production of product 1   = 20 units

Total (daily) cost of assigning plant 1 to product 1 = 20 ($41)

= $820

Cells D15:G17 give the total (daily) assignment costs, calculated in this way (see the equations at the bottom of the figure), for each combination of assigning a plant to a product.

Since plant 2 cannot produce product 3, the Solver dialogue box includes the constraint that F25 = 0. Either plant 1 or plant 2 (but not both) needs to be chosen to produce a second product, so these two plants are given a supply of 2 in cells H15:H16 and J24:J25. A ≤ sign is then used for the corresponding supply constraints, H24:H25 ≤ J24:J25. However, the supply constraint for plant 3 and the demand constraints are the usual one for an assignment problem.

After clicking on the Solve button, the optimal solution shown in the changing cells (D24:G26) is obtained, namely, plant 1 produces products 2 and 3, plant 2 produces product 1, and plant 3 produces product 4. The target cell (H27) gives the total daily cost of $3,290 for this production plan.

It is interesting to compare this solution with the one given in cells D15:G17 of Figure 5.4 when product splitting was permitted. Note that the assignments for plants 2 and 3 in Figure 5.4 are quite different than here. The total cost calculated for the production plan shown in that figure is $3,260 per day, or $30 per day less than for the plan in Figure 5.21.

However, the formulation of the original problem (product splitting permitted) as a variant of a transportation problem does not take into account *hidden costs* of product splitting (extra setup, distribution, and administration costs), which probably are considerably more than $30 per day. Therefore, management adopted the production plan based on this new formulation (product splitting prohibited) as a variant of an assignment problem.

Example 3: Designing School Attendance Zones

Now refer back to Section 5.4 for the problem faced by the management of the Middletown School District in designing school attendance zones. Table 5.12 gives the data for the problem and Figure 5.8 shows its formulation as a variant of a transportation problem.

The optimal solution obtained from this formulation has two problems that concern management. One is that this solution splits tract 5 between two schools (schools 1 and 2). Each tract is a cohesive neighborhood that has always stayed together in attending the same school prior to high school. The school district superintendent and the school board are in agreement that it would be much better to continue to keep each neighborhood (including tract 5) together in assigning it to a single school. The second problem with the solution is that it assigns the smallest number of students (1,200) to the school with the largest capacity (school 1, with a capacity of 1,800 students). Although this is marginally acceptable (the school board has chosen 1,200 as the minimum number of students it would allow to be assigned to school 1), a more even allocation of students to the schools would be preferable.

Therefore, the school district management has decided to prohibit splitting any tract between schools. To provide a relatively even allocation of students to schools, management also will require that exactly three tracts be assigned to each school.

New Problem Statement: Given the data in Table 5.12, minimize the total distance that all students must travel to school when each tract is assigned entirely to one school (no tract splitting) and each school is assigned exactly three tracts.

Formulation of a Spreadsheet Model.   Since tracts are being assigned to schools, this problem can be interpreted as a variant of an assignment problem where the tracts are the *assignees* and the schools are the *tasks*. It is only a variant because each school is to be assigned exactly three tracts, whereas assumption 3 for the assignment problem model specifies that each task is to be performed by exactly *one* assignee. Therefore, in the spreadsheet model shown in Figure 5.22, each task (school) is given a demand of 3 rather than 1. Otherwise, the constraints for this model are the same as for an assignment problem.

The objective for an assignment problem is to minimize the total cost of all the assignments made, but now *cost* is being measured in terms of the total *distance* that students travel. Therefore, the cost of assigning any tract to a particular school is the number of students in that tract *times* the distance to that school per student, where both of these quantities are given in the top left-hand table in Figure 5.22. To illustrate, consider the cost of assigning tract 1 to school 1.

Distance from tract 1 to school 1   = 2.2 miles

Number of students in tract 1   = 500

Cost of assigning tract 1 to school 1 = 500(2.2 miles)

= 1,100 miles

The top right-hand table shows the costs calculated in this way for all the combinations of assignees and tasks, using the equations given for cells K6:M14.

FIGURE 5.22

In contrast to Figure 5.8, tract splitting is no longer allowed, so the Middletown School District problem becomes a variant of an assignment problem. The cost table is in columns I to N and the optimal zoning plan found by the Solver is given by the changing cells (D21:F29).

Middletown School District Zoning Problem (Revised)

		Distance (Miles)						Cost (Miles)			
		School			Number of			Task (School)			
		1	2	3	Students			1	2	3	Supply
	1	2.2	1.9	2.5	500		1	1100	950	1250	1
	2	1.4	1.3	1.7	400		2	560	520	680	1
	3	0.5	1.8	1.1	450		3	225	810	495	1
	4	1.2	0.3	2.0	400	Assignee	4	480	120	800	1
Tract	5	0.9	0.7	1.0	500	(Tract)	5	450	350	500	1
	6	1.1	1.6	0.6	450		6	495	720	270	1
	7	2.7	0.7	1.5	450		7	1215	315	675	1
	8	1.8	1.2	0.8	400		8	720	480	320	1
	9	1.5	1.7	0.7	500		9	750	850	350	1
						Demand		3	3	3	

Assignments

		Task (School)					
		1	2	3	Totals		Supply
	1	0	1	0	1	=	1
	2	1	0	0	1	=	1
	3	1	0	0	1	=	1
Assignee	4	0	1	0	1	=	1
(Tract)	5	1	0	0	1	=	1
	6	0	0	1	1	=	1
	7	0	1	0	1	=	1
	8	0	0	1	1	=	1
	9	0	0	1	1	=	1
Totals		3	3	3	3560	=	Total Miles
		=	=	=			
Demand		3	3	3			

Solver Parameters

Set Target Cell: $G$30

Equal To: ○ Max ● Min ○ Valu

By Changing Cells:

$D$21:$F$29

Subject to the Constraints:

$D$30:$F$30 = $D$32:$F$32
$G$21:$G$29 = $I$21:$I$29

Solver Options

☑ Assume Linear Model
☑ Assume Non-Negative

	K	L	M
6	=D6*$G6	=E6*$G6	=F6*$G6
7	=D7*$G7	=E7*$G7	=F7*$G7
8	=D8*$G8	=E8*$G8	=F8*$G8
9	=D9*$G9	=E9*$G9	=F9*$G9
10	=D10*$G10	=E10*$G10	=F10*$G10
11	=D11*$G11	=E11*$G11	=F11*$G11
12	=D12*$G12	=E12*$G12	=F12*$G12
13	=D13*$G13	=E13*$G13	=F13*$G13
14	=D14*$G14	=E14*$G14	=F14*$G14

	G
21	=SUM(D21:F21)
22	=SUM(D22:F22)
23	=SUM(D23:F23)
24	=SUM(D24:F24)
25	=SUM(D25:F25)
26	=SUM(D26:F26)
27	=SUM(D27:F27)
28	=SUM(D28:F28)
29	=SUM(D29:F29)
30	=SUMPRODUCT(K6:M14,D21:F29)

	D	E	F
30	=SUM(D21:D29)	=SUM(E21:E29)	=SUM(F21:F29)

The changing cells (D21:F29) show the optimal assignments of tracts to schools obtained by clicking on the Solve button. As indicated in the target cell (G30), the resulting total distance traveled to school by all the students is 3,560 miles This amounts to an average of 0.879 mile per student.

This plan is very similar to the one obtained in Section 5.4 (see Figure 5.8) when tract splitting was permitted. The only difference is that the earlier plan splits tract 5, with 150 of its 500 students assigned to school 2 rather than to school 1, thereby reducing the distance traveled to school for each of these 150 students from 0.9 mile to 0.7 mile. However, the school district management feels that this small saving in distance traveled does not justify separating these 150 students from their neighbors who had always gone to school with them. Therefore, management adopted the new plan.

As this example and the preceding one illustrate, management often needs to have modifications made in the original model of the problem to better consider managerial concerns.

Review Questions

1. When formulating a spreadsheet model for a variant of an assignment problem where certain assignees are unable to perform certain tasks, how is this feature formulated in the model?

2. If an assignee will perform more than one task, how is this feature formulated in the spreadsheet model?

3. If a task will be performed jointly by more than one assignee, how is this feature formulated in the spreadsheet model?

5.8 Summary

Transportation problems and assignment problems (and their variants) are special types of linear programming problems that have a variety of important applications.

A transportation problem is concerned (literally or figuratively) with distributing a commodity from its *sources* to some *destinations*. Each source has a fixed supply and each destination has a fixed demand for the commodity. A basic assumption is that the cost of distribution from each source to each destination is directly proportional to the amount distributed. Formulating a transportation problem requires constructing a *parameter table* that gives the unit costs of distribution, the supplies, and the demands.

Given a set of *tasks* to be performed and a set of *assignees* who are available to perform the tasks (one assignee per task), an assignment problem deals with the question of which assignee should be assigned to each task so as to minimize the total cost of performing all the tasks. The assignees can be people, machines, vehicles, plants, and so on, so there are many applications. The formulation of the problem requires constructing a *cost table* that gives the cost for each possible assignment of an assignee to a task.

A variety of features that do not quite fit either the transportation problem format or the assignment problem format also can be readily formulated in a spreadsheet model.

The overriding goal of this chapter has been to enable you to recognize when a problem you might face as a future manager can be formulated and analyzed as a transportation or assignment problem, or as a variant of one of these problem types.

Glossary

Assignees   The entities (people, machines, vehicles, plants, etc.) that are to perform the tasks when formulating a problem as an assignment problem. (Section 5.6)   185

Cost table   The table that summarizes the formulation of an assignment problem by giving the cost for each possible assignment of an assignee to a task. (Section 5.6)   185

Demand at a destination   The number of units that need to be received by this destination from the sources. (Section 5.2)   158

Destinations   The receiving centers for a transportation problem. (Section 5.2)   158

Hungarian method   An algorithm designed specifically to solve assignment problems very efficiently. (Section 5.6)   186

Network simplex method   A streamlined version of the simplex method for solving distribution-network problems,

including transportation and assignment problems, very efficiently. (Section 5.2)   162

Parameter table   The table that summarizes the formulation of a transportation problem by giving all the unit costs, supplies, and demands. (Section 5.2)   159

Sources   The supply centers for a transportation problem. (Section 5.2)   158

Supply from a source   The number of units to be distributed from this source to the destinations. (Section 5.2)   158

Tasks   The jobs to be performed by the assignees when formulating a problem as an assignment problem. (Section 5.6)   185

Transportation simplex method   A streamlined version of the simplex method for solving transportation problems very efficiently. (Section 5.2)   162

Learning Aids for This Chapter in Your MS Courseware

"Ch. 5—Transp. & Assignment" Excel File:

P & T Case Study
Better Products Example

Nifty Example
Metro Example
Northern Airplane Example

Problems

We have inserted the symbol E* to the left of each problem (or its parts) where Excel should be used (unless your instructor gives you contrary instructions). An asterisk on the problem number indicates that at least a partial answer is given in the back of the book.

5.1. Consider the transportation problem having the following parameter table:

	Unit Cost ($)			
Destination:	*1*	*2*	*3*	*Supply*
Source				
1	9	6	8	4
2	7	12	10	3
3	6	7	6	2
Demand	4	2	3	

    a. Draw the network representation of this problem.
E* *b.* Display the problem on a spreadsheet.
E* *c.* Use the Excel Solver to obtain an optimal solution.

5.2. Consider the transportation problem having the following parameter table:

	Unit Cost ($)				
Destination:	*1*	*2*	*3*	*4*	*Supply*
Source					
1	3	7	6	4	5
2	2	4	3	2	2
3	4	3	8	5	3
Demand	3	3	2	2	

    a. Draw the network representation of this problem.
E* *b.* Display the problem on a spreadsheet.
E* *c.* Use the Excel Solver to obtain an optimal solution.

5.3. The Cost-Less Corp. supplies its four retail outlets from its four plants. The shipping cost per shipment from each plant to each retail outlet is given below.

	Unit Shipping Cost			
Retail Outlet: *1*	*2*	*3*	*4*	
Plant				
1	$500	$600	$400	$200
2	200	900	100	300
3	300	400	200	100
4	200	100	300	200

Plants 1, 2, 3, and 4 make 10, 20, 20, and 10 shipments per month, respectively. Retail outlets 1, 2, 3, and 4 need to receive 20, 10, 10, and 20 shipments per month, respectively.

The distribution manager, Randy Smith, now wants to determine the best plan for how many shipments to send from each plant to the respective retail outlets each month. Randy's objective is to minimize the total shipping cost.

    a. Formulate this problem as a transportation problem by constructing the appropriate parameter table.
E* *b.* Display the transportation problem on a spreadsheet.
E* *c.* Use the Excel Solver to obtain an optimal solution.

5.4. The Childfair Company has three plants producing child push chairs that are to be shipped to four distribution centers. Plants 1, 2, and 3 produce 12, 17, and 11 shipments per month, respectively. Each distribution center needs to receive 10 shipments per month. The distance from each plant to the respective distributing centers is given below:

	Distance to Distribution Center (Miles)			
	1	*2*	*3*	*4*
Plant				
1	800	1,300	400	700
2	1,100	1,400	600	1,000
3	600	1,200	800	900

The freight cost for each shipment is $100 plus 50 cents/mile.

How much should be shipped from each plant to each of the distribution centers to minimize the total shipping cost?

    a. Formulate this problem as a transportation problem by constructing the appropriate parameter table.
E* *b.* Display the transportation problem on a spreadsheet.
E* *c.* Use the Excel Solver to obtain an optimal solution.

E*5.5.* Tom would like 3 pints of home brew today and an additional 4 pints of home brew tomorrow. Dick is willing to sell a maximum of 5 pints total at a price of $3.00/pint today and $2.70/pint tomorrow. Harry is willing to sell a maximum of 4 pints total at a price of $2.90/pint today and $2.80/pint tomorrow.

Tom wishes to know what his purchases should be to minimize his cost while satisfying his thirst requirements. Formulate and solve a spreadsheet model for this problem.

E*5.6. The Versatech Corporation has decided to produce three new products. Five branch plants now have excess product capacity. The unit manufacturing cost of the first product would be $31, $29, $32, $28, and $29 in plants 1, 2, 3, 4, and 5, respectively. The unit manufacturing cost of the second product would be $45, $41, $46, $42, and $43 in plants 1, 2, 3, 4, and 5, respectively. The unit manufacturing cost of the third product would be $38, $35, and $40 in plants 1, 2, and 3, respectively, whereas plants 4 and 5 do not have the capability for producing this product. Sales forecasts indicate that 600, 1,000, and 800 units of products 1, 2, and 3, respectively, should be produced per day. Plants 1, 2, 3, 4, and 5 have the capacity to produce 400, 600, 400, 600, and 1,000 units daily, respectively, regardless of the product or combinations of products involved. Assume that any plant having the capability and capacity to produce them can produce any combination of the products in any quantity.

Management wishes to know how to allocate the new products to the plants to minimize total manufacturing cost. Formulate and solve a spreadsheet model for this problem.

E* 5.7. Suppose that England, France, and Spain produce all the wheat, barley, and oats in the world. The world demand for wheat requires 125 million acres of land devoted to wheat production. Similarly, 60 million acres of land are required for barley and 75 million acres of land for oats. The total amount of land available for these purposes in England, France, and Spain is 70 million acres, 110 million acres, and 80 million acres, respectively. The number of hours of labor needed in England, France, and Spain, respectively, to produce an acre of wheat is 18, 13, and 16; to produce an acre of barley is 15, 12, and 12; and to produce an acre of oats is 12, 10, and 16. The labor cost per hour in England, France, and Spain, respectively, for producing wheat is $9.00, $7.20, and $9.90; for producing barley is $8.10, $9.00, and $8.40; and for producing oats is $6.90, $7.50, and $6.30. The problem is to allocate land use in each country so as to meet the world food requirement and minimize the total labor cost. Formulate and solve a spreadsheet model for this problem.

E* 5.8. A contractor, Susan Meyer, has to haul gravel to three building sites. She can purchase as much as 18 tons at a gravel pit in the north of the city and 14 tons at one in the south. She needs 10, 5, and 10 tons at sites 1, 2, and 3, respectively. The purchase price per ton at each gravel pit and the hauling cost per ton are given in the table below.

	Hauling Cost per Ton at Site			
Pit	*1*	*2*	*3*	*Price per Ton*
North	$30	$60	$50	$100
South	60	30	40	120

Susan wishes to determine how much to haul from each pit to each site to minimize the total cost for purchasing and hauling gravel. Formulate and solve a spreadsheet model for this problem.

E* 5.9. Reconsider the P & T Co. case study presented in Sections 5.1 and 5.2. Refer to the spreadsheet in Figure 5.2, which shows the formulation as a transportation problem and displays an optimal solution. You now learn that one or more of the unit costs in the parameter table may change slightly before shipments begin.

Use the Excel Solver to generate the sensitivity report for this problem. Use this report to determine the range of optimality for each of the unit costs. What do these ranges of optimality tell P & T management?

E* 5.10. Reconsider the Metro Water District problem presented in Section 5.4. Refer to the spreadsheet in Figure 5.6, which shows the formulation as a variant of a transportation problem and displays an optimal solution.

The numbers given in the parameter table are only estimates that may be somewhat inaccurate, so management now wishes to do some what-if analysis. Use the Excel Solver to generate the sensitivity report. Then use this report to address the following questions. (In each case, assume that the indicated change is the only change in the model.)

a. Would the optimal solution in Figure 5.6 remain optimal if the cost per acre foot of shipping Calorie River water to San Go were actually $200 rather than $230?

b. Would this solution remain optimal if the cost per acre foot of shipping Sacron River water to Los Devils were actually $160 rather than $130?

c. Must this solution remain optimal if the costs considered in parts *a* and *b* were simultaneously changed from their original values to $215 and $145, respectively?

d. Suppose that the supply from the Sacron River and the demand at Hollyglass are decreased simultaneously by the same amount. Must the shadow prices for evaluating these changes remain valid if the decrease were 0.5 million acre feet?

E* 5.11. Reconsider the Metro Water District problem presented in Section 5.4, including the data given in Table 5.9.

The numbers in this table for the amount of water needed by the respective cities actually represent the absolute minimum that each city must have. Each city would like to have as much as 2 million additional acre feet beyond this minimum amount.

Since the amount of water available exceeds the sum of these minimum amounts by 3.5 million acre feet, Metro management has decided to distribute this additional water to the cities as well. The decisions on how much additional water the respective cities will receive beyond meeting their minimum needs will be based on minimizing Metro's total cost. Management wants to know which plan for distributing water from the rivers to the cities will achieve this objective. Formulate and solve a spreadsheet model for this problem.

E* 5.12. The Onenote Co. produces a single product at three plants for four customers. The three plants will produce 60, 80, and 40 units, respectively, during the next week. The firm has made a commitment to sell 40 units to customer 1, 60 units to customer 2, and at least 20 units to customer 3. Both customers 3 and 4 also want to buy as many of the remaining units as possible. The net profit associated with shipping a unit from plant *i* for sale to customer *j* is given by the following table:

	Customer			
	1	*2*	*3*	*4*
Plant				
1	$800	$700	$500	$200
2	500	200	100	300
3	600	400	300	500

Management wishes to know how many units to sell to customers 3 and 4 and how many units to ship from each of the plants to each of the customers to maximize profit. Formulate and solve a spreadsheet model for this problem.

E* 5.13. The Move-It Company has two plants building forklift trucks that then are shipped to three distribution centers. The production costs are the same at the two plants, and the cost of shipping each truck is shown below for each combination of plant and distribution center:

	Distribution Center		
	1	*2*	*3*
Plant			
A	$800	$700	$400
B	600	800	500

A total of 60 forklift trucks are produced and shipped per week. Each plant can produce and ship any amount up to a maximum of 50 trucks per week, so there is considerable flexibility on how to divide the total production between the two plants so as to reduce shipping costs. However, each distribution center must receive exactly 20 trucks per week.

Management's objective is to determine how many forklift trucks should be produced at each plant, and then what the overall shipping pattern should be to minimize total shipping cost. Formulate and solve a spreadsheet model for this problem.

E* 5.14. Redo Problem 5.13 when any distribution center may receive any quantity between 10 and 30 forklift trucks per week in order to further reduce total shipping cost, provided only that the total shipped to all three distribution centers must still equal 60 trucks per week.

E* 5.15. The Build-Em-Fast Company has agreed to supply its best customer with three widgits during *each* of the next three weeks, even though producing them will require some overtime work. The relevant production data are as follows:

	Maximum Production		
Week	*Regular Time*	*Overtime*	*Production Cost per Unit, Regular Time*
1	2	2	$300
2	3	2	500
3	1	2	400

The cost per unit produced with overtime for each week is $100 more than for regular time. The cost of storage is $50 per unit for each week it is stored. There is already an inventory of two widgets on hand currently, but the company does not want to retain any widgets in inventory after the three weeks.

Management wants to know how many units should be produced in each week to minimize the total cost of meeting the delivery schedule. Formulate and solve a spreadsheet model for this problem.

E* 5.16. The MJK Manufacturing Company must produce two products in sufficient quantity to meet contracted sales in each of the next three months. The two products share the same production facilities, and each unit of both products requires the same amount of production capacity. The available production and storage facilities are changing month by month, so the production capacities, unit production costs, and unit storage costs vary by month. Therefore, it may be worthwhile to overproduce one or both products in some months and store them until needed.

For each of the three months, the initial columns of the following table give the maximum number of units of the two products combined that can be produced on regular time (RT) and on overtime (O). For each of the two products, the subsequent columns give (1) the number of units needed for the contracted sales, (2) the cost (in thousands of dollars) per unit produced on regular time, (3) the cost (in thousands of dollars) per unit produced on overtime, and (4) the cost (in thousands of dollars) of storing each extra unit that is held over into the next month. In each case, the numbers for the two products are separated by a slash /, with the number for product 1 on the left and the number for product 2 on the right.

	Maximum Combined Production			**Product 1/Product 2**		
Month	*RT*	*OT*	*Sales*	*Unit Cost of Production ($1,000s)* RT	*OT*	*Unit Cost of Storage ($1,000s)*
1	10	3	5/3	15/16	18/20	1/2
2	8	2	3/5	17/15	20/18	2/1
3	10	3	4/4	19/17	22/22	

The production manager wants a schedule developed for the number of units of each of the two products to be produced on regular time and, if regular time production capacity is used up, on overtime in each of the three months. The objective is to minimize the total of the production and storage costs while meeting the contracted sales for each month. There is no initial inventory, and no final inventory is desired after the three months.

Formulate and solve a spreadsheet model for this problem.

5.17. Consider the transportation problem having the following parameter table:

Destination:	Unit Cost ($) 1	2	3	4	Supply
Source					
1	7	4	1	4	1
2	4	6	7	2	1
3	8	5	4	6	1
4	6	7	6	3	1
Demand	1	1	1	1	

a. What property ensures that this problem has feasible solutions?

b. What property ensures that this problem has an optimal solution with values of 0 or 1 for all the shipment amounts?

c. Explain how this problem can be interpreted to be an assignment problem.

d. Draw the network representation of this assignment problem.

E* e. Display the problem on a spreadsheet.

E* f. Use the Excel Solver to obtain an optimal solution.

5.18.*Consider the assignment problem having the following cost table.

Person	Job 1	2	3
A	$5	$7	$4
B	3	6	5
C	2	3	4

The optimal solution is A-3, B-1, C-2, with a total cost of $10.

a. Draw the network representation of this problem.

E* b. Formulate this problem on a spreadsheet.

E* c. Use the Excel Solver to obtain the optimal solution identified above.

5.19. Consider the assignment problem having the following cost table.

Assignee	Task 1	2	3	4
A	$8	$6	$5	$7
B	6	5	3	4
C	7	8	4	6
D	6	7	5	6

a. Draw the network representation of this assignment problem.

E* b. Formulate this problem on a spreadsheet.

E* c. Use the Excel Solver to obtain an optimal solution.

5.20. Four cargo ships will be used for shipping goods from one port to four other ports (labeled 1, 2, 3, 4). Any ship can be used for making any one of these four trips. However, because of differences in the ships and cargoes, the total cost of loading, transporting, and unloading the goods for the different ship–port combinations varies considerably, as shown in the following table:

Ship	Port 1	2	3	4
1	$500	$400	$600	$700
2	600	600	700	500
3	700	500	700	600
4	500	400	600	600

The objective is to assign the four ships to four different ports in such a way as to minimize the total cost for all four shipments.

a. Describe how this problem fits into the format for an assignment problem.

E* b. Formulate and solve this problem on a spreadsheet.

E* 5.21. Reconsider Problem 5.6. Suppose that the sales forecasts have been revised downward to 240, 400, and 320 units per day of products 1, 2, and 3, respectively. Thus, each plant now has the capacity to produce all that is required of any one product. Therefore, management has decided that each new product should be assigned to only one plant and that no plant should be assigned more than one product (so that three plants are each to be assigned one product, and two plants are to be assigned none). The objective is to make these assignments so as to minimize the *total* cost of producing these amounts of the three products. Formulate and solve a spreadsheet model for this problem.

5.22.* The coach of an age group swim team needs to assign swimmers to a 200-yard medley relay team to send to the Junior Olympics. Since most of his best swimmers are very fast in more than one stroke, it is not clear which swimmer should be assigned to each of the four strokes. The five fastest swimmers and the best times (in seconds) they have achieved in each of the strokes (for 50 yards) are

Stroke	Carl	Chris	David	Tony	Ken
Backstroke	37.7	32.9	33.8	37.0	35.4
Breaststroke	43.4	33.1	42.2	34.7	41.8
Butterfly	33.3	28.5	38.9	30.4	33.6
Freestyle	29.2	26.4	29.6	28.5	31.1

The coach wishes to determine how to assign four swimmers to the four different strokes to minimize the sum of the corresponding best times.

a. Describe how this problem fits into the format for a variant of an assignment problem even though it does not involve costs. What plays the role of costs?

E*   *b.* Formulate and solve this problem on a spreadsheet.

E* 5.23. Reconsider Problem 5.8. Now suppose that trucks (and their drivers) need to be hired to do the hauling, where each truck can only be used once to haul gravel from a single pit to a single site. Enough trucks are available to haul all the gravel that can be purchased at each site. Each truck can haul five tons, and the cost per truck is five times the hauling cost per ton given earlier. Only full trucks are to supply each site.

Formulate and solve a spreadsheet model for this problem.

E* 5.24. Reconsider Problem 5.13. Now distribution centers 1, 2, and 3 must receive exactly 10, 20, and 30 units per week, respectively. For administrative convenience, management has decided that each distribution center will be supplied totally by a single plant, so that one plant will supply one distribution center and the other plant will supply the other two distribution centers. The choice of these assignments of plants to distribution centers is to be made solely on the basis of minimizing total shipping cost.

Formulate and solve a spreadsheet model for this problem.

CASE 5.1
SHIPPING WOOD TO MARKET

Alabama Atlantic is a lumber company that has three sources of wood and five markets to be supplied. The annual availability of wood at sources 1, 2, and 3 is 15, 20, and 15 million board feet, respectively. The amount that can be sold annually at markets 1, 2, 3, 4, and 5 is 11, 12, 9, 10, and 8 million board feet, respectively.

In the past, the company has shipped the wood by train. However, because shipping costs have been increasing, the alternative of using ships to make some of the deliveries is being investigated. This alternative would require the company to invest in some ships. Except for these investment costs, the shipping costs in thousands of dollars per million board feet by rail and by water (when feasible) would be the following for each route:

	Unit Cost by Rail ($1,000s) to Market					Unit Cost by Ship ($1,000s) to Market				
Source	1	2	3	4	5	1	2	3	4	5
1	61	72	45	55	66	31	38	24	—	35
2	69	78	60	49	56	36	43	28	24	31
3	59	66	63	61	47	—	33	36	32	26

The capital investment (in thousands of dollars) in ships required for each million board feet to be transported annually by ship along each route is given as follows:

	Unit Investment for Ships ($1,000s) to Market				
Source	1	2	3	4	5
1	275	303	238	—	285
2	293	318	270	250	265
3	—	283	275	268	240

Considering the expected useful life of the ships and the time value of money, the equivalent uniform annual cost of these investments is one-tenth the amount given in the table. The objective is to determine the overall shipping plan that minimizes the total equivalent uniform annual cost (including shipping costs).

You are the head of the management science team that has been assigned the task of determining this shipping plan for each of the following three options.

Option 1: Continue shipping exclusively by rail.

Option 2: Switch to shipping exclusively by water (except where only rail is feasible).

Option 3: Ship by either rail or water, depending on which is less expensive for the particular route.

Present your results for each option. Compare.

Finally, consider the fact that these results are based on current shipping and investment costs, so that the decision on the option to adopt now should take into account management's projection of how these costs are likely to change in the future. For each option, describe a scenario of future cost changes that would justify adopting that option now.

CASE 5.2
PROJECT PICKINGS

Tazer, a pharmaceutical manufacturing company, entered the pharmaceutical market 12 years ago with the introduction of six new drugs. Five of the six drugs were simply permutations of existing drugs and therefore did not sell very heavily. The sixth drug, however, addressed hypertension and was a huge success. Since Tazer had a patent on the hypertension drug, it experienced no competition, and profits from the hypertension drug alone kept Tazer in business.

During the past 12 years, Tazer continued a moderate amount of research and development, but it never stumbled upon a drug as successful as the hypertension drug. One reason is that the company never had the motivation to invest heavily in innovative research and development. The company was riding the profit wave generated by its hypertension drug and did not feel the need to commit significant resources to finding new drug breakthroughs.

Now Tazer is beginning to fear the pressure of competition. The patent for the hypertension drug expires in five years,[1] and Tazer knows that once the patent expires, generic drug manufacturing companies will swarm into the market like vultures. Historical trends show that generic drugs decrease sales of branded drugs by 75 percent.

Tazer is therefore looking to invest significant amounts of money in research and development this year to begin the search for a new breakthrough drug that will offer the company the same success as the hypertension drug. Tazer believes that if the company begins extensive research and development now, the probability of finding a successful drug shortly after the expiration of the hypertension patent will be high.

As head of research and development at Tazer, you are responsible for choosing potential projects and assigning project directors to lead each of the projects. After researching the needs of the market, analyzing the shortcomings of current drugs, and interviewing numerous scientists concerning the promising areas of medical research, you have decided that your department will pursue five separate projects, which are listed below:

Project Up:	Develop a more effective antidepressant that does not cause serious mood swings.
Project Stable:	Develop a drug that addresses manic-depression.
Project Choice:	Develop a less intrusive birth control method for women.
Project Hope:	Develop a vaccine to prevent HIV infection.
Project Release:	Develop a more effective drug to lower blood pressure.

For each of the five projects, you are only able to specify the medical ailment the research should address since you do not know what compounds will exist and be effective without research.

You also have five senior scientists to lead the five projects. You know that scientists are very temperamental people and will only work well if they are challenged and motivated by the project. To ensure that the senior scientists are assigned to projects they find motivating, you have established a bidding system for the projects. You have given each of the five scientists 1,000 bid points. They assign bids to each project, giving a higher number of bid points to projects they most prefer to lead.

The following table provides the bids from the five senior scientists for the five individual projects:

Project	Dr. Kvaal	Dr. Zuner	Dr. Tsai	Dr. Mickey	Dr. Rollins
Project Up	100	0	100	267	100
Project Stable	400	200	100	153	33
Project Choice	200	800	100	99	33
Project Hope	200	0	100	451	34
Project Release	100	0	600	30	800

You decide to evaluate a variety of scenarios you think are likely.

a. Given the bids, you need to assign one senior scientist to each of the five projects to maximize the preferences of the scientists. What are the assignments?

b. Dr. Rollins is being courted by Harvard Medical School to accept a teaching position. You are fighting desperately to keep her at Tazer, but the prestige of Harvard may lure her away. If this were to happen, the company would give up the project with the least enthusiasm. Which project would not be done?

c. You do not want to sacrifice any project since researching only four projects decreases the probability of finding a breakthrough new drug. You decide that either Dr. Zuner or Dr. Mickey could lead two projects. Under these new conditions with just four senior scientists, which scientists will lead which projects to maximize preferences?

d. After Dr. Zuner was informed that she and Dr. Mickey are being considered for two projects, she decided to change her bids. Dr. Zuner's new bids for each of the projects are the following:

Project Up:	20
Project Stable:	450

---

[1]In general, patents protect inventions for 17 years. In 1995, GATT legislation extending the protection given by new pharmaceutical patents to 20 years became effective. The patent for Tazer's hypertension drug was issued prior to the GATT legislation, however. Thus, the patent only protects the drug for 17 years.

Project Choice: 451
Project Hope: 39
Project Release: 40

Under these new conditions with just four senior scientists, which scientists will lead which projects to maximize preferences?

e. Do you support the assignments found in part *d*? Why or why not?

f. Now you again consider all five scientists. You decide, however, that several scientists cannot lead certain projects. In particular, Dr. Mickey does not have experience with research on the immune system, so he cannot lead Project Hope. His family also has a history of manic-depression, and you feel that he would be too personally involved in Project Stable to serve as an effective project leader. Dr. Mickey therefore cannot lead Project Stable. Dr. Kvaal also does not have experience with research on the immune system and cannot lead Project Hope. In addition, Dr. Kvaal cannot lead Project Release because he does not have experience with research on the cardiovascular system. Finally, Dr. Rollins cannot lead Project Up because her family has a history of depression and you feel she would be too personally involved in the project to serve as an effective leader. Because Dr. Mickey and Dr. Kvaal cannot lead two of the five projects, they each have

only 600 bid points. Dr. Rollins has only 800 bid points because she cannot lead one of the five projects. The following table provides the new bids of Dr. Mickey, Dr. Kvaal and Dr. Rollins:

Project	Dr. Mickey	Dr. Kvaal	Dr. Rollins
Project Up	300	86	can't lead
Project Stable	can't lead	343	50
Project Choice	125	171	50
Project Hope	can't lead	can't lead	100
Project Release	175	can't lead	600

Which scientists should lead which projects to maximize preferences?

g. You decide that Project Hope and Project Release are too complex to be led by only one scientist. Therefore, each of these projects will be assigned two scientists as project leaders. You decide to hire two more scientists in order to staff all projects: Dr. Arriaga and Dr. Santos. Because of religious reasons, the two doctors both do not want to lead Project Choice. The following table lists all projects, scientists, and their bids.

Project	Kvaal	Zuner	Tsai	Mickey	Rollins	Arriaga	Santos
Up	86	0	100	300	can't lead	250	111
Stable	343	200	100	can't lead	50	250	1
Choice	171	800	100	125	50	can't lead	can't lead
Hope	can't lead	0	100	can't lead	100	250	333
Release	can't lead	0	600	175	600	250	555

Which scientists should lead which projects to maximize preferences?

h. Do you think it is wise to base your decision in part *g* only on an optimal solution for a variant of an assignment problem?

CHAPTER

6

NETWORK OPTIMIZATION PROBLEMS

Networks arise in numerous settings and in a variety of guises. Transportation, electrical, and communication networks pervade our daily lives. Network representations also are widely used for problems in such diverse areas as production, distribution, project planning, facilities location, resource management, and financial planning—to name just a few examples. In fact, a network representation provides such a powerful visual and conceptual aid for portraying the relationships between the components of systems that it is used in virtually every field of scientific, social, and economic endeavor.

One of the most exciting developments in management science in recent years has been the unusually rapid advance in both the methodology and application of network optimization problems. A number of algorithmic breakthroughs have had a major impact, as have ideas from computer science concerning data structures and efficient data manipulation. Consequently, algorithms and software now are available *and are being used* to solve huge problems on a routine basis that would have been completely intractable a couple of decades ago.

This chapter presents the network optimization problems that have been particularly helpful in dealing with managerial issues. We focus on the nature of these problems and their applications rather than on the technical details and the algorithms used to solve the problems.

Many network optimization problems actually are special types of *linear programming* problems. For example, both of the special types of linear programming problems discussed in the preceding chapter—transportation problems and assignment problems—also have network representations, presented in Figures 5.3 and 5.19.

The linear programming example presented in Section 3.4 also is a network optimization problem. This is the Distribution Unlimited Co. problem of how to distribute its goods through the distribution network shown in Figure 3.4. We return to this example in the next section because it illustrates an especially important type of network optimization problem called a *minimum-cost flow problem.* Minimum-cost flow problems are the special type of linear programming problem referred to in Section 3.4 as a *distribution-network problem.*

Section 6.3 presents *maximum flow problems,* which are concerned with such issues as how to maximize the flow of goods through a distribution network. Section 6.2 lays the groundwork by introducing a case study of a maximum flow problem.

Section 6.4 considers *shortest path problems.* In their simplest form, the objective is to find the shortest route between two locations.

Section 6.5 discusses *minimum spanning-tree problems,* which are concerned with minimizing the cost of providing connections between all users of a system. This is the only network optimization problem considered in this chapter (or the preceding chapter) that is not, in fact, a special type of linear programming problem.

6.1 Minimum-Cost Flow Problems

We begin with an example, which is just the example of a distribution-network problem presented in Section 3.4. (*Distribution-network problem* is another name for *minimum-cost flow problem.* We will use the latter, more common name hereafter.)

An Example: The Distribution Unlimited Co. Problem

As described in Section 3.4, the Distribution Unlimited Co. has two factories producing a product that needs to be shipped to two warehouses. Here are some details.

> Factory 1 is producing 80 units.
>
> Factory 2 is producing 70 units.
>
> Warehouse 1 needs 60 units.
>
> Warehouse 2 needs 90 units.

(Each unit corresponds to a full truckload of the product.)

Figure 6.1 shows the distribution network available for shipping this product, where F1 and F2 are the two factories, W1 and W2 are the two warehouses, and DC is a distribution center. The arrows show feasible shipping lanes. In particular, there is a rail link from factory 1 to warehouse 1 and another from factory 2 to warehouse 2. (Any amounts can be shipped along these rail links.) In addition, independent truckers are available to ship up to 50 units from each factory to the distribution center, and then to ship up to 50 units from the distribution center to each warehouse. (Whatever is shipped to the distribution center must subsequently be shipped on to the warehouses.)

The shipping costs differ considerably among these shipping lanes. The cost per unit shipped through each lane is shown above the corresponding arrow in Figure 6.2.

Management's objective is to determine the shipping plan (how many units to ship along each shipping lane) that will minimize the total shipping cost.

Except for its very small size, this problem is a typical *minimum-cost flow problem*. As described in Section 3.4, a full-fledged linear programming model can be formulated to represent this problem. However, there is no need to develop such a lengthy formulation. A network such as Figure 6.2 provides a simpler and more intuitive formulation.

FIGURE 6.1

The distribution network for the Distribution Unlimited Co. problem, where each feasible shipping lane is represented by an arrow.

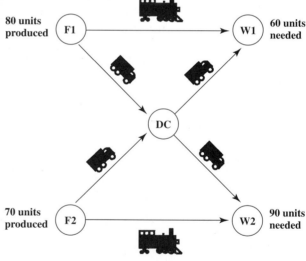

FIGURE 6.2

The data for the distribution network for the Distribution Unlimited Co. problem.

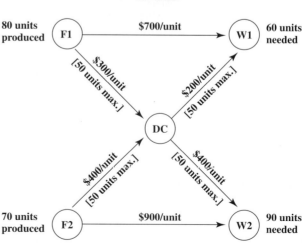

To make the network less crowded, the problem usually is presented even more compactly, as shown in Figure 6.3. The number in square brackets next to the location of each facility indicates the net number of units (outflow minus inflow) generated there. Thus, the number of units terminating at each warehouse is shown as a negative number. The number at the distribution center is 0 since the number of units leaving *minus* the number of units arriving must equal 0. The number on top of each arrow shows the unit shipping cost along that shipping lane. Any number in square brackets underneath an arrow gives the maximum number of units that can be shipped along that shipping lane. (The absence of a number in square brackets underneath an arrow implies that there is no limit on the shipping amount there.) This network provides a complete representation of the problem, including all the necessary data, so it constitutes a *network model* for this minimum-cost flow problem.

Since this is such a tiny problem, you probably can see what the optimal solution must be. (Try it.) This solution is shown in Figure 6.4, where the shipping amount along each shipping lane is given in parentheses there. (To avoid confusion, we delete the unit shipping costs and shipping capacities in this figure.) Combining these shipping amounts with the unit shipping costs given in Figures 6.2 and 6.3, the total shipping cost for this solution is

$$\text{Total shipping cost} = 30(\$700) + 50(\$300) + 50(\$400) + 50(\$200)$$
$$+ 50(\$400) + 20(\$900)$$

$$= \$104,000$$

FIGURE 6.3

A network model for the Distribution Unlimited Co. problem as a minimum-cost flow problem.

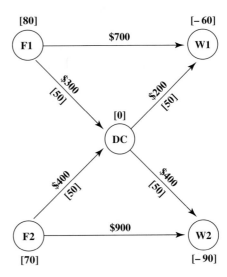

FIGURE 6.4

The optimal solution for the Distribution Unlimited Co. problem, where the shipping amounts are shown in parentheses over the arrows.

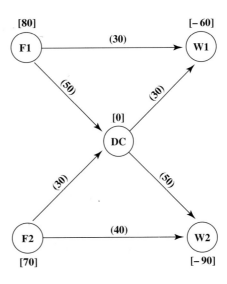

General Characteristics   This example possesses all the general characteristics of any minimum-cost flow problem. Before summarizing these characteristics, here is the terminology you will need.

Terminology

1. The model for any minimum-cost flow problem is represented by a *network* with flow passing through it.
2. The circles in the network are called **nodes.**
3. Each node where the net amount of flow generated (outflow minus inflow) is a fixed *positive* number is a **supply node.** (Thus, F1 and F2 are the supply nodes in Figure 6.3.)
4. Each node where the net amount of flow generated is a fixed *negative* number is a **demand node.** (Consequently, W1 and W2 are the demand nodes in the example.)
5. Any node where the net amount of flow generated is fixed at *zero* is a **transshipment node.** (Thus, DC is the transshipment node in the example.) Having the flow out of the node equal the flow in is referred to as **conservation of flow.**
6. The arrows in the network are called **arcs.**
7. The maximum amount of flow allowed through an arc is referred to as the **capacity** of that arc.

Using this terminology, the general characteristics of minimum-cost flow problems (the model for this type of problem) can be described in terms of the following assumptions.

Assumptions of a Minimum-Cost Flow Problem

1. *At least one* of the nodes is a *supply node.*
2. *At least one* of the other nodes is a *demand node.*
3. All the remaining nodes are *transshipment nodes.*
4. Flow through an arc is only allowed in the direction indicated by the arrowhead, where the maximum amount of flow is given by the *capacity* of that arc. (If flow can occur in both directions, this would be represented by a pair of arcs pointing in opposite directions.)
5. The network has enough arcs with sufficient capacity to enable all the flow generated at the *supply nodes* to reach all the *demand nodes.*
6. The cost of the flow through each arc is *proportional* to the amount of that flow, where the cost per unit flow is known.
7. The objective is to minimize the total cost of sending the available supply through the network to satisfy the given demand. (An alternative objective is to maximize the total profit from doing this.)

A *solution* for this kind of problem needs to specify how much flow is going through each arc. To be a *feasible* solution, the amount of flow through each arc cannot exceed the capacity of that arc and the net amount of flow generated at each node must equal the specified amount for that node. The following property indicates when the problem will have feasible solutions.

The Feasible Solutions Property: Under the above assumptions, a minimum-cost flow problem will have feasible solutions if and only if the sum of the supplies from its supply nodes *equals* the sum of the demands at its demand nodes.

Note that this property holds for the Distribution Unlimited Co. problem, because the sum of its supplies is $80 + 70 = 150$ and the sum of its demands also is $60 + 90 = 150$.

For many applications of minimum-cost flow problems, management desires a solution with *integer* values for all the flow quantities (e.g., integer numbers of *full* truckloads along each shipping lane). The model does not include any constraints that require this for feasible solutions. Fortunately, such constraints are not needed because of the following property.

Integer Solutions Property: As long as all its supplies, demands, and arc capacities have integer values, any minimum-cost flow problem with feasible solutions is guaranteed to have an optimal solution with integer values for all its flow quantities.

See in Figure 6.2 that this property holds for the Distribution Unlimited Co. problem. All the supplies (80 and 70), demands (60 and 90), and arc capacities (50) have integer values. Therefore, all the flow quantities in the optimal solution given in Figure 6.4 (30, 50 four times, and 20) have integer values. This ensures that only full truckloads will be shipped into and out of the distribution center. (Remember that each unit corresponds to a full truckload of the product.)

Now let us see how to obtain an optimal solution.

Using Excel to Solve Minimum-Cost Flow Problems

Section 3.4 describes the formulation of a full-fledged linear programming model for the Distribution Unlimited Co. problem. This involved developing a parameter table (Table 3.9) as the basis for a spreadsheet model (Figure 3.5). The Excel Solver then provided an optimal solution.

There is an easier method. Figure 6.5 shows a simpler spreadsheet model that is based directly on the network representation of the problem in Figure 6.3. The arcs are listed in columns B and C, along with their capacities (unless unlimited) in column F, and their costs per unit flow in column G. The changing cells (D4:D9) show the flow amounts through these arcs and the target cell (D11) provides the total cost of this flow by using the equation

$$D11 = \text{SUMPRODUCT(D4:D9,G4:G9)}$$

The first set of constraints in the Solver dialogue box, D5:D8 ≤ F5:F8, ensure that the arc capacities are not exceeded.

Similarly, column I lists the nodes and column L specifies the net amount of flow that is to be generated at each one. Column J then shows the actual net amount of flow generated at each node, given the flows in the changing cells, by using the equations displayed in the bottom right-hand side of Figure 6.5. The second set of constraints in the Solver dialogue box, J4:J8 = L4:L8, requires that the actual net amount of flow generated at each node must equal the specified amount.

The first Solver option selected (Assume Linear Model) acknowledges that this is still a linear programming problem (in a streamlined form). The second option (Assume Non-Negative) specifies that the flow amounts cannot be negative.

Clicking on the Solve button gives the optimal solution shown in cells D4:D9. This is the same solution as displayed in Figure 6.4.

FIGURE 6.5

A spreadsheet model for the Distribution Unlimited Co. minimum-cost flow problem, where the changing cells (D4:D9) show the optimal solution obtained by the Solver and the target cell (D11) gives the resulting total cost of the flow through the network.

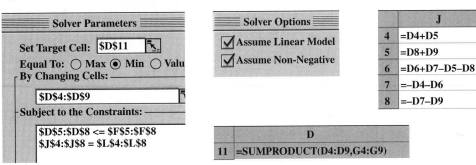

	A	B	C	D	E	F	G	H	I	J	K	L
1		Distribution Unlimited Co. Minimum-Cost Flow Problem										
2												
3		From	To	Ship		Capacity	Unit Cost		Nodes	Net Flow		Supply/Demand
4		F1	W1	30		–	$700		F1	80	=	80
5		F1	DC	50	≤	50	$300		F2	70	=	70
6		DC	W1	30	≤	50	$200		DC	0	=	0
7		DC	W2	50	≤	50	$400		W1	−60	=	−60
8		F2	DC	30	≤	50	$400		W2	−90	=	−90
9		F2	W2	40		–	$900					
10												
11			Total Cost =	$110,000								

Solver Parameters

Set Target Cell: $D$11

Equal To: ○ Max ● Min ○ Valu

By Changing Cells:

$D$4:$D$9

Subject to the Constraints:

$D$5:$D$8 <= $F$5:$F$8
$J$4:$J$8 = $L$4:$L$8

Solver Options

☑ Assume Linear Model
☑ Assume Non-Negative

	J
4	=D4+D5
5	=D8+D9
6	=D6+D7−D5−D8
7	=−D4−D6
8	=−D7−D9

	D
11	=SUMPRODUCT(D4:D9,G4:G9)

Solving Large Minimum-Cost Flow Problems More Efficiently

Because minimum-cost flow problems are a special type of linear programming problem, and the *simplex method* can solve any linear programming problem, it also can solve any minimum-cost flow problem in the standard way. For example, the Excel Solver uses the simplex method to solve this type (or any other type) of linear programming problem. This works fine for small problems, like the Distribution Unlimited Co. problem, and for considerably larger ones as well. Therefore, the approach illustrated in Figure 6.5 will serve you well for any minimum-cost flow problem encountered in this book and for many that you will encounter subsequently.

However, we should mention that a different approach is sometimes needed in practice to solve really big problems. Because of the special form of minimum-cost flow problems, it is possible to greatly *streamline* the simplex method to solve them far more quickly. In particular, rather than going through all the algebra of the simplex method, it is possible to execute the same steps far more quickly by working directly with the network for the problem.

This streamlined version of the simplex method is called the **network simplex method.** (As you may recall our mentioning in Section 5.2, the network simplex method also can be used to solve transportation problems.) The network simplex method can solve some huge problems that are much too large for the simplex method.

Like the simplex method, the network simplex method not only finds an optimal solution but also can be a valuable aid to managers in conducting the kinds of what-if analyses described in Chapter 4.

Many companies now use the network simplex method to solve their minimum-cost flow problems. Some of these problems are huge, with many tens of thousands of nodes and arcs. Occasionally, the number of arcs will even be far larger, perhaps into the millions.

Although the Excel Solver does not, other commercial software packages for linear programming commonly include the network simplex method.

An important advance in recent years has been the development of excellent *graphical interfaces* for modeling minimum-cost flow problems. These interfaces make the design of the model and the interpretation of the output of the network simplex method completely visual and intuitive with no mathematics involved. This is very helpful for managerial decision making.

Some Applications

Probably the most important kind of application of minimum-cost flow problems is to the operation of a distribution network, such as the one depicted in Figures 6.1–6.4 for the Distribution Unlimited Co. problem. (This is why minimum-cost flow problems were referred to as distribution-network problems in Section 3.4.) As summarized in the first row of Table 6.1, this kind of application always involves determining a plan for shipping goods from its *sources* (factories, etc.) to *intermediate storage facilities* (as needed) and then on to the *customers*.

However, the distribution network often is much more complicated than the one shown in Figures 6.1–6.4. For example, consider the distribution network for the **International Paper Company** (as described in the March–April 1988 issue of *Interfaces*). This company is the world's largest manufacturer of pulp, paper, and paper products, as well as a major producer of lumber and plywood. It also either owns or has rights over about 20 million acres of woodlands. The supply nodes in its distribution network are these woodlands in

TABLE 6.1   Typical Kinds of Applications of Minimum-Cost Flow Problems

Kind of Application	Supply Nodes	Transshipment Nodes	Demand Nodes
Operation of a distribution network	Sources of goods	Intermediate storage facilities	Customers
Solid waste management	Sources of solid waste	Processing facilities	Landfill locations
Operation of a supply network	Vendors	Intermediate warehouses	Processing facilities
Coordinating product mixes at plants	Plants	Production of a specific product	Market for a specific product
Cash-flow management	Sources of cash at a specific time	Short-term investment options	Needs for cash at a specific time

their various locations. However, before the company's goods can eventually reach the demand nodes (the customers), it must pass through a long sequence of transshipment nodes. A typical path through the distribution network is

woodlands → woodyards → sawmills

→ paper mills → converting plants

→ warehouses → customers

Another example of a complicated distribution network is the one for the **Citgo Petroleum Corporation** described in Section 2.1. Applying a minimum-cost flow problem formulation to improve the operation of this distribution network saved Citgo at least $16.5 million annually.

For some applications of minimum-cost flow problems, all the transshipment nodes are *processing facilities* rather than intermediate storage facilities. This is the case for *solid waste management,* as indicated in Table 6.1. Here, the flow of materials through the network begins at the sources of the solid waste, then goes to the facilities for processing these waste materials into a form suitable for landfill, and then sends them on to the various landfill locations. However, the objective still is to determine the flow plan that minimizes the total cost, where the cost now is for both shipping and processing.

In other applications, the *demand nodes* might be processing facilities. For example, in the third row of Table 6.1, the objective is to find the minimum-cost plan for obtaining supplies from various possible vendors, storing these goods in warehouses (as needed), and then shipping the supplies to the company's processing facilities (factories, etc.).

The July–August 1987 issue of *Interfaces* describes how, even back then, microcomputers were being used by **Marshalls, Inc.** (an off-price retail chain), to deal with a minimum-cost flow problem this way. In this application, Marshalls was optimizing the flow of freight from vendors to processing centers and then on to retail stores. Some of their networks had over 20,000 arcs.

The next kind of application in Table 6.1 (coordinating product mixes at plants) illustrates that arcs can represent something other than a shipping lane for a physical flow of materials. This application involves a company with several plants (the supply nodes) that can produce the same products but at different costs. Each arc from a supply node represents the production of one of the possible products at that plant, where this arc leads to the transshipment node that corresponds to this product. Thus, this transshipment node has an arc coming in from each plant capable of producing this product, and then the arcs leading out of this node go to the respective customers (the demand nodes) for this product. The objective is to determine how to divide each plant's production capacity among the products so as to minimize the total cost of meeting the demand for the various products.

The last application in Table 6.1 (cash-flow management) illustrates that different nodes can represent some event that occurs at different times. In this case, each supply node represents a specific time (or time period) when some cash will become available to the company (through maturing accounts, notes receivable, sales of securities, borrowing, etc.). The supply at each of these nodes is the amount of cash that will become available then. Similarly, each demand node represents a specific time (or time period) when the company will need to draw on its cash reserves. The demand at each such node is the amount of cash that will be needed then. The objective is to maximize the company's income from investing the cash between each time it becomes available and when it will be used. Therefore, each transshipment node represents the choice of a specific short-term investment option (e.g., purchasing a certificate of deposit from a bank) over a specific time interval. The resulting network will have a succession of flows representing a schedule for cash becoming available, being invested, and then being used after the maturing of the investment.

Special Types of Minimum-Cost Flow Problems

There are five important categories of network problems that turn out to be special types of minimum-cost flow problems.

One is the *transportation problems* discussed in the early part of the preceding chapter. Figure 5.3 in Section 5.2 shows the network representation of a typical transportation problem. In our current terminology, the sources and destinations of a transportation problem are the supply nodes and demand nodes, respectively. Thus, a transportation problem is just a minimum-cost flow problem without any transshipment nodes and without any capacity constraints on the arcs (all of which go directly from a supply node to a demand node).

A second category is the *assignment problems* discussed in Section 5.6. Recall that this kind of problem involves assigning a group of assignees to a group of tasks where each assignee is to perform a single task. The network representation of a typical assignment problem is displayed in Figure 5.19 in Section 5.6. We also pointed out in that section that an assignment problem can be viewed as a special type of transportation problem whose sources are the assignees and whose destinations are the tasks. This then makes the assignment problem also a special type of minimum-cost flow problem with the characteristics described in the preceding paragraph. In addition, each assignee is a supply node with a supply of 1 and each task is a demand node with a demand of 1.

A third special type of minimum-cost flow problem is **transshipment problems.** This kind of problem is just like a transportation problem except for the additional feature that the shipments from the sources (supply nodes) to the destinations (demand nodes) might also pass through intermediate transfer points (transshipment nodes) such as distribution centers. Like a transportation problem, there are no capacity constraints on the arcs. Consequently, any minimum-cost flow problem where each arc can carry any desired amount of flow is a transshipment problem. For example, if the data in Figure 6.2 were altered so that any amounts (within the ranges of the supplies and demands) could be shipped into and out of the distribution center, the Distribution Unlimited Co. would become just a transshipment problem.[1]

Because of their close relationship to a general minimum-cost flow problem, we will not discuss transshipment problems further.

The other two important special types of minimum-cost flow problems are *maximum flow problems* and *shortest path problems,* which will be described in Sections 6.3 and 6.4 after presenting a case study of a maximum flow problem in the next section.

In case you are wondering why we are bothering to point out that these five kinds of problems are special types of minimum-cost flow problems, here is one very important reason. It means that the *network simplex method* can be used to solve large problems of any of these types that might be difficult or impossible for the simplex method to solve. It is true that other efficient *special-purpose algorithms* also are available for each of these kinds of problems (such as the *transportation simplex method* for the transportation problem). However, recent implementations of the network simplex method have become so powerful that it now provides an excellent alternative to these other algorithms in most cases. This is especially valuable when the available software package includes the network simplex method but not another relevant special-purpose algorithm. Furthermore, even after finding an optimal solution, the network simplex method can continue to be helpful in aiding managerial what-if sessions along the lines discussed in Chapter 4.

Review Questions

1. Name and describe the three kinds of nodes in a minimum-cost flow problem.
2. What is meant by the *capacity* of an arc?
3. What is the usual objective for a minimum-cost flow problem?
4. What property is necessary for a minimum-cost flow problem to have feasible solutions?
5. What is the integer solutions property for minimum-cost flow problems?
6. What is the name of the streamlined version of the simplex method that is designed to solve minimum-cost flow problems very efficiently?
7. What are a few typical kinds of applications of minimum-cost flow problems?
8. Name five important categories of network optimization problems that turn out to be special types of minimum-cost flow problems.

---

[1]Be aware that a minimum-cost flow problem that does have capacity constraints on the arcs is sometimes referred to as a *capacitated transshipment problem.* We will not use this terminology.

6.2 A Case Study: The BMZ Co. Maximum Flow Problem

What a day! First being called into his boss's office and then receiving an urgent telephone call from the company president himself. Fortunately, he was able to reassure them that he has the situation under control.

Although his official title is Supply Chain Manager for the BMZ Company, Karl Schmidt often tells his friends that he really is the company's *crisis manager.* One crisis after another. The supplies needed to keep the production lines going haven't arrived yet. Or the supplies have arrived but are unusable because they are the wrong size. Or an urgent shipment to a key customer has been delayed. This current crisis is typical. One of the company's most important distribution centers—the one in Los Angeles—urgently needs an increased flow of shipments from the company.

Karl was chosen for this key position because he is considered a rising young star. Having just received his MBA degree from a top American business school four years ago, he is the youngest member of upper-level management in the entire company. His business school training in the latest management science techniques has proven invaluable in improving supply chain management throughout the company. The crises still occur, but the frequent chaos of past years has been eliminated.

Karl has a plan for dealing with the current crisis. This will mean calling on management science once again.

Background

The BMZ Company is a European manufacturer of luxury automobiles. Although its cars sell well in all the developed countries, its exports to the United States are particularly important to the company.

BMZ has a well-deserved reputation for providing excellent service. One key to maintaining this reputation is having a plentiful supply of automobile replacement parts readily available to the company's numerous dealerships and authorized repair shops. These parts are mainly stored in the company's distribution centers and then delivered promptly when needed. One of Karl Schmidt's top priorities is avoiding shortages at these distribution centers.

The company has several distribution centers in the United States. However, the closest one to the Los Angeles center is over 1,000 miles away in Seattle. Since BMZ cars are becoming especially popular in California, it is particularly important to keep the Los Angeles center well supplied. Therefore, the fact that supplies there are currently dwindling is a matter of real concern to BMZ top management—as Karl learned forcefully today.

Most of the automobile replacement parts are produced at the company's main factory in Stuttgart, Germany, along with the production of new cars. It is this factory that has been supplying the Los Angeles center with spare parts. Some of these parts are bulky, and very large numbers of certain parts are needed, so the total volume of the supplies has been relatively massive—over 300,000 cubic feet of goods arriving monthly. Now a much larger amount will be needed over the next month to replenish the dwindling inventory.

The Problem

Karl needs to execute a plan quickly for shipping as much as possible from the main factory to the distribution center in Los Angeles over the next month. He already has recognized that this is a *maximum flow problem*—a problem of maximizing the flow of replacement parts from the factory to this distribution center.

The factory is producing far more than can be shipped to this one distribution center. Therefore, the limiting factor on how much can be shipped is the limited capacity of the company's distribution network.

This distribution network is depicted in Figure 6.6, where the nodes labeled ST and LA are the factory in Stuttgart and the distribution center in Los Angeles, respectively. There is a rail head at the factory, so shipments first go by rail to one of three European ports: Rotterdam (node RO), Bordeaux (node BO), and Lisbon (node LI). They then go by ship to ports in the United States, either New York (node NY) or New Orleans (node NO). Finally, they are shipped by truck from these ports to the distribution center in Los Angeles.

The organizations operating these railroads, ships, and trucks are independently owned companies that ship goods for numerous firms. Because of prior commitments to their regular customers, these companies are unable to drastically increase the allocation of space

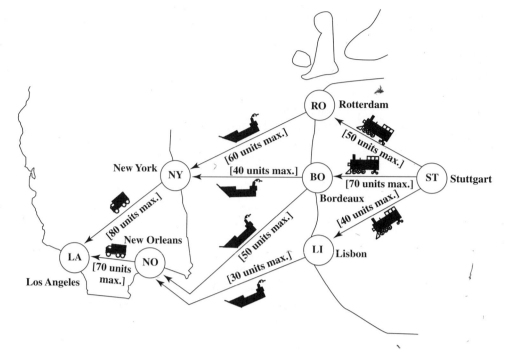

FIGURE 6.7

A network model for the BMZ problem as a maximum flow problem, where the number in square brackets below each arc is the capacity of that arc.

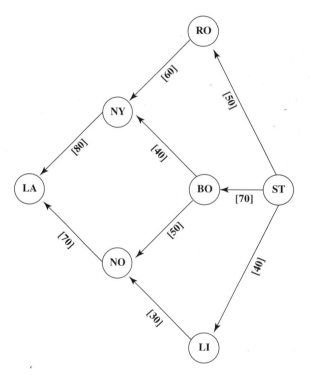

to any single customer on short notice. Therefore, the BMZ Co. is only able to secure a limited amount of shipping space along each shipping lane over the next month. The amounts available are given in Figure 6.6, using units of *hundreds of cubic meters*. (Since each unit of 100 cubic meters is a little over 3,500 cubic feet, these are large volumes of goods that need to be moved.)

Model Formulation   Figure 6.7 shows the *network model* for this maximum flow problem. Rather than showing the geographical layout of the distribution network, this network simply lines up the nodes (representing the cities) in evenly spaced columns. The arcs represent the shipping lanes, where the capacity of each arc (given in square brackets under the arc) is the amount of shipping space available along that shipping lane. The objective is to determine how much flow to send through each arc (how many units to ship through each shipping lane) to max-

FIGURE 6.8

A spreadsheet model for the BMZ Co. maximum flow problem, where the changing cells (D4:D12) show the optimal solution obtained by the Solver and the target cell (D14) gives the resulting flow through the network.

	A	B	C	D	E	F	G	H	I	J	K
1		BMZ Co. Maximum Flow Problem									
2											
3		From	To	Ship		Capacity		Nodes	Net Flow		Supply/Demand
4		Stuttgart	Rotterdam	50	≤	50		Stuttgart	150		
5		Stuttgart	Bordeaux	70	≤	70		Rotterdam	0	=	0
6		Stuttgart	Lisbon	30	≤	40		Bordeaux	0	=	0
7		Rotterdam	New York	50	≤	60		Lisbon	0	=	0
8		Bordeaux	New York	30	≤	40		New York	0	=	0
9		Bordeaux	New Orleans	40	≤	50		New Orleans	0	=	0
10		Lisbon	New Orleans	30	≤	30		Los Angeles	–150		
11		New York	Los Angeles	80	≤	80					
12		New Orleans	Los Angeles	70	≤	70					
13											
14			Maximum Flow =	150							

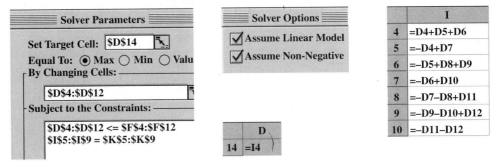

	Solver Parameters
	Set Target Cell: $D$14
	Equal To: ● Max ○ Min ○ Valu
	By Changing Cells:
	$D$4:$D$12
	Subject to the Constraints:
	$D$4:$D$12 <= $F$4:$F$12
	$I$5:$I$9 = $K$5:$K$9

	Solver Options
	☑ Assume Linear Model
	☑ Assume Non-Negative

	D
14	=I4

	I
4	=D4+D5+D6
5	=–D4+D7
6	=–D5+D8+D9
7	=–D6+D10
8	=–D7–D8+D11
9	=–D9–D10+D12
10	=–D11–D12

imize the total number of units flowing from the factory in Stuttgart to the distribution center in Los Angeles.

Figure 6.8 shows the corresponding spreadsheet model for this problem when using the format introduced in Figure 6.5. The main difference from the model in Figure 6.5 is the change in the objective. Since we are no longer minimizing the total cost of the flow through the network, column G in Figure 6.5 can be deleted here. The target cell (D14) now needs to give the total number of units flowing from Stuttgart to Los Angeles. Thus, the equations at the bottom of the figure include D14 = I4, where I4 = D4 + D5 + D6. The Solver dialogue box specifies that this target cell is to be maximized. After clicking on the Solve button, the optimal solution shown in the changing cells (D4:D12) is obtained for the amount that BMZ should ship through each shipping lane.

However, Karl is not completely satisfied with this solution. He has an idea for doing even better. This will require formulating and solving another maximum flow problem. (This story continues in the middle of the next section.)

Review Questions

1. What is the current crisis facing the BMZ Co.?
2. When formulating this problem in network terms, what is flowing through BMZ's distribution network? From where to where?
3. What is the objective of the resulting maximum flow problem?

6.3 Maximum Flow Problems

Like a minimum-cost flow problem, a maximum flow problem is concerned with *flow through a network*. However, the objective now is different. Rather than minimizing the cost of the flow, the objective now is to find a flow plan that maximizes the amount flowing through the network. This is how Karl Schmidt was able to find a flow plan that maximizes the number of units of automobile replacement parts flowing through BMZ's distribution network from its factory in Stuttgart to the distribution center in Los Angeles.

General Characteristics

Except for the difference in objective (maximize flow versus minimize cost), the characteristics of the maximum flow problem are quite similar to those for the minimum-cost flow problem. However, there are some minor differences, as we will discuss after summarizing the assumptions.

Assumptions of a Maximum Flow Problem

1. All flow through the network originates at one node, called the **source,** and terminates at one other node, called the **sink.** (The source and sink in the BMZ problem are the factory and the distribution center, respectively.)
2. All the remaining nodes are *transshipment nodes.* (These are nodes RO, BO, LI, NY, and NO in the BMZ problem.)
3. Flow through an arc is only allowed in the direction indicated by the arrowhead, where the maximum amount of flow is given by the *capacity* of that arc. At the *source,* all arcs point away from the node. At the *sink,* all arcs point into the node.
4. The objective is to maximize the total amount of flow from the source to the sink. This amount is measured in either of two equivalent ways, namely, either the amount *leaving the source* or the amount *entering the sink.* (Cells D14 and I4 in Figure 6.8 use the amount leaving the source.)

The source and sink of a maximum flow problem are analogous to the supply nodes and demand nodes of a minimum-cost flow problem. These are the only nodes in both problems that do not have conservation of flow (flow out equals flow in). Like the supply nodes, the source *generates flow.* Like the demand nodes, the sink *absorbs flow.*

However, there are two differences between these nodes in a minimum-cost flow problem and the corresponding nodes in a maximum flow problem.

One difference is that, whereas supply nodes have fixed supplies and demand nodes have fixed demands, the source and sink do not. The reason is that the objective is to maximize the flow leaving the source and entering the sink rather than fixing this amount.

The second difference is that, whereas the number of supply nodes and the number of demand nodes in a minimum-cost flow problem may be *more than one,* there can be *only one* source and *only one* sink in a maximum flow problem. However, variants of maximum flow problems that have multiple sources and sinks can still be solved by the Excel Solver, as you now will see illustrated by the BMZ case study introduced in the preceding section.

Continuing the Case Study with Multiple Supply Points and Multiple Demand Points

Here is Karl Schmidt's idea for how to improve upon the flow plan obtained at the end of Section 6.2 (as given in column D of Figure 6.8).

The company has a second, smaller factory in Berlin, north of its Stuttgart factory, for producing automobile parts. Although this factory normally is used to help supply distribution centers in northern Europe, Canada, and the northern United States (including one in Seattle), it also is able to ship to the distribution center in Los Angeles. Furthermore, the distribution center in Seattle has the capability of supplying parts to the customers of the distribution center in Los Angeles when shortages occur at the latter center.

In this light, Karl now has developed a better plan for addressing the current inventory shortages in Los Angeles. Rather than simply maximizing shipments from the Stuttgart factory to Los Angeles, he has decided to maximize shipments from both factories to the distribution centers in both Los Angeles and Seattle.

Figure 6.9 shows the network model representing the expanded distribution network that encompasses both factories and both distribution centers. In addition to the nodes shown in Figures 6.6 and 6.7, node BE is the second, smaller factory in Berlin; nodes HA and BN are additional ports used by this factory in Hamburg and Boston, respectively; and node SE is the distribution center in Seattle. As before, the arcs represent the shipping lanes, where the number in square brackets below each arc is the capacity of that arc, that is, the maximum number of units that can be shipped through that shipping lane over the next month.

The corresponding spreadsheet model is displayed in Figure 6.10. The format is the same as in Figure 6.8. However, the target cell (D21) now gives the total flow from Stuttgart

FIGURE 6.9

A network model for the expanded BMZ problem as a maximum flow problem, where the number in square brackets below each arc is the capacity of that arc.

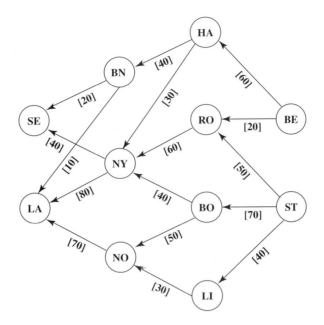

FIGURE 6.10

A spreadsheet model for the expanded BMZ Co. problem as a variant of a maximum flow problem, including the optimal solution obtained by the Solver.

	A	B	C	D	E	F	G	H	I	J	K
1		BMZ Co. Expanded Maximum Flow Problem									
2											
3		From	To	Ship		Capacity		Nodes	Net Flow		Supply/Demand
4		Stuttgart	Rotterdam	40	≤	50		Stuttgart	140		
5		Stuttgart	Bordeaux	70	≤	70		Berlin	80		
6		Stuttgart	Lisbon	30	≤	40		Hamburg	0	=	0
7		Berlin	Rotterdam	20	≤	20		Rotterdam	0	=	0
8		Berlin	Hamburg	60	≤	60		Bordeaux	0	=	0
9		Rotterdam	New York	60	≤	60		Lisbon	0	=	0
10		Bordeaux	New York	30	≤	40		Boston	0	=	0
11		Bordeaux	New Orleans	40	≤	50		New York	0	=	0
12		Lisbon	New Orleans	30	≤	30		New Orleans	0	=	0
13		Hamburg	New York	30	≤	30		Los Angeles	−160		
14		Hamburg	Boston	30	≤	40		Seattle	−60		
15		New Orleans	Los Angeles	70	≤	70					
16		New York	Los Angeles	80	≤	80					
17		New York	Seattle	40	≤	40					
18		Boston	Los Angeles	10	≤	10					
19		Boston	Seattle	20	≤	20					
20											
21			Maximum Flow =	220							

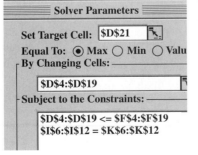

	I
4	=D4+D5+D6
5	=D7+D8
6	=−D8+D13+D14
7	=−D4−D7+D9
8	=−D5+D10+D11
9	=−D6+D12
10	=−D14+D18+D19
11	=−D9−D10−D13+D16+D17
12	=−D11−D12+D15
13	=−D15−D16−D18
14	=−D17−D19

	D
21	=I4+I5

and Berlin, so D21 = I4 + I5, where I4 = D4 + D5 + D6 and I5 = D7 + D8 (as shown at the bottom of the figure).

The changing cells (D4:D19) in this figure show the optimal solution obtained for the number of units to ship through each shipping lane over the next month. Comparing this solution with the one in Figure 6.8 shows the impact of Karl Schmidt's decision to expand the distribution network to include the second factory and the distribution center in Seattle. As indicated in column I of the two figures, the number of units going to Los Angeles directly has been increased from 150 to 160, in addition to the 60 units going to Seattle as a backup for the inventory shortage in Los Angeles. This plan solved the crisis in Los Angeles, and won Karl commendations from top management.

Some Applications

The applications of maximum flow problems and their variants are somewhat similar to those for minimum-cost flow problems described in the preceding section when management's objective is to *maximize flow* rather than to *minimize cost*. Here are some typical kinds of applications.

1. Maximize the flow through a distribution network, as for the BMZ problem.
2. Maximize the flow through a company's supply network from its vendors to its processing facilities.
3. Maximize the flow of oil through a system of pipelines.
4. Maximize the flow of water through a system of aqueducts.
5. Maximize the flow of vehicles through a transportation network.

Solving Very Large Problems

The expanded BMZ network in Figure 6.9 has 11 nodes and 16 arcs. However, the networks for most real applications are considerably larger, and occasionally vastly larger. As the number of nodes and arcs grows into the hundreds or thousands, the formulation and solution approach illustrated in Figures 6.8 and 6.10 quickly becomes impractical.

Fortunately, management scientists have other techniques available for formulating and solving huge problems with many tens of thousands of nodes and arcs. One technique is to reformulate a variant of a maximum flow problem so that an extremely efficient special-purpose algorithm for maximum flow problems still can be applied. Another is to reformulate the problem to fit the format for a minimum-cost flow problem so that the network simplex method can be applied. These special algorithms are available in some software packages, but not in the Excel Solver. Thus, if you should ever encounter a maximum flow problem or a variant that is beyond the scope of the Excel Solver (which won't happen in this book), rest assured that it probably can be formulated and solved in another way by a qualified management scientist.

Review Questions

1. How does the objective of a maximum flow problem differ from that for a minimum-cost flow problem?
2. What are the *source* and the *sink* for a maximum flow problem? For each, in what direction do all their arcs point?
3. What are the two equivalent ways in which the total amount of flow from the source to the sink can be measured?
4. The source and sink of a maximum flow problem are different from the supply nodes and demand nodes of a minimum-cost flow problem in what two ways?
5. What are a few typical kinds of applications of maximum flow problems?

6.4 Shortest Path Problems

The most common applications of shortest path problems are for what the name suggests—finding the *shortest path* between two points. Here is an example.

An Example: The Littletown Fire Department Problem

Littletown is a small town in a rural area. Its fire department serves a relatively large geographical area that includes many farming communities. Since there are numerous roads throughout the area, many possible routes may be available for traveling to any given farming community from the fire station. Since time is of the essence in reaching a fire, the fire chief wishes to determine in advance the *shortest path* from the fire station to each of the farming communities.

Figure 6.11 shows the road system connecting the fire station to one of the farming communities, including the mileage along each road. Can you find which route from the fire station to the farming community minimizes the total number of miles?

Model Formulation for the Littletown Problem. Figure 6.12 gives the network representation of this problem, which ignores the geographical layout and the curves in the roads. This network model is the usual way of representing a shortest path problem. The junctions now are nodes of the network, where the fire station and farming community are two additional nodes labeled as O (for *origin*) and T (for *destination*), respectively. Since travel (flow) can go in either direction between the nodes, the lines connecting the nodes now are referred to as **links**[2] instead of *arcs*. (Notice that the links do not have an arrowhead at either end.)

Have you found the shortest path from the origin to the destination yet? (Try it now before reading further.) It is

$$O \rightarrow A \rightarrow B \rightarrow E \rightarrow F \rightarrow T$$

with a total distance of 19 miles.

This problem (like any shortest path problem) can be thought of as a special kind of minimum-cost flow problem (Section 6.1) where the *miles traveled* now are interpreted to be the *cost* of flow through the network. A trip from the fire station to the farming community is interpreted to be a flow of 1 on the chosen path through the network, so minimizing

FIGURE 6.11

The road system between the Littletown Fire Station and a certain farming community, where A, B, . . . , H are junctions and the number next to each road shows its distance in miles.

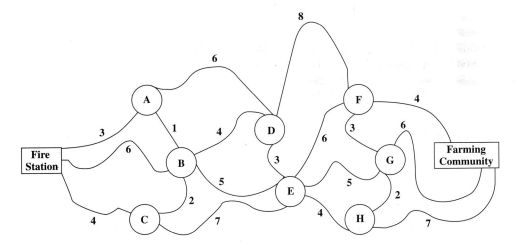

FIGURE 6.12

The network representation of Figure 6.11 as a shortest path problem.

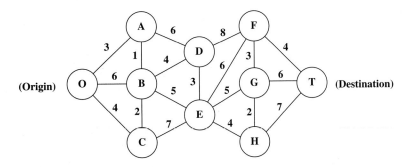

---

[2]Another name sometimes used is *undirected arc,* but we will not use this terminology.

FIGURE 6.13

A spreadsheet model for the Littletown Fire Department shortest path problem, where the changing cells (D4:D27) show the optimal solution obtained by the Solver and the target cell (D29) gives the total distance (in miles) of this shortest path.

	A	B	C	D	E	F	G	H	I	J
1		Littletown Fire Department Shortest Path Problem								
2										
3		From	To	On Route	Distance		Nodes	Net Flow		Supply/Demand
4		Fire St.	A	1	3		Fire St.	1	=	1
5		Fire St.	B	0	6		A	0	=	0
6		Fire St.	C	0	4		B	0	=	0
7		A	B	1	1		C	0	=	0
8		A	D	0	6		D	0	=	0
9		B	A	0	1		E	0	=	0
10		B	C	0	2		F	0	=	0
11		B	D	0	4		G	0	=	0
12		B	E	1	5		H	0	=	0
13		C	B	0	2		Farm Com.	–1	=	–1
14		C	E	0	7					
15		D	E	0	3					
16		D	F	0	8					
17		E	D	0	3					
18		E	F	1	6					
19		E	G	0	5					
20		E	H	0	4					
21		F	G	0	3					
22		F	Farm Com.	1	4					
23		G	F	0	3					
24		G	H	0	2					
25		G	Farm Com.	0	6					
26		H	G	0	2					
27		H	Farm Com.	0	7					
28										
29			Total Distance =	19						

Solver Parameters

Set Target Cell: $D$29

Equal To: ○ Max ● Min ○ Valu

By Changing Cells:

$D$4:$D$27

Subject to the Constraints:

$H$4:$H$13 = $J$4:$J$13

Solver Options

☑ Assume Linear Model
☑ Assume Non-Negative

	H
4	=D4+D5+D6
5	=-D4+D7+D8-D9
6	=-D5-D7+D9+D10+D11+D12-D13
7	=-D6-D10+D13+D14
8	=-D8-D11+D15+D16-D17
9	=-D12-D14-D15+D17+D18+D19+D20
10	=-D16-D18+D21+D22-D23
11	=-D19-D21+D23+D24+D25-D26
12	=-D20-D24+D26+D27
13	=-D22-D25-D27

	D
29	=SUMPRODUCT(D4:D27,E4:E27)

the cost of this flow is equivalent to minimizing the number of miles traveled. The fire station is considered to be the one supply node, with a supply of 1 to represent the start of this trip. The farming community is the one demand node, with a demand of 1 to represent the completion of this trip. All the other nodes in Figure 6.12 are transshipment nodes, so the net flow generated at each is 0.

Figure 6.13 shows the spreadsheet model that results from this interpretation. The format is basically the same as for the minimum-cost flow problem formulated in Figure 6.5, except now there are no arc capacity constraints and the unit cost column is replaced by a column of distances in miles. The flow quantities given by the changing cells (D4:D27) are 1 for each arc that is on the chosen path from the fire station to the farming community and 0 otherwise. The target cell (D29) gives the total distance of this path in miles. (See the equation for this cell at the bottom of the figure.) Columns B and C together list all the vertical links in Figure 6.12 twice, once as a downward arc and once as an upward arc, since either direction might be on the chosen path. The other links are only listed as left-to-right arcs, since this is the only direction of interest for choosing a shortest path from the origin to the destination.

Column J shows the net flow that needs to be generated at each of the nodes. Using the equations at the bottom of the figure, each column H cell then calculates the *actual* net flow at that node by adding the flow in and subtracting the flow out. The corresponding constraints, H4:H13 = J4:J13, are specified in the Solver dialogue box.

The solution shown in column D is the optimal solution obtained after clicking on the Solve button. It is exactly the same as the shortest path given earlier.

Just as for minimum-cost flow problems and maximum flow problems, special algorithms are available for solving large shortest path problems very efficiently, but these algorithms are not included in the Excel Solver. Using a spreadsheet formulation and the Solver are fine for problems of the size of the Littletown problem and somewhat larger, but you should be aware that vastly larger problems can still be solved by other means.

General Characteristics

Except for more complicated variations beyond the scope of this book, all shortest path problems share the characteristics illustrated by the Littletown problem. Here are the basic assumptions.

Assumptions of a Shortest Path Problem

1. You need to choose a path through the network that starts at a certain node, called the **origin,** and ends at another certain node, called the **destination.**
2. The lines connecting certain pairs of nodes commonly are *links* (which allow travel in either direction), although arcs (which only permit travel in one direction) also are allowed.
3. Associated with each link (or arc) is a nonnegative number called its **length.** (Be aware that the drawing of each link in the network typically makes no effort to show its true length other than giving the correct number next to the link.)
4. The objective is to find the shortest path (the path with the minimum total length) from the origin to the destination.

Some Applications

Not all applications of shortest path problems involve minimizing the distance traveled from the origin to the destination. In fact, they might not even involve travel at all. The links (or arcs) might instead represent activities of some other kind, so choosing a path through the network corresponds to selecting the best sequence of activities. The numbers giving the "lengths" of the links might then be, for example, the costs of the activities, in which case the objective would be to determine which sequence of activities minimizes the total cost.

Here are three categories of applications.

1. Minimize the total *distance* traveled, as in the Littletown example.
2. Minimize the total *cost* of a sequence of activities, as in the next example.
3. Minimize the total *time* of a sequence of activities, as in the example that follows the next one.

An Example of Minimizing Total Cost

Sarah has just graduated from high school. As a graduation present, her parents have given her a car fund of $21,000 to help purchase and maintain a certain three-year-old used car for college. Since operating and maintenance costs go up rapidly as the car ages, Sarah's parents tell her that she will be welcome to trade in her car on another three-year-old car one or more times during the next three summers if she determines that this would minimize her total net cost. They also inform her that they will give her a new car in four years as a college graduation present, so she should definitely plan to trade in her car then. (These are pretty nice parents!)

Table 6.2 gives the relevant data for *each* time Sarah purchases a three-year-old car. For example, if she trades in her car after two years, the next car will be in ownership year 1 during her junior year, and so forth.

TABLE 6.2 **Sarah's Data Each Time She Purchases a Three-Year-Old Car**

Purchase Price	Operating and Maintenance Costs for Ownership Year				Trade-in Value at End of Ownership Year			
	1	*2*	*3*	*4*	*1*	*2*	*3*	*4*
$12,000	$2,000	$3,000	$4,500	$6,500	$8,500	$6,500	$4,500	$3,000

FIGURE 6.14

Formulation of the problem of when Sarah should trade in her car as a shortest path problem. The node labels measure the number of years from now. Each arc represents purchasing a car and then trading it in later.

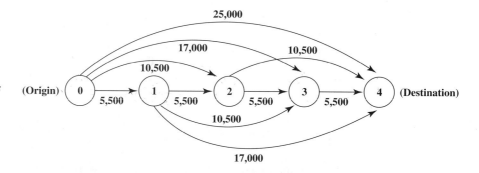

When should Sarah trade in her car (if at all) during the next three summers to minimize her total net cost of purchasing, operating, and maintaining the cars over her four years of college?

Figure 6.14 shows the network formulation of this problem as a shortest path problem. Nodes 1, 2, 3, and 4 are the end of Sarah's first, second, third, and fourth years of college, respectively. Node 0 is now, before starting college. Each arc from one node to a second node corresponds to the activity of purchasing a car at the time indicated by the first of these two nodes and then trading it in at the time indicated by the second node. Sarah begins by purchasing a car now, and she ends by trading in a car at the end of year 4, so node 0 is the *origin* and node 4 is the *destination*.

The number of arcs on the path chosen from the origin to the destination indicates how many times Sarah will purchase and trade in a car. For example, consider the path

This corresponds to purchasing a car now, then trading it in at the end of year 1 to purchase a second car, then trading in the second car at the end of year 3 to purchase a third car, and then trading in this third car at the end of year 4.

Since Sarah wants to minimize her total net cost from now (node 0) to the end of year 4 (node 4), each arc length needs to measure the net cost of that arc's cycle of purchasing, maintaining, and trading in a car. Therefore,

Arc length = Purchase price + Operating and maintenance costs − Trade-in value

For example, consider the arc from node 1 to node 3. This arc corresponds to purchasing a car at the end of year 1, operating and maintaining it during ownership years 1 and 2, and then trading it in at the end of ownership year 2. Consequently,

$$\text{Length of arc from } \textcircled{1} \text{ to } \textcircled{3} = 12{,}000 + 2{,}000 + 3{,}000 - 6{,}500$$
$$= 10{,}500 \quad \text{(in dollars)}$$

The arc lengths calculated in this way are shown next to the arcs in Figure 6.14. Adding up the lengths of the arcs on any path from node 0 to node 4 then gives the total net cost for that particular plan for trading in cars over the next four years. Therefore, finding the shortest path from the origin to the destination identifies the plan that will minimize Sarah's total net cost.

FIGURE 6.15

A spreadsheet model for Sarah's problem as a shortest path problem, where the changing cells (D4:D13) give the optimal solution obtained by the Solver and the target cell (D15) shows the resulting total cost of this shortest (least expensive) path.

	A	B	C	D	E	F	G	H	I	J
1		Sarah's Car Purchasing Problem								
2										
3		**From**	**To**	**On Route**	**Cost**		**Nodes**	**Net Flow**		**Supply/Demand**
4		Node 0	Node 1	0	$5,500		0	1	=	1
5		Node 0	Node 2	1	$10,500		1	0	=	0
6		Node 0	Node 3	0	$17,000		2	0	=	0
7		Node 0	Node 4	0	$25,000		3	0	=	0
8		Node 1	Node 2	0	$5,500		4	–1	=	–1
9		Node 1	Node 3	0	$10,500					
10		Node 1	Node 4	0	$17,000					
11		Node 2	Node 3	0	$5,500					
12		Node 2	Node 4	1	$10,500					
13		Node 3	Node 4	0	$5,500					
14										
15		**Total Distance =**		$21,000						

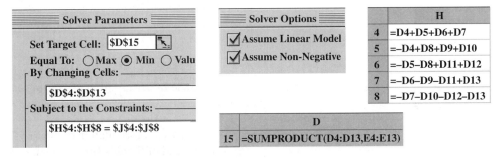

Solver Parameters

Set Target Cell: $D$15

Equal To: ○ Max ● Min ○ Valu

By Changing Cells:

$D$4:$D$13

Subject to the Constraints:

$H$4:$H$8 = $J$4:$J$8

Solver Options

☑ Assume Linear Model

☑ Assume Non-Negative

	H
4	=D4+D5+D6+D7
5	=–D4+D8+D9+D10
6	=–D5–D8+D11+D12
7	=–D6–D9–D11+D13
8	=–D7–D10–D12–D13

	D
15	=SUMPRODUCT(D4:D13,E4:E13)

Figure 6.15 shows the corresponding spreadsheet model, formulated in just the same way as for Figure 6.13 except that distances are now costs. Thus, the target cell (D15) now gives the total cost that is to be minimized. The changing cells (D4:D13) in the figure display the optimal solution obtained after having clicked on the Solve button. Since values of 1 indicate the path being followed, the shortest path turns out to be

Trade in the first car at the end of Year 2.

Trade in the second car at the end of Year 4.

The length of this path is 10,500 + 10,500 = 21,000, so Sarah's total net cost is $21,000, as given by the target cell. Recall that this is exactly the amount in Sarah's car fund provided by her parents. (These are *really* nice parents!)

An Example of Minimizing Total Time

The Quick Company has learned that a competitor is planning to come out with a new kind of product with a great sales potential. Quick has been working on a similar product that had been scheduled to come to market in 20 months. However, research is nearly complete and Quick's management now wishes to rush the product out to meet the competition.

There are four nonoverlapping phases left to be accomplished, including the remaining research that currently is being conducted at a normal pace. However, each phase can instead be conducted at a priority or crash level to expedite completion, and these are the levels that will be considered for the last three phases. The times required at these levels are shown in Table 6.3. (The times in parentheses at the normal level have been ruled out as too long.)

Management now has allocated $30 million for these four phases. The cost of each phase at the levels under consideration is shown in Table 6.4.

Management wishes to determine at which level to conduct each of the four phases to minimize the total time until the product can be marketed subject to the budget restriction of $30 million.

TABLE 6.3   Time Required for the Phases of Preparing Quick's New Product

Level	Remaining Research	Development	Design of Manufacturing System	Initiate Production and Distribution
Normal	5 months	(4 months)	(7 months)	(4 months)
Priority	4 months	3 months	5 months	2 months
Crash	2 months	2 months	3 months	1 month

TABLE 6.4   Cost for the Phases of Preparing Quick's New Product

Level	Remaining Research	Development	Design of Manufacturing System	Initiate Production and Distribution
Normal	$3 million	—	—	—
Priority	6 million	$6 million	$9 million	$3 million
Crash	9 million	9 million	12 million	6 million

FIGURE 6.16

Formulation of the Quick Co. problem as a shortest path problem. Except for the dummy destination, the arc labels indicate, first, the number of phases completed and, second, the amount of money left (in millions of dollars) for the remaining phases. Each arc length gives the time (in months) to perform that phase.

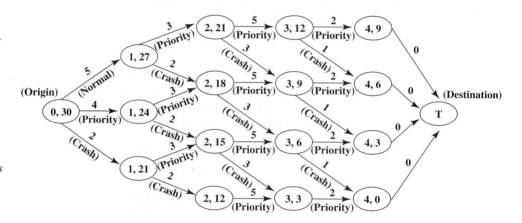

Figure 6.16 shows the network formulation of this problem as a shortest path problem. Each node indicates the situation at that point in time. Except for the destination, a node is identified by two numbers:

1. The number of phases completed.
2. The number of millions of dollars left for the remaining phases.

The origin is *now,* when 0 phases have been completed and the entire budget of $30 million is left. Each arc represents the choice of a particular level of effort (identified in parentheses below the arc) for that phase. The *time* (in months) required to perform the phase with this level of effort then is the *length* of the arc (shown above the arc). Time is chosen as the measure of arc length because the objective is to minimize the total time for all four phases. Summing the arc lengths for any particular path through the network gives the total time for the plan corresponding to that path. Therefore, the shortest path through the network identifies the plan that minimizes total time.

All four phases have been completed as soon as any one of the four nodes with a first label of 4 has been reached. So why doesn't the network just end with these four nodes rather than having an arc coming out of each one? The reason is that a shortest path problem is required to have only a single destination. Consequently, a dummy destination is added at the right-hand side.

> When real travel through a network can end at more than one node, an arc with length 0 is inserted from each of these nodes to a **dummy destination** so that the network will have just a single destination.

Since each of the arcs into the dummy destination has length 0, this addition to the network does not affect the total length of a path from the origin to its ending point.

Figure 6.17 displays the spreadsheet model for this problem. Once again, the format is the same as in Figures 6.13 and 6.15, except now the quantity of concern in column E and the target cell (D32) is time rather than distance or cost. Since the Solve button has already been clicked, the changing cells (D4:D30) indicate which arcs lie on the path that minimizes the total time. Thus, the shortest path is

$$(0, 30) \rightarrow (1, 21) \rightarrow (2, 15) \rightarrow (3, 3) \rightarrow (4, 0) \rightarrow T$$

with a total length of $2 + 3 + 3 + 2 + 0 = 10$ months (as given by cell D32). The resulting plan for the four phases is shown in Table 6.5. Although this plan does consume

FIGURE 6.17

A spreadsheet model for the Quick Co. problem as a shortest path problem, where the changing cells (D4:D30) show the optimal solution obtained by the Solver and the target cell (D32) gives the resulting total time for this shortest (quickest) path.

	A	B	C	D	E	F	G	H	I	J
1		Quick Co. Product Development Scheduling Problem								
2										
3		From	To	On Route	Time		Nodes	Net Flow		Supply/Demand
4		(0, 30)	(1, 27)	0	5		(0, 30)	1	=	1
5		(0, 30)	(1, 24)	0	4		(1, 27)	0	=	0
6		(0, 30)	(1, 21)	1	2		(1, 24)	0	=	0
7		(1, 27)	(2, 21)	0	3		(1, 21)	0	=	0
8		(1, 27)	(2, 18)	0	2		(2, 21)	0	=	0
9		(1, 24)	(2, 18)	0	3		(2, 18)	0	=	0
10		(1, 24)	(2, 15)	0	2		(2, 15)	0	=	0
11		(1, 21)	(2, 15)	1	3		(2, 12)	0	=	0
12		(1, 21)	(2, 12)	0	2		(3, 12)	0	=	0
13		(2, 21)	(3, 12)	0	5		(3, 9)	0	=	0
14		(2, 21)	(3, 9)	0	3		(3, 6)	0	=	0
15		(2, 18)	(3, 9)	0	5		(3, 3)	0	=	0
16		(2, 18)	(3, 6)	0	3		(4, 9)	0	=	0
17		(2, 15)	(3, 6)	0	5		(4, 6)	0	=	0
18		(2, 15)	(3, 3)	1	3		(4, 3)	0	=	0
19		(2, 12)	(3, 3)	0	5		(4, 0)	0	=	0
20		(3, 12)	(4, 9)	0	2		(T)	–1	=	–1
21		(3, 12)	(4, 6)	0	1					
22		(3, 9)	(4, 6)	0	2					
23		(3, 9)	(4, 3)	0	1					
24		(3, 6)	(4, 3)	0	2					
25		(3, 6)	(4, 0)	0	1					
26		(3, 3)	(4, 0)	1	2					
27		(4, 9)	(T)	0	0					
28		(4, 6)	(T)	0	0					
29		(4, 3)	(T)	0	0					
30		(4, 0)	(T)	1	0					
31										
32			Total Time=	10						

	H
4	=D4+D5+D6
5	=–D4+D7+D8
6	=–D5+D9+D10
7	=–D6+D11+D12
8	=–D7+D13+D14
9	=–D8–D9+D15+D16
10	=–D10–D11+D17+D18
11	=–D12+D19
12	=–D13+D20+D21
13	=–D14–D15+D22+D23
14	=–D16–D17+D24+D25
15	=–D18–D19+D26
16	=–D20+D27
17	=–D21–D22+D28
18	=–D23–D24+D29
19	=–D25–D26+D30
20	=–D27–D28–D29–D30

Solver Parameters

Set Target Cell: $D$32

Equal To: ○ Max ● Min ○ Valu

By Changing Cells:

$D$4:$D$30

Subject to the Constraints:

$H$4:$H$20 = $J$4:$J$20

Solver Options

☑ Assume Linear Model

☑ Assume Non-Negative

	D
32	=SUMPRODUCT(D4:D30,E4:E30)

TABLE 6.5   The Optimal Solution Obtained by the Excel Solver for Quick's Shortest Path Problem

Phase	Level	Time	Cost
Remaining research	Crash	2 months	$ 9 million
Development	Priority	3 months	6 million
Design of manufacturing system	Crash	3 months	12 million
Initiate production and distribution	Priority	2 months	3 million
Total		10 months	$30 million

the entire budget of $30 million, it does reduce the time until the product can be brought to market from the originally planned 20 months down to just 10 months.

Given this information, Quick's management now must decide whether this plan provides the best trade-off between time and cost. What would be the effect on total time of spending a few million more dollars? What would be the effect of reducing the spending somewhat instead? It is easy to provide management with this information as well by quickly solving some shortest path problems that correspond to budgets different from $30 million. The ultimate decision on which plan provides the best time–cost trade-off then is a judgment decision that only management can make.

Review Questions

1. What are the origin and the destination in the Littletown Fire Department example?
2. What is the distinction between an arc and a link?
3. What are the supply node and the demand node when a shortest path problem is interpreted as a minimum-cost flow problem? With what supply and demand?
4. What are three measures of the length of a link (or arc) that lead to three categories of applications of shortest path problems?
5. What is the objective for Sarah's shortest path problem?
6. When does a dummy destination need to be added to the formulation of a shortest path problem?
7. What kind of trade-off does the management of the Quick Co. need to consider in making its final decision about how to expedite its new product to market?

6.5 Minimum Spanning-Tree Problems

This chapter focuses on problems with *network representations.* Thus far, the networks already have been complete with both nodes and links (or arcs).

We now turn our attention to a different kind of problem where the objective is to *design the network.* The nodes are given, but we must decide which links to give to the network. Specifically, each *potential link* has a cost (different for different links) for inserting it into the network. We are required to provide enough links to provide a path between *every pair of nodes.* The objective is to do this in a way that minimizes the total cost of the links.

Such a problem is referred to as a *minimum spanning-tree problem,* as illustrated by the following example.

An Example: The Modern Corp. Problem

Management of the Modern Corporation has decided to have a state-of-the-art *fiber-optic network* installed to provide high-speed communications (data, voice, and video) between its major centers.

FIGURE 6.18

A display of Modern Corp.'s major centers (the nodes), the possible locations for fiber-optic cables (the dashed lines), and the cost in millions of dollars for those cables (the numbers).

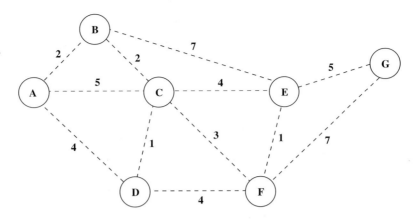

FIGURE 6.19

The fiber-optic network that provides the optimal solution for Modern's minimum spanning-tree problem.

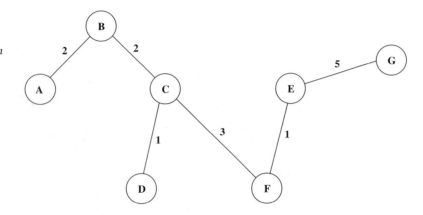

The nodes in Figure 6.18 show the geographical layout of the corporation's major centers (which include corporate headquarters, a supercomputer facility, and a research park, as well as production and distribution centers). The dashed lines are the potential locations of fiber-optic cables. (Other cables between pairs of centers also are possible but have been ruled out as uneconomical.) The number next to each dashed line gives the cost (in millions of dollars) if that particular cable is chosen as one to be installed.

Any pair of centers does not need to have a cable directly connecting them in order to take full advantage of the fiber-optic technology for high-speed communications between these centers. All that is necessary is to have a series of cables that connect the centers.

The problem is to determine which cables should be installed to minimize the total cost of providing high-speed communications between *every* pair of centers. This is, in fact, a *minimum spanning-tree problem.*

The optimal solution for this problem is shown in Figure 6.19, where the links in this network correspond to the possible cables in Figure 6.18 that should be chosen for installation. (Note that there is indeed a path between every pair of centers.) The resulting cost of this fiber-optic network is

$$\text{Total cost} = 2 + 2 + 1 + 3 + 1 + 5 = 14 \qquad (\$14 \text{ million})$$

Any other design of the network that connects every pair of centers would cost at least $1 million more.

What is the reason for the strange name, *minimum spanning-tree problem?* Here is the explanation. In the terminology of network theory, the network in Figure 6.19 is a **tree** because it does not have any paths that begin and end at the same node without backtracking (i.e., no paths that cycle). It also is a **spanning tree** because it is a tree that provides a path between every pair of nodes (so it spans all the nodes). Finally, it is a **minimum spanning tree** because it *minimizes* the total cost among all spanning trees.

General Characteristics   Just as for Modern's problem, every minimum spanning-tree problem satisfies the following assumptions.

Assumptions of a Minimum Spanning-Tree Problem

1. You are given the *nodes* of a network but *not* the *links.* Instead, you are given the *potential links* and the positive *cost* (or a similar measure) for each if it is inserted into the network.

2. You wish to design the network by inserting enough links to satisfy the requirement that there be a path between *every pair* of nodes.

3. The objective is to satisfy this requirement in a way that minimizes the total cost of doing so.

An optimal solution for this problem always is a *spanning tree.* Here is an easy way to recognize a spanning tree.

> The number of links in a spanning tree always is one less than the number of nodes. Furthermore, each node is directly connected by a single link to at least one other node.

See that this description fits the spanning tree in Figure 6.19, where there are six links and seven nodes (all directly connected to at least one other node). Remove any one of these links and assumption 2 above would be violated (no spanning tree). (Check this.) Incur the needless extra cost of adding another link instead (without removing one) and you again no longer have a spanning tree. (Check that adding any unused link from Figure 6.18 into Figure 6.19 would create a path that begins and ends at the same node without backtracking, which violates the definition of a tree.)

Finally, we should point out that, in contrast to transportation, assignment, maximum flow, and shortest path problems, a minimum spanning-tree problem is *not* a special type of minimum-cost flow problem. (It is not even a special type of linear programming problem.) Furthermore, it cannot be solved by the Excel Solver.

That is the bad news. The good news is that you can solve it very easily by the algorithm described below without even using a computer.

A Remarkably Simple Algorithm   Starting with no links in the network, each step of the algorithm selects one new link to insert from the list of potential links. As described below, the algorithm continues in this way until every node is touched by a link, at which point the selected nodes form a minimum spanning tree.

Algorithm for a Minimum Spanning-Tree Problem

1. Choice of the first link: Select the *cheapest* potential link.

2. Choice of the next link: Select the *cheapest* potential link between a node that already is touched by a link and a node that does not yet have such a link.

3. Repeat step 2 over and over until every node is touched by a link (perhaps more than one). At that point, an optimal solution (a minimum spanning tree) has been obtained.

[*Tie breaking*: Ties for the *cheapest* potential link may be broken arbitrarily without affecting the optimality of the final solution. However, ties in step 2 signal that there may also be (but need not be) other optimal solutions that would be obtained by breaking ties in another way.]

Application of the Algorithm to the Modern Corp. Problem   Now let us apply this algorithm to Modern's minimum spanning-tree problem as displayed in Figure 6.18.

Among all the potential links (the dashed lines), the one between node C and node D ties with the one between node E and node F as the cheapest (a cost of 1). Therefore, for step 1, we need to select one of these two potential links to be the first link inserted into the network. Breaking the tie arbitrarily, let us select the one between node C and node D (the other will be chosen later), as shown next.

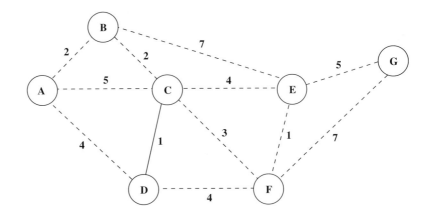

Next, we apply step 2 for the first time. The two nodes that are touched by a link are nodes C and D, so we need to compare the costs of the potential links between either of these nodes and a node that does not yet have a touching link. These potential links and their costs are

C----B : Cost = 2   C----F : Cost = 3
C----A : Cost = 5   D----A : Cost = 4
C----E : Cost = 4   D----F : Cost = 4

Since the cheapest of these is the one between node C and node B, with a cost of 2, it is selected to be the next link inserted into the network, as displayed below.

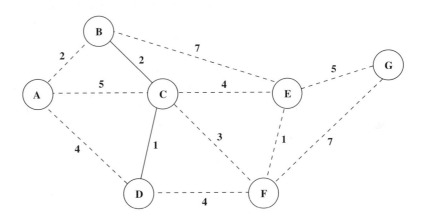

Now, nodes B, C, and D each are touched by a link (or two links in the case of node C), so the next execution of step 2 requires comparing the costs of the potential links between one of these nodes and one of the others.

C----A : Cost = 5   D----A : Cost = 4
C----E : Cost = 4   D----F : Cost = 4
C----F : Cost = 3   B----A : Cost = 2
                           B----E : Cost = 7

The cheapest of these is the potential link between node B and node A, so it becomes the next link added to the network.

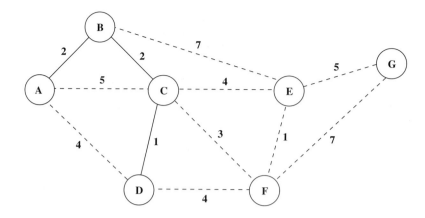

Nodes A, B, C, and D now all have touching links, so we next compare the costs of the potential links between one of these nodes and one of the others. (Actually, none of these potential links involve node A, since it does not have any potential links that go to a node that is not yet touched by a link.)

C----------E : Cost = 4   D----------F : Cost = 4

C----------F : Cost = 3   B----------E : Cost = 7

The cheapest is the potential link between node C and node F, so it is added next.

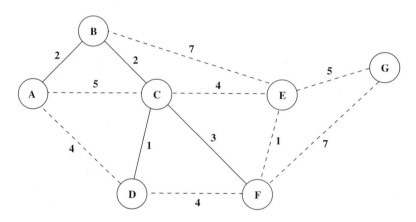

All but nodes E and G now are touched by a link. Therefore, the only potential links that need to be considered next are between either node E or G and one of the other nodes.

C----------E : Cost = 4   F----------E : Cost = 1

B----------E : Cost = 7   F----------G : Cost = 7

The cheapest by far is the potential link between node F and node E, so it finally gets inserted into the network. (Remember that this potential link was tied to be the initial link in step 1.)

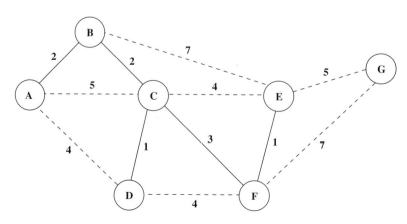

Since node G now is the only node untouched by a link, the only potential links to consider next are those between this node and the others.

(F)----------(G) : Cost = 7   (E)----------(G) : Cost = 5

The cheaper one is the potential link between node E and node G, so we insert it into the network.

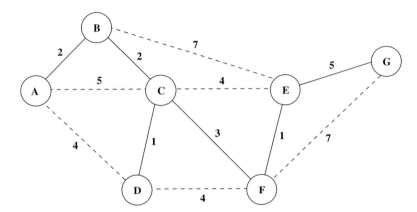

Every node now is touched by a link, so the algorithm is done and this is our optimal solution. All the links that have been inserted into the network form a *minimum spanning tree* with a total cost of $2 + 2 + 1 + 3 + 1 + 5 = 14$ ($14 million). All the remaining potential links (dashed lines) are rejected because the inserted links provide a path between every pair of nodes.

Notice that this optimal solution is the same as the one given in Figure 6.19. (There is only one optimal solution for this particular problem.)

What would have happened if the tie had been broken the other way in step 1 by selecting the potential link between node E and node F to be the initial link inserted into the network instead of the potential link between node C and node D? Go ahead and check this out by cranking through the algorithm from this point. You will find that exactly the same links get selected, but in a different order from before.

This algorithm is referred to as a **greedy algorithm** because it simply grabs the most favorable choice (the cheapest potential link) at each step without worrying about the effect of this choice on subsequent decisions. It is remarkable that such a quick and simpleminded procedure still is guaranteed to find an optimal solution. Rejoice this time, but beware. Greedy algorithms normally will not necessarily find optimal solutions for other management science problems.

Some Applications   In this age of the information superhighway, applications similar to the Modern Corp. example have become increasingly important. However, minimum spanning-tree problems have several other types of applications as well.

1. Design of telecommunication networks (computer networks, leased-line telephone networks, cable television networks, etc.)
2. Design of a lightly used transportation network to minimize the total cost of providing the links (rail lines, roads, etc.).
3. Design of a network of high-voltage electrical power transmission lines.
4. Design of a network of wiring on electrical equipment (e.g., a digital computer system) to minimize the total length of the wire.
5. Design of a network of pipelines to connect a number of locations.

Review Questions

1. In a minimum spanning-tree problem, what part of the network is given and what part remains to be designed?
2. What kind of network is being designed in the Modern Corp. example?

3. In the terminology of network theory, what is a tree? A spanning tree? A minimum spanning tree?

4. What is an easy way to recognize a spanning tree?

5. What is the objective of a minimum spanning-tree problem?

6. Is a minimum spanning-tree problem a special type of minimum-cost flow problem?

7. What kind of algorithm will solve a minimum spanning-tree problem (but very few other management science problems)?

8. What are a few types of applications of minimum spanning-tree problems?

6.6 Summary

Networks of some type arise in a wide variety of contexts. Network representations are very useful for portraying the relationships and connections between the components of systems. Each component is represented by a point in the network called a *node,* and then the connections between components (nodes) are represented by lines called *arcs* (for one-way travel) or *links* (for two-way travel).

Frequently, a flow of some type must be sent through a network, so a decision needs to be made about the best way to do this. The kinds of network optimization models introduced in this chapter provide a powerful tool for making such decisions.

The model for minimum-cost flow problems plays a central role among these network optimization models, both because it is so broadly applicable and because it can be readily solved. The Excel Solver solves spreadsheet formulations of reasonable size, and the network simplex method can be used to solve larger problems, including huge problems with tens of thousands of nodes and arcs. A minimum-cost flow problem typically is concerned with optimizing the flow of goods through a network from their points of origin (the *supply nodes*) to where they are needed (the *demand nodes*). The objective is to minimize the total cost of sending the available supply through the network to satisfy the given demand. One typical application (among several) is to optimize the operation of a distribution network.

Special types of minimum-cost flow problems include transportation problems and assignment problems (discussed in the preceding chapter) as well as two prominent types introduced in this chapter: maximum flow problems and shortest path problems.

Given the limited capacities of the arcs in the network, the objective of a maximum flow problem is to maximize the total amount of flow from a particular point of origin (the *source*) to a particular terminal point (the *sink*). For example, this might involve maximizing the flow of goods through a company's supply network from its vendors to its processing facilities.

A shortest path problem also has a beginning point (the *origin*) and an ending point (the *destination*), but now the objective is to find a path from the origin to the destination that has the minimum total *length.* For some applications, length refers to distance, so the objective is to minimize the total distance traveled. However, some applications instead involve minimizing either the total cost or the total time of a sequence of activities.

Whereas all these models are concerned with optimizing the operation of an existing network, minimum spanning-tree problems are a prominent example of a model for optimizing the design of a new network. In this case, the nodes are given, but decisions need to be made on which links to insert into the network. The objective is to minimize the total cost of the links while providing a path between every pair of nodes. For example, this is management's usual objective when designing a modern telecommunication network to link the company's various centers.

Glossary

Arc A channel through which flow may occur from one node to another, shown as an arrow between the nodes pointing in the direction in which flow is allowed. (Section 6.1)   204

Capacity of an arc The maximum amount of flow allowed through the arc. (Section 6.1)   204

Conservation of flow Having the amount of flow out of a node equal to the amount of flow into that node. (Section 6.1)   204

Demand node A node where the net amount of flow generated (outflow minus inflow) is a fixed negative number, so that flow is absorbed there. (Section 6.1)   204

Destination The node at which travel through the network is assumed to end for a shortest path problem. (Section 6.4)   217

Dummy destination A fictitious destination introduced into the formulation of a shortest path problem with multiple possible termination points to satisfy the requirement that there be just a single destination. (Section 6.4)   220

Greedy algorithm An algorithm that simply grabs the most favorable choice at each step without worrying about the effect of this choice on subsequent decisions. (Section 6.5)   227

Length of a link or arc The number (typically a distance, a cost, or a time) associated with including the link or arc in the selected path for a shortest path problem. (Section 6.4)   217

Link A channel through which flow may occur in either direction between a pair of nodes, shown as a line between the nodes. (Section 6.4)   215

Minimum spanning tree One among all spanning trees that minimizes total cost. (Section 6.5)   223

Network simplex method A streamlined version of the simplex method for solving minimum-cost flow problems very efficiently. (Section 6.1)   206

Node A junction point of a network, shown as a labeled circle. (Section 6.1)   204

Origin The node at which travel through the network is assumed to start for a shortest path problem. (Section 6.4)   217

Sink The node for a maximum flow problem at which all flow through the network terminates. (Section 6.3)   212

Source The node for a maximum flow problem at which all flow through the network originates. (Section 6.3)   212

Spanning tree A tree that provides a path between every pair of nodes. (Section 6.5)   223

Supply node A node where the net amount of flow generated (outflow minus inflow) is a fixed positive number. (Section 6.1)   204

Transshipment node A node where the amount of flow out equals the amount of flow in. (Section 6.1)   204

Transshipment problem A special type of minimum-cost flow problem where there are no capacity constraints on the arcs. (Section 6.1)   208

Tree A network that does not have any paths that begin and end at the same node without backtracking. (Section 6.5)   223

Learning Aids for This Chapter in Your MS Courseware

"Ch. 6—Network Opt Problems" Excel File:

Distribution Unlimited Example
BMZ Example
Expanded BMZ Example
Littletown Fire Department Example
Sarah Example
Quick Example

An Excel Add-in:

Premium Solver

Problems

We have inserted the symbol E* to the left of each problem (or its parts) where Excel should be used (unless your instructor gives you contrary instructions). An asterisk on the problem number indicates that at least a partial answer is given in the back of the book.

6.1. Consider the Distribution Unlimited Co. problem presented in both Sections 3.4 and 6.1. The same problem is formulated in two different ways in these two sections, but the two formulations must have the same optimal solution. Refer to the parameter table (Table 3.9) needed to formulate a complete linear programming model for this problem. Then refer to its network formulation as a minimum-cost flow problem in Figures 6.2 and 6.3.
  a. Compare how many numbers (including zeroes) are needed for the two formulations.
  b. Which formulation do you think more clearly depicts the problem? Why?
  c. Now compare the two different spreadsheet models for this same problem in Figures 3.5 and 6.5. Which model do you think more clearly depicts the problem? Why?

6.2.* Consider the transportation problem having the following parameter table.

	Destination			
	1	*2*	*3*	*Supply*
Source				
1	6	7	4	40
2	5	8	6	60
Demand	30	40	30	

  a. Formulate a network model for this problem as a minimum-cost flow problem by drawing a network similar to Figure 6.3.

E* b. Formulate and solve a spreadsheet model for this problem in the format used for transportation problems in Chapter 5.

E* c. Formulate and solve a spreadsheet model for this problem in the format of a minimum-cost flow problem.

6.3. The Makonsel Company is a fully integrated company that both produces goods and sells them at its retail outlets. After production, the goods are stored in the company's two warehouses until needed by the retail outlets. Trucks are used to transport the goods from the two plants to the warehouses, and then from the warehouses to the three retail outlets.

Using units of full truckloads, the following table shows each plant's monthly output, its shipping cost per truckload sent to each warehouse, and the maximum amount that it can ship per month to each warehouse.

To From	Unit Shipping Cost		Shipping Capacity		
	Warehouse 1	Warehouse 2	Warehouse 1	Warehouse 2	Output
Plant 1	$425	$560	125	150	200
Plant 2	510	600	175	200	300

For each retail outlet (RO), the next table shows its monthly demand, its shipping cost per truckload from each warehouse, and the maximum amount that can be shipped per month from each warehouse.

To From	Unit Shipping Cost			Shipping Capacity		
	RO1	RO2	RO3	RO1	RO2	RO3
Warehouse 1	$470	$505	$490	100	150	100
Warehouse 2	390	410	440	125	150	75
Demand	150	200	150	150	200	150

Management now wants to determine a distribution plan (number of truckloads shipped per month from each plant to each warehouse and from each warehouse to each retail outlet) that will minimize the total shipping cost.

a. Draw a network that depicts the company's distribution network. Identify the supply nodes, transshipment nodes, and demand nodes in this network.

b. Formulate a network model for this problem as a minimum-cost flow problem by inserting all the necessary data into the network drawn in part a. (Use the format depicted in Figure 6.3 to display these data.)

E* c. Formulate and solve a spreadsheet model for this problem.

6.4. The Audiofile Company produces boomboxes. However, management has decided to subcontract out the production of the speakers needed for the boomboxes. Three vendors are available to supply the speakers. Their price for each shipment of 1,000 speakers is shown below.

Vendor	Price
1	$22,500
2	22,700
3	22,300

Each shipment would go to one of the company's two warehouses. In addition to the price for each shipment, each vendor would charge a shipping cost for which it has its own formula based on the mileage to the warehouse. These formulas and the mileage data are shown below.

Vendor	Charge per Shipment	Warehouse 1	Warehouse 2
1	$300 + 40¢/mile	1,600 miles	400 miles
2	$200 + 50¢/mile	500 miles	600 miles
3	$500 + 20¢/mile	2,000 miles	1,000 miles

Whenever one of the company's two factories needs a shipment of speakers to assemble into the boomboxes, the company hires a trucker to bring the shipment in from one of the warehouses. The cost per shipment is given below, along with the number of shipments needed per month at each factory.

	Unit Shipping Cost	
	Factory 1	Factory 2
Warehouse 1	$200	$700
Warehouse 2	400	500
Monthly demand	10	6

Each vendor is able to supply as many as 10 shipments per month. However, because of shipping limitations, each vendor is only able to send a maximum of 6 shipments per month to each warehouse. Similarly, each warehouse is only able to send a maximum of 6 shipments per month to each factory.

Management now wants to develop a plan for each month regarding how many shipments (if any) to order from each vendor, how many of those shipments should go to each warehouse, and then how many shipments each warehouse should send to each factory. The objective is to minimize the sum of the purchase costs (including the shipping charge) and the shipping costs from the warehouses to the factories.

    a. Draw a network that depicts the company's supply network. Identify the supply nodes, transshipment nodes, and demand nodes in this network.

    b. This problem is only a *variant* of a minimum-cost flow problem because the supply from each vendor is a *maximum* of 10 rather than a fixed amount of 10. However, it can be converted to a full-fledged minimum-cost flow problem by adding a dummy demand node that receives (at zero cost) all the unused supply capacity at the vendors. Formulate a network model for this minimum-cost flow problem by inserting all the necessary data into the network drawn in part *a* supplemented by this dummy demand node. (Use the format depicted in Figure 6.3 to display these data.)

E*   *c.* Formulate and solve a spreadsheet model for the company's problem.

6.5.* Consider Figure 6.9 (in Section 6.3), which depicts the BMZ distribution network from its factories in Stuttgart and Berlin to the distribution centers in both Los Angeles

and Seattle. This figure also gives in brackets the maximum amount that can be shipped through each shipping lane.

    In the weeks following the crisis described in Section 6.2, the distribution center in Los Angeles has successfully replenished its inventory. Therefore, Karl Schmidt (the supply chain manager for the BMZ Co.) has concluded that it will be sufficient hereafter to ship 130 units per month to Los Angeles and 50 units per month to Seattle. (One unit is a hundred cubic meters of automobile replacement parts.) The Stuttgart factory (node ST in the figure) will allocate 130 units per month and the Berlin factory (node BE) will allocate 50 units per month out of their total production to cover these shipments. However, rather than resuming the past practice of supplying the Los Angeles distribution center from only the Stuttgart factory and supplying the Seattle distribution center from only the Berlin factory, Karl has decided to allow either factory to supply either distribution center. He feels that this additional flexibility is likely to reduce the total shipping cost.

    The following table gives the shipping cost per unit through each of these shipping lanes.

From \ To	LI	BO	RO	HA	NO	NY	BN	LA	SE
Node									
ST	$3,200	$2,500	$2,900	—	—	—	—	—	—
BE	—	—	$2,400	$2,000	—	—	—	—	—
LI	—	—	—	—	$6,100	—	—	—	—
BO	—	—	—	—	$6,800	$5,400	—	—	—
RO	—	—	—	—	—	$5,900	—	—	—
HA	—	—	—	—	—	$6,300	$5,700	—	—
NO	—	—	—	—	—	—	—	$3,100	—
NY	—	—	—	—	—	—	—	$4,200	$4,000
BN	—	—	—	—	—	—	—	$3,400	$3,000

Unit Shipping Cost to Node

Karl wants to determine the shipping plan that will minimize the total shipping cost.

    a. Formulate a network model for this problem as a minimum-cost flow problem by inserting all the necessary data into the distribution network shown in Figure 6.9. (Use the format depicted in Figure 6.3 to display these data.)

E*   *b.* Formulate and solve a spreadsheet model for this problem.

    c. What is the total shipping cost for this optimal solution?

6.6. Reconsider Problem 6.5. Suppose now that, for administrative convenience, management has decided that all 130 units per month needed at the distribution center in Los Angeles must come from the Stuttgart factory (node ST) and all 50 units per month needed at the distribution center in Seattle must come from the Berlin factory (node BE). For each of these distribution centers, Karl Schmidt wants to determine the shipping plan that will minimize the total shipping cost.

    a. For the distribution center in Los Angeles, formulate a network model for this problem as a minimum-cost flow problem by inserting all the necessary data into the distribution network shown in Figure 6.6. (Use the format depicted in Figure 6.3 to display these data.)

E*   *b.* Formulate and solve a spreadsheet model for the problem formulated in part *a.*

    c. For the distribution center in Seattle, draw its distribution network emanating from the Berlin factory at node BE.

    d. Repeat part *a* for the distribution center in Seattle by using the network drawn in part *c.*

E*   *e.* Formulate and solve a spreadsheet model for the problem formulated in part *d.*

    f. Add the total shipping costs obtained in parts *b* and *e.* Compare this sum with the total shipping cost obtained in part *c* of Problem 6.5 (as given in the back of the book).

6.7. Consider the maximum flow problem formulated in Figures 6.7 and 6.8 for the BMZ case study. Redraw Figure 6.7 and insert the optimal shipping quantities (cells D4:D12 in

Figure 6.8) in parentheses above the respective arcs. Examine the capacities of these arcs. Explain why these arc capacities ensure that the shipping quantities in parentheses must be an optimal solution because the maximum flow cannot exceed 150.

E* 6.8.* Formulate and solve a spreadsheet model for the maximum flow problem shown below, where node A is the source, node F is the sink, and the arc capacities are the numbers in square brackets shown next to the arcs.

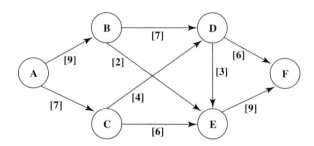

6.9. The diagram to the right depicts a system of aqueducts that originate at three rivers (nodes R1, R2, and R3) and

terminate at a major city (node T), where the other nodes are junction points in the system.

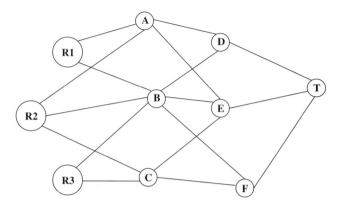

Using units of thousands of acre feet, the following tables show the maximum amount of water that can be pumped through each aqueduct per day.

To⎯⎯ From	A	B	C
R1	75	65	—
R2	40	50	60
R3	—	80	70

To⎯⎯ From	D	E	F
A	60	45	—
B	70	55	45
C	—	70	90

To⎯⎯ From	T
D	120
E	190
F	130

The city water manager wants to determine a flow plan that will maximize the flow of water to the city.

a. Formulate this problem as a maximum flow problem by identifying a source, a sink, and the transshipment nodes, and then drawing the complete network that shows the capacity of each arc.

E* b. Formulate and solve a spreadsheet model for this problem.

6.10. Refer back to Table 5.14, which gives the location of Texago Corporation's three oil fields, three refineries, and four distribution centers. In addition to these locations, Texago also imports oil from the Middle East and has opened a new refinery in St. Louis.

A major strike involving the transportation industries now has sharply curtailed Texago's capacity to ship oil from the four oil fields to the four refineries and to ship petroleum products from the refineries to the distribution centers. Using units of thousands of barrels of crude oil (and its equivalent in refined products), the following

tables show the maximum number of units that can be shipped per day from each oil field to each refinery and from each refinery to each distribution center.

Refinery	Pittsburgh	Atlanta	Kansas City	San Francisco
New Orleans	5	9	6	4
Charleston	8	7	9	5
Seattle	4	6	7	8
St. Louis	12	11	9	7

(Distribution Center header spans Pittsburgh, Atlanta, Kansas City, San Francisco.)

The Texago management now wants to determine a plan for how many units to ship from each oil field to each refinery and from each refinery to each distribution center that will maximize the total number of units reaching the distribution centers.

a. Draw a rough map that shows the location of Texago's oil fields, refineries, and distribution centers. Add arrows to show the flow of crude oil and then petroleum products through this distribution network.

b. Redraw this distribution network by lining up all the nodes representing oil fields in one column, all the nodes representing refineries in a second column, and all the nodes representing distribution centers in a third column. Then add arcs to show the possible flow.

Oil Field	New Orleans	Charleston	Seattle	St. Louis
Texas	11	7	2	8
California	5	4	8	7
Alaska	7	3	12	6
Middle East	8	9	4	15

(Refinery header spans New Orleans, Charleston, Seattle, St. Louis.)

c. Use the distribution network from part *b* to formulate a network model for Texago's problem as a variant of a maximum flow problem.

E*   d. Formulate and solve a spreadsheet model for this problem.

E*6.11. Reconsider the Littletown Fire Department problem presented in Section 6.4 and depicted in Figure 6.11. Due to maintenance work on the one-mile road between nodes A and B, a detour currently must be taken that extends the trip between these nodes to four miles.

Formulate and solve a spreadsheet model for this revised problem to find the new shortest path from the fire station to the farming community.

6.12. You need to take a trip by car to another town that you have never visited before. Therefore, you are studying a map to determine the shortest route to your destination. Depending on which route you choose, there are five other towns (call them A, B, C, D, E) through which you might pass on the way. The map shows the mileage along each road that directly connects two towns without any intervening towns. These numbers are summarized in the following table, where a dash indicates that there is no road directly connecting these two towns without going through any other towns.

Miles between Adjacent Towns

Town	A	B	C	D	E	Destination
Origin	40	60	50	—	—	—
A		10	—	70	—	—
B			20	55	40	—
C				—	50	—
D					10	60
E						80

a. Formulate a network model for this problem as a shortest path problem by drawing a network where nodes represent towns, links represent roads, and numbers indicate the length of each link in miles.

E*   b. Formulate and solve a spreadsheet model for this problem.

c. Use part *b* to identify your shortest route.

d. If each number in the table represented your *cost* (in dollars) for driving your car from one town to the next, would the answer in part *c* now give your minimum-cost route?

e. If each number in the table represented your *time* (in minutes) for driving your car from one town to the next, would the answer in part *c* now give your minimum-time route?

6.13.* At a small but growing airport, the local airline company is purchasing a new tractor for a tractor-trailer train to bring luggage to and from the airplanes. A new mechanized luggage system will be installed in three years, so the tractor will not be needed after that. However, because it will receive heavy use, so that the running and maintenance costs will increase rapidly as it ages, it may still be more economical to replace the tractor after one or two years. The following table gives the total net discounted cost associated with purchasing a tractor (purchase price minus trade-in allowance, plus running and maintenance costs) at the end of year *i* and trading it in at the end of year *j* (where year 0 is now).

		j	
	1	*2*	*3*
i			
0	$8,000	$18,000	$31,000
1		$10,000	$21,000
2			$12,000

Management wishes to determine at what times (if any) the tractor should be replaced to minimize the total cost for the tractors over three years.

a. Formulate a network model for this problem as a shortest path problem.

E*   b. Formulate and solve a spreadsheet model for this problem.

6.14. One of Speedy Airlines' flights is about to take off from Seattle for a nonstop flight to London. There is some flexibility in choosing the precise route to be taken, depending upon weather conditions. The following network depicts the possible routes under consideration, where SE and LN are Seattle and London, respectively, and the other nodes represent various intermediate locations.

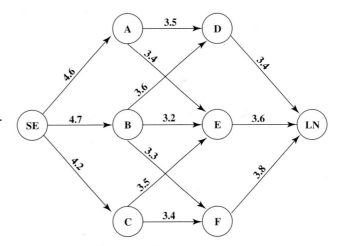

The winds along each arc greatly affect the flying time (and so the fuel consumption). Based on current meteorological reports, the flying times (in hours) for this particular flight are shown next to the arcs. Because the fuel consumed is so expensive, the management of Speedy Airlines has established a policy of choosing the route that minimizes the total flight time.

a. What plays the role of distances in interpreting this problem to be a shortest path problem?

E*   b. Formulate and solve a spreadsheet model for this problem.

6.15. Reconsider the Modern Corp. problem presented in Section 6.5. When the algorithm for a minimum spanning-tree problem was applied to this problem, there was a tie at step 1 for choosing the first link. This tie was broken arbitrarily by selecting the potential link between node C and node D.

Now break the tie the other way by selecting the potential link between node E and node F to be the first link and then reapply the rest of the algorithm. Show each step. (You again should obtain the minimum spanning tree shown in Figure 6.19.)

6.16.* Use the greedy algorithm presented in Section 6.5 to find a minimum spanning tree for a network with the following nodes and with the links still to be chosen. The dashed lines between pairs of nodes represent *potential* links and the number next to each dashed line represents the cost (in thousands of dollars) of inserting that link into the network.

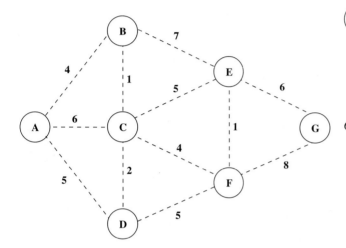

6.17. Use the greedy algorithm presented in Section 6.5 to find a minimum spanning tree for a network with the following nodes and with the links still to be chosen. The dashed lines between pairs of nodes represent *potential* nodes and the number next to each dashed line represents the cost (in millions of dollars) of inserting that link into the network.

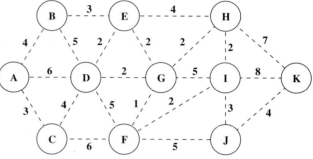

6.18. The Wirehouse Lumber Company will soon begin logging eight groves of trees in the same general area. Therefore, it must develop a system of dirt roads that makes each grove accessible from every other grove. The distance (in miles) between every pair of groves is as follows:

	Distance between Pairs of Groves							
Grove	1	2	3	4	5	6	7	8
1	—	1.3	2.1	0.9	0.7	1.8	2.0	1.5
2	1.3	—	0.9	1.8	1.2	2.6	2.3	1.1
3	2.1	0.9	—	2.6	1.7	2.5	1.9	1.0
4	0.9	1.8	2.6	—	0.7	1.6	1.5	0.9
5	0.7	1.2	1.7	0.7	—	0.9	1.1	0.8
6	1.8	2.6	2.5	1.6	0.9	—	0.6	1.0
7	2.0	2.3	1.9	1.5	1.1	0.6	—	0.5
8	1.5	1.1	1.0	0.9	0.8	1.0	0.5	—

Management now wants to determine between which pairs of groves the roads should be constructed to connect all groves with a minimum total length of road.

a. Describe how this problem fits the network description of a minimum spanning-tree problem.

b. Use the greedy algorithm presented in Section 6.5 to solve the problem.

6.19. The Premiere Bank soon will be hooking up computer terminals at each of its branch offices to the computer at its main office, using special phone lines with telecommunications devices. The phone line from a branch office need not be connected directly to the main office. It can be connected indirectly by being connected to another branch office that is connected (directly or indirectly) to the main office. The only requirement is that every branch office be connected by some route to the main office.

The charge for the special phone lines is $100 times the number of miles involved, where the distance (in miles) between every pair of offices is as follows:

Distance between Pairs of Offices

	Main	Branch 1	Branch 2	Branch 3	Branch 4	Branch 5
Main office	—	190	70	115	270	160
Branch 1	190	—	100	110	215	50
Branch 2	70	100	—	140	120	220
Branch 3	115	110	140	—	175	80
Branch 4	270	215	120	175	—	310
Branch 5	160	50	220	80	310	—

Management wishes to determine which pairs of offices should be directly connected by special phone lines in order to connect every branch office (directly or indirectly) to the main office at a minimum total cost.

a. Describe how this problem fits the network description of a minimum spanning-tree problem.

b. Use the greedy algorithm presented in Section 6.5 to solve the problem. What is the total cost for the special phone lines?

CASE 6.1
AIDING ALLIES

Commander Votachev steps into the cold October night and deeply inhales the smoke from his cigarette, savoring its warmth. He surveys the destruction surrounding him—shattered windows, burning buildings, torn roads—and smiles. His two years of work training revolutionaries east of the Ural Mountains has proven successful; his troops now occupy seven strategically important cities in the Russian Federation: Kazan, Perm, Yekaterinburg, Ufa, Samara, Saratov, and Orenburg. His siege is not yet over, however. He looks to the west. Given the political and economic confusion in the Russian Federation at this time, he knows that his troops will be able to conquer Saint Petersburg and Moscow shortly. Commander Votachev will then be able to rule with the wisdom and control exhibited by his communist predecessors Lenin and Stalin.

Across the Pacific Ocean, a meeting of the top security and foreign policy advisors of the United States is in progress at the White House. The president has recently been briefed about the communist revolution masterminded by Commander Votachev and is de-

termining a plan of action. The president reflects upon a similar October long ago in 1917, and he fears the possibility of a new age of radical Communist rule accompanied by chaos, bloodshed, escalating tensions, and possibly nuclear war. He therefore decides that the United States needs to respond and to respond quickly. Moscow has requested assistance from the United States military, and the president plans to send troops and supplies immediately.

The president turns to General Lankletter and asks him to describe the preparations being taken in the United States to send the necessary troops and supplies to the Russian Federation.

General Lankletter informs the president that along with troops, weapons, ammunition, fuel, and supplies, aircraft, ships, and vehicles are being assembled at two port cities with airfields: Boston and Jacksonville. The aircraft and ships will transfer all troops and cargo across the Atlantic Ocean to the Eurasian continent. The general hands the president a list of the types of aircraft, ships, and vehicles being assembled along with a description of each type. The list is shown below.

Transportation Type	Name	Capacity	Speed
Aircraft	C-141 Starlifter	150 tons	400 miles per hour
Ship	Transport	240 tons	35 miles per hour
Vehicle	Palletized Load System Truck	16,000 kilograms	60 miles per hour

All aircraft, ships, and vehicles are able to carry both troops and cargo. Once an aircraft or ship arrives in Europe, it stays there to support the armed forces.

The president then turns to Tabitha Neal, who has been negotiating with the NATO countries for the last several hours to use their ports and airfields as stops to refuel and resupply before heading to the Russian Federation. She informs the president that the following ports and airfields in the NATO countries will be made available to the U.S. military.

Ports	Airfields
Napoli	London
Hamburg	Berlin
Rotterdam	Istanbul

The president stands and walks to the map of the world projected on a large screen in the middle of the room. He maps the progress of troops and cargo from the United States to three strategic cities in the Russian Federation that have not yet been seized by Commander Votachev. The three cities are Saint Petersburg, Moscow, and Rostov. He explains that the troops and cargo will be used both to defend the Russian cities and to launch a counterattack against Votachev to recapture the cities he currently occupies. (The map is shown at the end of the case.)

The president also explains that all Starlifters and transports leave Boston or Jacksonville. All transports that have traveled across the Atlantic must dock at one of the NATO ports to unload. Palletized load system trucks brought over in the transports will then carry all troops and materials unloaded from the ships at the NATO ports to the three strategic Russian cities not yet seized by Votachev. All Starlifters that have traveled across the Atlantic must land at one of the NATO airfields for refueling. The planes will then carry all troops and cargo from the NATO airfields to the three Russian cities.

a. Draw a network showing the different routes troops and supplies may take to reach the Russian Federation from the United States.

b. Moscow and Washington do not know when Commander Votachev will launch his next attack. Leaders from the two countries therefore have agreed that troops should reach each of the three strategic Russian cities as quickly as possible. The president has determined that the situation is so dire that cost is no object—as many Starlifters, transports, and trucks as are necessary will be used to transfer troops and cargo from the United States to Saint Petersburg, Moscow, and Rostov. Therefore, no limitations exist on the number of troops and amount of cargo that can be transferred between any cities.

The president has been given the following information about the length of the available routes between cities.

From	To	(Kilometers)
Boston	Berlin	7,250 km
Boston	Hamburg	8,250
Boston	Istanbul	8,300
Boston	London	6,200
Boston	Rotterdam	6,900
Boston	Napoli	7,950
Jacksonville	Berlin	9,200
Jacksonville	Hamburg	9,800
Jacksonville	Istanbul	10,100
Jacksonville	London	7,900
Jacksonville	Rotterdam	8,900
Jacksonville	Napoli	9,400
Berlin	Saint Petersburg	1,280
Hamburg	Saint Petersburg	1,880
Istanbul	Saint Petersburg	2,040
London	Saint Petersburg	1,980
Rotterdam	Saint Petersburg	2,200
Napoli	Saint Petersburg	2,970
Berlin	Moscow	1,600
Hamburg	Moscow	2,120
Istanbul	Moscow	1,700

From	To	(Kilometers)
London	Moscow	2,300
Rotterdam	Moscow	2,450
Napoli	Moscow	2,890
Berlin	Rostov	1,730
Hamburg	Rostov	2,470
Istanbul	Rostov	990
London	Rostov	2,860
Rotterdam	Rostov	2,760
Napoli	Rostov	2,800

Given the distance and the speed of the transportation used between each pair of cities, how can the president most quickly move troops from the United States to each of the three strategic Russian cities? Highlight the path(s) on the network. How long will it take troops and supplies to reach Saint Petersburg? Moscow? Rostov?

c. The president encounters only one problem with his first plan: he has to sell the military deployment to Congress. Under the War Powers Act, the president is required to consult with Congress before introducing troops into hostilities or situations where hostilities will occur. If Congress does not give authorization to the president for such use of troops, the president must withdraw troops after 60 days. Congress also has the power to decrease the 60-day time period by passing a concurrent resolution.

The president knows that Congress will not authorize significant spending for another country's war, especially when voters have paid so much attention to decreasing the national debt. He therefore decides that he needs to find a way to get the needed troops and supplies to Saint Petersburg, Moscow, and Rostov at the minimum cost.

Each Russian city has contacted Washington to communicate the number of troops and supplies the city needs at a minimum for reinforcement. After analyzing the requests, General Lankletter has converted the requests from numbers of troops, gallons of gasoline, and so on, to tons of cargo for easier planning. The requirements are listed below.

City	Requirements
Saint Petersburg	320,000 tons
Moscow	440,000 tons
Rostov	240,000 tons

Both in Boston and Jacksonville, there are 500,000 tons of the necessary cargo available. When the United States decides to send a plane, ship, or truck between two cities, several costs occur: fuel costs, labor costs, maintenance costs, and appropriate port or airfield taxes and tariffs. These costs are listed next.

From	To	Cost
Boston	Berlin	$50,000 per Starlifter
Boston	Hamburg	$30,000 per transport
Boston	Istanbul	$55,000 per Starlifter
Boston	London	$45,000 per Starlifter
Boston	Rotterdam	$30,000 per transport
Boston	Napoli	$32,000 per transport
Jacksonville	Berlin	$57,000 per Starlifter
Jacksonville	Hamburg	$48,000 per transport
Jacksonville	Istanbul	$61,000 per Starlifter
Jacksonville	London	$49,000 per Starlifter
Jacksonville	Rotterdam	$44,000 per transport
Jacksonville	Napoli	$56,000 per transport
Berlin	Saint Petersburg	$24,000 per Starlifter
Hamburg	Saint Petersburg	$3,000 per truck
Istanbul	Saint Petersburg	$28,000 per Starlifter
London	Saint Petersburg	$22,000 per Starlifter
Rotterdam	Saint Petersburg	$3,000 per truck
Napoli	Saint Petersburg	$5,000 per truck
Berlin	Moscow	$22,000 per Starlifter
Hamburg	Moscow	$4,000 per truck
Istanbul	Moscow	$25,000 per Starlifter
London	Moscow	$19,000 per Starlifter
Rotterdam	Moscow	$5,000 per truck
Napoli	Moscow	$5,000 per truck
Berlin	Rostov	$23,000 per Starlifter
Hamburg	Rostov	$7,000 per truck
Istanbul	Rostov	$2,000 per Starlifter
London	Rostov	$4,000 per Starlifter
Rotterdam	Rostov	$8,000 per truck
Napoli	Rostov	$9,000 per truck

The president faces a number of restrictions when trying to satisfy the requirements. Early winter weather in northern Russia has brought a deep freeze with much snow. Therefore, General Lankletter is opposed to sending truck convoys in the area. He convinces the president to supply Saint Petersburg only through the air. Moreover, the truck routes into Rostov are quite limited, so that from each port, at most 2,500 trucks can be sent to Rostov. The Ukrainian government is very sensitive about American air planes flying through their air space. It restricts the U.S. military to at most 200 flights from Berlin to Rostov and to at most 200 flights from London to Rostov. (The U.S. military does not want to fly around the Ukraine and is thus restricted by the Ukrainian limitations.)

How does the president satisfy each Russian city's military requirements at minimum cost? Highlight the path to be used between the United States and the Russian Federation on the network.

d. Once the president releases the number of planes, ships, and trucks that will travel between the United States and the Russian Federation, Tabitha Neal contacts each of the American cities and NATO countries to indicate the number of planes to expect at the airfields, the number of ships to expect at the docks, and the number of trucks to expect traveling across the

roads. Unfortunately, Tabitha learns that several additional restrictions exist that cannot be immediately eliminated. Because of airfield congestion and unalterable flight schedules, only a limited number of planes may be sent between any two cities. These plane limitations are given below.

From	To	Maximum Number of Airplanes
Boston	Berlin	300
Boston	Istanbul	500
Boston	London	500
Jacksonville	Berlin	500
Jacksonville	Istanbul	700
Jacksonville	London	600
Berlin	Saint Petersburg	500
Istanbul	Saint Petersburg	0
London	Saint Petersburg	1,000
Berlin	Moscow	300
Istanbul	Moscow	100
London	Moscow	200
Berlin	Rostov	0
Istanbul	Rostov	900
London	Rostov	100

In addition, because some countries fear that citizens will become alarmed if too many military trucks travel the public highways, they object to a large number of trucks traveling through their countries. These objections mean that a limited number of trucks are able to travel between certain ports and Russian cities. These limitations are listed below.

From	To	Maximum Number of Trucks
Rotterdam	Moscow	600
Rotterdam	Rostov	750
Hamburg	Moscow	700
Hamburg	Rostov	500
Napoli	Moscow	1,500
Napoli	Rostov	1,400

Tabitha learns that all shipping lanes have no capacity limits due to the American control of the Atlantic Ocean.

The president realizes that due to all the restrictions, he will not be able to satisfy all the reinforcement requirements of the three Russian cities. He decides to disregard the cost issue and instead to maximize the total amount of cargo he can get to the Russian cities. How does the president maximize the total amount of cargo that reaches the Russian Federation? Highlight the path(s) used between the United States and the Russian Federation on the network.

e. Even before all American troops and supplies had reached Saint Petersburg, Moscow, and Rostov, infighting among Commander Votachev's troops about whether to make the next attack against Saint Petersburg or against Moscow split the revolutionaries. Troops from Moscow easily overcame the vulnerable revolutionaries. Commander Votachev was imprisoned, and the next step became re-building the seven cities razed by his armies.

The president's top priority is to help the Russian government to re-establish communications between the seven Russian cities and Moscow at minimum cost. The price of installing communication lines between any two Russian cities varies given the cost of shipping wire to the area, the level of destruction in the area, and the rough-ness of the terrain. Luckily, a city is able to communicate with all others if it is connected only indirectly to every other city. Saint Petersburg and Rostov are already connected to Moscow, so if any of the seven cities is connected to Saint Petersburg or Rostov, it will also be connected to Moscow. The cost of replacing communication lines between two given cities for which this is possible is shown to the right.

Where should communication lines be installed to minimize the total cost of re-establishing communications between Moscow and all seven Russian cities?

Between	Cost to Re-establish Communication Lines
Saint Petersburg and Kazan	$210,000
Saint Petersburg and Perm	185,000
Saint Petersburg and Ufa	225,000
Moscow and Ufa	310,000
Moscow and Samara	195,000
Moscow and Orenburg	440,000
Moscow and Saratov	140,000
Rostov and Saratov	200,000
Rostov and Orenburg	120,000
Kazan and Perm	150,000
Kazan and Ufa	105,000
Kazan and Samara	95,000
Perm and Yekaterinburg	85,000
Perm and Ufa	125,000
Yekaterinburg and Ufa	125,000
Ufa and Samara	100,000
Ufa and Orenburg	75,000
Saratov and Samara	100,000
Saratov and Orenburg	95,000

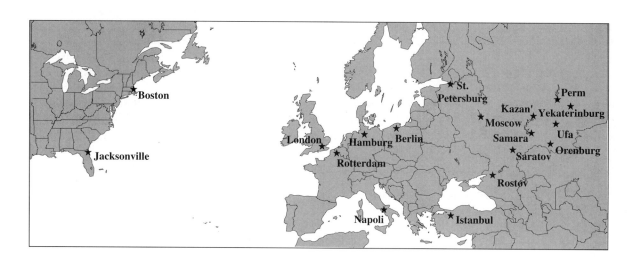

CASE 6.2
MONEY IN MOTION

Jake Nguyen runs a nervous hand through his once finely combed hair. He loosens his once perfectly knotted silk tie. And he rubs his sweaty hands across his once immaculately pressed trousers. To-day has certainly not been a good day.

Over the past few months, Jake had heard whispers circulating from Wall Street—whispers from the lips of investment bankers and stock brokers famous for their outspokenness. They had whis-pered about a coming Japanese economic collapse—whispered because they had believed that publicly vocalizing their fears would hasten the collapse.

And, today, their very fears have come true. Jake and his col-leagues gather around a small television dedicated exclusively to the Bloomberg channel. Jake stares in disbelief as he listens to the horrors taking place in the Japanese market. And the Japanese market is taking the financial markets in all other East Asian coun-tries with it on its tailspin. He goes numb. As manager of Asian foreign investment for Grant Hill Associates, a small West Coast investment boutique specializing in currency trading, Jake bears personal responsibility for any negative impacts of the collapse. And Grant Hill Associates will experience negative impacts.

Jake had not heeded the whispered warnings of a Japanese collapse. Instead, he had greatly increased the stake Grant Hill Associates held in the Japanese market. Because the Japanese market had performed better than expected over the past year, Jake had increased investments in Japan from $2.5 million to $15 million only one month ago. At that time, one dollar was worth 80 yen.

No longer. Jake realizes that today's devaluation of the yen means that one dollar is worth 125 yen. He will be able to liquidate these investments without any loss in yen, but now the dollar loss when converting back into U.S. currency would be huge. He takes a deep breath, closes his eyes, and mentally prepares himself for serious damage control.

Jake's meditation is interrupted by a booming voice calling for him from a large, corner office. Grant Hill, the president of Grant Hill Associates, yells, "Nguyen, get the hell in here!"

Jake jumps and looks reluctantly toward the corner office hiding the furious Grant Hill. He smooths his hair, tightens his tie, and walks briskly into the office.

Grant Hill meets Jake's eyes upon his entrance and continues yelling, "I don't want one word out of you, Nguyen! No excuses; just fix this debacle! Get all of our money out of Japan! My gut tells me this is only the beginning! Get the money into safe U.S. bonds! NOW! And don't forget to get our cash positions out of Indonesia and Malaysia ASAP with it!"

Jake has enough common sense to say nothing. He nods his head, turns on his heels, and practically runs out of the office.

Safely back at his desk, Jake begins formulating a plan to move the investments out of Japan, Indonesia, and Malaysia. His experiences investing in foreign markets have taught him that when playing with millions of dollars, how he gets money out of a foreign market is almost as important as when he gets money out of the market. The banking partners of Grant Hill Associates charge different transaction fees for converting one currency into another one and wiring large sums of money around the globe.

And now, to make matters worse, the governments in East Asia have imposed very tight limits on the amount of money an individual or a company can exchange from the domestic currency into a particular foreign currency and withdraw it from the country. The goal of this dramatic measure is to reduce the outflow of foreign investments out of those countries to prevent a complete collapse of the economies in the region. Because of Grant Hill Associates' cash holdings of 10.5 billion Indonesian rupiahs and 28 million Malaysian ringgits, along with the holdings in yen, it is not clear how these holdings should be converted back into dollars.

Jake wants to find the most cost-effective method to convert these holdings into dollars. On his company's Web site, he always can find on-the-minute exchange rates for most currencies in the world (see Table 1).

TABLE 1   Currency Exchange Rates

To From	Yen	Rupiah	Ringgit	U.S.Dollar	Canadian Dollar	Euro	Pound	Peso
Japanese yen	1	50	0.04	0.008	0.01	0.0064	0.0048	0.0768
Indonesian rupiah		1	0.0008	0.00016	0.0002	0.000128	0.000096	0.001536
Malaysian ringgit			1	0.2	0.25	0.16	0.12	1.92
U.S. dollar				1	1.25	0.8	0.6	9.6
Canadian dollar					1	0.64	0.48	7.68
European euro						1	0.75	12
English pound							1	16
Mexican peso								1

The table states that, for example, 1 Japanese yen equals 0.008 U.S. dollar. By making a few phone calls, he discovers the transaction costs his company must pay for large currency transactions during these critical times (see Table 2).

TABLE 2   Transaction Cost (Percent)

To From	Yen	Rupiah	Ringgit	U.S. Dollar	Canadian Dollar	Euro	Pound	Peso
Yen	—	0.5	0.5	0.4	0.4	0.4	0.25	0.5
Rupiah		—	0.7	0.5	0.3	0.3	0.75	0.75
Ringgit			—	0.7	0.7	0.4	0.45	0.5
U.S. dollar				—	0.05	0.1	0.1	0.1
Canadian dollar					—	0.2	0.1	0.1
Euro						—	0.05	0.5
Pound							—	0.5
Peso								—

Jake notes that exchanging one currency for another one results in the same transaction cost as a reverse conversion. Finally, Jake finds out the maximum amounts of domestic currencies his company is allowed to convert into other currencies in Japan, Indonesia, and Malaysia (see Table 3).

TABLE 3   Transaction Limits in Equivalent of 1,000 Dollars

To From	Yen	Rupiah	Ringgit	U.S. Dollar	Canadian Dollar	Euro	Pound	Peso
Yen	—	5,000	5,000	2,000	2,000	2,000	2,000	4,000
Rupiah	5,000	—	2,000	200	200	1,000	500	200
Ringgit	3,000	4,500	—	1,500	1,500	2,500	1,000	1,000

a. Formulate Jake's problem as a minimum-cost flow problem, and draw the network for his problem. Identify the supply and demand nodes for the network.

b. Which currency transactions must Jake perform to convert the investments from yens, rupiahs, and ringgits into U.S. dollars to ensure that Grant Hill Associates has the maximum dollar amount after all transactions have occurred? How much money does Jake have to invest in U.S. bonds?

c. The World Trade Organization forbids transaction limits because they promote protectionism. If no transaction limits exist, what method should Jake use to convert the Asian holdings from the respective currencies into dollars?

d. In response to the World Trade Organization's mandate forbidding transaction limits, the Indonesian government introduces a new tax to protect their currency that leads to a 500 percent increase in transaction costs for transactions of rupiahs. Given these new transaction costs but no transaction limits, what currency transactions should Jake perform to convert the Asian holdings from the respective currencies into dollars?

e. Jake realizes that his analysis is incomplete because he has not included all aspects that might influence his planned currency exchanges. Describe other factors that Jake should examine before he makes his final decision.

PROJECT MANAGEMENT WITH PERT/CPM

One of the most challenging jobs that any manager can take on is the management of a large-scale project that requires coordinating numerous activities throughout the organization. A myriad of details must be considered in planning how to coordinate all these activities, in developing a realistic schedule, and then in monitoring the progress of the project.

Fortunately, two closely related management science techniques, **PERT** (*program evaluation and review technique*) and **CPM** (*critical path method*), are available to assist the project manager in carrying out these responsibilities. These techniques make heavy use of *networks* (as introduced in the preceding chapter) to help plan and display the coordination of all the activities. They also normally use a *software package* to deal with all the data needed to develop schedule information and then to monitor the progress of the project. *Project management software,* such as MS Project in your MS Courseware, now is widely available for these purposes.

PERT and CPM have been widely used for a variety of projects, including the following types:

1. Construction of a new plant.
2. Research and development of a new product.
3. NASA space exploration projects.
4. Movie productions.
5. Building of a ship.
6. Government-sponsored projects for developing a new weapons system.
7. Relocation of a major facility.
8. Maintenance of a nuclear reactor.
9. Installation of a management information system.
10. Conducting of an advertising campaign.

PERT and CPM were independently developed in the late 1950s. Ever since, they have been among the most widely used management science techniques.

The original versions of PERT and CPM had some important differences, as we will point out later in the chapter. However, they also had a great deal in common, and the two techniques have gradually merged further over the years. In fact, today's software packages often include all the important options from both original versions.

Consequently, practitioners now commonly use the two names interchangeably, or combine them into the single acronym **PERT/CPM** as we often will do. We will make the distinction between them only when we are describing an option that was unique to one of the original versions.

The next section introduces a case study that will carry through the chapter to illustrate the various options for analyzing projects provided by PERT/CPM.

7.1 A Case Study: The Reliable Construction Co. Project

The Reliable Construction Company has just made the winning bid of $5.4 million to construct a new plant for a major manufacturer. The manufacturer needs the plant to go into operation within a year. Therefore, the contract includes the following provisions:

- A *penalty* of $300,000 if Reliable has not completed construction by the deadline 47 weeks from now.
- To provide additional incentive for speedy construction, a *bonus* of $150,000 to be paid to Reliable if the plant is completed within 40 weeks.

Reliable is assigning its best construction manager, David Perty, to this project to help ensure that it stays on schedule. Mr. Perty has earned the confidence of management through many years of exemplary performance with the company. He began as a carpenter fresh out of community college and soon became the youngest foreman in the company, so he knows the construction business from the ground up. While a foreman, he went back to college part time at night to earn his business degree. It was an arduous schedule that stretched out over five years, but he found that he enjoyed his business major and was good at it. His favorite course was a graduate-level elective in project management, and it was there that he thoroughly learned the techniques of PERT/CPM. Immediately after earning his business degree with honors, Mr. Perty was promoted to construction manager. He has been serving the company in this capacity now for 14 years, and rumors have it that he may be next in line to move into top management in a year when the retirement of the company president will cause some shuffling of the top positions. Although Mr. Perty would welcome this opportunity, he does not feel any hurry to move up. Despite its many stresses, he thoroughly enjoys the challenges of being a construction manager, including the opportunities to apply the latest project management techniques.

Mr. Perty is very pleased to receive this latest assignment as the project manager for such an important project. He looks forward to the challenge of bringing the project in on schedule, and perhaps earning a promotion in the process. However, since he is doubtful that it will be feasible to finish within 40 weeks without incurring excessive costs, he has decided to focus his initial planning on meeting the deadline of 47 weeks.

He will need to arrange for a number of crews to perform the various construction activities at different times. Table 7.1 shows his list of the various **activities**. The third column provides important additional information for coordinating the scheduling of the crews.

TABLE 7.1   Activity List for the Reliable Construction Co. Project

Activity	Activity Description	Immediate Predecessors	Estimated Duration (Weeks)
A	Excavate	—	2
B	Lay the foundation	A	4
C	Put up the rough wall	B	10
D	Put up the roof	C	6
E	Install the exterior plumbing	C	4
F	Install the interior plumbing	E	5
G	Put up the exterior siding	D	7
H	Do the exterior painting	E, G	9
I	Do the electrical work	C	7
J	Put up the wallboard	F, I	8
K	Install the flooring	J	4
L	Do the interior painting	J	5
M	Install the exterior fixtures	H	2
N	Install the interior fixtures	K, L	6

For any given activity, its **immediate predecessors** (as given in the third column of Table 7.1) are those activities that must be completed just prior to starting the given activity. (Similarly, the given activity is called an **immediate successor** of each of its immediate predecessors.)

For example, the top entries in this column indicate that

1. Excavation does not need to wait for any other activities.
2. Excavation must be completed before starting to lay the foundation.
3. The foundation must be completely laid before starting to put up the rough wall, and so on.

When a given activity has *more than one* immediate predecessor, all must be finished before the activity can begin.

In order to schedule the activities, Mr. Perty consults with each of the crew foremen to develop an estimate of how long each activity should take when it is done in the normal way. These estimates are given in the rightmost column of Table 7.1.

Adding up these times gives a grand total of 79 weeks, which is far beyond the deadline for the project. Fortunately, some of the activities can be done in parallel, which substantially reduces the project completion time.

Given all the information in Table 7.1, Mr. Perty now wants to develop answers to the following questions.

1. How can the project be displayed graphically to better visualize the flow of the activities? (Section 7.2)
2. What is the total time required to complete the project if no delays occur? (Section 7.3)
3. When do the individual activities need to start and finish (at the latest) to meet this project completion time? (Section 7.3)
4. When can the individual activities start and finish (at the earliest) if no delays occur? (Section 7.3)
5. Which are the critical bottleneck activities where any delays must be avoided to prevent delaying project completion? (Section 7.3)
6. For the other activities, how much delay can be tolerated without delaying project completion? (Section 7.3)
7. Given the uncertainties in accurately estimating activity durations, what is the probability of completing the project by the deadline (47 weeks)? (Section 7.4)
8. If extra money is spent to expedite the project, what is the least expensive way of attempting to meet the target completion time (40 weeks)? (Section 7.5)
9. How should ongoing costs be monitored to try to keep the project within budget? (Section 7.6)

Being a regular user of PERT/CPM, Mr. Perty knows that this technique will provide invaluable help in answering these questions (as you will see in the sections indicated in parentheses above).

Review Questions

1. What are the financial terms in the contract that the Reliable Construction Co. has just won?
2. What is the deadline that Mr. Perty is focusing on meeting?
3. What is meant by an *immediate predecessor* of an activity? An *immediate successor*?
4. What are the three types of information that Mr. Perty gathered regarding the project?

7.2 Using a Network to Visually Display a Project

The preceding chapter describes how valuable *networks* can be to represent and help analyze many kinds of problems. In much the same way, networks play a key role in dealing with projects. They enable showing the relationships between the activities and placing everything into perspective. They then are used to help analyze the project and answer the kinds of questions raised at the end of the preceding section.

Project Networks

A network used to represent a project is called a **project network.** A project network consists of a number of **nodes** (typically shown as small circles or rectangles) and a number of **arcs** (shown as arrows) that lead from some node to another. (If you have not previously studied Chapter 6, where nodes and arcs are discussed extensively, just think of them as the names given to the small circles or rectangles and to the arrows in the network.)

As Table 7.1 indicates, there are three types of information needed to describe a project.

1. Activity information: Break down the project into its individual activities (at the desired level of detail).
2. Precedence relationships: Identify the immediate predecessor(s) for each activity.
3. Time information: Estimate the duration of each activity.

The project network needs to convey all this information. There are two alternative types of project networks available for doing this.

One type is the **activity-on-arc (AOA) project network,** where each activity is represented by an *arc*. A node is used to separate an activity (an outgoing arc) from each of its immediate predecessors (an incoming arc). The sequencing of the arcs thereby shows the precedence relationships between the activities.

The second type is the **activity-on-node (AON) project network,** where each activity is represented by a *node*. The arcs then are used just to show the precedence relationships between the activities. In particular, the node for each activity with immediate predecessors has an arc coming in from each of these predecessors.

The original versions of PERT and CPM used AOA project networks, so this was the conventional type for some years. However, AON project networks have some important advantages over AOA project networks for conveying exactly the same information.

1. AON project networks are considerably easier to construct than AOA project networks.
2. AON project networks are easier to understand than AOA project networks for inexperienced users, including many managers.
3. AON project networks are easier to revise than AOA project networks when there are changes in the project.

For these reasons, AON project networks have become increasingly popular with practitioners. It appears somewhat likely that they will become the conventional type to use. Therefore, we now will focus solely on AON project networks.

Figure 7.1 shows the project network for Reliable's project.[1] Referring also to the third column of Table 7.1, note how there is an arc leading to each activity from each of its immediate predecessors. Because activity A has no immediate predecessors, there is an arc leading from the **start node** to this activity. Similarly, since activities M and N have no immediate successors, arcs lead from these activities to the **finish node.** Therefore, the project network nicely displays at a glance all the precedence relationships between all the activities (plus the start and finish of the project). Based on the rightmost column of Table 7.1, the number next to the node for each activity then records the estimated duration (in weeks) of that activity.

For projects of this size and larger, it is not always straightforward to construct the project network from the activity list. In case you have trouble doing this, we have included a supplement to this chapter on your CD-ROM that outlines and illustrates a systematic procedure for constructing the project network.

---

[1]Although project networks often are drawn from left to right, we go from top to bottom to better fit on the printed page.

FIGURE 7.1

The project network for the Reliable Construction Co. project.

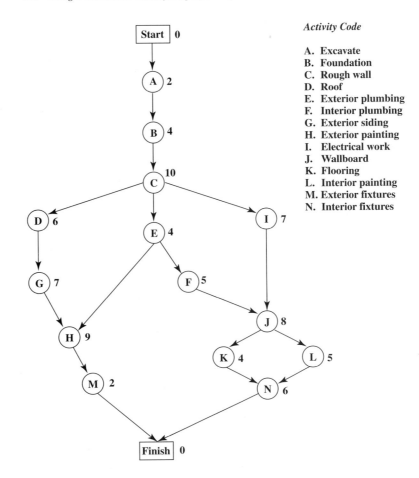

Activity Code

A. Excavate
B. Foundation
C. Rough wall
D. Roof
E. Exterior plumbing
F. Interior plumbing
G. Exterior siding
H. Exterior painting
I. Electrical work
J. Wallboard
K. Flooring
L. Interior painting
M. Exterior fixtures
N. Interior fixtures

In real applications, software commonly is used to construct the project network. We next describe how MS Project (in your MS Courseware) does this for Reliable's project.

Using MS Project

The first step with MS Project is to enter the information in the activity list (Table 7.1). Choose the View menu and then select its option called Table. From the resulting submenu, choose the option called Entry to bring up the table needed to enter the information. This table is displayed in Figure 7.2 for Reliable's project. You enter the task (activity) names, the duration of each, a starting date for the first activity, and the immediate predecessors of each, as shown in the figure. The program automatically builds up the rest of the table (including the chart on the right) as you enter this information.

The default duration is in units of days, but we have changed the units to weeks here. Such a change can be made by choosing Options under the Tools menu and then changing "Duration is entered in" under the Schedule options.

The default date format is a calendar date (e.g., 1/2/00). This can be changed by choosing Options from the Tools menu and then changing the Date Format option under the View options. We have chosen to count time from time 0. Thus, the start time for the first activity is given as W1/1, which is shorthand for Week 1, day 1. A five-day work week is assumed. For example, since the duration of the first activity is two weeks, its finish time is given as W2/5 (Week 2, day 5).

The chart on the right is referred to as a **Gantt chart.** This kind of chart is a popular one in practice for displaying a project schedule, because the bars nicely show the scheduled start and finish times for the respective activities. (This figure assumes that the project begins at the beginning of a calendar year.) The arrows show the precedence relationships between the activities. For example, since both activities 5 and 7 are immediate predecessors of activity 8, there are arrows from both activities 5 and 7 leading to activity 8.

This project entry table can be returned to at any time by choosing Table:Entry in the View menu.

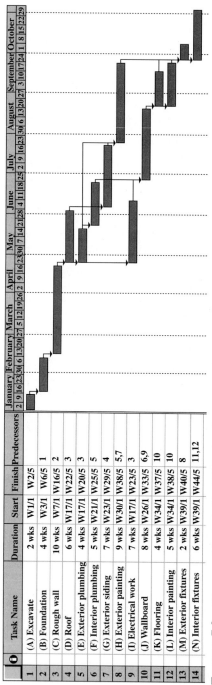

O	Task Name	Duration	Start	Finish	Predecessors
1	(A) Excavate	2 wks	W1/1	W2/5	
2	(B) Foundation	4 wks	W3/1	W6/5	1
3	(C) Rough wall	10 wks	W7/1	W16/5	2
4	(D) Roof	6 wks	W17/1	W22/5	3
5	(E) Exterior plumbing	4 wks	W17/1	W20/5	3
6	(F) Interior plumbing	5 wks	W21/1	W25/5	5
7	(G) Exterior siding	7 wks	W23/1	W29/5	4
8	(H) Exterior painting	9 wks	W30/1	W38/5	5,7
9	(I) Electrical work	7 wks	W17/1	W23/5	3
10	(J) Wallboard	8 wks	W26/1	W33/5	6,9
11	(K) Flooring	4 wks	W34/1	W37/5	10
12	(L) Interior painting	5 wks	W34/1	W38/5	10
13	(M) Exterior fixtures	2 wks	W39/1	W40/5	8
14	(N) Interior fixtures	6 wks	W39/1	W44/5	11,12

FIGURE 7.2 The spreadsheet used by MS Project for entering the activity list for the Reliable Construction Co. project. On the right is a Gantt chart showing the project schedule.

248

FIGURE 7.3

Reliable's project network as constructed with MS Project.

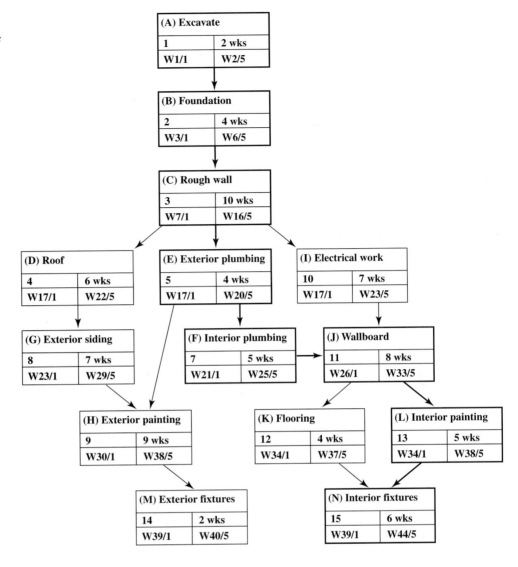

You can choose between various views with the view toolbar down the left side of the screen. The Gantt Chart view is the default. The PERT Chart view shows the project network. This view initially lines all the activity boxes up in a row, but they can be moved as desired by dragging the boxes with the mouse. Figure 7.3 shows this project network after placing the activity boxes in the same locations as the corresponding nodes in Figure 7.1 (except no boxes are included now for the start and finish of the project). Note that each box provides considerable information about the activity. After giving its name, the second row shows the activity number and duration. The last row then gives the scheduled start and finish times.

MS Project also provides additional information of the types described in some of the subsequent sections. We will point this out as it arises. However, rather than continuing to display the form of the output in the upcoming sections, we will show it in the MS Project file for this chapter in your MS Courseware.

Review Questions

1. What three types of information does a project network need to convey?
2. What is the difference between an activity-on-arc (AOA) project network and an activity-on-node (AON) project network? Which type is being used here?
3. What do the bars in a Gantt chart show?

7.3 Scheduling a Project with PERT/CPM

At the end of Section 7.1, we mentioned that Mr. Perty, the project manager for the Reliable Construction Co. project, wants to answer a series of questions and so will use PERT/CPM as the best method for obtaining answers. His first question has been answered in the preceding section. Here are the five questions that will be answered in this section.

> **Question 2:** What is the total time required to complete the project if no delays occur?
>
> **Question 3:** When do the individual activities need to start and finish (at the latest) to meet this project completion time?
>
> **Question 4:** When can the individual activities start and finish (at the earliest) if no delays occur?
>
> **Question 5:** Which are the critical bottleneck activities where any delays must be avoided to prevent delaying project completion?
>
> **Question 6:** For the other activities, how much delay can be tolerated without delaying project completion?

The project network in Figure 7.1 enables answering all these questions by providing two crucial pieces of information, namely, the *order* in which certain activities must be performed and the (estimated) *duration* of each activity. We begin by focusing on Questions 2 and 5.

The Critical Path

How long should the project take? We noted earlier that summing the durations of all the activities gives a grand total of 79 weeks. However, this isn't the answer to the question because some of the activities can be performed (roughly) simultaneously.

What is relevant instead is the *length* of each *path* through the network.

> A **path** through a project network is one of the routes following the arrows (arcs) from the start node to the finish node. The **length of a path** is the *sum* of the (estimated) *durations* of the activities on the path.

The six paths through the project network in Figure 7.1 are given in Table 7.2, along with the calculations of the lengths of these paths. The path lengths range from 31 weeks up to 44 weeks for the longest path (the fourth one in the table).

So given these path lengths, what do you think should be the (estimated) *project duration* (the total time required for the project)? Let us reason it out.

Since the activities on any given path must be done one after another with no overlap, the project duration cannot be *shorter* than the path length. However, the project duration can be *longer* because some activity on the path with multiple immediate predecessors might have to wait longer for an immediate predecessor *not* on the path to finish than for the one on the path. For example, consider the second path in Table 7.2 and focus on activity H. This activity has two immediate predecessors, one (activity G) *not* on the path and one (activity E) that is. After activity C finishes, only 4 more weeks are required for activity E but 13 weeks will be needed for activity D and then activity G to finish. Therefore, the project duration must be considerably longer than the length of the second path in the table.

TABLE 7.2 The Paths and Path Lengths through Reliable's Project Network

Path	Length (Weeks)
Start →A→B→C→D→G→H→M→ Finish	2 + 4 + 10 + 6 + 7 + 9 + 2 = 40
Start →A→B→C→E→H→M→ Finish	2 + 4 + 10 + 4 + 9 + 2 = 31
Start →A→B→C→E→F→J→K→N→ Finish	2 + 4 + 10 + 4 + 5 + 8 + 4 + 6 = 43
Start →A→B→C→E→F→J→L→N→ Finish	2 + 4 + 10 + 4 + 5 + 8 + 5 + 6 = 44
Start →A→B→C→I→J→K→N→ Finish	2 + 4 + 10 + 7 + 8 + 4 + 6 = 41
Start →A→B→C→I→J→L→N→ Finish	2 + 4 + 10 + 7 + 8 + 5 + 6 = 42

However, the project duration will not be longer than one particular path. This is the *longest path* through the project network. The activities on this path can be performed sequentially without interruption. (Otherwise, this would not be the longest path.) Therefore, the time required to reach the finish node equals the length of this path. Furthermore, all the shorter paths will reach the finish node no later than this.

Here is the key conclusion.

> The (estimated) *project duration* equals the *length of the longest path* through the project network. This longest path is called the **critical path.** (If more than one path tie for the longest, they all are critical paths.)

Thus, for the Reliable Construction Co. project, we have

Critical path: Start →A→B→C→E→F→J→L→N→Finish
(Estimated) project duration = 44 weeks

We now have answered Mr. Perty's Questions 2 and 5 given at the beginning of the section. If no delays occur, the total time required to complete the project should be about 44 weeks. Furthermore, the activities on this critical path are the critical bottleneck activities where any delays in their completion must be avoided to prevent delaying project completion. This is valuable information for Mr. Perty since he now knows that he should focus most of his attention on keeping these particular activities on schedule in striving to keep the overall project on schedule. Furthermore, if he decides to reduce the duration of the project (remember that bonus for completion within 40 weeks), these are the main activities where changes should be made to reduce their durations.

For small project networks like Figure 7.1, finding all the paths and determining the longest path is a convenient way to identify the critical path. However, this is not an efficient procedure for larger projects. PERT/CPM uses a considerably more efficient procedure instead.

Not only is this PERT/CPM procedure very efficient for larger projects, it also provides much more information than is available from finding all the paths. In particular, it answers *all five* of Mr. Perty's questions listed at the beginning of the section rather than just two. These answers provide the key information needed to schedule all the activities and then to evaluate the consequences should any activities slip behind schedule.

The components of this procedure are described in the remainder of this section.

Scheduling Individual Activities

The PERT/CPM scheduling procedure begins by addressing Question 4: When can the individual activities start and finish (at the earliest) if no delays occur? Having no delays means that (1) the *actual* duration of each activity turns out to be the same as its *estimated* duration and (2) each activity begins as soon as all its immediate predecessors are finished. The starting and finishing times of each activity if no delays occur anywhere in the project are called the **earliest start time** and the **earliest finish time** of the activity. These times are represented by the symbols

ES = Earliest start time for a particular activity
EF = Earliest finish time for a particular activity

where

EF = ES + (estimated) duration of the activity

Rather than assigning calendar dates to these times, we will use the convention of counting the number of time periods (weeks for Reliable's project) from when the project started. Thus,

Starting time for project = 0

Since activity A starts Reliable's project, we have

Activity A: ES = 0

EF = 0 + duration (2 weeks)

= 2

where the duration (in weeks) of activity A is given in Figure 7.1 as the boldfaced number next to this activity. Activity B can start as soon as activity A finishes, so

$$\text{Activity B:} \quad ES = EF \text{ for activity A}$$
$$= 2$$
$$EF = 2 + \text{duration (4 weeks)}$$
$$= 6$$

This calculation of ES for activity B illustrates our first rule for obtaining ES.

If an activity has only a *single* immediate predecessor, then

$$ES \text{ for the activity} = EF \text{ for the immediate predecessor}$$

This rule (plus the calculation of each EF) immediately gives ES and EF for activity C, then for activities D, E, I, and then for activities G, F as well. Figure 7.4 shows ES and EF for each of these activities to the right of its node. For example,

$$\text{Activity G:} \quad ES = EF \text{ for activity D}$$
$$= 22$$
$$EF = 22 + \text{duration (7 weeks)}$$
$$= 29$$

which means that this activity (putting up the exterior siding) should start 22 weeks and finish 29 weeks after the start of the project.

Now consider activity H, which has *two* immediate predecessors, activities G and E. Activity H must wait to start until *both* activities G and E are finished, which gives the following calculation.

FIGURE 7.4

Earliest start time (ES) and earliest finish time (EF) values for the initial activities in Figure 7.1 that have only a single immediate predecessor.

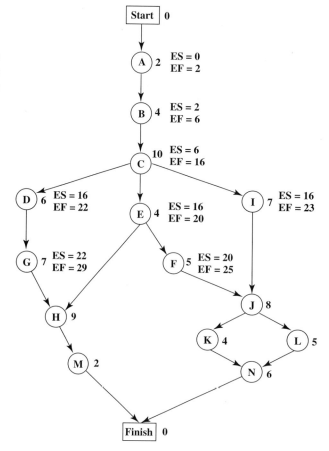

Immediate predecessors of activity H:

Activity G has EF = 29

Activity E has EF = 20

Larger EF = 29

Therefore,

$$\text{ES for activity H} = \text{larger EF above}$$

$$= 29$$

This calculation illustrates the general rule for obtaining the earliest start time for any activity.

EARLIEST START TIME RULE

The earliest start time of an activity is equal to the *largest* of the earliest finish times of its immediate predecessors. In symbols,

ES = largest EF of the immediate predecessors

When the activity has only a single immediate predecessor, this rule becomes the same as the first rule given earlier. However, it also allows any larger number of immediate predecessors as well. Applying this rule to the rest of the activities in Figure 7.4 (and calculating each EF from ES) yields the complete set of ES and EF values given in Figure 7.5.

Note that Figure 7.5 also includes ES and EF values for the start and finish nodes. The reason is that these nodes are conventionally treated as *dummy activities* that require no time. For the start node, ES = 0 = EF automatically. For the finish node, the earliest start time rule is used to calculate ES in the usual way, as illustrated on the next page.

FIGURE 7.5

Earliest start time (ES) and earliest finish time (EF) values for all the activities (plus the start and finish nodes) of the Reliable Construction Co. project.

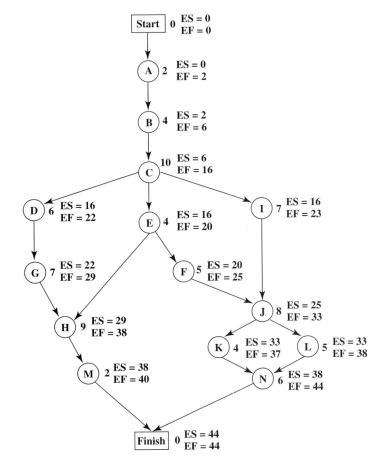

Immediate predecessors of the finish node:

$$\text{Activity M has EF} = 40$$

$$\text{Activity N has EF} = 44$$

$$\text{Larger EF} = 44$$

Therefore,

$$\text{ES for the finish node} = \text{larger EF above}$$

$$= 44$$

$$\text{EF for the finish node} = 44 + 0 = 44.$$

This last calculation indicates that the project should be completed in 44 weeks if everything stays on schedule according to the start and finish times for each activity given in Figure 7.5. (This answers Question 2.) Mr. Perty now can use this schedule to inform the crew responsible for each activity as to when it should plan to start and finish its work.

Here is a summary of the overall procedure for obtaining such a schedule for any project.

Procedure for Obtaining Earliest Times for All Activities

1. For each activity that starts the project (including the start node), set its earliest start time as ES = 0.

2. For each activity whose ES value has just been obtained, calculate its earliest finish time as

$$\text{EF} = \text{ES} + \text{(estimated) duration of the activity}$$

3. For each new activity whose immediate predecessors now have EF values, obtain its ES by applying the *earliest start time rule*. Then apply step 2 to calculate its EF.

4. Repeat step 3 over and over again until ES and EF have been obtained for *all* activities (including the finish node).

This process of starting with the initial activities and working *forward* in time toward the final activities is referred to as making a **forward pass** through the network.

Keep in mind that the schedule obtained from this procedure assumes that the *actual* duration of each activity will turn out to be the same as its *estimated* duration. What happens if some activity takes longer than expected? Would this delay project completion? Perhaps, but not necessarily. It depends on which activity and the length of the delay.

The next part of the procedure focuses on determining how much later than indicated in Figure 7.5 can an activity start or finish without delaying project completion.

Later Schedules That Avoid Delaying Project Completion

Having found *earliest* start and finish times for each activity, we next want to answer Question 3 by finding the *latest* start and finish times that will still enable completing the project in 44 weeks.

The **latest start time for an activity** is the latest possible time that it can start without delaying the completion of the project (so the finish node still is reached at its earliest finish time), assuming no subsequent delays in the project. The **latest finish time** has the corresponding definition with respect to finishing the activity.

In symbols,

LS = latest start time for a particular activity
LF = latest finish time for a particular activity

where

$$\text{LS} = \text{LF} - \text{(estimated) duration of the activity}$$

To find LF, we have the following rule.

LATEST FINISH TIME RULE

The latest finish time of an activity is equal to the *smallest* of the latest start times of its immediate successors. In symbols,

LF = smallest LS of the immediate successors

Since an activity's immediate successors cannot start until the activity finishes, this rule is saying that the activity must finish in time to enable *all* its immediate successors to begin by their latest start times.

For example, consider activity M in Figure 7.1. Its only immediate successor is the finish node. This node must be reached by time 44 to complete the project within 44 weeks, so we begin by assigning values to this node as follows.

$$\text{Finish node:} \quad \text{LF = its EF = 44}$$

$$\text{LS} = 44 - 0 = 44$$

Now we can apply the latest finish time rule to activity M.

$$\text{Activity M:} \quad \text{LF = LS for the finish node}$$

$$= 44$$

$$\text{LS} = 44 - \text{duration (2 weeks)}$$

$$= 42$$

(Since activity M is one of the activities that together complete the project, we also could have automatically set its LF equal to the earliest finish time of the finish node without applying the latest finish time rule.)

Since activity M is the only immediate successor of activity H, we now can apply the latest finish time rule to the latter activity.

$$\text{Activity H:} \quad \text{LF = LS for activity M}$$

$$= 42$$

$$\text{LS} = 42 - \text{duration (9 weeks)}$$

$$= 33$$

Note that the procedure being illustrated above is to start with the final activities and work *backward* in time toward the initial activities. Thus, in contrast to the *forward pass* used to find earliest start and finish times, we now are making a **backward pass** through the network, as summarized below.

Procedure for Obtaining Latest Times for All Activities

1. For each of the activities that together complete the project (including the finish node), set its latest finish time (LF) equal to the earliest finish time of the finish node.

2. For each activity whose LF value has just been obtained, calculate its latest start time as

   LS = LF − (estimated) duration of the activity

3. For each new activity whose immediate successors now have LS values, obtain its LF by applying the *latest finish time rule.* Then apply step 2 to calculate its LS.

4. Repeat step 3 over and over again until LF and LS have been obtained for *all* activities (including the start node).

Figure 7.6 shows the results of applying this procedure to its conclusion. For example, consider activity C, which has three immediate successors.

FIGURE 7.6

Latest start time (LS) and latest finish time (LF) for all the activities (plus the start and finish nodes) of the Reliable Construction Co. project.

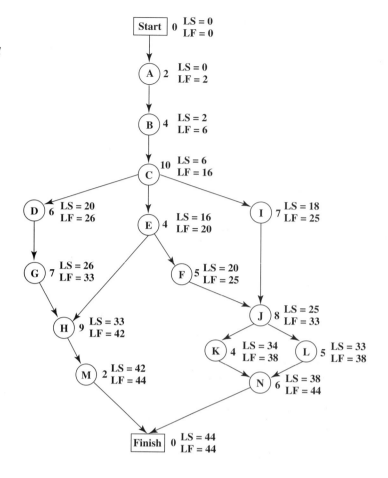

Immediate successors of activity C:

Activity D has LS = 20

Activity E has LS = 16

Activity I has LS = 18

Smallest LS = 16

Therefore,

LF for activity C = smallest LS above

= 16

Mr. Perty now knows that the schedule given in Figure 7.6 represents his "last chance schedule." Even if an activity starts and finishes as late as indicated in the figure, he still will be able to avoid delaying project completion beyond 44 weeks as long as there is no subsequent slippage in the schedule. However, to allow for unexpected delays, he would prefer to stick instead to the *earliest time schedule* given in Figure 7.5 whenever possible in order to provide some slack in parts of the schedule.

If the start and finish times in Figure 7.6 for a particular activity are later than the corresponding earliest times in Figure 7.5, then this activity has some slack in the schedule. The last part of the PERT/CPM procedure for scheduling a project is to identify this slack, and then to use this information to find the *critical path*. (This will answer both Questions 5 and 6.)

Identifying Slack in the Schedule

To identify slack, it is convenient to combine the latest times in Figure 7.6 and the earliest times in Figure 7.5 into a single figure. Using activity M as an example, this is done by displaying the information for each activity as follows.

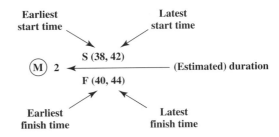

(Note that the S or F in front of each parenthesis will remind you of whether these are start times or finish times.) Figure 7.7 displays this information for the entire project.

This figure makes it easy to see how much slack each activity has.

The **slack for an activity** is the difference between its latest finish time and its earliest finish time. In symbols,

$$\text{Slack} = \text{LF} - \text{EF}$$

(Since LF − EF = LS − ES, either difference actually can be used to calculate slack.)

For example,

$$\text{Slack for activity M} = 44 - 40 = 4$$

This indicates that activity M can be delayed up to 4 weeks beyond the earliest time schedule without delaying the completion of the project at 44 weeks. This makes sense since the project is finished as soon as both activities M and N are completed and the earliest finish time for activity N (44) is 4 weeks later than for activity M (40). As long as activity N stays on schedule, the project still will finish at 44 weeks if any delays in starting activity M (perhaps due to preceding activities taking longer than expected) and in performing activity M do not cumulate more than 4 weeks.

FIGURE 7.7

The complete project network showing ES and LS (in the upper parentheses next to the node) and EF and LF (in the lower parentheses next to the node) for each activity of the Reliable Construction Co. project. The darker arrows show the critical path through the project network.

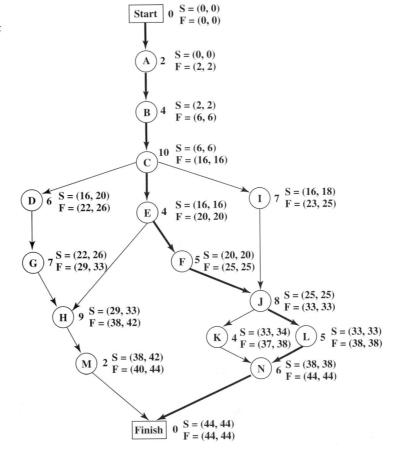

TABLE 7.3   Slack for Reliable's Activities

Activity	Slack (LF − EF)	On Critical Path?
A	0	Yes
B	0	Yes
C	0	Yes
D	4	No
E	0	Yes
F	0	Yes
G	4	No
H	4	No
I	2	No
J	0	Yes
K	1	No
L	0	Yes
M	4	No
N	0	Yes

Table 7.3 shows the slack for each of the activities. Note that some of the activities have *zero slack*, indicating that any delays in these activities will delay project completion. This is how PERT/CPM identifies the critical path(s).

> Each activity with *zero slack* is on a **critical path** through the project network such that any delay along this path will delay project completion.

Thus, the critical path is

$$\text{Start} \rightarrow A \rightarrow B \rightarrow C \rightarrow E \rightarrow F \rightarrow J \rightarrow L \rightarrow N \rightarrow \text{Finish}$$

just as we found by a different method at the beginning of the section. This path is highlighted in Figure 7.7 by the darker arrows. It is the activities on this path that Mr. Perty must monitor with special care to keep the project on schedule.

Review

Now let us review Mr. Perty's questions at the beginning of the section and see how all of them have been answered by the PERT/CPM scheduling procedure.

Question 2: What is the total time required to complete the project if no delays occur? This is the earliest finish time at the finish node (EF=44 weeks), as given at the bottom of Figures 7.5 and 7.7.

Question 3: When do the individual activities need to start and finish (at the latest) to meet this project completion time? These times are the latest start times (LS) and latest finish times (LF) given in Figures 7.6 and 7.7. These times provide a "last chance schedule" to complete the project in 44 weeks if no further delays occur.

Question 4: When can the individual activities start and finish (at the earliest) if no delays occur? These times are the earliest start times (ES) and earliest finish times (EF) given in Figures 7.5 and 7.7. These times usually are used to establish the initial schedule for the project. (Subsequent delays may force later adjustments in the schedule.)

Question 5: Which are the critical bottleneck activities where any delays must be avoided to prevent delaying project completion? These are the activities on the critical path shown by the darker arrows in Figure 7.7. Mr. Perty needs to focus most of his attention on keeping these particular activities on schedule in striving to keep the overall project on schedule.

Question 6: For the other activities, how much delay can be tolerated without delaying project completion? These tolerable delays are the positive slacks given in the middle column of Table 7.3.

FIGURE 7.8

The equations in the bottom half show how to develop the schedule for the Reliable Construction Co. project on a spreadsheet.

A	B	C	D	E	F	G	H	I	J
1		Reliable Construction Co. Project Scheduling Problem							
2									
3	Activity	Description	Time	ES	EF	LS	LF	Slack	Critical?
4	A	Excavate	2	0	2	0	2	0	Yes
5	B	Foundation	4	2	6	2	6	0	Yes
6	C	Rough Wall	10	6	16	6	16	0	Yes
7	D	Roof	6	16	22	20	26	4	No
8	E	Exterior Plumbing	4	16	20	16	20	0	Yes
9	F	Interior Plumbing	5	20	25	20	25	0	Yes
10	G	Exterior Siding	7	22	29	26	33	4	No
11	H	Exterior Painting	9	29	38	33	42	4	No
12	I	Electrical Work	7	16	23	18	25	2	No
13	J	Wallboard	8	25	33	25	33	0	Yes
14	K	Flooring	4	33	37	34	38	1	No
15	L	Interior Painting	5	33	38	33	38	0	Yes
16	M	Exterior Fixtures	2	38	40	42	44	4	No
17	N	Interior Fixtures	6	38	44	38	44	0	Yes
18									
19			Project Duration =	44					

	E	F	G	H	I	J
4	0	=E4+D4	=H4–D4	=MIN(G5)	=H4–F4	=IF(I4=0,"Yes","No")
5	=MAX(F4)	=E5+D5	=H5–D5	=MIN(G6)	=H5–F5	=IF(I5=0,"Yes","No")
6	=MAX(F5)	=E6+D6	=H6–D6	=MIN(G7,G8,G12)	=H6–F6	=IF(I6=0,"Yes","No")
7	=MAX(F6)	=E7+D7	=H7–D7	=MIN(G10)	=H7–F7	=IF(I7=0,"Yes","No")
8	=MAX(F6)	=E8+D8	=H8–D8	=MIN(G9,G11)	=H8–F8	=IF(I8=0,"Yes","No")
9	=MAX(F8)	=E9+D9	=H9–D9	=MIN(G13)	=H9–F9	=IF(I9=0,"Yes","No")
10	=MAX(F7)	=E10+D10	=H10–D10	=MIN(G11)	=H10–F10	=IF(I10=0,"Yes","No")
11	=MAX(F8,F10)	=E11+D11	=H11–D11	=MIN(G16)	=H11–F11	=IF(I11=0,"Yes","No")
12	=MAX(F6)	=E12+D12	=H12–D12	=MIN(G13)	=H12–F12	=IF(I12=0,"Yes","No")
13	=MAX(F9,F12)	=E13+D13	=H13–D13	=MIN(G14,G15)	=H13–F13	=IF(I13=0,"Yes","No")
14	=MAX(F13)	=E14+D14	=H14–D14	=MIN(G17)	=H14–F14	=IF(I14=0,"Yes","No")
15	=MAX(F13)	=E15+D15	=H15–D15	=MIN(G17)	=H15–F15	=IF(I15=0,"Yes","No")
16	=MAX(F11)	=E16+D16	=H16–D16	=F19	=H16–F16	=IF(I16=0,"Yes","No")
17	=MAX(F14,F15)	=E17+D17	=H17–D17	=F19	=H17–F17	=IF(I17=0,"Yes","No")
18						
19	Project Duration=	=MAX(F4:F17)				

Using a Computer to Answer These Questions

If you prefer to use a spreadsheet to do the work involved in answering these questions, Figure 7.8 shows how this can be done. The top half gives the answers. To obtain these answers, you need to enter the appropriate equations into the various cells (as shown in the bottom half of the figure) by applying the logic described in this section. The column E equations are directly based on the *earliest start time rule.* Column F uses the formula that EF = ES + duration of the activity, where the duration is given in column D. Similarly, column G uses the formula that LS = LF − duration of the activity. Column H directly applies the *latest finish time rule.* Column I uses the formula that Slack = LF − EF. Column J answers *Yes* if Slack = 0 and *No* otherwise.

It may take longer to set up the spreadsheet and enter all the equations than to mentally perform all the calculations directly on the project network. However, if you don't trust your arithmetic, Excel can be relied on to do that part of the job correctly. The spreadsheet also displays the results in a nice format.

After having entered the *project entry table* (Figure 7.2), you can use MS Project to generate a table similar to the top half of Figure 7.8 by choosing Table:Schedule under the View menu. As shown in the MS Project file for this chapter in your MS Courseware, this table labels ES, EF, LS, and LF as Start, Finish, Late Start, and Late Finish, respectively. Each of these times is displayed in the same format as in Figures 7.2 and 7.3. The table also shows two quantities, called *free slack* and *total slack,* for each activity. When multiple activities on the same path have the same slack, *free slack* only shows this slack once for the last of these activities. *Total slack* is what we (and others) have called slack. The critical path is identified by referring back to Figure 7.3 and identifying the path with the broader arrows. (With a color monitor and printer, the critical path is shown in red.)

Review Questions

1. What is meant by the following terms: (a) a path through the project network; (b) the length of a path; and (c) a critical path?
2. What needs to happen in order to meet a schedule based on earliest start times and earliest finish times?
3. What does the earliest start time rule say?
4. What is a forward pass through the project network?
5. Why is a schedule based on latest start times and latest finish times a "last chance schedule"?
6. What does the latest finish time rule say?
7. How does a backward pass through the project network differ from a forward pass?
8. What is the significance of a critical path for the project manager?
9. What are two methods of finding a critical path through the project network?

7.4 Dealing with Uncertain Activity Durations

Now we come to the next of Mr. Perty's questions posed at the end of Section 7.1.

Question 7: Given the uncertainties in accurately estimating activity durations, what is the probability of completing the project by the deadline (47 weeks)?

Recall that Reliable will incur a large penalty ($300,000) if this deadline is missed. Therefore, Mr. Perty needs to know the probability of meeting the deadline. If this probability is not very high, he will need to consider taking costly measures (using overtime, etc.) to shorten the duration of some of the activities.

It is somewhat reassuring that the PERT/CPM scheduling procedure in the preceding section obtained an estimate of 44 weeks for the project duration. However, Mr. Perty understands very well that this estimate is based on the assumption that the *actual* duration of each activity will turn out to be the same as its *estimated* duration for at least the activities on the critical path. Since the company does not have much prior experience with this kind of project, there is considerable uncertainty about how much time actually will be needed for each activity. In reality, the duration of each activity is a *random variable* having some probability distribution.

The original version of PERT took this uncertainty into account by using three different types of estimates of the duration of an activity to obtain basic information about its probability distribution, as described below.

The PERT Three-Estimate Approach

The three estimates to be obtained for each activity are

Most likely estimate (m) = estimate of the most likely value of the duration
Optimistic estimate (o) = estimate of the duration under the most favorable conditions
Pessimistic estimate (p) = estimate of the duration under the most unfavorable conditions

The intended location of these three estimates with respect to the probability distribution is shown in Figure 7.9.

Thus, the optimistic and pessimistic estimates are meant to lie at the extremes of what is possible, whereas the most likely estimate provides the highest point of the probability distribution. PERT also assumes that the *form* of the probability distribution is a *beta distribution* (which has a shape like that in the figure) in order to calculate the *mean* and *variance* of the probability distribution.

FIGURE 7.9

Model of the probability distribution of the duration of an activity for the PERT three-estimate approach: m = most likely estimate, o = optimistic estimate, and p = pessimistic estimate.

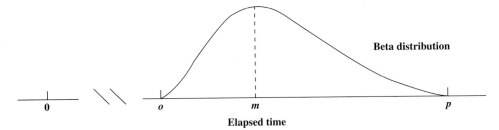

Let

μ = mean of the probability distribution in Figure 7.9
σ^2 = variance of the probability distribution in Figure 7.9

Thus, if the activity were to be performed numerous times and the duration recorded each time, μ would be essentially the *average* of these durations and σ^2 would be a measure of the *variability* of these durations. If $\sigma^2 = 0$, then all the durations would be exactly the same (no variability), whereas a large value of σ^2 indicates a lot of variability in the durations. The *standard deviation* σ (the square root of σ^2) also helps to measure the variability. Many of the durations would be spread out over the interval between $(\mu - \sigma)$ and $(\mu + \sigma)$, but some would be further from μ than this. However, for most probability distributions such as the beta distribution, essentially all the durations would lie inside the interval between $(\mu - 3\sigma)$ and $(\mu + 3\sigma)$. (For example, for a normal distribution, 99.73 percent of the distribution lies inside this interval.) In other words, the spread between the smallest and largest durations (essentially $p - o$) would be roughly 6σ. Therefore, an approximate formula for σ^2 is

$$\sigma^2 = \left(\frac{p - o}{6}\right)^2$$

Similarly, an approximate formula for μ is

$$\mu = \frac{o + 4m + p}{6}$$

Intuitively, this formula is placing most of the weight on the *most likely estimate* and then small equal weights on the other two estimates.

MS Project provides the option of calculating μ for each activity with this formula. Choosing Table:PA_PERT Entry under the View menu enables entering the three types of estimates for the respective activities (where the most likely estimate is labeled as the expected duration). Choosing Toolbars:PERT Analysis under the View menu then enables a toolbar that allows doing various types of analysis with these estimates. Using the Calculate PERT option on this toolbar recalculates Duration with the above formula to obtain μ. Another option is to show the Gantt charts based on each of the three kinds of estimates.

Mr. Perty now has contacted the foreman of each crew that will be responsible for one of the activities to request that these three estimates be made of the duration of the activity. The responses are shown in the first four columns of Table 7.4.

For example, the three estimates for activity C are

Activity C: $o = 6$ $m = 9$ $p = 18$

Therefore, applying the above formulas, the mean and variance of the duration of this activity are approximately

$$\mu = \frac{5 + 4(9) + 18}{6} = 10$$

$$\sigma^2 = \left(\frac{18 - 6}{6}\right)^2 = 4$$

Note that the value of the mean (μ) is not the same as the most likely estimate (m). This is not unusual (the possibility of *much* higher durations here pushes the mean up), but μ generally is at least fairly close to m.

TABLE 7.4 Expected Value and Variance of the Duration of Each Activity for Reliable's Project

Activity	Optimistic Estimate, o	Most Likely Estimate, m	Pessimistic Estimate, p	Mean, $\mu = \dfrac{o + 4m + p}{6}$	Variance, $\sigma^2 = \left(\dfrac{p - o}{6}\right)^2$
A	1	2	3	2	$\frac{1}{9}$
B	2	3½	8	4	1
C	6	9	18	10	4
D	4	5½	10	6	1
E	1	4½	5	4	$\frac{4}{9}$
F	4	4	10	5	1
G	5	6½	11	7	1
H	5	8	17	9	4
I	3	7½	9	7	1
J	3	9	9	8	1
K	4	4	4	4	0
L	1	5½	7	5	1
M	1	2	3	2	$\frac{1}{9}$
N	5	5½	9	6	$\frac{4}{9}$

TABLE 7.5 The Paths and Path Lengths through Reliable's Project Network When the Duration of Each Activity Equals Its Pessimistic Estimate

Path	Length (weeks)
Start→A→B→C→D→G→H→M→Finish	3 + 8 + 18 + 10 + 11 + 17 + 3 = 70
Start→A→B→C→E→H→M→Finish	3 + 8 + 18 + 5 + 17 + 3 = 54
Start→A→B→C→E→F→J→K→N→Finish	3 + 8 + 18 + 5 + 10 + 9 + 4 + 9 = 66
Start→A→B→C→E→F→J→L→N→Finish	3 + 8 + 18 + 5 + 10 + 9 + 7 + 9 = 69
Start→A→B→C→I→J→K→N→Finish	3 + 8 + 18 + 9 + 9 + 4 + 9 = 60
Start→A→B→C→I→J→L→N→Finish	3 + 8 + 18 + 9 + 9 + 7 + 9 = 63

The last two columns of Table 7.4 show the approximate mean and variance of the duration of each activity, calculated in this same way. In this example, all the means happen to be the same as the estimated duration obtained in Table 7.1 of Section 7.1. Therefore, if all the activity durations were to equal their means, the duration of the project still would be 44 weeks, so 3 weeks before the deadline. (See Figure 7.7 for the critical path requiring 44 weeks.)

However, this piece of information is not very reassuring to Mr. Perty. He knows that the durations fluctuate around their means. Consequently, it is inevitable that the duration of some activities will be larger than the mean, perhaps even nearly as large as the pessimistic estimate, which could greatly delay the project.

To check the *worst case scenario,* Mr. Perty reexamines the project network with the duration of each activity set equal to the *pessimistic estimate* (as given in the fourth column of Table 7.4). Table 7.5 shows the six paths through this network (as given previously in Table 7.2) and the length of each path using the pessimistic estimates. The fourth path, which was the critical path in Figure 7.7, now has increased its length from 44 weeks to 69 weeks. However, the length of the first path, which originally was 40 weeks (as given in Table 7.2), now has increased all the way up to 70 weeks. Since this is the longest path, it is the critical path with pessimistic estimates, which would give a project duration of 70 weeks.

Given this dire (albeit unlikely) worst case scenario, Mr. Perty realizes that it is far from certain that the deadline of 47 weeks will be met. But what is the probability of doing so?

PERT/CPM makes three *simplifying approximations* to help calculate this probability.

Three Simplifying Approximations

To calculate the probability that *project duration* will be no more than 47 weeks, it is necessary to obtain the following information about the probability distribution of project duration.

Probability Distribution of Project Duration

1. What is the *mean* (denoted by μ_p) of this distribution?
2. What is the *variance* (denoted by σ_p^2) of this distribution?
3. What is the *form* of this distribution?

Recall that project duration equals the *length* (total elapsed time) of the *longest path* through the project network. However, just about any of the six paths listed in Table 7.5 can turn out to be the longest path (and so the critical path), depending on what the duration of each activity turns out to be between its optimistic and pessimistic estimates. Since dealing with all these paths would be complicated, PERT/CPM focuses on just the following path.

> The **mean critical path** is the path through the project network that would be the critical path if the duration of each activity equals its *mean*.

Reliable's mean critical path is

$$\text{Start} \rightarrow A \rightarrow B \rightarrow C \rightarrow E \rightarrow F \rightarrow J \rightarrow L \rightarrow N \rightarrow \text{Finish}$$

as highlighted in Figure 7.7.

> **Simplifying Approximation 1:** Assume that the *mean critical path* will turn out to be the longest path through the project network. This is only a rough approximation since the assumption occasionally does not hold in the usual case where some of the activity durations do not equal their means. Fortunately, when the assumption does not hold, the true longest path commonly is not much longer than the mean critical path (as illustrated in Table 7.5).

Although this approximation will enable us to calculate μ_p, we need one more approximation to obtain σ_p^2.

> **Simplifying Approximation 2:** Assume that the durations of the activities on the mean critical path are *statistically independent*. Thus, the three estimates of the duration of an activity would never change after learning the durations of some of the other activities. This assumption should hold if the activities are performed truly independently of each other. However, the assumption becomes only a rough approximation if the circumstances that cause the duration of one activity to deviate from its mean also tend to cause similar deviations for some other activities.

We now have a simple method for computing μ_p and σ_p^2.

Calculation of μ_p and σ_p^2: Because of simplifying approximation 1, the *mean* of the probability distribution of project duration is approximately

$$\mu_p = \text{sum of the } means \text{ of the durations for the activities on the mean critical path}$$

Because of both simplifying approximations 1 and 2, the *variance* of the probability distribution of project duration is approximately

$$\sigma_p^2 = \text{sum of the } variances \text{ of the durations for the activities on the mean critical path}$$

Since the means and variances of the durations for all the activities of Reliable's project already are given in Table 7.4, we only need to record these values for the activities on the mean critical path, as shown in Table 7.6. Summing the second column and then summing the third column give

$$\mu_p = 44 \qquad \sigma_p^2 = 9$$

Now we just need an approximation for the *form* of the probability distribution of project duration.

> **Simplifying Approximation 3:** Assume that the form of the probability distribution of project duration is the *normal distribution*, which has the bell shape illustrated in Figure 7.10. By using simplifying approximations 1 and 2, there is some statistical theory (one version of the central limit theorem) that justifies this assumption as being a reasonable approximation if the number of activities on the mean critical path is not too small (say, at least five). The approximation becomes better as this number of activities increases.

TABLE 7.6 Calculation of μ_p and σ_p^2 for Reliable's Project

Activities on Mean Critical Path	Mean	Variance
A	2	1/9
B	4	1
C	10	4
E	4	4/9
F	5	1
J	8	1
L	5	1
N	6	4/9
Project duration	$\mu_p = 44$	$\sigma_p^2 = 9$

FIGURE 7.10

The three simplifying approximations lead to the probability distribution of the duration of Reliable's project being approximated by the normal distribution shown here. The shaded area is the portion of the distribution that meets the deadline of 47 weeks.

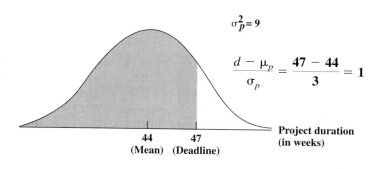

Now we are ready to determine (approximately) the probability of completing Reliable's project within 47 weeks.

Approximating the Probability of Meeting the Deadline

Let

$$d = \text{deadline for the project}$$
$$= 47 \text{ weeks}$$
$$P(T \le d) = \text{probability that the project duration } (T) \text{ does not exceed the deadline}$$
$$\text{(given the three simplifying approximations)}$$

To find $P(T \le d)$, first calculate the *standard deviation* of project duration as

$$\sigma_p = \sqrt{\sigma_p^2} = \sqrt{9} = 3$$

and then compute

$$\frac{d - \mu_p}{\sigma_p} = \frac{47 - 44}{3} = 1$$

$$= \text{number of standard deviations by which } d \text{ exceeds } \mu_p$$

Finally, use this latter number to read off the corresponding value of $P(T \le d)$ in Table 7.7, so

$$P(T \le d) = 0.84$$

(This table is an abbreviated table for the normal distribution.)

Warning: This $P(T \le d)$ is only a rough approximation of the true probability of meeting the project deadline. Furthermore, because of simplifying approximation 1, it usually overstates the true probability somewhat. Therefore, the project manager should view $P(T \le d)$ as only providing rough guidance on the best odds of meeting the deadline without taking new costly measures to try to reduce the duration of some activities.

To assist you in carrying out this procedure for calculating $P(T \le d)$, we have provided an Excel template (labeled PERT) in this chapter's Excel file in your MS Courseware. Figure 7.11 illustrates the use of this template for Reliable's project. The data for the problem

TABLE 7.7   Approximate Probability of Meeting a Project Deadline

$\dfrac{d - \mu_p}{\sigma_p}$	$P(T \le d)$	$\dfrac{d - \mu_p}{\sigma_p}$	$P(T \le d)$
−3.0	0.0014	0	0.50
−2.5	0.0062	0.25	0.60
−2.0	0.023	0.5	0.69
−1.75	0.040	0.75	0.77
−1.5	0.067	1.0	0.84
−1.25	0.11	1.25	0.89
−1.0	0.16	1.5	0.933
−0.75	0.23	1.75	0.960
−0.5	0.31	2.0	0.977
−0.25	0.40	2.5	0.9938
0	0.50	3.0	0.9986

FIGURE 7.11

This Excel template in your MS Courseware enables efficient application of the PERT three-estimate approach, as illustrated here for Reliable's project.

	A	B	C	D	E	F	G	H	I	J	K
1		Template for PERT Three–Estimate Approach									
2											
3				**Time Estimates**				**On Mean**			
4		**Activity**	**o**	**m**	**p**	μ	σ^2	**Critical Path**			
5		A	1	2	3	2	0.111	*		**Mean Critical**	
6		B	2	3.5	8	4	1	*		**Path**	
7		C	6	9	18	10	4	*		$\mu=$	44
8		D	4	5.5	10	6	1			$\sigma^2 =$	9
9		E	1	4.5	5	4	0.444	*			
10		F	4	4	10	5	1	*		$P(T\le d)=$	0.84134474
11		G	5	6.5	11	7	1			**where**	
12		H	5	8	17	9	4			**d =**	47
13		I	3	7.5	9	7	1				
14		J	3	9	9	8	1	*			
15		K	4	4	4	4	0				
16		L	1	5.5	7	5	1	*			
17		M	1	2	3	2	0.111				
18		N	5	5.5	9	6	0.444	*			
19											
20											
21				**Data**							
22				**Results**							

	F	G
5	=(C5+4*D5+E5)/6	=((E5–C5)/6)^2
6	=(C6+4*D6+E6)/6	=((E6–C6)/6)^2
7	=(C7+4*D7+E7)/6	=((E7–C7)/6)^2
8	=(C8+4*D8+E8)/6	=((E8–C8)/6)^2
9	:	:
10	:	:

	K
7	=SUMIF(H5:H18, "*",F5:F18)
8	=SUMIF(H5:H18, "*",G5:G18)
9	
10	=NORMDIST(K12,K7,SQRT(K8),1)

are entered in the light sections of the spreadsheet. After entering data, the results immediately appear in the dark sections. In particular, by entering the three time estimates for each activity, the spreadsheet will automatically calculate the corresponding estimates for the mean and variance. Next, by specifying the mean critical path (by entering * in column H for each activity on the mean critical path) and the deadline (in cell K12), the spreadsheet automatically calculates the mean and variance of the length of the mean critical path along with the probability that the project will be completed by the deadline. (If you are not sure which path is the mean critical path, the mean length of *any* path can be checked by entering a * for each activity on that path in column H. The path with the longest mean length then is the mean critical path.)

Realizing that $P(T \leq d) = 0.84$ is probably an optimistic approximation, Mr. Perty is somewhat concerned that he may have perhaps only a 70 to 80 percent chance of meeting the deadline with the current plan. Therefore, rather than taking the significant chance of the company incurring the late penalty of $300,000, he decides to investigate what it would cost to reduce the project duration down to about 40 weeks. If the *time–cost trade-off* for doing this is favorable, the company might then be able to earn the bonus of $150,000 for finishing within 40 weeks.

You will see this story unfold in the next section.

Review Questions

1. What are the names of the three estimates in the PERT three-estimate approach?
2. Where are these three estimates meant to be located in the probability distribution of the duration of an activity?
3. What simplifying approximation is made about which path will be the longest path through the project network?
4. What simplifying approximation is made about the relationship between the durations of different activities?
5. What is the formula for the mean (μ_p) of the probability distribution of project duration?
6. What is the formula for the variance (σ_p^2) of the probability distribution of project duration?
7. What simplifying approximation is made about the form of the probability distribution of project duration?
8. The approximation obtained for the probability of meeting the project deadline is likely to be on which side (higher or lower) of the true probability?

7.5 Considering Time–Cost Trade-Offs

Mr. Perty now wants to investigate how much extra it would cost to reduce the expected project duration down to 40 weeks (the deadline for the company earning a bonus of $150,000 for early completion). Therefore, he is ready to address the next of his questions posed at the end of Section 7.1.

> **Question 8:** If extra money is spent to expedite the project, what is the least expensive way of attempting to meet the target completion time (40 weeks)?

Mr. Perty remembers that CPM provides an excellent procedure for using *linear programming* to investigate such *time–cost trade-offs*, so he will use this approach again to address this question.

We begin with some background.

Time–Cost Trade-Offs for Individual Activities

The first key concept for this approach is that of *crashing*.

> **Crashing an activity** refers to taking special costly measures to reduce the duration of an activity below its normal value. These special measures might include using overtime, hiring additional temporary help, using special time-saving materials, obtaining special equipment, and so forth. **Crashing the project** refers to crashing a number of activities to reduce the duration of the project below its normal value.

The **CPM method of time–cost trade-offs** is concerned with determining how much (if any) to crash each of the activities to reduce the anticipated duration of the project down to a desired value.

FIGURE 7.12

A typical time–cost graph for an activity.

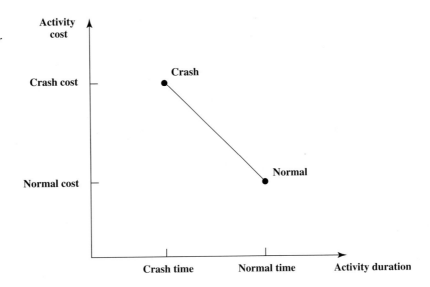

The data necessary for determining how much to crash a particular activity are given by the *time–cost graph* for the activity. Figure 7.12 shows a typical time–cost graph. Note the two key points on this graph labeled *normal* and *crash.*

> The **normal point** on the time–cost graph shows the time (duration) and cost of the activity when it is performed in the normal way. The **crash point** shows the time and cost when the activity is *fully crashed;* that is, it is fully expedited with no cost spared to reduce its duration as much as possible.

For most applications, it is assumed that *partially crashing* the activity at any level will give a combination of time and cost that will lie somewhere on the line segment between these two points. (For example, this assumption says that *half* of a full crash will give a point on this line segment that is midway between the normal and crash points.) This simplifying approximation reduces the necessary data gathering to estimating the time and cost for just two situations: *normal conditions* (to obtain the normal point) and a *full crash* (to obtain the crash point).

Using this approach, Mr. Perty has his staff and crew foremen working on developing these data for each of the activities of Reliable's project. For example, the foreman of the crew responsible for putting up the wallboard indicates that adding two temporary employees and using overtime would enable him to reduce the duration of this activity from eight weeks to six weeks, which is the minimum possible. Mr. Perty's staff then estimates the cost of fully crashing the activity in this way as compared to following the normal eight-week schedule, as shown below.

Activity J (Put up the wallboard)
Normal point: Time = 8 weeks, Cost = \$430,000
Crash point: Time = 6 weeks, Cost = \$460,000
Maximum reduction in time = 8 − 6 = 2 weeks

$$\text{Crash cost per week saved} = \frac{\$460,000 - \$430,000}{2}$$

$$= \$15,000$$

Table 7.8 gives the corresponding data obtained for all the activities.

Which Activities Should Be Crashed?

Summing the *normal cost* and *crash cost* columns of Table 7.8 gives

Sum of normal costs = \$4.55 million

Sum of crash costs   = \$6.15 million

Recall that the company will be paid \$5.4 million for doing this project. (This figure excludes the \$150,000 bonus for finishing within 40 weeks and the \$300,000 penalty for not

TABLE 7.8   Time–Cost Trade-Off Data for the Activities of Reliable's Project

Activity	Time (weeks) Normal	Crash	Cost Normal	Crash	Maximum Reduction in Time (weeks)	Crash Cost per Week Saved
A	2	1	$180,000	$ 280,000	1	$100,000
B	4	2	320,000	420,000	2	50,000
C	10	7	620,000	860,000	3	80,000
D	6	4	260,000	340,000	2	40,000
E	4	3	410,000	570,000	1	160,000
F	5	3	180,000	260,000	2	40,000
G	7	4	900,000	1,020,000	3	40,000
H	9	6	200,000	380,000	3	60,000
I	7	5	210,000	270,000	2	30,000
J	8	6	430,000	490,000	2	30,000
K	4	3	160,000	200,000	1	40,000
L	5	3	250,000	350,000	2	50,000
M	2	1	100,000	200,000	1	100,000
N	6	3	330,000	510,000	3	60,000

finishing within 47 weeks.) This payment needs to cover some *overhead costs* in addition to the costs of the activities listed in the table, as well as provide a reasonable profit to the company. When developing the (winning) bid of $5.4 million, Reliable's management felt that this amount would provide a reasonable profit as long as the total cost of the activities could be held fairly close to the normal level of about $4.55 million. Mr. Perty understands very well that it is now his responsibility to keep the project as close to both budget and schedule as possible.

As found previously in Figure 7.7, if all the activities are performed in the normal way, the anticipated duration of the project would be 44 weeks (if delays can be avoided). If *all* the activities were to be *fully crashed* instead, then a similar calculation would find that this duration would be reduced to only 28 weeks. But look at the prohibitive cost ($6.15 million) of doing this! Fully crashing all activities clearly is not an option that can be considered.

However, Mr. Perty still wants to investigate the possibility of partially or fully crashing just a few activities to reduce the anticipated duration of the project down to 40 weeks.

The problem: What is the least expensive way of crashing some activities to reduce project duration to the specified level (40 weeks)?

One way of solving this problem is **marginal cost analysis,** which uses the last column of Table 7.8 (along with Figure 7.7 in Section 7.3) to determine the least expensive way to reduce project duration one week at a time. The easiest way to conduct this kind of analysis is to set up a table like Table 7.9 that lists all the paths through the project network and the current length of each of these paths. To get started, this information can be copied directly from Table 7.2.

Since the fourth path listed in Table 7.9 has the longest length (44 weeks), the only way to reduce project duration by a week is to reduce the duration of the activities on this particular path by a week. Comparing the crash cost per week saved given in the last column of Table 7.8 for these activities, the smallest cost is $30,000 for activity J. (Note that activity I with this same cost is not on this path.) Therefore, the first change is to crash activity J enough to reduce its duration by a week.

This change results in reducing the length of each path that includes activity J (the third, fourth, fifth, and sixth paths in Table 7.9) by a week, as shown in the second row of Table 7.10. Because the fourth path still is the longest (43 weeks), the same process is repeated to find the least expensive activity to shorten on this path. This again is activity J, since the next-to-last column in Table 7.8 indicates that a maximum reduction of two weeks

TABLE 7.9   **The Initial Table for Starting Marginal Cost Analysis of Reliable's Project**

Activity to Crash	Crash Cost	Length of Path					
		ABCDGHM	ABCEHM	ABCEFJKN	ABCEFJLN	ABCIJKN	ABCIJLN
		40	31	43	44	41	42

TABLE 7.10   **The Final Table for Performing Marginal Cost Analysis on Reliable's Project**

Activity to Crash	Crash Cost	Length of Path					
		ABCDGHM	ABCEHM	ABCEFJKN	ABCEFJLN	ABCIJKN	ABCIJLN
		40	31	43	44	41	42
J	$30,000	40	31	42	43	40	41
J	$30,000	40	31	41	42	39	40
F	$40,000	40	31	40	41	39	40
F	$40,000	40	31	39	40	39	40

is allowed for this activity. This second reduction of a week for activity J leads to the third row of Table 7.10.

At this point, the fourth path still is the longest (42 weeks), but activity J cannot be shortened any further. Among the other activities on this path, activity F now is the least expensive to shorten ($40,000 per week) according to the last column of Table 7.8. Therefore, this activity is shortened by a week to obtain the fourth row of Table 7.10, and then (because a maximum reduction of two weeks is allowed) is shortened by another week to obtain the last row of this table.

The longest path (a tie between the first, fourth, and sixth paths) now has the desired length of 40 weeks, so we don't need to do any more crashing. (If we did need to go further, the next step would require looking at the activities on all three paths to find the least expensive way of shortening all three paths by a week.) The total cost of crashing activities J and F to get down to this project duration of 40 weeks is calculated by adding the costs in the second column of Table 7.10—a total of $140,000. Figure 7.13 shows the resulting project network.

Since $140,000 is slightly less than the bonus of $150,000 for finishing within 40 weeks, it might appear that Mr. Perty should proceed with this solution. However, he actually concludes that he probably should not crash the project at all, as we will discuss at the end of the section. (Meanwhile, be mulling over why his conclusion makes sense because of the preceding section on dealing with uncertain activity durations.)

Figure 7.13 shows that reducing the durations of activities F and J to their crash times has led to now having *three* critical paths through the network. The reason is that, as we found earlier from the last row of Table 7.10, the three paths tie for being the longest, each with a length of 40 weeks.

With larger networks, marginal cost analysis can become quite unwieldy. A more efficient procedure would be desirable for large projects.

For these reasons, the standard CPM procedure is to apply *linear programming* instead (commonly with a customized software package).

FIGURE 7.13

The project network if activities J and F are fully crashed (with all other activities normal) for Reliable's project. The darker arrows show the various critical paths through the project network.

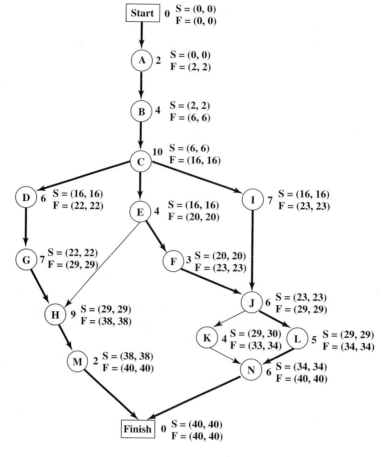

Using Linear Programming to Make Crashing Decisions

The problem of finding the least expensive way of crashing activities can be rephrased in a form more familiar to linear programming as follows.

> **Restatement of the problem:** Consider the total cost of the project, including the extra cost of crashing activities. The problem then is to minimize this total cost, subject to the constraint that project duration must be less than or equal to the time desired by the project manager.

The decisions to be made are the following:

1. The start time of each activity.
2. The reduction in the duration of each activity due to crashing.
3. The finish time of the project (must not exceed 40 weeks).

Figure 7.14 shows how this problem can be formulated as a linear programming model on a spreadsheet. The decisions to be made are shown in the changing cells, I6:J19 and J21. Columns B to H correspond to the columns in Table 7.8. As the equations in the bottom half of the figure indicate, columns G and H are calculated in a straightforward way. The equations for column K express the fact that the finish time for each activity is its start time *plus* its normal time *minus* its time reduction due to crashing. The equation entered into the target cell (J22) adds all the normal costs plus the extra costs due to crashing to obtain the total cost.

The last set of constraints in the Solver dialogue box (J6:J19 ≤ G6:G19) specifies that the time reduction for each activity cannot exceed its maximum time reduction given in column G. The two preceding constraints (J21 ≥ K18 and J21 ≥ K19) indicate that the project cannot finish until each of the two immediate predecessors (activities M and N) finish. The constraint that J21 ≤ 40 is a key one that specifies that the project must finish within 40 weeks.

The constraints involving cells I7:I19 all are *start-time constraints* that specify that an activity cannot start until each of its immediate predecessors have finished. For example, the first constraint shown (I10 ≥ K8) says that activity E cannot start until activity C (its

FIGURE 7.14

The spreadsheet displays the application of the CPM method of time–cost trade-offs to Reliable's project, where columns I and J show the optimal solution obtained by using the Excel Solver with the entries shown in the Solver Parameters dialogue box.

	A	B	C	D	E	F	G	H	I	J	K
1		Reliable Construction Co. Project Scheduling Problem with Time–Cost Trade–offs									
2											
3							Maximum	Crash Cost			
4			Time		Cost		Time	per Week	Start	Time	Finish
5		Activity	Normal	Crash	Normal	Crash	Reduction	saved	Time	Reduction	Time
6		A	2	1	$180000	$280000	1	$100000	0	0	2
7		B	4	2	$320000	$420000	2	$50000	2	0	6
8		C	10	7	$620000	$860000	3	$80000	6	0	16
9		D	6	4	$260000	$340000	2	$40000	16	0	22
10		E	4	3	$410000	$570000	1	$160000	16	0	20
11		F	5	3	$180000	$260000	2	$40000	20	2	23
12		G	7	4	$900000	$1020000	3	$40000	22	0	29
13		H	9	6	$200000	$380000	3	$60000	29	0	38
14		I	7	5	$210000	$270000	2	$30000	16	0	23
15		J	8	6	$430000	$490000	2	$30000	23	2	29
16		K	4	3	$160000	$200000	1	$40000	30	0	34
17		L	5	3	$250000	$350000	2	$50000	29	0	34
18		M	2	1	$100000	$200000	1	$100000	38	0	40
19		N	6	3	$330000	$510000	3	$60000	34	0	40
20											
21									Finish Time =	40	
22									Total Cost =	$4,690,000	

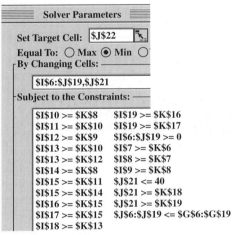

Solver Parameters

Set Target Cell: $J$22

Equal To: ○ Max ● Min ○

By Changing Cells:

$I$6:$J$19,$J$21

Subject to the Constraints:

$I$10 >= $K$8	$I$19 >= $K$16
$I$11 >= $K$10	$I$19 >= $K$17
$I$12 >= $K$9	$I$6:$J$19 >= 0
$I$13 >= $K$10	$I$7 >= $K$6
$I$13 >= $K$12	$I$8 >= $K$7
$I$14 >= $K$8	$I$9 >= $K$8
$I$15 >= $K$11	$J$21 <= 40
$I$15 >= $K$14	$J$21 >= $K$18
$I$16 >= $K$15	$J$21 >= $K$19
$I$17 >= $K$15	$J$6:$J$19 <= $G$6:$G$19
$I$18 >= $K$13	

Solver Options

☑ Assume Linear Model

☑ Assume Non-Negative

	G	H	K
6	=C6–D6	=(F6–E6)/G6	=I6+C6–J6
7	=C7–D7	=(F7–E7)/G7	=I7+C7–J7
8	=C8–D8	=(F8–E8)/G8	=I8+C8–J8
9	=C9–D9	=(F9–E9)/G9	=I9+C9–J9
10	=C10–D10	=(F10–E10)/G10	=I10+C10–J10
11	=C11–D11	=(F11–E11)/G11	=I11+C11–J11
12	=C12–D12	=(F12–E12)/G12	=I12+C12–J12
13	=C13–D13	=(F13–E13)/G13	=I13+C13–J13
14	=C14–D14	=(F14–E14)/G14	=I14+C14–J14
15	=C15–D15	=(F15–E15)/G15	=I15+C15–J15
16	=C16–D16	=(F16–E16)/G16	=I16+C16–J16
17	=C17–D17	=(F17–E17)/G17	=I17+C17–J17
18	=C18–D18	=(F18–E18)/G18	=I18+C18–J18
19	=C19–D19	=(F19–E19)/G19	=I19+C19–J19

	J
22	=SUM(E6:E19)+SUMPRODUCT(H6:H19,J6:J19)

immediate predecessor) finishes. When an activity has more than one immediate predecessor, there is one such constraint for each of them. To illustrate, activity H has both activities E and G as immediate predecessors. Consequently, activity H has two start-time constraints, I13 ≥ K10 and I13 ≥ K12.

You may have noticed that the ≥ form of the *start-time constraints* allows a delay in starting an activity after all its immediate predecessors have finished. Although such a delay is feasible in the model, it cannot be optimal for any activity on a critical path since this needless delay would increase the total cost (by necessitating additional crashing to meet the project duration constraint). Therefore, an optimal solution for the model will not have any such delays, except possibly for activities not on a critical path.

Columns I and J in Figure 7.14 show the optimal solution obtained after having clicked on the Solve button. (Note that this solution involves one delay—activity K starts at 30 even though its only immediate predecessor, activity J, finishes at 29—but this doesn't matter since activity K is not on a critical path.) This solution corresponds to the one displayed in Figure 7.13 that was obtained by marginal cost analysis.

*Mr. Perty's
Conclusions*

Mr. Perty always keeps a sharp eye on the bottom line. Therefore, when his staff brings him the above plan for crashing the project to try to reduce its duration from about 44 weeks to about 40 weeks, he first looks at the estimated total cost of $4.69 million. Since the estimated total cost without any crashing is $4.55 million, the additional cost from the crashing would be about $140,000. This is $10,000 less than the bonus of $150,000 that the company would earn by finishing within 40 weeks.

However, Mr. Perty knows from long experience what we discussed in the preceding section, namely, that there is considerable uncertainty about how much time actually will be needed for each activity and so for the overall project. Recall that the PERT three-estimate approach led to having a *probability distribution* for project duration. Without crashing, this probability distribution has a *mean* of 44 weeks but such a large *variance* that there is even a substantial probability (roughly 0.2) of not even finishing within 47 weeks (which would trigger a penalty of $300,000). With the new crashing plan reducing the mean to 40 weeks, there is as much chance that the actual project duration will turn out to exceed 40 weeks as being within 40 weeks. Why spend an extra $140,000 to obtain a 50 percent chance of earning the bonus of $150,000?

> **Conclusion 1:** The plan for crashing the project only provides a 50 percent chance of actually finishing the project within 40 weeks, so the extra cost of the plan ($140,000) is not justified. Therefore, Mr. Perty rejects any crashing at this stage.

Mr. Perty does note that the two activities that had been proposed for crashing (F and J) come about halfway through the project. Therefore, if the project is well ahead of schedule before reaching activity F, then implementing the crashing plan almost certainly would enable finishing the project within 40 weeks. Furthermore, Mr. Perty knows that it would be good for the company's reputation (as well as a feather in his own cap) to finish this early.

> **Conclusion 2:** The extra cost of the crashing plan can be justified if it almost certainly would earn the bonus of $150,000 for finishing the project within 40 weeks. Therefore, Mr. Perty will hold the plan in reserve to be implemented if the project is running well ahead of schedule before reaching activity F.

Mr. Perty is more concerned about the possibility that the project will run so far behind schedule that the penalty of $300,000 will be incurred for not finishing within 47 weeks. If this becomes likely without crashing, Mr. Perty sees that it probably can be avoided by crashing activity J (at a cost of $30,000 per week saved) and, if necessary, crashing activity F as well (at a cost of $40,000 per week saved). This will hold true as long as these activities remain on the critical path (as is likely) after the delays occurred.

> **Conclusion 3:** The extra cost of part or all of the crashing plan can be easily justified if it likely would make the difference in avoiding the penalty of $300,000 for not finishing the project within 47 weeks. Therefore, Mr. Perty will hold the crashing plan in reserve to be partially or wholly implemented if the project is running far behind schedule before reaching activity F or activity J.

In addition to carefully monitoring the schedule as the project evolves (and making a later decision about any crashing), Mr. Perty will be closely watching the costs to try to keep the project within budget. The next section describes how he plans to do this.

Review Questions

1. What are some ways of crashing an activity?
2. What are the two key points in a time–cost graph for an activity? What do these points show?
3. Does crashing an activity always reduce the duration of the project? Why?
4. What are the costs being examined when performing marginal cost analysis on a project?
5. What are the decisions to be made when using linear programming to make crashing decisions?
6. In the linear programming formulation, describe in words what each starting time constraint is saying.

7. Why did Mr. Perty decide to reject the proposed plan for crashing the project even though the extra cost of the plan is less than the bonus for early completion of the project?

7.6 Scheduling and Controlling Project Costs

Any good project manager like Mr. Perty carefully plans and monitors both the *time* and *cost* aspects of the project. Both schedule and budget are important.

Sections 7.3 and 7.4 have described how PERT/CPM deals with the *time* aspect in developing a schedule and taking uncertainties in activity or project durations into account. Section 7.5 then placed an equal emphasis on time and cost by describing the CPM method of time–cost trade-offs.

Mr. Perty now is ready to turn his focus to *costs* by addressing the last of his questions posed at the end of Section 7.1.

Question 9: How should ongoing costs be monitored to try to keep the project within budget?

Mr. Perty recalls that the PERT/CPM technique known as PERT/Cost is specifically designed for this purpose.

PERT/Cost is a systematic procedure (normally computerized) to help the project manager plan, schedule, and control project costs.

The PERT/Cost procedure begins with the hard work of developing an estimate of the cost of each activity when it is performed in the planned way (including any crashing). At this stage, Mr. Perty does not plan on any crashing, so the estimated costs of the activities in Reliable's project are given in the normal cost column of Table 7.8 in the preceding section. These costs then are displayed in the *project budget* shown in Table 7.11. This table also includes the estimated duration of each activity (as already given in Table 7.1 or in Figures 7.1–7.8 or in the normal time column of Table 7.8). Dividing the cost of each activity by its duration gives the amount in the rightmost column of Table 7.11.

Assumption: A common assumption when using PERT/Cost is that the costs of performing an activity are incurred at a constant rate throughout its duration. Mr. Perty is making this assumption, so the estimated cost during each week of an activity's duration is given by the rightmost column of Table 7.11.

TABLE 7.11   The Project Budget for Reliable's Project

Activity	Estimated Duration (weeks)	Estimated Cost	Cost per Week of Its Duration
A	2	$180,000	$ 90,000
B	4	320,000	80,000
C	10	620,000	62,000
D	6	260,000	43,333
E	4	410,000	102,500
F	5	180,000	36,000
G	7	900,000	128,571
H	9	200,000	22,222
I	7	210,000	30,000
J	8	430,000	53,750
K	4	160,000	40,000
L	5	250,000	50,000
M	2	100,000	50,000
N	6	330,000	55,000

When applying PERT/Cost to larger projects with numerous activities, it is common to combine each group of related activities into a "work package." Both the project budget and the schedule of project costs (described below) then are developed in terms of these work packages rather than the individual activities. Mr. Perty has chosen not to do this since his project only has 14 activities.

Scheduling Project Costs

Mr. Perty needs to know how much money is required to cover project expenses week by week. PERT/Cost provides this information by using the rightmost column of Table 7.11 to develop a weekly schedule of expenses when the individual activities begin at their earliest start times. Then, to indicate how much flexibility is available for delaying expenses, PERT/Cost does the same thing when the individual activities begin at their latest start times instead.

To do this, this chapter's Excel file in your MS Courseware includes an Excel template (labeled PERT Cost) for generating a project's schedule of costs for up to 45 time periods. (MS Project generates basically the same information by choosing Table:Cost and then Reports under the View menu, and next choosing the Costs ... option and selecting the Cash Flow report.) Figure 7.15 shows this Excel template (including the equations entered into its output cells) for the beginning of Reliable's project, based on earliest start times (column E) as first obtained in Figure 7.5, where Columns B, C, and D come directly from

FIGURE 7.15

This Excel template in your MS Courseware enables efficient application of the PERT/Cost procedure, as illustrated here for the beginning of Reliable's project when using earliest start times.

	A	B	C	D	E	F	G	H	I
1		Template for PERT/Cost							
2									
3			Estimated						
4			Duration	Estimated	Start	Cost per Week	Week	Week	...
5		Activity	(weeks)	Cost	Time	of Its Duration	1	2	
6		A	2	$180,000	0	$90,000	90000	90000	
7		B	4	$320,000	2	$80,000	0	0	
8		C	10	$620,000	6	$62,000	0	0	
9		D	6	$260,000	16	$43,333	0	0	...
10		E	4	$410,000	16	$102,500	0	0	
11		F	5	$180,000	20	$36,000	0	0	
12		G	7	$900,000	22	$128,571	0	0	
13		H	9	$200,000	29	$22,222	0	0	...
14		I	7	$210,000	16	$30,000	0	0	
15		J	8	$430,000	25	$53,750	0	0	
16		K	4	$160,000	33	$40,000	0	0	
17		L	5	$250,000	33	$50,000	0	0	...
18		M	2	$100,000	38	$50,000	0	0	
19		N	6	$330,000	38	$55,000	0	0	
20							0	0	
21									
22						Weekly Project Cost	90000	90000	...
23						Cumulative Project Cost	90000	180000	...
24									
25			Data						
26			Results						

	F	G	H	I
6	=D6/C6	=IF(AND(G5>E6,G5<=E6+C6),F6,0)	=IF(AND(H5>E6,H5<=E6+C6),F6,0)	
7	=D7/C7	=IF(AND(G5>E7,G5<=E7+C7),F7,0)	=IF(AND(H5>E7,H5<=E7+C7),F7,0)	
8	=D8/C8	=IF(AND(G5>E8,G5<=E8+C8),F8,0)	=IF(AND(H5>E8,H5<=E8+C8),F8,0)	
9	=D9/C9	=IF(AND(G5>E9,G5<=E9+C9),F9,0)	=IF(AND(H5>E9,H5<=E9+C9),F9,0)	...
10	:	:	:	
11	:	:	:	
21				
22		=SUM(G6:G20)	=SUM(H6:H20)	...
23		=G22	=G23+H22	...

Table 7.11. Figure 7.16 jumps ahead to show this same template for weeks 17 to 25. Since activities D, E, and I all have earliest start times of 16 (16 weeks after the commencement of the project), they all start in week 17, while activities F and G commence later during the period shown. Columns W through AE give the weekly cost (in dollars) of each of these activities, as obtained from column F (see Figure 7.15), for the duration of the activity (given by column C). Row 22 shows the sum of the weekly activity costs for each week.

Row 23 of this template gives the total project cost from week 1 on up to the indicated week. For example, consider week 17. Prior to week 17, activities A, B, and C all have been completed but no other activities have begun, so the total cost for the first 16 weeks (from the third column of Table 7.11) are $180,000 + $320,000 + $620,000 = $1,120,000. Adding the weekly project cost for week 17 then gives $1,120,000 + $175,833 = $1,295,833.

Thus, Figure 7.16 (and its extension to earlier and later weeks) shows Mr. Perty just how much money he will need to cover each week's expenses, as well as the cumulative amount, assuming the project can stick to the earliest start time schedule.

Next, PERT/Cost uses the same procedure to develop the corresponding information when each activity begins at its *latest* start times instead. These latest start times were first obtained in Figure 7.6 and are repeated here in column E of Figure 7.17. The rest of this figure then is generated in the same way as for Figure 7.16. For example, since activity D has a latest start time of 20 (versus an earliest start time of 16), its weekly cost of $43,333 now begins in week 21 rather than week 17. Similarly, activity G has a latest start time of 26, so it has no entries for the weeks considered in this figure.

Figure 7.17 (and its extension to earlier and later weeks) tells Mr. Perty what his weekly and cumulative expenses would be if he postpones each activity as long as possible without delaying project completion (assuming no unexpected delays occur). Comparing row 23 of Figures 7.16 and 7.17 indicates that fairly substantial *temporary* savings can be achieved by such postponements, which is very helpful if the company is incurring cash shortages. (However, such postponements would only be used reluctantly since they would remove any latitude for avoiding a delay in the completion of the project if any activities incur unexpected delays.)

To better visualize the comparison between row 23 of Figures 7.16 and 7.17, it is helpful to graph these two rows together over all 44 weeks of the project, as shown in Figure 7.18. Since the earliest start times and latest start times are the same for the first three activities (A, B, C), which encompass the first 16 weeks, the cumulative project cost is the same for the

FIGURE 7.16

This spreadsheet extends the template in Figure 7.15 to weeks 17 to 25.

	A	B	E	W	X	Y	Z	AA	AB	AC	AD	AE
1	Template for PERT/Cost											
2												
3												
4			Start	Week	Week	Week	Week	Week	Week	Week	Week	Week
5		Activity	Time	17	18	19	20	21	22	23	24	25
6		A	0	0	0	0	0	0	0	0	0	0
7		B	2	0	0	0	0	0	0	0	0	0
8		C	6	0	0	0	0	0	0	0	0	0
9		D	16	43333.3	43333.3	43333.3	43333.3	43333.3	43333.3	0	0	0
10		E	16	102500	102500	102500	102500	0	0	0	0	0
11		F	20	0	0	0	0	36000	36000	36000	36000	36000
12		G	22	0	0	0	0	0	0	128571	128571	128571
13		H	29	0	0	0	0	0	0	0	0	0
14		I	16	30000	30000	30000	30000	30000	30000	30000	0	0
15		J	25	0	0	0	0	0	0	0	0	0
16		K	33	0	0	0	0	0	0	0	0	0
17		L	33	0	0	0	0	0	0	0	0	0
18		M	38	0	0	0	0	0	0	0	0	0
19		N	38	0	0	0	0	0	0	0	0	0
21												
22	Weekly Project Cost=			175833	175833	175833	175833	109333	109333	194571	164571	164571
23	Cum. Project Cost=			1295833	1471667	1647500	1823333	1932667	2042000	2236571	2401143	2565714

FIGURE 7.17

The application of the PERT/Cost procedure to weeks 17 to 25 of Reliable's project when using latest start times.

	A	B	E	W	X	Y	Z	AA	AB	AC	AD	AE
1	Template for PERT/Cost											
2												
3												
4			Start	Week	Week	Week	Week	Week	Week	Week	Week	Week
5		Activity	Time	17	18	19	20	21	22	23	24	25
6		A	0	0	0	0	0	0	0	0	0	0
7		B	2	0	0	0	0	0	0	0	0	0
8		C	6	0	0	0	0	0	0	0	0	0
9		D	20	0	0	0	0	43333.3	43333.3	43333.3	43333.3	43333.3
10		E	16	102500	102500	102500	102500	0	0	0	0	0
11		F	20	0	0	0	0	36000	36000	36000	36000	36000
12		G	26	0	0	0	0	0	0	0	0	0
13		H	33	0	0	0	0	0	0	0	0	0
14		I	18	0	0	30000	30000	30000	30000	30000	30000	30000
15		J	25	0	0	0	0	0	0	0	0	0
16		K	34	0	0	0	0	0	0	0	0	0
17		L	33	0	0	0	0	0	0	0	0	0
18		M	42	0	0	0	0	0	0	0	0	0
19		N	38	0	0	0	0	0	0	0	0	0
20				0	0	0	0	0	0	0	0	0
21												
22	Weekly Project Cost=			102500	102500	132500	132500	109333	109333	109333	109333	109333
23	Cum. Project Cost=			1222500	1325000	1457500	1590000	1699333	1808667	1918000	2027333	2136667

FIGURE 7.18

The schedule of cumulative project costs when all activities begin at their earliest start times (the top cost curve) or at their latest start times (the bottom cost curve).

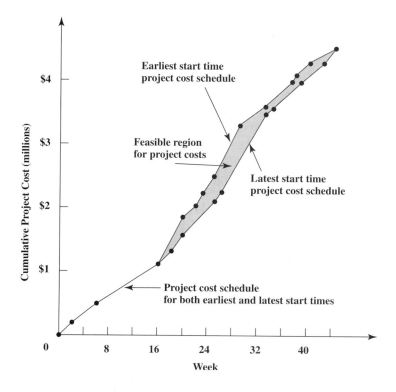

two kinds of start times over this period. After week 16, we obtain two distinct cost curves by plotting the values in row 23 of Figures 7.16 and 7.17 (and their extensions to later weeks). Since sticking to either earliest start times or latest start times leads to project completion at the end of 44 weeks, the two cost curves come together again at that point with a total project cost of $4.55 million. The dots on either curve are the points at which the weekly project costs change.

Naturally, the start times and activity costs that lead to Figure 7.18 are only estimates of what actually will transpire. However, the figure provides a *best forecast* of cumulative

TABLE 7.12 PERT/Cost Report after Week 22 of Reliable's Project

Activity	Budgeted Cost	Percent Completed	Value Completed	Actual Cost to Date	Cost Overrun to Date
A	$180,000	100%	$180,000	$200,000	$20,000
B	320,000	100	320,000	330,000	10,000
C	620,000	100	620,000	600,000	−20,000
D	260,000	75	195,000	200,000	5,000
E	410,000	100	410,000	400,000	−10,000
F	180,000	25	45,000	60,000	15,000
I	210,000	50	105,000	130,000	25,000
Total	2,180,000		1,875,000	1,920,000	45,000

project costs week by week when following a work schedule based on either earliest or latest start times. If either of these work schedules is selected, this best forecast then becomes a *budget* to be followed as closely as possible. A budget in the shaded area between the two cost curves also can be obtained by selecting a work schedule that calls for beginning each activity somewhere between its earliest and latest start times. The only *feasible* budgets for scheduling project completion at the end of week 44 (without any crashing) lie in this shaded area or on one of the two cost curves.

Reliable Construction Co. has adequate funds to cover expenses until payments are received. Therefore, Mr. Perty has selected a work schedule based on earliest start times to provide the best chance for prompt completion. (He is still nervous about the significant probability of incurring the penalty of $300,000 for not finishing within 47 weeks.) Consequently, his budget is provided by the top cost curve in Figure 7.18.

Controlling Project Costs

Once the project is under way, Mr. Perty will need to monitor carefully actual costs and take corrective action as needed to avoid serious cost overruns. One important way of monitoring costs is to compare actual costs to date with his budget provided by the top curve in Figure 7.18.

However, since deviations from the planned work schedule may occur, this method of monitoring costs is not adequate by itself. For example, suppose that individual activities have been costing more than budgeted, but delays have prevented some activities from beginning when scheduled. These delays might cause the total cost to date to be less than the budgeted cumulative project cost, thereby giving the illusion that project costs are well under control. Furthermore, regardless of whether the cost performance of the project as a whole seems satisfactory, Mr. Perty needs information about the cost performance of individual activities to identify trouble spots where corrective action is needed.

Therefore, PERT/Cost periodically generates a report that focuses on the cost performance of the individual activities. To illustrate, Table 7.12 shows the report that Mr. Perty received after the completion of week 22 (halfway through the project schedule). The first column lists the activities that have at least begun by this time. The next column gives the budgeted total cost of each activity (as given previously in the third column of Table 7.11). The third column indicates what percentage of the activity now has been completed. Multiplying the second and third columns then gives the fourth column, which thereby represents the budgeted value of the work completed on the activity.

The fourth column is the one that Mr. Perty wants to compare to the *actual cost* to date given in the fifth column. Subtracting the fourth column from the fifth gives the *cost overrun* to date of each activity, as shown in the rightmost column. (A negative number in the cost overrun column indicates a *cost underrun*.)

Mr. Perty pays special attention in the report to the activities that are not yet completed, since these are the ones that he can still affect. (He used earlier reports to monitor activities A, B, C, and E while they were under way, which led to meeting the total budget for these four activities.) Activity D is barely over budget (less than 3 percent), but Mr. Perty is very concerned about the large cost overruns to date for activities F and I. Therefore, he next will investigate these two activities and work with the foremen involved to improve their cost performances.

Note in the bottom row of Table 7.12 that the cumulative project cost after week 22 is $1.92 million. This is considerably less than Mr. Perty's *budgeted* cumulative project cost of $2.042 million given in cell AB23 of Figure 7.16. Without any further information, this comparison would suggest an excellent cost performance for the project so far. However, the real reason for being under budget is that the current activities all are behind schedule and so have not yet incurred some expenses that had been scheduled to occur earlier. Fortunately, the PERT/Cost report provides valuable additional information that paints a truer picture of cost performance to date. By focusing on individual activities rather than the overall project, the report identifies the current trouble spots (activities F and I) that require Mr. Perty's immediate attention. Thus, the report enables him to take corrective action while there is still time to reverse these cost overruns.

Review Questions

1. What is the purpose of PERT/Cost?
2. How does the PERT/Cost procedure begin?
3. What assumption is commonly made about how the cost of performing an activity is spread over the duration of the activity?
4. What is a work package?
5. Which two work schedules does PERT/Cost use as a basis for developing cost schedules?
6. What two types of information about project cost are provided for each time period by a PERT/Cost schedule of costs?
7. What information does a PERT/Cost report provide about the cost performance of each activity?
8. Why is a PERT/Cost report needed when the project manager already can evaluate the cost performance of the overall project by comparing the actual cost to date with the budgeted cumulative cost?

7.7 An Evaluation of PERT/CPM from a Managerial Perspective

PERT/CPM has stood the test of time. Despite being more than 40 years old, it continues to be one of the most widely used techniques of management science. It is a standard tool of project managers.

The Value of PERT/CPM

Much of the value of PERT/CPM derives from the basic framework it provides for planning a project. Recall its planning steps: (1) identify the activities that are needed to carry out the project; (2) estimate how much time will be needed for each activity; (3) determine the activities that must immediately precede each activity; and (4) develop the project network that visually displays the relationships between the activities. The discipline of going through these steps forces the needed planning to be done.

The scheduling information generated by PERT/CPM also is vital to the project manager. When can each activity begin if there are no delays? How much delay in an activity can be tolerated without delaying project completion? What is the critical path of activities where no delay can be tolerated? What is the effect of uncertainty in activity times? What is the probability of meeting the project deadline under the current plan? PERT/CPM provides the answers.

PERT/CPM also assists the project manager in other ways. Schedule and budget are key concerns. The CPM method of time–cost trade-offs enables investigating ways of reducing the duration of the project at an additional cost. PERT/Cost provides a systematic procedure for planning, scheduling, and controlling project costs.

In many ways, PERT/CPM exemplifies the application of management science at its finest. Its modeling approach focuses on the key features of the problem (activities, precedence relationships, time, and cost) without getting mired down in unimportant details. The resulting model (a project network and an optional linear programming formulation) are easy to understand and apply. It addresses the issues that are important to management (planning, scheduling, dealing with uncertainty, making time–cost trade-offs, and controlling costs). It assists the project manager in dealing with these issues in useful ways and in a timely manner.

Using the Computer

PERT/CPM continues to evolve to meet new needs. At its inception over 40 years ago, it was largely executed manually. The project network sometimes was spread out over the walls of the project manager. Recording changes in the plan became a major task. Communicating changes to crew foremen and subcontractors was cumbersome. The computer has changed all of that.

For many years now, PERT/CPM has become highly computerized. There has been a remarkable growth in the number and power of software packages for PERT/CPM that run on personal computers or workstations. *Project management software* (for example, Microsoft Project) now is a standard tool for project managers. This has enabled applications to numerous projects that each involve many millions of dollars and perhaps even thousands of activities. Possible revisions in the project plan now can be investigated almost instantaneously. Actual changes and the resulting updates in the schedule, and so forth, are recorded virtually effortlessly. Communications to all parties involved through computer networks and telecommunication systems also have become quick and easy.

Nevertheless, PERT/CPM still is not a panacea. It has certain major deficiencies for some applications. We briefly describe each of these deficiencies below along with how it is being addressed through research on improvements or extensions to PERT/CPM.

Approximating the Means and Variances of Activity Durations

The PERT three-estimate approach described in Section 7.4 provides a straightforward procedure for approximating the mean and variance of the probability distribution of the duration of each activity. Recall that this approach involved obtaining a most likely estimate, an optimistic estimate, and a pessimistic estimate of the duration. Given these three estimates, simple formulas were given for approximating the mean and variance. The means and variances for the various activities then were used to estimate the probability of completing the project by a specified time.

Unfortunately, considerable subsequent research has shown that this approach tends to provide a pretty rough approximation of the mean and variance. Part of the difficulty lies in aiming the optimistic and pessimistic estimates at the *end points* of the probability distribution. These end points correspond to very rare events (the best and worst that could ever occur) that typically are outside the estimator's realm of experience. The accuracy and reliability of such estimates are not as good as for points that are not at the extremes of the probability distribution. For example, research has demonstrated that much better estimates can be obtained by aiming them at the 10 percent and 90 percent points of the probability distribution. The optimistic and pessimistic estimates then would be described in terms of having 1 chance in 10 of doing better or 1 chance in 10 of doing worse. The middle estimate also can be improved by aiming it at the 50 percent point (the median value) of the probability distribution.

Revising the definitions of the three estimates along these lines leads to considerably more complicated formulas for the mean and variance of the duration of an activity. However, this is no problem since the analysis is computerized anyway. The important consideration is that much better approximations of the mean and variance are obtained in this way.[2]

Approximating the Probability of Meeting the Deadline

Of all the assumptions and simplifying approximations made by PERT/CPM, one is particularly controversial. This is simplifying approximation 1 in Section 7.4, which assumes that the *mean critical path* will turn out to be the longest path through the project network.

---

[2] For further information, see, for example, D. L. Keefer and W. A. Verdini, "Better Estimation of PERT Activity Time Parameters," *Management Science* 39 (September 1993), pp. 1086–91. Also see A. H.-L. Lau, H.-S. Lau, and Y. Zhang, "A Simple and Logical Alternative for Making PERT Time Estimates," *IIE Transactions* 28 (March 1996), pp. 183–92.

This approximation greatly simplifies the calculation of the approximate probability of completing the project by a specified deadline. Unfortunately, in reality, there usually is a significant chance, and sometimes a very substantial chance, that some other path or paths will turn out to be longer than the mean critical path. Consequently, the calculated probability of meeting the deadline usually overstates the true probability somewhat. PERT/CPM provides no information on the likely size of the error. (Research has found that the error often is modest, but can be very large.) Thus, the project manager who relies on the calculated probability can be badly misled.

Considerable research has been conducted to develop more accurate (albeit more complicated) analytical approximations of this probability. Of special interest are methods that provide both upper and lower bounds on the probability.[3]

Another alternative is to use the technique of computer simulation described in Chapter 15 to approximate this probability. This appears to be the most commonly used method in practice (when any is used) to improve upon the PERT/CPM approximation. We describe in Section 15.6 how this would be done for the Reliable Construction Co. project.

Dealing with Overlapping Activities

Another key assumption of PERT/CPM is that an activity cannot begin until all its immediate predecessors are completely finished. Although this may appear to be a perfectly reasonable assumption, it too is sometimes only a rough approximation of reality.

For example, in the Reliable Construction Co. project, consider activity H (do the exterior painting) and its immediate predecessor, activity G (put up the exterior siding). Naturally, this painting cannot begin until the exterior siding is there on which to paint. However, it certainly is possible to begin painting on one wall while the exterior siding still is being put up to form the other walls. Thus, activity H actually can begin before activity G is completely finished. Although careful coordination is needed, this possibility to overlap activities can significantly reduce project duration below that predicted by PERT/CPM.

The **precedence diagramming method (PDM)** has been developed as an extension of PERT/CPM to deal with such overlapping activities.[4] PDM provides four options for the relationship between an activity and any one of its immediate predecessors.

> Option 1: The activity cannot begin until the immediate predecessor has been in progress a certain amount of time.
>
> Option 2: The activity cannot finish until a certain amount of time after the immediate predecessor has finished.
>
> Option 3: The activity cannot finish until a certain amount of time after the immediate predecessor has started.
>
> Option 4: The activity cannot begin until a certain amount of time after the immediate predecessor has finished. (Rather than overlapping the activities, note that this option creates a lag between them such as, for example, waiting for the paint to dry before beginning the activity that follows painting).

Alternatively, the *certain amount of time* mentioned in each option also can be expressed as a certain percentage of the work content of the immediate predecessor.

After incorporating these options, PDM can be used much like PERT/CPM to determine earliest start times, latest start times, and the critical path and to investigate time–cost trade-offs, and so on.

Although it adds considerable flexibility to PERT/CPM, PDM is neither as well known nor as widely used as PERT/CPM. This should gradually change.

Incorporating the Allocation of Resources to Activities

PERT/CPM assumes that each activity has available all the resources (money, personnel, equipment, etc.) needed to perform the activity in the normal way (or on a crashed basis). In actuality, many projects have only limited resources for which the activities must com-

---

[3]See, for example, J. Kamburowski, "Bounding the Distribution of Project Duration in PERT Networks," *Operations Research Letters* 12 (July 1992), pp. 17–22.

[4]For an introduction to PDM, see pp. 136–44 in A. B. Badiru and P. S. Pulat, *Comprehensive Project Management: Integrating Optimization Models, Management Principles, and Computers* (Englewood Cliffs, NJ: Prentice-Hall, 1995).

pete. A major challenge in planning the project then is to determine how the resources should be allocated to the activities.

Once the resources have been allocated, PERT/CPM can be applied in the usual way. However, it would be far better to combine the allocation of the resources with the kind of planning and scheduling done by PERT/CPM so as to strive simultaneously toward a desired objective. For example, a common objective is to allocate the resources so as to minimize the duration of the project.

Much research has been conducted (and is continuing) to develop the methodology for simultaneously allocating resources and scheduling the activities of a project. This subject is beyond the scope of this book, but considerable reading is available elsewhere.[5]

The Future

Despite its deficiencies, PERT/CPM undoubtedly will continue to be widely used for the foreseeable future. It provides the project manager with most of what he or she wants: structure, scheduling information, tools for controlling schedule (latest start times, slacks, the critical path, etc.) and controlling costs (PERT/Cost), as well as the flexibility to investigate time–cost trade-offs.

Even though some of the approximations involved with the PERT three-estimate approach are questionable, these inaccuracies ultimately may not be too important. Just the process of developing estimates of the duration of activities encourages effective interaction between the project manager and subordinates that leads to setting mutual goals for start times, activity durations, project duration, and so forth. Striving together toward these goals may make them self-fulfilling prophecies despite inaccuracies in the underlying mathematics that led to these goals.

Similarly, possibilities for a modest amount of overlapping of activities need not invalidate a schedule generated by PERT/CPM, despite its assumption that no overlapping can occur. Actually having a small amount of overlapping may just provide the slack needed to compensate for the "unexpected" delays that inevitably seem to slip into a schedule.

Even when needing to allocate resources to activities, just using common sense in this allocation and then applying PERT/CPM should be quite satisfactory for some projects.

Nevertheless, it is unfortunate that the kinds of improvements and extensions to PERT/CPM described in this section have not been incorporated much into practice to date. Old comfortable methods that have proven their value are not readily discarded, and it takes awhile to learn about and gain confidence in new better methods. However, we anticipate that these improvements and extensions gradually will come into more widespread use as they prove their value as well. We also expect that the recent and current extensive research on techniques for project management and scheduling (much of it in Europe) will continue and will lead to further improvements in the future.

Review Questions

1. What are some important managerial issues in managing a project that PERT/CPM addresses?

2. What have been some benefits from changing from the original manual execution of PERT/CPM to its computer implementation in more recent years?

3. In the PERT three-estimate approach, what has research shown regarding how the accuracy of the optimistic and pessimistic estimates are affected by the choice of the points at which they are aimed in the probability distribution of the duration of the activity involved?

4. What is an alternative technique for improving the PERT/CPM approximation of the probability that the project will meet its deadline?

5. What is the name of a method for extending PERT/CPM to permit activities and their immediate predecessors to overlap?

---

[5]See, for example, ibid., pp. 162–209. Also see L. Özdamar and G. Ulusay, "A Survey on the Resource-Constrained Project Scheduling Problem," *IIE Transactions* 27 (October 1995), pp. 574–86.

6. What does PERT/CPM assume about the availability of the resources needed to perform each activity in the normal way?

7. Beyond the estimates themselves, what is an additional benefit of conducting the process of developing estimates of the duration of activities?

8. Considering that PERT/CPM has become such a well-established management science technique, are new improvements and extensions still being developed?

7.8 Summary

Ever since their inception in the late 1950s, PERT (program evaluation and review technique) and CPM (critical path method) have been used extensively to assist project managers in planning, scheduling, and controlling their projects. Over time, these two techniques gradually have merged, so PERT/CPM today refers to the combined version that includes all the various options of either of the original techniques.

The application of PERT/CPM begins by breaking the project down into its individual activities, identifying the immediate predecessors of each activity, and estimating the duration of each activity. The next step is to construct a project network to visually display all this information. The type of network that is becoming increasingly popular for this purpose is the activity-on-node (AON) project network, where each activity is represented by a node.

PERT/CPM then generates scheduling information for the project manager, including the earliest start time, the latest start time, and the slack for each activity. It also identifies the critical path of activities such that any delay along this path will delay project completion. Since the critical path is the longest path through the project network, its length determines the duration of the project, assuming all activities remain on schedule.

However, it is difficult for all activities to remain on schedule because there frequently is considerable uncertainty about what the duration of an activity will turn out to be. The PERT three-estimate approach addresses this situation by obtaining three different kinds of estimates (most likely, optimistic, and pessimistic) for the duration of each activity. This information is used to approximate the mean and variance of the probability distribution of this duration. It then is possible to approximate the probability that the project will be completed by the deadline.

The CPM method of time–cost trade-offs enables the project manager to investigate the effect on total cost of changing the estimated duration of the project to various alternative values. The data needed for this activity are the time and cost for each activity when it is done in the normal way and then when it is fully crashed (expedited). Either marginal cost analysis or linear programming can be used to determine how much (if any) to crash each activity to minimize the total cost of meeting any specified deadline for the project.

The PERT/CPM technique called PERT/Cost provides the project manager with a systematic procedure for planning, scheduling, and controlling project costs. It generates a complete schedule for what the project costs should be in each time period when activities begin at either their earliest start times or latest start times. It also generates periodic reports that evaluate the cost performance of the individual activities, including identifying those where cost overruns are occurring.

PERT/CPM does have some important deficiencies. These include questionable approximations made when estimating the mean and variance of activity durations as well as when estimating the probability that the project will be completed by the deadline. Another deficiency is that it does not allow an activity to begin until all its immediate predecessors are completely finished, even though some overlap is sometimes possible. In addition, PERT/CPM does not address the important issue of how to allocate limited resources to the various activities.

Nevertheless, PERT/CPM has stood the test of time in providing project mangers with most of the help they want. Furthermore, much progress is being made in developing improvements and extensions to PERT/CPM (such as the precedence diagramming method for dealing with overlapping activities) that address these deficiencies.

Glossary

Activity A distinct task that needs to be performed as part of a project. (Section 7.1) 244

Activity-on-arc (AOA) project network A project network where each activity is represented by an arc (arrow). (Section 7.2) 246

Activity-on-node (AON) project network A project network where each activity is represented by a node (small circle or rectangle) and the arcs (arrows) show the precedence relationships between the activities. (Section 7.2) 246

Arc An arrow in the project network. (Section 7.2) 246

Backward pass The process of moving backward through the project network to determine the latest finish time and latest start time of each activity. (Section 7.3) 255

CPM An acronym for critical path method, a technique for assisting project managers with carrying out their responsibilities. (Introduction) 243

CPM method of time–cost trade-offs A method of investigating the trade-off between the total cost of a project and its duration when various levels of crashing are used to reduce the duration. (Section 7.5) 266

Crash point The point on the time–cost graph for an activity that shows the time (duration) and cost when the activity is fully crashed; that is, it is fully expedited with no cost spared to reduce its duration as much as possible. (Section 7.5) 267

Crashing an activity Taking special costly measures to reduce the duration of an activity below its normal value. (Section 7.5) 266

Crashing the project Crashing a number of activities to reduce the duration of the project below its normal value. (Section 7.5) 266

Critical path The longest path through the project network, so the activities on this path are the critical bottleneck activities where any delays in their completion must be avoided to prevent delaying project completion. (Section 7.3) 251

Earliest finish time for an activity The time at which this activity will finish if there are no delays anywhere in the project. (Section 7.3) 251

Earliest start time for an activity The time at which this activity will begin if there are no delays anywhere in the project. (Section 7.3) 251

EF Abbreviation for the earliest finish time of an activity. (Section 7.3) 251

ES Abbreviation for the earliest start time of an activity. (Section 7.3) 251

Finish node The node (small rectangle) in the project network that represents the finish of the project. (Section 7.2) 246

Forward pass The process of moving forward through the project network to determine the earliest start time and earliest finish time of each activity. (Section 7.3) 254

Gantt chart A chart that uses bars to show the scheduled start and finish times of the various activities of a project. (Section 7.2) 247

Immediate predecessor The immediate predecessors of a given activity are those activities that must be completed just prior to starting the given activity. (Section 7.1) 245

Immediate successor Given the immediate predecessors of an activity, this activity then becomes the immediate successor of each of these immediate predecessors. (Section 7.1) 245

Latest finish time for an activity The latest possible time that this activity can finish without delaying project completion (assuming no subsequent delays in the project). (Section 7.3) 254

Latest start time for an activity The latest possible time that this activity can start without delaying project completion (assuming no subsequent delays in the project). (Section 7.3) 254

Length of a path The sum of the (estimated) durations of the activities on the path. (Section 7.3) 250

LF Abbreviation for the latest finish time of an activity. (Section 7.3) 254

LS Abbreviation for the latest start time of an activity. (Section 7.3) 254

Marginal cost analysis A method of using the marginal cost of crashing individual activities on the current critical path to determine the least expensive way of reducing project duration to a desired level. (Section 7.5) 268

Mean critical path The path through the project network that would be the critical path if the duration of each activity equals its mean. (Section 7.4) 263

Most likely estimate An estimate of the most likely value of the duration of an activity. (Section 7.4) 260

Node A small circle or rectangle that serves as a junction point in the project network. (Section 7.2) 246

Normal point The point on the time–cost graph for an activity that shows the time (duration) and cost of the activity when it is performed in the normal way. (Section 7.5) 267

Optimistic estimate An estimate of the duration of an activity under the most favorable conditions. (Section 7.4) 260

Path A path through a project network is one of the routes following the arrows (arcs) from the start node to the finish node. (Section 7.3) 250

PERT An acronym for program evaluation and review technique, a technique for assisting project managers with carrying out their responsibilities. (Introduction) 243

PERT/Cost A systematic procedure (normally computerized) to help the project manager plan, schedule, and control project costs. (Section 7.6) 273

PERT/CPM The merger of the two techniques originally known as PERT and CPM. (Introduction) 243

PERT three-estimate approach An approach to dealing with uncertainties in activity times by obtaining three different kinds of estimates (most likely, optimistic, and pessimistic) for the duration of each activity. (Section 7.4) 260

Pessimistic estimate An estimate of the duration of an activity under the most unfavorable conditions. (Section 7.4) 260

Precedence diagramming method (PDM) An extension of PERT/CPM that deals with overlapping activities. (Section 7.7) 280

Project network A network used to visually display a project. (Section 7.2) 246

Slack for an activity The amount of time that this activity can be delayed without delaying project completion (assuming no subsequent delays in the project); it is calculated as the difference between the latest finish time and the earliest finish time for the activity. (Section 7.3) 257

Start node The node (small rectangle) in the project network that represents the start of the project. (Section 7.2) 246

Learning Aids for This Chapter in Your MS Courseware

"Ch. 7—Project Management" Excel File:

Reliable Example (Project Schedule)
Template for PERT Three-Estimate Approach (labeled PERT)
Reliable Example (CPM Method of Time–Cost Trade-Offs)
Template for PERT/Cost (labeled PERT Cost)
Reliable's ES Schedule of Costs
Reliable's LS Schedule of Costs

Special Software:

MS Project

MS Project File:

Reliable's Schedule
Reliable's Three-Estimate Data
Reliable's Schedule of Costs Based on Earliest Start Times
(last 8 weeks)

An Excel Add-in:

Premium Solver

Supplement to Section 7.2 on the CD-ROM:

The Procedure for Constructing a Project Network

Problems

To the left of the problems (or their parts), we have inserted an E whenever Excel can be helpful. An asterisk on this symbol indicates that it definitely should be used (unless your instructor gives you contrary instructions). Your instructor might also suggest that you use MS Project on some of the problems. An asterisk on the problem number indicates that at least a partial answer is given in the back of the book.

7.1. Christine Phillips is in charge of planning and coordinating next spring's sales management training program for her company. Christine has listed the following activity information for this project:

Activity	Activity Description	Immediate Predecessors	Estimated Duration (weeks)
A	Select location	—	2
B	Obtain speakers	—	3
C	Make speaker travel plans	A, B	2
D	Prepare and mail brochure	A, B	2
E	Take reservations	D	3

a. Construct the project network for this project.
b. Find all the paths and path lengths through this project network. Which of these paths is a critical path?
c. Find the earliest times, latest times, and slack for each activity. Use this information to determine which of the paths is a critical path.
d. It is now one week later, and Christine is ahead of schedule. She has already selected a location for the sales meeting, and all the other activities are right on schedule. Will this shorten the length of the project? Why or why not?

7.2.* Reconsider Problem 7.1. Christine has done more detailed planning for this project and so now has the following expanded activity list:

Activity	Activity Description	Immediate Predecessors	Estimated Duration (weeks)
A	Select location	—	2
B	Obtain keynote speaker	—	1
C	Obtain other speakers	B	2
D	Make speaker travel plans for keynote speaker	A, B	2
E	Make travel plans for other speakers	A, C	3
F	Make food arrangements	A	2
G	Negotiate hotel rates	A	1
H	Prepare brochure	C, G	1
I	Mail brochure	H	1
J	Take reservations	I	3
K	Prepare handouts	C, F	4

Follow the instructions for Problem 7.1 with this expanded activity list.

7.3. Consider a project with the following activity list.

Activity	Immediate Predecessors	Estimated Duration (months)
A	—	1
B	A	2
C	B	4
D	B	3
E	B	2
F	C	3
G	D, E	5
H	F	1
I	G, H	4
J	I	2
K	I	3
L	J	3
M	K	5
N	L	4

a. Construct the project network for this project.
b. Find the earliest start time and earliest finish time for each activity.
c. Find the latest start time and latest finish time for each activity.
d. Find the slack for each activity. Which of the paths is a critical path?

7.4. You and several friends are about to prepare a lasagna dinner. The tasks to be performed, their immediate predecessors, and their estimated durations are as follows:

Task	Task Description	Tasks That Must Precede	Time (Minutes)
A	Buy the mozzarella cheese*	—	30
B	Slice the mozzarella	A	5
C	Beat 2 eggs	—	2
D	Mix eggs and ricotta cheese	C	3
E	Cut up onions and mushrooms	—	7
F	Cook the tomato sauce	E	25
G	Boil large quantity of water	—	15
H	Boil the lasagna noodles	G	10
I	Drain the lasagna noodles	H	2
J	Assemble all the ingredients	I, F, D, B	10
K	Preheat the oven	—	15
L	Bake the lasagna	J, K	30

*There is none in the refrigerator.

a. Construct the project network.
b. Find all the paths and path lengths through this project network. Which of these paths is a critical path?

c. Find the earliest start time and earliest finish time for each activity.
d. Find the latest start time and latest finish time for each activity.
e. Find the slack for each activity. Which of the paths is a critical path?
f. Because of a phone call, you were interrupted for 6 minutes when you should have been cutting the onions and mushrooms. By how much will the dinner be delayed? If you use your food processor, which reduces the cutting time from 7 to 2 minutes, will the dinner still be delayed?

7.5.* Ken Johnston, the data processing manager for Stanley Morgan Bank, is planning a project to install a new management information system. He now is ready to start the project and wishes to finish in 20 weeks. After identifying the 14 separate activities needed to carry out this project, as well as their precedence relationships and estimated durations (in weeks), Ken has constructed the following project network:

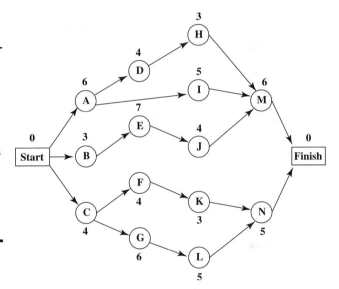

a. Find all the paths and path lengths through this project network. Which of these paths is a critical path?
b. Find the earliest times, latest times, and slack for each activity. Will Ken be able to meet his deadline if no delays occur?
c. Use the information from part *b* to determine which of the paths is a critical path. What does this tell Ken about which activities he should focus most of his attention on for staying on schedule?
d. Use the information from part *b* to determine what the duration of the project would be if the only delay is that activity I takes 2 extra weeks. What if the only delay is that activity H takes 2 extra weeks? What if the only delay is that activity J takes 2 extra weeks?

7.6. You are given the following information about a project consisting of six activities:

Activity	Immediate Predecessors	Estimated Duration (months)
A	—	5
B	—	1
C	B	2
D	A, C	4
E	A	6
F	D, E	3

a. Construct the project network for this project.

b. Find the earliest times, latest times, and slack for each activity. Which of the paths is a critical path?

c. If all other activities take the estimated amount of time, what is the maximum duration of activity D without delaying the completion of the project?

7.7. Reconsider the Reliable Construction Co. case study introduced in Section 7.1, including the complete project network obtained in Figure 7.7 at the end of Section 7.3. Note that the estimated durations of the activities in this figure turn out to be the same as the mean durations given in Table 7.4 (Section 7.4) when using the PERT three-estimate approach.

Now suppose that the *pessimistic* estimates in Table 7.4 are used instead to provide the estimated durations in Figure 7.7. Find the new earliest times, latest times, and slacks for all the activities in this project network. Also identify the critical path and the total estimated duration of the project. (Table 7.5 provides some clues.)

7.8.* Follow the instructions for Problem 7.7 except use the *optimistic* estimates in Table 7.4 instead.

7.9. Follow the instructions for Problem 7.7 except use the *crash times* given in Table 7.8 (Section 7.5) instead.

7.10.* Using the PERT three-estimate approach, the three estimates for one of the activities are as follows: optimistic estimate = 30 days, most likely estimate = 36 days, pessimistic estimate = 48 days. What are the resulting estimates of the mean and variance of the duration of the activity?

7.11. Alfred Lowenstein is the president of the Research Division for Better Health, Inc., a major pharmaceutical company. His most important project coming up is the development of a new drug to combat AIDS. He has identified 10 groups in his division that will need to carry out different phases of this research-and-development project. Referring to the work to be done by the respective groups as activities A, B, . . ., J, the precedence relationships for when these groups need to do their work are shown in the following project network.

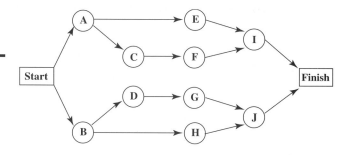

To beat the competition, Better Health's CEO has informed Alfred that he wants the drug ready within 22 months if possible.

Alfred knows very well that there is considerable uncertainty about how long each group will need to do its work. Using the PERT three-estimate approach, the manager of each group has provided a most likely estimate, an optimistic estimate, and a pessimistic estimate of the duration of that group's activity. Using PERT formulas, these estimates now have been converted into estimates of the mean and variance of the probability distribution of the duration of each group's activity, as given in the following table (after rounding to the nearest integer).

	Duration (months)	
Activity	Estimated Mean	Estimated Variance
A	4	5
B	6	10
C	4	8
D	3	6
E	8	12
F	4	6
G	3	5
H	7	14
I	5	8
J	5	7

a. Find the mean critical path for this project.

b. Use this mean critical path and Table 7.7 to find the approximate probability that the project will be completed within 22 months.

c. Now consider the other three paths through this project network. For each of these paths, use Table 7.7 to find the approximate probability that the path will be completed within 22 months.

d. What should Alfred tell his CEO about the likelihood that the drug will be ready within 22 months?

E* 7.12. Reconsider Problem 7.11. For each of the 10 activities, here are the three estimates that led to the estimates of the mean and variance of the duration of the activity (rounded to the nearest integer) given in the table for Problem 7.11.

Activity	Time Required (Months)		
	Optimistic Estimate	Most Likely Estimate	Pessimistic Estimate
A	1.5	2	15
B	2	3.5	21
C	1	1.5	18
D	0.5	1	15
E	3	5	24
F	1	2	16
G	0.5	1	14
H	2.5	3.5	25
I	1	3	18
J	2	3	18

(Note how the great uncertainty in the duration of these research activities causes each pessimistic estimate to be several times larger than either the optimistic estimate or the most likely estimate.)

Now use the Excel template in your MS Courseware (as depicted in Figure 7.11) to help you carry out the instructions for Problem 7.11. In particular, enter the three estimates for each activity and the template immediately will display the estimates of the means and variances of the activity durations. After indicating each path of interest, the template also will display the approximate probability that the path will be completed within 22 months.

7.13. Bill Fredlund, president of Lincoln Log Construction, is considering placing a bid on a building project. Bill has determined that five tasks would need to be performed to carry out the project. Using the PERT three-estimate approach, Bill has obtained the estimates in the table below for how long these tasks will take. Also shown are the precedence relationships for these tasks.

Task	Time Required (Weeks)			Immediate Predecessors
	Optimistic Estimate	Most Likely Estimate	Pessimistic Estimate	
A	3	4	5	—
B	2	2	2	A
C	3	5	6	B
D	1	3	5	A
E	2	3	5	B, D

There is a penalty of $500,000 if the project is not completed in 11 weeks. Therefore, Bill is very interested in how likely it is that his company could finish the project in time.

    a. Construct the project network for this project.
E   b. Find the estimate of the mean and variance of the duration of each activity.
E   c. Find the mean critical path.
E   d. Find the approximate probability of completing the project within 11 weeks.

    e. Bill has concluded that the bid he would need to make to have a realistic chance of winning the contract would earn Lincoln Log Construction a profit of about $250,000 if the project is completed within 11 weeks. However, because of the penalty for missing this deadline, his company would lose about $250,000 if the project takes more than 11 weeks. Therefore, he wants to place the bid only if he has at least a 50 percent chance of meeting the deadline. How would you advise him?

7.14.* Sharon Lowe, vice president for marketing for the Electronic Toys Company, is about to begin a project to design an advertising campaign for a new line of toys. She wants the project completed within 57 days in time to launch the advertising campaign at the beginning of the Christmas season.

Sharon has identified the six activities (labeled A, B, ... F) needed to execute this project. Considering the order in which these activities need to occur, she also has constructed the following project network.

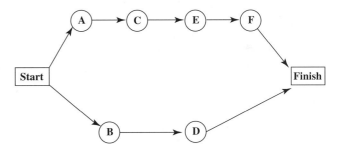

Using the PERT three-estimate approach, Sharon has obtained the following estimates of the duration of each activity.

Activity	Time Required (Days)		
	Optimistic Estimate	Most Likely Estimate	Pessimistic Estimate
A	12	12	12
B	15	21	39
C	12	15	18
D	18	27	36
E	12	18	24
F	2	5	14

E   a. Find the estimate of the mean and variance of the duration of each activity.
    b. Find the mean critical path.
E   c. Use the mean critical path to find the approximate probability that the advertising campaign will be ready to launch within 57 days.
E   d. Now consider the other path through the project network. Find the approximate probability that this path will be completed within 57 days.
    e. Since these paths do not overlap, a better estimate of the probability that the project will finish within 57 days can be obtained as follows. The project will finish within 57 days if both paths are completed within 57

days. Therefore, the approximate probability that the project will finish within 57 days is the *product* of the probabilities found in parts *c* and *d*. Perform this calculation. What does this answer say about the accuracy of the standard procedure used in part *c*?

7.15. The Lockhead Aircraft Co. is ready to begin a project to develop a new fighter airplane for the U.S. Air Force. The company's contract with the Department of Defense calls for project completion within 100 weeks, with penalties imposed for late delivery.

The project involves 10 activities (labeled A, B, . . . , J), where their precedence relationships are shown in the following project network.

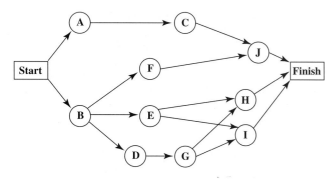

Using the PERT three-estimate approach, the usual three estimates of the duration of each activity have been obtained as given below.

	Time Required (Weeks)		
Activity	Optimistic Estimate	Most Likely Estimate	Pessimistic Estimate
A	28	32	36
B	22	28	32
C	26	36	46
D	14	16	18
E	32	32	32
F	40	52	74
G	12	16	24
H	16	20	26
I	26	34	42
J	12	16	30

E   *a.* Find the estimate of the mean and variance of the duration of each activity.

     b. Find the mean critical path.

E   *c.* Find the approximate probability that the project will finish within 100 weeks.

     d. Is the approximate probability obtained in part *c* likely to be higher or lower than the true value?

7.16. Label each of the following statements about the PERT three-estimate approach as true or false, and then justify your answer by referring to specific statements (with page citations) in the chapter.

     a. Activity durations are assumed to be no larger than the optimistic estimate and no smaller than the pessimistic estimate.

     b. Activity durations are assumed to have a normal distribution.

     c. The mean critical path is assumed to always require the minimum elapsed time of any path through the project network.

7.17. The Tinker Construction Company is ready to begin a project that must be completed in 12 months. This project has four activities (A, B, C, D) with the project network shown below.

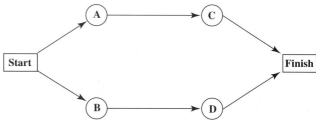

The project manager, Sean Murphy, has concluded that he cannot meet the deadline by performing all these activities in the normal way. Therefore, Sean has decided to use the CPM method of time–cost trade-offs to determine the most economical way of crashing the project to meet the deadline. He has gathered the following data for the four activities.

Activity	Normal Time (Months)	Crash Time (Months)	Normal Cost	Crash Cost
A	8	5	$25,000	$40,000
B	9	7	20,000	30,000
C	6	4	16,000	24,000
D	7	4	27,000	45,000

Use marginal cost analysis to solve the problem.

7.18. Reconsider the Tinker Construction Co. problem presented in Problem 7.17. While in college, Sean Murphy took a management science course that devoted a month to linear programming, so Sean has decided to use linear programming to analyze this problem.

     a. Consider the upper path through the project network. Formulate a two-variable linear programming model (in algebraic form) for the problem of how to minimize the cost of performing this sequence of activities within 12 months. Use the graphical method to solve this model.

     b. Repeat part *a* for the lower path through the project network.

     c. Combine the models in parts *a* and *b* into a single complete linear programming model (in algebraic form) for the problem of how to minimize the cost of completing the project within 12 months. What must an optimal solution for this model be.

E⁺   *d.* Formulate and solve a spreadsheet model in the format of Figure 7.14 for this problem.

E*   *e.* Check the effect of changing the deadline by re-solving this model with a deadline of 11 months and then with a deadline of 13 months.

7.19. Reconsider the Electronic Toys Co. problem presented in Problem 7.14. Sharon Lowe is concerned that there is a significant chance that the vitally important deadline of 57 days will not be met. Therefore, to make it virtually certain that the deadline will be met, she has decided to crash the project, using the CPM method of time–cost trade-offs to determine how to do this in the most economical way.

Sharon now has gathered the data needed to apply this method, as given below.

Activity	Normal Time (Days)	Crash Time (Days)	Normal Cost	Crash Cost
A	12	9	$210,000	$270,000
B	23	18	410,000	460,000
C	15	12	290,000	320,000
D	27	21	440,000	500,000
E	18	14	350,000	410,000
F	6	4	160,000	210,000

The normal times are the estimates of the means obtained from the original data in Problem 7.14. The mean critical path gives an estimate that the project will finish in 51 days. However, Sharon knows from the earlier analysis that some of the pessimistic estimates are far larger than the means, so the project duration might be considerably longer than 51 days. Therefore, to better ensure that the project will finish within 57 days, she has decided to require that the estimated project duration based on means (as used throughout the CPM analysis) must not exceed 47 days.

    a. Consider the lower path through the project network. Use marginal cost analysis to determine the most economical way of reducing the length of this path to 47 days.

    b. Repeat part *a* for the upper path through the project network. What is the total crashing cost for the optimal way of decreasing estimated project duration to 47 days?

E*   *c.* Formulate and solve a spreadsheet model that fits linear programming for this problem.

7.20.* Good Homes Construction Company is about to begin the construction of a large new home. The company's president, Michael Dean, is currently planning the schedule for this project. Michael has identified the five major activities (labeled A, B, . . . , E) that will need to be performed according to the following project network.

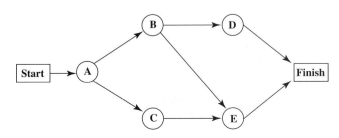

He also has gathered the following data about the normal point and crash point for each of these activities.

Activity	Normal Time (Weeks)	Crash Time (Weeks)	Normal Cost	Crash Cost
A	3	2	$54,000	$60,000
B	4	3	62,000	65,000
C	5	2	66,000	70,000
D	3	1	40,000	43,000
E	4	2	75,000	80,000

These costs reflect the company's direct costs for the material, equipment, and direct labor required to perform the activities. In addition, the company incurs indirect project costs such as supervision and other customary overhead costs, interest charges for capital tied up, and so forth. Michael estimates that these indirect costs run $5,000 per week. He wants to minimize the overall cost of the project. Therefore, to save some of these indirect costs, Michael concludes that he should shorten the project by doing some crashing to the extent that the crashing cost for each additional week saved is less than $5,000.

    a. To prepare for analyzing the effect of crashing, find the earliest times, latest times, and slack for each activity when they are done in the normal way. Also identify the corresponding critical path(s) and project duration.

    b. Use marginal cost analysis to determine which activities should be crashed and by how much to minimize the overall cost of the project. Under this plan, what is the duration and cost of each activity? How much money is saved by doing this crashing?

E*   *c.* Now formulate a spreadsheet model that fits linear programming and repeatedly solve it to do part *b* by shortening the deadline one week at a time from the project duration found in part *a*.

7.21.* The 21st Century Studios is about to begin the production of its most important (and most expensive) movie of the year. The movie's producer, Dusty Hoffmer, has decided to use PERT/CPM to help plan and control this key project. He has identified the eight major activities (labeled A, B, . . . , H) required to produce the movie. Their precedence relationships are shown in the project network below.

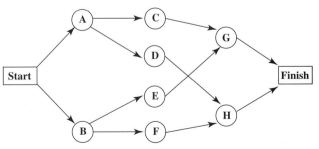

Dusty now has learned that another studio also will be coming out with a blockbuster movie during the middle of the upcoming summer, just when his movie was to be released. This would be very unfortunate timing. Therefore, he and the top management of 21st Century

Studios have concluded that they must accelerate production of their movie and bring it out at the beginning of the summer (15 weeks from now) to establish it as *the* movie of the year. Although this will require substantially increasing an already huge budget, management feels that this will pay off in much larger box office earnings both nationally and internationally.

Dusty now wants to determine the least costly way of meeting the new deadline 15 weeks hence. Using the CPM method of time–cost trade-offs, he has obtained the following data.

Activity	Normal Time (Weeks)	Crash Time (Weeks)	Normal Cost (Millions)	Crash Cost (Millions)
A	5	3	$20	$30
B	3	2	10	20
C	4	2	16	24
D	6	3	25	43
E	5	4	22	30
F	7	4	30	48
G	9	5	25	45
H	8	6	30	44

Formulate and solve a spreadsheet model that fits linear programming for this problem.

7.22. Reconsider the Lockhead Aircraft Co. problem presented in Problem 7.15 regarding a project to develop a new fighter airplane for the U.S. Air Force. Management is extremely concerned that current plans for this project have a substantial likelihood (roughly a probability of 0.5) of missing the deadline imposed in the Department of Defense contract to finish within 100 weeks. The company has a bad record of missing deadlines, and management is worried that doing so again would jeopardize obtaining future contracts for defense work. Furthermore, management would like to avoid the hefty penalties for missing the deadline in the current contract. Therefore, the decision has been made to crash the project using the CPM method of time–cost trade-offs to determine how to do this in the most economical way. The data needed to apply this method are given below.

Activity	Normal Time (Weeks)	Crash Time (Weeks)	Normal Cost (Millions)	Crash Cost (Millions)
A	32	28	$160	$180
B	28	25	125	146
C	36	31	170	210
D	16	13	60	72
E	32	27	135	160
F	54	47	215	257
G	17	15	90	96
H	20	17	120	132
I	34	30	190	226
J	18	16	80	84

These normal times are the rounded estimates of the means obtained from the original data in Problem 7.15. The corresponding mean critical path provides an estimate that the project will finish in 100 weeks. However, management understands well that the high variability of activity durations means that the actual duration of the project may be much longer. Therefore, the decision is made to require that the estimated project duration based on means (as used throughout the CPM analysis) must not exceed 92 weeks.

Formulate and solve a spreadsheet model that fits linear programming for this problem.

7.23. Reconsider Problem 7.20 involving the Good Homes Construction Co. project to construct a large new home. Michael Dean now has generated the plan for how to crash this project (as given as an answer in the back of the book). Since this plan causes all three paths through the project network to be critical paths, the earliest start time for each activity also is its latest start time.

Michael has decided to use PERT/Cost to schedule and control project costs.

a. Find the earliest start time for each activity and the earliest finish time for the completion of the project.

b. Construct a table like Table 7.11 to show the budget for this project.

c. Construct a table like Figure 7.16 (by hand) to show the schedule of costs based on earliest times for each of the eight weeks of the project.

E* d. Now use the corresponding Excel template in your MS Courseware to do parts *b* and *c* on a single spreadsheet.

e. After four weeks, activity A has been completed (with an actual cost of $65,000) and activity B has just now been completed (with an actual cost of $55,000), but activity C is just 33 percent completed (with an actual cost to date of $44,000). Construct a PERT/Cost report after week 4. Where should Michael concentrate his efforts to improve cost performances?

7.24.* The P-H Microchip Co. needs to undertake a major maintenance and renovation program to overhaul and modernize its facilities for wafer fabrication. This project involves six activities (labeled A, B, . . . , F) with the precedence relationships shown in the following network.

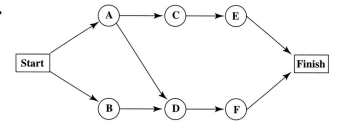

The estimated durations and costs of these activities are shown on the next page.

Activity	Estimated Duration (Weeks)	Estimated Cost
A	6	$420,000
B	2	180,000
C	4	540,000
D	5	360,000
E	7	590,000
F	9	630,000

Activity	Estimated Duration (Weeks)	Estimated Cost
A	6	$180,000
B	3	75,000
C	4	120,000
D	4	140,000
E	7	175,000
F	4	80,000
G	6	210,000
H	3	45,000
I	5	125,000
J	4	100,000
K	3	60,000
L	5	50,000
M	6	90,000
N	5	150,000

    a. Find the earliest times, latest times, and slack for each activity. What is the earliest finish time for the completion of the project?

E* *b.* Use the Excel template for PERT/Cost in your MS Courseware to display the budget and schedule of costs based on earliest start times for this project on a single spreadsheet.

E* *c.* Repeat part *b* except based on latest start times.

    d. Use these spreadsheets to draw a figure like Figure 7.18 to show the schedule of cumulative project costs when all activities begin at their earliest start times or at their latest start times.

    e. After four weeks, activity B has been completed (with an actual cost of $200,000), activity A is 50 percent completed (with an actual cost to date of $200,000), and activity D is 50 percent completed (with an actual cost to date of $210,000). Construct a PERT/Cost report after week 4. Where should the project manager focus her attention to improve cost performance?

7.25. Reconsider Problem 7.5 involving a project at Stanley Morgan Bank to install a new management information system. Ken Johnston already has obtained the earliest times, latest times, and slack for each activity. He now is getting ready to use PERT/Cost to schedule and control the costs for this project. The estimated durations and costs of the various activities are given in the following table.

E* *a.* Use the Excel template for PERT/Cost in your MS Courseware to display the budget and schedule of costs based on earliest start times for this project on a single spreadsheet.

E* *b.* Repeat part *a* except based on latest start times.

    c. Use these spreadsheets to draw a figure like Figure 7.18 to show the schedule of cumulative project costs when all activities begin at their earliest start times or at their latest start times.

    d. After eight weeks, activities A, B, and C have been completed with actual costs of $190,000, $70,000, and $150,000, respectively. Activities D, E, F, G, and I are under way, with the percent completed being 40 percent, 50 percent, 60 percent, 25 percent, and 20 percent, respectively. Their actual costs to date are $70,000, $100,000, $45,000, $50,000, and $35,000, respectively. Construct a PERT/Cost report after week 8. Which activities should Ken Johnston investigate to try to improve their cost performances?

CASE 7.1
STEPS TO SUCCESS

Janet Richards fixes her eyes on those of her partner Gilbert Baker and says firmly, "Alright. Let's do it."

And with those words, InterCat, a firm founded by Janet and Gilbert that specializes in the design and maintenance of Internet catalogues for small consumer businesses, will be going public. InterCat employs 30 individuals, with the majority of them computer programmers. Many of the employees have followed the high-technology market very closely and have decided that since high-technology firms are more understood and valued in the United States than in other countries, InterCat should issue its stock only in the United States. Five million shares of InterCat stock will comprise this new issue.

The task the company has ahead of itself is certainly daunting. Janet and Gilbert know that many steps have to be completed in the process of making an initial public offering. They also know

that they need to complete the process within 28 weeks because they need the new capital fairly soon to ensure that InterCat has the resources to capture valuable new business from its competitors and continue growing. They also value a speedy initial public offering because they believe that the window of opportunity for obtaining a good stock price is presently wide open—the public is wild about shopping on the Internet, and few companies offering Web page design services have gone public.

Because the 28-week deadline is breathing down their necks, Janet and Gilbert decide to map the steps in the process of making an initial public offering. They list each major activity that needs to be completed, the activities that directly precede each activity, the time needed to complete each activity, and the cost of each activity. This list is shown on the next page.

Activity	Preceding Activities	Time (Weeks)	Cost
Evaluate the prestige of each potential underwriter.		3	$8,000
Select a syndicate of underwriters.	Evaluate the prestige of each potential underwriter.	1.5	4,500
Negotiate the commitment of each member of the syndicate.	Select a syndicate of underwriters.	2	9,000
Negotiate the spread* for each member of the syndicate.	Select a syndicate of underwriters.	3	12,000
Prepare the registration statement including the proposed financing and information about the firm's history, existing business, and plans for the future.	Negotiate both the commitment and spread for each member of the syndicate.	5	50,000
Submit the registration statement to the Securities and Exchange Commission (SEC).	Prepare the registration statement.	1	1,000
Make presentations to institutional investors and develop the interest of potential buyers.	Submit the registration statement to the SEC.	6	25,000
Distribute the preliminary prospectus, affectionately termed the red herring.	Submit the registration statement to the SEC.	3	15,000
Calculate the issue price.	Submit the registration statement to the SEC.	5	12,000
Receive deficiency memorandum from the SEC.	Submit the registration statement to the SEC.	3	0
Amend the registration statement and resubmit it to the SEC.	Receive deficiency memorandum from the SEC.	1	6,000
Receive registration confirmation from the SEC.	Amend the registration statement and resubmit it to the SEC.	2	0
Confirm that the new issue complies with the "blue sky" laws of each state.	Make presentations to institutional investors and develop the interest of potential buyers. Distribute the preliminary prospectus, affectionately termed the red herring. Calculate the issue price. Receive registration confirmation from the SEC.	1	5,000
Appoint a registrar.	Receive registration confirmation from the SEC.	3	12,000
Appoint a transfer agent.	Receive registration confirmation from the SEC.	3.5	13,000
Issue final prospectus that includes the final offer price and any amendments to all purchasers offered securities through the mail.	Confirm that the new issue complies with the "blue sky" laws of each state. Appoint a registrar and transfer agent.	4.5	40,000
Phone interested buyers.	Confirm that the new issue complies with the "blue sky" laws of each state. Appoint a registrar and transfer agent.	4	9,000

*The spread is the payment an underwriter receives for services.

Janet and Gilbert present the list of steps to the employees of InterCat. The head of the finance department, Leslie Grey, is fresh out of business school. She remembers the various project management tools she has learned in business school and suggests that Janet and Gilbert use PERT/CPM analysis to understand where their priorities should lie.

a. Draw the project network for completing the initial public offering of InterCat stock. How long is the initial public offering process? What are the critical steps in the process?

b. How would the change in the following activities affect the time to complete the initial public offering? Please evaluate each change independently.

    i. Some members of the syndicate are playing hardball. Therefore, the time it takes to negotiate the commitment of each member of the syndicate increases from two to three weeks.

    ii. The underwriters are truly math geniuses. Therefore, the time it takes to calculate the issue price decreases to four weeks.

iii. Whoa! The SEC found many deficiencies in the initial registration statement. The underwriters must therefore spend 2.5 weeks amending the statement and resubmitting it to the SEC.

iv. The new issue does not comply with the "blue sky" laws of a handful of states. The time it takes to edit the issue for each state to ensure compliance increases to four weeks.

c. Janet and Gilbert hear through the grapevine that their most fierce competitor, Soft Sales, is also planning to go public. They fear that if InterCat does not complete its initial public offering before Soft Sales, the price investors are willing to pay for InterCat stock will drop since investors will perceive Soft Sales to be a stronger, more organized company. Janet and Gilbert therefore decide that they want to complete the process of issuing new stock within 22 weeks. They think such a goal is possible if they throw more resources—workers and money—into some activities. They list the activities that can be shortened, the time the activity will take when it is fully shortened, and the cost of shortening the activity this much. They also conclude that partially shortening each activity listed below is possible and will give a time reduction and cost proportional to the amounts when fully shortening.

Activity	Time (Weeks)	Cost
Evaluate the prestige of each potential underwriter.	1.5	$14,000
Select a syndicate of underwriters.	0.5	8,000
Prepare the registration statement including the proposed financing and information about the firm's history, existing business, and plans for the future.	4	95,000
Make presentations to institutional investors and develop the interest of potential buyers.	4	60,000
Distribute the preliminary prospectus, affectionately termed the red herring.	2	22,000
Calculate the issue price.	3.5	31,000
Amend the registration statement and resubmit it to the SEC.	0.5	9,000
Confirm that the new issue complies with the "blue sky" laws of each state.	0.5	8,300
Appoint a registrar.	1.5	19,000
Appoint a transfer agent.	1.5	21,000
Issue final prospectus that includes the final offer price and any amendments to all purchasers offered securities through the mail.	2	99,000
Phone interested buyers.	1.5	20,000

How can InterCat meet the new deadline set by Janet and Gilbert at minimum cost?

d. Janet and Gilbert learn that the investment bankers are two-timing scoundrels! They are also serving as lead underwriters for the Soft Sales new issue! To keep the deal with InterCat, the bankers agree to let Janet and Gilbert in on a little secret. Soft Sales has been forced to delay its public issue because the company's records are disorganized and incomplete. Given this new information, Janet and Gilbert decide that they can be more lenient on the initial public offering timeframe. They want to complete the process of issuing new stock within 24 weeks instead of 22 weeks. Assume that the cost and time to complete the appointment of the registrar and transfer agent are the same as in part *c.* How can InterCat meet this new deadline set by Janet and Gilbert at minimum cost?

CASE 7.2
"SCHOOL'S OUT FOREVER..."
Alice Cooper

Brent Bonnin begins his senior year of college filled with excitement and a twinge of fear. The excitement stems from his anticipation of being done with it all—professors, exams, problem sets, grades, group meetings, all-nighters... The list could go on and on. The fear stems from the fact that he is graduating in December and has only four months to find a job.

Brent is a little unsure about how he should approach the job search. During his sophomore and junior years, he had certainly heard seniors talking about their strategies for finding the perfect job, and he knows that he should first visit the Campus Career Planning Center to devise a search plan.

On September 1, the first day of school, he walks through the doors of the Campus Career Planning Center and meets Elizabeth Merryweather, a recent graduate overflowing with energy and comforting smiles. Brent explains to Elizabeth that since he is graduating in December and plans to begin work in January, he wants to leave all of November and December open for interviews. Such a plan means that by October 31 he has to have all his preliminary materials, such as cover letters and résumés, submitted to the companies where he wants to work.

Elizabeth recognizes that Brent has to follow a very tight schedule, if he wants to meet his goal within the next 60 days. She suggests that the two of them sit down together and decide the major milestones that need to be completed in the job search process. Elizabeth and Brent list the 19 major milestones. For each of the 19 milestones, they identify the other milestones that must be accomplished directly before Brent can begin this next milestone. They also estimate the time needed to complete each milestone. The list is shown below.

Milestone	Milestones Directly Preceding Each Milestone	Time to Complete Each Milestone
A. Complete and submit an on-line registration form to the career center.	None.	2 days (This figure includes the time needed for the career center to process the registration form.)
B. Attend the career center orientation to learn about the resources available at the center and the campus recruiting process.	None.	5 days (This figure includes the time Brent must wait before the career center hosts an orientation.)
C. Write an initial résumé that includes all academic and career experiences.	None.	7 days
D. Search the Internet to find job opportunities available outside of campus recruiting.	None.	10 days
E. Attend the company presentations hosted during the fall to understand the cultures of companies and to meet with company representatives.	None.	25 days
F. Review the industry resources available at the career center to understand the career and growth opportunities available in each industry. Take a career test to understand the career that provides the best fit with your skills and interests. Contact alumni listed in the career center directories to discuss the nature of a variety of jobs.	Complete and submit an on-line registration form to the career center. Attend the career center orientation.	7 days
G. Attend a mock interview hosted by the career center to practice interviewing and to learn effective interviewing styles.	Complete and submit an on-line registration form to the career center. Attend the career center orientation. Write the initial résumé.	4 days (This figure includes the time that elapses between the day that Brent signs up for the interview and the day that the interview takes place.)
H. Submit the initial résumé to the career center for review.	Complete and submit an on-line registration form to the career center. Attend the career center orientation. Write the initial résumé.	2 days (This figure includes the time the career center needs to review the résumé.)
I. Meet with a résumé expert to discuss improvements to the initial résumé.	Submit the initial résumé to the career center for review.	1 day
J. Revise the initial résumé.	Meet with a résumé expert to discuss improvements.	4 days
K. Attend the career fair to gather company literature, speak to company representatives, and submit résumés.	Revise the initial résumé.	1 day
L. Search campus job listings to identify the potential jobs that fit your qualifications and interests.	Review the industry resources, take the career test, and contact alumni.	5 days
M. Decide which jobs you will pursue given the job opportunities you found on the Internet, at the career fair, and through the campus job listings.	Search the Internet. Search the campus job listings. Attend the career fair.	3 days

Milestone	Milestones Directly Preceding Each Milestone	Time to Complete Each Milestone
N. Bid to obtain job interviews with companies that recruit through the campus career center and have open interview schedules.*	Decide which jobs you will pursue.	3 days
O. Write cover letters to seek jobs with companies that either do not recruit through the campus career center or recruit through the campus career center but have closed interview schedules.** Tailor each cover letter to the culture of each company.	Decide which jobs you will pursue. Attend company presentations.	10 days
P. Submit the cover letters to the career center for review.	Write the cover letters.	4 days (This figure includes the time the career center needs to review the cover letters.)
Q. Revise the cover letters.	Submit the cover letters to the career center for review.	4 days
R. For the companies that are not recruiting through the campus career center, mail the cover letter and résumé to the company's recruiting department.	Revise the cover letters.	6 days (This figure includes the time needed to print and package the application materials and the time needed for the materials to reach the companies.)
S. For the companies that recruit through the campus career center but that hold closed interview schedules, drop the cover letter and résumé at the career center.	Revise the cover letters.	2 days (This figure includes the time needed to print and package the application materials.)

*An open interview schedule occurs when the company does not select the candidates that it wants to interview. Any candidate may interview, but since the company has only a limited number of interview slots, interested candidates must bid points (out of their total allocation of points) for the interviews. The candidates with the highest bids win the interview slots.

**Closed interview schedules occur when a company requires candidates to submit their cover letters, résumés, and test scores so that the company is able to select the candidates it wants to interview.

In the evening after his meeting with Elizabeth, Brent meets with his buddies at the college coffee house to chat about their summer endeavors. Brent also tells his friends about the meeting he had earlier with Elizabeth. He describes the long to-do list he and Elizabeth developed and says that he is really worried about keeping track of all the major milestones and getting his job search organized. One of his friends reminds him of the cool management science class they all took together in the first semester of Brent's junior year and how they had learned about some techniques to organize large projects. Brent remembers this class fondly since he was able to use a number of the methods he studied in that class in his last summer job.

a. Draw the project network for completing all milestones before the interview process. If everything stays on schedule, how long will it take Brent until he can start with the interviews? What are the critical steps in the process?

b. Brent realizes that there is a lot of uncertainty in the times it will take him to complete some of the milestones. He expects to get really busy during his senior year, in particular since he is taking a demanding course load. Also, students sometimes have to wait quite a while before they get appointments with the counselors at the career center. In addition to the list estimating the most likely times that he and Elizabeth wrote down, he makes a list of optimistic and pessimistic estimates of how long the various milestones might take.

Milestone	Optimistic Estimate (Days)	Pessimistic Estimate (Days)
A	1	4
B	3	10
C	5	14
D	7	12
E	20	30
F	5	12
G	3	8
H	1	6
I	1	1
J	3	6
K	1	1
L	3	10
M	2	4
N	2	8
O	3	12
P	2	7
Q	3	9
R	4	10
S	1	3

How long will it take Brent to get everything done under the worst-case scenario? How long will it take if all his optimistic estimates are correct?

c. Determine the mean critical path for Brent's job search process. What is the variance of the project duration?

d. Give a rough estimate of the probability that Brent will be done within 60 days?

e. Brent realizes that he has made a serious mistake in his calculations so far. He cannot schedule the career fair to

fit his schedule. Brent read in the campus newspaper that the fair has been set 24 days from today on September 25th. Draw a revised project network that takes into account this complicating fact.

f. What is the mean critical path for the new network? What is the probability that Brent will complete his project within 60 days?

BEYOND LINEAR PROGRAMMING

In the previous chapters, you have seen how versatile and useful linear programming can be in a wide variety of applications. However, linear programming also has its limitations. There are many situations where, at first glance, linear programming appears to be applicable but further study reveals that it does not quite fit for some reason. Fortunately, several similar management science techniques are available that are designed for just such situations. We examine four of these techniques in this chapter.

Each technique resembles linear programming in many ways. In fact, you will find the procedure for formulating and solving a spreadsheet model to be nearly the same as for linear programming.

However, each technique moves beyond linear programming to deal with situations where one of the basic assumptions of linear programming is violated. Therefore, this chapter also focuses on highlighting these assumptions and illustrating how they can be violated.

8.1 Integer Programming

In an optimal solution for a linear programming problem, the decision variables sometimes will have an *integer value,* that is, a *whole number* (0, 1, 2, . . .). However, they sometimes instead will have a *fractional value* (e.g., 2¾ or 4.1353). None of the constraints of a linear programming model prohibit fractional values.

In some applications, the decision variables will make sense *only* if they have integer values. For example, it may be necessary to assign people, or machines, or vehicles to activities in integer quantities. This is the kind of situation that integer programming addresses.

One example of an application having this kind of decision variable is provided by the first-prize winner of the 1988 Franz Edelman Award for Management Science Achievement. This prestigious prize was awarded for a management science study done for the **San Francisco Police Department,** as described in the January–February 1989 issue of *Interfaces.* This study resulted in the development of a computerized system for optimally scheduling and deploying police patrol officers. The new system provided annual savings of $11 million, an annual $3 million increase in traffic citation revenues, and a 20 percent improvement in response times. The main decision variables in the mathematical model were the number of officers to schedule to go on duty at each of the shift start times. Since this number had to be an integer, these decision variables were restricted to having integer values.

Here is another example where integer decision variables arise.

An Example: The TBA Airlines Problem

TBA Airlines is a small regional company that specializes in short flights in small airplanes. The company has been doing well and management has decided to expand its operations.

The basic issue facing management now is whether to purchase more small airplanes to add some new short flights or to start moving into the national market by purchasing some large

TABLE 8.1   Data for the TBA Airlines Problem

	Small Airplane	Large Airplane	Capital Available
Net annual profit per airplane	$1 million	$5 million	
Purchase cost per airplane	$5 million	$50 million	$100 million
Maximum purchase quantity	2	No maximum	

airplanes for new cross-country flights (or both). Many factors will go into management's final decision, but the most important one is which strategy is likely to be most profitable.

The first row of Table 8.1 shows the estimated net annual profit (inclusive of capital recovery costs) from each airplane purchased of each type. The second row gives the purchase cost per airplane and also notes that the total amount of capital available for airplane purchases is $100 million. The third row records the fact that management does not want to purchase more than two small airplanes because of limited possibilities for adding lucrative short flights, whereas they have not specified a maximum number for large airplanes (other than that imposed by the limited capital available).

How many airplanes of each type should be purchased to maximize the total net annual profit?

Since only two decisions need to be made, this question can be addressed graphically. Before turning to a spreadsheet, we will use this approach first to add graphical insight into the comparisons between linear programming and integer programming.

A Linear Programming Formulation of the TBA Airlines Problem

Let us begin analyzing this problem by attempting to use a linear programming formulation. To apply the graphical method, we will formulate the model in algebraic form.

The decisions to be made are

S = number of small airplanes to purchase
L = number of large airplanes to purchase

The constraints on these decisions are the limited capital available and the maximum purchase quantity of small airplanes (along with nonnegativity constraints). The objective is to maximize the total net annual profit. Therefore, using units of millions of dollars, the data in Table 8.1 provide the following linear programming model:

$$\text{Maximize} \quad \text{Profit} = S + 5L$$

subject to

$$5S + 50L \leq 100$$
$$S \quad\quad \leq 2$$

and

$$S \geq 0 \quad\quad L \geq 0$$

Applying the graphical method, Figure 8.1 shows the optimal solution for this model, namely,

$S = 2$:   Purchase 2 small airplanes
$L = 1.8$: Purchase 1.8 large airplanes

for a total net profit of $11 million.

It is, of course, impossible for the company to purchase a fractional number of airplanes, so this solution is of little use for the real problem. About all we can do with it is round down the fractional value (1.8) to obtain the following *rounded solution:*

$S = 2$:   Purchase 2 small airplanes
$L = 1$:   Purchase 1 large airplane

FIGURE 8.1

Applying the graphical method to the linear programming model for the TBA Airlines problem yields (S, L) = (2, 1.8) as the optimal solution. Rounding L = 1.8 down then gives (2, 1) as a feasible integer solution.

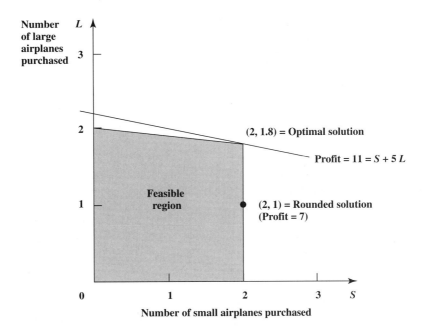

for a total net annual profit of $7 million. However, there is no guarantee that this rounded solution is the *optimal integer solution.* (In fact, you soon will see that it is far from optimal.)

What we need to do is add constraints to the model that restrict the values of the decision variables to *integer values* and then solve for the optimal solution for this *integer programming model.* This is exactly what we will do after highlighting the assumption of linear programming that is being violated by this problem.

The TBA Airlines Problem Violates the Divisibility Assumption of Linear Programming

One of the basic assumptions of linear programming is the following.

> **Divisibility Assumption of Linear Programming:** Decision variables in a linear programming model are allowed to have *any* values, including *fractional* values, that satisfy the functional and nonnegativity constraints. Thus, these variables are *not* restricted to just integer values. Since each decision variable represents the level of some activity, it is being assumed that the activities can be run at *fractional levels.* If this assumption is violated because the real problem requires that the decision variables have integer values, then *integer programming* should be used instead of linear programming.

For the TBA Airlines problem, the activities are the purchases of airplanes of different types, so the level of each activity is the number of airplanes of that type purchased. Since the number purchased must have an integer value, the divisibility assumption is violated.

There are some applications where linear programming can be used as a reasonable approximation even though the divisibility assumption is violated. This would be the case, for example, when the variable values are very big and, because of inevitable imprecision in the model, there is a bit of flexibility to violate the constraints slightly. Rounding then becomes a perfectly practical procedure. Thus, if the value of a variable were, say, $L = 101.8$, it should be fine to simply round it to the nearest integer, $L = 102$.

However, with $L = 1.8$ in the TBA Airlines problem, it is a different story. Rounding to $L = 2$ would require spending $10 million more capital than is available, which is unacceptable to TBA management. Therefore, we now abandon linear programming and turn to integer programming to deal with this problem.

An Integer Programming Formulation of the TBA Airlines Problem

The integer programming formulation of this problem is exactly the same as the linear programming formulation except for one crucial difference—constraints are added that require the decision variables to have integer values. Therefore, the algebraic form of the integer programming model is

$$\text{Maximize} \qquad \text{Profit} = S + 5L$$

subject to

$$5S + 50L \leq 100$$
$$S \qquad \leq \ \ 2$$

and

$$S \geq 0 \qquad L \geq 0$$

S, L are integers

The original linear programming model, without the addition of the last row above, is referred to as the **LP relaxation** of this integer programming problem. Its feasible region shown in Figure 8.1 is reproduced as the shaded region in Figure 8.2.

However, the only feasible solutions for the integer programming problem are the *integer solutions* (shown as dots in Figure 8.2) that lie within this shaded region, namely, (0, 0), (1, 0), (2, 0), (0, 1), (1, 1), (2, 1), and (0, 2). The *optimal solution* (i.e., the best of these seven feasible solutions) can be found by the following convenient method.

> **Graphical Method for Integer Programming:** When an integer programming problem has just two decision variables, its optimal solution can be found by applying the *graphical method for linear programming* (see Section 2.5) with just one change at the end. Thus, we begin as usual by graphing the feasible region for the LP relaxation, determining the slope of objective function lines, and moving a straight edge with this slope through this feasible region in the direction of improving values of the objective function. However, rather than stopping at the last instant that the straight edge still passes through this feasible region, we now stop at the last instant that the straight edge passes through an integer point that lies within this feasible region. This integer point is the optimal solution.

Figure 8.2 shows the result of applying this method to the TBA Airlines problem. When Profit = 0, the objective function line passes through the integer point (0, 0). When Profit (in millions of dollars) is increased in turn to 1, 2, 5, 6, and 7, the objective function line moves up to pass through the integer points (1, 0), (2, 0), (0, 1), (1, 1), and (2, 1), respectively. Finally, when Profit is increased to 10, the objective function line passes through the last feasible point (0, 2). Therefore, the optimal solution is

$S = 0$:   Purchase no small airplanes
$L = 2$:   Purchase 2 large airplanes

for a total net annual profit of $10 million.

FIGURE 8.2

Applying the graphical method for integer programming to the TBA Airlines problem yields (S, L) = (0, 2) as the optimal solution.

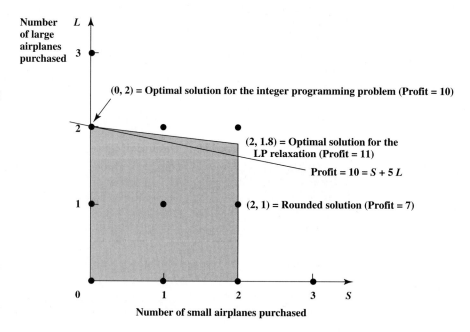

Note in Figure 8.2 how far away this optimal solution is from the optimal solution for the LP relaxation. We cannot reach the former solution simply by rounding the latter one, or even by moving to any of the four dots shown in Figure 8.2 that are closest to the latter solution. Therefore, first finding the optimal solution for the LP relaxation has done us little good in finding the optimal solution for the real problem, the integer programming problem.

Another interesting feature of this example is how markedly inferior the rounded solution in Figure 8.2 is to the optimal solution for the integer programming problem. Although the latter solution yields a total net annual profit of $10 million, the rounded solution would only provide $7 million per year. Rounding cannot be relied on to find an optimal solution, or even a good feasible integer solution. In fact, on bigger problems where a number of variables have fractional values, it may not be at all obvious how to round the variables to obtain *any* feasible integer solution. To guarantee finding an optimal solution, a procedure designed for this purpose should be used instead.

Formulating and Solving Spreadsheet Models for Integer Programming Problems

The spreadsheet procedure for integer programming is exactly the same as for linear programming except for adding one small step near the end. When specifying the constraints in the Solver dialogue box, you also need to include the constraints that the decision variables (changing cells) need to be integer.

Figure 8.3 shows how this is done for the TBA problem. Except for the second line of constraints in the Solver dialogue box, this entire formulation fits the linear programming formulation of the problem. Since C7 and D7 are the changing cells, and both need to be integer, you then enter C7:D7 = integer in the Solver dialogue box to convert this model into an integer programming model. These changing cells show the optimal solution, $(S, L) = (0, 2)$, obtained after clicking on the Solve button.

Algorithms for solving integer programming models (including the one in the Excel Solver) are not nearly as efficient as the simplex method for linear programming. This is the reason why a linear programming model (with rounding of the optimal solution) is sometimes used to approximate an integer programming model when this is considered a reasonable approximation. However, the Excel Solver is sometimes able to solve an integer programming model with well over 100 variables, depending on the difficulty of the problem.

The best commercial software (not using spreadsheets) occasionally have been successful in solving very large integer programming models ranging into the thousands of variables. This is an area of continuing research and progress.

FIGURE 8.3

A spreadsheet model for the TBA Airlines integer programming problem, where the changing cells (C7:D7) show the optimal airplane purchases obtained by the Solver and the target cell (E6) gives the resulting total profit in millions of dollars.

	A	B	C	D	E	F	G
1		TBA Airlines Airplane Purchasing Problem					
2							
3			Resource Usage per Unit of Each Activity				Resource
4		Resource	Small Airplane	Large Airplane	Totals		Available
5		Capital ($millions)	5	50	100	≤	100
6		Unit Profit ($millions)	1	5	10		
7		Solution	0	2			
8		Maximum	2	unlimited			

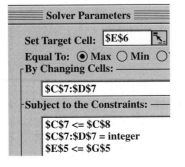

Solver Parameters

Set Target Cell: $E$6

Equal To: ● Max ○ Min ○

By Changing Cells:

$C$7:$D$7

Subject to the Constraints:

$C$7 <= $C$8
$C$7:$D$7 = integer
$E$5 <= $G$5

	E
5	=SUMPRODUCT(C5:D5,C7:D7)
6	=SUMPRODUCT(C6:D6,C7:D7)

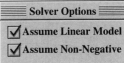

Solver Options

☑ Assume Linear Model
☑ Assume Non-Negative

Types of Integer Programming Problems

The TBA Airlines problem illustrates a situation where *all* the decision variables are required to have integer values. Some other applications will have a variety of decision variables where only *some* of them will have this restriction.

> **Pure integer programming** problems are those where all the decision variables must be integers. **Mixed integer programming** problems only require some of the variables to have integer values (so the divisibility assumption holds for the rest).

Many applications of integer programming (either pure or mixed) further restrict the integer variables to just the two values, 0 or 1.

> **Binary variables** are variables whose only possible values are 0 and 1. **Binary integer programming** problems are those where all the decision variables restricted to integer values are further restricted to be binary variables. Such problems can be further categorized as either *pure* or *mixed*, depending on whether *all* the decision variables or only *some* of them are binary variables.

Since binary variables only provide two choices, they are ideally suited to be the decision variables when dealing with yes-or-no decisions. In such a decision, the only two possible choices are yes and no, so the binary decision variable is assigned a value of 1 for choosing yes and a value of 0 for choosing no. Here are some examples of yes-or-no decisions.

1. Should we undertake a particular fixed project?
2. Should we make a particular fixed investment?
3. Should we locate a facility in a particular site?

Applications of binary integer programming for dealing with such decisions are so important that we devote the entire next chapter to this subject.

Review Questions

1. Why might a decision variable need to be restricted to integer values?
2. How does an integer programming model differ from a linear programming model?
3. What is the divisibility assumption of linear programming?
4. What is the LP relaxation of an integer programming problem?
5. How does the graphical method for integer programming differ from the graphical method for linear programming?
6. Can an optimal solution for an integer programming problem always be found by rounding the optimal solution for its LP relaxation?
7. What is the distinction between pure and mixed integer programming?
8. What are binary integer programming problems? How do they arise?

8.2 Separable Programming

Each term in the objective function of a linear programming model consists of a decision variable multiplied by its coefficient. The decision variable represents the level of an activity and the coefficient commonly is the *unit profit* from the activity or (in minimization problems) its *unit cost*.

Using the unit profit, say, for a coefficient implies that each additional unit of the activity provides the same profit (this unit profit) as the first unit. In other words, linear programming assumes that the profit from each activity is *proportional* to the level of that activity.

As the following example illustrates, this assumption sometimes is violated in real applications, in which case *separable programming* may be applicable.

An Example: The Wyndor Glass Co. Problem When Overtime Is Needed

As described in Section 2.2, the Wyndor Glass Co. produces high-quality glass products, where different parts of the production are performed in three plants. It now is launching two new products (a special kind of door and a special kind of window), where the anticipated profit has been estimated to be $300 per door and $500 per window. The company's *product-mix problem* addressed in much of Chapter 2 involved making the following two decisions:

D = number of doors to be produced per week
W = number of windows to be produced per week

When making these decisions, the objective was to maximize the total profit per week from the two products. Thus, the objective function to be maximized is

$$Profit = \$300D + \$500W$$

The decisions also needed to satisfy constraints on the number of hours of production time available per week for these products in each of the three plants.

To refresh your memory, Figure 8.4 shows the spreadsheet model that was formulated in Chapter 2 for this problem. Having clicked on the Solve button, the changing cells (C9 and D9) give the optimal solution, $(D, W) = (2, 6)$, which yields a weekly profit of \$3,600 (cell E8) according to the model.

However, a change now has occurred that invalidates this model. In particular, the company has accepted a special order for hand-crafted goods to be made in plants 1 and 2 throughout the next four months. Filling this order will require borrowing certain employees from the work crews for the regular products, so the remaining workers will need to work overtime to utilize the full production capacity of each plant's machinery and equipment for these products.

Thus, the constraints in the model still are valid, where overtime would be used to fill some of the hours of production time available in plants 1 and 2 as given by cells G5 and G6. However, the objective function no longer is valid because the additional cost of using overtime work reduces the profit obtained from each unit of product produced in this way.

For the portion of the work done in plants 1 and 2, Table 8.2 shows the maximum number of units of each product that can be produced per week on regular time and on overtime. Plant 3 does not need to use overtime, so its unchanged constraint is given in parentheses at the bottom. The fourth column is the sum of the second and third columns, where these sums are implied by the original constraints for plants 1 and 2 ($D \leq 4$ and $2W \leq 12$, so $W \leq 6$). The final two columns give the estimated profit for each unit produced on regular time and on overtime (in plants 1 and 2).

Figure 8.5 plots the weekly profit from each product versus its production rate. Note that the *slope* (steepness) of each profit graph decreases when the production rate is in-

FIGURE 8.4

The spreadsheet model that was formulated in Chapter 2 for the original Wyndor problem discussed there.

	A	B	C	D	E	F	G
1		Original Wyndor Glass Co. Product–Mix Problem					
2							
3			Hours Used per Unit Produced				Hours
4			Doors	Windows	Totals		Available
5		Plant 1	1	0	2	≤	4
6		Plant 2	0	2	12	≤	12
7		Plant 3	3	2	18	≤	18
8		Unit Profit	\$300	\$500	\$3,600		
9		Solution	2	6			

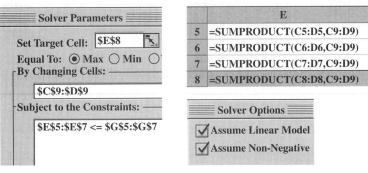

	E
5	=SUMPRODUCT(C5:D5,C9:D9)
6	=SUMPRODUCT(C6:D6,C9:D9)
7	=SUMPRODUCT(C7:D7,C9:D9)
8	=SUMPRODUCT(C8:D8,C9:D9)

FIGURE 8.5

Profit graphs for the Wyndor Glass Co. that show the total weekly profit from each product versus the production rate for that product when overtime is needed to exceed a production rate of three units per week.

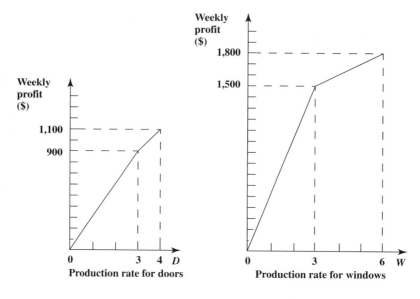

TABLE 8.2   Data for the Wyndor Problem When Overtime Is Needed

	Maximum Weekly Production			Profit per Unit Produced	
Product	*Regular Time*	*Overtime*	*Total*	*Regular Time*	*Overtime*
Doors	3	1	4	$300	$200
Windows	3	3	6	500	100
	(and $3D + 2W \leq 18$)				

creased sufficiently to require overtime, because the profit per unit produced shown in Table 8.2 is less on overtime than on regular time.

Management had considered hiring some temporary workers to avoid the extra expense of using overtime. However, this would mean incurring some training costs, as well as inefficiencies from using inexperienced workers. Therefore, because this is a temporary situation where regular production can resume in four months, management has decided to go ahead and use overtime.

However, management does insist that the work crew for each product be fully utilized on regular time before any overtime is used. Furthermore, it feels that the current production rates ($D = 2$ and $W = 6$) should be changed temporarily if this would improve overall profitability. Therefore, it has instructed the Management Science Group to review these products again to determine the most profitable product mix during the next four months.

This Problem Violates the Proportionality Assumption of Linear Programming

Here is a key assumption of linear programming.

Proportionality Assumption of Linear Programming: The contribution of each activity to the value of the objective function is *proportional* to the level of the activity.[1] In other words, the term in the objective function involving this activity consists of a coefficient times a decision variable, where the coefficient is the contribution per unit of this activity and the decision variable is the level of this activity.

The original Wyndor Glass Co. problem in Section 2.2 satisfies this assumption because the contribution to the objective function (Profit) of the two activities, producing doors and producing windows, were $300D$ and $500W$, respectively. Plotting the profit

---

[1]The same assumption also is made about the contribution of each activity to the left-hand side of each functional constraint, but we are focusing in this section on how to deal with a lack of proportionality in the objective function.

graph for each of these activities would give a straight line, which is the graphical signal that the proportionality assumption is satisfied.

By contrast, for the current problem with overtime needed, the profit graphs in Figure 8.5 are not straight lines. Each graph has a kink where the slope changes because the profit per unit produced is less when overtime is used instead of regular time. Therefore, the proportionality assumption is violated.

The profit graphs in Figure 8.5 illustrate having *decreasing marginal returns.*

> Consider any activity where a graph of its total profit versus the level of the activity is plotted. Suppose that the *slope* (steepness) of the graph never increases but sometimes decreases as the level of the activity increases. Then the activity is said to have **decreasing marginal returns.**

The slope of each profit graph in Figure 8.5 only decreases once as the level of the activity is increased, but that is enough to have decreasing marginal returns.

In problems where the objective is to minimize the total cost of the activities, an activity can still be said to have decreasing marginal returns if the slope of its *cost graph* never decreases but sometimes *increases* as the level of the activity is increased.

Having activities with a decreasing marginal return is not the only way in which the proportionality assumption can be violated. For example, another way is to have activities with *increasing* marginal returns, that is, where the slope of each *profit graph* never decreases but sometimes *increases* as the level of the activity increases. This can occur because of the greater efficiencies that sometimes can be achieved at higher levels of an activity.

However, *separable programming* is only applicable when activities have *decreasing* marginal returns (except for those activities that satisfy the proportionality assumption).

Applying Separable Programming to This Problem

Although each profit graph in Figure 8.5 is not a straight line, it does consist of *two* straight lines (line segments) that are connected together at the point where the slope changes. Thus, within each line segment, the profit graph looks like the proportionality assumption still holds. This suggests the following key idea.

> **The Separable Programming Technique:** For each activity that violates the proportionality assumption, separate its profit graph into parts, with a line segment in each part. Then, instead of using a single decision variable to represent the level of each such activity, introduce a separate new decision variable for each line segment on that activity's profit graph. Since the proportionality assumption holds for these new decision variables, formulate a linear programming model in terms of these variables.

For the Wyndor problem, these new decision variables are

D_R = number of doors produced per week on regular time
D_O = number of doors produced per week on overtime
W_R = number of windows produced per week on regular time
W_O = number of windows produced per week on overtime

The unit profits associated with these variables are given in the final two columns of Table 8.2, so these numbers become the coefficients in the objective function. The second and third columns give the maximum values of these variables, so corresponding constraints are introduced into the model. The three functional constraints in the model for the original Wyndor problem also need to hold, but with D replaced by $(D_R + D_O)$ and W replaced by $(W_R + W_O)$.

The resulting spreadsheet model is shown in Figure 8.6. Note that the Assume Linear Model option has been selected because the model now has been formulated to become a linear programming model. The proportionality assumption now is satisfied for the new decision variables. Therefore, the model can be solved very efficiently. This ability to reformulate the original model to make it fit linear programming is what makes separable programming a valuable technique.

However, there is one important factor that is not taken into account explicitly in this formulation. Recall that management insists that regular time production be fully utilized before using any overtime on each product. There are no constraints in the model that enforce this restriction. Consequently, it actually is feasible in the model to have $D_O > 0$ when $D_R < 3$, or to have $W_O > 0$ when $W_R < 3$.

FIGURE 8.6

A spreadsheet model for the Wyndor separable programming problem when overtime is needed, where the changing cells (C10:F10) give the optimal production rates obtained by the Solver and the target cell (G9) shows the resulting total profit per week.

	A	B	C	D	E	F	G	H	I
1		Wyndor Glass Co. Product–Mix Problem When Overtime is Needed							
2									
3				Hours Used per Unit Produced					
4			**Doors**	**Doors**	**Windows**	**Windows**			**Hours**
5		**Resource**	**Regular**	**Overtime**	**Regular**	**Overtime**	**Totals**		**Available**
6		Plant 1	1	1	0	0	4	≤	4
7		Plant 2	0	0	2	2	6	≤	12
8		Plant 3	3	3	2	2	18	≤	18
9		Unit Profit	$300	$200	$500	$100	$2,600.00		
10		Solution	3	1	3	0			
11		Maximum	3	1	3	3			

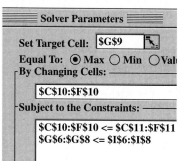

```
═══ Solver Parameters ═══

Set Target Cell: $G$9  [↖]
Equal To:  ● Max  ○ Min  ○ Val
─By Changing Cells:──────────
    $C$10:$F$10
─Subject to the Constraints:──
    $C$10:$F$10 <= $C$11:$F$11
    $G$6:$G$8 <= $I$6:$I$8
```

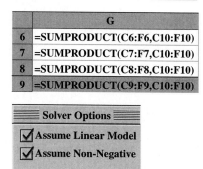

	G
6	=SUMPRODUCT(C6:F6,C10:F10)
7	=SUMPRODUCT(C7:F7,C10:F10)
8	=SUMPRODUCT(C8:F8,C10:F10)
9	=SUMPRODUCT(C9:F9,C10:F10)

```
═══ Solver Options ═══

☑ Assume Linear Model
☑ Assume Non-Negative
```

Fortunately, even though such a solution is feasible in the model, it cannot be optimal. The reason is that the activities (producing products 1 and 2) have *decreasing marginal returns,* since the unit profit on overtime is less than on regular time for each product. Therefore, to maximize the total profit, an optimal solution automatically will use up all regular time for a product before starting on overtime.

The key is to have decreasing marginal returns. Without it, the linear programming model with this approach may not provide a legitimate optimal solution. This is the reason that separable programming is only applicable when the activities have decreasing marginal returns (except for those activities that satisfy the proportionality assumption).

Figure 8.6 shows the changing cells (C10:F10) after using the Excel Solver to obtain an optimal solution. This optimal solution is

$D_R = 3, D_O = 1$:   Produce 4 doors per week
$W_R = 3, W_O = 0$:   Produce 3 windows per week

for a total profit of $2,600 per week (given by cell G9).

Applying Separable Programming with Smooth Profit Graphs

In some applications of separable programming, the profit graphs will be *curves* rather than a series of line segments. This occurs when the marginal return from an activity decreases on a continuous basis rather than just at certain points.

For example, the solid curve in Figure 8.7 shows such a profit graph for an activity. To apply separable programming, this curve can then be approximated by a series of line segments, such as the dashed line segments in the figure. By introducing a new decision variable for each of the line segments (and repeating this for other activities with such profit graphs), the approach just illustrated by the Wyndor example can again be used to convert the overall problem into a linear programming problem.

Although not quite as convenient as linear programming, the next section describes another approach to problems where the profit graphs are curves (or similar problems). This next approach has the advantage of using the curves directly rather than approximations.

FIGURE 8.7

The solid curve shows a profit graph for an activity whose marginal return decreases on a continuous basis. The dashed line segments display the kind of approximation used by separable programming.

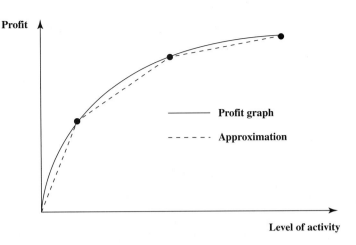

Review Questions

1. What is the proportionality assumption of linear programming?
2. What is meant by an activity having decreasing marginal returns?
3. For each activity that violates the proportionality assumption, what must be the shape of its profit graph (or at least an approximation of the profit graph) in order to apply separable programming?
4. What kind of mathematical model is eventually formulated when applying the separable programming technique?

8.3 Nonlinear Programming

In the preceding section, we discussed and illustrated the fact that some activities violate the proportionality assumption of linear programming. Thus, the contribution of each such activity to the value of the objective function is not proportional to the level of the activity. Consequently, this contribution cannot be expressed simply as a decision variable (the level of the activity) multiplied by a coefficient (the unit contribution), so the objective function does not fit linear programming.

However, sometimes each such contribution still can be expressed mathematically as a *nonlinear function,* in which case *nonlinear programming* is applicable instead. Let us look at a couple examples.

An Example: The Wyndor Problem with Nonlinear Marketing Costs

Consider another variation of the Wyndor Glass Co. problem discussed in the preceding section and Chapter 2. The constraints remain the same. In contrast to the preceding section, no overtime is needed. Instead, the change from the original problem is that *marketing costs* need to go up more than proportionally to attain increases in the level of sales for either product.

In particular, the doors can be sold at the rate of 1 per week ($D = 1$) with virtually no advertising. However, attaining sales to sustain a production rate of $D = 2$ would require a moderate amount of advertising, $D = 3$ would necessitate an extensive advertising campaign, and $D = 4$ would require also lowering the price. For any fractional or integer value of D permitted by the constraints, it is estimated that the weekly marketing costs required to sustain a production rate of D doors per week would be roughly

$$\text{Marketing cost for doors} = \$25\,D^2$$

Excluding marketing costs, the gross profit per door sold is about \$375. Therefore, the weekly net profit would be roughly

$$\text{Net profit for doors} = \$375\,D - \$25\,D^2$$

FIGURE 8.8

The smooth curves are the profit graphs for Wyndor's doors and windows for the version of its problem where nonlinear marketing costs must be considered.

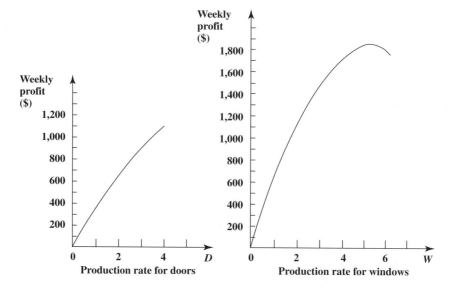

Weekly profit ($)

Production rate for doors

Production rate for windows

The corresponding estimates per week for windows are

$$\text{Marketing cost for windows} = \$66\tfrac{2}{3}\,W^2$$

$$\text{Gross profit for windows} \quad = \$700W$$

$$\text{Net profit for windows} \quad\;\; = \$700W - \$66\tfrac{2}{3}\,W^2$$

Figure 8.8 shows the resulting profit graphs for both products. Note that both curves show decreasing marginal returns, where this becomes particularly pronounced for larger values of W.

Combining the net profit for doors and for windows, the new objective function to be maximized for this problem is

$$\text{Profit} = \$375D - \$25D^2 + \$700W - \$66\tfrac{2}{3}\,W^2$$

subject to the same constraints as before. Because the terms involving D^2 and W^2 have exponents different from 1 for these decision variables, this objective function is a *nonlinear* function. Therefore, the overall problem is a *nonlinear programming* problem.

A Spreadsheet Formulation

Figure 8.9 shows the formulation of a spreadsheet model for this problem. It is interesting to compare this model with the one for the original Wyndor problem in Figure 8.4. At first glance, they appear to be virtually the same. A closer examination reveals only three significant differences.

First, the unit profit row (row 8) in Figure 8.4 has been deleted here because it is no longer applicable, so row 8 in Figure 8.9 includes both the changing cells (C8 and D8) and the target cell (E8).

Second, a more fundamental difference lies in the equation entered into the target cell. In Figure 8.4, the equation is expressed in terms of the SUMPRODUCT function that is characteristic of linear programming. In Figure 8.9, something else is needed because the objective function now is a nonlinear function. For example, consider the term involving D^2. Because the value of D appears in cell C8, Excel expresses D^2 as C8^2, where the symbol ^ indicates that the number following (2) is the exponent of the number in cell C8. Therefore, the overall equation entered into the target cell is

$$\text{E8} = 375*\text{C8} - 25*(\text{C8}^2) + 700*\text{D8} - 66.667*(\text{D8}^2)$$

The third difference arises in the selection of the Solver options at the bottom of Figures 8.4 and 8.9. In contrast to Figure 8.4, note that the Assume Linear Model option is *not* selected in Figure 8.9, because the model is not a linear programming model.

Before solving any nonlinear programming model, you should click on the Option button and make sure that the Assume Linear Model option has not been selected.

FIGURE 8.9

A spreadsheet model for the Wyndor nonlinear programming problem with nonlinear marketing costs, where the changing cells (C8:D8) show the optimal production rates and the target cell (E8) gives the resulting total profit per week.

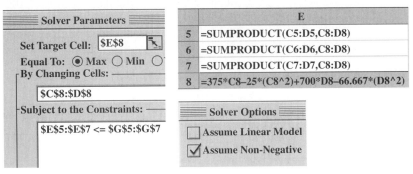

	A	B	C	D	E	F	G
1		Wyndor Glass Co. Product–Mix Problem With Marketing Costs (Nonlinear)					
2							
3			Hours Used per Unit Produced				Hours
4		Resource	Doors	Windows	Totals		Available
5		Plant 1	1	0	3.214	≤	4
6		Plant 2	0	2	8.357	≤	12
7		Plant 3	3	2	18	≤	18
8		Solution	3.214	4.179	$2708	=	Profit

Solver Parameters

Set Target Cell: $E$8

Equal To: ● Max ○ Min ○

By Changing Cells:

$C$8:$D$8

Subject to the Constraints:

$E$5:$E$7 <= $G$5:$G$7

	E
5	=SUMPRODUCT(C5:D5,C8:D8)
6	=SUMPRODUCT(C6:D6,C8:D8)
7	=SUMPRODUCT(C7:D7,C8:D8)
8	=375*C8–25*(C8^2)+700*D8–66.667*(D8^2)

Solver Options

☐ Assume Linear Model

☑ Assume Non-Negative

FIGURE 8.10

Graphical display of the nonlinear programming formulation of the Wyndor problem with nonlinear marketing costs. The curves are objective function curves for some sample values of Profit and the one (Profit = $2,708) that passes through the optimal solution, (D, W) = (3³/₁₄, 4⁵/₂₈).

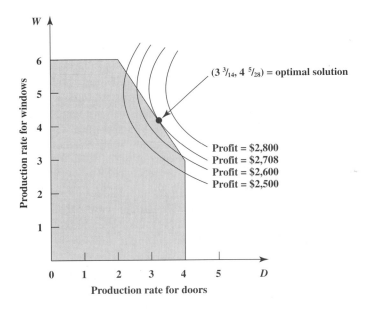

$(3 \frac{3}{14}, 4 \frac{5}{28})$ = optimal solution

Profit = $2,800
Profit = $2,708
Profit = $2,600
Profit = $2,500

Production rate for windows

Production rate for doors

For this particular model, clicking on the Solve button provides the optimal solution shown in cells C8 and D8, namely,

$D = 3.214$ (produce an average of 3.214 doors per week)
$W = 4.179$ (produce an average of 4.179 windows per week)

where cell E8 shows a resulting weekly profit of $2,708. These strange values of D and W certainly are not intuitive. Figure 8.10 conveys some graphical intuition into why this answer was obtained. The feasible region is the same as for the original Wyndor problem in Chapter 2. However, instead of having objective function *lines* with which to search for an optimal solution, plotting the points that give any constant value for our nonlinear objective function now gives an objective function *curve* instead. Thus, when using the objective function to calculate Profit for various feasible and infeasible values of (D, W), each of the four curves in the figure shows all the values of (D, W) that give the fixed value of Profit indicated for that curve. (Plotting these points is a tedious and difficult process, so we will not bother you with the details of how it is done.) The figure shows that increasing Profit moves the objective function curve to the right. The largest value of Profit such that the objective function curve still passes through any points in the feasible region is Profit = $2,708. Therefore, using fractions, the one feasible point that the Profit = $2,708 curve passes through,

$$(D, W) = (3\tfrac{3}{14}, 4\tfrac{5}{28})$$

is the optimal solution.

Since these are not particularly convenient fractions with which to plan production schedules, they should be adjusted slightly. The curve for Profit = $2,708 in Figure 8.10 indicates that any point on the slanting line at the boundary of the feasible region that is close to the optimal solution will provide a weekly profit very close to $2,708. For example,

$$(D, W) = (3\tfrac{1}{5}, 4)$$

gives a weekly profit of $2,706.

Characteristics of Nonlinear Programming Problems

In this example, the problem has the following characteristics:

1. The same constraints as for a linear programming model.
2. A nonlinear function for the objective function.
3. Each activity that violates the proportionality assumption of linear programming has *decreasing marginal returns.*

This is a particularly simple type of nonlinear programming problem. The Excel Solver can readily solve such problems.

However, nonlinear programming problems come in many guises and forms. Some might have *increasing* marginal returns for certain activities. Some might have nonlinear functions in the constraints. Some might have profit graphs with several disconnected curves. These other kinds of nonlinear programming problems often are much more difficult, if not impossible, to solve. There also is a danger with such problems that the Solver will provide an incorrect solution. Managers dealing with these kinds of problems would be well advised to enlist the assistance of a trained management scientist.

Of the three characteristics listed above for the simple type of nonlinear programming problem, the only one that is sometimes difficult to verify is the third one. This is particularly true when the objective function includes cross-product terms involving the product of two or more decision variables. In this case, whenever all but one of the decision variables are fixed at particular values, the effect on the value of the objective function of increasing the one decision variable must still satisfy either proportionality or decreasing marginal returns for the third characteristic to hold.

In addition to violating the proportionality assumption of linear programming, nonlinear programming problems with cross-product terms also violate the following assumption.

Additivity Assumption of Linear Programming: Each term in the objective function only contains a single decision variable, where this term represents the contribution of the corresponding activity to the value of the objective function. Therefore, this value is obtained simply by *adding* these contributions for all the activities. This assumption also is required for separable programming, but can be violated by nonlinear programming problems because of cross-product terms involving the product of two or more variables.

We next look at an example that has cross-product terms but still fits all three characteristics to be a simple type of nonlinear programming problem.

Applying Nonlinear Programming to Portfolio Selection

It now is common practice for professional managers of large stock portfolios to use computer models based partially on nonlinear programming to guide them. Because investors are concerned about both the *expected return* (gain) and the *risk* associated with their investments, nonlinear programming is used to determine a portfolio that, under certain assumptions, provides an optimal trade-off between these two factors. This approach is based largely on path-breaking research done by Harry Markowitz and William Sharpe that helped them win the 1990 Nobel Prize in economics.

One way of formulating their approach is as a nonlinear version of the *cost–benefit trade-off problems* discussed in Section 3.3. In this case, the cost involved is the risk associated with the investments. The benefit is the expected return from the portfolio of investments. Therefore, the general form of the model is

$$\text{Minimize} \quad \text{Risk}$$

subject to

$$\text{Expected return} \geq \text{minimum acceptable level}$$

The measure of risk used here is a basic quantity from probability theory called the *variance* of the return. Using standard formulas from probability theory, the objective function then can be expressed as a nonlinear function of the decision variables (the number of shares of the respective stocks to purchase) that yields decreasing marginal returns for the stocks. By adding the constraint on expected return, as well as nonnegativity constraints and a constraint that the amount to be invested in the portfolio cannot exceed the budgeted amount, we thereby obtain a simple type of nonlinear programming model for optimizing the selection of the portfolio.

To illustrate the approach, we now will focus on a small numerical example where just three stocks (securities) are being considered for inclusion in the portfolio. Thus, the decision variables are

S_1 = number of blocks of shares of stock 1 to purchase
S_2 = number of blocks of shares of stock 2 to purchase
S_3 = number of blocks of shares of stock 3 to purchase

where each block consists of 1,000 shares. Table 8.3 gives the needed data (in units of thousands of dollars) for each block of shares of the three stocks. In addition, the investor specifies the following two quantities:

Budgeted amount to invest = 1,000   ($1 million)
Minimum acceptable expected return = 300   ($300,000)

Since the amount to invest cannot exceed 1,000, the second column of Table 8.3 gives the constraint

$$60S_1 + 40S_2 + 50S_3 \leq 1,000$$

The third column provides the coefficients for the expected return for the portfolio

$$\text{Expected return} = 25S_1 + 20S_2 + 9S_3$$

However, the risk for the portfolio cannot be obtained solely from the fourth column, since this column only gives the risk for each individual stock considered in isolation. The risk for the portfolio also is affected by whether the particular stocks tend to move up and down together (increased risk) or tend to move in opposite directions (decreased risk). In the rightmost column of Table 8.3, the *positive* joint risk for stocks 1 and 2 indicates that these two stocks have some tendency to move in the same direction. However, the *negative* joint risk for the other two pairs of stocks shows that stock 3 tends to go up when either stock 1 or 2 goes down, and vice versa. (In the terminology of probability theory, the joint risk for two stocks is the *covariance* of the return from one block of shares of each of these

TABLE 8.3 **Data per Block of Shares for the Stocks of the Portfolio Selection Example**

Stock	Price ($000)	Expected Return ($000)	Risk	Pair of Stocks	Joint Risk
1	60	25	4	1 and 2	2
2	40	20	9	1 and 3	−1
3	50	9	1	2 and 3	−1.5

FIGURE 8.11

A spreadsheet model for the portfolio selection example of nonlinear programming, where the changing cells (C8:E8) give the optimal portfolio and the target cell (F7) shows the resulting risk.

	A	B	C	D	E	F	G	H
1		Portfolio Selection Problem (Nonlinear Programming)						
2								
3				Amount per Block				Right-Hand
4		Factors	Stock 1	Stock 2	Stock 3	Totals		Side
5		Budget	60	40	50	1000	≤	1000
6		Expected Return	25	20	9	300.00	≥	300
7		Risk	4	9	1	246.76		
8		Solution	6.416	2.257	10.495			
9								
10								
11		Joint Risk	Stock 1	Stock 2	Stock 3			
12		Stock 1		2	−1			
13		Stock 2			−1.5			
14		Stock 3						

	F
5	=SUMPRODUCT(C5:E5,C8:E8)
6	=SUMPRODUCT(C6:E6,C8:E8)
7	=C7*C8^2+D7*D8^2+E7*E8^2+D12*C8*D8+E12*C8*E8+E13*D8*E8

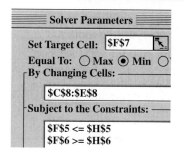

Solver Parameters

Set Target Cell: $F$7

Equal To: ○ Max ● Min ○

By Changing Cells: ───

$C$8:$E$8

Subject to the Constraints: ───

$F$5 <= $H$5
$F$6 >= $H$6

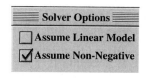

Solver Options

☐ Assume Linear Model
☑ Assume Non-Negative

stocks.) Using the formula from probability theory for calculating the overall variance from individual variances and covariances, the risk for the entire portfolio is

$$\text{Risk} = 4S_1^2 + 9S_2^2 + S_3^2 + 2S_1S_2 - S_1S_3 - 1.5S_2S_3$$

Therefore, the algebraic form of the nonlinear programming model for this example is

Minimize $\text{Risk} = 4S_1^2 + 9S_2^2 + S_3^2 + 2S_1S_2 - S_1S_3 - 1.5S_2S_3$

subject to

$$25S_1 + 20S_2 + 9S_3 \geq 300$$
$$60S_1 + 40S_2 + 50S_3 \leq 1{,}000$$

and

$$S_1 \geq 0 \qquad S_2 \geq 0 \qquad S_3 \geq 0$$

Figure 8.11 shows the corresponding spreadsheet model after having applied the Solver. The Solution row indicates that the optimal solution is

$S_1 = 6.416$:   Purchase 6,416 shares of stock 1
$S_2 = 2.257$:   Purchase 2,257 shares of stock 2
$S_3 = 10.495$:   Purchase 10,495 shares of stock 3

with an expected return of 300 ($300,000). Thus, despite its relatively low return, including a substantial amount of stock 3 in the portfolio is worthwhile to counteract the high risk associated with stocks 1 and 2. (Problem 8.13 asks you to explore this model further to see the effect of reducing the purchases of stock 3.)

    This is an example of a cost–benefit trade-off problem since it involves finding the best trade-off between cost (risk) and a benefit (expected return). Except for the form of the ob-

FIGURE 8.12

A data table that shows the trade-off between expected return and risk when the model of Figure 8.11 is altered by varying the minimum acceptable expected return.

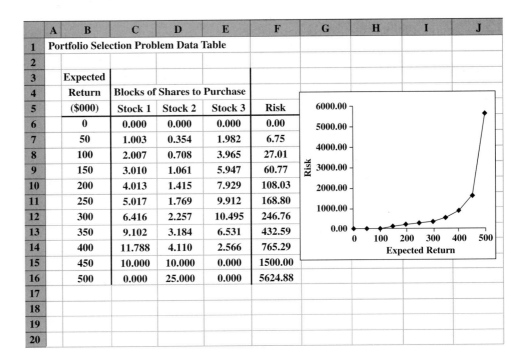

	A	B	C	D	E	F	G	H	I	J
1		Portfolio Selection Problem Data Table								
2										
3		Expected								
4		Return	Blocks of Shares to Purchase							
5		($000)	Stock 1	Stock 2	Stock 3	Risk				
6		0	0.000	0.000	0.000	0.00				
7		50	1.003	0.354	1.982	6.75				
8		100	2.007	0.708	3.965	27.01				
9		150	3.010	1.061	5.947	60.77				
10		200	4.013	1.415	7.929	108.03				
11		250	5.017	1.769	9.912	168.80				
12		300	6.416	2.257	10.495	246.76				
13		350	9.102	3.184	6.531	432.59				
14		400	11.788	4.110	2.566	765.29				
15		450	10.000	10.000	0.000	1500.00				
16		500	0.000	25.000	0.000	5624.88				
17										
18										
19										
20										

jective function, it is analogous to the cost–benefit trade-off problems discussed in Section 3.3. As discussed further in Chapter 4, analysis of such a problem seldom ends with finding an optimal solution for the original version of the model. The minimum acceptable level stated in the model for the benefit (or benefits) involved is a tentative policy decision. After learning the resulting cost, further analysis is needed to find the best trade-off between costs and benefits. This analysis involves varying the minimum acceptable level for the benefit and seeing what the effect is on the cost. If a lot more benefit can be obtained for relatively little cost, this probably should be done. On the other hand, if decreasing the benefit a little would save a lot of cost, the minimum acceptable level probably should be decreased.

One way of applying this approach to the current example is to develop a *data table* that gives the expected return and risk provided by an optimal solution for the model for a range of values of the minimum acceptable expected return. Figure 8.12 shows such a data table. In the parlance of the world of finance, the pairs of values in columns B and F are referred to as points on the *efficient frontier*. In fact, the right-hand side of Figure 8.12 shows a plot of this efficient frontier. After examining enough such points, the investor then can make a personal decision about which one provides the best trade-off between expected return and risk. Since the risk begins rising significantly faster above an expected return of 300, an investor with a strong aversion to risk might stick with this expected return. Someone who is considerably less risk-averse might choose to go out to an expected return of about 400. A risk-seeker probably would go out somewhat further.

Review Questions

1. How does a nonlinear programming model differ from a linear programming model?
2. What are the three characteristics of a simple type of nonlinear programming problem that can be readily solved by the Excel Solver?
3. For this simple type of nonlinear programming problem, how does the graphical display for a two-variable problem differ from that for a two-variable linear programming problem?
4. What is the additivity assumption of linear programming? In what way might it be violated by a nonlinear programming problem?
5. When applying nonlinear programming to portfolio selection, a trade-off is being sought between which two factors?

8.4 A Case Study: The Dewright Co. Goal-Programming Problem

"What's the matter, honey? A rough day at the office?"

"Well, it really wasn't all that bad." Kathleen responds to her husband Scott. "Mainly just frustrating. Ever since I got this job as head of Dewright's Management Science Department, I have emphasized making sure that everything we do is responding to management's needs. Understand what management's objectives are for the decisions they need to make based on our studies. Then address those objectives rather than what we think the goals should be. I preach that all the time."

"So what happened?"

"Well, we've just been handed an extremely important new project, a really juicy management science study. So I made the rounds today interviewing the key people in top management to clarify just what they wanted to get out of our study. What is the basic objective for the decisions they need to make? Usually this goes pretty smoothly, with a lot of consensus about what the overriding objective should be. But not today. First I was told that we should focus on such and such as the main goal of the study. Then the next person I interviewed said no, the key goal was something completely different. Then the next guy had an entirely new slant on it. I've never seen so much disagreement. Each one was only protecting his or her own interests instead of looking at the big picture of what is best for the company as a whole. So now we're stymied. I've already selected the members of the team to work on this study. But we can't really get started until we receive much clearer direction from management. And, of course, management needs the study completed quickly. One jokester said they would like our report the day before yesterday. I laughed politely, but I felt like kicking him. Don't they realize that our output from the study can only be as good as their input!?! And that we can only act as quickly as they give us the direction we need!"

"Wow, no wonder you're frustrated," Scott responds. "It sounds like management really dropped the ball on this one."

"Yes, they did. It was clear that they hadn't talked to each other about this issue, even though they knew I would be interviewing all of them about this today. It's management's responsibility to thrash this out and come to a common understanding of what they want out of a management science study, and then give us clear direction. They really didn't do their job this time!"

"So what's the next step?"

"I've already called our CEO late this afternoon. Direction needs to come from the top. Actually, Gary was pretty sympathetic. He even volunteered that he thought his people had let me down this time."

"So did he give you the direction you need?" Scott asks Kathleen.

"No, I really wasn't asking for that at this point. He wasn't involved with requesting this management science study, so I was hitting him cold. But he understood right away what had gone wrong. Even before I could suggest it, he said that the managers involved with this project should be brought together in a meeting to thrash out what the main goals should be. He even said he would chair the meeting himself. He also wants me and key members of my team there. He says it is very important that we have a clear understanding of management's thinking on this issue. And I certainly agreed."

"Great! So it sounds to me like all you have to do is attend the meeting and listen carefully. Let them do their homework and then come to a meeting of the minds. Press them if necessary to get the clarity you need. Then you'll be off and running."

Background

The Dewright Company is one of the largest producers of power tools in the United States. The company has had its ups and downs, but has managed to maintain its position as one of the market leaders for over 20 years. This is largely due to superior products produced by a skilled and loyal workforce, many of whom have been with the company for most of its existence. One of management's priorities has been to maintain a relatively stable employment level to retain the high morale and loyalty of this workforce.

The company has just gone through one of its leaner years. Sales were down slightly from the preceding year and earnings dipped as well (much to the discontent of the company's stockholders). One consequence is that the company now has less capital available than usual with which to invest in new product development. Management also is concerned that some downsizing may be needed if sales don't improve soon.

Fortunately, help is on the way. The company is preparing to replace its current product line with the next generation of products—specifically, three exciting new power tools with the latest state-of-the-art features, so they are expected to sell well for at least a year or two. Because of the limited amount of capital available, management needs to make some difficult choices about how much to invest in each of these products. Another concern is the effect of these decisions on the company's ability to maintain a relatively stable employment level. A competitor is known to be developing similar new products, so decisions must be made quickly.

These kinds of considerations recently led the company's president, Tasha Johnson, to call Kathleen Donaldson, head of the Management Science Department, to request an urgent management science study to analyze what the product mix should be. Tasha asked Kathleen to come see her for a briefing on management's objectives in making the product-mix decisions. Tasha also suggested that Kathleen talk with Vijay Shah (vice president for manufacturing) and Hien Nguyen (the chief financial officer).

Kathleen has just completed these interviews, with the unsatisfactory results reported to her husband.

Gary Lang, the company's CEO, now has arranged for the meeting to bring these parties together with Kathleen and key members of her team.

The Management Science Team Meets with Top Management	After some pleasantries, the meeting gets under way.

Gary Lang (CEO): I've called this meeting to clarify what we want to accomplish when we introduce these three new products. What are our main goals? I have some thoughts on that. But first I want to hear your thinking. Then we can work this out together. Once this is settled, planning can get under way to accomplish what we want accomplished. As you know, Tasha has asked Kathleen to personally head a management science team from her department to analyze how we can best meet our goals. Before the team can do that, they need some clear direction from us on just what our goals and priorities are. Kathleen, is that a fair summary of what you want to get out of this meeting?

Kathleen Donaldson (head of Management Science Department): Yes, it is, Gary. Thank you.

Gary: OK. Let's make the rounds then and get your thinking. Tasha, let's start with you.

Tasha Johnson (president): Well, as usual, I think we need to focus on the bottom line. If we do that, everything else will fall into place. After the year we just went through, we've got to get our earnings up. That's certainly the message our board of directors has been giving us. You'll recall the plan I presented at the last board meeting. To get our earnings headed up where we want them, we need to generate a total profit of at least $125 million from these three products until they're replaced by the next generation of products. And I think that's doable. I've already told Kathleen that I would like her team to find the mix of the three products that would maximize our long-run profit. And to make sure that it is at least $125 million, as I promised the board of directors. I think that should be our main focus.

Gary: Thank you, Tasha. It's certainly true that the board has been pressing us to substantially improve earnings. And they were encouraged by your plan to generate profits of at least $125 million from these products. Vijay, what is your take on this issue of where our focus should be?

Vijay Shah (vice president for manufacturing): Well, I'm certainly not going to argue against making profits. But there are different ways of accomplishing that. By and large, we've been a very profitable company for over 20 years. And despite our occasional off years like last year, I think we will continue to be a very successful company as long as we don't forget what got us here. Our number one asset is our workforce. They're the best in the business and we all know it. Beside our strong leadership at the top, they're our main reason for success. If we simply go scrambling after big profits in the short run to satisfy the board of directors for a little while, I think that's going to mean some downsizing. That would ruin morale! And cause all kinds of disruption. I know a lot of companies have been doing it, often to their regret, but it would be a huge mistake in our case. Let's not kill the goose that's been laying our golden eggs. We have great morale and an exceptionally efficient workforce largely because we've kept them together all these years. We're going to have larger profits in the long run if we maintain a stable employment level and continue developing new products to keep them fully utilized. I told Kathleen that I thought her team should develop a plan for the current new products that would maintain our present employment level, and then profits would take care of themselves.

Tasha: But in this global economy, the companies that are surviving are those that downsize quickly when they need to in order to stay competitive.

Vijay: That would be shortsighted, especially in our situation.

Gary: Vijay, I do agree that we have a terrific workforce and we should try to maintain it if possible. It is my hope that these three new products will enable us to do just that. We currently have 4,000 employees. We might even be able to increase that if everything falls into place. When you talk about the disadvantages of changing the employment level, how would you feel about an increase rather than a decrease.

Vijay: An increase wouldn't be so bad. But it still would cause some problems, especially since the increase probably would be temporary as these products wind down. First, we would incur the expense and disruption of training these inexperienced workers. Then we would turn around and need to lay them off because we have so little attrition here. Any layoffs are not good for morale. I think we're better off sticking pretty close to the 4,000 employees.

Gary: OK. Thanks, Vijay. Now I'm anxious to hear from Hien, especially after our financial downturn this past year.

Hien Nguyen (chief financial officer): Yes. You know well that we're not in a good financial situation. We seldom have been as strapped for capital as we are right now.

Gary: Unfortunately, we're going to need a lot of capital to launch these new products properly. And it is very important to the future of this company to have a good launch. I'm going to need to depend on you to work your usual magic to come up with at least the minimum amounts necessary to invest in the production facilities, marketing campaigns, and so forth, that we need for these products. How much do you think we can do?

Hien: I've been looking into that pretty carefully. I think we can scrape together something close to $55 million. However, I wouldn't advise trying to go beyond that. If we get that overextended, I fear that our corporate bonds will be downgraded into the junk bond category. And then we would be paying through the nose in high interest rates for all our debt. So when Kathleen saw me recently, I advised her to stick with plans that would hold the capital investment down to no more than $55 million.

Gary: I hear you. OK, here is my conclusion so far. I think all three of you have raised very valid concerns. You each have enunciated a goal: achieve a total profit from these products of at least $125 million, maintain the current employment level of 4,000 employees, and hold the capital investment down to no more than $55 million. These all are legitimate goals. I seriously doubt that we can fully achieve all of them. However, rather than selecting just one of them, I think we need to try to come as close to meeting all three goals simultaneously as we can.

Kathleen: I have a question.

Gary: Shoot.

Kathleen: Do you see any way of combining all three goals into a single overriding objective—one objective that would encompass all three?

Gary: Such as?

Kathleen: Well, perhaps maximizing *long-run* profit. The problems associated with either changing the employment level or overextending our capital outlays affect our profit in the long run. Can we measure these effects on long-run profits and combine them with the direct profit from the new products?

Gary: Hmmm. An interesting idea. But no, I don't think so. You're really comparing apples and oranges. There are too many intangibles involved in the impact of missing either the second or third goal. I don't see how you can develop any reasonable estimate of the long-run profit that would result from all this.

Kathleen: Yes, that was my reaction too. But yours is the one that counts. So it sounds like we should consider all three goals as separate goals, but then analyze them simultaneously.

Gary: Yes, I think so. Do you have a good way of doing this?

Kathleen: Well, I can think of two possibilities. But we need further guidance from all of you to determine the approach we should use.

Gary: Go ahead.

Kathleen: One possibility is to use a linear programming approach. You'll recall that we've conducted several linear programming studies for you recently.

Gary: Yes.

Kathleen: This would involve maximizing the total profit from the new products, subject to constraints that the second and third goals are met. But this would mean requiring that the second and third goals are completely satisfied. Would that requirement seem reasonable to you?

Tasha: No, no, no! I think the first goal is the most important. We should make sure we meet it even if that means missing the second and third goals somewhat.

Vijay: But we also should permit missing the first goal somewhat to avoid missing the other goals by a large amount.

Gary: Well, there you have it. I agree that we shouldn't require any of the goals to be completely satisfied if they can't all be satisfied simultaneously.

Kathleen: OK, fine. So formulating a linear programming model would not be appropriate to meet your needs. But now it sounds to me like the second approach would be perfect for you.

Gary: What's that?

Kathleen: It's a management science technique called **goal programming.** It is designed to find the best way of striving toward several goals simultaneously.

Gary: Yes, that sounds like just the ticket. So now you have what you need from us to start your study?

Kathleen: Not quite. I need to ask your indulgence for a few minutes to elicit a little more input we need from you—information we need to be able to use goal programming.

Gary: This is important. We'll take as long as you need.

Kathleen: Thank you. What we need is your collective assessment of the relative importance of these three goals.

Gary: I would like to take a crack at that. I've been thinking hard about this during our discussion here. I must say that Tasha, Vijay, and Hien all have made strong cases. I think all three goals are important. However, I don't think we have any choice but to put top priority on achieving our profit goal. That is the engine that drives everything else. And our board of directors has made it very clear that this needs to be our top priority. But I also resonate with what Vijay had to say about our workforce being our number one asset. However, I would divide his goal of maintaining a stable employment level into two parts—avoiding a *decrease* in the employment level and avoiding an *increase* in the employment level. I think the negative impact of laying off some of our loyal long-time employees would be much more serious than from hiring new people and perhaps laying them off in a year or two. Therefore, I would place a pretty strong second priority on avoiding layoffs, but not on avoiding new hiring. Then sorry, Hien, but I think we can only give third priority to the goal of holding our capital investment under $55 million. We mustn't ignore your very legitimate concerns. However, we are in a hole that we need to dig out of, even if that means stretching our finances more than we normally would be willing to do. Then finally, I would put fourth priority on the second part of Vijay's goal—avoiding an increase in our employment level since it might need to be temporary.

What do the rest of you think? Does this seem reasonable?

Tasha: Definitely.

Vijay: I can live with it.

Hien: You're the one that needs to set priorities. But we do need to be cautious about getting overextended financially.

Gary: I hear you. OK, Kathleen, does this give you everything you need?

Kathleen: Nearly. This has been extremely helpful. But here is how goal programming works. It assigns penalties to not achieving goals. The more you miss a goal, the larger the penalty. The top priority goals get the largest penalties for missing them and the lowest priority goals get the smallest penalties. Then goal programming finds the set of decisions—in this case the production rates for the three products—that minimizes the total number of penalty points incurred by missing goals.

Gary: Sounds like a good approach.

Kathleen: Yes. But what this means is that we need to assign penalty weights that measure the relative seriousness of missing the respective goals. Now we could try to assign the penalty weights based on the discussion here and the priorities you have set. But that really isn't our place. These penalty weights need to reflect *your* assessment, not ours, of the relative seriousness of missing these goals.

Gary: I agree. How do we go about that?

Kathleen: Well, the first step is that we assign any old number as the penalty weight for missing one of the goals, just to establish a standard of comparison. Then you would scale this penalty weight up or down for each of the other goals, depending on whether you think the seriousness of missing that goal is larger or smaller than for missing the first goal. OK, since our top priority is on the goal of achieving a total profit from these new products of at least $125 million, let's assign a penalty weight of 5 for each $1 million you undershoot this goal. In other words, if the estimated total profit resulting from the selected profit mix is $124 million, 5 penalty points would be assessed. If the estimated total profit is $115 million, undershooting the goal by $10 million, then 50 penalty points would be assessed. Ten times five is 50."

Gary: I get it.

Kathleen: OK. With this penalty weight of 5 as a standard of comparison, now we're ready for the hard questions. Going down your priorities, what should the penalty weight be for each 100 employees we *undershoot* the goal of maintaining the current employment level at 4,000 employees? For each $1 million we miss the goal of holding the capital investment down to no more than $55 million? For each 100 employees we *overshoot* the goal of sticking with 4,000 employees?

Gary: Hmmm. Good questions. Hmmm. Well, I think I would go 5, 4, 3, 2. Five for the first goal, and then 4, 3, 2 for your three questions.

Kathleen: Great. Understood. That gives us exactly what we need. We can launch into our study immediately now.

Gary: Very good. You understand that we'll need your report quite soon.

Kathleen: Yes, I think we can finish in a month. I'll tell you what our biggest job is going to be. Gathering data. We're going to need to get good data on the effect of each product's production rate toward meeting each of the three goals. How much profit will each product generate? How much employment level? How much capital investment is needed? We'll have to get a lot of help from various staff people.

Gary: I'll see it to that everybody makes this their top priority.

Kathleen: Then we can do it. I don't think any of us will see much of our families for the next month, but I'll make sure that we get it done in time.

Gary: Good for you, Kathleen. Thank you so much. And let us know whenever you need more input or help from any of us.

Kathleen: I will. Thank you.

The meeting concludes, except for a somewhat heated private conversation between Tasha and Vijay.

The Conclusions from This Meeting

To summarize, here are the key conclusions from this meeting.

The management science team led by Kathleen Donaldson will conduct a study to be completed within the next month. The study will focus on determining the mix of the company's three new products that would best meet management's goals. The specific decisions to be made are the production rates for the three products.

In addressing these decisions, management wants primary consideration given to three factors: total profit, stability in the workforce, and the level of capital investment needed to launch these products. In particular, management has established the following goals.

Goal 1: Achieve a total profit (net present value) from these products of at least $125 million.

Goal 2: Maintain the current employment level of 4,000 employees.

Goal 3: Hold the capital investment down to no more than $55 million.

However, management realizes that it probably will not be possible to attain all these goals simultaneously, and so they evaluated the relative importance of the goals. All are important, but by small margins their order of importance is

Order of Importance: Goal 1, part of Goal 2 (avoid decreasing the employment level), Goal 3, and the other part of Goal 2 (avoid increasing the employment level).

To further quantify this ordering, **penalty weights** were assigned to indicate the relative seriousness of missing these goals. Discussions between management and Kathleen led to the choice of the penalty weights shown in Table 8.4.

Relevant Data

What the long-run profit, employment level, and capital investment level will be depends on the *production rates* (number of units produced per day) of the three products. Each product's contribution to each of these three quantities is *proportional* to the rate of production of the product. Therefore, for each of the three products, the management science team focuses on estimating the contribution to each of these quantities *per unit* rate of production of the product. Much of these data are not readily available, so the team has to do considerable digging with much help from knowledgeable staff. Based on the limited information they can uncover, the team then makes the best estimates that they can of each product's contribution to each of the three quantities.

These estimated contributions per unit rate of production are shown in Table 8.5, where the contributions are in the units indicated (in parentheses) in the first column. Thus, for example, producing one unit per day of product 1 would contribute $12 million toward total profit, 500 employees to the employment level, and $5 million to the capital investment level.

The story of how the team uses these data to complete its study continues in the next section after we introduce the general subject of goal programming.

TABLE 8.4   Penalty Weights That Measure the Relative Seriousness of Missing the Goals for the Dewright Co. Problem

Goal	Factor	Penalty Weight for Missing Goal
1	Total profit	5 (per $1 million under the goal)
2	Employment level	4 (per 100 employees under the goal)
		2 (per 100 employees over the goal)
3	Capital investment	3 (per $1 million over the goal)

TABLE 8.5   Contributions to the Goals per Unit Rate of Production of Each Product for the Dewright Co. Problem

Factor	Unit Contribution of Product			Goal
	1	*2*	*3*	
Total profit (millions of dollars)	12	9	15	≥ 125
Employment level (hundreds of employees)	5	3	4	$= 40$
Capital investment (millions of dollars)	5	7	8	≤ 55

Review Questions

1. What is the problem that Dewright's management science team has been asked to address?
2. What are the three goals that management has established for addressing this problem?
3. What is to be minimized when using a goal-programming approach?

8.5 Goal Programming

One common characteristic of all the different kinds of mathematical models introduced so far (linear programming, integer programming, separable programming, and nonlinear programming) is that they have a single objective function. This implies that all the managerial objectives for the problem being studied can be encompassed within a single overriding objective, such as maximizing total profit or minimizing total cost. However, this is not always possible, as you have just seen in the Dewright case study.

For example, consider again the prize-winning study for the **San Francisco Police Department** described at the beginning of Section 8.1. One managerial objective was to minimize the sum of the *shortages* (the deficit in the number of police patrol officers on duty below the goal for a given hour) over all the hours of the week. Another objective was to make the *maximum shortage* over the week as small as possible. Since these two objectives could not be combined into a single overriding one, a way had to be found to strive toward both objectives simultaneously.

When managing a for-profit organization, the managerial objectives might well include some of the following:

1. Maintain stable profits.
2. Increase market share.
3. Diversify the product line.
4. Maintain stable prices.
5. Improve worker morale.
6. Maintain family control of the business.
7. Increase company prestige.

These objectives are so different in nature that it really is not realistic to combine them into a single overriding objective. Instead, analysis of the problem of concern requires individual consideration of the separate objectives.

Goal programming provides a way of striving toward several such objectives simultaneously. The basic approach is to establish a specific numeric goal for each of the objectives and then to seek a solution that balances how close this solution comes to each of these goals. **Penalty weights** are assigned to the objectives to measure the relative seriousness of missing their numeric goals. An objective function is formulated for each of the objectives. The overall objective is to minimize the weighted sum of deviations of these objective functions from their respective goals. Assuming that all the individual objective functions and the constraints of the problem fit the format for linear programming, the overall problem then can be formulated as a linear programming problem.

Now let us see how Dewright's management science team does this for the case study introduced in the preceding section.

Formulation of a Goal-Programming Model for the Dewright Co. Problem

The decisions that need to be made for the Dewright Co. problem are the production rates for the three new products that will be introduced soon. Therefore, the decision variables are

P_1 = number of units of product 1 to produce per day
P_2 = number of units of product 2 to produce per day
P_3 = number of units of product 3 to produce per day

Using the unit contributions given in Table 8.5, the three goals can be expressed in terms of these decision variables as

Goal 1:	$12P_1 + 9P_2 + 15P_3 \geq 125$	(Total profit goal)
Goal 2:	$5P_1 + 3P_2 + 4P_3 = 40$	(Employment level goal)
Goal 3:	$5P_1 + 7P_2 + 8P_3 \leq 55$	(Capital investment goal)

These mathematical expressions for the goals look like linear programming constraints. However, they cannot be used as constraints in a mathematical model because constraints definitely must be satisfied whereas Dewright management already has concluded that it probably will not be possible to attain all these goals simultaneously. For a goal-programming model, the overall objective instead is to come as close as possible to satisfying all these goals simultaneously.

More precisely, using the penalty weights given in Table 8.4, let

W = Weighted sum of deviations from the goals
= Number of penalty points incurred by missing the goals

For each goal that is missed, the number of penalty points incurred is the penalty weight *times* the deviation from the goal. Therefore, the overall objective then is to choose the values of P_1, P_2, and P_3 so as to

$$\text{Minimize} \quad W = 5 \text{ (amount under goal 1)} + 2 \text{ (amount over goal 2)}$$
$$+ 4 \text{ (amount under goal 2)} + 3 \text{ (amount over goal 3)}$$

where no penalty points are incurred for being over goal 1 (exceeding the target for total profit is fine) or for being under goal 3 (underexpending the capital investment budget is satisfactory).

Figure 8.13 shows one way of formulating the spreadsheet model for this problem. Three of the changing cells (C8:E8) display the values of the decision variables (P_1, P_2, and P_3). Given these values, the equations entered into cells F5:F7 provide the levels achieved toward meeting the goals expressed in columns B, G, and H.

The most subtle part of this formulation involves columns I, J, K, and M. The column M cells are data cells giving the right-hand sides of the respective goals. Cells I5:J7 are additional changing cells that display the decisions on the amounts over and amounts under the respective goals. Cell J10 is the target cell giving the value of W, where the Solver dialogue box specifies that the objective is to minimize this value. Using the expression for W given above, the equation entered into this target cell is

$$\text{J10} = 5*\text{J5} + 2*\text{I6} + 4*\text{J6} + 3*\text{I7}$$

The Solver options selected at the bottom of Figure 8.13 specify that this model now has been formulated in a way that fits linear programming (which enables solving the model) and that all the changing cells need to be nonnegative. In addition, the constraints in the Solver dialogue box (K5:K7 = M5:M7) need to be satisfied. However, there are no constraints involving the output cells in column F since these cell values are not required to fully satisfy the goals specified in columns B, G, and H.

Finally, we need to clarify the key role played by the output cells in column K. For example, consider cell K6. Since M6 = 40, the second of the constraints in the Solver dialogue box (K6 = M6) specifies that K6 = 40 for any feasible solution. The equation entered into this cell (as shown near the bottom of Figure 8.13) is

$$\text{K6} = \text{F6} - \text{I6} + \text{J6}$$

Given the value of 48.3333 in the figure for output cell F6, this equation becomes

$$40 = 48.3333 - \text{I6} + \text{J6}$$

for any feasible solution. This equation reduces algebraically to

$$\text{I6} - \text{J6} = 8.3333$$

To minimize the target cell, the smallest nonnegative values of I6 and J6 that satisfy this equation need to be chosen, which yields I6 = 8.3333 and J6 = 0.

FIGURE 8.13

A spreadsheet model for the Dewright Co. goal programming problem formulated as a linear programming problem, where the changing cells C8:E8 show the optimal production rates and the changing cells I5:J7 show the optimal amounts over and under the goals. The target cell (J10) gives the resulting weighted sum of deviations from the goals.

	A	B	C	D	E	F	G	H	I	J	K	L	M
1		Dewright Co. Goal–Programming Problem											
2			Unit Contribution per Unit										
3			of Each Activity			Level			Amount	Amount			Right-Hand
4		Goals	Product 1	Product 2	Product 3	Achieved	Goal		Over	Under	Totals		Side
5		Profit	12	9	15	125	≥	125	0	0	125	=	125
6		Employment	5	3	4	48.3333	=	40	8.3333	0	40	=	40
7		Investment	5	7	8	55	≤	55	0	0	55	=	55
8		Solution	8.3333333	0	1.6666667								
9													
10						Weighted Sum of Deviations =		16.667					

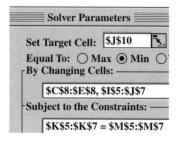

Solver Parameters

Set Target Cell: **$J$10**

Equal To: ○ Max ◉ Min ○

By Changing Cells:

   $C$8:$E$8, $I$5:$J$7

Subject to the Constraints:

   $K$5:$K$7 = $M$5:$M$7

Solver Options

☑ Assume Linear Model

☑ Assume Non-Negative

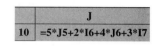
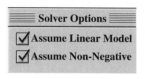

	F	K
5	=SUMPRODUCT(C5:E5,C8:E8)	=F5−I5+J5
6	=SUMPRODUCT(C6:E6,C8:E8)	=F6−I6+J6
7	=SUMPRODUCT(C7:E7,C8:E8)	=F7−I7+J7

	J
10	=5*J5+2*I6+4*J6+3*I7

Based on similar reasoning, clicking on the Solve button yields the optimal solution for all the changing cells shown in Figure 8.13. Since the units being used in the spreadsheet are those given in the first column of Table 8.5, this solution thereby provides the following.

Production rate for product 1 = 8⅓ units per day
Production rate for product 2 = 0
Production rate for product 3 = 1⅔ units per day
Total profit = $125 million
Employment level = 4,833 employees
Capital investment = $55 million

The only deviation from management's goals is the one considered least serious (exceeding the employment level goal of 4,000 employees).

Epilogue to the Dewright Case Study

Exactly one month after their first meeting, Gary Lang called the same group together again to hear the report of the management science team. The night before, Kathleen Donaldson had made sure that all the parties received the team's written report via courier service. Based on the above analysis, the report recommended that the company focus most of its efforts on producing and marketing large quantities of product 1 ($P_1 = 8⅓$), while providing some diversification with a much smaller output of product 3 ($P_3 = 1⅔$). Another recommendation was that any production of product 2 be postponed indefinitely ($P_2 = 0$), but that further development work be done on this product to see if it could be made sufficiently attractive for release with the next generation of products. The report then highlighted the fact that this plan would enable meeting all of management's more important goals.

Everybody had read the written report with this wonderful news before entering the meeting. This completely changed the mood from the usual one that Kathleen encountered when presenting an oral report and recommendations to Dewright management. Gone was the usual probing and skeptical questioning of the presentation. (In the privacy of her home with her husband Scott, Kathleen referred to these sessions as her inquisitions.) Also missing was the zealous guarding of territory by some Dewright managers that Kathleen had observed in the past. (Kathleen marveled to Scott afterward that she actually spotted Tasha and Vijay smiling at each other for the first time in months.) Vijay did suggest, with nods all around, that some of the new employees be brought in as "temps" (temporary workers) and that the development of the next generation of new products be accelerated a little to try to avoid any future layoffs of permanent employees. Otherwise, the presentation was virtually uninterrupted. Following a quick pro forma vote to approve the plan recommended by the management science team, Gary had champagne brought in. He then offered a toast to the very fine work done by Kathleen and her team.

Thus began a very good year for the Dewright Company. However, some very rocky times—and managerial changes—awaited the company further down the road. Shortly before the downturn, Kathleen left Dewright to head up her own management science consulting firm. Her firm is doing very well.

Review Questions

1. What is the one common characteristic of the mathematical models introduced in previous sections and chapters that is not possessed by goal-programming problems?
2. What is the basic approach of goal-programming?
3. What is represented by the objective function in a goal-programming model?
4. What is shown by the changing cells (other than those displaying the values of the decision variables for the original problem) in the spreadsheet model for a goal-programming problem?
5. To enable solving a goal-programming problem, it can be formulated to fit what kind of spreadsheet model?

8.6 Summary

This chapter introduces four management science techniques for dealing with problems that do not satisfy some particular assumption of linear programming.

The *divisibility assumption* of linear programming allows the decision variables to have any values, including fractional values, that satisfy the functional and nonnegativity constraints. When this assumption is violated because some or all of the variables need to be restricted to integer values, then *integer programming* should be used instead. The Excel Solver can readily solve integer programming problems of reasonable size.

The *proportionality assumption* of linear programming requires that the contribution of each activity to the value of the objective function be proportional to the level of that activity. When this assumption is violated because at least some of the activities have decreasing marginal returns, the *separable programming* technique becomes applicable. This technique introduces some new variables that enable formulating a linear programming model that at least closely approximates the original problem while satisfying the proportionality assumption in terms of the new variables.

Nonlinear programming provides another approach to problems that violate the proportionality assumption of linear programming. The nonlinear objective function is allowed to include cross-product terms that involve the product of two or more variables, even though this violates the *additivity assumption* that is needed for both linear programming and separable programming. Some types of nonlinear programming problems can be readily solved by the Excel Solver while others cannot.

All these techniques, as well as linear programming, make the basic assumption that a single objective function is available that encompasses the overriding objective of management for the problem. However, management sometimes will instead have a variety of rather different objectives that require separate consideration. As illustrated by the Dewright case study, *goal programming* provides a way of striving toward several such objectives simultaneously. The basic approach is to establish a specific numeric goal for each of the objectives and then to seek a solution that balances how close it comes to each of these goals. By introducing some new variables that represent the amounts over or under the respective goals, this approach eventually succeeds in formulating a linear programming model where the objective is to minimize the weighted sum of the deviations from the goals.

Glossary

Additivity assumption   A basic assumption of both linear programming and separable programming that requires that each term in the objective function only contains a single variable. (Section 8.3)   312

Binary integer programming   Integer programming where all the decision variables restricted to integer values are further restricted to be binary variables. (Section 8.1)   304

Binary variable   A variable whose only possible values are 0 and 1. (Section 8.1)   304

Decreasing marginal returns   An activity has decreasing marginal returns if the slope (steepness) of its profit graph never increases but sometimes decreases as the level of the activity increases. (Section 8.2)   307

Divisibility assumption   A basic assumption of linear programming that allows the decision variables to have any values, including fractional values, that satisfy the functional and nonnegativity constraints. (Section 8.1)   301

Goal programming   A technique designed to find the best way of striving toward several goals simultaneously. (Sections 8.4 and 8.5)   319, 322

Graphical method for integer programming   A method for solving integer programming problems that have only two decision variables by graphing the problem on a two-dimensional graph. (Section 8.1)   302

LP relaxation   The linear programming problem obtained by deleting from the current integer programming problem the constraints that require the decision variables to have integer values. (Section 8.1)   302

Mixed integer programming   Integer programming where only some of the decision variables are required to have integer values. (Section 8.1)   304

Penalty weights   Values assigned to the goals of a goal-programming problem that measure the relative seriousness of missing these goals. (Sections 8.4 and 8.5)   321, 322

Proportionality assumption   A basic assumption of linear programming that requires that the contribution of each activity to the value of the objective function must be proportional to the level of that activity. (Section 8.2)   306

Pure integer programming   Integer programming where all the decision variables are required to have integer values. (Section 8.1)   304

Learning Aids for This Chapter in Your MS Courseware

"Ch. 8—Beyond LP" Excel File:

TBA Airlines Example
Original Wyndor Example
Wyndor Example with Overtime
Wyndor Example with Marketing Costs

Portfolio Selection Example
Dewright Case Study

An Excel Add-in:

Premium Solver

Problems

To the left of each of the following problems (or their parts), we have inserted an E* whenever Excel should be used (unless your instructor gives you contrary instructions). An asterisk on the problem number indicates that at least a partial answer is given in the back of the book.

8.1. Vincent Cardoza is the owner and manager of a machine shop that does custom order work. This Wednesday afternoon, he has received calls from two customers who would like to place rush orders. One is a trailer hitch company that would like some custom-made heavy-duty tow bars. The other is a mini-car-carrier company that needs some customized stabilizer bars. Both customers would like as many as possible by the end of the week (two working days). Since both products would require the use of the same two machines, Vincent needs to decide and inform the customers this afternoon about how many of each product he will agree to make over the next two days.

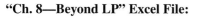

Each tow bar requires 3.2 hours on machine 1 and 2 hours on machine 2. Each stabilizer bar requires 2.4 hours on machine 1 and 3 hours on machine 2. Machine 1 will be available for 16 hours over the next two days and machine 2 will be available for 15 hours. The profit for each tow bar produced would be $130 and the profit for each stabilizer bar produced would be $150.

Vincent now wants to determine the mix of these production quantities that will maximize the total profit.

   a. Formulate an integer programming model in algebraic form for this problem.
   b. Use the graphical method for integer programming to solve this model.
E*   *c.* Display the model on a spreadsheet.
E*   *d.* Solve the model.

8.2. Pawtucket University is planning to buy new copier machines for its library. Three members of its Management Science Department are analyzing what to buy. They are considering two different models: Model A, a high-speed copier, and Model B, a lower-speed but less expensive copier. Model A can handle 20,000 copies a day and costs $6,000. Model B can handle 10,000 copies a day but only costs $4,000. They would like to have at least six copiers so that they can spread them throughout the library. They also would like to have at least one high-speed copier. Finally, the copiers need to be able to handle a capacity of at least 75,000 copies per day. The objective is to determine the mix of these two copiers that will handle all these requirements at minimum cost.

E* a. Formulate and solve a spreadsheet model for this problem.
  b. Formulate this same model in algebraic form.
  c. Use the graphical method for integer programming to solve this model.

8.3.* Consider the following algebraic form of an integer programming model:

$$\text{Maximize} \quad \text{Profit} = 5x_1 + x_2$$

subject to

$$-x_1 + 2x_2 \leq 4$$
$$x_1 - x_2 \leq 1$$
$$4x_1 + x_2 \leq 12$$

and

$$x_1 \geq 0 \qquad x_2 \geq 0$$
$$x_1, x_2 \text{ are integers}$$

  a. Use the graphical method for integer programming to solve this model.
  b. Use the graphical method for linear programming to solve the LP relaxation of the model. Round this solution to the *nearest* integer solution and check whether it is feasible. Then enumerate *all* the rounded solutions by rounding this solution for the LP relaxation in *all* possible ways (i.e., by rounding each noninteger value both up and down). For each rounded solution, check for feasibility and, if feasible, calculate Profit. Are any of these feasible rounded solutions optimal for the integer programming model?

8.4. Follow the instructions of Problem 8.3 for the following algebraic form of an integer programming model:

$$\text{Maximize} \quad \text{Profit} = 220x_1 + 80x_2,$$

subject to

$$5x_1 + 2x_2 \leq 16$$
$$2x_1 - x_2 \leq 4$$
$$-x_1 + 2x_2 \leq 4$$

and

$$x_1 \geq 0 \qquad x_2 \geq 0$$
$$x_1, x_2 \text{ are integers}$$

8.5.* Northeastern Airlines is considering the purchase of new long-, medium-, and short-range jet passenger airplanes. The purchase price would be $67 million for each long-range plane, $50 million for each medium-range plane, and $35 million for each short-range plane. The board of directors has authorized a maximum commitment of $1.5 billion for these purchases. Regardless of which airplanes are purchased, air travel of all distances is expected to be sufficiently large that these planes would be utilized at essentially maximum capacity. It is estimated that the net annual profit (after capital recovery costs are subtracted)

would be $4.2 million per long-range plane, $3 million per medium-range plane, and $2.3 million per short-range plane.

It is predicted that enough trained pilots will be available to the company to crew 30 new airplanes. If only short-range planes were purchased, the maintenance facilities would be able to handle 40 new planes. However, each medium-range plane is equivalent to $1\frac{1}{3}$ short-range planes, and each long-range plane is equivalent to $1\frac{2}{3}$ short-range planes in terms of their use of the maintenance facilities.

The information given here was obtained by a preliminary analysis of the problem. A more detailed analysis will be conducted subsequently. However, using the preceding data as a first approximation, management wishes to know how many planes of each type should be purchased to maximize profit.

E* a. Formulate and solve a spreadsheet model for this problem.
  b. Formulate this model in algebraic form.

8.6. Reconsider Problem 5.8 involving a contractor (Susan Meyer) who needs to arrange for hauling gravel from two pits to three building sites.

Susan now needs to hire the trucks (and their drivers) to do the hauling. Each truck can only be used to haul gravel from a single pit to a single site. In addition to the hauling and gravel costs specified in Problem 5.8, there now is a fixed cost of $50 associated with hiring each truck. A truck can haul five tons, but it is not required to go full. For each combination of pit and site, there now are two decisions to be made: the number of trucks to be used and the amount of gravel to be hauled.

  a. Formulate a mixed integer programming model in algebraic form for this problem.
E* b. Display the formulation of the model on a spreadsheet.
E* c. Solve this model.

8.7. The B.J. Jensen Company specializes in the production of power saws and power drills for home use. Sales are relatively stable throughout the year except for a jump upward during the Christmas season. Since the production work requires considerable work and experience, the company maintains a stable employment level and then uses overtime to increase production in November. The workers also welcome this opportunity to earn extra money for the holidays.

B.J. Jensen Jr., the current president of the company, is overseeing the production plans being made for the upcoming November. He has obtained the following data.

	Maximum Monthly Production*		Profit per Unit Produced	
	Regular Time	*Overtime*	*Regular Time*	*Overtime*
Power saws	3,000	2,000	$150	$50
Power drills	5,000	3,000	100	75

*Assuming adequate supplies of materials from the company's vendors.

However, Mr. Jensen now has learned that, in addition to the limited number of labor hours available, two other factors will limit the production levels that can be achieved this November. One is that the company's vendor for power supply units will only be able to provide 10,000 of these units for November (2,000 more than his usual monthly shipment). Each power saw and each power drill requires one of these units. Second, the vendor who supplies a key part for the gear assemblies will only be able to provide 15,000 for November (4,000 more than for other months). Each power saw requires two of these parts and each power drill requires one.

Mr. Jensen now wants to determine how many power saws and how many power drills to produce in November to maximize the company's total profit.

     a. Draw the profit graph for each of these two products.

E*   *b.* Use separable programming to formulate a linear programming model on a spreadsheet for this problem.

E*   *c.* Solve the model. What does this say about how many power saws and how many power drills to produce in November?

8.8.* The Dorwyn Company has two new products (special kinds of doors and windows) that will compete with the two new products for the Wyndor Glass Co. (described in Section 2.2). Using units of hundreds of dollars for the objective function, the linear programming model in algebraic form shown below has been formulated to determine the most profitable product mix.

$$\text{Maximize} \quad \text{Profit} = 4D + 6W$$

subject to

$$D + 3W \leq 8$$
$$5D + 2W \leq 14$$

and

$$D \geq 0 \qquad W \geq 0$$

However, because of the strong competition from Wyndor, Dorwyn management now realizes that the company will need to make a strong marketing effort to generate substantial sales of these products. In particular, it is estimated that achieving a production and sales rate of D doors per week will require weekly marketing costs of D^3 hundred dollars (so \$100 for $D = 1$, \$800 for $D = 2$, \$2,700 for $D = 3$, etc.). The corresponding marketing costs for windows are estimated to be $2W^2$ hundred dollars. Thus, the objective function in the model should be

$$\text{Profit} = 4D + 6W - D^3 - 2W^2$$

Dorwyn management now would like to use the revised model to determine the most profitable product mix.

     a. Construct tables to show the profit data for each product when the production rate is 0, 1, 2, 3.

     b. Draw a figure that plots the weekly profit points for each product when the production rate is 0, 1, 2, 3. Connect the pairs of consecutive points with (dashed) line segments.

E*   *c.* Use separable programming based on this figure to formulate an approximate linear programming model on a spreadsheet for this problem.

E*   *d.* Solve the model. What does this say to Dorwyn management about which product mix to use?

8.9. The MFG Corporation is planning to produce and market three different products. Let x_1, x_2, and x_3 denote the number of units of the three respective products to be produced. The preliminary estimates of their potential profitability are as follows.

For the first 15 units produced of product 1, the unit profit would be approximately \$360. The unit profit would be only \$30 for any additional units of product 1. For the first 20 units produced of product 2, the unit profit is estimated at \$240. The unit profit would be \$120 for each of the next 20 units and \$90 for any additional units. For the first 10 units of product 3, the unit profit would be \$450. The unit profit would be \$300 for each of the next 5 units and \$180 for any additional units.

Certain limitations on the use of needed resources impose the following constraints on the production of the three products:

$$x_1 + x_2 + x_3 \leq 60$$
$$3x_1 + 2x_2 \qquad \leq 200$$
$$x_1 \qquad + 2x_3 \leq 70$$

Management wants to know what values of x_1, x_2, and x_3 should be chosen to maximize the total profit.

     a. Plot the profit graph for each of the three products.

E*   *b.* Use separable programming to formulate a linear programming model on a spreadsheet for this problem.

E*   *c.* Solve the model. What is the resulting recommendation to management about the values of x_1, x_2, and x_3 to use?

8.10. Reconsider the production scheduling problem of the Build-Em-Fast Company described in Problem 5.15. The *special restriction* for such a situation is that overtime should not be used in any particular period unless regular time in that period is completely used up. Explain why the logic of *separable programming* implies that this restriction will be satisfied automatically by any optimal solution for the transportation problem formulation of the problem.

8.11. Suppose that separable programming has been applied to a certain problem (the "original problem") to convert it to the following equivalent linear programming model in algebraic form:

$$\text{Maximize} \quad \text{Profit} = 5x_{11} + 4x_{12} + 2x_{13} + 4x_{21} + x_{22}$$

subject to

$$3x_{11} + 3x_{12} + 3x_{13} + 2x_{21} + 2x_{22} \leq 25$$
$$2x_{11} + 2x_{12} + 2x_{13} - x_{21} - x_{22} \leq 10$$

and

$$0 \leq x_{11} \leq 2 \qquad\qquad 0 \leq x_{21} \leq 3$$
$$0 \leq x_{12} \leq 3 \qquad\qquad 0 \leq x_{22} \leq 1$$
$$0 \leq x_{13}$$

What was the mathematical model for the original problem? Answer this by plotting the profit graph for each of the original activities and then writing the constraints for the original problem in terms of the original decision variables.

8.12. Jim Matthews, vice president for marketing of the J.R. Nickel Company, is planning advertising campaigns for two unrelated products. These two campaigns need to use some of the same resources. Therefore, Jim knows that his decisions on the levels of the two campaigns need to be made jointly after considering these resource constraints. In particular, letting x_1 and x_2 denote the levels of campaigns 1 and 2, respectively, these constraints are $4x_1 + x_2 \leq 20$ and $x_1 + 4x_2 \leq 20$.

In facing these decisions, Jim is well aware that there is a point of diminishing returns when raising the level of an advertising campaign too far. At that point, the cost of additional advertising becomes larger than the increase in net revenue (excluding advertising costs) generated by the advertising. After careful analysis, he and his staff estimate that the net profit from the first product (including advertising costs) when conducting the first campaign at level x_1 would be $3x_1 - (x_1 - 1)^2$ in millions of dollars. The corresponding estimate for the second product is $3x_2 - (x_2 - 2)^2$.

Letting P be total net profit, this analysis led to the following nonlinear programming model for determining the levels of the two advertising campaigns:

Maximize $P = 3x_1 - (x_1 - 1)^2 + 3x_2 - (x_2 - 2)^2$

subject to

$$4x_1 + x_2 \leq 20$$

$$x_1 + 4x_2 \leq 20$$

and

$$x_1 \geq 0 \qquad x_2 \geq 0$$

a. Construct tables to show the profit data for each product when the level of its advertising campaign is $x_1 = 0, 1, 2, 2.5, 3, 4, 5$ (for the first product) or $x_2 = 0, 1, 2, 3, 3.5, 4, 5$ (for the second product).

b. Use these profit data to draw rough-hand a smooth profit graph for each product. (Note that these profit graphs start at negative values when $x_1 = 0$ or $x_2 = 0$ because the products would lose money if there is no advertising to support them.)

c. On the profit graph for the first product, draw an approximation of this profit graph by inserting a dashed line segment between the profit at $x_1 = 0$ and $x_1 = 2$, between the profit at $x_1 = 2$ and $x_1 = 4$, and between the profit at $x_1 = 4$ and $x_1 = 5$. Then do the same on the profit graph for the second product with $x_2 = 0, 2, 4, 5$.

E*   d. Use separable programming with the approximation of the profit graphs obtained in part *c* to formulate an approximate linear programming model on a spreadsheet for Jim Matthews's problem.

E*   e. Solve this model. What does this solution say the levels of the advertising campaigns should be? What would the total net profit from the two products be?

E*   f. Repeat parts *c*, *d*, and *e* except using $x_1 = 0, 2, 2.5, 3, 5$ and $x_2 = 0, 3, 3.5, 4, 5$ for the approximations of the profit graphs in part *c*. (These particular

approximations actually lead to the exact optimal solution for Jim Matthews's problem.)

E*   g. Use Excel and its Solver to formulate and solve the original nonlinear programming model directly. Compare with the answers obtained after completing part *f*.

h. Use calculus to find the value of x_1 that maximizes $3x_1 - (x_1 - 1)^2$, the net profit from the first product. Also use calculus to find the value of x_2 that maximizes $3x_2 - (x_2 - 2)^2$, the net profit from the second product. Show that these values satisfy the constraints for the nonlinear programming model. Then compare these values with the answers obtained in parts *f* and *g*.

E* 8.13. Reconsider the portfolio selection example, including its spreadsheet model in Figure 8.11, given in Section 8.3. Note in Table 8.3 that stock 2 has the highest ratio of expected return to price and stock 3 has by far the lowest ratio. Nevertheless, the changing cells (C8:E8) provide an optimal solution that calls for purchasing far more shares of stock 3 than any other and far less shares of stock 2 than any other.

You now are being asked to explore this puzzling phenomenon by using this same spreadsheet model (one is provided in the Excel file for this chapter in your MS Courseware) to check on the effect of changing from the given optimal portfolio to more intuitively appealing portfolios.

a. How would the expected return and risk change if you were to change the optimal portfolio by only purchasing 5 blocks of stock 3?

b. Repeat part *a* if stock 3 were completely eliminated from the portfolio.

c. Because of the price differential, each reduction of 2 blocks of stock 3 purchased enables purchasing 2.5 more blocks of stock 2 without exceeding the budgeted amount to invest. Develop a data table that shows how the expected return and risk vary as the purchases of stocks 3 and 2 are changed by 0, 1, 2, 3, 4, and 5 times these amounts.

8.14.* A stockbroker, Richard Smith, has just received a call from his most important client, Ann Hardy. Ann has $50,000 to invest and wants to use it to purchase two stocks. Stock 1 is a solid blue-chip security with a respectable growth potential and little risk involved. Stock 2 is much more speculative. It is being touted in two investment newsletters as having outstanding growth potential, but also is considered very risky. Ann would like a large return on her investment, but also has considerable aversion to risk. Therefore, she has instructed Richard to analyze what mix of investments in the two stocks would be appropriate for her.

Ann is used to talking in units of thousands of dollars and 1,000-share blocks of stocks. Using these units, the price per block is 20 for stock 1 and 30 for stock 2. After doing some research, Richard has made the following estimates. The expected return per block is 5 for stock 1 and 10 for stock 2. The variance of the return on each block is 4 for stock 1 and 100 for stock 2. The covariance of the return on one block each of the two stocks is 5.

a. Without yet assigning a specific numerical value to the minimum acceptable expected return, formulate a nonlinear programming model in algebraic form for this problem.

E*   *b.* Display this model on a spreadsheet.

E*   *c.* Solve this model for four cases: Minimum acceptable expected return = 13, 14, 15, and 16.

   d. Ann was a statistics major in college and so understands well that the *expected return* and *risk* in this model represent estimates of the *mean* and *variance* of the probability distribution of the return on the corresponding portfolio. The square root of the variance is the standard deviation. Ann uses the notation μ and σ^2 for the mean and variance. She recalls that, for typical probability distributions, the probability is fairly high (about 0.8 or 0.9) that the return will exceed $\mu - \sigma$, and the probability is extremely high (often close to 0.999) that the return will exceed $\mu - 3\sigma$. Calculate $\mu - \sigma$ and $\mu - 3\sigma$ for her for the four portfolios obtained in part *c*. Which portfolio will give her the highest μ among those that also give $\mu - \sigma \geq 0$?

8.15. Reconsider the portfolio selection example given in Section 8.3. A fourth stock (stock 4) now has been found that gives a good balance between expected return and risk. Using the same units as in Table 8.3, its price is 45, its expected return is 18, and its risk is 3. Its joint risk with stocks 1, 2, and 3 is -1, -2, and 0.5, respectively.

   a. Still using a minimum acceptable expected return of 300 ($300,000), formulate the revised nonlinear programming model in algebraic form for this problem.

E*   *b.* Display this model on a spreadsheet.

E*   *c.* Solve the model.

E*   *d.* Develop a revision of the data table shown in Figure 8.12 for this revised problem.

8.16. The following table shows the estimated daily profit from a new product for several of the alternative choices for the production rate.

Production Rate (R)	Profit per Day (P)
0	0
1	$95
2	184
3	255
4	320

Because the profit goes up less than proportionally with the production rate, the management science team analyzing what this production rate (and the production rates of some other products) should be has decided to approximate the profit (P) by a simple *nonlinear function* of the production rate R.

   a. One such approximation is $P = \$100R - \$5R^2$. How closely does this nonlinear function approximate the five values of P given in the table?

   b. Repeat part *a* for the approximation, $P = \$104R - \$6R^2$.

   c. Which of these two nonlinear functions provides the better fit to all the data?

8.17. The management of the Albert Hanson Company is trying to determine the best product mix for two new products.

Because these products would share the same production facilities, the total number of units produced of the two products combined cannot exceed two per hour. Because of uncertainty about how well these products will sell, the profit from producing each product provides decreasing marginal returns as the production rate is increased. In particular, with a production rate of R_1 units per hour, it is estimated that product 1 would provide a profit per hour of $\$200R_1 - \$100R_1^2$. If the production rate of product 2 is R_2 units per hour, its estimated profit per hour would be $\$300R_2 - \$100R_2^2$.

   a. Formulate a nonlinear programming model in algebraic form for determining the product mix that maximizes the total profit per hour.

E*   *b.* Formulate and solve this model on a spreadsheet.

8.18.* One of management's goals in a goal-programming problem is to maintain the company's employment level next year at its current level of 60 full-time equivalents (60 FTEs). Each FTE under this goal is considered three times as serious as each FTE over the goal. Suppose that the *amount over* appears in cell K7 of the spreadsheet model and the *amount under* appears in cell L7. (Both cells are changing cells.) What is the relationship between the coefficients of K7 and L7 in the equation entered into the target cell?

8.19. Management of the Albert Franko Co. has established goals for the market share it wants each of the company's two new products to capture in their respective markets. Specifically, management wants product 1 to capture at least 15 percent of its market and product 2 to capture at least 10 percent of its market. Three advertising campaigns are being planned to try to achieve these market shares. One is targeted directly on the first product. The second targets the second product. The third is intended to enhance the general reputation of the company and its products. Letting x_1, x_2, and x_3 be the amount of money allocated (in millions of dollars) to these respective campaigns, the resulting market share (expressed as a percentage) for the two products are estimated to be

$$\text{Market share for product 1} = 0.5x_1 + 0.2x_3$$

$$\text{Market share for product 2} = 0.3x_2 + 0.2x_3$$

A total of $55 million is available for the three advertising campaigns, but management wants at least $10 million devoted to the third campaign. If both market share goals cannot be achieved, management considers each 1 percent decrease in the market share from the goal to be equally serious for the two products. In this light, management wants to know how to most effectively allocate the available money to the three campaigns.

   a. Describe why this problem is a goal-programming problem by giving quantitative expressions for the goals and the overall objective.

E*   *b.* Formulate and solve this problem as a linear programming model on a spreadsheet.

   c. Interpret this solution to management in its language.

8.20.* The Research and Development Division of the Emax Corporation has developed three new products. A decision now needs to be made on which mix of these products should be produced. Management wants primary consideration given to three factors: total profit, stability in the workforce, and achieving an increase in the company's earnings next year from the $75 million achieved this year. In particular, using the units given in the table below, they want to

$$\text{Maximize} \quad M = P - 6C - 3D$$

where

M = overall measure of performance combining the three factors

P = total (discounted) profit over the life of the new products

C = change (in either direction) in the current level of employment

D = decrease (if any) in next year's earnings from the current year's level

The amount of any increase in earnings does not enter into M, because management is concerned primarily with just achieving some increase to keep the stockholders happy. (It has mixed feelings about a large increase that then would be difficult to surpass in subsequent years.)

The impact of each of the new products (per unit rate of production) on each of these factors is shown in the following table:

E*   *a.* Formulate and solve a spreadsheet model for this problem.

     b. Interpret this solution to management in its language.

	Unit Contribution of Product				
Factor	*1*	*2*	*3*	*Goal*	*(Units)*
Total profit	20	15	25	Maximize	(millions of dollars)
Employment level	6	4	5	= 50	(hundreds of employees)
Earnings next year	8	7	5	≥ 75	(millions of dollars)

8.21. Reconsider the Dewright Co. case study presented in Sections 8.4 and 8.5. After further reflection about the plan recommended by the management science team, management now is asking some what-if questions.

     a. Gary Lang wonders what would happen if the penalty weights in the rightmost column of Table 8.4 were to be changed to 7, 4, 1, and 3, respectively. Would you expect the optimal solution to change? Why?

E*   *b.* Tasha Johnson is wondering what would happen if the total profit goal were to be increased to wanting at least $140 million (without any change in the original penalty weights). Solve the revised model with this change.

E*   *c.* Solve the revised model if both Gary's and Tasha's changes are made.

8.22. Montega is a developing country that has 15,000,000 acres of publicly controlled agricultural land in active use. Its government currently is planning a way to divide this land among three basic crops (labeled 1, 2, and 3) next year. A certain percentage of each of these crops is exported to obtain badly needed foreign capital (dollars), and the rest of each of these crops is used to feed the populace. Raising these crops also provides employment for a significant proportion of the population. Therefore, the main factors to be considered in allocating the land to these crops are (1) the amount of foreign capital generated, (2) the number of citizens fed, and (3) the number of citizens employed in raising these crops. The following table shows how much each 1,000 acres of each crop contributes toward these factors, and the last column

gives the goal established by the government for each of these factors.

	Contribution per 1,000 Acres of Crop			
Factor	*1*	*2*	*3*	*Goal*
Foreign capital	$3,000	$5,000	$4,000	≥ $70,000,000
Citizens fed	150	75	100	≥ 1,750,000
Citizens employed	10	15	12	= 200,000

In evaluating the relative seriousness of *not* achieving these goals, the government has concluded that the following deviations from the goals should be considered *equally undesirable:* (1) each $100 under the foreign-capital goal, (2) each person under the citizens-fed goal, and (3) each deviation of one (in either direction) from the citizens-employed goal.

     a. Describe why this problem is a goal-programming problem by giving quantitative expressions for the goals and the overall objective.

E*   *b.* Formulate and solve this problem as a linear programming model on a spreadsheet.

     c. Interpret this solution to management in its language.

CASE 8.1
CAPACITY CONCERNS

Bentley Hamilton throws the business section of *The New York Times* onto the conference room table and watches as his associates jolt upright in their overstuffed chairs.

Mr. Hamilton wants to make a point.

He throws the front page of the *The Wall Street Journal* on top of *The New York Times* and watches as his associates widen their eyes once heavy with boredom.

Mr. Hamilton wants to make a big point.

He then throws the front page of the *Financial Times* on top of the newspaper pile and watches as his associates dab the fine beads of sweat off their brows.

Mr. Hamilton wants his point indelibly etched into his associates' minds.

"I have just presented you with three leading financial newspapers carrying today's top business story," Mr. Hamilton declares in a tight, angry voice. "My dear associates, our company is going to hell in a hand basket! Shall I read you the headlines? From *The New York Times,* 'CommuniCorp stock drops to lowest in 52 weeks.' From *The Wall Street Journal,* 'CommuniCorp loses 25 percent of the pager market in only one year.' Oh, and my favorite, from the *Financial Times,* 'CommuniCorp cannot CommuniCate: CommuniCorp stock drops because of internal communications disarray.' How did our company fall into such dire straits?"

Mr. Hamilton throws a transparency showing a line sloping slightly upward onto the overhead projector. "This is a graph of our productivity over the last 12 months. As you can see from the graph, productivity in our pager production facility has increased steadily over the last year. Clearly, productivity is not the cause of our problem."

Mr. Hamilton throws a second transparency showing a line sloping steeply upward onto the overhead projector. "This is a graph of our missed or late orders over the last 12 months." Mr. Hamilton hears an audible gasp from his associates. "As you can see from the graph, our missed or late orders have increased steadily and significantly over the past 12 months. I think this trend explains why we have been losing market share, causing our stock to drop to its lowest level in 52 weeks. We have angered and lost the business of retailers, our customers who depend upon on-time deliveries to meet the demand of consumers."

"Why have we missed our delivery dates when our productivity level should have allowed us to fill all orders?" Mr. Hamilton asks. "I called several departments to ask this question."

"It turns out that we have been producing pagers for the hell of it!" Mr. Hamilton says in disbelief. "The marketing and sales departments do not communicate with the manufacturing department, so manufacturing executives do not know what pagers to produce to fill orders. The manufacturing executives want to keep the plant running, so they produce pagers regardless of whether the pagers have been ordered. Finished pagers are sent to the warehouse, but marketing and sales executives do not know the number and styles of pagers in the warehouse. They try to communicate with warehouse executives to determine if the pagers in inventory can fill the orders, but they rarely receive answers to their questions."

Mr. Hamilton pauses and looks directly at his associates. "Ladies and gentlemen, it seems to me that we have a serious in-

ternal communications problem. I intend to correct this problem immediately. I want to begin by installing a companywide computer network to ensure that all departments have access to critical documents and are able to easily communicate with each other through e-mail. Because this intranet will represent a large change from the current communications infrastructure, I expect some bugs in the system and some resistance from employees. I therefore want to phase in the installation of the intranet."

Mr. Hamilton passes the following timeline and requirements chart to his associates (IN = intranet).

	Month 1	Month 2	Month 3	Month 4	Month 5
IN education					
		Install IN in sales			
			Install IN in manufacturing		
				Install IN in warehouse	
					Install IN in marketing

Department	Number of Employees
Sales	60
Manufacturing	200
Warehouse	30
Marketing	75

Mr. Hamilton proceeds to explain the timeline and requirements chart. "In the first month, I do not want to bring any department onto the intranet; I simply want to disseminate information about it and get buy-in from employees. In the second month, I want to bring the sales department onto the intranet since the sales department receives all critical information from customers. In the third month, I want to bring the manufacturing department onto the intranet. In the fourth month, I want to install the intranet at the warehouse, and in the fifth and final month, I want to bring the marketing department onto the intranet. The requirements chart under the timeline lists the number of employees requiring access to the intranet in each department."

Mr. Hamilton turns to Emily Jones, the head of Corporate Information Management. "I need your help in planning for the installation of the intranet. Specifically, the company needs to purchase servers for the internal network. Employees will connect to company servers and download information to their own desktop computers."

Mr. Hamilton passes Emily the following chart detailing the types of servers available, the number of employees each server supports, and the cost of each server.

Type of Server	Number of Employees Server Supports	Cost of Server
Standard Intel Pentium PC	Up to 30 Employees	$2,500
Enhanced Intel Pentium PC	Up to 80 Employees	5,000
SGI Workstation	Up to 200 Employees	10,000
Sun Workstation	Up to 2,000 Employees	25,000

"Emily, I need you to decide what servers to purchase and when to purchase them to minimize cost and to ensure that the company possesses enough server capacity to follow the intranet implementation timeline," Mr. Hamilton says. "For example, you may decide to buy one large server during the first month to support all employees, or buy several small servers during the first month to support all employees, or buy one small server each month to support each new group of employees gaining access to the intranet."

"There are several factors that complicate your decision," Mr. Hamilton continues. "Two server manufacturers are willing to offer discounts to CommuniCorp. SGI is willing to give you a discount of 10 percent off each server purchased, but only if you purchase servers in the first or second month. Sun is willing to give you a 25 percent discount off all servers purchased in the first two months. You are also limited in the amount of money you can spend during the first month. CommuniCorp has already allocated much of the budget for the next two months, so you only have a total of $9,500 available to purchase servers in months 1 and 2. Finally, the manufacturing department requires at least one of the three more powerful servers. Have your decision on my desk at the end of the week."

a. Emily first decides to evaluate the number and type of servers to purchase on a month-to-month basis. For each month, formulate an integer programming problem to determine which servers Emily should purchase in that month to minimize costs in that month and support the new users. How many and which types of servers should she purchase in each month? How much is the total cost of the plan?

b. Emily realizes that she could perhaps achieve savings if she bought a larger server in the initial months to support users in the final months. She therefore decides to evaluate the number and type of servers to purchase over the entire planning period. Formulate an integer programming problem to determine which servers Emily should purchase in which months to minimize total cost and support all new users. How many and which types of servers should she purchase in each month? How much is the total cost of the plan?

c. Why is the answer using the first method different from that using the second method?

d. Are there other costs for which Emily is not accounting in her problem formulation? If so, what are they?

e. What further concerns might the various departments of CommuniCorp have regarding the intranet?

CASE 8.2
INTERNATIONAL INVESTMENTS

Charles Rosen relaxes in a plush, overstuffed recliner by the fire, enjoying the final vestiges of his week-long winter vacation. As a financial analyst working for a large investment firm in Germany, Charles has very few occasions to enjoy these private moments since he is generally catching red-eye flights around the world to evaluate various investment opportunities. Charles pats the loyal golden retriever lying at his feet and takes a swig of brandy, enjoying the warmth of the liquid. He sighs and realizes that he must begin attending to his own financial matters while he still has the time during the holiday. He opens a folder placed conspicuously on the top of a large stack of papers. The folder contains information about an investment Charles made when he graduated from college four years ago . . .

Charles remembers his graduation day fondly. He obtained a degree in business administration and was full of investment ideas that were born while he had been daydreaming in his numerous finance classes. Charles maintained a well-paying job throughout college, and he was able to save a large portion of the college fund that his parents had invested for him.

Upon graduation, Charles decided that he should transfer the college funds to a more lucrative investment opportunity. Since he had signed to work in Germany, he evaluated investment opportunities in that country. Ultimately, he decided to invest 30,000 German marks (DM) in so-called B bonds that would mature in seven years. Charles purchased the bonds just four years ago last week (in early January of what will be called the "first year" in this discussion). He considered the bonds an excellent investment opportunity since they offered high interest rates (see Table 1) that would rise over the subsequent seven years and because he could sell the bonds whenever he wanted after the first year. He calculated the amount that he would be paid if he sold bonds originally worth DM 100 on the last day of any of the seven years (see Table 2). The amount paid included the principle plus the interest. For example, if he sold bonds originally worth DM 100 on December 31 of the sixth year, he would be paid DM 163.51 (the principle is DM 100 and the interest is DM 63.51).

TABLE 1   Interest Rates Over the Seven Years

Year	Interest Rate	Annual Percentage Yield
1	7.50%	7.50%
2	8.50	8.00
3	8.50	8.17
4	8.75	8.31
5	9.00	8.45
6	9.00	8.54
7	9.00	8.61

TABLE 2   Total Return on 100 DM

Year	DM
1	107.50
2	116.64
3	126.55
4	137.62
5	150.01
6	163.51
7	178.23

Charles did not sell any of the bonds during the first four years. Last year, however, the German federal government introduced a capital gains tax on interest income. The German government designated that the first DM 6,100 a single individual earns in interest per year would be tax-free. Any interest income beyond DM 6,100 would be taxed at a rate of 30 percent. For example, if Charles earned interest income of DM 10,100, he would be required to pay 30 percent of DM 4,000 (DM 10,100 − DM 6,100) in taxes, or DM 1,200. His after-tax income would therefore be DM 8,900.

Because of the new tax implemented last year, Charles has decided to reevaluate the investment. He knows that the new tax affects his potential return on the B bonds, but he also knows that most likely a strategy exists for maximizing his return on the bonds. He might be able to decrease the tax he has to pay on interest income by selling portions of his bonds in different years. Charles considers his strategy viable because the government requires investors to pay taxes on interest income only when they sell their B bonds. For example, if Charles were to sell one-third of his B bonds on December 31 of the sixth year, he would have to pay taxes on the interest income of DM (6,351 − 6,100).

Charles asks himself several questions. Should he keep all the bonds until the end of the seventh year? If so, he would earn 0.7823 times DM 30,000 in interest income, but he would have to pay very substantial taxes for that year. Considering these tax payments, Charles wonders if he should sell a portion of the bonds at the end of this year (the fifth year) and at the end of next year?

If Charles sells his bonds, his alternative investment opportunities are limited. He could purchase a certificate of deposit (CD) paying 4.0 percent interest, so he investigates this alternative. He meets with an investment advisor from the local branch of a bank, and the advisor tells him to keep the B bonds until the end of the

seventh year. She argues that even if he had to pay 30 percent in taxes on the 9.00 percent rate of interest that the B bonds would be paying in their last year (see Table 1), this strategy would still result in a net rate of 6.30 percent interest, which is much better than the 4.0 percent interest he could obtain on a CD.

Charles concludes that he would make all his transactions on December 31, regardless of the year. Also, since he intends to attend business school in the United States in the fall of the seventh year and plans to pay his tuition for his second, third, and fourth semester with his investment, he does not plan to keep his money in Germany beyond December 31 of the seventh year.

(For the first three parts, assume that if Charles sells a portion of his bonds, he will put the money under his mattress earning zero percent interest. For the subsequent parts, assume that he could invest the proceeds of the bonds in the certificate of deposit.)

a. Identify one of the four techniques described in this chapter that is applicable to this problem, and then formulate a model of this kind to be used in the following parts.

b. What is the optimal investment strategy for Charles?

c. What is fundamentally wrong with the advice Charles got from the investment advisor at the bank?

d. Now that Charles is considering investing in the certificate of deposit, what is his optimal investment strategy?

e. What would his optimal investment strategy for the fifth, sixth, and seventh years have been if he had originally invested DM 50,000?

f. Charles and his fiancée have been planning to get married after his first year in business school. However, Charles learns that for married couples, the tax-free amount of interest earnings each year is DM 12,200. How much money could Charles save on his DM 30,000 investment by getting married this year (the fifth year for his investment)?

g. Due to a recession in Germany, interest rates are low and are expected to remain low. However, since the American economy is booming, interest rates are expected to rise in the United States. A rise in interest rates would lead to a rise of the dollar in comparison to the mark. Analysts at Charles' investment bank expect the dollar to remain at the current exchange rate of DM 1.50 per dollar for the fifth year and then to rise to DM 1.80 per dollar by the end of the seventh year. Therefore, Charles is considering investing at the beginning of the sixth year in a two-year American municipal bond paying 3.6 percent tax-exempt interest to help pay tuition. How much money should he plan to convert into dollars by selling B bonds for this investment?

CASE 8.3
SAVVY STOCK SELECTION

Ever since the day she took her first economics class in high school, Lydia wondered about the financial practices of her parents. They worked very hard to earn enough money to live a comfortable middle-class life, but they never made their money work for them. They simply deposited their hard-earned paychecks in savings accounts earning a nominal amount of interest. (Fortunately, there always was enough money available when it came time to pay her college bills.) She promised herself that when she became an adult, she would not follow the same financially conservative practices as her parents.

And Lydia kept this promise. She took every available finance course in her business program at college. Since landing a coveted job on Wall Street upon graduation, she begins every morning by watching the CNN financial reports. She plays investment games on the World Wide Web, finding portfolios that maximize her return while minimizing her risk. And she reads *The Wall Street Journal* and *Financial Times*.

Lydia also reads the investment advice columns of the financial magazines. She decides to follow the current advice given by her two favorite columnists. In his monthly column, editor

Jonathan Taylor recommends three stocks that he believes will rise far above market average. In addition, the well-known mutual fund guru Donna Carter advocates the purchase of three more stocks that she thinks will outperform the market over the next year.

Bigbell (ticker symbol on the stock exchange: BB), one of the nation's largest telecommunications companies, trades at a price–earnings ratio well below market average. Huge investments over the last eight months have depressed earnings considerably. However, with their new cutting-edge technology, the company is expected to significantly raise their profit margins. Taylor predicts that the stock will rise from its current price of $60 per share to $72 per share within the next year.

Lotsofplace (LOP) is one of the leading hard drive manufacturers in the world. The industry recently underwent major consolidation, as fierce price wars over the last few years were followed by many competitors going bankrupt or being bought by Lotsofplace and its competitors. Due to reduced competition in the hard drive market, revenues and earnings are expected to rise considerably over the next year. Taylor predicts a one-year increase of 42 percent in the stock of Lotsofplace from the current price of $127 per share.

Internetlife (ILI) has survived the many up and downs of Internet companies. With the next Internet frenzy just around the corner, Taylor expects a doubling of this company's stock price from $4 to $8 within a year.

Healthtomorrow (HEAL) is a leading biotechnology company that is about to get approval for several new drugs from the Food and Drug Administration, which will help earnings to grow 20 percent over the next few years. In particular, a new drug to significantly reduce the risk of heart attacks is supposed to reap huge profits. Also, due to several new great-tasting medications for children, the company has been able to build an excellent image in the media. This public relations coup will surely have positive effects for the sale of its over-the-counter medications. Carter is convinced that the stock will rise from $50 to $75 per share within a year.

Quicky (QUI) is a fast-food chain that has been vastly expanding its network of restaurants all over the United States. Carter has followed this company closely since it went public some 15 years ago when it only had a few dozen restaurants on the West Coast of the United States. Since then the company has expanded, and it now has restaurants in every state. Due to its emphasis on healthy foods, it is capturing a growing market share. Carter believes that the stock will continue to perform well-above market average for an increase of 46 percent in one year from its current stock price of $150.

Automobile Alliance (AUA) is a leading car manufacturer from the Detroit area that just recently introduced two new models. These models show very strong initial sales, and therefore the company's stock is predicted to rise from $20 to $26 over the next year.

On the World Wide Web, Lydia found data about the risk involved in the stocks of these companies. The historical variances of return of the six stocks and their covariances are shown below.

Company	BB	LOP	ILI	HEAL	QUI	AUA
Variance	0.032	0.1	0.333	0.125	0.065	0.08

Covariances	LOP	ILI	HEAL	QUI	AUA
BB	0.005	0.03	−0.031	−0.027	0.01
LOP		0.085	−0.07	−0.05	0.02
ILI			−0.11	−0.02	0.042
HEAL				0.05	−0.06
QUI					−0.02

a. At first, Lydia wants to ignore the risk of all the investments. Given this strategy, what is her optimal investment portfolio; that is, what fraction of her money should she invest in each of the six different stocks? What is the total risk of her portfolio?

b. Lydia decides that she doesn't want to invest more than 40 percent in any individual stock. While still ignoring risk, what is her new optimal investment portfolio? What is the total risk of her new portfolio?

c. Now Lydia wants to take into account the risk of her investment opportunities. Identify one of the four techniques described in this chapter that is applicable to her problem, and then formulate a model of this kind to be used in the following parts.

d. What fractions of her money should Lydia put into the various stocks if she decides to maximize the expected return minus beta times the risk of her investment for beta = 0.25?

e. Lydia recently received a bonus at work, $15,000 after taxes, that she wishes to invest. For the investment policy in part *d,* how much money does she invest in the various stocks? How many shares of each stock does she buy?

f. How does the solution in part *e* change if beta = 0.5? If beta = 1? If beta = 2?

g. Give an intuitive explanation for the change in the expected return and the risk in part *f* as beta changes.

h. Lydia wants to ensure that she receives an expected return of at least 35 percent. She wants to reach this goal at minimum risk. What investment portfolio allows her to do that?

i. What is the minimum risk Lydia can achieve if she wants an expected return of at least 25 percent? Of at least 40 percent?

j. Do you see any problems or disadvantages with Lydia's approach to her investment strategy?

CASE 8.4
A CURE FOR CUBA

Fulgencio Batista led Cuba with a cold heart and iron fist—greedily stealing from poor citizens, capriciously ruling the Cuban population that looked to him for guidance, and violently murdering the innocent critics of his politics. In 1958, tired of watching his fellow Cubans suffer from corruption and tyranny, Fidel Castro led a guerrilla attack against the Batista regime and wrested power from Batista in January 1959. Cubans, along with members of the international community, believed that political and economic freedom had finally triumphed on the island. The next two years showed, however, that Castro was leading a Communist dictatorship—killing his political opponents and nationalizing all privately held assets. The United States responded to Castro's leadership in 1961 by invoking a trade embargo against Cuba. The embargo forbade any country from selling Cuban products in the United States and forbade businesses from selling American products to Cuba. Cubans did not feel the true impact of the embargo until 1989 when the Soviet economy collapsed. Prior to the disintegration of the Soviet Union, Cuba had received an average of $5 billion in annual economic assistance from the Soviet Union. With the disappearance of the economy that Cuba had almost exclusively depended upon for trade, Cubans had few avenues from which to purchase food, clothes, and medicine. The avenues narrowed even further when the United States passed the Torricelli Act in 1992 that forbade American subsidiaries in third countries from doing business with Cuba that had been worth a total of $700 million annually.

Since 1989, the Cuban economy has certainly felt the impact from decades of frozen trade. Today poverty ravages the island of Cuba. Families do not have money to purchase bare necessities, such as food, milk, and clothing. Children die from malnutrition or exposure. Disease infects the island because medicine is unavailable. Optical neuritis, tuberculosis, pneumonia, and influenza run rampant among the population.

Few Americans hold sympathy for Cuba, but Robert Baker, director of Helping Hand, leads a handful of tender souls on Capitol Hill who cannot bear to see politics destroy so many human lives. His organization distributes humanitarian aid annually to needy countries around the world. Mr. Baker recognizes the dire situation in Cuba, and he wants to allocate aid to Cuba for the coming year.

Mr. Baker wants to send numerous aid packages to Cuban citizens. Three different types of packages are available. The basic package contains only food, such as grain and powdered milk. Each basic package costs $300, weighs 120 pounds, and aids 30 people. The advanced package contains food and clothing, such as blankets and fabrics. Each advanced package costs $350, weighs 180 pounds, and aids 35 people. The supreme package contains food, clothing, and medicine. Each supreme package costs $720, weighs 220 pounds, and aids 54 people.

Mr. Baker has several goals he wants to achieve when deciding upon the number and types of aid packages to allocate to Cuba. First, he wants to aid at least 20 percent of Cuba's 11 million citizens. Second, because disease runs rampant among the Cuban population, he wants at least 30 percent of the aid packages sent to Cuba to be the supreme packages. Third, because he knows many other nations also require humanitarian aid, he wants to keep the cost of aiding Cuba below $20 million.

Mr. Baker places different levels of importance on his three goals. He believes the most important goal is keeping costs

down since low costs mean that his organization is able to aid a larger number of needy nations. He decides to penalize his plan by one point for every $1 million above his $20 million goal. He believes the second most important goal is ensuring that at least 3,000 of the aid packages sent to Cuba are supreme packages since he does not want to see an epidemic develop and completely destroy the Cuban population. He decides to penalize his plan by one point for every 1,000 packages below his goal of 3,000 packages. Finally, he believes the least important goal is reaching at least 20 percent of the population since he would rather give a smaller number of individuals all they need to thrive instead of a larger number of individuals only some of what they need to thrive. He therefore decides to penalize his plan by seven points for every 100,000 people below his 20 percent goal.

Mr. Baker realizes that he has certain limitations on the aid packages that he delivers to Cuba. Each type of package is approximately the same size, and because only a limited number of cargo flights from the United States are allowed into Cuba, he is only able to send a maximum of 40,000 packages. Along with a size limitation, he also encounters a weight restriction. He cannot ship more that six million pounds of cargo. Finally, he has a safety restriction. When sending medicine, he needs to ensure that the Cubans know how to use the medicine properly. Therefore, for every 100 supreme packages, Mr. Baker must send one doctor to Cuba at a cost of $33,000 per doctor.

a. Identify one of the four techniques described in this chapter that is applicable to Mr. Baker's problem.

b. How many basic, advanced, and supreme packages should Mr. Baker send to Cuba?

c. Mr. Baker reevaluates the levels of importance he places on each of the three goals. To sell his efforts to potential donors, he must show that his program is effective. Donors generally judge the effectiveness of a program on the number of people reached by aid packages. Mr. Baker therefore decides that he must put more importance on the goal of reaching at least 20 percent of the population. He decides to penalize his plan by 10 points for every half a percentage point below his 20 percent goal. The penalties for his other two goals remain the same. Under this scenario, how many basic, advanced, and supreme packages should Mr. Baker send to Cuba? How sensitive is the plan to changes in the penalty weights?

d. Mr. Baker realizes that sending more doctors along with the supreme packages will improve the proper use and distribution of the packages' contents, which in turn will increase the effectiveness of the program. He therefore decides to send one doctor with every 75 supreme packages. The penalties for the goals remain the same as in part c. Under this scenario, how many basic, advanced, and supreme packages should Mr. Baker send to Cuba?

e. The aid budget is cut, and Mr. Baker learns that he definitely cannot allocate more than $20 million in aid to Cuba. Due to the budget cut, Mr. Baker decides to stay with his original policy of sending one doctor with every 100 supreme packages. How many basic, advanced, and supreme packages should Mr. Baker send to Cuba assuming that the penalties for not meeting the other two goals remain the same as in part b?

USING BINARY INTEGER PROGRAMMING TO DEAL WITH YES-OR-NO DECISIONS

Section 8.1 introduced *integer programming,* which is just linear programming except for the one additional restriction that certain decision variables (perhaps all of them) must have an *integer value* (0, 1, 2, . . .). Thus, the mathematical model for an integer programming problem is a linear programming model except for this one additional restriction. Integer programming is very useful for dealing with applications where it is necessary to assign people, machines, or vehicles to activities in integer quantities.

Section 8.1 also pointed out that many applications of integer programming further restrict the integer variables to just two values, 0 or 1. Variables whose only possible values are 0 and 1 are called **binary variables.** Thus, **binary integer programming** problems are those where all the variables restricted to integer values are further restricted to be binary variables. (We hereafter will use the abbreviation **BIP** for *binary integer programming.*)

Such a problem where *all* the variables are binary variables is referred to as a **pure BIP problem.** It also is quite common to have a *mixture* of variables, where some are binary variables and the rest are so-called *continuous variables* that have no special restriction (as in linear programming). A problem of this type is called a **mixed BIP problem.**

Binary variables are ideally suited to be the decision variables when dealing with **yes-or-no decisions.** A yes-or-no decision arises when a particular option is being considered and the only two possible choices are yes, go ahead with this option, or no, decline this option. The binary decision variable then is assigned a value of 1 for choosing yes and a value of 0 for choosing no.

A BIP problem considers many options simultaneously, with a binary decision variable for each one. The overall objective is to choose the best combination of options to approve.

You will see in this chapter that both pure and mixed BIP problems arise with considerable frequency in a wide variety of important applications. We begin with a case study and then present a survey of some of the applications. The third and fourth sections focus on how to formulate BIP models to fit such applications.

In addition, a supplement to this chapter entitled Some Perspectives on Solving Binary Integer Programming Problems is provided on the CD-ROM. The algorithms available for solving BIP problems are not nearly as efficient as those for linear programming, so this supplement discusses some of the difficulties and pitfalls involved in solving large BIP problems. One option with any integer programming problem is to use a linear programming approximation (by ignoring the integer constraints) and then rounding the optimal solution for this approximation to integer values. As discussed in Section 8.1, this is a reasonable option in some cases but not in others. The supplement emphasizes that this is a particularly dangerous shortcut with BIP problems.

9.1 A Case Study: The California Manufacturing Co. Problem

"OK, Steve, here is the situation. With our growing business, we are strongly considering building a new factory. Maybe even two. The factory needs to be close to a large, skilled

labor force, so we are looking at Los Angeles and San Francisco as the potential sites. We also are considering building one new warehouse. Not more than one. This warehouse would make sense in saving shipping costs only if it is in the same city as the new factory. Either Los Angeles or San Francisco. If we decide not to build a new factory at all, we definitely don't want the warehouse either. Is this clear, so far?"

"Yes, Armando, I understand," Steve Chan responds. "What are your criteria for making these decisions?"

"Well, all the other members of top management have joined me in addressing this issue, " Armando Ortega replies. "We have concluded that these two potential sites are very comparable on nonfinancial grounds. Therefore, we feel that these decisions should be based mainly on financial considerations. We have $10 million of capital available for this expansion and we want it to go as far as possible in improving our bottom line. Which feasible combination of investments in factories and warehouses in which locations will be most profitable for the company in the long run? In your language, we want to maximize the total net present value of these investments."

"That's very clear. It sounds like a classical management science problem."

"That's why I called you in, Steve. I would like you to conduct a quick management science study to determine the most profitable combination of investments. I need your input within the next couple weeks. Can you do it?"

"Well, Armando, as usual, the one question is whether we can gather all the necessary data that quickly. We'll need to get good estimates of the net present value of each of the possible investments. I'll need a lot of help in digging out that information."

"I thought you would say that. I already have my staff working hard on developing these estimates. I can get you together with them this afternoon."

"Great. I'll get right on it."

As president of the California Manufacturing Company, Armando Ortega has had many similar conversations in the past with Steve Chan, the company's top management scientist. Armando is confident that Steve will come through for him again.

Background

The California Manufacturing Company is a diversified company with several factories and warehouses throughout California, but none yet in Los Angeles or San Francisco. Because the company is enjoying increasing sales and earnings, management feels that the time may be ripe to expand into one or both of those prime locations. A basic issue is whether to build a new factory in either Los Angeles or San Francisco, or perhaps even in both cities. Management also is considering building at most one new warehouse, but will restrict the choice of location to a city where a new factory is being built.

The decisions to be made are listed in the second column of Table 9.1 in the form of yes-or-no questions. In each case, giving an answer of yes to the question corresponds to the decision to make the investment to build the indicated facility (a factory or a warehouse) in the indicated location (Los Angeles or San Francisco). The capital required for the investment is given in the rightmost column, where the total capital available for all the investments is $10 million. (Note that this amount is inadequate for some of the combinations of investments.) The fourth column shows the estimated *net present value* (net long-run profit considering the time value of money) if the corresponding investment is made. (The net present value is 0 if the investment is not made.) Much of the work of Steve Chan's man-

TABLE 9.1   Data for the California Manufacturing Co. Problem

Decision Number	Yes-or-No Question	Decision Variable	Net Present Value (Millions)	Capital Required (Millions)
1	Build a factory in Los Angeles?	x_1	$9	$6
2	Build a factory in San Francisco?	x_2	5	3
3	Build a warehouse in Los Angeles?	x_3	6	5
4	Build a warehouse in San Francisco?	x_4	4	2

Capital available: $10 million

agement science study (with substantial help from the president's staff) goes into developing these estimates of the net present values. As specified by the company's president, Armando Ortega, the objective now is to find the feasible combination of investments that maximizes the total net present value.

Introducing Binary Decision Variables for the Yes-or-No Decisions

As summarized in the second column of Table 9.1, the problem facing management is to make four interrelated *yes-or-no decisions.* To formulate a mathematical model for this problem, Steve Chan needs to introduce a decision variable for each of these decisions. Since each decision has just two alternatives, choose yes or choose no, the corresponding decision variable only needs to have two values (one for each alternative). Therefore, Steve uses a *binary variable,* whose only possible values are 0 and 1, where 1 corresponds to the decision to choose yes and 0 corresponds to choosing no.

These decision variables are shown in the second column of Table 9.2. The final two columns give the interpretation of a value of 1 and 0, respectively.

Dealing with Interrelationships between the Decisions

Recall that management wants no more than one new warehouse to be built. In terms of the corresponding decision variables, x_3 and x_4, this means that no more than one of these variables is allowed to have the value 1. Therefore, these variables must satisfy the constraint

$$x_3 + x_4 \leq 1$$

as part of the mathematical model for the problem.

These two alternatives (build a warehouse in Los Angeles or build a warehouse in San Francisco) are referred to as **mutually exclusive alternatives** because choosing one of these alternatives excludes choosing the other. Groups of two or more mutually exclusive alternatives arise commonly in BIP problems. For each such group where at most one of the alternatives can be chosen, the constraint on the corresponding binary decision variables has the form shown above, namely, the sum of these variables must be *less than or equal to* 1. For some groups of mutually exclusive alternatives, management will exclude the possibility of choosing *none* of the alternatives, in which case the constraint will set the sum of the corresponding binary decision variables *equal* to 1.

The California Manufacturing Co. problem also has another important kind of restriction. Management will allow a warehouse to be built in a particular city only if a factory also is being built in that city. For example, consider the situation for Los Angeles (LA).

If decide no, do not build a factory in LA (i.e., if choose $x_1 = 0$),

then cannot build a warehouse in LA (i.e., must choose $x_3 = 0$).

If decide yes, do build a factory in LA (i.e., if choose $x_1 = 1$),

then can either build a warehouse in LA or not (i.e., can choose either $x_3 = 1$ or 0).

How can these interrelationships between the factory and warehouse decisions for LA be expressed in a constraint for a mathematical model? The key is to note that, for either value of x_1, the permissible value or values of x_3 are less than or equal to x_1. Since x_1 and x_3 are binary variables, the constraint

$$x_3 \leq x_1$$

forces x_3 to take on a permissible value given the value of x_1.

TABLE 9.2 Binary Decision Variables for the California Manufacturing Co. Problem

Decision Number	Decision Variable	Possible Value	Interpretation of a Value of 1	Interpretation of a Value of 0
1	x_1	0 or 1	Build a factory in Los Angeles	Do not build this factory
2	x_2	0 or 1	Build a factory in San Francisco	Do not build this factory
3	x_3	0 or 1	Build a warehouse in Los Angeles	Do not build this warehouse
4	x_4	0 or 1	Build a warehouse in San Francisco	Do not build this warehouse

Exactly the same reasoning leads to

$$x_4 \le x_2$$

as the corresponding constraint for San Francisco. Just as for Los Angeles, this constraint forces having no warehouse in San Francisco ($x_4 = 0$) if a factory will not be built there ($x_2 = 0$), whereas going ahead with the factory there ($x_2 = 1$) leaves open the decision on the warehouse there ($x_4 = 0$ or 1).

For either city, the warehouse decision is referred to as a **contingent decision,** because the decision depends on a prior decision regarding whether to build a factory there. In general, one yes-or-no decision is said to be contingent on another yes-or-no decision if it is allowed to be yes *only if* the other is yes. As above, the mathematical constraint expressing this relationship requires that the binary variable for the former decision must be less than or equal to the binary variable for the latter decision.

The rightmost column of Table 9.1 reveals one more interrelationship between the four decisions, namely, that the amount of capital expended on the four facilities under consideration cannot exceed the amount available ($10 million). Using units of millions of dollars, the amount of capital expended will be

$$6x_1 + 3x_2 + 5x_3 + 2x_4$$

since the amount shown in the table for any particular facility is expended only if the facility is built (i.e., only if the corresponding decision variable has a value of 1 rather than 0). Therefore, the constraint expressing this interrelationship is

$$6x_1 + 3x_2 + 5x_3 + 2x_4 \le 10$$

The BIP Model

As indicated by Armando Ortega in his conversation with Steve Chan, management's objective is to find the feasible combination of investments that *maximizes* the total net present value of these investments. Thus, the value of the objective function should be

$$\text{NPV} = \text{total net present value}$$

If the investment is made to build a particular facility (so that the corresponding decision variable has a value of 1), the estimated net present value from that investment is given in the fourth column of Table 9.1. If the investment is not made (so the decision variable equals 0), the net present value is 0. Therefore, continuing to use units of millions of dollars,

$$\text{NPV} = 9x_1 + 5x_2 + 6x_3 + 4x_4$$

is the quantity to enter into the target cell to be maximized.

Incorporating the constraints developed in the preceding subsection, the complete BIP model then is shown in Figure 9.1. The format is basically the same as for linear programming models. The one key difference arises when using the Solver dialogue box. Each of the decision variables (cells C9, E9:F9, and H9) is constrained to be binary. This is accomplished in the Add Constraint dialogue box by choosing the range of variables as the left-hand side, and then choosing bin from the pop-up menu. [Note that earlier versions of Excel do not include the bin option. In these versions, binary variables can still be specified by constraining the variables to be integer (by choosing int), and then adding two further sets of constraints that specify that each of these variables must be greater than or equal to zero *and* less than or equal to one.] Also note that the contingent-decision constraints are incorporated into the model as C9 ≤ E9 and F9 ≤ H9. For convenience, the equations entered into the output cells in column I use a SUMPRODUCT function that include columns D and G because the blanks or ≤ signs in these columns are interpreted as zeroes by the Solver.

The Excel Solver gives the optimal solution shown in row 9 of the spreadsheet, namely, build factories in *both* Los Angeles and San Francisco, but do not build any warehouses. The target cell (I8) indicates that the total net present value from building these two factories is estimated to be $14 million.

Steve Chan's report with this recommended plan was delivered to Armando Ortega within the two-week deadline. After careful consideration by Armando and other members of top management, the decision was made to proceed with this plan.

FIGURE 9.1

A spreadsheet formulation of the BIP model for the California Manufacturing Co. case study, where row 9 gives the optimal solution obtained by using the Excel Solver.

	A	B	C	D	E	F	G	H	I	J	K
1		California Manufacturing Co. Facility Location Problem									
2											
3			Yes-or-No Question								
4			Warehouse		Factory	Warehouse		Factory			Right-Hand
5		Constraint	in LA?		in LA?	in SF?		in SF?	Totals		Side
6		Capital ($millions)	5		6	2		3	9	≤	10
7		≤ 1 Warehouse	1		0	1		0	0	≤	1
8		NPV ($millions)	6		9	4		5	14		
9		Solution	0	≤	1	0	≤	1			

Solver Parameters

Set Target Cell: $I$8

Equal To: ● Max ○ Min ○
By Changing Cells:

$C$9,$E$9:$F$9,$H$9

Subject to the Constraints:

$C$9 <= $E$9
$C$9 = binary
$E$9:$F$9 = binary
$F$9 <= $H$9
$H$9 = binary
$I$6:$I$7 <= $K$6:$K$7

	I
6	=SUMPRODUCT(C6:H6,C9:H9)
7	=SUMPRODUCT(C7:H7,C9:H9)
8	=SUMPRODUCT(C8:H8,C9:H9)

Solver Options

☑ Assume Linear Model
☑ Assume Non-Negative

Review Questions

1. What are the four interrelated decisions that need to be made by the management of the California Management Co.?
2. Why are binary decision variables appropriate to represent these decisions?
3. What is the objective specified by management for this problem?
4. What are the mutually exclusive alternatives in this problem? What is the form of the resulting constraint in the BIP model?
5. What are the contingent decisions in this problem? For each one, what is the form of the resulting constraint in the BIP model?

9.2 Some Other Applications

Just as in the California Manufacturing Co. case study, managers frequently must face yes-or-no decisions. Therefore, binary integer programming (BIP) is widely used to aid in these decisions.

We now will introduce various types of yes-or-no decisions. We also will mention some examples of actual applications where binary integer programming was used to address these decisions.

Each of these applications is fully described in an article in the journal *Interfaces*. In each case, we will mention the specific issue in which the article appears in case you want to read further.

Capital Budgeting with Fixed Investment Proposals

In Section 3.2, the example of the Think-Big Development Co. investing in commercial real-estate development projects illustrates how linear programming can be used to make capital budgeting decisions about how much to invest in various projects. However, as the California Manufacturing Co. case study demonstrates, some capital budgeting decisions do not involve *how much* to invest but, rather, *whether* to invest a fixed amount. Specifically, the four decisions in the case study were whether to invest the fixed amount of capital required to build a certain kind of facility (factory or warehouse) in a certain location (Los Angeles or San Francisco).

Management often must face decisions about whether to make fixed investments (those where the amount of capital required has been fixed in advance). Should we acquire a certain subsidiary being spun off by another company? Should we purchase a certain source of raw materials? Should we add a new production line to produce a certain input item ourselves rather than continuing to obtain it from a supplier?

In general, capital budgeting decisions about fixed investments are yes-or-no decisions of the following type.

Each yes-or-no decision:

Should we make a certain fixed investment?

$$\text{Its decision variable} = \begin{cases} 1, & \text{if yes} \\ 0, & \text{if no} \end{cases}$$

The July–August 1990 issue of *Interfaces* describes how the **Turkish Petroleum Refineries Corporation** used BIP to analyze capital investments worth tens of millions of dollars to expand refinery capacity and conserve energy.

A rather different example that still falls somewhat into this category is described in the January–February 1997 issue of *Interfaces*. A major management science study was conducted for the top military management of the **South African National Defense Force** to upgrade its capabilities with a smaller budget. The "investments" under consideration in this case were acquisition costs and ongoing expenses that would be required to provide specific types of military capabilities. A mixed BIP model was formulated to choose those specific capabilities that would maximize the overall effectiveness of the Defense Force while satisfying a budget constraint. The model had over 16,000 variables (including 256 binary variables) and over 5,000 functional constraints. The resulting optimization of the size and shape of the defense force provided savings of over $1.1 billion per year as well as vital nonmonetary benefits. The impact of this study won it the prestigious first prize among the 1996 Franz Edelman Awards for Management Science Achievement.

Site Selection

In this global economy, many corporations are opening up new plants in various parts of the world to take advantage of lower labor costs, and so on. Before selecting a site for a new plant, many potential sites may need to be analyzed and compared. (The California Manufacturing Co. case study had just two potential sites for each of two kinds of facilities.) Each of the potential sites involves a yes-or-no decision of the following type.

Each yes-or-no decision:

Should a certain site be selected for the location of a certain new facility?

$$\text{Its decision variable} = \begin{cases} 1, & \text{if yes} \\ 0, & \text{if no} \end{cases}$$

In many cases, the objective is to select the sites so as to minimize the total cost of the new facilities that will provide the required output.

As described in the January–February 1990 issue of *Interfaces*, **AT&T** used a BIP model to help dozens of their customers select the sites for their telemarketing centers. The model minimizes labor, communications, and real-estate costs while providing the desired level of coverage by the centers. In one year alone (1988), this approach enabled 46 AT&T customers to make their yes-or-no decisions on site locations swiftly and confidently, while committing to $375 million in annual network services and $31 million in equipment sales from AT&T.

We next describe an important type of problem for many corporations where site selection plays a key role.

Designing a Production and Distribution Network

Manufacturers today face great competitive pressure to get their products to market more quickly as well as to reduce their production and distribution costs. Therefore, any corporation that distributes its products over a wide geographical area (or even worldwide) must pay continuing attention to the design of its production and distribution network.

This design involves addressing the following kinds of yes-or-no decisions.

Should a certain plant remain open?

Should a certain site be selected for a new plant?

Should a certain distribution center remain open?

Should a certain site be selected for a new distribution center?

If each market area is to be served by a single distribution center, then we also have another kind of yes-or-no decision for each combination of a market area and a distribution center.

Should a certain distribution center be assigned to serve a certain market area?

For each of the yes-or-no decisions of any of these kinds,

$$\text{Its decision variable} = \begin{cases} 1, & \text{if yes} \\ 0, & \text{if no} \end{cases}$$

Ault Foods Limited (July–August 1994 issue of *Interfaces*) used this approach to design its production and distribution center. Management considered 10 sites for plants, 13 sites for distribution centers, and 48 market areas. This application of BIP was credited with saving the company $200,000 per year.

Digital Equipment Corporation (January–February 1995 issue of *Interfaces*) provides another example of an application of this kind. At the time, this large multinational corporation was serving one-quarter million customer sites, with more than half of its $14 billion annual revenues coming from 81 countries outside the United States. Therefore, this application involved restructuring the corporation's entire *global supply chain,* consisting of its suppliers, plants, distribution centers, potential sites, and market areas all around the world. The restructuring generated annual cost reductions of $500 million in manufacturing and $300 million in logistics, as well as a reduction of over $400 million in required capital assets.

Dispatching Shipments   Once a production and distribution network has been designed and put into operation, daily operating decisions need to be made about how to send the shipments. Some of these decisions again are yes-or-no decisions.

For example, suppose that trucks are being used to transport the shipments and each truck typically makes deliveries to several customers during each trip. It then becomes necessary to select a route (sequence of customers) for each truck, so each candidate for a route leads to the following yes-or-no decision.

Should a certain route be selected for one of the trucks?

$$\text{Its decision variable} = \begin{cases} 1, & \text{if yes} \\ 0, & \text{if no} \end{cases}$$

The objective would be to select the routes that would minimize the total cost of making all the deliveries.

Various complications also can be considered. For example, if different truck sizes are available, each candidate for selection would include both a certain route and a certain truck size. Similarly, if timing is an issue, a time period for the departure also can be specified as part of the yes-or-no decision. With both factors, each yes-or-no decision would have the form shown below.

Should all the following be selected simultaneously for a delivery run:

1. a certain route,

2. a certain size of truck, and

3. a certain time period for the departure?

$$\text{Its decision variable} = \begin{cases} 1, & \text{if yes} \\ 0, & \text{if no} \end{cases}$$

Here are a few of the companies that use BIP to help make these kinds of decisions. A Michigan-based retail chain called **Quality Stores** (March–April 1987 issue of *Interfaces*) makes the routing decisions for its delivery trucks this way, thereby saving about $450,000 per year. **Air Products and Chemicals, Inc.** (December 1983 issue of *Interfaces*) saves approximately $2 million annually (about 8 percent of its prior distribution costs) by using this approach to produce its daily delivery schedules. The **Reynolds Metals Co.** (January–February 1991 issue of *Interfaces*) achieves savings of over $7 million annually with an automated dispatching system based partially on BIP for its freight shipments from over 200 plants, warehouses, and suppliers.

Scheduling Interrelated Activities

We all schedule interrelated activities in our everyday lives, even if it is just scheduling when to begin our various homework assignments. So, too, managers must schedule various kinds of interrelated activities. When should we begin production for various new orders? When should we begin marketing various new products? When should we make various capital investments to expand our production capacity?

For any such activity, the decision about when to begin can be expressed in terms of a series of yes-or-no decisions, with one of these decisions for each of the possible time periods in which to begin, as shown below.

Should a certain activity begin in a certain time period?

$$\text{Its decision variable} = \begin{cases} 1, & \text{if yes} \\ 0, & \text{if no} \end{cases}$$

Since a particular activity can begin in only one time period, the choice of the various time periods provides a group of *mutually exclusive alternatives,* so the decision variable for only one time period can have a value of 1.

For example, this approach was used to schedule the building of a series of seven office buildings on the property adjacent to **Texas Stadium** (home of the Dallas Cowboys) over a seven-year planning horizon. In this case, the model had 49 binary decision variables, seven for each office building corresponding to each of the seven years in which its construction could begin. This application of BIP was credited with increasing the profit by $6.3 million. (See the October 1983 issue of *Interfaces*.)

A somewhat similar application on a vastly larger scale occurred in **China** recently (January–February 1995 issue of *Interfaces*). China was facing at least $240 billion in new investments over a 15-year horizon to meet the energy needs of its rapidly growing economy. Shortages of coal and electricity required developing new infrastructure for transporting coal and transmitting electricity, as well as building new dams and plants for generating thermal, hydro, and nuclear power. Therefore, the Chinese State Planning Commission and the World Bank collaborated in developing a huge mixed BIP model to guide the decisions on which projects to approve and when to undertake them over the 15-year planning period to minimize the total discounted cost. It is estimated that this application of management science is saving China about $6.4 billion over the 15 years.

Scheduling Asset Divestitures

This next application actually is another example of the preceding one (scheduling interrelated activities). However, rather than dealing with such activities as constructing office buildings or investing in hydroelectric plants, the activities now are *selling* (divesting) *assets* to generate income. The assets can be either *financial* assets, such as stocks and bonds, or *physical* assets, such as real estate. Given a group of assets, the problem is to determine when to sell each one to maximize the net present value of total profit from these assets while generating the desired income stream.

In this case, each yes-or-no decision has the following form.

Should a certain asset be sold in a certain time period?

$$\text{Its decision variable} = \begin{cases} 1, & \text{if yes} \\ 0, & \text{if no} \end{cases}$$

One company that deals with these kinds of yes-or-no decisions is **Homart Development Company** (January–February 1987 issue of *Interfaces*), which ranks among the largest commercial land developers in the United States. One of its most important strategic issues is scheduling divestiture of shopping malls and office buildings. At any particular time, well over 100 assets will be under consideration for divestiture over the next 10 years. Applying BIP to guide these decisions is credited with adding $40 million of profit from the divestiture plan.

Airline Applications

The airline industry is an especially heavy user of management science throughout its operations. For example, one large consulting firm called SABRE (spun off by American Airlines) employs several hundred management science professionals solely to focus on the problems of companies involved with transportation, including especially airlines. We will mention here just two of the applications that specifically use BIP.

One is the *fleet assignment problem.* Given several different types of airplanes available, the problem is to assign a specific type to each flight leg in the schedule so as to maximize the total profit from meeting the schedule. The basic trade-off is that if the airline uses an airplane that is too small on a particular flight leg, it will leave potential customers behind, while if it uses an airplane that is too large, it will suffer the greater expense of the larger airplane to fly empty seats.

For each combination of an airplane type and a flight leg, we have the following yes-or-no decision.

Should a certain type of airplane be assigned to a certain flight leg?

$$\text{Its decision variable} = \begin{cases} 1, & \text{if yes} \\ 0, & \text{if no} \end{cases}$$

Delta Air Lines (January–February 1994 issue of *Interfaces*) flies over 2,500 domestic flight legs every day, using about 450 airplanes of 10 different types. They use a huge integer programming model (about 40,000 functional constraints, 20,000 binary variables, and 40,000 general integer variables) to solve their fleet assignment problem each time a change is needed. This application saves Delta approximately $100 million per year.

A fairly similar application is the *crew scheduling problem.* Here, rather than assigning airplane types to flight legs, we are instead assigning sequences of flight legs to crews of pilots and flight attendants. Thus, for each feasible sequence of flight legs that leaves from a crew base and returns to the same base, the following yes-or-no decision must be made.

Should a certain sequence of flight legs be assigned to a crew?

$$\text{Its decision variable} = \begin{cases} 1, & \text{if yes} \\ 0, & \text{if no} \end{cases}$$

The objective is to minimize the total cost of providing crews that cover each flight leg in the schedule.

American Airlines (July–August 1989 and January–February 1991 issues of *Interfaces*) achieves annual savings of over $20 million by using BIP to solve its crew scheduling problem on a monthly basis.

A full-fledged formulation example of this type will be presented at the end of Section 9.4.

Review Questions

1. How is the binary decision variable defined for each yes-or-no decision?
2. What is the nature of each yes-or-no decision for capital budgeting with fixed investment proposals?
3. What is the nature of each yes-or-no decision when applying BIP to site selection?
4. What kinds of yes-or-no decisions involving site selection also arise when designing a company's production and distribution network?
5. How can the assignment of routes to delivery trucks be posed as yes-or-no decisions?

6. How much is China estimated to be saving by applying BIP to guide the decisions on which projects to approve and when to undertake them over a 15-year planning period?

7. What is the form of each yes-or-no decision when scheduling asset divestitures?

8. What are two kinds of applications of BIP in the airline industry?

9.3 Some Other Formulation Possibilities with Binary Variables

The two preceding sections give various examples of how yes-or-no decisions can arise. Each such decision is represented by a *binary decision variable* in a BIP model.

In addition to any such binary decision variables, other binary variables sometimes are introduced simply to help formulate the model. Here is the terminology to distinguish between the two kinds of binary variables.

> A **binary decision variable** is a binary variable that represents a yes-or-no decision. An **auxiliary binary variable** is an additional binary variable that is introduced into the model, not to represent a yes-or-no decision, but simply to help formulate the model as a (pure or mixed) BIP problem. Auxiliary binary variables will be denoted by $y_1, y_2, \ldots$.

This section illustrates three of the ways in which auxiliary binary variables can play a crucial role in being able to formulate the model to fit a standard problem so that the model can be solved. To facilitate focusing on the role of the auxiliary binary variables, all three examples are variations of the familiar Wyndor Glass Co. problem introduced in Section 2.2 and formulated as a linear programming model on a spreadsheet in Section 2.3. This spreadsheet model also is shown in Figure 8.4 in Section 8.2. To further refresh your memory, Figure 9.2 shows the graphical solution originally developed in Section 2.5 for this problem, where the symbol P represents the weekly profit in dollars.

This original Wyndor problem has no yes-or-no decisions and so no binary decision variables. However, each variation presented below introduces a complication that can be overcome by using auxiliary binary variables to formulate a model that can be readily solved. (Because the Wyndor problem has only two decision variables, we will be able to use graphical analysis to help introduce and analyze each variation before showing how auxiliary binary variables can be used with any number of decision variables.)

FIGURE 9.2

This graph summarizes the application of the graphical method to the original Wyndor problem that was presented in Section 2.5.

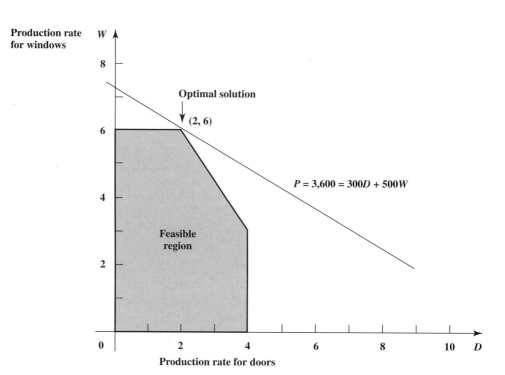

Variation 1: Wyndor with Setup Costs for Initiating Production

Now suppose that the following two changes are made in the original problem.

Change 1 for variation 1: For each product, producing any units requires incurring a substantial one-time *setup cost* for setting up the production facilities for the entire production run for this product. These setup costs are $700 for doors and $1,300 for windows. Otherwise, each door and window still contributes $300 and $500, respectively, to profit.

Change 2 for variation 1: The production runs for these products will be ended after one week, so D and W in the original model now represent the *total* number of doors and windows produced, respectively, rather than production rates. Therefore, these two variables need to be restricted to integer values.

Table 9.3 shows the resulting net profit from producing any feasible quantity for either product. Note that the large setup cost for either product makes it unprofitable to produce less than three units of that product.

The dots in Figure 9.3 show the feasible solutions for this problem. By adding the appropriate entries in Table 9.3, the figure also shows the calculation of the total net profit P for each of the corner points. The optimal solution turns out to be

$$(D, W) = (0, 6) \qquad \text{with} \qquad P = 1{,}700$$

TABLE 9.3   Net Profit ($) for Variation 1 of the Wyndor Problem

	Net Profit	
Number of Units Produced	*Doors*	*Windows*
0	0 (300) − 0 = 0	0 (500) − 0 = 0
1	1 (300) − 700 = −400	1 (500) − 1,300 = −800
2	2 (300) − 700 = −100	2 (500) − 1,300 = −300
3	3 (300) − 700 = 200	3 (500) − 1,300 = 200
4	4 (300) − 700 = 500	4 (500) − 1,300 = 700
5	Not feasible	5 (500) − 1,300 = 1200
6	Not feasible	6 (500) − 1,300 = 1700

FIGURE 9.3

The dots are the feasible solutions for Variation 1 of the Wyndor problem. Also shown is the calculation of the total net profit P for each corner point from the net profits given in Table 9.3.

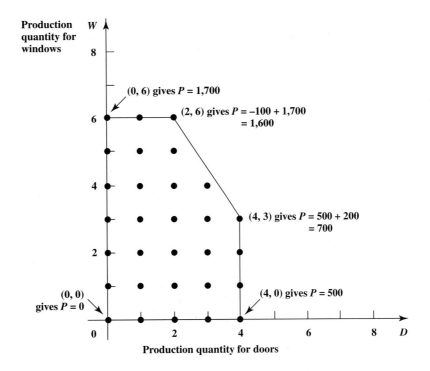

By contrast, the original solution

$$(D, W) = (2, 6) \quad \text{with} \quad P = 1,600$$

now gives a smaller value of P. The reason that this original solution (which gave $P = 3,600$ for the original problem) is no longer optimal is that the setup costs reduce the total net profit so much:

$$P = 3,600 - 700 - 1,300 = 1,600$$

Therefore, the graphical method for linear programming can no longer be used to find the optimal solution for this new problem with setup costs.

How can we formulate a model for this problem so that it fits a standard kind of model that can be solved by an available algorithm? Table 9.3 shows that the net profit for either product is no longer *directly proportional* to the number of units produced. Therefore, as it stands, the problem no longer fits either linear or integer programming. Before, for the original problem without setup costs, the objective function was simply $P = 300D + 500W$. Now we need to subtract from this expression each setup cost *if* the corresponding product will be produced, but we should not subtract the setup cost if the product will not be produced. There appears to be no way to fit such an objective function to the requirements of linear programming (or the equivalent requirements of integer programming). This is where *auxiliary binary variables* come to the rescue.

Formulation with Auxiliary Binary Variables.   For each setup cost, there are just two possibilities. Either it will be incurred or it will not. A binary variable has just two values. Therefore, we can introduce an *auxiliary binary variable* for each setup cost and associate each value of the binary variable with one of the two possibilities for the setup cost. In particular, let

$$y_1 = \begin{cases} 1, & \text{if perform the setup to produce doors} \\ 0, & \text{if not} \end{cases}$$

$$y_2 = \begin{cases} 1, & \text{if perform the setup to produce windows} \\ 0, & \text{if not} \end{cases}$$

Therefore, the objective function now can be written as

$$P = 300D + 500W - 700y_1 - 1,300y_2$$

which fits the format for integer programming.

Since a setup is required to produce the corresponding product, these auxiliary binary variables can be related directly to the production quantities as follows.

$$y_1 = \begin{cases} 1, & \text{if } D > 0 \text{ can hold (can produce doors)} \\ 0, & \text{if } D = 0 \text{ must hold (cannot produce doors)} \end{cases}$$

$$y_2 = \begin{cases} 1, & \text{if } W > 0 \text{ can hold (can produce windows)} \\ 0, & \text{if } W = 0 \text{ must hold (cannot produce windows)} \end{cases}$$

We need to include constraints in the model that will ensure that these relationships will hold. (An algorithm solving the model only recognizes the objective function and the constraints, not the definitions of the variables.)

So what are the constraints of the model for variation 1? We still need all the constraints of the original model. We also need constraints that D and W are integers (because of change 2) and that y_1 and y_2 are binary. In addition, we need some ordinary linear programming constraints that will ensure the following relationships.

If $y_1 = 0$,   then $D = 0$.
If $y_2 = 0$,   then $W = 0$.

(If $y_1 = 1$ or $y_2 = 1$, no restrictions are placed on D or W other than those already imposed by the other constraints.)

It is possible with Excel to use the IF function to represent this relationship between y_1 and D and between y_2 and W.[1] Unfortunately, the IF function does not fit into a linear programming (or integer programming) format. Consequently, the Excel Solver has difficulty solving spreadsheet models that use this function. This is why another formulation with ordinary linear programming constraints is needed instead to express these relationships.

Since the other constraints impose bounds on D and W of $0 \leq D \leq 4$ and $0 \leq W \leq 6$, here are some ordinary linear programming constraints that ensure these relationships.

$$D \leq 4 y_1$$

$$W \leq 6 y_2$$

Note that setting $y_1 = 0$ gives $D \leq 0$, which forces the nonnegative D to be $D = 0$, whereas setting $y_1 = 1$ gives $D \leq 4$, which allows all the values of D already allowed by the other constraints. Then check that the same conclusions apply for W when setting $y_2 = 0$ and $y_2 = 1$.

It was not necessary to choose 4 and 6 for the respective coefficients of y_1 and y_2 in these two constraints. Any coefficients *larger* than 4 and 6 would have the same effect. You just need to avoid *smaller* coefficients, since this would impose undesired restrictions on D and W when $y_1 = 1$ and $y_2 = 1$.

On larger problems, it is sometimes difficult to determine the smallest acceptable coefficients for these auxiliary binary variables. Therefore, it is common to formulate the model by just using a reasonably large number (say, 99 in this case) that is safely larger than the smallest acceptable coefficient.

Figure 9.4 shows one way of formulating this model when using the number 99. The format for the first nine rows is the same as for the original problem, so the difference arises in rows 10–13 of the spreadsheet. The values of the auxiliary binary variables, y_1 and y_2, appear in the new changing cells, C12 and D12. The bottom right side of the figure identifies the equations entered into the output cells in row 11, C11 = 99*C12 and D11 = 99*D12. Consequently, the constraints, C9:D9 $\leq$ C11:D11, impose the relationships that $D \leq 99y_1$ and $W \leq 99y_2$.

The shaded cells in this spreadsheet show the optimal solution obtained after applying the Excel Solver. Thus, this solution is to not produce any doors ($y_1 = 0$ and $D = 0$) but to perform the setup to enable producing 6 windows ($y_2 = 1$ and $W = 6$) to obtain a net profit of $1,700.

Note that this optimal solution does indeed satisfy the requirements that $D=0$ must hold when $y_1 = 0$ and that $W > 0$ can hold when $y_2 = 1$. The constraints do permit performing a setup to produce a product and then not producing any units ($y_1 = 1$ with $D = 0$ or $y_2 = 1$ with $W = 0$), but the objective function causes an optimal solution automatically to avoid this foolish option of incurring the setup cost for no purpose. None of this would have been possible without introducing the auxiliary binary variables y_1 and y_2.

Variation 2: Wyndor with Mutually Exclusive Products

Instead of the changes in variation 1, suppose now that the only change from the original Wyndor problem is the following.

> **Change for variation 2:** The two potential new products (doors and windows) would compete for the same customers. Therefore, management has decided not to produce both of them together. At most one can be chosen for production, so

$$\text{either} \quad D = 0 \quad \text{or} \quad W = 0 \quad \text{(or both)}$$

Thus, we now are dealing with *mutually exclusive products*.

Figure 9.5 shows the feasible region for this problem, namely, the line segment from $(0, 0)$ to $(4, 0)$ and the line segment from $(0, 0)$ to $(0, 6)$. These are the only solutions from the feasible region for the original problem for which either $x_1 = 0$ or $x_2 = 0$. For this tiny

---

[1]This is not straightforward since, for example, in the case where y_1 is not equal to 0 in the IF function, D needs to be set equal to a cell that is constrained to equal the changing cell holding the value of D.

FIGURE 9.4

A spreadsheet model for Variation 1 of the Wyndor problem, where the Excel Solver gives the optimal solution shown in the changing cells (C9:D9 and C12:D12).

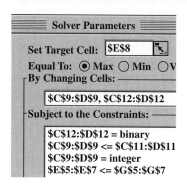

	A	B	C	D	E	F	G
1		Wyndor Glass Co. Problem with Setup Costs					
2							
3							Right-Hand
4		Constraint	Doors	Windows	Totals		Side
5		Plant 1	1	0	0	≤	4
6		Plant 2	0	2	12	≤	12
7		Plant 3	3	2	12	≤	18
8		Unit Profit	$300	$500	$1700		
9		Solution	0	6			
10			≤	≤			
11			0	99			
12		Set Up?	0	1			
13		Setup Cost	$700	$1,300			

	E
5	=SUMPRODUCT(C5:D5,C9:D9)
6	=SUMPRODUCT(C6:D6,C9:D9)
7	=SUMPRODUCT(C7:D7,C9:D9)
8	=SUMPRODUCT(C8:D8,C9:D9)–SUMPRODUCT(C13:D13,C12:D12)

Solver Parameters

Set Target Cell: $E$8

Equal To: ● Max ○ Min ○ V

By Changing Cells:

$C$9:$D$9, $C$12:$D$12

Subject to the Constraints:

$C$12:$D$12 = binary
$C$9:$D$9 <= $C$11:$D$11
$C$9:$D$9 = integer
$E$5:$E$7 <= $G$5:$G$7

	C	D
11	=99*C12	=99*D12

Solver Options

☑ Assume Linear Model
☑ Assume Non-Negative

FIGURE 9.5

The dark line segments show the feasible solutions for Variation 2 of the Wyndor problem.

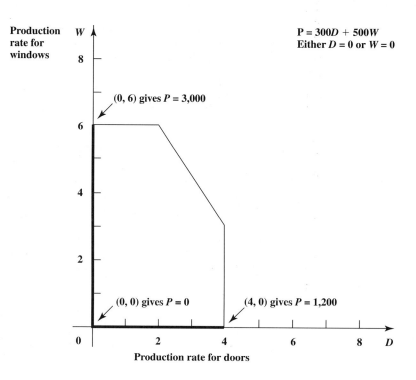

$P = 300D + 500W$
Either $D = 0$ or $W = 0$

(0, 6) gives $P = 3,000$

(0, 0) gives $P = 0$ (4, 0) gives $P = 1,200$

Production rate for windows   W

Production rate for doors

problem, it can be seen from the figure that the feasible solution that maximizes P (i.e., the optimal solution) is

$$(D, W) = (0, 6) \quad \text{with} \quad P = 3{,}000$$

Linear or integer programming models do not permit an **either-or constraint** such as *either $D = 0$ or $W = 0$*. How can we rewrite this constraint in a standard form to fit such a model so that the model can be solved by available algorithms (including those in the Excel Solver)?

As illustrated by the case study in Section 9.1, if D and W were binary variables, we would only need to rewrite the constraint as $D + W \leq 1$. However, D and W represent production rates that can take on various values besides 0 and 1, so this constraint does not work.

Now watch auxiliary binary variables come to the rescue again.

Formulation with Auxiliary Binary Variables. For each product, there are just two possibilities regarding the decision of whether it can be produced. Either it can or it cannot. Therefore, we can associate each of the two values of an auxiliary binary variable with one of these possibilities. Specifically, let the auxiliary binary variables be

$$y_1 = \begin{cases} 1, & \text{if } D > 0 \text{ can hold (can produce doors)} \\ 0, & \text{if } D = 0 \text{ must hold (cannot produce doors)} \end{cases}$$

$$y_2 = \begin{cases} 1, & \text{if } W > 0 \text{ can hold (can produce windows)} \\ 0, & \text{if } W = 0 \text{ must hold (cannot produce windows)} \end{cases}$$

The relationships between y_1 and D, as well as between y_2 and W, are identical to the ones for variation 1. Therefore, Figure 9.6 demonstrates that exactly the same constraints (C9:D9 $\leq$ C11:D11 and C12:D12 = binary) can be used to ensure that these relationships

FIGURE 9.6

A spreadsheet model for Variation 2 of the Wyndor problem, where the Excel Solver provides the optimal solution shown in the changing cells (C9:D9 and C12:D12).

	A	B	C	D	E	F	G
1		Wyndor Glass Co. with Mutually Exclusive Products					
2							
3							Right-Hand
4		Constraint	Doors	Windows	Totals		Side
5		Plant 1	1	0	0	$\leq$	4
6		Plant 2	0	2	12	$\leq$	12
7		Plant 3	3	2	12	$\leq$	18
8		Unit Profit	300	500	$3000		
9		Solution	0	6			
10			$\leq$	$\leq$			
11			0	99			
12		Produce?	0	1	1	$\leq$	1

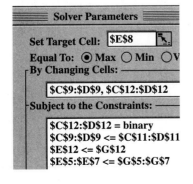

	E
5	=SUMPRODUCT(C5:D5,C9:D9)
6	=SUMPRODUCT(C6:D6,C9:D9)
7	=SUMPRODUCT(C7:D7,C9:D9)
8	=SUMPRODUCT(C8:D8,C9:D9)

	C	D	E
11	=99*C12	=99*D12	
12	0	1	=C12+D12

Solver Parameters

Set Target Cell: $E$8

Equal To: ● Max ○ Min ○V

By Changing Cells:

$C$9:$D$9, $C$12:$D$12

Subject to the Constraints:

$C$12:$D$12 = binary
$C$9:$D$9 <= $C$11:$D$11
$E$12 <= $G$12
$E$5:$E$7 <= $G$5:$G$7

Solver Options

☑ Assume Linear Model

☑ Assume Non-Negative

hold. To make the products mutually exclusive, we now add the usual kind of constraint for mutually exclusive alternatives with regard to these two binary variables,

$$y_1 + y_2 \leq 1$$

which gives the constraint, E12 ≤ G12, in the spreadsheet model. This forces either C12 = 0 or D12 = 0 (or both).

These are the only new constraints needed along with the constraints of the original model. Since D and W now have their original definitions as *production rates* (change 2 for variation 1 no longer applies), these variables do not need to have integer values, so the model in Figure 9.6 is a mixed BIP model.

In contrast to variation 1, there are no extra costs associated with any values of y_1 and y_2. The original objective function, without y_1 and y_2, still applies, as indicated by the equation entered into the target cell (E8).

The Excel Solver gives the optimal solution shown in the changing cells, namely, the windows are the product chosen to be produced, and then they are produced at the maximum rate ($W = 6$) allowed by the original constraints.

For such a small problem, we were able to find this optimal solution from Figure 9.5 without introducing auxiliary binary variables. However, auxiliary binary variables become necessary when dealing with larger problems. For example, if this pair of mutually exclusive products is just part of a larger group of products under consideration, then the larger model would need to add the constraints involving y_1 and y_2.

You will see this same approach included again in the first example of the next section when there are *three* potential new products and *at most two* can be chosen to be produced.

Variation 3: Wyndor with Either-Or Constraints

Now suppose that the only change from the original Wyndor problem is the one spelled out below.

> **Change for variation 3:** The company has just opened a new plant (plant 4) that is similar to plant 3, so the new plant can perform the same operations as plant 3 to help produce the two new products (doors and windows). However, for administrative reasons, management wants just one of the plants to be chosen to work on these products. The plant chosen should be the one that provides the most profitable product mix.

Table 9.4 gives the data for this problem. This table is identical to Table 2.1 for the original problem except for the addition of the data for plant 4. Although the hours of production time are different for plants 3 and 4 (because of differences in the types of production facilities being used), the costs of the operations for each product are essentially the same for the two plants. Therefore, the unit profits in the last row of the table are unaffected by the choice of which plant to use for these products.

The data for plant 4 indicate that if this plant is chosen, then we must satisfy the constraint

$$2D + 4W \leq 28$$

when solving for the most profitable product mix. However, if plant 3 is chosen instead, then this constraint is irrelevant and we must instead satisfy the original constraint for plant 3,

$$3D + 2W \leq 18$$

TABLE 9.4   Data for Variation 3 of the Wyndor Problem

Plant	Production Time Used for Each Unit Produced (Hours)		Production Time Available per Week (Hours)
	Doors	*Windows*	
1	1	0	4
2	0	2	12
3	3	2	18
4	2	4	28
Unit profit	$300	$500	

In other words, the relevant constraint is

$$\text{Either} \quad 3D + 2W \le 18$$

$$\text{Or} \quad 2D + 4W \le 28$$

depending upon whether plant 3 or plant 4 is chosen. The choice of which plant depends on which one allows the largest total profit when considering all the constraints of the model.

Figure 9.7 shows the effect of these two choices. If plant 3 were chosen to help produce these two products (so $3D + 2W \le 18$ is relevant but $2D + 4W \le 28$ is not), then we would have the linear programming problem on the left side of the figure. Since this problem is identical to the original Wyndor problem shown in Figure 9.2, the best available solution would be

$$(D, W) = (2, 6) \quad \text{with} \quad P = 3,600$$

However, if plant 4 were chosen instead (so $2D + 4W \le 28$ is relevant but $3D + 2W \le 18$ is not), then we would have the linear programming problem on the right side of the figure. The best available solution for this problem would be

$$(D, W) = (4, 5) \quad \text{with} \quad P = 3,700$$

Since $P = 3,700$ is larger than $P = 3,600$, the largest possible weekly profit is $3,700, which is only obtainable by choosing plant 4 instead of plant 3 to help produce the two new products.

Despite its either-or constraint, we have just managed to solve the complete model for variation 3 by solving and comparing two linear programming problems. However, solving larger models with several either-or constraints in this way would require solving and comparing numerous linear programming problems. We would much prefer to be able to apply a standard algorithm just once to solve the model.

Unfortunately, the model for variation 3 is not a linear programming model, since either-or constraints are not allowed in linear or integer programming. In fact, this model does not fit the format for *any* kind of standard model. Therefore, we cannot use a standard algorithm once to find an optimal solution for this model in its current form.

How can we reformulate this model into a standard format where a standard algorithm can be used one time to find an optimal solution? Once again, auxiliary binary variables come to the rescue.

FIGURE 9.7

These two graphs for Variation 3 of the Wyndor problem show the linear programming problem and its optimal solution that would result if the plant chosen to help produce the two new products were (a) plant 3 or (b) plant 4.

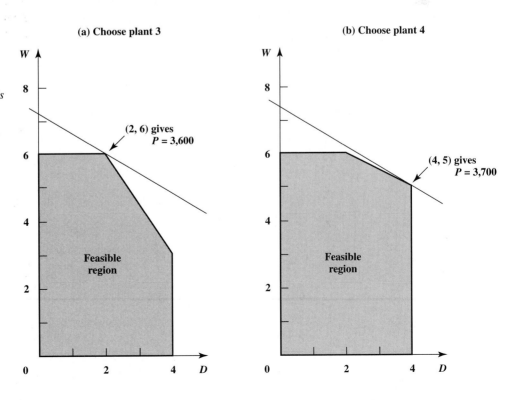

Formulation with an Auxiliary Binary Variable.   There are just two possibilities: either $3D + 2W \leq 18$ must hold (due to choosing plant 3) or $2D + 4W \leq 28$ must hold (due to choosing plant 4). Therefore, we can introduce an auxiliary binary variable y to indicate which possibility is chosen by defining y as

$$y = \begin{cases} 1, & \text{if } 2D + 4W \leq 28 \text{ must hold (choose plant 4)} \\ 0, & \text{if } 3D + 2W \leq 18 \text{ must hold (choose plant 3)} \end{cases}$$

This definition is enforced by introducing an extremely large positive number (we will use 99 again) and then making the following changes in the model.

	Replace	by
Either	$3D + 2W \leq 18$	$3D + 2W \leq 18 + 99y$
Or	$2D + 4W \leq 28$	$2D + 4W \leq 28 + 99(1 - y)$
		y is binary

To see why these new constraints work, check what happens when $y = 0$.

$y = 0$ gives $3D + 2W \leq 18$

and $2D + 4W \leq 28 + 99$ (a relatively huge number)

so

$3D + 2W \leq 18$ must hold

but $2D + 4W \leq 28$ does not need to hold

Since the other constraints in the model prevent $2D + 4W$ from being much larger than 28, having $y = 0$ give $2D + 4W \leq 28 + 99$ has the same effect as eliminating this constraint from the model. Similarly,

$y = 1$ gives $3D + 2W \leq 18 + 99$ (a relatively huge number)

and $2D + 4W \leq 28$

so

$3D + 2W \leq 18$ does not need to hold

but $3D + 4W \leq 28$ must hold

Again, adding 99 to the right-hand side of $3D + 2W \leq 18$ is equivalent to eliminating the constraint.

Figure 9.8 shows how this approach can be incorporated into a spreadsheet model. An additional changing cell (F13) displays the value of y. As indicated in the figure by the equations entered into cells G8 and G9, these cells give the modified right-hand sides of the plants 3 and 4 constraints that result from the value of y. With the constraints included in the Solver dialogue box, we now have a mixed BIP model that can be solved by the Excel Solver.

Clicking on the Solve button causes the Solver to simultaneously choose the value of y and the production rates (D and W) that maximize the total profit given in the target cell (E10). Since $y = 1$ in this optimal solution, plant 4 should be chosen to help produce the new products, with $D = 4$ and $W = 5$. This choice of plant provides a weekly profit of $3,700 rather than the $3,600 obtainable by choosing plant 3 instead.

Review Questions

1. What is the distinction between a binary decision variable and an auxiliary binary variable?

2. Why is a linear programming formulation no longer valid for a product-mix problem when there are setup costs for initiating production?

3. How can an auxiliary binary variable be defined in terms of whether a setup is performed to initiate the production of a certain product?

FIGURE 9.8

A spreadsheet model for Variation 3 of the Wyndor problem, where the Excel Solver gives the optimal solution shown in the changing cells (C11:D11 and F13).

	A	B	C	D	E	F	G	H
1		Wyndor Glass Co. Problem with Either-Or Constraints						
2								
3							Modified	Original
4							Right-Hand	Right-Hand
5		Constraint	Doors	Windows	Totals		Side	Side
6		Plant 1	1	0	4	≤	4	4
7		Plant 2	0	2	10	≤	12	12
8		Plant 3	3	2	22	≤	117	18
9		Plant 4	2	4	28	≤	28	28
10		Unit Profit	$300	$500	$3700			
11		Solution	4	5				
12								
13		Which Plant to Use? (0=Plant 3, 1=Plant 4)				1		

	E	F	G
6	=SUMPRODUCT(C6:D6,C11:D11)	≤	=H6
7	=SUMPRODUCT(C7:D7,C11:D11)	≤	=H7
8	=SUMPRODUCT(C8:D8,C11:D11)	≤	=H8+99*F13
9	=SUMPRODUCT(C9:D9,C11:D11)	≤	=H9+99*(1–F13)
10	=SUMPRODUCT(C10:D10,C11:D11)		

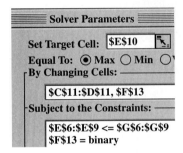

Solver Parameters

Set Target Cell: $E$10
Equal To: ⦿ Max ◯ Min ◯
By Changing Cells:
$C$11:$D$11, $F$13
Subject to the Constraints:
$E$6:$E$9 <= $G$6:$G$9
$F$13 = binary

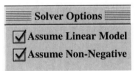

Solver Options

☑ Assume Linear Model
☑ Assume Non-Negative

4. What is meant by *mutually exclusive products*?

5. How can an auxiliary binary variable be defined in terms of whether to allow the production of a certain product?

6. How does an either-or constraint arise in variation 3 of the Wyndor problem?

7. When two individual constraints are paired together as an either-or constraint, how can an auxiliary binary variable be defined in terms of which one of these individual constraints is chosen as the one that must hold?

9.4 Some Formulation Examples

We now present a series of examples that illustrate a variety of formulation techniques with binary variables, including those discussed in the preceding sections. For the sake of clarity, these examples have been kept very small. In actual applications, these formulations typically would be just a small part of a vastly larger model.

Example 1: Imposing Managerial Restrictions

The Research and Development Division of the Good Products Company has developed three possible new products. However, to avoid undue diversification of the company's product line, management has imposed the following restriction:

Restriction 1: From the three possible new products, *at most two* should be chosen to be produced.

Each of these products can be produced in either of two plants. For administrative reasons, management has imposed a second restriction in this regard:

Restriction 2: Just one of the two plants should be chosen to be the sole producer of the new products.

TABLE 9.5   Data for Example 1 (The Good Products Co. Problem)

	Production Time Used for Each Unit Produced (Hours)			Production Time Available per Week (Hours)
	Product 1	*Product 2*	*Product 3*	
Plant				
1	3	4	2	30
2	4	6	2	40
Unit profit	5	7	3	(thousands of dollars)
Sales potential	7	5	9	(units per week)

The production cost per unit of each product would be essentially the same in the two plants. However, because of differences in their production facilities, the number of hours of production time needed per unit of each product might differ between the two plants. These data are given in Table 9.5 along with other relevant information, including marketing estimates of the number of units of each product that could be sold per week if it is produced. According to management, the objective is to choose the products, the plant, and the production rates of the chosen products so as to maximize the total profit.

In some ways, this problem resembles a standard *product-mix problem* such as the Wyndor Glass Co. example described in Section 2.2. In fact, if we changed the problem by dropping the two restrictions *and* by requiring each unit of a product to use the production hours given in Table 9.5 in *both plants* (so the two plants now perform different operations needed by the products), it would become just such a problem. In particular, let x_1, x_2, and x_3 be the production rates of the respective products. Displaying the values of these decision variables in changing cells C12:E12, the spreadsheet model then would become the one shown in rows 3–12 of Figure 9.9 if column H and the subsequent rows were omitted.

For the real problem, however, restriction 1 necessitates adding to the model the constraint:

No more than two of the decision variables (x_1, x_2, x_3) can have a value greater than zero.

This constraint does not fit into a linear or integer programming format, so the key question is how to convert it to such a format so that a corresponding algorithm can be used to solve the overall model. If the decision variables were binary variables, then the constraint would be expressed in this format as $x_1 + x_2 + x_3 \leq 2$. However, with *continuous* decision variables, a more complicated approach involving the introduction of auxiliary binary variables is needed.

Restriction 2 necessitates replacing the first two functional constraints ($3x_1 + 4x_2 + 2x_3 \leq 30$ and $4x_1 + 6x_2 + 2x_3 \leq 40$) by the restriction

$$\text{Either} \quad 3x_1 + 4x_2 + 2x_3 \leq 30$$

$$\text{Or} \quad 4x_1 + 6x_2 + 2x_3 \leq 40$$

must hold, where the choice of which constraint must hold corresponds to the choice of which plant will be used to produce the new products. Variation 3 of the Wyndor problem in the preceding section illustrated how such an either-or constraint can be converted to a linear or integer programming format, again with the help of an auxiliary binary variable.

Formulation with Auxiliary Binary Variables.   Except for involving more products and choices, restriction 1 is similar to the restriction imposed in variation 2 of the Wyndor problem in the preceding section. For variation 2, there were just *two* new products, and the restriction was that *at most one* could be chosen to be produced. Following the formulation approach used there, we can deal with restriction 1 by introducing *three* auxiliary binary variables (y_1, y_2, y_3) with the interpretation that

$$y_j = \begin{cases} 1, & \text{if } x_j > 0 \text{ can hold (can produce product } j) \\ 0, & \text{if } x_j = 0 \text{ must hold (cannot produce product } j) \end{cases}$$

	A	B	C	D	E	F	G	H	I
1		Good Products Co. with Managerial Restrictions							
2									
3								Modified	Original
4								Right-Hand	Right-Hand
5		Constraint	Product 1	Product 2	Product 3	Totals		Side	Side
6		Max Sales Product 1	1	0	0	5.5	≤	7	7
7		Max Sales Product 2	0	1	0	0	≤	5	5
8		Max Sales Product 3	0	0	1	9	≤	9	9
9		Plant 1	3	4	2	34.5	≤	129	30
10		Plant 2	4	6	2	40	≤	40	40
11		Unit Profit ($thousands)	5	7	3	54.5			
12		Solution	5.5	0	9				
13			≤	≤	≤				
14			99	0	99				
15		Produce?	1	0	1	2	≤	2	
16									
17		Which Plant to Use? (0=Plant 1, 1=Plant 2)			1				

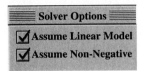

Solver Options
- ☑ Assume Linear Model
- ☑ Assume Non-Negative

	F	G	H
6	=SUMPRODUCT(C6:E6,C12:E12)	≤	=I6
7	=SUMPRODUCT(C7:E7,C12:E12)	≤	=I7
8	=SUMPRODUCT(C8:E8,C12:E12)	≤	=I8
9	=SUMPRODUCT(C9:E9,C12:E12)	≤	=I9+99*E17
10	=SUMPRODUCT(C10:E10,C12:E12)	≤	=I10+99*(1–E17)
11	=SUMPRODUCT(C11:E11,C12:E12)		

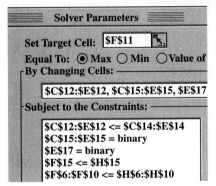

Solver Parameters

Set Target Cell: $F$11

Equal To: ● Max ○ Min ○ Value of
By Changing Cells:

$C$12:$E$12, $C$15:$E$15, $E$17

Subject to the Constraints:

$C$12:$E$12 <= $C$14:$E$14
$C$15:$E$15 = binary
$E$17 = binary
$F$15 <= $H$15
$F$6:$F$10 <= $H$6:$H$10

	C	D	E	F
14	=99*C15	=99*D15	=99*E15	
15	1	0	1	=SUM(C15:E15)

for $j = 1, 2, 3$. To enforce this interpretation in the model with the help of an extremely large positive number (say, 99 once again), we add the constraints

$$x_1 \leq 99y_1$$

$$x_2 \leq 99y_2$$

$$x_3 \leq 99y_3$$

$$y_1 + y_2 + y_3 \leq 2$$

$$y_j \text{ is binary,} \quad \text{for } j = 1, 2, 3$$

Because 99 is extremely large relative to the numbers in column I of Figure 9.9, the other constraints in the model already ensure that each decision variable x_j satisfies $0 \leq x_j \leq 99$ throughout the feasible region. Therefore, in each $x_j \leq 99 y_j$ constraint, $y_j = 1$ allows any value of x_j in the feasible region, whereas $y_j = 0$ forces $x_j = 0$. (Conversely, $x_j > 0$ forces $y_j = 1$, whereas $x_j = 0$ allows either value of y_j.) Consequently, when the fourth new constraint forces choosing at most two of the y_j to equal 1, this amounts to choosing at most two of the new products as the ones that can be produced.

To deal with restriction 2, we use the same approach as for variation 3 of the Wyndor problem in the preceding section. Therefore, we introduce another auxiliary binary variable y_4 with the interpretation that

$$y_4 = \begin{cases} 1, & \text{if } 4x_1 + 6x_2 + 2x_3 \le 40 \text{ must hold (choose plant 2)} \\ 0, & \text{if } 3x_1 + 4x_2 + 2x_3 \le 30 \text{ must hold (choose plant 1)} \end{cases}$$

This interpretation is enforced by adding the constraints

$$3x_1 + 4x_2 + 2x_3 \le 30 + 99y_4$$

$$4x_1 + 6x_2 + 2x_3 \le 40 + 99(1 - y_4)$$

$$y_4 \text{ is binary}$$

Both column H and rows 13–17 of Figure 9.9 show how all of this can be incorporated into the spreadsheet model in an intuitive way. The additional changing cells, C15:E15 and E17, give the values of the four auxiliary binary variables, so all four cells are constrained to be binary. The constraint that F15 ≤ H15 forces choosing at most two of the new products to be produced. The equations entered into cells C14:E14—as shown near the bottom of the figure—give the values of $99y_1$, $99y_2$, and $99y_3$, so the constraints that C12:E12 ≤ C14:E14 force the production rate of a product to be 0 in row 12 if the decision has been made in row 15 not to produce that product. With the equations that are shown for cells H9 and H10, the constraints that F9:F10 ≤ H9:H10 correspond to the algebraic constraints given at the end of the preceding paragraph.

This spreadsheet model now is a mixed BIP model, with three decision variables (cells C12:E12) not required to be integer and four auxiliary binary variables (cells C15:E15 and E17), so now the problem is formulated in a form that can be solved. Using the Excel Solver gives the optimal solution shown in the changing cells in Figure 9.9, namely, choose products 1 and 3 to produce, choose plant 2 for the production, and choose the production rates of 5½ units per week for product 1 and 9 units per week for product 3. The resulting total profit given in the target cell (F11) is $54,500 per week.

Example 2: Violating Proportionality

The Supersuds Corporation is developing its marketing plans for next year's new products. For three of these products, the decision has been made to purchase a total of five TV spots for commercials on national television networks. Each spot will feature a single product. Therefore, the problem on which we will focus is how to allocate the five spots to these three products, with a maximum of three spots (and a minimum of zero) for each product.

Table 9.6 shows the estimated impact of allocating zero, one, two, or three spots to each product. This impact is measured in terms of the *profit* from the *additional sales* that would result from the spots, considering also the cost of producing the commercial and purchasing the spots. The objective is to allocate five spots to the products so as to maximize the total profit.

This problem is small enough that it can be solved easily by trial and error. (The optimal solution is to allocate two spots to product 1, no spots to product 2, and three spots to product 3.) However, we will show one formulation with auxiliary binary variables for illustrative purposes. Such a formulation would become necessary if this small problem needed to be incorporated into a larger model involving the allocation of resources to marketing activities for all the corporation's new products.

TABLE 9.6   Data for Example 2 (the Supersuds Corp. Problem)

	Profit (Millions)		
Number of TV Spots	*Product 1*	*Product 2*	*Product 3*
0	0	0	0
1	$1	0	− $1
2	3	$2	2
3	3	3	4

A Formulation with Auxiliary Binary Variables. A natural formulation would be to let

x_1 = number of TV spots allocated to product 1
x_2 = number of TV spots allocated to product 2
x_3 = number of TV spots allocated to product 3
P = total profit (in millions of dollars)

The contribution of each of these integer decision variables (x_1, x_2, x_3) to P then would be given by the corresponding column in Table 9.6. However, each column indicates that profit is *not* proportional to the number of TV spots allocated to that product. Therefore, we cannot write a legitimate objective function in terms of these decision variables to fit integer programming. Using the algebraic form, the best that we can do with these decision variables is to formulate an incomplete integer programming model (not a *binary* integer programming model) that includes all the needed constraints but not an objective function.

$$\text{Maximize} \quad P = ?$$

subject to

$$x_1 \leq 3$$

$$x_2 \leq 3$$

$$x_3 \leq 3$$

$$x_1 + x_2 + x_3 = 5$$

and

$$x_1 \geq 0 \qquad x_2 \geq 0 \qquad x_3 \geq 0$$

$$x_1, x_2, x_3 \text{ are integers}$$

Now see what happens when we introduce nine auxiliary binary variables with the following interpretations:

$$y_{11} = \begin{cases} 1, & \text{if } x_1 = 1 \\ 0, & \text{otherwise} \end{cases} \quad y_{12} = \begin{cases} 1, & \text{if } x_1 = 2 \\ 0, & \text{otherwise} \end{cases} \quad y_{13} = \begin{cases} 1, & \text{if } x_1 = 3 \\ 0, & \text{otherwise} \end{cases}$$

$$y_{21} = \begin{cases} 1, & \text{if } x_2 = 1 \\ 0, & \text{otherwise} \end{cases} \quad y_{22} = \begin{cases} 1, & \text{if } x_2 = 2 \\ 0, & \text{otherwise} \end{cases} \quad y_{23} = \begin{cases} 1, & \text{if } x_2 = 3 \\ 0, & \text{otherwise} \end{cases}$$

$$y_{31} = \begin{cases} 1, & \text{if } x_3 = 1 \\ 0, & \text{otherwise} \end{cases} \quad y_{32} = \begin{cases} 1, & \text{if } x_3 = 2 \\ 0, & \text{otherwise} \end{cases} \quad y_{33} = \begin{cases} 1, & \text{if } x_3 = 3 \\ 0, & \text{otherwise} \end{cases}$$

For example, look at the definitions of y_{11}, y_{12}, and y_{13}. These definitions imply that

$$(y_{11}, y_{12}, y_{13}) = (0, 0, 0) \quad \text{if} \quad x_1 = 0$$

$$(y_{11}, y_{12}, y_{13}) = (1, 0, 0) \quad \text{if} \quad x_1 = 1$$

$$(y_{11}, y_{12}, y_{13}) = (0, 1, 0) \quad \text{if} \quad x_1 = 2$$

$$(y_{11}, y_{12}, y_{13}) = (0, 0, 1) \quad \text{if} \quad x_1 = 3$$

These four alternative values of x_1 are the only possible values. Since these alternative values are mutually exclusive alternatives, y_1, y_2, and y_3 need to satisfy the constraints

$$y_{11} + y_{12} + y_{13} \leq 1$$

$$y_{11}, y_{12}, y_{13} \text{ are binary}$$

Selecting values of y_{11}, y_{12}, and y_{13} that satisfy these constraints is equivalent to selecting a value of x_1 that satisfies the constraints

$$x_1 \leq 3$$
$$x_1 \geq 0$$
$$x_1 \text{ is integer}$$

In just the same way, the other auxiliary binary variables need to satisfy the constraints

$$y_{21} + y_{22} + y_{23} \leq 1$$

$$y_{31} + y_{32} + y_{33} \leq 1$$

$$y_{21}, y_{22}, y_{23}, y_{31}, y_{32}, y_{33} \text{ are binary}$$

Selecting values of these variables that satisfy these constraints is equivalent to selecting values of x_2 and x_3 that satisfy the constraints

$$x_2 \leq 3$$
$$x_3 \leq 3$$
$$x_2 \geq 0, \quad x_3 \geq 0$$
$$x_2, x_3 \text{ are integers}$$

Therefore, we now can formulate a model for the Supersuds problem in terms of these auxiliary binary variables by including the above constraints on these variables. We also need to add a constraint that will ensure that the original constraint,

$$x_1 + x_2 + x_3 = 5$$

still will hold. The key here is to note that the definitions of the auxiliary binary variables imply that

$$x_1 = y_{11} + 2y_{12} + 3y_{13}$$

$$x_2 = y_{21} + 2y_{22} + 3y_{23}$$

$$x_3 = y_{31} + 2y_{32} + 3y_{33}$$

Therefore, the original constraint can be replaced by the constraint

$$y_{11} + 2y_{12} + 3y_{13} + y_{21} + 2y_{22} + 3y_{23} + y_{31} + 2y_{32} + 3y_{33} = 5$$

Finally, we come to the whole reason for bothering with all of this, namely, that the auxiliary binary variables enable us to formulate a legitimate objective function. Using monetary units of millions of dollars, the three profit columns of Table 9.6 respectively indicate that

$$\text{Profit from product } 1 = y_{11} + 3y_{12} + 3y_{13}$$

$$\text{Profit from product } 2 = 2y_{22} + 3y_{23}$$

$$\text{Profit from product } 3 = -y_{31} + 2y_{32} + 4y_{33}$$

Therefore, adding these three profits, the total profit is

$$P = y_{11} + 3y_{12} + 3y_{13} + 2y_{22} + 3y_{23} - y_{31} + 2y_{32} + 4y_{33}$$

Consequently, the complete BIP model for the Supersuds problem can be formulated on a spreadsheet as shown in Figure 9.10, where the changing cells (C10:K10) display the values of the auxiliary binary variables. Clicking on the Solve button then provides the optimal solution shown in these changing cells in the figure, namely,

$y_{11} = 0$	$y_{12} = 1$	$y_{13} = 0$	so	$x_1 = 2$	(allocate 2 TV spots to product 1)
$y_{21} = 0$	$y_{22} = 0$	$y_{23} = 0$	so	$x_2 = 0$	(allocate 0 TV spots to product 2)
$y_{31} = 0$	$y_{32} = 0$	$y_{33} = 1$	so	$x_3 = 3$	(allocate 3 TV spots to product 3)

which yields a profit of $P = 7$ ($7 million), according to the target cell (L9).

Example 3: Airline Crew Scheduling

Southwestern Airways needs to assign its crews to cover all its upcoming flights. We will focus on the problem of assigning three crews based in San Francisco (SFO) to the 11 flights shown in Figure 9.11. These same flights are listed in the first column of Table 9.7. The other 12 columns show the 12 feasible sequences of flights for a crew. (The numbers in each column indicate the order of the flights.) Exactly three of the sequences need to be chosen (one per crew) in such a way that every flight is covered. (It is permissible to have more than one crew on a flight, where the extra crews would fly as passengers, but union

FIGURE 9.10

A spreadsheet formulation of the BIP model for the Supersuds problem, where the optimal solution obtained by the Excel Solver is given in row 10.

	A	B	C	D	E	F	G	H	I	J	K	L	M	N
1		Supersuds Corp. Marketing Plan												
2														
3				Product 1			Product 2			Product 3				Right-Hand
4		Constraint	1 Spot	2 Spots	3 Spots	1 Spot	2 Spots	3 Spots	1 Spot	2 Spots	3 Spots	Totals		Side
5		Product 1	1	1	1	0	0	0	0	0	0	1	≤	1
6		Product 2	0	0	0	1	1	1	0	0	0	0	≤	1
7		Product 3	0	0	0	0	0	0	1	1	1	1	≤	1
8		Total Spots	1	2	3	1	2	3	1	2	3	5	=	5
9		Profit ($millions)	1	3	3	0	2	3	–1	2	4	7		
10		Solution	0	1	0	0	0	0	0	0	1			

Solver Parameters

Set Target Cell: $L$9

Equal To: ● Max ○ Min ○

By Changing Cells:

$C$10:$K$10

Subject to the Constraints:

$C$10:$K$10 = binary
$L$5:$L$7 <= $N$5:$N$7
$L$8 = $N$8

	L
5	=SUMPRODUCT(C5:K5,C10:K10)
6	=SUMPRODUCT(C6:K6,C10:K10)
7	=SUMPRODUCT(C7:K7,C10:K10)
8	=SUMPRODUCT(C8:K8,C10:K10)
9	=SUMPRODUCT(C9:K9,C10:K10)

Solver Options

☑ Assume Linear Model
☑ Assume Non-Negative

FIGURE 9.11

The arrows show the 11 Southwestern Airways flights that need to be covered by the three crews based in San Francisco.

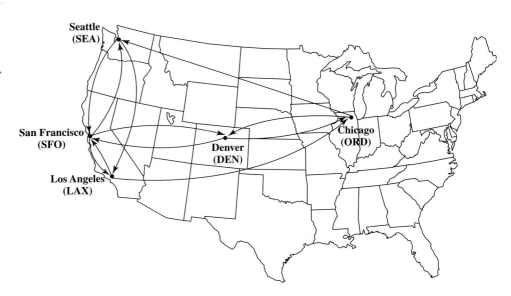

contracts require that the extra crews still be paid for their time as if they were working.) The cost of assigning a crew to a particular sequence of flights is given (in thousands of dollars) in the bottom row of the table. The objective is to minimize the total cost of the three crew assignments that cover all the flights.

Formulation with Binary Variables.   With 12 feasible sequences of flights, we have 12 yes-or-no decisions:

Should sequence j be assigned to a crew?   ($j = 1, 2, \ldots, 12$)

Therefore, we use 12 binary variables to represent these respective decisions:

$$x_j = \begin{cases} 1, & \text{if sequence } j \text{ is assigned to a crew} \\ 0, & \text{otherwise} \end{cases}$$

The most interesting part of this formulation is the nature of each constraint that ensures that a corresponding flight is covered. For example, consider the last flight in Table 9.7 (Seattle to Los Angeles). Five sequences (namely, sequences 6, 9, 10, 11, and 12)

TABLE 9.7 Data for Example 3 (the Southwestern Airways Problem)

Flight	|Feasible Sequence of Flights											
	1	*2*	*3*	*4*	*5*	*6*	*7*	*8*	*9*	*10*	*11*	*12*
1. San Francisco to Los Angeles (SFO–LAX)	1			1			1			1		
2. San Francisco to Denver (SFO–DEN)		1			1			1			1	
3. San Francisco to Seattle (SFO–SEA)			1			1			1			1
4. Los Angeles to Chicago (LAX–ORD)				2			2		3	2		3
5. Los Angeles to San Francisco (LAX–SFO)	2					3				5	5	
6. Chicago to Denver (ORD–DEN)				3	3				4			
7. Chicago to Seattle (ORD–SEA)							3	3		3	3	4
8. Denver to San Francisco (DEN–SFO)		2		4	4				5			
9. Denver to Chicago (DEN–ORD)					2			2			2	
10. Seattle to San Francisco (SEA–SFO)			2				4	4				5
11. Seattle to Los Angeles (SEA–LAX)						2			2	4	4	2
Cost, $1,000s	2	3	4	6	7	5	7	8	9	9	8	9

include this flight. Therefore, at least one of these five sequences must be chosen. The resulting constraint is

$$x_6 + x_9 + x_{10} + x_{11} + x_{12} \geq 1$$

Using similar constraints for the other 10 flights, Figure 9.12 shows a spreadsheet formulation of the complete BIP model for this problem. The Excel Solver provides the optimal solution shown in row 19. In terms of the x_j variables, this solution is

$$
\begin{aligned}
x_3 &= 1 \quad \text{(assign sequence 3 to a crew)} \\
x_4 &= 1 \quad \text{(assign sequence 4 to a crew)} \\
x_{11} &= 1 \quad \text{(assign sequence 11 to a crew)}
\end{aligned}
$$

and all other $x_j = 0$, for a total cost of $18,000 as given by cell O18. (Another optimal solution is $x_1 = 1$, $x_5 = 1$, $x_{12} = 1$, and all other $x_j = 0$.)

As discussed at the end of Section 9.2, airline crew scheduling has become one important application of BIP in recent years. Problems involving thousands of possible flight sequences now are being solved by using models similar to the one shown above but with thousands of binary variables rather than just a dozen.

Review Questions

1. How does restriction 1 for Example 1 relate to the restriction imposed in variation 2 of the Wyndor problem in the preceding section?
2. After introducing auxiliary binary variables for Example 1, what constraint on these variables forces choosing at most two of the possible new products as the ones that can be produced?

FIGURE 9.12

A spreadsheet formulation of the BIP model for the Southwestern Airways crew scheduling problem, where row 19 shows the optimal solution obtained by the Excel Solver. Under the solution is the list of flight sequences under consideration.

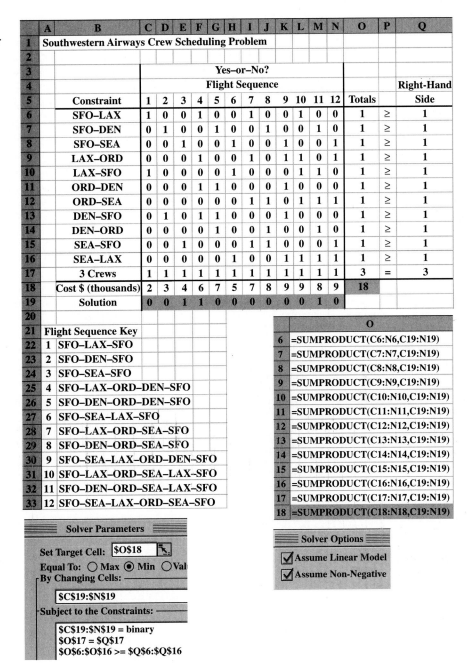

	A	B	C	D	E	F	G	H	I	J	K	L	M	N	O	P	Q
1	Southwestern Airways Crew Scheduling Problem																
2																	
3						Yes–or–No?											
4						Flight Sequence											Right-Hand
5		Constraint	1	2	3	4	5	6	7	8	9	10	11	12	Totals		Side
6		SFO–LAX	1	0	0	1	0	0	1	0	0	1	0	0	1	≥	1
7		SFO–DEN	0	1	0	0	1	0	0	1	0	0	1	0	1	≥	1
8		SFO–SEA	0	0	1	0	0	1	0	0	1	0	0	1	1	≥	1
9		LAX–ORD	0	0	0	1	0	0	1	0	1	1	0	1	1	≥	1
10		LAX–SFO	1	0	0	0	0	1	0	0	0	1	1	0	1	≥	1
11		ORD–DEN	0	0	0	1	1	0	0	0	1	0	0	0	1	≥	1
12		ORD–SEA	0	0	0	0	0	0	1	1	0	1	1	1	1	≥	1
13		DEN–SFO	0	1	0	1	1	0	0	0	1	0	0	0	1	≥	1
14		DEN–ORD	0	0	0	0	1	0	0	1	0	0	1	0	1	≥	1
15		SEA–SFO	0	0	1	0	0	0	1	1	0	0	0	1	1	≥	1
16		SEA–LAX	0	0	0	0	0	1	0	0	1	1	1	1	1	≥	1
17		3 Crews	1	1	1	1	1	1	1	1	1	1	1	1	3	=	3
18		Cost $ (thousands)	2	3	4	6	7	5	7	8	9	9	8	9	18		
19		Solution	0	0	1	1	0	0	0	0	0	0	1	0			

Flight Sequence Key

1	SFO–LAX–SFO
2	SFO–DEN–SFO
3	SFO–SEA–SFO
4	SFO–LAX–ORD–DEN–SFO
5	SFO–DEN–ORD–DEN–SFO
6	SFO–SEA–LAX–SFO
7	SFO–LAX–ORD–SEA–SFO
8	SFO–DEN–ORD–SEA–SFO
9	SFO–SEA–LAX–ORD–DEN–SFO
10	SFO–LAX–ORD–SEA–LAX–SFO
11	SFO–DEN–ORD–SEA–LAX–SFO
12	SFO–SEA–LAX–ORD–SEA–SFO

	O
6	=SUMPRODUCT(C6:N6,C19:N19)
7	=SUMPRODUCT(C7:N7,C19:N19)
8	=SUMPRODUCT(C8:N8,C19:N19)
9	=SUMPRODUCT(C9:N9,C19:N19)
10	=SUMPRODUCT(C10:N10,C19:N19)
11	=SUMPRODUCT(C11:N11,C19:N19)
12	=SUMPRODUCT(C12:N12,C19:N19)
13	=SUMPRODUCT(C13:N13,C19:N19)
14	=SUMPRODUCT(C14:N14,C19:N19)
15	=SUMPRODUCT(C15:N15,C19:N19)
16	=SUMPRODUCT(C16:N16,C19:N19)
17	=SUMPRODUCT(C17:N17,C19:N19)
18	=SUMPRODUCT(C18:N18,C19:N19)

Solver Parameters

Set Target Cell: $O$18

Equal To: ○ Max ● Min ○ Val

By Changing Cells:

$C$19:$N$19

Subject to the Constraints:

$C$19:$N$19 = binary
$O$17 = $Q$17
$O$6:$O$16 >= $Q$6:$Q$16

Solver Options

☑ Assume Linear Model
☑ Assume Non-Negative

3. When using the natural (integer) decision variables (x_1, x_2, x_3) defined for Example 2, why is it not possible to write a legitimate objective function in terms of these decision variables to fit integer programming?

4. What are the groups of mutually exclusive alternatives that arise when introducing the auxiliary binary variables for Example 2?

5. For Example 3, there is a constraint for each flight to ensure that this flight is covered by a crew. Describe the mathematical form of this constraint. Then explain in words what this constraint is saying.

9.5 Summary

Managers frequently must make yes-or-no decisions, where the only two possible choices are yes, go ahead with a particular option, or no, decline this option. A binary integer programming (BIP) model considers many options simultaneously, with a binary decision variable for each one. Mixed BIP models include some continuous decision variables as well.

Many companies have saved millions of dollars by formulating and solving BIP models for such diverse applications as capital budgeting, site selection, designing of production and distribution networks, dispatching of shipments, scheduling of interrelated activities, scheduling of asset divestitures, and various airline applications.

In addition to binary decision variables, *auxiliary binary variables* sometimes can be very useful in helping reformulate a model that cannot be solved into a BIP model that is readily solvable. For example, these variables can be used to deal with (1) setup costs for initiating production, (2) mutually exclusive products, and (3) either-or constraints.

Section 9.4 presents a series of examples that illustrate a variety of formulation techniques with binary variables.

Glossary

Auxiliary binary variable   A binary variable that is introduced into the model, not to represent a yes-or-no decision, but simply to help formulate the model as a (pure or mixed) BIP problem. (Section 9.3)   348

Binary decision variable   A binary variable that represents a yes-or-no decision by assigning a value of 1 for choosing yes and a value of 0 for choosing no. (Section 9.3)   348

Binary integer programming   The model for a binary integer programming (BIP) problem is identical to that for a linear programming problem except that the nonnegativity constraints for at least some of the variables are replaced by the constraints that these variables are binary variables. (Section 8.1 and Chapter 9)   339

Binary variable   A variable whose only possible values are 0 and 1. (Introduction)   339

BIP   Abbreviation for binary integer programming. (Introduction)   339

Contingent decision   A yes-or-no decision is a contingent decision if it can be yes only if a certain other yes-or-no decision is yes. (Section 9.1)   342

Either-or constraints   A pair of constraints such that either one can be chosen to be observed and then the other one would be ignored. (Section 9.3)   354

Mixed BIP problem   A BIP problem where some of the variables are restricted to be binary variables but the rest have no special restriction. (Introduction)   339

Mutually exclusive alternatives   A group of alternatives where choosing any one excludes choosing all the others. (Section 9.1)   341

Pure BIP problem   A BIP problem where all the variables are restricted to be binary variables. (Introduction)   339

Yes-or-no decision   A decision whose only possible choices are (1) yes, go ahead with a certain option, or (2) no, decline this option. (Introduction)   339

Learning Aids for This Chapter in Your MS Courseware

"Ch. 9—Using BIP" Excel File:

California Mfg. Case Study
Three Variants of Wyndor Example
Good Products Example
Supersuds Example
Southwestern Airways Example

An Excel Add-In:

Premium Solver

Supplement to This Chapter on the CD-ROM:

Some Perspectives on Solving Binary Integer Programming Problems

Problems

To the left of the problems (or their parts), we have inserted the symbol E* (for Excel) whenever Excel should be used (unless your instructor gives you contrary instructions). An asterisk on the problem number indicates that at least a partial answer is given in the back of the book.

9.1. Reconsider the California Manufacturing Co. case study presented in Section 9.1. The mayor of San Diego now has contacted the company's president, Armando Ortega, to try to persuade him to build a factory and perhaps a warehouse in that city. With the tax incentives being offered the company, Armando's staff estimates that the net present value of building a factory in San Diego would be $7 million and the amount of capital required to do this would be $4 million. The net present value of building a warehouse there would be $5 million and the capital

required would be $3 million. (This option would only be considered if a factory also is being built there.)

Armando has asked Steve Chan to revise his previous management science study to incorporate these new alternatives into the overall problem. The objective still is to find the feasible combination of investments that maximizes the total net present value, given that the amount of capital available for these investments is $10 million.

   a. Formulate a BIP model in algebraic form for this problem.

E* *b.* Formulate and solve this model on a spreadsheet.

9.2. Select one of the actual applications of BIP by a company mentioned in Section 9.2. Read the article describing the application in the referenced issue of *Interfaces*. Write a two-page summary of the application and its benefits.

9.3.* A young couple, Eve and Steven, want to divide their main household chores (marketing, cooking, dish washing, and laundering) between them so that each has two tasks but the total time they spend on household duties is kept to a minimum. Their efficiencies on these tasks differ, where the time each would need to perform the task is given by the following table:

	Time Needed per Week (Hours)			
	Marketing	*Cooking*	*Dish washing*	*Laundry*
Eve	4.5	7.8	3.6	2.9
Steven	4.9	7.2	4.3	3.1

    a. Formulate a BIP model in algebraic form for this problem.

E* *b.* Formulate and solve this model on a spreadsheet.

9.4. A real-estate development firm, Peterson and Johnson, is considering five possible development projects. Using units of millions of dollars, the following table shows the estimated long-run profit (net present value) that each project would generate, as well as the amount of investment required to undertake the project.

	Development Project (Millions)				
	1	*2*	*3*	*4*	*5*
Estimated profit	$1	$ 1.8	$ 1.6	$0.8	$1.4
Capital required	6	12	10	4	8

The owners of the firm, Dave Peterson and Ron Johnson, have raised $20 million of investment capital for these projects. Dave and Ron now want to select the combination of projects that will maximize their total estimated long-run profit (net present value) without investing more than $20 million.

    a. Formulate a BIP model in algebraic form for this problem.

E* *b.* Formulate and solve this model on a spreadsheet.

E* 9.5. The board of directors of General Wheels Co. is considering seven large capital investments. Each investment can be made only once. These investments differ in the estimated long-run profit (net present value) that they will generate as well as in the amount of capital required, as shown by the following table:

Investment Opportunity	Estimated Profit (Millions)	Capital Required (Millions)
1	$17	$43
2	10	28
3	15	34
4	19	48
5	7	17
6	13	32
7	9	23

The total amount of capital available for these investments is $100 million. Investment opportunities 1 and 2 are mutually exclusive, and so are 3 and 4. Furthermore, neither 3 nor 4 can be undertaken unless one of the first two opportunities is undertaken. There are no such restrictions on investment opportunities 5, 6, and 7. The objective is to select the combination of capital investments that will maximize the total estimated long-run profit (net present value). Formulate and solve a BIP model on a spreadsheet for this problem.

E* 9.6. Reconsider Problem 5.22, where a swim team coach needs to assign swimmers to the different legs of a 200-yard medley relay team. Formulate and solve a BIP model on a spreadsheet for this problem. Identify the groups of mutually exclusive alternatives in this formulation.

E* 9.7.* The Research and Development Division of the Progressive Company has been developing four possible new product lines. Management must now make a decision as to which of these four products actually will be produced and at what levels. Therefore, a management science study has been requested to find the most profitable product mix.

A substantial cost is associated with beginning the production of any product, as given in the first row of the following table. Management's objective is to find the product mix that maximizes the total profit (total net revenue minus start-up costs).

	Product			
	1	*2*	*3*	*4*
Start-up cost	$50,000	$40,000	$70,000	$60,000
Marginal revenue	70	60	90	80

Let the continuous decision variables x_1, x_2, x_3, and x_4 be the total number of units produced of products 1, 2, 3, and 4, respectively. Management has imposed the following policy constraints on these variables:

1. No more than two of the products can be produced.
2. Either product 3 or 4 can be produced only if either product 1 or 2 is produced.
3. Either $5x_1 + 3x_2 + 6x_3 + 4x_4 \leq 6,000$

    or $4x_1 + 6x_2 + 3x_3 + 5x_4 \leq 6,000$

Use auxiliary binary variables to formulate and solve a mixed BIP model on a spreadsheet for this problem.

E* 9.8. The Toys-R-4-U Company has developed two new toys for possible inclusion in its product line for the upcoming Christmas season. Setting up the production facilities to begin production would cost $50,000 for toy 1 and $80,000 for toy 2. Once these costs are covered, the toys would generate a unit profit of $10 for toy 1 and $15 for toy 2.

The company has two factories that are capable of producing these toys. However, to avoid doubling the start-up costs, just one factory would be used, where the choice would be based on maximizing profit. For administrative reasons, the same factory would be used for both new toys if both are produced.

Toy 1 can be produced at the rate of 50 per hour in factory 1 and 40 per hour in factory 2. Toy 2 can be produced at the rate of 40 per hour in factory 1 and 25 per hour in factory 2. Factories 1 and 2, respectively, have 500 hours and 700 hours of production time available before Christmas that could be used to produce these toys.

It is not known whether these two toys would be continued after Christmas. Therefore, the problem is to determine how many units (if any) of each new toy should be produced before Christmas to maximize the total profit. Formulate and solve a mixed BIP model on a spreadsheet for this problem.

E* 9.9. The Fly-Right Airplane Company builds small jet airplanes to sell to corporations for the use of their executives. To meet the needs of these executives, the company's customers sometimes order a custom design of the airplanes being purchased. When this occurs, a substantial start-up cost is incurred to initiate the production of these airplanes.

Fly-Right has recently received purchase requests from three customers with short deadlines. However, because the company's production facilities already are almost completely tied up filling previous orders, it will not be able to accept all three orders. Therefore, a decision now needs to be made on the number of airplanes the company will agree to produce (if any) for each of the three customers.

The relevant data are given in the table below. The first row gives the start-up cost required to initiate the production of the airplanes for each customer. Once production is under way, the marginal net revenue (which is the purchase price minus the marginal production cost) from each airplane produced is shown in the second row. The third row gives the percentage of the available production capacity that would be used for each airplane produced. The last row indicates the maximum number of airplanes requested by each customer (but less will be accepted).

	Customer 1	Customer 2	Customer 3
Start-up cost	$3 million	$2 million	0
Marginal net revenue	$2 million	$3 million	$0.8 million
Capacity used per plane	20%	40%	20%
Maximum order	3 planes	2 planes	5 planes

Fly-Right now wants to determine how many airplanes to produce for each customer (if any) to maximize the company's total profit (total net revenue minus start-up costs). Formulate and solve a spreadsheet model with both integer variables and binary variables for this problem.

E* 9.10. Reconsider the Fly-Right Airplane Co. problem introduced in Problem 9.9. A more detailed analysis of the various cost and revenue factors now has revealed

that the potential profit from producing airplanes for each customer cannot be expressed simply in terms of a start-up cost and a fixed marginal net revenue per airplane produced. Instead, the profits are given by the following table.

Airplanes Produced	Profit (Millions)		
	Customer 1	Customer 2	Customer 3
0	0	0	0
1	−$1	$1	$1
2	2	5	3
3	4		5
4			6
5			7

Use auxiliary binary variables to formulate and solve a BIP model on a spreadsheet for this new version of the problem.

E* 9.11.* Reconsider Problem 3.5, where the management of the Omega Manufacturing Company is considering devoting excess production capacity to one or more of three products. (See the Partial Answers to Selected Problems in the back of the book for the linear programming model for this problem.) Management now has decided to add the restriction that no more than two of the three prospective products should be produced. Use auxiliary binary variables to formulate and solve a mixed BIP model on a spreadsheet for this new version of the problem.

9.12. Consider the following algebraic form of an integer nonlinear programming model:

Maximize   Profit $= 4x_1^2 - x_1^3 + 10x_2^2 - x_2^4$

subject to

$$x_1 + x_2 \le 3$$

and

$$x_1 \ge 0 \qquad x_2 \ge 0$$

x_1 and x_2 are integers

a. Reformulate this model in algebraic form as a pure BIP model with six binary variables.

E* b. Display and solve this model on a spreadsheet.

c. Reexpress the optimal solution obtained in part *b* in terms of the variables, x_1 and x_2, for the original model.

E* 9.13.* Consider the following special type of shortest-path problem (discussed in Section 6.4) where the nodes are in columns and the only paths considered always move forward one column at a time.

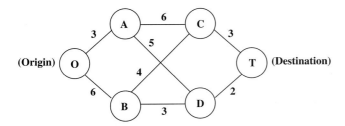

The numbers along the links represent distances (in miles), and the objective is to find the shortest path from the origin to the destination.

This problem also can be formulated as a BIP model involving both mutually exclusive alternatives and contingent decisions. Formulate and solve this BIP model on a spreadsheet. Identify the constraints that are for mutually exclusive alternatives and that are for contingent decisions.

E* 9.14. Speedy Delivery provides two-day delivery service of large parcels across the United States. Each morning at each collection center, the parcels that have arrived overnight are loaded onto several trucks for delivery throughout the area. Since the competitive battlefield in this business is speed of delivery, the parcels are divided among the trucks according to their geographical destinations to minimize the average time needed to make the deliveries.

On this particular morning, the dispatcher for the Blue River Valley Collection Center, Sharon Lofton, is hard at work. Her three drivers will be arriving in less than an hour to make the day's deliveries. There are nine parcels to be delivered, all at locations many miles apart. As usual, Sharon has loaded these locations into her computer. She is using her company's special software package, a decision support system called Dispatcher. The first thing Dispatcher does is use these locations to generate a considerable number of attractive possible routes for the individual delivery trucks. These routes are shown in the following table (where the numbers in each column indicate the order of the deliveries), along with the estimated time required to traverse the route.

	Attractive Possible Route									
Delivery Location	1	2	3	4	5	6	7	8	9	10
A	1				1				1	
B		2		1		2			2	2
C			3	3			3		3	
D	2					1		1		
E			2	2		3				
F		1			2					
G	3						1	2		3
H			1		3					1
I			3	4			2			
Time (in hours)	6	4	7	5	4	6	5	3	7	6

Dispatcher is an interactive system that shows these routes to Sharon for her approval or modification. (For example, the computer may not know that flooding has made a particular route infeasible.) After Sharon approves these routes as attractive possibilities with reasonable time estimates, Dispatcher next formulates and solves a BIP model for selecting three routes that minimize their total time while including each delivery location on exactly one route.

Using the data in the table, demonstrate how Dispatcher can formulate and solve this BIP model on a spreadsheet.

E* 9.15. An increasing number of Americans are moving to a warmer climate when they retire. To take advantage of this trend, Sunny Skies Unlimited is undertaking a major real-estate development project. The project is to develop a completely new retirement community (to be called Pilgrim Haven) that will cover several square miles. One of the decisions to be made is where to locate the two fire stations that have been allocated to the community. For planning purposes, Pilgrim Haven has been divided into five tracts, with no more than one fire station to be located in any given tract. Each station is to respond to *all* the fires that occur in the tract in which it is located as well as in the other tracts that are assigned to this station. Thus, the decisions to be made consist of (1) the tracts to receive a fire station and (2) the assignment of each of the other tracts to one of the fire stations. The objective is to minimize the overall average of the *response times* to fires.

The following table gives the average response time to a fire in each tract (the columns) if that tract is served by a station in a given tract (the rows). The bottom row gives the forecasted average number of fires that will occur in each of the tracts per day.

Assigned Station Located in Tract	Response Times (Minutes) to Fire in Tract				
	1	2	3	4	5
1	5	12	30	20	15
2	20	4	15	10	25
3	15	20	6	15	12
4	25	15	25	4	10
5	10	25	15	12	5
Average frequency of fires per day	2	1	3	1	3

Formulate and solve a BIP model on a spreadsheet for this problem. Identify any constraints that correspond to mutually exclusive alternatives or contingent decisions.

9.16 Reconsider Problem 9.15. The management of Sunny Skies Unlimited now has decided that the decision on the locations of the fire stations should be based mainly on costs.

The cost of locating a fire station in a tract is $200,000 for tract 1, $250,000 for tract 2, $400,000 for tract 3, $300,000 for tract 4, and $500,000 for tract 5. Management's objective now is the following:

Determine which tracts should receive a station to minimize the total cost of stations while ensuring that each tract has at least one station close enough to respond to a fire in no more than 15 minutes (on the average).

In contrast to the original problem, note that the total number of fire stations is no longer fixed. Furthermore, if a tract without a station has more than one station within 15 minutes, it is no longer necessary to assign this tract to just one of these stations.

    a. Formulate the algebraic form of a pure BIP model with five binary variables for this problem.

E*   *b.* Display and solve this model on a spreadsheet.

CASE 9.1
ASSIGNING ART

It had been a dream come true for Ash Briggs, a struggling artist living in the San Francisco Bay Area. He had made a trip to the corner grocery store late one Friday afternoon to buy some milk, and, on impulse, he had also purchased a California lottery ticket. One week later, he was a multimillionaire.

Ash did not want to squander his winnings on materialistic, trivial items. Instead he wanted to use his money to support his true passion: art. Ash knew all too well the difficulties of gaining recognition as an artist in this post-industrial, technological society where artistic appreciation is rare and financial support even rarer. He therefore decided to use the money to fund an exhibit of up-and-coming modern artists at the San Francisco Museum of Modern Art.

Ash approached the museum directors with his idea, and the directors became excited immediately after he informed them that he would fund the entire exhibit in addition to donating $1 million to the museum. Celeste McKenzie, a museum director, was assigned to work with Ash in planning the exhibit . The exhibit was slated to open one year from the time Ash met with the directors, and the exhibit pieces would remain on display for two months.

Ash began the project by combing the modern art community for potential artists and pieces. He presented a list (see next page) of artists, their pieces, and the price of displaying each piece[2] to Celeste.

Ash possesses certain requirements for the exhibit. He believes the majority of Americans lack adequate knowledge of art and artistic styles, and he wants the exhibit to educate Americans. Ash wants visitors to become aware of the collage as an art form, but he believes collages require little talent. He therefore decides to include only one collage. Additionally, Ash wants viewers to compare the delicate lines in a three-dimensional wire mesh sculpture to the delicate lines in a two-dimensional computer-generated drawing. He therefore wants at least one wire-mesh sculpture displayed if a computer-generated drawing is displayed. Alternatively, he wants at least one computer-generated drawing displayed if a wire-mesh sculpture is displayed. Furthermore, Ash wants to expose viewers to all painting styles, but he wants to limit the number of paintings displayed to achieve a balance in the exhibit between paintings and other art forms. He therefore decides to include at least one photo-realistic painting, at least one cubist painting, at least one expressionist painting, at least one water-color painting, and at least one oil painting. At the same time, he

wants the number of paintings to be no greater than twice the number of other art forms.

Ash wants all his own paintings included in the exhibit since he is sponsoring the exhibit and since his paintings celebrate the San Francisco Bay area, the home of the exhibit.

Ash possesses personal biases for and against some artists. Ash is currently having a steamy affair with Candy Tate, and he wants both of her paintings displayed. Ash counts both David Lyman and Rick Rawls as his best friends, and he does not want to play favorites among these two artists. He therefore decides to display as many pieces from David Lyman as from Rick Rawls and to display at least one piece from each of them. Although Ziggy Lite is very popular within art circles, Ash believes Ziggy makes a mockery of art. Ash will therefore only accept one display piece from Ziggy, if any at all.

Celeste also possesses her own agenda for the exhibit. As a museum director, she is interested in representing a diverse population of artists, appealing to a wide audience, and creating a politically correct exhibit. To advance feminism, she decides to include at least one piece from a female artist for every two pieces included from a male artist. To advance environmentalism, she decides to include either one or both of the pieces "Aging Earth" and "Wasted Resources." To advance Native American rights, she decides to include at least one piece by Bear Canton. To advance science, she decides to include at least one of the following pieces: "Chaos Reigns," "Who Has Control," "Beyond," and "Pioneers."

Celeste also understands that space is limited at the museum. The museum only has enough floor space for four sculptures and enough wall space for 20 paintings, collages, and drawings.

Finally, Celeste decides that if "Narcissism" is displayed, "Reflection" should also be displayed since "Reflection" also suggests narcissism.

Please explore the following questions independently except where otherwise indicated.

   a. Ash decides to allocate $4 million to fund the exhibit. Given the pieces available and the specific requirements from Ash and Celeste, formulate and solve a binary integer programming problem to maximize the number of pieces displayed in the exhibit without exceeding the budget. How many pieces are displayed? Which pieces are displayed?

   b. To ensure that the exhibit draws the attention of the public, Celeste decides that it must include at least 20 pieces. Formulate and solve a binary integer programming problem to minimize the cost of the exhibit while displaying at least 20 pieces and meeting the requirements set by Ash

---

[2]The display price includes the cost of paying the artist for loaning the piece to the museum, transporting the piece to San Francisco, constructing the display for the piece, insuring the piece while it is on display, and transporting the piece back to its origin.

Artist	Piece	Description of Piece	Price
Colin Zweibell	"Perfection"	A wire-mesh sculpture of the human body	$300,000
	"Burden"	A wire-mesh sculpture of a mule	250,000
	"The Great Equalizer"	A wire-mesh sculpture of a gun	125,000
Rita Losky	"Chaos Reigns"	A series of computer-generated drawings	400,000
	"Who Has Control?"	A computer-generated drawing intermeshed with lines of computer code	500,000
	"Domestication"	A pen-and-ink drawing of a house	400,000
	"Innocence"	A pen-and-ink drawing of a child	550,000
Norm Marson	"Aging Earth"	A sculpture of trash covering a larger globe	700,000
	"Wasted Resources"	A collage of various packaging materials	575,000
Candy Tate	"Serenity"	An all-blue watercolor painting	200,000
	"Calm before the Storm"	A painting with an all-blue watercolor background and a black watercolor center	225,000
Robert Bayer	"Void"	An all-black oil painting	150,000
	"Sun"	An all-yellow oil painting	150,000
David Lyman	"Storefront Window"	A photo-realistic painting of a jewelry store display window	850,000
	"Harley"	A photo-realistic painting of a Harley-Davidson motorcycle	750,000
Angie Oldman	"Consumerism"	A collage of magazine advertisements	400,000
	"Reflection"	A mirror (considered a sculpture)	175,000
	"Trojan Victory"	A wooden sculpture of a condom	450,000
Rick Rawls	"Rick"	A photo-realistic self-portrait (painting)	500,000
	"Rick II"	A cubist self-portrait (painting)	500,000
	"Rick III"	An expressionist self-portrait (painting)	500,000
Bill Reynolds	"Beyond"	A science fiction oil painting depicting Mars colonization	650,000
	"Pioneers"	An oil painting of three astronauts aboard the space shuttle	650,000
Bear Canton	"Wisdom"	A pen-and-ink drawing of an Apache chieftain	250,000
	"Superior Powers"	A pen-and-ink drawing of a traditional Native American rain dance	350,000
	"Living Land"	An oil painting of the Grand Canyon	450,000
Helen Row	"Study of a Violin"	A cubist painting of a violin	400,000
	"Study of a Fruit Bowl"	A cubist painting of a bowl of fruit	400,000
Ziggy Lite	"My Namesake"	A collage of Ziggy cartoons	300,000
	"Narcissism"	A collage of photographs of Ziggy Lite	300,000
Ash Briggs	"All That Glitters"	A watercolor painting of the Golden Gate Bridge	50,000*
	"The Rock"	A watercolor painting of Alcatraz	50,000
	"Winding Road"	A watercolor painting of Lombard Street	50,000
	"Dreams Come True"	A watercolor painting of the San Francisco Museum of Modern Art	50,000

*Ash does not require personal compensation, and the cost for moving his pieces to the museum from his home in San Francisco is minimal. The cost of displaying his pieces therefore only includes the cost of constructing the display and insuring the pieces.

and Celeste. How much does the exhibit cost? Which pieces are displayed?

c. An influential patron of Rita Losky's work who chairs the Museum Board of Directors learns that Celeste requires at least 20 pieces in the exhibit. He offers to pay the mini-

mum amount required on top of Ash's $4 million to ensure that exactly 20 pieces are displayed in the exhibit and that all of Rita's pieces are displayed. How much does the patron have to pay? Which pieces are displayed?

CASE 9.2
STOCKING SETS

Daniel Holbrook, an expediter at the local warehouse for Furniture City, sighed as he moved boxes and boxes of inventory to the side to reach the shelf where the particular item he needed was located. He dropped to his hands and knees and squinted at the inventory numbers lining the bottom row of the shelf. He did not find the number he needed. He worked his way up the shelf until he found the number matching the number on the order

slip. Just his luck! The item was on the top row of the shelf! Daniel walked back through the warehouse to find a ladder, stumbling over boxes of inventory littering his path. When he finally climbed the ladder to reach the top shelf, his face crinkled in frustration. Not again! The item he needed was not in stock! All he saw above the inventory number was an empty space covered with dust!

Daniel trudged back through the warehouse to make the dreadful phone call. He dialed the number of Brenda Sims, the saleswoman on the kitchen showroom floor of Furniture City, and informed her that the particular light fixture the customer had requested was not in stock. He then asked her if she wanted him to look for the rest of the items in the kitchen set. Brenda told him that she would talk to the customer and call him back.

Brenda hung up the phone and frowned. Mr. Davidson, her customer, would not be happy. Ordering and receiving the correct light fixture from the regional warehouse would take at least two weeks.

Brenda then paused to reflect upon business during the last month and realized that over 80 percent of the orders for kitchen sets could not be filled because items needed to complete the sets were not in stock at the local warehouse. She also realized that Furniture City was losing customer goodwill and business because of stockouts. The furniture megastore was gaining a reputation for slow service and delayed deliveries, causing customers to turn to small competitors that sold furniture directly from the showroom floor.

Brenda decided to investigate the inventory situation at the local warehouse. She walked the short distance to the building next door and gasped when she stepped inside the warehouse. What she saw could only be described as chaos. Spaces allocated for some items were overflowing into the aisles of the warehouse while other spaces were completely bare. She walked over to one of the spaces overflowing with inventory to determine what item was overstocked. She could not believe her eyes! The warehouse had at least 30 rolls of pea-green wallpaper! No customer had ordered pea-green wallpaper since 1973!

Brenda marched over to Daniel demanding an explanation. Daniel said that the warehouse had been in such a chaotic state since his arrival one year ago. He said the inventory problems occurred because management had a policy of stocking every furniture item on the showroom floor in the local warehouse. Management only replenished inventory every three months, and when inventory was replenished, management ordered every item regardless of whether it had been sold. Daniel also said that he had tried to make management aware of the problems with overstocking unpopular items and understocking popular items, but management would not listen to him because he was simply an expediter.

Brenda understood that Furniture City required a new inventory policy. Not only was the megastore losing money by making customers unhappy with delivery delays, but it was also losing money by wasting warehouse space. By changing the inventory policy to stock only popular items and replenish them immediately when they are sold, Furniture City would ensure that the majority of customers receive their furniture immediately and that the valuable warehouse space was utilized effectively.

Brenda needed to sell her inventory policy to management. Using her extensive sales experience, she decided that the most effective sales strategy would be to use her kitchen department as a model for the new inventory policy. She would identify all kitchen sets comprising 85 percent of customer orders. Given the fixed amount of warehouse space allocated to the kitchen department, she would identify the items Furniture City should stock to satisfy the greatest number of customer orders. She would then calculate the revenue from satisfying customer orders under the new inventory policy, using the bottom line to persuade management to accept her policy.

Brenda analyzed her records over the past three years and determined that 20 kitchen sets were responsible for 85 percent of the customer orders. These 20 kitchen sets were composed of up to eight features in a variety of styles. Brenda listed each feature and its popular styles.

Brenda then created a table (given on the next page) showing the 20 kitchen sets and the particular features composing each set. To simplify the table, she used the codes shown in parentheses below to represent the particular feature and style. For example, kitchen set 1 consists of floor tile T2, wallpaper W2, light fixture L4, cabinet C2, countertop O2, dishwasher D2, sink S2, and range R2. Notice that sets 14 through 20 do not contain dishwashers.

Floor Tile	Wallpaper	Light Fixtures	Cabinets
(T1) White textured tile	(W1) Plain ivory paper	(L1) One large rectangular frosted fixture	(C1) Light solid wood cabinets
(T2) Ivory textured tile	(W2) Ivory paper with dark brown pinstripes	(L2) Three small square frosted fixtures	(C2) Dark solid wood cabinets
(T3) White checkered tile with blue trim	(W3) Blue paper with marble texture	(L3) One large oval frosted fixture	(C3) Light-wood cabinets with glass doors
(T4) White checkered tile with light yellow trim	(W4) Light yellow paper with marble texture	(L4) Three small frosted globe fixtures	(C4) Dark-wood cabinets with glass doors

Countertops	Dishwashers	Sinks	Ranges
(O1) Plain light-wood countertops	(D1) White energy-saving dishwasher	(S1) Sink with separate hot and cold water taps	(R1) White electric oven
(O2) Stained light-wood countertops	(D2) Ivory energy-saving dishwasher	(S2) Divided sink with separate hot and cold water taps and garbage disposal	(R2) Ivory electric oven
(O3) White lacquer-coated countertops		(S3) Sink with one hot and cold water tap	(R3) White gas oven
(O4) Ivory lacquer-coated countertops		(S4) Divided sink with one hot and cold water tap and garbage disposal	(R4) Ivory gas oven

	T1	T2	T3	T4	W1	W2	W3	W4	L1	L2	L3	L4	C1	C2	C3	C4	O1	O2	O3	O4	D1	D2	S1	S2	S3	S4	R1	R2	R3	R4
Set 1		X				X						X		X						X		X		X				X		
Set 2		X	X		X				X							X				X		X				X		X		
Set 3	X						X			X			X		X	X	X				X				X				X	
Set 4			X				X				X				X				X	X	X		X				X			
Set 5				X				X	X				X					X			X			X			X			
Set 6		X				X				X						X				X		X			X					X
Set 7	X						X					X			X			X			X		X				X			
Set 8		X			X						X		X				X					X			X					X
Set 9		X			X					X					X			X				X		X				X		
Set 10					X				X				X						X		X					X			X	
Set 11			X		X						X				X		X				X		X						X	
Set 12		X				X			X					X				X				X				X		X		
Set 13			X	X			X	X			X				X		X				X			X					X	
Set 14				X				X				X	X						X				X				X			
Set 15			X		X				X				X				X								X				X	
Set 16			X				X	X				X	X						X					X			X			
Set 17	X									X					X				X	X						X			X	
Set 18		X					X				X			X						X	X		X					X		
Set 19		X						X		X		X				X				X	X			X				X		X
Set 20		X					X						X					X							X					X

373

Brenda knew she had only a limited amount of warehouse space allocated to the kitchen department. The warehouse could hold 50 square feet of tile and 12 rolls of wallpaper in the inventory bins. The inventory shelves could hold two light fixtures, two cabinets, three countertops, and two sinks. Dishwashers and ranges are similar in size, so Furniture City stored them in similar locations. The warehouse floor could hold a total of four dishwashers and ranges.

Every kitchen set always includes exactly 20 square feet of tile and exactly five rolls of wallpaper. Therefore, 20 square feet of a particular style of tile and five rolls of a particular style of wallpaper are required for the styles to be in stock.

a. Formulate and solve a binary integer programming problem to maximize the total number of kitchen sets (and thus the number of customer orders) Furniture City stocks in the local warehouse. Assume that when a customer orders a kitchen set, all the particular items composing that kitchen set are replenished at the local warehouse immediately.

b. How many of each feature and style should Furniture City stock in the local warehouse? How many different kitchen sets are in stock?

c. Furniture City decides to discontinue carrying nursery sets, and the warehouse space previously allocated to the nursery department is divided between the existing departments at Furniture City. The kitchen department receives enough additional space to allow it to stock both styles of dishwashers and three of the four styles of ranges. How does the optimal inventory policy for the kitchen department change with this additional warehouse space?

d. Brenda convinces management that the kitchen department should serve as a testing ground for future inventory policies. To provide adequate space for testing, management decides to allocate all the space freed by the nursery department to the kitchen department. The extra space means that the kitchen department can store not only the dishwashers and ranges from part c, but also all sinks, all countertops, three of the four light fixtures, and three of the four cabinets. How much does the additional space help?

e. How would the inventory policy be affected if the items composing a kitchen set could not be replenished immediately? Under what conditions is the assumption of immediate replenishment nevertheless justified?

CASE 9.3
ASSIGNING STUDENTS TO SCHOOLS (REVISITED)

Reconsider Case 3.3. The Springfield School Board now has made the decision to prohibit the splitting of residential areas among multiple schools. Thus, each of the six areas must be assigned to a single school.

a. Formulate a BIP model for this problem under the current policy of providing bussing for all middle school students who must travel more than approximately a mile.

b. Referring to part a of Case 3.3, explain why that linear programming model and the BIP model just formulated

are so different when they are dealing with nearly the same problem.

c. Solve the BIP model formulated in part a.

d. Referring to part c of Case 3.3, determine how much the total bussing cost increases because of the decision to prohibit the splitting of residential areas among multiple schools.

e, f, g, h. Repeat parts e, f, g, h of Case 3.3 under the new school board decision to prohibit splitting of residential areas among multiple schools.

10

DECISION ANALYSIS

The previous chapters have focused mainly on managerial decision making when the consequences of alternative decisions are known with a reasonable degree of certainty. This decision-making environment enabled formulating helpful mathematical models (linear programming, integer programming, etc.) with objective functions that specify the estimated consequences of any combination of decisions. Although these consequences usually cannot be predicted with complete certainty, they could at least be estimated with enough accuracy to justify using such models (along with sensitivity analysis, etc.).

However, managers often must make decisions in environments that are much more fraught with uncertainty. Here are a few examples.

1. A manufacturer introducing a new product into the marketplace. What will be the reaction of potential customers? How much should be produced? Should the product be test marketed in a small region before deciding upon full distribution? How much advertising is needed to launch the product successfully?

2. A financial firm investing in securities. Which are the market sectors and individual securities with the best prospects? Where is the economy headed? How about interest rates? How should these factors affect the investment decisions?

3. A government contractor bidding on a new contract. What will be the actual costs of the project? Which other companies might be bidding? What are their likely bids?

4. An agricultural firm selecting the mix of crops and livestock for the upcoming season. What will be the weather conditions? Where are prices headed? What will costs be?

5. An oil company deciding whether to drill for oil in a particular location. How likely is oil there? How much? How deep will they need to drill? Should geologists investigate the site further before drilling?

These are the kinds of decision making in the face of great uncertainty that *decision analysis* is designed to address. Decision analysis provides a framework and methodology for rational decision making when the outcomes are uncertain.

The first section introduces a case study that will be carried throughout the chapter to illustrate the various phases involved in applying decision analysis. Sections 10.2 and 10.3 focus on formulating the problem and choosing an appropriate decision criterion. The subsequent two sections deal with whether it would be worthwhile to obtain more information and, if so, how to use this information. Sections 10.6 and 10.7 then describe how to analyze the problem while calibrating the possible outcomes to reflect their true value to the decision maker. Finally, Section 10.8 discusses the practical application of decision analysis and summarizes a variety of applications that have been very beneficial to the organizations involved.

10.1 A Case Study: The Goferbroke Company Problem

Max Flyer is the founder and sole owner of the Goferbroke Company, which develops oil wells in unproven territory. Max's friends refer to him affectionately as a wildcatter. However, he prefers to think of himself as an entrepreneur. He has poured his life's savings into the company in the hope of making it big with a large strike of oil.

Now his chance possibly has come. His company has purchased various tracts of land that larger oil companies have spurned as unpromising even though they are near some large oil fields. Now Max has received an exciting report about one of these tracts. A consulting geologist has just informed Max that he believes there is one chance in four of oil there.

Max has learned from bitter experience to be skeptical about the chances of oil reported by consulting geologists. Drilling for oil on this tract would require an investment of about $100,000. If the land turns out to be dry (no oil), the entire investment would be lost. Since his company does not have much capital left, this loss would be quite serious.

On the other hand, if the tract does contain oil, the consulting geologist estimates that there would be enough there to generate a net revenue of approximately $800,000, leaving an approximate profit of

$$\text{Profit if find oil} = \text{revenue if find oil} - \text{drilling cost}$$

$$= \$800,000 - \$100,000$$

$$= \$700,000$$

Although this wouldn't be quite the big strike for which Max has been waiting, it would provide a very welcome infusion of capital into the company to keep it going until he hopefully can hit the really big gusher.

There is another option. Another oil company has gotten wind of the consulting geologist's report and so has offered to purchase the tract of land from Max for $90,000. This is very tempting. This too would provide a welcome infusion of capital into the company, but without incurring the large risk of a very substantial loss of $100,000.

Table 10.1 summarizes the decision alternatives and prospective payoffs that face Max.

So Max is in a quandary about what to do. Fortunately, help is at hand. Max's daughter Jennifer has recently earned her degree from a fine business school and now has come to work for her proud dad. He asks her to apply her business training to help him analyze the problem. Having studied management science in college, she recommends applying decision analysis. Having paid for her fine education, he agrees to give it a try.

Jennifer begins by interviewing her dad about the problem.

Jennifer: How much faith do you put in the consulting geologist's assessment that there is one chance in four of oil on this tract?
Max: Not too much. These guys sometimes seem to pull numbers out of the air. He has convinced me that there is some chance of oil there. But it could just as well be one chance in three, or one chance in five. They don't really know.
Jennifer: Is there a way of getting more information to pin these odds down better? This is an important option with the decision analysis approach.
Max: Yes. We could arrange for a detailed seismic survey of the land. That would pin down the odds somewhat better. But you don't really find out until you drill. Furthermore, these seismic surveys cost you an arm and a leg. I got a quote for this

TABLE 10.1   **Prospective Profits for the Goferbroke Company**

Alternative	Status of Land	Profit	
		Oil	Dry
Drill for oil		$700,000	−$100,000
Sell the land		90,000	90,000
Chance of status		1 in 4	3 in 4

tract. 30,000 bucks! Then it might say oil is likely, so we drill and we might not find anything. Then I'm out another 100,000 bucks! Losing $130,000 would almost put us out of business.

Jennifer: OK. Let's put the seismic survey on the back burner for now. Here is another key consideration. It sounds like we need to go beyond dollars and cents to look at the consequences of the possible outcomes. Losing $130,000 would hurt a lot more than gaining $130,000 would help.

Max: That's for sure!

Jennifer: Well, decision analysis has a way of taking this into account by using what are called utilities. The **utility** of an outcome measures the true value to you of that outcome rather than just the monetary value.

Max: Sounds good.

Jennifer: Now this is what I suggest we do. We'll start out simple, without considering the option of the seismic survey and without getting into utilities. I'll introduce you to how decision analysis organizes our problem and to the options it provides for the criterion to use for making your decision. You'll be able to choose the criterion that feels right to you. Then we'll look at whether it might be worthwhile to do the seismic survey and, if so, how to best use its information. After that, we'll get into the nitty gritty of carefully analyzing the problem, including incorporating utilities. I think when we finish the process and you make your decision, you'll feel quite comfortable that you are making the best one.

Max: Good. Let's get started.

Review Questions

1. What are the decision alternatives being considered by Max?
2. What is the consulting geologist's assessment of the chances of oil on the tract of land?
3. How much faith does Max put in the consulting geologist's assessment of the chances of oil?
4. What option is available for obtaining more information about the chances of oil?

10.2 Formulating the Problem

Here is the tutorial that Jennifer provided her dad about the logical way in which decision analysis organizes a problem.

Terminology

Decision analysis has a few special terms.

The **decision maker** is the individual or group responsible for making the decision (or sequence of decisions) under consideration. For the Goferbroke Co. problem, the decision maker is Max. Jennifer (the management scientist) can help perform the analyses, but the objective is to assist the decision maker in identifying the best possible decision from the decision maker's perspective.

The **alternatives** are the options for the decision to be made by the decision maker. Max's alternatives at this point are to drill for oil or to sell the tract of land.

The outcome of the decision to be made will be affected by random factors that are outside the control of the decision maker. These random factors determine the situation that will be found when the decision is executed. Each of these possible situations is referred to as a possible **state of nature.** For the Goferbroke Co. problem, the possible states of nature are that the tract contains oil or that it is dry (no oil).

The decision maker generally will have some information about the relative likelihood of the possible states of nature. This information may just be in the form of subjective estimates based on the experience or intuition of an individual, or there may be some degree of hard evidence involved (such as is contained in the consulting geologist's report). When these estimates are expressed in the form of probabilities, they are referred to as the **prior**

probabilities of the respective states of nature. For the Goferbroke Co. problem, the consulting geologist has provided the prior probabilities given in Table 10.2. Although these are unlikely to be the true probabilities based on more information (such as through a seismic survey), they are the best available estimates of the probabilities *prior* to obtaining more information.

Each combination of a decision alternative and a state of nature results in some outcome. The **payoff** is a quantitative measure of the value to the decision maker of the consequences of the outcome. In most cases, the payoff is expressed as a monetary value, such as the profit. As indicated in Table 10.1, the payoff for the Goferbroke Co. at this stage is profit. (In Section 10.7, the company's payoffs will be reexpressed in terms of utilities.)

The Payoff Table

When formulating the problem, it is important to identify *all* the relevant decision alternatives and the possible states of nature. After identifying the appropriate measure for the *payoff* from the perspective of the decision maker, the next step is to estimate the payoff for each combination of a decision alternative and a state of nature. These payoffs then are displayed in a **payoff table.**

Table 10.3 shows the payoff table for the Goferbroke Co. problem. The payoffs are given in units of thousands of dollars of profit. Note that the bottom row also shows the prior probabilities of the states of nature, as given earlier in Table 10.2.

The Decision Tree

This same information also can be displayed graphically in what is called a **decision tree.** The decision tree for the Goferbroke Co. problem is shown in Figure 10.1. Starting on the

---

TABLE 10.2   Prior Probabilities for the Goferbroke Co. Problem

State of Nature	Prior Probability
The tract of land contains oil	0.25
The tract of land is dry (no oil)	0.75

TABLE 10.3   Payoff Table (Profit in $1,000s) for the Goferbroke Problem

	State of Nature	
Alternative	Oil	Dry
Drill for oil	700	−100
Sell the land	90	90
Prior probability	0.25	0.75

FIGURE 10.1

The decision tree for the Goferbroke Co. problem presented in Table 10.3.

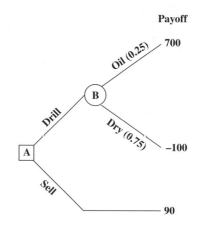

left side and moving to the right side shows the progression of events. First, a decision is made as to whether to drill for oil or sell the land. If the decision is to drill, the next event is to learn whether the state of nature is that the land contains oil or it is dry. Finally, the payoff is obtained that results from these events.

In the terminology of decision trees, the junction points are called **nodes** (or forks) and the lines emanating from the nodes are referred to as **branches.** A distinction is then made between the following two types of nodes.

> A **decision node,** represented by a *square,* indicates that a decision needs to be made at that point in the process. A **chance node,** represented by a *circle,* indicates that a random event occurs at that point.

Thus, node A in Figure 10.1 is a decision node since the decision on whether to drill or sell occurs there. Node B is a chance node since a random event, the occurrence of one of the possible states of nature, takes place there. Each of the two branches emanating from this node corresponds to one of the possible random events, where the number in parentheses along the branch gives the probability that this event will occur.

A decision tree can be very helpful for visualizing and analyzing a problem. When the problem is as small as the one in Figure 10.1, using the decision tree in the analysis process is optional, and we will not explicitly do so in the next few sections. However, one nice feature of decision trees is that they also can be used for more complicated problems where a sequence of decisions needs to be made. You will see this illustrated for the Goferbroke Co. problem in Sections 10.6 and 10.7 when a decision on whether to conduct a seismic survey is made before deciding whether to drill or sell.

Spreadsheet Software for Decision Trees

We will describe and illustrate how to use either of two Excel add-ins for constructing and analyzing decision trees on a spreadsheet. One of these add-ins is the academic version of *TreePlan,* which is shareware developed by Professor Michael Middleton. It is available to you in your MS Courseware. (If you want to continue to use it after this course, you should register and pay the shareware fee.) The other add-in is PrecisionTree, which has been developed by Palisade Corporation. The professional version of PrecisionTree is available from Palisade for a free trial period of 10 days. It can either be downloaded from the Palisade web site, www.Palisade.com, or ordered on a CD-ROM from this web site. Like any Excel add-ins, these add-ins need to be installed before they will show up in Excel.

To begin creating a decision tree using PrecisionTree, select the Create New Tree command in the menu. This will create a single branch for starting the tree, followed by a single *end node* (represented by a blue triangle). Clicking on the New Tree label on this branch brings up the Tree Settings dialogue box (as shown in Figure 10.2).

The Optimum Path entry can be set at either Maximum (indicates that the objective is to maximize the payoff) or Minimum (for an objective of minimizing the cost), so

FIGURE 10.2

The Tree Settings dialogue box used by PrecisionTree to initiate the construction of the Goferbroke decision tree.

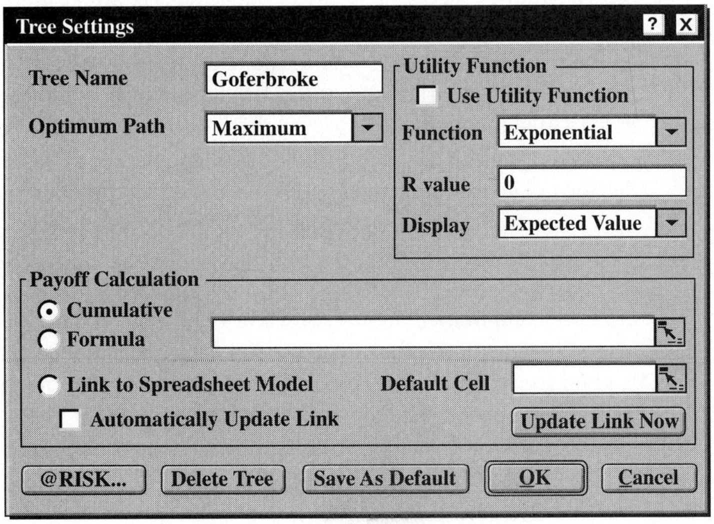

FIGURE 10.3

The Node Settings dialogue box used by PrecisionTree to create nodes in a decision tree.

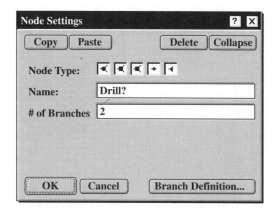

FIGURE 10.4

The Branch Settings dialogue box used by PrecisionTree to give names to branches in a decision tree.

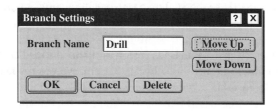

FIGURE 10.5

The decision tree constructed and solved by the professional version of PrecisionTree for the first Goferbroke Co. problem (no consideration of doing a seismic survey).

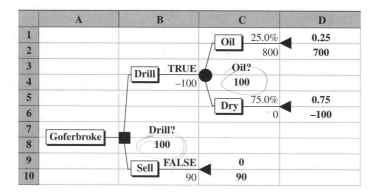

Maximum is chosen here. After entering the tree name (Goferbroke), you can just leave the other settings at their default values and click OK.

To create a decision node for starting the tree, click on the single end node that was obtained when you created the new tree. Clicking on the decision node icon—a green square—in the Node Settings dialogue box changes the end node to a decision node. Figure 10.3 shows the Node Settings dialogue box after entering the node name (Drill?) and the number of branches (2) emanating from that node.

Clicking OK enables you to move on to deal with each branch by clicking on its box in the tree. Figure 10.4 shows the Branch Settings dialogue box that is being used in this case to give the name Drill to one of the branches.

To create a chance node, click on the end node it is replacing, which brings up the Node Settings dialogue box. Then, click on the chance node icon—a red circle—next to Node Type. Next, enter the node's name (Oil?) and the number of branches (2). After clicking OK, click on each branch box to give it a name with the Branch Settings dialogue box.

Applying this procedure to the Goferbroke Co. problem leads to creating all the nodes, branches, and branch names shown in Figure 10.5. At this point, each branch would show a default value of 0 for the net cash flow being generated there and each of the two branches leading from the chance node in column C also would display default values of 50 percent for the prior probabilities (expressed as a percentage). Therefore, you next should click on these default values and replace them with the correct numbers, namely,

B4 = −100 (the cost of drilling is $100,000)
B10 = 90 (the profit from selling is $90,000)
C1 = 25% (the prior probability of oil is 0.25)
C2 = 800 (the net revenue after finding oil is $800,000)
C5 = 75% (the prior probability of dry is 0.75)
C6 = 0 (the net revenue after finding dry is 0)

as shown in the figure.

At each stage in constructing a decision tree, PrecisionTree automatically solves for the optimal policy with the current tree when using *Bayes' decision rule,* described in the next section. Thus, for the final decision tree in Figure 10.5, the word TRUE in cell B3 indicates that the Drill alternative should be chosen, whereas the word FALSE in cell B9 says that the Sell alternative should not be chosen. The two numbers to the right of each end node are, first, the probability of reaching that node under the indicated policy and, second, the payoff if that node is reached. The number 100 in cells B8 and C4 is the *expected payoff* (the measure of performance to be described for Bayes' decision rule) at those stages in the process.

This description of PrecisionTree may seem somewhat complicated. However, we think that you will find the procedure quite intuitive when you execute it on a computer. If you spend considerable time with PrecisionTree, you also will find that it has many helpful features (including nice ways of performing sensitivity analysis) that haven't been described in this brief introduction.

The second Excel add-in, TreePlan (academic version), constructs and analyzes decision trees in much the same way as PrecisionTree. Since it is shareware rather than a commercial product, it lacks some of the bells and whistles (including special capabilities for sensitivity analysis) of PrecisionTree. However, a companion software package, called *SensIt,* provides these capabilities for sensitivity analysis. The academic version of this Excel add-in also is included in your MS Courseware, and we will show its dialogue box near the end of the next section (Figure 10.15).

To construct a decision tree with TreePlan, go to its Tools menu and choose Decision Tree, which brings up the TreePlan . . . New dialogue box shown in Figure 10.6. Clicking on New Tree then adds a tree to the spreadsheet that initially consists of a single (square) decision node with two branches. Clicking just to the right of a terminal node (displayed by a vertical hash mark at the end of a branch) brings up the TreePlan . . . Terminal dialogue box (see Figure 10.6), which enables you to change the terminal node into either a decision node or an event (chance) node with the desired number of branches (between 1 and 5). (TreePlan refers to chance nodes as *event* nodes.) At any time, you also can click on any existing decision node (a square) or event node (circle) to bring up the corresponding dialogue box—TreePlan . . . Decision or TreePlan . . . Event—to make any of the modifications listed in Figure 10.6 at that node.

Figure 10.7 shows the decision tree that would be constructed with TreePlan for the Goferbroke Co. problem. For the various branches, the names (cells D4, D12, H2, and H7), the cash flows (cells D6, D14, H4, and H9), and the probabilities (cells H1 and H6) are typed directly into the spreadsheet. TreePlan automatically adds the cash flows (e.g., I4 = D6 + H4) to obtain the total cash flows shown twice at each end node. As in Figure 10.5, the number 100 (in cells A10 and E6) is the *expected payoff* (the measure of performance to be described for Bayes' decision rule) at those stages in the process. The number 1 in cell B9 signifies that the first branch named (the Drill branch) is the one that should be chosen for the decision at this node.

Review Questions

1. What is meant by the possible states of nature?
2. What is meant by prior probabilities?
3. What are represented by the payoffs in a payoff table?

FIGURE 10.6

The dialogue boxes used by TreePlan for constructing a decision tree.

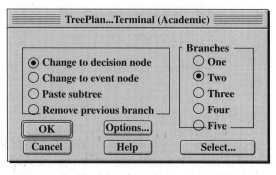

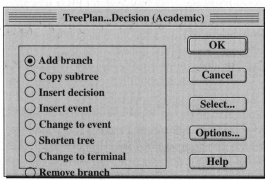

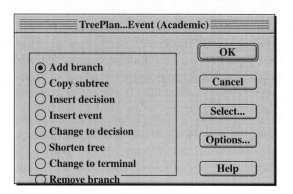

FIGURE 10.7

The decision tree constructed and solved by the academic version of TreePlan for the first Goferbroke Co. problem.

	A	B	C	D	E	F	G	H	I	J	K
1								0.25			
2								Oil			
3											700
4				Drill				800	700		
5							◯				
6				−100	100			0.75			
7								Dry			
8											−100
9			1					0	−100		
10		100									
11											
12				Sell							
13											90
14				90	90						

4. What is a decision tree?

5. What is a decision node in a decision tree? A chance node?

6. What symbols are used to represent decision nodes and chance nodes?

10.3 Decision Criteria That Use Probabilities

Based on the consulting geologist's report for the Goferbroke Company, Table 10.2 gives the prior probabilities of the two possible states of nature (oil and dry) as 0.25 and 0.75, respectively. The company owner, Max Flyer, would prefer to make his decision on whether to drill or sell the tract of land without relying on these prior probabilities if there is a good way of doing so. In fact, several different criteria were proposed decades ago for making such a decision without using probabilities. Unfortunately, all these criteria were found to have major deficiencies. A supplement to this chapter on your CD-ROM describes these criteria, their deficiencies, and how Jennifer Flyer was able to persuade Max that he instead should adopt some decision criterion that uses probabilities without relying on the numbers being exactly correct. We describe three such criteria below.

The Maximum Likelihood Criterion

The **maximum likelihood criterion** says to focus on the *most likely* state of nature as follows.

1. Identify the state of nature with the largest prior probability.

2. Choose the decision alternative that has the largest payoff for this state of nature.

Your MS Courseware includes an Excel template for applying this criterion. Figure 10.8 shows how this would be done for Goferbroke's problem. Since dry is the state of nature with the larger prior probability, we only consider the payoffs in column D (-100 and 90). The larger of these two payoffs is 90, so we choose the corresponding alternative, sell the land.

The rationale for this criterion is a simple one. The final payoff will depend partially on which state of nature will turn out to be the true one. Although we don't know which state of nature will occur, we do know which one probably has the maximum likelihood. By basing our decision on the assumption that this state of nature will occur, we are giving ourselves a better chance of a favorable outcome than by assuming any other state of nature.

This criterion also has received a number of criticisms.

1. This criterion chooses an alternative without considering its payoffs for states of nature other than the most likely one. What if any of these other payoffs would be disastrous? (Fortunately, this is not the case for Goferbroke's problem, where the payoff from selling the land is the same for both states of nature.)

2. For alternatives that are not chosen, this criterion also ignores their payoffs for states of nature other than the most likely one. What if any of these payoffs would be far better than could be obtained with the chosen alternative? Shouldn't we

FIGURE 10.8

The application of the Excel template for the maximum likelihood criterion to the first Goferbroke Co. problem.

	A	B	C	D	E	F	G	H
1		Maximum Likelihood Criterion for the Goferbroke Co. Problem						
2								
3				State of Nature				
4		Alternative	Oil	Dry				
5		Drill	700	–100				
6		Sell	90	90				Maximum
7								
8								
9								
10		Prior Probability	0.25	0.75				
11			Maximum					

consider the fact that Goferbroke's payoff from drilling for oil and finding it is much, much more than from selling the land?

3. If the differences in the payoffs for the most likely state of nature are much less than for another somewhat likely state of nature, then it might make more sense to focus on this latter state of nature instead. For Goferbroke, the difference between the payoffs for drilling and selling when the land is dry is only 190, whereas it is 610 when the land contains oil, so perhaps it is more crucial to choose the best alternative for this latter state of nature instead.

4. If there are many states of nature and they are nearly equally likely, then the probability that the most likely state of nature will be the true one is fairly low. In this case, would it make sense to make the decision based on just one state of nature that has a fairly low probability?

Max's Reaction

Max: It sounds like this criterion won't fit some situations very well. But I kind of like it for my problem. It is simple for one thing. But more importantly, it doesn't require me to use the consulting geologist's numbers, which I know are pulled somewhat out of the air. I do have enough faith in his report to believe it is more likely that the land is dry than that there is oil there. So I am pretty comfortable in providing the information the criterion needs by specifying which is more likely.
Jennifer: Sure, you can do that. But is it making the decision the way you want?
Max: What do you mean?
Jennifer: When you buy your tracts of land, is your main goal to find oil there? Or are you mostly interested in reselling the land?
Max: Finding oil, of course. That is the whole point.
Jennifer: Typically, for a tract of land you buy, will it be more likely that it is dry or that it contains oil?
Max: Dry. That's the nature of our business. You have to try a lot of sites to find that one big strike.
Jennifer: So what do you think this criterion will tell you to do on those sites?
Max: Oh, you're right! Now I see your point. Because it normally is more likely that the land is dry, it will keep telling me time after time to sell rather than drill for oil. That is no way to run an oil-prospecting business.
Jennifer: Exactly! The key is the second and third criticisms I gave earlier. You really need to take into account how large the payoff might be if you do find oil.
Max: I agree. This is not a good criterion for an oil prospector to use. I hope the next one is better.
Jennifer: You'll be the judge of that.

The Equally Likely Criterion

It usually is difficult to place a lot of faith in the prior probabilities of the possible states of nature. Therefore, the **equally likely criterion** says to not even try to assign meaningful numbers to these probabilities. In the absence of further information, simply assume instead that the states of nature are *equally likely* and proceed as follows.

1. For each decision alternative, calculate the *average* of its payoffs over all the states of nature. (With equally likely states of nature, this average is the expected payoff in the statistical sense.)
2. Choose the alternative with the *largest* average payoff.

Using the corresponding Excel template in your MS Courseware, Figure 10.9 shows the application of this criterion to Goferbroke's problem. The average payoff for each alternative is given in column H. Since drilling for oil has an average payoff of 300, versus only 90 for selling the land, the choice is to drill.

This criterion is sometimes called the *Laplace Principle,* because it was first enunciated (to our knowledge) about 200 years ago by the famous French mathematician, the Marquis Pierre-Simon de Laplace. (Sometimes called the Isaac Newton of France, Laplace was a key founder of the modern theory of probability.)

FIGURE 10.9

The application of the Excel template for the equally likely criterion to the first Goferbroke Co. problem.

	A	B	C	D	E	F	G	H	I
1		Equally Likely Criterion for the Goferbroke Co. Problem							
2									
3				State of Nature				Row	
4		Alternative	Oil	Dry				Average	
5		Drill	700	–100				300	Maximum
6		Sell	90	90				90	
7									
8									
9									
10		Prior Probability	0.25	0.75					

	H	I
5	=AVERAGE(C5:G5)	=IF(H5=MAX($H$5:$H$9),"Maximum","")
6	=AVERAGE(C6:G6)	=IF(H6=MAX($H$5:$H$9),"Maximum","")
7	=AVERAGE(C7:G7)	=IF(H7=MAX($H$5:$H$9),"Maximum","")
8	=AVERAGE(C8:G8)	=IF(H8=MAX($H$5:$H$9),"Maximum","")
9	=AVERAGE(C9:G9)	=IF(H9=MAX($H$5:$H$9),"Maximum","")

Some modern decision makers agree with Laplace that decision making should be based on the reality that it is impossible to accurately predict the future. Events occur randomly. A typical random event is the occurrence of a state of nature. It is unrealistic to try to assign prior probabilities to states of nature, since this would go beyond our ability to predict the future. Nature gives us no advance information that it will do anything but randomize over its states. Therefore, to stay within the bounds of rationality, we should simply assume that the states of nature are equally likely.

Critics of this line of reasoning make three main points.

1. Treating the states of nature as equally likely amounts to assigning each one the following prior probability:

$$\text{Prior probability} = \frac{1}{\text{number of states of nature}}$$

Assigning this value to each prior probability is just as arbitrary as assigning any other values to these probabilities.

2. In some situations, there is good evidence that certain states of nature are more likely than others. Using this information should improve the decision.

3. There often are alternative ways of itemizing the possible states of nature. For example, the state of having oil could be broken down into several states involving different amounts of oil. Changing the number of states changes the prior probability of each one, which might then change the resulting decision. It is undesirable to have the decision depend on the arbitrary way in which the possible states of nature are itemized.

Max's Reaction

Max: I like the fact that this criterion doesn't force me to rely on the consulting geologist's numbers.

Jennifer: You mean his estimate that there is one chance in four of having oil on this tract of land?

Max: Yes. I just don't trust his numbers.

Jennifer: Would you have any more faith in his numbers if he had said one chance in two of oil?

Max: No, not particularly. Whatever numbers he comes up with, the real chance of oil could be quite a bit lower or quite a bit higher.

Jennifer: But if one chance in two of oil is the right ballpark, would you want to drill?

Max: Certainly. Those are great odds in this business. Why?

Jennifer: Because this criterion is always giving you odds of one chance in two of oil.

Max: Really? I didn't catch that. You mean it would tell me to drill regardless of how promising or unpromising the land looked?

Jennifer: Yes, pretty automatically. I guess I didn't make clear that this equally likely business says to assume that the odds of having oil are the same as for being dry.

Max: Whoa. Now I get it. That won't do at all! I may not trust the consulting geologist's numbers completely, but this criterion's numbers seem completely worthless in my business. I need real odds based on solid evidence, not numbers pulled completely out of the air.

Jennifer: If one chance in two of oil is not the right ballpark, then you certainly are correct. So you prefer the consulting geologist's numbers?

Max: Definitely. But I don't want my decision to depend on his numbers being exactly correct.

Jennifer: OK. Let's look at a criterion that uses his numbers. Then we'll talk about how to analyze the situation if his numbers are off some.

Max: Good.

Bayes' Decision Rule

Bayes' decision rule directly uses the prior probabilities of the possible states of nature as summarized below.

1. For each decision alternative, calculate the *weighted average* of its payoffs by multiplying each payoff by the prior probability of the corresponding state of nature and then summing these products. Using statistical terminology, refer to this weighted average as the **expected payoff (EP)** for this decision alternative.

2. Bayes' decision rule says to choose the alternative with the *largest* expected payoff.

Figure 10.10 shows the application of the Excel template for this criterion to Goferbroke's problem. This template executes step 1 of the procedure by using the equations entered into cells H5 and H6, namely,

$$H5 = SUMPRODUCT (C5:G5, C10:G10),$$

$$H6 = SUMPRODUCT (C6:G6, C10:G10),$$

where the blanks in columns E, F, and G are interpreted as zeroes. Since expected payoff = 100 for the drilling alternative (cell H5), versus a smaller value of expected payoff = 90

FIGURE 10.10

The application of the Excel template for Bayes' decision rule to the first Goferbroke Co. problem.

	A	B	C	D	E	F	G	H	I
1		Bayes' Decision Rule for the Goferbroke Co. Problem							
2									
3				State of Nature				Expected	
4		Alternative	Oil	Dry				Payoff	
5		Drill	700	–100				100	Maximum
6		Sell	90	90				90	
7									
8									
9									
10		Prior Probability	0.25	0.75					

	H	I
5	=SUMPRODUCT(C5:G5,C10:G10)	=IF(H5=MAX($H$5:$H$9),"Maximum","")
6	=SUMPRODUCT(C6:G6,C10:G10)	=IF(H6=MAX($H$5:$H$9),"Maximum","")
7	=SUMPRODUCT(C7:G7,C10:G10)	=IF(H7=MAX($H$5:$H$9),"Maximum","")
8	=SUMPRODUCT(C8:G8,C10:G10)	=IF(H8=MAX($H$5:$H$9),"Maximum","")
9	=SUMPRODUCT(C9:G9,C10:G10)	=IF(H9=MAX($H$5:$H$9),"Maximum","")

for selling the land (cell H6), this criterion says to drill for oil, as indicated by the word *Maximum* entered into cell I5.

Referring back to the decision trees in Figures 10.5 and 10.7, both PrecisionTree and TreePlan use this same procedure to select the alternative of drilling for oil. The number 100 in cells B8 and C4 of Figure 10.5 and in cells A10 and E6 of Figure 10.7 is the expected payoff for this alternative.

Like all the others, this criterion cannot guarantee that the selected alternative will turn out to have been the best one after learning the true state of nature. However, it does provide another guarantee described below.

> The expected payoff for a particular decision alternative can be interpreted as what the *average* payoff would become if the same situation were to be repeated numerous times. Therefore, *on the average,* repeatedly using Bayes' decision rule to make decisions will lead to larger payoffs in the long run than any other criterion (assuming the prior probabilities are valid).

Thus, if the Goferbroke Co. owned many tracts of land with this same payoff table, drilling for oil on all of them would provide an average payoff of about 100 ($100,000), versus only 90 ($90,000) for selling. As the following calculations indicate, this is the average payoff from drilling that results from having oil in an average of one tract out of every four (as indicated by the prior probabilities).

$$\text{Oil found in one tract:} \qquad \text{Payoff} = 700$$

$$\text{Three tracts are dry:} \qquad \text{Payoff} = 3\,(-100) = -300$$

$$\text{Total payoff} = 400$$

$$\text{Average payoff} = \frac{400}{4} = 100$$

However, achieving this average payoff might require going through a long stretch of dry tracts until the "law of averages" can prevail to reach 25 percent of the tracts having oil. Surviving a long stretch of bad luck may not be feasible if the company does not have adequate financing.

This criterion also has its share of critics. Here are the main criticisms.

1. There usually is considerable uncertainty involved in assigning values to prior probabilities, so treating these values as true probabilities will not reveal the true range of possible outcomes. (The end of this section discusses how *sensitivity analysis* can address this concern.)

2. Prior probabilities inherently are at least largely subjective in nature, whereas sound decision making should be based on objective data and procedures. (Section 10.5 describes how new information sometimes can be obtained to improve prior probabilities and make them more objective.)

3. By focusing on average outcomes, expected (monetary) payoffs ignore the effect that the amount of variability in the possible outcomes should have on the decision making. For example, since Goferbroke does not have the financing to sustain a large loss, selling the land to assure a payoff of 90 ($90,000) may be preferable to an expected payoff of 100 ($100,000) from drilling. Selling would avoid the risk of a large loss from drilling when the land is dry. (Section 10.7 will discuss how utilities can be used to better reflect the value of payoffs.)

So why is this criterion commonly referred to as Bayes' decision rule? The reason is that it is often credited to the Reverend Thomas Bayes, a nonconforming 18th century English minister who won renown as a philosopher and mathematician, although the same basic idea has even longer roots in the field of economics. (Yes, some management science techniques have *very* long roots!) Bayes' philosophy of decision making still is very influential today, and some management scientists even refer to themselves as Bayesians because of their devotion to this philosophy.

Because of its popularity, the rest of the chapter focuses on procedures that are based on this criterion.

Max's Reaction

Max: So most management scientists feel that this is the right criterion to use?

Jennifer: There really is no such thing as a right or wrong criterion for everybody. An appropriate criterion for one person might not fit another at all. It really depends on the individual's own temperament and attitude toward decision making. It might also depend on the situation: how much is known about the decision alternatives and whether meaningful prior probabilities can be obtained for the possible states of nature. All that sort of thing.

Max: So where does this leave us?

Jennifer: Well, now you need to decide which criterion seems most appropriate to you in this situation.

Max: Well, I can't say that I am very excited about any of the criteria. But it sounded like this one is a popular one.

Jennifer: Yes, it is.

Max: Why?

Jennifer: Really, two reasons. First, this is the criterion that uses all the available information. The prior probabilities may not be as accurate as we would like, but they do give us valuable information about roughly how likely each of the possible states of nature is. Many management scientists feel that using this key information should lead to better decisions.

Max: I'm not ready to accept that yet. But what is the second reason?

Jennifer: Remember that this is the criterion that focuses on what the average payoff would be if the same situation were repeated numerous times. We called this the expected payoff. Consistently selecting the decision alternative that provides the best expected payoff would provide the most payoff to the company in the long run. Doing what is best in the long run seems like rational decision making for a manager.

Max: Yes, that makes some sense. But before Goferbroke can get to the long run, we need to survive the short run. We can't take many more of these losses from drilling when the land is dry.

Jennifer: You're right. Considering the short run can be really important as well. But remember that I mentioned utilities awhile ago. A little later, I'll explain how using utilities will enable us to give full consideration to the short run as well.

Max: Good. But one thing still really bothers me about this criterion.

Jennifer: I think I can guess.

Max: Yes. I've made it pretty plain that I don't want to make my decision based on believing the consulting geologist's numbers. One chance in four of oil. Hah! I've seen these guys operate too much in the past. I don't mean they don't know what they're doing. They're good at spotting favorable signs for oil. The trouble comes when you ask for some numbers. They'll stare into space for awhile, and then out pops the numbers. It's just an educated guess.

Jennifer: Well, let me ask this. What is the key factor in deciding whether to drill for oil or sell the land?

Max: How likely that there is oil there.

Jennifer: Doesn't the consulting geologist help in determining this?

Max: Definitely. I hardly ever drill without their input.

Jennifer: So shouldn't your criterion for deciding whether to drill be based directly on this input?

Max: Yes, it should.

Jennifer: But then I don't understand why you keep objecting to using the consulting geologist's numbers.

Max: I'm not objecting to using his input. This input is vital to my decision. What I object to is using his numbers, one chance in four of oil, as being the gospel truth. That is what this Bayes' decision rule seems to do. We both saw what a close decision this was, 100 versus 90. What happens if his numbers are off some, as they probably are. This is too important a decision to be based on some numbers that are largely pulled out of the air.

Jennifer: OK, I see. Now he says that there is one chance in four of oil, a 25 percent chance. Do you think that is the right ballpark at least?

Max: Yes. I believe him that there is a decent chance of oil there.

Jennifer: If 25 percent isn't the right number, what do you think it might be?

Max: Who knows?

Jennifer: What I mean is, you have seen the consulting geologist's report and the evidence he gives to support his numbers. Based on this report and your past experience, can you give me a range for what the right number is likely to be? If not 25 percent, how much lower might it be? Or how much higher?

Max: I usually add and subtract 10 percent from whatever the consulting geologist says. So I suppose the chance of oil is likely to be somewhere between 15 percent and 35 percent.

Jennifer: Good. Now we're getting somewhere. I think I know exactly what we should do next.

Max: What's that?

Jennifer: There is a management science technique that is designed for just this kind of situation. It is called *sensitivity analysis.* It will allow us to investigate what happens if the consulting geologist's numbers are off.

Max: Great! Let's do it.

Sensitivity Analysis with Bayes' Decision Rule

Sensitivity analysis commonly is used with various applications of management science to study the effect if some of the numbers included in the mathematical model are not correct. In this case, the mathematical model is represented by the payoff table shown in Figure 10.10. The numbers in this table that are most questionable are the prior probabilities in cells C10 and D10. We will focus the sensitivity analysis on these numbers, although a similar approach could be applied to the payoffs given in cells C5:D6.

The sum of the two prior probabilities must equal one, so increasing one of these probabilities automatically decreases the other one by the same amount, and vice versa. Max has concluded that the true chances of having oil on the tract of land are likely to lie somewhere between 15 and 35 percent. In other words, the true prior probability of having oil is likely to be in the range from 0.15 to 0.35, so the corresponding prior probability of the land being dry would range from 0.85 to 0.65.

Sensitivity analysis begins by reapplying Bayes' decision rule twice, once when the prior probability of oil is at the lower end of this range (0.15) and next when it is at the upper end (0.35). Figure 10.11 shows the results from doing this. When the prior probability

FIGURE 10.11

Performing sensitivity analysis by trying alternative values of the prior probability of oil.

	A	B	C	D	E	F	G	H	I
1		Bayes' Decision Rule for the Goferbroke Co. Problem							
2									
3					State of Nature			Expected	
4		Alternative	Oil	Dry				Payoff	
5		Drill	700	–100				20	
6		Sell	90	90				90	Maximum
7									
8									
9									
10		Prior Probability	0.15	0.85					

	A	B	C	D	E	F	G	H	I
1		Bayes' Decision Rule for the Goferbroke Co. Problem							
2									
3					State of Nature			Expected	
4		Alternative	Oil	Dry				Payoff	
5		Drill	700	–100				180	Maximum
6		Sell	90	90				90	
7									
8									
9									
10		Prior Probability	0.35	0.65					

of oil is only 0.15, the decision swings over to selling the land by a wide margin (an expected payoff of 90 versus only 20 for drilling). However, when this probability is 0.35, the decision is to drill by a wide margin (expected payoff = 180 versus only 90 for selling). Thus, the decision is very *sensitive* to the prior probability of oil. This sensitivity analysis has revealed that it is important to do more, if possible, to pin down just what the true value of the probability of oil is.

This is a good start on sensitivity analysis, but much more can be done. We mentioned near the end of the preceding section that one of the Excel add-ins for decision analysis, PrecisionTree, has nice ways of performing sensitivity analysis, so let us see how this is done.

It is helpful to start this process by constructing a spreadsheet as in Figure 10.12 that contains all the data for the problem as well as the results. This spreadsheet accompanies the decision tree spreadsheet shown in Figure 10.5. Therefore, as indicated by the equations at the bottom of Figure 10.12, the cells giving the results on this spreadsheet make reference to the corresponding output cells on the Tree spreadsheet. Similarly, the data cells on the Tree spreadsheet now would make reference to the corresponding data cells on this spreadsheet. Consequently, the user can experiment with various alternative values in the data cells on this spreadsheet and the results would simultaneously change on this spreadsheet and on the decision tree to reflect the new data.

In addition to "playing" with the data, PrecisionTree provides several ways of displaying the results from systematically performing sensitivity analysis. For example, let us again explore what happens when the prior probability of oil varies from its original estimate of 0.25. To begin, we select the Sensitivity Analysis command from the Analysis submenu on the PrecisionTree menu (or click on the Sensitivity Analysis icon—an inverted pyramid—on the PrecisionTree toolbar). This brings up the dialogue box displayed in Figure 10.13. To analyze how the expected payoff (cell C17 in Figure 10.12) varies as one data cell (C12) changes (which automatically changes cell C13 accordingly), we make the entries shown in the figure. The choice of One Way Analysis Type indicates that *one* data cell is being varied at a time. The big white box in the center indicates that the original prior probability of oil of 0.25 is being varied from 0 to 1 in 20 steps. This number of steps is the number of equally spaced values across the minimum–maximum range (excluding the minimum value) that

FIGURE 10.12

This spreadsheet uses the decision tree in Figure 10.5 as a worksheet to perform sensitivity analysis on the data for the first Goferbroke Co. problem.

	A	B	C	D	E
1	Decision Analysis for Goferbroke Co. Problem				
2					
3		Cost of Data			
4		Cost of Drilling	100		
5		Revenue if Oil	800		
6		Revenue if Dry	0		
7		Revenue if Sell	90		
8					
9		Probability Data			
10		State of	Prior		
11		Nature	Probability		
12		Oil	0.25		
13		Dry	0.75		
14					
15		Results			
16		Action:	Drill		
17		Expected Payoff:	100		

	C
13	=1–C12
14	
15	
16	=IF(Tree!B3,"Drill","Sell")
17	=Tree!B8

will be tested, so the values to be checked are 0, 0.05, 0.1, . . . , 1. These entries in the big white box are entered in the Input Editor by individually typing in the name (Prior Probability of Oil), the cell being varied (C12), the minimum value being considered (0), the "base value" (0.25), the maximum value (1), and the number of steps (20). (If you want to vary a series of data cells one at a time, you would click on Add after entering the information for each one to clear the Input Editor for starting on the next one.) After completing the dialogue box, click on Run Analysis.

When PrecisionTree runs a one-way sensitivity analysis, a number of graphs and reports are generated. One of these is the *sensitivity graph* in Figure 10.14 that shows how the expected payoff varies as the selected data cell (the prior probability of oil in this case) changes. The fact that the expected payoff varies all the way from 90 to 700 in this graph emphasizes how sensitive the expected payoff is to the prior probability of oil. (We will display some other graphs and reports at the end of Section 10.6 when further sensitivity analysis is conducted for the full-fledged Goferbroke Co. problem where a decision on whether to conduct a seismic survey must be made.)

At the end of the preceding section, we mentioned that an Excel add-in in your MS Courseware called SensIt (academic version) also has excellent capabilities for sensitivity

FIGURE 10.13

The Sensitivity Analysis dialogue box used by PrecisionTree to initiate an investigation of how Goferbroke's expected payoff varies as the prior probability of oil varies.

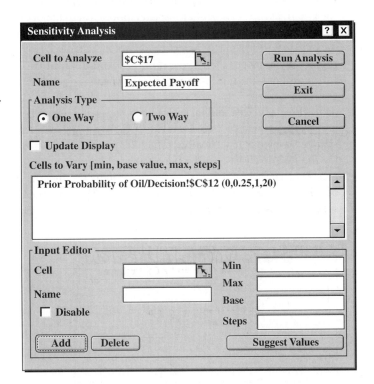

FIGURE 10.14

The sensitivity graph shows how Goferbroke's expected payoff (when using Bayes' decision rule) depends on the prior probability of oil.

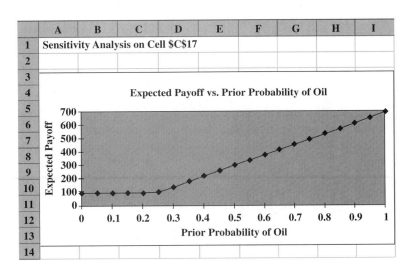

analysis. As indicated in the courseware, it operates much like PrecisionTree in this regard. To generate the sensitivity graph in Figure 10.14 with SensIt, you would choose Plot under the Sensitivity Analysis option under the Tools menu. This brings up the dialogue box shown in Figure 10.15. Referring to the cells in Figure 10.12, you choose the cell (C12) and label (cell B12) for the input variable (the data cell being varied) and then the cell (C17) and label (cell B17) for the output variable (the expected payoff in this case). The entries on the right side of the dialogue box indicate that the plot is to be made by increasing cell C12 (the prior probability of oil) from 0 to 1 in increments of 0.05. Clicking OK then generates the sensitivity graph. Since the output for SensIt is so similar to that for PrecisionTree, we will not describe it further at this point.

The sensitivity graph in Figure 10.14 does not explicitly show how the prior probability of oil affects the decision of whether to drill or sell the land. By choosing the value of this decision node (cell B8) in Figure 10.5 as the cell to analyze in Figure 10.13, the professional version of PrecisionTree (the one on the Palisade web site) will generate the *strategy region graph* in Figure 10.16 that focuses on this issue. The flat line gives the fixed payoff of 90 for the alternative of selling the land, whereas the slanting line shows how the expected payoff from drilling would vary with the prior probability of oil. (This same graph could be drawn by hand by drawing the lines through the points identified in Figure 10.11.) The point where the two lines intersect is the **crossover point** where the decision shifts from one alternative (sell the land) to the other (drill for oil) as the prior probability increases.

You can see in this strategy region graph that the crossover point occurs where the prior probability of oil is slightly under 0.25. Algebra can be used to solve for the exact value of this prior probability as follows.

Let p = prior probability of oil.
For the alternative of drilling for oil,

$$\text{Expected payoff} = p(700) + (1-p)(-100)$$

$$= 700p - 100 + 100p$$

$$= 800p - 100$$

FIGURE 10.15

The dialogue box that would be used by the academic version of SensIt to plot the sensitivity graph in Figure 10.14 by referencing the cells in Figure 10.12.

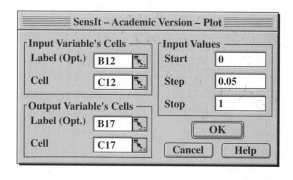

FIGURE 10.16

The strategy region graph generated by the professional version (only) of PrecisionTree to show how Goferbroke's decision of whether to drill or sell depends on the prior probability of oil.

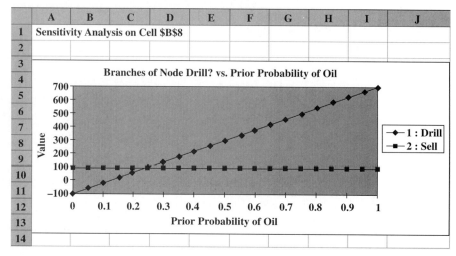

Set Expected payoff = 90 (the payoff for selling the land).

$$800p - 100 \ = \ 90$$

$$800p = 190$$

$$p = \frac{190}{800} = 0.2375$$

Conclusion: Should sell the land if $p < 0.2375$.
Should drill for oil if $p > 0.2375$.

For other problems that have more than two decision alternatives, the same kind of graphical analysis can be applied. The main difference is that there now would be more than two lines (one per alternative) in the graphical display corresponding to Figure 10.16. However, the top line for any particular value of the prior probability still indicates which alternative should be chosen. With more than two lines, there might be more than one crossover point where the decision shifts from one alternative to another.

For a problem with more than two possible states of nature, the most straightforward approach is to focus the sensitivity analysis on only two states at a time as described above. This again would involve investigating what happens when the prior probability of one state increases as the prior probability of the other state decreases by the same amount, holding fixed the prior probabilities of the remaining states. This procedure then can be repeated for as many other pairs of states as desired.

Max's Reaction

Max: That strategy region graph paints a pretty clear picture. I think I'm getting a much better handle on the problem.
Jennifer: Good.
Max: I like that crossover point idea. Less than a 23¾ percent chance of oil, I should sell. If it's more, I should drill. Right?
Jennifer: That's right.
Max: That really pins it down.
Jennifer: Yes.
Max: It confirms what I suspected all along. This is a close decision, and it all boils down to picking the right number for the chances of oil. I sure wish I had more to go on than the consulting geologist's numbers.
Jennifer: You talked earlier about the possibility of paying $30,000 to get a detailed seismic survey of the land.
Max: Yes, I might have to do that. But 30,000 bucks! I'm still not sure that it's worth that much dough.
Jennifer: I have a quick way of checking that. It's another technique I learned in my management science course. It's called finding the **expected value of perfect information (EVPI).** The expected value of perfect information is the increase in the expected payoff you would get if the seismic survey could tell you for sure if there is oil there.
Max: But it can't tell you for sure.
Jennifer: Yes, I know. But finding out for sure if oil is there is what we refer to as perfect information. So the increase in the expected payoff if you find out for sure is the expected value of perfect information. We know that's better than you actually can do with a seismic survey.
Max: Right.
Jennifer: OK, suppose we find that the expected value of perfect information is less than $30,000. Since that is better than we can do with a seismic survey, that tells us right off the bat that it wouldn't pay to do the seismic survey.
Max: OK, I get it. But what if this expected value of perfect information is more than $30,000?
Jennifer: Then you don't know for sure whether the seismic survey is worth it until you do some more analysis. This analysis takes some time, whereas it is very quick to calculate the expected value of perfect information. So it is well worth simply

checking whether the expected value of perfect information is less than $30,000 and, if so, saving a lot of additional work.

Max: OK. Let's do it.

Review Questions

1. On which state of nature does the maximum likelihood criterion focus?
2. What are some criticisms of the maximum likelihood criterion?
3. What assumption about the states of nature is made by the equally likely criterion?
4. What are some criticisms of the equally likely criterion?
5. How does Bayes' decision rule select a decision alternative?
6. How is the expected payoff for a decision alternative calculated?
7. What are some criticisms of Bayes' decision rule?
8. Why might it be helpful to use sensitivity analysis with Bayes' decision rule?
9. What does a crossover point represent when graphically displaying the expected payoffs for the decision alternatives?

10.4 Checking Whether to Obtain More Information

Prior probabilities may provide somewhat inaccurate estimates of the true probabilities of the states of nature. Might it be worthwhile for Max to spend some money for a seismic survey to obtain better estimates? The quickest way to check this is to pretend that it is possible for the same amount of money to actually determine which state is the true state of nature ("perfect information") and then determine whether obtaining this information would make this expenditure worthwhile. If having perfect information would not be worthwhile, then it definitely would not be worthwhile to spend this money just to learn more about the probabilities of the states of nature.

The key quantities for performing this analysis are

EP (without more info) = expected payoff from applying Bayes' decision rule with
 the original prior probabilities
 = 100 (as given in Figure 10.10)
C = cost of obtaining more information
 = 30 (cost of the seismic survey in thousands of dollars)
EP (with perfect info) = expected payoff if the decision could be made after
 learning the true state of nature
EVPI = expected value of perfect information

This last quantity is calculated as

$$\text{EVPI} = \text{EP (with perfect info)} - \text{EP (without more info)}$$

After calculating EP (with perfect info) and then EVPI, the last step is to compare EVPI with *C*.

If $\text{EVPI} < C$, then it is not worthwhile to obtain more information.

If $\text{EVPI} \geq C$, then it might be worthwhile to obtain more information.

The Excel template in Figure 10.17 demonstrates the procedure for calculating EP (with perfect info). Since we are pretending that the decision can be made after learning the true state of nature, we automatically would choose the alternative with the maximum payoff for that state (drill if oil is there and sell if not). The prior probabilities still give the probability that each state of nature will turn out to be the true one. Therefore, EP (with perfect info) is calculated in cell F13 with the equation

$$\text{F13} = \text{SUMPRODUCT (C10:G10, C11:G11)},$$

where the blanks in columns E, F, and G are treated as zeroes.

FIGURE 10.17

This Excel template for obtaining the expected payoff with perfect information is applied here to the first Goferbroke Co. problem.

	A	B	C	D	E	F	G
1		Expected Payoff with Perfect Information for Goferbroke					
2							
3				State of Nature			
4		Alternative	Oil	Dry			
5		Drill	700	–100			
6		Sell	90	90			
7							
8							
9							
10		Prior Probability	0.25	0.75			
11		Maximum Payoff	700	90			
12							
13		Expected Payoff with Perfect Information=		242.5			

	C	D	E	F	G
11	=MAX(C5:C9)	=MAX(D5:D9)	=MAX(E5:E9)	=MAX(F5:F9)	=MAX(G5:G9)

	F
13	=SUMPRODUCT(C10:G10,C11:G11)

FIGURE 10.18

By starting with a chance node involving the states of nature, PrecisionTree uses this decision tree to obtain the expected payoff with perfect information for the first Goferbroke Co. problem.

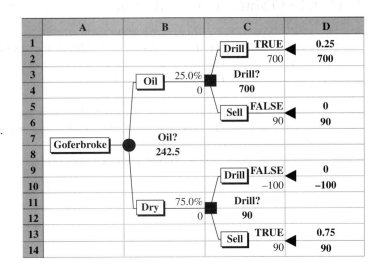

PrecisionTree (or TreePlan) also can be used to calculate EP (with perfect info) by constructing and solving the decision tree shown in Figure 10.18. The clever idea here is to *start* the decision tree with a *chance* node whose branches are the various states of nature (oil and dry in this case). Since a decision node follows each of these branches, the decision is being made with perfect information about the true state of nature. Therefore, the expected payoff of 242.5 obtained by PrecisionTree in cell B8 is the expected payoff with perfect information. This approach is more versatile than the Excel template in Figure 10.17 because it can also be used when a sequence of decisions needs to be made.

Since either Figure 10.17 or 10.18 gives EP (with perfect info) = 242½, we now can calculate the expected value of perfect information as

$$EVPI = EP \text{ (with perfect info)} - EP \text{ (without more info)}$$

$$= 242\tfrac{1}{2} - 100$$

$$= 142\tfrac{1}{2}$$

Conclusion: EVPI > C, since 142½ > 30. Therefore, it might be worthwhile to do the seismic survey.

Max's Reaction

Max: So you're telling me that if the seismic survey could really be definitive in determining whether oil is there, doing the survey would increase my average payoff by about $142,500?

Jennifer: That's right.

Max: So after subtracting the $30,000 cost of the survey, I would be ahead $112,500?

Jennifer: You got it. But remember that the $112,500 is an average. That's roughly the average amount you would be ahead if you did this on many similar tracts of land. There are no guarantees on this one tract. But it does indicate that we might want to get more information.

Max: OK. Well, too bad the surveys aren't that good. In fact, they're not all that reliable.

Jennifer: Tell me more. How reliable are they?

Max: Well, they come back with seismic soundings. If the seismic soundings are favorable, then oil is fairly likely. If they are unfavorable, then oil is pretty unlikely. But you can't tell for sure.

Jennifer: OK. Suppose oil is there. How often would you get favorable seismic soundings?

Max: Oh, a little over half the time.

Jennifer: Can you give me a percentage?

Max: I can't give you an exact number. Maybe 60 percent.

Jennifer: OK, good. Now suppose that the land is dry. How often would you still get favorable seismic soundings?

Max: Too often! I've lost a lot of money drilling when the seismic survey said to and then nothing was there. That's why I don't like to spend the 30,000 bucks.

Jennifer: Sure. So it tells you to drill when you shouldn't close to half the time?

Max: No. It's not that bad. But fairly often.

Jennifer: Can you give me a percentage?

Max: I don't like to give those numbers. I'm no better at it than those consulting geologists.

Jennifer: I understand. But a ballpark figure would be helpful.

Max: OK. Maybe 20 percent.

Jennifer: Good. Thanks. Now I think we can do some analysis to determine whether it is really worthwhile to do the seismic survey.

Max: How do you do the analysis?

Jennifer: Well, I'll describe the process in detail pretty soon. But here is the general idea. We'll do some calculations to determine what the chances of oil would be if the seismic soundings turn out to be favorable. Then we'll calculate the chances if the soundings are unfavorable.

Max: You can do that?

Jennifer: Yes, there is something called Bayes' theorem that enables us to do it.

Max: Hmm, that Reverend Bayes fellow again?

Jennifer: Yep.

Max: Pretty smart guy.

Jennifer: Yes, he was. Anyway, we'll use his theorem to improve the consulting geologist's numbers on the chances of oil for each possible outcome of the seismic survey.

Max: Good.

Jennifer: We called the consulting geologist's numbers prior probabilities because they were prior to obtaining more information. The improved numbers are referred to as **posterior probabilities.**

Max: OK.

Jennifer: Then we'll use these posterior probabilities to determine the average payoff, after subtracting the $30,000 cost, if we do the seismic survey. If this payoff is better than we would do without the seismic survey, then we should do it. Otherwise, not.

Max: That makes sense.

Jennifer: Shall we get started?

Max: OK.

Review Questions

1. What is meant by perfect information regarding the states of nature?
2. How can the expected payoff with perfect information be calculated from the payoff table?
3. How should a decision tree be constructed to obtain the expected payoff with perfect information by solving the tree?
4. What is the formula for calculating the expected value of perfect information?
5. What is the conclusion if the cost of obtaining more information is more than the expected value of perfect information?
6. What is the conclusion if the cost of obtaining more information is less than the expected value of perfect information?
7. Which of these two cases occurs in the Goferbroke Co. problem?

10.5 Using New Information to Update the Probabilities

The prior probabilities of the possible states of nature often are quite subjective in nature, so they may be only very rough estimates of the true probabilities. Fortunately, it frequently is possible to do some additional testing or surveying (at some expense) to improve these estimates. These improved estimates are called **posterior probabilities.**

In the case of the Goferbroke Co., these improved estimates can be obtained at a cost of $30,000 by conducting a detailed seismic survey of the land. The possible findings from such a survey are summarized below.

Possible Findings from a Seismic Survey

FSS: Favorable seismic soundings; oil is fairly likely.

USS: Unfavorable seismic soundings; oil is quite unlikely.

To use either finding to calculate the posterior probability of oil (or of being dry), it is necessary to estimate the probability of obtaining this finding for each state of nature. During the conversation at the end of the preceding section, Jennifer elicited these estimates from Max, as summarized in Table 10.4. (Max actually only estimated the probability of favorable seismic soundings, but subtracting this number from one gives the probability of unfavorable seismic soundings.) The symbol used in the table for each of these estimated probabilities is

P(finding | state) = probability that the indicated finding will occur, given that the state of nature is the indicated one.

This kind of probability is referred to as a *conditional probability,* because it is conditioned on being given the state of nature.

Recall that the prior probabilities are

P(Oil) = 0.25
P(Dry) = 0.75

The next step is to use these probabilities and the probabilities in Table 10.4 to obtain a combined probability called a *joint probability.* Each combination of a state of nature and

TABLE 10.4 **Probabilities of the Possible Findings from the Seismic Survey, Given the State of Nature, for the Goferbroke Co. Problem**

	P(finding | state)	
State of Nature	Favorable (FSS)	Unfavorable (USS)
Oil	P(FSS | Oil) = 0.6	P(USS | Oil) = 0.4
Dry	P(FSS | Dry) = 0.2	P(USS | Dry) = 0.8

a finding from the seismic survey will have a joint probability that is determined by the following formula.

$$P(\text{state and finding}) = P(\text{state})\, P(\text{finding} \mid \text{state})$$

For example, the joint probability that the state of nature is Oil *and* the finding from the seismic survey is favorable (FSS) is

$$P(\text{Oil and FSS}) = P(\text{Oil})\, P(\text{FSS} \mid \text{Oil})$$

$$= 0.25(0.6)$$

$$= 0.15$$

The calculation of all these joint probabilities is shown in the third column of the **probability tree diagram** given in Figure 10.19. The case involved is identified underneath each branch of the tree and the probability is given over the branch. The first column gives the prior probabilities and then the probabilities from Table 10.4 are shown in the second column. Multiplying each probability in the first column by a probability in the second column gives the corresponding joint probability in the third column.

Having found each joint probability of both a particular state of nature and a particular finding from the seismic survey, the next step is to use these probabilities to find each probability of just a particular finding without specifying the state of nature. Since any finding can be obtained with any state of nature, the formula for calculating the probability of just a particular finding is

$$P(\text{finding}) = P(\text{Oil and finding}) + P(\text{Dry and finding})$$

For example, the probability of a favorable finding (FSS) is

$$P(\text{FSS}) = P(\text{Oil and FSS}) + P(\text{Dry and FSS})$$

$$= 0.15 + 0.15 = 0.3$$

FIGURE 10.19

Probability tree diagram for the Goferbroke Co. problem showing all the probabilities leading to the calculation of each posterior probability of the state of nature given the finding of the seismic survey.

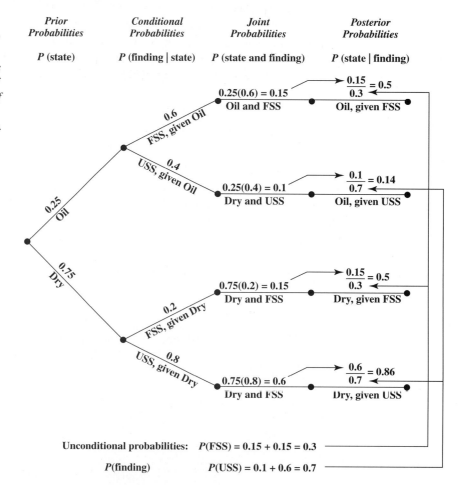

where the two joint probabilities on the right-hand side of this equation are found on the first and third branches of the third column of the probability tree diagram. The calculation of both P(FSS) and P(USS) is shown underneath the diagram. (These are referred to as *unconditional* probabilities to differentiate them from the *conditional* probabilities of a finding given the state of nature, shown in the second column.)

Finally, we now are ready to calculate each *posterior probability* of a particular state of nature given a particular finding from the seismic survey. The formula involves combining the joint probabilities in the third column with the unconditional probabilities underneath the diagram as follows.

$$P(\text{state} \mid \text{finding}) = \frac{P(\text{state and finding})}{P(\text{finding})}$$

For example, the posterior probability that the true state of nature is oil, given a favorable finding (FSS) from the seismic survey, is

$$P(\text{Oil} \mid \text{FSS}) = \frac{P(\text{Oil and FSS})}{P(\text{FSS})}$$

$$= \frac{0.15}{0.3} = 0.5$$

The fourth column of the probability tree diagram shows the calculation of all the posterior probabilities. The arrows indicate how each numerator comes from the corresponding joint probability in the third column and the denominator comes from the corresponding unconditional probability below the diagram.

By using the formulas given earlier for the joint probabilities and unconditional probabilities, each posterior probability also can be calculated directly from the prior probabilities (first column) and the conditional probabilities (second column) as follows.

$$P(\text{state} \mid \text{finding}) = \frac{P(\text{state}) \, P(\text{finding} \mid \text{state})}{P(\text{Oil}) \, P(\text{finding} \mid \text{Oil}) + P(\text{Dry}) \, P(\text{finding} \mid \text{Dry})}$$

For example, the posterior probability of oil, given a favorable finding (FSS), is

$$P(\text{Oil} \mid \text{FSS}) = \frac{P(\text{Oil}) \, P(\text{FSS} \mid \text{Oil})}{P(\text{Oil}) \, P(\text{FSS} \mid \text{Oil}) + P(\text{Dry}) \, P(\text{FSS} \mid \text{Dry})}$$

$$= \frac{0.25(0.6)}{0.25(0.6) + 0.75(0.2)}$$

$$= 0.5$$

This formula for a posterior probability is known as **Bayes' theorem,** in honor of its discovery by the Reverend Bayes. The clever Reverend Bayes found that any posterior probability can be found in this way for any decision analysis problem, regardless of how many states of nature it has. The denominator in the formula would contain one such term for each of the states of nature. Note that the probability tree diagram also is applying Bayes' theorem, but in smaller steps rather than a single long formula.

Table 10.5 summarizes all the posterior probabilities calculated in Figure 10.19.

TABLE 10.5   Posterior Probabilities of the States of Nature, Given the Finding from the Seismic Survey, for the Goferbroke Co. Problem

	P(state | finding)	
Finding	*Oil*	*Dry*
Favorable (FSS)	P(Oil | FSS) = 1/2	P(Dry | FSS) = 1/2
Unfavorable (USS)	P(Oil | USS) = 1/7	P(Dry | USS) = 6/7

FIGURE 10.20

This Posterior Probabilities template in your MS Courseware enables efficient calculation of posterior probabilities, as illustrated here for the Goferbroke Co. problem.

	A	B	C	D	E	F	G	H
1		Posterior Probabilities						
2								
3		Data:		P(Finding | State)				
4		State of	Prior	Finding				
5		Nature	Probability	FSS	USS			
6		Oil	0.25	0.6	0.4			
7		Dry	0.75	0.2	0.8			
8								
9								
10								
11								
12		Posterior		P(State | Finding)				
13		Probabilities:		State of Nature				
14		Finding	P(Finding)	Oil	Dry			
15		FSS	0.3	0.5	0.5			
16		USS	0.7	0.1429	0.8571			
17								
18								
19								

	B	C	D
14	Finding	P(Finding)	=B6
15	=D5	=SUMPRODUCT(C6:C10,D6:D10)	=C6*D6/SUMPRODUCT(C6:C10,D6:D10)
16	=E5	=SUMPRODUCT(C6:C10,E6:E10)	=C6*E6/SUMPRODUCT(C6:C10,E6:E10)
17	=F5	=SUMPRODUCT(C6:C10,F6:F10)	=C6*F6/SUMPRODUCT(C6:C10,F6:F10)
18	=G5	=SUMPRODUCT(C6:C10,G6:G10)	=C6*G6/SUMPRODUCT(C6:C10,G6:G10)
19	=H5	=SUMPRODUCT(C6:C10,H6:H10)	=C6*H6/SUMPRODUCT(C6:C10,H6:H10)

After you learn the logic of calculating posterior probabilities, we suggest that you use the computer to perform these rather lengthy calculations. We have provided an Excel template (labeled Posterior Probabilities) for this purpose in this chapter's Excel file in your MS Courseware. Figure 10.20 illustrates the use of this template for the Goferbroke Co. problem. All you do is enter the prior probabilities and the conditional probabilities from the first two columns of Figure 10.19 into the top half of the template. The posterior probabilities then immediately appear in the bottom half. (The equations entered into the cells in columns E through H are similar to those for column D shown at the bottom of the figure.)

Max's Reaction

Max: So this is saying that even with favorable seismic soundings, I still only have one chance in two of finding oil.

Jennifer: Yes. Assuming you start off with the consulting geologist giving you one chance in four, that is correct.

Max: No wonder I've been disappointed so often in the past when I've drilled after receiving a favorable seismic survey. I thought those surveys were supposed to be more reliable than that. So now I'm even more unenthusiastic about paying 30,000 bucks to get a survey done.

Jennifer: But one chance in two of oil. Those are good odds.

Max: Yes, they are. But I'm likely to lay out 30,000 bucks and then just get an unfavorable survey back.

Jennifer: My calculations indicate that you have about a 70 percent chance of that happening.

Max: See what I mean?

Jennifer: But even an unfavorable survey tells you a lot. Just one chance in seven of oil then. That might rule out drilling.

Max: Yes, it might not pay to drill with those odds.

Jennifer: So a seismic survey really does pin down the odds of oil a lot better. Either one chance in two or one chance in seven instead of the ballpark estimate of one chance in four from the consulting geologist.

Max: Yes, I suppose that's right. I really would like to improve the consulting geologist's numbers. It sounds like you're recommending that we do the seismic survey.

Jennifer: Well, actually, I'm not quite sure yet. We still need to do just a little more analysis. Then I think we'll have all the information you need to make a confident decision. Remember I was talking earlier about finding what the average payoff would be if we do the seismic survey and then comparing that with what we would get without the survey?

Max: Yes, I remember. But I'm still not clear on how we do that.

Jennifer: Well, what we'll do is sketch out a decision tree, showing the decision on whether to do the seismic survey and then the decision on whether to drill or sell. Then we'll work out the average payoffs for these decisions on the decision tree. Do you remember my mentioning decision trees at the beginning?

Max: Vaguely.

Jennifer: We'll go over that again, and then work out the rest.

Max: OK, let's do it. I want to make a decision soon.

Review Questions

1. What are posterior probabilities of the states of nature?
2. What are the possible findings from a seismic survey for the Goferbroke Co.?
3. What probabilities need to be estimated in addition to prior probabilities in order to begin calculating posterior probabilities?
4. What five kinds of probabilities are considered in a probability tree diagram?
5. What is the formula for calculating P(state and finding)?
6. What is the formula for calculating P(finding)?
7. What is the formula for calculating a posterior probability, P(state | finding), from P(state and finding) and P(finding).
8. What is the name of the famous theorem for how to calculate posterior probabilities?

10.6 Using a Decision Tree to Analyze the Problem with a Sequence of Decisions

As described in Section 10.2, a **decision tree** provides a graphical display of the progression of decisions and random events for the problem. Figure 10.1 in that section shows the decision tree for the Goferbroke problem when the only decision under consideration was whether to drill for oil or sell the land. Figures 10.5 and 10.7 then show the same decision tree as it would be constructed and solved with PrecisionTree and TreePlan, respectively.

Constructing the Decision Tree

Now that a prior decision needs to be made on whether to conduct a seismic survey, this same decision tree needs to be expanded as shown in Figure 10.21 (before including any numbers). Recall that each *square* in the tree represents a *decision node,* where a decision needs to be made, and each *circle* represents a *chance node,* where a random event will occur.

Thus, the first decision (should we have a seismic survey done?) is represented by decision node *a* in Figure 10.21. The two branches leading out of this node correspond to the two alternatives for this decision. Node *b* is a chance node representing the random event of the outcome of the seismic survey. The two branches emanating from node *b* represent the two possible outcomes of the survey. Next comes the second decision (nodes *c, d,* and *e*) with its two possible choices. If the decision is to drill for oil, then we come to another chance node (nodes *f, g,* and *h*), where its two branches correspond to the two possible states of nature.

Figure 10.21

The decision tree for the Goferbroke Co. problem (before including any numbers) when first deciding whether to conduct a seismic survey.

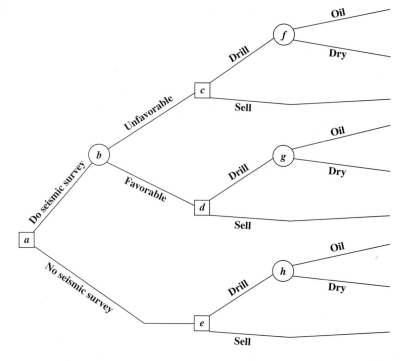

Figure 10.22

The decision tree in Figure 10.21 after adding both the probabilities of random events and the payoffs.

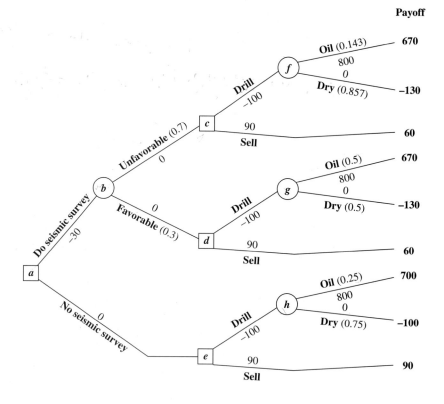

The next step is to insert numbers into the decision tree as shown in Figure 10.22. The numbers under or over the branches that are *not* in parentheses are the cash flows (in thousands of dollars) that occur at those branches. For each path through the tree from node *a* to a final branch, these same numbers then are added to obtain the resulting total payoff shown in boldface to the right of that branch. The last set of numbers is the probabilities of random events. In particular, since each branch emanating from a chance node represents a possible random event, the probability of this event occurring from this node has been inserted in parentheses along this branch. From chance node *h*, the probabilities are the *prior*

probabilities of these states of nature, since no seismic survey has been conducted to obtain more information in this case. However, chance nodes *f* and *g* lead out of a decision to do the seismic survey (and then to drill). Therefore, the probabilities from these chance nodes are the *posterior probabilities* of the states of nature, given the outcome of the seismic survey, where these numbers are obtained from Table 10.5 or from cells D15:E16 in Figure 10.20. Finally, we have the two branches emanating from chance node *b*. The numbers here are the probabilities of these findings from the seismic survey, Favorable (FSS) or Unfavorable (USS), as given underneath the probability tree diagram in Figure 10.19 or in cells C15:C16 of Figure 10.20.

Performing the Analysis

Having constructed the decision tree, including its numbers, we now are ready to analyze the problem by using the following procedure.

1. Start at the right side of the decision tree and move left one column at a time. For each column, perform either step 2 or step 3 depending on whether the nodes in that column are chance nodes or decision nodes.

2. For each chance node, calculate its *expected payoff* by multiplying the expected payoff of each branch (shown in boldface to the right of the branch) by the probability of that branch and then summing these products. Record this expected payoff for each decision node in boldface next to the node, and designate this quantity as also being the expected payoff for the branch leading to this node.

3. For each decision node, compare the expected payoffs of its branches and choose the alternative whose branch has the largest expected payoff. In each case, record the choice on the decision tree.

To begin the procedure, consider the rightmost column of nodes, namely, chance nodes *f, g,* and *h*. Applying step 2, their expected payoffs (EP) are calculated as

$$EP = \frac{1}{7}(670) + \frac{6}{7}(-130) = -15.7 \qquad \text{for node } f$$

$$EP = \frac{1}{2}(670) + \frac{1}{2}(-130) = 270 \qquad \text{for node } g$$

$$EP = \frac{1}{4}(700) + \frac{3}{4}(-100) = 100 \qquad \text{for node } h$$

These expected payoffs then are placed above these nodes, as shown in Figure 10.23.

Next, we move one column to the left, which consists of decision nodes *c, d,* and *e*. The expected payoff for a branch that leads to a chance node now is recorded in boldface over that chance node. Therefore, step 3 can be applied as follows.

Node *c:*   Drill alternative has EP = − 15.7

Sell alternative has EP = 60

60 > −15.7, so choose the Sell alternative.

Node *d:*   Drill alternative has EP = 270

Sell alternative has EP = 60

270 > 60, so choose the Drill alternative

Node *e:*   Drill alternative has EP = 100

Sell alternative has EP = 90

100 > 90, so choose the Drill alternative

The expected payoff for each chosen alternative now would be recorded in boldface over its decision node, as already shown in Figure 10.23. The chosen alternative also is indicated by inserting a double dash as a barrier through each rejected branch.

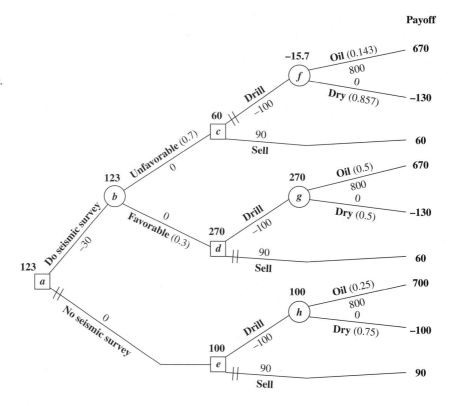

Next, moving one more column to the left brings us to node *b*. Since this is a chance node, step 2 of the procedure needs to be applied. The expected payoff for each of its branches is recorded over the following decision node. Therefore, the expected payoff is

$$EP = 0.7\,(60) + 0.3(270) = 123 \qquad \text{for node } b$$

as recorded over this node in Figure 10.23.

Finally, we move left to node *a,* a decision node. Applying step 3 yields

> Node *a:*   Do seismic survey has EP = 123
>
> No seismic survey has EP = 100

123 > 100, so choose Do seismic survey.

This expected payoff of 123 now would be recorded over the node, and a double dash inserted to indicate the rejected branch, as already shown in Figure 10.23.

This procedure has moved from right to left for analysis purposes. However, having completed the decision tree in this way, the decision maker now can read the tree from left to right to see the actual progression of events. The double dashes have closed off the undesirable paths. Therefore, given the payoffs for the final outcomes shown on the right side, *Bayes' decision rule* says to follow only the open paths from left to right to achieve the largest possible expected payoff.

Following the open paths from left to right in Fig. 10.23 yields the following optimal policy, according to Bayes' decision rule.

Optimal Policy

Do the seismic survey.

If the result is unfavorable, sell the land.

If the result is favorable, drill for oil.

The expected payoff (including the cost of the seismic survey) is 123 ($123,000).

Using PrecisionTree or TreePlan

Using the procedures described at the end of Section 10.2, either PrecisionTree or TreePlan can be used to construct and solve this same decision tree on a spreadsheet. Figure 10.24 shows the one obtained with PrecisionTree. Although the form is somewhat different, note

FIGURE 10.24

The decision tree constructed and solved by PrecisionTree for the full Goferbroke Co. problem that also considers whether to do a seismic survey.

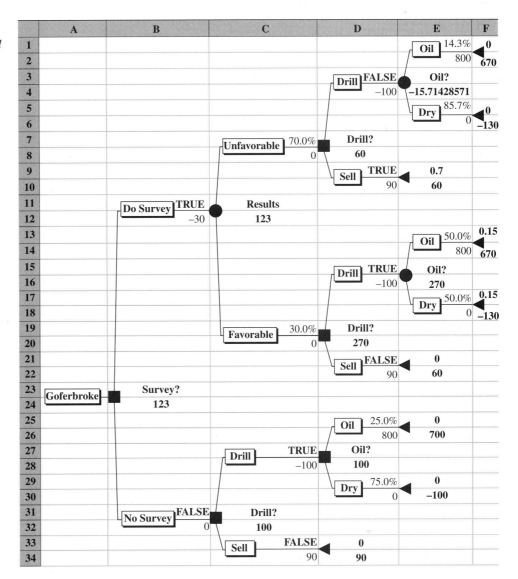

that this decision tree is completely equivalent to the one in Figure 10.23. Besides the convenience of constructing the tree directly on a spreadsheet, PrecisionTree also provides the key advantage of automatically solving the decision tree. Rather than relying on hand calculations as in Figure 10.23, PrecisionTree instantaneously calculates all the boldfaced numbers in Figure 10.24 as soon as the decision tree is constructed. Instead of using double dashes, PrecisionTree inserts the word FALSE to record a rejected branch as well as the word TRUE to record an accepted branch. Based on these choices, the top number to the right of each end node is the probability of reaching that node at the end of the process.

TreePlan also automatically solves the decision tree. However, as was illustrated by Figure 10.7 in Section 10.2, it provides a less elaborate decision tree than does PrecisionTree.

In addition to its decision tree, PrecisionTree also can provide some supplementary analysis of the problem. Using the Decision Analysis command on the Analysis submenu brings up the dialogue box shown in the upper left-hand corner of Figure 10.25. As one possibility, making the entries shown in this box and clicking OK then generates the other three reports in the figure. The Policy Suggestion in the lower right-hand corner summarizes the optimal policy by displaying the corresponding portion of the decision tree. The Statistics Report in the lower left-hand corner gives some statistics about the payoff obtained under this optimal policy. The most interesting statistics shown there are the mean (the expected payoff), the minimum possible payoff, the maximum possible payoff, the mode (the most likely payoff), and the standard deviation of the probability distribution of payoffs. The bottom of the statistics report also gives the complete probability distribution of payoffs by

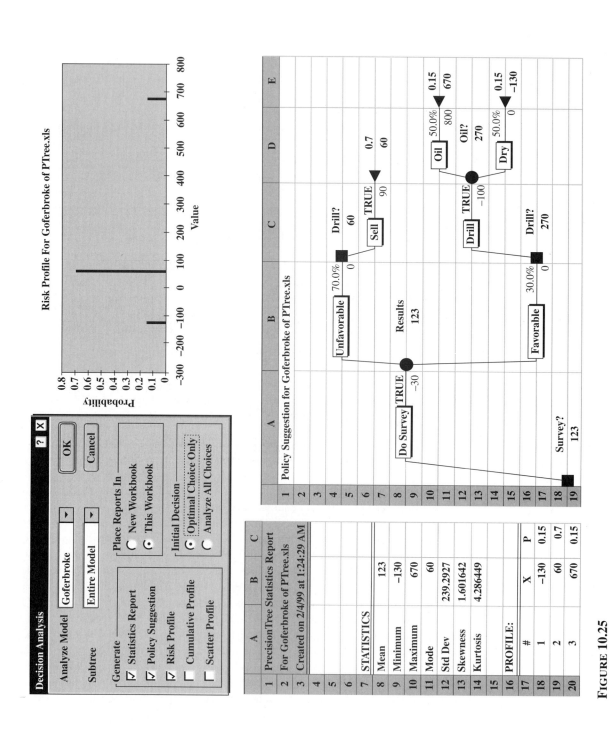

FIGURE 10.25

PrecisionTree's Decision Analysis dialogue box and the resulting reports generated for the full Goferbroke Co. problem.

listing the possible payoffs (in cells B18:B20) and the corresponding probabilities (in cells C18:C20). This probability distribution then is displayed graphically in the Risk Profile in the upper right-hand corner.

Max's Reaction

Max: I like this decision tree thing. It puts everything into perspective.

Jennifer: Good.

Max: It also gives me some numbers to compare alternatives. But how reliable are those numbers?

Jennifer: Well, you have to remember that these average payoffs for the alternatives at the decision nodes are based on both the payoffs on the right and the probabilities at the chance nodes. These probabilities are based in turn on the consulting geologist's numbers and the numbers you gave me on how frequently you get favorable seismic soundings when you have oil or when the land is dry.

Max: That doesn't sound so good. You know what I think about the consulting geologist's numbers. And the numbers I gave you were pretty rough estimates.

Jennifer: True. So the average payoffs shown in the decision tree are only approximations. This is when some sensitivity analysis can be helpful, like we did earlier before we considered doing the seismic survey.

Max: So shouldn't we do some sensitivity analysis now?

Jennifer: Yes, it generally is a good idea to do some sensitivity analysis until you are comfortable with your decision.

Max: OK. So let's do it.

Performing Sensitivity Analysis

At the end of Section 10.2, we described how PrecisionTree performs sensitivity analysis. We next apply this procedure with the current decision tree.

To begin, it is helpful to construct the spreadsheet shown in Figure 10.26 to summarize all the data and results. Sensitivity analysis then can be conducted by changing the data as desired on this spreadsheet. Therefore, the data cells on the Tree spreadsheet (Figure 10.24) now would make reference to the data cells on this spreadsheet. Similarly, the cells giving results on this spreadsheet make reference to the output cells on the Tree spreadsheet, as indicated by the equations at the bottom of Figure 10.26. At the same time, the data cells of the Posterior Probabilities template (Figure 10.20) now would refer to the probability data cells in this spreadsheet. The appropriate data cells on the Tree spreadsheet then refer to the output cells in the Posterior Probabilities template. Consequently, after making any changes in the cost data, revenue data, or probability data in Figure 10.26, this spreadsheet nicely summarizes the new results after the actual work to obtain these results is instantly done entirely in the background on two other worksheets (the Tree spreadsheet and the Posterior Probabilities template). Experimenting with alternative data values in this way is one useful way of performing sensitivity analysis.

By using this same spreadsheet (Figure 10.26) and the accompanying worksheets (Figures 10.24 and 10.20), PrecisionTree also provides some ways of performing sensitivity analysis systematically. The Sensitivity Analysis dialogue box back in Figure 10.13, including the same entries (except that the expected payoff now is in cell C22 and the prior probability of oil now is in cell C13), leads to the graph shown in Figure 10.27. This *one-way sensitivity graph* shows the relationship between the prior probability of oil and the expected payoff that results from using the optimal policy given this probability.

This graph indicates that the expected payoff starts increasing when the prior probability is a little over 0.15 and then starts increasing more rapidly when this probability is around 0.3. This suggests that the optimal policy changes at roughly these values of the prior probability. To check this out, the spreadsheet in Figure 10.26 can be used to see how the results change when the prior probability of oil is slowly increased in the vicinity of these values. This kind of trial-and-error analysis soon leads to the following conclusions about how the optimal policy depends on this probability.

Optimal policy

Let p = prior probability of oil.

If $p \leq 0.168$, then sell the land (no seismic survey).

If $0.169 \leq p \leq 0.308$, then do the survey: drill if favorable and sell if not.

If $p \geq 0.309$, then drill for oil (no seismic survey).

FIGURE 10.26

This spreadsheet uses the decision tree in Figure 10.24 and the posterior probabilities template in Figure 10.20 as worksheets to perform sensitivity analysis on the data for the full Goferbroke Co. problem.

	A	B	C	D	E
1		**Decision Analysis for Goferbroke Co. Problem**			
2					
3		**Cost Data**			
4		**Cost of Survey**	30		
5		**Cost of Drilling**	100		
6		**Revenue if Oil**	800		
7		**Revenue if Dry**	0		
8		**Revenue if Sell**	90		
9					
10		**Probability Data**			
11		**State of**	**Prior**	**P(Finding | State)**	
12		**Nature**	**Probability**	**FSS**	**USS**
13		**Oil**	0.25	0.6	0.4
14		**Dry**	0.75	0.2	0.8
15					
16		**Results**			
17		**Do Survey?**	**Yes**		
18		**If Favorable:**	**Drill**		
19		**If Unfavorable:**	**Sell**		
20		**If No Survey:**	**Drill**		
21					
22		**Expected Payoff:**	123		

	C
14	=1–C13
15	
16	
17	=IF(Tree!B11,"Yes","No")
18	=IF(Tree!D15,"Drill","Sell")
19	=IF(Tree!D3,"Drill","Sell")
20	=IF(Tree!C27,"Drill","Sell")
21	
22	=Tree!B24

FIGURE 10.27

This sensitivity graph for the full Goferbroke Co. problem shows how the expected payoff (when using Bayes' decision rule) depends on the prior probability of oil.

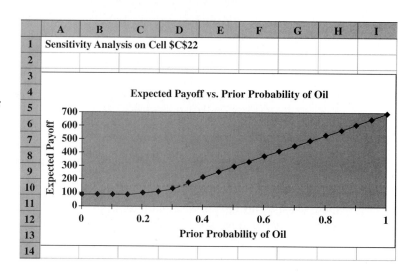

This sensitivity analysis has focused so far on investigating the effect if the true probability of finding oil is different from the original prior probability of 0.25. Similar analysis could be done with respect to the probabilities in cells D13:D14 of Figure 10.26. However, since there is significant uncertainty about some of the cost and revenue data in cells C4:C8, we turn next to performing sensitivity analysis with respect to these data.

Suppose we want to investigate how the expected payoff would change if one of the costs or revenues in cells C4:C6 and C8 were to change by up to *plus or minus 10 percent.* Figure 10.28 then shows the entries that should be made in the Sensitivity Analysis dialogue box (when accepting the default value of 10 for the number of steps to take over each range of values). Clicking on Run Analysis then leads to a variety of graphs. One type that you already have seen is the *one-way sensitivity graph* in Figure 10.27, except now the horizontal axis for each one would represent one of the costs or revenues rather than the prior probability of oil. Two other interesting types of graphs that you haven't yet seen are the *spider graph* and the *tornado diagram* shown in Figure 10.29.

Each line in the **spider graph** in this figure plots the expected payoff as one of the selected data cells (C4:C6 and C8) is changed from its original value by the percentage indicated along the bottom of the graph. (The diamonds for the *cost of survey line* are hidden under the squares for the *cost of drilling line.*) The fact that the *revenue if oil line* is the steepest one reveals that the expected payoff is particularly sensitive to the estimate of the revenue if oil is found, so any additional work on refining the estimates should focus the most attention on this one.

The **tornado diagram** in the figure provides a similar message in a different form. Each bar in this graph shows the range of percentage changes in the expected payoff from its original value (123) as the corresponding cost or revenue is varied over the range that was specified in the Sensitivity Analysis dialogue box (Figure 10.28). Although the label for the horizontal axis (% Change from Base Value) is the same as for the spider graph, this percentage change now refers to the change in the expected payoff rather than the change in the cost or revenue involved. Therefore, the width of each bar measures how sensitive the expected payoff is to changes in that bar's cost or revenue. Once again, *revenue if oil* stands out as causing much more sensitivity than the other costs or revenues.

When TreePlan is being used instead of PrecisionTree, its companion Excel add-in SensIt can also provide a spider graph and tornado diagram, as well as plots of sensitivity graphs like the one in Figure 10.27. Generating these graphs requires choosing Spider, Tornado, and Plot, respectively, under the Sensitivity Analysis option under the Tools menu.

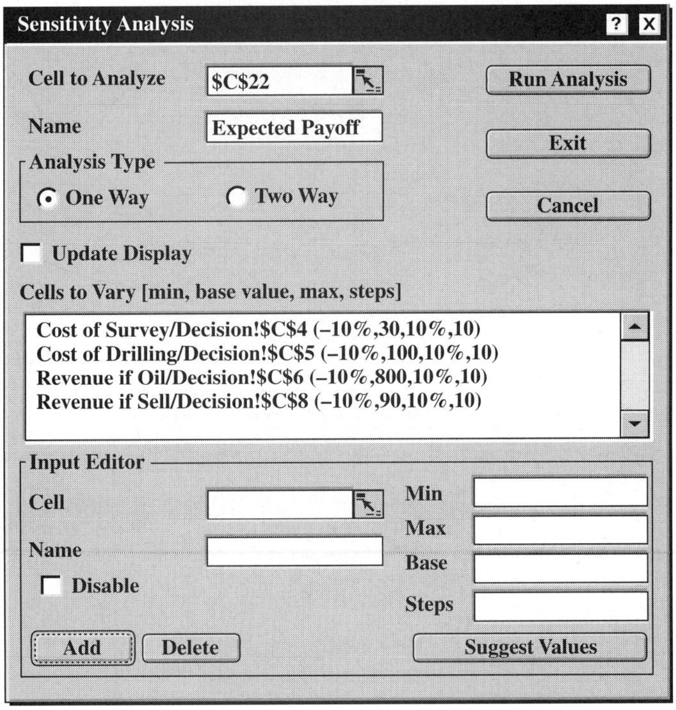

FIGURE 10.28

The Sensitivity Analysis dialogue box used by PrecisionTree to initiate an investigation for the full Goferbroke Co. problem of how the expected payoff varies as each of the costs or revenues varies one at a time.

FIGURE 10.29

The spider graph and tornado diagram generated by PrecisionTree to perform sensitivity analysis on the full Goferbroke Co. problem.

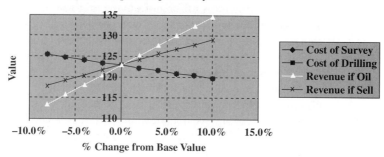

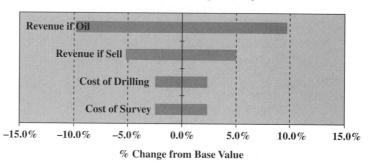

FIGURE 10.30

The dialogue boxes that would be used by SensIt to generate Figures 10.27 and 10.29 by referencing the cells in Figure 10.26 (after adding data in columns D, E, and F from Figure 10.28).

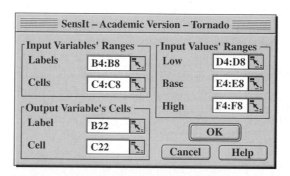

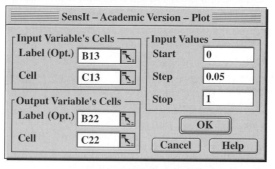

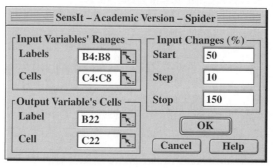

Figure 10.30 shows the corresponding dialogue boxes, where the cells being referenced are those in the Decision Analysis spreadsheet in Figure 10.26. (Although cells D4:F8 are blank in this figure, the right side of the Tornado dialogue box assumes that these cells now have been filled in with the range information given in the center of Figure 10.28.) The Plot dialogue box was previously discussed in Section 10.3 and illustrated in Figure 10.15. The output cell and label are chosen in the same way in the other two dialogue boxes. However, the input cells and the optional labels are chosen by dragging across them, so the cells in each of these sets need to be contiguous. Clicking OK on each dialogue box then generates the corresponding graph.

Max's Reaction

Max: Very interesting. I especially liked the way we were able to use that decision analysis spreadsheet to see immediately what would happen when we change some of the numbers. And there was one thing that I found particularly encouraging.

Jennifer: What was that?

Max: When we changed that prior probability of oil to nearly every other plausible value, it kept coming back with the same answer. Do the seismic survey and then drill only if the survey is favorable. Otherwise, sell. So the consulting geologist's numbers can be off by quite a bit and we still would be doing the right thing.

Jennifer: Yes, that was a key finding, wasn't it. What did you think of the sensitivity analysis involving the cost and revenue data?

Max: Those spider and tornado graph things were pretty clever. However, what they were saying didn't particularly surprise me. Sure, my payoff will depend much more on the revenue we get if we find oil than on anything else.

Jennifer: But what that is telling us is that it is especially important to try to better pin down what that revenue would be.

Max: Yes, I got that message. Unfortunately, that revenue number is particularly difficult to pin down. The geology suggests that we should have a pretty good-sized pocket of oil there if we have anything there at all. But you never know exactly how much will be there if you're lucky enough to strike oil. And, of course, the revenue depends on the amount of oil.

Jennifer: So from where did the estimate of $800,000 in revenue come?

Max: That was based mainly on an estimate of the size of the pocket that we hope contains oil. This estimate could be off some in either direction, but it represents what we think is the most likely outcome if, in fact, any oil is there. I don't think we have any way of improving much upon this estimate.

Jennifer: Too bad. But having this kind of uncertainty in the data is pretty common in applications of decision analysis. All you can do is develop a good solid estimate of what the average revenue would be, assuming oil is found, in situations resembling this one.

Max: I think we did that.

Jennifer: Good. Then we next should do what we did with the prior probability of oil. Try various plausible values of what the revenue would be if oil is found and see if the answer remains the same about what to do. If we quickly get some different results, you should take another look at the estimate of the revenue and also think hard about these alternative courses of action before you make your decision. However, if the results basically stay the same, then we can just go with the estimate of $800,000 in revenue if oil is found.

Max: That makes sense.

Jennifer: OK, let me save you some time in doing this. Based on both the decision tree and the sensitivity results we've already gotten, I can tell you right now that the Decision Analysis spreadsheet will give us the same results for what to do even if we make fairly substantial changes in the estimate of the revenue if oil is found. The boldfaced numbers in the decision tree indicate that the suggested policy is far from a close call. If the revenue from oil were considerably less than $800,000, then the question would become whether to do the seismic survey or simply sell the land immediately. However, the trend in the spider graph tells me that the revenue if oil is found could be as much as 25 percent less than the estimate of $800,000 and our expected payoff from the suggested policy still would exceed the $90,000 we could get from selling the land immediately.

Max: It's pretty unlikely that the revenue would be that much less than our estimate. So I am satisfied with going ahead with $800,000 as our estimate.

Jennifer: OK. Does this mean that you are comfortable now with a decision to proceed with the seismic survey and then either drill or sell depending on the outcome of the survey?

Max: Not quite. There is still one thing that bothers me.

Jennifer: What's that?

Max: Suppose the seismic survey gives us a favorable seismic sounding, so we drill. If the land turns out to be dry, then I'm out 130,000 bucks! As I said at the beginning, that would nearly put us out of business. That scares me.

Jennifer: Yes, you're right. There are about 3 chances in 20 of all that happening. But you have about the same odds of both getting a favorable seismic sounding and finding oil. If that happens, you would clear about $670,000, which would be a great boost to the company. Then there is about a 70 percent chance of obtaining unfavorable seismic soundings, in which case you would sell and clear $60,000. A nice profit. This approach is basically saying that these odds for the various possible outcomes, including the chance to clear $670,000, gives you the best available gamble.

Max: Yes, it does sound like a good gamble. I don't mind taking a small chance of a substantial loss when there is a reasonable chance of getting a much larger profit instead. That's the nature of this business. But here is my point. I currently am shorter of working capital than I normally am. Therefore, losing $130,000 now would hurt more than it normally does. It doesn't look like this approach is really taking that into account.

Jennifer: No, you're right. It really doesn't. This approach just looks at average *monetary* values. That isn't good enough when you're dealing with such large amounts. You wouldn't be willing to flip a coin to determine whether you win or lose $130,000, right?

Max: No, I sure wouldn't.

Jennifer: OK, that's the tipoff. As I mentioned the first time we talked about this problem, I think the circumstances here indicate that we need to go beyond dollars and cents to look at the consequences of the possible outcomes. Fortunately, decision analysis has a way of doing this by introducing utilities.

Max: Yes, I remember your mentioning utilities. What are they again?

Jennifer: Well, the basic idea is that the utility of an outcome measures the true value to you of that outcome rather than just the monetary value. So by expressing payoffs in terms of utilities, the decision tree analysis would find the average utility at each node instead of the average monetary value. So now the decisions would be based on giving you the highest possible average utility. In other words, they would give the highest true value to you on the average.

Max: Sounds reasonable. But I'm still not very clear on what these utilities are.

Jennifer: OK, get ready and I'll give you some background on utilities next.

Review Questions

1. What does a decision tree display?
2. What is happening at a decision node?
3. What is happening at a chance node?
4. What kinds of numbers need to be inserted into a decision tree before beginning the analysis?
5. When performing the analysis, where do you begin on the decision tree and in which direction do you move for dealing with the nodes?
6. What calculation needs to be performed at each chance node?

7. What comparison needs to be made at each decision node?
8. What kinds of graphs can either PrecisionTree or SensIt provide to assist with sensitivity analysis?

10.7 Using Utilities to Better Reflect the Values of Payoffs

Thus far, when applying Bayes' decision rule, we have assumed that the expected payoff in *monetary terms* is the appropriate measure of the consequences of taking an action. However, in many situations where very large amounts of money are involved, this assumption is inappropriate.

For example, suppose that an individual is offered the choice of (1) accepting a 50–50 chance of winning $100,000 or (2) receiving $40,000 with certainty. Many people would prefer the $40,000 even though the expected payoff on the 50–50 chance of winning $100,000 is $50,000. A company may be unwilling to invest a large sum of money in a new product, even when the expected profit is substantial, if there is a risk of losing its investment and thereby becoming bankrupt. People buy insurance even though it is a poor investment from the viewpoint of the expected payoff.

Do these examples invalidate Bayes' decision rule? Fortunately, the answer is no, because there is a way of transforming monetary values to an appropriate scale that reflects the decision maker's preferences. This scale is called the *utility function for money.*

Utility Functions for Money

Figure 10.31 shows a typical **utility function $U(M)$ for money** M. It indicates that an individual having this utility function would value obtaining $30,000 twice as much as $10,000 and would value obtaining $100,000 twice as much as $30,000. This reflects the fact that the person's highest-priority needs would be met by the first $10,000. Having this decreasing slope of the function as the amount of money increases is referred to as having a *decreasing marginal utility for money.* Such an individual is referred to as being **risk averse.**

However, not all individuals have a decreasing marginal utility for money. Some people are **risk seekers** instead of *risk averse,* and they go through life looking for the "big score." The slope of their utility function *increases* as the amount of money increases, so they have an *increasing marginal utility for money.*

Figure 10.32 compares the shape of the utility function for money for risk-averse and risk-seeking individuals. Also shown is the intermediate case of a **risk-neutral** individual,

FIGURE 10.31

A typical utility function for money, where U(M) *is the utility of obtaining an amount of money* M.

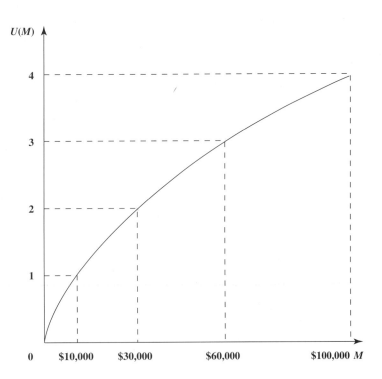

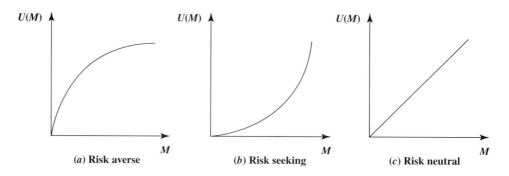

(a) Risk averse   (b) Risk seeking   (c) Risk neutral

who prizes money at its face value. Such an individual's utility for money is simply proportional to the amount of money involved. Although some people appear to be risk neutral when only small amounts of money are involved, it is unusual to be truly risk neutral with very large amounts.

It also is possible to exhibit a mixture of these kinds of behavior. For example, an individual might be essentially risk neutral with small amounts of money, then become a risk seeker with moderate amounts, and then turn risk averse with large amounts. In addition, one's attitude toward risk can shift over time depending on circumstances.

Managers of a business firm need to consider the company's circumstances and the collective philosophy of top management in determining the appropriate attitude toward risk when making managerial decisions.

The fact that different people have different utility functions for money has an important implication for decision making in the face of uncertainty.

When a *utility function for money* is incorporated into a decision analysis approach to a problem, this utility function must be constructed to fit the current preferences and values of the decision maker involved. (The decision maker can be either a single individual or a group of people.)

The key to constructing the utility function for money to fit the decision maker is the following fundamental property of utility functions.

Fundamental Property: Under the assumptions of utility theory, the decision maker's *utility function for money* has the property that the decision maker is *indifferent* between two alternative courses of action if the two alternatives have the *same expected utility.*

To illustrate, suppose that the decision maker has the utility function shown in Fig. 10.31. Further suppose that the decision maker is offered the following opportunity.

Offer: An opportunity to obtain either $100,000 (utility = 4) with probability p or nothing (utility = 0) with probability $(1 - p)$.

Thus, by weighting the two possible utilities (4 and 0) by their probabilities, the expected utility is

$$E(\text{utility}) = 4p + 0\,(1 - p)$$

$$= 4p \qquad \text{for this offer}$$

Therefore, for *each* of the following three pairs of alternatives, the above fundamental property indicates that the decision maker is indifferent between the first and second alternatives.

1. First alternative: The offer with $p = 0.25$, so $E(\text{utility}) = 1$.
   Second alternative: Definitely obtain $10,000, so utility = 1.
2. First alternative: The offer with $p = 0.5$, so $E(\text{utility}) = 2$.
   Second alternative: Definitely obtain $30,000, so utility = 2.
3. First alternative: The offer with $p = 0.75$, so $E(\text{utility}) = 3$.
   Second alternative: Definitely obtain $60,000, so utility = 3.

This example also illustrates one way in which the decision maker's utility function for money can be constructed in the first place. The decision maker would be made the same hypothetical offer to obtain a large amount of money (e.g., $100,000) with probability p, or nothing otherwise. Then, for each of a few smaller amounts of money (e.g., $10,000,

$30,000, and $60,000), the decision maker would be asked to choose a value of p that would make him or her *indifferent* between the offer and definitely obtaining that amount of money. The utility of the smaller amount of money then is p times the utility of the large amount.

The *scale* of the utility function is irrelevant. In other words, it doesn't matter whether the values of $U(M)$ at the dashed lines in Figure 10.31 are 1, 2, 3, 4 (as shown) or 10,000, 20,000, 30,000, 40,000, or whatever. All that matters is that these second, third, and fourth values of $U(M)$ should 2, 3, and 4 times the first value, respectively. All the utilities can be multiplied by any positive constant without affecting which decision alternative will have the largest expected utility. Therefore, in addition to having $U(0) = 0$, the value of $U(M)$ can be set arbitrarily for one nonzero value of M (with a positive utility for a positive M and a negative utility for a negative M).

Now we are ready to summarize the basic role of utility functions in decision analysis.

When the decision maker's utility function for money is used to measure the relative worth of the various possible monetary outcomes, *Bayes' decision rule* replaces monetary payoffs by the corresponding utilities. Therefore, the optimal decision (or series of decisions) is the one that *maximizes the expected utility.*

Only utility functions *for money* have been discussed here. However, we should mention that utility functions can sometimes still be constructed when some or all of the important consequences of the decision alternatives are *not* monetary in nature. (For example, the consequences of a doctor's decision alternatives in treating a patient involve the future health of the patient.) This is not necessarily easy, since it may require making value judgments about the relative desirability of rather intangible consequences. Nevertheless, under these circumstances, it is important to incorporate such value judgments into the decision process.

Dealing with the Goferbroke Co. Problem

Recall that the Goferbroke Co. is operating without much capital, so a loss of $100,000 would be quite serious. As the owner of the company, Max already has gone heavily into debt to keep going. The worst-case scenario would be to come up with $30,000 for a seismic survey and then still lose $100,000 by drilling when there is no oil. This scenario would not bankrupt the company at this point, but definitely would leave it in a precarious financial position.

On the other hand, striking oil is an exciting prospect, since earning $700,000 finally would put the company in a fairly solid financial footing.

Max is the decision maker for this problem. Therefore, to prepare for using utilities to analyze the problem, it is necessary to construct Max's utility function for money, $U(M)$, where we will express the amount of money M in units of thousands of dollars.

As a starting point, it is natural to let the utility of *zero* money be zero, so $U(0) = 0$. Recall that we can also arbitrarily set the value of $U(M)$ for one nonzero value of M. We will do this for the smallest possible value of M for this problem, namely, $M = -130$ (a loss of $130,000), by setting

$$U(-130) = -150$$

Although the choice of -150 is completely arbitrary (except for being negative), this will be a convenient choice since it will make $U(M)$ approximately equal to M when M is in the vicinity of 0. This will enable us to better see how the utilities compare with monetary values (M) over the entire range of M.

To determine the utilities for other possible monetary payoffs, it is necessary to probe Max's attitude toward risk. Especially important are his feelings about the consequences of the worst possible loss ($130,000) and the best possible gain ($700,000), as well as how he compares these consequences. Let us eavesdrop as Jennifer probes these feelings with Max.

Interviewing Max

Jennifer: Well now, these utilities are intended to reflect your feelings about the true value to you of these various possible payoffs. Therefore, to pin down what your utilities are, we need to talk some about how you feel about these payoffs and their consequences for the company.

Max: Fine.

Jennifer: A good place to begin would be the best and worst possible cases. The possibility of gaining $700,000 or losing $130,000.

Max: Those are the big ones all right.

Jennifer: OK, suppose you drill without paying for a seismic survey and then you find oil, so your profit is about $700,000. What would that do for the company?

Max: A lot. That would finally give me the capital I need to become more of a major player in this business. I then could take a shot at finding a big oil field. That big strike I've talked about.

Jennifer: Yes, that's always been your dream, hasn't it? To get your big strike.

Max: It sure has. That's why I've gone through all those rough times all these years. It's been exciting when we got some small strikes, but scary too when we've gone through some dry patches. Fortunately, I've had some decent luck and managed to keep going. But I won't be satisfied until I get that big strike.

Jennifer: And you think that clearing $700,000 on this drill would give you a good shot at that big strike soon?

Max: A decent shot. That's all you can ask for in this business.

Jennifer: OK, good. Now let's talk about the consequences if you were to get that biggest possible loss instead. Suppose you pay for a seismic survey, then you drill and the land is dry. So you're out about $130,000. How bad would that be? What kind of future would the company have?

Max: Well, let me put it this way. It would put the company in a pretty uncomfortable financial position. I would need to work hard on getting some more financing. Then we would need to cautiously work our way out of the hole by forming some partnerships for some low-risk, low-gain drilling. But I think we could do it. I've been in that position a couple times before and come out of it. We'd be OK.

Jennifer: It sounds like you wouldn't be overly worried about such a loss as long as you have reasonable odds for a big payoff to justify this risk.

Max: That's right.

Jennifer: OK, now let's talk about those odds. What I'm going to do is set up a simpler hypothetical situation. Suppose you don't have the option of selling. So here are your alternatives. One is to drill. If you find oil, you clear $700,000. If the land is dry, you're out $130,000. The only other alternative is to do nothing, so you would neither gain nor lose anything. I know this isn't your actual situation. But let's pretend that it is.

Max: I don't understand why you want to talk about a situation that is different from what we are facing.

Jennifer: Trust me. This is going to enable us to determine your utilities.

Max: OK.

Jennifer: Now presumably if you had a 50–50 chance of either clearing $700,000 or losing $130,000, you would drill.

Max: Sure.

Jennifer: But if you had only a very small chance, say, a 10 percent chance of gaining $700,000, versus a 90 percent chance of losing $130,000, you presumably wouldn't drill.

Max: True.

Jennifer: OK, let's improve your odds a little. Suppose you have a 15 percent chance of getting the $700,000. In this case, if you look at the average payoff, you would be just a shade short of coming out even. So if you had an unlimited amount of money, you would be at just about your break-even point for going ahead and drilling.

Max: Well, I sure don't have an unlimited amount of money! I would need to do quite a bit better than breaking even on the average to justify the risk of crippling the company by losing $130,000.

Jennifer: I was guessing you would feel that way. OK, let's improve your odds some more. Suppose now that you have a 25 percent chance of gaining $700,000 versus a 75 percent chance of losing $130,000. Would you do it?

Max: I like those odds a lot better. $700,000 is over five times as large as $130,000, whereas 75 percent is only three times as large as 25 percent, so that average payoff you're always talking about must be pretty large in this case.
Jennifer: Yes, it would be over $75,000.
Max: That's a lot. Well, that $700,000 sure would give a huge boost to the future of the company. I don't relish the hard times we would go through if we lost $130,000, but yes, I think a 25 percent chance of clearing $700,000 would justify that risk. You have to take those kinds of chances in this business.
Jennifer: OK, so now we know that the point at which you would be indifferent between going ahead or not is somewhere between having a 15 percent chance and a 25 percent chance of gaining $700,000 rather than losing $130,000. Let's see if we can pin down just where your **point of indifference** is within this range from 15 percent to 25 percent. Let's try 20 percent. Would you go ahead and drill with a 20 percent chance of gaining $700,000 versus an 80 percent chance of losing $130,000?
Max: Hmm. That's not so clear. What would be the average payoff in this case?
Jennifer: $36,000.
Max: Not bad. Hmm, one chance in five of gaining $700,000. That's tempting. But four chances in five of losing $130,000 with all the problems involved with that. I don't know. That's a tough one.
Jennifer: OK, let's try this. Suppose your chances of gaining $700,000 were a little better than 20 percent. Would you do it?
Max: Yes, I think so.
Jennifer: And if your chances were a little under 20 percent?
Max: Then I don't think I would do it.
Jennifer: OK. You've convinced me that your point of indifference is 20 percent. That's exactly what I needed to know.

Finding U*(700)*

Max has indeed given Jennifer just the information she needs to determine $U(700)$, Max's utility for a payoff of 700 (a gain of $700,000). Recall that $U(-130)$ already has been set at $U(-130) = -150$. Given this value, the procedure for finding $U(700)$ is summarized below. The decision maker (Max) is offered two alternatives, A_1 and A_2.

A_1: Obtain a payoff of 700 with probability p.
   Obtain a payoff of -130 with probability $(1 - p)$.
A_2: Definitely obtain a payoff of 0.

Question to the decision maker: What value of p makes you *indifferent* between these two alternatives?
The decision maker's choice: $p = 0.2$.

Set

E(utility for A_1) $= E$(utility for A_2)
and solve this equation for the unknown, $U(700)$.

Since $U(0) = 0$, we have E(utility for A_2) $= 0$. The expected utility for A_1 is

$$E\text{(utility for } A_1) = pU(700) + (1 - p)U(-130)$$

$$= 0.2U(700) + 0.8\,(-150)$$

$$= 0.2U(700) - 120$$

Because the fundamental property of utility functions says that the expected utilities for the two alternatives are the same at the decision maker's point of indifference, $p = 0.2$, we have

$$0.2U(700) - 120 = 0$$

$$0.2U(700) = 120$$

$$U(700) = 600$$

The General Procedure for Finding a Utility

The above procedure for finding $U(700)$ illustrates that the key is having the decision maker select a *point of indifference* between two alternatives where one of them (A_1) involves a *lottery*. Here is the general version of this **lottery procedure**.

Lottery Procedure

1. We are given three possible monetary payoffs—M_1, M_2, M_3 ($M_1 < M_2 < M_3$)—where the utility is known for two of them and we wish to find the utility for the third one.

2. The decision maker is offered the following two hypothetical alternatives:

   A_1: Obtain a payoff of M_3 with probability p.
       Obtain a payoff of M_1 with probability $(1 - p)$.
   A_2: Definitely obtain a payoff of M_2.

3. Question to the decision maker: What value of p makes you *indifferent* between these two alternatives?

4. Using this value of p, write the *fundamental property equation,*

$$E(\text{utility for } A_1) = E(\text{utility for } A_2),$$

so

$$pU(M_3) + (1 - p)U(M_1) = U(M_2).$$

5. Solve this equation for the unknown utility.

When finding $U(700)$, we actually were applying this lottery procedure with $M_1 = -130$, $M_2 = 0$, and $M_3 = 700$. When finding the next two utilities, we will have $M_3 = 0$ in the first case and then $M_1 = 0$ in the second case instead. (Although not required, it is common to include 0 as one of the three payoffs to enable focusing better on the comparison between the other two.) We also will have the middle payoff M_2 be the one with the unknown utility, although any position (smallest, middle, largest) is allowed.

Finding U(−100)

We now will illustrate the lottery procedure by applying it step by step to find the utility for another of Goferbroke's possible payoffs, namely, -100 (a loss of $100,000). However, we will not bother to eavesdrop this time on Jennifer's interview of Max to determine his point of indifference between the two hypothetical alternatives in this case.

We now have three payoffs ($-130, 0, 700$) with known utilities, so any two can be chosen for this procedure. The two actually selected were -130 and 0, since they can be compared to -100 somewhat more easily than can 700.

1. The three given payoffs are

   $M_1 = -130$ with $U(-130) = -150$ known
   $M_2 = -100$ with $U(-100)$ unknown
   $M_3 = 0$ with $U(0) = 0$ known

2. The two hypothetical alternatives are

   A_1: Obtain a payoff of 0 with probability p.
       Obtain a payoff of -130 with probability $(1 - p)$.
   A_2: Definitely obtain a payoff of -100.

3. Max chooses $p = 0.3$ as his point of indifference between these two alternatives.
4. The fundamental property equation is

$$pU(0) + (1 - p) U(-130) = U(-100)$$

so

$$0.3 (0) + 0.7 (-150) = U(-100)$$

5. The solution is $U(-100) = -105$.

Finding U(90)

In addition to $U(0) = 0$, we now have found Max's utilities for Goferbroke's possible negative payoffs (-130 and -100) and the largest possible positive payoff (700). For our last calculation, we now will find the utility for a relatively small positive payoff (90), using 0 and 700 in the procedure as two payoffs with known utilities.

1. The three given payoffs are

   $M_1 = 0$ with $U(0) = 0$ known
   $M_2 = 90$ with $U(90)$ unknown
   $M_3 = 700$ with $U(700) = 600$ known

2. The two hypothetical alternatives are

   A_1: Obtain a payoff of 700 with probability p.
       Obtain a payoff of 0 with probability $(1 - p)$.
   A_2: Definitely obtain a payoff of 90.

3. Max chooses $p = 0.15$ as his point of indifference between these two alternatives.

4. The fundamental property equation is

   $$pU(700) + (1 - p)\, U(0) = U(90)$$

   so

   $$0.15(600) + 0.85\,(0) = U(90).$$

5. The solution is $U(90) = 90$.

Constructing Max's Utility Function for Money

We now have found the utilities for five representative possible payoffs (-130, -100, 0, 90, 700) for Goferbroke. Plotting these values on a graph of the utility $U(M)$ versus the monetary payoff M and then drawing a smooth curve through these points gives the curve shown in Figure 10.33.

This curve is our best estimate of Max's utility function for money. The values on this curve at $M=60$ and $M = 670$ provide the corresponding utilities, $U(60) = 60$ and $U(670) = 580$, for these last two possible payoffs. (The lottery procedure also could have been applied to find these utilities, but there is no need since these payoffs are so close to others with known utilities.) Table 10.6 gives the complete list of possible payoffs and their utilities.

FIGURE 10.33

Max's utility function for money as the owner of Goferbroke Co.

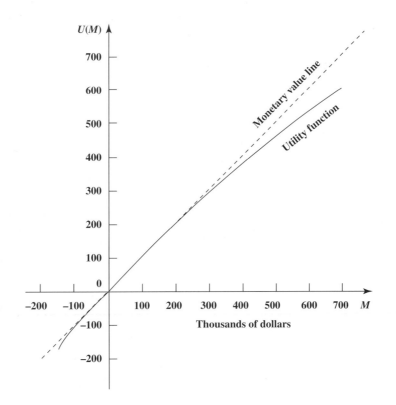

TABLE 10.6   Utilities for the Goferbroke Co. Problem

Monetary Payoff, M	Utility, U(M)
−130	−150
−100	−105
0	0
60	60
90	90
670	580
700	600

For comparative purposes, the dashed line in Figure 10.33 shows the monetary value (in thousands of dollars) along the vertical axis for any payoff M along the horizontal axis. (Since this line is drawn at 45°, the value along the vertical axis always is the same as the value along the horizontal axis for any point on the line.) This dashed line would have been the utility function $U(M) = M$ if Max were completely *risk neutral*, since then monetary payoffs would be equivalent to utilities. However, note how the actual utility function $U(M)$ given by the smooth curve essentially equals M for small values (positive or negative) of M, and then $U(M)$ gradually falls off M for larger values of M. This is typical for a moderately risk-averse individual.

By nature, Max is inclined to be a risk seeker. However, the difficult financial circumstances of his company that he badly wants to keep solvent has forced him to adopt a moderately risk-averse stance in addressing his current decisions.

***Summary of the Procedure for Constructing* U(M)**

Here is a summary of the general procedure that we have just followed in constructing Max's utility function $U(M)$.

Procedure for Constructing a Utility Function for Money
1. List all the possible monetary payoffs for the problem, including 0 (whether possible or not).
2. Set $U(0) = 0$ and then arbitrarily choose a utility value for one other payoff (with a negative value for a negative payoff and a positive value for a positive payoff).
3. Choose three of the payoffs where the utility is known for two of them.
4. Apply the lottery procedure to find the utility for the third payoff.
5. Repeat steps 3 and 4 for as many other representative payoffs with unknown utilities as desired.
6. Then plot the utilities found on a graph of the utility $U(M)$ versus the payoff M. Draw a smooth curve through these points to obtain the utility function.

***Another Approach for Estimating* U(M)**

The above procedure for constructing $U(M)$ asks the decision maker to repeatedly apply the lottery procedure, which requires him (or her) each time to make a difficult decision about which probability would make him indifferent between two alternatives. Many managers would be uncomfortable with making this kind of decision. Therefore, an alternative approach is sometimes used instead to estimate the utility function for money.

This approach is to assume that the utility function has a certain mathematical form, and then adjust this form to fit the decision maker's attitude toward risk as closely as possible. For example, one particularly popular form to assume (because of its relative simplicity) is the **exponential utility function,**

$$U(M) = R\left(1 - e^{-\frac{M}{R}}\right)$$

where R is the decision maker's *risk tolerance*. This utility function has the kind of shape shown in Figure 10.32(*a*), so it is designed to fit a *risk-averse* individual. A great aversion to risk corresponds to a small value of R (which would cause the curve in this figure to bend sharply), whereas a small aversion to risk corresponds to a large value of R (which gives a much more gradual bend in the curve).

Since Max has a relatively small aversion to risk, his utility function curve in Figure 10.33 bends quite slowly. The value of R that would give Max's utilities of $U(670) = 580$ and $U(700) = 600$ is approximately R = 2,250. On the other hand, Max becomes much more risk averse when large losses can occur, since this now would threaten bankruptcy, so the value of R that would give his utility of $U(-130) = -150$ is only about $R = 465$.

Unfortunately, it is not possible to use two different values of R for the same utility function. A drawback of the exponential utility function is that it assumes a constant aversion to risk (a fixed value of R), regardless of how much (or how little) money the decision maker currently has. This doesn't fit Max's situation, since his current shortage of money makes him much more concerned about incurring a large loss than usual. This is why Jennifer never raised the possibility of using an exponential utility function.

In other situations where the consequences of the potential losses are not as severe, assuming an exponential utility function may provide a reasonable approximation. In such a case, here is an easy way of estimating the appropriate value of R. The decision maker would be asked to choose the number R that would make him indifferent between the following two alternatives.

A_1: A 50–50 gamble where he would gain R dollars with probability 0.5 and lose $R/2$ dollars with probability 0.5.

A_2: Neither gain nor lose anything.

Both PrecisionTree and TreePlan include the option of using the exponential utility function. In fact, the upper right-hand side of the Tree Settings dialogue box for Precision-Tree displayed in Figure 10.2 shows that exponential is the default choice for the utility function. All you need to do is click on using a utility function and then enter the desired value of R in this dialogue box. With TreePlan, you click on the Options button in the TreePlan dialogue box and then select Use Exponential Utility Function. TreePlan uses a different form for the exponential utility function that requires specifying the values of three constants (by choosing Define Name under the Insert menu and entering the values). By choosing the value of R for all three of these constants, this utility function becomes the same as the exponential utility function used by PrecisionTree.

Using a Decision Tree to Analyze the Problem with Utilities

Now that Max's utility function for money has been constructed in Table 10.6 (and Figure 10.33), this information can be used with a decision tree as summarized below.

> The procedure for using a decision tree to analyze the problem now is *identical* to that described in Section 10.6 *except* for substituting utilities for monetary payoffs. Therefore, the value obtained to evaluate each node of the tree now is the *expected utility* there rather than the expected (monetary) payoff. Consequently, the optimal policy selected by Bayes' decision rule maximizes the expected utility for the overall problem.

Thus, using PrecisionTree once again, our final decision tree with utilities shown in Figure 10.34 closely resembles the one in Figure 10.24 given in the preceding section. The nodes and branches are exactly the same, as are the probabilities for the branches emanating from the chance nodes. However, the key difference from Figure 10.24 is that the monetary payoff to the right of each terminal node now has been replaced by the corresponding utility from Table 10.6. (This was accomplished with PrecisionTree by entering this same utility as the "cash flow" at the terminal branch and then entering "cash flows" of 0 at all the preceding branches.) It is these utilities that have been used by PrecisionTree to compute the *expected utilities* given next to all the nodes.

These expected utilities lead to the same decisions as in Figure 10.24 at all decision nodes except the bottom one in cells C31:C32. The decision at this node now switches to sell instead of drill. However, the solution procedure still leaves this node on a closed path, as indicated by FALSE in cell B31. Therefore, the overall optimal policy remains the same as obtained in Figure 10.24 (do the seismic survey; sell if the result is unfavorable; drill if the result is favorable).

FIGURE 10.34

The final decision tree constructed and solved by PrecisionTree for the full Goferbroke Co. problem when using Max's utility function for money to maximize expected utility.

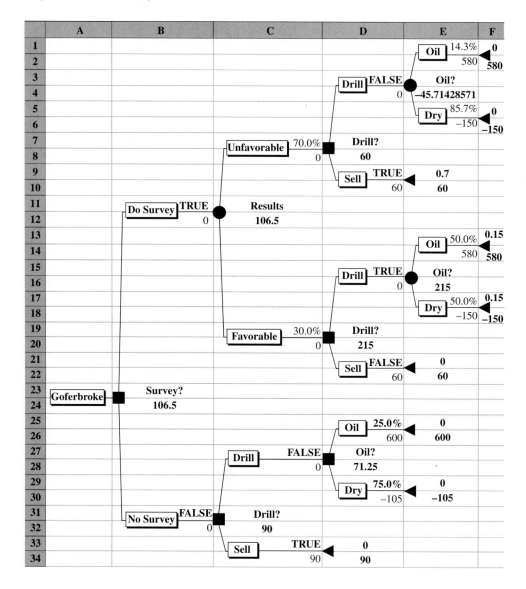

The approach used in the preceding sections of maximizing the expected monetary payoff was equivalent to assuming that the decision maker is neutral toward risk so that $U(M) = M$. By using utility theory with an appropriate utility function, the optimal solution now reflects the decision maker's attitude about risk. Because Max adopted only a moderately risk-averse stance, the optimal policy did not change from before. For a somewhat more risk-averse decision maker, the optimal solution would switch to the more conservative approach of immediately selling the land (no seismic survey).

Jennifer and Max are to be commended for incorporating utilities into a decision analysis approach to his problem. Utilities help to provide a rational approach to decision making in the face of uncertainty. However, many managers are not sufficiently comfortable with the relatively abstract notion of utilities, or with working with probabilities to construct a utility function, to be willing to use this approach. Consequently, utilities are not used nearly as widely in practice as some of the other techniques of decision analysis described in this chapter, including Bayes' decision rule (with monetary payoffs) and decision trees.

Max's Reaction

> *Max:* Whew! I haven't had to do that much hard thinking since I was in school. That management science stuff really forces you to follow a very disciplined, logical approach, doesn't it?

Jennifer: That's true. What did you think of using utilities?

Max: Well, those utilities still are a little mysterious to me. But the numbers we ended up with for the utilities made sense. I can see what this is driving at and I think these utilities do better reflect my feelings about the true value of these payoffs.

Jennifer: Good. So are you comfortable with your decisions?

Max: Yes, I am. I'm more than satisfied that we've thought it through carefully enough. And I like the fact that there are no close calls. Even if the numbers are off some, these probably are still the best decisions.

Jennifer: Right. Otherwise, I would urge you to do some more sensitivity analysis.

Max: No, I'm satisfied. It's pretty clear we should do the seismic survey. Then it certainly makes sense to drill if we get favorable seismic soundings and to sell if we don't. All this analysis has really clarified my thinking.

Jennifer: Great. That's the idea.

Max: I must say that I'm impressed with this management science stuff, even if it is a lot of work. Glad to see that all that tuition I paid for you was so worthwhile.

Jennifer: I liked my management science class. A lot of it seemed very useful.

Max: Well, you've just done a great job for me applying that stuff. Thanks a lot, sweetheart.

Jennifer: You're welcome, Dad.

Review Questions

1. What are utilities intended to reflect?
2. What is the shape of the utility function for money for a risk-averse individual? A risk-seeking individual? A risk-neutral individual?
3. What is the fundamental property of utility functions?
4. What is the lottery involved with the lottery procedure?
5. Given two hypothetical alternatives where one of them involves a probability *p,* what is meant by the point of indifference between these two alternatives?
6. When using utilities with a decision tree, what kind of value is obtained to evaluate each node of the tree?
7. What decisions did Max make regarding the Goferbroke Co. problem?

10.8 The Practical Application of Decision Analysis

In one sense, the Goferbroke Co. problem is a very typical application of decision analysis. Like other applications, Max needed to make his decisions (Do a seismic survey? Drill for oil or sell the land?) in the face of great uncertainty. The decisions were difficult because their payoffs were so unpredictable. The outcome depended on factors that were outside Max's control (does the land contain oil or is it dry?). He needed a framework and methodology for rational decision making in this uncertain environment. These are the usual characteristics of applications of decision analysis.

However, in other ways, the Goferbroke problem is not such a typical application. It was oversimplified to include only two possible states of nature (oil and dry), whereas there actually would be a considerable number of distinct possibilities. For example, the actual state might be dry, a small amount of oil, a moderate amount, a large amount, and a huge amount, plus different possibilities concerning the depth of the oil and soil conditions that impact the cost of drilling to reach the oil. Max also was considering only two alternatives for each of two decisions. Real applications commonly involve more decisions, more alternatives to be considered for each one, and many possible states of nature.

Problems as tiny as the Goferbroke problem can readily be analyzed and solved by hand. However, real applications typically involve large decision trees, whose construction and analysis require the use of a software package (such as PrecisionTree or TreePlan introduced in this chapter). In some cases, the decision tree can explode in size with many thousand terminal branches. Special algebraic techniques are being developed and incorporated into the solvers for dealing with such large problems.[1]

Sensitivity analysis also can become unwieldy on large problems. Although it normally is supported by the computer software, the amount of data generated can easily overwhelm an analyst or decision maker. Therefore, some graphical techniques, such as the spider graph and tornado diagram introduced in Figure 10.29, have been developed to organize the data in a readily understandable way.[2]

Other kinds of graphical techniques also are available to complement the decision tree in representing and solving decision analysis problems. One that has become quite popular is called the **influence diagram,** and researchers continue to develop others as well.[3]

Although the Goferbroke problem only involved a single decision maker (Max) assisted by a single analyst (Jennifer), many strategic business decisions are made collectively by management. One technique for group decision making is called **decision conferencing.** This is a process where the group comes together for discussions in a decision conference with the help of an analyst and a group facilitator. The facilitator works directly with the group to help it structure and focus discussions, think creatively about the problem, bring assumptions to the surface, and address the full range of issues involved. The analyst uses decision analysis to assist the group in exploring the implications of the various decision alternatives. With the assistance of a computerized *group decision support system,* the analyst builds and solves models on the spot, and then performs sensitivity analysis to respond to what-if questions from the group.[4]

Applications of decision analysis commonly involve a partnership between the managerial decision maker (whether an individual or a group) and an analyst (whether an individual or a team) with training in management science. Some managers are not as fortunate as Max in having a staff member (let alone a daughter) like Jennifer who is qualified to serve as the analyst. Therefore, a considerable number of management consulting firms specializing in decision analysis have been formed to fill this role. (For example, a few large ones are located in Silicon Valley next to Stanford University, with names such as Applied Decision Analysis, Decision Focus, and the Strategic Decisions Group.)

Decision analysis is widely used around the world. For proprietary reasons (among others), companies usually do not publish articles in professional journals to describe their applications of management science techniques, including decision analysis. Fortunately, such articles do filter out once in awhile, with some of them appearing in the journal called *Interfaces.* The articles about decision analysis provide valuable insights about the practical application of this technique in practice.

Table 10.7 briefly summarizes the nature of some of the applications of decision analysis that have appeared in *Interfaces.* The rightmost column identifies the specific issue of the journal for each application. Note in the other columns the wide diversity of organizations and applications (with public utilities as the heaviest users). For each specific application, think about how uncertainties in the situation make decision analysis a natural technique to use.

If you would like to do more reading about the practical application of decision analysis, a good place to begin would be the November–December 1992 issue of *Interfaces.* This is a special issue devoted entirely to decision analysis and the related area of risk analysis. It includes many interesting articles, including descriptions of basic methods, sensitivity analysis, and decision conferencing. Also included are several of the articles on applications that are listed in Table 10.7.

---

[1] For example, see C. W. Kirkwood, "An Algebraic Approach to Formulating and Solving Large Models for Sequential Decisions under Uncertainty," *Management Science* 39 (July 1993), pp. 900–13.

[2] For further information, see T. G. Eschenbach, "Spiderplots versus Tornado Diagrams for Sensitivity Analysis," *Interfaces* 22 (November–December 1992), pp. 40–46.

[3] For example, see P. P. Schnoy, "A Comparison of Graphical Techniques for Decision Analysis," *European Journal of Operational Research* 78 (October 13, 1994), pp. 1–21. Also see Z. Covaliu and R. M. Oliver, "Representation and Solution of Decision Problems Using Sequential Decision Diagrams," *Management Science* 41 (December 1995), pp. 1860–81, as well as Chapters 4 and 9 in K. T. Marshall and R. M. Oliver, *Decision Making and Forecasting* (New York: McGraw-Hill, 1995).

[4] For further information, see the two articles on decision conferencing in the November–December 1992 issue of *Interfaces,* where one describes an application in Australia and the other summarizes the experience of 26 decision conferences in Hungary.

TABLE 10.7   Some Applications of Decision Analysis

Organization	Nature of Application	Issue of Interfaces
Amoco Oil Co.	Used utilities to evaluate strategies for marketing its products through full-facility service stations.	Dec. 1982
Ohio Edison Co.	Evaluated and selected particulate emission control equipment for a coal-fired power plant.	Feb. 1983
New England Electric System	Determined an appropriate bid for the salvage rights to a grounded ship.	March–April 1984
National Weather Service	Developed a plan for responding to flood forecasts and warnings.	May–June 1984
National Forest Administrations	Planned prescribed fires to improve forest and rangeland ecosystems.	Sept.–Oct. 1984
Tomco Oil Corp.	Chose between two site locations for drilling an oil well, with 74 states of nature.	March–April 1986
Personal decision	Used decision criteria without probabilities to choose between adjustable-rate and fixed-rate mortgages.	May–June 1986
U.S. Postal Service	Chose between six alternatives for a postal automation program, saving $200 million.	March–April 1987; Jan.–Feb. 1988
Santa Clara University	Evaluated whether to implement a drug-testing program for their intercollegiate athletes.	May–June 1990
Independent Living Center (Australia)	A decision conference developed a strategic plan for reorganizing the center.	Nov.–Dec. 1992
DuPont Corp.	Many applications to strategic planning; one added $175 million in value.	Nov.–Dec. 1992
British Columbia Hydro and Power Authority	Elicited a utility function for clarifying value trade-offs for many strategic issues.	Nov.–Dec. 1992
U.S. Department of Defense	Improved the decision process for the acquisition of weapon systems.	Nov.–Dec. 1992
Electric utility industry	Considered health and environmental risks in dealing with utility-generated solid wastes and air emissions.	Nov.–Dec. 1992
An anonymous international bank	Developed a contingency-planning program against fire and power failure for all services.	Nov.–Dec. 1992
General Motors	More than 40 major decision analysis projects over five years.	Nov.–Dec. 1992
Southern Company (electric utility)	Evaluated alternative preventive maintenance programs for motor vehicle and construction equipment fleets.	May–June 1993
ICI Americas	Selected research and development projects with little data available for assessing them.	Nov.–Dec. 1993
Federal National Mortgage Association	Used utilities to select the composition of a portfolio of home mortgage assets.	May–June 1994
Oglethorpe Power Corp.	Evaluated whether to invest in a major transmission system and how to finance it.	March–April 1995
Phillips Petroleum Co.	Evaluated oil exploration opportunities with a consistent risk-taking policy.	Nov.–Dec. 1995
Energy Electric System	Evaluated schedules for preventive maintenance for electrical generator units.	July–Aug. 1996

Review Questions

1. How does the Goferbroke Co. problem compare with typical applications of decision analysis?
2. What is the purpose of an influence diagram?
3. Who are the typical participants in a decision-conferencing process?
4. Where can a manager go for expert help in applying decision analysis if a qualified analyst is not available on staff?
5. How much is decision analysis actually used?

10.9 Summary

Decision analysis is a valuable technique for decision making in the face of great uncertainty. It provides a framework and methodology for rational decision making when the outcomes are uncertain.

In a typical application, a decision maker needs to make either a single decision or a short sequence of decisions (with additional information perhaps becoming available between decisions). A number of alternatives are available for each decision. Uncontrollable random factors affect the payoff that would be obtained from a decision alternative. The possible outcomes of the random factors are referred to as the possible *states of nature.*

Which state of nature actually occurs will only be learned after making the decisions. However, prior to the decisions, it often is possible to estimate *prior probabilities* of the respective states of nature.

Decision criteria that use these probabilities in some way include the *maximum likelihood* and *equally likely* criteria. Another is the popular *Bayes' decision rule,* which uses the prior probabilities to determine the expected payoff for each decision alternative and then chooses the one with the largest expected payoff. This is the criterion (accompanied by sensitivity analysis) that is mostly used in practice, so it is the focus of much of the chapter.

It sometimes is possible to pay for a test or survey to obtain additional information about the probabilities of the various states of nature. Calculating the *expected value of perfect information* provides a quick way of checking whether doing this might be worthwhile.

When more information is obtained, the updated probabilities are referred to as *posterior probabilities.* A *probability tree diagram* is helpful for calculating these new probabilities.

For problems involving a sequence of decisions (including perhaps a decision on whether to obtain more information), a decision tree commonly is used to graphically display the progression of decisions and random events. The calculations for applying Bayes' decision rule can then be performed directly on the decision tree one chance node or decision node at a time. Spreadsheet packages, such as PrecisionTree and TreePlan, are very helpful for constructing and solving decision trees.

When the problem involves the possibility of uncomfortably large losses, utilities provide a way of incorporating the decision maker's attitude toward risk into the analysis. Bayes' decision rule then is applied by expressing payoffs in terms of utilities rather than monetary values.

Decision analysis is widely used. Versatile software packages for personal computers have become an integral part of the practical application of decision analysis.

Glossary

Alternatives   The options available to the decision maker for the decision under consideration. (Section 10.2)   379

Bayes' decision rule   A popular criterion for decision making that uses probabilities to calculate the expected payoff for each decision alternative and then chooses the one with the largest expected payoff. (Section 10.3)   388

Bayes' theorem   A formula for calculating a posterior probability of a state of nature. (Section 10.5)   401

Branch   A line emanating from a node in a decision tree. (Section 10.2)   381

Chance node   A point in a decision tree where a random event will occur. (Section 10.2)   381

Crossover point   A point at which the decision shifts when increasing the prior probability of a state of nature during sensitivity analysis. (Section 10.3)   394

Decision conferencing   A process used for group decision making. (Section 10.8)   426

Decision maker   The individual or group responsible for making the decision under consideration. (Section 10.2)   379

Decision node   A point in a decision tree where a decision needs to be made. (Section 10.2)   381

Decision tree   A graphical display of the progression of decisions and random events to be considered. (Sections 10.2 and 10.6)   380, 403

Equally likely criterion   A criterion for decision making that assigns equal probabilities to all the states of nature. (Section 10.3)   386

Expected payoff (EP)   For a decision alternative, it is the weighted average of the payoffs, using the probabilities of the states of nature as the weights. (Section 10.3)   388

Expected value of perfect information (EVPI)   The increase in the expected payoff that could be obtained if it were possible to learn the true state of nature before making the decision. (Sections 10.3 and 10.4)   395

Exponential utility function A utility function designed to fit a risk-averse individual. (Section 10.7) 422

Influence diagram A diagram that complements the decision tree for representing and analyzing decision tree problems. (Section 10.8) 426

Lottery procedure The procedure for finding the decision maker's utility for a specific amount of money by comparing two hypothetical alternatives where one involves a gamble. (Section 10.7) 420

Maximum likelihood criterion A criterion for decision making with probabilities that focuses on the most likely state of nature. (Section 10.3) 385

Node A junction point in a decision tree. (Section 10.2) 381

Payoff A quantitative measure of the outcome from a decision alternative and a state of nature. (Section 10.2) 380

Payoff table A table giving the payoff for each combination of a decision alternative and a state of nature. (Section 10.2) 380

Point of indifference The point where the decision maker is indifferent between the two hypothetical alternatives in the lottery procedure. (Section 10.7) 419

Posterior probabilities Revised probabilities of the states of nature after doing a test or survey to improve the prior probabilities. (Sections 10.4 and 10.5) 398, 399

Prior probabilities The estimated probabilities of the states of nature prior to obtaining additional information through a test or survey. (Section 10.2) 379–380

Probability tree diagram A diagram that is helpful for calculating the posterior probabilities of the states of nature. (Section 10.5) 400

Risk-averse individual An individual whose utility function for money has a decreasing slope as the amount of money increases. (Section 10.7) 415

Risk-neutral individual An individual whose utility for money is proportional to the amount of money. (Section 10.7) 415

Risk-seeking individual An individual whose utility function for money has an increasing slope as the amount of money increases. (Section 10.7) 415

Sensitivity analysis The study of how other plausible values for the probabilities of the states of nature (or for the payoffs) would affect the recommended decision alternative. (Sections 10.3 and 10.6) 391, 409

Spider graph A graph that provides helpful comparisons for sensitivity analysis. (Section 10.6) 411

States of nature The possible outcomes of the random factors that affect the payoff that would be obtained from a decision alternative. (Section 10.2) 379

Tornado diagram A diagram that organizes the data from sensitivity analysis in a readily understandable way. (Section 10.6) 411

Utility The utility of an outcome measures the true value to the decision maker of that outcome. (Sections 10.1 and 10.7) 379

Utility function for money, *U(M)* A plot of utility versus the amount of money *M* being received. (Section 10.7) 415

Learning Aids for This Chapter in Your MS Courseware

"Ch. 10—Dec Anal (PrecTree)" Excel File and "Ch. 10—Dec Anal (TreePlan)" Excel File:

Decision Trees for Goferbroke Problems
Decision Analysis Spreadsheets for Goferbroke Problems
Sensitivity Analysis Graphs for Goferbroke Problems
Decision Tree for Goferbroke's EP with Perfect Information

"Ch. 10—Dec Anal (Templates)" Excel File:

Template for Maximum Likelihood Criterion
Template for Equally Likely Criterion
Template for Bayes' Decision Rule
Template for Expected Payoff with Perfect Information
Template for Posterior Probabilities

Excel Add-Ins:

TreePlan (academic version)
SensIt (academic version)
(*PrecisionTree* is on the web site, www.Palisade.com.)

Supplement to This Chapter on the CD-ROM:

Decision Criteria without Probabilities

"Ch. 10 Supplement" Excel File:

Template for Maximax Criterion
Template for Maximin Criterion
Template for Realism Criterion
Template for Minimax Regret Criterion

Problems

To the left of the following problems (or their parts), we have inserted the symbol E whenever Excel (including any of the above templates) can be helpful. The symbol A (for Add-in) has been inserted instead whenever one of the Excel add-ins listed above can be used. Your instructor may give you instructions on which, if any, of these add-ins to use. An asterisk on the problem

number indicates that at least a partial answer is given in the back of the book.

10.1.* Silicon Dynamics has developed a new computer chip that will enable it to begin producing and marketing a personal computer if it so desires. Alternatively, it can sell the rights to the computer chip for $15 million. If the company chooses to build computers, the profitability of the venture depends on the company's ability to market the computer during the first year. It has sufficient access to retail outlets that it can guarantee sales of 10,000 computers. On the other hand, if this computer catches on, the company can sell 100,000 machines. For analysis purposes, these two levels of sales are taken to be the two possible outcomes of marketing the computer, but it is unclear what their prior probabilities are. The cost of setting up the assembly line is $6 million. The difference between the selling price and the variable cost of each computer is $600.

    a. Develop a decision analysis formulation of this problem by identifying the decision alternatives, the states of nature, and the payoff table.

    b. Construct a decision tree for this problem by hand.

A   *c.* Assuming the prior probabilities of the two levels of sales are both 0.5, use PrecisionTree or TreePlan to construct and solve this decision tree. According to this analysis, which decision alternative should be chosen?

A   *d.* Use PrecisionTree or SensIt to develop a sensitivity graph that plots the expected payoff (when using Bayes' decision rule) versus the prior probability of selling 10,000 computers.

A   *e.* Develop a strategy region graph that plots the expected payoff for each of the decision alternatives versus the prior probability of selling 10,000 computers. (*Note:* PrecisionTree can generate this graph, but, if you are using TreePlan, you will need to plot this graph by hand.)

    f. Referring to this strategy region graph, use algebra to solve for the crossover point. Explain the significance of this point.

10.2. Jean Clark is the manager of the Midtown Saveway Grocery Store. She now needs to replenish her supply of strawberries. Her regular supplier can provide as many cases as she wants. However, because these strawberries already are very ripe, she will need to sell them tomorrow and then discard any that remain unsold. Jean estimates that she will be able to sell 10, 11, 12, or 13 cases tomorrow. She can purchase the strawberries for $3 per case and sell them for $8 per case. Jean now needs to decide how many cases to purchase.

Jean has checked the store's records on daily sales of strawberries. On this basis, she estimates that the prior probabilities are 0.2, 0.4, 0.3, and 0.1 for being able to sell 10, 11, 12, and 13 cases of strawberries tomorrow.

    a. Develop a decision analysis formulation of this problem by identifying the decision alternatives, the states of nature, and the payoff table.

E   *b.* How many cases of strawberries should Jean purchase if she uses the maximum likelihood criterion?

E   *c.* If Jean is dubious about the accuracy of these prior probabilities and so uses the equally likely criterion, how many cases of strawberries should be purchased?

E   *d.* How many cases should be purchased according to Bayes' decision rule?

E   *e.* Jean thinks she has the prior probabilities just about right for selling 10 cases and selling 13 cases, but is uncertain about how to split the prior probabilities for 11 cases and 12 cases. Reapply Bayes' decision rule when the prior probabilities of 11 and 12 cases are (*i*) 0.2 and 0.5, (*ii*) 0.3 and 0.4, and (*iii*) 0.5 and 0.2.

E 10.3.* Warren Buffy is an enormously wealthy investor who has built his fortune through his legendary investing acumen. He currently has been offered three major investments and he would like to choose one. The first one is a *conservative investment* that would perform very well in an improving economy and only suffer a small loss in a worsening economy. The second is a *speculative investment* that would perform extremely well in an improving economy but would do very badly in a worsening economy. The third is a *counter-cyclical investment* that would lose some money in an improving economy but would perform well in a worsening economy.

    Warren believes that there are three possible scenarios over the lives of these potential investments: (1) an improving economy, (2) a stable economy, and (3) a worsening economy. He is pessimistic about where the economy is headed, and so has assigned prior probabilities of 0.1, 0.5, and 0.4, respectively, to these three scenarios. He also estimates that his profits under these respective scenarios are those given by the following table:

	Improving Economy	Stable Economy	Worsening Economy
Conservative investment	$30 million	$5 million	−$10 million
Speculative investment	40 million	10 million	−30 million
Counter-cyclical investment	−10 million	0	15 million
Prior probability	0.1	0.5	0.4

Which investment should Warren make under each of the following criteria?

    a. Maximum likelihood criterion.

    b. Equally likely criterion.

    c. Bayes' decision rule.

10.4. Reconsider Problem 10.3. Warren Buffy decides that Bayes' decision rule is his most reliable decision criterion.

He believes that 0.1 is just about right as the prior probability of an improving economy, but is quite uncertain about how to split the remaining probabilities between a stable economy and a worsening economy. Therefore, he now wishes to do sensitivity analysis with respect to these latter two prior probabilities.

E *a.* Reapply Bayes' decision rule when the prior probability of a stable economy is 0.3 and the prior probability of a worsening economy is 0.6.

E *b.* Reapply Bayes' decision rule when the prior probability of a stable economy is 0.7 and the prior probability of a worsening economy is 0.2.

    c. Graph the expected profit for each of the three investment alternatives versus the prior probability of a stable economy (with the prior probability of an improving economy fixed at 0.1). Use this graph to identify the crossover points where the decision shifts from one investment to another.

    d. Use algebra to solve for the crossover points identified in part *c*.

A *e.* Use PrecisionTree or TreePlan to construct and solve a decision tree for this problem with the original prior probabilities.

A *f.* Using this decision tree spreadsheet as a worksheet, formulate a decision analysis spreadsheet similar to Figure 10.12 for this problem. Then use this spreadsheet to do parts *a* and *b*.

A *g.* Generate a sensitivity graph that plots the expected profit (when using Bayes' decision rule) versus the prior probability of a stable economy (with the prior probability of an improving economy fixed at 0.1).

A *h.* Use PrecisionTree to generate the strategy region graph requested in part *c*. Use this graph to describe how the choice of the investment depends on the prior probability of a stable economy.

E *i.* Identify the crossover points in this strategy region graph within 0.01 by using trial and error with the decision analysis spreadsheet.

10.5.* Consider a decision analysis problem whose payoffs (in units of thousands of dollars) are given by the following payoff table:

	State of Nature	
Alternative	S_1	S_2
A_1	80	25
A_2	30	50
A_3	60	40
Prior probability	0.4	0.6

E *a.* Which alternative should be chosen under the maximum likelihood criterion?

E *b.* Which alternative should be chosen under the equally likely criterion?

E *c.* Which alternative should be chosen under Bayes' decision rule?

A *d.* Using Bayes' decision rule, do sensitivity analysis graphically with respect to the prior probabilities to determine the crossover points where the decision shifts from one alternative to another.

    e. Use algebra to solve for the crossover points identified in part *d*.

10.6. You are given the following payoff table (in units of thousands of dollars) for a decision analysis problem:

	State of Nature		
Alternative	S_1	S_2	S_3
A_1	220	170	110
A_2	200	180	150
Prior probability	0.6	0.3	0.1

E *a.* Which alternative should be chosen under the maximum likelihood criterion?

E *b.* Which alternative should be chosen under the equally likely criterion?

E *c.* Which alternative should be chosen under Bayes' decision rule?

A *d.* Using Bayes' decision rule, do sensitivity analysis graphically with respect to the prior probabilities of states S_1 and S_2 (without changing the prior probability of state S_3) to determine the crossover point where the decision shifts from one alternative to the other. Then use algebra to calculate this crossover point.

A *e.* Repeat part *d* for the prior probabilities of states S_1 and S_3.

A *f.* Repeat part *d* for the prior probabilities of states S_2 and S_3.

    g. If you feel that the true probabilities of the states of nature should be within 10 percent of the given prior probabilities, which alternative would you choose?

10.7. Dwight Moody is the manager of a large farm with 1,000 acres of arable land. For greater efficiency, Dwight always devotes the farm to growing one crop at a time. He now needs to make a decision on which one of four crops to grow during the upcoming growing season. For each of these crops, Dwight has obtained the following estimates of crop yields and net incomes per bushel under various weather conditions.

	Expected Yield, Bushels/Acre			
Weather	Crop 1	Crop 2	Crop 3	Crop 4
Dry	20	15	30	40
Moderate	35	20	25	40
Damp	40	30	25	40
Net income per bushel	$1.00	$1.50	$1.00	$0.50

After referring to historical meteorological records, Dwight also estimated the following prior probabilities for the weather during the growing season:

Dry	0.3
Moderate	0.5
Damp	0.2

    a. Develop a decision analysis formulation of this problem by identifying the decision alternatives, the states of nature, and the payoff table.

A *b.* Construct a decision tree for this problem.

E   c. Use Bayes' decision rule to determine which crop to grow.

E   d. Using Bayes' decision rule, do sensitivity analysis with respect to the prior probabilities of moderate weather and damp weather (without changing the prior probability of dry weather) by re-solving when the prior probability of moderate weather is 0.2, 0.3, 0.4, and 0.6.

10.8. Barbara Miller makes decisions according to Bayes' decision rule. For her current problem, Barbara has constructed the following payoff table (in units of hundreds of dollars) and she now wishes to maximize the expected payoff.

	State of Nature		
Alternative	S_1	S_2	S_3
A_1	$2x$	50	10
A_2	25	40	90
A_3	35	$3x$	30
Prior probability	0.4	0.2	0.4

The value of x currently is 50, but there is an opportunity to increase x by spending some money now.

What is the maximum amount Barbara should spend to increase x to 75?

10.9.* Reconsider Problem 10.1. Management of Silicon Dynamics now is considering doing full-fledged market research at a cost of $1 million to predict which of the two levels of demand is likely to occur. Previous experience indicates that such market research is correct two-thirds of the time.

E   a. Find the expected value of perfect information for this problem.

b. Does the answer in part a indicate that it might be worthwhile to perform this market research?

c. Develop a probability tree diagram to obtain the posterior probabilities of the two levels of demand for each of the two possible outcomes of the market research.

E   d. Use the corresponding Excel template to check your answers in part c.

10.10. You are given the following payoff table (in units of thousands of dollars) for a decision analysis problem:

	State of Nature		
Alternative	S_1	S_2	S_3
A_1	4	0	0
A_2	0	2	0
A_3	3	0	1
Prior probability	0.2	0.5	0.3

E   a. According to Bayes' decision rule, which alternative should be chosen?

E   b. Find the expected value of perfect information.

A   c. Check your answer in part b by recalculating it with the help of a decision tree.

d. You are given the opportunity to spend $1,000 to obtain more information about which state of nature is likely to occur. Given your answer to part b, might it be worthwhile to spend this money?

10.11.* Betsy Pitzer makes decisions according to Bayes' decision rule. For her current problem, Betsy has constructed the following payoff table (in units of dollars):

	State of Nature		
Alternative	S_1	S_2	S_3
A_1	50	100	−100
A_2	0	10	−10
A_3	20	40	−40
Prior probability	0.5	0.3	0.2

E   a. Which alternative should Betsy choose?

E   b. Find the expected value of perfect information.

c. Check your answer in part b by recalculating it with the help of a decision tree.

d. What is the most that Betsy should consider paying to obtain more information about which state of nature will occur?

10.12. Using Bayes' decision rule, consider the decision analysis problem having the following payoff table (in units of thousands of dollars):

	State of Nature		
Alternative	S_1	S_2	S_3
A_1	−100	10	100
A_2	−10	20	50
A_3	10	10	60
Prior probability	0.2	0.3	0.5

E   a. Which alternative should be chosen? What is the resulting expected payoff?

b. You are offered the opportunity to obtain information that will tell you with certainty whether the first state of nature S_1 will occur. What is the maximum amount you should pay for the information? Assuming you will obtain the information, how should this information be used to choose an alternative? What is the resulting expected payoff (excluding the payment)?

c. Now repeat part b if the information offered concerns S_2 instead of S_1.

d. Now repeat part b if the information offered concerns S_3 instead of S_1.

E   e. Now suppose that the opportunity is offered to provide information that will tell you with certainty which state of nature will occur (perfect information). What is the maximum amount you should pay for the information? Assuming you will obtain the information, how should this information be used to choose an alternative? What is the resulting expected payoff (excluding the payment)?

    f. If you have the opportunity to do some testing that will give you partial additional information (not perfect information) about the state of nature, what is the maximum amount you should consider paying for this information?

10.13. Reconsider the Goferbroke Co. case study, including its analysis in Sections 10.5 and 10.6. With the help of the consulting geologist, Jennifer Flyer now has obtained some historical data that provides more precise information than Max could supply on the likelihood of obtaining favorable seismic soundings on similar tracts of land. Specifically, when the land contains oil, favorable seismic soundings are obtained 80 percent of the time. This percentage changes to 40 percent when the land is dry.

    a. Revise Figure 10.19 to find the new posterior probabilities.

E   *b.* Use the corresponding Excel template to check your answers in part *a.*

    c. Revise Figure 10.23 to find the new decision tree. What is the resulting optimal policy?

A   *d.* Use PrecisionTree or TreePlan to construct and solve this new decision tree.

A 10.14. Reconsider Problem 10.13. Max is skeptical that his estimates (60 percent and 20 percent) could be so far off the percentages (80 percent and 40 percent) obtained by Jennifer, so he requests that sensitivity analysis be conducted regarding these percentages.

    a. Set up the decision analysis spreadsheet in Figure 10.26 (with constraints added that E13 = 1 − D13 and E14 = 1 − D14) with the decision tree in Figure 10.24 and template in Figure 10.20 as worksheets.

    b. Obtain the results when Jennifer's probabilities are used.

    c. Generate two sensitivity graphs like Figure 10.27 where the horizontal axis for one is the probability in cell D13, P(FSS|Oil), and the horizontal axis for the other is the probability in cell D14, P(FSS|Dry).

    d. Generate the spider graph and tornado diagram corresponding to Figure 10.29 when Jennifer's probabilities are used instead of Max's estimates.

10.15.* Vincent Cuomo is the credit manager for the Fine Fabrics Mill. He is currently faced with the question of whether to extend $100,000 of credit to a potential new customer, a dress manufacturer. Vincent has three categories for the creditworthiness of a company—poor risk, average risk, and good risk—but he does not know which category fits this potential customer. Experience indicates that 20 percent of companies similar to this dress manufacturer are poor risks, 50 percent are average risks, and 30 percent are good risks. If credit is extended, the expected profit for poor risks is −$15,000, for average risks $10,000, and for good risks $20,000. If credit is not extended, the dress manufacturer will turn to another mill. Vincent is able to consult a credit-rating organization for a fee of $5,000 per company evaluated. For companies whose

actual credit record with the mill turns out to fall into each of the three categories, the following table shows the percentage that were given each of the three possible credit evaluations by the credit-rating organization.

	Actual Credit Record		
Credit Evaluation	*Poor*	*Average*	*Good*
Poor	50%	40%	20%
Average	40	50	40
Good	10	10	40

    a. Develop a decision analysis formulation of this problem by identifying the decision alternatives, the states of nature, and the payoff table when the credit-rating organization is not used.

E   *b.* Assuming the credit-rating organization is not used, use Bayes' decision rule to determine which decision alternative should be chosen.

E   *c.* Find the expected value of perfect information. Does this answer indicate that consideration should be given to using the credit-rating organization?

    d. Assume now that the credit-rating organization is used. Develop a probability tree diagram to find the posterior probabilities of the respective states of nature for each of the three possible credit evaluations of this potential customer.

E   *e.* Use the corresponding Excel template to obtain the answers for part *d.*

    f. Draw the decision tree for this entire problem by hand. Use this decision tree to determine Vincent's optimal policy.

A   *g.* Use PrecisionTree or TreePlan to construct and solve this decision tree.

10.16. You are given the following payoff table (in units of dollars):

	State of Nature	
Alternative	S_1	S_2
A_1	400	−100
A_1	0	100
Prior probability	0.4	0.6

You have the option of paying $100 to have research done to better predict which state of nature will occur. When the true state of nature is S_1, the research will accurately predict S_1 60 percent of the time (but will inaccurately predict S_2 40 percent of the time). When the true state of nature is S_2, the research will accurately predict S_2 80 percent of the time (but will inaccurately predict S_1 20 percent of the time).

E   *a.* Given that the research is not done, use Bayes' decision rule to determine which decision alternative should be chosen.

A   b. Use a decision tree to help find the expected value of perfect information. Does this answer indicate that it might be worthwhile to do the research?

     c. Given that the research is done, find the joint probability of each of the following pairs of outcomes: (*i*) the state of nature is S_1 and the research predicts S_1, (*ii*) the state of nature is S_1 and the research predicts S_2, (*iii*) the state of nature is S_2 and the research predicts S_1, and (*iv*) the state of nature is S_2 and the research predicts S_2.

     d. Find the unconditional probability that the research predicts S_1. Also find the unconditional probability that the research predicts S_2.

     e. Given that the research is done, use your answers in parts *c* and *d* to determine the posterior probabilities of the states of nature for each of the two possible predictions of the research.

E   f. Use the corresponding Excel template to obtain the answers for part *e*.

E   g. Given that the research predicts S_1, use Bayes' decision rule to determine which decision alternative should be chosen and the resulting expected payoff.

E   h. Repeat part *g* when the research predicts S_2.

E   i. Given that research is done, what is the expected payoff when using Bayes' decision rule?

     j. Use the preceding results to determine the optimal policy regarding whether to do the research and the choice of the decision alternative.

A   k. Construct and solve the decision tree to show the analysis for the entire problem. (Using an Excel add-in is optional.)

10.17. An athletic league does drug testing of its athletes, 10 percent of whom use drugs. The test, however, is only 95 percent reliable. That is, a drug user will test positive with probability 0.95 and negative with probability 0.05, and a nonuser will test negative with probability 0.95 and positive with probability 0.05.

     Develop a probability tree diagram to determine the posterior probability of each of the following outcomes of testing an athlete.

     a. The athlete is a drug user, given that the test is positive.

     b. The athlete is not a drug user, given that the test is positive.

     c. The athlete is a drug user, given that the test is negative.

     d. The athlete is not a drug user, given that the test is negative.

E   e. Use the corresponding Excel template to check your answers in the preceding parts.

10.18. Management of the Telemore Company is considering developing and marketing a new product. It is estimated to be twice as likely that the product would prove to be successful as unsuccessful. If it were successful, the expected profit would be $1,500,000. If unsuccessful, the expected loss would be $1,800,000. A marketing survey can be conducted at a cost of $100,000 to predict whether the product would be successful. Past experience with such surveys indicates that successful products have been predicted to be successful 80 percent of the time, whereas unsuccessful products have been predicted to be unsuccessful 70 percent of the time.

     a. Develop a decision analysis formulation of this problem by identifying the decision alternatives, the states of nature, and the payoff table when the market survey is not conducted.

E   b. Assuming the market survey is not conducted, use Bayes' decision rule to determine which decision alternative should be chosen.

E   c. Find the expected value of perfect information. Does this answer indicate that consideration should be given to conducting the market survey?

E   d. Assume now that the market survey is conducted. Find the posterior probabilities of the respective states of nature for each of the two possible predictions from the market survey.

A   e. Use PrecisionTree to construct and solve the decision tree for this entire problem.

A   f. Use PrecisionTree to generate the policy suggestion, statistics report, and risk profile.

A   g. Generate a spider graph and tornado diagram with respect to the profit, loss, and cost data when each can vary as much as 25 percent in either direction from its base value.

10.19. The Hit-and-Miss Manufacturing Company produces items that have a probability p of being defective. These items are produced in lots of 150. Past experience indicates that p for an entire lot is either 0.05 or 0.25. Furthermore, in 80 percent of the lots produced, p equals 0.05 (so p equals 0.25 in 20 percent of the lots). These items are then used in an assembly, and ultimately their quality is determined before the final assembly leaves the plant. Initially the company can *either* screen each item in a lot at a cost of $10 per item and replace defective items *or* use the items directly without screening. If the latter action is chosen, the cost of rework is ultimately $100 per defective item. Because screening requires scheduling of inspectors and equipment, the decision to screen or not screen must be made two days before the screening is to take place. However, one item can be taken from the lot and sent to a laboratory for inspection, and its quality (defective or nondefective) can be reported before the screen/no-screen decision must be made. The cost of this initial inspection is $125.

     a. Develop a decision analysis formulation of this problem by identifying the decision alternatives, the states of nature, and the payoff table if the single item is not inspected in advance.

E   b. Assuming the single item is not inspected in advance, use Bayes' decision rule to determine which decision alternative should be chosen.

E   c. Find the expected value of perfect information. Does this answer indicate that consideration should be given to inspecting the single item in advance?

E   d. Assume now that the single item is inspected in advance. Find the posterior probabilities of the respective states of nature for each of the two possible outcomes of this inspection.

A   e. Construct and solve the decision tree for this entire problem.

A 10.20.* Reconsider Problem 10.9. The management of Silicon Dynamics now wants to see a decision tree displaying the entire problem.

a. Use PrecisionTree or TreePlan to construct and solve this decision tree.

b. There is some uncertainty in the financial data ($15 million, $6 million, and $600) stated in Problem 10.1. Each could vary from its base value by as much as 10 percent. For each one, generate a sensitivity graph that plots the expected profit over this range of variation.

c. Generate the corresponding spider graph and tornado diagram.

10.21. You are given the following decision tree, where the numbers in parentheses are probabilities and the numbers on the right are payoffs at these terminal points.

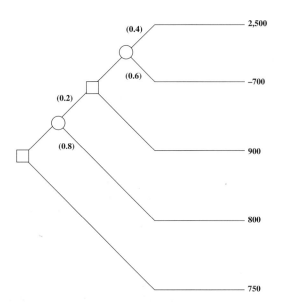

a. Analyze this decision tree to obtain the optimal policy.

A b. Use PrecisionTree to construct and solve the same decision tree.

A c. Use PrecisionTree to generate the policy suggestion, statistics report, and risk profile.

10.22. You are given the following decision tree, with the probabilities at chance nodes shown in parentheses and with the payoffs at terminal points shown on the right. Analyze this decision tree to obtain the optimal policy.

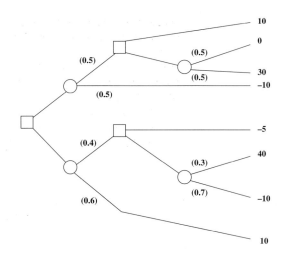

10.23.* The Athletic Department of Leland University is considering whether to hold an extensive campaign next year to raise funds for a new athletic field. The response to the campaign depends heavily on the success of the football team this fall. In the past, the football team has had winning seasons 60 percent of the time. If the football team has a winning season (W) this fall, then many of the alumnae and alumni will contribute and the campaign will raise $3 million. If the team has a losing season (L), few will contribute and the campaign will lose $2 million. If no campaign is undertaken, no costs are incurred. On September 1, just before the football season begins, the Athletic Department needs to make its decision about whether to hold the campaign next year.

a. Develop a decision analysis formulation of this problem by identifying the decision alternatives, the states of nature, and the payoff table.

E b. According to Bayes' decision rule, should the campaign be undertaken?

E c. What is the expected value of perfect information?

E d. A famous football guru, William Walsh, has offered his services to help evaluate whether the team will have a winning season. For $100,000, he will carefully evaluate the team throughout spring practice and then throughout preseason workouts. William then will provide his prediction on September 1 regarding what kind of season, W or L, the team will have. In similar situations in the past when evaluating teams that have winning seasons 50 percent of the time, his predictions have been correct 75 percent of the time. Considering that this team has more of a winning tradition, if William predicts a winning season, what is the posterior probability that the team actually will have a winning season? What is the posterior probability of a losing season? If William predicts a losing season instead, what is the posterior probability of a winning season? Of a losing season? Show how these answers are obtained from a probability tree diagram.

e. Use the corresponding Excel template to obtain the answers requested in part *d*.

f. Draw the decision tree for this entire problem by hand. Analyze this decision tree to determine the optimal policy regarding whether to hire William and whether to undertake the campaign.

A g. Use PrecisionTree or TreePlan to construct and solve this decision tree.

10.24. The comptroller of the Macrosoft Corporation has $100 million of excess funds to invest. She has been instructed to invest the entire amount for one year in either stocks or bonds (but not both) and then to reinvest the entire fund in either stocks or bonds (but not both) for one year more. The objective is to maximize the expected monetary value of the fund at the end of the second year.

The annual rates of return on these investments depend on the economic environment, as shown in the following table:

Economic Environment	Rate of Return	
	Stocks	*Bonds*
Growth	20%	5%
Recession	−10	10
Depression	−50	20

The probabilities of growth, recession, and depression for the first year are 0.7, 0.3, and 0, respectively. If growth occurs in the first year, these probabilities remain the same for the second year. However, if a recession occurs in the first year, these probabilities change to 0.2, 0.7, and 0.1, respectively, for the second year.

    a. Construct by hand the decision tree for this problem.

    b. Analyze the decision tree to identify the optimal policy.

A   *c.* Use PrecisionTree or TreePlan to construct and solve the decision tree.

10.25. On Monday, a certain stock closed at $10 per share. On Tuesday, you expect the stock to close at $9, $10, or $11 per share, with respective probabilities 0.3, 0.3, and 0.4. On Wednesday, you expect the stock to close 10 percent lower, unchanged, or 10 percent higher than Tuesday's close, with the following probabilities:

Today's Close	10 Percent Lower	Unchanged	10 Percent Higher
$ 9	0.4	0.3	0.3
10	0.2	0.2	0.6
11	0.1	0.2	0.7

On Tuesday, you are directed to buy 100 shares of the stock before Thursday. All purchases are made at the end of the day, at the known closing price for that day, so your only options are to buy at the end of Tuesday or at the end of Wednesday. You wish to determine the optimal strategy for whether to buy on Tuesday or defer the purchase until Wednesday, given the Tuesday closing price, to minimize the expected purchase price.

    a. Develop and evaluate a decision tree by hand for determining the optimal strategy.

A   *b.* Use PrecisionTree or TreePlan to construct and solve the decision tree.

A 10.26. Jose Morales manages a large outdoor fruit stand in one of the less affluent neighborhoods of San Jose, California. To replenish his supply, Jose buys boxes of fruit early each morning from a grower south of San Jose. About 90 percent of the boxes of fruit turn out to be of satisfactory quality, but the other 10 percent are unsatisfactory. A satisfactory box contains 80 percent excellent fruit and will earn $200 profit for Jose. An unsatisfactory box contains 30 percent excellent fruit and will produce a loss of $1,000. Before Jose decides to accept a box, he is given the opportunity to sample one piece of fruit to test whether it is excellent. Based on that sample, he then has the option of rejecting the box without paying for it. Jose wonders (1) whether he should continue buying from this grower, (2) if so, whether it is worthwhile sampling just one piece of fruit from a box, and (3) if so, whether he should be accepting or rejecting the box based on the outcome of this sampling.

Use PrecisionTree or TreePlan (and the Excel template for posterior probabilities) to construct and solve the decision tree for this problem.

10.27.* The Morton Ward Company is considering the introduction of a new product that is believed to have a 50–50 chance of being successful. One option is to try out the product in a test market, at a cost of $5 million, before making the introduction decision. Past experience shows that ultimately successful products are approved in the test market 80 percent of the time, whereas ultimately unsuccessful products are approved in the test market only 25 percent of the time. If the product is successful, the net profit to the company will be $40 million; if unsuccessful, the net loss will be $15 million.

E   *a.* Discarding the test market option, develop a decision analysis formulation of the problem by identifying the decision alternatives, states of nature, and payoff table. Then apply Bayes' decision rule to determine the optimal decision alternative.

E   *b.* Find the expected value of perfect information.

A   *c.* Now including the option of trying out the product in a test market, use PrecisionTree or TreePlan (and the Excel template for posterior probabilities) to construct and solve the decision tree for this problem.

A   *d.* There is some uncertainty in the stated profit and loss figures ($40 million and $15 million). Either could vary from its base by as much as 25 percent in either direction. Use PrecisionTree or SensIt to generate a sensitivity graph for each that plots the expected payoff over this range of variability.

A   *e.* Generate the corresponding spider graph and tornado diagram. Interpret each one.

A 10.28. Chelsea Bush is an emerging candidate for her party's nomination for president of the United States. She now is considering whether to run in the high-stakes Super Tuesday primaries. If she enters the Super Tuesday (S.T.) primaries, she and her advisers believe that she will either do well (finish first or second) or do poorly (finish third or worse) with probabilities 0.4 and 0.6, respectively. Doing well on Super Tuesday will net the candidate's campaign approximately $16 million in new contributions, whereas a poor showing will mean a loss of $10 million after numerous TV ads are paid for. Alternatively, she may choose not to run at all on Super Tuesday and incur no costs.

Chelsea's advisers realize that her chances of success on Super Tuesday may be affected by the outcome of the smaller New Hampshire (N.H.) primary occurring three weeks before Super Tuesday. Political analysts feel that the results of New Hampshire's primary are correct two-thirds of the time in predicting the results of the Super Tuesday primaries. Among Chelsea's advisers is a decision analysis expert who uses this information to calculate the following probabilities:

P(Chelsea does well in S.T. primaries, given she does well in N.H.) = ⅔

P(Chelsea does well in S.T. primaries, given she does poorly in N.H.) = ¼

P(Chelsea does well in N.H. primary) = 7⁄15

The cost of entering and campaigning in the New Hampshire primary is estimated to be $1.6 million.

Chelsea feels that her chance of winning the nomination depends largely on having substantial funds available after the Super Tuesday primaries to carry on a vigorous campaign the rest of the way. Therefore, she wants to choose the strategy (whether to run in the New Hampshire primary and then whether to run in the Super Tuesday primaries) that will maximize her expected funds after these primaries.

   a. Construct and solve the decision tree for this problem.

   b. There is some uncertainty in the estimates of a gain of $16 million or a loss of $10 million depending on the showing on Super Tuesday. Either amount could differ from this estimate by as much as 25 percent in either direction. Generate a sensitivity graph for each amount that plots the expected payoff over this range of variability.

   c. Generate the corresponding spider graph and tornado diagram. Interpret each one.

A 10.29. The executive search being conducted for Western Bank by Headhunters Inc. may finally be bearing fruit. The position to be filled is a key one—vice president for Information Processing—because this person will have responsibility for developing a state-of-the-art management information system that will link together Western's many branch banks. However, Headhunters feels they have found just the right person, Matthew Fenton, who has an excellent record in a similar position for a mid-sized bank in New York.

After a round of interviews, Western's president believes that Matthew has a probability of 0.7 of designing the management information system successfully. If Matthew is successful, the company will realize a profit of $2 million (net of Matthew's salary, training, recruiting costs, and expenses). If he is not successful, the company will realize a net loss of $400,000.

For an additional fee of $20,000, Headhunters will provide a detailed investigative process (including an extensive background check, a battery of academic and psychological tests, etc.) that will further pinpoint Matthew's potential for success. This process has been found to be 90 percent reliable, that is, a candidate who would successfully design the management information system will pass the test with probability 0.9, and a candidate who would not successfully design the system will fail the test with probability 0.9.

Western's top management needs to decide whether to hire Matthew and whether to have Headhunters conduct the detailed investigative process before making this decision.

   a. Construct the decision tree for this problem.

E *b.* Find the probabilities for the branches emanating from the chance nodes.

   c. Analyze the decision tree to identify the optimal policy.

   d. Now suppose that the Headhunters' fee for administering its detailed investigative process is negotiable. What is the maximum amount that Western Bank should pay?

10.30. Reconsider the Goferbroke Co. case study, including the application of utilities in Section 10.7. Max Flyer now has decided that, given the company's precarious financial situation, he needs to take a much more risk-averse approach to the problem. Therefore, he has revised the utilities given in Table 10.6 as follows: $U(-130) = -200$, $U(-100) = -130$, $U(60) = 60$, $U(90) = 90$, $U(670) = 440$, and $U(700) = 450$.

   a. Analyze the revised decision tree corresponding to Figure 10.34 by hand to obtain the new optimal policy.

A *b.* Use PrecisionTree or TreePlan to construct and solve this revised decision tree.

10.31.* You live in an area that has a possibility of incurring a massive earthquake, so you are considering buying earthquake insurance on your home at an annual cost of $180. The probability of an earthquake damaging your home during one year is 0.001. If this happens, you estimate that the cost of the damage (fully covered by earthquake insurance) will be $160,000. Your total assets (including your home) are worth $250,000.

E *a.* Apply Bayes' decision rule to determine which alternative (take the insurance or not) maximizes your expected assets after one year.

   b. You now have constructed a utility function that measures how much you value having total assets worth x dollars ($x \geq 0$). This utility function is $U(x) = \sqrt{x}$. Compare the utility of reducing your total assets next year by the cost of the earthquake insurance with the expected utility next year of not taking the earthquake insurance. Should you take the insurance?

10.32. For your graduation present from college, your parents are offering you your choice of two alternatives. The first alternative is to give you a money gift of $19,000. The second alternative is to make an investment in your name. This investment will quickly have the following two possible outcomes:

Outcome	Probability
Receive $10,000	0.3
Receive $30,000	0.7

Your utility for receiving M thousand dollars is given by the utility function $U(M) = \sqrt{M+6}$. Which choice should you make to maximize expected utility?

10.33.* Reconsider Problem 10.32. You now are uncertain about what your true utility function for receiving money is, so you are in the process of constructing this utility function. So far, you have found that $U(19) = 16.7$ and $U(30) = 20$ are the utility of receiving $19,000 and $30,000, respectively. You also have concluded that you are indifferent between the two alternatives offered to you by your parents. Use this information to find $U(10)$.

10.34. You wish to construct your personal utility function $U(M)$ for receiving M thousand dollars. After setting $U(0) = 0$, you next set $U(1) = 1$ as your utility for receiving $1,000. You next want to find $U(10)$ and then $U(5)$.

a. You offer yourself the following two hypothetical alternatives:

A_1: Obtain $10,000 with probability p.
    Obtain 0 with probability $(1 - p)$.
A_2: Definitely obtain $1,000.

You then ask yourself the question: What value of p makes you indifferent between these two alternatives? Your answer is $p = 0.125$. Find $U(10)$.

b. You next repeat part a except for changing the second alternative to definitely receiving $5,000. The value of p that makes you indifferent between these two alternatives now is $p = 0.5625$. Find $U(5)$.

c. Repeat parts a and b, but now use *your* personal choices for p.

10.35. You are given the following payoff table:

| | State of Nature | |
Alternative	S_1	S_2
A_1	25	36
A_2	100	0
A_3	0	49
Prior probability	p	$1-p$

a. Assume that your utility function for the payoffs is $U(x) = \sqrt{x}$. Plot the expected utility of each decision alternative versus the value of p on the same graph. For each decision alternative, find the range of values of p over which this alternative maximizes the expected utility.

A   b. Now assume that your utility function is the exponential utility function with a risk tolerance of $R = 50$. Use PrecisionTree or TreePlan to construct and solve the resulting decision tree in turn for $p = 0.25$, $p = 0.5$, and $p = 0.75$.

A 10.36. Dr. Switzer has a seriously ill patient but has had trouble diagnosing the specific cause of the illness. The doctor now has narrowed the cause down to two alternatives: disease A or disease B. Based on the evidence so far, she feels that the two alternatives are equally likely.

Beyond the testing already done, there is no test available to determine if the cause is disease B. One

test is available for disease A, but it has two major problems. First, it is very expensive. Second, it is somewhat unreliable, giving an accurate result only 80 percent of the time. Thus, it will give a positive result (indicating disease A) for only 80 percent of patients who have disease A, whereas it will give a positive result for 20 percent of patients who actually have disease B instead.

Disease B is a very serious disease with no known treatment. It is sometimes fatal, and those who survive remain in poor health with a poor quality of life thereafter. The prognosis is similar for victims of disease A if it is left untreated. However, there is a fairly expensive treatment available that eliminates the danger for those with disease A, and it may return them to good health. Unfortunately, it is a relatively radical treatment that always leads to death if the patient actually has disease B instead.

The probability distribution for the prognosis for this patient is given for each case in the following table, where the column headings (after the first one) indicate the disease for the patient.

| | Outcome Probabilities | | | |
| | No Treatment | | Receive Treatment for Disease A | |
Outcome	A	B	A	B
Die	0.2	0.5	0	1.0
Survive with poor health	0.8	0.5	0.5	0
Return to good health	0	0	0.5	0

The patient has assigned the following utilities to the possible outcomes:

Outcome	Utility
Die	0
Survive with poor health	10
Return to good health	30

In addition, these utilities should be incremented by -2 if the patient incurs the cost of the test for disease A and by -1 if the patient (or the patient's estate) incurs the cost of the treatment for disease A.

Use decision analysis with a complete decision tree to determine if the patient should undergo the test for disease A and then how to proceed (receive the treatment for disease A?) to maximize the patient's expected utility.

10.37. Consider the following decision tree, where the probabilities for each chance node are shown in parentheses.

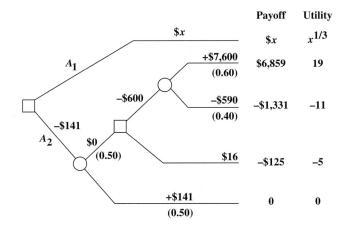

	Payoff	Utility
x	x	$x^{1/3}$
+$7,600 (0.60)	$6,859	19
−$590 (0.40)	−$1,331	−11
$16	−$125	−5
+$141 (0.50)	0	0

The dollar amount given next to each branch is the cash flow generated along that branch, where these intermediate cash flows add up to the total net cash flow shown to the right of each terminal branch. (The unknown amount for the top branch is represented by the variable x.) The decision maker has a utility function $U(y) = y^{1/3}$ where y is the total net cash flow after a terminal branch. The resulting utilities for the various terminal branches are shown to the right of the decision tree.

Use these utilities to analyze the decision tree. Then determine the value of x for which the decision maker is indifferent between decision alternatives A_1 and A_2.

A 10.38. Reconsider the Goferbroke Co. case study when using utilities, as presented in Section 10.7.

   a. Use PrecisionTree to construct the decision tree shown in Figure 10.34 again.

   b. Use PrecisionTree to generate the policy suggestion, statistics report, and risk profile in terms of these utilities.

   c. Perform sensitivity analysis by re-solving the decision tree (after using the Excel template for posterior probabilities to revise these probabilities) when the prior probability of oil is changed in turn to 0.15, 0.2, 0.3, and 0.35.

10.39. Select one of the applications of decision analysis listed in Table 10.7. Read the article describing the application in the indicated issue of *Interfaces*. Write a two-page summary of the application and the benefits it provided.

10.40. Select three of the applications of decision analysis listed in Table 10.7. Read the articles describing the applications in the indicated issues of *Interfaces*. For each one, write a one-page summary of the application and the benefits it provided.

CASE 10.1
BRAINY BUSINESS

While El Niño is pouring its rain on northern California, Charlotte Rothstein, CEO, major shareholder, and founder of Cerebrosoft, sits in her office, contemplating the decision she faces regarding her company's newest proposed product, Brainet. This has been a particularly difficult decision. Brainet might catch on and sell very well. However, Charlotte is concerned about the risk involved. In this competitive market, marketing Brainet also could lead to substantial losses. Should she go ahead anyway and start the marketing campaign? Or just abandon the product? Or perhaps buy additional marketing research information from a local market research company before deciding whether to launch the product. She has to make a decision very soon and so, as she slowly drinks from her glass of high-protein-power multivitamin juice, she reflects on the events of the past few years.

Cerebrosoft was founded by Charlotte and two friends after they had graduated from business school. The company is located in the heart of Silicon Valley. Charlotte and her friends managed to make money in their second year in business and have continued to do so every year since. Cerebrosoft was one of the first companies to sell software over the World Wide Web and to develop PC-based software tools for the multimedia sector. Two of the products generate 80 percent of the company's revenues: Audiatur and Videatur. Each product has sold more than 100,000 units during the past year. Business is done over the Web: customers can download a trial version of the software, test it, and if they are satisfied with what they see, they can purchase the product (by using a password that enables them to disable the time

counter in the trial version). Both products are priced at $75.95 and are sold exclusively over the Web.

Although the World Wide Web is a network of computers of different types, running different kinds of software, a standardized protocol between the computers enables them to communicate. Users can surf the Web and visit computers many thousands of miles away, accessing information available at the site. Users also can make files available on the Web, and this is how Cerebrosoft generates its sales. Selling software over the Web eliminates many of the traditional cost factors of consumer products: packaging, storage, distribution, sales force, and so on. Instead, potential customers can download a trial version, take a look at it (that is, use the product) before its trial period expires, and then decide whether to buy it. Furthermore, Cerebrosoft can always make the most recent files available to the customer, avoiding the problem of having outdated software in the distribution pipeline.

Charlotte is interrupted in her thoughts by the arrival of Jeannie Korn. Jeannie is in charge of marketing for on-line products and Brainet has had her particular attention from the beginning. She is more than ready to provide the advice that Charlotte has requested. "Charlotte, I think we should really go ahead with Brainet. The software engineers have convinced me that the current version is robust and we want to be on the market with this as soon as possible! From the data for our product launches during the past two years, we can get a rather reliable estimate of how the market will respond to the new product, don't you think? And look!" She pulls out some presentation slides. "During that time period we launched 12 new products altogether and 4 of them sold more than 30,000 units during the first six months alone! Even better: the last two we launched even sold more than 40,000 copies during the first two quarters!" Charlotte knows these numbers as well as Jeannie does. After all, two of these launches have been products she herself helped to develop. But she feels uneasy about this particular product launch. The company has grown rapidly during the past three years and its financial capabilities are already rather stretched. A poor product launch for Brainet would cost the company a lot of money, something that isn't available right now due to the investments Cerebrosoft has recently made.

Later in the afternoon, Charlotte meets with Reggie Ruffin, a jack of all trades and the production manager. Reggie has a solid track record in his field and Charlotte wants his opinion on the Brainet project.

"Well, Charlotte, quite frankly, I think that there are three main factors that are relevant to the success of this project: competition, units sold, and cost—ah, and, of course, our pricing. Have you decided on the price yet?"

"I am still considering which of the three strategies would be most beneficial to us. Selling for $50.00 and trying to maximize revenues—or selling for $30.00 and trying to maximize market share. Of course, there is still your third alternative; we could sell for $40.00 and try to do both."

At this point, Reggie focuses on the sheet of paper in front of him. "And I still believe that the $40.00 alternative is the best one. Concerning the costs, I checked the records; basically we have to amortize the development costs we incurred for Brainet. So far we have spent $800,000 and we expect to spend another $50,000 per year for support and shipping the CDs to those who want a hardcopy on top of their downloaded software." Reggie next hands a report to Charlotte. "Here we have some data on the industry. I just received that yesterday, hot off the press. Let's see what we can learn about the industry here." He shows Charlotte some of the highlights. Reggie then agrees to compile the most relevant information contained in the report and have it ready for Charlotte the following morning. It takes him long into the night to gather the data from the pages of the report, but in the end he produces three tables, one for each of the three alternative pricing strategies. Each table shows the corresponding probability of various amounts of sales given the level of competition (severe, moderate, or weak) that develops from other companies.

TABLE 1   Probability Distribution of Unit Sales, Given a High Price ($50)

Sales	Severe	Moderate	Weak
50,000 units	0.2	0.25	0.3
30,000 units	0.25	0.3	0.35
20,000 units	0.55	0.45	0.35

TABLE 2   Probability Distribution of Unit Sales, Given a Medium Price ($40)

Sales	Severe	Moderate	Weak
50,000 units	0.25	0.30	0.40
30,000 units	0.35	0.40	0.50
20,000 units	0.40	0.30	0.10

TABLE 3   Probability Distribution of Unit Sales, Given a Low Price ($30)

Sales	Severe	Moderate	Weak
50,000 units	0.35	0.40	0.50
30,000 units	0.40	0.50	0.45
20,000 units	0.25	0.10	0.05

The next morning, Charlotte is sipping from another power drink. Jeannie and Reggie will be in her office any moment now and, with their help, she will have to decide what to do with Brainet. Should they launch the product? If so, at what price?

When Jeannie and Reggie enter the office, Jeannie immediately bursts out: "Guys, I just spoke to our marketing research company. They say that they could do a study for us about the competitive situation for the introduction of Brainet and deliver the results within a week."

"How much do they want for the study?"

"I knew you'd ask that, Reggie. They want $10,000, and I think it's a fair deal."

At this point, Charlotte steps into the conversation. "Do we have any data on the quality of the work of this marketing research company?"

"Yes, I do have some reports here. After analyzing them, I have come to the conclusion that the predictions of the marketing research company are pretty good: given that the competition turned out to be severe, they predicted it correctly 80 percent of the time, while 15 percent of the time they predicted moderate competition in that setting. Given that the competition turned out to be moderate, they predicted severe competition 15 percent of the time and moderate competition 80 percent of the time. Finally, for the case of weak competition, the numbers were 90 percent of the time a correct prediction, 7 percent of the time a 'moderate' prediction and 3 percent of the time a 'severe' prediction."

Charlotte feels that all these numbers are too much for her. "Don't we have a simple estimate of how the market will react?"

"Some prior probabilities, you mean? Sure, from our past experience, the likelihood of facing severe competition is 20 percent, whereas it is 70 percent for moderate competition and 10 percent for weak competition," Jeannie has her numbers always ready when needed.

All that is left to do now is to sit down and make sense of all this . . .

 a. For the initial analysis, ignore the opportunity of obtaining more information by hiring the marketing research company. Identify the decision alternatives and the states of nature. Construct the payoff table. Then formulate the decision problem in a decision tree. Clearly distinguish between decision and chance nodes and include all the relevant data.

 b. What is Charlotte's decision if she uses the maximum likelihood criterion? The equally likely criterion?

 c. What is Charlotte's decision if she uses Bayes' decision rule?

 d. Now consider the possibility of doing the market research. Develop the corresponding decision tree. Calculate the relevant probabilities and analyze the decision tree. Should Cerebrosoft pay the $10,000 for the marketing research? What is the overall optimal policy?

CASE 10.2
SMART STEERING SUPPORT

On a sunny May morning, Marc Binton, CEO of Bay Area Automobile Gadgets (BAAG), enters the conference room on the 40th floor of the Gates building in San Francisco, where BAAG's offices are located. The other executive officers of the company have already gathered. The meeting has only one item on its agenda: planning a Research and Development project to develop a new driver support system (DSS). Brian Huang, manager of Research and Development, is walking around nervously. He has to inform the group about the R&D strategy he has developed for the DSS. Marc has identified DSS as the strategic new product for the company. Julie Aker, vice president of Marketing, will speak after Brian. She will give detailed information about the target segment, expected sales, and marketing costs associated with the introduction of the DSS.

BAAG builds electronic nonaudio equipment for luxury cars. Founded by a group of Stanford graduates, the company sold its first product—a car routing system relying on a technology called Global Positioning Satellites (GPS)—a few years ago. Such routing systems help drivers to find directions to their desired destinations using satellites to determine the exact position of the car. To keep up with technology and to meet the wishes of their customers, the company has added a number of new features to its router during the last few years. The DSS will be a completely new product, incorporating recent developments in GPS as well as voice recognition and display technologies. Marc strongly supports this product, as it will give BAAG a competitive advantage over its Asian and European competitors.

Driver support systems have been a field of intense research for more than a decade. These systems provide the driver with a wide range of information, such as directions, road conditions, traffic updates, and so forth. The information exchange can take place verbally or via projection of text onto the windscreen. Other features help the driver avoid obstacles that have been identified by cars ahead on the road (these cars transmit the information to the following vehicles). Marc wants to incorporate all these features and other technologies into one support system that would then be sold to BAAG's customers in the automobile industry.

After all the attendees have taken their seats, Brian starts his presentation: "Marc asked me to inform you about our efforts with the driver support system, particularly the road scanning device. We have reached a stage where we basically have to make a go or no-go decision concerning the research for this device, which, as you all know by now, is a key feature in the DSS. We have already integrated the other devices, such as the GPS-based positioning

and direction system. The question with which we have to deal is whether to fund basic research into the road scanning device. If this research were successful, we then would have to decide if we want to develop a product based on these results—or if we just want to sell the technology without developing a product. If we do decide to develop the product ourselves, there is a chance that the product development process might not be successful. In that case, we could still sell the technology. In the case of successful product development, we would have to decide whether to market the product. If we decide not to market the developed product, we could at least sell the product concept that was the result of our successful research and development efforts. Doing so would earn more than just selling the technology prematurely. If, on the other hand, we decide to market the driver support system, then we are faced with the uncertainty of how the product will be received by our customers. "

"You completely lost me," snipes Marc.

Max, Julie's assistant, just shakes his head and murmurs, "those techno-nerds. . . ."

Brian starts to explain: "Sorry for the confusion. Let's just go through it again, step by step."

"Good idea—and perhaps make smaller steps!" Julie obviously dislikes Brian's style of presentation.

"OK, the first decision we are facing is whether to invest in research for the road scanning device."

"How much would that cost us?" asks Marc.

"Our estimated budget for this is $300,000. Once we invest that money, the outcome of the research effort is somewhat uncertain. Our engineers assess the probability of successful research at 80 percent."

"That's a pretty optimistic success rate, don't you think?" Julie remarks sarcastically. She still remembers the disaster with Brian's last project, the fingerprint-based car-security-system. After spending half a million dollars, the development engineers concluded that it would be impossible to produce the security system at an attractive price.

Brian senses Julie's hostility and shoots back: "In engineering, we are quite accustomed to these success rates—something we can't say about marketing. . ."

"What would be the next step?" intervenes Marc.

"Hm, sorry. If the research is not successful, then we can only sell the DSS in its current form."

"The profit estimate for that scenario is $2 million," Julie throws in.

"If, however, the research effort is successful, then we will have to make another decision, namely, whether to go on to the development stage."

"If we wouldn't want to develop a product at that point, would that mean that we would have to sell the DSS as it is now?" asks Max.

"Yes, Max. Except that additionally we would earn some $200,000 from selling our research results to GM. Their research division is very interested in our work and they have offered me that money for our findings."

"Ah, now that's good news," remarks Julie.

Brian continues, "If, however, after successfully completing the research stage, we decide to develop a new product, then we'll have to spend another $800,000 for that task, at a 35 percent chance of not being successful."

"So you are telling us we'll have to spend $800,000 for a ticket in a lottery where we have a 35 percent chance of not winning anything?" asks Julie.

"Julie, don't focus on the losses but on the potential gains! The chance of winning in this lottery, as you call it, is 65 percent. I believe that that's much more than with a normal lottery ticket," says Marc.

"Thanks, Marc," says Brian. "Once we invest that money in development, we have two possible outcomes: either we will be successful in developing the road scanning device or we won't. If we fail, then once again we'll sell the DSS in its current form and cash in the $200,000 from GM for the research results. If the development process is successful, then we have to decide whether to market the new product."

"Why wouldn't we want to market it after successfully developing it?" asks Marc.

"That's a good question. Basically what I mean is that we could decide not to sell the product ourselves but instead give the right to sell it to somebody else, to GM for example. They would pay us $1 million for it."

"I like those numbers!" remarks Julie.

"Once we decide to build the product and market it, we will face the market uncertainties and I'm sure that Julie has those numbers ready for us. Thanks."

At this point, Brian sits down and Julie comes forward to give her presentation. Immediately some colorful slides are projected on the wall behind her as Max operates the computer.

"Thanks, Brian. Well, here's the data we have been able to gather from some marketing research. The acceptance of our new product in the market can be high, medium, or low." Julie is pointing to some figures projected on the wall behind her. "Our estimates indicate that high acceptance would result in profits of $8.0 million and that medium acceptance would give us $4.0 million. In the unfortunate case of a poor reception by our customers, we still expect $2.2 million in profit. I should mention that these profits do not include the additional costs of marketing or R&D expenses."

"So, you are saying that in the worst case we'll make barely more money than with the current product?" asks Brian.

"Yes, that's what I am saying."

"What budget would you need for the marketing of our DSS with the road scanner?" asks Marc.

"For that we would need an additional $200,000 on top of what has already been included in the profit estimates," Julie replies.

"What are the chances of ending up with a high, medium, or low acceptance of the new DSS?" asks Brian.

"We can see those numbers at the bottom of the slide," says Julie, while she is turning toward the projection behind her. "There is a 30 percent chance of high market acceptance and a 20 percent chance of low market acceptance.

At this point, Marc moves in his seat and asks: "Given all these numbers and bits of information, what are you suggesting that we do?"

a. Organize the available data on cost and profit estimates in a table.
b. Formulate the problem in a decision tree. Clearly distinguish between decision and chance nodes.
c. Calculate the expected payoffs for each node in the decision tree.
d. What is BAAG's optimal policy according to Bayes' decision rule?
e. What would be the expected value of perfect information on the outcome of the research effort?
f. What would be the expected value of perfect information on the outcome of the development effort?
g. Marc is a risk-averse decision maker. In a number of interviews, his utility function for money was assessed to be

$$U(M) = \frac{1 - e^{-\frac{M}{12}}}{1 - e^{-\frac{1}{12}}}$$

where M is the company's net profit in units of hundreds of thousands of dollars (e.g., $M = 8$ would imply a net profit of $800,000). Using Marc's utility function, calculate the utility for each terminal branch of the decision tree.
h. Determine the expected utilities for all nodes in the decision tree.
i. Based on Marc's utility function, what is BAAG's optimal policy?
j. Based on Marc's utility function, what would be the expected value of perfect information on the outcome of the research effort?
k. Based on Marc's utility function, what would be the expected value of perfect information on the outcome of the development effort?

CHAPTER

11

INVENTORY MANAGEMENT WITH KNOWN DEMAND

"Sorry, we're out of that item." How often have you heard that during shopping trips? In many of these cases, what you have encountered are stores that aren't doing a very good job of managing their **inventories** (stocks of goods being held for future use or sale). They aren't placing orders to replenish inventories soon enough to avoid shortages. These stores could benefit from the kinds of techniques for scientific inventory management that are described in this chapter.

It isn't just retail stores that must manage inventories. In fact, inventories pervade the business world. Maintaining inventories is necessary for any company dealing with physical products, including manufacturers, wholesalers, and retailers. For example, manufacturers need inventories of the materials required to make their products. They also need inventories of the finished products awaiting shipment. Similarly, both wholesalers and retailers need to maintain inventories of goods to be available for purchase by customers.

The total value of all inventory—including finished goods, partially finished goods, and raw materials—in the United States is more than a *trillion* dollars. This is more than $4,000 each for every man, woman, and child in the country.

The costs associated with storing ("carrying") inventory are also very large, perhaps a quarter of the value of the inventory. Therefore, the costs being incurred for the storage of inventory in the United States run into the hundreds of billions of dollars. Reducing storage costs by avoiding unnecessarily large inventories can enhance any firm's competitiveness.

Some Japanese companies were pioneers in introducing the *just-in-time inventory system*—a system that emphasizes planning and scheduling so that the needed materials arrive just-in-time for their use. Huge savings are thereby achieved by reducing inventory levels to a bare minimum.

Many companies in other parts of the world also have been revamping the way in which they manage their inventories. The application of management science techniques in this area (sometimes called *scientific inventory management*) is providing a powerful tool for gaining a competitive edge. (For example, Section 2.1 describes how Citgo Petroleum Corporation used management science to reduce their inventory levels by $116.5 million in the mid-1980s.)

How do managers use management science to improve their **inventory policy** for when and how much to replenish their inventory? They use **scientific inventory management,** which involves the following steps:

1. Formulate a *mathematical model* describing the behavior of the inventory system.
2. Seek an *optimal* inventory policy with respect to this model.
3. Use a computerized *information processing system* to maintain a record of the current inventory levels.
4. Using this record of current inventory levels, apply the optimal inventory policy to signal when and how much to replenish inventory.

The purpose of this chapter, together with Chapter 12, is to provide an introduction to scientific inventory management from a managerial perspective. The two chapters consider, in turn, two categories of inventory problems—those with known demand and those with unknown demand. The **demand** for a product in inventory is the number of units that will need to be withdrawn from inventory for some use (e.g., sales) during a specific period. If the demand in future periods can be forecast with considerable precision, it is reasonable to use an inventory policy that assumes that all forecasts will always be completely accurate. This is the case of *known demand,* considered in this chapter.

Beginning with a case study, we shall investigate models of inventory problems where the demand for the product is essentially the same each period, so the product is being withdrawn from inventory at a fixed rate (e.g., 50 units per month).

11.1 A Case Study: The Atlantic Coast Tire Corp. (ACT) Problem

"I have a problem, Nick. And I think maybe you're just the person who can help me with it."

"I hope so. Tell me more, Ashley."

"Well, here is the situation. I am getting all kinds of pressure from upstairs to cut down on our inventory levels. They say that there is far too much of the company's capital tied up in our inventory. They complain about the high cost of tying up all this capital, along with all the other costs of maintaining such large inventories. They say that I need to run a leaner operation."

"Yes, a lot of companies are cutting back on their inventories these days. It's another way to cut costs to stay competitive."

"But having too little inventory can be costly also. These guys are the first to complain when we have shortages because we weren't carrying enough inventory. Then I hear about how costly it is to lose future customers because they won't come back again if we make them wait too long to fill their orders. And my people already are spending too much of their time processing orders to replenish inventory. That is only going to get worse and drive up my department's costs if we carry less inventory. As ACT's inventory manager, I need to consider all these cost factors and achieve a good balance—not just focus on the cost of holding inventory."

"Yes, I agree with you, Ashley. You need to consider these trade-offs. Carrying too little inventory can be just as costly as having too much. But where do I come in on all this?"

"Well, as I say, I want to achieve a good balance between all these cost factors. I think we can cut back on our inventory levels somewhat. But I don't want to cut back too far. That's where I need your help. I am not quite sure on how to get a handle on finding the right balance. I hear that you management scientists have ways of using mathematics to do this."

"Yes, we do. But mathematics is just a small part of it. We spend most of our time digging out good estimates of all the cost factors involved. Then we add them up and see what the total cost would be for various inventory policies. Check how the total cost would change if you change your **order quantity**—the number of units you purchase each time you replenish your inventory. That sort of thing. At that point, we use mathematics to determine which inventory policy would minimize your total cost."

"Sounds good. How soon can you start?"

As the conversation ends, Nicholas Relich agrees to start a management science study next week. Ashley Collins asks him to begin by focusing on her biggest headache—the inventory of 185/70 R13 Eversafe tires. She also promises to provide all the help he needs to dig out good estimates of the various cost factors.

Background

The Atlantic Coast Tire Corporation (ACT) is the East Coast distributor of Eversafe tires. ACT supplies 1,500 retail stores and auto service stations with a dozen different sizes of Eversafes, and so must maintain an inventory of each. ACT stores the tires in its warehouse, from which shipments are continually being made to its various customers. Ashley Collins is the inventory manager overseeing this operation. When the inventory level of a particular size of tire gets low, ACT places a large order by fax with Eversafe to replenish the inventory. Eversafe then ships the tires by truck to arrive nine working days after the placement of the order.

FIGURE 11.1

The pattern of inventory levels over time for the 185/70 R13 Eversafe tire under ACT's current inventory policy.

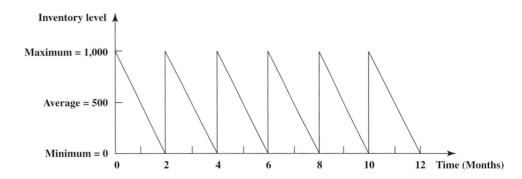

Ashley gets Nicholas Relich started by providing him with the following information about the 185/70 R13 size of Eversafe tires. These tires have been selling at a regular rate of about 500 per month. Therefore, Ashley's policy has been to place an order with Eversafe for 1,000 tires as needed every couple months. The order is placed just in time to have the delivery arrive as the inventory runs out. Consequently, the inventory level roughly follows the saw-toothed pattern over a year's time, shown in Figure 11.1. The graph begins at time 0 when a delivery has just arrived. Then, over each two-month cycle, the inventory level drops at a steady rate from 1,000 to 0, so that the average inventory level is 500.

Nick comments to Ashley that this saw-toothed pattern is a common one for inventory levels. This looks like a reasonable inventory policy. However, the key question is whether 1,000 is the right amount for the *order quantity*. Cutting this number down somewhat would reduce the average inventory level by a proportional amount, but at the cost of increasing the frequency of placing orders. What the order quantity should be will depend on the various cost factors.

Nick and Ashley next turn their attention to estimating the values of these various costs.

The Cost Components of Maintaining ACT's Inventory of 185/70 R13 Eversafe Tires

One major cost associated with maintaining the inventory of 185/70 R13 size tires is ACT's cost for purchasing the tires. Eversafe charges ACT $20 per tire.

$$\text{Purchase price} = \$20 \text{ per tire} \tag{1}$$

In addition to this purchase price, ACT incurs some additional administrative costs each time it places an order with Eversafe. A purchase order must be initiated and processed. The shipment must be received, placed into storage, and recorded in the computerized information processing system that monitors the status of the inventory. Then the payment to Eversafe must be processed.

All these steps triggered by placing an order require a significant amount of time from various employees of ACT. Ashley estimates that the labor charges (including both wages and benefits) average $15 per hour and that approximately six hours of labor are associated with placing an order, resulting in a labor cost of $90. In addition to these direct labor charges, there also are associated overhead costs (supervision, office space, etc.), which are estimated to be $25. The sum of these two figures is $115.

$$\text{Administrative cost for placing an order} = \$115. \tag{2}$$

Note that this administrative cost remains the same regardless of how many tires are ordered. For example, considering both the purchase price and administrative cost, the total cost for placing an order is

$$\$115 + \$20(1) = \$135 \qquad \text{if 1 tire is ordered}$$

$$\$115 + \$20 \,(1,000) = \$20,115 \qquad \text{if 1,000 tires are ordered}$$

so that the total cost per tire decreases sharply from $135 to barely over $20 when the order size is increased. Thus, the administrative cost provides a strong incentive to place larger orders on an infrequent basis instead of small orders on a frequent basis.

When ACT receives a shipment of tires from Eversafe, there are a number of additional costs associated with holding these tires in inventory until they are sold. The most important of these costs is the *cost of capital tied up in inventory*. For example, suppose that there currently are 1,000 of the 185/70 R13 tires in inventory. The purchase of these 1,000 tires required an expenditure of 1,000($20) = $20,000 (plus a bit more in administrative costs), and this money will not be regained until the tires are sold. If this capital of $20,000 were not tied up in these tires, ACT would have other opportunities to use the money that would earn an attractive return. This lost return because alternate opportunities must be forgone is referred to as the **opportunity cost** of this capital. Regardless of whether the $20,000 has been borrowed or comes from the company's own funds (or a combination), it is this opportunity cost that reflects the true cost of tying up this capital in the inventory of tires.

The ACT comptroller gives Nick his estimate that the cost of capital tied up is 15 percent per annum. For example, if the average number of tires of this size in inventory during one year is 500, then the cost of capital tied up in this inventory that year is

$$0.15(500 \text{ tires})(\$20 \text{ per tire}) = \$1,500$$

The other kinds of costs associated with holding tires in inventory include

1. The cost of leasing the warehouse space for storing the tires.
2. The cost of insurance against loss of inventory by fire, theft, vandalism, and so on.
3. The cost of personnel who oversee and protect the inventory.
4. Taxes that are based on the value of inventory.

On an annual basis, the sum of these costs is estimated to be 6 percent of the average value (based on ACT's purchase price) of the inventory being held. (This is only a rough estimate since some of these costs may not change when small changes occur in the average inventory level.)

Adding this 6 percent to the 15 percent for the cost of capital tied up in inventory gives 21 percent per year. Therefore, the total annual cost associated with holding tires in inventory is 21 percent of the average value of these tires ($20 times the average number of tires). In other words, for the tire size under consideration, this total annual cost per tire is 0.21($20 per tire) = $4.20 per tire.

$$\text{Annual cost of holding tires in inventory} = \$4.20 \times \text{the average number of tires in inventory throughout the year} \qquad (3)$$

The last major kind of cost that can be incurred as a result of ACT's inventory policy is the cost incurred when a shortage occurs. (Although the idealized pattern of inventory levels shown in Figure 11.1 indicates that shortages do not occur, they actually can happen due to either a delay in Eversafe's delivery or larger-than-usual sales orders while the delivery is in transit.) What are the cost consequences when there are not enough tires in inventory to fill immediately the incoming orders from ACT's customers? Nearly all these customers are willing to wait a reasonable period for the tires to become available again, so lost sales in the short run is not a major consequence. Instead, the important consequences are

1. Customer dissatisfaction that results in the loss of good will and perhaps the loss of some future sales.
2. The potential necessity for ACT to drop its price for tires being delivered late in order to placate its customers so that they will accept a delay.
3. The acceptance of late payments for tires being delivered late, resulting in delayed revenue.
4. The costs of additional record keeping, and other labor costs, required for out-of-stock tires.

The total cost resulting from these consequences is roughly proportional to the number of tires short and to the length of time the shortage continues. After consulting with upper management, Ashley estimates that this cost on an annual basis is $7.50 *times* the average number of tires short throughout the year.

For example, in a typical year, suppose that ACT is out of stock for a total of 30 days (essentially $\frac{1}{12}$ of the year) and that the average number of tires short during these 30 days is 120. Since there is no shortage during the remainder of the year, the average number of tires short throughout the year is 120($\frac{1}{12}$) = 10, so the annual cost is 10($7.50) = $75.

$$\text{Annual cost of being out of stock} = \$7.50 \times \text{the average number of tires} \qquad (4)$$
$$\text{short throughout the year}$$

Section 11.4 will describe how Nick uses all this information to determine what Ashley's order quantity should be. Meanwhile, the next two sections provide further background.

Review Questions

1. When a wholesaler (like ACT) places an order for goods, what can cause the cost to exceed the purchase price?
2. Why is there a cost associated with tying up capital in inventory? Why is this cost also referred to as an opportunity cost?
3. What are some other kinds of costs associated with holding inventory?
4. What are some cost consequences when a wholesaler incurs an inventory shortage and so cannot fill immediately incoming orders from its customers?

11.2 Cost Components of Inventory Models

There are four kinds of costs that are included in many inventory models. The precise nature of these costs depends on the type of organization involved. Retailers and wholesalers (such as ACT) replenish their inventory by *purchasing* the product. Manufacturers (such as Eversafe) replenish their inventory of finished products for subsequent sale to their customers by *manufacturing* more of the product involved. However, inventory models use the same terminology to identify the costs in both types of situations.

Let us now examine these four cost components that may be included in an inventory model.

Acquisition Cost

Whether a product is purchased or manufactured, there is a direct cost associated with bringing it into inventory, an **acquisition cost.** The cost incurred may be a fixed *unit cost,* as with the tires ACT purchases from Eversafe ($20 per tire no matter how many are purchased). Or there might be a *quantity discount* that lowers the purchase price per unit for larger orders. A model for quantity discounts is presented in Section 11.6. However, most of the models considered in this chapter will have a fixed unit cost for acquiring the product.

> *Cost Component 1:* The direct cost of replenishing inventory, whether through purchasing or manufacturing of the product.
> *Notation:* c = unit acquisition cost
> *ACT Example:* c = $20 per tire

Setup Cost

In addition to the direct cost of replenishing inventory, there may be an additional **setup cost** incurred by initiating the replenishment.

When the replenishment is done by purchasing the product, this setup cost consists of the various administrative costs (including overhead) associated with initiating and processing the purchase order, receiving the shipment, and processing the payment. These kinds of administrative costs were illustrated in the ACT example.

When a manufacturer is replenishing its inventory of a finished product by manufacturing more of the product, the setup cost consists of the cost of setting up the manufacturing process for another production run. For example, if the production facilities currently are being used to produce another product, some retooling of the factory equipment may be required to shift over to producing the product under consideration.

> *Cost Component 2:* The setup cost to initiate the replenishing of inventory, whether through purchasing or manufacturing of the product.
> *Notation:* K = setup cost
> *ACT Example:* K = $115

Holding Cost

When units are placed into inventory, there is a **holding cost** incurred (sometimes referred to as a *storage cost*). This component represents the costs associated with holding the items in inventory until they are needed elsewhere (e.g., for shipment to a customer). As described for the ACT example, this kind of cost includes the cost of capital tied up in inventory, as well as the cost of space, insurance, protection, and taxes attributed to storage.

> *Cost Component 3:* The cost of holding units in inventory.
> *Notation:* h = annual holding cost per unit held
> = unit holding cost
> *ACT Example:* h = $4.20

The quantity h assumes that the value of each unit held in inventory is fixed regardless of the inventory policy used. This assumption is violated when the supplier provides *quantity discounts* so that the cost of purchasing each unit depends on the order quantity. Section 11.6 discusses how to evaluate this cost component when quantity discounts are available.

Shortage Cost

The **shortage cost** is the cost incurred when there is a need to withdraw units from inventory and there are none available. Typically, such shortages occur when more orders come in from customers than can be filled from the current inventory. One possible consequence of not being able to fill orders immediately is that sales may be lost because these customers will take their business elsewhere. Even if customers are willing to wait for the inventory to be replenished again (as is the case for ACT), there are several other potentially costly consequences that were described for the ACT example. For example, there may be lost *future* sales because these dissatisfied customers do not return again.

> *Cost Component 4:* The cost of having a shortage of units, that is, of needing units from inventory when there are none there.
> *Notation:* p = annual shortage cost per unit short
> = unit shortage cost
> *ACT Example:* p = $7.50

To help remember the symbol p, think of it as representing the *penalty* for incurring the shortage of a unit.

Combining These Cost Components

Inventory models focus on determining an optimal **inventory policy,** which prescribes both when inventory should be replenished and by how much. The objective is to minimize the *total inventory cost* per unit time. This unit time commonly is taken to be a *year* (as we will do). Minimizing the *annual* total inventory cost requires expressing each of the above cost components on an annual basis. To do this, each of the specific costs identified above (c, k, h, and p) needs to be multiplied by the number of times the cost is incurred per year, as summarized below.

Annual acquisition cost = c × number of units added to inventory per year

Annual setup cost = K × number of setups per year

Annual holding cost = h × average number of units in inventory throughout a year

Annual shortage cost = p × average number of units short throughout a year

(These latter two annual costs were illustrated in the preceding section for the ACT case study.) Therefore, the total cost to be minimized to find an optimal inventory policy is

$$\text{TC} = \text{total inventory cost per year}$$

$$= \text{sum of the above four annual costs}$$

It is sometimes not necessary to consider the first of the above four annual costs—the annual acquisition cost—to determine an optimal inventory policy. This cost does not need to be considered when it is a **fixed cost**—a cost that remains the same regardless of the decisions made. And the *annual* acquisition cost will indeed be a fixed cost if the *unit* acquisition cost is fixed (since the number of units that need to be added to inventory per year also is a given quantity). The only relevant costs are the **variable costs**—those costs that are affected by the decisions made—since these are the only costs that can be decreased by improving the decisions. Therefore, to find an optimal inventory policy, inventory models focus on minimizing

$$\text{TVC} = \text{total } \textit{variable} \text{ inventory cost per year}$$

$$= \text{sum of the variable annual costs}$$

The next several sections will show TVC for each of several inventory models. In Section 11.6, when the unit acquisition cost is not fixed (because of quantity discounts), the annual acquisition cost will be included in TVC.

Estimating the Costs

To find the optimal inventory policy for any specific inventory system, it is first necessary to estimate the relevant unit costs—such as K, h, and p. Estimating these unit costs is nearly all that is needed to apply the models in this chapter to many real inventory problems. These models enable you to identify an inventory policy that achieves an optimal trade-off between these kinds of costs.

In applications, estimating K is relatively straightforward, and estimating h is not much more difficult. However, estimating p is quite challenging, because it is difficult to predict the consequences of shortages with much precision. Nevertheless, deriving a rational inventory policy demands examining these consequences and comparing them with the other kinds of costs. Are these consequences so severe that shortages should be eliminated as much as possible (as for the model in the next section)? Or can total costs be minimized by allowing occasional planned shortages? In the latter case, it is important to develop at least a rough estimate of p. Doing so enables using scientific inventory management to find an appropriate trade-off between the consequences of shortages and the other kinds of costs.

Review Questions

1. What are the four cost components that may be included in an inventory model?
2. What are the two alternative ways of incurring a direct cost of replenishing inventory, depending on the type of organization involved?
3. What are the two alternative ways of incurring a setup cost to replenish inventory, depending on the type of organization involved?
4. What does an inventory policy prescribe?
5. What needs to be minimized to determine an optimal inventory policy?
6. What is the difference between a fixed cost and a variable cost? Why are the variable costs the only relevant costs for finding an optimal inventory policy?

11.3 The Basic Economic Order Quantity (EOQ) Model

Nicholas Relich has concluded that ACT's inventory problem described by Ashley Collins can be analyzed by using the basic EOQ model. Let us take a look at this model.

The basic *EOQ model* (short for *economic order quantity model*) has long been the most widely used inventory model. Its popularity is due to a combination of simplicity and wide applicability. First introduced in 1913 by Ford W. Harris, an engineer with the Westinghouse Corporation, it has continued to be a key tool of inventory management for nearly a century.

For example, one of the *classic* applications of the EOQ model (described in the December 1981 issue of *Interfaces*) won a coveted Franz Edelman Award for Management Science Achievement for **Standard Brands Inc.** a couple decades ago. This application revamped the way the company managed its finished-goods inventories of over 100 Planters Peanuts products at 12 warehouses. Because of the simplicity of the EOQ model, the calculations for applying the model only required the use of a hand-held calculator. This application resulted in annual savings of $3.8 million for the company.

***Where the Model Is
Applicable***

This model is designed for the kind of situation where the product needs to be withdrawn from inventory at essentially a *constant rate.* Day after day, week after week, month after month, the units continue being withdrawn at this fixed rate. This is referred to as having a **constant demand rate.** In this case, the symbol D is used to denote this demand rate:

$$D = \text{annual demand rate}$$

$$= \text{number of units being withdrawn from inventory per year}$$

Many inventory systems have a constant demand rate, at least as a reasonable approximation. This is the case when the inventory of a particular subassembly feeds into an assembly line for assembly into a final product, provided the assembly line continues operating at a fixed rate, since then the subassemblies would be withdrawn from inventory at this same fixed rate. It also is the case for a manufacturer's finished-goods inventory when the product is being purchased at a fixed rate. Similarly, if a wholesaler's or retailer's customers are purchasing a product at roughly a fixed rate, then its inventory of this product has roughly a constant demand rate.

In the case of the ACT inventory system described in Section 11.1, we saw that ACT's customers purchase approximately 500 of its Eversafe tires of the 185/70 R13 size each month. Although there are fairly small fluctuations from month to month, the sales pattern is sufficiently regular to treat it as a constant demand rate. Thus, on an annual basis, this demand rate is

$$D = 12(500) = 6{,}000 \text{ tires sold per year}$$

***The Assumptions of the
Model***

Along with a constant demand rate, the basic EOQ model also makes two other key assumptions:

Assumptions

1. A constant demand rate.
2. The order quantity to replenish inventory arrives all at once just when desired.
3. Planned shortages are not allowed.

The second assumption also is satisfied by ACT's inventory system. As indicated in Section 11.1, when ACT places an order to replenish its inventory of tires, Eversafe ships the tires on a truck. Thus, the tires arrive all at once. Furthermore, Eversafe schedules its delivery to arrive nine working days after the placement of the order. Therefore, by faxing its order nine working days before the inventory will be depleted, ACT receives its shipment of tires when desired—just before a shortage will occur.

The amount of time between the placement of an order and its receipt is referred to as the **lead time.** Thus, ACT's lead time is nine working days.

The inventory level at which the order is placed is called the **reorder point.** For this model, the reorder point can be calculated as

$$\text{Reorder point} = (\text{daily demand}) \times (\text{lead time})$$

Since ACT has 250 working days per year, its daily demand is

$$\text{Daily demand} = \frac{D}{250 \text{ days}} = \frac{6{,}000 \text{ tires sold per year}}{250 \text{ working days per year}}$$

$$= 24 \text{ tires sold per day}$$

Consequently, ACT's reorder point is

$$\text{Reorder point} = (24 \text{ tires/day}) \, (9 \text{ days})$$

$$= 216 \text{ tires}$$

As depicted in Figure 11.2, each time the inventory level drops down to having 216 tires remaining, ACT faxes an order to Eversafe.

FIGURE 11.2

During each two-month inventory cycle depicted in Figure 11.1, ACT places a new order when the inventory level drops to 216 tires, just in time for the delivery to occur when the inventory level drops to 0. The lead time for the delivery is nine working days.

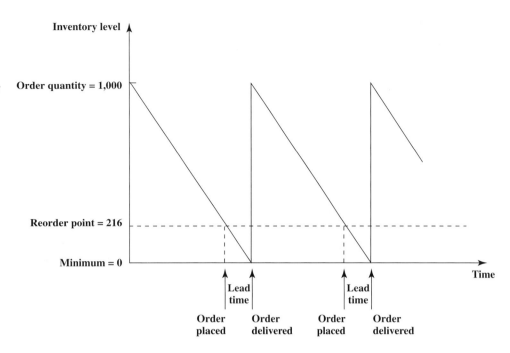

A Broader Perspective of the Model

If ACT sold *exactly* 24 tires each and every working day (as the model assumes), it would be possible to predict weeks in advance exactly when the inventory level will drop down to the reorder point. However, the model is only intended to provide an approximate representation of the real inventory system. Naturally, the number of tires sold does fluctuate somewhat from day to day. Therefore, it is necessary to keep track of the current inventory level on a continuous basis to detect exactly when the reorder point is reached. ACT accomplishes this through its computerized information processing system. Each sale (as well as each delivery from Eversafe) is recorded immediately in the computer, which then adjusts the current inventory level accordingly. This enables the computer to signal as soon as the reorder point is reached.

An inventory system whose current inventory level is monitored on a continuous basis like this is referred to as a **continuous-review system.** By contrast, a system whose inventory level is only checked periodically (e.g., at the end of each week) is called a **periodic-review system.** Because computerized information processing systems now are widely used to monitor inventory levels, continuous-review inventory systems have become increasingly prevalent for systems of significant size. This is the kind of inventory system assumed by the EOQ model, so it is classified as a *continuous-review inventory model.*

According to the model, the inventory level will drop to 0 at the same instant that a delivery occurs. This is only an approximation of how most real inventory systems operate. Since ACT's sales do fluctuate somewhat from day to day, its inventory level normally will reach 0 either shortly before or shortly after the delivery. However, the delivery normally arrives within a day of the inventory's depletion, which is fine for all practical purposes.

The fact that ACT can incur an inventory shortage very briefly does not contradict the third assumption (*planned shortages are not allowed*) of the basic EOQ model. This assumption really means that, if everything stays precisely on schedule (exactly a constant demand rate and deliveries exactly on schedule), the inventory level will not be allowed to drop below 0.

Some Continuous-Review Inventory Systems That Do Not Fit the Model

If ACT had a less reliable supplier than Eversafe, so that late deliveries causing substantial inventory shortages often occur, a different approach would be needed. In this situation, the inventory manager usually would increase the reorder point somewhat to provide some leeway for a late delivery. This extra inventory being carried to safeguard against delivery delays is referred to as **safety stock.** The amount of safety stock is the difference between the reorder point and the expected demand during the scheduled lead time.

Maintaining a substantial amount of safety stock also is appropriate when there is considerable uncertainty about what the demand will be from one time period to the next. This situation will be discussed in detail in the latter part of the next chapter.

The Objective of the Model

As its name (*economic order quantity* model) implies, the purpose of the EOQ model is to choose the *order quantity* that is most economical. Thus, this model has just one decision variable:

$$Q = \text{order quantity}$$

which is the number of units being ordered (whether through purchasing or manufacturing of the product) each time that the inventory needs to be replenished. Since the model assumes that the order arrives at the same moment that the inventory level drops to 0, this delivery immediately jumps the inventory level up from 0 to Q. With the constant demand rate, the inventory level then gradually drops down over time at this rate until the level reaches 0 again, at which point the process is repeated. This saw-toothed pattern is depicted in Figure 11.3. The pattern is the same as in Figure 11.1, where $Q = 1,000$, but now we want to choose the best value of Q.

The specific objective in choosing Q is to

Minimize   TVC = total variable inventory cost per year

TVC excludes the cost of the product, since this is a fixed cost. TVC also does not include any shortage costs, since the model assumes that shortages never occur. Therefore,

TVC = annual setup cost + annual holding cost

where

Annual setup cost = $K \times$ number of setups per year

Annual holding cost = $h \times$ average inventory level

As described in the preceding section,

K = setup cost each time an order occurs
h = unit holding cost

For example, for ACT's inventory of 185/70 R13 Eversafe tires, Figure 11.1 shows that currently the number of setups (order placements) per year is six and the average inventory level is 500. Consequently, since $K = \$115$ and $h = \$4.20$, TVC for ACT's current inventory policy is

$$TVC = 6K + 500h$$

$$= 6(\$115) + 500(\$4.20)$$

$$= \$2,790$$

FIGURE 11.3

The pattern of inventory levels over time assumed by the basic EOQ model, where the order quantity Q is the decision variable.

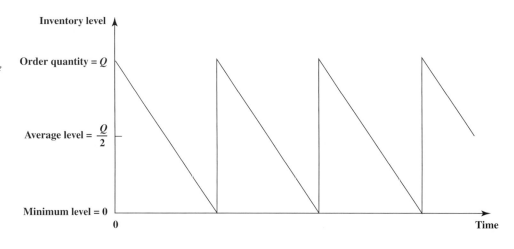

Changing the current order quantity, $Q = 1{,}000$, will change these numbers. Nicholas Relich now needs to express TVC in terms of Q, and then find the value of Q that minimizes TVC.

Review Questions

1. Why is the basic EOQ model such a popular inventory model?
2. What are the assumptions of the model? Is the model sometimes used when these assumptions are not completely satisfied?
3. What is meant by *lead time*? By *reorder point*?
4. What is the distinction between a continuous-review inventory system and a periodic-review inventory system?
5. When can a continuous-review inventory system not fit the basic EOQ model?
6. What is the single decision variable for the model?
7. What is the shape of the pattern of inventory levels over time for the model?

11.4 The Optimal Inventory Policy for the Basic EOQ Model

There is a simple *square root formula* that gives the order quantity that minimizes the total variable cost for any application of the basic EOQ model. Nicholas Relich has used this formula many times in the past and will do so again for the current ACT problem. However, he doesn't begin this way. Let us see what he does before we describe the square root formula.

Analysis of the ACT Problem

Having dealt with managers for many years, Nicholas Relich realizes that he needs to do more than simply plug into a mysterious "square root formula" to persuade them of the validity of his recommendation. Therefore, before turning to this formula, he begins by developing some supporting analysis in a form that will be persuasive to Ashley Collins and her superiors.

His first step is to set up a spreadsheet that shows the data (in column C) for the problem and what the resulting variable costs (in column G) would be for any choice of the order quantity. He then plugs in the order quantity under the current policy ($Q = 1{,}000$), as shown in Figure 11.4. This will be Exhibit A in his case to management, first, to show the current situation and, second, to enable management to experiment with other order quantities.

FIGURE 11.4

A spreadsheet formulation of the basic EOQ model for the ACT problem when using the current order quantity of Q = 1,000.

	A	B	C	D	E	F	G
1		**Basic EOQ Model for Atlantic Coast Tire Corp. (Before Solving)**					
2							
3			**Data**			**Results**	
4		**D =**	6000	(demand/year)		**Reorder Point =**	216
5		**K =**	$115	(setup cost)			
6		**h =**	$4.20	(unit holding cost)		**Annual Setup Cost =**	$690.00
7		**L =**	9	(lead time in days)		**Annual Holding Cost =**	$2,100.00
8		**WD =**	250	(working days/year)		**Total Variable Cost =**	$2,790.00
9							
10			**Decision**				
11		**Q =**	1000	(order quantity)			

	G
4	=C7*C4/C8
5	
6	=C5*C4/C11
7	=C6*C11/2
8	=SUM(G6:G7)

For Exhibit B, Nick wants to demonstrate the effect of reducing average inventory levels by decreasing the order quantity. To do this, he uses this same spreadsheet to generate the data table shown in Figure 11.5. (The equations given at the bottom of the figure for row 18 refer to the cells in the spreadsheet in Figure 11.4.) This table is generated by building a column of input data (the various order quantities) in column B, then selecting the data cells for the table (cells B18:E27), then choosing Table under the Data menu, and then entering the input cell (the order quantity) in the Column input cell.

Nick is pleased with how well this data table and the corresponding graph on the right demonstrate the effect of varying the order quantity. Clearly, the total variable cost is very high for an overly small order quantity ($Q = 100$) and then rapidly decreases as Q increases

FIGURE 11.5

A data table for the ACT problem that shows the variable costs that would be incurred with various order quantities.

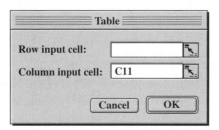

	Order Quantity	Setup Cost	Holding Cost	Total Cost
14	Data Table for Atlantic Coast Tire Corp. (Cost vs. Order Quantity)			
18	1000	$690	$2,100	$2,790
19	900	$767	$1,890	$2,657
20	800	$863	$1,680	$2,543
21	700	$986	$1,470	$2,456
22	600	$1,150	$1,260	$2,410
23	500	$1,380	$1,050	$2,430
24	400	$1,725	$840	$2,565
25	300	$2,300	$630	$2,930
26	200	$3,450	$420	$3,870
27	100	$6,900	$210	$7,110

Column input cell: C11

	C	D	E
18	=G6	=G7	=G8

FIGURE 11.6

The results obtained by applying the Excel Solver to the spreadsheet model in Figure 11.4.

	B	C	D	E	F	G
1	Basic EOQ Model for Atlantic Coast Tire Corp. (After Solving)					
3		Data			Results	
4	D =	6000	(demand/year)		Reorder Point =	216
5	K =	$115	(setup cost)			
6	h =	$4.20	(unit holding cost)		Annual Setup Cost =	$1,203.74
7	L =	9	(lead time in days)		Annual Holding Cost =	$1,203.74
8	WD =	250	(working days/year)		Total Variable Cost =	$2,407.49
10		Decision				
11	Q =	573.21	(order quantity)			

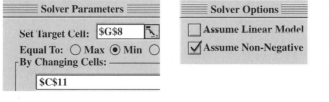

Solver Parameters — Set Target Cell: $G$8 — Equal To: Max ● Min — By Changing Cells: $C$11

Solver Options — ☐ Assume Linear Model ☑ Assume Non-Negative

	G
4	=C7*C4/C8
6	=C5*C4/C11
7	=C6*C11/2
8	=SUM(G6:G7)

until reaching a minimum somewhere between $Q = 500$ and $Q = 600$, after which it begins climbing fairly slowly. However, this doesn't yet answer the question of precisely which order quantity between 500 and 600 will minimize the total variable cost.

By having the data table raise this question, Nick reasons that this Exhibit B will provide the foundation for the coup de grace of his recommendation to management—Exhibit C. By and large, managers are very comfortable with Excel, have some experience with its Solver, and have gained confidence in the validity of this Solver. Therefore, for Exhibit C, Nick chooses Figure 11.6, which shows that the Excel Solver has found that $Q = 573$ (after rounding) is the order quantity that minimizes the total variable cost.[1] (This same figure, or Figure 11.4, can be obtained immediately by using one of the Excel templates—the Solver version for the basic EOQ model—in your MS Courseware.)

The Square Root Formula for the Optimal Order Quantity

The square root formula provides a considerably quicker way of finding the optimal order quantity shown in Figure 11.6. Let us see how this formula is obtained.

For any inventory system fitting the basic EOQ model, here are some key formulas.

$$\text{Number of setups per year} = \frac{\text{annual demand rate}}{\text{order quantity}} = \frac{D}{Q}$$

$$\text{Average inventory level} = \frac{\text{maximum level} + \text{minimum level}}{2}$$

$$= \frac{Q + 0}{2} = \frac{Q}{2}$$

$$\text{TVC (Total Variable Cost)} = \text{annual setup cost} + \text{annual holding cost}$$

$$= K\frac{D}{Q} + h\frac{Q}{2}$$

The right side of Figure 11.5 illustrates how the annual setup cost and the annual holding cost vary with the order quantity Q. The annual setup cost goes down as Q increases because this cost equals a constant (KD) *times* $1/Q$. By contrast, the annual holding cost goes up proportionally as Q increases because this cost equals a constant ($h/2$) *times* Q. Above these two curves is a plot of TVC versus Q. For each value of Q, the value on the TVC curve is the sum of the values on the two lower curves. The value of Q that gives the minimum value on the TVC curve is the optimal order quantity Q^*.

The right side of Figure 11.5 also illustrates that Q^* occurs at the point where the two lower curves intersect. (This is verified by the fact that the numbers in cells G6 and G7 in Figure 11.6 are identical.) In contrast to many other models, this *always* happens at the minimum of the TVC curve for the basic EOQ model. This is a fortunate coincidence because it provides a straightforward way of finding Q^*. All we need to do is solve for the value of Q such that

$$\text{Annual holding cost} = \text{Annual setup cost}$$

$$h\frac{Q}{2} = K\frac{D}{Q}$$

$$\frac{h}{2}Q = KD\frac{1}{Q}$$

$$Q = \frac{2KD}{h}\frac{1}{Q}$$

$$Q^2 = \frac{2KD}{h}$$

---

[1]By adding the constraint in the Solver dialogue box that C11 = integer, the Solver could have obtained the rounded solution of $Q = 573$ directly. This was not done here because the Solver can have difficulty with integer constraints when the equation entered into the target cell is a nonlinear function.

This yields the following formula for Q^*:

$$Q^* = \sqrt{\frac{2KD}{h}}$$

where

D = annual demand rate
K = setup cost
h = unit holding cost

This is the **square root formula** for Q^*. It is the most famous formula in inventory theory.

It is interesting to observe how Q^* changes when a change is made in K, D, or h. As K increases, Q^* *increases* in order to decrease the number of times this setup cost will be incurred per year. As D increases, Q^* *increases* to avoid an overly large increase in the number of setup costs incurred per year. As h increases, Q^* *decreases* to drive down the average inventory level on which this unit holding cost rate will be charged.

Applying the Square Root Formula to ACT's Problem

Your MS Courseware includes an Excel template (the analytical version for the basic EOQ model) that directly solves for the optimal order quantity. When applied to the ACT problem, this template looks identical to Figure 11.6 except for one key difference. Instead of taking the time to set up and use the Solver to find this quantity, the template enters the square root formula into the order quantity cell (C11 in this case). Naturally, the results are exactly the same as in Figure 11.6.

To illustrate, the ACT data needed for the square root formula are

$D = 6,000$
$K = \$115$
$h = \$4.20$

Thus, the formula gives

$$Q^* = \sqrt{\frac{2(115)(6,000)}{4.20}} = \sqrt{328,571}$$

$$= 573 \qquad \text{(after rounding)}$$

Therefore, rather than the current policy of ordering 1,000 tires each time, it is most economical to order 573 tires each time instead. Although this increases the annual number of setups to place orders from the current 6 to

$$\text{Number of setups per year} = \frac{D}{Q} = \frac{6,000}{573} = 10.47$$

it decreases the average inventory level from 500 tires to

$$\text{Average inventory level} = \frac{Q}{2} = \frac{573}{2} = 286.5$$

As indicated in Figures 11.4 and 11.6, this results in a reduction in the total variable cost per year from the current $2,790 to

$$\text{TVC} = \$115(10.47) + \$4.20(286.5)$$

$$= \$2,407$$

a 14 percent reduction.

Sensitivity Analysis

When Nicholas Relich presents the results in Figures 11.4, 11.5, and 11.6 to Ashley Collins, he points out that the accuracy of these results depends on the accuracy of the data that went into the analysis. After spending so much time together developing estimates of these data, they both recognize that these numbers are not exact. This is especially true of the cost estimates, $K = \$115$ and $h = \$4.20$. They agree that each of these estimates could be off by as much as 10 percent in either direction. Thus, the true value of each of these costs could lie anywhere within the following ranges.

	Range of Possible Values
Setup cost:	$103.50 to $126.50
Unit holding cost:	$3.78 to $4.62

Consequently, Nick decides to do some *sensitivity analysis* to see how sensitive the original solution of $Q^* = 573$ tires is to changes in the original estimates to other possible values in these ranges. He wants to address two questions:

1. How much can the optimal order quantity Q^* change from 573 if the true values of these costs lie elsewhere in these ranges?
2. If the true values do lie elsewhere, but $Q = 573$ is used as the order quantity anyway (since the true values are not known), how much can the resulting total variable cost (TVC) exceed the value of TVC when using the order quantity Q^* that would be optimal for the true values of the costs?

To address these two questions, Nick generates the data tables shown in Figure 11.7 in basically the same way as Figure 11.5 was generated. (The third data table is generated from the spreadsheet in Figure 11.6 whereas the other two use the template version of this spreadsheet that applies the square root formula.) The top table directly addresses the first question. It shows that, as the setup cost and unit holding cost vary over their ranges of possible values, the optimal order quantity can vary all the way from 518 to 634. Therefore, the value of Q^* obtained from the square root formula is fairly *sensitive* to the estimates of K and h used in the formula.

However, the cases on the diagonal that have the constant value of 573 do not show this same sensitivity. The reason lies in the square root formula that gives Q^*. The fraction inside the square root sign has h in the denominator and a constant (2D) *times* K in the numerator. Therefore, when both K and h are changed by the same proportional amount, the value of the fraction and of its square root (Q^*) remain unchanged.

Both the second and third data tables show the obvious fact that, as either the setup cost or unit holding cost (or both) increases, the total variable cost also increases, and vice versa for decreases. What is interesting about these tables is how their comparison directly addresses the second question. The second table gives the total variable cost (TVC) when using the correct optimal order quantity (given in the first table) based on the indicated true values of the two costs. The third table shows TVC when using $Q = 573$ based on the estimates ($K = \$115$ and $h = \$4.20$) rather than the (unknown) true values of the two costs. Thus, for each pair of K and h values considered, the difference between TVC in the third table and TVC in the second table is the extra cost being incurred due to the estimates of K and h being wrong. For example, comparing cells D42 and D32 indicates that this extra cost is ($\$2,408 - \$2,395) = \$13$ when the true value of the two costs are $K = \$126.50$ and $h = \$3.78$. Now note for the other cases that this extra cost is never more than $13 (less than 0.6 percent), and it often is much less. Therefore, very little extra cost is incurred if the true values of K and/or h differ from their estimated values by as much as 10 percent. The Total Variable Cost curve on the right side of Figure 11.5 provides an explanation. This curve is so flat in the vicinity of its minimum that even a significant error in pinpointing the true point at which the minimum occurs (due to errors in estimating K and/or h) cannot increase the value of TVC much from its minimum. Having the curve this flat is common for inventory problems. This is reassuring, since it is often difficult to estimate K and h with great precision.

One of the Excel add-ins in your MS Courseware—SensIt—is sometimes helpful for performing sensitivity analysis. One of its features is that it will plot the values of one spreadsheet cell (e.g., the optimal order quantity) for a range of values for another cell (e.g., the unit holding cost).

FIGURE 11.7

Data tables for performing sensitivity analysis on the ACT problem.

	A	B	C	D	E	F	G	H
14	Sensitivity Analysis for Atlantic Coast Tire Corp.							
15								
16					Unit Holding Cost			
17			573	$3.78	$3.99	$4.20	$4.41	$4.62
18			$103.50	573	558	544	531	518
19		Setup	$109.25	589	573	559	545	533
20		Cost	$115.00	604	588	573	559	547
21			$120.75	619	603	587	573	560
22			$126.50	634	617	601	587	573
23					Optimal Order Quantity			
24								
25								
26					Unit Holding Cost			
27			$2,407.49	$3.78	$3.99	$4.20	$4.41	$4.62
28			$103.50	$2,167	$2,226	$2,284	$2,340	$2,395
29		Setup	$109.25	$2,226	$2,287	$2,347	$2,404	$2,461
30		Cost	$115.00	$2,284	$2,347	$2,407	$2,467	$2,525
31			$120.75	$2,340	$2,404	$2,467	$2,528	$2,587
32			$126.50	$2,395	$2,461	$2,525	$2,587	$2,648
33					Total Variable Cost (with Q = Q*)			
34								
35								
36					Unit Holding Cost			
37			$2,407.49	$3.78	$3.99	$4.20	$4.41	$4.62
38			$103.50	$2,167	$2,227	$2,287	$2,347	$2,407
39		Setup	$109.25	$2,227	$2,287	$2,347	$2,407	$2,468
40		Cost	$115.00	$2,287	$2,347	$2,407	$2,468	$2,528
41			$120.75	$2,347	$2,408	$2,468	$2,528	$2,588
42			$126.50	$2,408	$2,468	$2,528	$2,588	$2,648
43					Total Variable Cost (with Q = 573)			

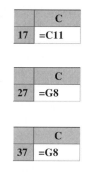

Table

Row input cell: C6

Column input cell: C5

Cancel   OK

	C
17	=C11

	C
27	=G8

	C
37	=G8

The Reaction of ACT Management to the Proposed Inventory Policy

After seeing Nicholas Relich's sensitivity analysis in Figure 11.7, Ashley Collins is satisfied that the proposed order quantity of 573 tires will at least essentially minimize her total variable cost. She also is happy that this reduction from the current order quantity of 1,000 will reduce the current cost by approximately 14 percent.

This analysis of the inventory policy for the 185/70 R13 size tires is a trial run before dealing with all the other size tires. Ashley now would like Nick to use the same approach with the other sizes as well. However, before proceeding, Ashley makes a progress report to her superiors in upper management about the direction in which they are heading. After showing them Figures 11.4 and 11.5, she uses the spreadsheet in Figure 11.6 to summarize the proposed inventory policy for this first size of tire, while emphasizing the nearly 43 percent reduction in average inventory levels (due to decreasing the order quantity by nearly 43 percent) and the 14 percent reduction in the total variable cost.

The reaction of the members of upper management is mixed. They are somewhat pleased to see this much reduction in the inventory levels and costs. However, their goal had been to cut the amount of capital tied up in inventory by a full 50 percent, not just nearly

43 percent. Therefore, they ask Ashley to go back and see if she and Nick can modify their approach in some way to decrease average inventory levels a little further without increasing the total variable cost.

Ashley asks Nick if there is a way of doing this. Nick responds that there is, but he is not sure if management will like it any better. It involves planning to have occasional small inventory shortages—as you will see in the next section.

Review Questions

1. For the basic EOQ model, what are the two types of costs included in the total variable cost? What is the relationship between these two costs at the point where the order quantity equals its optimal value.
2. Does the optimal order quantity increase or decrease if the demand rate is increased? If the setup cost is increased? If the unit holding cost is increased? In each case, what is the intuitive explanation?
3. Can the optimal order quantity change fairly significantly if a fairly small (say, 10 percent) change is made in *either* the setup cost or the unit holding cost? How about if the change is made in *both* costs in *opposite* directions?
4. What happens to the optimal order quantity if *both* the setup cost and the unit holding cost are changed by the same percentage amount in the *same* direction?
5. Would a fairly small (say, 10 percent) error in estimating *either* the setup cost or the unit holding cost increase the total variable cost very much? How about if the error occurs in *both* costs?

11.5 The EOQ Model with Planned Shortages

One of the banes of any inventory manager is the occurrence of an *inventory shortage* (sometimes referred to as a *stockout*)—demand that cannot be met currently because the inventory is depleted. This causes a variety of headaches, including dealing with unhappy customers and having extra record keeping to arrange for filling the demand later (**backorders**) when the inventory can be replenished. By assuming that planned shortages are not allowed, the basic EOQ model satisfies the common desire of managers to avoid shortages as much as possible. (Nevertheless, unplanned shortages can still occur if the demand rate and deliveries do not stay on schedule.)

However, there are situations where permitting limited planned shortages makes sense from a managerial perspective. The most important requirement is that the customers generally are able and willing to accept a reasonable delay in filling their orders if need be. If so, the costs of incurring shortages described in Sections 11.1 and 11.2 (including lost future business) should not be exorbitant. If the cost of holding inventory is high relative to these shortage costs, then lowering the average inventory level by permitting occasional brief shortages may be a sound business decision.

The model described next addresses this kind of situation.

The Assumptions of the Model

This model is a variation of the basic EOQ model described in the preceding two sections. The difference arises in the third of its key assumptions:

Assumptions
1. A constant demand rate.
2. The order quantity to replenish inventory arrives all at once just when desired.
3. Planned shortages are allowed. When a shortage occurs, the affected customers will wait for the product to become available again. Their backorders are filled immediately when the order quantity arrives to replenish inventory.

Under these assumptions, the pattern of inventory levels over time has the appearance shown in Figure 11.8. Compare this pattern with the one in Figure 11.3 for the basic EOQ

FIGURE 11.8

The pattern of inventory levels over time assumed by the EOQ model with planned shortages, where both the order quantity Q and the maximum shortage S are the decision variables.

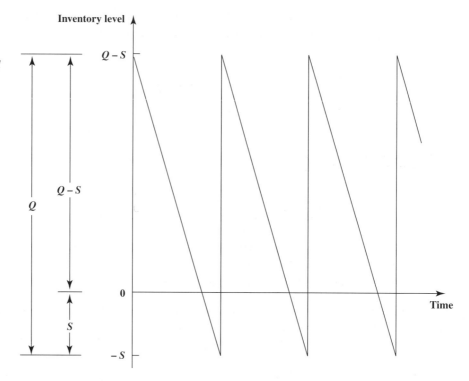

model. The saw-toothed appearance is the same. However, now the inventory levels extend down to negative values that reflect the number of units of the product that are backordered. Letting

    S = maximum shortage (units backordered)

the inventory level is allowed to go down to $-S$, at which point an order quantity Q arrives. S units out of the Q are used to fill the backorders, so the maximum inventory level is $Q - S$.

The Objective of the Model

This model has two decision variables—the order quantity Q and the maximum shortage S. The objective in choosing Q and S is to

        Minimize   TVC = total variable inventory cost per year

This TVC needs to include the same kinds of costs as for the basic EOQ model *plus* the cost of incurring the shortages. Thus,

        TVC = annual setup cost + annual holding cost + annual shortage cost

As for the basic EOQ model,

$$\text{Annual setup cost} = K\frac{D}{Q}$$

where K is the cost of each setup to place an order and D is the total demand per year. Since the unit holding cost h is only incurred on units when the inventory level is positive,

    Annual holding cost = $h \times$ (average inventory level when the level is positive)
                                $\times$ (fraction of time inventory level is positive)

$$= h\left(\frac{Q - S}{2}\right)\left(\frac{Q - S}{Q}\right) = h\frac{(Q - S)^2}{2Q}$$

To obtain a similar expression for the shortage costs described in Sections 11.1 and 11.2, recall that

    p = annual shortage cost per unit short

where the symbol p is used to indicate that this is the *penalty* for incurring the shortage of a unit. Since this unit shortage cost only is incurred during the fraction of the year when a shortage is occurring,

$$\text{Annual shortage cost} = p \times (\text{average shortage level when a shortage occurs})$$
$$\times (\text{fraction of time shortage is occurring})$$

$$= p\left(\frac{S}{2}\right)\left(\frac{S}{Q}\right) = p\,\frac{S^2}{2Q}$$

Combining these expressions gives

$$TVC = K\frac{D}{Q} + h\frac{(Q-S)^2}{2Q} + p\,\frac{S^2}{2Q}$$

The Optimal Inventory Policy

Calculus[2] now can be used to find the values of Q and S that minimize TVC. This leads to the following formulas for their optimal values, Q^* and S^*.

$$Q^* = \sqrt{\frac{h+p}{p}}\,\sqrt{\frac{2KD}{h}}$$

$$S^* = \left(\frac{h}{h+p}\right)Q^*$$

where

D = annual demand rate
K = setup cost
h = unit holding cost
p = unit shortage cost

Note that the second square root in the formula for Q^* is just the *square root formula* given in the preceding section for the basic EOQ model. Thus, the value of Q^* when planned shortages are not allowed is being multiplied here by the first square root. Since $(h+p)$ is larger than p, this first square root is larger than 1. How much larger than 1 depends on how large the unit holding cost h is compared to the unit shortage cost p. In many inventory systems, h is somewhat smaller than p, so Q^* for this model will not be much larger than Q^* for the basic EOQ model.

The formula for S^* indicates that its size compared to Q^* also depends on the relative sizes of h and p. S^* always will be smaller than Q^*, which ensures that the order quantity will be sufficient to cover all the backorders. If h is somewhat smaller than p, S^* will be fairly small compared to Q^*.

After some algebra, these two formulas also yield

$$\text{Maximum inventory level} = Q^* - S^*$$

$$= \sqrt{\frac{p}{h+p}}\,\sqrt{\frac{2KD}{h}}$$

Since the first square root is less than 1 and the second square root is the value of Q^* when planned shortages are not allowed, the maximum inventory level for this model always will be less than for the basic EOQ model. This level can be considerably less if h is fairly large compared to p. This is good, since we want the inventory levels to come down when the unit holding cost goes up. Having shortages a significant fraction of the time also helps to drive down the annual holding cost.

Therefore, this model does a good job of reducing the annual holding cost well below that for the basic EOQ model when h is fairly large compared to p. When p is considerably

---

[2]This involves taking the partial derivatives of TVC with respect to Q and S, setting these partial derivatives equal to 0, and then solving this system of two equations for the two unknowns.

larger than h instead, the trade-offs between the cost factors will lead to an optimal inventory policy that is not much different than for the basic EOQ model.

Application to the ACT Case Study

Nicholas Relich begins the application of this model by pinning down the following estimates of the cost factors given in Section 11.1:

$$K = \$115 \qquad h = \$4.20 \qquad p = \$7.50$$

Plugging these costs into the two formulas then gives the following results:

$$Q^* = 716 \text{ tires} \qquad \text{(order quantity)}$$

$$S^* = 257 \text{ tires} \qquad \text{(maximum shortage)}$$

$$Q^* - S^* = 459 \text{ tires} \qquad \text{(maximum inventory level)}$$

The resulting total variable inventory cost per year is

$$\text{TVC} = \$1,928$$

The value of S^* also leads to identifying the reorder point for this inventory policy.

$$\text{Reorder point} = -S^* + \text{(daily demand) (lead time)}$$

$$= -257 \text{ tires} + (24 \text{ tires/day}) (9 \text{ days})$$

$$= -41 \text{ tires}$$

Thus, according to this (unusual) policy, the order for purchasing another 716 tires from Eversafe should be placed when the number of tires backordered reaches 41. The delivery then should arrive nine working days later when the number of tires backordered reaches approximately 257.

Your MS Courseware includes two Excel templates for performing all these calculations (and more) for this model. Figure 11.9 illustrates the use of either template for the ACT problem. Both templates use the spreadsheet and the equations for column G shown in the figure. One template (the Solver version) enables you to experiment with various values in the changing cells and then to use the Excel Solver to obtain the optimal values. The other template (the analytical version) instead uses the formulas for Q^* and S^* (see the

FIGURE 11.9

The results obtained for the ACT problem by applying either of the Excel templates (Solver version or analytical version) for the EOQ model with planned shortages.

	A	B	C	D	E	F	G
1		EOQ Model with Planned Shortages for Atlantic Coast Tire Corp.					
2							
3			Data			Results	
4		D =	6000	(demand/year)		Max Inventory Level =	458.94
5		K =	$115	(setup cost)			
6		h =	$4.20	(unit holding cost)		Annual Setup Cost =	$963.77
7		p =	$7.50	(unit shortage cost)		Annual Holding Cost =	$617.80
8						Annual Shortage Cost =	$345.97
9			Decision			Total Variable Cost =	$1,927.53
10		Q =	715.94	(order quantity)			
11		S =	257.00	(maximum shortage)			

Solver Parameters

Set Target Cell: $G$9

Equal To: ○ Max ● Min ○

By Changing Cells:

$C$10:$C$11

Solver Options

☐ Assume Linear Model

☑ Assume Non-Negative

	G
4	=C10–C11
5	
6	=C5*C4/C10
7	=C6*(G4^2)/(2*C10)
8	=C7*((C10–G4)^2)/(2*C10)
9	=SUM(G6:G8)

Analytical Version:

	C
10	=SQRT(2*C4*C5/C6)*SQRT((C7+C6)/C7)
11	=(C6/(C6+C7))*C10

equations entered into cells C10 and C11 in the lower right-hand corner of the figure) to automatically calculate the optimal values for the changing cells, as shown in the figure.

Table 11.1 compares this problem's optimal inventory policies and costs (rounded to the nearest dollar) for the basic EOQ model (as obtained in Figure 11.6) and the current EOQ model with planned shortages. Note the rather substantial changes that result from having planned shortages. A sizable increase in the order quantity leads to a corresponding reduction in the annual setup cost (the administrative cost of placing orders). Despite the larger order quantity, the maximum inventory level goes down considerably because this level of 459 *equals* the order quantity of 716 *minus* the maximum shortage of 257. The combination of a smaller maximum inventory level and a large maximum shortage (so the inventory is depleted much of the time) yields nearly a 50 percent reduction in the annual holding cost. The price that is paid for the reductions in the annual setup cost and the annual holding cost is the new annual shortage cost of $346. Nevertheless, the total variable cost goes down from $2,407 to $1,928, a 20 percent reduction.

As ACT's inventory manager, Ashley Collins always has tried to avoid inventory shortages. Therefore, when Nicholas Relich shows her these results, she is surprised to see the cost reductions achieved by having planned shortages. Nick explains that the additional flexibility from allowing shortages enables finding the best trade-off from all three cost factors—setup costs, holding costs, and shortage costs. When shortages are very undesirable, so the unit shortage cost is extremely high, the results from this model will be virtually the same as for the basic EOQ model, with only a tiny maximum shortage included. However, when the unit shortage cost is only modestly larger than the unit holding cost, as for this ACT problem, then the kinds of substantial changes shown in Table 11.1 will result from having planned shortages.

When Ashley shows these results to the interested members of upper management, their reaction is mainly skepticism and concern. Although they like the large reduction in inventory levels, they are very dubious that intentionally causing substantial shortages can be a rational policy. The company has built up a long-standing reputation for providing good service to its customers, and management does not want to throw this away by suddenly forcing some of ACT's customers to wait a substantial time to have their orders filled. Ashley's boss expressed this feeling pungently: "We already have more shortages than I like because of larger-than-usual orders from our customers or delays in the deliveries from Eversafe. But at least these are brief unavoidable shortages that don't upset our customers too much. I certainly don't want to alienate a lot of our customers by purposely making them wait. How do I explain to them that we care more about our inventory costs than the quality of service we are providing? Regardless of what your mathematics might say, the company's reputation for good service is one of our most precious assets and we need to preserve it!"

Upon hearing about this reaction, Nick remarks to Ashley that they apparently have greatly underestimated the true value of the unit shortage cost. With a good estimate that

TABLE 11.1 **Comparison of the Basic EOQ Model and the EOQ Model with Planned Shortages for the ACT Problem**

Quantity	Basic EOQ Model	EOQ Model with Planned Shortages
Order quantity	573	716
Maximum shortage	0	257
Maximum inventory level	573	459
Reorder point	216	−41
Annual setup cost	$1,204	$ 964
Annual holding cost	1,204	618
Annual shortage cost	0	346
Total variable cost	2,407	1,928

accurately reflects management's feelings about the long-range damage done by incurring shortages, the optimal inventory policy according to this model can indeed be a very rational policy. However, it is management's prerogative to decide whether to have any planned shortages, and they have decided against them in this case, so this particular model should not be used further. Instead, Ashley's boss tells her to go ahead with the kind of inventory policies generated by the basic EOQ model—policies with no planned shortages.

Review Questions

1. When does it make sense from a managerial perspective to permit planned inventory shortages?
2. How do the assumptions for the EOQ model with planned shortages differ from those for the basic EOQ model?
3. What are the decision variables for the EOQ model with planned shortages?
4. What are the kinds of costs included in the total variable cost for this model?
5. Is the optimal order quantity for this model larger or smaller than this quantity for the basic EOQ model? What is the corresponding comparison for the maximum inventory level?
6. What is the objection of ACT management to having planned shortages?

11.6 The EOQ Model with Quantity Discounts

Now we see an important new development in the ACT case study. Eversafe management has reacted quickly after receiving the bad news from Ashley Collins that ACT soon will be substantially reducing its individual order quantities for the various Eversafe tire sizes. Although Eversafe's annual sales to ACT will remain the same, achieving these sales through many more, but smaller, deliveries than before would significantly increase Eversafe's costs. Therefore, to try to persuade ACT from reducing its order quantities so much, Eversafe management has decided to offer ACT **quantity discounts** for placing relatively large orders.

Quantity Discounts

Table 11.2 shows how these discounts would work for the 185/70 R13 size of Eversafe tires. The discounts begin with order quantities of at least 750 tires. Ordering between 750 and 1,999 tires reduces ACT's purchase cost per tire by 1 percent from the standard $20 price down to $19.80. Ordering at least 2,000 tires provides a 2 percent discount down to $19.60 for each tire. For example, ordering 2,000 tires would cost 2,000 ($19.60) = $39,200, whereas obtaining the same 2,000 tires through placing a sequence of four orders for 500 tires each would cost 4(500)($20) = $40,000.

The drawback of placing larger orders is that this increases the average inventory level and thereby increases the holding cost. Therefore, Nicholas Relich and Ashley Collins need to do a careful cost analysis to determine whether it is worthwhile to take advantage of these quantity discounts.

Cost Analysis

For the basic EOQ model, the only components of the total variable inventory cost per year (TVC) are the annual setup cost and the annual holding cost, since the annual cost of purchasing the product is a *fixed cost*. Now, with quantity discounts, this annual acquisition

TABLE 11.2   The Quantity Discounts Being Offered to ACT

Discount Quantity	Order Quantity	Discount	Unit Cost
1	0 to 749	0	$20.00
2	750 to 1,999	1%	19.80
3	2,000 or more	2%	19.60

cost becomes a *variable cost.* Even though ACT will continue to purchase a fixed total of 6,000 tires of the 185/70 R13 size per year, the annual acquisition cost now depends on the size of the individual order quantities. Therefore, to adapt the basic EOQ model (as presented in Section 11.3) to incorporate quantity discounts, the total variable cost now is

$$\text{TVC} = \text{annual acquisition cost} + \text{annual setup cost} + \text{annual holding cost}$$

$$= cD + K\frac{D}{Q} + h\frac{Q}{2}$$

where

c = unit acquisition cost (as given in Table 11.2)
D = annual demand rate = 6,000
K = setup cost = \$115
Q = order quantity (the decision variable)
h = unit holding cost

As described in Section 11.1, ACT's unit holding cost has been estimated to be 21 percent of the average value of the tires. Thus,

$$I = \text{inventory holding cost rate}$$

$$= 0.21$$

Now, the value of a tire (its purchase price) depends on which discount category is being used, so

$$h = Ic = 0.21c$$

Table 11.3 shows the calculation of this unit holding cost for each of the discount categories.

Given the values in Table 11.3, Figure 11.10 plots the total variable cost TVC versus the order quantity Q for each of the discount categories. For each curve, the value of Q that gives the minimum value of TVC can be calculated from the *square root formula* for the basic EOQ model, $Q = \sqrt{2KD/h}$, namely, $Q = 573$ for category 1 (as before), $Q = 576$ for category 2, and $Q = 579$ for category 3. However, only the solid part of each curve extends over the range of feasible values of Q (as given in the second column of Table 11.2) for that category. The feasible part of the category 1 curve includes its minimum (at $Q = 573$), but this is not the case for the other two curves. The feasible part of the category 2 curve continually increases over its entire feasible range from $Q = 750$ to $Q = 1,999$, so the *feasible* minimum of this curve is at $Q = 750$. Similarly, the feasible part of the category 3 curve continually increases from its starting point of $Q = 2,000$ onward, so its *feasible* minimum is at $Q = 2,000$.

The goal is to find the value of Q that gives the overall minimum cost. This requires comparing the total variable cost at the *feasible* minimum of the respective curves in Figure 11.10. The calculations needed to make this comparison are summarized in Table 11.4, where the values of c and h are taken from Table 11.3. The rightmost column of Table 11.4 shows that the minimum *total variable cost* is obtained by using discount category 2 with an order quantity of 750 tires, which yields TVC = \$121,279.

TABLE 11.3   The Unit Holding Cost for ACT's Various Discount Categories

Discount Category	Price c	Unit Holding Cost $h = Ic = 0.21c$
1	\$20	0.21(\$20) = \$4.20
2	19.80	0.21(\$19.80) = \$4.158
3	19.60	0.21(\$19.60) = \$4.116

FIGURE 11.10

The curve of total variable cost (TVC) versus order quantity (Q) for each discount category, where the solid part of the curve extends over the feasible range of order quantities. The feasible minimum occurs at Q = 750, with TVC = $121,279.

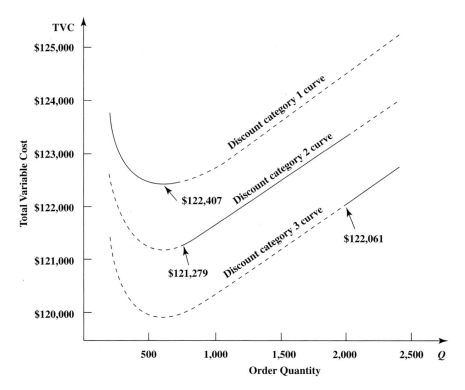

TABLE 11.4   A Cost Comparison of the Best Order Quantities for the Respective Discount Categories

		Annual Costs			
Discount Category	Best Order Quantity	Acquisition Cost $= 6{,}000c$	Setup Cost $= \$115\dfrac{6{,}000}{Q}$	Holding Cost $= h\dfrac{Q}{2}$	Total (TVC) $= Sum$
1	Q = 573	$120,000	$1,204	$1,204	$122,407
2	Q = 750	118,800	920	1,559	121,279
3	Q = 2,000	117,600	345	4,116	122,061

An Excel template is available in your MS Courseware for performing all these calculations for you automatically. Figure 11.11 illustrates its use on this same problem. (Although the template's equations are not included in this figure, they can be viewed in this chapter's Excel file.) In addition to all the results in Table 11.4, the template also includes a column labeled EOQ (economic order quantity) that uses the *square root formula* to calculate the value of Q at the minimum of each discount category curve (including its dashed part) in Figure 11.10. The bottom of the template then gives the optimal order quantity and the corresponding total variable cost.

The Conclusion of the ACT Case Study

When Ashley Collins presents these results to the relevant members of upper management, she points out three immediate benefits of the proposed inventory policy.

1. A substantial reduction in the order quantity (from the current 1,000 down to 750) would provide a substantial reduction in the average inventory level (which is half of the order quantity) and a substantial reduction in the resulting holding cost.

2. The threat to reduce the order quantity even further (as suggested by the basic EOQ model) has prodded Eversafe into providing quantity discounts to ACT.

FIGURE 11.11

The application of the Excel template (analytical) for the EOQ model with quantity discounts to the ACT problem.

	A	B	C	D	E	F	G	H	I	J	K
1			EOQ Model with Quantity Discounts (Analytical) for Atlantic Coast Tire Corp.								
2											
3			Data								
4		D =	6000	(demand/year)							
5		K =	$115	(setup cost)							
6		I =	0.21	(inventory holding cost rate)							
7		N =	3	(number of discount categories)							
8											
9								Annual	Annual	Annual	Total
10				Range of order quantities				Purchase	Setup	Holding	Variable
11		Category	Price	Lower Limit	Upper Limit	EOQ	Q*	Cost	Cost	Cost	Cost
12		1	$20.00	0	749	573.21	573.21	$120,000	$1,204	$1,204	$122,407
13		2	$19.80	750	1999	576.10	750.00	$118,800	$920	$1,559	$121,279
14		3	$19.60	2000	10000000	579.03	2000.00	$117,600	$345	$4,116	$122,061
15											
16											
17											
18				Results							
19				Optimal Q =		750					
20			Total Variable Cost =			$121,279					

3. The resulting reduction in the total annual inventory cost from that for the current policy ($120,000 in acquisition cost plus the $2,790 in setup and holding costs calculated at the end of Section 11.3) would exceed $1,500 for just this one size of tire. Extending this approach to the other tire sizes should greatly multiply this saving.

Although some members of upper management express mild disappointment that the original goal of reducing average inventory levels by at least 50 percent has not been reached, they are very pleased by the quantity discount obtained from Eversafe. Even a 1 percent saving in acquisition costs adds substantially to ACT's profit margin, and the additional saving in overall setup and holding costs also is welcome. Consequently, upper management asks Ashley to continue working with Nicholas Relich to extend the same approach throughout the remainder of the inventory system as well.

Review Questions

1. What is a quantity discount?
2. When quantity discounts are offered, what additional type of cost needs to be included in the total variable inventory cost?
3. What is the relationship between the unit holding cost and the price paid for the items in inventory?
4. What is the best order quantity for a discount category whose *minimum* order quantity exceeds the order quantity calculated from the square root formula for the basic EOQ model? What would it be for a discount category whose *maximum* order quantity is less than the order quantity given by the square root formula?

11.7 The EOQ Model with Gradual Replenishment

One of the assumptions of the basic EOQ model is that the order quantity to replenish inventory arrives *all at once* just when desired. Having the order delivered all at once is common for retailers or wholesalers (such as ACT), or even for manufacturers receiving raw materials from their vendors. However, the situation often is different with manufacturers

FIGURE 11.12

The pattern of inventory levels over time—rising during a production run and dropping afterward—for the EOQ model with gradual replenishment.

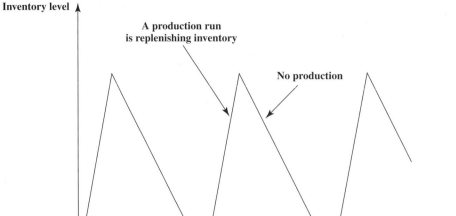

when they replenish their finished-goods and intermediate-goods inventories internally by conducting intermittent production runs. Assuming the production run takes a significant period of time and the items are transferred to inventory as they are produced (rather than all at once at the end of the run), this assumption does not hold. The *EOQ model with gradual replenishment* is designed to fit this situation instead.

This model assumes that the pattern of inventory levels over time is the one shown in Figure 11.12. When a production run is under way, the inventory is being replenished at the rate of production while withdrawals are simultaneously occurring at the demand rate. However, once the production run concludes, the inventory level drops according to the demand rate. Later, the production facilities are set up again to start another production run when the inventory level drops to 0. This pattern continues indefinitely.

In this context, the *order quantity Q* is the number of units produced during a production run. This number is commonly referred to as the **production lot size.**

Except for the change in how inventory is replenished, the assumptions for this model are the same as for the basic EOQ model—as summarized below.

Assumptions
1. A constant demand rate.
2. A production run is scheduled to begin each time the inventory level drops to 0, and this production replenishes inventory at a constant rate throughout the duration of the run.
3. Planned shortages are not allowed.

An Example: The SOCA Problem

SOCA, a television manufacturing company, produces its own speakers for assembly into its television sets. To maintain its production schedule for television sets, the company needs to have 1,000 speakers available for assembly per day. Each time an order is placed to produce more speakers, the rate of production is 3,000 speakers per day until the order is filled, after which the production facilities are used for other purposes until another production run for speakers is needed. Since this production rate is three times the rate at which the speakers are needed, speakers are being produced only one-third of the time.

The current policy for managing SOCA's inventory of speakers is summarized below.

Current Inventory Policy
1. Daily demand rate = 1,000 speakers per day.
2. Daily production rate = 3,000 speakers per day (when producing).
3. The production facilities get set up to start a production run each time the inventory level is scheduled to drop to 0.
4. Each production run produces 30,000 speakers over a period of 10 working days, so another 20 working days elapse before the next production run is needed.

This policy leads to the pattern of inventory levels over time shown in Figure 11.12. Thus, the inventory level fluctuates between 0 and a maximum inventory level that is somewhat under 30,000 speakers. The reason for not reaching 30,000 is that speakers also are being withdrawn from inventory for assembly into television sets while a production run is under way. Consequently,

$$\text{Maximum inventory level} = \text{production lot size} - \text{demand during production run}$$

$$= 30{,}000 \text{ speakers} - (10 \text{ days})(1{,}000 \text{ speakers/day})$$

$$= 30{,}000 \text{ speakers} - 10{,}000 \text{ speakers}$$

$$= 20{,}000 \text{ speakers}$$

Therefore,

$$\text{Average inventory level} = \frac{1}{2}(\text{maximum inventory level})$$

$$= 10{,}000 \text{ speakers}$$

SOCA's costs associated with this inventory policy are summarized below.

c = unit production cost = \$12 per speaker produced
K = setup cost for a production run = \$12,000
h = unit holding cost = \$3.60 per speaker in inventory per year

With 250 working days per year, the number of speakers needed per year is

$$D = \text{annual demand rate}$$

$$= (1{,}000 \text{ speakers/day})(250 \text{ days})$$

$$= 250{,}000 \text{ speakers}$$

Excluding setup costs, the annual cost of producing these speakers is fixed at (\$12/speaker) (250,000 speakers) = \$3 million, regardless of the choice of the production lot size. One cost that does depend on this lot size is

$$\text{Annual setup cost} = K\frac{D}{Q}$$

$$= (\$12{,}000/\text{setup})\ \frac{250{,}000 \text{ speakers}}{30{,}000 \text{ speakers/setup}}$$

$$= \$100{,}000$$

The other variable cost is

$$\text{Annual holding cost} = h\ (\text{average inventory level})$$

$$= (\$3.60/\text{speaker})(10{,}000 \text{ speakers})$$

$$= \$36{,}000$$

Therefore, SOCA's total variable inventory cost per year is

$$\text{TVC} = \text{annual setup cost} + \text{annual holding cost}$$

$$= \$136{,}000$$

SOCA management now wants to determine whether this total cost can be decreased by adjusting the production lot size appropriately.

The Optimal Inventory Policy for This Model

SOCA's optimal production lot size can be obtained directly from a *square root formula* that is similar to the one for the basic EOQ model. The new formula is

$$Q^* = \sqrt{\frac{2KD}{h\left(1 - \dfrac{D}{R}\right)}}$$

where

D = annual demand rate
R = annual production rate if producing continuously
K = setup cost
h = unit holding cost

For the SOCA example, the only new symbol is

$$R = \text{(daily production rate) (number of working days per year)}$$

$$= (3{,}000)\,(250)$$

$$= 750{,}000$$

Therefore, its optimal production lot size is

$$Q^* = \sqrt{\frac{2(12{,}000)(250{,}000)}{3.60\left(1 - \dfrac{250{,}000}{750{,}000}\right)}}$$

$$= 50{,}000$$

Rather than producing only 30,000 speakers over each production run of 10 days, SOCA should extend the run length to 16⅔ days to produce this larger quantity.

The corresponding total variable inventory cost per year is calculated from the following formula:

$$\text{TVC} = \text{annual setup cost} + \text{annual holding cost}$$

$$= K\frac{D}{Q} + h\frac{Q}{2}\left(1 - \frac{D}{R}\right)$$

so SOCA's cost for using $Q = 50{,}000$ is

$$\text{TVC} = \$12{,}000\,\frac{250{,}000}{50{,}000} + \$3.60(25{,}000)\left(1 - \frac{250{,}000}{750{,}000}\right)$$

$$= \$60{,}000 + \$60{,}000$$

$$= \$120{,}000$$

a reduction of $16,000 from the cost for the current inventory policy.

The new square root formula is derived in the same way as described for the basic EOQ model at the end of Section 11.4. The only reason the new formula differs from the one for the basic EOQ model is that the annual holding cost for the basic EOQ model now is being multiplied by the factor $(1 - D/R)$. The reason for this factor is that the maximum inventory level has changed from Q to

Maximum inventory level = production lot size − demand during production run

$$= Q - \frac{D}{R}Q$$

$$= \left(1 - \frac{D}{R}\right)Q$$

Your MS Courseware includes two Excel templates for this model. Since they use the same spreadsheet, both templates are illustrated in Figure 11.13 for the SOCA example. One template (the Solver version) allows you to enter any production lot size into the changing cell (C10) and then, if desired, use the Solver to find the optimal value. The other template (the analytical version) uses the formula for Q^* (entered into cell C10) to solve for the optimal production lot size automatically.

A Broader Perspective of the SOCA Example

The ACT case study considered in the preceding sections focused on managing the inventory of one type of tire. The demand for this product is generated by the company's cus-

FIGURE 11.13

The results obtained for the SOCA problem by applying either of the Excel templates (Solver version or analytical version) for the EOQ model with gradual replenishment.

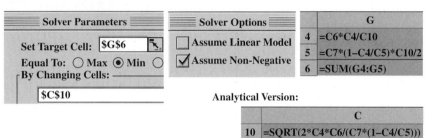

	A	B	C	D	E	F	G
1		EOQ Model with Gradual Replenishment for SOCA					
2							
3			Data			Results	
4		D =	250000	(demand/year)		Annual Setup Cost =	$60,000.00
5		R =	750000	(production rate)		Annual Holding Cost =	$60,000.00
6		K =	$12,000	(unit setup cost)		Total Variable Cost =	$120,000.00
7		h =	$3.60	(unit holding cost)			
8							
9			Decision				
10		Q =	50000	(production lot size)			

Solver Parameters

Set Target Cell: $G$6

Equal To: ○ Max ● Min ○
By Changing Cells:

$C$10

Solver Options

☐ Assume Linear Model
☑ Assume Non-Negative

	G
4	=C6*C4/C10
5	=C7*(1–C4/C5)*C10/2
6	=SUM(G4:G5)

Analytical Version:

	C
10	=SQRT(2*C4*C6/(C7*(1–C4/C5)))

tomers (various retailers) that purchase the tire to replenish their inventories according to their own schedules. ACT has no control over this demand. Because the tire is sold separately from other products, its demand does not even depend on the demand for any of the company's other products. Such demand is referred to as **independent demand.**

The situation is different for the SOCA example. Here, the product under consideration—television speakers—is just one component being assembled into the company's final product—television sets. Consequently, the demand for the speakers depends on the demand for the television set. The pattern of this demand for the speakers is determined internally by the production schedule that the company establishes for the television sets. Such demand is referred to as **dependent demand.**

SOCA produces a considerable number of products—various parts and subassemblies—that become components of the television sets. Like the speakers, these various products also are *dependent-demand products.*

Because of the dependencies and interrelationships involved, managing the inventories of dependent-demand products can be considerably more complicated than for independent-demand products. A popular technique for assisting in this task is **material requirements planning,** abbreviated as **MRP.** MRP is a computer-based system for planning, scheduling, and controlling the production of all the components of a final product. The system begins by "exploding" the product by breaking it down into all its subassemblies and then into all its individual component parts. A production schedule is then developed, using the demand and lead time for each component to determine the demand and lead time for the subsequent component in the process. In addition to a *master production schedule* for the final product, a *bill of materials* provides detailed information about all its components. Inventory status records give the current inventory levels, number of units on order, and so on, for all the components. When more units of a component need to be ordered, the MRP system automatically generates either a purchase order to the vendor or a work order to the internal department that produces the component.

When the new square root formula was used to calculate the optimal production lot size for SOCA's speakers, a very large quantity (50,000 speakers) was obtained. This enables having relatively infrequent setups to initiate production runs (only once every 50 working days). However, it also causes large average inventory levels (16,667 speakers), which leads to a large total variable inventory cost per year of $120,000.

The basic reason for this large cost is the high setup cost of $K = \$12,000$ for each production run. The setup cost is so sizable because the production facilities need to be set up again from scratch each time. Consequently, even with only five production runs per year, the annual setup cost is $60,000, and the large inventories lead to another $60,000 in annual holding costs.

Rather than continuing to tolerate a $12,000 setup cost in the future, another option for SOCA is to seek ways to reduce this setup cost. One possibility is to develop methods for quickly transferring machines from one use to another. Another is to dedicate a group of production facilities to the production of speakers so they would remain set up between production runs in preparation for beginning another run whenever needed.

Suppose the setup cost could be drastically reduced from $12,000 all the way down to $K = \$120$. This would reduce the optimal production lot size from 50,000 speakers down to $Q^* = 5,000$ speakers, so a new production run lasting $1\frac{2}{3}$ working days would be initiated every 5 working days. This also would reduce the total variable inventory cost per year from $120,000 down to only $12,000. By having such frequent (but inexpensive) production runs, the speakers would be produced *just in time* for their assembly into television sets.

Just in time actually is a well-developed philosophy for managing inventories. A **just-in-time (JIT) inventory system** places great emphasis on reducing inventory levels to a bare minimum, and so providing the items just in time as they are needed. This philosophy was first developed in Japan, beginning with the Toyota Company in the late 1950s, and is given part of the credit for the remarkable gains in Japanese productivity through much of the late 20th century. The philosophy also has become popular in other parts of the world, including the United States, in more recent years.

Although the just-in-time philosophy sometimes is misinterpreted as being incompatible with using an EOQ model (since the latter gives a large order quantity when the setup cost is large), they actually are complementary. A JIT inventory system focuses on finding ways to greatly reduce the setup costs so that the optimal order quantity will be small. Such a system also seeks ways to reduce the lead time for the delivery of an order, since this reduces the uncertainty about the number of units that will be needed when the delivery occurs. Another emphasis is on improving preventive maintenance so that the required production facilities will be available to produce the units when they are needed. Still another emphasis is on improving the production process to guarantee good quality. Providing just the right number of units just in time does not provide any leeway for including defective units.

In more general terms, the focus of the just-in-time philosophy is on *avoiding waste* wherever it might occur in the production process. One form of waste is unnecessary inventory. Others are unnecessarily large setup costs, unnecessarily long lead times, production facilities that are not operational when they are needed, and defective items. Minimizing these forms of waste are key components of superior inventory management.

Review Questions

1. In what type of situation is it common to have the replenishment of inventory occur over a period of time rather than instantaneously?

2. In what way do the assumptions for the model in this section differ from those for the basic EOQ model?

3. For the current model, why is the maximum inventory level less than the production lot size?

4. In what way does the square root formula for this model differ from the square root formula for the basic EOQ model?

5. What is the distinction between *independent-demand* and *dependent-demand* products?

6. What is the name of a popular technique for planning, scheduling, and controlling the production of the components of a final product?

7. What is the emphasis of a just-in-time inventory system in regard to inventory levels?

8. In more general terms, what is the focus of the just-in-time philosophy?

11.8 Summary

Scientific inventory management in this modern age involves using mathematical models to seek an optimal inventory policy. With the help of a computerized information processing system to maintain a record of current inventory levels, this policy signals when and how much to replenish inventory.

Determining the appropriate order quantity for replenishing inventory of a particular product each time involves examining the trade-off between the setup cost incurred by initiating the replenishment and the costs associated with holding the product in inventory (including the cost of capital tied up in inventory). When planned inventory shortages are allowed, the costs associated with such shortages (including lost future sales because of dissatisfaction with the service) also need to be considered. The direct cost of acquiring units of the product is not relevant if the annual acquisition cost is fixed. However, if quantity discounts that lower the purchase price for larger orders are available, the annual acquisition cost becomes part of the total variable inventory cost per year that is to be minimized.

The basic *economic order quantity* (EOQ) model is a particularly popular inventory model because of its simplicity and wide applicability. It assumes a constant demand rate, instantaneous replenishment of inventory when desired, and no planned shortages. Although these assumptions seldom are completely satisfied, they do provide reasonable approximations of many inventory systems. These assumptions lead to a relatively simple *square root formula* for calculating the optimal order quantity.

Three variations of the basic EOQ model also are considered here. One allows planned shortages. Another considers quantity discounts. The third variation deals with gradual replenishment of inventory, such as occurs when a manufacturer replenishes its inventory internally by conducting a production run over a period of time.

All the EOQ models are based on having a fixed known demand, at least as an approximation. In many inventory systems, there actually is considerable uncertainty about what the demand will be. The next chapter focuses on that kind of situation.

Glossary

Acquisition cost   The direct cost of acquiring units of a product, either through purchasing or manufacturing, to replenish inventory. (Section 11.2)   449

Backorder   An order that cannot be filled currently because the inventory is depleted, but will be filled later when the inventory is replenished. (Section 11.5)   461

Constant demand rate   A fixed rate at which units need to be withdrawn from inventory. (Section 11.3)   452

Continuous-review system   An inventory system whose current inventory level is monitored on a continuous basis. (Section 11.3)   453

Demand   The number of units of a product that will need to be withdrawn from inventory during a specific period. (Introduction)   446

Dependent demand   Demand for a product that is dependent upon the demand for another product, generally because the former product is a component of the latter product. (Section 11.7)   473

Fixed cost   A cost that remains the same regardless of the decisions made. (Section 11.2)   450

Holding cost   The cost associated with holding units of a product in inventory. (Section 11.2)   450

Independent demand   Demand for a product that is independent of the demand for all other products. (Section 11.7)   473

Inventory   Goods being stored for future use or sale. (Introduction)   445

Inventory policy   A rule that specifies when to replenish inventory and by how much. (Introduction, Section 11.2)   445, 450

Just-in-time (JIT) inventory system   A system that places great emphasis on reducing inventory levels to a bare minimum, as well as eliminating other forms of waste in the production process. (Section 11.7)   474

Lead time   The amount of time between the placement of an order and the delivery of the order quantity. (Section 11.3)   452

Material requirements planning (MRP)   A computer-based system for planning, scheduling, and controlling the production of all the components of a final product. (Section 11.7)   473

Opportunity cost   When capital is used in a certain way, its opportunity cost is the lost return because alternate opportunities for using this capital must be forgone. (Section 11.1)   448

Order quantity   The number of units of a product being acquired, either through purchasing or manufacturing, to replenish inventory. (Section 11.1)   446

Periodic-review system   An inventory system whose inventory level is only checked periodically. (Section 11.3)   453

Production lot size   The number of units of a product being produced during a production run. (Section 11.7)   470

Quantity discounts   Reductions in the unit acquisition cost of a product that are offered for ordering a relatively large quantity. (Section 11.6)   468

Reorder point   The inventory level at which an order is placed. (Section 11.3)   452

Safety stock   Extra inventory being carried to safeguard against delivery delays. (Section 11.3)   453

Scientific inventory management   A management science approach to inventory management that involves using a mathematical model to seek and implement an optimal inventory policy. (Introduction)   445

Setup cost   The fixed cost associated with initiating the replenishment of inventory, whether the administrative cost of purchasing the product or the cost of setting up a production run to manufacture the product. (Section 11.2)   449

Shortage cost   The cost incurred when there is a need to withdraw units from inventory and there are none available. (Section 11.2)   450

Square root formula   The formula for calculating the optimal order quantity for the basic EOQ model. (Section 11.4)   458

Variable cost   A cost that is affected by the decisions made. (Section 11.2)   450

Learning Aids for This Chapter in Your MS Courseware

"Ch. 11—Known Demand Inventories" Excel File:

Template for the *Basic EOQ Model* (Solver version)
Template for the *Basic EOQ Model* (Analytical version)
Template for the *EOQ Model with Planned Shortages* (Solver version)
Template for the *EOQ Model with Planned Shortages* (Analytical version)
Template for the *EOQ Model with Quantity Discounts* (Analytical version only)

Template for the *EOQ Model with Gradual Replenishment* (Solver version)
Template for the *EOQ Model with Gradual Replenishment* (Analytical version)

Excel Add-In:

SensIt (can be useful for sensitivity analysis)

Problems

To the left of the following problems (or their parts), we have inserted the symbol E (for Excel) whenever one of the above templates can be helpful. The symbol E* indicates that a template (or an equivalent spreadsheet) should definitely be used (unless your instructor gives you contrary instructions). An asterisk on the problem number indicates that at least a partial answer is given in the back of the book.

11.1.* Tim Madsen is the purchasing agent for Computer Center, a large discount computer store. He has recently added the hottest new computer, the Power model, to the store's stock of goods. Sales of this model now are running at about 13 per week. Tim purchases these computers directly from the manufacturer at a unit cost of $3,000, where each shipment takes half a week to arrive.

   Tim routinely uses the basic EOQ model to determine the store's inventory policy for each of its more important products. For this purpose, he estimates that the annual cost of holding items in inventory is 20 percent of their purchase cost. He also estimates that the administrative cost associated with placing each order is $75.

E*   a. Tim currently is using the policy of ordering five Power model computers at a time, where each order is timed to have the shipment arrive just about when the inventory of these computers is being depleted. Use the Solver version of the Excel template for the basic EOQ model to determine the various annual costs being incurred with this policy.

E*   b. Use this same spreadsheet to generate a data table that shows how these costs would change if the order quantity were changed to the following values: 5, 7, 9, . . . , 25.

E*   c. Use the Solver to find the optimal order quantity.

E*   d. Now use the analytical version of the Excel template for the basic EOQ model (which applies the square root formula) to find the optimal order quantity. Compare the results (including the various costs) with those obtained in part c.

   e. Verify your answer for the optimal order quantity obtained in part d by applying the square root formula by hand.

   f. With the optimal order quantity obtained above, how frequently will orders need to be placed on the average? What should the approximate inventory level be when each order is placed?

   g. How much does the optimal inventory policy reduce the total variable inventory cost per year for Power model computers from that for the policy described in part a? What is the percentage reduction?

11.2. The Blue Cab Company is the primary taxi company in the city of Maintown. It uses gasoline at the rate of 8,500 gallons per month. Because this is such a major cost, the company has made a special arrangement with the Amicable Petroleum Company to purchase a huge quantity of gasoline at a reduced price of $1.05 per gallon every few months. The cost of arranging for each order, including placing the gasoline into storage, is $1,000. The cost of holding the gasoline in storage is estimated to be $0.01 per gallon per month.

E*   a. Use the Solver version of the Excel template for the basic EOQ model to determine the costs that would be incurred annually if the gasoline were to be ordered monthly.

E*   b. Use this same spreadsheet to generate a data table that shows how these costs would change if the number of months between orders were to be changed to the following values: 1, 2, 3, . . . , 10.

E*   c. Use the Solver to find the optimal order quantity.

E*   d. Now use the analytical version of the Excel template for the basic EOQ model to find the optimal order quantity. Compare the results (including the various costs) with those obtained in part c.

   e. Verify your answer for the optimal order quantity obtained in part d by applying the square root formula by hand.

E 11.3. Computronics is a manufacturer of calculators, currently producing 200 per week. One component for every calculator is a liquid crystal display (LCD), which the company purchases from Displays, Inc. (DI), for $1 per LCD. Computronics management wants to avoid any shortage of LCDs, since this would disrupt production, so DI guarantees a delivery time of ½ week on each order. The placement of each order is estimated to require one hour of clerical time, with a direct cost of $15 per hour plus overhead costs of another $5 per hour. A rough estimate has been made that the annual cost of capital tied up in Computronics's inventory is 15 percent of the value of the inventory. Other costs associated with storing and protecting the LCDs in inventory amount to 5¢ per LCD per year.

a. What should the order quantity and reorder point be for the LCDs? What is the corresponding total variable inventory cost per year (TVC)?

b. Suppose the true annual cost of capital tied up in Computronics's inventory actually is 10 percent of the value of the inventory. Then what should the order quantity and TVC be? What is the difference between this order quantity and the one obtained in part *a*? How much more would TVC be if the order quantity obtained in part *a* still were used here because of the incorrect estimate of the cost of capital tied up in inventory?

c. Repeat part *b* if the true annual cost of capital tied up in Computronics's inventory actually is 20 percent of the value of the inventory.

d. Perform sensitivity analysis systematically on the unit holding cost by generating a data table that shows what the optimal order quantity would be if the true annual cost of capital tied up in Computronics's inventory were each of the following percentages of the value of the inventory: 10, 12, 14, 16, 18, 20.

e. Assuming that the rough estimate of 15 percent is correct for the cost of capital, perform sensitivity analysis on the setup cost by generating a data table that shows what the optimal order quantity would be if the true number of hours of clerical time required to place each order were each of the following: 0.5, 0.75, 1, 1.25, 1.5.

f. Perform sensitivity analysis simultaneously on the unit holding cost and the setup cost by generating a data table that shows the optimal order quantity for the various combinations of values considered in parts *d* and *e*.

E 11.4. Reconsider the sensitivity analysis done for the ACT case study in Section 11.4. Suppose now that the estimates of K and h could each be off by as much as 25 percent in either direction. Repeat the sensitivity analysis done in Figure 11.7 over this wider range of possible values of K and h by considering the cases of being off by 0, 10, 20, and 25 percent. How do the conclusions change (if at all) from the original sensitivity analysis when each of the estimates could only be off by as much as 10 percent in either direction?

11.5. For the basic EOQ model, use the square root formula to determine how Q^* would change for each of the following

changes in the costs or the demand rate. (Unless otherwise noted, consider each change by itself.)

a. The setup cost is reduced to 25 percent of its original value.

b. The annual demand rate becomes four times as large as its original value.

c. Both changes in parts *a* and *b*.

d. The unit holding cost is reduced to 25 percent of its original value.

e. Both changes in parts *a* and *d*.

11.6.* Kris Lee, the owner and manager of the Quality Hardware Store, is reassessing his inventory policy for hammers. He sells an average of 50 hammers per month, so he has been placing an order to purchase 50 hammers from a wholesaler at a cost of $20 per hammer at the end of each month. However, Kris does all the ordering for the store himself and finds that this is taking a great deal of his time. He estimates that the value of his time spent in placing each order for hammers is $75.

a. What would the unit holding cost for hammers need to be for Kris's current inventory policy to be optimal according to the basic EOQ model? What is this unit holding cost as a percentage of the unit acquisition cost?

E b. What is the optimal order quantity if the unit holding cost actually is 20 percent of the unit acquisition cost? What is the corresponding value of TVC? What is TVC for the current inventory policy?

E c. If the wholesaler typically delivers an order of hammers in 5 working days (out of 25 working days in an average month), what should the reorder point be (according to the basic EOQ model)?

d. Kris doesn't like to incur inventory shortages of important items. Therefore, he has decided to add a safety stock of five hammers to safeguard against late deliveries and larger-than-usual sales. What is his new reorder point? How much does this safety stock add to TVC?

11.7. Cindy Stewart and Misty Whitworth graduated from business school together. They now are inventory managers for competing wholesale distributors, making use of the scientific inventory management techniques they learned in school. Both of them are purchasing 85-horsepower speedboat engines for their inventories from the same manufacturer. Cindy has found that the setup cost for initiating each order is $200 and the unit holding cost is $400.

Cindy has learned that Misty is ordering 10 engines each time. Cindy assumes that Misty is using the basic EOQ model and has the same setup cost and unit holding cost as Cindy. Show how Cindy can use this information to deduce what the annual demand rate must be for Misty's company for these engines.

11.8. Use calculus to derive the square root formula for the basic EOQ model.

11.9.* Speedy Wheels is a wholesale distributor of bicycles for the western United States. Its inventory manager, Ricky Sapolo, is currently reviewing the inventory policy for one popular model—a small, one-speed girl's bicycle that is selling at the rate of 250 per month. The administrative cost for placing an order for this model from the manufacturer is $200 and the purchase price is $70 per bicycle. The annual cost of the capital tied up in inventory is 20 percent of the value of these bicycles. The additional cost of storing the bicycles—including leasing warehouse space, insurance, taxes, and so on—is $6 per bicycle per year.

E   *a.* Use the basic EOQ model to determine the optimal order quantity and the total variable inventory cost per year.

E   *b.* Speedy Wheels's customers (retail outlets) generally do not object to short delays in having their orders filled. Therefore, management has agreed to a new policy of having small planned shortages occasionally to reduce the variable inventory cost. After consultations with management, Ricky estimates that the annual shortage cost (including lost future business) would be $30 times the average number of bicycles short throughout the year. Use the EOQ model with planned shortages to determine the new optimal inventory policy.

  c. Construct a table with the same rows and columns as in Table 11.1 to compare the results from parts *a* and *b.*

11.10. Reconsider the application of the EOQ model with planned shortages to the ACT case study as presented in Section 11.5. ACT management objected to the substantial planned shortages that would result from using a unit shortage cost of $p = \$7.50$, even though the corresponding total variable inventory cost per year is only TVC = $1,928 as compared to TVC = $2,407 for the basic EOQ model where planned shortages are not allowed. Nicholas Relich feels that he and Ashley Collins have greatly underestimated the true value of the unit shortage cost and that a better estimate might have led to management accepting the resulting inventory policy with smaller planned shortages.

E   *a.* Find the optimal inventory policy and TVC for each of the following estimates of the unit shortage cost: $p = \$15$, $p = \$30$, $p = \$60$, and $p = \$120$.

  b. For each of the cases considered in part *a,* calculate the percentage reduction in TVC from TVC = $2,407 for the basic EOQ model.

  c. For each of the cases considered in part *a,* calculate the maximum number of working days that customers would need to wait to have their orders filled (assuming everything stays on schedule). If ACT management were willing for this maximum to be as much as two working days, which of these cases would be acceptable to management?

E* 11.11. Reconsider Problem 11.1. Because of the popularity of the Power model computer, Tim Madsen has found that customers are willing to purchase a computer even when none are currently in stock as long as they can be assured that their order will be filled in a reasonable period of time. Therefore, Tim has decided to switch from the basic EOQ model to the EOQ model with planned shortages, using a unit shortage cost of $200.

  a. Use the Solver version of the Excel template for the EOQ model with planned shortages (with

constraints added in the Solver dialogue box that C10:C11 = integer) to find the new optimal inventory policy and its total variable inventory cost per year (TVC). What is the reduction in the value of TVC found for Problem 11.1 (and given in the back of the book) when planned shortages were not allowed?

  b. Use this same spreadsheet to generate a data table that shows how TVC and its components would change if the maximum shortage were kept the same as found in part *a* but the order quantity were changed to the following values: 15, 17, 19, . . . , 35.

  c. Use this same spreadsheet to generate a data table that shows how TVC and its components would change if the order quantity were kept the same as found in part *a* but the maximum shortage were changed to the following values: 10, 12, 14, . . . , 30.

E 11.12. You have been hired as a management science consultant by a company to reevaluate the inventory policy for one of its products. The company currently uses the basic EOQ model. Under this model, the optimal order quantity for this product is 1,000 units, so the maximum inventory level also is 1,000 units and the maximum shortage is 0.

  You have decided to recommend that the company switch to using the EOQ model with planned shortages instead after determining how large the unit shortage cost (p) is compared to the unit holding cost (h). Prepare a data table for management that shows what the optimal order quantity, maximum inventory level, and maximum shortage would be under this model for each of the following ratios of p to h: $\frac{1}{3}$, 1, 2, 3, 5, 10.

11.13. MBI is a manufacturer of personal computers. All its personal computers use a 3.5″ high-density floppy disk drive that it purchases from Ynos. MBI operates its factory 52 weeks per year, which requires assembling 100 of these floppy disk drives into computers per week. MBI's annual holding cost rate is 20 percent of the value of the inventory. Regardless of order size, the administrative cost of placing an order with Ynos has been estimated to be $50. A quantity discount is offered by Ynos for large orders as shown below:

Discount Category	Quantity Purchased	Price (per disk drive)
1	1 to 99	$100
2	100 to 499	95
3	500 or more	90

E   *a.* Determine the optimal order quantity according to the EOQ model with quantity discounts. What is the resulting total variable inventory cost per year?

  b. With this order quantity, how many orders need to be placed per year? What is the time interval between orders?

11.14. The Gilbreth family drinks a case of Royal Cola every day, 365 days a year. Fortunately, a local distributor offers quantity discounts for large orders, as shown in the next table. Considering the cost of gasoline, Mr. Gilbreth estimates it costs him about $5 to go pick up an order of Royal Cola. Mr. Gilbreth also is an investor in the stock market, where he has been earning a 20 percent average annual return. He considers this opportunity cost to be the only holding cost for the Royal Cola.

Discount Category	Quantity Purchased	Price (per case)
1	1 to 49	$4.00
2	50 to 99	3.90
3	100 or more	3.80

E   a. Determine the optimal order quantity according to the EOQ model with quantity discounts. What is the resulting total variable inventory cost per year?

   b. With this order quantity, how many orders need to be placed per year? What is the time interval between orders?

11.15. Kenichi Kaneko is the manager of a production department that uses 400 boxes of rivets per year. To hold down his inventory level, Kenichi has been ordering only 50 boxes each time. However, the supplier of rivets now is offering a discount for higher quantity orders according to the following price schedule.

Discount Category	Quantity	Price (per box)
1	1 to 99	$8.50
2	100 to 999	8.00
3	1,000 or more	7.50

The company uses an annual holding cost rate of 20 percent of the price of the item. The total cost associated with placing an order is $80 per order.

Kenichi has decided to use the EOQ model with quantity discounts to determine his optimal inventory policy for rivets.

   a. For each discount category, write an expression for the total variable cost TVC as a function of the order quantity Q.

E   b. For each discount category, use the square root formula for the basic EOQ model to calculate the value of Q (feasible or infeasible) that gives the minimum value of TVC. (You may use the analytical version of the Excel template for the basic EOQ model to perform this calculation if you wish.)

   c. For each discount category, use the results from parts *a* and *b* to determine the *feasible* value of Q that gives the *feasible* minimum value of TVC and to calculate this value of TVC.

   d. Draw rough hand curves of TVC versus Q for each of the discount categories. Use the same format as in Figure 11.10 (a solid curve where feasible and a dashed curve where infeasible). Show the points found in parts *b* and *c*. However, you don't need to perform any additional calculations to make the curves particularly accurate at other points.

   e. Use the results from parts *c* and *d* to determine the optimal order quantity and the corresponding value of TVC.

E*   f. Use the Excel template for the EOQ model with quantity discounts to check your answers in parts *b, c,* and *e.*

   g. For discount category 2, the value of Q that minimizes TVC turns out to be feasible. Explain why learning this fact would allow you to rule out discount category 1 as a candidate for providing the optimal order quantity without even performing the calculations for this category that were done in parts *b* and *c.*

   h. Given the optimal order quantity from parts *e* and *f,* how many orders need to be placed per year? What is the time interval between orders?

11.16. Sarah operates a concession stand at a downtown location throughout the year. One of her most popular items is circus peanuts, selling about 200 bags per month.

Sarah purchases the circus peanuts from Peter's Peanut Shop. She has been purchasing 100 bags at a time. However, to encourage larger purchases, Peter now is offering her discounts for larger order sizes according to the following price schedule.

Discount Category	Order Quantity	Price (per bag)
1	1 to 199	$1.00
2	200 to 499	0.95
3	500 or more	0.90

Sarah wants to use the EOQ model with quantity discounts to determine what her order quantity should be. For this purpose, she estimates an annual holding cost rate of 17 percent of the value of the peanuts. She also estimates a setup cost of $4 for placing each order.

Follow the instructions of Problem 11.15 to analyze Sarah's problem.

11.17.* Color View is a manufacturer of color monitors for personal computers. The company uses the EOQ model with gradual replenishment to determine the production lot sizes for its various models.

Color View's newest monitor is the X-435 model. The company expects sales of this model to run at the rate of 6,000 per year for awhile. The facilities for producing this model are shared with several other models. While these production facilities are devoted to the X-435 model, the production rate is 2,000 monitors per month. The cost each time the facilities are set up for a production run for this model is $7,500. The annual cost of holding each of these monitors in inventory is estimated to be $120.

E   a. Determine what the production lot size should be according to the EOQ model with gradual replenishment. Also find the corresponding annual setup cost, annual holding cost, and total variable inventory cost per year.

   b. How long should each production run last and how frequently should they occur?

c. What is the maximum inventory level? Why is this less than the production lot size?

11.18. The Heavy Duty Company produces a variety of industrial machinery. One of its vendors is Fine Bearings, which supplies Heavy Duty with all of its ball bearings—approximately 52,000 per year. Since Fine Bearings is a small company, it fills large orders gradually rather than in a single delivery. Each time Keith Graham, Heavy Duty's inventory manager, places an order for ball bearings, Fine Bearings begins delivering them a week later at the rate of 2,000 per week. Keith estimates that, in addition to the purchase cost, the cost of placing each order (including shipping costs, the cost of processing and paying for the order, and the cost of inspecting the deliveries and putting them into storage) is $1,000. He also estimates that the cost of holding each ball bearing in inventory is $13 per year.

E   *a.* Use the EOQ model with gradual replenishment to determine the order quantity that Keith should place with Fine Bearings each time. What is the resulting total variable inventory cost per year?

  b. How frequently will Keith need to place orders? Over what period of time will the deliveries from a single order take place?

  c. What is Keith's reorder point?

11.19. Reconsider the SOCA example presented in Section 11.7 to illustrate the application of the EOQ model with gradual replenishment. SOCA management has not yet decided to implement the inventory policy prescribed by this model (a production lot size of $Q^* = 50,000$) because of concerns that the estimates of the setup cost ($K = \$12,000$) and the unit holding cost ($h = \$3.60$) may not be accurate. The feeling is that each of these estimates could be off by as much as 25 percent so that the ranges of possible values are from $9,000 to $15,000 for the setup cost and from $2.70 to $4.50 for the unit holding cost. Therefore, management would like sensitivity analysis conducted on these two parameters of the model.

E   *a.* Find Q^* and TVC from the model for each of the four cases where one of the cost estimates is accurate but the other cost lies at one of the endpoints of its range

of possible values. For each case, also calculate the difference between the new value of Q^* and the original value ($Q^* = 50,000$) obtained with the original cost estimates.

E   *b.* Repeat part *a* for each of the four cases where *both* of the costs lie at one of the endpoints of their ranges of possible values.

  c. Given the results obtained in parts *a* and/or *b*, what is your conclusion about how sensitive Q^* is to the two cost estimates?

E*   *d.* Generate three data tables that are analogous to those in Figure 11.7, namely, (1) Q^*, (2) TVC with $Q = Q^*$, and (3) TVC with $Q = 50,000$, for the combination of cases where $K = \$9,000$, $K = \$12,000$, $K = \$15,000$, and $h = \$2.70$, $h = \$3.60$, $h = \$4.50$.

  e. For each of the nine cases considered in part *d*, calculate by how much TVC with $Q = 50,000$ exceeds TVC with $Q = Q^*$.

  f. Given the results obtained in part *e*, what is your conclusion about how important it would be to try to improve upon the original cost estimates?

11.20. Reconsider the SOCA example involving the EOQ model with gradual replenishment presented in Section 11.7. SOCA management is unhappy that the inventory policy prescribed by the model costs so much (TVC = $120,000). Therefore, management is considering two options to try to improve the situation. Option 1 is to provide additional production facilities that would enable increasing the production rate from 3,000 to 6,000 speakers per day (when producing) with no change in the setup cost. Option 2 is to use only a portion of the current facilities but to use them on a continuous basis with a production rate of 1,000 speakers per day that would match the demand rate of 1,000 speakers per day.

E   *a.* Determine Q^* and TVC under Option 1. Does this look like a good alternative to the status quo?

  b. What would TVC be under Option 2? Does this look like a good alternative to the status quo?

  c. What is the common name given to the type of inventory system envisioned under Option 2?

CASE 11.1
BRUSHING UP ON INVENTORY CONTROL

Robert Gates rounds the corner of the street and smiles when he sees his wife pruning rose bushes in their front yard. He slowly pulls his car into the driveway, turns off the engine, and falls into his wife's open arms.

"How was your day?" she asks.

"Great! The drugstore business could not be better!" Robert replies. "Except for the traffic coming home from work! That traffic can drive a sane man crazy! I am so tense right now. I think I will go inside and make myself a relaxing martini."

Robert enters the house and walks directly into the kitchen. He sees the mail on the kitchen counter and begins flipping through the various bills and advertisements until he comes across the new issue of *OR/MS Today.* He prepares his drink, grabs the magazine,

treads into the living room, and settles comfortably into his recliner. He has all that he wants —except for one thing. He sees the remote control lying on the top of the television. He sets his drink and magazine on the coffee table and reaches for the remote control. Now, with the remote control in one hand, the magazine in the other, and the drink on the table near him, Robert is finally the master of his domain.

Robert turns on the television and flips the channels until he finds the local news. He then opens the magazine and begins reading an article about scientific inventory management. Occasionally he glances at the television to learn the latest in business, weather, and sports.

As Robert delves deeper into the article, he becomes distracted by a commercial on television about toothbrushes. His pulse quickens slightly in fear because the commercial for Totalee toothbrushes reminds him of the dentist. The commercial concludes that the customer should buy a Totalee toothbrush because the toothbrush is Totalee revolutionary and Totalee effective. It certainly is effective; it is the most popular toothbrush on the market!

At that moment, with the inventory article and the toothbrush commercial fresh in his mind, Robert experiences a flash of brilliance. He knows how to control the inventory of Totalee toothbrushes at Nightingale Drugstore!

As the inventory control manager at Nightingale Drugstore, Robert has been experiencing problems keeping Totalee toothbrushes in stock. He has discovered that customers are very loyal to the Totalee brand name since Totalee holds a patent on the toothbrush endorsed by 9 out of 10 dentists. Customers are willing to wait for the toothbrushes to arrive at Nightingale Drugstore since the drugstore sells the toothbrushes for 20 percent less than other local stores. This demand for the toothbrushes at Nightingale means that the drugstore is often out of Totalee toothbrushes. The store is able to receive a shipment of toothbrushes several hours after an order is placed to the Totalee regional warehouse because the warehouse is only 20 miles away from the store. Nevertheless, the current inventory situation causes problems because numerous emergency orders cost the store unnecessary time and paperwork and because customers become disgruntled when they must return to the store later in the day.

Robert now knows a way to prevent the inventory problems through scientific inventory management! He grabs his coat and car keys and rushes out of the house.

As he runs to the car, his wife yells, "Honey, where are you going?"

"I'm sorry, darling," Robert yells back. "I have just discovered a way to control the inventory of a critical item at the drugstore. I am really excited because I am able to apply my management science degree to my job! I need to get the data from the store and work out the new inventory policy! I will be back before dinner!"

Because rush hour traffic has dissipated, the drive to the drugstore takes Robert no time at all. He unlocks the darkened store and heads directly to his office where he rummages through file cabinets to find demand and cost data for Totalee toothbrushes over the past year.

Aha! Just as he suspected! The demand data for the toothbrushes are almost constant across the months. Whether in winter or summer, customers have teeth to brush, and they need toothbrushes. Since a toothbrush will wear out after a few months of use, customers will always return to buy another toothbrush. The demand data show that Nightingale Drugstore customers purchase an average of 250 Totalee toothbrushes per month (30 days).

After examining the demand data, Robert investigates the cost data. Because Nightingale Drugstore is such a good customer, Totalee charges its lowest wholesale price of only $1.25 per toothbrush. Robert spends about 20 minutes to place each order with Totalee. His salary and benefits add up to $18.75 per hour. The annual holding cost for the inventory is 12 percent of the capital tied up in the inventory of Totalee toothbrushes.

a. Robert decides to create an inventory policy that normally fulfills all demand since he believes that stock-outs are just not worth the hassle of calming customers or the risk of losing future business. He therefore does not allow any planned shortages. Since Nightingale Drugstore receives an order several hours after it is placed, Robert makes the simplifying assumption that delivery is instantaneous. What is the optimal inventory policy under these conditions? How many Totalee toothbrushes should Robert order each time and how frequently? What is the total variable inventory cost per year with this policy?

b. Totalee has been experiencing financial problems because the company has lost money trying to branch into producing other personal hygiene products, such as hairbrushes and dental floss. The company has therefore decided to close the warehouse located 20 miles from Nightingale Drugstore. The drugstore must now place orders with a warehouse located 350 miles away and must wait six days after it places an order to receive the shipment. Given this new lead time, how many Totalee toothbrushes should Robert order each time, and when should he order?

c. Robert begins to wonder whether he would save money if he allows planned shortages to occur. Customers would wait to buy the toothbrushes from Nightingale since they have high brand loyalty and since Nightingale sells the toothbrushes for less. Even though customers would wait to purchase the Totalee toothbrush from Nightingale, they would become unhappy with the prospect of having to return to the store again for the product. Robert decides that he needs to place a dollar value on the negative ramifications from shortages. He knows that an employee would have to calm each disgruntled customer and track down the delivery date for a new shipment of Totalee toothbrushes. Robert also believes that customers would become upset with the inconvenience of shopping at Nightingale and would perhaps begin looking for another store providing better service. He estimates the costs of dealing with disgruntled customers and losing customer goodwill and future sales as $1.50 per unit short per year. Given the six-day lead time and the shortage allowance, how many Totalee toothbrushes should Robert order each time, and when should he order? What is the maximum shortage under this optimal inventory policy? What is the total variable inventory cost per year?

d. Robert realizes that his estimate for the shortage cost is simply that—an estimate. He realizes that employees sometimes must spend several minutes with each customer who wishes to purchase a toothbrush when none is currently available. In addition, he realizes that the cost of losing customer goodwill and future sales could vary within a wide range. He estimates that the cost of dealing with disgruntled customers and losing customer goodwill and future sales could range from 85 cents to $25 per unit short per year. What effect would changing the estimate of the unit shortage cost have on the inventory policy and total variable inventory cost per year found in part *c*?

e. Closing warehouses has not improved Totalee's bottom line significantly, so the company has decided to institute a discount policy to encourage more sales. Totalee will charge $1.25 per toothbrush for any order of up to 500 toothbrushes, $1.15 per toothbrush for orders of more than 500 but less than 1,000 toothbrushes, and $1 per toothbrush for orders of 1,000 toothbrushes or more. Robert still assumes a five-day lead time, but he does not want planned shortages to occur. Under the new discount policy, how many Totalee toothbrushes should Robert order each time, and when should he order? What is the total inventory cost (including purchase costs) per year?

12

INVENTORY MANAGEMENT WITH UNCERTAIN DEMAND

We now continue the focus of the preceding chapter on inventory management, but with one key difference. We have been assuming that the product under consideration in inventory has a *known demand,* that is, we can predict with reasonable certainty when units will need to be withdrawn from inventory. We drop this assumption in this chapter, so we now will consider products with an *uncertain demand.*

The predictability of **demand** depends greatly on the situation. We certainly have known demand when the product is being withdrawn from inventory at a fixed rate because it actually is one of several components being assembled into a larger product on an assembly line. Similarly, a manufacturer has a known demand for a custom product in inventory when it is producing the product (replenishing inventory) only to satisfy a schedule of orders already received from a particular customer. A wholesaler also has roughly a known demand for a product after its retail customers have developed a well-established pattern for purchasing the product month after month. These are the types of situations considered in the preceding chapter.

By contrast, a retail store manager does not have the luxury of knowing when customers will come in to purchase a given product. If the product is a new one, predicting how well it will catch on may be particularly difficult. Similarly, a wholesaler supplying a number of retailers with a new product may have considerable uncertainty about what the demand will be. Sales can fluctuate widely from one month to the next. Consequently, a manufacturer selling the product to a number of wholesalers (perhaps in competition with other manufacturers) also can have significant uncertainty about the demand. We are considering these kinds of situations in this chapter.

Even with uncertainty, it is necessary to make some kind of forecast of the expected demand and what the variability might be. For example, you might use something like the *PERT three-estimate approach* described in Section 7.4 (making a most likely estimate, an optimistic estimate, and a pessimistic estimate, and then converting these estimates into a probability distribution). In some way, the forecast should be expressed in probabilistic terms. The probabilities might be quite subjective in nature, as with the typical *prior probabilities* of decision analysis discussed in Chapter 10, or they might be based on considerable historical experience and data. At any rate, the models in this chapter assume that an estimate has been made of the *probability distribution* of what the demand will be over a given period.

A very important consequence of uncertain demand is the great risk of incurring shortages unless the inventory is managed carefully. An order to replenish the inventory needs to be placed while some inventory still remains, because of the lag until the order can be filled. Even the amount of lead time needed to fill the order may be uncertain. However, if too much inventory is replenished too soon, a heavy price is paid because of the high cost of holding a large inventory. A constant theme throughout the chapter is the need to find the best trade-off between the consequences of having too much inventory and of having too little.

We will separately discuss inventory management for two types of products. One type is a **perishable product,** which can be carried in inventory for only a very limited period of time before it can no longer be sold. The second type is a **stable product,** which will remain sellable indefinitely. These two types need to be handled quite differently.

The first two sections present a case study and then a general model for perishable products. Sections 12.3 and 12.4 discuss a case study that involves a stable product. The inventory model that underlies this case study is summarized in Section 12.5. Section 12.6 describes the large inventory systems that commonly arise in practice, including massive systems that have been installed at IBM and Hewlett-Packard.

12.1 A Case Study for Perishable Products: Freddie the Newsboy's Problem

This case study concerns a newsstand in a prominent downtown location of a major city. The newsstand has been there longer than most people can remember. It has always been run by a well-known character named Freddie. (Nobody seems to know his last name.) His many customers refer to him affectionately as Freddie the newsboy, even though he is considerably older than most of them.

Freddie sells a wide variety of newspapers and magazines. The most expensive of the newspapers is a large national daily called the *Financial Journal.* Our case study involves this newspaper.

Freddie's Problem

The day's copies of the *Financial Journal* are brought to the newsstand early each morning by a distributor. Any copies unsold at the end of the day are returned to the distributor the next morning. (This is indeed a *perishable product*). However, to encourage ordering a large number of copies, the distributor does give a small refund for unsold copies.

Here are Freddie's cost figures.

Freddie pays $1.50 per copy delivered.
Freddie sells it at $2.50 per copy.
Freddie's refund is $0.50 per unsold copy.

Partially because of the refund, Freddie always has taken a plentiful supply. However, he has become concerned about paying so much for copies that then have to be returned unsold, particularly since this has been occurring nearly every day. He now thinks he might be better off by ordering only a minimal number of copies and saving this extra cost.

To investigate this further, Freddie has been keeping a record of his daily sales. This is what he has found.

Freddie sells 9 copies on 30 percent of the days.
Freddie sells 10 copies on 40 percent of the days.
Freddie sells 11 copies on 30 percent of the days.

So how many copies should Freddie order from the distributor per day? (Think about it before reading on.)

Applying Bayes' Decision Rule to Freddie's Problem

One approach to this problem is to apply decision analysis as described in Chapter 10. Specifically, Bayes' decision rule introduced in Section 10.3 is used as outlined below.

The procedure involves filling out the *payoff table* shown in Figure 12.1. Column B lists the decision alternatives that deserve consideration, namely, to order 9, 10, or 11 copies per day from the distributor. For each of these alternatives, Freddie's profit on a given day is determined by how many requests to purchase a copy of the *Financial Journal* occur that day, so these possible numbers of purchase requests (the possible *states of nature*) are listed in cells C4:E4. The relative likelihood of these numbers of purchase requests are entered in row 10 as the *prior probabilities* of these states of nature.

The payoff from Freddie's decision, given the state of nature, is the profit for that day. This profit is

$$\text{Profit} = \text{sales income} - \text{purchase cost} + \text{refund}$$

FIGURE 12.1

This Excel template in your MS Courseware shows that Freddie the newsboy maximizes his expected profit by ordering 10 copies each day.

	A	B	C	D	E	F	G	H	I
1		Bayes' Decision Rule (with Profits) for Freddie the Newboy's Problem							
2									
3			State of Nature (Purchase Requests)					Expected	
4		Alternative	9	10	11			Payoff	
5		Order 9 copies	$9	$9	$9			$9.00	
6		Order 10 copies	$8	$10	$10			$9.40	Maximum
7		Order 11 Copies	$7	$9	$11			$9.00	
8									
9									
10		Prior Probability	0.3	0.4	0.3				

	H	I
5	=SUMPRODUCT(C5:G5,C10:G10)	=IF(H5=MAX($H$5:$H$9),"Maximum","")
6	=SUMPRODUCT(C6:G6,C10:G10)	=IF(H6=MAX($H$5:$H$9),"Maximum","")
7	=SUMPRODUCT(C7:G7,C10:G10)	=IF(H7=MAX($H$5:$H$9),"Maximum","")
8	=SUMPRODUCT(C8:G8,C10:G10)	=IF(H8=MAX($H$5:$H$9),"Maximum","")
9	=SUMPRODUCT(C9:G9,C10:G10)	=IF(H9=MAX($H$5:$H$9),"Maximum","")

For example, if Freddie orders 11 copies from the distributor and the state of nature turns out to be 9 for that day (9 copies are sold), his profit is

$$\text{Profit} = 9\ (\$2.50) - 11\ (\$1.50) + 2\ (\$0.50) = \$7.00$$

Calculating the profit in this way for each of the combinations of a decision alternative and a possible state of nature yields the payoff table shown in columns B, C, D, and E of Figure 12.1. Applying Bayes' decision rule with this Excel template (first introduced in Figure 10.10) involves calculating the *expected payoff* (EP) for each alternative by using the indicated equations entered into cells H5:H7. (If you haven't studied this topic in Chapter 10, note that each of these equations is simply calculating the *statistical average* of the payoffs.) The rule then selects the alternative with the largest expected payoff, as indicated in cell I6.

Conclusion: Freddie's most profitable alternative in the long run is to order 10 copies, since this will provide an average daily profit of $9.40, versus $9.00 for either of the other alternatives.

In the next section, you will see a shortcut for drawing this same conclusion.

Review Questions

1. What is the trade-off that Freddie the newsboy should consider in making his decision?
2. Why are Freddie's decision alternatives limited to ordering 9, 10, or 11 copies?
3. What is the *state of nature* when using decision analysis to formulate Freddie's problem? Why?

12.2 An Inventory Model for Perishable Products

Freddie the newsboy's problem illustrates an application of a widely used inventory model for perishable products. Newspapers are just one of the many types of such products to which it can be applied. After summarizing its assumptions and applying Bayes' decision rule, we will show you a shortcut for solving the model and then describe the various types of perishable products.

The Assumptions of the Model

1. Each application involves a single perishable product.
2. Each application involves a single time period because the product cannot be sold later.

3. However, it will be possible to dispose of any units of the product remaining at the end of the period, perhaps even receiving a *salvage value* for the units.

4. The only decision to be made is how many units to order (the **order quantity**) so they can be placed into inventory at the beginning of the period.

5. The *demand* for withdrawing units from inventory to sell them (or for any other purpose) during the period is *uncertain*. However, the probability distribution of demand is known (or at least estimated).

6. If the demand exceeds the order quantity, a **cost of underordering** is incurred. In particular, the cost for each unit short is

$$C_{\text{under}} = \text{unit cost of underordering}$$

$$= \text{decrease in profit that results from failing to order a unit that could have been sold during the period}$$

7. If the order quantity exceeds the demand, a **cost of overordering** is incurred. In particular, the cost for each extra unit is

$$C_{\text{over}} = \text{unit cost of overordering}$$

$$= \text{decrease in profit that results from ordering a unit that could not be sold during the period}$$

These assumptions certainly fit Freddie the newsboy's problem. The day's newspaper of concern (the *Financial Journal*) is a single perishable product that cannot be sold after the day (the single time period), although it can be returned to the distributor for a small refund (the salvage value). Freddie's only decision is how many copies to order from the distributor for each day, given the probability distribution of how many can be sold (shown in row 10 of Figure 12.1). The last two assumptions also fit, since the definitions of the two unit costs imply that

$$C_{\text{under}} = \text{unit sale price} - \text{unit purchase cost}$$

$$= \$2.50 - \$1.50$$

$$= \$1.00$$

$$C_{\text{over}} = \text{unit purchase cost} - \text{unit salvage value}$$

$$= \$1.50 - \$0.50$$

$$= \$1.00$$

for this problem.

These expressions for C_{under} and C_{over} will fit any analogous problem where the only cost factors are the unit sale price, unit purchase cost, and unit salvage value. However, the definitions of C_{under} and C_{over} have been expressed more generally as a decrease in profit in order to fit other situations as well. For example, if there is a concern about losing future business due to ill will caused by underordering, then a unit cost of ill will could be added to the expression for C_{under}. Similarly, C_{over} might include an additional term for something like the extra holding cost associated with storing a unit all the way to the end of the period. Another possibility is that it might be necessary to add a unit disposal cost rather than having a refund to subtract.

As in Freddie's problem, it often is not feasible to place and receive an additional order before the period ends if a shortage occurs. However, if it is very important to fill all the demand, arrangements sometimes can be made to do this at an extra cost. In this case, C_{under} would equal the extra cost per unit of placing this emergency order plus any reduction in the unit selling price to pacify the customers who had to wait.

A key part of assumptions 6 and 7 is that C_{under} must be the same for each unit short and C_{over} must be the same for each extra unit.

One way of solving this model is to apply *Bayes' decision rule,* as described in the box. Another simple method is presented next.

Applying Bayes' Decision Rule

Any application of this model can be solved in much the same way as we solved Freddie the newsboy's problem in the preceding section, namely, by applying Bayes' decision rule (first introduced in Section 10.3). One alternative is to express the payoffs in terms of profits and then proceed as in Figure 12.1. However, in light of assumptions 6 and 7, a completely equivalent but more direct approach is to focus on just the costs of underordering and overordering. This is what is done in Figure 12.2 for Freddie's problem.

Note that the numbers in cells C5, D6, and E7 are 0, because the order quantity equals the demand in these cases. The costs (in dollars) in cells D5, E5, and E6 are solely the cost of underordering and those in cells C6, C7, and D7 are solely the cost of overordering. The expected cost for each alternative is calculated in column H with the equations given in Figure 12.1. Since we wish to *minimize* expected cost, the equations in column I now use the MIN function instead of the MAX function, so the conclusion again is that Freddie should order 10 copies.

The conclusion here must be the same as in Figure 12.1 since the two approaches are equivalent. All we have done here is eliminate the revenues and cost factors that don't affect the decision and focus on just those that do, namely, the cost of underordering and the cost of overordering. Both approaches are applying Bayes' decision rule, but with different payoffs, where one is to be maximized and the other minimized.

FIGURE 12.2

This Excel template finds that Freddie the newsboy minimizes his expected cost of underordering or overordering by ordering 10 copies each day.

	A	B	C	D	E	F	G	H	I
1		Bayes' Decision Rule (with Costs) for Freddie the Newboy's Problem							
2									
3			State of Nature (Purchase Requests)					Expected	
4		Alternative	9	10	11			Cost	
5		Order 9 copies	$0	$1	$2			$1.00	
6		Order 10 copies	$1	$0	$1			$0.60	Minimum
7		Order 11 copies	$2	$1	$0			$1.00	
8									
9									
10		Prior Probability	0.3	0.4	0.3				

A Simple Formula for Solving the Model

The drawback with relying on Bayes' decision rule as the method for solving the model is that most applications involve many more decision alternatives and states of nature than Freddie's problem formulated in Figures 12.1 and 12.2. In fact, if Freddie were to apply the same approach to another more popular newspaper where the number of copies sold in a day range from 100 to 200, he then would have 101 decision alternatives and 101 states of nature to consider. Other applications might have thousands. Using Bayes' decision rule to deal with such large problems would be extremely cumbersome.

A Quicker Approach.   Fortunately, a much quicker way to solve problems of any size has been found. It involves using the **service level,** defined as follows:

$$\text{Service level} = \text{probability that } no \text{ shortage will occur}$$

A shortage occurs when the demand for the product exceeds the number of units available in inventory, so one or more customers suffer the disappointment of not immediately obtaining the units they wanted. Therefore, the probability of avoiding a shortage is a key measure of the level of service being provided to the customers. Given the prior probabilities in cells C10:E10 of Figure 12.2, the service levels for Freddie's three alternatives are

Service level if order 9 copies   = C10 = 0.3
Service level if order 10 copies = C10 + D10 = 0.3 + 0.4 = 0.7
Service level if order 11 copies = C10 + D10 + E10 = 0.3 + 0.4 + 0.3 = 1

Here is the simple formula for solving this model.

Ordering Rule for the Model for Perishable Products

1. Optimal service level $= \dfrac{C_{under}}{C_{under} + C_{over}}$

2. Choose the smallest order quantity that provides at least this service level.

Since $C_{under} = \$1.00$ and $C_{over} = \$1.00$ for Freddie's problem, this formula gives

$$\text{Optimal service level} = \frac{\$1.00}{\$1.00 + \$1.00} = 0.5$$

Referring to the service levels for Freddie's three alternative order quantities, the smallest one that provides at least this optimal service level is to order 10 copies. This, of course, is the same answer as provided by Bayes' decision rule.

An Excel template is available in your MS Courseware for applying this model for perishable products to any situation where, as for Freddie's problem, the only cost factors are the unit sale price, unit purchase cost, and unit salvage value. As illustrated in Figure 12.3 for Freddie's problem, all you need to do is enter these three cost factors. The template then calculates C_{over}, C_{under}, and the optimal service level. What remains is for you to use the probability distribution of demand for your specific problem to apply step 2 of the ordering rule.

Applying Step 2 of the Ordering Rule Graphically.   For any given order quantity, the definition of service level can be restated in another equivalent way as

Service level = probability that the demand is less than or equal to the order quantity

= P(demand ≤ order quantity)

The probability on the right for each of Freddie's three alternative order quantities is

$$P(\text{demand} \leq 9) = 0.3$$
$$P(\text{demand} \leq 10) = 0.7$$
$$P(\text{demand} \leq 11) = 1$$

Figure 12.4 shows a graph where the horizontal axis is x and the vertical axis is $P(\text{demand} \leq x)$. Since demand is a random variable, this graph is referred to as the *cumulative distribution function* (or CDF for short) of demand. The point at which the optimal service level of 0.5 (see the horizontal dashed line) hits this CDF gives the optimal order quantity of 10.

FIGURE 12.3

The Excel template for the inventory model for perishable products in your MS Courseware applies step 1 of the ordering rule, as illustrated here for Freddie's problem.

	A	B	C	D	E	F
1	Optimal Service Level for Perishable Products (Freddie's Problem)					
2						
3		Data			Results	
4		Unit sale price =	$2.50		Cost of overordering =	$1.00
5		Unit purchase cost =	$1.50		Cost of underordering =	$1.00
6		Unit salvage value =	$0.50		Optimal Service Level =	0.5

	F
4	=C5–C6
5	=C4–C5
6	=F5/(F4+F5)

The figure enables visualizing the ordering rule graphically. Furthermore, on larger problems, this graphical approach may find the optimal order quantity more quickly than enumerating the service levels for all the alternatives. This is illustrated by the following example.

A Variation of Freddie's Problem

Freddie now wishes to find the optimal order quantity for another of his newspapers. This is a more popular newspaper whose daily sales range from 100 copies to 200 copies, with roughly equal probabilities over this range. In this case, the relevant unit costs are $C_{under} = \$0.75$ and $C_{over} = \$0.25$.

Since the probabilities of the various possible demands from 100 to 200 are roughly equal, a good estimate of the probability distribution of demand is the uniform distribution from 100 to 200. The solid lines in Figure 12.5 show the CDF of this distribution.

FIGURE 12.4

Graphical application of the ordering rule to Freddie the newsboy's problem. The solid lines give the cumulative distribution function of demand, P (demand ≤ x). The point at which the optimal service level hits the cumulative distribution function gives the optimal order quantity.

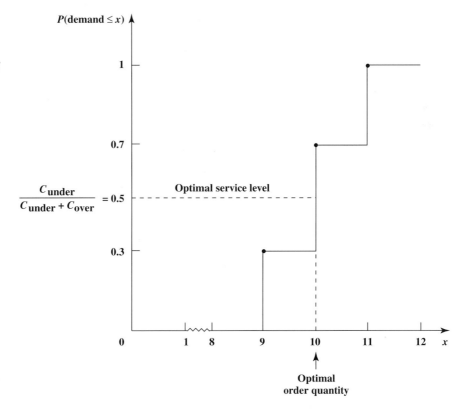

FIGURE 12.5

Graphical application of the ordering rule to the variation of Freddie's problem where demand has a uniform distribution from 100 to 200, $C_{under} = 0.75$ and $C_{over} = 0.25$.

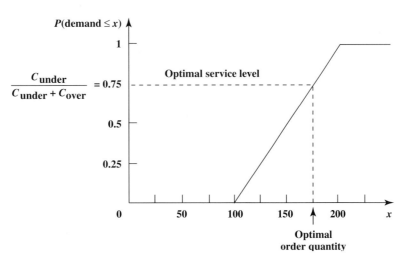

With the given unit costs, the ordering rule says that

$$\text{Optimal service level} = \frac{C_{\text{under}}}{C_{\text{under}} + C_{\text{over}}} = \frac{\$0.75}{\$0.75 + \$0.25} = 0.75$$

The corresponding dashed lines in the figure show that the optimal order quantity is 175.

Some Types of Perishable Products

The model presented in this section has traditionally been called the **newsboy problem**[1] because it fits the problems of newsboys like Freddie so well. However, it has always been recognized that the model is just as applicable to other perishable products as to newspapers. In fact, most of the applications have been to perishable products other than newspapers.

As you read through the list below of various types of **perishable products,** think about how the inventory management of such products is analogous to Freddie's problem since these products also cannot be sold after a single time period. All that may differ is that the length of this time period may be a week, a month, or even several months rather than just one day.

1. Periodicals, such as newspapers and magazines.
2. Flowers being sold by a florist.
3. The makings of fresh food to be prepared in a restaurant.
4. Produce, including fresh fruits and vegetables, to be sold in a grocery store.
5. Christmas trees.
6. Seasonal clothing, such as winter coats, where any goods remaining at the end of the season must be sold at highly discounted prices to clear space for the next season.
7. Seasonal greeting cards.
8. Fashion goods that will be out of style soon.
9. New cars at the end of a model year.
10. Any product that will be obsolete soon.
11. Vital spare parts that must be produced during the last production run of a certain model of a product (e.g., an airplane) for use as needed throughout the lengthy field life of that model.
12. Reservations provided by an airline for a particular flight. Reservations provided in excess of the number of seats available (overbooking) can be viewed as the inventory of a perishable product (they cannot be sold after the flight has occurred), where the demand then is the number of no-shows. With this interpretation, the cost of underordering (too little overbooking) would be the lost profit from empty seats and the cost of overordering (too much overbooking) would be the cost of compensating bumped customers.

This last type is a particularly interesting one because major airlines now are making extensive use of this section's model to analyze how much overbooking to do. For example, an article in the January–February 1992 issue of *Interfaces* describes how **American Airlines** is dealing with overbooking in this way. In addition, the article describes how the company is also using management science to address some related issues (such as the fare structure). These applications of management science are credited with increasing American Airline's annual revenues by over $500 million.

When managing the inventory of these various types of perishable products, it is occasionally necessary to deal with some considerations beyond those discussed in this section. Extensive research has been conducted to extend the model to encompass these considerations, and considerable progress has been made. Further information is available in the footnoted references.[2]

---

[1] Recently, some writers have been substituting the name *newsvendor problem.* Other names include the *single-period probabilistic model* and *single-period stochastic model.*

[2] See H.-S. Lau and A. H.-L. Lau, "The Newsstand Problem: A Capacitated Multiple Product Single-Period Inventory Problem," *European Journal of Operational Research* 94 (October 11, 1996), pp. 29–42, and its references. Also see pp. 610–28 in E. L. Porteus, "Stochastic Inventory Theory," in D. P. Heyman and M. J. Sobel (eds.), *Stochastic Models* (Amsterdam: North Holland, 1990).

Review Questions

1. Why does this model for perishable products need only a single time period?
2. What is the only decision to be made with this model?
3. What assumption is made about the demand for the product?
4. How is the unit cost of underordering C_{under} defined? The unit cost of overordering C_{over}?
5. Will Bayes' decision rule make the same decision when expressing the payoffs in terms of profits to be maximized or in terms of the costs of underordering and overordering to be minimized?
6. What is the definition of *service level*?
7. What is the formula for the optimal service level?
8. For the graphical application of the ordering rule, what is the point that gives the optimal order quantity?
9. Are there many types of perishable products in addition to newspapers?

12.3 A Case Study for Stable Products: The Niko Camera Corp. Problem

The Niko Camera Corporation is a major Japanese company that specializes in producing high quality cameras with an especially fine lens. It sells many different models to meet the various needs of discriminating photographers (both amateur and professional) around the world.

Background on the Product of Concern

One of Niko's newer models is an inexpensive disposable panoramic camera. Very light and compact, this camera is designed to be especially convenient for a traveler who wants to take high quality panoramic shots of beautiful scenery without carrying the usual photographic equipment required to do this. The key to this convenience is that the camera is designed to be used for just one series of shots. It comes with special film already loaded at the factory and no provision is made for reloading by the customer. Therefore, the camera is given back to the camera store when the customer wants to have the film developed after completing the allotment of 27 shots. After removing the film, the camera store then returns the camera to the factory so that most of its components can be reused in a recycled camera. The special design for one-time use by the customer (but recycling of the expensive components by the factory) enables selling the camera so cheaply that many customers now think of repeated purchases as a good alternative to repeatedly buying rolls of film to use in an expensive and inconvenient permanent camera.

Although the cameras are produced initially in Japan, North American camera stores return the cameras for recycling to a factory in the United States run by Niko's North American Division. Our focus will be on this factory. Niko's American factory has been selling an average of 8,000 of these recycled cameras per month to a number of wholesale distributors. However, since these distributors only submit purchase orders on a very occasional basis, sales fluctuate widely from month to month (but *without* any noticeable *seasonal pattern*). Figure 12.6 shows the pattern of monthly sales over the past year. Note that some months are nearly double the monthly average (e.g., 15,800 in March) while others are almost nil (e.g., 700 in August). This same kind of random fluctuation, with no particular trend or seasonal pattern, also has been observed in the months prior to last year.

Because of these fluctuations, the camera is only produced on a sporadic basis. Every few months, the needed production facilities are set up to produce this particular model. In one concentrated production run lasting just a few days, a very large number of cameras are produced and placed into final inventory. This run size has been set at 20,000, which covers sales for 2½ months on the average. (As indicated in the preceding chapter, the number produced or ordered to replenish inventory is called the **order quantity**.)

Although it is only possible to produce these recycled cameras from the cameras returned by camera stores, the factory always has had a plentiful supply of these returned cameras for its production runs.

FIGURE 12.6

Niko's sales of disposable panoramic cameras in each month of the past year.

	A	B	C	D	E
1		Monthly Sales of Niko's Disposable Cameras			
2					
3		Month	Sales		
4		January	7,000		
5		February	1,500		
6		March	15,800		
7		April	8,600		
8		May	9,900		
9		June	4,200		
10		July	13,600		
11		August	700		
12		September	14,100		
13		October	6,200		
14		November	5,000		
15		December	9,400		

Once the decision has been made to initiate a production run, some time is needed to clear the required production facilities from other uses and set them up for this run. (Recall that this time between ordering a product and receiving it is referred to as the **lead time.**) The lead time for this camera generally is about *one month.*

Since average sales over a lead time of one month are 8,000, it has become routine to order another production run when the number of cameras in inventory drops to 8,000. (Recall that this inventory level at which an order to replenish is placed is called the **reorder point.**)

To summarize, here are the key data for how the inventory of this camera is being managed.

Order quantity = 20,000
Lead time = 1 month
Reorder point = 8,000

Last Year's Experience   Last year began with 16,500 disposable panoramic cameras in inventory. The January sales of 7,000 reported in Figure 12.6 reduced this inventory level to 9,500 by the end of the month. The February sales of 1,500 then reduced it to 8,000. Since 8,000 is the reorder point, an order was given at the end of February to initiate a production run of 20,000. After the lead time of one month, these 20,000 cameras were received and placed into inventory at the end of March. Since March sales of 15,800 already had depleted the 8,000 in inventory and left 7,800 in **backorders,** part of the production run immediately was used to fill these backorders. This left 12,200 in inventory to begin April.

Figure 12.7 shows the record of what happened throughout the year, where the diamonds in the plot record the beginning inventories in those months. Five orders were placed for production runs of 20,000 (although the last run hadn't quite been set up by the end of December). Therefore, the beginning-of-month inventory levels fluctuated widely, with some values near 15,000 and some others near 0. Only one month (August) had a shortage (called a **stockout**) at the beginning of the month. This inventory level of −4,100 indicates that backorders for 4,100 cameras had accumulated in late July after the depletion of the inventory and that these backorders would need to be filled from the upcoming production run of 20,000 cameras. (Holding backorders when shortages occur and then filling them when the inventory is replenished is referred to as **backlogging.**)

However, this figure does not show the full story, because columns D and E only give the inventory levels at the change of a month. Furthermore, the plot at the bottom simply connects the beginning-of-month inventories with line segments. By contrast, whereas Figure 12.8 uses dots to show these same inventory levels, the dashed lines then display approximately how the inventory level varied within each month as well. (This still is an approximation since it assumes that each month's sales occurred evenly throughout the month rather than recording the actual individual sales during the month.) Note that four stockouts

FIGURE 12.7

Niko's record of sales, inventories, and orders for each month last year, where the graph shows how the beginning inventory changes from month to month.

	A	B	C	D	E	F
1		Monthly Record of Niko's Inventory of Disposable Cameras				
2						
3				Beginning	Ending	
4		Month	Sales	Inventory	Inventory	Action
5		January	7,000	16,500	9,500	None
6		February	1,500	9,500	8,000	Ordered 20,000 at end of month
7		March	15,800	8,000	12,200	Order received at end of month
8		April	8,600	12,200	3,600	Ordered 20,000 during month
9		May	9,900	3,600	13,700	Order received during month
10		June	4,200	13,700	9,500	None
11		July	13,600	9,500	– 4,100	Ordered 20,000 during month
12		August	700	– 4,100	15,200	Order received during month
13		September	14,100	15,200	1,100	Ordered 20,000 during month
14		October	6,200	1,100	14,900	Order received during month
15		November	5,000	14,900	9,900	None
16		December	9,400	9,900	500	Ordered 20,000 during month
17						

(Rows 18–28 contain the embedded chart of Inventory Level vs. Time, with the inventory level plotted for each month January through December.)

FIGURE 12.8

A smoothed display of how Niko's inventory level varied throughout the past year, where sales within each month are shown as occurring evenly throughout the month. (The detailed display reflecting any sales each day actually has a very jagged appearance.)

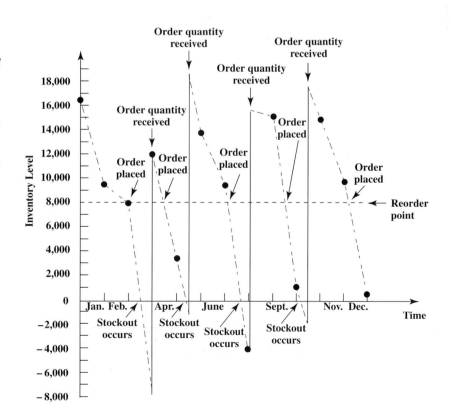

occurred during the year. Their sizes ranged from 1,235 to 7,800 cameras backordered. The durations ranged from a few days to a couple weeks. The distributors affected by the longer stockouts were not happy with this shoddy service, and several of them registered complaints with Niko management.

Management's Concerns

Niko's management has always taken pride in both the quality of its cameras and the quality of the company's service to its customers. Therefore, the recent complaints from several distributors about delays in shipping one of the company's most popular models, the disposable panoramic camera, has caused considerable concern. The North American Division's vice president for marketing, in particular, is urging that something be done about this problem. She is suggesting having more frequent production runs to keep the inventory better stocked.

At the same time, complaints have been received from the production floor about the relatively frequent interruptions in the production of other models caused by setting up for a production run for the disposable panoramic camera every two or three months. Although a production run is quick once the setup is completed, the process of setting up is quite complicated. A significant part of the expense in producing this camera is the direct cost of setting up and the additional cost attributable to disrupting other production. Therefore, the vice president for production strongly disagrees with the vice president for marketing. He recommends instead having much longer production runs much less frequently. He argues that this will solve two problems at once. First, it would provide larger inventories for longer periods of time and thereby greatly reduce the frequency of delayed shipments due to stockouts. Second, it would substantially reduce the annual cost of setting up for production runs, including the cost associated with disrupting other production.

However, because it would increase inventory levels, the president of the North American Division is quite skeptical about this recommendation. For some time, he has been pushing the just-in-time philosophy of minimizing inventory by using careful planning and coordinating to provide items just in time to serve their purpose. This philosophy has enabled the company to greatly reduce its work-in-process inventories while also improving the efficiency of its production processes. Although it has been necessary to maintain some inventories of finished products until they could be sold, the president is proud of the fact that even these inventories have been considerably reduced in recent years. The reductions in inventories throughout the company have provided substantial cost savings, including in the cost of capital tied up in inventory. These economies have been one of the key factors in maintaining Niko's place as one of the world's leading producers of cameras. Therefore, the president feels that it should be possible to solve the current problems without increasing the average inventory levels of disposable panoramic cameras.

So what should be done? The president has called upon the North American Division's Management Science Department many times in the past to address similar problems, with excellent results. Therefore, he has instructed this department to form a team to study this problem.

The next section describes the management science team's approach to the problem.

Review Questions

1. What has been happening in Niko's North American Division that is causing considerable managerial concern?
2. What is the concern of the vice president for marketing of the North American Division about the current situation? What recommendation is she making?
3. What is the main concern of the Division vice president for production about the current situation? What recommendation is he making?
4. Why is the Division president skeptical about his vice president for production's recommendation? What company philosophy has he been promoting that relates to the current situation?

12.4 The Management Science Team's Analysis of the Case Study

The management science team begins by trying to diagnose why the frequent stockouts were occurring under the current inventory policy (order a production run of 20,000 when the inventory level drops to 8,000). Was this just a string of bad luck? Or did the current policy naturally lead to a high probability of a stockout occurring before the production run takes place? Just what is this probability? If a stockout occurs, what is the probability distribution of the size of the stockout (the number of cameras backordered when the stockout ends)?

Assessing the Stockout Problem

Since the lead time for a production run is approximately one month, the key to answering these questions is to estimate the underlying *probability distribution* of the number of cameras sold in a month. Examining the pattern of monthly sales over the past year shown in Figure 12.6 (along with similar data for other recent years), the team notes that these sales ranged pretty uniformly from almost nothing up to about 16,000. Therefore, the team's best estimate is that the number of cameras sold in a month has a *uniform distribution* over the range from 0 to 16,000. Since this assumes that all the values over this range are equally likely, but that there is no chance of values outside this range, this distribution has the appearance shown in Figure 12.9. The mean of this distribution is 8,000, which corresponds to the observed average monthly sales.

When a production run is ordered with 8,000 cameras left in inventory, and the new cameras arrive a month later, the probability of a stockout occurring is just the probability that a month's sales exceeds 8,000. With this uniform distribution, these probabilities are

$$P(\text{stockout}) = P(\text{monthly sales} > 8,000)$$

$$= 0.5$$

With just a 50-50 chance of incurring a stockout after ordering a production run, having this occur four times in a row last year (as shown in Figure 12.8) was indeed a string of bad luck. This should occur only two times out of four *on the average*.

This uniform distribution also indicates that there was further bad luck in terms of the size of the stockouts last year. The inventory level *just* before the order for the 20,000 new cameras is received is 8,000 minus the month's sales. Therefore, the probability distribution of this inventory level also is a uniform distribution, but over the range from −8,000 (= 8,000 − 16,000) to 8,000 (= 8,000 − 0), as shown in Figure 12.10. The probability that this inventory level would fall as low as −7,800 is extremely small (0.0125), but this did indeed occur at the end of March last year.

However, given management's desire to provide high-quality service to the company's customers, it seems unacceptable to have a probability of a stockout as high as 0.5 and to have the size of stockouts range as high as 8,000. Even without the bad luck of last year, such high numbers would inevitably lead to occasional significant delays in filling customer orders. Although customers would accept brief delays every once in a while, such frequent and lengthy delays need to be avoided.

Conclusion: Both the probability of a stockout and the maximum size of a stockout are too large.

FIGURE 12.9

The estimated probability distribution of the number of disposable panoramic cameras that Niko sells in a month is a uniform distribution from 0 to 16,000.

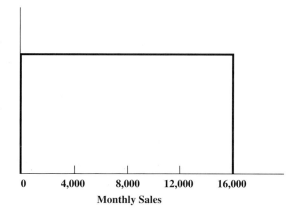

Monthly Sales

FIGURE 12.10

Based on Figure 12.9, the estimated probability distribution of Niko's inventory level just before receiving 20,000 new cameras from a production run is a uniform distribution from −8,000 to 8,000.

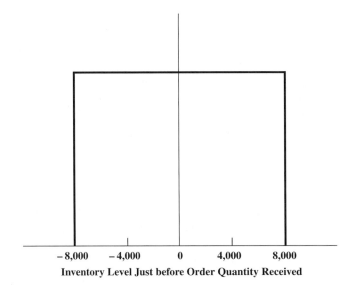

Inventory Level Just before Order Quantity Received

FIGURE 12.11

If the reorder point were reset to 12,000, then the estimated probability distribution of Niko's inventory level just before receiving 20,000 new cameras from a production run would be a uniform distribution from −4,000 to 12,000.

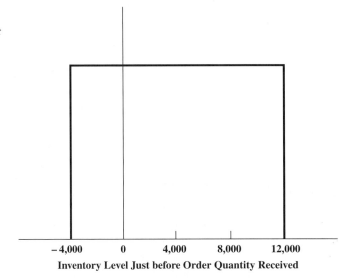

Inventory Level Just before Order Quantity Received

Alleviating Stockouts

Why is the probability of a stockout so high? The reason is that the method that was used to set the *reorder point* is faulty. This point was only set equal to the average sales (8,000) during the lead time (one month) for producing the next batch of cameras. No provision was made for the month's sales exceeding the average, even though this should be expected to occur half the time.

> **Conclusion:** When reordering, a cushion of extra inventory needs to be provided in addition to the amount needed to cover the average sales during the lead time. (This extra inventory is referred to as **safety stock.**)

With safety stock, the formula for setting the reorder point then is

Reorder point = average sales during lead time + amount of safety stock

= 8,000 + amount of safety stock

For example,

Reorder point = 12,000   if   amount of safety stock = 4,000

Changing the reorder point from 8,000 to 12,000 would change the probability distribution of the inventory level at the end of the lead time from the one shown in Figure 12.10 to that given in Figure 12.11. Since this new distribution is a uniform distribution over the range

FIGURE 12.12

A smoothed display of how Niko's inventory level would have varied throughout the past year if the reorder point had been set at 12,000 instead of 8,000 (as in Figure 12.8).

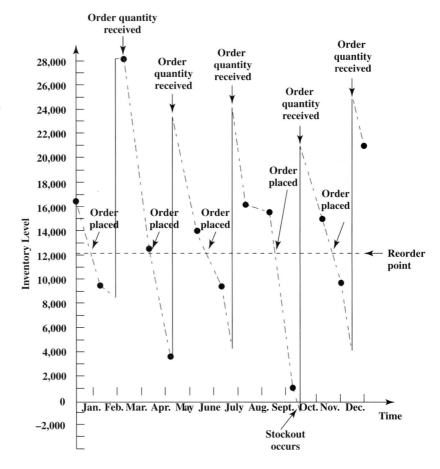

from −4,000 to 12,000, the probability of a stockout now would be 0.25, with a maximum possible size of 4,000. Thus, stockouts now would occur only about once every four times a production run is ordered, on the average, and those shortages that do occur would tend to be somewhat smaller than before.

Figure 12.12 shows approximately how the inventory level would have evolved throughout the past year if the reorder point had been 12,000. (As with Figure 12.8, the dashed lines in this graph approximate the evolution within each month by treating the month's sales as having occurred evenly throughout the month.) Under this scenario, an order is fortuitously placed in mid-January and received in mid-February, in time to cover the unusually large sales of 15,800 in March. Consequently, a substantial number of cameras remain in inventory throughout the entire year, except for one very small and brief stockout in October.

Now compare this figure to Figure 12.8. Note the dramatic improvement in avoiding stockouts and thereby avoiding delays in filling customer orders. It is true that part of the improvement was a matter of luck. Nevertheless, even under the worst circumstances, the higher reorder point of 12,000 would have avoided the more serious stockout problems shown in Figure 12.8. With a maximum possible stockout size of 4,000 instead of 8,000, the stockouts that do occur would tend to be both smaller and briefer, thereby causing much less damage to customer relations.

> **Conclusion:** Even when the amount of safety stock provided still permits occasional short stockouts, this safety stock can dramatically improve the service to customers by greatly reducing both the number and length of the delays in filling customer orders.

Choosing the Amount of Safety Stock

You have just seen that providing a safety stock of 4,000 cameras is much better than providing none at all. But is 4,000 the right amount? Note that the inventory levels shown in Figure 12.12 are much higher than in Figure 12.8, whereas the president wants to keep inventories down as much as reasonably possible. What is the best trade-off between the costs of holding inventory and the consequences of stockouts?

Since choosing such a trade-off is ultimately a management decision, the management science team consults with management about their feelings regarding stockouts. These are the key questions posed to management.

1. How important is it to reduce delays in filling customer orders?
2. Considering that larger inventories would be needed to reduce delays, how would you compare the importance of reducing delays with the importance of holding inventory levels down?
3. Considering that unacceptably large inventories would be needed to completely eliminate any delays, what would you consider tolerable in terms of the frequency, size, and length of stockouts?

To help make these questions more concrete to management, the management science team describes the frequency, size, and length of stockouts that would be expected for each of several alternative amounts of safety stock. For example, here is the description for a safety stock of 4,000 cameras.

> With a safety stockout of 4,000 disposable panoramic cameras, a new production run would be ordered when the inventory level drops to 12,000 cameras. Since the average sales during the lead time for the production run (one month) are 8,000 cameras, the inventory would be adequate to cover sales in most cases. However, since a month's sales can range as high as 16,000 cameras, and about a quarter of the months have sales between 12,000 and 16,000 cameras, a stockout would occur about once every four times on the average. With the current production runs of 20,000 cameras occurring about four times every 10 months, this means that a stockout would occur about once every 10 months. When it does occur, the size would range from very small to about 4,000 cameras backordered, so about 2,000 on the average. Since we sell about 80,000 cameras over 10 months, this means that about 2.5 percent of our customers would incur a delay in having their orders filled. The delays would range from very short (in most cases) up to about a week, with an estimated average of about a third of a week. (The full week would result from a month's sales of 16,000 cameras after ordering a production run, with the last 4,000 sales occurring during the last week of the month.) Beware, however, that these numbers assume that we can continue holding to a lead time of about one month. If an unexpected delay in a production run should occur, the possible shortages and delays would be extended accordingly.

After the management science team elicits management's views about this scenario and the several alternatives, the following conclusion is drawn.

> **Conclusion:** Management feels that providing a safety stock of roughly 4,000 cameras is needed to provide an adequate level of service to customers in minimizing delays in filling their orders. Considering the company's just-in-time philosophy regarding the need to hold down inventories, management does not want the safety stock raised higher than this.

Having established that the reorder point should be increased from 8,000 to 12,000, the management science team next wants to investigate what the *order quantity* (the size of each production run) should be. Realizing that this issue involves a trade-off between several types of costs, the team first turns to estimating these costs.

The Cost Factors

All the relevant cost factors for analyzing inventory problems were described in Section 11.2. The four types are (1) acquisition costs, (2) setup costs, (3) holding costs, and (4) shortage costs.

The *acquisition cost* in this case is the cost of producing the disposable panoramic cameras (when using the recycled components). Excluding setup costs, this production cost is just $7 per camera. However, this cost turns out to be irrelevant for choosing the order quantity. The reason is that the order quantity does not affect sales, and it is sales that determine the number (and so the production cost) of cameras that will be produced eventually. The order quantity only affects the timing of when the fixed production costs will be incurred.

However, **setup costs** are very relevant. The cost of setting up for a production run, plus additional costs associated with disrupting other production in the process, is estimated to be $12,000. The order quantity (size of the production run) determines how frequently this cost will be incurred.

The **holding costs** encompass all the costs associated with holding the cameras in inventory. One important component is the cost of capital tied up in the inventory. The company pays an annual interest rate of about 10 percent on money borrowed to pay for the production of cameras that are not yet sold. The production cost (including setup cost) per camera is about $7.50, and the company's cost invested in each set of recycled components of a camera is another $16.50, for a total of $24. Therefore, the cost of capital tied up for each camera in inventory is about $2.40 per year, or 20¢ per month. (This seemingly insignificant cost does add up when there are many thousands of cameras in inventory.)

Holding costs also include all the costs directly involved with storing the cameras, including the cost of the space, record keeping, protection, insurance, and taxes. When 12,500 cameras are in inventory (a roughly average level), these costs are estimated to add up to just about $1,250 per month, so about 10¢ per camera. Adding in the cost of capital tied up gives a total holding cost per camera of about 30¢ per month. Certain storage costs (e.g., space and protection) may not be directly proportional to the inventory level. However, as an approximation, it is assumed that the total holding cost per month is 30¢ *times* the current inventory level (except for ignoring negative levels that represent shortages).

The **shortage costs** are more difficult to quantify. The main component is lost future profit from lost future sales caused by customer dissatisfaction with delays in filling current orders. This is difficult to estimate. Other minor components might include the cost of additional record keeping and handling for dealing with backordered cameras.

Estimating shortage costs requires a managerial assessment of the seriousness of making customers wait to have their orders filled. To obtain this managerial input, the management science team poses the following question to the vice president for marketing.

> *Question:* We have discussed the fact that the worst case scenario with a safety stock of 4,000 cameras would be to incur a stockout of about 4,000 cameras with a delay in filling the orders of about one week. If you were to put a dollar figure on the damage that such a stockout would cause the company in terms of lost profit from lost future business, and so forth, what would that figure be? In other words, if it were possible for the company to pay some money to prevent this one stockout completely, how much should we be willing to pay to do so? We realize that it is difficult to pin down an exact dollar figure, but we are only asking you to apply your judgment as best you can in responding to this question.
> *Response:* $10,000.

As a rough approximation, the management science team assumes that the shortage cost from any stockout should be *proportional* to both the size of the stockout and the resulting average delay in filling the orders. Thus, with a cost of $10,000 for a shortage of 4,000 cameras for one week, the cost for extending the average delay to one month (four weeks) is assumed to be about $40,000, or about $10 per camera per month of delay.

This assumption is definitely questionable. The actual shortage cost for a delay of a month (*infuriating* the customers) might be considerably more than four times that for a delay of a week (mildly concerning the customers). However, the management science team feels that the assumption of proportionality is a reasonable one over the range of actual delays (up to roughly one week) that would be incurred with a safety stock of 4,000 cameras.

Table 12.1 summarizes all these cost factors and their estimated values. The symbols in the table are the same as introduced in Chapter 11 for these types of cost except that the management science team now is measuring costs on a monthly rather than annual basis.

TABLE 12.1 **The Cost Factors for Niko's Inventory Problem**

Type of Cost	Symbol	Value
Setup cost for a production run	K	$12,000
Holding cost per camera per month	h	$0.30
Shortage cost per camera per month of delay in filling the customer order	p	$10

Choosing the Order Quantity

With these cost factors pinned down, the management science team now is ready to address the problem of determining what order quantity (number of cameras to be produced in a production run) would minimize the sum of all these costs. (Recall from Chapter 11 that the order quantity that minimizes the total average cost is commonly referred to as the **economic order quantity** or **EOQ** for short.)

Here are the trade-offs involved in making this decision.

1. The average monthly setup costs are decreased by increasing the order quantity, because this decreases the average number of setups required per month.
2. However, the average monthly holding costs are decreased by decreasing the order quantity, since this decreases the average inventory level.
3. However, the average monthly shortage costs are decreased by increasing the order quantity, because this decreases the average number of opportunities for stockouts per month.

Section 11.5 presented the **EOQ model with planned shortages** to address exactly these same trade-offs. In fact, that model completely fits Niko's inventory problem with just one important exception: the model's assumption that sales occur at a constant rate, with no variation from month to month. Thus, for the Niko problem, the model would assume that the average monthly sales of 8,000 disposable panoramic cameras are the actual sales spread evenly through the month for each and every month. The reality, of course, is that Niko's sales of these cameras vary greatly from month to month.

How much effect does this month-to-month variation have on the *average* total monthly cost that needs to be minimized to determine the economic order quantity? The effect on the average monthly shortage costs is rather considerable, since the month-to-month variation tends to increase the frequency and size of the shortages. However, the effect on the average monthly holding cost is only slight. The fact that no holding costs are incurred during shortages has a slight effect, but otherwise the average inventory level is not significantly affected. Furthermore, there is no effect on the average monthly setup costs, since the variation does not affect the average frequency of setups for production runs. Consequently, the overall effect of the month-to-month variation in sales on the average total monthly cost is modest. Therefore, using the model from Section 11.5 to calculate the economic order quantity (but not the reorder point) for Niko's problem provides a pretty good approximation. The management science team decides to adopt this approach.

To review, the important notation from Section 11.5 (now expressed on a monthly rather than annual basis) is

K, h, p as defined in Table 12.1

$$D = \text{monthly sales rate}$$

$$= 8,000 \text{ as the average for Niko's problem}$$

$$Q = \text{order quantity}$$

$$S = \text{shortage } just \text{ before an order quantity is received}$$

Using an asterisk to indicate the *optimal* value of Q and S, their formulas given in Section 11.5 are

$$Q^* = \sqrt{\frac{h + p}{p}} \sqrt{\frac{2KD}{h}}$$

$$S^* = \left(\frac{h}{h + p}\right)Q^*$$

An Excel template is available in your MS Courseware for performing these calculations for you. For Niko's problem, plugging the values of K, h, and p given in Table 12.1 (plus $D = 8,000$) into this template gives the results shown in Figure 12.13. Since $Q^* = 25,675$ cameras and $S^* = 748$ cameras, the inventory level jumps from a shortage of 748 cameras to a level of

$$Q^* - S^* = 24,927 \text{ cameras}$$

when the order quantity (the output of a production run) arrives.

FIGURE 12.13

The Excel template for the EOQ model with planned shortages (analytical version) in your MS Courseware is applied here to find the order quantity for the Niko problem.

	A	B	C	D	E	F	G
1		EOQ Model with Planned Shortages (Niko Case Study)					
2							
3			Data			Results	
4		D =	8000	(demand/year)		Max Inventory Level =	24927.08
5		K =	$12,000	(setup cost)			
6		h =	$0.30	(unit holding cost)		Annual Setup Cost =	$3,739.06
7		p =	$10	(unit shortage cost)		Annual Holding Cost =	$3,630.16
8						Annual Shortage Cost =	$108.90
9			Decision			Total Variable Cost =	$7,478.12
10		Q =	25675	(order quantity)			
11		S =	748	(maximum shortage)			

	C
10	=SQRT(2*C4*C5/C6)*SQRT((C7+C6)/C7)
11	=(C6/(C6+C7))*C10

	G
4	=C10–C11
5	
6	=C5*C4/C10
7	=C6*(G4^2)/(2*C10)
8	=C7*((C10–G4)^2)/(2*C10)
9	=SUM(G6:G8)

FIGURE 12.14

A hypothetical display of how Niko's inventory level is assumed to evolve under the EOQ model with planned shortages, including the assumption of a constant rate of sales of 8,000 cameras per month.

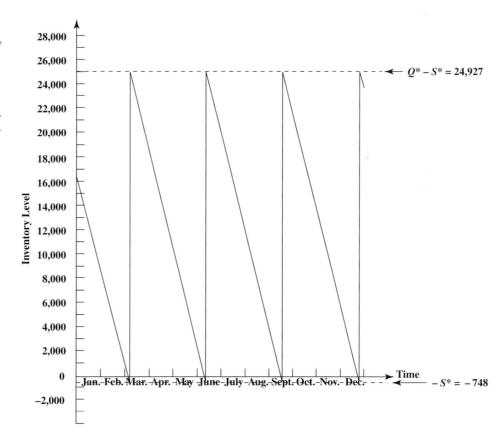

Using these quantities, Figure 12.14 shows how the EOQ model with planned shortages assumes Niko's inventory level would evolve over a year, starting with last year's initial inventory of 16,500 cameras. (Keep in mind that this model assumes that sales occur at a constant rate, which does not fit Niko's situation.) With a lead time of one month, the model orders a production run each time just one month before a shortage of 748 cameras occurs. Since the assumed sales over this lead time are 8,000 cameras, the model thereby sets the reorder point at 8,000 − 748 = 7,252 cameras.

FIGURE 12.15

A smoothed display of how Niko's inventory level would have evolved throughout the past year under the inventory policy recommended by the management science team.

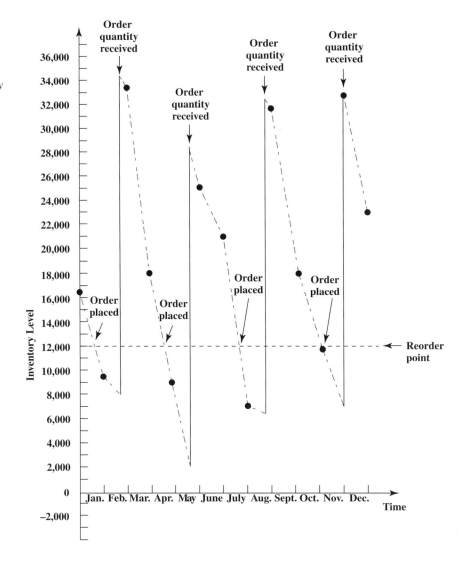

However, it is crucial that *only Q** and *not* this reorder point be used from the model. Because Niko's actual sales do vary considerably from month to month, a substantial safety stock is needed as a cushion against the sales during the lead time being much higher than average. Therefore, based on the earlier analysis of how much safety stock is needed, the management science team makes the following recommendation.

> **Recommended inventory policy:** Whenever the number of disposable panoramic cameras in inventory drops to 12,000, order a production run of 25,675 cameras.

Figure 12.15 depicts how this inventory policy would have performed throughout the past year. (Once again, the dashed lines approximate the evolution of the inventory level throughout each month by treating the sales as having occurred evenly throughout the month.) A substantial inventory, ranging from 2,513 to 34,211 cameras, would have been maintained throughout the year. However, in light of the probability distribution shown in Figure 12.11, a bit of good luck was involved. Despite having a probability of 0.25 that a stockout will occur before an order is received, this never happened in the four chances during the year.

Management's Reaction to the Recommended Inventory Policy

This recommended inventory policy provides at least a good approximation of an optimal policy (an optimal combination of a reorder point and an order quantity) that minimizes the total average monthly cost. Or at least it is an "approximately optimal" policy under the conditions given to the management science team (a lead time of one month, the cost factors in Table 12.1, etc.). But is it really a sound policy from a managerial perspective?

The three members of management dealing with this problem have expressed their reservations about the recommendation. The president is unhappy about the large increase in inventory levels that would result from the substantial increases in both the reorder point and order quantity. He realizes the need for some safety stock, but feels that there should be a better approach to the problem that is more in line with the company's just-in-time philosophy of minimizing the use of inventories.

The vice president for marketing is happy that the new safety stock will considerably alleviate the stockout problem. However, she is somewhat concerned that shortages of various magnitudes still can be expected to occur about once per year. She continues to emphasize that high priority needs to be placed on maintaining and building the company's reputation for good and prompt service to its customers.

The vice president for production is quite unhappy. He had emphasized the problems caused in disrupting other production by shifting facilities over so frequently to set up for production runs of the disposable panoramic camera. Although the recommendation would slightly decrease the frequency of production runs, he does not feel that the disruption problems have yet been dealt with adequately.

The costs associated with this "approximately optimal" policy are indeed disturbingly high. The profit margin on each camera sold is only about $2, due partially to these high costs. Here is a breakdown of each of the costs of major concern to one of the members of management under the recommended inventory policy.

HOLDING COST CALCULATIONS

Average Inventory Levels:

Just before an order is received
$$= 12,000 - 8,000$$
$$= 4,000$$

Just after an order is received
$$= 4,000 + 25,675$$
$$= 29,675$$

Overall average
$$= \frac{4,000 + 29,675}{2}$$
$$= 16,837$$

Holding cost per camera per month, $h = \$0.30$

Average monthly holding cost[3]
$$= 16,837 \ (\$0.30)$$
$$= \$5,051$$

SHORTAGE COST CALCULATIONS

Average number of orders per month
$$= \frac{\text{sales}}{\text{order quantity}}$$
$$= \frac{8,000}{25,675} = 0.31$$

Probability of a stockout before order received $= 0.25$

Expected number of stockouts per month
$$= 0.25 \ (0.31)$$
$$= 0.078$$

Average stockout size
$$= \frac{4,000}{2} = 2,000$$

---

[3]Actually, this calculation slightly understates the true average montly holding cost because it charges a negative holding cost instead of zero when the inventory level is negative because of shortages.

$$\text{Estimate of average delay per camera delayed}^4 = \tfrac{1}{3} \text{ week}$$

$$= 0.08 \text{ month}$$

$$\text{Shortage cost per camera per month, } p = \$10$$

$$\text{Average monthly shortage cost} = 0.078(2,000)(0.08)(\$10)$$

$$= \$125$$

SETUP COST CALCULATIONS

$$\text{Average number of setups per month} = \frac{\text{sales}}{\text{order quantity}}$$

$$= \frac{8,000}{25,675} = 0.31$$

$$\text{Cost per setup, } K = \$12,000$$

$$\text{Average monthly setup cost} = 0.31(\$12,000)$$

$$= \$3,720$$

Adding these three average monthly costs gives

$$\text{Average total monthly cost} = \$5,051 + \$125 + \$3,720$$

$$= \$8,896$$

Since an average of 8,000 cameras are sold per month, this cost amounts to about $1.11 per camera. Thus, a substantial decrease in this cost would add significantly to the company's current profit margin of about $2 per camera sold.

In light of these considerations, management instructs the management science team to go back and study the problem anew from a broader perspective. Rather than focusing on the reorder point and the order quantity, the team is to investigate what fundamental changes might be made to drive these costs down.

Additional Recommendations from the Management Science Team

The management science team begins this phase of their study by diagnosing the factors that are forcing the cost of even an "optimal" inventory policy to be so unusually high for such an inexpensive product. They identify the following three.

1. The *high setup cost* ($12,000), including a substantial component for the disruption of other production. The average monthly setup cost is nearly half of the average total monthly cost. Furthermore, the high setup cost is forcing large production runs that are driving up the average inventory levels.

2. The *long lead time* (about one month). This is a major factor in the disruption of other production while facilities are being shifted to both continue that production and set up for a production run for the disposable panoramic camera. Furthermore, the long lead time is a major factor in needing a large safety stock while still incurring a substantial risk of a stockout.

3. The *high variability in monthly sales.* Because of this variability, the inventory level just before the order quantity from the production run is received can range anywhere from 12,000 to −4,000 (4,000 cameras backordered). Thus, the variability is both driving up the average inventory level and causing significant shortage costs.

The team devotes considerable time to analyzing these three factors and what can be done to counteract them. This process leads to the following four recommendations to management.

---

[4]Although the *maximum* delay is about a week, most delayed camera orders do not wait nearly this long, either because they come in during the latter part of a shortage or because the shortage is much briefer than this maximum duration. Based on calculus, the management science team has calculated that the average delay per camera delayed should be one-third of the maximum delay.

Recommendation 1: Acquire some additional production facilities that would be used solely for production runs of the disposable panoramic camera as needed. Although some modest shifting of other facilities and personnel still would be needed for these production runs, having these dedicated facilities permanently set up for the runs would eliminate most of the setup cost and reduce the lead time to less than a week. The new facilities are estimated to cost about $50,000, plus an overall increase of about $2,000 monthly in maintenance and space costs. However, these costs will be recovered in about a year by the great decreases in setup, holding, and shortage costs.

Recommendation 2: Provide a small price incentive to the company's customers (wholesale distributors) to place a standing order for regular monthly purchases of the disposable panoramic camera, with an option to make additional purchases as needed. The resulting reduced variability in the sales pattern should substantially reduce the risk of stockouts and thereby decrease the amount of safety stock needed.

Recommendation 3: Develop a system for coordinating sales of the disposable panoramic camera as needed with the company's divisions in other parts of the world. Specifically, the system should enable another division with excess inventory to quickly fill a large order we have received when we are unable to do so. Conversely, we can do the same for another division and reduce our inventory level in the process.

Recommendation 4: A study also should be conducted of the raw material inventories, including especially the returned reusable components, for the disposable panoramic camera. These inventory levels have been running very high. An attempt should be made to coordinate these inventory levels with production decisions for the camera. In line with recommendation 3, the new system should include a provision for some shifting of raw material inventories between divisions as needed. Finally, when these inventory levels are too high, strong consideration should be given to temporarily providing a rebate coupon with each camera to generate increased sales and thereby help work down these expensive inventories.

After further discussion between management and the management science team, management accepts all four recommendations with considerable enthusiasm. The president is very pleased about all the steps being taken to drive down inventory levels in line with the company's just-in-time philosophy. The vice president for marketing applauds the creative proposals for greatly reducing the risk of not being able to fill customer orders promptly. The vice president for production is especially happy that recommendation 1 will largely solve his problem that shifting facilities to start a production run for the disposable panoramic camera has somewhat disrupted other production.

The president commends the management science team for continuing in the fine tradition of the Management Science Department by effectively looking at the big picture in creatively addressing management's concerns. As usual, he also instructs the team to work with management on explaining and selling the recommendations to the affected personnel and on overseeing the implementation of the recommendations.

Finally, he asks the team to go back to the drawing board to develop a new recommended policy (reorder point and order quantity) for the finished product inventory of disposable panoramic cameras after the four recommendations have been implemented. He also remarks, somewhat ominously, that he wants to be shown much smaller average inventory levels this time under the new policy. The team leader smiles, realizing that the four recommendations will enable the team to do just that. (See Problem 12.9.)

Review Questions

1. How did the management science team begin their analysis?
2. What conclusion was drawn about the probability of a stockout and the maximum size of a stockout under the old inventory policy?
3. After the amount of safety stock is chosen, what is the formula for setting the reorder point?

4. What conclusion was drawn about the value of safety stock?

5. Did management or the management science team make the decision on how much safety stock to provide?

6. What are the relevant cost factors for choosing the order quantity?

7. What is the main component of shortage costs?

8. What effect does increasing the order quantity have on average monthly setup costs? On average monthly holding costs? On average monthly shortage costs?

9. Which inventory model from Chapter 11 did the management science team use to find the approximately optimal order quantity?

10. Why was management unhappy with the recommended inventory policy?

11. What were the three factors that caused the cost of this inventory policy to be unusually high for such an inexpensive product?

12. What recommendation was made that would greatly reduce the setup cost and the lead time?

12.5 A Continuous-Review Inventory Model for Stable Products

The management science team was not starting from scratch in their analysis of Niko's inventory problem with the disposable panoramic camera. A widely used inventory model is available for dealing with such problems, and the management science team was using this model to guide its analysis as well. We now will provide an overview of this model.

The model is for **stable products** (products that will remain sellable indefinitely) as opposed to *perishable products* (sellable for only a very limited time). So which type is the *disposable* panoramic camera? Customers would think of it as perishable since it is, after all, a disposable camera. However, what is relevant is the company's viewpoint. From Niko's perspective, it is a *stable* product because each camera in inventory will remain sellable indefinitely.

The model is designed for a **continuous-review inventory system,** because it assumes that the inventory level is monitored on a continuous basis so that a new order can be placed as soon as the inventory level drops to the reorder point, as opposed to a **periodic-review inventory system** where the inventory level is only monitored periodically such as at the end of each week. (Recall that the distinction between continuous-review and periodic-review inventory systems was discussed earlier in Section 11.3.)

The traditional method of implementing a continuous-review inventory system was to use a **two-bin system.** All the units for a particular product would be held in two bins. The capacity of one bin would equal the reorder point. The units would first be withdrawn from the other bin. Therefore, the emptying of this second bin would trigger placing a new order. During the lead time until this order is received, units would then be withdrawn from the first bin.

In more recent years, two-bin systems have been largely replaced by **computerized inventory systems.** Each addition to inventory and each sale causing a withdrawal are recorded electronically, so the current inventory level is always available from the computer. (For example, the modern scanning devices at retail store checkout stands may both itemize your purchases and record the sales of stable products for purposes of adjusting the current inventory levels.) Therefore, the computer will trigger a new order as soon as the inventory level has dropped to the reorder point. Several excellent software packages are available from software companies for implementing such a system.

Because of the extensive use of computers for modern inventory management, continuous-review inventory systems have become increasingly prevalent for stable products that are sufficiently important to warrant a formal inventory policy.

A continuous-review inventory system for a particular stable product normally will be based on two critical numbers:

R = reorder point
Q = order quantity

For a manufacturer managing its finished products inventory, as with the Niko case study, the order will be for a *production run* of size Q. For a wholesaler or retailer (or a manufacturer replenishing its raw materials inventory from a supplier), the order will be a *purchase order* for Q units of the product.

An inventory policy based on these two critical numbers is a simple one.

> **Inventory policy:** Whenever the inventory level of the product drops to R units, place an order for Q more units to replenish the inventory.

Such a policy is often called a *reorder-point, order-quantity policy,* or **(R, Q) policy** for short. (Consequently, the overall model might be referred to as the (R, Q) model. Other variations of these names, such as (Q, R) policy, (Q, R) model, etc., also are sometimes used.)

After summarizing the model's assumptions, we will outline how R and Q can be determined.

The Assumptions of the Model

1. Each application involves a single stable product.
2. The inventory level is under *continuous review,* so its current value always is known.
3. An (R, Q) policy is to be used, so the only decisions to be made are to choose R and Q.
4. There is a *lead time* between when the order is placed and when the order quantity is received. This lead time can be either fixed or variable.
5. The *demand* for withdrawing units from inventory to sell them (or for any other purpose) during this lead time is uncertain. However, the probability distribution of demand is known (or at least estimated).
6. If a stockout occurs before the order is received, the excess demand is *backlogged,* so that the backorders are filled once the order arrives.
7. A fixed *setup cost* (denoted by K) is incurred each time an order is placed.
8. Except for this setup cost, the cost of the order is proportional to the order quantity Q.
9. A certain holding cost (denoted by h) is incurred for each unit in inventory per unit time.
10. When a stockout occurs, a certain shortage cost (denoted by p) is incurred for each unit backordered per unit time until the backorder is filled.

All these assumptions fit the Niko case study quite closely, so the management science team had no hesitation in using this model to guide its analysis.

As already mentioned in the preceding section, this model also is closely related to the *EOQ model with planned shortages* presented in Section 11.5. In fact, all these assumptions also are consistent with that model, with the one key exception of assumption 5. Rather than having uncertain demand, that model assumed *known demand* with a fixed rate.

Because of the close relationship between these two models, their results should be fairly similar. The main difference is that, because of the uncertain demand for the current model, some safety stock needs to be added when setting the reorder point to provide some cushion for having well-above-average demand during the lead time. Otherwise, the trade-offs between the various cost factors are basically the same, so the order quantities from the two models should be similar.

Choosing the Order Quantity **Q**

The most straightforward approach to choosing Q for the current model is to simply use the formula given in Section 11.5 for the EOQ model with planned shortages. This formula is

$$Q = \sqrt{\frac{h + p}{p}} \sqrt{\frac{2KD}{h}}$$

where D now is the average demand per unit time and K, h, and p are defined in assumptions 7, 9, and 10, respectively.

This Q will be only an approximation of the optimal order quantity for the current model. However, no formula is available for the exact value of the optimal order quantity, so an approximation is needed. Fortunately, the approximation given above is a fairly good one.[5]

Choosing the Reorder Point R

A common approach to choosing the reorder point R is to base it on management's desired level of service to customers. Thus, the starting point is to obtain a managerial decision on service level. (Problem 12.12 analyzes the factors involved in this managerial decision.)

Service level can be defined in a number of different ways in this context, as outlined below.

Alternative Measures of Service Level

1. The probability that a stockout will not occur between the time an order is placed and the order quantity is received. (This is the definition used for the inventory model for perishable products presented in Section 12.2.)
2. The average number of stockouts per year.
3. The average percentage of annual demand that can be satisfied immediately (no stockout).
4. The average delay in filling backorders when a stockout occurs.
5. The overall average delay in filling orders (where the delay without a stockout is 0).

Measures 1 and 2 are closely related. For example, suppose that the order quantity Q has been set at 10 percent of the annual demand, so an average of 10 orders are placed per year. If the probability is 0.2 that a stockout *will* occur during the lead time until an order is received, then the average number of stockouts per year would be 10 (0.2) = 2.

Measures 2 and 3 also are related. For example, suppose an average of two stockouts occur per year and the average length of a stockout is nine days. Since 2(9) = 18 days of stockout per year are essentially 5 percent of the year, the average percentage of annual demand that can be satisfied immediately would be 95 percent.

In addition, measures 3, 4, and 5 are related. For example, suppose that the average percentage of annual demand that can be satisfied immediately is 95 percent and the average delay in filling backorders when a stockout occurs is five days. Since only 5 percent of the customers incur this delay, the overall average delay in filling orders then would be 0.05(5) = 0.25 day per order.

A managerial decision needs to be made on the desired value of at least one of these measures of service level. After selecting one of these measures on which to focus primary attention, it is useful to explore the implications of several alternative values of this measure on some of the other measures before choosing the best alternative. This is basically the approach that was used by the management science team with Niko management in the case study—measure 1 was the primary measure but considerable attention was given to several others as well. (See the subsection entitled "Choosing the Amount of Safety Stock" in Section 12.4.)

Measure 1 probably is the most convenient one to use as the primary measure, so we now will focus on this case. We will denote the desired level of service under this measure by L, so

L = management's desired probability that a stockout will not occur between the time an order quantity is placed and the order quantity is received

Using measure 1 involves working with the estimated probability distribution of the demand during the lead time in filling an order. For example, for the Niko case study, this distribution is the *uniform distribution* from 0 to 16,000 (as shown in Figure 12.9 at the beginning of Section 12.4).

With a uniform distribution, the formula for choosing the reorder point R is a simple one.

If the probability distribution of the demand during the lead time is a *uniform distribution* over the interval from a to b, set

$$R = a + L(b - a)$$

---

[5]For further information about the quality of this approximation, see S. Axsäter, "Using the Deterministic EOQ Formula in Stochastic Inventory Control," *Management Science* 42 (1996), pp. 830–34. Also see Y.-S. Zheng, "On Properties of Stochastic Systems," *Management Science* 38 (1992), pp. 87–103.

FIGURE 12.16

Calculation of the reorder point R *when* L = 0.75 *and the probability distribution of the demand over the lead time is a uniform distribution over the range from* a *to* b.

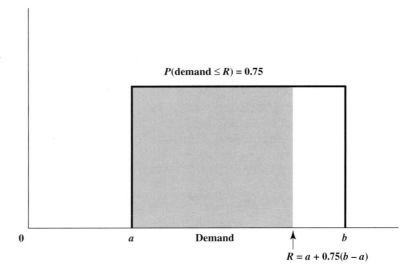

because then

$$P(\text{demand} \leq R) = L$$

Figure 12.16 shows such a distribution and the calculation of R for the case where $L = 0.75$. Since the mean of this distribution is

$$\text{Mean} = \frac{a + b}{2}$$

the amount of safety stock provided by the reorder point R is

$$\text{Safety stock} = R - \text{mean} = a + L(b - a) - \frac{a + b}{2}$$

$$= (L - \tfrac{1}{2})(b - a)$$

For the Niko case study, where $a = 0$ and $b = 16,000$, choosing $L = 0.75$ gave

$$R = 0 + 0.75(16,000 - 0)$$

$$= 12,000$$

as the reorder point that was adopted. This provided

$$\text{Safety stock} = (0.75 - 0.5)(16,000 - 0) = 4,000$$

When the demand distribution is something other than a uniform distribution, the procedure for choosing R is similar.

General Procedure for Choosing *R* under Service Level Measure 1

1. Choose *L*.
2. Solve for *R* such that

$$P(\text{demand} \leq R) = L$$

For example, suppose that the demand distribution is a normal distribution with some mean μ and variance σ^2 (and so standard deviation σ), as shown in Figure 12.17. Given the value of *L*, a standard table for the normal distribution then can be used to determine the value of *R*. Alternatively, the needed values from such a table also are given in the K_L column of Table 12.2 for various values of *L*. After choosing the desired value of *L*, you just need to find the corresponding value of K_L in Table 12.2 and then plug into the following formula to find *R*.

$$R = \mu + K_L \sigma$$

FIGURE 12.17

Calculation of the reorder point R when L = 0.75 and the probability distribution of the demand over the lead time is a normal distribution with mean μ and standard deviation σ.

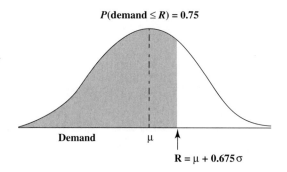

$P(\text{demand} \leq R) = 0.75$

Demand   μ

$R = \mu + 0.675\sigma$

TABLE 12.2   **Data for Choosing the Reorder Point When the Demand Distribution Is a Normal Distribution**

L	K_L	L	K_L
0.5	0	0.9	1.282
0.6	0.253	0.95	1.645
0.7	0.524	0.975	1.960
0.75	0.675	0.99	2.327
0.8	0.842	0.995	2.576
0.85	1.037	0.999	3.098

The resulting amount of safety stock is

$$\text{Safety stock} = R - \text{mean} = \mu + K_L \sigma - \mu$$

$$= K_L \sigma$$

To illustrate, if $L = 0.75$, then $K_L = 0.675$, so

$$R = \mu + 0.675\sigma$$

as shown in Figure 12.17. This provides

$$\text{Safety stock} = 0.675\sigma$$

As illustrated in Figure 12.18, your MS Courseware includes an Excel template that will calculate both the order quantity Q and the reorder point R for you. You need to enter the average demand per unit time, the costs (K, h, and p), and the service level based on measure 1. You also indicate whether the probability distribution of the demand during the lead time is a uniform distribution or a normal distribution. For a uniform distribution, you specify the interval over which the distribution extends by entering the lower endpoint and upper endpoint of this interval. For a normal distribution, you instead enter the mean μ and standard deviation σ of the distribution. After you provide all this information, the template immediately calculates Q and R and displays these results on the right side.

Figure 12.18 shows how this template could have been applied to the first stage of the Niko case study, which assumed a uniform distribution for demand. The results for Q and R correspond to the *recommended inventory policy* obtained in the middle of Section 12.4 while the management science team still was focusing on these quantities.

The choice of the distribution to use as the demand distribution can have a substantial effect on the reorder point R, and so on the amount of safety stock carried in inventory. Even with the same mean and standard deviation, the normal distribution can yield a substantially different amount of safety stock than the uniform distribution. To illustrate, consider the data of monthly sales over the past year for the Niko case study given in Figure 12.6 (beginning of Section 12.3). There is some underlying probability distribution for these monthly sales. It appears plausible from the data that this distribution is indeed a uniform distribution, as was assumed by the management science team. However, it also is quite possible that the underlying distribution is a normal distribution instead.

FIGURE 12.18

The Excel template for the continuous-review inventory model for stable products in your MS Courseware is being applied here to verify the recommended inventory policy presented in the middle of Section 12.4 for the first stage of the Niko case study.

	A	B	C	D	E	F	G
1		**Optimal Ordering Policy for Stable Products (Niko Case Study)**					
2							
3			**Data**				**Results**
4		D =	8000	(average demand/unit time)		Q =	25675
5		K =	$12,000	(setup cost)		R =	12000
6		h =	$0.30	(unit holding cost)			
7		p =	$10	(unit shortage cost)			
8		L =	0.75	(service level)			
9							
10							
11			**Demand During Lead Time**				
12		Distribution =	Uniform				
13		a =	0	(lower endpoint)			
14		b =	16000	(upper endpoint)			

	G
4	=SQRT(2*C4*C5/C6)*SQRT((C7+C6)/C7)
5	=IF(C12="Uniform",C13+C8*(C14–C13),NORMINV(C8,C13,C14))

FIGURE 12.19

The variation of Figure 12.18 where the probability distribution of Niko's monthly sales now is assumed to be a normal distribution with the same mean and standard deviation as before.

	A	B	C	D	E	F	G
1		**Optimal Ordering Policy for Stable Products (Normal Distribution)**					
2							
3			**Data**				**Results**
4		D =	8000	(average demand/unit time)		Q =	25675
5		K =	$12,000	(setup cost)		R =	11115
6		h =	$0.30	(unit holding cost)			
7		p =	$10	(unit shortage cost)			
8		L =	0.75	(service level)			
9							
10							
11			**Demand During Lead Time**				
12		Distribution =	Normal				
13		mean =	8000				
14		stand. dev. =	4619				

Suppose that further examination of the monthly sales data for both the past year and other recent years led to choosing a normal distribution (except for excluding negative values) as the best estimate of the underlying distribution of sales. Also suppose that calculating the *sample average* and *sample variance* from all these data provided the following estimates of the mean and standard deviation of the underlying distribution:

$$\mu = 8,000 \qquad \sigma = 4,619$$

(These are the same mean and standard deviation as for the uniform distribution from 0 to 16,000 that was previously used.) Then, with $L = 0.75$ and so $K_L = 0.675$, the reorder point would be

$$R = \mu + 0.675\sigma$$

$$= 8,000 + 0.675(4,619)$$

$$= 11,118$$

Using more decimal places for K_L, the Excel template in Figure 12.19 refines this calculation to obtain $R = 11,115$.

Note that this reorder point would provide a safety stock of only 3,115 cameras, versus the safety stock of 4,000 cameras when using the uniform distribution as the underlying distribution of sales. Thus, the decision on which type of distribution provides the best estimate of this underlying distribution makes a considerable difference.

So how should this decision on the distribution be made? The management science team in the Niko case study did this by simply making a judgment decision after "eyeballing" the data. However, we would advise you to take more care with such an important decision. A mathematical statistician can be very helpful in dealing with this issue. There is a statistical procedure called the *chi-square goodness-of-fit test* for checking whether a particular distribution (with mean and variance equal to the sample mean and sample variance, respectively) provides a good fit to the available data. (Beware, however, that this test is not very discriminating without a substantial amount of data—far more than the 12 months of sales figures given in Figure 12.6.) This test also can be used informally to check which of several alternative distributions provides the best fit.

Review Questions

1. Why is the disposable panoramic camera considered a *stable* product rather than a *perishable* product from Niko's perspective?
2. What is meant by a continuous-review inventory system?
3. What is the traditional method of implementing a continuous-review inventory system?
4. What is the common modern method of implementing a continuous-review inventory system?
5. What is an (R, Q) inventory policy?
6. What are the cost assumptions of the model for stable products?
7. What model from Chapter 11 is used to approximate the optimal order quantity?
8. What is the key difference in the assumptions of this model from Chapter 11 and the model in this section? What is the resulting main difference in the results from the two models?
9. What is a convenient measure of the service level?
10. What is the general formula needed to solve for the reorder point R when using this measure of the service level?

12.6 Larger Inventory Systems in Practice

All the inventory models presented in these two chapters have been concerned with the management of the inventory of a single product at a single geographical location. Such models provide the basic building blocks of scientific inventory management.

Multiproduct Inventory Systems

However, it is important to recognize that many inventory systems must deal simultaneously with many products, sometimes even hundreds or thousands of products. Furthermore, the inventory of each product often is dispersed geographically, perhaps even globally.

With multiple products, it commonly is possible to apply the appropriate single-product model to each of the products individually. However, companies may not bother to do this for the less important products because of the costs involved in regularly monitoring the inventory level to implement such a model. One popular approach in practice is the **ABC control method.** This involves dividing the products into three groups called the A group, B group, and C group. The products in the A group are the particularly important ones that are to be carefully monitored according to a formal inventory model. Products in the C group are the least important, so they are only monitored informally on a very occasional basis. Group B products receive an intermediate treatment.

It occasionally is not appropriate to apply a single-product inventory model because of interactions between the products. Various interactions are possible. Perhaps similar products can be substituted for each other as needed. For a manufacturer, perhaps its products must compete for production time when ordering production runs. For a wholesaler or retailer, perhaps its setup cost for ordering a product can be reduced by placing a joint order for a number of products simultaneously. Perhaps there also are joint budget limitations involving all the products. Perhaps the products need to compete for limited storage space.

It is common in practice to have a little bit of such interactions between products and still apply a single-product inventory model as a reasonable approximation. However, when an interaction is playing a major role, further analysis is needed. Some research has been conducted already to develop *multiproduct inventory models* to deal with some of these interactions.

Multiechelon Inventory Systems

Our growing global economy has caused a dramatic shift in inventory management entering the 21st century. Now, as never before, the inventory of many manufacturers is scattered throughout the world. Even the inventory of an individual product may be dispersed globally.

This inventory may be stored initially at the point or points of manufacture (one *echelon* of the inventory system), then at national or regional warehouses (a second echelon), then at field distribution centers (a third echelon), and so on. Such a system with multiple echelons of inventory is referred to as a **multiechelon inventory system.** In the case of a fully integrated corporation that both manufactures its products and sells them at the retail level, its echelons will extend all the way down to its retail outlets.

Some coordination is needed between the inventories of any particular product at the different echelons. Since the inventory at each echelon (except the top one) is replenished from the next higher echelon, the inventory level currently needed at the higher echelon is affected by how soon replenishment will be needed at the various locations for the lower echelon.

Considerable research (with roots tracing back to the middle of the 20th century) is being conducted to develop multiechelon inventory models.

Now let us see how one major corporation has been managing one of its multiechelon inventory systems.

Multiechelon Inventory Management at IBM[6]

IBM has roughly 1,000 products in service. Therefore, it employs over 15,000 customer engineers who are trained to repair and maintain all the installed computer systems sold or leased by IBM throughout the United States.

To support this effort, IBM maintains a huge multiechelon inventory system of spare parts. This system controls over 200,000 part numbers, with the total inventory valued in the billions of dollars. Millions of parts transactions are processed annually.

The echelons of this system start with the manufacture of the parts, then national or regional warehouses, then field distribution centers, then parts stations, and finally many thousand outside locations (including customer stock locations and the car trunks or tool chests of the company's customer engineers).

To coordinate and control all these inventories at the different echelons, a huge computerized system called *Optimizer* was developed. Optimizer consists of four major modules. A forecasting system module contains a few programs for estimating the failure rates of individual types of parts. A data delivery system module consists of approximately 100 programs that process over 15 gigabytes of data to provide the needed input into Optimizer. A decision system module then optimizes control of the inventories on a weekly basis. The fourth module includes six programs that integrate Optimizer into IBM's Parts Inventory Management System (PIMS). PIMS is a sophisticated information and control system that contains millions of lines of code.

Optimizer tracks the inventory level for each part number at all stocking locations (except at the outside locations, where only parts costing more than a certain threshold are tracked). An (R, Q) type of inventory policy is used for each part at each location and echelon in the system.

Careful planning was required to implement such a complex system after it had been designed. Three factors proved to be especially important in achieving a successful implementation. The first was the inclusion of a *user team* (consisting of operational managers)

---

[6]M. Cohen, P. V. Kamesam, P. Kleindorfer, H. Lee, and A. Tekerian, "Optimizer: IBM's Multi-Echelon Inventory System for Managing Service Logistics," *Interfaces* 20 (January–February 1990), pp. 65–82.

as advisers to the project team throughout the study. By the time of the implementation phase, these operational managers had a strong sense of ownership and so had become ardent supporters for installing Optimizer in their functional areas. A second success factor was a very extensive *user acceptance test* whereby users could identify problem areas that needed rectifying prior to full implementation. The third key was that the new system was phased in gradually, with careful testing at each phase, so the major bugs would be eliminated before the system went live nationally.

This new multiechelon inventory system proved to be extremely successful. It provided savings of about $20 million per year through improved operational efficiency. It also gave even larger annual savings in holding costs (including the cost of capital tied up in inventory) by reducing the value of IBM's inventories by over $250 million. Despite this large reduction in inventories, the improved inventory management still enabled providing better service to IBM's customers. Specifically, the new system yielded a 10 percent improvement in parts availability at the lower echelons (where the customers are affected) while maintaining the parts availability levels at the higher echelons.

Supply Chain Management

Another key concept that has emerged in this global economy is that of supply chain management. This concept pushes the management of a multiechelon inventory system one step further by also considering what needs to happen to bring a product into the inventory system in the first place. However, as with inventory management, a main purpose still is to win the competitive battle against other companies in bringing the product to the customers as promptly as possible.

A **supply chain** is a network of facilities that procure raw materials, transform them into intermediate goods and then final products, and finally deliver the products to customers through a distribution system that includes a (probably multiechelon) inventory system. Thus, it spans procurement, manufacturing, and distribution, with effective inventory management as one key element. To fill orders efficiently, it is necessary to understand the linkages and interrelationships of all the key elements of the supply chain. Therefore, integrated management of the supply chain has become a key success factor for some of today's leading companies.

We summarize below the experience of one of the companies that have led the way in making supply chain management part of their corporate culture.

Supply Chain Management at Hewlett-Packard[7]

Hewlett-Packard (HP) is one of today's leading high-technology companies. Its scope is truly global. Nearly half of its employees are outside the United States. In 1993, it had manufacturing or research and development sites in 16 countries, as well as sales and service offices in 110 countries. Its total number of catalog products exceeded 22,000.

Late in the 1980s, HP faced inventories mounting into the billions of dollars and alarming customer dissatisfaction with its order fulfillment process. Management was very concerned since order fulfillment was becoming a major battlefield in the high-technology industries. Recognizing the need for management science models to support top management decision making, HP formed a group known as Strategic Planning and Modeling (SPaM) in 1988. Management charged the group with developing and introducing innovations in management science and industrial engineering.

In 1989, SPaM began bringing supply chain management concepts into HP. HP's supply chain includes manufacturing integrated circuits, board assembly, final assembly, and delivery to customers on a global basis. With such diverse and complex products, grappling with supply chain issues can be very challenging. Variabilities and uncertainties are prevalent all along the chain. Suppliers can be late in their shipments, or the incoming materials may be flawed. The production process may break down, or the production yield may be imperfect. Finally, product demands also are highly uncertain.

Much of SPaM's initial focus was on inventory modeling. This effort led to the development of HP's *Worldwide Inventory Network Optimizer* (WINO). Like IBM's Optimizer described earlier in this section, WINO manages a multiechelon inventory system. How-

---

[7]H. L. Lee and C. Billington, "The Evolution of Supply-Chain Management Models and Practices at Hewlett-Packard," *Interfaces* 25 (September–October 1995), pp. 42–63.

ever, rather than dealing just with inventories of finished products, WINO also considers the inventories of incoming goods and departing goods at each site along the supply chain.

WINO uses a discrete-review inventory model to determine the reorder point and order quantities for each of these inventories. By introducing more frequent reviews of inventories, better balancing of related inventories, elimination of redundant safety stocks, and so forth, inventory reductions of 10 to 30 percent typically were obtained.

WINO was even extended to include the inventory systems of some key dealers. This enabled reducing the inventories of finished products at both HP's distribution centers and the dealers while maintaining the same service target for the customers.

SpaM's initial focus on inventory modeling soon broadened to dealing with distribution strategy issues. For example, its realignment of the distribution network in Europe reduced the total distribution cost there by $18 million per year.

SpaM's work also evolved into other functional areas, including design and engineering, finance, and marketing.

The importance of supply chain management now is recognized throughout HP. Several key divisions have formalized such positions as supply chain project managers, supply chain analysts, and supply chain coordinators. These individuals work closely with SPaM to ensure that supply chain models are used effectively and to identify new problems that feed SpaM's research and development effort.

The work of SPaM in applying management science to integrate supply chain management into HP has paid tremendous dividends. SPaM has often identified cost savings of $10 million to $40 million per year from just a single project. Therefore, total cost savings now run into the hundreds of millions of dollars annually. There have been key intangible benefits as well, including enhancing HP's reputation as a progressive company that can be counted on by its customers to fill their orders promptly.

Review Questions

1. How does the ABC control method categorize the products in inventory?
2. Why is it occasionally not appropriate to apply a single-product inventory model to each of the important products in inventory?
3. What is a multiechelon inventory system?
4. What are the echelons in IBM's multiechelon inventory system for spare parts?
5. What were the three factors that proved to be especially important in achieving a successful implementation of IBM's new multiechelon inventory system for spare parts?
6. What were the cost savings achieved by this new inventory system?
7. What are the business areas that are spanned by a supply chain?
8. What were the problems faced by Hewlett-Packard in the late 1980s that led to the introduction of supply chain management?
9. What kinds of inventories are included in Hewlett-Packard's Worldwide Inventory Network Optimizer?
10. What was a key intangible benefit of integrating supply chain management into Hewlett-Packard?

12.7 Summary

The preceding chapter discussed inventory management when each product under consideration in inventory has a known demand. The current chapter has turned the focus to the case of *uncertain* demand, where only a *probability distribution* of demand is available.

A constant theme throughout the chapter is the need to find the best trade-off between the consequences of having too much inventory (high holding costs) and of having too little (a great risk of incurring shortages).

A *perishable product* is one that can be carried in inventory for only a very limited period of time before it can no longer be sold. An inventory model for such products is presented for deciding how many units to order so they can be placed into inventory. A simple formula, based on just the unit cost of underordering and the unit cost of overordering, is given for making this decision. A case study involving Freddie the newsboy is used to introduce and illustrate this approach.

A *stable product* is one that will remain sellable indefinitely. The Niko Camera Corp. case study deals with how to manage the inventory of such a product. The product in this case is Niko's disposable panoramic camera, which has highly variable sales from month to month. Management has been very concerned about the frequent stockouts that have been occurring.

Niko's management science team worked with management to analyze this problem. One conclusion was that a substantial *safety stock* needed to be added to inventory. This led to substantially increasing the *reorder point* (the inventory level at which an order for a production run should be placed). By considering the relevant cost factors, the team then adapted the *EOQ model with planned shortages* to determine an appropriate *order quantity* (the size of a production run in this case). Finally, the team studied the problem from a broader perspective and developed four fundamental recommendations for how to address management's continuing concerns about high inventory levels and other problem areas.

The management science team used a *continuous-review model for stable products.* Following the case study, an overview of this model was presented. The model leads to an (R, Q) *inventory policy,* where R is the reorder point and Q is the order quantity.

Inventory systems arising in practice often are very large, perhaps involving hundreds or thousands of products. The inventories may also be dispersed geographically. This may result in a *multiechelon inventory system,* where the inventory at each echelon is used to replenish the inventories at different sites in the next lower echelon. Such a system is illustrated by IBM's far-flung inventories of spare parts, which are coordinated and controlled by a huge computerized system called Optimizer.

A supply chain spans procurement, manufacturing, and distribution, including all the inventories accumulated along the way. Thus, supply chain management extends the management of a multiechelon inventory system one step further by also considering all the linkages and interrelationships throughout the supply chain. Hewlett-Packard's experience has been described as one example of successful supply chain management.

Glossary

ABC control method   A method for controlling an inventory system with many products where the products are divided into three groups according to their level of importance. (Section 12.6)   512

Backlogging   Holding backorders when shortages occur and then filling them when the inventory is replenished. (Section 12.3)   492

Backorders   Demand for a product that cannot be satisfied currently because the inventory has been completely depleted. (Section 12.3)   492

Computerized inventory system   An inventory system where all additions and withdrawals are recorded electronically so that the computer can trigger the placement of orders to replenish the inventory. (Section 12.5)   506

Continuous-review inventory system   A system where the inventory level of a stable product is monitored on a continuous basis so that a new order can be placed as soon as the inventory level drops to the reorder point. (Section 12.5)   506

Cost of overordering   The lost profit incurred when the order quantity for a perishable product exceeds the demand. (Section 12.2)   486

Cost of underordering   The lost profit incurred when the demand for a perishable product exceeds the order quantity. (Section 12.2)   486

Demand   The demand for a product over a particular period of time is the number of units of that product that need to be withdrawn from inventory to sell them (or for any other purpose) over that period. (Introduction)   483

Economic order quantity   The order quantity that minimizes the total average cost. (Section 12.4)   500

EOQ   An acronym for economic order quantity. (Section 12.4)   500

EOQ model with planned shortages   The inventory model presented in Section 11.5. (Sections 11.5 and 12.4)   459, 500

Holding cost   Cost incurred by holding a product in inventory. (Sections 11.2 and 12.4)   448, 498

Lead time   The elapsed time between ordering a product and its delivery. (Section 12.3)   492

Multiechelon inventory system   A system with multiple echelons of inventory where each echelon (except the bottom one) is used to replenish the inventories at the various sites of the next lower echelon. (Section 12.6)   513

Newsboy problem The traditional name that has been given to the problem of determining the appropriate order quantity for a perishable product. Also known as the *newsvendor problem* or the *single-period probabilistic model*. (Sections 12.1 and 12.2) 484, 490

Order quantity The number of units of a product that are produced or ordered at one time to replenish inventory. (Sections 12.2 and 12.3) 486, 491

Periodic-review inventory system A system where the inventory level of a stable product is only monitored periodically. (Section 12.5) 506

Perishable product A product that can be carried in inventory for only a very limited period of time before it can no longer be sold. (Introduction and Section 12.2) 484, 490

(R, Q) policy A policy for controlling a continuous-review inventory system by using a fixed reorder point R and a fixed order quantity Q. (Section 12.5) 507

Reorder point The inventory level of a stable product at which an order is to be placed to replenish inventory. (Section 12.3) 492

Safety stock A cushion of extra inventory in addition to the amount needed to cover the average demand during the lead time. (Section 12.4) 496

Service level The service level for a perishable product is the probability that no shortage will occur. Five alternative measures are given for the service level for a stable product. (Sections 12.2 and 12.5) 487, 508

Setup cost The cost incurred by placing an order for a product (whether it be a purchase order or an order for a production run) that is in addition to the cost of the product. (Sections 11.2 and 12.4) 447, 498

Shortage cost Cost incurred by having demand for a product occur when the inventory is completely depleted. (Sections 11.2 and 12.4) 448, 499

Stable product A product that will remain sellable indefinitely. (Introduction and Section 12.5) 484, 506

Stockout The condition where the inventory of a product is completely depleted and additional demand cannot be immediately satisfied. (Section 12.3) 492

Supply chain A network of facilities that spans procurement, manufacturing, and distribution, including all the inventories accumulated along the way. (Section 12.6) 514

Two-bin system The traditional method of implementing a continuous-review inventory system. (Section 12.5) 506

Learning Aids for This Chapter in Your MS Courseware

"Ch. 12—Uncertain Demand Inv Mgmt" Excel File:

Template for *Bayes' Decision Rule* (with Profits)
Template for *Bayes' Decision Rule* (with Costs)
Template for the *Perishable Products Model*

Template for the *EOQ Model with Planned Shortages* (Analytical Version)
Template for the *Stable Products Model*

Problems

To the left of the following problems (or their parts), we have inserted the symbol E (for Excel) whenever one of the above templates can be helpful. An asterisk on the problem number indicates that at least a partial answer is given in the back of the book.

12.1. Reconsider Freddie the newsboy's problem presented in Section 12.1. A new financial services office has just opened near Freddie's newsstand. This has resulted in increased requests to purchase a copy of the *Financial Journal* from Freddie each day. The number of requests now range from 15 to 18 copies per day. Freddie estimates that there are 15 requests on 40 percent of the days, 16 requests on 20 percent of the days, 17 requests on 30 percent of the days, and 18 requests on the remaining days.

   E   *a.* Use Bayes' decision rule to determine what Freddie's new order quantity should be to maximize his average daily profit.

   E   *b.* Repeat part *a* with the criterion of minimizing Freddie's average daily cost of underordering or overordering.

   E   *c.* Use the ordering rule for the model for perishable products to determine Freddie's new order quantity.

        d. Draw a graph to show the application of step 2 of this ordering rule.

12.2. Jennifer's Donut House serves a large variety of doughnuts, one of which is a blueberry filled, chocolate-covered, super-sized doughnut supreme with sprinkles. This is an extra large doughnut that is meant to be shared by a whole family. Since the dough requires so long to rise, preparation of these doughnuts begins at 4:00 in the morning, so a decision on how many to prepare must be made long before learning how many will be needed. The cost of the ingredients and labor required to prepare each of these doughnuts is $1. Their sale price is $3 each. Any not sold that day are sold to a local discount grocery store for $0.50. Over the last several weeks, the number of these doughnuts sold for $3 each day has been tracked. These data are summarized on the next page.

Number Sold	Percentage of Days
0	10%
1	15
2	20
3	30
4	15
5	10

  a. What is the unit cost of underordering? The unit cost of overordering?

E b. Use Bayes' decision rule to determine how many of these doughnuts should be prepared each day to minimize the average daily cost of underordering or overordering.

E c. Use the ordering rule for the model for perishable products, including its graphical procedure, to determine how many of these doughnuts to prepare each day.

  d. Given the answer in part *c*, what will be the probability of running short of these doughnuts on any given day?

  e. Some families make a special trip to the Donut House just to buy this special doughnut. Therefore, Jennifer thinks that the cost when they run short might be greater than just the lost profit. In particular, there may be a cost for lost customer goodwill each time a customer orders this doughnut but none are available. How high would this cost have to be before they should prepare one more of these doughnuts each day than was found in part *c*?

12.3.* Swanson's Bakery is well-known for producing the best fresh bread in the city, so the sales are very substantial. The daily demand for its fresh bread has a uniform distribution between 300 and 600 loaves. The bread is baked in the early morning, before the bakery opens for business, at a cost of $2 per loaf. It then is sold that day for $3 per loaf. Any bread not sold on the day it is baked is relabeled as day-old bread and sold subsequently at a discount price of $1.50 per loaf.

E a. Apply step 1 of the ordering rule for the model for perishable products to determine the optimal service level.

  b. Apply step 2 of this ordering rule graphically to estimate the optimal number of loaves to bake each morning.

  c. With such a wide range of possible values in the demand distribution, it is difficult to draw the graph in part *b* carefully enough to determine the exact value of the optimal number of loaves. Use algebra to calculate this exact value.

  d. Given your answer in part *a*, what is the probability of incurring a shortage of fresh bread on any given day?

E e. Because the bakery's bread is so popular, its customers are quite disappointed when a shortage occurs. The owner of the bakery, Ken Swanson, places high priority on keeping his customers satisfied, so he doesn't like having shortages. Rather than using an inventory policy that simply maximizes his current average daily profit (as in the preceding parts), he feels that the analysis also should consider the loss of

customer goodwill due to shortages. Since this loss of goodwill can have a negative effect on future sales, he estimates that a cost of $1.50 per loaf should be assessed each time a customer cannot purchase fresh bread because of a shortage. Determine the new optimal number of loaves to bake each day with this change. What is the new probability of incurring a shortage of fresh bread on any given day?

12.4. Reconsider Problem 12.3. The bakery owner, Ken Swanson, now wants you to conduct a financial analysis of various inventory policies. You are to begin with the policy obtained in the first four parts of Problem 12.3 (ignoring any cost for the loss of customer goodwill). As given with the answers in the back of the book, this policy is to bake 500 loaves of bread each morning, which gives a probability of incurring a shortage of ⅓.

  a. For any day that a shortage *does* occur, calculate the revenue from selling fresh bread.

  b. For those days where shortages do *not* occur, use the probability distribution of demand to determine the average number of loaves of fresh bread sold. Use this number to calculate the average daily revenue from selling fresh bread on those days.

  c. Multiply your answer in part *a* by the probability of incurring a shortage. Then multiply your answer for average daily revenue in part *b* by the probability of *not* incurring a shortage. Add these two products to obtain the average daily revenue from selling fresh bread when the average is taken over *all* days.

  d. For those days where shortages do *not* occur, use the probability distribution of demand to determine the average number of loaves of fresh bread not sold. Multiply this number by the probability of *not* incurring a shortage to determine the average daily number of loaves of *day-old* bread obtained when the average is taken over all days. Use this number to calculate the average daily revenue from selling day-old bread.

  e. Add your final answers in parts *c* and *d* to obtain the average total daily revenue. Then subtract the daily cost of baking the bread to obtain the average daily profit (excluding overhead).

  f. Now consider the inventory policy of baking 600 loaves each morning, so that shortages never occur. Calculate the average daily profit (excluding overhead) from this policy.

  g. Consider the inventory policy found in part *e* of Problem 12.3. As given with the answers in the back of the book, this policy is to bake 550 loaves each morning, which gives a probability of incurring a shortage of ⅙. Since this policy is midway between the policy considered here in parts *a–e* and the one considered in part *f*, its average daily profit (excluding overhead and the cost of the loss of customer goodwill) also is midway between the average daily profit for those two policies. Use this fact to determine its average daily profit.

  h. Now consider the cost of the loss of customer goodwill for the inventory policy analyzed in part *g*. For those days where shortages *do* occur, use the probability distribution of demand to determine the average size of the shortage. Then multiply this number by the probability of a shortage to obtain the average daily size of a shortage when the average is taken over all days. Multiply this number by the cost per loaf short to obtain the average daily cost of the loss of customer goodwill. Subtract this average daily cost from the answer in part *g* to obtain the average daily profit when considering this cost.

   i. Repeat part *h* for the inventory policy considered in parts *a–e.*

12.5. Reconsider Problem 12.3 (including its answers in the back of the book). The bakery owner, Ken Swanson, now has developed a new plan to decrease the size of shortages. The bread will be baked twice a day, once before the bakery opens (as before) and the other during the day after it becomes clearer what the demand for that day will be. The first baking will produce 300 loaves to cover the minimum demand for the day. The size of the second baking will be based on an estimate of the remaining demand for the day. This remaining demand is assumed to have a uniform distribution from *a* to *b,* where the values of *a* and *b* are chosen each day based on the sales so far. It is anticipated that $b - a$ typically will be approximately 75, as opposed to the range of 300 for the distribution of demand in Problem 12.3.

   a. Ignoring any cost of the loss of customer goodwill (as in parts *a–d* of Problem 12.3), write a formula for how many loaves should be produced in the second baking in terms of *a* and *b.*

   b. What is the probability of still incurring a shortage of fresh bread on any given day? How should this answer compare to the corresponding probability in Problem 12.3?

   c. When $b - a = 75$, what is the maximum size of a shortage that can occur? What is the maximum number of loaves of fresh bread that will not be sold? How do these answers compare to the corresponding numbers for the situation in Problem 12.3 where only one (early morning) baking occurs per day?

   d. Given your answers in part *c,* how should the average total daily cost of underordering and overordering for this new plan compare with that for the situation in Problem 12.3? What does this say in general about the value of obtaining as much information as possible about what the demand will be before placing the final order for a perishable product?

   e. Repeat parts *a, b,* and *c* when including the cost of the loss of customer goodwill as in part *e* of Problem 12.3.

12.6.* A college student, Stan Ford recently took a course in management science. He now enjoys applying what he learned to optimize his personal decisions. He is analyzing one such decision currently, namely, how much money (if any) to take out of his savings account to buy $100 traveler's checks before leaving on a short vacation trip to Europe next summer.

   Stan already has used the money he had in his checking account to buy traveler's checks worth $1,200, but this may not be enough. In fact, he has estimated the probability distribution of what he will need as shown in the following table:

Amount needed ($)	1,000	1,100	1,200	1,300	1,400	1,500	1,600	1,700
Probability	0.05	0.10	0.15	0.25	0.20	0.10	0.10	0.05

If he turns out to have less than he needs, then he will have to leave Europe one day early for every $100 short. Because he places a value of $150 on each day in Europe, each day lost would thereby represent a net loss of $50 to him. However, every $100 traveler's check costs an extra $1. Furthermore, each such check left over at the end of the trip (which would be redeposited in the savings account) represents a loss of $2 in interest that could have been earned in the savings account during the trip, so he does not want to purchase too many.

   a. Describe how this problem can be interpreted to be an inventory problem with uncertain demand for a perishable product. Also, identify the unit cost of underordering and the unit cost of overordering.

E *b.* Use Bayes' decision rule to determine how many additional $100 traveler's checks Stan should purchase to minimize his expected cost of underordering or overordering.

E *c.* Use the ordering rule for the model for perishable products to make Stan's decision.

   d. Draw a graph to show the application of step 2 of this ordering rule.

12.7. Henry Edsel is the owner of Honest Henry's, the largest car dealership in its part of the country. Henry's most popular car model this year is the Triton. In fact, the Tritons are selling so well that Henry now realizes that he probably will run out before the end of the model year. Fortunately, he still has time to place one more order to replenish his inventory of Tritons.

   Henry now needs to decide how many Tritons to order from the factory. Each one costs him $20,000. He then is able to sell them at an average price of $23,000, provided they are sold before the end of the model year. However, any of these Tritons left at the end of the model year would then need to be sold at a special sale price of $19,500. Furthermore, Henry estimates that the extra cost of the capital tied up by holding these cars such an unusually long time would be $500 per car, so his net revenue would be only $19,000. Since he would lose $1,000 on each of these cars left at the end of the model year, Henry concludes that he needs to be cautious to avoid ordering too many cars, but he also wants to avoid running out of cars to sell before the end of the model year if possible. Therefore, he asks his general manager, Ruby Willis, to examine past sales data and then develop a careful estimate of how many Tritons being ordered now could be sold before the end of the model year.

   Ruby has graduated from business school and so realizes that this demand has a probability distribution. She decides that the bell-shaped curve of the normal distribution should have the right shape to fit this distribution. Based on past data, she then estimates that the mean of this distribution is $\mu = 50$ and the standard deviation is $\sigma = 15$.

E   a. Use step 1 of the ordering rule for the model for perishable products to determine the optimal service level.

    b. Let L denote the optimal service level found in part *a*. Explain why step 2 of the ordering rule amounts to finding the value of the order quantity Q that satisfies the following equation: $P(\text{demand} \leq Q) = L$.

    c. Since demand has a normal distribution, this equation is satisfied when $Q = \mu + K_L\sigma$, where K_L is a constant based on L that is obtained from a table for the normal distribution. Use such a table (e.g., Table 12.2 in Section 12.5) to solve for Q, the number of Tritons Henry should order from the factory.

12.8. The management of Quality Airlines has decided to base its overbooking policy on the inventory model for perishable products presented in Section 12.2, since this will maximize expected profit. This policy now needs to be applied to a new flight from Seattle to Atlanta. The airplane has 125 seats available for a fare of $250. However, since there commonly are a few no-shows, the airline should accept a few more than 125 reservations. On those occasions when more than 125 people arrive to take the flight, the airline will find volunteers who are willing to be put on a later flight in return for being given a certificate worth $150 toward any future travel on this airline.

    Based on previous experience with similar flights, it is estimated that the relative frequency of the number of no-shows will be as shown below.

Number of No-Shows	Relative Frequency
0	5%
1	10
2	15
3	15
4	15
5	15
6	10
7	10
8	5

    a. When interpreting this problem as an inventory problem, what are the units of a perishable product being placed into inventory?

    b. Identify the unit cost of underordering and the unit cost of overordering.

E   c. Use the ordering rule for the model for perishable products to determine how many overbooked reservations to accept.

    d. Draw a graph to show the application of step 2 of this ordering rule.

E 12.9. The final recommendations of the management science team presented at the end of Section 12.4 for the Niko case study are expected to result in the following changes:

Change 1: Reduce the setup cost from $12,000 to $3,000.

Change 2: Decrease the variability of the number of cameras sold in a month so that this number will have a uniform distribution from 4,000 to 12,000 instead of from 0 to 16,000.

Change 3: Reduce the lead time from 1 month to 0.2 month. The demand during this reduced lead time is assumed to have a uniform distribution from 200 to 3,000.

    However, management does not want any change in the current probability of 0.25 that a stockout will occur during the lead time.

    a. Determine the effect of change 1 alone (without the other changes) on the order quantity and the reorder point. Will this reduce the average monthly holding cost? The average monthly shortage cost? The average monthly setup cost?

    b. Repeat part *a* for change 2 alone.

    c. Repeat part *a* for change 3 alone.

    d. Repeat part *a* if both changes 1 and 3 occur.

    e. Calculate the average total monthly cost when both changes 1 and 3 occur. Compare with this cost before the changes occur.

12.10.* Reconsider Problem 12.7. The new model year now is almost here, so Henry Edsel will have many opportunities to order the new Tritons throughout the coming year. Henry was impressed with the analysis Ruby Willis did in dealing with Problem 12.7. Therefore, Henry asks Ruby to use her business school training again to develop a cost-effective policy for when to place these orders and how many to order each time.

    Ruby decides to use the inventory model for stable products to determine an (R, Q) policy. After some investigation, she estimates that the administrative cost for placing each order is $1,500 (a lot of paperwork is needed for ordering cars), the holding cost for each car is $3,000 per year (15 percent of the agency's purchase price of $20,000), and the shortage cost per car short is $1,000 per year (an estimated probability of ⅓ of losing a car sale and its profit of about $3,000). After considering both the seriousness of incurring shortages and the high holding cost, Ruby and Henry agree to use a 75 percent service level (a probability of 0.75 of not incurring a shortage between the time an order is placed and the delivery of the cars ordered). Based on the past year's experience, they also estimate that about 900 Tritons should be sold over the next model year.

    After an order is placed, the cars are delivered in about two-thirds of a month. This is about the same length of time for which Ruby had estimated a demand distribution in Problem 12.7. Therefore, her best estimate of the probability distribution of demand during the lead time before a delivery arrives is a normal distribution with a mean of 50 and a standard deviation of 15.

    a. Solve by hand for the order quantity.

    b. Use Table 12.2 to solve for the reorder point.

E   c. Use the Excel template for this model in your MS Courseware to check your answers in parts *a* and *b*.

    d. Given your previous answers, how much safety stock does this inventory policy provide?

e. This policy can lead to placing a new order before the delivery from the preceding order arrives. Indicate when this would happen.

12.11. One of the largest selling items in J.C. Ward's Department Store is a new model of refrigerator that is highly energy efficient. About 40 of these refrigerators are being sold per month. It takes about a week for the store to obtain more refrigerators from a wholesaler. The demand during this time has a uniform distribution between 5 and 15. The administrative cost of placing each order is $40. For each refrigerator, the holding cost per month is $8 and the shortage cost per month is estimated to be $1.

The store's inventory manager has decided to use the inventory model for stable products presented in Section 12.5, with a service level (measure 1) of 0.8, to determine an (R, Q) policy.

a. Solve by hand for R and Q.

E   *b.* Use the corresponding Excel template to check your answer in part *a.*

c. What will be the average number of stockouts per year with this inventory policy?

12.12. When using the inventory model for stable products presented in Section 12.5, a difficult managerial judgment decision needs to be made on the level of service to provide to customers. The purpose of this problem is to enable you to explore the trade-off involved in making this decision.

Assume that the measure of service level being used is L = probability that a stockout will not occur during the lead time. Since management generally places a high priority on providing excellent service to customers, the temptation is to assign a very high value to L. However, this would result in providing a very large amount of safety stock, which runs counter to management's desire to eliminate unnecessary inventory. (Remember the *just-in-time philosophy* discussed in Section 11.7 that is heavily influencing managerial thinking today.) What is the best trade-off between providing good service and eliminating unnecessary inventory?

Assume that the probability distribution of demand during the lead time is a normal distribution with mean μ and standard deviation σ. Then the reorder point R is $R = \mu + K_L \sigma$, where K_L is given in Table 12.2 for various values of L. The amount of safety stock provided by this reorder point is $K_L \sigma$. Thus, if h denotes the holding cost for each unit held in inventory per year, the *average annual holding cost for safety stock* (denoted by C) is $C = hK_L \sigma$.

a. Construct a table with five columns. The first column is the service level L, with values 0.5, 0.75, 0.9, 0.95, 0.99, and 0.999. The next four columns give C for four cases. Case 1 is $h = \$1$ and $\sigma = 1$. Case 2 is $h = \$100$ and $\sigma = 1$. Case 3 is $h = \$1$ and $\sigma = 100$. Case 4 is $h = \$100$ and $\sigma = 100$.

b. Construct a second table that is based on the table obtained in part *a.* The new table has five rows and the same five columns as the first table. Each entry in the new table is obtained by subtracting the corresponding entry in the first table from the entry in the next row of the first table. For example, the entries in the first column of the new table are $0.75 - 0.5 = 0.25$, $0.9 - 0.75 = 0.15$, $0.95 - 0.9 = 0.05$, $0.99 - 0.95 = 0.04$, and $0.999 - 0.99 = 0.009$. Since these entries represent increases in the service level L, each entry in the next four columns represents the increase in C that would result from increasing L by the amount shown in the first column.

c. Based on these two tables, what advice would you give a manager who needs to make a decision on the value of L to use.

12.13. The preceding problem describes the factors involved in making a managerial decision on the service level L to use. It also points out that for any given values of L, h (the unit holding cost per year), and σ (the standard deviation when the demand during the lead time has a normal distribution), the average annual holding cost for the safety stock would turn out to be $C = hK_L \sigma$, where C denotes this holding cost and K_L is given in Table 12.2. Thus, the amount of variability in the demand, as measured by σ, has a major impact on this holding cost C.

The value of σ is substantially affected by the duration of the lead time. In particular, σ increases as the lead time increases. The purpose of this problem is to enable you to explore this relationship further.

To make this more concrete, suppose that the inventory system under consideration currently has the following values: $L = 0.9$, $h = \$100$, and $\sigma = 100$ with a lead time of four days. However, the vendor being used to replenish inventory is proposing a change in the delivery schedule that would change your lead time. You want to determine how this would change σ and C.

We assume for this inventory system (as is commonly the case) that the demands on separate days are statistically independent. In other words, the fact that demand is larger (or smaller) than usual on one day has no influence on whether demand will turn out to be larger (or smaller) than usual on another day. In this case, the relationship between σ and the lead time is given by the formula:

$$\sigma = \sqrt{d}\,\sigma_1$$

where

d = number of days in the lead time

σ_1 = standard deviation if $d = 1$

a. Calculate C for the current inventory system.

b. Determine σ_1. Then find how C would change if the lead time were reduced from four days to one day.

c. How would C change if the lead time were doubled, from four days to eight days?

d. How long would the lead time need to be in order for C to double from its current value with a lead time of four days?

12.14. What is the effect on the amount of safety stock provided by the inventory model for stable products when the following change is made in the inventory system. (Consider each change independently.)

a. The lead time is reduced to 0 (instantaneous delivery).

b. The service level (measure 1) is decreased.

c. The unit shortage cost is doubled.

d. The mean of the probability distribution of demand during the lead time is increased (with no other change to the distribution).

e. The probability distribution of demand during the lead time is a uniform distribution from a to b, but now b − a has been doubled.

f. The probability distribution of demand during the lead time is a normal distribution with mean μ and standard deviation σ, but now σ has been doubled.

12.15.* Jed Walker is the manager of Have a Cow, a hamburger restaurant in the downtown area. Jed has been purchasing all the restaurant's beef from Ground Chuck (a local supplier) but is considering switching to Chuck Wagon (a national warehouse) because its prices are lower.

Weekly demand for beef averages 500 pounds, with some variability from week to week. Jed estimates that the annual holding cost is 30¢ per pound of beef. When he runs out of beef, Jed is forced to buy from the grocery store next door. The high purchase cost and the hassle involved are estimated to cost him about $3 per pound of beef short. To help avoid shortages, Jed has decided to keep enough safety stock to prevent a shortage before the delivery arrives during 95 percent of the order cycles. Placing an order only requires sending a simple fax, so the administrative cost is negligible.

Have a Cow's contract with Ground Chuck is as follows: The purchase price is $1.49 per pound. A fixed cost of $25 per order is added for shipping and handling. The shipment is guaranteed to arrive within two days. Jed estimates that the demand for beef during this lead time has a uniform distribution from 50 to 150 pounds.

The Chuck Wagon is proposing the following terms: The beef will be priced at $1.35 per pound. The Chuck Wagon ships via refrigerated truck, and so charges additional shipping costs of $200 per order plus $0.10 per pound. The shipment time will be roughly a week, but is guaranteed not to exceed 10 days. Jed estimates that the probability distribution of demand during this lead time will be a normal distribution with a mean of 500 pounds and a standard deviation of 200 pounds.

E   a. Use the inventory model for stable products presented in Section 12.5 to obtain an (R, Q) policy for Have a Cow for each of the two alternatives of which supplier to use.

b. Show how the reorder point is calculated for each of these two policies.

c. Determine and compare the amount of safety stock provided by the two policies obtained in part a.

d. Determine and compare the average annual holding cost under these two policies.

e. Determine and compare the average annual acquisition cost (combining purchase price and shipping cost) under these two policies.

f. Since shortages are very infrequent, the only important costs for comparing the two suppliers are those obtained in parts d and e. Add these costs for each supplier. Which supplier should be selected?

g. Jed likes to use the beef (which he keeps in a freezer) within a month of receiving it. How would this influence his choice of supplier?

12.16. MicroApple is a manufacturer of personal computers. It currently manufactures a single model—the MacinDOS—on an assembly line at a steady rate of 500 per week. MicroApple orders the floppy disk drives for the MacinDOS (one per computer) from an outside supplier at a cost of $30 each. Additional administrative costs for placing an order total $30. The annual holding cost is $6 per drive. If MicroApple stocks out of floppy disk drives, production is halted, costing $100 per drive short. Because of the seriousness of stockouts, management wants to keep enough safety stock to prevent a shortage before the delivery arrives during 99 percent of the order cycles.

The supplier now is offering two shipping options. With option 1, the lead time would have a normal distribution with a mean of 0.5 week and a standard deviation of 0.1 week. For each order, the shipping cost charged to MicroApple would be $100 plus $3 per drive. With option 2, the lead time would have a uniform distribution from 1.0 week to 2.0 weeks. For each order, the shipping cost charged to MicroApple would be $20 plus $2 per drive.

E   a. Use the inventory model for stable products presented in Section 12.5 to obtain an (R, Q) policy under each of these two shipping options.

b. Show how the reorder point is calculated for each of these two policies.

c. Determine and compare the amount of safety stock provided by these two policies.

d. Determine and compare the average annual holding cost under these two policies.

e. Determine and compare the average annual acquisition cost (combining purchase price and shipping cost) under these two policies.

f. Since shortages are very infrequent (and very small when they do occur), the only important costs for comparing the two shipping options are those obtained in parts d and e. Add these costs for each option. Which option should be selected?

CASE 12.1
TNT: TACKLING NEWSBOY'S TEACHINGS

Howie Rogers sits in an isolated booth at his favorite coffee shop completely immersed in the classified ads of the local newspaper. He is searching for his next get-rich-quick venture. As he meticu-

lously reviews each ad, he absent-mindedly sips his lemonade and wonders how he will be able to exploit each opportunity to his advantage.

He is becoming quite disillusioned with his chosen vocation of being an entrepreneur looking for high-flying ventures. These past few years have not dealt him a lucky hand. Every project on which he has embarked has ended in utter disaster, and he is slowly coming to the realization that he just might have to find a real job.

He reads the date at the top of the newspaper. June 18. Ohhhhh. No need to look for a real job until the end of the summer.

Each advertisement Howie reviews registers as only a minor blip on his radar screen until the word Corvette jumps out at him. He narrows his eyes and reads:

> WIN A NEW CORVETTE AND EARN CASH AT THE SAME TIME! Fourth of July is fast approaching, and we need YOU to sell firecrackers. Call 1-800-555-3426 to establish a firecracker stand in your neighborhood.
>
> Earn fast money AND win the car of your dreams!

Well, certainly not a business that will make him a millionaire, but a worthwhile endeavor nonetheless! Howie tears the advertisement out of the newspaper and heads to the payphone in the back.

A brief—but informative—conversation reveals the details of the operation. Leisure Limited, a large wholesaler that distributes holiday products—Christmas decorations, Easter decorations, firecrackers, and so on—to small independents for resale, is recruiting entrepreneurs to run local firecracker stands for the Fourth of July. The wholesaler is offering to rent wooden shacks to entrepreneurs who will purchase firecrackers from Leisure Limited and will subsequently resell the firecrackers in these shacks on the side of the road to local customers for a higher price. The entrepreneurs will sell firecrackers until the Fourth of July, but after the holiday, customers will no longer want to purchase firecrackers until New Year's Eve. Therefore, the entrepreneurs will return any firecrackers not sold by the Fourth of July while keeping the revenues from all firecrackers sold. Leisure Limited will refund only part of the cost of the returned firecrackers, however, since returned firecrackers must be restocked and since they lose their explosiveness with age. And the Corvette? The individual who sells the greatest number of Leisure Limited firecrackers in the state will win a new Corvette.

Before Howie hangs up the phone, the Leisure Limited representative reveals one hitch—once an entrepreneur places an order for firecrackers, seven days are required for the delivery of the firecrackers. Howie realizes that he better get started quickly so that he will be able to sell firecrackers during the week preceding the Fourth of July when most of the demand occurs.

People could call Howie many things, but 'pokey' they could not. Howie springs to action by reserving a wooden shack and scheduling a delivery seven days hence. He then places another quarter in the payphone to order firecracker sets, but as he starts dialing the phone, he realizes that he has no idea how many sets he should order.

How should he solve this problem? If he orders too few firecracker sets, he will not have time to place and receive another order before the holiday and will therefore lose valuable sales (not to mention the chance to win the Corvette). If he orders too many firecracker sets, he will simply throw away money since he will not obtain a full refund for the cost of the surplus sets.

Quite a dilemma! He hangs up the phone and bangs his head against the hard concrete wall. After several bangs, he stands up straight with a thought. Of course! His sister would help him. She graduated from college several years ago with a business degree, and he is sure that she will agree to help him.

Howie calls Talia, his sister, at her work and explains his problem. Once she hears the problem, she is confident that she will be able to tell Howie how many sets he should order. Her dedicated management science teacher in college had taught her well. Talia asks Howie to give her the number for Leisure Limited, and she would then have the answer for him the next day.

Talia calls Leisure Limited and asks to speak to the manager on duty. Buddy Williams, the manager, takes her call, and Talia explains to him that she wants to run a firecracker stand. To decide the number of firecracker sets she should order, however, she needs some information from him. She persuades Buddy that he should not hesitate to give her the information since a more informed order is better for Leisure Limited—the wholesaler will not lose too many sales and will not have to deal with too many returns.

Talia receives the following information from Buddy. Entrepreneurs purchase firecracker sets from Leisure Limited at a cost of $3.00 per set. Entrepreneurs are able to sell the firecracker sets for any price that they deem reasonable. In addition to the wholesale price of the firecracker sets, entrepreneurs also have to pay administrative and delivery fees for each order they place. These fees average approximately $20.00 per order. After the Fourth of July, Leisure Limited returns only half of the wholesale cost for each firecracker set returned. To return the unsold firecracker sets, entrepreneurs also have to pay shipping costs that average $0.50 per firecracker set.

Finally, Talia asks about the demand for firecracker sets. Buddy is not able to give her very specific information, but he is able to give her general information about last year's sales. Data compiled from last year's stand sales throughout the state indicate that stands sold between 120 and 420 firecracker sets. The stands operated any time between June 20 and July 4 and sold the firecracker sets for an average of $5.00 per set.

Talia thanks Buddy, hangs up the phone, and begins making assumptions to help her overcome the lack of specific data. Even though Howie will operate his stand only during the week preceding the Fourth of July, she decides to use the demands quoted by Buddy for simplicity. She assumes that the demand follows a uniform distribution. She decides to use the average of $5.00 for the unit sale price.

a. How many firecracker sets should Howie purchase from Leisure Limited to maximize his expected profit?

b. How would Howie's order quantity change if Leisure Limited refunds 75 percent of the wholesale price for returned firecracker sets? How would it change if Leisure Limited refunds 25 percent of the wholesale price for returned firecracker sets?

c. Howie is not happy with selling the firecracker sets for $5.00 per set. He needs to make some serious dough! Suppose Howie wants to sell the firecracker sets for $6.00 per set instead. What factors would Talia have to take into account when recalculating the optimal order quantity?

d. What do you think of Talia's strategy for estimating demand?

CASE 12.2
JETTISONING SURPLUS STOCK

Scarlett Windermere cautiously approaches the expansive gray factory building and experiences a mixture of fear and excitement. The first day of a new consulting assignment always leaves her fighting conflicting emotions. She takes a deep breath, clutches her briefcase, and marches into the small, stuffy reception area of American Aerospace.

"Scarlett Windermere here to see Bryan Zimmerman," she says to the bored security guard behind the reception desk.

The security guard eyes Scarlett suspiciously and says, "Ya don't belong here, do ya? Of course, ya don't. Then ya gotta fill out this paperwork for a temporary security pass."

As Scarlett completes the necessary paperwork, Bryan exits through the heavy door leading to the factory floor and enters the reception area. His eyes roam the reception area and rest upon Scarlett. He approaches Scarlett booming, "So you must be the inventory expert—Scarlett Windermere. So glad to finally meet you face to face! They already got you pouring out your life story, huh? Well, there will be enough time for that. Right now, let's get you back to the factory floor to help me solve my inventory problem!"

And with that, Bryan stuffs a pair of safety glasses in Scarlett's right hand, stuffs the incomplete security forms in her left hand, and hustles her through the heavy security door.

As Scarlett walks through the security door, she feels as though she has entered another world. Machines twice the size of humans line the aisles as far as the eye can see. These monsters make high-pitched squeals or low, horrifying rumbles as they cut and grind metal. Surrounding these machines are shelves piled with metal pieces.

As Bryan leads Scarlett down the aisles of the factory, he yells to her over the machines, "As you well know from the proposal stage of this project, this factory produces the stationary parts for the military jet engines American Aerospace sells. Most people think the aerospace industry is real high-tech. Well, not this factory. This factory is as dirty as they come. Jet engines are made out of a lot of solid metal parts, and this factory cuts, grinds, and welds those parts.

"This factory produces over 200 different stationary parts for jet engines. Each jet engine model requires different parts. And each part requires different raw materials. Hence, the factory's current inventory problem.

"We hold all kinds of raw materials—from rivets to steel sheets—here on the factory floor, and we currently mismanage our raw materials inventory. We order enough raw materials to produce a year's worth of some stationary parts, but only enough raw materials to produce a week's worth of others. We waste a ton of money stocking raw materials that are not needed and lose a ton of money dealing with late deliveries of orders. We need you to tell us how to control the inventory—how many raw materials we need to stock for each part, how often we need to order additional raw materials, and how many we should order."

As she walks down the aisle, Scarlett studies the shelves and shelves of inventory. She has quite a mission to accomplish in this factory!

Bryan continues, "Let me tell you how we receive orders for this factory. Whenever the American Aerospace sales department gets an order for a particular jet engine, the order is transferred to its assembly plant here on the site. The assembly plant then sub-

mits an order to this factory here for the stationary parts required to assemble the engine. Unfortunately, because this factory is frequently running out of raw materials, it takes us an average of a month between the time we receive an order and the time we deliver the finished order to the assembly plant. The finished order includes all the stationary parts needed to assemble that particular jet engine. BUT—and that's a big but—the delivery time really depends upon which stationary parts are included in the order."

Scarlett interrupts Bryan and says, "Then I guess now would be as good a time as any to start collecting the details of the orders and solving your inventory problem!"

Bryan smiles and says, "That's the attitude I like to see—chomping at the bit to solve the problem! Well, I'll show you to your computer. We just had another consulting firm complete a data warehouse started by American Aerospace three years ago, so you can access any of the data you need right from your desktop!" And with a flurry, Bryan heads back down the aisle.

Scarlett realizes that the inventory system is quite complicated. She remembers a golden rule from her consulting firm: break down a complex system into simple parts. She therefore decides to analyze the control of inventory for each stationary part independently. But with 200 different stationary parts, where should she begin?

She remembers that when the assembly plant receives an order for a particular jet engine, it places an order with the factory for the stationary parts required to assemble the engine. The factory delivers an order to the assembly plant when all stationary parts for that order have been completed. The stationary part that takes the longest to complete in a given order therefore determines the delivery date of the order.

Scarlett decides to begin her analysis with the most time-intensive stationary part required to assemble the most popular jet engine. She types a command into the computer to determine the most popular jet engine. She learns that the MX332 has received the largest number of orders over the past year. She types another command to generate the following printout of the monthly orders for the MX332.

Month	Number of MX332 Ordered
June	25
July	31
August	18
September	22
October	40
November	19
December	38
January	21
February	25
March	36
April	34
May	28
June	27

She enters the monthly order quantities for the MX332 into a computerized statistical program to estimate the underlying distribution. She learns that the orders roughly follow a normal distribution. It appears to Scarlett that the number of orders in a particular month does not depend on the number of orders in the previous or following months.

a. What is the sample mean and sample variance of the set of monthly orders for the MX332?

Scarlett next researches the most time-intensive stationary part required to assemble the MX332. She types a command into the computer to generate a list of parts required to assemble the MX332. She then types a command to list the average delivery time for each part. She learns that part 10003487 typically requires the longest time to complete, and that this part is only used for the MX332. She investigates the pattern for the part further and learns that over the past year, part 10003487 has taken an average of one month to complete once an order is placed. She also learns that the factory can produce the part almost immediately if all the necessary raw materials for the production process are on hand. So the completion time actually depends on how long it takes to obtain these raw materials from the supplier. On those unusual occasions when all the raw materials already are available in inventory, the completion time for the part is essentially zero. But typically the completion time is one and a half months.

Scarlett performs further analysis on the computer and learns that each MX332 jet engine requires two parts numbered 10003487. Each part 10003487 accepts one solid steel part molded into a cylindrical shape as its main raw material input. The data shows that several times the delivery of all the stationary parts for the MX332 to the assembly plant got delayed for up to one and a half months only because a part 10003487 was not completed. And why wasn't it completed? The factory had run out of those steel parts and had to wait for another shipment from its supplier! It takes the supplier one and a half months to produce and deliver the steel parts after receiving an order from the factory. Once an order of steel parts arrives, the factory quickly sets up and executes a production run to use all the steel parts for producing part 10003487. Apparently the production problems in the factory are mainly due to the inventory management for those unassuming steel parts. And that inventory management appears to be completely out of whack. The only good news is that there is no

significant administrative cost associated with placing an order for the steel parts with the supplier.

After Scarlett has finished her work on the computer, she heads to Bryan's office to obtain the financials needed to complete her analysis. A short meeting with Bryan yields the following financial information.

Now Scarlett has all of the information necessary to perform her inventory analysis for part 10003487!

Setup cost for a production run to produce part 10003487:	$5,800
Holding cost for machine part 10003487:	$750 per part per year
Shortage cost for part 10003487 (includes outsourcing cost, cost of production delay, and cost of the loss of future orders):	$3,250 per part per year
Desired probability that a shortage for machine part 10003487 will not occur between the time an order for the steel parts is placed and the time the order is delivered.	0.85

b. What is the inventory policy that American Aerospace should implement for part 10003487?
c. What are the average annual holding costs and setup costs associated with this inventory policy?
d. How do the average annual holding costs and setup costs change if the desired probability that a shortage will not occur between the time an order is placed and the time the order is delivered is increased to 0.95?
e. Do you think Scarlett's independent analysis of each stationary part could generate inaccurate inventory policies? Why or why not?
f. Scarlett knows that the aerospace industry is very cyclical—the industry experiences several years of high sales, several years of mediocre sales, and several years of low sales. How would you recommend incorporating this fact into the analysis?

FORECASTING

How much will the economy grow over the next year? Where is the stock market headed? What about interest rates? How will consumer tastes be changing? What will be the hot new products?

Forecasters have answers to all these questions. Unfortunately, these answers will more than likely be wrong. Nobody can accurately predict the future every time.

Nevertheless, the future success of any business depends heavily on how savvy its management is in spotting trends and developing appropriate strategies. The leaders of the best companies often seem to have a sixth sense for when to change direction to stay a step ahead of the competition. These companies seldom get into trouble by badly misestimating what the demand will be for their products. Many other companies do. The ability to forecast well makes the difference.

The preceding two chapters have presented a considerable number of models for the management of inventories. All these models are based on a forecast of future demand for a product, or at least a probability distribution for that demand. Therefore, the missing ingredient for successfully implementing these inventory models is an approach for forecasting demand.

Fortunately, when historical sales data are available, some proven **statistical forecasting methods** have been developed for using these data to forecast future demand. Such a method assumes that historical trends will continue, so management then needs to make any adjustments to reflect current changes in the marketplace.

Several **judgmental forecasting methods** that solely use expert judgment also are available. These methods are especially valuable when little or no historical sales data are available or when major changes in the marketplace make these data unreliable for forecasting purposes.

Forecasting product demand is just one important application of these forecasting methods. A variety of applications are surveyed in the first section.

Section 13.2 introduces a case study that will be carried through much of the chapter. Sections 13.3–13.5 focus on statistical forecasting methods and Section 13.6 on judgmental forecasting methods. The chapter then concludes by surveying forecasting practices in U.S. corporations.

13.1 Some Applications of Forecasting

We now will discuss some main areas in which forecasting is widely used. In each case, we will illustrate this use by mentioning one or more actual applications that have been described in published articles. A summary table at the end of the section will tell you where these articles can be found in case you want to read further.

Sales Forecasting

Any company engaged in selling goods needs to forecast the demand for those goods. Manufacturers need to know how much to produce. Wholesalers and retailers need to know how much to stock. Substantially underestimating demand is likely to lead to many lost sales, unhappy customers, and perhaps allowing the competition to gain the upper hand in the marketplace. On the other hand, significantly overestimating demand also is very costly due to (1) excessive inventory costs, (2) forced price reductions, (3) unneeded production or storage capacity, and (4) lost opportunities to market more profitable goods. Successful marketing and production managers understand very well the importance of obtaining good sales forecasts.

The **Merit Brass Company** is a family-owned company that supplies several thousand products to the pipe, valve, and fittings industry. In 1990, Merit Brass embarked on a modernization program that emphasized installing management science methodologies in statistical sales forecasting and finished-goods inventory management (two activities that go hand in glove). This program led to major improvements in customer service (as measured by product availability) while simultaneously achieving substantial cost reductions.

A major Spanish electric utility, **Hidroeléctrica Español,** has developed and implemented a hierarchy of management science models to assist in managing its system of reservoirs used for generating hydroelectric power. All these models are driven by forecasts of both energy demand (this company's sales) and reservoir inflows. A sophisticated statistical forecasting method is used to forecast energy demand on both a short-term and long-term basis. A hydrological forecasting model generates the forecasts of reservoir inflows.

Airline companies now depend heavily on the high fares paid by businesspeople traveling on short notice while providing discount fares to others to help fill the seats. The decision on how to allocate seats to the different fare classes is a crucial one for maximizing revenue. **American Airlines,** for example, uses statistical forecasting of the demand at each fare to make this decision.

Forecasting the Need for Spare Parts

Although effective sales forecasting is a key for virtually any company, some organizations must rely on other types of forecasts as well. A prime example involves forecasts of the need for spare parts.

Many companies need to maintain an inventory of spare parts to enable them to quickly repair either their own equipment or their products sold or leased to customers. In some cases, this inventory is huge. For example, IBM's spare-parts inventory described in Section 12.6 is valued in the billions of dollars and includes many thousand different parts.

Just as for a finished-goods inventory ready for sale, effective management of a spare-parts inventory depends on obtaining a reliable forecast of the demand for that inventory. Although the types of costs incurred by misestimating demand are somewhat different, the consequences may be no less severe for spare parts. For example, the consequence for an airline not having a spare part available on location when needed to continue flying an airplane probably is at least one canceled flight.

To support its operation of several hundred aircraft, **American Airlines** maintains an extensive inventory of spare parts. Included are over 5,000 different types of *rotatable* parts (e.g., landing gear and wing flaps) with an average value of $5,000 per item. When a rotatable part on an airplane is found to be defective, it is immediately replaced by a corresponding part in inventory so the airplane can depart. However, the replaced part then is repaired and placed back into inventory for subsequent use as a replacement part.

American Airlines uses a PC-based forecasting system called the Rotatables Allocation and Planning System (RAPS) to forecast demand for the rotatable parts and to help allocate these parts to the various airports. The statistical forecast uses an 18-month history of parts usage and flying hours for the fleet, and then projects ahead based on planned flying hours.

Forecasting Production Yields

The *yield* of a production process refers to the percentage of the completed items that meet quality standards (perhaps after rework) and so do not need to be discarded. Particularly with high technology products, the yield frequently is well under 100 percent.

If the forecast for the production yield is somewhat under 100 percent, the size of the production run probably should be somewhat larger than the order quantity to provide a good chance of fulfilling the order with acceptable items. (The difference between the run size and the order quantity is referred to as the *reject allowance*.) If an expensive setup is required for each production run, or if there is only time for one production run, the reject allowance may need to be quite large. However, an overly large value should be avoided to prevent excessive production costs.

Obtaining a reliable forecast of production yield is essential for choosing an appropriate value of the reject allowance.

This was the case for **Albuquerque Microelectronics Operation,** a dedicated production source for radiation-hardened microchips. The first phase in the production of its microchips, the *wafer fabrication process,* was continuing to provide erratic production yields. For a given product, the yield typically would be quite small (0 to 40 percent) for the first several lots and then would gradually increase to a higher range (35 to 75 percent) for later lots. Therefore, a statistical forecasting method that considered this increasing trend was used to forecast the production yield.

Forecasting Economic Trends

With the possible exception of sales forecasting, the most extensive forecasting effort is devoted to forecasting economic trends on a regional, national, or even international level. How much will the nation's gross domestic product grow next quarter? Next year? What is the forecast for the rate of inflation? The unemployment rate? The balance of trade?

Statistical models to forecast economic trends (commonly called **econometric models**) have been developed in a number of governmental agencies, university research centers, large corporations, and consulting firms, both in the United States and elsewhere. Using historical data to project ahead, these econometric models typically consider a very large number of factors that help drive the economy. Some models include hundreds of variables and equations. However, except for their size and scope, these models resemble some of the statistical forecasting methods used by businesses for sales forecasting, and so forth.

These econometric models can be very influential in determining governmental policies. For example, the forecasts provided by the U.S. Congressional Budget Office strongly guide Congress in developing the federal budgets. These forecasts also help businesses in assessing the general economic outlook.

As an example on a smaller scale, the **U.S. Department of Labor** contracted with a consulting firm to develop the *unemployment insurance econometric forecasting model* (UIEFM). The model is now in use by state employment security agencies around the nation. By projecting such fundamental economic factors as unemployment rates, wage levels, the size of the labor force covered by unemployment insurance, and so on, UIEFM forecasts how much the state will need to pay in unemployment insurance. By projecting tax inflows into the state's unemployment insurance trust fund, UIEFM also forecasts trust fund balances over a 10-year period. Therefore, UIEFM has proven to be invaluable in managing state unemployment insurance systems and in guiding related legislative policies.

Forecasting Staffing Needs

One of the major trends in the American economy is a shifting emphasis from manufacturing to *services.* More and more of our manufactured goods are being produced outside the country (where labor is cheaper) and then imported. At the same time, an increasing number of American business firms are specializing in providing a service of some kind (e.g., travel, tourism, entertainment, legal aid, health services, financial, educational, design, maintenance, etc.). For such a company, forecasting "sales" becomes forecasting the *demand for services,* which then translates into forecasting staffing needs to provide those services.

For example, one of the fastest-growing service industries in the United States today is *call centers.* A call center receives telephone calls from the general public requesting a particular type of service. Depending on the center, the service might be providing technical assistance over the phone, making a travel reservation, filling a telephone order for goods, or booking services to be performed later, as well as other types of assistance. There now are more than 350,000 call centers in the United States, with over $25 billion invested to date and an annual growth rate of 20 percent.

As with any service organization, an erroneous forecast of staffing requirements for a call center has serious consequences. Providing too few agents to answer the telephone leads to unhappy customers, lost calls, and perhaps lost business. Too many agents cause excessive personnel costs.

Section 2.1 described a major management science study that involved personnel scheduling at **United Airlines.** With over 4,000 reservations sales representatives and support

TABLE 13.1   Some Applications of Statistical Forecasting Methods

Organization	Quantity Being Forecasted	Issue of Interfaces
Merit Brass Co.	Sales of finished goods	January–February 1993
Hidroeléctrica Español	Energy demand	January–February 1990
American Airlines	Demand for different fare classes	January–February 1992
American Airlines	Need for spare parts to repair airplanes	July–August 1989
Albuquerque Microelectronics	Production yield in wafer fabrication	March–April 1994
U.S. Department of Labor	Unemployment insurance payments	March–April 1988
United Airlines	Demand at reservations offices and airports	January–February 1986
L. L. Bean	Staffing needs at call center	November–December 1995

personnel at its 11 reservations offices, and about 1,000 customer service agents at its 10 largest airports, a computerized planning system was developed to design the work schedules for these employees. Although several other management science techniques (including linear programming) were incorporated into this system, *statistical forecasting* of staffing requirements also was a key ingredient. This system provided annual savings of over $6 million as well as improved customer service and reduced support staff requirements.

L.L. Bean is a major retailer of high-quality outdoor goods and apparel. Over 70 percent of its total sales volume is generated through orders taken at the company's call center. Two 800 numbers are provided, one for placing orders and the second for making inquiries or reporting problems. Each of the company's agents is trained to answer just one of the 800 numbers. Therefore, separate statistical forecasting models were developed to forecast staffing requirements for the two 800 numbers on a weekly basis. The improved precision of these models is estimated to have saved L.L. Bean $300,000 annually through enhanced scheduling efficiency. (The case study introduced in the next section is based largely on this application.)

Other

Table 13.1 summarizes the actual applications of statistical forecasting methods presented in this section. The last column cites the issue of *Interfaces* that includes the article that describes each application in detail.

All five categories of forecasting applications discussed in this section use the types of statistical forecasting methods presented in the subsequent sections. There also are other important categories (including forecasting weather, the stock market, and prospects for new products before market testing) that use specialized techniques that are not discussed here.

Review Questions

1. When doing sales forecasting, what are the consequences of underestimating demand? Of overestimating demand?
2. When a company leases its products to customers, what kind of forecasting is needed to provide good maintenance service to these customers?
3. What is the purpose of forecasting production yield?
4. What is the common name for statistical models used to forecast economic trends?
5. What are the consequences of an erroneous forecast of staffing needs for a call center?

13.2 A Case Study: The Computer Club Warehouse (CCW) Problem

The Computer Club Warehouse (commonly referred to as CCW) sells various computer products at bargain prices by taking telephone orders (as well as Web site and fax orders) directly from customers. Its products include desktop and laptop computers, peripherals, hardware accessories, supplies, software (including games), and computer-related furniture. The company mails catalogs to its customers and numerous prospective customers several times per year, as well as publishing minicatalogs in computer magazines. These catalogs prominently display the 800 toll-free telephone number to call to place an order. These calls come into the company's *call center.*

The CCW Call Center

The call center is never closed. During busy hours, it is staffed by dozens of agents. Their sole job is to take and process customer orders over the telephone. (A second, much smaller call center uses another 800 number that is for making inquiries or reporting problems. This case study focuses on just the main call center.)

New agents receive a week's training before beginning work. This training emphasizes how to efficiently and courteously process an order. An agent is expected not to average more than five minutes per call. Records are kept and an agent who does not meet this target by the end of the probationary period will not be retained. Although the agents are well-paid, the tedium and time pressure associated with the job leads to a fairly high turnover rate.

A large number of telephone trunks are provided for incoming calls. If an agent is not free when the call arrives, it is placed on hold with a recorded message and background music. If all the trunks are in use (referred to as *saturation*), an incoming call receives a busy signal instead.

Although some customers who receive a busy signal, or who hang up after being on hold too long, will try again later until they get through, many do not. Therefore, it is very important to have enough agents on duty to minimize these problems. On the other hand, because of the high labor costs for the agents, CCW tries to avoid having so many on duty that they have significant idle time.

Consequently, obtaining forecasts of the demand for the agents is crucial to the company.

The Call Center Manager, Lydia Weigelt

The current manager of the call center is Lydia Ann Weigelt. As the top student in her graduating class from business school, she was wooed by several top companies before choosing CCW. Extremely bright and hard driving, she is being groomed to enter top management at CCW in the coming years.

When Lydia was hired a little over three years ago, she was assigned to her current position in order to learn the business from the ground up. The call center is considered to be the nerve center of the entire CCW operation.

Before Lydia's arrival, the company had suffered from serious management problems with the call center. Orders were not being processed efficiently. A few were even misdirected. Staffing levels never seemed to be right. Management directives to adjust the levels kept overcompensating in the opposite direction. Data needed to get a handle on the staffing level problem hadn't been kept. Morale was low.

All that changed when Lydia arrived. One of her first moves was to install procedures for gathering the data needed to make decisions on staffing levels. The key data included a detailed record of call volume and how much of the volume was being handled by each agent. Efficiency improved substantially. Despite running a tight ship, Lydia took great pains to praise and reward good work. Morale increased dramatically.

Although gratified by the great improvement in the operation of the call center, Lydia still has one major frustration. At the end of each quarter, when she knows how many agents are not being retained at the end of their probationary period, she makes a decision on how many new agents to hire to go through the next training session (held at the beginning of each quarter). She has developed an excellent procedure for estimating how much staffing level would be needed to cover any particular call volume. However, each time she has used this procedure to set the staffing level for the upcoming quarter, based on her forecast of the call volume, the forecast usually turned out to be considerably off. Therefore, she still isn't getting the right staffing levels.

Lydia has concluded that her next project should be to develop a better forecasting method to replace the current one.

Lydia's Current Forecasting Method

Thanks to Lydia's data-gathering procedures installed shortly after her arrival, reliable data on call volume now are available for the past three years. Figure 13.1 shows the average number of calls received per day in each of the four quarters of these years. The right side

FIGURE 13.1

The average number of calls received per day at the CCW call center in each of the four quarters of the past three years.

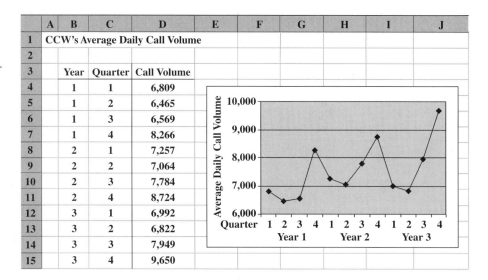

	A	B	C	D	E	F	G	H	I	J
1	CCW's Average Daily Call Volume									
2										
3		Year	Quarter	Call Volume						
4		1	1	6,809						
5		1	2	6,465						
6		1	3	6,569						
7		1	4	8,266						
8		2	1	7,257						
9		2	2	7,064						
10		2	3	7,784						
11		2	4	8,724						
12		3	1	6,992						
13		3	2	6,822						
14		3	3	7,949						
15		3	4	9,650						

also displays these same data to show the pattern graphically. (This graph was generated from the data by choosing "Chart" under the Insert menu, selecting the Line chart type, and following the directions of the Chart Wizard.)

Note that the sales in Quarter 4 jump up each year due to Christmas purchases. When Lydia first joined CCW, the president told her about the "25 percent rule" that the company had traditionally used to forecast call volume (and sales).

The 25 Percent Rule: Since sales are relatively stable through the year except for a substantial increase during the Christmas season, assume that each quarter's call volume will be the same as for the preceding quarter, except for adding 25 percent for quarter 4. Thus,

Forecast for Quarter 2 = Call volume for Quarter 1
Forecast for Quarter 3 = Call volume for Quarter 2
Forecast for Quarter 4 = 1.25(Call volume for Quarter 3)

The forecast for the next year's Quarter 1 then would be obtained from the current year's Quarter 4 by

$$\text{Forecast for next Quarter 1} = \frac{\text{Call volume for Quarter 4}}{1.25}$$

This is the forecasting method that Lydia has been using.

Figure 13.2 shows the forecasts that Lydia obtained with this method. Column F gives the **forecasting error** (the deviation of the forecast from what then turned out to be the true value of the call volume) in each case. Since the total of the 11 forecasting errors is 4,662, the average is

$$\text{Average forecasting error} = \frac{4,662}{11}$$

$$= 424$$

The average forecasting error is commonly called **MAD,** which stands for **mean absolute deviation.** Its formula is

$$\text{MAD} = \frac{\text{Sum of forecasting errors}}{\text{Number of forecasts}}$$

Thus, in this case, cell I5 gives

$$\text{MAD} = 424$$

MAD is only one of several measures of the accuracy of forecasting methods, but it is the most straightforward. We will use MAD as our measure.

To put this value of MAD = 424 into perspective, note that 424 is over 5 percent of the average daily call volume in most quarters. With forecasting errors ranging as high as

FIGURE 13.2

This spreadsheet records the results of applying the 25 percent rule over the past three years to forecast the average daily call volume for the upcoming quarter.

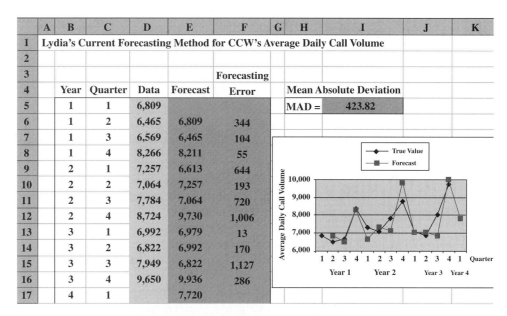

	E	F		I
6	=D5	=ABS(D6–E6)	5	=AVERAGE(F6:F16)
7	=D6	=ABS(D7–E7)		
8	=1.25*D7	=ABS(D8–E8)		
9	=D8/1.25	=ABS(D9–E9)		
10	=D9	=ABS(D10–E10)		
11	:	:		
12	:	:		

1,127, two of the errors are well over 10 percent. Although errors of this size are common in typical applications of forecasting, greater accuracy is needed for this particular application. Errors of 5 and 10 percent make it impossible to properly set the staffing level for a quarter. No wonder Lydia is *mad* about the poor job that the 25 percent rule is doing. A better forecasting method is needed.

The Plan to Find a Better Forecasting Method

Lydia had taken a management science course in college. She recalls that one of the topics in the course had been *forecasting*, so she decides to review her textbook and class notes on this topic.

This review reminds her that she is dealing with what is called a *time series*.

A **time series** is a series of observations over time of some quantity of interest. For example, the series of observations of average daily call columns for the most recent 12 quarters, as given in Figure 13.1, constitute a time series.

She also is reminded that a variety of statistical methods are available for using the historical data from a time series to forecast a future observation in the series. Her task now is to review these methods and assess which one is best suited for her particular forecasting problem.

To assist her in this task for a few weeks, Lydia gains approval from the CCW president to contract for the services of a consultant (a former classmate) from a management science consulting firm that specializes largely in forecasting.

The next section describes their approach to the problem.

Review Questions

1. How does the Computer Club Warehouse (CCW) operate?
2. What are the consequences of not having enough agents on duty in the CCW call center? Of having too many?

3. Who is the call center manager? What is her current major frustration?
4. What is CCW's 25 percent rule?
5. What is MAD?
6. What is a time series?

13.3 Applying Time-Series Forecasting Methods to the Case Study

Figure 13.1 in the preceding section highlights the seasonal pattern of CCW's call volumes, with a large jump up each fourth quarter due to Christmas shopping. Therefore, before considering specific forecasting methods, Lydia and the consultant begin by addressing how to deal with this seasonal pattern.

Considering Seasonal Effects

For many years, the folklore at CCW has been that the call volume (and sales) will be pretty stable over the first three quarters of a year and then will jump up by about 25 percent in Quarter 4. This has been the basis for the 25 percent rule.

To check how close this folklore still is to reality, the consultant uses the data previously given in Figure 13.1 to calculate the average daily call volume for each quarter over the past three years. For example, the average for Quarter 1 is

$$\text{Average(Quarter 1)} = \frac{6{,}809 + 7{,}257 + 6{,}992}{3}$$

$$= 7{,}019$$

These averages for all four quarters are shown in the second column of Table 13.2. Underneath this column, the *overall average* over all four quarters is calculated to be 7,529. Dividing the average for each quarter by this overall average gives the *seasonal factor* shown in the third column.

In general, the **seasonal factor** for any period of a year (a quarter, a month, etc.) measures how that period compares to the overall average for an entire year. Specifically, using historical data, the seasonal factor is calculated to be

$$\text{Seasonal factor} = \frac{\text{Average for the period}}{\text{Overall average}}$$

Your MS Courseware includes an Excel template for calculating these seasonal factors. Figure 13.3 shows this template applied to the CCW problem.

Note the significant differences in the seasonal factors for the first three quarters, with Quarter 3 considerably above the other two. This makes sense to Lydia, who has long suspected that back-to-school buying should give a small boost to sales in Quarter 3.

TABLE 13.2 Calculation of the Seasonal Factors for the CCW Problem

Quarter	Three–Year Average	Seasonal Factor
1	7,019	$\frac{7{,}019}{7{,}529} = 0.93$
2	6,784	$\frac{6{,}784}{7{,}529} = 0.90$
3	7,434	$\frac{7{,}434}{7{,}529} = 0.99$
4	8,880	$\frac{8{,}880}{7{,}529} = 1.18$

Total = 30,117

$$\text{Average} = \frac{30{,}117}{4} = 7{,}529$$

In contrast to the 25 percent rule, the seasonal factor for Quarter 4 is only 19 percent higher than that for Quarter 3. (However, the Quarter 4 factor *is* about 25 percent above 0.94, which is the *average* of the seasonal factors for the first three quarters.)

Although data on call volumes are not available prior to the most recent three years, reliable sales data have been kept. Upon checking these data several years back, Lydia finds the same seasonal patterns occurring.

> **Conclusion:** The seasonal factors given in Table 13.2 appear to accurately reflect subtle but important differences in all the seasons. Therefore, these factors now will be used, instead of the 25 percent rule, to indicate seasonal patterns until such time as future data indicate a shift in these patterns.

The Seasonally Adjusted Time Series

It is much easier to analyze sales data and detect new trends if the data are first adjusted to remove the effect of seasonal patterns. To remove the seasonal effects from the time series shown in Figure 13.1, each of these average daily call volumes needs to be divided by the corresponding seasonal factor given in Table 13.2 and Figure 13.3. Thus, the formula is

$$\text{Seasonally adjusted call volume} = \frac{\text{Actual call volume}}{\text{Seasonal factor}}$$

Applying this formula to all 12 call volumes in Figure 13.1 gives the seasonally adjusted call volumes shown in column F of the Excel template in Figure 13.4.

In effect, these seasonally adjusted call volumes show what the call volumes would have been if the calls that occur because of the time of the year (Christmas shopping, back-to-school shopping, etc.) had been spread evenly throughout the year instead. Compare the plots in Figures 13.4 and 13.1. After considering the smaller vertical scale in Figure 13.4, note how much less fluctuation this figure has than Figure 13.1 because of removing seasonal effects. However, this figure still is far from completely flat because fluctuations in call volume occur for other reasons besides just seasonal effects. For example, hot new products attract a flurry of calls. A jump also occurs just after the mailing of a catalog. Some random fluctuations occur without any apparent explanation. Figure 13.4 enables seeing and analyzing these fluctuations in sales volumes that are not caused by seasonal effects.

FIGURE 13.3

The Excel template in your MS Courseware for calculating seasonal factors is applied here to the CCW problem.

	A	B	C	D	E	F	G
1	Estimating Seasonal Factors for CCW						
2							
3							
4				True			
5		Year	Quarter	Value		Type of Seasonality	
6		1	1	6809		Quarterly	
7		1	2	6465			
8		1	3	6569			
9		1	4	8266			Estimate for
10		2	1	7257		Quarter	Seasonal Factor
11		2	2	7064		1	0.9323
12		2	3	7784		2	0.9010
13		2	4	8724		3	0.9873
14		3	1	6992		4	1.1794
15		3	2	6822			
16		3	3	7949			
17		3	4	9650			

	G
11	=AVERAGE(D6,D10,D14)/AVERAGE($D$6:$D$17)
12	=AVERAGE(D7,D11,D15)/AVERAGE($D$6:$D$17)
13	=AVERAGE(D8,D12,D16)/AVERAGE($D$6:$D$17)
14	=AVERAGE(D9,D13,D17)/AVERAGE($D$6:$D$17)

FIGURE 13.4

The seasonally adjusted time series for the CCW problem obtained by dividing each actual average daily call volume in Figure 13.1 by the corresponding seasonal factor obtained in Figure 13.3.

	A	B	C	D	E	F	G	H	I	J
1	Seasonally Adjusted Time Series for CCW									
2						Seasonally				
3				Seasonal	Actual	Adjusted				
4		Year	Quarter	Factor	Call Volume	Call Volume				
5		1	1	0.93	6809	7322				
6		1	2	0.90	6465	7183				
7		1	3	0.99	6569	6635				
8		1	4	1.18	8266	7005				
9		2	1	0.93	7257	7803				
10		2	2	0.90	7064	7849				
11		2	3	0.99	7784	7863				
12		2	4	1.18	8724	7393				
13		3	1	0.93	6992	7518				
14		3	2	0.90	6822	7580				
15		3	3	0.99	7949	8029				
16		3	4	1.18	9650	8178				

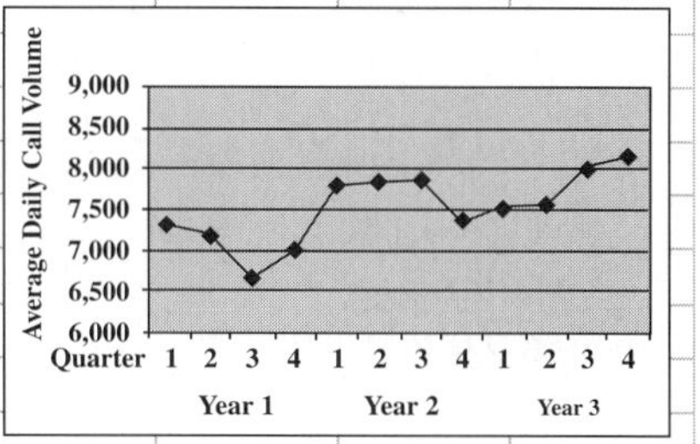

	F
5	=E5/D5
6	=E6/D6
7	=E7/D7
8	=E8/D8
9	:
10	:

The pattern in these remaining fluctuations in the **seasonally adjusted time series** (especially the pattern for the most recent data points) is particularly helpful for forecasting where the next data point will fall. Thus, in Figure 13.4, the data points fall in the range between 6,635 and 8,178, with an average of 7,530. However, the last few data points are trending upward above this average, and the last point is the highest in the entire time series. This suggests that the next data point for the upcoming quarter probably will be above the 7,530 average and may well be near or even above the last data point of 8,178.

The various time series forecasting methods use different approaches to projecting forward the pattern in the seasonally adjusted time series to forecast the next data point. The main methods will be presented in this section.

After obtaining a forecast for the seasonally adjusted time series, all these methods then convert this forecast to a forecast of the actual call volume (without seasonal adjustments), as outlined below.

Outline for Forecasting Call Volume

1. Select a time series forecasting method.
2. Apply this method to the seasonally adjusted time series to obtain a forecast of the seasonally adjusted call volume for the next quarter.[1]
3. Multiply this forecast by the corresponding seasonal factor in Table 13.2 to obtain a forecast of the actual call volume (without seasonal adjustment).

The following descriptions of the methods focus on how to perform step 2, that is, how to forecast the next data point for a given time series. We also include a spreadsheet in each case that applies steps 2 and 3 throughout the past three years and then calculates MAD (the average forecasting error). Lydia and the consultant are paying particular attention to the MAD values to assess which method seems best suited for forecasting CCW call volumes.

---

[1]This forecast also can be projected ahead to subsequent quarters, but we are focusing on just the next quarter.

FIGURE 13.5

The Excel template in your MS Courseware for the last-value method with seasonal adjustments is applied here to the CCW problem.

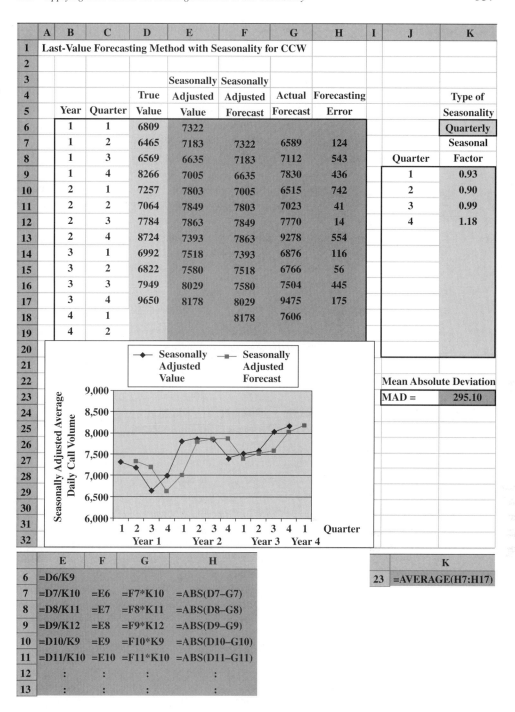

	A	B	C	D	E	F	G	H	I	J	K
1		Last-Value Forecasting Method with Seasonality for CCW									
2											
3					Seasonally	Seasonally					
4				True	Adjusted	Adjusted	Actual	Forecasting			Type of
5		Year	Quarter	Value	Value	Forecast	Forecast	Error			Seasonality
6		1	1	6809	7322						Quarterly
7		1	2	6465	7183	7322	6589	124			Seasonal
8		1	3	6569	6635	7183	7112	543		Quarter	Factor
9		1	4	8266	7005	6635	7830	436		1	0.93
10		2	1	7257	7803	7005	6515	742		2	0.90
11		2	2	7064	7849	7803	7023	41		3	0.99
12		2	3	7784	7863	7849	7770	14		4	1.18
13		2	4	8724	7393	7863	9278	554			
14		3	1	6992	7518	7393	6876	116			
15		3	2	6822	7580	7518	6766	56			
16		3	3	7949	8029	7580	7504	445			
17		3	4	9650	8178	8029	9475	175			
18		4	1			8178	7606				
19		4	2								
20											
21											
22											Mean Absolute Deviation
23										MAD =	295.10

	E	F	G	H
6	=D6/K9			
7	=D7/K10	=E6	=F7*K10	=ABS(D7–G7)
8	=D8/K11	=E7	=F8*K11	=ABS(D8–G8)
9	=D9/K12	=E8	=F9*K12	=ABS(D9–G9)
10	=D10/K9	=E9	=F10*K9	=ABS(D10–G10)
11	=D11/K10	=E10	=F11*K10	=ABS(D11–G11)
12	:	:	:	:
13	:	:	:	:

	K
23	=AVERAGE(H7:H17)

The Last-Value Forecasting Method

The **last-value forecasting method** ignores all the data points in a time series except the last one. It then uses this last value as the forecast of what the next data point will turn out to be, so the formula is simply

$$\text{Forecast} = \text{Last value}$$

Figure 13.5 shows what would have happened if this method had been applied to the CCW problem over the past three years. (We are supposing that the seasonal factors given in Table 13.2 already were being used then.) Column E gives the true values of the seasonally adjusted call volumes from column F of Figure 13.4. Each of these values then becomes the seasonally adjusted forecast for the *next* quarter, as shown in column F.

Rows 23–30 show separate plots of these values in columns E and F. Note how the plot of the seasonally adjusted forecasts follows exactly the same path as the plot of the seasonally adjusted call volumes but shifted to the right by one quarter. Therefore, each time there is a large shift up or down in the call volume, the forecasts are one quarter late in catching up with the shift.

Multiplying each seasonally adjusted forecast in column F by the corresponding seasonal factor in column K gives the forecast of the actual call volume (without seasonal adjustment) presented in column G. The difference between this forecast and the actual call volume in column D gives the forecasting error in column H.

Thus, column G is using the following formula:

$$\text{Actual forecast} = \text{Seasonal factor} \times \text{Seasonally adjusted forecast}$$

as indicated by the equations at the bottom of the figure. For example, since cell K9 gives 0.93 as the seasonal factor for Quarter 1, the forecast of the actual call volume for Year 2, Quarter 1 given in cell G10 is

$$\text{Actual forecast} = (0.93)(7,257) = 6,515$$

Since the true value of this call volume turned out to be 7,257, the forecasting error calculated in cell H10 for this quarter is

$$\text{Forecasting error} = 7,257 - 6,515 = 742$$

Summing these forecasting errors over all 11 quarters of forecasts gives a total of 3,246, so the average forecasting error given in cell K23 is

$$\text{MAD} = \frac{3,246}{11} = 295$$

This compares with MAD = 424 for the 25 percent rule that Lydia has been using (as described in the preceding section).

Except for its graph, Figure 13.5 displays one of the templates in this chapter's Excel file. In fact, your MS Courseware includes two Excel templates for each of the forecasting methods presented in this section. One template performs all the calculations for you for the case where no seasonal adjustments are needed. The second template does the same when seasonal adjustments are included, as illustrated by this figure. With all templates of the second type, you have complete flexibility for what to enter as the seasonal factors. One option is to *calculate* these factors based on historical data (as was done with another Excel template in Figure 13.3). Another is to *estimate* them based on historical experience, as with the 25 percent rule.

The 25 percent rule actually is a *last-value forecasting method* as well, but with different seasonal factors. Since this rule that the call volume in the fourth quarter will average 25 percent more than *each* of the first three quarters, its seasonal factors are essentially 0.94 for Quarters 1, 2, 3 and 1.18 (25 percent more than 0.94) for Quarter 4. Thus, the lower value of MAD in Figure 13.5 is entirely due to refining the seasonal factors in Table 13.2.

Lydia is enthusiastic to see the substantial improvement obtained by simply refining the seasonal factors. However, the consultant quickly adds a note of caution. The forecasts obtained in Figure 13.5 are using the same data that were used to calculate these refined seasonal factors, which creates some bias for these factors to tend to perform better than on new data (future call volumes). Fortunately, Lydia also has checked older sales data to confirm that these seasonal factors seem quite accurate. The consultant agrees that it appears that these factors should provide a significant improvement over the 25 percent rule.

The last-value forecasting method sometimes is called the **naive method,** because statisticians consider it naive to use just a *sample size of one* when additional relevant data are available. However, when conditions are changing rapidly, it may be that the last value is the only relevant data point for forecasting the next value under current conditions. Therefore, managers who are anything but naive do occasionally use this method under such circumstances.

The Averaging Forecasting Method

The **averaging forecasting method** goes to the other extreme. Rather than using just a sample size of one, this method uses *all* the data points in the time series and simply *averages* these points. Thus, the forecast of what the next data point will turn out to be is

$$\text{Forecast} = \text{average of all data to date}$$

FIGURE 13.6

The Excel template in your MS Courseware for the averaging method with seasonal adjustments is applied here to the CCW problem.

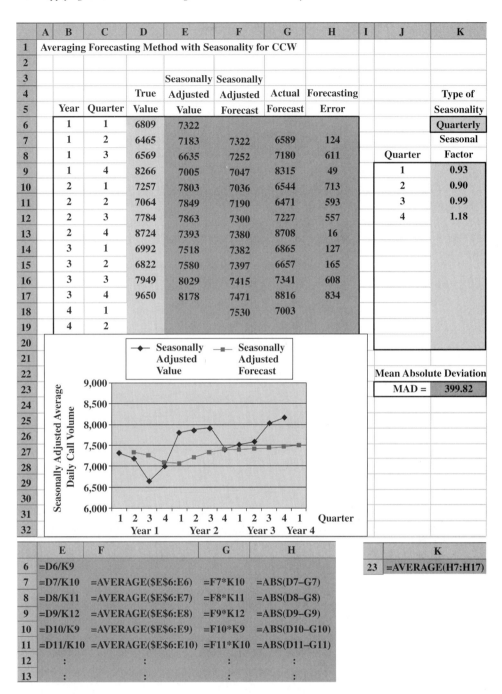

	A	B	C	D	E	F	G	H	I	J	K
1	Averaging Forecasting Method with Seasonality for CCW										
2											
3					Seasonally	Seasonally					
4				True	Adjusted	Adjusted	Actual	Forecasting			Type of
5		Year	Quarter	Value	Value	Forecast	Forecast	Error			Seasonality
6		1	1	6809	7322						Quarterly
7		1	2	6465	7183	7322	6589	124			Seasonal
8		1	3	6569	6635	7252	7180	611		Quarter	Factor
9		1	4	8266	7005	7047	8315	49		1	0.93
10		2	1	7257	7803	7036	6544	713		2	0.90
11		2	2	7064	7849	7190	6471	593		3	0.99
12		2	3	7784	7863	7300	7227	557		4	1.18
13		2	4	8724	7393	7380	8708	16			
14		3	1	6992	7518	7382	6865	127			
15		3	2	6822	7580	7397	6657	165			
16		3	3	7949	8029	7415	7341	608			
17		3	4	9650	8178	7471	8816	834			
18		4	1			7530	7003				
19		4	2								
20											
21											
22											Mean Absolute Deviation
23										MAD =	399.82

	E	F	G	H
6	=D6/K9			
7	=D7/K10	=AVERAGE($E$6:E6)	=F7*K10	=ABS(D7–G7)
8	=D8/K11	=AVERAGE($E$6:E7)	=F8*K11	=ABS(D8–G8)
9	=D9/K12	=AVERAGE($E$6:E8)	=F9*K12	=ABS(D9–G9)
10	=D10/K9	=AVERAGE($E$6:E9)	=F10*K9	=ABS(D10–G10)
11	=D11/K10	=AVERAGE($E$6:E10)	=F11*K10	=ABS(D11–G11)
12	:	:	:	:
13	:	:	:	:

	K
23	=AVERAGE(H7:H17)

Using the corresponding Excel template to apply this method to the CCW problem over the past three years gives the seasonally adjusted forecasts shown in column F of Figure 13.6. At the bottom of the figure, the equation entered into each of the column F cells is just the average of the column E cells in the preceding rows. The middle of the figure shows a plot of these seasonally adjusted forecasts for all three years next to the true values of the seasonally adjusted call volumes. Note how each forecast lies at the average of the preceding call volumes. Therefore, each time there is a large shift in the call volume, the subsequent forecasts are very slow in catching up with the shift.

Multiplying all the seasonally adjusted forecasts in column F by the corresponding seasonal factors in column K then gives the *forecasts of the actual call volumes* shown in column G. Based on the resulting forecasting errors given in column H, the average forecasting error in this case (cell K23) is

$$MAD = 400$$

considerably larger than the 295 obtained for the last-value forecasting method.

Lydia is quite surprised, since she expected an average to do much better than a sample size of one. The consultant agrees that averaging should perform considerably better if conditions remain the same throughout the time series. However, it appears that the conditions affecting the CCW call volume were changing significantly over the past three years. The call volume was quite a bit higher in Year 2 than in Year 1, and then jumped up again late in Year 3, apparently as popular new products became available. Therefore, the Year 1 values were not very relevant for forecasting under the changed conditions of Years 2 and 3. Including the Year 1 call volumes in the overall average caused *every* forecast for Years 2 and 3 to be too low, sometimes by large amounts.

The Moving-Average Forecasting Method

Rather than using old data that may no longer be relevant, the **moving-average forecasting method** averages the data for only the most recent time periods. Let

n = number of most recent periods considered particularly relevant for forecasting the next period

Then the forecast for the next period is

$$\text{Forecast} = \text{average of last } n \text{ values}$$

Lydia and the consultant decide to use $n = 4$, since conditions appear to be relatively stable for only about four quarters (one year) at a time.

With $n = 4$, the first forecast becomes available after four quarters of call volumes have been observed. Thus, the initial seasonally adjusted forecasts in cells F10:F12 of Figure 13.7 are

Y2, Q1: Seas. adj. forecast $= \dfrac{7{,}311 + 7{,}183 + 6{,}635 + 7{,}005}{4} = 7{,}036$

Y2, Q2: Seas. adj. forecast $= \dfrac{7{,}183 + 6{,}635 + 7{,}005 + 7{,}803}{4} = 7{,}157$

Y2, Q3: Seas. adj. forecast $= \dfrac{6{,}635 + 7{,}005 + 7{,}803 + 7{,}849}{4} = 7{,}323$

Note how each forecast is updated from the preceding one by lopping off one observation (the oldest one) and adding one new one (the most recent observation).

Column F of Figure 13.7 shows all the seasonally adjusted forecasts obtained in this way with the equations at the bottom. For each of these forecasts, note in the plot how it lies at the average of the four preceding (seasonally adjusted) call volumes. Consequently, each time there is a large shift in the call volume, it takes four quarters for the forecasts to fully catch up with this shift (by which time another shift may already have occurred). Consequently, the average of the eight forecasting errors in column H is

$$\text{MAD} = 437$$

the highest of any of the methods so far, including even the 25 percent rule.

Lydia is very puzzled about this surprisingly high MAD value. The moving-average method seemed like a very sensible approach to forecasting, with more rationale behind it than any of the previous methods. (It uses only recent history *and* it uses multiple observations.) So why should it do so poorly?

The consultant explains that this is indeed a very good forecasting method when conditions remain pretty much the same over n time periods (or four quarters in this case). For example, the seasonally adjusted call volumes remained reasonably stable throughout Year 2 and the first half of Year 3. Consequently, the forecasting error dropped all the way down to 68 (cell H15) for the last of these six quarters. However, when conditions shift sharply, as with the big jump up in call volumes at the beginning of Year 2, and then again in the middle of Year 3, the next few forecasting errors tend to be very large.

Thus, the moving-average method is somewhat slow to respond to changing conditions. One reason is that it places the *same* weight on each of the last n values in the time series even though the older values may be less representative of current conditions than the last value observed.

The next method corrects this weighting defect.

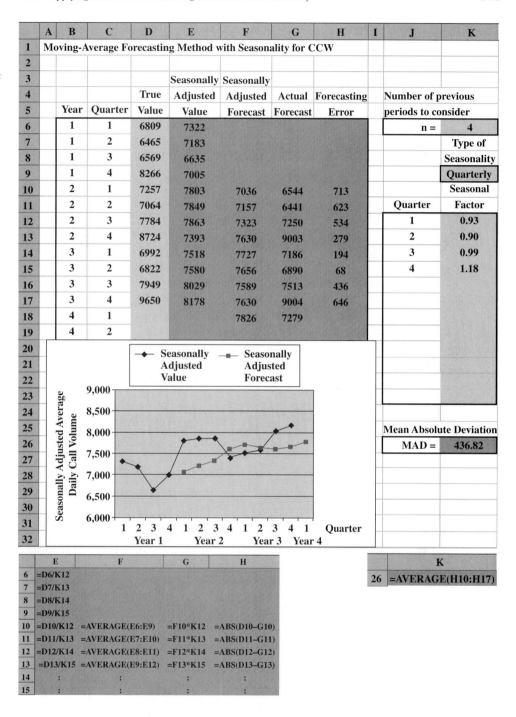

FIGURE 13.7

The Excel template in your MS Courseware for the moving-average method with seasonal adjustments is applied here to the CCW problem.

The Exponential Smoothing Forecasting Method

The **exponential smoothing forecasting method** modifies the moving-average method by placing the greatest weight on the last value in the time series and then progressively smaller weights on the older values. However, rather than needing to calculate a *weighted average* each time, it uses a simpler formula to obtain the same result.

This formula for forecasting the next value in the time series combines the *last value* and the *last forecast* (the one used one time period ago to forecast this last value) as follows:

$$\text{Forecast} = \alpha(\text{last value}) + (1 - \alpha)(\text{last forecast})$$

where α (the Greek letter alpha) is a constant between 0 and 1 called the **smoothing constant**. For example, if the last value in a time series (not the CCW time series) is 24, the last forecast is 20, and $\alpha = 0.25$, then

$$\text{Forecast} = 0.25(24) + 0.75(20)$$

$$= 21$$

Two Excel templates (one without seasonal adjustments and one with) are available in your MS Courseware for applying this formula to generate a series of forecasts (period by period) for a time series when you specify the value of α.

The choice of the value for the smoothing constant α has a substantial effect on the forecast, so the choice should be made with care. A small value (say, $\alpha = 0.1$) is appropriate if conditions are remaining relatively stable. However, a larger value (say, $\alpha = 0.3$) is needed if significant changes in the conditions are occurring relatively frequently. Because of the frequent shifts in the CCW seasonally adjusted time series, Lydia and the consultant conclude that $\alpha=0.5$ would be an appropriate value. (The values selected for most applications are between 0.1 and 0.3, but a larger value can be used in this kind of situation.)

When making the first forecast, there is no *last forecast* available to plug into the right-hand side of the above formula. Therefore, to get started, a reasonable approach is to make an *initial estimate* of the average value anticipated for the time series. This initial estimate is used as the forecast for the first value, and then the formula is used to forecast the second value onward.

CCW call volumes have averaged just over 7,500 for the past three years, and the level of business just prior to Year 1 was comparable. Consequently, Lydia and the consultant decide to use

$$\text{Initial estimate} = 7,500$$

to begin retrospectively generating the forecasts over the past three years. Recall that the first few seasonally adjusted call volumes are 7,322, 7,183, and 6,635. Thus, using the above formula with $\alpha=0.5$ for the second quarter onward, the first few seasonally adjusted forecasts are

Y1, Q1:	Seas. adj. forecast = 7,500
Y1, Q2:	Seas. adj. forecast = 0.5 (7,322) + 0.5 (7,500) = 7,411
Y1, Q3:	Seas. adj. forecast = 0.5 (7,183) + 0.5 (7,411) = 7,297
Y1, Q4:	Seas. adj. forecast = 0.5 (6,635) + 0.5 (7,297) = 6,966

To see why these forecasts are weighted averages of the time series values to date, look at the calculations for Quarters 2 and 3. Since

$$0.5(7,322) + 0.5(7,500) = 7,411$$

the forecast for Quarter 3 can be written as

$$
\begin{aligned}
\text{Seas. adj. forecast} &= 0.5(7,183) + 0.5(7,411) \\
&= 0.5(7,183) + 0.5[0.5(7,322) + 0.5(7,500)] \\
&= 0.5(7,183) + 0.25(7,322) + 0.25(7,500) \\
&= 7,297
\end{aligned}
$$

Similarly, the forecast for Quarter 4 is

$$
\begin{aligned}
\text{Seas. adj. forecast} &= 0.5(6,635) + 0.5(7,297) \\
&= 0.5(6,635) + 0.5[0.5(7,183) + 0.25(7,322) + 0.25(7,500)] \\
&= 0.5(6,635) + 0.25(7,183) + 0.125(7,322) + 0.125(7,500) \\
&= 6,966
\end{aligned}
$$

Thus, this latter forecast places a weight of 0.5 on the last value, 0.25 on the next-to-last value, and 0.125 on the next prior value (the first one), with the remaining weight on the initial estimate. With other values of α, these weights would be α, $\alpha(1 - \alpha)$, $\alpha(1-\alpha)^2$, and so forth.

Therefore, choosing the value of α amounts to using this pattern to choose the desired progression of weights on the time series values. With frequent shifts in the time series, a large weight needs to be placed on the most recent value, with rapidly decreasing weights on older values. However, with a relatively stable time series, it is desirable to place a significant weight on many values in order to have a large sample size.

Further insight into the choice of α is provided by an alternative form of the forecasting formula.

$$\text{Forecast} = \alpha(\text{last value}) + (1 - \alpha)(\text{last forecast})$$

$$= \alpha(\text{last value}) + \text{last forecast} - \alpha(\text{last forecast})$$

$$= \text{last forecast} + \alpha(\text{last value} - \text{last forecast})$$

where the absolute value of (last value − last forecast) is just the last forecasting error. Therefore, the bottom form of this formula indicates that each new forecast is adjusting the last forecast by adding or subtracting the quantity α *times* the last forecasting error. If the forecasting error usually is mainly due to random fluctuations in the time-series values, then only a small value of α should be used for this adjustment. However, if the forecasting error often is largely due to a shift in the time series, then a large value of α is needed to make a substantial adjustment quickly.

Using $\alpha = 0.5$, the Excel template in Figure 13.8 provides all the results for CCW with this forecasting method. Rows 23–30 show a plot of all the seasonally adjusted forecasts next to the true values of the seasonally adjusted call volumes. Note how each forecast lies midway between the preceding call volume and the preceding forecast. Therefore, each time there is a large shift in the call volume, the forecasts largely catch up with the shift rather quickly. The resulting average of the forecasting errors in column H is given in cell K29 as

$$\text{MAD} = 324$$

This is significantly smaller than for the previous forecasting methods, except for the value of MAD = 295 for the last-value forecasting method.

Lydia is somewhat frustrated at this point. She feels that she needs a method with average forecasting errors well below 295. Realizing that the last-value forecasting method is considered the *naive* method, she had expected that such a popular and sophisticated method as exponential smoothing would beat it easily.

The consultant is somewhat surprised also. However, he points out that the difference between MAD = 324 for exponential smoothing and MAD = 295 for last-value forecasting is really too small to be statistically significant. If the same two methods were to be applied the *next* three years, exponential smoothing might come out ahead. Lydia is not impressed.

Although he isn't ready to mention it to Lydia yet, the consultant is beginning to develop an idea for a whole new approach that might give her the forecasting precision she needs. But first he has one more time-series forecasting method to present.

To lay the groundwork for this method, the consultant explains a major reason why exponential smoothing had not fared well in this case. Look at the plot of seasonally adjusted call volumes in Figure 13.8. Note the distinct trend downward in the first three quarters, then a sharp trend upward for the next two, and finally a major trend upward for the last five quarters. Also note the large gap between the two plots (meaning large forecasting errors) by the end of each of these trends. The reason for these large errors is that exponential smoothing forecasts lag well behind such a trend because they place significant weight on values near the beginning of the trend. Although a large value of $\alpha=0.5$ helps, exponential smoothing forecasts tend to lag further behind such a trend than last-value forecasts.

The next method adjusts exponential smoothing by also estimating the current trend and then projects this trend forward to help forecast the next value in the time series.

Exponential Smoothing with Trend

Exponential smoothing with trend uses the recent values in the time series to estimate any current upward or downward **trend** in these values. It is especially designed for the kind of time series depicted in Figure 13.9 where an upward (or downward) trend tends to continue for a considerable number of periods (but not necessarily indefinitely). This particular figure shows the estimated population of a certain state at mid-year over a series of years. The line in the figure (commonly referred to as a *trend line*) shows the basic trend that the time series is following, but with fluctuations on both sides of the line. Because the basic trend is upward in this case, forecasts based on any of the preceding forecasting methods would tend to be considerably too low. However, by developing an estimate of the current slope

FIGURE 13.8

The Excel template in your MS Courseware for the exponential smoothing method with seasonal adjustments is applied here to the CCW problem.

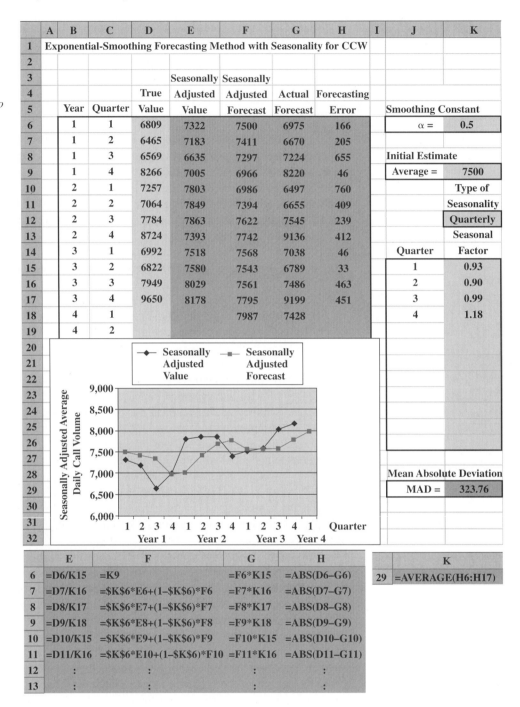

	A	B	C	D	E	F	G	H	I	J	K
1		Exponential-Smoothing Forecasting Method with Seasonality for CCW									
2											
3					Seasonally	Seasonally					
4				True	Adjusted	Adjusted	Actual	Forecasting			
5		Year	Quarter	Value	Value	Forecast	Forecast	Error		Smoothing Constant	
6		1	1	6809	7322	7500	6975	166		$\alpha =$	0.5
7		1	2	6465	7183	7411	6670	205			
8		1	3	6569	6635	7297	7224	655		Initial Estimate	
9		1	4	8266	7005	6966	8220	46		Average =	7500
10		2	1	7257	7803	6986	6497	760			Type of
11		2	2	7064	7849	7394	6655	409			Seasonality
12		2	3	7784	7863	7622	7545	239			Quarterly
13		2	4	8724	7393	7742	9136	412			Seasonal
14		3	1	6992	7518	7568	7038	46		Quarter	Factor
15		3	2	6822	7580	7543	6789	33		1	0.93
16		3	3	7949	8029	7561	7486	463		2	0.90
17		3	4	9650	8178	7795	9199	451		3	0.99
18		4	1			7987	7428			4	1.18
19		4	2								
28										Mean Absolute Deviation	
29										MAD =	323.76

	E	F	G	H		K
6	=D6/K15	=K9	=F6*K15	=ABS(D6–G6)	29	=AVERAGE(H6:H17)
7	=D7/K16	=$K$6*E6+(1–$K$6)*F6	=F7*K16	=ABS(D7–G7)		
8	=D8/K17	=$K$6*E7+(1–$K$6)*F7	=F8*K17	=ABS(D8–G8)		
9	=D9/K18	=$K$6*E8+(1–$K$6)*F8	=F9*K18	=ABS(D9–G9)		
10	=D10/K15	=$K$6*E9+(1–$K$6)*F9	=F10*K15	=ABS(D10–G10)		
11	=D11/K16	=$K$6*E10+(1–$K$6)*F10	=F11*K16	=ABS(D11–G11)		
12	:	:	:	:		
13	:	:	:	:		

of this trend line, and then adjusting the forecast to consider this slope, considerably more accurate forecasts should be obtained. This is the basic idea behind exponential smoothing with trend.

Trend is defined as

Trend = average change from one time-series value to the next if the current pattern continues

The formula for forecasting the next value in the time series, then, is modified from the preceding method by *adding the estimated trend.* Thus, the new formula is

Forecast = α(last value) + $(1 - \alpha)$(last forecast) + estimated trend

(A separate box describes how this formula can be easily modified to forecast *beyond* the next value in the time series as well.)

FIGURE 13.9

A time series that gives the estimated population of a certain state over a series of years. The trend line shows the basic upward trend of the population.

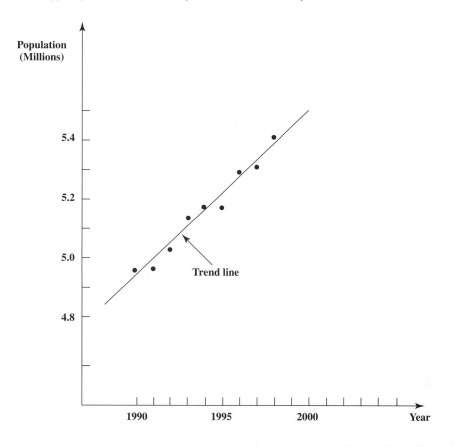

Forecasting More Than One Time Period Ahead

We have focused thus far on forecasting what will happen in the *next* time period (the next quarter in the case of CCW). However, managers sometimes need to forecast further into the future. How can the various time series forecasting methods be adapted to do this?

In the case of the last-value, averaging, moving-average, and exponential smoothing methods, the forecast for the next period also is the best available forecast for subsequent periods as well. However, when there is a *trend* in the data, it is important to take this trend into account for long-range forecasts. *Exponential smoothing with trend* provides a way of doing this. In particular, after determining the *estimated trend*, this method's forecast for *n* time periods into the future is

Forecast for *n* periods from now = α(last value) + (1 − α)(last forecast) + *n* × (estimated trend)

Exponential smoothing also is used to obtain and update *estimated trend* each time. The formula is

Estimated trend = β(latest trend) + (1 − β)(last estimate of trend)

where β (the Greek letter beta) is the **trend smoothing constant,** which, like α, must be between 0 and 1. *Latest trend* refers to the trend based on just the last two values in the time series and the last two forecasts. Its formula is

Latest trend = α(last value − next-to-last value)

+ (1 − α)(last forecast − next-to-last forecast)

Getting started with this forecasting method requires making two initial estimates about the status of the time series just prior to beginning forecasting. These initial estimates are

1. Initial estimate of the *average value* of the time series if the conditions just prior to beginning forecasting were to remain unchanged without any trend.
2. Initial estimate of the *trend* of the time series just prior to beginning forecasting.

The forecast for the first period being forecasted then is

First forecast = initial estimate of average value + initial estimate of trend

The second forecast is obtained from the above formulas, where the *initial estimate of trend* is used as the last estimate of trend in the formula for estimated trend and the *initial estimate of average value* is used as both the next-to-last value and the next-to-last forecast in the formula for latest trend. The above formulas then are used directly to obtain subsequent forecasts.

Since the calculations involved with this method are relatively involved, a computer commonly is used to implement the method. Your MS Courseware includes two Excel templates (one without seasonal adjustments and one with) for this method.

The considerations involved in choosing the trend smoothing constant β are similar to those for α. A large value of β (say, $\beta = 0.3$) is more responsive to recent changes in the trend, whereas a relatively small value (say, $\beta = 0.1$) uses more data in a significant way to estimate trend.

After trying various combinations of α and β on the CCW problem, the consultant concludes that $\alpha=0.3$ and $\beta=0.3$ perform about as well as any. Both values are on the high end of the typically used range (0.1 to 0.3), but the frequent changes in the CCW time series call for large values. However, lowering α from the 0.5 value used with the preceding method seems justified since incorporating trend into the analysis would help respond more quickly to changes.

When applying exponential smoothing *without* trend earlier, Lydia and the consultant had chosen 7,500 as the initial estimate of the average value of the seasonally adjusted call volumes. They now note that there was no noticeable trend in these call volumes just prior to the retrospective generation of forecasts three years ago. Therefore, to apply exponential smoothing with trend, they decide to use

Initial estimate of average value = 7,500
Initial estimate of trend = 0

Working with the seasonally adjusted call volumes given in several recent figures, these initial estimates lead to the following seasonally adjusted forecasts.

Y1, Q1:   Seas. adj. forecast = 7,500 + 0 = 7,500

Y1, Q2:   Latest trend = 0.3(7,322 − 7,500) + 0.7(7,500 − 7,500) = −53.4

Estimated trend = 0.3(−53.4) + 0.7(0) = −16

Seas. adj. forecast = 0.3(7,322) + 0.7(7,500) − 16 = 7,431

Y1, Q3:   Latest trend = 0.3(7,183 − 7,322) + 0.7(7,431 − 7,500) = −90

Estimated trend = 0.3(−90) + 0.7(−16) = −38.2

Seas. adj. forecast = 0.3(7,183) + 0.7(7,431) − 38.2 = 7,318

The Excel template in Figure 13.10 shows the results from these calculations for all 12 quarters over the past three years, as well as for the upcoming quarter. The middle of the figure shows the plots of all the seasonally adjusted call volumes and seasonally adjusted forecasts. Note how each trend up or down in the call volumes causes the forecasts to gradually trend in the same direction, but then the trend in the forecasts takes a couple quarters to turn around when the trend in call volumes suddenly reverses direction. The resulting forecasting errors in column J then give an average forecasting error (cell M31) of

$$\text{MAD} = 345$$

a little above the 324 value for regular exponential smoothing and 295 for last-value forecasting.

FIGURE 13.10

The Excel template in your MS Courseware for the exponential smoothing with trend method with seasonal adjustments is applied here to the CCW problem.

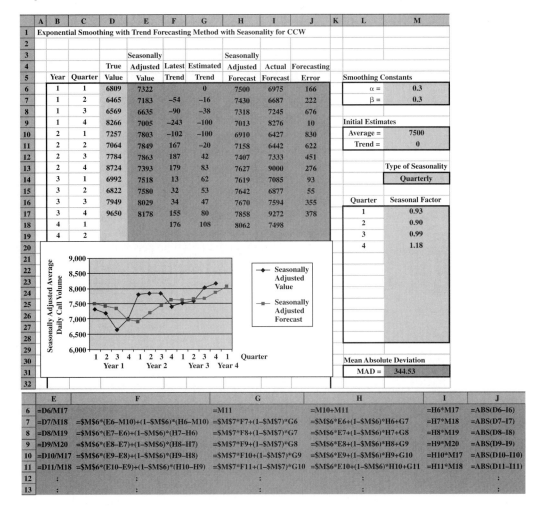

	E	F	G	H	I	J
6	=D6/M17		=M11	=M10+M11	=H6*M17	=ABS(D6–I6)
7	=D7/M18	=$M$6*(E6–M10)+(1–$M$6)*(H6–M10)	=$M$7*F7+(1–$M$7)*G6	=$M$6*E6+(1–$M$6)*H6+G7	=H7*M18	=ABS(D7–I7)
8	=D8/M19	=$M$6*(E7–E6)+(1–$M$6)*(H7–H6)	=$M$7*F8+(1–$M$7)*G7	=$M$6*E7+(1–$M$6)*H7+G8	=H8*M19	=ABS(D8–I8)
9	=D9/M20	=$M$6*(E8–E7)+(1–$M$6)*(H8–H7)	=$M$7*F9+(1–$M$7)*G8	=$M$6*E8+(1–$M$6)*H8+G9	=H9*M20	=ABS(D9–I9)
10	=D10/M17	=$M$6*(E9–E8)+(1–$M$6)*(H9–H8)	=$M$7*F10+(1–$M$7)*G9	=$M$6*E9+(1–$M$6)*H9+G10	=H10*M17	=ABS(D10–I10)
11	=D11/M18	=$M$6*(E10–E9)+(1–$M$6)*(H10–H9)	=$M$7*F11+(1–$M$7)*G10	=$M$6*E10+(1–$M$6)*H10+G11	=H11*M18	=ABS(D11–I11)
12	:	:	:	:	:	:
13	:	:	:	:	:	:

TABLE 13.3   The Average Forecasting Error (MAD) for the Various Time-Series Forecasting Methods When Forecasting CCW Call Volumes

Forecasting Method	MAD
CCW's 25 percent rule	424
Last-value method	295
Averaging method	400
Moving-average method	437
Exponential smoothing	324
Exponential smoothing with trend	345

Table 13.3 summarizes the values of MAD for all the forecasting methods so far. Here is Lydia's reaction to the large MAD value for exponential smoothing with trend.

Lydia: I'm very discouraged. These time-series forecasting methods just aren't doing the job I need. I thought this one would. It sounded like an excellent method that also would deal with the trends we keep encountering.

Consultant: Yes, it is a very good method under the right circumstances. When you have trends that may occasionally shift some over time, it should do a great job.

Lydia: So what went wrong here?

Consultant: Well, look at the trends you have here in the seasonally adjusted time series. You have a fairly sharp downward trend the first three quarters and then suddenly a very sharp upward trend for a couple quarters. Then it flattens out before a big drop in the eighth quarter. Then suddenly it is going up again. It is really tough to keep up with such abrupt big shifts in the trends. This method is better suited for much more gradual shifts in the trends.

Lydia: OK. But aren't there any other methods? None of these will do.

Consultant: There is one other main time-series forecasting method. It is called the **ARIMA** method, which is an acronym for AutoRegressive Integrated Moving Average. It also is sometimes called the Box-Jenkins method, in honor of its founders. It is a very sophisticated method, but some excellent software is available for implementing it. Another nice feature is that it is well-suited for dealing with strong seasonal patterns.

Lydia: Sounds good. So shouldn't we be trying this ARIMA method?

Consultant: Not at this point. It is such a sophisticated method that it requires a great amount of past data, say, a minimum of 50 time periods. We don't have nearly enough data.

Lydia: A pity. So what are we going to do? I haven't seen anything that will do the job.

Consultant: Cheer up. I have an idea for how we can use one of these time-series forecasting methods in a different way that may do the job you want.

Lydia: Really? Tell me more.

Consultant: Well, let me hold off on the details until we can check out whether this is going to work.

Lydia: OK. But how do we check it out?

Consultant: Well, what I would like you to do is contact CCW's marketing manager and set up a meeting between the three of us. Also, send him your data on call volumes for the past three years. Ask him to dig out his sales data for the same period and compare it to your data.

Lydia: OK. What should I tell him is the purpose of the meeting?

Consultant: Explain what we're trying to accomplish here about forecasting call volumes. Then tell him that we're trying to understand better what has been causing these sudden shifts in call volumes. He knows more about what has been driving sales up or down than anybody. We just want to pick his brain about this.

Lydia: OK. Will do.

The Meeting with the Marketing Manager

This meeting takes place a few days later. As you eavesdrop (after the preliminaries), you will find it helpful to refer to the call volume data in one of the recent spreadsheets, such as Figure 13.10.

Lydia: Did you receive the call volume data I mailed to you?

Marketing manager: Yes, I did.

Consultant: How does it compare with your own sales data for these three years?

Marketing manager: Your data track mine pretty closely. I see the same ups and downs in both sets of data.

Lydia: That makes sense, since it's the calls to my call center that generate those sales.

Marketing manager: Right.

Consultant: Now, let me check on what caused the ups and downs. Three years ago, what we labeled as Year 1 in our data, there was a definite trend down for most of the year. What caused that?

Marketing manager: Yes, I remember that year all too well. It wasn't a very good year. The new Klugman operating system had been scheduled to come out early that year. Then they kept pushing the release date back. People kept waiting. They didn't manage to get it out until the beginning of the next year, so we even missed the Christmas sales.

Lydia: But our call volume did jump up a little more than usual during that holiday season.

Marketing manager: Yes. So did sales. I remember that we came out with a new networking tool, one with faster data transfer, in time for the holiday season. It turned out to be very popular for a few months. It really bailed us out during that slow period.

Consultant: Then the Klugman operating system was released and sales jumped the next year.

Marketing manager: Right.

Lydia: What happened late in the year? We weren't as busy as we expected to be.

Marketing manager: I assume that most people already had updated to the new operating system by then. There wasn't any major change in our product mix during that period.

Consultant: Then sales moved back up the next year. Last year.

Marketing manager: Yes, last year was a rather good year. We had a couple new products that did very well. One was a new data storage device that came out early in the year. Very inexpensive. The other was a color plain-paper printer that was released in July. We were able to offer it at a very competitive price and our customers gobbled it up.

Consultant: Thanks. That really clarifies what lies behind those call volume numbers we've been working with. Now I have another key question for you. When you look at your sales data and do your own forecasting, what do you see as the key factors that drive total sales up or down?

Marketing manager: There really is just one big factor. Do we have any hot new products out there. We have well over a hundred products. But most of them just fill a small niche in the market. Many of them are old standbys that, with updates, just keep going indefinitely. All these small-niche products together provide most of our total sales. A nice stable market base. Then, in addition, we should have three or four major new products out there. Maybe a couple that have been out for a few months but still have some life left in them. Then one or two just coming out that we hope will do very well.

Consultant: I see. A large market base and then three or four major new products.

Marketing manager: That's what we shoot for.

Consultant: Are you able to predict how well a major new product will do?

Marketing manager: I try. I've gotten better at it. I'm usually fairly close on what the initial response will be, but it is difficult to predict how long the product will hold up. I would like to have a better handle on it.

Consultant: Thanks very much for all your information. It has verified what I've been suspecting for awhile now.

Lydia: What's that?

Consultant: That we really need to coordinate directly with what is driving sales in order to do a better job of forecasting call volumes.

Lydia: Good thought!

Consultant: How would the two of you feel about coordinating in developing better procedures for forecasting both sales and call volumes?

Lydia: You bet.

Marketing manager: I would need to see what you have in mind. But as I said, I would like to have a better handle on my forecasting.

Lydia: OK, let us work out some details and then we'll send you a specific proposal.

Marketing manager: Sounds good.

Lydia: Thanks again for all your help.

Marketing manager: Any time.

The marketing manager leaves.

Lydia: I'm beginning to see where you are headed with all this. And I really like it. Are you ready to give me the details yet?

Consultant: Almost. I am convinced now that what I have in mind is probably going to work. But let me first spend a little time using the marketing manager's

information to put the time-series forecasting methods into better perspective for you. Then I'll give you my recommended plan.
Lydia: OK, let's do it.

Review Questions

1. What does a seasonal factor measure?
2. What is the formula for calculating the seasonally adjusted call volume from the actual call volume and the seasonal factor?
3. What is the formula for calculating the forecast of the actual call volume from the seasonal factor and the seasonally adjusted forecast?
4. Why is the last-value forecasting method sometimes called the *naive method*?
5. Why did the averaging forecasting method not perform very well on the case study?
6. What is the rationale for replacing the averaging forecasting method by the moving-average forecasting method?
7. How does the exponential smoothing forecasting method modify the moving-average forecasting method?
8. With exponential smoothing, when is a small value of the smoothing constant appropriate? A larger value?
9. What is the formula for obtaining the next forecast with exponential smoothing? What is added to this formula when using exponential smoothing with trend?
10. What does the marketing manager say is the one big factor that drives total sales up or down?

13.4 The Time-Series Forecasting Methods in Perspective

The preceding section presented several methods for forecasting the next value of a time series in the context of the CCW case study. We now will take a step back to place into perspective just what these methods are trying to accomplish. After providing this perspective, CCW's consultant then will give his recommendation for setting up a forecasting system.

The Goal of the Forecasting Methods

It actually is something of a misnomer to talk about forecasting *the* value of the next observation in a time series (such as CCW's call volume in the next quarter). It is impossible to predict *the value* precisely, because this next value can turn out to be anything over some range. What it will be depends upon future circumstances that are beyond our control.

In other words, the next value that will occur in a time series is a *random variable.* It has some *probability distribution.* For example, Figure 13.11 shows a typical probability distribution for the CCW call volume in a future quarter in which the mean of this distribution happens to be 7,500. This distribution indicates the relative likelihood of the various possible values of the call volume. Nobody can say in advance which value actually will occur.

So what is the meaning of the single number that is selected as the "forecast" of the next value in the time series? If possible, we would like this number to be the *mean* of the distribution. The reason is that random observations from the distribution tend to cluster around the mean of the distribution. Therefore, using the mean as the forecast would tend to minimize the average forecasting error.

Unfortunately, we don't actually know what this probability distribution is, let alone its mean. The best we can do is use all the available data (past values from the time series) to estimate the mean as closely as possible.

The goal of time-series forecasting methods is to estimate the *mean* of the underlying probability distribution of the next value of the time series as closely as possible.

Given some random observations from a single probability distribution, the best estimate of its mean is the *sample average* (the average of all these observations). Therefore,

FIGURE 13.11

A typical probability distribution of what the average daily call volume will be for CCW in a quarter when the mean is 7,500.

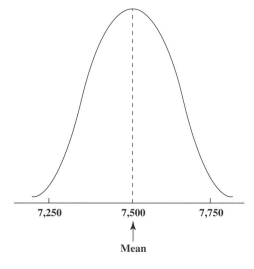

FIGURE 13.12

Typical probability distributions of CCW's average daily call volumes in the four quarters of a year in which the overall average is 7,500.

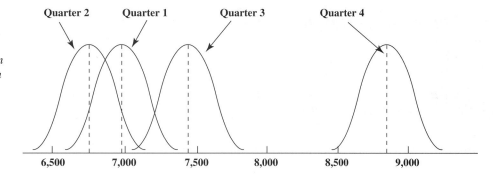

if a time series has exactly the same distribution for each and every time period, then the *averaging forecasting method* provides the best estimate of the mean.

However, other forecasting methods commonly are used instead because the distribution may be changing over time.

Problems Caused by Shifting Distributions

Section 13.3 began by considering seasonal effects. This then led to estimating CCW's seasonal factors as 0.93, 0.90, 0.99, and 1.18 for Quarters 1, 2, 3, and 4, respectively.

If the overall average daily call volume for a year is 7,500, these seasonal factors imply that the probability distributions for the four quarters of that year fall roughly as shown in Figure 13.12. Since these distributions have different means, we should no longer simply average the random observations (observed call volumes) from all four quarters to estimate the mean for any one of these distributions.

This complication is why the preceding section seasonally adjusted the time series. Dividing each quarter's call volume by its seasonal factor shifts the distribution of this seasonally adjusted call volume over to basically the distribution shown in Figure 13.11 with a mean of 7,500. This allows averaging the seasonally adjusted values to estimate this mean.

Unfortunately, even after seasonally adjusting the time series, the probability distribution may not remain the same from one year to the next (or even from one quarter to the next). For example, as CCW's marketing manager explained, total sales jumped very substantially at the beginning of Year 2 when the new Klugman operating system became available. This also caused the average daily call volume to increase by about 10 percent, from just over 7,000 in Year 1 to over 7,700 in Year 2. Figure13.13 compares the resulting distributions for typical quarters (seasonally adjusted) in the two years.

Random observations from the Year 1 distribution in this figure provide a poor basis for estimating the mean of the Year 2 distribution. Yet, except for the last-value method, *each* of the forecasting methods presented in the preceding section placed at least some weight on these observations from Year 1 to estimate the mean for *each* quarter in Year 2. This was a major part of the reason why the average forecasting errors (MAD) were higher for these methods than for the last-value method.

FIGURE 13.13

Comparison of typical probability distributions of CCW's average daily call volumes (seasonally adjusted) in Years 1 and 2.

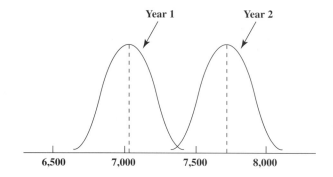

Judging from the marketing manager's information, it appears that some shift in the distribution also occurred several times from just one quarter to the next. This further added to the forecasting errors.

Comparison of the Forecasting Methods

Section 13.3 presented five methods for forecasting the next value in a time series. Which of these methods is particularly suitable for a given application depends greatly on how *stable* the time series is.

> A time series is said to be **stable** if its underlying probability distribution usually remains the same from one time period to the next. (Any shifts that do occur in the distribution are both infrequent and small.) A time series is **unstable** if both frequent and sizable shifts in the distribution tend to occur.

CCW's seasonally adjusted time series shown in Figure 13.4 (and many subsequent figures) appears to have had several shifts in the distribution, including the sizable one depicted in Figure 13.13. Therefore, this time series is an example of a relatively *unstable* one.

Here is a summary of which type of time series fits each of the forecasting methods.

Last-value method: Suitable for a time series that is so unstable that even the next-to-last value is not considered relevant for forecasting the next value.

Averaging method: Suitable for a very stable time series where even its first few values are considered relevant for forecasting the next value.

Moving-average method: Suitable for a moderately stable time series where the last few values are considered relevant for forecasting the next value. The number of values included in the moving average reflects the anticipated degree of stability in the time series.

Exponential smoothing method: Suitable for a time series in the range from somewhat unstable to rather stable, where the value of the smoothing constant needs to be adjusted to fit the anticipated degree of stability. Refines the moving-average method by placing the greatest weight on the most recent values, but is not as readily understood by managers as the moving-average method.

Exponential smoothing with trend: Suitable for a time series where the mean of the distribution tends to follow a trend either up or down, provided that changes in the trend occur only occasionally and gradually.

Unfortunately for CCW, its seasonally adjusted time series proved to be a little too unstable for any of these methods except the last-value method, which is considered to be the least powerful of these forecasting methods. Even when using exponential smoothing with trend, the changes in the trend occurred too frequently and sharply.

In light of these considerations, the consultant now is ready to present his recommendations to Lydia for a new forecasting procedure.

The Consultant's Recommendations

1. Forecasting should be done monthly rather than quarterly in order to respond more quickly to changing conditions.

2. Hiring and training of new agents also should be done monthly instead of quarterly in order to fine-tune staffing levels to meet changing needs.

3. Recently retired agents should be offered the opportunity to work part time on an on-call basis to help meet current staffing needs more closely.

4. Since sales drive call volume, the forecasting process should begin by forecasting sales.

5. For forecasting purposes, total sales should be broken down into the major components described by the marketing manager, namely, (1) the relatively stable market base of numerous small-niche products and (2) *each* of the few (perhaps three or four) major new products whose success or failure can significantly drive total sales up or down. These major new products would be identified by the marketing manager on an ongoing basis.

6. Exponential smoothing with a relatively small smoothing constant is suggested for forecasting sales of the marketing base of numerous small-niche products. However, before making a final decision on the forecasting method, retrospective testing should be conducted to check how well this particular method would have performed over the past three years. This testing also should guide selection of the value of the smoothing constant.

7. Exponential smoothing with trend, with relatively large smoothing constants, is suggested for forecasting sales of *each* of the major new products. Once again, retrospective testing should be conducted to check this decision and to guide choosing values for the smoothing constants. The marketing manager should be asked to provide the initial estimate of anticipated sales in the first month for a new product. He also should be asked to check the subsequent exponential smoothing forecasts and make any adjustments he feels are appropriate based on his knowledge of what is happening in the marketplace.

8. Because of the strong seasonal sales pattern, seasonally adjusted time series should be used for each application of these forecasting methods.

9. After separately obtaining forecasts of actual sales for each of the major components of total sales identified in recommendation 5, these forecasts should be summed to obtain a forecast of total sales.

10. *Causal forecasting with linear regression* (as described in the next section) should be used to obtain a forecast of *call volume* from this forecast of total sales.

Lydia accepts these recommendations with considerable enthusiasm. She also agrees to work with the marketing manager to gain his cooperation.

Read on to see how the last recommendation is implemented.

Review Questions

1. What kind of variable is the next value that will occur in a time series?
2. What is the goal of time-series forecasting methods?
3. Is the probability distribution of CCW's average daily call volume the same for every quarter?
4. What is the explanation for why the average forecasting errors were higher for the other time-series forecasting methods than for the supposedly less powerful last-value method?
5. What is the distinction between a *stable* time series and an *unstable* time series?
6. What is the consultant's recommendation regarding what should be forecasted instead of call volumes to begin the forecasting process?
7. What are the major components of CCW's total sales?

13.5 Causal Forecasting with Linear Regression

We have focused so far on *time-series forecasting methods,* that is, methods that forecast the next value in a time series based on its previous values. These methods have been used retrospectively in Section 13.3 to forecast CCW's call volume in the next quarter based on its previous call volumes.

Causal Forecasting

However, the consultant's last recommendation suggests another approach to forecasting. It is really sales that drive call volume, and sales can be forecasted considerably more precisely than call volume. Therefore, it should be possible to obtain a better forecast of call volume by relating it directly to forecasted sales. This kind of approach is called *causal forecasting*.

> **Causal forecasting** obtains a forecast of the quantity of interest (the **dependent variable**) by relating it directly to one or more other quantities (the **independent variables**) that drive the quantity of interest.

Table 13.4 shows some examples of the kinds of situations where causal forecasting sometimes is used. In each of the first four cases, the indicated dependent variable can be expected to go up or down rather directly with the independent variable(s) listed in the rightmost column. The last case also applies when some quantity of interest (e.g., sales of a product) tends to follow a steady trend upward (or downward) with the passage of time (the independent variable that drives the quantity of interest).

As one specific example, Section 13.1 includes a description of American Airline's elaborate system for forecasting its need for expensive spare parts (its "rotatable" parts) to continue operating its fleet of several hundred airplanes. This system uses causal forecasting, where the demand for spare parts is the dependent variable and the number of flying hours is the independent variable. This makes sense because the demand for spare parts should be roughly proportional to the number of flying hours for the fleet.

Linear Regression

At Lydia's request, the marketing manager brought sales data for the past three years to their recent meeting. These data are summarized in Figure 13.14. In particular, column D gives the average daily sales (in units of thousands of dollars) for each of the 12 past quarters. Column E repeats the data given previously on average daily call volumes. None of the data have been seasonally adjusted.

TABLE 13.4   Possible Examples of Causal Forecasting

Type of Forecasting	Possible Dependent Variable	Possible Independent Variables
Sales	Sales of a product	Amount of advertising
Spare parts	Demand for spare parts	Usage of equipment
Economic trends	Gross domestic product	Various economic factors
CCW call volume	Call volume	Sales
Any quantity	This same quantity	Time

FIGURE 13.14

The data needed to do causal forecasting for the CCW problem by relating call volume to sales.

	A	B	C	D	E	F	G	H	I	J
1	CCW's Average Daily Sales and Call Volume									
2										
3				Sales	Call					
4		Year	Quarter	($thousands)	Volume					
5		1	1	4894	6809					
6		1	2	4703	6465					
7		1	3	4748	6569					
8		1	4	5844	8266					
9		2	1	5192	7257					
10		2	2	5086	7064					
11		2	3	5511	7784					
12		2	4	6107	8724					
13		3	1	5052	6992					
14		3	2	4985	6822					
15		3	3	5576	7949					
16		3	4	6647	9650					

The right side of the figure was generated by choosing Chart under the Insert menu, selecting an XY (Scatter) chart type, and following the directions of the Chart Wizard. This graph shows a plot of the data in columns D and E on a two-dimensional graph. Thus, each of the 12 points in the graph shows the combination of sales and call volume for one of the 12 quarters (without identifying which quarter).

This graph shows a close relationship between call volume and sales. Each increase or decrease in sales is accompanied by a roughly proportional increase or decrease in call volume. This is not surprising since the sales are being made through the calls to the call center.

It appears from this graph that the relationship between call volume and sales can be approximated by a straight line. Figure 13.15 shows such a line. (This line was generated by clicking on the graph in Figure 13.14, selecting Add Trendline under the Chart menu, and then selecting Linear trend under the Options tab. The equation above the line was added by choosing Display equation on chart under the Options tab.) This line is referred to as a *linear regression line.*

> When doing causal forecasting with a single independent variable, **linear regression** involves approximating the relationship between the dependent variable (call volume for CCW) and the independent variable (sales for CCW) by a straight line. This line is drawn on a graph with the independent variable on the horizontal axis and the dependent variable on the vertical axis. The line is constructed after plotting a number of points showing each observed value of the independent variable and the corresponding value of the dependent variable.

Thus, the linear regression line in Figure 13.15 can be used to estimate what the call volume should be for a particular value of sales. In general, the equation for the linear regression line has the form

$$y = a + bx$$

where

y = estimated value of the dependent variable, as given by the linear regression line

a = intercept of the linear regression line with the y-axis

b = slope of the linear regression line

x = value of the independent variable

(If there is more than one independent variable, then this **regression equation** has a term, a constant times the variable, added on the right-hand side for *each* of these variables.) For the linear regression line in this figure, the exact values of a and b happen to be

$$a = -1223.86 \qquad b = 1.6324$$

FIGURE 13.15

Figure 13.14 has been modified here by adding a trend line to the graph.

	A	B	C	D	E	F	G	H	I	J
1	CCW's Average Daily Sales and Call Volume									
2										
3				**Sales**	**Call**					
4		**Year**	**Quarter**	**($thousands)**	**Volume**					
5		1	1	4894	6809					
6		1	2	4703	6465					
7		1	3	4748	6569					
8		1	4	5844	8266					
9		2	1	5192	7257					
10		2	2	5086	7064					
11		2	3	5511	7784					
12		2	4	6107	8724					
13		3	1	5052	6992					
14		3	2	4985	6822					
15		3	3	5576	7949					
16		3	4	6647	9650					

FIGURE 13.16

The Excel template in your MS Courseware for doing causal forecasting with linear regression, as illustrated here for the CCW problem.

	A	B	C	D	E	F	G	H	I	J
1		Linear Regression of Call Volume vs. Sales Volume for CCW								
2										
3		Time	Independent	Dependent		Estimation	Square		Linear Regression Line	
4		Period	Variable	Variable	Estimate	Error	of Error		y = a + bx	
5		1	4894	6809	6765	43.85	1923		a =	–1223.86
6		2	4703	6465	6453	11.64	136		b =	1.63
7		3	4748	6569	6527	42.18	1780			
8		4	5844	8266	8316	49.93	2493			
9		5	5192	7257	7252	5.40	29		Estimator	
10		6	5086	7064	7079	14.57	212		If x =	5000
11		7	5511	7784	7772	11.66	136		then y =	6938.18
12		8	6107	8724	8745	21.26	452			
13		9	5052	6992	7023	31.07	965			
14		10	4985	6822	6914	91.70	8408			
15		11	5576	7949	7878	70.55	4977			
16		12	6647	9650	9627	23.24	540			

	E	F	G	H	I	J
5	=$J$5+$J$6*C5	=ABS(D5–E5)	=F5^2		a =	=INTERCEPT(D5:D16,C5:C16)
6	=$J$5+$J$6*C6	=ABS(D6–E6)	=F6^2		b =	=SLOPE(D5:D16,C5:C16)
7	=$J$5+$J$6*C7	=ABS(D7–E7)	=F7^2			
8	=$J$5+$J$6*C8	=ABS(D8–E8)	=F8^2			
9	=$J$5+$J$6*C9	=ABS(D9–E9)	=F9^2		Estimator	
10	:	:	:		If x =	5000
11	:	:	:		then y =	=J5+J6*J10

Figure 13.16 shows the Excel template in your MS Courseware that can be used to find these values of *a* and *b,* and so on. You need to input all the observed values of the independent variable (sales) and of the dependent variable (call volume) in columns C and D, and then the template performs all the calculations. On the right, note that you have the option of inserting a value for *x* (sales) in cell J10 and then the template calculates the corresponding value of *y* (call volume) that lies on the linear regression line. This calculation can be repeated for as many values of *x* as desired. In addition, column E already shows these calculations for each value of *x* in column C, so each cell in column E gives the estimate of call volume provided by the linear regression line for the corresponding sales level in column C. The difference between this estimate and the actual call volume in column D gives the estimation error in column F. The *square* of this error is shown in column G.

The procedure used to obtain *a* and *b* is called the **method of least squares.** This method chooses the values of *a* and *b* that *minimize* the sum of the *square of the estimation errors* given in column G of Figure 13.16. Thus, the sum of the numbers in column G (22,051) is the minimum possible. Any significantly different values of *a and b* would give different estimation errors that would cause this sum to be larger.

The numbers in column F also are interesting. Averaging these numbers reveals that the *average estimation error* for the 12 quarters is only 35. This indicates that if the sales for a quarter were known in advance (or could be predicted exactly), then using the linear regression line to forecast call volume would give an average forecasting error (MAD) of only 35. This is only about 10 percent of the values of MAD obtained for the various time-series forecasting methods in Section 13.3.

For some applications of causal forecasting, the value of the independent variable will be known in advance. This is not the case here, where the independent variable is the sales for the upcoming time period. However, the consultant is confident that a very good forecast of sales can be obtained by following his recommendations. This forecast can then be used as the value of the independent variable for obtaining a good forecast of call volume from the linear regression line.

CCW's New Forecasting Procedure

1. Obtain a forecast of total (average daily) sales for the upcoming month by implementing the consultant's recommendations.

2. Use this forecast as the value of sales for then forecasting the average daily call volume for the upcoming month from the linear regression line identified in Figures 13.15 and 13.16.

The CCW Case Study a Year Later

A year after implementing the consultant's recommendations, Lydia gives him a call.

Lydia: I just wanted to let you know how things are going. And to congratulate you on the great job you did for us.

Consultant: Thanks. So my recommended forecasting procedure is performing well?

Lydia: Extremely well. Remember that the 25 percent rule was giving us MAD values over 400? And then the various time-series forecasting methods were doing almost as badly?

Consultant: Yes, I do remember. You were pretty discouraged there for awhile.

Lydia: I sure was! But I'm feeling a lot better now. I just calculated MAD for the first year under your new procedure.

Consultant: Oh. What did you get?

Lydia: 120. Only 120!

Consultant: Great. That's the kind of improvement we like to see. What do you think has made the biggest difference?

Lydia: I think the biggest factor was tying our forecasting into forecasting sales. We never had much feeling for where call volumes were headed. But we have a much better handle on what sales will be because, with the marketing manager's help, we can see what is causing the shifts.

Consultant: Yes. I think that is a real key to successful forecasting. You saw that we can get a lot of garbage by simply applying a time-series forecasting method to historical data without understanding what is causing the shifts. You have to get behind the numbers and see what is really going on, then design the forecasting procedure to catch the shifts as they occur, like we did by having the marketing manager identify the major new products that impact total sales and then separately forecasting sales for each of them.

Lydia: Right. Bringing the marketing manager in on this was a great move. He's a real supporter of the new procedure now, by the way. He says it is giving him valuable information as well.

Consultant: Good. Is he making adjustments in the statistical forecasts, based on his knowledge of what is going on in the marketplace, like I recommended?

Lydia: Yes, he is. He says he isn't ready to be replaced by a computer yet.

Consultant: He sure isn't. He's a savvy guy. A good forecasting procedure needs somebody like him overseeing things and making appropriate adjustments in the forecasts. That's a great combination: a well-constructed statistical forecasting procedure and a savvy manager who understands what is driving the numbers.

Lydia: Well, it's really working. Anyway, you have a couple fans here. We really appreciate the great job you did for us.

Review Questions

1. What is causal forecasting?

2. When applying causal forecasting to the CCW problem, what is the dependent variable and what is the independent variable?

3. When doing causal forecasting with a single independent variable, what does linear regression involve?

4. What is the form of the equation for a linear regression line with a single independent variable? With more than one independent variable?

5. What is the name of the method for obtaining the value of the constants, *a* and *b*, for a linear regression line?

6. How does the MAD value for CCW's new forecasting procedure compare with that for the old procedure that used the 25 percent rule?

13.6 Judgmental Forecasting Methods

We have focused so far on *statistical* forecasting methods that base the forecast on historical data. However, such methods cannot be used if no data are available, or if the data are not representative of current conditions. In such cases, **judgmental forecasting methods** can be used instead.

Even when good data are available, some managers prefer a judgmental method instead of a formal statistical method. In many other cases, a combination of the two may be used. For example, in the CCW case study, the marketing manager uses his judgment, based on his long experience and his knowledge of what is happening in the marketplace, to adjust the sales forecasts obtained from time-series forecasting methods.

Here is a brief overview of the main judgmental forecasting methods.

1. **Manager's opinion:** This is the most informal of the methods, because it simply involves a single manager using his or her best judgment to make the forecast. In some cases, some data may be available to help make this judgment. In others, the manager may be drawing solely on experience and an intimate knowledge of the current conditions that drive the forecasted quantity.

2. **Jury of executive opinion:** This method is similar to the first one, except now it involves a small group of high-level managers who pool their best judgment to collectively make the forecast. This method may be used for more critical forecasts for which several executives share responsibility and can provide different types of expertise.

3. **Salesforce composite:** This method is often used for sales forecasting when a company employs a sales force to help generate sales. It is a *bottom-up approach* whereby each salesperson provides an estimate of what sales will be in his or her region. These estimates then are sent up through the corporate chain of command, with managerial review at each level, to be aggregated into a corporate sales forecast.

4. **Consumer market survey:** This method goes even further than the preceding one in adopting a *grass-roots approach* to sales forecasting. It involves surveying customers and potential customers regarding their future purchasing plans and how they would respond to various new features in products. This input is particularly helpful for designing new products and then in developing the initial forecasts of their sales. It also is helpful for planning a marketing campaign.

5. **Delphi method:** This method employs a panel of experts in different locations who independently fill out a series of questionnaires. However, the results from each questionnaire are provided with the next one, so each expert then can evaluate this group information in adjusting his or her responses next time. The goal is to reach a relatively narrow spread of conclusions from most of the experts. The decision makers then assess this input from the panel of experts to develop the forecast. This involved process normally is used only at the highest levels of a corporation or government to develop long-range forecasts of broad trends.

Review Questions

1. Statistical forecasting methods cannot be used under what circumstances?

2. Are judgmental forecasting methods only used when statistical forecasting methods cannot be used?

3. How does the jury of executive opinion method differ from the manager's opinion method?

4. How does the salesforce composite method begin?

5. When is a consumer market survey particularly helpful?
6. When might the Delphi method be used?

13.7 Forecasting in Practice

You now have seen the major forecasting methods used by managers. We conclude with a brief look at how widely the various methods are used.

To begin, consider the actual forecasting applications discussed in Section 13.1 and summarized in Table 13.1 there. Most of this table is repeated here in Table 13.5, but the rightmost column now identifies which forecasting method was used in each application. Not surprisingly, these major forecasting projects chose one of the more sophisticated statistical forecasting methods. (The most sophisticated is the ARIMA method, commonly called the Box-Jenkins method, that the consultant introduced to Lydia in a conversation near the end of Section 13.3.)

Every company needs to do at least some forecasting, but their methods often are not as sophisticated as with these major projects. Some insight into their general approach was provided by a survey conducted a few years ago[2] of sales forecasting practices at 500 U.S. corporations.

This survey indicates that, generally speaking, *judgmental* forecasting methods are somewhat more widely used than *statistical* methods. The main reasons given for using judgmental methods were accuracy and difficulty in obtaining the data required for statistical methods. Comments also were made that upper management is not familiar with quantitative techniques, that judgmental methods create a sense of ownership, and that these methods add a common-sense element to the forecast.

Among the judgmental methods, the most popular is a *jury of executive opinion*. This is especially true for companywide or industry sales forecasts, but also holds true by a small margin over *manager's opinion* when forecasting sales of individual products or families of products.

Statistical forecasting methods also are fairly widely used, especially in companies with high sales. Compared to earlier surveys, familiarity with such methods is increasing. However, many survey respondents cited better data availability as the improvement they most wanted to see in their organizations. The availability of good data is crucial for the use of these methods.

The survey indicates that the *moving-average method* and *linear regression* are the most widely used statistical forecasting methods. The moving-average method is more popular for short- and medium-range forecasts (less than a year), as well as for forecasting sales of individual products and families of products. Linear regression is more popular for longer-range forecasts and for forecasting either companywide or industry sales.

TABLE 13.5 **The Forecasting Methods Used in the Actual Applications Presented in Section 13.1**

Organization	Quantity Being Forecasted	Forecasting Method
Merit Brass Co.	Sales of finished goods	Exponential smoothing
Hidroeléctrica Español	Energy demand	ARIMA (Box-Jenkins), etc.
American Airlines	Demand for different fare classes	Exponential smoothing
American Airlines	Need for spare parts to repair airplanes	Causal forecasting with linear regression
Albuquerque Microelectronics	Production yield in wafer fabrication	Exponential smoothing with trend
U.S. Department of Labor	Unemployment insurance payments	Causal forecasting with linear regression
United Airlines	Demand at reservation offices and airports	ARIMA (Box-Jenkins)
L.L. Bean	Staffing needs at call center	ARIMA (Box-Jenkins)

[2]N. R. Sanders and K. B. Manrodt, "Forecasting Practices in U.S. Corporations: Survey Results," *Interfaces* 24 (March–April 1994), pp. 92–100.

Both exponential smoothing and the last-value method also receive considerable use. However, the highest dissatisfaction is with the last-value method, and its popularity is decreasing compared to earlier surveys.

When statistical forecasting methods are used, it is fairly common to also use judgmental methods to adjust the forecasts.

As managers become more familiar with statistical methods, and more used to using the computer to compile data and implement management science techniques, we anticipate a continuing increase in the usage of statistical forecasting methods. However, there always will be an important role for judgmental methods, both alone and in combination with statistical methods.

Review Questions

1. According to a recent survey of sales forecasting practices, are judgmental or statistical forecasting methods more widely used?

2. What does this survey indicate are the most popular judgmental forecasting methods?

3. What does the survey indicate are the most popular statistical forecasting methods?

13.8 Summary

The future success of any business depends heavily on the ability of its management to forecast well. Forecasting may be needed in several areas, including sales, the need for spare parts, production yields, economic trends, and staffing needs.

The Computer Club Warehouse (CCW) case study illustrates a variety of approaches to forecasting, some of which prove unsatisfactory in this case. Ultimately, it becomes necessary to get behind the CCW data to understand just what is driving the call volumes at its call center in order to develop a good forecasting system.

A time series is a series of observations over time of some quantity of interest. Several statistical forecasting methods use these observations in some way to forecast what the next value will be. These methods include the last-value method, the averaging method, the moving-average method, the exponential smoothing method, and exponential smoothing with trend.

The goal of all these methods is to estimate the mean of the underlying probability distribution of the next value of the time series as closely as possible. This may require using seasonal factors to seasonally adjust the time series, as well as identifying other factors that may cause this underlying probability distribution to shift from one time period to the next.

Another statistical forecasting approach is called causal forecasting. This approach obtains a forecast of the quantity of interest (the dependent variable) by relating it directly to one or more other quantities (the independent variables) that drive the quantity of interest. Frequently, this involves using linear regression to approximate the relationship between the dependent variable and each independent variable by a straight line.

Still another key category of forecasting methods is judgmental methods. This category involves basing the forecast on a manager's opinion, a jury of executive opinion, a salesforce composite, a consumer market survey, or the Delphi method. A recent survey indicates that judgmental methods are used even more widely for sales forecasting than statistical methods. Frequently, both types of methods are used in complementary ways.

Glossary

ARIMA An acronym for the AutoRegressive Integrated Moving Average method, a sophisticated time-series forecasting method commonly referred to as the Box-Jenkins method. (Section 13.3) 548

Averaging forecasting method A method that uses the average of the past observations from a time series as a forecast of the next value. (Section 13.3) 538

Causal forecasting Obtaining a forecast of the dependent variable by relating it directly to one or more independent variables. (Section 13.5) 554

Consumer market survey A judgmental forecasting method that uses surveys of customers and potential customers. (Section 13.6) 558

Delphi method A judgmental forecasting method that uses input from a panel of experts in different locations. (Section 13.6) 558

Dependent variable The quantity of interest when doing causal forecasting. (Section 13.5) 554

Econometric model A statistical model used to forecast economic trends. (Section 13.1) 529

Exponential smoothing forecasting method A method that uses a weighted average of the last value from a time series and the last forecast to obtain the forecast of the next value. (Section 13.3) 541

Exponential smoothing with trend An adjustment of the exponential smoothing forecasting method that projects the current trend forward to help forecast the next value of a time series (and perhaps subsequent values as well). (Section 13.3) 543

Forecasting error The deviation of the forecast from the realized quantity. (Section 13.2) 532

Independent variable A quantity that drives the value of the dependent variable in causal forecasting. (Section 13.5) 554

Judgmental forecasting methods Methods that use expert judgment to make forecasts. (Introduction and Section 13.6) 527

Jury of executive opinion A judgmental forecasting method that involves a small group of high-level managers pooling their best judgment to collectively make the forecast. (Section 13.6) 558

Last-value forecasting method A method that uses the last value of a time series as the forecast of the next value. (Section 13.3) 537

Linear regression Approximating the relationship between the dependent variable and each independent variable by a straight line. (Section 13.5) 555

MAD An acronym for mean absolute deviation, the average forecasting error. (Section 13.2) 532

Manager's opinion A judgmental forecasting method that involves using a single manager's best judgment to make the forecast. (Section 13.6) 558

Mean absolute deviation The average forecasting error. (Section 13.2) 532

Method of least squares The procedure used to obtain the constants in the equation for a linear regression line. (Section 13.5) 556

Moving-average forecasting method A method that uses the average of the last n observations from a time series as a forecast of the next value. (Section 13.3) 540

Naive method Another name for the last-value forecasting method. (Section 13.3) 538

Regression equation The equation for a linear regression line. (Section 13.5) 555

Salesforce composite A judgmental forecasting method that aggregates the sales forecasts of the sales force from their various regions. (Section 13.6) 558

Seasonal factor A factor for any period of a year that measures how that period compares to the overall average for an entire year. (Section 13.3) 534

Seasonally adjusted time series An adjustment of the original time series that removes seasonal effects. (Section 13.3) 536

Smoothing constant A parameter of the exponential smoothing forecasting method that gives the weight to be placed on the last value in the time series. (Section 13.3) 541

Stable time series A time series whose underlying probability distribution usually remains the same from one time period to the next. (Section 13.4) 552

Statistical forecasting methods Methods that use historical data to forecast future quantities. (Introduction and Sections 13.2–13.5) 527

Time series A series of observations over time of some quantity of interest. (Section 13.2) 533

Time-series forecasting methods Methods that use the past observations in a time series to forecast what the next value will be. (Sections 13.3 and 13.4) 534

Trend The average change from one time series value to the next if the current pattern continues. (Section 13.3) 543

Trend smoothing constant A smoothing constant for estimating the trend when using exponential smoothing with trend. (Section 13.3) 545

Unstable time series A time series that has frequent and sizable shifts in its underlying probability distribution. (Section 13.4) 552

Summary of Key Formulas

Forecasting error = Difference between a forecasted value and the true value then obtained   (Section 13.2)

$$\text{MAD} = \frac{\text{Sum of forecasting errors}}{\text{Number of forecasts}} \quad \text{(Section 13.2)}$$

$$\text{Seasonal factor} = \frac{\text{Average for the period}}{\text{Overall average}} \quad \text{(Section 13.3)}$$

$$\text{Seasonally adjusted value} = \frac{\text{Actual value}}{\text{Seasonal factor}} \quad \text{(Section 13.3)}$$

Last-Value Method: (Section 13.3)

$$\text{Forecast} = \text{last value}$$

Averaging Method: (Section 13.3)

$$\text{Forecast} = \text{average of all data to date}$$

Moving-Average Method: (Section 13.3)

$$\text{Forecast} = \text{average of last } n \text{ values}$$

Exponential Smoothing Method: (Section 13.3)

$$\text{Forecast} = \alpha(\text{last value}) + (1 - \alpha)(\text{last forecast})$$

Exponential Smoothing with Trend: (Section 13.3)

$$\text{Forecast} = \alpha(\text{last value}) + (1 - \alpha)(\text{last forecast}) + \text{estimated trend}$$

$$\text{Estimated trend} = \beta(\text{latest trend}) + (1 - \beta)(\text{last estimate of trend})$$

$$\text{Latest trend} = \alpha(\text{last value} - \text{next-to-last value}) + (1 - \alpha)(\text{last forecast} - \text{next-to-last forecast})$$

Linear Regression Line: (Section 13.5)

$$y = a + bx$$

Learning Aids for This Chapter in Your MS Courseware

"Ch. 13—Forecasting" Excel File:

Template for *Seasonal Factors*
Templates for *Last-Value Method* (with and without Seasonality)
Templates for *Averaging Method* (with and without Seasonality)
Templates for *Moving-Average Method* (with and without Seasonality)

Templates for *Exponential Smoothing Method* (with and without Seasonality)
Templates for *Exponential Smoothing with Trend* (with and without Seasonality)
Template for *Linear Regression*

Problems

The first 16 problems should be done by hand without using the above templates. To the left of the subsequent problems (or their parts), we have inserted the symbol E (for Excel) to indicate that one of the above templates can be helpful. An asterisk on the problem number indicates that at least a partial answer is given in the back of the book.

13.1.* The Hammaker Company's newest product has had the following sales during its first five months: 5, 17, 29, 41, 39. The sales manager now wants a forecast of sales in the next month.

    a. Use the last-value method.
    b. Use the averaging method.
    c. Use the moving-average method with the three most recent months.
    d. Given the sales pattern so far, do any of these methods seem inappropriate for obtaining the forecast? Why?

13.2. Sales of stoves have been going well for the Good-Value Department Store. These sales for the past five months have been 15, 18, 12, 17, 13. Use the following methods to obtain a forecast of sales for the next month.

    a. The last-value method.
    b. The averaging method.
    c. The moving-average method with three months.
    d. If you feel that the conditions affecting sales next month will be the same as in the last five months, which of these methods do you prefer for obtaining the forecast? Why?

13.3.* You have been forecasting sales the last four quarters. These forecasts and the true values that subsequently were obtained are shown below.

Quarter	Forecast	True Value
1	327	345
2	332	317
3	328	336
4	330	311

Calculate the forecasting error for each quarter. Then calculate MAD.

13.4. Sharon Johnson, sales manager for the Alvarez-Baines Company, is trying to choose between two methods for forecasting sales that she has been using during the past five months. During these months, the two methods obtained the forecasts shown below for the company's most important product, where the subsequent actual sales are shown on the right.

	Forecast		
Month	*Method 1*	*Method 2*	*Actual Sales*
1	5,324	5,208	5,582
2	5,405	5,377	4,906
3	5,195	5,462	5,755
4	5,511	5,414	6,320
5	5,762	5,549	5,153

a. Calculate and compare MAD for these two forecasting methods.

b. Sharon is uncomfortable with choosing between these two methods based on such limited data, but she also does not want to delay further before making her choice. She does have similar sales data for the three years prior to using these forecasting methods the past five months. How can these older data be used to further help her evaluate the two methods and choose one?

13.5. Figure 13.1 shows CCW's average daily call volume for each quarter of the past three years and Figure 13.4 gives the seasonally adjusted call volumes. Lydia Weigelt now wonders what these seasonally adjusted call volumes would have been if she had started using seasonal factors two years ago rather than applying them retrospectively now.

a. Use only the call volumes in Year 1 to determine the seasonal factors for Year 2 (so that the "average" call volume for each quarter is just the actual call volume for that quarter in Year 1).

b. Use these seasonal factors to determine the seasonally adjusted call volumes for Year 2.

c. Use the call volumes in Years 1 and 2 to determine the seasonal factors for Year 3.

d. Use the seasonal factors obtained in part *c* to determine the seasonally adjusted call volumes for Year 3.

13.6. Even when the economy is holding steady, the unemployment rate tends to fluctuate because of seasonal effects. For example, unemployment generally goes up in Quarter 3 (summer) as students (including new graduates) enter the labor market. The unemployment rate then tends to go down in Quarter 4 (fall) as students return to school and temporary help is hired for the Christmas season. Therefore, using seasonal factors to obtain a seasonally adjusted unemployment rate is helpful for painting a truer picture of economic trends.

Over the past 10 years, one state's average unemployment rates (not seasonally adjusted) in Quarters 1, 2, 3, and 4 have been 6.2 percent, 6.0 percent, 7.5 percent, and 5.5 percent, respectively. The overall average has been 6.3 percent.

a. Determine the seasonal factors for the four quarters.

b. Over the next year, the unemployment rates (not seasonally adjusted) for the four quarters turn out to be 7.8 percent, 7.4 percent. 8.7 percent, and 6.1 percent. Determine the seasonally adjusted unemployment rates for the four quarters. What does this progression of rates suggest about whether the state's economy is improving?

13.7. Ralph Billett is the manager of a real estate agency. He now wishes to develop a forecast of the number of houses that will be sold by the agency over the next year.

The agency's quarter-by-quarter sales figures over the last three years are shown below.

Quarter	*Year 1*	*Year 2*	*Year 3*
1	23	19	21
2	22	21	26
3	31	27	32
4	26	24	28

a. Determine the seasonal factors for the four quarters.

b. After considering seasonal effects, use the last-value method to forecast sales in Quarter 1 of next year.

c. Assuming that each of the quarterly forecasts is correct, what would the last-value method forecast as the sales in each of the four quarters next year?

d. Based on his assessment of the current state of the housing market, Ralph's best judgment is that the agency will sell 100 houses next year. Given this forecast for the year, what is the quarter-by-quarter forecast according to the seasonal factors?

13.8.* You are using the moving-average forecasting method based on the last four observations. When making the forecast for the last period, the oldest of the four observations was 1,945 and the forecast was 2,083. The true value for the last period then turned out to be 1,977. What is your new forecast for the next period?

13.9. You are using the moving-average forecasting method based on sales in the last three months to forecast sales for the next month. When making the forecast for last month, sales for the third month before were 805. The forecast for last month was 782 and then the actual sales turned out to be 793. What is your new forecast for next month?

13.10. After graduating from college with a degree in mathematical statistics, Ann Preston has been hired by the Monty Ward Company to apply statistical methods for forecasting the company's sales. For one of the company's products, the moving-average method based on sales in the 10 most recent months already is being used. Ann's first task is to update last month's forecast to obtain the forecast for next month. She learns that the forecast for last month was 1,551 and that the actual sales then turned out to be 1,532. She also learns that the sales for the 10th month before last month was 1,632. What is Ann's forecast for next month?

13.11. The J.J. Bone Company uses exponential smoothing to forecast the average daily call volume at its call center. The forecast for last month was 782, and then the actual value turned out to be 792. Obtain the forecast for next month for each of the following values of the smoothing constant: $\alpha = 0.1, 0.3, 0.5$.

13.12.* You are using exponential smoothing to obtain monthly forecasts of the sales of a certain product. The forecast for last month was 2,083, and then the actual sales turned out to be 1,973. Obtain the forecast for next month for each of the following values of the smoothing constant: $\alpha = 0.1, 0.3, 0.5$.

13.13. Three years ago, the Admissions Office for Ivy College began using exponential smoothing with a smoothing constant of 0.25 to forecast the number of applications for admission each year. Based on previous experience, this process was begun with an initial estimate of 5,000 applications. The actual number of applications then turned out to be 4,600 in the first year. Thanks to new favorable ratings in national surveys, this number grew to 5,300 in the second year and 6,000 last year.

   a. Determine the forecasts that were made for each of the past three years.

   b. Calculate MAD for these three years.

   c. Determine the forecast for next year.

13.14. Reconsider Problem 13.13. Notice the steady trend upward in the number of applications over the past three years—from 4,600 to 5,300 to 6,000. Suppose now that the Admissions Office of Ivy College had been able to foresee this kind of trend and so had decided to use exponential smoothing with trend to do the forecasting. Suppose also that the initial estimates just over three years ago had been *average value = 3,900* and *trend = 700*. Then, with any values of the smoothing constants, the forecasts obtained by this forecasting method would have been exactly correct for all three years.

   Illustrate this fact by doing the calculations to obtain these forecasts when the smoothing constant is $\alpha = 0.25$ and the trend smoothing constant is $\beta = 0.25$.

13.15.* Exponential smoothing with trend, with a smoothing constant of $\alpha = 0.2$ and a trend smoothing constant of $\beta = 0.3$, is being used to forecast values in a time series. At this point, the last two values have been 535 and then 550. The last two forecasts have been 530 and then 540. The last estimate of trend has been 10. Use this information to forecast the next value in the time series.

13.16. The Healthwise Company produces a variety of exercise equipment. Healthwise management is very pleased with the increasing sales of its newest model of exercise bicycle. The sales during the last two months have been 4,655 and then 4,935.

   Management has been using exponential smoothing with trend, with a smoothing constant of $\alpha = 0.1$ and a trend smoothing constant of $\beta = 0.2$, to forecast sales for the next month each time. The forecasts for the last two months were 4,720 and then 4,975. The last estimate of trend was 240.

   Calculate the forecast of sales for next month.

13.17.* Ben Swanson, owner and manager of Swanson's Department Store, has decided to use statistical forecasting to get a better handle on the demand for his major products. However, Ben now needs to decide which forecasting method is most appropriate for each category of product. One category is major household appliances, such as washing machines, which have a relatively stable sales level. Monthly sales of washing machines last year are shown below.

Month	Sales	Month	Sales	Month	Sales
January	23	May	22	September	21
February	24	June	27	October	29
March	22	July	20	November	23
April	28	August	26	December	28

   a. Considering that the sales level is relatively stable, which of the most basic forecasting methods—the last-value method, the averaging method, or the moving-average method—do you feel would be most appropriate for forecasting future sales? Why?

E b. Use the last-value method retrospectively to determine what the forecasts would have been for the last 11 months of last year. What is MAD?

E c. Use the averaging method retrospectively to determine what the forecasts would have been for the last 11 months of last year. What is MAD?

E d. Use the moving-average method with $n = 3$ retrospectively to determine what the forecasts would have been for the last nine months of last year. What is MAD?

   e. Use their MAD values to compare the three methods.

   f. Do you feel comfortable in drawing a definitive conclusion about which of the three forecasting methods should be the most accurate in the future based on these 12 months of data?

E 13.18. Reconsider Problem 13.17. Ben Swanson now has decided to use the exponential smoothing method to forecast future sales of washing machines, but he needs to decide on which smoothing constant to use. Using an initial estimate of 24, apply this method retrospectively to the 12 months of last year with $\alpha = 0.1, 0.2, 0.3, 0.4$, and 0.5. Compare MAD for these five values of the smoothing constant α.

13.19. Management of the Jackson Manufacturing Corporation wishes to choose a statistical forecasting method for forecasting total sales for the corporation. Total sales (in millions of dollars) for each month of last year are shown below.

Month	Sales	Month	Sales	Month	Sales
January	126	May	153	September	147
February	137	June	154	October	151
March	142	July	148	November	159
April	150	August	145	December	166

   a. Note how the sales level is shifting significantly from month to month—first trending upward and then dipping down before resuming an upward trend. Assuming that similar patterns would continue in the future, evaluate how well you feel each of the five forecasting methods introduced in Section 13.3 would perform in forecasting future sales.

E   b. Apply the last-value method, the averaging method, and the moving-average method (with $n=3$) retrospectively to last year's sales and compare their MAD values.

E   c. Using an initial estimate of 120, apply the exponential smoothing method retrospectively to last year's sales with $\alpha=0.1, 0.2, 0.3, 0.4$, and 0.5. Compare MAD for these five values of the smoothing constant α.

E   d. Using initial estimates of 120 for the average value and 10 for the trend, apply exponential smoothing with trend retrospectively to last year's sales. Use all combinations of the smoothing constants where $\alpha=0.1, 0.3$, or 0.5 and $\beta=0.1, 0.3$, or 0.5. Compare MAD for these nine combinations.

   e. Which one of the above forecasting methods would you recommend that management use? Using this method, what is the forecast of total sales for January of the new year?

13.20. Reconsider Problem 13.19. Use the lessons learned from the CCW case study to address the following questions.

   a. What might be causing the significant shifts in total sales from month to month that were observed last year?

   b. Given your answer to part *a*, how might the basic statistical approach to forecasting total sales be improved?

   c. Describe the role of managerial judgment in applying the statistical approach developed in part *b*.

E 13.21. Choosing an appropriate value of the smoothing constant α is a key decision when applying the exponential smoothing method. When relevant historical data exist, one approach to making this decision is to apply the method retrospectively to these data with different values of α and then choose the value of α that gives the smallest MAD. Use this approach for choosing α with each of the following time series representing monthly sales. In each case, use an initial estimate of 50 and compare $\alpha=0.1, 0.2, 0.3, 0.4$, and 0.5.

   a. 51, 48, 52, 49, 53, 49, 48, 51, 50, 49
   b. 52, 50, 53, 51, 52, 48, 52, 53, 49, 52
   c. 50, 52, 51, 55, 53, 56, 52, 55, 54, 53

E 13.22. The choice of the smoothing constants, α and β, have a considerable effect on the accuracy of the forecasts obtained by using exponential smoothing with trend. For each of the following time series, set $\alpha=0.2$ and then compare MAD obtained with $\beta = 0.1, 0.2, 0.3, 0.4$, and 0.5. Begin with initial estimates of 50 for the average value and 2 for the trend.

   a. 52, 55, 55, 58, 59, 63, 64, 66, 67, 72, 73, 74
   b. 52, 55, 59, 61, 66, 69, 71, 72, 73, 74, 73, 74
   c. 52, 53, 51, 50, 48, 47, 49, 52, 57, 62, 69, 74

13.23. The Andes Mining Company mines and ships copper ore. The company's sales manager, Juanita Valdes, has been using the moving-average method based on the last three years of sales to forecast the demand for the next year. However, she has become dissatisfied with the inaccurate forecasts being provided by this method.

   The annual demands (in tons of copper ore) over the past 10 years are 382, 405, 398, 421, 426, 415, 443, 451, 446, 464.

E   a. Explain why this pattern of demands inevitably led to significant inaccuracies in the moving-average forecasts.

E   b. Determine the moving-average forecasts for the past seven years. What is MAD? What is the forecast for next year?

E   c. Determine what the forecasts would have been for the past 10 years if the exponential smoothing method had been used instead with an initial estimate of 380 and a smoothing constant of $\alpha=0.5$. What is MAD? What is the forecast for next year?

E   d. Determine what the forecasts would have been for the past 10 years if exponential smoothing with trend had been used instead. Use initial estimates of 370 for the average value and 10 for the trend, with smoothing constants $\alpha=0.25$ and $\beta=0.25$.

E   e. Based on the MAD values, which of these three methods do you recommend using hereafter?

E 13.24.* The Pentel Microchip Company has started production of its new microchip. The first phase in this production is the wafer fabrication process. Because of the great difficulty in fabricating acceptable wafers, many of these tiny wafers must be rejected because they are defective. Therefore, management places great emphasis on continually improving the wafer fabrication process to increase its *production yield* (the percentage of wafers fabricated in the current lot that are of acceptable quality for producing microchips).

   So far, the production yields of the respective lots have been 15 percent, 21 percent, 24 percent, 32 percent, 37 percent, 41 percent, 40 percent, 47 percent, 51 percent, 53 percent. Use exponential smoothing with trend to forecast the production yield of the next lot. Begin with initial estimates of 10 percent for the average value and 5 percent for the trend. Use smoothing constants of $\alpha=0.2$ and $\beta=0.2$.

13.25. The Centerville Water Department provides water for the entire town and outlying areas. The number of acre-feet of water consumed in each of the four seasons of the three preceding years is shown below.

Season	Year 1	Year 2	Year 3
Winter	25	27	24
Spring	47	46	49
Summer	68	72	70
Fall	42	39	44

E   a. Determine the seasonal factors for the four seasons.
E   b. After considering seasonal effects, use the last-value method to forecast water consumption next winter.

   c. Assuming that each of the forecasts for the next three seasons is correct, what would the last-value method forecast as the water consumption in each of the four seasons next year.

E   d. After considering seasonal effects, use the averaging method to forecast water consumption next winter.

E   *e.* After considering seasonal effects, use the moving-average method based on four seasons to forecast water consumption next winter.

E   *f.* After considering seasonal effects, use the exponential smoothing method with an initial estimate of 46 and a smoothing constant of $\alpha=0.1$ to forecast water consumption next winter.

E   *g.* Compare the MAD values of these four forecasting methods when they are applied retrospectively to the last three years.

13.26. Reconsider Problem 13.7. Ralph Billett realizes that the last-value method is considered to be the naive forecasting method, so he wonders whether he should be using another method. Therefore, he has decided to use the available Excel templates that consider seasonal effects to apply various statistical forecasting methods retrospectively to the past three years of data and compare their MAD values.

E*   *a.* Determine the seasonal factors for the four quarters.

E*   *b.* Apply the last-value method.

E*   *c.* Apply the averaging method.

E*   *d.* Apply the moving-average method based on the four most recent quarters of data.

E*   *e.* Apply the exponential smoothing method with an initial estimate of 25 and a smoothing constant of $\alpha=0.25$.

E*   *f.* Apply exponential smoothing with trend with smoothing constants of $\alpha=0.25$ and $\beta=0.25$. Use initial estimates of 25 for the average value and 0 for the trend.

E*   *g.* Compare the MAD values for these methods. Use the one with the smallest MAD to forecast sales in Quarter 1 of next year.

     h. Use the forecast in part *g* and the seasonal factors to make long-range forecasts now of the sales in the remaining quarters of next year.

E 13.27. Transcontinental Airlines maintains a computerized forecasting system to forecast the number of customers in each fare class who will fly on each flight in order to allocate the available reservations to fare classes properly. For example, consider *economy-class customers* flying in midweek on the noon flight from New York to Los Angeles. The following table shows the average number of such passengers during each month of the year just completed. The table also shows the seasonal factor that has been assigned to each month based on historical data.

Month	Average Number	Seasonal Factor	Month	Average Number	Seasonal Factor
January	68	0.90	July	94	1.17
February	71	0.88	August	96	1.15
March	66	0.91	September	80	0.97
April	72	0.93	October	73	0.91
May	77	0.96	November	84	1.05
June	85	1.09	December	89	1.08

     a. After considering seasonal effects, compare the MAD values for the last-value method, the averaging method, the moving-average method (based on the most recent three months), and the exponential smoothing method (with an initial estimate of 80 and a smoothing constant of $\alpha=0.2$) when they are applied retrospectively to the past year.

     b. Use the forecasting method with the smallest MAD value to forecast the average number of these passengers flying in January of the new year.

13.28. Reconsider Problem 13.27. The economy is beginning to boom so the management of Transcontinental Airlines is predicting that the number of people flying will steadily increase this year over the relatively flat (seasonally adjusted) level of last year. Since the forecasting methods considered in Problem 13.27 are relatively slow in adjusting to such a trend, consideration is being given to switching to exponential smoothing with trend.

     Subsequently, as the year goes on, management's prediction proves to be true. The following table shows the average number of the passengers under consideration in each month of the new year.

Month	Average Number	Month	Average Number	Month	Average Number
January	75	May	85	September	94
February	76	June	99	October	90
March	81	July	107	November	106
April	84	August	108	December	110

E   *a.* Repeat part *a* of Problem 13.27 for the two years of data.

E   *b.* After considering seasonal effects, apply exponential smoothing with trend to just the new year. Use initial estimates of 80 for the average value and 2 for the trend, along with smoothing constants of $\alpha=0.2$ and $\beta=0.2$. Compare MAD for this method to the MAD values obtained in part *a*.

E   *c.* Repeat part *b* when exponential smoothing with trend is begun at the beginning of the first year and then applied to both years, just like the other forecasting methods in part *a*. Use the same initial estimates and smoothing constants except change the initial estimate of trend to 0.

     d. Based on these results, which forecasting method would you recommend that Transcontinental Airlines use hereafter?

13.29. Quality Bikes is a wholesale firm that specializes in the distribution of bicycles. In the past, the company has maintained ample inventories of bicycles to enable filling orders immediately, so informal rough forecasts of demand were sufficient to make the decisions on when to replenish inventory. However, the company's new president, Marcia Salgo, intends to run a tighter ship. Scientific inventory management is to be used to reduce inventory levels and minimize total variable inventory costs. At the same time, Marcia has ordered the development of a computerized forecasting system based on statistical forecasting that considers seasonal effects. The system is to generate three sets of forecasts—one based on the moving-average method, a second based on the exponential smoothing method, and a third based on exponential smoothing with trend. The average of these three forecasts for each month is to be used for inventory management purposes.

The following table gives the available data on monthly sales of 10-speed bicycles over the past three years. The last column also shows monthly sales this year, which is the first year of operation of the new forecasting system.

	Past Sales			Current Sales
Month	*Year 1*	*Year 2*	*Year 3*	*This Year*
January	352	317	338	364
February	329	331	346	343
March	365	344	383	391
April	358	386	404	437
May	412	423	431	458
June	446	472	459	494
July	420	415	433	468
August	471	492	518	555
September	355	340	309	387
October	312	301	335	364
November	567	629	594	662
December	533	505	527	581

E   a. Determine the seasonal factors for the 12 months based on past sales.

E   b. After considering seasonal effects, apply the moving-average method based on the most recent three months to forecast monthly sales for each month of this year.

E   c. After considering seasonal effects, apply the exponential smoothing method to forecast monthly sales this year. Use an initial estimate of 420 and a smoothing constant of $\alpha = 0.2$.

E   d. After considering seasonal effects, apply exponential smoothing with trend to forecast monthly sales this year. Use initial estimates of 420 for the average value and 0 for the trend, along with smoothing constants of $\alpha = 0.2$ and $\beta = 0.2$.

   e. Compare the MAD values obtained in parts *b*, *c*, and *d*.

   f. Calculate the combined forecast for each month by averaging the forecasts for that month obtained in parts *b*, *c*, and *d*. Then calculate MAD for these combined forecasts.

   g. Based on these results, what is your recommendation for how to do the forecasts next year?

13.30.* Long a market leader in the production of heavy machinery, the Spellman Corporation recently has been enjoying a steady increase in the sales of its new lathe. The sales over the past 10 months are shown below.

Month	*Sales*	*Month*	*Sales*
1	430	6	514
2	446	7	532
3	464	8	548
4	480	9	570
5	498	10	591

Because of this steady increase, management has decided to use *causal forecasting*, with the month as the independent variable and sales as the dependent variable, to forecast sales in the coming months.

   a. Plot these data on a two-dimensional graph with the month on the horizontal axis and sales on the vertical axis.

E   b. Find the formula for the linear regression line that fits these data.

   c. Plot this line on the graph constructed in part *a*.

   d. Use this line to forecast sales in month 11.

   e. Use this line to forecast sales in month 20.

   f. What does the formula for the linear regression line indicate is roughly the average growth in sales per month?

13.31. Reconsider Problems 13.13 and 13.14. Since the number of applications for admission submitted to Ivy College has been increasing at a steady rate, causal forecasting can be used to forecast the number of applications in future years by letting the year be the independent variable and the number of applications be the dependent variable.

   a. Plot the data for Years 1, 2, and 3 on a two-dimensional graph with the year on the horizontal axis and the number of applications on the vertical axis.

   b. Since the three points in this graph line up in a straight line, this straight line is the linear regression line. Draw this line.

E   c. Find the formula for this linear regression line.

   d. Use this line to forecast the number of applications for each of the next five years (Years 4 through 8).

   e. As these next years go on, conditions change for the worse at Ivy College. The favorable ratings in the national surveys that had propelled the growth in applications turn unfavorable. Consequently, the number of applications turn out to be 6,300 in Year 4 and 6,200 in Year 5, followed by sizable drops to 5,600 in Year 6 and 5,200 in Year 7. Does it still make sense to use the forecast for Year 8 obtained in part *d*? Explain.

E   f. Plot the data for all seven years. Find the formula for the linear regression line based on all these data and plot this line. Use this formula to forecast the number of applications for Year 8. Does the linear regression line provide a close fit to the data? Given this answer, do you have much confidence in the forecast it provides for Year 8? Does it make sense to continue to use a linear regression line when changing conditions cause a large shift in the underlying trend in the data?

E   g. Apply exponential smoothing with trend to all seven years of data to forecast the number of applications in Year 8. Use initial estimates of 3,900 for the average and 700 for the trend, along with smoothing constants of $\alpha = 0.5$ and $\beta = 0.5$. When the underlying trend in the data stays the same, causal forecasting provides the best possible linear regression line (according to the method of least squares) for making forecasts. However, when changing conditions cause a shift in the underlying trend, what advantage does exponential smoothing with trend have over causal forecasting?

13.32. Reconsider Problem 13.23. Despite some fluctuations from year to year, note that there has been a basic trend upward in the annual demand for copper ore over the past 10 years. Therefore, by projecting this trend forward, causal forecasting can be used to forecast demands in future years by letting the year be the independent variable and the demand be the dependent variable.

    a. Plot the data for the past 10 years (Years 1 through 10) on a two-dimensional graph with the year on the horizontal axis and the demand on the vertical axis.

E   *b.* Find the formula for the linear regression line that fits these data.

    c. Plot this line on the graph constructed in part *a*.

    d. Use this line to forecast demand next year (Year 11).

    e. Use this line to forecast demand in Year 15.

    f. What does the formula for the linear regression line indicate is roughly the average growth in demand per year?

13.33. Luxury Cruise Lines has a fleet of ships that travel to Alaska repeatedly every summer (and elsewhere during other times of the year). A considerable amount of advertising is done each winter to help generate enough passenger business for that summer. With the coming of a new winter, a decision needs to be made about how much advertising to do this year.

    The following table shows the amount of advertising (in thousands of dollars) and the resulting sales (in thousands of passengers booked for a cruise) for each of the past five years.

Amount of advertising ($1,000s)	225	400	350	275	450
Sales (thousands of passengers)	16	21	20	17	23

    a. To use causal forecasting to forecast sales for a given amount of advertising, which need to be the dependent variable and the independent variable?

    b. Plot the data on a graph.

E   *c.* Find the formula for the linear regression line that fits these data. Then plot this line on the graph constructed in part *b*.

    d. Forecast the sales that would be attained by expending $300,000 on advertising.

    e. Estimate the amount of advertising that would need to be done to attain a booking of 22,000 passengers.

    f. According to the linear regression line, about how much increase in sales can be attained on the average per $1,000 increase in the amount of advertising?

13.34. To support its large fleet, North American Airlines maintains an extensive inventory of spare parts, including wing flaps. The number of wing flaps needed in inventory to replace damaged wing flaps each month depends partially on the number of flying hours for the fleet that month, since increased usage increases the chances of damage.

    The following table shows both the number of replacement wing flaps needed and the number of thousands of flying hours for the entire fleet for each of several recent months.

Thousands of flying hours	162	149	185	171	138	154
Number of wing flaps needed	12	9	13	14	10	11

    a. Identify the dependent variable and the independent variable for doing causal forecasting of the number of wing flaps needed for a given number of flying hours.

    b. Plot the data on a graph.

E   *c.* Find the formula for the linear regression line.

    d. Plot this line on the graph constructed in part *b*.

    e. Forecast the average number of wing flaps needed in a month in which 150,000 flying hours are planned.

    f. Repeat part *e* for 200,000 flying hours.

E 13.35. Joe Barnes is the owner of Standing Tall, one of the major roofing companies in town. Much of the company's business comes from building roofs on new houses. Joe has learned that general contractors constructing new houses typically will subcontract the roofing work about two months after construction begins. Therefore, to help him develop long-range schedules for his work crews, Joe has decided to use county records on the number of housing construction permits issued each month to forecast the number of roofing jobs on new houses he will have two months later.

    Joe has now gathered the following data for each month over the past year, where the second column gives the number of housing construction permits issued in that month and the third column shows the number of roofing jobs on new houses that were subcontracted out to Standing Tall in that month.

Month	Permits	Jobs	Month	Permits	Jobs
January	323	19	July	446	34
February	359	17	August	407	37
March	396	24	September	374	33
April	421	23	October	343	30
May	457	28	November	311	27
June	472	32	December	277	22

Use a causal forecasting approach to develop a forecasting procedure for Joe to use hereafter.

CASE 13.1
FINAGLING THE FORECASTS

Mark Lawrence has been pursuing a vision for more than two years. This pursuit began when he became frustrated in his role as director of Human Resources at Cutting Edge, a large company manufacturing computers and computer peripherals. At that time, the Human Resources Department under his direction provided records and benefits administration to the 60,000 Cutting Edge employees throughout the United States, and 35 separate records and benefits administration centers existed across the country. Employees contacted these records and benefits centers to obtain information about dental plans and stock options, change tax forms and personal information, and process leaves of absence and retirements. The decentralization of these administration centers caused numerous headaches for Mark. He had to deal with employee complaints often since each center interpreted company policies differently—communicating inconsistent and sometimes inaccurate answers to employees. His department also suffered high operating costs since operating 35 separate centers created inefficiency.

His vision? To centralize records and benefits administration by establishing one administration center. This centralized records and benefits administration center would perform two distinct functions: data management and customer service. The data management function would include updating employee records after performance reviews and maintaining the human resource management system. The customer service function would include establishing a call center to answer employee questions concerning records and benefits and to process records and benefits changes over the phone.

One year after proposing his vision to management, Mark received the go-ahead from Cutting Edge corporate headquarters. He prepared his "to do" list—specifying computer and phone systems requirements, installing hardware and software, integrating data from the 35 separate administration centers, standardizing record-keeping and response procedures, and staffing the administration center. Mark delegated the systems requirements, installation, and integration jobs to a competent group of technology specialists. He took on the responsibility of standardizing procedures and staffing the administration center.

Mark had spent many years in human resources and therefore had little problem with standardizing record-keeping and response procedures. He encountered trouble in determining the number of representatives needed to staff the center, however. He was particularly worried about staffing the call center since the representatives answering phones interact directly with customers—the 60,000 Cutting Edge employees. The customer service representatives would receive extensive training so that they would know the records and benefits policies backwards and forwards—enabling them to answer questions accurately and process changes efficiently. Overstaffing would cause Mark to suffer the high costs of training unneeded representatives and paying the surplus representatives the high salaries that go along with such an intense job. Understaffing would cause Mark to continue to suffer the headaches from customer complaints—something he definitely wanted to avoid.

The number of customer service representatives Mark needed to hire depended on the number of calls that the records and benefits call center would receive. Mark therefore needed to forecast the number of calls that the new centralized center would receive. He approached the forecasting problem by using judgmental forecasting. He studied data from one of the 35 decentralized administration centers and learned that the decentralized center had serviced 15,000 customers and had received 2,000 calls per month. He concluded that since the new centralized center would service four times the number of customers—60,000 customers—it would receive four times the number of calls—8,000 calls per month.

Mark slowly checked off the items on his "to do" list, and the centralized records and benefits administration center opened one year after Mark had received the go-ahead from corporate headquarters.

Now, after operating the new center for 13 weeks, Mark's call center forecasts are proving to be terribly inaccurate. The number of calls the center receives is roughly three times as large as the 8,000 calls per month that Mark had forecasted. Because of demand overload, the call center is slowly going to hell in a handbasket. Customers calling the center must wait an average of five minutes before speaking to a representative, and Mark is receiving numerous complaints. At the same time, the customer service representatives are unhappy and on the verge of quitting because of the stress created by the demand overload. Even corporate headquarters has become aware of the staff and service inadequacies, and executives have been breathing down Mark's neck demanding improvements.

Mark needs help, and he approaches you to forecast demand for the call center more accurately.

Luckily, when Mark first established the call center, he realized the importance of keeping operational data, and he provides you with the number of calls received on each day of the week over the last 13 weeks. The data (shown next) begins in week 44 of the last year and continues to week 5 of the current year.

	Monday	*Tuesday*	*Wednesday*	*Thursday*	*Friday*
Week 44	1130	851	859	828	726
Week 45	1085	1042	892	840	799
Week 46	1303	1121	1003	1113	1005
Week 47	2652	2825	1841	0	0
Week 48	1949	1507	989	990	1084
Week 49	1260	1134	941	847	714
Week 50	1002	847	922	842	784
Week 51	823	0	0	401	429
Week 52/1	1209	830	0	1082	841
Week 2	1362	1174	967	930	853
Week 3	924	954	1346	904	758
Week 4	886	878	802	945	610
Week 5	910	754	705	729	772

Mark indicates that the days where no calls were received were holidays.

a. Mark first asks you to forecast daily demand for the next week using the data from the past 13 weeks. You should make the forecasts for all the days of the next week now (at the end of week 5), but you should provide a different forecast for each day of the week by treating the forecast for a single day as being the actual call volume on that day.

1. From working at the records and benefits administration center, you know that demand follows "seasonal" patterns within the week. For example, more employees call at the beginning of the week when they are fresh and productive than at the end of the week when they are planning for the weekend. You therefore realize that you must account for the seasonal patterns and adjust the data that Mark gave you accordingly. What is the seasonally adjusted call volume for the past 13 weeks?

2. Using the seasonally adjusted call volume, forecast the daily demand for the next week using the last-value forecasting method.

3. Using the seasonally adjusted call volume, forecast the daily demand for the next week using the averaging forecasting method.

4. Using the seasonally adjusted call volume, forecast the daily demand for the next week using the moving-average forecasting method. You decide to use the five most recent days in this analysis.

5. Using the seasonally adjusted call volume, forecast the daily demand for the next week using the exponential smoothing forecasting method. You decide to use a smoothing constant of 0.1 because you believe that demand without seasonal effects remains relatively stable. Use the daily call volume average over the past 13 weeks for the initial estimate.

b. After one week, the period you have forecasted passes. You realize that you are able to determine the accuracy of your forecasts because you now have the actual call volumes from the week you had forecasted. The actual call volumes are shown below.

	Monday	*Tuesday*	*Wednesday*	*Thursday*	*Friday*
Week 6	723	677	521	571	498

For each of the forecasting methods, calculate the mean absolute deviation for the method and evaluate the performance of the method. When calculating the mean absolute deviation, you should use the actual forecasts you found in part *a* above. You should not recalculate the forecasts based on the actual values. In your evaluation, provide an explanation for the effectiveness or ineffectiveness of the method.

You realize that the forecasting methods that you have investigated do not provide a great degree of accuracy, and you decide to use a creative approach to forecasting that combines the statistical and judgmental approaches. You know that Mark had used data from one of the 35 decentralized records and benefits administration centers to perform his original forecasting. You therefore suspect that call volume data exists for this decentralized center. Because the decentralized centers performed the same functions as the new centralized center currently performs, you decide that the call volumes from the decentralized center will help you forecast the call volumes for the new centralized center. You simply need to understand how the decentralized volumes relate to the new centralized volumes. Once you understand this relationship, you can use the call volumes from the decentralized center to forecast the call volumes for the centralized center.

You approach Mark and ask him whether call center data exist for the decentralized center. He tells you that data exist, but data do not exist in the format that you need. Case volume data—not call volume data—exist. You do not understand the distinction, so Mark continues his explanation. There are two types of demand data—case volume data and call volume data. Case volume data count the actions taken by the representatives at the call center. Call volume data count the number of calls answered by the representatives at the call center. A case may require one call or multiple calls to resolve it. Thus, the number of cases is always less than or equal to the number of calls.

You know you only have case volume data for the decentralized center, and you certainly do not want to compare apples and oranges. You therefore ask if case volume data exist for the new centralized center. Mark gives you a wicked grin and nods his head. He sees where you are going with your forecasts, and he tells you that he will have the data for you within the hour.

c. At the end of the hour, Mark arrives at your desk with two data sets: weekly case volumes for the decentralized center and weekly case volumes for the centralized center. You ask Mark if he has data for daily case volumes, and he tells you that he does not. You therefore first have to forecast the weekly demand for the next week and then break this weekly demand into daily demand.

The decentralized center was shut down last year when the new centralized center opened, so you have the decentralized case data spanning from week 44 of two years ago to week 5 of last year. You compare this decentralized data to the centralized data spanning from week 44 of last year to week 5 of this year. The weekly case volumes are shown in the table below.

	Decentralized Case Volume	Centralized Case Volume
Week 44	612	2,052
Week 45	721	2,170
Week 46	693	2,779
Week 47	540	2,334
Week 48	1,386	2,514
Week 49	577	1,713
Week 50	405	1,927
Week 51	441	1,167
Week 52/1	655	1,549
Week 2	572	2,126
Week 3	475	2,337
Week 4	530	1,916
Week 5	595	2,098

1. Find a mathematical relationship between the decentralized case volume data and the centralized case volume data.
2. Now that you have a relationship between the weekly decentralized case volume and the weekly centralized case volume, you are able to forecast the weekly case volume for the new center. Unfortunately, you do not need the weekly case volume; you need the daily call volume. To calculate call volume from case volume, you perform further analysis and determine that each case generates an average of 1.5 calls. To calculate daily call volume from weekly call volume, you decide to use the seasonal factors as conversion factors. Given the following case volume data from the decentralized center for week 6 of last year, forecast the daily call volume for the new center for week 6 of this year.

	Week 6
Decentralized case volume	613

3. Using the actual call volumes given in part *b*, calculate the mean absolute deviation and evaluate the effectiveness of this forecasting method.

d. Which forecasting method would you recommend Mark use and why? As the call center continues its operation, how would you recommend improving the forecasting procedure?

QUEUEING MODELS

Queues (waiting lines) are a part of everyday life. We all wait in queues to buy a movie ticket, make a bank deposit, pay for groceries, mail a package, obtain food in a cafeteria, start a ride in an amusement park, and so on. We have become accustomed to considerable amounts of waiting, but still get annoyed by unusually long waits.

However, having to wait is not just a petty personal annoyance. The amount of time that a nation's populace wastes by waiting in queues is a major factor in both the quality of life there and the efficiency of the nation's economy. For example, before its dissolution, the USSR was notorious for the tremendously long queues that its citizens frequently had to endure just to purchase basic necessities. Even in the United States today, it has been estimated that Americans spend 37,000,000,000 hours per year waiting in queues. If this time could be spent productively instead, it would amount to nearly 20 million person-years of useful work each year!

Even this staggering figure does not tell the whole story of the impact of causing excessive waiting. Great inefficiencies also occur because of other kinds of waiting than people standing in line. For example, making *machines* wait to be repaired may result in lost production. *Vehicles* (including ships and trucks) that need to wait to be unloaded may delay subsequent shipments. *Airplanes* waiting to take off or land may disrupt later travel schedules. Delays in *telecommunication* transmissions due to saturated lines may cause data glitches. Causing *manufacturing jobs* to wait to be performed may disrupt subsequent production. Delaying *service jobs* beyond their due dates may result in lost future business.

Queueing theory is the study of waiting in all these various guises. It uses *queueing models* to represent the various types of *queueing systems* (systems that involve queues of some kind) that arise in practice. Formulas for each model indicate how the corresponding queueing system should perform, including the average amount of waiting that will occur, under a variety of circumstances.

Therefore, these queueing models are very helpful for determining how to operate a queueing system in the most effective way. Providing too much service capacity to operate the system involves excessive costs. But not providing enough service results in excessive waiting and all its unfortunate consequences. The models enable finding an appropriate balance between the cost of service and the amount of waiting.

The first three sections describe the elements of queueing models, give various examples of important queueing systems to which these models can be applied, and present measures of performance for these queueing systems. Section 14.4 then introduces a case study that will be carried through most of the chapter. Three subsequent sections present the most important queueing models in the context of analyzing the case study. Section 14.8 summarizes some key insights from the case study for designing queueing systems. After describing how economic analysis can be used to determine the number of servers to provide in a queueing system, the chapter then concludes by describing some award-winning applications of queueing theory.

14.1 Elements of a Queueing Model

We begin by describing the basic type of queueing system assumed by the queueing models in this chapter.

A Basic Queueing System

Figure 14.1 depicts a typical **queueing system. Customers** arrive individually to receive some kind of service. If an arrival cannot be served immediately, that customer joins a **queue** (waiting line) to await service. (The queue does not include the customers who are currently being served.) One or more **servers** at the service facility provide the service. Each customer is individually served by one of the servers and then departs.

For some queueing systems, the customers are *people.* However, in other cases, the customers might be *vehicles* (e.g., airplanes waiting to take off on a runway), *machines* (e.g., machines waiting to be repaired), or other *items* (e.g., jobs waiting for a manufacturing operation).

A server commonly is an individual person. However, it might instead be a crew of people working together to serve each customer. The server can also be a machine, a vehicle, an electronic device, and so forth.

In most cases, the queue is just an ordinary waiting line. However, it is not necessary for the customers to be standing in line in front of a physical structure that constitutes the service facility. They might be sitting in a waiting room. They might even be scattered throughout an area waiting for a server to come to them (e.g., stationary machines needing repair).

The next section presents many more examples of important queueing systems that fit Figure 14.1 and the above description. All the queueing models in this chapter also are based on this figure.

However, we also should mention that more complicated kinds of queueing systems sometimes do arise in practice. For example, a server might serve a group of customers simultaneously. Customers also might arrive in a group rather than individually. Impatient customers might leave before receiving service. The queueing system might include multiple queues, one for each server, with customers occasionally switching queues. It might include multiple service facilities, where some customers need to go to more than one of the facilities to obtain all the required service. (This last type of queueing system is referred to as a *queueing network.*) Such queueing systems also are quite important, but we will not delve into the more complicated queueing models that have been developed to deal with them. The next chapter will describe another technique (computer simulation) that often is used to analyze complex queueing systems.

An Example

Herr Cutter is a German barber who runs a one-man barber shop. Thus, his shop is a basic queueing system for which he is the only server.

Herr Cutter opens his shop at 8:00 A.M. each weekday morning. Table 14.1 shows his queueing system in action over the beginning of a typical morning. For each of his first five customers, the table indicates when the customer arrived, when his haircut began, how long the haircut took, and when the haircut was finished.

FIGURE 14.1

A basic queueing system, where each customer is indicated by C *and each server by* S.

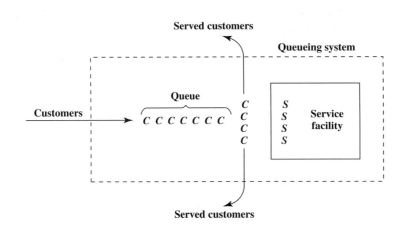

TABLE 14.1 The Data for Herr Cutter's First Five Customers

Customer	Time of Arrival	Haircut Begins	Duration of Haircut	Haircut Ends
1	8:03	8:03	17 minutes	8:20
2	8:15	8:20	21 minutes	8:41
3	8:25	8:41	19 minutes	9:00
4	8:30	9:00	15 minutes	9:15
5	9:05	9:15	20 minutes	9:35
6	9:43	—	—	—

FIGURE 14.2

The evolution of the number of customers in Herr Cutter's barber shop over the first 100 minutes (from 8:00 to 9:40), given the data in Table 14.1.

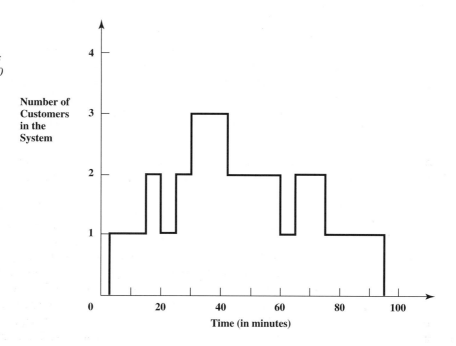

Figure 14.2 plots the number of customers in this queueing system over the first 100 minutes. This number includes both the customers waiting to begin a haircut and the one already under way. Thus, the number of customers in the queue (only those waiting to begin) is one less (unless already zero).

Referring to this example, let us now look at the kinds of assumptions that the queueing models make about the different parts of a basic queueing system.

Arrivals

The times between consecutive arrivals to a queueing system are called the **interarrival times.** For Herr Cutter's barber shop, the second column of Table 14.1 indicates that the interarrival times on this particular morning are 12 minutes, 10 minutes, 5 minutes, 35 minutes, and 38 minutes.

This high variability in the interarrival times is common for queueing systems. As with Herr Cutter, it usually is impossible to predict just how long until the next customer will arrive.

However, after gathering a lot more data such as in the second column of Table 14.1, it does become possible to do two things:

1. Estimate the *expected number* of arrivals per unit time. This quantity is normally referred to as the **mean arrival rate.** (The symbol for this quantity is λ, which is the Greek letter lambda.)
2. Estimate the *form* of the probability distribution of interarrival times.

The mean of this distribution actually comes directly from item 1. Since

$$\lambda = \text{mean arrival rate for customers coming to the queueing system}$$

the mean is

$$\frac{1}{\lambda} = \text{expected interarrival time}$$

For example, after gathering more data, Herr Cutter finds that 300 customers have arrived over a period of 100 hours.[1] Therefore, the estimate of λ is

$$\lambda = \frac{300 \text{ customers}}{100 \text{ hours}} = 3 \text{ customers per hour on the average}$$

The corresponding estimate of the expected interarrival time is

$$\frac{1}{\lambda} = \frac{1}{3} \text{ hour between customers on the average}$$

Most queueing models assume that the *form* of the probability distribution of interarrival times is an *exponential distribution*, as explained below.

The Exponential Distribution for Interarrival Times

Figure 14.3 shows the shape of an exponential distribution, where the height of the curve at various times represents the relative likelihood of those times occurring. Note in the figure how the highest points on the curve are at very small times and then the curve drops down "exponentially" as time increases. This indicates a high likelihood of small interarrival times, well under the mean. However, the long tail of the distribution also indicates a small chance of a very large interarrival time, much larger than the mean. All this is characteristic of interarrival times observed in practice. Several customers may arrive quickly. Then there may be a long pause until the next arrival.

This variability in interarrival times makes it impossible to predict just when future arrivals will occur. When the variability is as large as for the exponential distribution, this is referred to as having *random arrivals*.

> For most queueing systems, the servers have no control over when customers will arrive. In this case, the customers generally arrive *randomly*. Having *random arrivals* means that arrival times are completely unpredictable in the sense that the chance of an arrival in the next minute always is just the same (no more and no less) as for any other minute. It does not matter how long it has been since the last arrival occurred. The only distribution of interarrival times that fits having random arrivals is the exponential distribution.

The fact that the probability of an arrival in the next minute is completely uninfluenced by when the last arrival occurred is called the **lack-of-memory property** (or the *Markovian property*). This is a strange property, because it implies that the probability distribution of

FIGURE 14.3

The shape of an exponential distribution, commonly used in queueing models as the distribution of interarrival times (and sometimes as the distribution of service times as well).

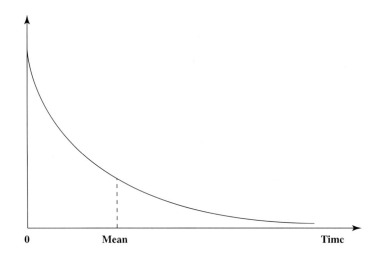

---

[1]The count of 300 arrivals includes those customers who enter the barber shop but decide not to stay because the wait would be too long. The effect of these immediate departures is analyzed in the supplement to this chapter on the CD-ROM.

the *remaining time from now* until the next arrival occurs always is the same, regardless of whether the last arrival occurred just now or a long time ago. Therefore, this distribution of the remaining time from now is the same as the distribution of the *total interarrival time* given in Figure 14.2. (This is what causes the probability of an arrival in the next minute to always be the same.) Although this concept of a lack-of-memory property takes some getting used to, it is an integral part of what is meant by having random arrivals.

The Queue

The queue is where customers wait before being served. For Herr Cutter's barber shop, the customers in the queue sit in chairs (other than the barber's chair) while waiting to begin a haircut.

Because there are two ways of counting the customers, queueing models distinguish between them with the following terminology.

> The **number of customers in the queue** (or *queue size* for short) is the number of customers waiting for service to begin. The **number of customers in the system** is the number in the queue *plus* the number currently being served.

For example, Figure 14.1 shows 7 customers in the queue plus 4 more being served by the 4 servers, so a total of 11 customers are in the system. Since Herr Cutter is the only server for his queueing system, the number of customers in his queue is one less than the number of customers in the system shown in Figure 14.2 (except when both are zero).

The **queue capacity** is the maximum number of customers that can be held in the queue. An **infinite queue** is one in which, for all practical purposes, an unlimited number of customers can be held there. When the capacity is small enough that it needs to be taken into account, then the queue is called a **finite queue.** During those times when a finite queue is full, any arriving customers will immediately leave.

Herr Cutter's queue actually is a finite queue. The queue capacity is three since he provides only three chairs (other than the barber's chair) for waiting. (He has found that his customers typically are unwilling to wait for a haircut when there already are three customers waiting in front of them.)

Unless specified otherwise, queueing models conventionally assume that the queue is an *infinite* queue. (All the models in this chapter make this assumption, but the chapter supplement on the CD-ROM introduces a model that assumes a finite queue. This model is used to analyze Herr Cutter's barber shop.)

The **queue discipline** refers to the order in which members of the queue are selected to begin service. The most common is *first-come, first-served* (FCFS). However, other possibilities include *random selection,* some *priority procedure,* or even *last-come, first-served.* (This last possibility occurs, for example, when jobs brought to a machine are piled on top of the preceding jobs and then the machine operator takes the next job to be performed off the top of the pile.)

Section 14.7 will focus on priority queueing models. Otherwise, the queueing models throughout the chapter make the conventional assumption that the queue discipline is first-come, first-served.

Service

For a basic queueing system, each customer is served individually by one of the servers. A system with more than one server is called a *multiple-server system,* whereas a *single-server system* has just one server (as for Herr Cutter's barber shop).

When a customer enters service, the elapsed time from the beginning to the end of the service is referred to as the **service time.** Service times generally vary from one customer to the next. However, basic queueing models assume that the service time has a particular probability distribution, independent of which server is providing the service.

The symbol used for the *mean* of the service-time distribution is

$$\frac{1}{\mu} = \text{expected service time}$$

where μ is the Greek letter mu. The interpretation of μ itself is

> μ = expected number of service completions per unit time for a single continuously busy server

where this quantity is called the **mean service rate.** For example, Herr Cutter's expected time to give a haircut is

$$\frac{1}{\mu} = 20 \text{ minutes} = \frac{1}{3} \text{ hour per customer}$$

so his mean service rate is

$$\mu = 3 \text{ customers per hour}$$

Different queueing models provide a choice of service-time distributions, as described next.

Some Service-Time Distributions

The most popular choice for the probability distribution of service times is the **exponential distribution,** which has the shape already shown in Figure 14.3. The main reason for this choice is that this distribution is *much* easier to analyze than any other. Although this distribution provides an excellent fit for *interarrival times* for most situations, this is much less true for *service times.* Depending on the nature of the queueing system, the exponential distribution can provide either a reasonable approximation or a gross distortion of the true service-time distribution. Caution is needed.

As suggested by Figure 14.3, the exponential distribution implies that many of the service times are quite short (considerably less than the mean) but occasional service times are very long (far more than the mean). This accurately describes the kind of queueing system where many customers have just a small amount of business to transact with the server but occasional customers have a lot of business. For example, if the server is a bank teller, many customers have just a single check to deposit or cash, but occasional customers have many transactions.

However, the exponential distribution is a poor fit for the kind of queueing system where service consists basically of a fixed sequence of operations that require approximately the same time for every customer. For example, this describes the situation where the server is an ATM machine. Although there may be small variations in service times from one customer to the next, these times generally are just about the same.

For the latter kind of queueing system, a much better approximation would be to assume **constant service times,** that is, the same service time for every customer. (This also is referred to as having a *degenerate distribution* for service times.)

The exponential and degenerate distributions represent two rather extreme cases regarding the amount of variability in the service times. A standard measure of the amount of variability is the *standard deviation* of the distribution, denoted by σ. For example, a value of σ that is nearly as large as the mean $(1/\mu)$ of a service-time distribution is a large standard deviation indicating a high degree of variability. For the two distributions considered above, the standard deviations are

$$\sigma = \text{mean} \qquad \text{for the exponential distribution}$$

$$\sigma = 0 \qquad \text{for the degenerate distribution (constant service times)}$$

For many queueing systems, the amount of variability in the service times falls somewhere between those for the exponential and degenerate distributions. Another service-time distribution that fills this middle ground is the **Erlang distribution.** (It is named after A. K. Erlang, a Danish mathematician in the early 20th century whose work for the Copenhagen Telephone Company in analyzing the waiting of telephone calls began the development of queueing theory.) This distribution has a parameter k, called the *shape parameter,* that determines the standard deviation σ. In particular,

$$\sigma = \frac{1}{\sqrt{k}} \text{ mean}$$

where k is allowed to be any positive integer $(k=1,2,3,\ldots)$. Figure 14.4 shows the shape of this distribution for several values of k.

When $k = 1$, this figure indicates that the shape of the Erlang distribution is the same as for the exponential distribution. This is no coincidence, because the two distributions ac-

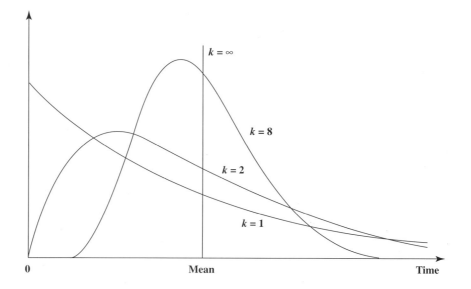

FIGURE 14.4

The shape of several Erlang distributions with the same mean but with different values of the shape parameter k.

TABLE 14.2   **The Relationship between the Standard Deviation and the Mean for Service-Time Distributions**

Distribution	Standard Deviation
Exponential	mean
Degenerate (constant)	0
Erlang, any k ($k = 1, 2, \dots$)	$\dfrac{1}{\sqrt{k}}$ mean
Erlang, $k = 2$	$\dfrac{1}{\sqrt{2}}$ mean
Erlang, $k = 4$	$\dfrac{1}{2}$ mean
Erlang, $k = 8$	$\dfrac{1}{2\sqrt{2}}$ mean
Erlang, $k = 16$	$\dfrac{1}{4}$ mean

tually are the same for $k = 1$. For larger values of k, the figure shows that the high point of the distribution (called the *mode*) no longer is at 0. In fact,

$$\text{mode} = \left(\frac{k - 1}{k} \right) \text{mean}$$

Thus, as k increases, the mode moves closer and closer to the mean and, simultaneously, the spread (standard deviation) of the distribution decreases. When $k = \infty$, so $\sigma = 0$, the Erlang distribution coincides with the degenerate distribution. Consequently, both of the previous service-time distributions can be thought of as special cases of the Erlang distribution.

Certain queueing models use still other service-time distributions, but these three are the most important.

Table 14.2 compares the standard deviation of these three service-time distributions for several values of k. Note that quadrupling k decreases the standard deviation by a factor of ½.

When choosing a service-time distribution for a queueing model to redesign a queueing system that is already in operation, a good approach is to take some observations of the actual service times. The sample average provides an estimate of the mean of the distribution. Similarly, the square root of the sample variance estimates the standard deviation. The right column of Table 14.2 then can be used to determine the distribution and (for the Erlang distribution) the integer value of k that gives the column value closest to this estimate of the standard deviation.

When designing a new queueing system, it becomes necessary to estimate what the mean and standard deviation of the service-time distribution will be, based on previous experience with similar systems.

If the standard deviation is expected to be reasonably close to the mean, practitioners normally choose the exponential distribution because of its convenience.

Labels for Queueing Models

To identify which probability distribution is being assumed for service times (and for interarrival times), a queueing model for a basic queueing system conventionally is labeled as follows:

$$\text{Distribution of service times}$$
$$\downarrow$$
$$-/\overset{}{-}/- \; \leftarrow \text{Number of servers}$$
$$\uparrow$$
$$\text{Distribution of interarrival times}$$

The symbols used for the possible distributions (for either service times or interarrival times) are

M = exponential distribution (Markovian)
D = degenerate distribution (constant times)
E_k = Erlang distribution (shape parameter = k)

For example, the *M/M*/1 model is the single-server model that assumes that both interarrival times and service times have an exponential distribution. The *M/M*/2 model is the corresponding model with two servers. Letting *s* be the symbol that represents the number of servers, the *M/M/s* model is the corresponding model that permits any number of servers. Similarly, the *M/D/s* model has exponential interarrival times, constant service times, and any desired number of servers. The $M/E_k/2$ model has exponential interarrival times, Erlang service times (with any desired value of k), and two servers.

Interarrival times also can have either a degenerate or Erlang distribution instead of an exponential distribution. The *D/M/s* model has constant interarrival times, exponential service times, and any desired number of servers. The $E_k/M/2$ has Erlang interarrival times, exponential service times, and two servers.

All the queueing models mentioned above will be considered at least briefly later in the chapter, along with results on how well such queueing systems perform.

There even are queueing models (with limited results) that permit choosing *any* probability distribution for the interarrival times or for the service times. The symbols used in these cases are

GI = general independent interarrival-time distribution (any arbitrary distribution allowed)
G = general service-time distribution (any arbitrary distribution allowed).

Thus, the *GI/M/s* model allows any interarrival-time distribution (with independent interarrival times), exponential service times, and any desired number of servers. The *M/G/*1 model has exponential interarrival times and one server but allows any service-time distribution. (We will touch later on just the latter model.)

Summary of Model Assumptions

To summarize, we list below the assumptions generally made by queueing models of a basic queueing system. Each of these assumptions should be taken for granted unless a model explicitly states otherwise.

1. Interarrival times are independent and identically distributed according to a specified probability distribution.
2. All arriving customers enter the queueing system and remain there until service has been completed.
3. The queueing system has a single *infinite queue,* so that the queue will hold an unlimited number of customers (for all practical purposes).
4. The queue discipline is first-come, first-served.

5. The queueing system has a specified number of servers, where each server is capable of serving any of the customers.

6. Each customer is served individually by any one of the servers.

7. Service times are independent and identically distributed according to a specified probability distribution.

Review Questions

1. What might the customers of a queueing system be other than people?

2. What might the server of a queueing system be other than an individual person?

3. What is the relationship between the mean arrival rate and the mean of the probability distribution of interarrival times?

4. What is the shape of the exponential distribution?

5. What is the relationship between the mean and the standard deviation of the exponential distribution?

6. What is meant by customers arriving *randomly*? Which distribution of interarrival times corresponds to random arrivals?

7. What is the distinction between the number of customers in the queue and the number in the system?

8. What is the conventional assumption made by most queueing models about the queue capacity? About the queue discipline?

9. What is the relationship between the mean of the service-time distribution and the mean service rate for a single continuously busy server?

10. What are the three most important service-time distributions? How do their standard deviations compare?

11. What information is provided by the three parts of the label for queueing models?

14.2 Some Examples of Queueing Systems

Our description of queueing systems in the preceding section may appear relatively abstract and applicable to only rather special practical situations. On the contrary, queueing systems are surprisingly prevalent in a wide variety of contexts. To broaden your horizons on the applicability of queueing models, let us take a brief look at a variety of examples of real queueing systems.

One important class of queueing systems that we all encounter in our daily lives is **commercial service systems,** where outside customers receive service from commercial organizations. The first column of Table 14.3 lists a sampling of typical commercial service systems. Each of these is a queueing system whose customers and servers are identified in the second and third columns.

Most of these examples involve the customers coming to the server at a fixed location, where a physical queue forms if customers need to wait to begin service. However, for the plumbing services and roofing services examples, the server comes to the customers, so the customers in the queue are geographically dispersed. In several other cases, the service is performed over the telephone, perhaps after some customers have been placed on hold (the queue).

Organizations also have their own **internal service systems,** where the customers receiving service are internal to the organization. As the examples in Table 14.4 indicate, these too are queueing systems. In some cases, the customers are employees of the organizations. In other examples, the customers are loads to be moved, machines to be repaired, items to be inspected, jobs to be performed, and so forth.

TABLE 14.3   Examples of Commercial Service Systems That Are Queueing Systems

Type of System	Customers	Server(s)
Barber shop	People	Barber
Bank teller service	People	Teller
ATM machine service	People	ATM machine
Checkout at a store	People	Checkout clerk
Plumbing services	Clogged pipes	Plumber
Ticket window at a movie theater	People	Cashier
Check-in counter at an airport	People	Airline agent
Brokerage service	People	Stock broker
Gas station	Cars	Pump
Call center for ordering goods	People	Telephone agent
Call center for technical assistance	People	Technical representative
Travel agency	People	Travel agent
Automobile repair shop	Car owners	Mechanic
Vending services	People	Vending machine
Dental services	People	Dentist
Roofing services	Roofs	Roofer

TABLE 14.4   Examples of Internal Service Systems That Are Queueing Systems

Type of System	Customers	Server(s)
Secretarial services	Employees	Secretary
Copying services	Employees	Copy machine
Computer programming services	Employees	Programmer
Mainframe computer	Employees	Computer
First-aid center	Employees	Nurse
Faxing services	Employees	Fax machine
Materials-handling system	Loads	Materials-handling unit
Maintenance system	Machines	Repair crew
Inspection station	Items	Inspector
Production system	Jobs	Machine
Semi-automatic machines	Machines	Operator
Tool crib	Machine operators	Clerk

Transportation service systems provide another important category of queueing systems. Table 14.5 gives some examples. For several of the cases, the vehicles involved are the customers. For others, each vehicle is a server. A few of the examples go beyond the basic kind of queueing system described in the preceding section. In particular, the airline service and elevator service examples involve a server that serves a group of customers simultaneously rather than just one at a time. The queue in the parking lot example has zero capacity because arriving cars (customers) go elsewhere to park if all the parking spaces are occupied (all the servers are busy).

There are many additional examples of important queueing systems that may not fit nicely into any of the above categories. For example, a judicial system is a queueing network, where the courts are service facilities, the judges (or panels of judges) are the servers, and the cases waiting to be tried are the customers. Various health-care systems, such as hospital emergency rooms, also are queueing systems. For example, x-ray machines and hospital beds can be viewed as servers in their own queueing systems. The initial applications of queueing theory (thanks to A. K. Erlang with the Copenhagen Telephone Company) were to telephone engineering, and the general area of telecommunications continues to be a very important area of application. Furthermore, we all have our own personal queues—

TABLE 14.5   **Examples of Transportation Service Stations That Are Queueing Systems**

Type of System	Customers	Server(s)
Highway tollbooth	Cars	Cashier
Truck loading dock	Trucks	Loading crew
Port unloading area	Ships	Unloading crew
Airplanes waiting to take off	Airplanes	Runway
Airplanes waiting to land	Airplanes	Runway
Airline service	People	Airplane
Taxicab service	People	Taxicab
Elevator service	People	Elevator
Fire department	Fires	Fire truck
Parking lot	Cars	Parking space
Ambulance service	People	Ambulance

homework assignments, books to be read, and so forth. Queueing systems do indeed pervade many areas of society.

Review Questions

1. What are commercial service systems? Also give a new example (not in Table 14.3) of such a system, including identifying the customers and server.
2. What are internal service systems? Also give a new example (not in Table 14.4) of such a system, including identifying the customers and server.
3. What are transportation service systems? Also give a new example (not in Table 14.5) of such a system, including identifying the customers and server.

14.3 Measures of Performance for Queueing Systems

Managers who oversee queueing systems are mainly concerned with two types of measures of performance:

1. How many customers typically are waiting in the queueing system?
2. How long do these customers typically have to wait?

These measures are somewhat related, since how long a customer has to wait is partially determined by how many customers are already there when this customer arrives. Which measure is of greater concern depends on the situation.

Choosing a Measure of Performance

When the customers are internal to the organization providing the service (internal service systems), the first measure tends to be more important. In this situation, forcing customers to wait causes them to be unproductive members of the organization during the wait. For example, this is the case for machine operators waiting at a tool crib or for machines that are down waiting to be repaired. Having such customers wait causes *lost productivity,* where the amount of lost productivity is directly related to the number of waiting customers. The active members of the organization may be able to fill in for one or two idle members, but not for more.

Commercial service systems (where outside customers receive service from commercial organizations) tend to place greater importance on the second measure. For such queueing systems, an important goal is to keep customers happy so they will return again. Customers are more concerned with how long they have to wait than with how many other customers are there. The consequence of making customers wait too long may be *lost profit from lost future business.*

Defining the Measures of Performance

The two measures commonly are expressed in terms of their *expected values* (in the statistical sense). To do this, it is necessary to clarify whether we are counting customers only while they are in the queue (i.e., before service begins) or while they are anywhere in the queueing system (i.e., either in the queue or being served). These two ways of defining the two types of measures thereby give us four measures of performance. These four measures and their symbols are shown below.

L = expected **number of customers in the system**, including those being served (the symbol L comes from *Line Length*)

L_q = expected **number of customers in the queue**, which excludes customers being served

W = expected **waiting time in the system** (includes service time) for an individual customer (the symbol W comes from *Waiting* time)

W_q = expected **waiting time in the queue** (excludes service time) for an individual customer

These definitions assume that the queueing system is in a **steady-state condition,** that is, the system is in its normal condition after operating for some time. During the initial *start-up period* after a queueing system opens up with no customers there, it takes awhile for the expected number of customers to reach its normal level. After essentially reaching this level, the system is said to be in a steady-state condition. (This condition also rules out such abnormal operating conditions as a temporary "rush hour" jump in the mean arrival rate.)

The choice of whether to focus on the entire queueing system (L or W) or just on the queue (L_q or W_q) depends on the nature of the queueing system. For a hospital emergency room or a fire department, the queue (the time until service can begin) probably is more important. For an internal service system, the entire queueing system (the total number of members of the organization that are idle there) may be more important.

Relationships between
L, W, L_q, and W_q

The only difference between W and W_q is that W includes the expected service time and W_q does not. Therefore, since $1/\mu$ is the symbol for the expected service time (where μ is called the *mean service rate*),

$$W = W_q + \frac{1}{\mu}$$

For example, if

W_q = ¾ hour waiting in the queue on the average

$\dfrac{1}{\mu}$ = ¼ hour service time on the average

then

W = ¾ hour + ¼ hour

= 1 hour waiting in the queueing system on the average

Perhaps the most important formula in queueing theory provides a direct relationship between L and W. This formula is

$$L = \lambda W$$

where

λ = mean arrival rate for customers coming to the queueing system

This is called **Little's formula,** in honor of the eminent management scientist John D. C. Little (a long-time faculty member at MIT), who provided the first rigorous proof of the formula in 1961.

To illustrate the formula, suppose that

W = 1 hour waiting in the queueing system on the average

λ = 3 customers per hour arrive on the average

It then follows that

$$L = (3 \text{ customers/hour})(1 \text{ hour})$$

$$= 3 \text{ customers in the queueing system on the average}$$

Here is an intuitive way to view Little's formula. Since L is the expected number of customers in the queueing system at any time, a customer looking back at the system after completing service should see L customers there on the average. With a first-come, first-served queue discipline, all L customers there normally would have arrived during this customer's waiting time in the queueing system. This waiting time is W on the average. Since λ is the expected number of arrivals per unit time, λW is the expected number of arrivals during this customer's waiting time in the system. Therefore, $L = \lambda W$.

Professor Little's proof that $L = \lambda W$ also applies to the relationship between L_q and W_q. Therefore, another version of Little's formula is

$$L_q = \lambda W_q$$

For example, if

$W_q = \frac{3}{4}$ hour waiting in the queue on the average
$\lambda = 3$ customers per hour arrive on the average

then

$$L_q = (3 \text{ customers/hour})(\tfrac{3}{4} \text{ hour})$$

$$= 2\tfrac{1}{4} \text{ customers in the queue on the average.}$$

Combining the above relationships also gives the following direct relationship between L and L_q.

$$L = \lambda W = \lambda \left(W_q + \frac{1}{\mu} \right)$$

$$= L_q + \frac{\lambda}{\mu}$$

For example, if $L_q = 2\tfrac{1}{4}$, $\lambda = 3$, and $\mu = 4$, then

$$L = 2\tfrac{1}{4} + \tfrac{3}{4} = 3 \text{ customers in the system on the average}$$

These relationships are extremely important because they enable all four of the fundamental quantities—L, W, L_q, and W_q—to be immediately determined as soon as one is found analytically. This situation is fortunate because some of these quantities often are much easier to find than others when a queueing model is solved from basic principles.

Using Probabilities as Measures of Performance

Managers frequently are interested in more than what happens *on the average* in a queueing system. In addition to wanting L, L_q, W, and W_q not to exceed target values, they also may be concerned with *worst-case scenarios*. What will be the *maximum* number of customers in the system (or in the queue) that will only be exceeded a small fraction of the time (that is, with a small probability)? What will be the *maximum* waiting time of customers in the system (or in the queue) that will only be exceeded a small fraction of the time? A manager might specify that the queueing system should be designed in such a way that these maximum numbers do not exceed certain values.

Meeting such a goal requires using the steady-state *probability distribution* of these quantities (the number of customers and the waiting time). For example, suppose that the goal is to have no more than three customers in the system at least 95 percent of the time. Using the notation

P_n = steady-state probability of having exactly n customers in the system
(for $n = 0, 1, 2, \ldots$)

meeting this goal requires that

$$P_0 + P_1 + P_2 + P_3 \geq 0.95$$

Similarly, suppose that another goal is that the waiting time in the system should not exceed two hours for at least 95 percent of the customers. Let the *random variable* $\mathcal{W}$ be the waiting time in the system for an individual customer while the system is in a steady-state condition. (Thus, W is the expected value of this random variable.) Using the probability distribution for this random variable, meeting the goal requires that

$$P(\mathcal{W} \leq 2 \text{ hours}) \geq 0.95$$

If the goal is stated in terms of the waiting time in the *queue* instead, then a different random variable $\mathcal{W}_q$ representing this waiting time would be used in the same way.

Formulas are available for calculating at least some of these probabilities for several of the queueing models considered later in the chapter. Excel templates in your MS Courseware will perform these calculations for you.

Review Questions

1. Which type of measure of performance of queueing systems tends to be more important when the customers are internal to the organization?
2. Which type of measure of performance tends to be more important for commercial service systems?
3. What are the four basic measures of performance based on expected values? What are their symbols?
4. What is meant by a queueing system being in a steady-state condition?
5. What is the formula that relates W and W_q?
6. What is Little's formula that relates L and W? That relates L_q and W_q?
7. What is the formula that relates L and L_q?
8. What kinds of probabilities can also be used as measures of performance of queueing systems?

14.4 A Case Study: The Dupit Corp. Problem

The Dupit Corporation is a long-time leader in the office photocopier marketplace. One reason for this leadership position is the service the company provides its customers. Dupit has enjoyed a reputation of excellent service and intends to maintain that reputation.

Some Background

Dupit has a service division that is responsible for providing high-quality support to the company's customers by promptly repairing the Dupit machines when needed. This work is done on the customer's site by the company's *service technical representatives,* more commonly known as **tech reps.**

Each tech rep is given responsibility for a specified territory. This enables providing personalized service, since a customer sees the same tech rep on each service call. The tech rep generally feels like a one-person territory manager and takes pride in this role.

John Phixitt is the Dupit senior vice president in charge of the service division. He has spent his entire career with the company, and actually began as a tech rep. While in this initial position, John took classes in the evening for several years to earn his business degree. Since then, he has moved steadily up the corporate ladder. He is well respected for his sound judgment and his thorough understanding of the company's business from the ground up.

John's years as a tech rep impressed upon him the importance of the tech rep's role as an ambassador of the company to its customers. He continues to preach this message regularly. He has established high personnel standards for becoming and remaining a tech rep and has built up the salaries accordingly. The morale in the division is quite high, largely through his efforts.

John also emphasizes obtaining regular feedback from a random sample of the company's customers on the quality of the service being provided. He likes to refer to this as keeping his ear to the ground. The customer feedback is channeled to both the tech reps and management for their information.

Another of John's themes is the importance of not overloading the tech reps. When he was a tech rep himself, the company policy had been to assign each tech rep enough machines in his or her territory that the tech rep would be active repairing machines 90 percent of the time (during an eight-hour working day). The intent was to maintain a high utilization of expensive personnel while providing some slack so that customers would not have to wait very long for repairs. John's own experience was that this did not work very well. He did have his idle periods about 10 percent of the time, which was helpful for catching up on his paperwork and maintaining his equipment. However, he also had frequent busy periods with many repair requests, including some long ones, and a large backlog of unhappy customers waiting for repairs would build up.

Therefore, when he was appointed to his current position, one of his first moves was to make the case to Dupit top management that tech reps needed to have more slack time to ensure providing prompt service to customers. A major part of his argument was that customer feedback indicated that the company was failing to deliver on the second and third part of the company slogan given below.

1. High-quality products.
2. High-quality service.
3. All delivered efficiently.

The company president had been promoting this slogan for years and so found this argument persuasive. Despite continuing pressure to hold costs down, John won approval for changing company policy regarding tech reps as summarized below.

> **Current Policy**: Each tech rep's territory should be assigned enough machines so that the tech rep will be active repairing machines (or traveling to the repair site) approximately 75 percent of the time. When working continuously, each tech rep should be able to repair an average of four machines per day (an average of two hours per machine, including travel time). Therefore, to minimize customer waiting times, the goal is to have an average of three repair calls per working day. Since the company's machines now are averaging 50 work days between needing repairs, the target is to assign approximately 150 machines to each tech rep's territory.

Under this policy, the company now has nearly 10,000 tech reps, with a total payroll (including benefits) of approximately $600 million per year.

The Issue Facing Top Management

Dupit has had a long succession of very successful products that has maintained its position as a market leader for many years. Furthermore, its latest product has been a particularly big winner. It is a color printer-copier that collates, staples, and so on, as well as having faxing capabilities. Thus, it is a state-of-the-art, all-in-one copier for the modern office. Sales have even exceeded the optimistic predictions made by the vice president for marketing.

However, this success also has brought its problems. The fact that the machine performs so many key functions makes it a vital part of the purchaser's office. The owner has great difficulty in getting along without it for even a few hours when it is down requiring repair. Consequently, even though the tech reps are giving the same level of service as they have in the past, complaints about intolerable waits for repairs have skyrocketed.

This crisis has led to an emergency meeting of top management, with John Phixitt the man on the spot. He assures his colleagues that service has not deteriorated in the least. There is agreement that the company is a victim of its own success. The new machine is so valuable that a much higher level of service is required.

After considerable discussion about how to achieve the needed service, Dupit's president suggests the following four-step approach to dealing with the problem.

1. Agree on a tentative new standard for the level of service that needs to be provided.
2. Develop some proposals for alternative approaches that might achieve this standard.

3. Have a management science team work with John Phixitt to analyze these alternative approaches in detail to evaluate the effectiveness and cost of each one.

4. Reconvene this group of top management to make a final decision on what to do.

The group agrees.

Discussion then turns to what the new standard should be for the level of service. John proposes that this standard should specify that a customer's average waiting time before the tech rep can respond to the request for a repair should not exceed some maximum quantity. The customer relations manager agrees and argues that this average waiting time should not exceed two hours (versus about six hours now). The group agrees to adopt two hours as the tentative standard, pending further analysis by the management science team.

> **Proposed New Service Standard**: The average waiting time of customers before the tech rep begins the trip to the customer site to repair the machine should not exceed two hours.

Alternative Approaches to the Problem

After further discussion of various ideas about how to meet this service standard, the meeting concludes. The president asks the participants who had proposed some approach to think further about their idea. If they conclude that their idea should be a particularly sound approach to the problem, they are to send him a memorandum supporting that approach.

The president subsequently receives four memoranda supporting the approaches summarized below.

> **Approach Suggested by John Phixitt:** Modify the current policy by decreasing the percentage of time that tech reps are expected to be active repairing machines. This involves simply decreasing the number of machines assigned to each tech rep and adding more tech reps. This approach would enable continuing the mode of operation for the service division that has served the company so well in the past while increasing the level of service to meet the new demands of the marketplace.

> **Approach Suggested by the Vice President for Engineering:** Provide new state-of-the-art equipment to the tech reps that would substantially reduce the time required for the longer repairs. Although expensive, this would significantly reduce the average repair time. Perhaps more importantly, it would greatly reduce the variability of repair times, which might decrease average waiting times for repairs.

> **Approach Suggested by the Chief Financial Officer:** Replace the current one-person tech rep territories by larger territories that would be served by multiple tech reps. Having teams of tech reps to back each other up during busy periods might decrease average waiting times for repairs enough that the company would not need to hire additional tech reps.

> **Approach Suggested by the Vice President for Marketing:** Give owners of the new printer-copier priority for receiving repairs over the company's other customers. Since the complaints about slow service are coming mainly from these owners, this approach might give them the service they require while still giving adequate service to other customers.

The president is pleased to have four promising approaches to consider. As previously agreed, his next step is to set up a team of management scientists (three from the company plus an outside consultant) to work with John Phixitt in analyzing these approaches in detail. They are to report back to top management with their results and recommendations in six weeks.

Before reading further, we suggest that you think about these four alternative approaches and decide which one seems most promising. You then will be able to compare with the results from the management science study.

The Management Science Team's View of the Problem

The management science team quickly recognizes that *queueing theory* will be a key technique for analyzing this problem. In particular, each tech rep's territory can be viewed as including the basic queueing system described below.

The Queueing System for Each Tech Rep

1. **The customers**: The machines needing repair.

2. **Customer arrivals**: The calls to the tech rep on his or her cellular telephone requesting repairs.

3. **The queue**: The machines waiting for repair to begin at their sites.

4. **The server**: The tech rep.

5. **Service time**: The total time the tech rep is tied up with a machine, either traveling to the machine site or repairing the machine. (Thus, a machine is viewed as leaving the queue and entering service when the tech rep begins the trip to the machine site.)

With the approach suggested by the Chief Financial Officer (enlarge the territories with multiple tech reps for each territory), this single-server queueing system would be changed to a multiple-server queueing system.

The management science team now needs to decide which specific queueing model is most appropriate for analyzing each of the four approaches. You will see this story unfold in the next few sections while we are presenting various important queueing models.

Review Questions

1. What is the company's current policy regarding the workload for tech reps?
2. What is the issue currently facing top management?
3. What is the proposed new service standard?
4. How many alternative approaches have been suggested for dealing with the issue facing top management?
5. Who now will be analyzing these approaches?
6. In the queueing system interpretation of this problem, what are the customers? The server?

14.5 Some Single-Server Queueing Models

Using the background on the elements of queueing models presented in Section 14.1, this section focuses on models of basic queueing systems having just one server. Key symbols introduced in Section 14.1 that will continue to be used here (and throughout the remainder of the chapter) are

$$\lambda = \text{mean arrival rate for customers coming to the queueing system}$$

$$= \text{expected number of arrivals per unit time}$$

$$\mu = \text{mean service rate (for a continuously busy server)}$$

$$= \text{expected number of service completions per unit time}$$

Also recall that $1/\lambda$ is the *expected interarrival time* (the average time between the arrival of consecutive customers) and $1/\mu$ is the *expected service time* for each customer.

A new symbol for this section is

$$\rho = \frac{\lambda}{\mu}$$

where ρ is the Greek letter rho. This quantity ρ is referred to as the **utilization factor,** because it represents the average fraction of time that the server is being utilized serving customers.

In the Dupit Corp. case study, under the company's current policy, a typical tech rep experiences

$\lambda = 3$ customers (machines needing repair) arriving per day on the average

$\mu = 4$ service completions (repair completions) per day on the average when the tech rep is continuously busy

Since

$$\rho = \frac{3}{4} = 0.75$$

the tech rep is active repairing machines 75 percent of the time.

For each of the queueing models, we will consider the measures of performance introduced in Section 14.3. Because of the relationships between the four basic measures—L, L_q, W, and W_q—including Little's formula given in that section, recall that all four quantities can be calculated easily as soon as one of their values has been determined. Therefore, we sometimes will be focusing on just one of these measures of performance for the following models.

The M/M/1 Model

Using the labels for queueing models given near the end of Section 14.1, recall that the first symbol (M) in the $M/M/1$ label identifies the probability distribution of *interarrival times,* the second symbol (M) indicates the distribution of *service times,* and the third symbol (1) gives the number of servers. Since M is the symbol used for the *exponential distribution,* the $M/M/1$ model makes the following assumptions.

Assumptions

1. *Interarrival times* have an exponential distribution with a mean of $1/\lambda$. (See Figure 14.3 and the description of this distribution in Section 14.1.)
2. *Service times* have an exponential distribution with a mean of $1/\mu$.
3. The queueing system has 1 server.

As discussed in Section 14.1, the first assumption corresponds to having customers arrive *randomly.* Consequently, this assumption commonly is a valid one for real queueing systems.

The second assumption also is a reasonable one for those queueing systems where many service times are quite short (well under the mean) but occasional service times are very long. Some queueing systems fit this description, but some others do not even come close.

Along with its multiple-server counterpart (considered in Section 14.6), the $M/M/1$ model is the most widely used queueing model. (It is even sometimes used for queueing systems that don't fit the second assumption very well.) A key reason is that this model has the most results readily available. Because the formulas are relatively simple, we give them for all the measures of performance below. (All these measures assume that the queueing system is in a *steady-state condition.*)

Two equivalent formulas for the *expected number of customers in the system* are

$$L = \frac{\rho}{1 - \rho} = \frac{\lambda}{\lambda - \mu}$$

Because of Little's formula ($L = \lambda W$), the *expected waiting time in the system* is

$$W = \frac{1}{\lambda}L = \frac{1}{\mu - \lambda}$$

Therefore, the *expected waiting time in the queue* (excludes service time) is

$$W_q = W - \frac{1}{\mu} = \frac{1}{\mu - \lambda} - \frac{1}{\mu} = \frac{\mu - (\mu - \lambda)}{\mu(\mu - \lambda)}$$

$$= \frac{\lambda}{\mu(\mu - \lambda)}$$

Applying the other version of Little's formula again ($L_q = \lambda W_q$), the *expected number of customers in the queue* (excludes customers being served) is

$$L_q = \lambda W_q = \frac{\lambda^2}{\mu(\mu - \lambda)} = \frac{\rho^2}{1 - \rho}$$

Even the formulas for the various probabilities are relatively simple. The probability of having exactly n customers in the system is

$$P_n - (1 - \rho)\rho^n \qquad \text{for } n = 0, 1, 2, \ldots$$

Thus,

$$P_0 = 1 - \rho$$

$$P_1 = (1 - \rho)\rho$$

$$P_2 = (1 - \rho) \rho^2$$

.

.

.

The probability that the *waiting time in the system* exceeds some amount of time t is

$$P(\mathcal{W} > t) = e^{-\mu(1-\rho)t} \qquad \text{for } t \geq 0$$

The corresponding probability that the *waiting time in the queue* exceeds t is

$$P(\mathcal{W}_q > t) = \rho e^{-\mu(1-\rho)t} \qquad \text{for } t \geq 0$$

Since this waiting time in the queue is 0 if there are no customers in the system when an arrival occurs,

$$P(\mathcal{W}_q = 0) = P_0 = 1 - \rho$$

All these formulas assume that the server has a manageable utilization factor ($\rho = \lambda/\mu$), that is, that

$$\rho < 1$$

(*All* single-server queueing models make this same assumption.) When $\rho > 1$, so that the mean arrival rate λ exceeds the mean service rate μ, the server is not able to keep up with the arrivals so the queueing system never reaches a steady-state condition. (This is even technically true when $\rho = 1$.)

There is an Excel template for the *M/M/s* model in your MS Courseware that will calculate all these measures of performance for you if you wish. All you have to do is set $s = 1$ and then specify the values of λ and μ. Since λ and μ are the *estimated* values of the mean arrival rate and mean service rate, respectively, you then can conduct sensitivity analysis on λ and μ by rerunning the template for various other possible values. All this can be done in a matter of seconds.

Applying the* M/M/1 *Model to the Case Study under the Current Policy

The Dupit management science team begins their study by gathering some data on the experiences of some representative tech reps. They determine that the company's current policy regarding tech rep workloads (they are supposed to be busy repairing machines 75 percent of the time) is operating basically as intended. Although there is some variation from one tech rep to the next, they typically are averaging about three calls requesting repairs per day. They also are averaging about two hours per repair (including a little travel time), and so can average four repairs for each eight-hour working day that they are continuously repairing machines. This verifies that the best estimates of the daily rates for a typical tech rep's queueing system (where the tech rep is the server and the machines needing repairs are the customers) are a mean arrival rate of $\lambda = 3$ customers per day and a mean service rate of $\mu = 4$ customers per day (so $\rho = \lambda/\mu = 0.75$), just as assumed under the current policy. (Other time units, such as *hourly* rates rather than *daily* rates, could be used for λ and μ, but it is essential that the *same* time units be used for both.)

The team also concludes that the customer arrivals (calls requesting repairs) are occurring *randomly,* so the first assumption of the *M/M/1* model (an exponential distribution for interarrival times) is a good one for this situation. The team is less comfortable with the second assumption (an exponential distribution for service times), since the *total service time* (travel time plus repair time) never is extremely short as allowed by the exponential distribution. However, many service times are at least fairly short (well under the mean) and occasional service times are very long, which does fit the exponential distribution reasonably well. Furthermore, calculations with the data gathered on service times indicate that the standard deviation of the service-time distribution is just about as large as the mean (they are equal for the exponential distribution). Therefore, the team decides that it is reasonable to use the *M/M/1* model to represent a typical tech rep's queueing system under the current policy.

The Excel template in Figure 14.5 shows the results from applying the various formulas for this model to this queueing system. Look first at the results at the top of column G. The expected number of machines needing repairs is $L = 3$. When excluding any machine

FIGURE 14.5

This Excel template for the M/M/s model shows the results from applying the M/M/1 model to the Dupit case study by setting $\lambda = 3$, $\mu = 4$, and $s = 1$.

	A	B	C	D	E	F	G
1		M/M/1 Queueing Model for the Dupit Corp. Problem					
2							
3			Data			Results	
4		$\lambda =$	3	(mean arrival rate)		L =	3
5		$\mu =$	4	(mean service rate)		$L_q =$	2.25
6		s =	1	(# servers)			
7						W =	1
8		Pr(W>t) =	0.368			$W_q =$	0.75
9		when t =	1				
10						$\rho =$	0.75
11		Prob(W$_q$>t) =	0.276				
12		when t =	1			$P_0 =$	0.25
13						$P_1 =$	0.188
14						$P_2 =$	0.141
15						$P_3 =$	0.105
16						$P_4 =$	0.0791
17						$P_5 =$	0.0593
18						$P_6 =$	0.0445
19						$P_7 =$	0.0334
20						$P_8 =$	0.0250
21						$P_9 =$	0.0188
22						$P_{10} =$	0.0141

	G
4	=C4/(C5–C4)
5	=C4*G8
6	
7	=G4/C4
8	=G7–1/C5
9	
10	=C4/C5
11	
12	=1–G10
13	=(1–G10)*G10
14	=(1–G10)*G10^2
15	=(1–G10)*G10^3
16	=(1–G10)*G10^4
17	=(1–G10)*G10^5
18	=(1–G10)*G10^6
19	=(1–G10)*G10^7
20	=(1–G10)*G10^8
21	=(1–G10)*G10^9
22	=(1–G10)*G10^10

	C
8	=EXP(–C5*(1–G10)*C9)

	C
11	=G10*EXP(–C5*(1–G10)*C12)

that is currently being repaired, the expected number of machines waiting to begin service is $L_q = 2.25$. The expected waiting time of a machine, measured from when the service request is submitted to the tech rep until the repair is completed, is $W = 1$ day. When excluding the repair time, the expected waiting time to begin service is $W_q = 0.75$ day. (These results are treating a machine as moving from the queue into service when the tech rep begins the trip to the site of the machine.)

While gathering data, the management science team had found that the average waiting time of customers until service begins on their failed machines is approximately six hours of an eight-hour workday (i.e., ¾ of a workday). The fact that this time agrees with the value of W_q yielded by the model gives further credence to the validity of the model for this application.

Now look at the results in column G for the P_n (the probability of having exactly n customers in the system). With $P_0 = 0.25$, the tech rep will only be busy repairing machines 75 percent of the time (as indicated by the utilization factor of $\rho = 0.75$). Since $P_0 + P_1 + P_2 = 0.58$, the tech rep will have no more than two machines needing repair (including the one being worked on) well over half the time. However, he or she also will have *much* larger backlogs with some frequency. For example, $P_0 + P_1 + P_2 + \ldots + P_7 = 0.9$, which indicates that the tech rep will have *at least* eight machines needing repair (about two days' work or more) 10 percent of the time. With all the randomness inherent in such a queueing system (the great variability in both interarrival times and service times), these very big backlogs (and many unhappy customers) will occur occasionally despite the tech rep only having a utilization factor of 0.75.

Finally, look at the results in cells C8:C12. By setting $t = 1$, the probability that a customer has to wait more than one day (eight work hours) before a failed machine is operational again is given as $P(W > 1 \text{ day}) = 0.368$. The probability of waiting more than one day before the repair begins is $P(W_q > 1 \text{ day}) = 0.276$.

Upon being shown all these results, John Phixitt comments that he understands better now why the complaints have been pouring in. No owner of such a vital machine as the new printer-copier should be expected to go more than a day (or even most of a day) before it is repaired.

Applying the* M/M/1 *Model to John Phixitt's Suggested Approach

The management science team now is ready to begin analyzing each of the suggested approaches for lowering to two hours (¼ workday) the average waiting time before service begins. Thus, the new constraint is that

$$W_q \leq \text{¼ day}$$

The first approach, suggested by John Phixitt, is to modify the current policy by lowering a tech rep's utilization factor sufficiently to meet this new service requirement. This involves decreasing the number of machines assigned to each tech rep from about 150 to some smaller number. Since each machine needs repair about once every 50 work days on the average, decreasing the number of machines in a tech rep's territory results in decreasing the mean arrival rate λ from 3 to

$$\lambda = \frac{\text{number of machines assigned to tech rep}}{50}$$

With μ fixed at four, this decrease in λ will decrease the utilization factor, $\rho = \lambda/\mu$.

Since decreasing λ decreases W_q, the largest value of λ that has $W_q \leq$ ¼ day is the one that makes W_q *equal* to ¼ day. The easiest way to find this λ is by trial and error with the Excel template, trying various values of λ until one is found where $W_q = 0.25$. Figure 14.6 shows the template that gives this value of W_q by setting $\lambda = 2$. (By using the formula for W_q, it also is possible to solve algebraically to find $\lambda = 2$.)

Decreasing λ from three to two would require decreasing the target for the number of machines assigned to each tech rep from 150 to 100. This 100 is the *maximum* number that would satisfy the requirement that $W_q \leq$ ¼ day. With $\lambda = 2$ and $\mu = 4$, the utilization factor for each tech rep would be only

$$\rho = \frac{\lambda}{\mu} = \frac{2}{4} = 0.5$$

Recall that the company's payroll (including benefits) for its nearly 10,000 tech reps currently is about $600 million annually. Decreasing the number of machines assigned to each tech rep from 150 to 100 would require hiring nearly 5,000 more tech reps to cover all the machines. The additional payroll cost would be about $270 million annually. (It is a little less than half the current payroll cost because the new tech reps would have less seniority than the current ones.) However, the management science team estimates that the additional costs of hiring and training the new tech reps, covering their work expenses, providing them with equipment, and adding more field service managers to administer them would be equivalent to about $30 million annually.

Total Additional Cost of the Approach Suggested by John Phixitt: Approximately $300 million annually.

FIGURE 14.6

This Excel template shows that, when $\mu = 4$ and s = 1, the M/M/1 model gives an expected waiting time to begin service of $W_q = 0.25$ day (the largest value that satisfies Dupit's proposed new service standard) when $\lambda = 2$.

	A	B	C	D	E	F	G
1		M/M/1 Model for John Phixitt's Approach (Reduce Machines/Rep)					
2							
3				Data			Results
4		$\lambda =$	2	(mean arrival rate)		L =	1
5		$\mu =$	4	(mean service rate)		Lq =	0.5
6		s =	1	(# servers)			
7						W =	0.5
8		Pr(W>t) =	0.135			Wq =	0.25
9		when t =	1				
10						$\rho =$	0.5
11		Prob(Wq>t) =	0.0677				
12		when t =	1			P0 =	0.5
13						P1 =	0.25
14						P2 =	0.125
15						P3 =	0.0625
16						P4 =	0.0313
17						P5 =	0.0156

The* M/G/1 *Model

This queueing model differs from the *M/M/*1 model only in the second of its assumptions summarized below.

Assumptions

1. *Interarrival times* have an exponential distribution with a mean of $1/\lambda$.
2. *Service times* can have *any* probability distribution. It is not even necessary to determine the form of this distribution. You just need to estimate the mean ($1/\mu$) and standard deviation (σ) of the distribution.
3. The queueing system has one server.

Thus, this is an extremely flexible model that only requires the common situation of *random arrivals* (equivalent to the first assumption) and a single server, plus estimates of $1/\mu$ and σ.

Here are the available formulas for this model.

$$P_0 = 1 - \rho$$

$$L_q = \frac{\lambda^2\sigma^2 + \rho^2}{2(1 - \rho)}$$

$$L = L_q + \rho$$

$$W_q = \frac{L_q}{\lambda}$$

$$W = W_q + \frac{1}{\mu}$$

These steady-state measures of performance only require that $\rho < 1$, which allows the queueing system to reach a steady-state condition.

To illustrate the formulas, suppose that the service-time distribution is the exponential distribution with mean $1/\mu$. Then, since the standard deviation σ is

$$\sigma = \text{mean} = \frac{1}{\mu} \qquad \text{for the exponential distribution}$$

the formula for L_q indicates that

$$L_q = \frac{\lambda^2\left(\dfrac{1}{\mu^2}\right) + \rho^2}{2(1 - \rho)} = \frac{\rho^2 + \rho^2}{2(1 - \rho)}$$

$$= \frac{\rho^2}{(1 - \rho)}$$

just as for the *M/M/*1 model. Having $\sigma = 1/\mu$ also causes the formulas for *L*, W_q, and *W* to reduce algebraically to those given earlier for the *M/M/*1 model. In fact, the *M/M/*1 model is just the special case of the *M/G/*1 model where $\sigma = 1/\mu$. (However, the *M/M/*1 model yields some results that are not available from the *M/G/*1 model.)

Table 14.6 gives the value of the standard deviation σ for each of the service-time distributions discussed in Section 14.1. The fourth column shows the label for the special case of the *M/G/*1 model with this service-time distribution. The rightmost column then indicates to what the L_q formula for the *M/G/*1 model reduces for this special case. Individual Excel templates are available in your MS Courseware for calculating both L_q and the other available results for each of these special cases listed in the fourth column. In addition, a template is available for the general *M/G/*1 model.

Note in the third column of the table that the value of σ for the Erlang distribution lies in the inclusive range between the values for the other two distributions (as do most real queueing systems). The value of *k* determines just where σ lies in this range. (The Erlang distribution with *k*=1 is identical to the exponential distribution.) The rightmost column shows that the value of L_q with the Erlang distribution also lies within the inclusive range between the values obtained with the other service-time distributions.

The L_q formula for the *M/G/*1 model is an enlightening one, because it reveals even more clearly than the table what effect the variability of the service-time distribution has on

TABLE 14.6   **The Values of σ and L_q for the *M/G/*1 Model with Various Service-Time Distributions**

Distribution	Mean	σ	Model	L_q
Exponential	$\dfrac{1}{\mu}$	$\dfrac{1}{\mu}$	*M/M/*1	$\dfrac{\rho^2}{1-\rho}$
Degenerate (constant service times)	$\dfrac{1}{\mu}$	0	*M/D/*1	$\dfrac{1}{2}\dfrac{\rho^2}{1-\rho}$
Erlang, with shape parameter k ($k=1,2,\ldots$)	$\dfrac{1}{\mu}$	$\dfrac{1}{\sqrt{k}}\dfrac{1}{\mu}$	$M/E_k/1$	$\dfrac{k+1}{2k}\dfrac{\rho^2}{1-\rho}$

this measure of performance. With fixed values of λ, μ, and ρ, decreasing this variability (i.e., decreasing σ) definitely decreases L_q. The same thing happens with L, W, and W_q. Thus, the consistency of the server has a major bearing on the performance of the queueing system. Given the choice between two servers with the same average speed (the same value of $1/\mu$), the one with less variability (smaller σ) definitely should be preferred over the other one. (We will discuss this further in Section 14.8.)

Considering the complexity involved in analyzing a model that permits *any* service-time distribution, it is remarkable that such a simple formula can be obtained for L_q. This formula is one of the most important results in queueing theory because of its ease of use and the prevalence of *M/G/*1 queueing systems in practice. This equation for L_q (or its counterpart for W_q) commonly is referred to as the Pollaczek-Khintchine formula, named after two pioneers in the development of queueing theory who derived the formula independently in the early 1930s.

Applying the M/G/1 Model to the Approach Suggested by the Vice President for Engineering	Dupit's vice president for engineering has suggested providing the tech reps with new state-of-the-art equipment that would substantially reduce the time required for the longer repairs. This would decrease the average repair time a little, and also would substantially decrease the variability of the repair times.

After gathering more information from this vice president and analyzing it further, the management science team makes the following estimates about the effect this approach would have on the service-time distribution.

The mean would decrease from ¼ day to ⅕ day.

The standard deviation would decrease from ¼ day to ¹⁄₁₀ day.

Thus, the standard deviation would decrease from equaling the previous mean (as for the exponential distribution) to being just half the new mean (as for the Erlang distribution with shape parameter $k=4$). Since $\mu = 1/\text{mean}$, we now have $\mu = 5$ instead of $\mu = 4$.

With $\sigma = 0.1$, the Excel template for the *M/G/*1 model yields the results shown in Figure 14.7. Note that $W_q = 0.188$ day. This big reduction from $W_q = 0.75$ day under the current policy (as given in Figure 14.5) is largely due to the big decrease in σ. If the service-time distribution continued to be an exponential distribution, then increasing μ from 4 to 5 would decrease W_q from 0.75 day to 0.3 day. The additional reduction from 0.3 day to 0.188 day is because of the large reduction in the variability of service times.

Recall that the proposed new service standard is $W_q \leq 0.25$ day. Therefore, the approach suggested by the vice president for engineering would satisfy this standard.

Unfortunately, the management science team also determines that this approach would be expensive, as summarized below.

Total Additional Cost of the Approach Suggested by the Vice President for Engineering: A one-time cost of approximately $500 million (about $50,000 for new equipment per tech rep).

Review Questions

1. What are represented by the symbols λ and μ? By $1/\lambda$ and $1/\mu$? By ρ?
2. What are the assumptions of the *M/M/*1 model?

FIGURE 14.7

This Excel template for the M/G/1 model shows the results from applying this model to the approach suggested by Dupit's vice president for manufacturing to use new state-of-the-art equipment.

	A	B	C	D	E	F	G
1		**M/G/1 Model for VP of Engineering's Approach (New Equipment)**					
2							
3			**Data**			**Results**	
4		$\lambda =$	3	(mean arrival rate)		L =	1.163
5		$1/\mu =$	0.2	(expected service time)		$L_q =$	0.563
6		$\sigma =$	0.1	(standard deviation)			
7		s =	1	(# servers)		W =	0.388
8						$W_q =$	0.188
9							
10						$\rho =$	0.6
11							
12						$P_0 =$	0.4

	G
4	=G5+C4*C5
5	=((C4^2)*(C6^2)+(G10^2))/2*(1−G10))
6	
7	=G4/C4
8	=G5/C4
9	
10	=C4*C5
11	
12	=1−G10

3. For which measures of performance (both expected values and probabilities) are formulas available for the *M/M/*1 model?

4. Which values of ρ correspond to the server in a single-server queueing system having a manageable utilization factor that allows the system to reach a steady-state condition?

5. Under Dupit's current policy, what is the average waiting time of customers until service begins on their failed machines?

6. How much more would it cost Dupit to reduce this average waiting time to ¼ workday by decreasing the number of machines assigned to each tech rep?

7. How does the *M/G/*1 model differ from the *M/M/*1 model?

8. Which service-time distribution is assumed by the *M/D/*1 model? By the *M/E$_k$/*1 model?

9. For the *M/G/*1 model, what is the effect on L_q, L, W, and W_q of decreasing the standard deviation of the service-time distribution?

10. What is the total additional cost of the approach suggested by Dupit's vice president for engineering?

14.6 Some Multiple-Server Queueing Models

Many queueing systems have more than one server, so we now turn our attention to multiple-server queueing models. In particular, we will discuss what results are available for the multiple-server counterparts of the single-server models introduced in the preceding section.

Recall that the third symbol in the label for a queueing model indicates the number of servers. For example, the *M/M/*2 model has two servers. The *M/M/s* model allows the choice of any number of servers, where *s* is the symbol for this number.

Also recall that $\rho(=\lambda/\mu)$ was the symbol used for the *utilization factor* for the server in a single-server queueing system. With multiple servers, the formula for this symbol changes to

$$\rho = \frac{\lambda}{s\mu} \quad \text{(\textbf{utilization factor})}$$

where λ continues to be the mean arrival rate (so $1/\lambda$ still is the expected interarrival time) and μ continues to be the mean service rate for a single continuously busy server (so $1/\mu$ still is the expected service time). The models assume that all the servers have the same service-time distribution, so μ is the same for every server. Since

λ = expected number of arrivals per unit time

$s\mu$ = expected number of service completions per unit time when all s servers are continuously busy

it follows that $\rho = \lambda/s\mu$ is indeed the average fraction of time that individual servers are being utilized serving customers.

In order for the servers to have a manageable utilization factor, it is again necessary that

$$\rho < 1$$

All the models make this assumption to enable the queueing system to reach a steady-state condition.

Of the four previously considered single-server models ($M/M/1$, $M/G/1$, $M/D/1$, and $M/E_k/1$), the $M/G/1$ model is the only one whose multiple-server counterpart yields no useful analytical results. Combining the complication of multiple servers with the complication of allowing the choice of any service-time distribution is too much to handle.

We begin with the $M/M/s$ model, including its application to the Dupit case study. We then mention the limited results available for the $M/D/s$ and $M/E_k/s$ models.

The M/M/s Model

Except for the last one, the assumptions are the same as for the $M/M/1$ model.

Assumptions
1. Interarrival times have an exponential distribution with a mean of $1/\lambda$.
2. Service times have an exponential distribution with a mean of $1/\mu$.
3. Any number of servers (denoted by s) can be chosen for the queueing system.

Explicit formulas are available for all the measures of performance (including the probabilities) considered for the $M/M/1$ model. However, when $s>1$, the formulas are too tedious to want to do by hand. Therefore, you should use the Excel template for the $M/M/s$ model (as demonstrated earlier in Figures 14.5 and 14.6) to generate all these results.

Another alternative is to use Figure 14.8, which shows the values of L versus the utilization factor for various values of s. (Be aware that the vertical axis uses a logarithmic scale, so you need to refer to the notches to determine the value along this axis.) By estimating L from this graph, you then can use Little's formula ($L = \lambda W$ and $L_q = \lambda W_q$), plus $W = W_q + \frac{1}{\mu}$ to calculate W, W_q, and L_q.

Applying These Models to the Approach Suggested by the Chief Financial Officer

Dupit's chief financial officer has suggested combining the current one-person tech rep territories into larger territories that would be served jointly by multiple tech reps. The hope is that, without changing the total number of tech reps, this reorganization might decrease W_q sufficiently from its current value ($W_q = 0.75$ day) to satisfy the proposed new service standard ($W_q \leq 0.25$ day).

Let us first try it with *two* tech reps assigned to each territory.

A Territory with Two Tech Reps

Number of machines:	300	(versus 150 before)
Mean arrival rate:	$\lambda = 6$	(versus $\lambda = 3$ before)
Mean service rate:	$\mu = 4$	(same as before)
Number of servers:	$s = 2$	(versus $s = 1$ before)
Utilization factor:	$\rho = \dfrac{\lambda}{s\mu} = 0.75$	(same as before)

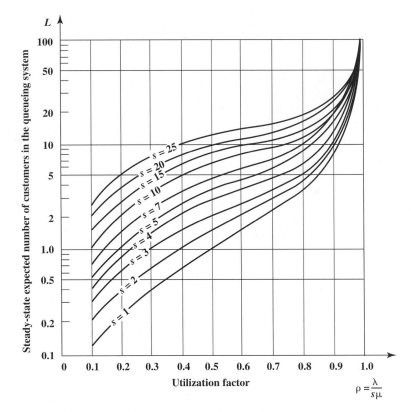

Applying the Excel template for the *M/M/s* model with these data yields the results shown in Figure 14.9, including $W_q = 0.321$ day. (The equations entered into the output cells are not given in this figure because they are very complicated, but they can be viewed in this chapter's Excel file.)

This is a very big improvement on the current value of $W_q = 0.75$ day, but does not quite satisfy the service standard of $W_q \leq 0.25$ day. So let us next see what would happen if *three* tech reps were assigned to each territory.

A Territory with Three Tech Reps

Number of machines:	450	(versus 150 before)
Mean arrival rate:	$\lambda = 9$	(versus $\lambda = 3$ before)
Mean service rate:	$\mu = 4$	(same as before)
Number of servers:	$s = 3$	(versus $s = 1$ before)
Utilization factor:	$\rho = \dfrac{\lambda}{s\mu} = 0.75$	(same as before)

With this utilization factor, Figure 14.8 indicates that L is very close to 4. Using 4 as the approximate value, and applying the relationships given in Section 14.3 (Little's formula, etc.),

$$W = \frac{L}{\lambda} = \frac{4}{9} = 0.44 \text{ day}$$

$$W_q = W - \frac{1}{\mu} = 0.44 - 0.25 = 0.19 \text{ day}$$

More precisely, the Excel template in Figure 14.10 gives $L = 3.953$ and $W_q = 0.189$ day. Since a workday is eight hours, this expected waiting time converts to just over one hour and 30 minutes.

Consequently, three-person territories would easily satisfy the proposed new service standard of $W_q \leq 0.25$ workday (two hours). Even considering that these larger territories would modestly increase the travel times for the tech reps, they still would comfortably satisfy the service standard.

FIGURE 14.9

This Excel template for the M/M/s model shows the results from applying this model to the approach suggested by Dupit's chief financial officer with two tech reps assigned to each territory.

	A	B	C	D	E	F	G
1		M/M/s Model for CFO's Approach (Combine into Teams of Two)					
2							
3			Data			Results	
4		$\lambda =$	6	(mean arrival rate)		L =	3.429
5		$\mu =$	4	(mean service rate)		Lq =	1.929
6		s =	2	(# servers)			
7						W =	0.571
8		Pr(W>t) =	0.169			Wq =	0.321
9		when t =	1				
10						$\rho =$	0.75
11		Prob(W_q>t) =	0.0870				
12		when t =	1			$P_0 =$	0.143
13						$P_1 =$	0.214
14						$P_2 =$	0.161
15						$P_3 =$	0.121
16						$P_4 =$	0.0904
17						$P_5 =$	0.0678

FIGURE 14.10

This Excel template modifies the results in Figure 14.9 by assigning three tech reps to each territory.

	A	B	C	D	E	F	G
1		M/M/s Model for CFO's Approach (Combine into Teams of Three)					
2							
3			Data			Results	
4		$\lambda =$	9	(mean arrival rate)		L =	3.953
5		$\mu =$	4	(mean service rate)		Lq =	1.703
6		s =	3	(# servers)			
7						W =	0.439
8		Pr(W>t) =	0.0898			Wq =	0.189
9		when t =	1				
10						$\rho =$	0.75
11		Prob(W_q>t) =	0.0283				
12		when t =	1			$P_0 =$	0.0748
13						$P_1 =$	0.1682
14						$P_2 =$	0.1893
15						$P_3 =$	0.1419
16						$P_4 =$	0.1065
17						$P_5 =$	0.1798

TABLE 14.7 **Comparison of W_q Values with Territories of Different Sizes for the Dupit Problem**

Number of Tech Reps	Number of Machines	λ	μ	s	ρ	W_q
1	150	3	4	1	0.75	0.75 workday (6 hours)
2	300	6	4	2	0.75	0.321 workday (2.57 hours)
3	450	9	4	3	0.75	0.189 workday (1.51 hours)

Table 14.7 summarizes the data and values of W_q for territories with one, two, and three tech reps. Note how sharply W_q decreases as the number of tech reps (servers) increases without changing the utilization factor. In fact, W_q for $s = 2$ is well under *half* that for $s = 1$, and W_q for $s = 3$ is about a *fourth* of that for $s = 1$.

These results suggest that further enlarging the territories by assigning four or more tech reps to each one would decrease W_q even further. However, there also are disadvantages to enlarging the territories. One is the possibility of a significant increase in the average time required for a tech rep to travel to the site of a failed machine. When combining only two or three one-person tech rep territories into a single joint territory, the average travel times should not increase much since the tech reps can effectively coordinate in dividing up the repair jobs based on the proximity of the jobs to the current locations of the tech reps. However, this becomes more difficult with even more tech reps in an even larger territory, so occasional travel times might become excessive. Since time traveling to a repair site is part of the total time a tech rep must devote to a repair, the *mean service rate* μ may decrease slightly from the four repairs per day assumed in Table 14.7 when the number of tech reps is more than three. For any given number of tech reps, decreasing μ increases W_q. Therefore, it is unclear how much further W_q can be decreased, if at all, by increasing the number of tech reps per territory beyond three.

Assigning a large number of tech reps to each territory has a number of practical drawbacks as well. Coordination between tech reps becomes more difficult. Customers lose the feeling of receiving personalized service when they are visited by so many different tech reps. Furthermore, tech reps lose the pride of ownership in managing their own territory and dealing with "their" customers. Personal or professional conflicts between tech reps also can arise when they share the same territory, and the opportunities for such conflicts increase with larger teams.

For all these reasons, John Phixitt concludes that normally assigning three tech reps to each territory would provide the best trade-off between minimizing these disadvantages of large territories and reducing W_q to a satisfactory level.

> **Conclusion:** The approach suggested by the chief financial officer would indeed satisfy the proposed new service standard ($W_q \leq 0.25$ day) if each three contiguous one-person tech rep territories are combined into a larger territory served jointly by the same three tech reps. Since the total number of tech reps does not change, there would be no significant additional cost from implementing this approach other than the disadvantages of larger territories cited above. To minimize these disadvantages, the territories should not be enlarged any further than having three tech reps per territory.

The M/D/s Model

The service times in many queueing systems have much less variability than is assumed by the *M/M/s* model. In some cases, there may be no variability (or almost no variability) at all in the service times. The *M/D/s* model is designed for these cases.

> **Assumptions:** Same as for the *M/M/s* model, except now all the service times are the *same*. This *constant service time* is denoted by $1/\mu$. (This is referred to as having a *degenerate* service-time distribution, which provides the symbol D for the model label.)

Constant service times arise when exactly the same work is being performed to serve each customer. When the servers are *machines,* there may literally be no variability at all in the service times. The assumption of constant service times also can be a reasonable approximation with *human servers* if they are performing the same routine task for all customers.

Table 14.6 in the preceding section reveals that, when $s = 1$, the value of L_q for the *M/D/1* model is only *half* that for the *M/M/1* model. Similar differences in L_q between the two models also occur when $s > 1$ (especially with larger values of the utilization factor ρ). Substantial differences between the models also occur for W_q, W, and L.

These large differences emphasize the importance of using the model that best fits the queueing system under study. Because the *M/M/s* model is the most convenient one, it is common practice to routinely use this model for most applications. However, doing so when there is little or no variability in the service times causes a large error in some measures of performance.

The procedures for calculating the various measures of performance for the *M/D/s* model are far more complicated than for the *M/M/s* model, so no Excel template is available in the case when $s > 1$. However, special projects have been conducted to calculate the measures. Figure 14.11 shows the values of L versus ρ for many values of s. The other

FIGURE 14.11

Values of L *for the* M/D/s *model for various values of* s, *the number of servers.*

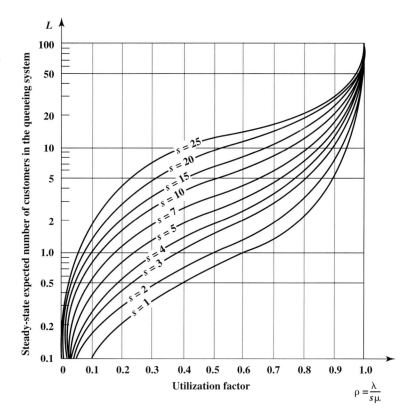

main measures (W, W_q, and L_q) then can be obtained from L by using Little's formula, and so forth (as described in Section 14.3).

The $M/E_k/s$ ***Model***

When the service times have some variability, but less so than for the exponential distribution, the $M/E_k/s$ model provides a welcome middle ground between the $M/M/s$ and $M/D/s$ models.

> **Assumptions:** Same as for the $M/M/s$ model, except now service times have an Erlang distribution with a mean of $1/\mu$ and shape parameter k ($k=1,2,\ldots$). (See Section 14.1 and Figure 14.4 there for a description of this distribution.)

As indicated in Table 14.6 in the preceding section, the standard deviation σ for the Erlang distribution with shape parameter k is

$$\sigma = \frac{1}{\sqrt{k}} \text{ mean } = \frac{1}{\sqrt{k}} \frac{1}{\mu}$$

The ability to choose any positive integer value for k provides considerable flexibility to match σ in this model quite closely to the anticipated standard deviation for the queueing system under study.

The procedures for obtaining the measures of performance for the $M/E_k/s$ model are even more complicated than for the M/D/s model. However, considerable numerical results have been generated.[2] Figure 14.12 compares the values of L for three values of k for the case of two servers ($s = 2$). The values of W, W_q, and L_q then can be obtained from L. (The percentage differences in the values of $L_q = L - \lambda/\mu$ between the cases of $k = 1$, $k = 2$, and $k = 8$ are considerably larger than these differences in L shown in the figure).

---

[2]Extensive tables and graphs for both the $M/E_k/s$ and $M/D/s$ models are available in F. S. Hillier and O. S. Yu, with D. Avis, L. Fossett, F. Lo, and M. Reiman, *Queueing Tables and Graphs* (New York: 1981), Elsevier North-Holland.

FIGURE 14.12

Values of L *for the* M/E$_k$/2 *model for various values of the shape parameter* k.

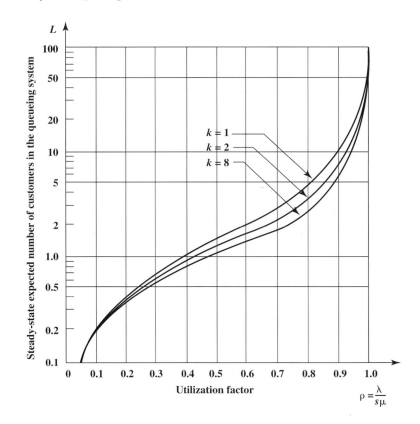

$$\rho = \frac{\lambda}{s\mu}$$

Review Questions

1. For multiple-server queueing models, what is the formula for the utilization factor ρ? What is the interpretation of ρ in terms of how servers use their time?

2. Which values of ρ correspond to the servers having a manageable utilization factor that allows the system to reach a steady-state condition?

3. Are there any measures of performance that can be calculated for the *M/M/*1 model but cannot for the *M/M/s* model?

4. How many one-person tech rep territories need to be combined into a larger territory in order to satisfy Dupit's proposed new service standard?

5. Compare the *M/M/s*, *M/D/s*, and *M/E$_k$/s* models in terms of the amount of variability in the service times.

14.7 Priority Queueing Models

All the queueing models presented so far assume that the customers are served on a first-come, first-served basis. Not all queueing systems operate that way. In some systems, the more important customers are served ahead of others who have waited longer. Management may want certain special customers to be given priority over others. In some cases, the customers in the queueing system are jobs to be performed, and the different deadlines for the jobs dictate the order in which these customers are served. Rush jobs need to be done before routine jobs.

A *hospital emergency room* is an example of a queueing system where priorities automatically are used. An arriving patient who is in critical condition naturally will be treated ahead of a routine patient who was already there waiting.

The models for such queueing systems generally make the following general assumptions.

General Assumptions

1. There are two or more categories of customers. Each category is assigned to a **priority class.** Customers in priority class 1 are given priority for receiving

service over customers in priority class 2. If there are more than two priority classes, customers in priority class 2 then are given priority over customers in priority class 3, and so on.

2. After deferring to higher priority customers, the customers within each priority class are served on a first-come, first-served basis. Thus, within a priority class, priority for receiving service is based on the time already spent waiting in the queueing system.

There actually are two types of priorities, as described below.

> **Nonpreemptive priorities:** Once a server has begun serving a customer, the service must be completed without interruption even if a higher priority customer arrives while this service is in process. However, once service is completed, if there are customers in the queue, priorities are applied to select the one to begin service. In particular, the one selected is that member of the *highest* priority class represented in the queue who has waited longest.

> **Preemptive priorities:** The lowest-priority customer being served is *preempted* (ejected back into the queue) whenever a higher-priority customer enters the queueing system. A server is thereby freed to begin serving the new arrival immediately. Whenever a server does succeed in *finishing* a service, the next customer to begin receiving service is selected just as described above for *nonpreemptive* priorities. (The preempted customer becomes the member of its priority class in the queue who has waited longest, so it hopefully will get back into service soon and, perhaps after additional preemptions, will eventually finish.)

This section includes a basic queueing model for each of these two types of priorities.

A Preemptive Priorities Queueing Model

Along with the general assumptions about priorities given above, this model makes the following assumptions.

Additional Assumptions

1. Preemptive priorities are used as just described. (Let *n* denote the number of priority classes.)
2. For priority class i ($i = 1, 2, \ldots, n$), the *interarrival times* of customers in that class have an *exponential* distribution with a mean of $1/\lambda_i$.
3. All *service times* have an *exponential* distribution with a mean of $1/\mu$, regardless of the priority class involved.
4. The queueing system has a single server.

Thus, except for the complication of using preemptive priorities, the assumptions are the same as for the *M/M/*1 model.

Since λ_i is the mean arrival rate for customers in priority class i ($i = 1, 2, \ldots, n$), $\lambda = (\lambda_1 + \lambda_2 + \ldots + \lambda_n)$ is the overall mean arrival rate for all customers. Therefore, the *utilization factor* for the server is

$$\rho = \frac{\lambda_1 + \lambda_2 + \ldots + \lambda_n}{\mu}$$

As with the previous models, $\rho < 1$ is required to enable the queueing system to reach a steady-state condition for all priority classes.

The reason for using priorities is to *decrease* the waiting times for high-priority customers. This is accomplished at the expense of *increasing* the waiting times for low-priority customers.

Assuming $\rho < 1$, formulas are available for calculating the main measures of performance (L, W, L_q, and W_q) for *each* of the priority classes. An Excel template in your MS Courseware quickly performs all these calculations for you.

A Nonpreemptive Priorities Queueing Model

Along with the general assumptions given earlier, the assumptions for this model are the ones shown next.

Additional Assumptions

1. Nonpreemptive priorities are used as described earlier in the section. (Again, let n be the number of priority classes.)

2 and 3. Same as for the preemptive priorities queueing model.

4. The queueing system can have any number of servers.

Except for using nonpreemptive priorities, these assumptions are the same as for the *M/M/s* model.

The utilization factor for the servers is

$$\rho = \frac{\lambda_1 + \lambda_2 + \dots + \lambda_n}{s\mu}$$

Again, $\rho < 1$ is needed to enable the queueing system to reach a steady-state condition for all the priority classes.

As before, an Excel template is available in your MS Courseware to calculate all the main measures of performance for *each* of the priority classes.

Applying the Nonpreemptive Priorities Queueing Model to the Approach Suggested by the Vice President for Marketing

Now we come to the last of the four approaches being investigated by Dupit's management science team. The vice president for marketing has proposed giving the printer-copiers priority over other machines for receiving service. In other words, whenever a tech rep finishes a repair, if there are *both* printer-copiers and other machines still waiting to be repaired, the tech rep *always* should choose a printer-copier (the one that has waited longest) to be repaired next, even if other machines have waited longer.

The rationale for this proposal is that the printer-copier performs so many vital functions that its owners cannot tolerate being without it as long as other machines. Indeed, nearly all the complaints about excessive waiting for repairs have come from these owners even though other machines wait just as long. Therefore, the vice president for marketing feels that the proposed new service standard ($W_q \leq 2$ hours) only needs to be applied to the printer-copiers. Giving them priority for service hopefully will result in meeting this standard while still providing satisfactory service to other machines.

To investigate this, the management science team is applying the nonpreemptive priorities queueing model. There are two priority classes.

Priority class 1:   Printer-copiers.
Priority class 2:   Other machines.

Therefore, a distinction is made between these two types of arriving customers (machines needing repairs) for the queueing system in each tech rep territory. To determine the *mean arrival rate* for each of these two priority classes (denoted by λ_1 and λ_2, respectively), the team has ascertained that about a third of the machines assigned to tech reps currently are printer-copiers. Each printer-copier requires service with about the same frequency (approximately once every 50 workdays) as other machines. Consequently, since the *total* mean arrival rate for all the machines in a one-person tech rep territory typically is three machines per day,

$$\lambda_1 = 1 \text{ customer per workday} \qquad \text{(now)}$$

$$\lambda_2 = 2 \text{ customers per workday} \qquad \text{(now)}$$

However, the proportion of the machines that are printer-copiers is expected to gradually increase until it peaks at about *half* in a couple years. At that point, the mean arrival rates will have changed to

$$\lambda_1 = 1.5 \text{ customers per workday} \qquad \text{(later)}$$

$$\lambda_2 = 1.5 \text{ customers per workday} \qquad \text{(later)}$$

The *mean service rate* for each tech rep is unchanged by applying priorities, so its best estimate continues to be $\mu = 4$ customers per workday. Under the company's current policy of one-person tech rep territories, the queueing system for each territory has a single server

($s = 1$). Since ($\lambda_1 + \lambda_2$) = 3 both now and later, the value of the utilization factor will continue to be

$$\rho = \frac{\lambda_1 + \lambda_2}{s\mu} = \frac{3}{4}$$

Figure 14.13 shows the results obtained by applying the Excel template for the non-preemptive priorities model to this queueing system *now* ($\lambda_1 = 1$ and $\lambda_2 = 2$). Figure 14.14 does the same under the conditions expected *later* ($\lambda_1 = 1.5$ and $\lambda_2 = 1.5$).

The management science team is particularly interested in the values of W_q, the expected waiting time in the queue, given in the last column of these two figures. These values are summarized in Table 14.8, where the first row comes from Figure 14.13 and the second comes from Figure 14.14.

For the printer-copiers, note that $W_q = 0.25$ workday now, which barely meets the proposed new service standard of $W_q \leq 0.25$ workday, but this expected waiting time would

FIGURE 14.13

This Excel template applies the nonpreemptive priorities queueing model to the Dupit problem now *under the approach suggested by the vice president for marketing to give priority to the printer-copiers.*

	A	B	C	D	E	F	G
1		Nonpreemptive Priorities Model for VP of Marketing's Approach					
2		(Current Arrival Rates)					
3							
4		n =	2	(# of priority classes)			
5		μ =	4	(mean service rate)			
6		s =	1	(# servers)			
7							
8							
9			λ_i	L	L_q	W	W_q
10		Priority Class 1	1	0.5	0.25	0.5	0.25
11		Priority Class 2	2	2.5	2	1.25	1
12							
13							
14							
15		λ =	3				
16		ρ =	0.75				

FIGURE 14.14

The modification of Figure 14.13 that applies the same model to the later *version of the Dupit problem.*

	A	B	C	D	E	F	G
1		Nonpreemptive Priorities Model for VP of Marketing's Approach					
2		(Future Arrival Rates)					
3							
4		n =	2	(# of priority classes)			
5		μ =	4	(mean service rate)			
6		s =	1	(# servers)			
7							
8							
9			λ_i	L	L_q	W	W_q
10		Priority Class 1	1.5	0.825	0.45	0.55	0.3
11		Priority Class 2	1.5	2.175	1.8	1.45	1.2
12							
13							
14							
15		λ =	3				
16		ρ =	0.75				

TABLE 14.8   **Expected Waiting Times* when Nonpreemptive Priorities Are Applied to the Dupit Problem**

s	When	λ_1	λ_2	μ	ρ	W_q for Printer-Copiers	W_q for Other Machines
1	Now	1	2	4	0.75	0.25 workday (2 hrs.)	1 workday (8 hrs.)
1	Later	1.5	1.5	4	0.75	0.3 workday (2.4 hrs.)	1.2 workdays (9.6 hrs.)
2	Now	2	4	4	0.75	0.107 workday (0.86 hr.)	0.429 workday (3.43 hrs.)
2	Later	3	3	4	0.75	0.129 workday (1.03 hrs.)	0.514 workday (4.11 hrs.)
3	Now	3	6	4	0.75	0.063 workday (0.50 hr.)	0.252 workday (2.02 hrs.)
3	Later	4.5	4.5	4	0.75	0.076 workday (0.61 hr.)	0.303 workday (2.42 hrs.)

*These times are obtained in units of *workdays,* consisting of eight hours each, and then converted to hours.

deteriorate later to 0.3 workday. Thus, this approach falls a little short. Furthermore, the expected waiting time before service begins for the other machines would go from $W_q = 1$ workday now to $W_q = 1.2$ workdays later. This large increase from the average waiting times being experienced under the current policy of $W_q = 0.75$ workday (as given in Figure 14.5) is likely to alienate a considerable number of customers.

Table 14.7 in the preceding section demonstrated what a great impact combining one-person tech rep territories into larger territories has on decreasing expected waiting times. Therefore, the management science team decides to investigate combining this approach with applying nonpreemptive priorities.

Combining pairs of one-person tech rep territories into single two-person tech rep territories doubles the mean arrival rates for both priority classes (λ_1 and λ_2) for each new territory. Since the number of servers also doubles (from $s = 1$ to $s = 2$) without any change in μ (the mean service rate for each server), the utilization factor ρ remains the same. These values now and later are shown in the third and fourth rows of Table 14.8. Applying the nonpreemptive priorities queueing model then yields the expected waiting times given in the last two columns.

These large reductions in the W_q values from the $s = 1$ case result in rather reasonable waiting times. Both now and later, W_q for printer-copiers is only about *half* of the maximum under the proposed new service standard ($W_q \leq 2$ hours). Although W_q for the other machines is somewhat over this maximum both now and later, these waiting times also are somewhat under the average waiting times currently being experienced (6 hours) without many complaints from members of this priority class. John Phixitt's reaction is favorable. He feels that the service standard of $W_q \leq 2$ hours really had been proposed with the printer-copiers in mind and that the other members of top management probably will also be satisfied with the values of W_q shown in the third and fourth rows of Table 14.8.

Since the analytical results reported in Table 14.7 had been so favorable for three-person tech rep territories without priorities, the management science team decides to investigate this option *with priorities* as well. The last two rows of Table 14.8 show the results for this case. Note that these W_q values for $s = 3$ are even smaller than for $s = 2$. In fact, even the W_q values for other machines nearly satisfy the proposed new service standard at this point. However, John Phixitt points out that three-person territories have substantial disadvantages compared to two-person territories. One is longer travel times to machine sites. Another is that customers would feel that service is considerably less personalized when they are seeing three different tech reps coming for repairs instead of just two. Another perhaps more important disadvantage is that three tech reps would have considerably more difficulty coordinating their work than two. John does not feel that the decreases in W_q values for $s = 3$ are worth these (and related) disadvantages.

Conclusion: Since the high-priority need is to improve service for the printer-copiers, strong consideration should be given to giving these machines priority over others for receiving repairs. However, the waiting times for both printer-copiers and other machines still would be unsatisfactory if the current one-person tech rep territories continue to be used. Enlarging to two-person territories would reduce these waiting times to levels that appear to be satisfactory, with-

TABLE 14.9   The Four Approaches Being Considered by Dupit Management

Proposer	Proposal	Additional Cost
John Phixitt	Maintain one-person territories, but reduce number of machines assigned to each from 150 to 100	$300 million per year
Vice president for engineering	Keep current one-person territories, but provide new state-of-the-art equipment to the tech reps	One-time cost of $500 million
Chief financial officer	Change to three-person territories	None, except disadvantages of larger territories
Vice president for marketing	Change to two-person territories, with priority given to the printer-copiers for repairs	None, except disadvantages of larger territories

out any significant additional (monetary) costs. Enlarging the territories even further probably would not be worthwhile in light of the disadvantages of large territories.

Management's Conclusions

After the management science team had been set up by Dupit's president to work with John Phixitt in studying this problem, the team and John had been asked to report back to the top management group dealing with the problem in six weeks. They now do so by sending their report to each member of the group. The report presents their conclusions (as stated above and in the preceding sections) on each of the four approaches they were asked to investigate. Also included are the projected measures of performance (such as in Tables 14.7 and 14.8) for these approaches.

Table 14.9 summarizes the four approaches as they now have been refined by the management science team.

At this point, the president reconvenes his top management group (including John Phixitt). The meeting begins with a brief (and well-rehearsed) presentation by the head of the management science team summarizing the analysis and conclusions of the team. The presentation is interrupted frequently by comments and questions from the group. The president next asks John Phixitt to present his recommendations.

John begins by emphasizing the many advantages of the current system of one-person territories. The first two proposals in Table 14.9 would enable continuing this system, but at a very high cost. He then concedes that he has concluded that the cost would be too high and that the time has come to modify the system in order to efficiently deliver the service that the marketplace now is demanding. (A brief discussion reveals strong agreement from the group on this point.)

This leaves the third and fourth proposals in Table 14.9 under consideration. John repeats the arguments he had given earlier to the management science team about the important advantages of two-person territories over three-person territories. He then points out that the fourth proposal not only would provide two-person territories but also would result in the printer-copiers having smaller average waiting times for repairs than under the third proposal. When the customer relations manager objects that the average waiting times of *other machines* would not meet the proposed new service standard (a maximum of two hours), John emphasizes that these waiting times still would decrease substantially from current levels and that the owners of these machines aren't even complaining now. In conclusion, John recommends adoption of the fourth proposal.

Some minor concerns are raised in the subsequent discussion, including the possibility that owners of other machines might feel that they are being treated as second-class customers. However, John indicates that the new policy would not be publicized, but, if discovered, could be easily justified to a customer. The group soon concurs with John's recommendation.

Decision: Adopt the fourth proposal in Table 14.9.

Finally, John points out that there currently are a relatively few one-person territories that are so sparsely populated that combining them into two-person territories would cause excessive travel times for the tech reps. Since this would defeat the purpose of the new policy, he suggests adopting the second proposal for these territories and then using the experience with the new equipment to make future decisions on which equipment to provide to all tech reps as service demands further increase. The group agrees.

> **Decision:** As an exception to the new policy, the second proposal in Table 14.9 is adopted just for current one-person territories that are particularly sparsely populated. The experience with the new equipment will be closely monitored to help guide future equipment purchase decisions for all tech reps.

The president thanks John Phixitt and the management science team for their outstanding work in pointing the way toward what appears to be an excellent resolution of a critical problem for the company. John graciously states that the real key was the insights obtained by the management science team by making effective use of the appropriate queueing models. The president smiles, and makes a mental note to seek John's advice more often.

Review Questions

1. How does using priorities differ from serving customers on a first-come, first-served basis?
2. What is the difference between nonpreemptive priorities and preemptive priorities?
3. Except for using preemptive priorities, the assumptions of the preemptive priorities model are the same as for which basic queueing model?
4. Except for using nonpreemptive priorities, the assumptions of the nonpreemptive priorities model are the same as for which basic queueing model?
5. For these models, which values of the utilization factor ρ enable the queueing system to reach a steady-state condition for all priority classes?
6. When applying the nonpreemptive priorities queueing model to the Dupit case study, what are the two priority classes?
7. For this application, what is the conclusion about the minimum number of tech reps per territory needed to reduce waiting times for repairs to levels that appear to be satisfactory?
8. What is the decision of Dupit's top management regarding which of the four proposed approaches will be adopted (except for particularly sparsely populated territories)?

14.8 Some Insights about Designing Queueing Systems

The Dupit case study illustrates some key insights that queueing models provide about how queueing systems should be designed. This section highlights these insights in a broader context.

There are four insights presented here. Each one was first seen when analyzing one of the four approaches proposed for the Dupit problem. After summarizing each insight, we will briefly review its application to the case study and then describe the insight in general terms.

> **Insight 1:** When designing a single-server queueing system, beware that giving a relatively high utilization factor (workload) to the server provides surprisingly poor measures of performance for the system.[3]

---

[3]The one exception is a queueing system that has *constant* (or nearly constant) interarrival times and service times. Such a system will perform very well with a high utilization factor.

FIGURE 14.15

This data table demonstrates Insight 1 in Section 14.8.

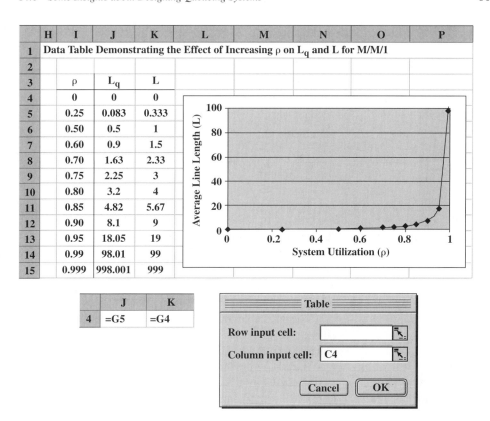

	H	I	J	K	L	M	N	O	P
1		Data Table Demonstrating the Effect of Increasing ρ on L_q and L for M/M/1							
2									
3		ρ	L_q	L					
4		0	0	0					
5		0.25	0.083	0.333					
6		0.50	0.5	1					
7		0.60	0.9	1.5					
8		0.70	1.63	2.33					
9		0.75	2.25	3					
10		0.80	3.2	4					
11		0.85	4.82	5.67					
12		0.90	8.1	9					
13		0.95	18.05	19					
14		0.99	98.01	99					
15		0.999	998.001	999					

	J	K
4	=G5	=G4

Table

Row input cell: [   ]

Column input cell: [C4]

[Cancel] [OK]

This insight arose in Section 14.5 when analyzing John Phixitt's suggested approach of decreasing the utilization factor ρ for each tech rep sufficiently to meet the proposed new service standard (a maximum average waiting time for repairs of two hours). The current $\rho=0.75$ gave average waiting times of six hours, which falls far short of this standard. It was necessary to decrease ρ all the way down to $\rho=0.5$ to meet this standard.

To further demonstrate this insight, we have used the Excel template for the *M/M/s* model (previously shown in Figures 14.5, 14.6, 14.9, and 14.10), with $s = 1$ and $\mu = 1$ (so the utilization factor ρ equals λ), to generate the data table in Figure 14.15. For any single-server queueing system fitting the basic *M/M/*1 model, this spreadsheet tabulates the expected number of customers in the queue (L_q) and in the system (L) for various values of ρ, and then plots L versus ρ on the right. (From Little's formula, the corresponding values of W_q and W are obtained by dividing L_q and L by the mean arrival rate λ.) Note how rapidly L_q and L increase with even small increases in ρ. For example, L triples when ρ is increased from 0.5 to 0.75, and then triples again when increasing ρ from 0.75 to 0.9. As ρ is increased above 0.9, L_q and L grow astronomically.

Managers normally strive for a high utilization factor for their employees, machines, equipment, and so on. This is an important part of running an efficient business. A utilization factor of 0.9 or higher would be considered desirable. However, all this should change when the employee or machine or piece of equipment is the server in a single-server queueing system that has considerable variability in its interarrival times and service times (such as for an *M/M/*1 system). For most such systems, the cognizant manager would consider it unacceptable to *average* having nine customers wait in the system (L = 9 with ρ = 0.9). If so, a utilization factor somewhat less (perhaps much less) than 0.9 would be needed. For example, we just mentioned that meeting Dupit's proposed service standard with John Phixitt's original suggested approach required reducing the utilization factor all the way down to ρ = 0.5.

Insight 2: Decreasing the *variability* of service times (without any change in the mean) improves the performance of a single-server queueing system substantially. (This also tends to be true for multiple-server queueing systems, especially with higher utilization factors.)

This insight was found in the Dupit study while analyzing the proposal by the vice president for engineering to provide new state-of-the-art equipment to all the tech reps. As

FIGURE 14.16

This data table demonstrates Insight 2 in Section 14.8.

	H	I	J	K	L	M	N
1		Data Table Demonstrating the Effect of Decreasing σ on L_q for M/G/1					
2							
3				L_q			
4							
5		ρ	σ = mean	σ = mean/2	σ = 0		
6		0.50	0.500	0.313	0.250		
7		0.75	2.250	1.406	1.125		
8		0.90	8.100	5.063	4.050		
9		0.99	98.100	61.256	49.005		

described at the end of Section 14.5, this approach would decrease both the *mean* and *standard deviation* of the service-time distribution. Decreasing the mean also decreased the utilization factor, which decreased the expected waiting time W_q. Decreasing the standard deviation σ (which measures the amount of variability) then provided an *additional* 37.5 percent reduction in W_q. Insight 2 refers to this latter substantial improvement in W_q (and in the other measures of performance).

The data table in Figure 14.16 demonstrates the effect on L_q of decreasing the standard deviation σ of the service-time distribution for any *M/G/1* queueing system. (This table was generated from the Excel template introduced in Figure 14.7 for the *M/G/1* model.) As you read the table from left to right, σ decreases from equaling the mean of the distribution (as for the *M/M/1* model) to being *half* the mean (as for the *M/E_k/1* model with $k = 4$) and then to σ = 0 (as for the *M/D/1* model).

In each row of this table, the value in the fourth column is only *half* that in the second column, so completely eliminating the variability of the service times gives a large improvement. However, the value in the third column is only 62.5 percent of that in the second column, so even cutting the variability in half provides most of the improvement from completely eliminating the variability. Therefore, whatever can be done to reduce the variability even modestly is going to improve the performance of the system significantly.

Insight 3: *Multiple-server* queueing systems can perform satisfactorily with somewhat higher utilization factors than can single-server queueing systems. For example, *pooling servers* by combining separate single-server queueing systems into one multiple-server queueing system (without changing the utilization factor) greatly improves the measures of performance.

This insight was gained during the Dupit study while investigating the proposal by the chief financial officer to combine one-person territories into larger territories served jointly by multiple tech reps. Table 14.7 in Section 14.6 summarizes the great impact that this approach would have on improving average waiting times to begin repairs (W_q). In particular, W_q for two-person territories is well under *half* that for one-person territories, and W_q for three-person territories is about a *fourth* of that for one-person territories, even though the utilization factor is the same for all these cases.

These dramatic improvements are not unusual. In fact, it has been found that pooling servers as described below *always* provides similar improvements.

The Impact of Pooling Servers: Suppose you have a number (denoted by *n*) of identical single-server queueing systems that fit the *M/M/1* model. Suppose you then combine these *n* systems (without changing the utilization factor) into a single queueing system that fits the *M/M/s* model, where the number of servers is $s = n$. This change *always* improves the value of W_q by *more* than dividing by *n*, that is,

$$W_q(\text{for combined system}) < \frac{W_q(\text{for each single–server system})}{n}$$

Although this inequality is not guaranteed to hold if these queueing systems do not fit the *M/M/1* and *M/M/s* models, the improvement in W_q by combining systems still will be very substantial for other models as well.

Insight 4: Applying *priorities* when selecting customers to begin service can greatly improve the measures of performance for high-priority customers.

This insight became evident during the Dupit study while investigating the proposal by the vice president for marketing to give higher (nonpreemptive) priority to repairing the printer-copiers than to repairing other machines. Table 14.8 in the preceding section gives the values of W_q for the printer-copiers and for the other machines under this proposal. Comparing these values to those in Table 14.7 without priorities shows that giving priority to the printer-copiers would reduce their waiting times now dramatically (but would also increase the waiting times for other machines). Later, as printer-copiers become a larger proportion of the machines being serviced (half instead of a third), the reduction in their waiting times would not be quite as large.

For other queueing systems as well, the impact of applying priorities depends somewhat on the proportion of the customers in the respective priority classes. If the proportion in the top priority class is small, the measures of performance for these customers will improve tremendously. If the proportion is large, the improvement will be more modest.

Preemptive priorities give an even stronger preference to high-priority customers than do the *nonpreemptive* priorities used for the Dupit problem. Therefore, applying preemptive priorities improves the measures of performance for customers in the top priority class even more than applying nonpreemptive priorities.

Review Questions

1. What is the effect of giving a relatively large utilization factor (workload) to the server in a single-server queueing system?
2. What happens to the values of L_q and L for the $M/M/1$ model when ρ is increased well above 0.9?
3. What is the effect of decreasing the variability of service times (without any change in the mean) on the performance of a single-server queueing system?
4. For an $M/G/1$ queueing system, does cutting the variability (standard deviation) of service times in half provide most of the improvement from completely eliminating the variability?
5. What is the effect of combining separate single-server queueing systems into one multiple-server queueing system (without changing the utilization factor)?
6. What is the effect of applying priorities when selecting customers to begin service?
7. Do preemptive priorities or nonpreemptive priorities give the greater improvement in the measures of performance for customers in the top priority class?

14.9 Economic Analysis of the Number of Servers to Provide

When designing a queueing system, a key question often is how many servers to provide. Providing too many causes excessive costs. Providing too few causes excessive waiting by the customers. Therefore, choosing the number of servers involves finding an appropriate trade-off between the cost of the servers and the amount of waiting.

In many cases, the consequences to an organization of making its customers wait can be expressed as a **waiting cost.** This is especially true when the customers are *internal* to the organization, such as the employees of a company. Making one's own employees wait causes *lost productivity,* which results in *lost profit.* This lost profit is the waiting cost.

A manager is interested in minimizing the total cost. Let

TC = expected total cost per unit time
SC = expected service cost per unit time
WC = expected waiting cost per unit time

Then the objective is to choose the number of servers so as to

$$\text{Minimize} \quad \text{TC} = \text{SC} + \text{WC}$$

When each server costs the same, the **service cost** is

$$SC = C_s s$$

where

    C_s = cost of a server per unit time
    s = number of servers

When the waiting cost is proportional to the amount of waiting, this cost can be expressed as

$$WC = C_w L$$

where

    C_w = Waiting cost per unit time for each customer in the queueing system
    L = expected number of customers in the queueing system

Therefore, after estimating the constants C_s and C_w, the goal is to choose the value of s so as to

$$\text{Minimize} \qquad TC = C_s s + C_w L$$

By choosing the queueing model that fits the queueing system, the value of L can be obtained for various values of s. Increasing s decreases L, at first rapidly and then gradually more slowly.

Figure 14.17 shows the general shape of the SC, WC, and TC curves versus the number of servers s. (For better conceptualization, we have drawn these as smooth curves even though the only feasible values of s are $s = 1, 2, \ldots$.) By calculating TC for consecutive values of s until TC stops decreasing and starts increasing instead, it is straightforward to find the number of servers that minimizes total cost. The following example illustrates this process.

An Example

The Acme Machine Shop has a tool crib to store tools required by the shop mechanics. Two clerks run the tool crib. The tools are handed out by the clerks as the mechanics arrive and request them and are returned to the clerks when they are no longer needed. There have been

FIGURE 14.17

The shape of the cost curves for determining the number of servers to provide.

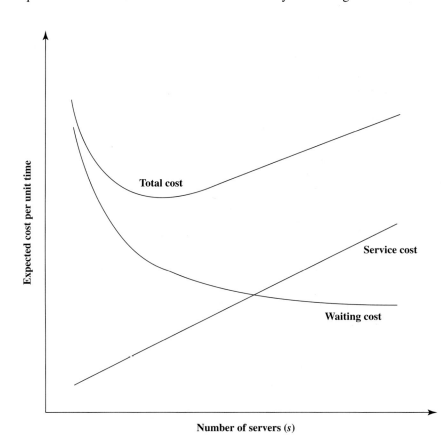

complaints from supervisors that their mechanics have had to waste too much time waiting to be served at the tool crib, so it appears that there should be *more* clerks. On the other hand, management is exerting pressure to reduce overhead in the plant, and this reduction would lead to *fewer* clerks. To resolve these conflicting pressures, a management science study is being conducted to determine just how many clerks the tool crib should have.

The tool crib constitutes a queueing system, with the clerks as its servers and the mechanics as its customers. After gathering some data on interarrival times and service times, the management science team has concluded that the queueing model that fits this queueing system best is the *M/M/s* model. The estimates of the mean arrival rate λ and the mean service rate (per server) μ are

$\lambda = 120$ customers per hour
$\mu = 80$ customers per hour

so the utilization factor for the two clerks is

$$\rho = \frac{\lambda}{s\mu} = \frac{120}{2(80)} = 0.75$$

The total cost to the company of each tool crib clerk is about \$20 per hour, so $C_s = \$20$. While a mechanic is busy, the value to the company of his or her output averages about \$48 per hour, so $C_w = \$48$. Therefore, the management science team now needs to find the number of servers (tool crib clerks) *s* that will

$$\text{Minimize} \quad TC = \$20s + \$48L$$

An Excel template has been provided in your MS Courseware for calculating these costs with the *M/M/s* model. All you need to do is enter the data for the model along with the unit service cost C_s, the unit waiting cost C_w, and the number of servers *s* you want to try. The template then calculates SC, WC, and TC. This is illustrated in Figure 14.18 with $s = 3$ for this example. By repeatedly entering alternative values of *s*, the template then can reveal which value minimizes TC in a matter of seconds.

Figure 14.19 shows a data table that has been generated from this template by repeating these calculations for $s = 1, 2, 3, 4,$ and 5. Since the utilization factor for $s = 1$ is

FIGURE 14.18

This Excel template for using economic analysis to choose the number of servers with the M/M/s model is applied here to the Acme Machine Shop example with s = 3.

	A	B	C	D	E	F	G
1		**Economic Analysis of Acme Machine Shop Example**					
2							
3			**Data**				**Results**
4		$\lambda =$	120	(mean arrival rate)		**L =**	1.737
5		$\mu =$	80	(mean service rate)		**L$_q$ =**	0.23684
6		s =	3	(# servers)			
7						**W =**	0.0145
8		Pr(W>t) =	0.1353			**W$_q$ =**	0.0019737
9		when t =	0.05				
10						$\rho =$	0.5
11		Prob(W_q>t) =	0.0677				
12		when t =	0.05			P$_0$ =	0.211
13						P$_1$ =	0.118
14		C$_S$ =	\$20	(cost/server/unit time)		P$_2$ =	0.0592
15		C$_W$ =	\$48	(waiting cost/unit time)		P$_3$ =	0.0296
16		Cost of Service =	\$60.00			P$_4$ =	0.01480
17		Cost of Waiting =	\$83.37			P$_5$ =	0.00740
18		Total Cost =	\$143.37			P$_6$ =	0.003701

	C
16	=C14*C6
17	=C15*G4
18	=C16+C17

FIGURE 14.19

*This data table compares
the expected hourly costs
with various alternative
numbers of clerks assigned to
the Acme Machine Shop
tool crib.*

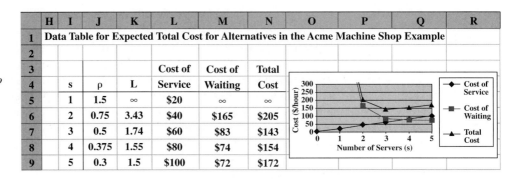

	H	I	J	K	L	M	N	O	P	Q	R
1	Data Table for Expected Total Cost for Alternatives in the Acme Machine Shop Example										
2											
3					Cost of	Cost of	Total				
4		s	ρ	L	Service	Waiting	Cost				
5		1	1.5	∞	$20	∞	∞				
6		2	0.75	3.43	$40	$165	$205				
7		3	0.5	1.74	$60	$83	$143				
8		4	0.375	1.55	$80	$74	$154				
9		5	0.3	1.5	$100	$72	$172				

$\rho = 1.5$, a single clerk would be unable to keep up with the customers, so this option is ruled out. All larger values of s are feasible, but $s = 3$ has the smallest total cost. Furthermore, $s = 3$ would decrease the current total cost for $s = 2$ by $62 per hour. Therefore, despite management's current drive to reduce overhead (which includes the cost of tool crib clerks), the management science team recommends that a third clerk be added to the tool crib. Note that this recommendation would decrease the utilization factor for the clerks from an already modest 0.75 all the way down to 0.5. However, because of the large improvement in the productivity of the mechanics (who are much more expensive than the clerks) through decreasing their time wasted waiting at the tool crib, management adopts the recommendation.

Review Questions

1. What is the trade-off involved in choosing the number of servers for a queueing system?
2. What is the nature of the waiting cost when the customers for the queueing system are the company's own employees?
3. When the waiting cost is proportional to the amount of waiting, what is an expression for the waiting cost?
4. What does the Acme Machine Shop example demonstrate about the advisability of always maintaining a relatively high utilization factor for the servers in a queueing system?

14.10 Some Award-Winning Applications of Queueing Models

Section 1.2 describes the prestigious Franz Edelman Awards for Management Science Achievement that are awarded annually. A rather substantial number of these awards have been given for innovative applications of queueing models. We briefly describe some of these applications below.

One of the early first-prize winners (November 1975 issue, Part 2, of *Interfaces*) was the **Xerox Corporation.** The company had recently introduced a major new duplicating system that was proving to be particularly valuable for its owners. Consequently, these customers were demanding that Xerox's tech reps reduce the waiting times to repair the machines. A management science team then applied queueing models to study how best to meet the new service requirements. This resulted in replacing the previous one-person tech rep territories by larger three-person tech rep territories. This change had the dramatic effect of both substantially reducing the average waiting times of the customers and increasing the utilization of the tech reps by over 50 percent.

Yes, the Dupit case study is based on this award-winning application (with some new enhancements). Although this application occurred many years ago, the case study demonstrates that the same principles for how to apply queueing models are equally valid today.

In Sections 2.1 and 3.8, we described an award-winning application by **United Airlines** (January 1986 issue of *Interfaces*) that resulted in annual savings of over $6 million. This application involved scheduling the work assignments of United's 4,000 reservations sales representatives and support personnel at its 11 reservations offices and the 1,000 customer service agents at its 10 largest airports. After determining how many employees are needed at each location during each half hour of the week, we discussed in these earlier sections how linear programming was applied to design the work schedules for all the employees to meet these service requirements most efficiently. However, we never mentioned how these service requirements on the number of employees needed each half hour were determined.

We now are in a position to point out that these service requirements were determined by applying *queueing models*. Each specific location (e.g., the check-in counters at an airport) constitutes a queueing system with the employees as the servers. After forecasting the mean arrival rate during each half hour of the week, queueing models are used to find the minimum number of servers that will provide satisfactory measures of performance for the queueing system.

L.L. Bean, Inc., the large telemarketer and mail-order catalog house, relied mainly on queueing models for its award winning study of how to allocate its telecommunications resources. (The article describing this study is in the January 1991 issue of *Interfaces,* and other articles giving additional information are in the November 1989 and March–April 1993 issues of this journal.) The telephone calls coming in to its call center to place orders are the customers in a large queueing system, with the telephone agents as the servers. The key questions being asked during the study were the following.

1. How many telephone trunk lines should be provided for incoming calls to the call center?
2. How many telephone agents should be scheduled at various times?
3. How many hold positions should be provided for customers waiting for a telephone agent? (Note that the limited number of hold positions causes the system to have a *finite queue.*)

For each interesting combination of these three quantities, queueing models provide the measures of performance of the queueing system. Given these measures, the management science team carefully assessed the cost of lost sales due to making some customers either incur a busy signal or be placed on hold too long. By adding the cost of the telemarketing resources, the team then was able to find the combination of the three quantities that minimizes the expected total cost. This resulted in cost savings of $9 to $10 million per year.

New York City has a long-standing tradition of using management science techniques in planning and operating many of its complex urban service systems. Starting in the late 1960s, award-winning studies involving queueing models have been conducted for its Fire Department and its Police Department. (Fires and police emergencies are the customers in these respective queueing systems.) Subsequently, major management science studies (including several more involving queueing models) have been conducted for its Department of Sanitation, Department of Transportation, Department of Health and Hospitals, Department of Environmental Protection, Office of Management and Budget, and Department of Probation. Because of the success of these studies, many of these departments now have their own in-house management science groups.

The award-winning study in New York City that we will describe here involves its *arrest-to-arraignment system.* This system consists of the process from when individuals are arrested until they are arraigned (the first court appearance before an arraignment judge, who determines whether there was probable cause for the arrest). Before the study, the city's arrestees (the customers in a queueing system) were in custody waiting to be arraigned for an average of 40 hours (occasionally more than 70 hours). These waiting times were considered excessive, because the arrestees were being held in crowded, noisy conditions that were emotionally stressful, unhealthy, and often physically dangerous. Therefore, a two-year management science study was conducted to overhaul the system. Both queueing models and computer simulation (the subject of the next chapter) were used. This led to sweeping operational and policy changes that *simultaneously* reduced average waiting times until arraignment to 24 hours or less and provided annual savings of $9.5 million. (See the January–February 1993 issue of *Interfaces* for details.)

The first prize in the 1993 competition was won by **AT&T** for a study that (like the preceding one) also combined the use of queueing models and computer simulation (January–February 1994 issue of *Interfaces*). The models are of both AT&T's telecommunication network and the call center environment for the typical business customers of AT&T that have such a center. The purpose of the study was to develop a user-friendly PC-based system that AT&T's business customers can use to guide them in how to design or redesign their call centers. Since call centers comprise one of the United States' fastest growing industries, this system had been used about 2,000 times by AT&T's business customers by 1992. This resulted in more than $750 million in annual profit for these customers.

There have been many other award winning applications of queueing models, as well as numerous additional articles describing other successful applications. However, the several examples presented in this section hopefully have given you a feeling for the kinds of applications that are occurring and for the impact they sometimes have.

Review Questions

1. What change in tech rep territories was made as a result of the award-winning application of queueing models at the Xerox Corporation?
2. What was found by using queueing models in the award-winning study at United Airlines?
3. Decisions needed to be made on which three quantities in the award-winning study at L.L. Bean, Inc.?
4. Who are the customers in the queueing system that was studied in the award-winning application in New York City?
5. How much additional annual profit was obtained by the business customers of AT&T by using its system to guide the design or redesign of their call centers?

14.11 Summary

Queueing systems are prevalent throughout society. The adequacy of these systems can have an important effect on the quality of life and the productivity of the economy.

Key components of a queueing system are the *arriving customers,* the *queue* in which they wait for service, and the *servers* that provide the service. A queueing model representing a queueing system needs to specify the number of servers, the distribution of interarrival times, and the distribution of service times. An *exponential* distribution usually is chosen for the distribution of interarrival times because this corresponds to the common phenomenon of arrivals occurring randomly. An exponential distribution sometimes provides a reasonable fit to the service-time distribution as well, and is a particularly convenient choice in terms of ease of analysis. Other probability distributions sometimes used for the service-time distribution include the *degenerate* distribution (constant service times) and the *Erlang* distribution.

Key measures of performance of queueing systems are the expected values of the number of customers in the queue or in the system (the latter adds on customers currently being served) and of the waiting time of a customer in the queue or in the system. General relationships between these expected values, including Little's formula, enable all four values to be determined immediately as soon as one has been found. In addition to the expected values, the probability distributions of these quantities are sometimes used as measures of performance as well.

This chapter's case study has the top management of the Dupit Corporation grappling with a difficult issue. The company's customers now are demanding a much higher level of service in promptly repairing the photo copiers (and particularly a new printer-copier) purchased from the company. Dupit already is spending $600 million per year servicing these machines. Each tech rep territory includes a queueing system with the tech rep as the server and the machines needing repairs as the customers. A management science team finds that the *M/M/*1 model, the *M/G/*1 model, the *M/M/s* model, and a nonpreemptive priorities model enable analyzing the alternative approaches to redesigning this queueing system. This analysis leads to top management adopting a policy of combining pairs of one-person tech rep territories into two-person territories that give priority to repairing the printer copiers. This provides the needed level of service without a significant increase in cost.

Other queueing models discussed in the chapter include the *M/D/*1 and *M/D/s* models, the *M/E_k/*1 and *M/E_k/s* models, and a preemptive priorities model. A supplement to this chapter on the CD-ROM also introduces the finite queue variation and the finite calling population variation of the *M/M/s* model.

Section 14.8 presents four key insights that queueing models provide about how queueing systems should be designed. Each of these insights also is illustrated by the Dupit case study.

The chapter concludes with a description of five award-winning applications of queueing models. Each of these applications led to annual savings of many millions of dollars.

Glossary

Commercial service system A queueing system where a commercial organization provides a service to customers from outside the organization. (Section 14.2) 581

Constant service times Every customer has the same service time. (Section 14.1) 578

Customers A generic term that refers to whichever kind of entity (people, vehicles, machines, items, etc.) is coming to the queueing system to receive service. (Section 14.1) 574

Erlang distribution A common service-time distribution whose shape parameter k specifies the amount of variability in the service times. Figure 14.4 shows its shape. (Section 14.1) 578

Exponential distribution The most popular choice for the probability distribution of both interarrival times and service times. Its shape is shown in Figure 14.3. (Section 14.1) 578

Finite queue A queue that can hold only a limited number of customers. (Section 14.1) 577

Infinite queue A queue that can hold an essentially unlimited number of customers. (Section 14.1) 577

Interarrival time The elapsed time between consecutive arrivals to a queueing system. (Section 14.1) 575

Internal service system A queueing system where the customers receiving service are internal to the organization providing the service. (Section 14.2) 581

Lack-of-memory property When referring to arrivals, this property is that the time of the next arrival is completely uninfluenced by when the last arrival occurred. Also called the Markovian property. (Section 14.1) 576

Little's formula The formula $L = \lambda W$, or $L_q = \lambda W_q$. (Section 14.3) 584

Mean arrival rate The expected number of arrivals to a queueing system per unit time. (Section 14.1) 575

Mean service rate The expected number of service completions per unit time for a single continuously busy server. (Section 14.1) 578

Nonpreemptive priorities Priorities for selecting the next customer to begin service when a server becomes free. However, these priorities do not affect customers who already have begun service. (Section 14.7) 603

Number of customers in the queue The number of customers who are waiting for service to begin. (Sections 14.1, 14.3) 577, 584

Number of customers in the system The total number of customers in the queueing system, either waiting for service to begin or currently being served. (Sections 14.1, 14.3) 577, 584

Preemptive priorities Priorities for serving customers that include ejecting the lowest-priority customer being served back into the queue in order to serve a higher-priority customer that has just entered the queueing system. (Section 14.7) 603

Priority classes Categories of customers that are given different priorities for receiving service. (Section 14.7) 602

Queue The waiting line in a queueing system. The queue does not include customers who are already being served. (Section 14.1) 574

Queue capacity The maximum number of customers that can be held in the queue. (Section 14.1) 577

Queue discipline The rule for determining the order in which members of the queue are selected to begin service. (Section 14.1) 577

Queueing system A place where customers receive some kind of service from a server, perhaps after waiting in a queue. (Section 14.1) 574

Server An entity that is serving the customers coming to a queueing system. (Section 14.1) 574

Service cost The cost associated with providing the servers in a queueing system. (Section 14.9) 612

Service time The elapsed time from the beginning to the end of a customer's service. (Section 14.1) 577

Steady-state condition The normal condition that a queueing system is in after operating for some time with a fixed utilization factor less than one. (Section 14.3) 584

Tech rep An abbreviated name for the service technical representatives in the Dupit case study. (Section 14.4) 586

Transportation service system A queueing system involving transportation, so that either the customers or the server(s) are vehicles. (Section 14.2) 582

Utilization factor The average fraction of time that the servers are being utilized serving customers. (Sections 14.5, 14.6) 589, 597

Waiting cost The cost associated with making customers wait in a queueing system. (Section 14.9)   611

Waiting time in the queue The elapsed time that an individual customer spends in the queue waiting for service to begin. (Section 14.3)   584

Waiting time in the system The elapsed time that an individual customer spends in the queueing system both before service begins and during service. (Section 14.3)   584

Key Symbols

λ = mean arrival rate   (Section 14.1)

μ = mean service rate   (Section 14.1)

s = number of servers   (Section 14.1)

L = expected number of customers in the system

(Section 14.3)

L_q = expected number of customers in the queue

(Section 14.3)

W = expected waiting time in the system   (Section 14.3)

W_q = expected waiting time in the queue   (Section 14.3)

ρ = utilization factor for the servers

(Sections 14.5 and 14.6)

Learning Aids for This Chapter in Your MS Courseware

"Ch. 14—Queueing Models" Excel File:

Template for *M/M/s Model*
Template for *M/G/1 Model*
Template for *M/D/1 Model*
Template for *M/E_k/1 Model*
Template for *Nonpreemptive Priorities Model*
Template for *Preemptive Priorities Model*
Template for *M/M/s Economic Analysis of Number of Servers*

Supplement to This Chapter on the CD-ROM:

The Finite Queue and Finite Calling Population Variations of the M/M/s Model

"Ch. 14 Supplement" Excel File:

Template for *Finite Queue Variation of M/M/s Model*
Template for *Finite Calling Population Variation of M/M/s Model*

Problems

To the left of the following problems (or their parts), we have inserted the symbol E (for Excel) whenever one of the above templates can be helpful. An asterisk on the problem number indicates that at least a partial answer is given in the back of the book.

14.1. Consider a typical hospital emergency room.

    a. Describe why it is a queueing system.

    b. What is the *queue* in this case? Describe how you would expect the queue discipline to operate.

    c. Would you expect *random arrivals*?

    d. What are *service times* in this context? Would you expect much variability in the service times?

14.2. Identify the customers and the servers in the queueing system in each of the following situations.

    a. The checkout stand in a grocery store.

    b. A fire station.

    c. The toll booth for a bridge.

    d. A bicycle repair shop.

    e. A shipping dock.

    f. A group of semiautomatic machines assigned to one operator.

    g. The materials-handling equipment in a factory area.

    h. A plumbing shop.

    i. A job shop producing custom orders.

    j. A secretarial word processing pool.

14.3.* For each of the following statements about using the exponential distribution as the probability distribution of interarrival times, label the statement as true or false and then justify your answer by referring to a specific statement in the chapter.

    a. It is the only distribution of interarrival times that fits having random arrivals.

    b. It has the lack-of-memory property because it cannot remember when the next arrival will occur.

    c. It provides an excellent fit for interarrival times for most situations.

14.4. For each of the following statements about using the exponential distribution as the probability distribution of service times, label the statement as true or false and then justify your answer by referring to a specific statement in the chapter.

    a. It generally provides an excellent approximation of the true service-time distribution.

    b. Its mean and variance are always equal.

    c. It represents a rather extreme case regarding the amount of variability in the service times.

14.5. For each of the following statements about the queue in a queueing system, label the statement as true or false and then justify your answer by referring to a specific statement in the chapter.

a. The queue is where customers wait in the queueing system until their service is completed.

b. Queueing models conventionally assume that the queue can hold only a limited number of customers.

c. The most common queue discipline is first-come, first-served.

14.6. Midtown Bank always has two tellers on duty. Customers arrive to receive service from a teller at a mean rate of 40 per hour. A teller requires an average of two minutes to serve a customer. When both tellers are busy, an arriving customer joins a single line to wait for service. Experience has shown that customers wait in line an average of one minute before service begins.

a. Describe why this is a queueing system.

b. Determine the basic measures of performance—W_q, W, L_q, and L—for this queueing system. (*Hint:* We don't know the probability distributions of interarrival times and service times for this queueing system, so you will need to use the relationships between these measures of performance to help answer the question.)

14.7. Mom-and-Pop's Grocery Store has a small adjacent parking lot with three parking spaces reserved for the store's customers. During store hours, when the lot is not full, cars enter the lot and use one of the spaces at a mean rate of two per hour. When the lot is full, arriving cars leave and do not return. For $n = 0, 1, 2, 3$, the probability P_n that exactly n spaces currently are being used is $P_0 = 0.2$, $P_1 = 0.3$, $P_2 = 0.3$, $P_3 = 0.2$.

a. Describe how this parking lot can be interpreted as being a queueing system. In particular, identify the customers and the servers. What is the service being provided? What constitutes a service time? What is the queue capacity? (*Hint:* See Table 14.5.)

b. Determine the basic measures of performance—L, L_q, W, and W_q—for this queueing system. (*Hint:* You can use the given probabilities to determine the average number of parking spaces that are being used.)

c. Use the results from part *b* to determine the average length of time that a car remains in a parking space.

14.8.* Newell and Jeff are the two barbers in a barber shop they own and operate. They provide two chairs for customers who are waiting to begin a haircut, so the number of customers in the shop varies between 0 and 4. For $n = 0, 1, 2, 3, 4$, the probability P_n that exactly n customers are in the shop is $P_0 = \frac{1}{16}$, $P_1 = \frac{4}{16}$, $P_2 = \frac{6}{16}$, $P_3 = \frac{4}{16}$, $P_4 = \frac{1}{16}$.

a. Use the formula $L = 0P_0 + 1P_1 + 2P_2 + 3P_3 + 4P_4$ to calculate L. How would you describe the meaning of L to Newell and Jeff?

b. For each of the possible values of the number of customers in the queueing system, specify how many customers are in the queue. For each of the possible numbers in the queue, multiply by its probability, and then add these products to calculate L_q. How would you describe the meaning of L_q to Newell and Jeff?

c. Given that an average of four customers per hour arrive and stay to receive a haircut, determine W and W_q. Describe these two quantities in terms meaningful to Newell and Jeff.

d. Given that Newell and Jeff are equally fast in giving haircuts, what is the average duration of a haircut?

14.9. Explain why the utilization factor ρ for the server in a single-server queueing system must equal $1 - P_0$, where P_0 is the probability of having 0 customers in the system.

14.10. The Friendly Neighbor Grocery Store has a single checkout stand with a full-time cashier. Customers arrive randomly at the stand at a mean rate of 30 per hour. The service-time distribution is exponential, with a mean of 1.5 minutes. This situation has resulted in occasional long lines and complaints from customers. Therefore, because there is no room for a second checkout stand, the manager is considering the alternative of hiring another person to help the cashier by bagging the groceries. This help would reduce the expected time required to process a customer to 1 minute, but the distribution still would be exponential.

The manager would like to have the percentage of time that there are more than two customers at the checkout stand down below 25 percent. She also would like to have no more than 5 percent of the customers needing to wait at least five minutes before beginning service, or at least seven minutes before finishing service.

a. Use the formulas for the *M/M/*1 model to calculate L, W, W_q, L_q, P_0, P_1, and P_2 for the current mode of operation. What is the probability of having more than two customers at the checkout stand?

E   b. Use the Excel template for this model to check your answers in part *a*. Also, find the probability that the waiting time before beginning service exceeds five minutes, and the probability that the waiting time before finishing service exceeds seven minutes.

c. Repeat part *a* for the alternative being considered by the manager.

d. Repeat part *b* for this alternative.

e. Which approach should the manager use to satisfy her criteria as closely as possible?

14.11.* The 4M Company has a single turret lathe as a key work center on its factory floor. Jobs arrive randomly at this work center at a mean rate of two per day. The processing time to perform each job has an exponential distribution with a mean of 1/4 day. Because the jobs are bulky, those not being worked on are currently being stored in a room some distance from the machine. However, to save time in fetching the jobs, the production manager is proposing to add enough in-process storage space next to the turret lathe to accommodate three jobs in addition to the one being processed. (Excess jobs will continue to be stored temporarily in the distant room.) Under this proposal, what proportion of the time will this storage space next to the turret lathe be adequate to accommodate all waiting jobs?

a. Use available formulas to calculate your answer.

E   b. Use an Excel template to obtain the information needed to answer the question.

14.12. Jerry Jansen, materials handling manager at the Casper-Edison Corporation's new factory, needs to decide whether to purchase a small tractor-trailer train or a heavy-duty forklift truck for transporting heavy goods between certain producing centers in the factory. Calls for the materials-handling unit to move a load would come essentially at random at a mean rate of four per hour. The total time required to move a load has an exponential distribution, where the expected time would be 12 minutes for the tractor-trailer train and 9 minutes for the forklift truck. The total equivalent uniform hourly cost (capital recovery cost plus operating cost) would be $50 for the tractor-trailer train and $150 for the forklift truck. The estimated cost of idle goods (waiting to be moved or in transit) because of increased in-process inventory is $20 per load per hour.

Jerry also has established certain criteria that he would like the materials-handling unit to satisfy in order to keep production flowing on schedule as much as possible. He would like to average no more than half an hour for completing the move of a load after receiving the call requesting the move. He also would like the time for completing the move to be no more than one hour 80 percent of the time. Finally, he would like to have no more than three loads waiting to start their move at least 80 percent of the time.

E   *a.* Obtain the various measures of performance if the tractor-trailer train were to be chosen. Evaluate how well these measures meet the above criteria.

E   *b.* Repeat part *a* if the forklift truck were to be chosen.

c. Compare the two alternatives in terms of their expected total cost per hour (including the cost of idle goods).

d. Which alternative do you think Jerry should choose?

E 14.13. Suppose a queueing system fitting the *M/M/*1 model has *W*=120 minutes and *L* = 8 customers. Use these facts (and the formula for *W*) to find λ and μ. Then find the various other measures of performance for this queueing system.

14.14.* The Seabuck and Roper Company has a large warehouse in southern California to store its inventory of goods until they are needed by the company's many furniture stores in that area. A single crew with four members is used to unload and/or load each truck that arrives at the loading dock of the warehouse. Management currently is downsizing to cut costs, so a decision needs to be made about the future size of this crew.

Trucks arrive randomly at the loading dock at a mean rate of one per hour. The time required by a crew to unload and/or load a truck has an exponential distribution (regardless of crew size). The mean of this distribution with the four-member crew is 15 minutes. If the size of the crew were to be changed, it is estimated that the mean service rate of the crew (now μ = 4 customers per hour) would be *proportional* to its size.

The cost of providing each member of the crew is $20 per hour. The cost that is attributable to having a truck not in use (i.e., a truck standing at the loading dock) is estimated to be $30 per hour.

a. Identify the customers and servers for this queueing system. How many servers does it currently have?

E   *b.* Find the various measures of performance of this queueing system with four members on the crew. (Set *t* = 1 hour in the Excel template for the waiting-time probabilities.)

E   *c.* Repeat *b* with three members.

E   *d.* Repeat part *b* with two members.

e. Should a one-member crew also be considered? Explain.

f. Given the previous results, which crew size do you think management should choose?

g. Use the cost figures to determine which crew size would minimize the expected total cost per hour.

14.15. Jake's Machine Shop contains a grinder for sharpening the machine cutting tools. A decision must now be made on the speed at which to set the grinder.

The grinding time required by a machine operator to sharpen the cutting tool has an exponential distribution, where the mean $1/\mu$ can be set at 1 minute, 1.5 minutes, or 2 minutes, depending upon the speed of the grinder. The running and maintenance costs go up rapidly with the speed of the grinder, so the estimated cost per minute is $1.60 for providing a mean of 1 minute, $0.90 for a mean of 1.5 minutes, and $0.40 for a mean of 2 minutes.

The machine operators arrive randomly to sharpen their tools at a mean rate of one every two minutes. The estimated cost of an operator being away from his or her machine to the grinder is $0.80 per minute.

E   *a.* Obtain the various measures of performance for this queueing system for each of the three alternative speeds for the grinder. (Set *t* = 5 minutes in the Excel template for the waiting time probabilities.)

b. Use the cost figures to determine which grinder speed minimizes the expected total cost per minute.

E 14.16. The Centerville International Airport has two runways, one used exclusively for takeoffs and the other exclusively for landings. Airplanes arrive randomly in the Centerville air space to request landing instructions at a mean rate of 10 per hour. The time required for an airplane to land after receiving clearance to land has an exponential distribution with a mean of three minutes, and this process must be completed before giving clearance to land to another airplane. Airplanes awaiting clearance must circle the airport.

The Federal Aviation Administration has a number of criteria regarding the safe level of congestion of airplanes waiting to land. These criteria depend on a number of factors regarding the airport involved, such as the number of runways available for landing. For Centerville, the criteria are (1) the average number of airplanes waiting to receive clearance to land should not exceed one, (2) 95 percent of the time, the actual number of airplanes waiting to receive clearance to land should not exceed four, (3) for 99 percent of the airplanes, the amount of time spent circling the airport before receiving clearance to land should not exceed 30 minutes (since exceeding this amount of time often would require rerouting the plane to another airport for an emergency landing before its fuel runs out).

a. Evaluate how well these criteria are currently being satisfied.

b. A major airline is considering adding this airport as one of its hubs. This would increase the mean arrival rate to 15 airplanes per hour. Evaluate how well the above criteria would be satisfied if this happens.

c. To attract additional business (including the major airline mentioned in part *b*), airport management is considering adding a second runway for landings. It is estimated that this eventually would increase the mean arrival rate to 25 airplanes per hour. Evaluate how well the above criteria would be satisfied if this happens.

14.17.* Consider the $M/G/1$ model. What is the effect on L_q and W_q if $1/\lambda$, $1/\mu$, and σ are all reduced by half?

14.18. Consider the $M/G/1$ model with $\lambda = 0.2$ and $\mu = 0.25$.

E   a. Use the Excel template for this model to find the main measures of performance—L, L_q, W, W_q—for each of the following values of σ: 4, 3, 2, 1, 0.

      b. What is the ratio of L_q with $\sigma = 4$ to L_q with $\sigma = 0$? What does this say about the importance of reducing the variability of the service times?

      c. Calculate the reduction in L_q when σ is reduced from 4 to 3, from 3 to 2, from 2 to 1, and from 1 to 0. Which is the largest reduction? Which is the smallest?

E   d. Use trial and error with the template to see approximately how much μ would need to be increased with $\sigma=4$ to achieve the same L_q as with $\mu = 0.25$ and $\sigma = 0$.

14.19. Consider the following statements about the $M/G/1$ queueing model, where σ^2 is the variance of service times. Label each statement as true or false, and then justify your answer.

      a. Increasing σ^2 (with fixed λ and μ) will increase L_q and L, but will not change W_q and W.

      b. When the choice is between a tortoise (small μ and σ^2) and a hare (large μ and σ^2) to be the server, the tortoise always wins by providing a smaller L_q.

      c. With λ and μ fixed, the value of L_q with an exponential service-time distribution is twice as large as with constant service times.

14.20. Marsha operates an espresso stand. Customers arrive randomly at a mean rate of 30 per hour. The time needed by Marsha to serve a customer has an exponential distribution with a mean of 75 seconds.

E   a. Use the Excel template for the $M/G/1$ model to find L, L_q, W, and W_q.

E   b. Suppose Marsha is replaced by an espresso vending machine that requires exactly 75 seconds for each customer to operate. Find L, L_q, W, and W_q.

      c. What is the ratio of L_q in part b to L_q in part a?

E   d. Use trial and error with the template to see approximately how much Marsha would need to reduce her expected service time to achieve the same L_q as with the espresso vending machine.

14.21.* The production of tractors at the Jim Buck Company involves producing several subassemblies and then using an assembly line to assemble the subassemblies and other parts into finished tractors. Approximately three tractors per day are produced in this way. An in-process inspection station is used to inspect the subassemblies before they enter the assembly line. At present, there are two inspectors at the station, and they work together to inspect each subassembly. The inspection time has an exponential distribution, with a mean of 15 minutes. The cost of providing this inspection system is $40 per hour.

A proposal has been made to streamline the inspection procedure so that it can be handled by only one inspector. This inspector would begin by visually inspecting the exterior of the subassembly, and she would then use new efficient equipment to complete the inspection. Although this process with just one inspector would slightly increase the mean of the distribution of inspection times from 15 minutes to 16 minutes, it also would reduce the variance of this distribution to only 40 percent of its current value.

The subassemblies arrive randomly at the inspection station at a mean rate of three per hour. The cost of having the subassemblies wait at the inspection station (thereby increasing in-process inventory and possibly disrupting subsequent production) is estimated to be $20 per hour for each subassembly.

Management now needs to make a decision about whether to continue the status quo or adopt the proposal.

E   a. Find the main measures of performance—L, L_q, W, W_q—for the current queueing system.

E   b. Repeat part a for the proposed queueing system.

      c. What conclusions can you draw about what management should do from the results in parts a and b?

      d. Determine and compare the expected total cost per hour for the status quo and the proposal.

14.22. Antonio runs a shoe repair store by himself. Customers arrive randomly to bring a pair of shoes to be repaired at a mean rate of one per hour. The time Antonio requires to repair each *individual* shoe has an exponential distribution with a mean of 15 minutes. According to statistical theory, this implies that the time required to repair a *pair* of shoes has an Erlang distribution with a mean of 30 minutes and a shape parameter of $k = 2$.

      a. Calculate the average number of pairs of shoes in the shop?

      b. Calculate the average amount of time from when a customer drops off a pair of shoes until they are repaired and ready to be picked up?

E   c. Use the Excel template for the $M/G/1$ model to check your answers in parts a and b.

E   d. Repeat part c with the Excel template for the $M/E_k/1$ model.

14.23.* The maintenance base for Friendly Skies Airline has facilities for overhauling only one airplane engine at a time. Therefore, to return the airplanes to use as soon as possible, the policy has been to stagger the overhauling of the four engines of each airplane. In other words, only one engine is overhauled each time an airplane comes into the shop. Under this policy, airplanes have arrived randomly at a mean rate of one per day. The time required for an engine overhaul (once work has begun) has an exponential distribution with a mean of ½ day.

A proposal has been made to change the policy so that all four engines are overhauled consecutively each time an airplane comes into the shop. This would mean that each plane would need to come to the maintenance base only one-fourth as often. Since the time required to overhaul one engine has an exponential distribution, statistical theory indicates that the time required to overhaul four engines has an Erlang distribution with a mean four times as large and with a shape parameter of $k = 4$.

Management now needs to decide whether to continue the status quo or adopt the proposal. The objective is to minimize the average amount of flying time lost by the entire fleet per day due to engine overhauls.

E   a. Compare the two alternatives with respect to the average amount of flying time lost by an airplane each time it comes to the maintenance base.

E   b. Compare the two alternatives with respect to the average number of airplanes losing flying time due to being at the maintenance base.

      c. Which of these two comparisons is the appropriate one for making management's decision? Explain.

E 14.24. The Security & Trust bank employs four tellers to serve its customers. Customers arrive randomly at a mean rate of two per minute. However, business is growing and management projects that the mean arrival rate will be three per minute a year from now. The transaction time between the teller and customer has an exponential distribution with a mean of one minute.

Management has established the following guidelines for a satisfactory level of service to customers. The average number of customers waiting in line to begin service should not exceed one. At least 95 percent of the time, the number of customers waiting in line should not exceed five. For at least 95 percent of the customers, the time spent in line waiting to begin service should not exceed five minutes.

      a. Use the *M/M/s* model to determine how well these guidelines are currently being satisfied.

      b. Evaluate how well the guidelines will be satisfied a year from now if no change is made in the number of tellers.

      c. Determine how many tellers will be needed a year from now to completely satisfy these guidelines.

E 14.25. Consider the *M/M/s* model.

      a. Suppose there is one server and the expected service time is one minute. Compare L for the cases where the mean arrival rate is 0.5, 0.9, and 0.99 customer per minute, respectively. Do the same for L_q, W, W_q, and $P\{\mathcal{W} > 5\}$. What conclusions do you draw about the impact of increasing the utilization factor ρ from small values (e.g., $\rho = 0.5$) to fairly large values (e.g., $\rho = 0.9$) and then to even larger values very close to 1 (e.g., $\rho = 0.99$)?

      b. Now suppose there are two servers and the expected service time is two minutes. Follow the instructions for part *a.*

E 14.26. Consider the *M/M/s* model with a mean arrival rate of 10 customers per hour and an expected service time of five minutes. Use the Excel template for this model to print out the various measures of performance (with $t = 10$ and $t = 0$, respectively, for the two waiting time probabilities) when the number of servers is one, two, three, four, and five. Then, for each of the following possible criteria for a satisfactory level of service (where the unit of time is one minute), use the printed results to determine how many servers are needed to satisfy this criterion.

      a. $L_q \leq 0.25$
      b. $L \leq 0.9$
      c. $W_q \leq 0.1$
      d. $W \leq 6$
      e. $P\{\mathcal{W}_q > 0\} \leq 0.01$
      f. $P\{\mathcal{W} > 10\} \leq 0.2$
      g. $\sum_{n=0}^{s} P_n \geq 0.95$

14.27. Greg is making plans to open a new fast-food restaurant soon. He is estimating that customers will arrive randomly at a mean rate of 150 per hour during the busiest times of the day. He is planning to have three employees directly serving the customers. He now needs to make a decision about how to organize these employees.

Option 1 is to have three cash registers with one employee at each to take the orders and get the food and drinks. In this case, it is estimated that the average time to serve each customer would be one minute, and the distribution of service times is assumed to be exponential.

Option 2 is to have one cash register with the three employees working together to serve each customer. One would take the order, a second would get the food, and the third would get the drinks. Greg estimates that this would reduce the average time to serve each customer down to 20 seconds, with the same assumption of exponential service times.

Greg wants to choose the option that would provide the best service to his customers. However, since Option 1 has three cash registers, both options would serve the customers at a mean rate of three per minute when everybody is busy serving customers, so it is not clear which option is better.

E   a. Use the main measures of performance—L, L_q, W, W_q—to compare the two options.

      b. Explain why these comparisons make sense intuitively.

      c. Which measure do you think would be most important to Greg's customers? Why? Which option is better with respect to this measure?

E 14.28.* In the Blue Chip Life Insurance Company, the deposit and withdrawal functions associated with a certain investment product are separated between two clerks. Deposit slips arrive randomly at Clerk Clara's desk at a mean rate of 16 per hour. Withdrawal slips arrive randomly at Clerk Clarence's desk at a mean rate of 14 per hour. The time required to process either transaction has an exponential distribution with a mean of three minutes. In order to reduce the expected waiting time in the system for both deposit slips and withdrawal slips, the Actuarial Department has made the following recommendations: (1) Train each clerk to handle both deposits and withdrawals; (2) put both deposit and withdrawal slips into a single queue that is accessed by both clerks.

      a. Determine the expected waiting time in the system under current procedures for each type of slip. Then combine these results (multiply W for deposit slips by $^{16}\!/_{30}$, multiply W for withdrawal slips by ¹⁴⁄₃₀, and add these two products) to calculate the expected waiting time in the system for a random arrival of either type of slip.

b. If the recommendations are adopted, determine the expected waiting time in the system for arriving slips.

c. Now suppose that adopting the recommendations would result in a slight increase in the expected processing time. Use the Excel template for this model to determine by trial and error the expected processing time (within 0.01 minute) that would cause the expected waiting time in the system for a random arrival to be essentially the same under current procedures and under the recommendations.

E 14.29. People's Software Company has just set up a call center to provide technical assistance on its new software package. Two technical representatives are taking the calls, where the time required by either representative to answer a customer's questions has an exponential distribution with a mean of eight minutes. Calls are arriving randomly at a mean rate of 10 per hour.

By next year, the mean arrival rate of calls is expected to decline to five per hour, so the plan is to reduce the number of technical representatives to one then. Determine L, L_q, W, and W_q for both the current queueing system and next year's system. For each of these four measures of performance, which system yields the smaller value?

14.30. The McAllister Company factory currently has two tool cribs, each with a single clerk, in its manufacturing area. One tool crib handles only the tools for the heavy machinery; the second one handles all other tools. However, for each crib, the mechanics arrive randomly to obtain tools at a mean rate of 24 per hour, and the expected service time is two minutes.

Because of complaints that the mechanics coming to the tool cribs have to wait too long, it has been proposed that the two tool cribs be combined so that either clerk can handle either kind of tool as the demand arises. It is believed that the mean arrival rate to the combined two-clerk tool crib would double to 48 per hour and that the expected service time would continue to be two minutes. However, information is not available on the *form* of the probability distribution for service times, so it is not clear which queueing model would be most appropriate.

E a. Compare the status quo and the proposal with respect to the total expected number of mechanics at the tool crib(s) and the expected waiting time (including service) for each mechanic. Do this by tabulating these data for the four queueing models where the distribution of service times is (1) exponential, (2) Erlang with shape parameter $k=2$, (3) Erlang with shape parameter $k=8$, and (4) degenerate (constant service times). Use available Excel templates, as well as Figures 14.11 and 14.12, as needed.

b. Given these results, which alternative should be chosen?

c. Which of the four insights presented in Section 14.8 is illustrated by these results?

14.31. The Southern Railroad Company has been subcontracting for the painting of its railroad cars as

needed. However, management has decided that the company can save money by doing this work itself. A decision now needs to be made to choose between two alternative ways of doing this.

Alternative 1 is to provide two paint shops, where painting is done by hand (one car at a time in each shop), for a total hourly cost of $70. The painting time for a car would be six hours. Alternative 2 is to provide one spray shop involving an hourly cost of $100. In this case, the painting time for a car (again done one at a time) would be three hours. For both alternatives, the cars arrive randomly with a mean rate of 1 every 5 hours. The cost of idle time per car is $100 per hour.

a. Use Figure 14.11 to estimate L, L_q, W, and W_q for Alternative 1.

E b. Find these same measures of performance for Alternative 2.

c. Determine and compare the expected total cost per hour for these alternatives.

14.32. The car rental company, Try Harder, has been subcontracting for the maintenance of its cars in St. Louis. However, due to long delays in getting its cars back, the company has decided to open its own maintenance shop to do this work more quickly. This shop will operate 42 hours per week.

Alternative 1 is to hire two mechanics (at a cost of $1,500 per week each), so that two cars can be worked on at a time. The time required by a mechanic to service a car has an Erlang distribution with a mean of five hours and a shape parameter of $k=8$.

Alternative 2 is to hire just one mechanic (for $1,500 per week) but to provide some additional special equipment (at a capitalized cost of $1,250 per week) to speed up the work. In this case, the maintenance work on each car is done in two stages, where the time required for each stage has an Erlang distribution with the shape parameter $k=4$, where the mean is two hours for the first stage and one hour for the second stage. This implies that the probability distribution of the total time for both stages has a mean of three hours and a variance equal to the sum of the variances of the times for the individual stages. However, the form of this distribution is unknown. (It is not Erlang.)

For both alternatives, the cars arrive randomly at a mean rate of 0.3 car per hour (during work hours). The company estimates that its net lost revenue due to having its cars unavailable for rental is $150 per week per car.

a. Use Figure 14.12 to estimate L, L_q, W, and W_q for alternative 1.

E b. Find these same measures of performance for Alternative 2.

c. Determine and compare the expected total cost per week for these alternatives.

14.33.* Southeast Airlines is a small commuter airline serving primarily the state of Florida. Their ticket counter at the Orlando airport is staffed by a single ticket agent. There are two separate lines—one for first-class passengers and one for coach-class passengers. When the ticket agent is ready for another customer, the next first-class passenger is served if there are any in line. If not, the next coach-class passenger is served. Service times have an exponential distribution with a mean of three minutes for both types of customers. During the 12 hours per day that the ticket counter is open, passengers arrive randomly at a mean rate of 2 per hour for first-class passengers and 10 per hour for coach-class passengers.

a. What kind of queueing model fits this queueing system?

E b. Find the main measures of performance—L, L_q, W, and W_q—for both first-class passengers and coach-class passengers.

c. What is the expected waiting time before service begins for first-class customers as a fraction of this waiting time for coach-class customers?

d. Determine the average number of hours per day that the ticket agent is busy.

14.34. The County Hospital emergency room always has one doctor on duty. In the past, having just a single doctor there has been sufficient. However, because of a growing tendency for emergency cases to use these facilities rather than go to a private doctor, the number of emergency room visits has been steadily increasing. By next year, it is estimated that patients will arrive randomly at a mean rate of two per hour during peak usage hours (the early evening). Therefore, a proposal has been made to assign a second doctor to the emergency room next year during those hours. Hospital management (an HMO) is resisting this proposal, but has asked a management scientist (you) to analyze whether a single doctor will continue to be sufficient next year.

The patients are not treated on a first-come, first-served basis. Rather, the admitting nurse divides the patients into three categories: (1) *critical* cases, where prompt treatment is vital for survival; (2) *serious* cases, where early treatment is important to prevent further deterioration; and (3) *stable* cases, where treatment can be delayed without adverse medical consequences. Patients are then treated in this order of priority, where those in the same category are normally taken on a first-come, first-served basis. A doctor will interrupt treatment of a patient if a new case in a higher-priority category arrives. Approximately 10 percent of the patients fall into the first category, 30 percent into the second, and 60 percent into the third. Because the more serious cases will be sent to the hospital for further care after receiving emergency treatment, the average treatment time by a doctor in the emergency room actually does not differ greatly among these categories. For all of them, the treatment time can be approximated by an exponential distribution with a mean of 20 minutes.

Hospital management has established the following guidelines. The average waiting time in the emergency room before treatment begins should not exceed 2 minutes for critical cases, 15 minutes for serious cases, and 2 hours for stable cases.

a. What kind of queueing model fits this queueing system?

E b. Use this model to determine if the management guidelines would be satisfied next year by continuing to have just a single doctor on duty.

c. Use the formula for W_q for the *M/M/1* model to determine if these guidelines would be satisfied if

treatment were given on a first-come, first-served basis instead.

E d. The mean arrival rate of two patients per hour during peak usage hours next year is only an estimate. Perform sensitivity analysis by repeating part *b* if this mean arrival rate were to turn out to be 2.25 patients per hour instead.

E 14.35. The Becker Company factory has been experiencing long delays in jobs going through the turret lathe department because of inadequate capacity. The head of this department contends that five machines are required, as opposed to the three machines that he now has. However, because of pressure from management to hold down capital expenditures, only one additional machine will be authorized unless there is solid evidence that a second one is necessary.

This shop does three kinds of jobs, namely, government jobs, commercial jobs, and standard products. Whenever a turret lathe operator finishes a job, he starts a government job if one is waiting; if not, he starts a commercial job if any are waiting; if not, he starts on a standard product if any are waiting. Jobs of the same type are taken on a first-come, first-served basis.

Although much overtime work is required currently, management wants the turret lathe department to operate on an eight-hour, five-day-per-week basis. The probability distribution of the time required by a turret lathe operator for a job appears to be approximately exponential, with a mean of 10 hours. Jobs come into the shop randomly at a mean rate of six per week for government jobs, four per week for commercial jobs, and two per week for standard products. (These figures are expected to remain the same for the indefinite future.)

Management feels that the average waiting time before work begins in the turret lathe department should not exceed 0.25 (working) day for government jobs, 0.5 day for commercial jobs, and 2 days for standard products.

a. Determine how many additional turret lathes need to be obtained to satisfy these management guidelines.

b. It is worth about $750, $450, and $150 to avoid a delay of one additional (working) day in a government, commercial, and standard job, respectively. The incremental capitalized cost of providing each turret lathe (including the operator and so on) is estimated to be $250 per working day. Determine the number of additional turret lathes that should be obtained to minimize the expected total cost.

E 14.36. When describing economic analysis of the number of servers to provide in a queueing system, Section 14.9 introduces a cost model where the objective is to minimize $TC = C_s s + C_w L$. The purpose of this problem is to enable you to explore the effect that the relative sizes of C_s and C_w have on the optimal number of servers.

Suppose that the queueing system under consideration fits the *M/M/s* model with $\lambda = 8$

customers per hour and $\mu = 10$ customers per hour. Use the Excel template for economic analysis with the $M/M/s$ model to find the optimal number of servers for each of the following cases.

  a. $C_s = \$100$ and $C_w = \$10$.
  b. $C_s = \$100$ and $C_w = \$100$.
  c. $C_s = \$10$ and $C_w = \$100$.

E 14.37.* Jim McDonald, manager of the fast-food hamburger restaurant McBurger, realizes that providing fast service is a key to the success of the restaurant. Customers who have to wait very long are likely to go to one of the other fast-food restaurants in town next time. He estimates that each minute a customer has to wait in line before completing service costs him an average of 30¢ in lost future business. Therefore, he wants to be sure that enough cash registers always are open to keep waiting to a minimum. Each cash register is operated by a part-time employee who obtains the food ordered by each customer and collects the payment. The total cost for each such employee is $9 per hour.

During lunch time, customers arrive randomly at a mean rate of 66 per hour. The time needed to serve a customer is estimated to have an exponential distribution with a mean of two minutes.

Determine how many cash registers Jim should have open during lunch time to minimize his expected total cost per hour.

E 14.38. The Garrett-Tompkins Company provides three copy machines in its copying room for the use of its employees. However, due to recent complaints about considerable time being wasted waiting for a copier to become free, management is considering adding one or more additional copy machines.

During the 2,000 working hours per year, employees arrive randomly at the copying room at a mean rate of 30 per hour. The time each employee needs with a copy machine is believed to have an exponential distribution with a mean of five minutes. The lost productivity due to an employee spending time in the copying room is estimated to cost the company an average of $25 per hour. Each copy machine is leased for $3,000 per year.

Determine how many copy machines the company should have to minimize its expected total cost per hour.

CASE 14.1
QUEUEING QUANDARY

(A sequel to Case 13.1)

Never dull. That is how you would describe your job at the centralized records and benefits administration center for Cutting Edge, a large company manufacturing computers and computer peripherals. Since opening the facility six months ago, you and Mark Lawrence, the director of Human Resources, have endured one long roller-coaster ride. Receiving the go-ahead from corporate headquarters to establish the centralized records and benefits administration center was definitely an up. Getting caught in the crossfire of angry customers (all employees of Cutting Edge) because of demand overload for the records and benefits call center was definitely a down. Accurately forecasting the demand for the call center provided another up.

And today you are faced with another down. Mark approaches your desk with a not altogether attractive frown on his face.

He begins complaining immediately, "I just don't understand. The forecasting job you did for us two months ago really allowed us to understand the weekly demand for the center, but we still have not been able to get a grasp on the staffing problem. We used both historical data and your forecasts to calculate the average weekly demand for the call center. We transformed this average weekly demand into average hourly demand by dividing the weekly demand by the number of hours in the workweek. We then staffed the center to meet this average hourly demand by taking into account the average number of calls a representative is able to handle per hour.

But something is horribly wrong. Operational data records show that over 35 percent of the customers wait over four minutes for a representative to answer the call! Customers are still sending me numerous complaints, and executives from corporate headquarters are still breathing down my neck! I need help!"

You calm Mark down and explain to him that you think you know the problem: the number of calls received in a certain hour can be much greater (or much less) than the average because of the stochastic nature of the demand. In addition, the number of calls a representative is able to handle per hour can be much less (or much greater) than the average depending upon the types of calls received.

You then tell him to have no fear; you have the problem under control. You have been reading about the successful application of queueing theory to the operation of call centers, and you decide that the queueing models you learned in school will help you determine the appropriate staffing level.

  a. You ask Mark to describe the demand and service rate. He tells you that calls are randomly received by the call center and that the center receives an average of 70 calls per hour. The computer system installed to answer and hold the calls is so advanced that its capacity far exceeds the demand. Because the nature of a call is random, the time required to process a call is random, where the time frequently is small but occasionally can be much longer. On average, however, representatives can handle six calls per hour. Which queueing model seems appropriate for this situation? Given that slightly more than 35 percent of customers wait over four minutes before a representative answers the call, use this model to estimate how many representatives Mark currently employs.

  b. Mark tells you that he will not be satisfied unless 95 percent of the customers wait only one minute or less for a representative to answer the call. Given this customer service level and the average arrival rates and service rates from part *a,* how many representatives should Mark employ?

c. Each representative receives an annual salary of $30,000, and Mark tells you that he simply does not have the resources available to hire the number of representatives required to achieve the customer service level desired in part *b*. He asks you to perform sensitivity analysis. How many representatives would he need to employ to ensure that 80 percent of customers wait one minute or less? How many would he need to employ to ensure that 95 percent of customers wait 90 seconds or less? How would you recommend Mark choose a customer service level? Would the decision criteria be different if Mark's call center were to serve external customers (not connected to the company) instead of internal customers (employees)?

d. Mark tells you that he is not happy with the number of representatives required to achieve a high customer service level. He therefore wants to explore alternatives to simply hiring additional representatives. The alternative he considers is instituting a training program that will teach representatives to more efficiently use computer tools to answer calls. He believes that this alternative will increase the average number of calls a representative is able to handle per hour from six calls to eight calls. The training program will cost $2,500 per employee per year since employees' knowledge will have to be updated yearly. How many representatives will Mark have to employ and train to achieve the customer service level desired in part *b*? Do you prefer this alternative to simply hiring additional representatives? Why or why not?

e. Mark realizes that queueing theory helps him only so much in determining the number of representatives needed. He realizes that the queueing models will not provide accurate answers if the inputs used in the models are inaccurate. What inputs do you think need reevaluation? How would you go about estimating these inputs?

CASE 14.2
REDUCING IN-PROCESS INVENTORY

Jim Wells, vice-president for manufacturing of the Northern Airplane Company, is exasperated. His walk through the company's most important plant this morning has left him in a foul mood. However, he now can vent his temper at Jerry Carstairs, the plant's production manager, who has just been summoned to Jim's office.

"Jerry, I just got back from walking through the plant, and I am very upset."

"What is the problem, Jim?"

"Well, you know how much I have been emphasizing the need to cut down on our in-process inventory."

"Yes, we've been working hard on that," responds Jerry.

"Well, not hard enough!" Jim raises his voice even higher. "Do you know what I found by the presses?"

"No."

"Five metal sheets still waiting to be formed into wing sections. And then, right next door at the inspection station, 13 wing sections! The inspector was inspecting one of them, but the other 12 were just sitting there. You know we have a couple hundred thousand dollars tied up in each of those wing sections. So between the presses and the inspection station, we have a few million bucks' worth of terribly expensive metal just sitting there. We can't have that!"

The chagrined Jerry Carstairs tries to respond. "Yes, Jim, I am well aware that that inspection station is a bottleneck. It usually isn't nearly as bad as you found it this morning, but it is a bottleneck. Much less so for the presses. You really caught us on a bad morning."

"I sure hope so," retorts Jim, "but you need to prevent anything nearly this bad happening even occasionally. What do you propose to do about it?"

Jerry now brightens noticeably in his response. "Well, actually, I've already been working on this problem. I have a couple proposals on the table and I have asked a management scientist on my staff to analyze these proposals and report back with recommendations."

"Great," responds Jim, "glad to see you are on top of the problem. Give this your highest priority and report back to me as soon as possible."

"Will do," promises Jerry.

Here is the problem that Jerry and his management scientist are addressing. Each of 10 identical presses is being used to form wing sections out of large sheets of specially processed metal. The sheets arrive randomly at a mean rate of seven per hour. The time required by a press to form a wing section out of a sheet has an exponential distribution with a mean of one hour. When finished, the wing sections arrive randomly at an inspection station at the same mean rate as the metal sheets arrived at the presses (seven per hour). A single inspector has the full-time job of inspecting these wing sections to make sure they meet specifications. Each inspection takes her 7½ minutes, so she can inspect eight wing sections per hour. This inspection rate has resulted in a substantial average amount of in-process inventory at the inspection station (i.e., the average number of wing sheets waiting to complete inspection is fairly large), in addition to that already found at the group of machines.

The cost of this in-process inventory is estimated to be $8 per hour for each metal sheet at the presses or each wing section at the inspection station. Therefore, Jerry Carstairs has made two alternative proposals to reduce the average level of in-process inventory.

Proposal 1 is to use slightly less power for the presses (which would increase their average time to form a wing section to 1.2 hours), so that the inspector can keep up with their output better. This also would reduce the cost for each machine (operating cost plus capital recovery cost) from $7.00 to $6.50 per hour. (By contrast, increasing to maximum power would increase this cost to $7.50 per hour while decreasing the average time to form a wing section to 0.8 hour.)

Proposal 2 is to substitute a certain younger inspector for this task. He is somewhat faster (albeit with some variability in his inspection times because of less experience), so he should keep up better. (His inspection time would have an Erlang distribution with a mean of 7.2 minutes and a shape parameter $k=2$.) This inspector is in a job classification that calls for a total compensation (including benefits) of $19 per hour, whereas the current inspector is in a lower job classification where the compensation is $17 per hour. (The inspection times for each of these inspectors are typical of those in the same job classification.)

You are the management scientist on Jerry Carstair's staff who has been asked to analyze this problem. He wants you to "use the latest management science techniques to see how much each proposal would cut down on in-process inventory and then make your recommendations."

 a. To provide a basis of comparison, begin by evaluating the status quo. Determine the expected amount of in-process inventory at the presses and at the inspection station. Then calculate the expected total cost per hour of the in-process inventory, the presses, and the inspector.
 b. What would be the effect of proposal 1? Why? Make specific comparisons to the results from part *a*. Explain this outcome to Jerry Carstairs.
 c. Determine the effect of proposal 2. Make specific comparisons to the results from part *a*. Explain this outcome to Jerry Carstairs.
 d. Make your recommendations for reducing the average level of in-process inventory at the inspection station and at the group of machines. Be specific in your recommendations, and support them with quantitative analysis like that done in part *a*. Make specific comparisons to the results from part *a*, and cite the improvements that your recommendations would yield.

CASE 14.3
KEYCORP[4]

KeyCorp, with over 1,300 branches from Maine to Alaska, was one of the largest bank holding companies in the United States. Building from a long history of strong financial performance, KeyCorp's vision was to become the first choice of those seeking world-class financial products and services. However, increased competition from conventional banks, and nonbank competitors who operated under fewer regulations, forced KeyCorp to rethink and restructure its retail branch franchise.

Electronic banking continued to gain in consumer acceptance, but branch banking continued to dominate the financial services industry. The branch teller was the primary bank contact, representing 95 percent of customer contacts at KeyCorp branches. Because of the volume of customers and transactions, and the costs associated with this service, branch managers had to continuously improve branch productivity. A fundamental problem facing Key-Corp's branch managers was figuring out how to improve customer service (defined primarily as reduced customer wait time) while still providing cost-effective staffing.

KeyCorp Executive Vice President Robert G. Jones emphasized the importance of continuously improving customer service: "We have 150 million moments of truth taking place every year . . . and it takes every one of us at KeyCorp to make those moments of truth come out in the customers' favor."

The Company and the Industry

Headquartered in Cleveland, Ohio, KeyCorp recorded record earnings of $854 million in 1994, with assets of $66.8 billion and equity capital of $4.7 billion at the end of the year. The consumer banking franchise, which comprised over 1,300 branches across 14 states and affiliate offices in 25 states, ranked in the top five in size within the United States. Through its full-service commercial

banks and specialized subsidiaries, KeyCorp provided such services as consumer banking, investment management and trust, corporate finance, security brokerage, and private banking, as well as customized financial services to individuals, investors, and small, medium, and large corporations.

KeyCorp possessed a long history of superior financial performance, ranking it in the top five in both ROA and ROE among its peers. KeyCorp's performance was even more impressive because the banking industry was in a state of uncertain evolution. Industry consolidation, increased competition, regulatory constraints, and increasing pressures on profitability presented industry leaders with a multitude of major challenges. Over the past 15 years, banking had seen a consolidation from over 200 major banks to fewer than 50. After the next five years, industry experts projected there would be fewer than a dozen major banks nationwide.

In contrast, banking regulations had not changed materially since the 1930s when new rules were introduced to solve the problems of the Great Depression. As a result, the regulations fell short in aiding the industry with respect to the global competition of the 1990s. Regulations continued to limit the rate at which banks could enter new lines of business and offer new products, and limited the banking industry's ability to compete with nonbanking entities such as Merrill Lynch and American Express. In addition, there was further competitive pressure from alternative delivery competitors, such as Microsoft with its popular PC-based home financial program, which opened the floodgates for home banking services.

Bankers faced increased competition within their traditional ranks, antiquated rules, and new, less regulated aggressive competitors. To meet these challenges, KeyCorp had to evolve from a traditional bank into a provider of financial services.

The Customer Service Problem

In response to the increased competition, KeyCorp introduced First Choice 2000, which would ultimately reconfigure its distribution system from branch banking to such alternatives as ATMs, telephone banking, and PC banking. However, despite the increasing popularity of electronic banking, branch banking continued to dominate the industry. While the industry continued to

[4]This is one of the INFORMS Teaching Cases that have been prepared to provide material for class discussion. This particular case was prepared by Binu Koshy under the supervision of Professor Peter Bell, Richard Ivey School of Business, The University of Western Ontario, Canada. Copyright 1998, by the Institute for Operations Research and the Management Sciences. In press. Reproduced by permission of INFORMS, the copyright owner.

evolve, KeyCorp had to focus on delivering quality service to its customers. Quality service included friendly, accurate tellers and fast, efficient service.

KeyCorp's branches were currently an indispensable component of the consumer franchise and would continue to play an integral role as the corporation grew. Rethinking and restructuring the retail branch franchise were critical to KeyCorp becoming a world-class provider of financial services. Two hundred ten million customer transactions were performed by branch tellers at KeyCorp every year, representing 63 percent of its total customer transactions. A survey performed by KeyCorp pointed to customer waiting times as the most frequently cited reason for customer dissatisfaction. The high volume of customers and transactions, and the costs associated with this service, led branch managers to want to continually enhance branch productivity, but if service was to be improved by reducing customer waiting times, then staffing levels and costs had to be tightly controlled. Given the dynamics of consolidation, increased competition, and the bank's continued expansion through merger and acquisition, KeyCorp wanted to control service quality rather than allow it to fall victim to industry events, and to do that it wanted to apply a systems approach.

KeyCorp viewed the management of customer service as a holistic system with all components working together towards a common goal. It emphasized the interrelationships among the component parts of the system, affirming that modifying one component would affect the others and ultimately the final outcome. KeyCorp set out the following goals for a new system:

- To empower line managers to manage those elements of service under their control while at the same time isolating and stabilizing those variables outside their control.
- To create a measurement and feedback system that was continuous and could change with the organization.
- To automate the collection of data.
- To generate fact-based output.
- To foster competition among branches and create pride and ownership in superior results.

Unlike many industries, banking was a human system. Service was provided by and consumed by human beings with the result that the environment was unpredictable and, if not managed properly, could quickly become unstable. To deal with this, KeyCorp aimed to provide managers with information to enable them to respond to the variations that inevitably occurred in this people-intensive service business. KeyCorp thought that this would foster ownership in both the approach and the results.

Eliminating Transaction-Processing Impediments Outside the Control of Branch Managers

KeyCorp management, agreeing that it was not possible to manage that which was impossible to measure, set out to break down the elements of each customer session with a branch teller. This would allow them to identify each area of opportunity to improve performance, and to identify which activities were within the control of the branch manager and which were not.

Accordingly, KeyCorp developed the Performance Capture System to collect data about each discrete component of the customer session, defined as time spent at the teller window. This system provided KeyCorp with the ability to measure individual transactions on a continuous basis, by capturing the beginning and ending times for each discrete component of the transaction: host-response time, network-response time, teller-controlled time, customer-controlled time, and branch-hardware time. KeyCorp was now able to dissect transactions into their most basic components and compare categories of transactions, allowing it to identify those components that offered the greatest opportunity for improvement. KeyCorp could also collect data on customer-session times down to the level of an individual transaction for a given teller on a particular day at a specific time.

The first transaction report published in April 1992 was based on 15,000 service sessions in five branches over 36 business days and revealed a 246-second average customer processing time, which was thought to be unacceptable.

KeyCorp performed a preliminary analysis, which defined a service objective of 90 percent of customers who had to wait less than five minutes on all days. The analysis also estimated the change in teller staffing needed to deliver service at the targeted level in a cost-effective and consistent manner, and indicated that it would require an additional 502 tellers (a 30 percent increase) at a cost of over $10 million annually to meet the 90 percent objective. KeyCorp would either have to increase the pool of tellers or reduce processing time. Adding tellers was impractical for reasons of cost and because the branches simply could not physically accommodate the required increase in staff; therefore, improved management of staff and reengineering of the customer session were required if the new service quality objective was to be met.

Analysis of the detailed transaction data identified an unacceptable response time on the part of the host computer for processing an information request from the teller system, and an unacceptable network response time (the time it takes to transmit an information request from the branch modem to the host modem), even though the average host and network response times were apparently low (2.0 seconds and 2.8 seconds respectively per request). There were large variations from the average with cases of upwards of 60 seconds per request.

The first step KeyCorp took to reduce the 246-second customer session time was to reengineer the transaction process. This stabilized and streamlined the operating environment and reduced transaction-processing time by 66 seconds, or 27 percent. After eliminating or reducing all the transaction-processing impediments outside the control of branch managers, KeyCorp challenged its branch managers to better manage teller productivity and customer wait time. KeyCorp asked them to focus on two areas:

1. Improving teller proficiency and productivity.
2. Scheduling tellers so that they were available when customer traffic required them.

The Teller Productivity System

KeyCorp management introduced the teller productivity module to the branch management in July 1992. This module used the data captured by the Performance Capture System to allow branch managers to identify the number of customers being served at any time, the associated transactions processed, and the time required to process each. The data module compiled the data and provided branch managers with four reports to help them in staffing, scheduling, and identifying tellers who needed additional training.

Report P1. The teller processing proficiency summary provided details on the number of customers each teller served, the total number of transactions processed, and the average number of transactions per customer. The report also compared the teller's average transaction-processing time for a given set of transactions to the top quartile processing time of all tellers for the same set of transactions.

Report P1—Teller Processing Proficiency Summary Report

**BANK—DISTRICT
BRANCH #—NAME
Month Year**

Teller	Customers Served	Transactions Processed	Average Number of Transactions/Customer	Average Time per (Sec)		Average Processing Time/Transaction		
				Customer	Transaction	Actual	Top Quartile	Proficiency
Drive up	5524	7704	1.39	82	59	44	60	134
Lobby	7465	11971	1.60	149	93	76	77	101
Total	12989	19675	1.51	120	79	64	70	110
11122333	1342	1984	1.48	127	86	69	76	110
***	***	***	***	***	***	***	***	***
***	***	***	***	***	***	***	***	***
77788999	3802	5302	1.39	79	57	43	59	138

Report P2.   The transaction type processing time summary provided managers with information about the most frequently processed transactions at their branches and the associated processing times. By sorting this information in descending order according to frequency of transaction, managers could better understand the needs of their branch customers and identify opportunities for software enhancements and strategies to move transactions from tellers to such alternatives as ATMs. Using reports P1 and P2, the manager had the tools to manage teller proficiency and productivity.

Report P2—Transaction Type Processing Time Summary

**BANK—DISTRICT
BRANCH #—NAME
Month Year**

Trancode	Transaction Description	Transactions Processed	Average Time per (Sec)	
			Actual	Top Quartile
0003	DDA deposit	9504	80	80
0010	Cash on US check	3898	70	66
0091	Inquiry	2317	76	71
0002	Cash not on US check	1579	58	53
0084	Installment loan payment	322	81	79
***	***	***	***	***
***	***	***	***	***
0074	Loc direct advance	1	213	91
Total		19675	79	76

Report P3.   Managers needed a forecast of patterns of peak and slow customer activity to schedule tellers. Report P₃, the summary of customers and transactions by day, provided daily transaction volumes by day of the week and by calendar day to facilitate effective staffing for such peak days as pay day, social security check-cashing day, and other high-volume days.

Report P3—Summary of Customers and Transactions by Day

BANK—DISTRICT
BRANCH #—NAME
Month Year

Weekday	Date	Customers Served	Transactions Processed	Average Number of Transactions/Customer	Average Time per (Sec) Transaction	Average Time per (Sec) Customer
Thursday	09/01/94	672	1035	1.54	78	120
Friday	09/02/94	966	1426	1.48	78	115
***	***	***	***	***	***	***
***	***	***	***	***	***	***
Friday	09/30/94	954	1472	1.54	76	117
Total		12989	19675	1.51	79	120

Report P4. Report P4 showed the average number of customers and transactions processed every half hour for a specific weekday. It also showed the average time taken to process a transaction and the average time for a customer session. Using reports P_3 and P_4, branch managers could determine daily schedules to match staffing levels with the anticipated transaction volumes.

KeyCorp believed that the teller productivity module provided branch managers with tools to measure and manage teller proficiency and to anticipate customer arrivals so that they could achieve the targeted level of service.

Report P4—Customer and Transaction Volumes by Weekday by Half Hour

BANK—DISTRICT
BRANCH #—NAME
Month Year

Time Interval	Average Number of Customers Served	Average Number of Transactions	Average Number of Transactions/Customer	Average Time per (Sec) Transaction	Average Time per (Sec) Customer
08:30 A.M.–08:59 A.M.	8	12	1.48	81	119
09:00 A.M.–09:29 A.M.	26	35	1.38	78	107
***	***	***	***	***	***
***	***	***	***	***	***
05:30 P.M.–05:59 P.M.	32	50	1.55	79	122
Total	899	1334	1.48	78	115

A System to Monitor Customer Waiting Times

KeyCorp next wanted to monitor customer waiting times to see if the defined service objective of 90 percent of customers waiting less than five minutes on all days was being met. In order to do this, KeyCorp collected two more sets of data. First, it collected data regarding queue lengths. In the first attempt to do this, the teller would set a mechanical kitchen timer to ring every 30 minutes, at which prompting the teller would record the number of customers standing in line. This primitive approach was soon replaced by a statistical prompt screen that automatically appeared on the teller's main menu screen (that is, between transactions) at the beginning of each half-hour interval. Once the number of customers in the queue was entered, the screen disappeared until the next half-hour interval.

Second, KeyCorp collected data on the average number of tellers working in each half hour interval. For example, this number could be 3.5 for the interval between 11:00 and 11:30 A.M. if three tellers worked the full half hour and a fourth started at 11:15, or if four tellers were working at 11:00, one left for lunch at 11:25, and another left to perform administrative duties at 11:20.

If KeyCorp was to establish separate service level targets for individual branches by day of week or by calendar day or for any combination, customer waiting times would need to be determined and reported. How could KeyCorp determine the expected customer waiting-time experience at KeyCorp branches for specific time intervals and determine whether the defined service objective was being met?

a. Address the following general issue: How can KeyCorp provide a report for branch managers that details customer waiting times and reviews branch performance against KeyCorp's service objectives?

b. Discuss the following specific questions:

1. Could KeyCorp collect customer waiting time data directly?
2. How can waiting times be estimated from the available data?
3. What assumptions are necessary to make these estimates?

CHAPTER

15

COMPUTER SIMULATION

In this concluding chapter, we now are ready to focus on the last of the key techniques of management science. *Computer simulation* ranks very high among the most widely used of these techniques. Furthermore, because it is such a flexible, powerful, and intuitive tool, it is continuing to rapidly grow in popularity. Many managers consider it one of their most valuable decision-making aids.

This technique involves using a computer to *imitate* (simulate) the operation of an entire process or system. For example, computer simulation is frequently used to perform risk analysis on financial processes by repeatedly imitating the evolution of the transactions involved to generate a profile of the possible outcomes. Computer simulation also is widely used to analyze systems that will continue operating indefinitely. For such systems, the computer randomly generates and records the occurrences of the various events that drive the system just as if it were physically operating. Because of its speed, the computer can simulate even years of operation in a matter of seconds. Recording the performance of the simulated operation of the system for a number of alternative designs or operating procedures then enables evaluating and comparing these alternatives before choosing one. For many processes and systems, all this now can be done with spreadsheet software.

The first section describes and illustrates the essence of computer simulation. The case study for this chapter (a revisit of Herr Cutter's barber shop from the preceding chapter) is discussed and analyzed in Sections 15.2 and 15.3. The following section then presents a variety of common applications of computer simulation and Section 15.5 outlines the overall procedure for applying computer simulation. The chapter concludes by describing how to apply @RISK, a prominent Excel add-in for efficiently performing fairly complicated computer simulations on spreadsheets.

15.1 The Essence of Computer Simulation

The technique of *simulation* has long been an important tool of the designer. For example, simulating airplane flight in a wind tunnel is standard practice when a new airplane is designed. Theoretically, the laws of physics could be used to obtain the same information about how the performance of the airplane changes as design parameters are altered, but, as a practical matter, the analysis would be too complicated to do it all. Another alternative would be to build real airplanes with alternative designs and test them in actual flight to choose the final design, but this would be far too expensive (as well as unsafe). Therefore, after some preliminary theoretical analysis is performed to develop a *rough* design, simulating flight in a wind tunnel is a vital tool for experimenting with *specific* designs. This simulation amounts to *imitating* the performance of a real airplane in a controlled environment in order to *estimate* what its actual performance will be. After a detailed design is developed in this way, a prototype model can be built and tested in actual flight to fine-tune the final design.

The Role of Computer Simulation

Computer simulation plays essentially this same role in many management science studies. However, rather than designing an airplane, the management science team is concerned with developing a design or operating procedure for some system. In many cases, the system is a *stochastic system,* as defined below.

> A **stochastic system** is a system that evolves over time according to one or more probability distributions. For example, the queueing systems described in the preceding chapter are stochastic systems because both the interarrival times and service times occur according to probability distributions.

Computer simulation imitates the operation of such a system by using the corresponding probability distributions to *randomly generate* the various events that occur in the system (e.g., the arrivals and service completions in a queueing system). However, rather than literally operating a physical system, the computer is just recording the occurrences of the *simulated* events and the resulting performance of this simulated system.

When computer simulation is used as part of a management science study, commonly it is preceded and followed by the same steps described earlier for the design of an airplane. In particular, some preliminary analysis is done first (perhaps with approximate mathematical models) to develop a rough design of the system (including its operating procedures). Then computer simulation is used to experiment with specific designs to estimate how well each will perform. After a detailed design is developed and selected in this way, the system probably is tested in actual use to fine-tune the final design.

When dealing with relatively complex systems, computer simulation tends to be a relatively expensive procedure. To get started, a detailed model must be formulated to describe the operation of the system of interest and how it is to be simulated. Then considerable time often is required to develop and debug the computer programs needed to run the simulation. Next, many long computer runs may be needed to obtain good estimates of how well all the alternative designs of the system would perform. Finally, all these data should be carefully analyzed before drawing any final conclusions. This entire process typically takes a lot of time and effort. Therefore, computer simulation should not be used when a less-expensive procedure is available that can provide the same information.

Computer simulation typically is used when the stochastic system involved is too complex to be analyzed satisfactorily by the kinds of mathematical models (e.g., queueing models) described in the preceding chapters. One of the main strengths of a mathematical model is that it abstracts the essence of the problem and reveals its underlying structure, thereby providing insight into the cause-and-effect relationships within the system. Therefore, if the modeler is able to construct a mathematical model that is both a reasonable idealization of the problem and amenable to solution, this approach usually is superior to computer simulation. However, many problems are too complex to permit this approach. Thus, computer simulation often provides the only practical approach to a problem.

Now let us look at a few examples to illustrate the basic ideas of computer simulation. These examples have been kept considerably simpler than the usual application of this technique in order to highlight the main ideas more readily. This also will enable us to obtain analytical solutions for the performance of the systems involved to compare with the estimates of the performance provided by computer simulation.

Example 1: A Coin-Flipping Game

You are the lucky winner of a sweepstakes contest. Your prize is an all-expense-paid vacation at a major hotel in Las Vegas, including some chips for gambling in the hotel casino.

Upon entering the casino, you find that, in addition to the usual games (blackjack, roulette, etc.), they are offering an interesting new game with the following rules.

Rules of the Game
1. Each play of the game involves repeatedly flipping an unbiased coin until the *difference* between the number of heads tossed and the number of tails is three.
2. If you decide to play the game, you are required to pay $1 for each flip of the coin. You are not allowed to quit during a play of the game.
3. You receive $8 at the end of each play of the game.

Thus, you win money if the number of flips required is fewer than eight, but you lose money if more than eight flips are required. Here are some examples (where H denotes a head and T a tail).

HHH	3 flips	You win $5.
THTTT	5 flips	You win $3.
THHTHTHTTTT	11 flips	You lose $3.

How would you decide whether to play this game?

Many people would base this decision on *simulation,* although they probably would not call it by that name. In this case, simulation amounts to nothing more than playing the game alone many times until it becomes clear whether it is worthwhile to play for money. Half an hour spent in repeatedly flipping a coin and recording the earnings or losses that would have resulted might be sufficient. This is a true simulation because you are *imitating* the actual play of the game *without* actually winning or losing any money.

Since the topic of this chapter is *computer* simulation, let us see now how a computer can be used to perform this same *simulated experiment.* Although a computer cannot flip coins, it can *simulate* doing so. It accomplishes this by generating a sequence of *random numbers,* as defined below.

A number is a **random number** between 0 and 1 if it has been generated in such a way that *every* possible number within this interval has an equal chance of occurring. For example, if numbers with four decimal places are being used, every one of the 10,000 numbers between 0.0000 and 0.9999 has an equal chance of occurring. Thus, a random number between 0 and 1 is a *random observation* from a *uniform* distribution between 0 and 1. (Hereafter, we will delete the phrase *between 0 and 1* when referring to these random numbers.)

An easy way to generate random numbers is to use the **RAND()** function in Excel. For example, the lower left-hand corner of Figure 15.1 indicates that = RAND() has been entered into cell C10 and then copied into the range C11:C59. (The parentheses need to be included with this function, but nothing is inserted between them.) This causes Excel to generate the random numbers shown in cells C10:C59 of the spreadsheet. (Rows 24–53 have been hidden to save space in the figure.)

The probabilities for the outcome of flipping a coin are

$$P(\text{heads}) = \tfrac{1}{2} \qquad P(\text{tails}) = \tfrac{1}{2}$$

Therefore, to simulate the flipping of a coin, the computer can just let *any half* of the possible random numbers correspond to *heads* and the *other half* correspond to *tails.* To be specific, we will use the following correspondence.

$$0.0000 \text{ to } 0.4999 \quad \text{correspond to} \quad \textit{heads}$$

$$0.5000 \text{ to } 0.9999 \quad \text{correspond to} \quad \textit{tails}$$

By using the formula

$$= \text{IF(RAND()} < 0.5, 1, 0)$$

in each of the column D cells in Figure 15.1, Excel inserts a 1 (to indicate heads) if the random number is less than 0.5 and inserts a 0 (to indicate tails) otherwise. Consequently, the first 11 random numbers generated in column C yield the following sequence of heads (H) and tails (T):

THHTTHTHTTT

at which point the game stops because the number of tails (seven) exceeds the number of heads (four) by three. Cells D4 and D5 record the total number of flips (11) and resulting winning ($8 − $11 = −$3).

FIGURE 15.1

A spreadsheet model for a computer simulation of the coin-flipping game (Example 1).

	A	B	C	D	E	F	G
1	Coin Flipping Game						
2							
3		Summary of Game					
4		Number of Flips =		11			
5		Winnings =		–$3			
6							
7				Result			
8			Random	(0=Tails,	Total	Total	
9		Flip	Number	1=Heads)	Heads	Tails	Stop?
10		1	0.7520	0	0	1	
11		2	0.4184	1	1	1	
12		3	0.4189	1	2	1	
13		4	0.5982	0	2	2	
14		5	0.9559	0	2	3	
15		6	0.1403	1	3	3	
16		7	0.9345	0	3	4	
17		8	0.0801	1	4	4	
18		9	0.6892	0	4	5	
19		10	0.5146	0	4	6	
20		11	0.6290	0	4	7	Stop
21		12	0.1612	1	5	7	NA
22		13	0.0989	1	6	7	NA
23		14	0.1155	1	7	7	NA
54		45	0.1898	1	25	20	NA
55		46	0.3814	1	26	20	NA
56		47	0.7810	0	26	21	NA
57		48	0.5110	0	26	22	NA
58		49	0.9735	0	26	23	NA
59		50	0.0881	1	27	23	NA

	D
4	=COUNTBLANK(G10:G59)+1
5	=8–D4

	C	D	E	F	G
10	=RAND()	=IF(C10<0.5,1,0)	=D10	=B10–E10	
11	=RAND()	=IF(C11<0.5,1,0)	=E10+D11	=B11–E11	
12	=RAND()	=IF(C12<0.5,1,0)	=E11+D12	=B12–E12	=IF(ABS(E12–F12)>=3,"STOP","")
13	=RAND()	=IF(C13<0.5,1,0)	=E12+D13	=B13–E13	=IF(G12="",IF(ABS(E13–F13)>=3,"STOP",""),"NA")
14	=RAND()	=IF(C14<0.5,1,0)	=E13+D14	=B14–E14	=IF(G13="",IF(ABS(E14–F14)>=3,"STOP",""),"NA")
15	=RAND()	=IF(C15<0.5,1,0)	=E14+D15	=B15–E15	=IF(G14="",IF(ABS(E15–F15)>=3,"STOP",""),"NA")
16	:	:	:	:	:
17	:	:	:	:	:

Thus, Figure 15.1 records the computer simulation of one complete play of the game. To virtually ensure that the game will be completed, 50 flips of the coin have been simulated. Columns E and F record the cumulative number of heads and tails after each flip. The equations entered into the column G cells leave each cell blank until the difference in the numbers of heads and tails reaches 3, at which point Stop is inserted into the cell. Thereafter, NA (for Not Applicable) is inserted instead.

Such simulations of plays of the game can be repeated as often as desired with this spreadsheet. Each time, Excel will generate a new sequence of random numbers, and so a new sequence of heads and tails. (Excel will repeat a sequence of random numbers only if you select the range of numbers you want to repeat, copy this range with the Copy command, select Paste Special from the Edit menu, choose the Values option, and click on OK.)

Computer simulations normally are repeated many times to obtain a more reliable estimate of an average outcome. Therefore, this same spreadsheet has been used to generate the data table in Figure 15.2 for 14 plays of the game. As indicated to the right, after choosing row 6 from Figure 15.2 as the prototype row, a *blank* cell E4 has been chosen as the column input cell (*any* blank cell will do).

FIGURE 15.2

A data table that records the results of performing 14 replications of a computer simulation with the spreadsheet in Figure 15.1.

	H	I	J	K
1		**Data Table for Coin Flipping Game**		
2		(14 Replications)		
3				
4			**Number**	
5		**Play**	**of Flips**	**Winnings**
6			7	$1
7		1	11	–$3
8		2	5	$3
9		3	5	$3
10		4	9	–$1
11		5	7	$1
12		6	7	$1
13		7	5	$3
14		8	3	$5
15		9	17	–$9
16		10	5	$3
17		11	5	$3
18		12	3	$5
19		13	9	–$1
20		14	7	$1
21				
22		Average	7	$1.00

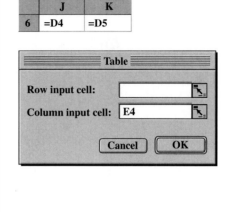

	J	K
6	=D4	=D5

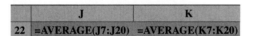

	J	K
22	=AVERAGE(J7:J20)	=AVERAGE(K7:K20)

Cell J22 shows that this sample of 14 plays of the game gives a sample average of seven flips. The sample average provides an *estimate* of the true *mean* of the underlying probability distribution of the number of flips required for a play of the game. Hence, this sample average of seven would seem to indicate that, on the average, you should win about $1 (cell K22) each time you play the game. Therefore, if you do not have a relatively high aversion to risk, it appears that you should choose to play this game, preferably a large number of times.

However, *beware!* One common error in the use of computer simulation is that conclusions are based on overly small samples, because statistical analysis was inadequate or totally lacking. It is very important to use a qualified statistician to help design the experiments to be performed with computer simulation. In this case, careful statistical analysis (using confidence intervals, etc.) would indicate that hundreds of simulated plays of the game would be needed before any conclusions should be drawn about whether you are likely to win or lose by playing this game numerous times.

It so happens that the true mean of the number of flips required for a play of this game is nine. (This mean can be found analytically, but not easily.) Thus, in the long run, you actually would average losing about $1 each time you played the game. Part of the reason that the above simulated experiment failed to draw this conclusion is that you have a small chance of a very large loss on any play of the game, but you can never win more than $5 each time. However, 14 simulated plays of the game were not enough to obtain any observations far out in the tail of the probability distribution of the amount won or lost on one play of the game. Only one simulated play gave a loss of more than $3, and that was only $9.

Figure 15.3 gives the results of running the simulation for 1,000 plays of the games (with rows 17–1,000 not shown). Cell J1008 records the average number of flips as 8.98, very close to the true mean of 9. With this number of replications, the average winnings of −$0.98 in cell K1008 now provides a reliable basis for concluding that this game will not win you money in the long run. (You can bet that the casino already has used computer simulation to verify this fact in advance.)

FIGURE 15.3

This data table improves the reliability of the computer simulation recorded in Figure 15.2 by performing 1,000 replications instead of only 14.

	H	I	J	K
1		Data Table for Coin-Flipping Game		
2		(1000 Replications)		
3				
4			Number	
5		Play	of Flips	Winnings
6			3	$5
7		1	15	–$7
8		2	9	–$1
9		3	11	–$3
10		4	9	–$1
11		5	3	$5
12		6	7	$1
13		7	11	–$3
14		8	9	–$1
15		9	11	–$3
16		10	7	$1
1001		995	3	$5
1002		996	15	–$7
1003		997	7	$1
1004		998	11	–$3
1005		999	7	$1
1006		1000	3	$5
1007				
1008		Average	8.98	–$0.98

TABLE 15.1   The Probability Distribution of Breakdowns for Heavy Duty's Motors, and the Corresponding Random Numbers

Day	Probability of a Breakdown	Corresponding Random Numbers
1, 2, 3	0	
4	0.25	0.0000 to 0.2499
5	0.5	0.2500 to 0.7499
6	0.25	0.7500 to 0.9999
7 or more	0	

Example 2: Corrective Maintenance versus Preventive Maintenance

The Heavy Duty Company has just purchased a large machine for a new production process. The machine is powered by a motor that occasionally breaks down and requires a major overhaul. Therefore, the manufacturer of the machine also provides a second stand-by motor. The two motors are rotated in use, with each one remaining in the machine until it is removed for an overhaul and replaced by the other one.

Given the planned usage of the machine, its manufacturer has provided the company with information about the *durability* of the motors (the number of days of usage until a breakdown occurs). This information is shown in the first two columns of Table 15.1. The first column lists the number of days the current machine has been in use. For each of these days, the second column then gives the probability that the breakdown will occur on that day. Since these probabilities are 0 except for days 4, 5, and 6, the breakdown always occurs on the fourth, fifth, or sixth day.

Fortunately, the time required to overhaul a motor never exceeds three days, so a replacement motor always is ready when a breakdown occurs. When this happens, the remainder of the day (plus overtime if needed) is used to remove the failed motor and install the replacement motor, so the machine then is ready to begin operation again at the beginning of the next day.

FIGURE 15.4

A spreadsheet model for a computer simulation of performing corrective maintenance on the Heavy Duty Co. motors.

	A	B	C	D	E	F	G	H	I	J	K
1		Heavy Duty Company Corrective Maintenance Simulation									
2											
3			Random	Time Since Last	Cumulative		Cumulative		Distribution of		
4		Breakdown	Number	Breakdown	Day	Cost	Cost		Time Between Breakdowns		
5		1	0.4871	5	5	$11,000	$11,000				Number
6		2	0.3611	5	10	$11,000	$22,000		Probability	Cumulative	of Days
7		3	0.1249	4	14	$11,000	$33,000		0.25	0	4
8		4	0.2439	4	18	$11,000	$44,000		0.5	0.25	5
9		5	0.7743	6	24	$11,000	$55,000		0.25	0.75	6
10		6	0.9157	6	30	$11,000	$66,000				
11		7	0.1998	4	34	$11,000	$77,000				
12		8	0.4170	5	39	$11,000	$88,000				
13		9	0.7533	6	45	$11,000	$99,000				
14		10	0.2436	4	49	$11,000	$110,000				
30		26	0.5289	5	131	$11,000	$286,000				
31		27	0.6148	5	136	$11,000	$297,000				
32		28	0.8597	6	142	$11,000	$308,000				
33		29	0.6120	5	147	$11,000	$319,000				
34		30	0.8045	6	153	$11,000	$330,000				
35											
36					Average Cost per Day=		$2,157				

	C	D	E	F	G
5	=RAND()	=VLOOKUP(C5,$J$7:$K$9,2)	=D5	11000	=F5
6	=RAND()	=VLOOKUP(C6,$J$7:$K$9,2)	=E5+D6	11000	=G5+F6
7	=RAND()	=VLOOKUP(C7,$J$7:$K$9,2)	=E6+D7	11000	=G6+F7
8	=RAND()	=VLOOKUP(C8,$J$7:$K$9,2)	=E7+D8	11000	=G7+F8
9	=RAND()	=VLOOKUP(C9,$J$7:$K$9,2)	=E8+D9	11000	=G8+F9
10	:	:	:	:	:
11	:	:	:	:	:

	G
36	=G34/E34

The average costs incurred during each *replacement cycle* (the time from when a replacement of a motor begins until just before another replacement is needed) are summarized below.

Cost of a Replacement Cycle That Begins with a Breakdown

Replace a motor	$ 2,000
Lost production during replacement	5,000
Overhaul a motor	4,000
Total	$11,000

Using Computer Simulation. Computer simulation can be used to estimate what the *average daily cost* will be for replacing the motors as needed. This requires using random numbers to determine when breakdowns occur in the *simulated* process. Using the probabilities in the second column of Table 15.1, 25 percent of the possible random numbers need to correspond to a breakdown on day 4, 50 percent to a breakdown on day 5, and the remaining 25 percent to a breakdown on day 6. The rightmost column of Table 15.1 shows the natural way of doing this.

Excel provides a convenient VLOOKUP function for implementing this correspondence between a random number and the associated event. Figure 15.4 illustrates how it works. One step is to create the table shown in columns I, J, and K, where columns K and I come directly from the first two columns of Table 15.1. Column J gives the cumulative probability *prior* to the number of days in column K, so J8 = I7 and J9 = I7 + I8. Cells J7:K9 then constitute the lookup table for the VLOOKUP function. The bottom of the figure displays how the VLOOKUP command has been entered into the column D cells. The first argument of this function identifies the cell in column C that provides the random number being used. The second argument gives the range for the lookup table. The third argument (2) indicates that column 2 of the lookup table is providing the number being entered into this cell in column D. The choice of the number in column 2 of the lookup table is based on where the random number falls within the ranges between rows in column 1 of this table. In particular, the three possible choices are

$$\text{if} \qquad 0 \le \text{RAND}() < 0.25 \qquad \text{choose 4 days}$$

$$\text{if} \qquad 0.25 \le \text{RAND}() < 0.75 \qquad \text{choose 5 days}$$

$$\text{if} \qquad 0.75 \le \text{RAND}() < 1 \qquad \text{choose 6 days}$$

which is precisely the correspondence indicated in Table 15.1.

By generating 30 simulated breakdowns in this way in column D of Figure 15.4, columns E, F, and G then show the resulting cumulative number of days, the estimated cost for each replacement cycle, and the cumulative cost for the corresponding replacement cycles. (In a more detailed computer simulation, random numbers also could be used to generate the exact costs with each simulated breakdown.) Since the total number of days in this simulation (cell E34) is 153 and the cumulative cost (cell G34) is $330,000, the average daily cost is calculated in cell G36 as

$$\text{Average cost per day} = \frac{\$330,000}{153} = \$2,157$$

Comparisons with Example 1.   Comparing this computer simulation with the ones run for the coin-flipping game reveal a couple interesting differences. One is that the IF function was used to generate each simulated coin flip from a random number (see the equations entered into the column D cells in Figure 15.1), whereas the VLOOKUP function has just been used here to generate the simulated results. Actually, the VLOOKUP function could have been used instead for the coin flips, but the IF function was more convenient. Conversely, a nested IF function could have been used instead for the current example, but the VLOOKUP function was more convenient. In general, we prefer using the IF function to generate a random observation from a probability distribution that has only two possible values, whereas we prefer the VLOOKUP function when the distribution has more than two possible values.

A second difference arose in the way the replications of the two computer simulations were recorded. For the coin-flipping game, simulating a single play of the game involved using the spreadsheet with 59 rows shown in Figure 15.1. Therefore, to record many replications, this same spreadsheet was used to generate the data table in Figure 15.2, which summarized the results of each replication in a single row. For the current example, no separate data table was needed because each replication could be executed and displayed in a single row of the original spreadsheet in Figure 15.4.

However, one similarity between the two examples is that we purposely kept each one sufficiently simple that an analytical solution is available to compare with the simulation results. In fact, it is quite straightforward to obtain the analytical solution for the current version of the Heavy Duty Co. problem. Using the probabilities in Table 15.1, the *expected* number of days until a breakdown occurs is

$$E \text{ (time until a breakdown)} = 0.25(4 \text{ days}) + 0.5(5 \text{ days}) + 0.25(6 \text{ days})$$

$$- 5 \text{ days}$$

Therefore, the *expected value* (in the statistical sense) of the cost per day is

$$E \text{ (cost per day)} = \frac{\$11,000}{5 \text{ days}} = \$2,200 \text{ per day}$$

The average cost of $2,157 per day obtained by computer simulation (cell G36 of Figure 15.4) is an estimate of this true expected value.

The fact that computer simulation actually was not needed to analyze this version of the Heavy Duty Co. problem illustrates a possible pitfall with this technique. Computer simulation is easy enough to use that there occasionally is a tendency to rush into using this technique when a bit of careful thought and analysis first could provide all the needed information more precisely (and perhaps more quickly) than computer simulation. In other cases, starting with a simple analytical model sometimes can provide important insights as a prelude to using computer simulation to refine the analysis with a more precise formulation of the problem.

Some Preventive Maintenance Options.   So far, we have assumed that the company will use a *corrective maintenance* policy. This means that the motor in the machine will be removed and overhauled only after it has broken down. However, many companies use a *preventive maintenance* policy instead. Such a policy in this case would involve *scheduling* the motor to be removed (and replaced) for an overhaul at a certain time even if a breakdown has not occurred. The goal is to provide maintenance early enough to prevent a breakdown. Scheduling the overhaul also enables removing and replacing the motor at a convenient time when the machine would not be in use otherwise, so that no production is lost. For example, by paying overtime wages for the removal and replacement, this work can be done after the normal workday ends so that the machine will be ready by the beginning of the next day. One possibility is to do this at the end of day 3, which would definitely be in time to prevent a breakdown. Other options are to do it at the end of day 4 or day 5 (if a breakdown has not yet occurred) in order to prevent disrupting production with a breakdown in the very near future. Computer simulation can be used to evaluate and compare each of these options (along with a corrective maintenance policy) when analytical solutions are not available.

Consider the option of removing (and replacing) the motor for an overhaul at the end of day 3. The average cost each time this is done happens to be the following.

Cost of a Replacement Cycle That Begins without a Breakdown

Replace a motor on overtime	$3,000
Lost production during replacement	0
Overhaul a motor before a breakdown	3,000
Total	$6,000

Since this total cost of $6,000 occurs every three days, the expected cost per day of this option would be

$$E \text{ (cost per day)} = \frac{\$6,000}{3 \text{ days}} = \$2,000 \text{ per day}$$

Since this cost has been obtained analytically, computer simulation is not needed in this case.

Now consider the remaining two options of removing (and replacing) the motor after day 4 or after day 5 if a breakdown has not yet occurred. Since it is somewhat more difficult to find the expected cost per day analytically for these options, we now will use computer simulation. For either case, the average cost during a replacement cycle depends on whether the replacement began before or after a breakdown occurred. As outlined earlier, these average costs are

Cost of a replacement cycle that begins with a breakdown   = $11,000

Cost of a replacement cycle that begins without a breakdown = $6,000

Figure 15.5 shows the use of computer simulation for the option of scheduling the replacement of each motor after four days. The times until 30 consecutive motors would have

FIGURE 15.5

A spreadsheet model for a computer simulation of performing preventive maintenance (replace after four days) on the Heavy Duty Co. motors.

	A	B	C	D	E	F	G	H	I	J	K	L	M
1		Heavy Duty Company Preventive Maintenance Simulation (Replace After 4 Days)											
2													
3			Random	Time Until	Scheduled Time	Event That	Cumulative		Cumulative		Distribution of		
4		Cycle	Number	Breakdown	Until Replacement	Initiates Cycle	Day	Cost	Cost		Time Between Breakdowns		
5		1	0.5311	5	4	Replacement	4	$6,000	$6,000				Number
6		2	0.8138	6	4	Replacement	8	$6,000	$12,000		Probability	Cumulative	of Days
7		3	0.5914	5	4	Replacement	12	$6,000	$18,000		0.25	0	4
8		4	0.3464	5	4	Replacement	16	$6,000	$24,000		0.5	0.25	5
9		5	0.7329	5	4	Replacement	20	$6,000	$30,000		0.25	0.75	6
10		6	0.2593	5	4	Replacement	24	$6,000	$36,000				
11		7	0.1147	4	4	Breakdown	28	$11,000	$47,000				
12		8	0.0193	4	4	Breakdown	32	$11,000	$58,000				
13		9	0.1572	4	4	Breakdown	36	$11,000	$69,000				
14		10	0.8020	6	4	Replacement	40	$6,000	$75,000				
30		26	0.1110	4	4	Breakdown	104	$11,000	$206,000				
31		27	0.3465	5	4	Replacement	108	$6,000	$212,000				
32		28	0.8552	6	4	Replacement	112	$6,000	$218,000				
33		29	0.9452	6	4	Replacement	116	$6,000	$224,000				
34		30	0.2937	5	4	Replacement	120	$6,000	$230,000				
35												I	
36							Average Cost per Day=		$1,917		36	=I34/G34	

	C	D	E	F	G	H	I
5	=RAND()	=VLOOKUP(C5,$L$7:$M$9,2)	4	=IF(D5<=E5,"Breakdown","Replacement")	=MIN(D5,E5)	=IF(F5="Breakdown",11000,6000)	=H5
6	=RAND()	=VLOOKUP(C6,$L$7:$M$9,2)	4	=IF(D6<=E6,"Breakdown","Replacement")	=G5+MIN(D6,E6)	=IF(F6="Breakdown",11000,6000)	=I5+H6
7	=RAND()	=VLOOKUP(C7,$L$7:$M$9,2)	4	=IF(D7<=E7,"Breakdown","Replacement")	=G6+MIN(D7,E7)	=IF(F7="Breakdown",11000,6000)	=I6+H7
8	=RAND()	=VLOOKUP(C8,$L$7:$M$9,2)	4	=IF(D8<=E8,"Breakdown","Replacement")	=G7+MIN(D8,E8)	=IF(F8="Breakdown",11000,6000)	=I7+H8
9	=RAND()	=VLOOKUP(C9,$L$7:$M$9,2)	4	=IF(D9<=E9,"Breakdown","Replacement")	=G8+MIN(D9,E9)	=IF(F9="Breakdown",11000,6000)	=I8+H9
10	:	:	:	:	:	:	:
11	:	:	:	:	:	:	:

broken down without the replacements are obtained from column D (except rows 15–29 are hidden). The cases where this time is four (indicating a breakdown *during* day 4) correspond to a motor breaking down before it is replaced. (This occurs in row 11 and in six of the hidden rows.) The first full replacement cycle begins with the replacement of the first motor after four days, as shown in row 5, and column G gives the cumulative number of days for the beginning of each cycle. (Since cycle 30 actually *begins* $120 - 4 = 116$ days after cycle 1 begins, we add the four days until the first replacement or breakdown to obtain the full time of 120 days for 30 cycles). Column F indicates whether each cycle begins with a breakdown or with a replacement that is soon enough to avoid a breakdown, and column H gives the resulting cost. Column I then cumulates these costs. Since the 30 cycles last 120 days (cell G34) and have a total cost of $230,000 (cell I34), this simulation yields

$$\text{Average cost per day} = \frac{\$230,000}{120} = \$1,917$$

as the *estimate* of the expected cost per day (which actually is $1,812 per day) for this option.

Figure 15.6 shows the corresponding simulation for the option of scheduling the replacement of each motor after five days. Thus, if the time until a breakdown would be on the sixth day (as indicated in column D), the replacement is made in time to avoid the breakdown (as indicated in column F). Since most of the times in column D are four or five instead, most of the cycles begin with a breakdown. This leads to a much higher total cost for the 30 cycles of $305,000, along with a somewhat longer total time of 144 days. Therefore, the *estimate* of the expected cost per day for this option is

$$\text{Average cost per day} = \frac{\$305,000}{144} = \$2,118$$

FIGURE 15.6

A revision of Figure 15.5 to schedule the replacement of the motors after five days instead of four.

	A	B	C	D	E	F	G	H	I	J	K	L	M
1		Heavy Duty Company Preventive Maintenance Simulation (Replace After 5 Days)											
2													
3			Random	Time Until	Scheduled Time	Event That	Cumulative		Cumulative		Distribution of		
4		Cycle	Number	Breakdown	Until Replacement	Initiates Cycle	Day	Cost	Cost		Time Between Breakdowns		
5		1	0.4877	5	5	Breakdown	5	$11,000	$11,000				Number
6		2	0.1944	4	5	Breakdown	9	$11,000	$22,000		Probability	Cumulative	of Days
7		3	0.6701	5	5	Breakdown	14	$11,000	$33,000		0.25	0	4
8		4	0.4791	5	5	Breakdown	19	$11,000	$44,000		0.5	0.25	5
9		5	0.0172	4	5	Breakdown	23	$11,000	$55,000		0.25	0.75	6
10		6	0.5189	5	5	Breakdown	28	$11,000	$66,000				
11		7	0.7737	6	5	Replacement	33	$6,000	$72,000				
12		8	0.6867	5	5	Breakdown	38	$11,000	$83,000				
13		9	0.7433	5	5	Breakdown	43	$11,000	$94,000				
14		10	0.0343	4	5	Breakdown	47	$11,000	$105,000				
30		26	0.5823	5	5	Breakdown	125	$11,000	$266,000				
31		27	0.9511	6	5	Replacement	130	$6,000	$272,000				
32		28	0.3529	5	5	Breakdown	135	$11,000	$283,000				
33		29	0.4421	5	5	Breakdown	140	$11,000	$294,000				
34		30	0.0239	4	5	Breakdown	144	$11,000	$305,000				
35													
36							Average Cost per Day=	$2,118					

(The true expected cost per day is $2,053.)

Based on all the above results, the clear choice for the least expensive option is the one that schedules the replacement of each motor after four days, since its estimated expected cost per day is only $1,917. Although this estimate based on the simulation in Figure 15.5 overestimates the true expected cost per day by $105, this option still is the least expensive one by a wide margin.

In practice, the simulation runs usually would be considerably longer than those shown in Figures 15.4, 15.5, and 15.6 in order to obtain more precise estimates of the true costs for the alternative options. The simulations typically also would include more details, such as when during a day a breakdown occurs and the resulting cost of lost production that day.

Both Examples 1 and 2 used random numbers to generate random observations from *discrete* probability distributions. Many computer simulations require generating random observations from *continuous* distributions instead. We next describe a general method for doing this with *either* continuous or discrete distributions.

Generating Random Observations from a Probability Distribution

The method for generating these observations is called the **inverse transformation method.** To explain and apply the method, we will use the following notation.

r is a random number.

F(x) is the *cumulative distribution function* (CDF) of the distribution from which we wish to generate a random observation. Thus, for each possible value of *x*, *F(x)* is the probability of being less than or equal to *x*.

For example, Figure 15.7 shows a random number, $r = 0.5271$, and also plots $F(x)$ versus *x* for an arbitrary probability distribution.

Generating each random observation then requires the following two steps.

The Inverse Transformation Method

1. Generate a random number *r*.
2. Find the value of *x* such that $F(x) = r$. This value of *x* is the desired random observation from the probability distribution.

Figure 15.7 illustrates the graphical application of this method. After locating the value of *r* along the vertical axis, a horizontal dashed line is drawn over to $F(x)$. When this line hits

FIGURE 15.7

Illustration of the inverse transformation method for obtaining a random observation from a given probability distribution.

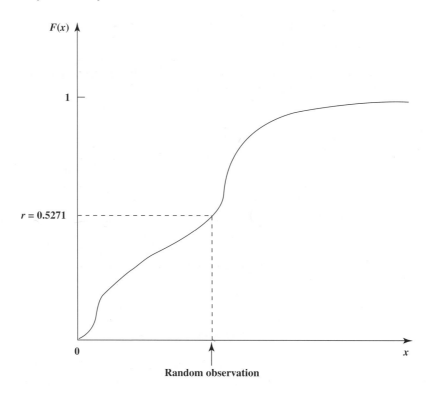

FIGURE 15.8

Applying the inverse transformation method to obtain a random observation from the discrete probability distribution for Example 2 given in Table 15.1.

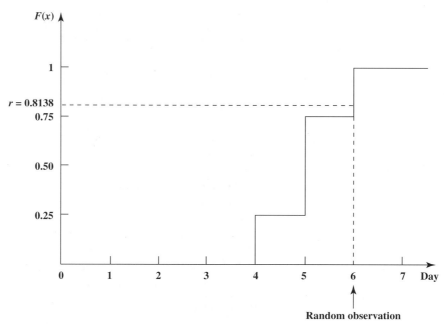

the $F(x)$ curve, a vertical dashed line then is dropped down to the horizontal axis. This point on the horizontal axis is the desired random observation because it is the value of x such that $F(x) = r$.

Although the probability distribution shown in Figure 15.7 is a *continuous* distribution, the inverse transformation method also can be used to generate random observations from *discrete* distributions. For example, consider the discrete distribution given in Table 15.1 for Example 2. Since the probability that a motor will break down on days 4, 5, and 6 is 0.25, 0.5, and 0.25, respectively, the CDF of this distribution is the one shown in Figure 15.8. Using the random number in cell C6 of Figure 15.5 ($r = 0.8138$) then generates the random observation that the breakdown occurs on day 6.

Excel's VLOOKUP function is designed specifically for applying the inverse transformation method to any discrete distribution. This function also can be applied to a continuous distribution by entering an extensive *lookup table* that closely approximates the distribution.

For certain common continuous distributions, the equation that $F(x) = r$ has an analytical solution for x. In such cases, the inverse transformation method enables Excel to quickly generate random observations from these distributions. Two examples of such distributions are the uniform distribution and the exponential distribution. We will illustrate the method with these two distributions in the next section in the context of a case study.

Unfortunately, when $F(x)$ is a relatively complicated function, the inverse transformation method becomes more difficult to apply *analytically*. One example is the *normal distribution*. The option of using the VLOOKUP function after entering an extensive *lookup table* always is available for such a distribution. However, the normal distribution is such an important one that more convenient special methods have been developed to generate random observations from this distribution. In particular, Excel uses the function

$$\text{NORMINV(RAND(), } \mu, \sigma)$$

to do this after you substitute the numerical values for the mean μ and standard deviation σ of the distribution.

Review Questions

1. How does computer simulation imitate the operation of a stochastic system?
2. Why does computer simulation tend to be a relatively expensive procedure?
3. When is computer simulation typically used despite being relatively expensive?
4. What is a random number? For what purpose is it used?
5. What is the purpose of the inverse transformation method? What are its two steps?

15.2 A Case Study: Herr Cutter's Barber Shop (Revisited)

If you have already studied the preceding chapter, you hopefully recall the brief description in Section 14.1 of Herr Cutter's barber shop as an example of a basic kind of queueing system. As indicated there, Herr Cutter is a German barber who runs a one-man barber shop. He opens his shop at 8:00 A.M. each weekday morning. His customers arrive randomly at an average rate of two customers per hour. He requires an average of 20 minutes for each haircut.

The case study concerns the problem described below.

The Decision Facing
Herr Cutter

Herr Cutter has run his barber shop in the same location for nearly 25 years. Although his parents had wanted him to follow in his father's footsteps as a medical doctor, he has never regretted his decision to follow this more modest career path. He enjoys the relaxed working environment, the regular hours, and the opportunity to visit with his customers.

Over the years, he has built up a loyal clientele. He is a fine barber who takes pride in his work. As his business has increased, his customers now often need to wait awhile (sometimes over half an hour) to begin a haircut. However, his long-time customers are willing to do so.

The shop is in a growing city. As the pace of life has increased, Herr Cutter has noticed that new customers are much less likely to return than in the early years, especially if they had to wait very long. He attributes this to a decreasing tolerance for waiting. However, since he is not gaining many new regular customers, his volume of business has leveled off at a steady average of two customers per hour.

As he has grown older, Herr Cutter has wondered increasingly about whether he should add an associate to share the workload. He also would enjoy the company, as well as the additional flexibility. A second barber should reduce the waiting times of the customers considerably, so an additional benefit would be that the total volume of business for the shop should increase somewhat.

However, what has always held him back from adding an associate is the fear of decreasing his personal income from the business. He needs to be putting away considerable money toward retirement and really can't afford a significant decrease in his already modest income. Given the salary and commission he would need to pay an associate, business would need to almost double just to maintain his current level of income. (We will spell out the financial details in the next section when the analysis takes place.) He is doubtful that business would increase nearly this much.

But now opportunity has come knocking on the door. A fellow barber (and friend) in the city has decided to retire and close his shop. This friend has had the same associate for several years, and he now has invited Herr Cutter to hire this fine young man. The friend highly recommends him, and also points out that the associate would bring considerable business with him.

So now Herr Cutter is in a quandary as to whether he should take the plunge in hiring this associate.

Fortunately, help is at hand for making this decision. This friend has shown Herr Cutter an interesting recent article in *The Barber's Journal.* The article describes a study that has been done of barber shops and how long customers now are willing to wait for haircuts to begin. The article concludes with two rules of thumb.

> **First Rule of Thumb:** In a well-run barber shop with a long-established clientele, these loyal customers are willing to tolerate an average waiting time of about 20 minutes until the haircut begins.

Herr Cutter feels that this description fits his situation. He has never tried to estimate the waiting times of his customers, but guesses that an average of 20 minutes sounds about right.

> **Second Rule of Thumb:** In a well-run barber shop, new customers are willing to tolerate an average waiting time of about 10 minutes before the haircut begins. (With longer waits, they tend to take their business elsewhere in the future.)

Again, Herr Cutter feels that this rule of thumb agrees with his own experience.

This second rule of thumb has given Herr Cutter a good idea about how to view his decision. With his current clientele, adding an associate probably would reduce their average waiting time to less than 10 minutes. This prompt service then should help to gradually attract and retain new customers (including some of the associate's customers from the barber shop that is closing). According to the rule of thumb, the level of business should increase until it reaches the point where the average waiting time before the haircut begins has increased to about 10 minutes. Estimating the level of business at that point would indicate the new level of income to the shop and his share of that income. The dilemma is that he does not see how to estimate this level of business in advance.

Herr Cutter asks for advice from his nephew Fritz (a university student majoring in business) about how to resolve this dilemma. Fritz excitedly responds that he thinks he knows just the right approach to use. Computer simulation.

Fritz recently took a course in management science. In fact, he has a copy of MS Courseware, including its Queueing Simulator for simulating queueing systems like his uncle's barber shop. Although not as sophisticated as expensive commercial software packages for performing computer simulations, Fritz explains to his uncle how this routine can indeed provide a good estimate in advance of what the level of business would be with an associate.

Fritz proposes spending a little time with his uncle to gather some data and develop a *simulation model* in preparation for performing the computer simulations. His first simulation will be of the barber shop under its current mode of operation (without an associate) to estimate the current average waiting time. Comparing the results from this simulation with what is actually happening in the barber shop also will help to test the validity of the simulation model. If necessary, the model will be adjusted to better represent the real system. The subsequent simulations will be run of the barber shop *with* an associate. These simulations will assume that the associate's speed in giving a haircut is the same as Herr Cutter's. Different means of the interarrival-time distribution will be tried to determine which mean (i.e., which level of business) would lead to an average waiting time of 10 minutes before the haircut begins.

Fritz asks his uncle if he should proceed with this plan. Herr Cutter urges him to do so.

The remainder of this section describes the execution of this plan, including the mechanics of how these simulations are performed. The next section then presents the results of the actual computer simulations and the analysis of what Herr Cutter should do.

Gathering Data

As with other basic queueing systems, the key events for this barber shop are *service (haircut) completions* and *customer arrivals.* Table 14.1 (in Section 14.1) records the times at which these events occurred over a typical early morning. Figure 14.2 displays these data in a different form by plotting the number of customers in the system (a basic measure of performance) over this same early morning.

By observing the barber shop over an extended period of time, extensive data of the same kind could be gathered to estimate various measures of performance for the barber shop under its current mode of operation. However, it is not necessary to spend months or years gathering such data. Once it has been set up on a computer, computer simulation can accomplish the same thing in a matter of seconds by *simulating* the operation of the barber shop over a lengthy period (even years if desired). However, performing this simulation does require gathering a bit of other data first.

In particular, it is necessary to estimate the *probability distributions* involving the random events (service completions and customer arrivals) in the system. These probability distributions are the distribution of *service times* (the times required to give a haircut) and the distribution of *interarrival times* (the times between consecutive arrivals).

Herr Cutter has found that the time required to give a haircut varies between 15 and 25 minutes, depending on the customer's amount of hair, the desired hair style, and so forth. Furthermore, his best estimate is that the times between 15 and 25 minutes are *equally likely,* which indicates the following distribution.

> **Estimated distribution of service times:** The *uniform distribution* over the interval from 15 minutes to 25 minutes.

The *cumulative distribution function* (CDF) for this distribution is plotted in Figure 15.9.

Since the barber shop has *random arrivals* of customers, Section 14.1 points out that the distribution of interarrival times must be an exponential distribution.

> **Estimated distribution of interarrival times:** An *exponential distribution* (described in Section 14.1) with a mean of 30 minutes.

The shape of an exponential distribution is shown in Figure 14.3 (Section 14.1). Using time units of *minutes,* the CDF for an exponential distribution with this mean of 30 minutes is

$$P(\text{interarrival time} \leq x) = 1 - e^{-x/30} \qquad \text{for } x \geq 0$$

as plotted in Figure 15.10. (Recall that the numerical value of the transcendental number e is slightly over 2.718.)

Generating Random Observations from These Probability Distributions

A computer simulation of the operation of the barber shop requires generating a series of *random observations* from the distributions shown in Figures 15.9 and 15.10. As usual, *random numbers* will be used to do this. However, since these probability distributions are *continuous* distributions, it is not very convenient to use random numbers in the ways described for the *discrete* distributions in Examples 1 and 2 (which employed Excel's IF and VLOOKUP functions, respectively). Instead, we will directly apply the *inverse transformation method* as described at the end of Section 15.1.

Figure 15.11 shows this approach being applied graphically to the probability distribution given in Figure 15.9, namely, the distribution of the duration of Herr Cutter's haircuts. In this case, the random number happens to be $r = 0.7270$. The resulting random observation from this uniform distribution between 15 and 25 is 22.27.

This graphical approach is not very convenient for a computer simulation, so we instead will apply the inverse transformation method *algebraically.* The latter procedure involves solving the equation $F(x) = r$ algebraically for x. For example, the formula for $F(x)$ in Figure 15.11 is

FIGURE 15.9

The cumulative distribution function (CDF) of the duration (in minutes) of haircuts given by Herr Cutter, so the CDF at any duration gives the probability that the time required to give a haircut will be less than or equal to this duration.

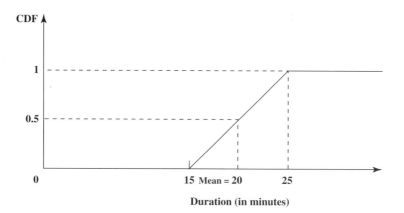

FIGURE 15.10

The cumulative distribution function (CDF) of the interarrival times (in minutes) for Herr Cutter's barber shop, so the CDF at any duration gives the probability that the time between consecutive arrivals is less than or equal to this duration.

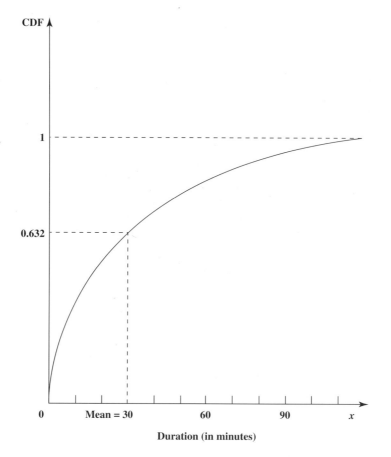

$$F(x) = \begin{cases} 0 & \text{for } x \leq 15 \\ \dfrac{x-15}{10} & \text{for } 15 \leq x \leq 25 \\ 1 & \text{for } x \geq 25 \end{cases}$$

Therefore, the $F(x) = r$ equation becomes

$$\frac{x-15}{10} = 0.7270$$

so

$$x - 15 = 10(0.7270) = 7.27$$

$$x = 15 + 7.27 = 22.27$$

FIGURE 15.11

Applying the inverse transformation method to obtain a random observation from the uniform distribution over the interval from 15 to 25 (which is the distribution of the duration in minutes of Herr Cutter's haircuts given in Figure 15.9).

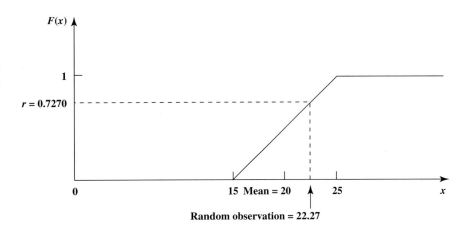

FIGURE 15.12

Applying the inverse transformation method to obtain a random observation from the exponential distribution with a mean of 30 (the distribution of interarrival times in minutes given in Figure 15.10 for Herr Cutter's barber shop).

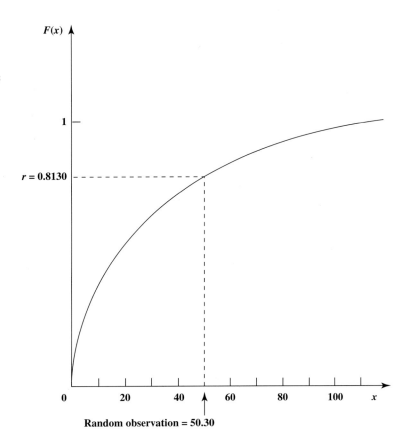

When using Excel, the equation to be entered into each cell receiving a random observation from this uniform distribution is

$$= 15 + 10*RAND()$$

For a uniform distribution with lower and upper bounds different from 15 and 25, the lower bound would be substituted for 15 in this equation and the difference between the two bounds would be substituted for 10.

Although the exponential distribution is more complicated than the uniform distribution, it is one of the distributions to which either the graphical or algebraic version of the inverse transformation method can be applied. Figure 15.12 shows the application of the graphical procedure to the exponential distribution in Figure 15.10 (the distribution of interarrival times in Herr Cutter's barber shop). The random number in this case happens to be $r = 0.8130$. Plotting carefully gives a random observation close to the exact value of 50.30.

As indicated earlier for Figure 15.10, the CDF for this distribution is

$$F(x) = 1 - e^{-x/30} \qquad \text{for } x \geq 0$$

Therefore, applying the algebraic procedure requires solving the equation

$$1 - e^{-x/30} = 0.8130$$

To start,

$$1 - 0.813 = e^{-x/30}$$

so

$$e^{-x/30} = 0.187$$

The tricky step is to next take the *natural logarithm* (denoted by ln) of both sides,

$$\ln e^{-x/30} = \ln 0.187$$

Since $\ln 0.187 = -1.67665$ and the natural logarithm of e to any power is just this power, this equation reduces to

$$-\frac{x}{30} = -1.67665$$

so

$$x = 30 \, (1.67665) = 50.30$$

is the random observation.

In the same manner, the Excel equation for the random observation generated by *any* random number is

$$= -30*LN(1 - RAND()).$$

Since $1 - RAND()$ also is a random number, it is conventional to save performing this subtraction by instead using the equation

$$= -30*LN(RAND())$$

For an exponential distribution with a different mean, this mean would be substituted for 30 in this equation.

The Building Blocks of a Simulation Model for a Stochastic System

With its multiple probability distributions, the case study has some of the complications that are typical of the stochastic systems for which many computer simulations are performed. When preparing for a relatively complex simulation of this type, it is sometimes helpful to develop a formal *simulation model*.

> A **simulation model** is a representation of the system to be simulated that also describes how the simulation will be performed.

> Here are the basic building blocks of a typical simulation model for a stochastic system.

> 1. A description of the components of the system, including how they are assumed to operate and interrelate.
> 2. A simulation clock.
> 3. A definition of the state of the system.
> 4. A method for randomly generating the (simulated) events that occur over time.
> 5. A method for changing the state of the system when an event occurs.
> 6. A procedure for advancing the time on the simulation clock.

We will use the case study to illustrate each of these building blocks.

As first described in Section 14.1, Herr Cutter's barber shop is a basic kind of single-server queueing system. The *components* of this system are the customers, the queue, and Herr Cutter as the server. The assumed distributions of service times and interarrival times were presented in Figures 15.9 and 15.10.

Once a computer simulation is under way, it is necessary to keep track of the passage of time in the system being simulated. Starting at time 0, let

t = amount of *simulated* time that has elapsed so far

The variable t in the computer program is referred to as the **simulation clock.** The program continually updates the current value of this variable as the simulation proceeds. With today's powerful computers, simulated time typically proceeds millions of time faster than running time on the computer.

For Herr Cutter's barber shop, the simulation clock records the amount of simulated time (in minutes) that has elapsed so far since the shop opened at 8:00 A.M. A precise simulation then would start anew for each successive day of simulated operation of the shop. (The next section describes a simplifying assumption that Fritz makes at this point.) A small amount of running time can simulate years of operation.

The key information that defines the current status of the system is called the **state of the system.** For Herr Cutter's barber shop, the state of the system is

$N(t)$ = number of customers in the system at time t.

The computer program for the simulation typically records the cumulative amount of time that the system spends in each state, as well as other measures of performance (e.g., the waiting times of the customers).

For queueing systems such as this barber shop, the key events are the arrivals of customers and the completions of service (haircuts). The preceding subsection describes how these events are randomly generated in a computer simulation by generating random observations from the distributions of interarrival times and service times.

Both of these types of events change the state of the system. The method used to adjust the state accordingly is to

$$\text{Reset} \quad N(t) = \begin{cases} N(t) + 1 & \text{if an arrival occurs at time } t \\ N(t) - 1 & \text{if a service completion occurs at time } t \end{cases}$$

The main procedure for advancing the time on the simulation clock is called **next-event time advance.** Here is how it works.

The Next-Event Time-Advance Procedure

1. Observe the current time t on the simulation clock and the randomly generated times of the next occurrence of each event type that can occur next. Determine which event will occur first.
2. Advance the time on the simulation clock to the time of this next event.
3. Update the system by determining its new state that results from this event and by randomly generating the time until the next occurrence of any event type that can occur from this state (if not previously generated). Also record desired information about the performance of the system. Then return to step 1.

This process continues until the computer simulation has gone as long as desired.

Illustrating the Computer Simulation Process

The Excel spreadsheet in Figure 15.13 shows a computer simulation of the operation of Herr Cutter's barber shop (without an associate) over a period when 100 customers arrive. The pertinent data regarding each customer is recorded on a single row of the spreadsheet (where the rows for customers 11–95 are hidden). All the times are in minutes. As indicated by the equations at the bottom of the figure, the inverse transformation method is being used to generate random observations for the interarrival times and service times in columns C and F. These two times then enable calculating the other pertinent times for each customer in order. Column H records the waiting time *before* the haircut begins for each customer and column I gives the total waiting time in the barber shop (including the haircut) for the customer.

The next-event time-advance procedure is used to carry out this simulation. The procedure focuses on the two key types of events—arrivals and service completions—being recorded in columns D and G, and then moves chronologically through these events. To start, $t = 0$ and $N(t) = 0$ (no customers are in the shop at the instant it opens). Since no service

FIGURE 15.13

A computer simulation of Herr Cutter's barber shop (as currently operated) over a period of 100 customer arrivals.

	A	B	C	D	E	F	G	H	I
1		Herr Cutter's Barber Shop							
2								E	
3		Average Time in Line (Wq) =			18.5 minutes		3	=AVERAGE(H9:H108)	
4		Average Time in System (W) =			38.3 minutes		4	=AVERAGE(I9:I108)	
5									
6				Time	Time		Time	Time	Time
7		Customer	Interarrival	of	Service	Service	Service	in	in
8		Arrival	Time	Arrival	Begins	Time	Ends	Line	System
9		1	4.0	4.0	4.0	19.6	23.5	0.0	19.6
10		2	15.6	19.5	23.5	24.9	48.4	4.0	28.8
11		3	1.4	20.9	48.4	15.7	64.0	27.5	43.1
12		4	36.0	56.9	64.0	20.9	84.9	7.1	28.0
13		5	41.4	98.3	98.3	16.0	114.3	0.0	16.0
14		6	30.2	128.6	128.6	18.9	147.5	0.0	18.9
15		7	10.0	138.6	147.5	20.6	168.1	8.9	29.5
16		8	35.8	174.4	174.4	23.4	197.8	0.0	23.4
17		9	13.0	187.4	197.8	18.8	216.6	10.4	29.2
18		10	12.0	199.4	216.6	19.2	235.8	17.2	36.4
104		96	63.8	2453.1	2453.1	23.9	2477.0	0.0	23.9
105		97	12.8	2465.9	2477.0	17.1	2494.0	11.0	28.1
106		98	1.0	2467.0	2494.0	23.9	2517.9	27.1	50.9
107		99	17.8	2484.7	2517.9	17.6	2535.5	33.2	50.7
108		100	9.3	2494.0	2535.5	20.9	2556.4	41.5	62.4

	C	D	E	F	G	H	I
9	=-30*LN(RAND())	=C9	=D9	=15+10*RAND()	=E9+F9	=E9-D9	=G9-D9
10	=-30*LN(RAND())	=D9+C10	=MAX(G9,D10)	=15+10*RAND()	=E10+F10	=E10-D10	=G10-D10
11	=-30*LN(RAND())	=D10+C11	=MAX(G10,D11)	=15+10*RAND()	=E11+F11	=E11-D11	=G11-D11
12	=-30*LN(RAND())	=D11+C12	=MAX(G11,D12)	=15+10*RAND()	=E12+F12	=E12-D12	=G12-D12
13	=-30*LN(RAND())	=D12+C13	=MAX(G12,D13)	=15+10*RAND()	=E13+F13	=E13-D13	=G13-D13
14	:	:	:	:	:	:	:
15	:	:	:	:	:	:	:

completions can occur without any customers there, the only type of event that can occur next is a customer arrival, so the time on the simulation clock is advanced next to $t = 4.0$ minutes (cell E9), the time when the first customer arrives. Subsequently, the clock is moved ahead to $t = 19.5$ minutes (arrival of customer 2), then to $t = 20.9$ minutes (arrival of customer 3), then to $t = 23.5$ minutes (service completion for customer 1), and so forth.

Figure 15.14 shows the evolution of the state of this system (the number of customers in the barber shop) throughout the first 200 minutes of simulated operation. Thus, the number of customers in the barber shop fluctuates mainly between 0 and 2, plus a couple minutes at 3, during this period.

Estimating Measures of Performance

The purpose of performing a computer simulation of a system is to estimate the measures of performance of the system. The most important measure of performance for Herr Cutter's barber shop (the system of interest here) is the expected waiting time of his customers before beginning a haircut. By averaging the waiting times in column H, cell E3 in Figure 15.13 provides an estimate of 18.5 minutes for this quantity. Similarly, cell E4 averages the times in column I to give an estimate of 38.3 minutes for the expected total waiting time in the shop, including the haircut. (In the notation introduced for queueing models in the preceding chapter, these expected waiting times are W_q and W, respectively.)

Various other measures of performance also could be estimated from this simulation. For example, the probability that a customer has to wait more than 20 minutes to begin a haircut is estimated by the fraction of the customers with a time greater than 20 in column H. An estimate of the expected number of customers in the system (including receiving a haircut) is estimated by summing the numbers in column I and dividing by the total simu-

FIGURE 15.14

This graph shows the evolution of the number of customers in Herr Cutter's barber shop over the first 200 minutes of the computer simulation in Figure 15.13.

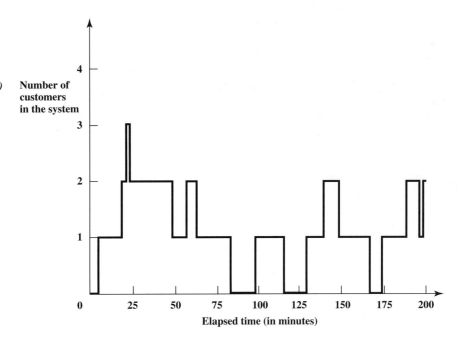

lated time. The expected number of customers waiting to begin a haircut is estimated from column H in the same way.

The probability distribution of the number of customers in the system also might be of interest. As suggested by Figure 15.14, the probability of any particular number of customers in the system can be estimated by the fraction of time that the simulated system spends in that state.

The computer simulation displayed in Figure 15.13 is a rather short one, so it only provides fairly rough estimates of the desired measures of performance. To obtain relatively precise estimates, a computer simulation might run for some years of simulated operation (as we will demonstrate in the next section).

Simulating the Barber Shop with an Associate

Figures 15.13 and 15.14 have illustrated the simulation of the barber shop under its current mode of operation (*without* an associate). In most respects, the procedure for the shop *with* an associate is the same. Each time an arrival occurs (or the shop opens), the next interarrival time needs to be randomly generated. Similarly, each time a customer enters service (begins a haircut), this service time needs to be randomly generated.

The only difference comes when the next-event time-advance procedure is determining which event occurs next. Instead of just two possibilities for this next event, there now are the following three:

1. A departure because Herr Cutter completes a haircut.
2. A departure because the associate completes a haircut.
3. An arrival.

However, other than needing to separately keep track of the time until the next departure of each of these two kinds, the simulation proceeds in basically the same way.

The next section presents the results of several lengthy computer simulations of the barber shop, both with and without an associate.

Review Questions

1. What is the decision facing Herr Cutter?
2. What are the two rules of thumb that will help guide this decision?
3. Which probability distributions need to be estimated in order to apply computer simulation to this case study?

4. What method is used to generate random observations from these distributions?
5. What is a simulation clock?
6. What is the name of the main procedure used to advance the time on the simulation clock?
7. What is the state of the system for Herr Cutter's barber shop?
8. What is the basic difference in the procedure between simulating Herr Cutter's barber shop without an associate and with an associate?

15.3 Analysis of the Case Study

Recall that the decision facing Herr Cutter is whether to add an associate to work with him as a second barber in his shop. The basic issue is whether he would still be able to at least maintain his current income level if he were to add the associate.

The Financial Factors

Here are the main financial factors (converted from German currency to American dollars) for addressing this decision.

Revenue = $15 per haircut

Average tip = $2 per haircut

Cost of maintaining the shop (with or without an associate) = $50 per working day

Salary of an associate = $120 per working day

Commission for an associate = $5 per haircut given by the associate

In addition to his salary and commission, the associate would keep his own tips. Otherwise, the revenue would go to Herr Cutter.

The shop opens at 8:00 A.M. and closes its door to new customers at 5:00 P.M., so it admits customers for nine hours. Herr Cutter and any associate eat their sack lunches and take other breaks only during times when no customers are waiting. Thus, any customer who wants to enter the shop at any time during the nine hours is welcomed by a barber on duty.

Analysis of Continuing without an Associate

As indicated in the preceding section (and depicted in Figure 15.10), the current distribution of interarrival times has a mean of 30 minutes. Thus, Herr Cutter is averaging two customers per hour, so an average of 18 customers per working day. Therefore, after subtracting the cost of maintaining the shop, his average net income per working day is

$$\text{Net daily income} = (\$15 + \$2)(18 \text{ customers}) - \$50$$

$$= \$306 - \$50$$

$$= \$256$$

Herr Cutter's nephew Fritz is helping his uncle analyze his decision by using the Queueing Simulator in your MS Courseware to run computer simulations of the barber shop. This routine is specifically designed to efficiently run long simulations for a variety of queueing systems. It operates basically as illustrated in Figure 15.13, but with more flexibility on the type of system and with far more output. The system can have either a single server or multiple servers. Several options are available for the probability distributions for interarrival times and service times.

Largely to help test the validity of his simulation model (described in the preceding section), Fritz is beginning by simulating the current operation of the shop. Although Figure 15.13 already did this for roughly a week of simulated operation (100 customer arrivals), he now wishes to simulate several years of operation (100,000 arrivals).

Figure 15.15 shows the output that Fritz obtains from this computer simulation. If you wish, you can duplicate this simulation run by using the Queueing Simulator yourself. You should obtain very similar results, but slightly different because different random numbers are used each time.

The measures of performance in column E are the same as those defined for any queueing system at the end of Section 14.3. Column F gives the **point estimate,** the single number that is the best estimate of the measure from this simulation run. Using statistical theory, columns G and H then provide a 95 percent **confidence interval** for each measure. Thus, there is a 95 percent chance that the *true* value of the measure lies within this interval. Because the simulation run was so long (100,000 arrivals), each of these confidence intervals is quite narrow.

Testing the Validity of the Simulation Model

When starting a management science study that will use computer simulation, it is a good idea to first run the simulation model on a simple version of the system for which analytical results are available (if such a version exists). Comparing the results from this simulation run with the analytical results then provides a good test of the validity of the simulation model.

Fritz recalls that the *M/G/*1 queueing model presented in Section 14.5 provides some exact analytical results for the same queueing system that has been assumed for the simulation run in Figure 15.15. This queueing model uses four parameters:

$$\lambda = \text{mean arrival rate}$$

$$= \tfrac{1}{30} \text{ customer per minute} \qquad \text{(from Figure 15.10)}$$

$$\mu = \text{mean service rate}$$

$$= \tfrac{1}{20} \text{ customer per minute} \qquad \text{(from Figure 15.9)}$$

$$\rho = \frac{\lambda}{\mu} = \frac{1/30}{1/20} = \frac{2}{3}$$

$$\sigma = \text{standard deviation of the distribution of service times}$$

Because the standard deviation of the uniform distribution from 0 to 1 is $1/\sqrt{12}$, the standard deviation of the service-time distribution given in Figure 15.9 is

$$\sigma = \frac{10}{\sqrt{12}} = 2.887$$

After entering these values of λ, $1/\mu$, and σ, the Excel template for the *M/G/*1 model in your MS Courseware yields the results shown in Figure 15.16. Note how each of these exact results for the measures of performance fall well within the corresponding 95 percent confidence interval in Figure 15.15. This provides some reassurance that the simulation model and the computer simulation are operating as intended.

FIGURE 15.15

The output obtained by using the Queueing Simulator in this chapter's Excel file to perform a computer simulation of Herr Cutter's barber shop (without an associate) over a period of 100,000 customer arrivals.

	A	B	C	D	E	F	G	H
1		Queueing Simulator for Herr Cutter's Barbershop						
2								
3			Data				Results	
4		Number of Servers =	1			Point	95% Confidence Interval	
5						Estimate	Low	High
6		Interarrival Times			L =	1.358	1.332	1.385
7		Distribution =	Exponential		L_q =	0.689	0.666	0.712
8		Mean =	30		W =	40.582	39.983	41.180
9					W_q =	20.577	19.980	21.174
10								
11		Service Times			P_0 =	0.330	0.326	0.335
12		Distribution =	Uniform		P_1 =	0.310	0.307	0.313
13		Minimum =	15		P_2 =	0.183	0.180	0.185
14		Maximum =	25		P_3 =	0.0942	0.0920	0.0963
15					P_4 =	0.0451	0.0433	0.0469
16		Length of Simulation Run			P_5 =	0.0206	0.0192	0.0220
17		Number of Arrivals =	100,000		P_6 =	0.00950	0.00849	0.0105
18					P_7 =	0.00432	0.00360	0.00503
19					P_8 =	0.00219	0.00163	0.00274
20		Run Simulation			P_9 =	0.000876	0.000540	0.00121
21					P_{10} =	0.000372	0.000165	0.000579

FIGURE 15.16

This Excel template for the M/G/1 model shows the basic measures of performance for Herr Cutter's barber shop without an associate.

	A	B	C	D	E	F	G
1		**Analytical M/G/1 Queueing Results for Herr Cutter**					
2							
3			**Data**			**Results**	
4		$\lambda =$	0.0333	(mean arrival rate)		**L =**	1.347
5		$1/\mu =$	20	(expected service time)		**L$_q$ =**	0.681
6		$\sigma =$	2.887	(standard deviation)			
7		**s =**	1	(# servers)		**W =**	40.417
8						**W$_q$ =**	20.417
9							
10						$\rho =$	0.667
11							
12						**P$_0$ =**	0.333

	G
4	=G5+C4*C5
5	=((C4^2)*(C6^2)+(G10^2))/(2*(1-G10))
6	
7	=G4/C4
8	=G5/C4
9	
10	=C4*C5
11	
12	=1-G10

To further test the validity of the simulation model, Fritz shows the results in column F of Figure 15.15 to Herr Cutter and asks whether these numbers seem consistent with what he has been experiencing in the barber shop. Although Herr Cutter has not been keeping such data, his impression is that the numbers seem about right. He also points out that the average waiting time of about 20 minutes before beginning a haircut is consistent with the first rule of thumb in the article in *The Barber's Journal* (described at the beginning of the preceding section).

Unfortunately, no queueing model yielding useful analytical results is available for the *two-server* queueing system that corresponds to Herr Cutter's barber shop *with* an associate. (None of the multiple-server queueing models presented in Chapter 14 allow a service-time distribution even close to the one in this barber shop.) Therefore, it will be necessary to use computer simulation to obtain good estimates of how the barber shop would perform with an associate. However, after the above testing of the validity of his simulation model, Fritz now is confident that this model will indeed provide good estimates.

Fritz does recognize that his simulation model (just like the *M/G/1* queueing model) does make two simplifying assumptions that are only approximations of how the barber shop actually operates. (These assumptions are incorporated into the Queueing Simulator.)

Simplifying Assumptions

1. The system (barber shop) has an *infinite queue,* so arriving customers always enter the system regardless of how many customers already are there. (In reality, Herr Cutter has found that arriving customers normally do not stay if three customers already are there waiting to begin a haircut, so he now only provides three chairs for waiting customers.)

2. Once started, the system operates continually without ever closing and reopening. (In reality, the barber shop closes its door at 5:00 P.M. each working day and reopens at 8:00 A.M. the next day.)

To evaluate the effect of the first assumption, Fritz notes that the results in Figure 15.15 estimate that

$$P_0 + P_1 + P_2 + P_3 + P_4 = 0.330 + 0.310 + 0.183 + 0.094 + 0.045$$

$$= 0.962$$

Thus, the simulation run exceeds the actual maximum of four customers in the barber shop (one receiving a haircut and three waiting to begin) less than 4 percent of the time. The effect of exceeding the actual maximum so infrequently is to slightly inflate the estimates of L, L_q, W, and W_q above their true values for the barber shop. Thus, the numbers in Figure 15.15 provide conservative estimates (which are preferable to overly optimistic estimates). If Herr Cutter does add an associate, he would provide three additional chairs for waiting customers. There also would be less waiting to begin a haircut, so having arriving customers not stay would become very unusual. Therefore, the first simplifying assumption seems very reasonable for simulating the barber shop with an associate.

The effect of the second simplifying assumption also is to slightly inflate the estimates of L, L_q, W, and W_q above their true values. The reason is that the barber shop begins empty each morning and then gradually builds up to a steady-state condition, whereas the simulation model has the shop operating in a steady-state condition for all but the very beginning of the simulation run. Fortunately, adding an associate would tend to keep the number of customers in the shop down to minimal levels, even in a steady-state condition (which would be nearly reached early in the day). Therefore, the estimation errors from using this assumption to simulate the shop with an associate should be reasonably small.

By obtaining a more expensive computer simulation package and devoting additional preparation time, Fritz would be able to closely simulate the actual operation of the barber shop without making these two approximations. A key advantage of computer simulation is the ability to incorporate as many realistic features into the model as desired.

However, just as with the mathematical model for any other management science technique, there always is a trade-off between the amount of realism incorporated into a model and the ease with which the model can be used. A simulation model does not need to be a completely realistic representation of the real system. Many simulation models err on the side of being overly realistic rather than overly idealistic. An overly realistic model includes unimportant details that do not significantly affect the estimates obtained from the simulation runs. Such a model often is very difficult to debug, and may never be completely debugged. It also is likely to require a great deal of programming and computer time to obtain a small amount of information. The goal should be to just incorporate the important features of the system into the model in order to generate reasonably accurate information that enables management to make well-informed decisions in a timely fashion.

Fritz feels that his current simulation model meets this goal.

Analysis of the Option of Adding an Associate

As described near the beginning of Section 15.2, Herr Cutter and his nephew Fritz have agreed on a plan for analyzing the option of adding an associate. They assume that the probability distribution of service times (the times required to give a haircut) for the associate would be the same as for Herr Cutter. Based on the second rule of thumb given in Section 15.2, they also are assuming that adding the associate would (1) reduce the average waiting time before a haircut begins to less than 10 minutes and (2) then gradually attract new business until this average waiting time reaches about 10 minutes. The level of business (say, the average number of customers per day) determines the mean of the probability distribution of interarrival times. Therefore, a number of computer simulations will be run with different means of this distribution to determine which mean would result in an average waiting time of about 10 minutes. Given the corresponding level of business, a financial analysis can then be conducted.

As depicted in Figure 15.10 in the preceding section, the current mean (without an associate) of the distribution of interarrival times is 30 minutes. Therefore, proceeding by trial and error, Fritz tries the series of means shown in the first column of Table 15.2. To quickly hone in on the neighborhood for the right mean, he uses the Queueing Simulator to run computer simulations of only moderate length, namely, 10,000 arrivals each (roughly half a year of simulated operation). The point estimates of W_q (the average waiting time until a haircut begins) in the second column indicates that the mean that gives a true value of W_q of 10 minutes should be somewhere close to 14.3 minutes. The 95 percent confidence intervals for W_q in the rightmost column further suggest that this mean should be within about half a minute of 14.3 minutes.

To check this further, Fritz next does a long simulation run (100,000 arrivals) with a mean of 14.3 minutes for the interarrival-time distribution. The complete results for all the

TABLE 15.2 The Estimates of W_q Obtained by Using the Queueing Simulator to Simulate Herr Cutter's Barber Shop with an Associate for 10,000 Arrivals for Different Means of the Distribution of Interarrival Times

Mean of Interarrival Times	*Point Estimate of* W_q	*95 percent Confidence Interval for* W_q
20 minutes	3.33 minutes	3.05 to 3.61 minutes
15 minutes	8.10 minutes	6.98 to 9.22 minutes
14 minutes	10.80 minutes	9.51 to 12.08 minutes
14.2 minutes	9.83 minutes	8.83 to 10.84 minutes
14.3 minutes	9.91 minutes	8.76 to 11.05 minutes

FIGURE 15.17

The results obtained by using the Queueing Simulator to perform a computer simulation of Herr Cutter's barber shop with an associate over a period of 100,000 customer arrivals.

	A	B	C	D	E	F	G	H
1	Queueing Simulator for Herr Cutter's Barbershop with an Associate							
2								
3			Data				Results	
4		Number of Servers =	2			Point	95% Confidence Interval	
5						Estimate	Low	High
6		Interarrival Times			L =	2.126	2.090	2.163
7		Distribution =	Exponential		L_q =	0.719	0.689	0.748
8		Mean =	14.3		W =	30.212	29.833	30.591
9					W_q =	10.211	9.834	10.588
10								
11		Service Times			P_0 =	0.163	0.160	0.166
12		Distribution =	Uniform		P_1 =	0.266	0.262	0.270
13		Minimum =	15		P_2 =	0.233	0.230	0.235
14		Maximum =	25		P_3 =	0.154	0.152	0.156
15					P_4 =	0.0877	0.0855	0.0898
16		Length of Simulation Run			P_5 =	0.0467	0.0448	0.0487
17		Number of Arrivals =	100,000		P_6 =	0.0242	0.0226	0.0257
18					P_7 =	0.0128	0.0116	0.0140
19					P_8 =	0.00634	0.00546	0.00722
20		Run Simulation			P_9 =	0.00321	0.00253	0.00389
21					P_{10} =	0.00155	0.00108	0.00202

measures of performance are shown in Figure 15.17. The point estimate of W_q (and most of the 95 percent confidence interval for W_q) now is slightly over 10. However, Fritz also recalls that the two simplifying assumptions discussed in the preceding subsection cause this estimate to slightly overstate the true value of W_q for the barber shop. Therefore, he concludes that 14.3 minutes is the best available estimate of the mean that would result in an average waiting time of about 10 minutes.

Fritz realizes that he could spend more time running long computer simulations with means slightly different from 14.3 minutes in order to pin down this estimate even better. However, he already knows from the confidence intervals in Table 15.2 that 14.3 minutes is at least very close. Furthermore, given the slight inaccuracies known to be in the simulation model due to the two simplifying assumptions, there is no point in trying to obtain an estimate of the mean that is more precise than the model is. This would only give a false sense of accuracy. He is content that 14.3 minutes provides a very adequate and conservative estimate of the mean for purposes of analysis.

Based on this estimate, Fritz concludes that having his uncle add an associate should gradually increase the level of business to around the point where

$$\text{Average interarrival time} = 14.3 \text{ minutes}$$

which would yield

$$\text{Mean arrival rate} = \frac{60}{14.3} \text{ customers per hour}$$

$$= 4.2 \text{ customers per hour}$$

$$= 4.2(9) \text{ customers per day}$$

$$= 37.8 \text{ customers per day}$$

This level of business would be more than double the current average of 18 customers per day for the shop. Herr Cutter would plan to divide the customers equally with the associate, so each would average 18.9 customers per day.

Therefore, using the cost factors given at the beginning of this section, Herr Cutter's average net income per working day would become

$$
\begin{aligned}
\text{Net daily income} = 37.8(\$15) \quad & \text{(shop revenue)} \\
+ 18.9(\$2) \quad & \text{(his tips)} \\
- \$50 \quad & \text{(shop maintenance)} \\
-\$120 \quad & \text{(associate's salary)} \\
- 18.9(\$5) \quad & \text{(associate's commission)} \\
= \$567 + \$37.80 - \$50 - \$120 - \$94.50 \\
= \$340.30
\end{aligned}
$$

This compares with Herr Cutter's current net daily income of $256. Thus, it is estimated that the change in his net daily income from adding an associate would eventually become

$$\text{Change in net daily income} = \$340.30 - \$256$$

$$= \$84.30$$

Thus, he actually would increase his income significantly.

When presenting this analysis to his uncle, Fritz emphasizes that this $84.30 figure is just an *estimate* of what will happen *after* the level of business gradually increases to its new level. It may take awhile, even a year or two, to reach this new level. Meanwhile, Herr Cutter's income may start off less than it has been before gradually increasing. Furthermore, the optimistic conclusion of a substantial increase in income eventually is based largely on the rather shaky premise that the second rule of thumb in the article in *The Barber's Journal* will prove to be valid and applicable to his shop. This premise leads to an estimate that his level of business would more than double eventually. Achieving this big increase in business would seem realistic only if the associate is able to bring a considerable number of customers with him from his current shop and then the two of them are able to attract many additional new customers.

Herr Cutter feels confident that they can accomplish this. This associate was highly recommended by his friend. Furthermore, he feels that his own skill as a barber would already have attracted many new customers if he didn't already have as much business as he can handle alone. In this growing city, the opportunity is there. He also likes the fact that adding an associate would enable him to improve the level of service for his current loyal clientele by substantially decreasing their average waiting time before beginning a haircut. Finally, he also sees many personal advantages to having a good associate that cannot be measured in monetary terms. Therefore, he wouldn't mind a temporary decrease in income as long as he probably would at least equal his current income level in a year or two. Actually increasing his income would be a pleasant bonus.

On these grounds, Herr Cutter decides to hire the associate. He also thanks his nephew for the invaluable help that Fritz's computer simulations provided him in making his decision.

Review Questions

1. What did Fritz simulate in his first simulation run? For what purpose?
2. What are the two types of estimates of a measure of performance obtained by the Queueing Simulator?

3. What were the two ways with which Fritz tested the validity of his simulation model?

4. Does Fritz's simulation model make any simplifying assumptions? Is it necessary for a simulation model to be a completely realistic representation of the real system?

5. Does Fritz's analysis estimate that Herr Cutter's income would eventually increase or decrease (compared to its current level) if he added an associate?

15.4 Some Common Types of Applications

Computer simulation is an exceptionally versatile technique. It can be used (with varying degrees of difficulty) to investigate virtually any kind of stochastic system, as well as simpler systems involving probability distributions. This versatility has made computer simulation the most widely used management science technique for studies dealing with such systems, and its popularity is continuing to increase. The ability of Excel and Excel add-ins to perform many of these computer simulations has given further impetus to the use of this technique.

Because of the tremendous diversity of its applications, it is impossible to enumerate all the specific areas in which computer simulation has been used. However, we will briefly describe here some particularly important categories of applications.

The first three categories concern types of stochastic systems considered in some preceding chapters. It is common to use the kinds of mathematical models described in those chapters to analyze simplified versions of the system and then to apply computer simulation to refine the results.

Design and Operation of Queueing Systems

Section 14.2 gives several dozen examples of commonly encountered queueing systems that illustrate how such systems pervade many areas of society. Many mathematical models are available (including several presented in Chapter 14) for analyzing relatively simple types of queueing systems. Unfortunately, these models can only provide rough approximations at best of more complicated queueing systems. However, computer simulation is well-suited for dealing with even very complicated queueing systems, so many of its applications fall into this category.

For example, this chapter's case study is of this type. Although a mathematical model (the *M/G/*1 model) is available to provide some of the measures of performance of Herr Cutter's barber shop under its current mode of operation (without an associate), this is not the case for the option of adding an associate. Therefore, computer simulation was needed for the key part of the study.

Because applications in this category are so pervasive, the Queueing Simulator in your MS Courseware has been designed specifically for simulating queuing systems.

Among the five award-winning applications of queueing models presented in Section 14.10, two of these also made heavy use of computer simulation. One was the study of **New York City's** arrest-to-arraignment system that led to great improvements in the efficiency of this system plus annual savings of $9.5 million. The other was **AT&T** developing a PC-based system to help its business customers design or redesign their call centers, resulting in more than $750 million in annual profit for these customers.

Managing Inventory Systems

Chapter 12 discusses the management of inventory systems when the products involved have uncertain demand. Two mathematical models are presented to guide the management of basic systems of this type. Section 12.6 then describes the kinds of larger inventory systems that commonly arise in practice. Although mathematical models sometimes can help analyze these more complicated systems, computer simulation often plays a key role as well.

As one example, an article in the April 1996 issue of *OR/MS Today* describes a management science study of this kind that was done for the **IBM PC Company** in Europe. Facing unrelenting pressure from increasingly agile and aggressive competitors, the company had to find a way to greatly improve its performance in quickly filling customer orders. The management science team analyzed how to do this by simulating various redesigns of the company's entire *supply chain* (the network of facilities that spans procurement, manufacturing, and distribution, including all the inventories accumulated along the way). This led to major changes in the design and operation of the supply chain (including its inventory systems) that greatly improved the company's competitive position. Direct cost savings of $40 million per year also were achieved.

Estimating the Probability of Completing a Project by the Deadline

One of the key concerns of a project manager is whether his or her team will be able to complete the project by the deadline. Section 7.4 describes how the PERT three-estimate approach can be used to obtain a rough estimate of the probability of meeting the deadline with the current project plan. That section also describes three simplifying approximations made by this approach to be able to estimate this probability. Unfortunately, because of these approximations, the resulting estimate always is overly optimistic, and sometimes by a considerable amount.

Consequently, it is becoming increasingly common now to use computer simulation to obtain a better estimate of this probability. This involves generating random observations from the probability distributions of the duration of the various activities in the project. By using the project network, it then is straightforward to simulate when each activity begins and ends, and so when the project finishes. By repeating this simulation thousands of times (in one computer run), a very good estimate can be obtained of the probability of meeting the deadline. (You will see an example in Section 15.6.)

Design and Operation of Manufacturing Systems

Surveys consistently show that a large proportion of the applications of computer simulation involve manufacturing systems. Many of these systems can be viewed as a queueing system of some kind (e.g., a queueing system where the machines are the servers and the jobs to be processed are the customers). However, various complications inherent in these systems (e.g., occasional machine breakdowns, defective items needing to be reworked, and multiple types of jobs) go beyond the scope of the usual queueing models. Such complications are no problem for computer simulation.

Here are a few examples of the kinds of questions that might be addressed.

1. How many machines of each type should be provided?
2. How many materials-handling units of each type should be provided?
3. Considering their due dates for completion of the entire production process, what rule should be used to choose the order in which the jobs currently at a machine should be processed?
4. What are realistic due dates for jobs?
5. What will be the bottleneck operations in a new production process as currently designed?
6. What will be the throughput (production rate) of a new production process?

Design and Operation of Distribution Systems

Any major manufacturing corporation needs an efficient *distribution system* for distributing its goods from its factories and warehouses to its customers. There are many uncertainties involved in the operation of such a system. When will vehicles become available for shipping the goods? How long will a shipment take? What will be the demands of the various customers? By generating random observations from the relevant probability distributions, computer simulation can readily deal with these kinds of uncertainties. Thus, it is used quite often to test various possibilities for improving the design and operation of these systems.

One award-winning application of this kind is described in the January–February 1991 issue of *Interfaces*. **Reynolds Metals Company** spends over $250 million annually to deliver its products and receive raw materials. Shipments are made by truck, rail, ship, and air across a network of well over a hundred shipping locations including plants, warehouses, and suppliers. A combination of mixed binary integer programming (Chapter 9) and computer simulation was used to design a new distribution system with central dispatching. The new system both improved on-time delivery of shipments and reduced annual freight costs by over $7 million.

The study for the IBM PC Company in Europe mentioned earlier (under "Managing Inventory Systems") also encompassed the design and operation of distribution systems as well.

Financial Risk Analysis

Financial risk analysis was one of the earliest application areas of computer simulation, and it continues to be a very active area. For example, consider the evaluation of a proposed capital investment with uncertain future cash flows. By generating random observations from the probability distributions for the cash flow in each of the respective time periods (and considering relationships between time periods), computer simulation can generate thousands of scenarios for how the investment will turn out. This provides a *probability distribution* of the return (e.g., net present value) from the investment. This distribution (sometimes called the *risk profile*) enables management to assess the risk involved in making the investment. (You will see an example in Section 15.6.)

A similar approach enables analyzing the risk associated with investing in various securities, including the more exotic financial instruments such as puts, calls, futures, stock options, and so on.

Health Care
Applications

Health care is another area where, like the evaluation of risky investments, analyzing future uncertainties is central to current decision making. However, rather than dealing with uncertain future cash flows, the uncertainties now involve such things as the evolution of human diseases.

Here are a few examples of the kinds of computer simulations that have been performed to guide the design of health care systems.

1. Simulating the use of hospital resources when treating patients with coronary heart disease.
2. Simulating health expenditures under alternative insurance plans.
3. Simulating the cost and effectiveness of screening for the early detection of a disease.
4. Simulating the use of the complex of surgical services at a medical center.
5. Simulating the timing and location of calls for ambulance services.
6. Simulating the matching of donated kidneys with transplant recipients.
7. Simulating the operation of an emergency room.

Applications to Other
Service Industries

Like health care, other service industries also have proven to be fertile fields for the application of computer simulation. These industries include government services, banking, hotel management, restaurants, educational institutions, disaster planning, the military, amusement parks, and many others. In many cases, the systems being simulated are, in fact, queueing systems of some type.

The January–February 1992 issue of *Interfaces* describes an award-winning application in this category. The **U.S. Postal Service** had identified *automation technology* as the only way it would be able to handle its increasing mail volume while remaining price competitive and satisfying service goals. Extensive planning over several years was required to convert to a largely automated system that would meet these goals. The backbone of the analysis leading to the adopted plan was performed with a comprehensive simulation model called META (Model for Evaluating Technology Alternatives). This model was first applied extensively at the national level, and then it was moved down to the local level for detailed planning. The resulting plan required a cumulative capital investment of $12 billion, but also was projected to achieve labor savings of over $4 billion per year. Another consequence of this highly successful application of computer simulation was that the value of management science tools now is recognized at the highest levels of the Postal Service. Management science techniques continue to be used by the planning staff both at headquarters and in the field divisions.

New Applications

More new innovative applications of computer simulation are being made each year. Many of these applications are first announced publicly at the annual Winter Simulation Conference, held each December in some U.S. city. Since its beginning in 1967, this conference has been an institution in the computer simulation field. It now is attended by nearly a thousand participants, divided roughly equally between academics and practitioners. Hundreds of papers are presented to announce both methodological advances and new innovative applications.

Review Questions

1. This chapter's case study falls into which category of computer simulation applications?
2. What was simulated in the management science study done for the IBM PC Company in Europe?
3. What is the quantity being estimated when computer simulation is used to supplement the PERT three-estimate approach?
4. What is an example of the kind of question that might be addressed when simulating a manufacturing system?
5. What was being designed when computer simulation was applied in the award-winning application at Reynolds Metal Company?
6. What can computer simulation provide to enable management to assess the risk involved in making a capital investment with uncertain future cash flows?
7. What is an example of the kind of computer simulation that has been performed to guide the design of health care systems?
8. What was being planned during the award-winning application of computer simulation performed for the U.S. Postal Service? What were the projected labor savings from the resulting plan?

15.5 Outline of a Major Computer Simulation Study

Thus far, this chapter has focused mainly on the *process* of performing a computer simulation and some applications from doing so. We now place this material into broader perspective by briefly outlining all the typical steps involved in a major management science study that is based on applying computer simulation. (Nearly the same steps also apply when the study is applying other management science techniques instead.)

We should emphasize that some applications of computer simulation do not require all the effort described in the following steps. The advent of Excel and Excel add-ins for efficiently performing basic computer simulations on a spreadsheet now often enables conducting the study with far less time and expense than previously. Managers now can sometimes perform the studies that previously were done by management science specialists.

However, major applications of computer simulation still require the extended effort of management science teams, as described below.

Step 1: Formulate the Problem and Plan the Study

The management science team needs to begin by meeting with management to address the following kinds of questions.

1. What is the problem that management wants studied?
2. What are the overall objectives for the study?
3. What specific issues should be addressed?
4. What kinds of alternative system configurations should be considered?
5. What measures of performance of the system are of interest to management?
6. What are the time constraints for performing the study?

In addition, the team also will meet with engineers and operational personnel to learn the details of just how the system would operate. (The team generally will also include one or more members with a firsthand knowledge of the system.) If a current version of the system is in operation, the team will observe the system to identify its components and the linkages between them.

For the case study involving Herr Cutter's barber shop, the components of this queueing system are the arriving customers, the queue, and the barber(s) as the server(s). Because this was a small informal study, the management science team consisted of just Herr Cutter's nephew Fritz, with Herr Cutter as the lone member of management.

Before concluding this step, the head of the management science team also needs to plan the overall study in terms of the number of people, their responsibilities, the schedule, and a budget for the study.

Step 2: Collect the Data and Formulate the Simulation Model

The types of data needed depend on the nature of the system to be simulated. For Herr Cutter's barber shop, the key pieces of data were the distribution of *interarrival times* and the distribution of *service times* (times needed to give a haircut). For a single-product inventory system, the team would need the distribution of *demand* for the product and the distribution of the *lead time* between placing an order to replenish inventory and receiving the amount ordered. For a PERT project network where the activity durations are uncertain, distributions of the *durations of the activities* are needed. For a manufacturing system involving machines that occasionally break down, the team needs to determine the distribution of the *time until a machine breaks down* and the distribution of *repair times.*

In each of these examples, note that it is the *probability distributions* of the relevant quantities that are needed. In order to generate representative scenarios of how a system would perform, it is essential that a computer simulation generate *random observations* from these distributions rather than simply using averages.

Generally, it will only be possible to *estimate* these distributions. This is done after taking direct observations from an existing version of the system under study, or from a similar system. If no such system exists, other possible sources of information include industrial engineering time studies, engineering records, operating manuals, machine specifications, and interviews with individuals who have experience with similar kinds of operations.

A simulation model often is formulated in terms of a *flow diagram* that links together the various components of the system. Operating rules are given for each component, including the probability distributions that control when events will occur there. The model only needs to contain enough detail to capture the essence of the system. For a large study, it is a good idea to begin by formulating and debugging a relatively simple version of the model before adding important details.

Step 3: Check the Accuracy of the Simulation Model

Before constructing a computer program, the management science team should engage the people most intimately familiar with how the system will operate in checking the accuracy of the simulation model. This often is done by performing a structured walk-through of the conceptual model, using an overhead project, before an audience of all the key people. At a typical such meeting, several erroneous model assumptions will be discovered and corrected, a few new assumptions will be added, and some issues will be resolved about how much detail is needed in the various parts of the model.

In addition to helping to ensure the accuracy of the simulation model, this process tends to provide the key people with some sense of ownership of the model and the study.

Step 4: Select the Software and Construct a Computer Program[1]

There are four major classes of software used for computer simulations. One is *spreadsheet software.* Section 15.1 described how Excel is able to perform some basic computer simulations on a spreadsheet. In addition, some excellent Excel add-ins now are available to enhance this kind of spreadsheet modeling. The next section focuses on the use of one of these add-ins in your MS Courseware.

The other three classes of software for computer simulations are intended for more extensive applications where it is no longer convenient to use spreadsheet software. One such class is a *general-purpose programming language,* such as C, FORTRAN, PASCAL, BASIC, and so on. Such languages (and their predecessors) often were used in the early history of the field because of their great flexibility for programming any sort of simulation. However, because of the considerable programming time required, they are not used nearly as much now.

The third class is a **general-purpose simulation language.** These languages provide many of the features needed to program a simulation model, and so may reduce the required

---

[1] This subsection does not attempt to enumerate or describe the individual simulation software packages that currently are available. For details about 54 such packages, see the 1999 Simulation Software Survey on pp. 38–51 of the February 1999 issue of *OR/MS Today.*

programming time substantially. They also provide a natural framework for simulation modeling. Although less flexible than a general-purpose programming language, they are capable of programming almost any kind of simulation model. However, some degree of expertise in the language is needed.

Prominent general-purpose simulation languages include the current version of GPSS, SIMSCRIPT, SLAM, and SIMAN. The initial versions of these languages date back to 1961, 1963, 1979, and 1983, respectively, but all have stood the test of time.

A key development in the 1980s and 1990s has been the emergence of the fourth class of software, called **applications-oriented simulators** (or just **simulators** for short). Each of these simulators is designed for simulating fairly specific types of systems, such as certain types of manufacturing, computer, and communications systems. Some are very specific (e.g., for oil and gas production engineering, nuclear power plant analysis, or cardiovascular physiology). Their *goal* is to be able to construct a simulation "program" by the use of menus and graphics, without the need for programming. They are relatively easy to learn and have modeling constructs closely related to the system of interest.

A simulator can be wonderful if the system you wish to simulate fits right into the prescribed category for the simulator. However, the prescription of allowable system features tends to be fairly narrow. Therefore, the major drawback of many simulators is that they are limited to modeling only those system configurations that are allowed by their standard features. Some simulators do allow the option of incorporating routines written in a general-purpose programming language to handle nonstandard features. This option is frequently needed when simulating relatively complex systems.

Another key development in recent years has been the development of **animation** capabilities for displaying computer simulations in action. In an animation, key elements of a system are represented in a computer display by icons that change shape, color, or position when there is a change in the state of the simulation system. Most simulation software vendors now offer a version of their software with animation capabilities. Furthermore, the animation is becoming increasingly elaborate, including even three-dimensional capabilities in some cases.

The major reason for the popularity of animation is its ability to communicate the essence of a simulation model (or of a computer simulation run) to managers and other key personnel. This greatly increases the credibility of the computer simulation approach. In addition, animation can be helpful in debugging the computer program for a computer simulation program.

Step 5: Test the Validity of the Simulation Model

After the computer program has been constructed and debugged, the next key step is to test whether the simulation model incorporated into the program is providing valid results for the system it is representing. Specifically, will the measures of performance for the real system be closely approximated by the values of these measures generated by the simulation model?

This question usually is difficult to answer because most versions of the "real" system do not currently exist. Typically, the purpose of computer simulation is to investigate and compare various proposed system configurations to help choose the best one.

However, some version of the real system may currently be in operation. If so, its performance data should be compared with the corresponding output measures generated by pilot runs of the simulation model.

In some cases, a mathematical model may be available to provide results for a simple version of the system. If so, these results also should be compared with the simulation results.

For example, in the case study, the barber shop currently is in operation with Herr Cutter as the only barber. Therefore, as described in Section 15.3 (see the subsection entitled "Testing the Validity of the Simulation Model"), Fritz compared the results from an applicable queueing model with a simulation of this current version of the barber shop. (Because this was a small informal simulation study, he and Herr Cutter did not take the time to gather detailed performance data for the actual operation of the shop.)

When no real data are available to compare with simulation results, one possibility is to conduct a *field test* to collect such data. This would involve constructing a small prototype of some version of the proposed system and placing it into operation. This prototype might also be used after the simulation study has been completed to fine-tune the design of the system before the real system is installed.

Another useful validation test is to have knowledgeable operational personnel check the credibility of how the simulation results change as the configuration of the simulated system is changed. Even when no basis exists for checking the reasonableness of the measures of performance obtained for a particular version of the system, some conclusions often can be drawn about how the *relative* performance of the system should change as its parameters are changed.

Watching animations of simulation runs is another way of checking the validity of the simulation model. Once the model is operating properly, animations also generate interest and credibility in the simulation study for both management and operational personnel.

Step 6: Plan the Simulations to Be Performed

At this point, you need to begin making decisions on which system configurations to simulate. This often is an evolutionary process, where the initial results for a range of configurations help you to hone in on which specific configurations warrant detailed investigation.

Decisions also need to be made now on such issues as the lengths of simulation runs. Keep in mind that computer simulation does not produce *exact* values for the measures of performance of a system. Instead, each simulation run can be viewed as a *statistical experiment* that is generating *statistical observations* of the performance of the simulated system. These observations are used to produce *statistical estimates* of the measures of performance. Increasing the length of a run increases the precision of these estimates.

The statistical theory for designing statistical experiments conducted through computer simulation is little different than for experiments conducted by directly observing the performance of a physical system.[2] Therefore, the services of a professional statistician (or at least an experienced simulation analyst with a strong statistical background) can be invaluable at this step.

Step 7: Conduct the Simulation Runs and Analyze the Results

The output from the simulation runs now provides statistical estimates of the desired measures of performance for each system configuration of interest. In addition to a *point estimate* of each measure, a *confidence interval* normally should be obtained to indicate the range of likely values of the measure (just as was done for the case study).

These results might immediately indicate that one system configuration is clearly superior to the others. More often, they will identify the few strong candidates to be the best one. In the latter case, some longer simulation runs would be conducted to better compare these candidates. Additional runs also might be used to fine-tune the details of what appears to be the best configuration.

Step 8: Present Recommendations to Management

After completing its analysis, the management science team needs to present its recommendations to management. This usually would be done through both a written report and a formal oral presentation to the managers responsible for making the decisions regarding the system under study.

The report and presentation should summarize how the study was conducted, including documentation of the validation of the simulation model. A demonstration of the *animation* of a simulation run might be included to better convey the simulation process and add credibility. Numerical results that provide the rationale for the recommendations need to be included.

Management usually involves the management science team further in the initial implementation of the new system, including the indoctrination of the affected personnel.

Review Questions

1. When beginning a computer simulation study, with whom should a management science team meet to address some key questions and then to learn the details of how the system would operate?

2. What kind of diagram is often used to formulate a simulation model?

3. Who should the team engage to help check the accuracy of the simulation model?

---

[2]For details about the relevant statistical theory, see Chapters 9–12 in A. M. Law and W. W. Kelton, *Simulation Modeling and Analysis,* 2nd ed. (New York: McGraw-Hill, 1991).

4. What is the difference between a general-purpose simulation language and an applications-oriented simulator?

5. When using animation to display a computer simulation in action, how are the key elements of the system represented?

6. What is the specific question being addressed when testing the validity of a simulation model?

7. A simulation run can be viewed as what kind of statistical experiment?

8. What kinds of estimates are obtained from simulation runs?

9. What are the two ways in which a management science team usually presents its recommendations to management?

15.6 Performing Computer Simulations with @RISK

The preceding section outlines the typical steps involved in major computer simulation studies of complex systems. However, not all computer simulation studies are nearly that involved. In fact, when studying relatively basic systems, it usually is possible to run the needed simulations quickly and easily on spreadsheets.

Whenever a spreadsheet model would be used to analyze a problem without taking uncertainties into account (except through sensitivity analysis), the tools now are available to use computer simulation to consider the effect of the uncertainties. As described in Section 15.1, the standard Excel package has some basic simulation capabilities, including the ability to generate uniform random numbers and to generate random observations from some probability distributions. Furthermore, some simulation add-ins for Excel have been developed that make it even easier to analyze spreadsheet models by efficiently performing computer simulations and generating the output in a variety of useful forms. Two prominent simulation add-ins with similar capabilities are @RISK, developed by Palisade Corporation, and Crystal Ball, developed by Decisioneering. Other simulation add-ins also are available as shareware. One is RiskSim, developed by Professor Michael Middleton.

We have provided the academic version of RiskSim for you in your MS Courseware. (If you want to continue to use it after this course, you should register and pay the shareware fee.) In addition, the full version of @RISK can be obtained from the Palisade Corp. for a free trial period of ten days in either of two ways. It can be downloaded directly from the Palisade web site, www.Palisade.com. Alternatively, it can be ordered on a CD-ROM from this web site. Like any Excel add-ins, these add-ins need to be installed before they will show up in Excel.

This section focuses on the use of @RISK to illustrate what can be done with any of these simulation add-ins. However, if you decide to use RiskSim, its documentation is included in the CD-ROM.

Business spreadsheets typically include some *data cells* that display key data (e.g., the various costs associated with producing or marketing a product) and one or more *output cells* that show measures of performance (e.g., the profit from producing or marketing the product). The user writes Excel equations to link the inputs to the outputs so that the output cells will show the values that correspond to the values that are entered into the data cells. In some cases, there will be uncertainty about what the correct values for the input cells will turn out to be. Sensitivity analysis can be used to check how the outputs change as the values in the data cells change. However, if there is considerable uncertainty about the values in some data cells, a more systematic approach to analyzing the effect of the uncertainty would be helpful. This is where computer simulation enters the picture.

With a simulation add-in, instead of entering a single number in a data cell where there is uncertainty, a *probability distribution* that describes the uncertainty is entered instead. By generating a *random observation* from the probability distribution for each such data cell, the spreadsheet can calculate the output values in the usual way. Each time this is done is referred to as an *iteration* by @RISK. By running the number of iterations specified by the user (typically hundreds or thousands), the computer simulation thereby generates the same number of random observations of the output values. The @RISK program records all this information and then gives you the choice of printing out detailed statistics in tabular or graphical form (or both) that roughly show the underlying *probability distribution* of the output values. A summary of the results also includes estimates of the mean and standard deviation of this distribution.

Now let us look at three examples (all drawn from spreadsheet models in previous chapters) that illustrate this process.

Inventory Management— Revisiting the Case Study of Freddie the Newsboy's Problem

You may recall a case study involving Freddie the newsboy in Sections 12.1 and 12.2. Here is what you need to know for the current example. One of the daily newspapers that Freddie sells from his newsstand is the *Financial Journal*. He pays $1.50 per copy delivered to him at the beginning of the day, sells it at $2.50 per copy, and then receives a refund of $0.50 per copy unsold at the end of the day. He has 9 requests to purchase a copy on 30 percent of the days, 10 requests on 40 percent of the days, and 11 requests on 30 percent of the days. The decision Freddie needs to make is how many copies (9, 10, or 11) per day to order from the distributor.

Figure 15.18 shows the @RISK spreadsheet for this problem. Since the only uncertain input quantity is the day's demand for this newspaper, its probability distribution is entered in the range E4:F6. Because this is a *discrete* probability distribution, the RiskDiscrete function is used to generate random observations from this distribution. This involves entering the formula = RiskDiscrete(E4:E6, F4:F6) in cell C12 (which shows a typical random observation in this figure). The computer simulation eventually needs to be run three times, once for each of the three order quantities under consideration, so we start with one of these order quantities (9) in cell C9. The regular Excel functions are used to calculate the simulated quantities in cells C14, C15, and C16 as C14 = C4*MIN (C9,C12), C15 = C5*C9, and C16 = C6*MAX(C9−C12,0). Similarly, the total profit in cell C18 (the one output cell) is calculated as C18 = C14 − C15 + C16.

Given this spreadsheet, the @RISK toolbar buttons shown in Figure 15.19 are used to run the simulation. The first seven buttons show up in the Excel toolbar. These buttons enable you in turn to open a previously saved simulation file, save a new simulation file, ad-

FIGURE 15.18

The @RISK spreadsheet for Freddie the newsboy's problem.

	A	B	C	D	E	F
1		Simulating Freddie the Newsboy's Problem				
2						
3			Data		Demand Distribution	
4		Unit sale price =	$2.50		9	0.3
5		Unit purchase cost =	$1.50		10	0.4
6		Unit salvage value =	$0.50		11	0.3
7						
8		Decision Variable				
9		Order Quantity =	9			
10						
11		Simulated Quantities				
12		Demand =	10			
13						
14		Sales Revenue =	$22.50			
15		Purchasing Cost =	$13.50			
16		Salvage Value =	$0.00			
17						
18		Total Profit =	$9.00			

	C
12	=RiskDiscrete(E4:E6,F4:F6)
13	
14	=C4*MIN(C9,C12)
15	=C5*C9
16	=C6*MAX(C9−C12,0)
17	
18	=C14−C15+C16

just the simulation settings, add an output cell, list the inputs and outputs, start the simulation, and switch to @RISK to view the results. The last three buttons only become available after running a simulation. The first two of these enable you to view the results in graphical or summary form. The Hide button takes you back to Excel from @RISK.

Three steps are needed to use the spreadsheet in Figure 15.18 to perform the computer simulation. To indicate that profit is the only output of interest, select cell C18 and click on the + Output button. Next, click on the Sim Sett button to select the number of iterations (we chose 250) and the number of simulations (1 for this first order quantity) in the dialogue box displayed in Figure 15.20. Finally, click on the Simulate button to run the simulation.

Once the iterations have been completed, you see an @RISK screen with a new menu bar, an expanded toolbar, a Results window, and a Summary Statistics window. The Results window is a good place to start to see a summary of the simulation results, and then the Summary Statistics window can be used if you want to see more detailed statistics. Figure 15.21

FIGURE 15.19

The toolbar for @RISK. The last three buttons become available only after running a simulation.

FIGURE 15.20

The Simulation Settings dialogue box for @RISK.

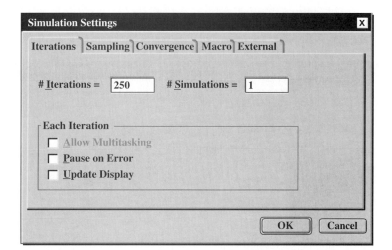

FIGURE 15.21

The summary of results obtained by @RISK after running the computer simulations in Figure 15.18 for all three order quantities under consideration.

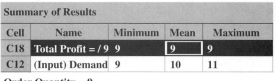

Summary of Results

Cell	Name	Minimum	Mean	Maximum
C18	Total Profit = / 9	9	9	9
C12	(Input) Demand	9	10	11

Order Quantity = 9

Summary of Results

Cell	Name	Minimum	Mean	Maximum
C18	Total Profit = / 9	8	9.4	10
C12	(Input) Demand	9	10	11

Order Quantity = 10

Summary of Results

Cell	Name	Minimum	Mean	Maximum
C18	Total Profit = / 9	7	9	11
C12	(Input) Demand	9	10	11

Order Quantity = 11

shows the summary of the results obtained for all three simulations with the respective order quantities. Look first at the top table (Order Quantity = 9). The C18 (Total Profit) row indicates that the minimum profit obtained on any of the 250 iterations (simulated days) was $9, the maximum also was $9, and so the mean over all 250 iterations was $9. (This occurred because all nine newspapers ordered *always* were sold, so the profit was $9 every time.) The C12 (Demand) row points out that the demand over the 250 iterations varied between 9 and 11, with a mean of 10. The second table (Order Quantity = 10) indicates that the total profit on each of the 250 simulated days varied between $8 and $10, with a mean of $9.40. The third simulation (Order Quantity = 11) gave a larger maximum profit ($11) on the best days, but also gave a lower minimum ($7) and a lower overall mean ($9). Therefore, these results indicate that an order quantity of 10 is the best choice for Freddie since it gives the largest mean profit per day (as was also concluded in Sections 12.1 and 12.2).

Referring next to the Summary Statistics window, the left side of Figure 15.22 gives the detailed statistics for the simulation with an order quantity of 10. The Total Profit column starts with the minimum, maximum, and mean already shown in the middle table of Figure 15.21. Next come such statistics as the standard deviation and variance of the 250 daily profits, as well as the mode (the most frequently observed profit). Finally, this column gives the *percentiles* of the *frequency distribution* of the 250 daily profits. The percentile for each percentage gives the profit such that this percentage of the observed profits were

FIGURE 15.22

The Simulation Statistics table and Output Graph generated by @RISK after running the computer simulation in Figure 15.18 with an order quantity of 10.

Simulation Statistics		
Name	**Total Profit = /**	**Demand = / Simulated**
Description	Output	Discrete(E4:E6,F4:F6)
Cell	'[Simulation.xls]	[Simulation.xls]Freddie
Minimum =	8	9
Maximum =	10	11
Mean =	9.4	10
Std Deviation =	0.9165151	0.7745967
Variance =	0.84	0.6
Skewness =	–0.8728716	0
Kurtosis =	1.761905	1.666667
Errors Calculated =	0	0
Mode =	10	10
5% Perc =	8	9
10% Perc =	8	9
15% Perc =	8	9
20% Perc =	8	9
25% Perc =	8	9
30% Perc =	10	10
35% Perc =	10	10
40% Perc =	10	10
45% Perc =	10	10
50% Perc =	10	10
55% Perc =	10	10
60% Perc =	10	10
65% Perc =	10	10
70% Perc =	10	11
75% Perc =	10	11
80% Perc =	10	11
85% Perc =	10	11
90% Perc =	10	11
95% Perc =	10	11

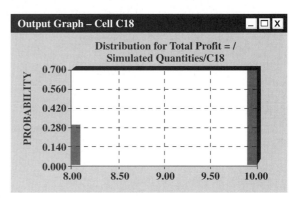

Output Graph – Cell C18

Distribution for Total Profit = / Simulated Quantities/C18

less than or equal to this amount. For example, the value for the 30 percent percentile ($10) means that the profits from 30 percent of the iterations of the simulation were $10 or less.

The right side of Figure 15.22 shows the *histogram* that graphically depicts the frequency with which the various daily profits ($8 and $10 in this case) were generated in this simulation. (This histogram was obtained by selecting the output cell C18 in the Results window and clicking on the Graph button in the @RISK toolbar.) Thus, very close to 30 percent of the iterations gave a profit of $8 and the remaining 70 percent or so yielded a profit of $10. (However, @RISK will not produce a histogram if the output value never changes during the simulation, which was the case with an order quantity of 9, since this order quantity always gives Freddie a daily profit of $9.)

Because a mathematical model is available that yields an exact analytical solution for Freddie's problem (as demonstrated in Sections 12.1 and 12.2), computer simulation is not the only feasible way of studying this problem. However, the situation will be somewhat different in the next example, which deals with finding the probability of completing a project by its deadline. In this case, there is again an analytical method available (through the PERT three-estimate approach), but this method only provides a rough, overly optimistic approximation of the true probability. Therefore, computer simulation frequently is used to obtain a much more precise estimate of this probability. This illustrates a common role for computer simulation—refining the results from a preliminary analysis conducted with approximate mathematical models.

Project Management—Revisiting the Case Study of the Reliable Construction Co. Project

This is the case study that is introduced in Section 7.1 and then continued through most of Chapter 7. Here are the essential facts needed for the current example. The Reliable Construction Company has just made the winning bid to construct a new plant for a major manufacturer. However, the contract includes a large penalty if construction is not completed by the deadline 47 weeks from now. Therefore, a key element in evaluating alternative construction plans is the *probability of meeting this deadline* under each plan. There are 14 major activities involved in carrying out this construction project, as listed on the right-hand side of Figure 15.23 (which repeats Figure 7.1 for your convenience). The project network

FIGURE 15.23

The project network for the Reliable Construction Co. project.

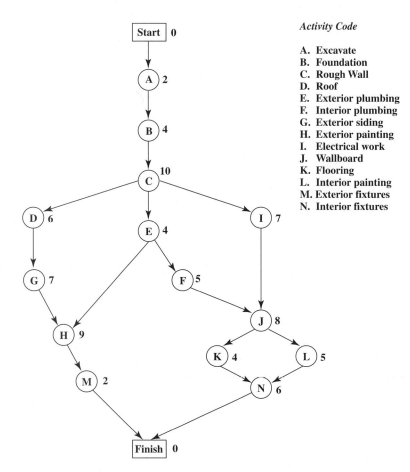

Activity Code

A. **Excavate**
B. **Foundation**
C. **Rough Wall**
D. **Roof**
E. **Exterior plumbing**
F. **Interior plumbing**
G. **Exterior siding**
H. **Exterior painting**
I. **Electrical work**
J. **Wallboard**
K. **Flooring**
L. **Interior painting**
M. **Exterior fixtures**
N. **Interior fixtures**

in this figure depicts the precedence relationships between the activities. Thus, there are six sequences of activities (paths through the network), all of which must be completed to finish the project. These six sequences are listed below.

Path 1:   Start → A → B → C → D → G → H → M → Finish

Path 2:   Start → A → B → C → E → H → M → Finish

Path 3:   Start → A → B → C → E → F → J → K → N → Finish

Path 4:   Start → A → B → C → E → F → J → L → N → Finish

Path 5:   Start → A → B → C → I → J → K → N → Finish

Path 6:   Start → A → B → C → I → J → L → N → Finish

The numbers next to the activities in the project network represent the *estimates* of the number of weeks the activities will take if they are carried out in the normal manner with the usual crew sizes, and so forth. Adding these times over each of the paths (as was done in Table 7.2) reveals that path 4 is the *longest path,* requiring a total of 44 weeks. Since the project is finished as soon as its longest path is completed, this indicates that the project can be completed in 44 weeks, 3 weeks before the deadline.

Now we come to the crux of the problem. The times for the activities in Figure 15.23 are only estimates, and there actually is considerable uncertainty about what the duration of each activity will be. Therefore, the duration of the entire project could well differ substantially from the estimate of 44 weeks, so there is a distinct possibility of missing the deadline of 47 weeks. What is the *probability* of missing this deadline? To estimate this probability, we need to learn more about the probability distribution of the duration of the project.

This is the reason for the PERT three-estimate approach described in Section 7.4. This approach involves obtaining three estimates—a *most likely estimate,* an *optimistic estimate,* and a *pessimistic estimate*—of the duration of each activity. (Table 7.4 lists these estimates for all 14 activities for the project under consideration.) These three quantities are intended to estimate the most likely duration, the minimum duration, and the maximum duration, respectively. Using these three quantities, PERT assumes (somewhat arbitrarily) that the form of the probability distribution of the duration of an activity is a *beta distribution.* By also making three simplifying approximations (described in Section 7.4), this leads to an analytical method for roughly approximating the probability of meeting the project deadline.

One key advantage of computer simulation is that it does not need to make most of the simplifying approximations that may be required by analytical methods. Another is that there is great flexibility about which probability distributions to use. It is not necessary to choose an analytically convenient one.

When dealing with the duration of an activity, computer simulations commonly use a *triangular distribution* as the distribution of this duration. A triangular distribution has the shape shown in Figure 15.24, where *o, m,* and *p* are the labels for the optimistic estimate, the most likely estimate, and the pessimistic estimate, respectively. The @RISK formula for this distri-

FIGURE 15.24

The shape of a triangular distribution for the duration of an activity, where the minimum lies at the optimistic estimate o, *the most likely value lies at the most likely estimate* m, *and the maximum lies at the pessimistic estimate* p.

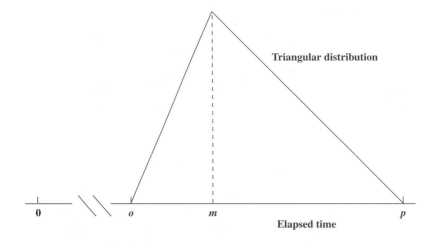

bution is = RiskTriang(*o,m,p*). [Other popular distributions are the *normal distribution* with mean μ and standard deviation σ, which has the @RISK formula = RiskNormal(μ,σ), and the *uniform distribution* from *a* to *b,* which has the @RISK formula = RiskUniform(*a,b*).]

Figure 15.25 shows the @RISK spreadsheet for simulating the duration of the Reliable Construction Company's project. The formula = RiskTriang(*o,m,p*) is inserted into each cell representing the duration of an activity (cells H5:H18), where the values of *o, m,* and *p* in columns D, E, and F are obtained from Table 7.4. The equations entered into the cells in columns G and I give the start times and finish times for the respective activities. For each iteration of the simulation, the maximum of the finish times for the last two activities (M and N) gives the duration of the project (in weeks). One output cell (I20) gives this duration and the other (I22) indicates whether this duration meets the deadline by not exceeding 47 weeks (where 1 indicates yes and 0 indicates no).

To run this simulation, we chose 1,000 as the number of iterations and 1 as the number of simulations (since only one construction plan is being simulated here). Figure 15.26 shows the results. The most crucial piece of information here is the mean for the output cell

FIGURE 15.25

A spreadsheet model for a computer simulation of the Reliable Construction Co. project.

	A	B	C	D	E	F	G	H	I
1		Simulation of Reliable Construction Co. Project							
2									
3			Immediate	Time Estimates			Start	Activity	Finish
4		Activity	Predecessor	o	m	p	Time	Time	Time
5		A	–	1	2	3	0	2	2
6		B	A	2	3.5	8	2	4.5	6.5
7		C	B	6	9	18	6.5	11	17.5
8		D	C	4	5.5	10	17.5	6.5	24
9		E	C	1	4.5	5	17.5	3.5	21
10		F	E	4	4	10	21	6	27
11		G	D	5	6.5	11	24	7.5	31.5
12		H	E,G	5	8	17	31.5	10	41.5
13		I	C	3	7.5	9	17.5	6.5	24
14		J	F,I	3	9	9	27	7	34
15		K	J	4	4	4	34	4	38
16		L	J	1	5.5	7	34	4.5	38.5
17		M	H	1	2	3	41.5	2	43.5
18		N	K,L	5	5.5	9	38.5	6.5	45
19									
20							Project Completion =		45
21							Project Deadline =		47
22							Deadline met (1=yes, 0=no)?		1

	G	H	I
5	0	=RiskTriang(D5,E5,F5)	=G5+H5
6	=I5	=RiskTriang(D6,E6,F6)	=G6+H6
7	=I6	=RiskTriang(D7,E7,F7)	=G7+H7
8	=I7	=RiskTriang(D8,E8,F8)	=G8+H8
9	=I7	=RiskTriang(D9,E9,F9)	=G9+H9
10	=I9	=RiskTriang(D10,E10,F10)	=G10+H10
11	=I8	=RiskTriang(D11,E11,F11)	=G11+H11
12	=MAX(I9,I11)	=RiskTriang(D12,E12,F12)	=G12+H12
13	=I7	=RiskTriang(D13,E13,F13)	=G13+H13
14	=MAX(I10,I13)	=RiskTriang(D14,E14,F14)	=G14+H14
15	=I14	=RiskTriang(D15,E15,F15)	=G15+H15
16	=I14	=RiskTriang(D16,E16,F16)	=G16+H16
17	=I12	=RiskTriang(D17,E17,F17)	=G17+H17
18	=MAX(I15,I16)	=RiskTriang(D18,E18,F18)	=G18+H18
19			
20		Project Completion =	=MAX(I17,I18)
21		Project Deadline =	47
22		Deadline met (1=yes, 0=no)?	=IF(I20<=I21,1,0)

FIGURE 15.26

The various outputs generated by @RISK after running the Reliable Construction Co. computer simulation in Figure 15.25 for 1,000 iterations.

Simulation Statistics		
Name	Project Completion	Deadline Met
Description	Output	Output
Cell	'[Reliable.xls]Reliab	'[Reliable.xls]R
Minimum =	36.98942	0
Maximum =	58.48365	1
Mean =	46.24534	0.591
Std Deviation =	3.63146	0.4916493
Variance =	13.1875	0.241719
Skewness =	0.1696594	−0.3701826
Kurtosis =	2.707775	1.137035
Errors Calculated =	0	0
Mode =	47.2127	1
5% Perc =	40.31811	0
10% Perc =	41.5235	0
15% Perc =	42.4042	0
20% Perc =	43.09111	0
25% Perc =	43.75802	0
30% Perc =	44.31891	0
35% Perc =	44.79782	0
40% Perc =	45.15918	0
45% Perc =	45.56504	1
50% Perc =	45.96362	1
55% Perc =	46.60467	1
60% Perc =	47.05931	1
65% Perc =	47.50695	1
70% Perc =	48.17402	1
75% Perc =	48.7167	1
80% Perc =	49.44214	1
85% Perc =	50.19196	1
90% Perc =	51.19381	1
95% Perc =	52.36878	1

Summary of Results					
Cell	Name	Minimum	Mean	Maximum
I20	Project Completion = / Time in	36.98942	46.24534	58.48365
I22	Deadline met (1=yes, 0=no)	0	0.591	1

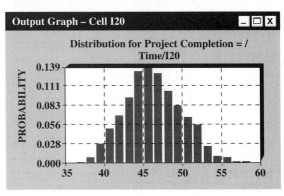

that indicates whether the deadline has been met, because this mean gives the proportion of the 1,000 iterations where the deadline was met. This mean is in the bottom row of the Summary of Results in the upper right-hand corner of the figure. This estimate of the probability of meeting the deadline is 0.591. Note how much smaller this relatively precise estimate is than the rough estimate of 0.84 obtained by the PERT three-estimate approach in Section 7.4. Thus, the simulation estimate provides much better guidance to management in deciding whether the construction plan should be changed to improve the chances of meeting the deadline. This illustrates how useful computer simulation can be in refining the results obtained by approximate analytical methods.

In addition to the probability of meeting the deadline, management also will be interested in the overall probability distribution of the duration of the project. What computer simulation has provided is 1,000 random observations from this distribution, so the *frequency distribution* from these random observations provides a close approximation to the true probability distribution. Among other information, the Simulation Statistics window gives the various *percentiles* of the frequency distribution, as shown on the left-hand side of Figure 15.26. The histogram on the lower right-hand side of the figure graphically depicts this frequency distribution.

TABLE 15.3   **Think-Big's Estimated Cash Flows per Share Taken in the Hotel and Shopping Center Projects**

Hotel Project		Shopping Center Project	
Year	Cash Flow ($1,000s)	Year	Cash Flow ($1,000s)
0	− 800	0	−900
1	Normal (− 800, 50)	1	Normal (− 600, 50)
2	Normal (− 800, 100)	2	Normal (− 200, 50)
3	Normal (− 700, 150)	3	Normal (− 600, 100)
4	Normal (+ 300, 200)	4	Normal (+ 250, 150)
5	Normal (+ 400, 200)	5	Normal (+ 350, 150)
6	Normal (+ 500, 200)	6	Normal (+ 400, 150)
7	Uniform (+ 2,000, 8,440)	7	Uniform (+ 1,600, 6,000)

Financial Risk Analysis—Revisiting the Think-Big Development Co. Problem

As introduced in Section 3.2, the Think-Big Development Co. is a major investor in commercial real estate development projects. It has been considering taking a share in three large construction projects—a high-rise office building, a hotel, and a shopping center. In each case, the partners in the project would spend three years with the construction, then retain ownership for three years while establishing the property, and then sell the property in the seventh year. By using estimates of expected cash flows, Section 3.2 describes how linear programming has been applied to obtain the following proposal for how many 1 percent shares Think-Big should take in each of these projects.

Proposal

Do not take any shares of the high-rise building project.

Take 16.5 shares of the hotel project.

Take 13.1 shares of the shopping center project.

This proposal is estimated to return a *net present value* (NPV) of $18.1 million to Think-Big.

However, Think-Big management understands very well that such decisions should not be made without taking risk into account. These are very risky projects since it is unclear how well these properties will compete in the marketplace when they go into operation in a few years. Although the construction costs during the first three years can be estimated fairly closely, the net incomes during the following three years of operation are very uncertain. Consequently, there is an extremely wide range of possible values for each sale price in year 7. Therefore, management wants *risk analysis* to be performed in the usual way (with computer simulation) to obtain a *risk profile* of what the total NPV might actually turn out to be with this proposal.

To perform this risk analysis, Think-Big staff now has devoted considerable time to estimating the amount of uncertainty in the cash flows for each project over the next seven years. These data are summarized in Table 15.3 (in units of thousands of dollars per share taken in each project). In years 1 through 6 for each project, the probability distribution of cash flow is assumed to be a *normal distribution,* where the first number shown is the estimated *mean* and the second number is the estimated *standard deviation* of the distribution. In year 7, the income from the sale of the property is assumed to have a *uniform distribution* over the range from the first number shown to the second number shown.

To compute NPV, a cost of capital of 10 percent per annum is being used. Thus, the cash flow in year n is divided by 1.1^n before adding these discounted cash flows to obtain NPV.

Figure 15.27 shows the @RISK spreadsheet for using computer simulation to perform risk analysis on the proposal. (The numbers currently in cells J22 and G22:G29 are expected values computed by @RISK.) For each iteration of the simulation, @RISK uses its functions, RiskNormal(μ, σ) and RiskUniform(a, b), to generate a random observation

FIGURE 15.27

A spreadsheet model for using computer simulation to perform risk analysis on the proposed real estate investments by the Think-Big Development Co.

	A	B	C	D	E	F	G	H	I	J	K	L	M	N
1		Simulation of Think-Big Development Co. Problem												
2														
3		Hotel Project:												
4														
5		Construction Costs per Share ($1,000s)						Revenue per Share ($1,000s)					Selling Price per Share ($1,000s)	
6		(Normal Distribution)						(Normal Distribution)					(Uniform Distribution)	
7			Year 0	Year 1	Year 2	Year 3			Year 4	Year 5	Year 6			Year 7
8		Mean	−800	−800	−800	−700		Mean	300	400	500		Minimum	2000
9		St. Dev.	0	50	100	150		St. Dev.	200	200	200		Maximum	8440
10														
11														
12		Shopping Center Project:												
13														
14		Construction Costs per Share ($1,000s)						Revenue per Share ($1,000s)					Selling Price per Share ($1,000s)	
15		(Normal Distribution)						(Normal Distribution)					(Uniform Distribution)	
16			Year 0	Year 1	Year 2	Year 3			Year 4	Year 5	Year 6			Year 7
17		Mean	−900	−600	−200	−600		Mean	250	350	400		Minimum	1600
18		St. Dev.	0	50	50	100		St. Dev.	150	150	150		Maximum	6000
19														
20														
21		Number of Shares:					Cash Flow ($1,000s):		Net Present Value ($1,000s):					
22			Hotel =	16.5			Year 0	−24,990		18.128				
23		Shopping Center =		13.1			Year 1	−21,060						
24							Year 2	−15,820						
25		Cost of Capital:		10%			Year 3	−19,410						
26							Year 4	8,225						
27							Year 5	11,185						
28							Year 6	13,490						
29							Year 7	135,910						

	G
22	=D22*RiskNormal(C8,C9)+D23*RiskNormal(C17,C18)
23	=D22*RiskNormal(D8,D9)+D23*RiskNormal(D17,D18)
24	=D22*RiskNormal(E8,E9)+D23*RiskNormal(E17,E18)
25	=D22*RiskNormal(F8,F9)+D23*RiskNormal(F17,F18)
26	=D22*RiskNormal(I8,I9)+D23*RiskNormal(I17,I18)
27	=D22*RiskNormal(J8,J9)+D23*RiskNormal(J17,J18)
28	=D22*RiskNormal(K8,K9)+D23*RiskNormal(K17,K18)
29	=D22*RiskNormal(N8,N9)+D23*RiskNormal(N17,N18)

	J
22	=G22+NPV(D25,G23:G29)

from each of the normal distributions and uniform distributions specified in Table 15.3. (@RISK provides numerous such functions for a wide variety of probability distributions.) These simulated cash flows then are used to calculate the total NPV for both projects in cell J22. By repeating this process for 1,000 iterations, we thereby obtain 1,000 random observations from the underlying probability distribution of the total NPV. These 1,000 observations constitute a *frequency distribution* of the total NPV that is virtually identical to the underlying probability distribution.

Figure 15.28 provides information about this frequency distribution in the usual variety of forms. The Summary of Results on the top of the figure indicates that the values of NPV over the 1,000 iterations ranged from about −$35 million to over $65 million, with a mean of $18.13 million. (The subsequent rows in this table show the corresponding statistics for

FIGURE 15.28

The various risk analysis outputs generated by @RISK after running the Think-Big Development Co. computer simulation in Figure 15.27 for 1,000 iterations.

Summary of Results

Cell	Name	Minimum	Mean	Maximum
J22	Year 0 / Net Present Value ($1,000's): in ('[Think-Big.xls]Think-Big')	–35081.42	18130.33	65575.85
G22	(Input)Year 0 in ([Think-Big.xls]Think-Big)	–800	–800	–800
G22	(Input)Year 0 in ([Think-Big.xls]Think-Big)	–900	–900	–900
G23	(Input)Year 1 / Year 1 in ([Think-Big.xls]Think-Big)	–991.5456	–800.0345	–639.1625
G23	(Input)Year 1 / Year 1 in ([Think-Big.xls]Think-Big)	–770.6567	–600.0127	–440.2328
G24	(Input)Year 2 / Year 2 in ([Think-Big.xls]Think-Big)	–1132.84	–799.9891	–457.1893
G24	(Input)Year 2 / Year 2 in ([Think-Big.xls]Think-Big)	–360.6227	–199.9776	–23.98881
G25	(Input)Year 3 / Year 3 in ([Think-Big.xls]Think-Big)	–1163.719	–699.9891	–189.6448
G25	(Input)Year 3 / Year 3 in ([Think-Big.xls]Think-Big)	–923.2188	–599.9961	–289.8651
G26	(Input)Year 4 / Year 4 in ([Think-Big.xls]Think-Big)	–322.4218	300.1159	1017.854
G26	(Input)Year 4 / Year 4 in ([Think-Big.xls]Think-Big)	–284.7605	250.0473	826.9261
G27	(Input)Year 5 / Year 5 in ([Think-Big.xls]Think-Big)	–227.1319	400.0233	1043.294
G27	(Input)Year 5 / Year 5 in ([Think-Big.xls]Think-Big)	–130.6366	350.0098	840.8525
G28	(Input)Year 6 / Year 6 in ([Think-Big.xls]Think-Big)	–127.4213	500.0163	1162.403
G28	(Input)Year 6 / Year 6 in ([Think-Big.xls]Think-Big)	–144.3892	400.022	925.3484
G29	(Input)Year 7 / Year 7 in ([Think-Big.xls]Think-Big)	2004.445	5219.979	8436.119
G29	(Input)Year 7 / Year 7 in ([Think-Big.xls]Think-Big)	1600.293	3800.036	5999.864

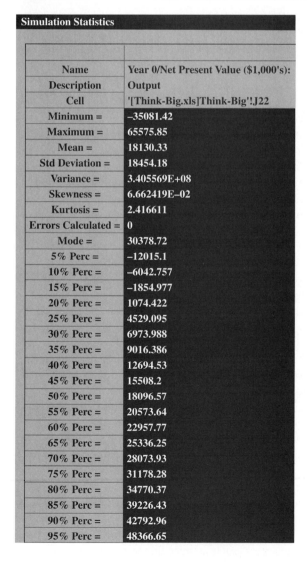

Simulation Statistics

Name	Year 0/Net Present Value ($1,000's):
Description	Output
Cell	'[Think-Big.xls]Think-Big'!J22
Minimum =	–35081.42
Maximum =	65575.85
Mean =	18130.33
Std Deviation =	18454.18
Variance =	3.405569E+08
Skewness =	6.662419E–02
Kurtosis =	2.416611
Errors Calculated =	0
Mode =	30378.72
5% Perc =	–12015.1
10% Perc =	–6042.757
15% Perc =	–1854.977
20% Perc =	1074.422
25% Perc =	4529.095
30% Perc =	6973.988
35% Perc =	9016.386
40% Perc =	12694.53
45% Perc =	15508.2
50% Perc =	18096.57
55% Perc =	20573.64
60% Perc =	22957.77
65% Perc =	25336.25
70% Perc =	28073.93
75% Perc =	31178.28
80% Perc =	34770.37
85% Perc =	39226.43
90% Perc =	42792.96
95% Perc =	48366.65

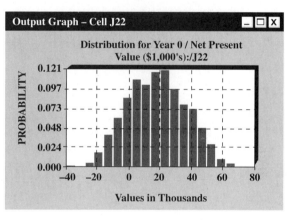

Output Graph – Cell J22

Distribution for Year 0 / Net Present Value ($1,000's):/J22

Values in Thousands

the cash flows per share in each year for each project.) The *Simulation Statistics* on the lower left give detailed information about the frequency distribution. For example, the fact that the 15 percent percentile has a negative NPV while it is positive at the 20 percent percentile reveals that the probability of incurring a loss by adopting the proposal is between 0.15 and 0.20. The *histogram* in the lower right-hand corner displays the frequency distribution graphically. This histogram provides management with the *risk profile* for the proposal. With this information, a managerial decision now needs to be made about whether the likelihood of a sizable profit justifies the significant risk of incurring a loss and perhaps even a very substantial loss.

Thus, as when using other management science techniques, management makes the decision but computer simulation provides the information needed for making a sound decision.

Review Questions

1. What are the names of three simulation add-ins for Excel?
2. What should be entered in a data cell where there is uncertainty about what its true value will turn out to be?
3. What does a spreadsheet computer simulation do to generate the output values for each iteration of the simulation?
4. What is the @RISK function for generating random observations from a discrete probability distribution?
5. What are two key advantages of computer simulation over approximate analytical methods?

15.7 Summary

Computer simulation is one of the most popular management science techniques because it is such a flexible, powerful, and intuitive tool. It involves using a computer to *imitate* (simulate) the operation of an entire process or system. For a system that evolves over time according to one or more probability distributions, random observations are generated from these distributions to generate the various events that occur in the simulated system over time. (The inverse transformation method uses *random numbers* to generate these random observations.) This provides a relatively quick way of investigating how well a proposed system configuration would perform without incurring the great expense of actually constructing and operating the system. Therefore, many alternative system configurations can be investigated and compared in advance before choosing the one to use.

Herr Cutter's barber shop provides a case study of how computer simulation was able to provide the needed information to decide whether to change this stochastic system by adding a second barber. Like so many others, this stochastic system is a *queueing system,* but one that is too complicated to be analyzed solely by using queueing models.

This case study also illustrates the building blocks of a *simulation model* that represents the system to be simulated and describes how the simulation will be performed. One key building block is a *simulation clock,* which is the variable in the computer program that records the amount of simulated time that has elapsed so far. The *next-event time-advance procedure* advances the time on the simulation clock by repeatedly moving from the current event to the next event that will occur in the simulated system.

In a matter of seconds or minutes, a computer simulation can simulate even years of operation of a typical system. Each simulation run generates a series of statistical observations about the performance of the system over the period of time simulated. These observations then are used to estimate the interesting measures of performance of the system. Both a *point estimate* and a *confidence interval* can be obtained for each measure.

Because of its exceptional versatility, computer simulation has been applied to a wide variety of areas. Some of these applications have involved investigating the kinds of stochastic systems introduced in recent chapters, such as queueing systems, inventory systems, and PERT projects. Other prominent areas of application include manufacturing systems, distribution systems, financial risk analysis, health care systems, and other systems in service industries.

Some computer simulation studies can be done relatively quickly by a single individual, who might be the manager concerned with the problem. For a more extensive study, however, the manager might want to assign a staff member, or even a full-fledged management science team, to the project. A major management science study based on computer simulation requires a series of important steps before the team is ready to obtain results from simulation runs. A series of questions must be addressed to management to properly define the problem from their viewpoint. Collecting good data generally is a difficult and time-consuming process. Another big task is formulating the simulation model, checking its accuracy, and then testing the validity of the model for closely approximating the system being simulated. One of the team's most important decisions is the choice of the software to be used. Several excellent *general-purpose simulation languages* are available. *Simulators* designed for simulating rather specific types of systems also have come on the market. Most simulation software vendors also now offer a version of their software with *animation* capabilities. Animation is very useful for displaying what a computer simulation is doing to managers and other key personnel, which can add much credibility to the study.

Even after the computer program is ready to go, the management science team needs to design the statistical experiments to be conducted through computer simulation. Then the simulation runs can be conducted and the results analyzed. Finally, the team usually needs to both prepare a written report and make a formal oral presentation to present its recommendations to management.

Spreadsheet software is increasingly being used to perform basic computer simulations. The standard Excel package often is sufficient to do this. Some Excel add-ins that add considerable functionality also are now available. For example, the add-in @RISK can generate the output of a computer simulation in a variety of useful forms. The availability of this kind of software now enables managers to add computer simulation to their personal tool kit of management science techniques for analyzing some key managerial problems.

Glossary

Animation   A computer display with icons that shows what is happening in a computer simulation. (Section 15.5)   665

Applications-oriented simulator   A software package designed for simulating a fairly specific type of stochastic system. (Section 15.5)   665

Confidence interval   An interval within which the true value of a measure of performance is likely to lie. (Section 15.3)   655

General-purpose simulation language   A general-purpose language for programming almost any kind of simulation model. (Section 15.5)   664

Inverse transformation method   A method for generating random observations from a probability distribution. (Section 15.1)   643

Next-event time advance   A procedure for advancing the time on the simulation clock by repeatedly moving from the current event to the next event that will occur in the simulated system. (Section 15.2)   651

Point estimate   The single number that provides the best estimate of a measure of performance. (Section 15.3)   654

Random number   A random observation from the uniform distribution over the interval from 0 to 1. (Section 15.1)   635

Simulation clock   A variable in the computer program that records how much simulated time has elapsed so far. (Section 15.2)   651

Simulation model   A representation of the system to be simulated that also describes how the simulation will be performed. (Section 15.2)   650

Simulator   The common short name for *applications-oriented simulator* (defined above). (Section 15.5)   665

State of the system   The key information that defines the current status of the system. (Section 15.2)   651

Stochastic system   A system that evolves over time according to one or more probability distributions. (Section 15.1)   634

Learning Aids for This Chapter in Your MS Courseware

"Ch. 15—Computer Simulation" Excel File:

Coin-Flipping Game Example
Heavy Duty Co. Examples (3)
Herr Cutter's Barber Shop Case Study
Queueing Simulator

Template for M/G/1 *Queueing Model*
Freddie the Newsboy Example
Reliable Construction Co. Example
Think-Big Development Co. Example

Excel Add-Ins:

   (@RISK is on the web site, www.Palisade.com)

   RiskSim

Routine:

Queueing Simulator (in the Excel file)

Problems

The symbols to the left of some of the problems (or their parts) have the following meaning:

   E*:   Use Excel.

   Q*:   Use the Queueing Simulator.

   R*:   Use @RISK (as an add-in to Excel).

An asterisk on the problem number indicates that at least a partial answer is given in the back of the book.

15.1.*   Use the random numbers in cells C10:C15 of Figure 15.1 to generate six random observations for each of the following situations.

    a.   Throwing an unbiased coin.

    b.   A baseball pitcher who throws a strike 60 percent of the time and a ball 40 percent of the time.

    c.   The color of a traffic light found by a randomly arriving car when it is green 40 percent of the time, yellow 10 percent of the time, and red 50 percent of the time.

15.2.   Reconsider the coin-flipping game introduced in Section 15.1 and analyzed with computer simulation in Figures 15.1, 15.2, and 15.3.

    a.   Simulate one play of this game by repeatedly flipping your own coin until the game ends. Record your results in the format shown in columns B, D, E, F, and G of Figure 15.1. How much would you have won or lost if this had been a real play of the game?

  E*   *b.*   Revise the spreadsheet model in Figure 15.1 by using Excel's VLOOKUP function instead of the IF function to generate each simulated flip of the coin. Then perform a computer simulation of one play of the game.

  E*   *c.*   Use this revised spreadsheet model to generate a data table with 14 replications like Figure 15.2.

  E*   *d.*   Repeat part *c* with 1,000 replications (like Figure 15.3).

15.3.   Each time an unbiased coin is flipped three times, the probability of getting 0, 1, 2, and 3 heads is ⅛, ⅜, ⅜, and ⅛, respectively. Therefore, with eight groups of three flips each, *on the average,* one group will yield no heads, three groups will yield one head, three groups will yield two heads, and one group will yield three heads.

    a.   Using your own coin, flip it 24 times divided into eight groups of three flips each, and record the number of groups with no head, with one head, with two heads, and with three heads.

    b.   Use random numbers in the order in which they are given in column C of Figure 15.4 and then in cells C5:C13 of Figure 15.5 to simulate the flips specified in part *a* and record the information indicated in part *a.*

  E*   *c.*   Formulate a spreadsheet model for performing a computer simulation of three flips of the coin and recording the number of heads. Perform one replication of this simulation.

  E*   *d.*   Use this spreadsheet to generate a data table with eight replications of the simulation. Compare this frequency distribution of the number of heads with the probability distribution of the number of heads with three flips.

  E*   *e.*   Repeat part *d* with 800 replications.

15.4.   The weather can be considered a stochastic system, because it evolves in a probabilistic manner from one day to the next. Suppose for a certain location that this probabilistic evolution satisfies the following description:

    The probability of rain tomorrow is 0.6 if it is raining today. The probability of its being clear (no rain) tomorrow is 0.8 if it is clear today.

    a.   Use the random numbers in cells C14:C23 of Figure 15.1 to simulate the evolution of the weather for 10 days, beginning the day after a clear day.

  E*   *b.*   Now use a computer with the random numbers generated by Excel to perform the simulation requested in part *a* on a spreadsheet.

15.5.*   The game of craps requires the player to throw two dice one or more times until a decision has been reached as to whether he (or she) wins or loses. He wins if the first throw results in a sum of seven or 11 or, alternatively, if the first sum is 4, 5, 6, 8, 9, or 10 and the same sum reappears before a sum of seven has appeared. Conversely, he loses if the first throw results in a sum of 2, 3, or 12 or, alternatively, if the first sum is 4, 5, 6, 8, 9, or 10 and a sum of 7 appears before the first sum reappears.

  E*   *a.*   Formulate a spreadsheet model for performing a computer simulation of the throw of two dice. Perform one replication.

  E*   *b.*   Perform 25 replications of this simulation.

    c.   Trace through these 25 replications to determine the number of times the simulated player would have won the game of craps when each play starts with the next throw after the previous play ends.

15.6.   Jessica Williams, manager of kitchen appliances for the Midtown Department Store, feels that her inventory levels of stoves have been running higher than necessary. Before revising the inventory policy for stoves, she records the number sold each day over a period of 25 days, as summarized below.

Number sold	2	3	4	5	6
Number of days	4	7	8	5	1

    a.   Use these data to estimate the probability distribution of daily sales.

    b.   Calculate the mean of the distribution obtained in part *a.*

    c.   Describe how random numbers can be used to simulate daily sales.

    d.   Use the random numbers 0.4476, 0.9713, and 0.0629 to simulate daily sales over three days. Compare the average with the mean obtained in part *b.*

E*   *e.* Formulate a spreadsheet model for performing a computer simulation of the daily sales. Perform 300 replications and obtain the average of the sales over the 300 simulated days.

15.7.* Apply the inverse transformation method as indicated below to generate three random observations from the uniform distribution between −10 and 40 by using the following random numbers: 0.0965, 0.5692, 0.6658.

    a. Apply this method graphically.

    b. Apply this method algebraically.

    c. Write the equation that Excel would use to generate each such random observation.

15.8. Eddie's Bicycle Shop has a thriving business repairing bicycles. Trisha runs the reception area where customers check in their bicycles to be repaired and then later pick up their bicycles and pay their bills. She estimates that the time required to serve a customer on each visit has a uniform distribution between three minutes and eight minutes.

    Apply the inverse transformation method as indicated below to simulate the service times for five customers by using the following five random numbers: 0.6505, 0.0740, 0.8443, 0.4975, 0.8178.

    a. Apply this method graphically.

    b. Apply this method algebraically.

    c. Calculate the average of the five service times and compare it to the mean of the service-time distribution.

E*   *d.* Use Excel to generate 500 random observations and calculate the average. Compare this average to the mean of the service-time distribution.

15.9.* Reconsider Eddie's Bicycle Shop described in the preceding problem. Forty percent of the bicycles require only a minor repair. The repair time for these bicycles has a uniform distribution between zero and one hour. Sixty percent of the bicycles require a major repair. The repair time for these bicycles has a uniform distribution between one hour and two hours. You now need to estimate the mean of the overall probability distribution of the repair times for all bicycles by using the following alternative methods.

    a. Use the random numbers 0.7256, 0.0817, and 0.4392 to simulate whether each of three bicycles requires minor repair or major repair. Then use the random numbers 0.2243, 0.9503, and 0.6104 to simulate the repair times of these bicycles. Calculate the average of these repair times to estimate the mean of the overall distribution of repair times.

    b. Draw the cumulative distribution function (CDF) for the overall probability distribution of the repair times for all bicycles. (*Hint:* This CDF = 0.4 at one hour.)

    c. Use the inverse transformation method with the latter three random numbers given in part *a* to generate three random observations from the overall distribution considered in part *b*. Calculate the average of these observations to estimate the mean of this distribution.

    d. Repeat part *c* with the complements of the random numbers used there, so the new random numbers are 0.7757, 0.0497, and 0.3896.

    e. Combine the random observations from parts *c* and *d* and calculate the average of these six observations to estimate the mean of the overall distribution of

repair times. (This is referred to as the *method of complementary random numbers.*)

    f. The true mean of the overall probability distribution of repair times is 1.1. Compare the estimates of this mean obtained in parts *a, c, d,* and *e.* For the method that provides the closest estimate, give an intuitive explanation for why it performed so well.

E*   *g.* Formulate a spreadsheet model to apply the method of complementary random numbers described in part *e.* Use 300 random numbers to generate 600 random observations from the distribution considered in part *b* and calculate the average of these random observations. Compare this average with the true mean of the distribution.

15.10. The employees of General Manufacturing Corp. receive health insurance through a group plan issued by Wellnet. During the past year, 40 percent of the employees did not file any health insurance claims, 40 percent filed only a small claim, and 20 percent filed a large claim. The small claims were spread uniformly between 0 and $2,000, whereas the large claims were spread uniformly between $2,000 and $20,000.

    Based on this experience, Wellnet now is negotiating the corporation's premium payment per employee for the upcoming year. You are a management science analyst for the insurance carrier, and you have been assigned the task of estimating the average cost of insurance coverage for the corporation's employees.

    Follow the instructions of Problem 15.9, where the size of an employee's health insurance claim (including zero if no claim was filed) now plays the role that the repair time for a bicycle did in Problem 15.9. [For part *f,* the true mean of the overall probability distribution of the size of an employee's health insurance claim is $2,600.]

15.11. Richard Collins, manager and owner of Richard's Tire Service, wishes to use computer simulation to analyze the operation of his shop. One of the activities to be included in the computer simulation is the installation of automobile tires (including balancing the tires). Richard estimates that the cumulative distribution function (CDF) of the probability distribution of the time (in minutes) required to install a tire has the graph shown below.

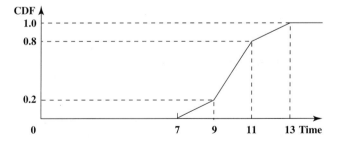

    a. Use the inverse transformation method to generate five random observations from this distribution when using the following five random numbers: 0.2655, 0.3472, 0.0248, 0.9205, 0.6130.

    b. Use a nested IF function to write an equation that Excel can use to generate each random observation from this distribution.

15.12.* Consider the probability distribution whose cumulative distribution function is

$$F(x) = x^2 \quad \text{if } 0 \le x \le 1$$

Suppose you need to generate random observations from this distribution to help perform a computer simulation.

   a. Derive an expression for each random observation in terms of the random number r.
   b. Generate five random observations for this distribution by using the following random numbers: 0.0956, 0.5629, 0.6695, 0.7634, 0.8426.
   c. The inverse transformation method was applied to generate the following three random observations from this distribution: 0.09, 0.64, 0.49. Identify the three random numbers that were used.
   d. Write an equation that Excel can use to generate each random observation from this distribution.

15.13. The William Graham Entertainment Company will be opening a new box office where customers can come to make ticket purchases in advance for the many entertainment events being held in the area. Computer simulation is being used to analyze whether to have one or two clerks on duty at the box office.

   While simulating the beginning of a day at the box office, the first customer arrives five minutes after it opens and then the interarrival times for the next four customers (in order) are three minutes, nine minutes, one minute, and four minutes, after which there is a long delay until the next customer arrives. The service times for these first five customers (in order) are eight minutes, six minutes, two minutes, four minutes, and seven minutes.

   a. For the alternative of a single clerk, draw a figure like Figure 15.14 that shows the evolution of the number of customers at the box office over this period.
   b. Use this figure to estimate the usual measures of performance—L, L_q, W, W_q, and the P_n (as defined in Section 14.3)—for this queueing system.
   c. Repeat part a for the alternative of two clerks.
   d. Repeat part b for the alternative of two clerks.

15.14. The Rustbelt Manufacturing Company employs a maintenance crew to repair its machines as needed. Management now wants a computer simulation study done to analyze what the size of the crew should be, where the crew sizes under consideration are two, three, and four. The time required by the crew to repair a machine has a uniform distribution over the interval from zero to twice the mean, where the mean depends on the crew size. The mean is four hours with two crew members, three hours with three crew members, and two hours with four crew members. The time between breakdowns of some machine has an exponential distribution with a mean of five hours. When a machine breaks down and so requires repair, management wants its average waiting time before repair begins to be no more than three hours. Management also wants the crew size to be no larger than necessary to achieve this.

   a. Develop a simulation model for this problem by describing its six basic building blocks listed in Section 15.2 as they would be applied to this situation.

E* b. Formulate a spreadsheet model to perform a computer simulation to estimate the average waiting time before repair begins. Perform this simulation over a period of 100 breakdowns for each of the three crew sizes under consideration. What do these results suggest the crew size should be?

Q* c. Use the Queueing Simulator to perform this computer simulation over 10,000 breakdowns for each of the three crew sizes.

E* d. Use the Excel template for the $M/G/1$ queueing model in this chapter's Excel file to obtain the expected waiting time analytically for each of the three crew sizes. Which crew size should be used?

15.15. Refer to the first 200 minutes of the computer simulation of the current operation of Herr Cutter's barber shop presented in Figure 15.13 and summarized in Figure 15.14. Now consider the alternative of adding an associate. Perform a simulation of this alternative by hand by using exactly the same interarrival times (in the same order) and exactly the same service times (in the same order) as in Figure 15.13.

   a. Determine the new waiting time before beginning a haircut for each of the 10 customers who arrive in the first 200 minutes. Use these results to estimate W_q, the expected waiting time before the haircut.
   b. Plot the new version of Figure 15.14 to show the evolution of the number of customers in the barber shop over these 200 minutes.

15.16. While performing a computer simulation of a single-server queueing system, the number of customers in the system is zero for the first 10 minutes, one for the next 17 minutes, two for the next 24 minutes, one for the next 15 minutes, two for the next 16 minutes, and one for the next 18 minutes. After this total of 100 minutes, the number becomes 0 again. Based on these results for the first 100 minutes, perform the following analysis (using the notation for queueing models introduced in Section 14.3).

   a. Draw a figure like Figure 15.14 showing the evolution of the number of customers in the system.
   b. Develop estimates of P_0, P_1, P_2, P_3.
   c. Develop estimates of L and L_q.
   d. Develop estimates of W and W_q.

15.17. A major banking institution, Best Bank, plans to open a new branch office in Littletown. Preliminary estimates suggest that two tellers (and teller windows) should be provided, but this decision now awaits further analysis.

   Marketing surveys indicate that the new Littletown bank will attract enough business that customers requiring teller service will enter the bank at the rate of about one per minute on the average. Thus, the average time between consecutive customer arrivals is estimated to be one minute.

   No parking is available near the bank, so a special parking lot for bank customers only will be provided. A parking lot attendant will be on duty to validate each customer's parking before he or she leaves the car to enter the bank. This validation process takes at least 0.5 minute, so the *minimum* time between consecutive arrivals of customers into the bank is 0.5 minute. The amount by which the interarrival time exceeds 0.5 minute is estimated to have an *exponential* distribution with a mean of 0.5 minute. Therefore, the total interarrival time has a *translated exponential* distribution with a mean of (0.5 + 0.5) = 1.0 minute. (A translated exponential distribution is just an exponential distribution with a constant added.)

Based on past experience in other branch offices, it is known that the time required by a teller to serve a customer will vary widely from customer to customer, but the average time is about 1.5 minutes. This experience also indicates that service time has approximately an *Erlang* distribution with a mean of 1.5 minutes and a shape parameter of $k = 4$, which provides a standard deviation of 0.75 minute (half that for an exponential distribution with the same mean).

These data suggest that two tellers should be able to keep up with the customers quite well. However, management wants to be sure that customers will not frequently encounter a long waiting line and an excessive wait before receiving service. Therefore, computer simulation will be used to study these measures of performance.

Q*   a. Use the Queueing Simulator with 5,000 customer arrivals to estimate the usual measures of performance for this queueing system if two tellers are provided.

Q*   b. Repeat part *a* if three tellers are provided.

Q*   c. Now perform some sensitivity analysis by checking the effect if the level of business turns out to be even higher than projected. In particular, assume that the average time between customer arrivals turns out to be only 0.9 minute (0.5 minute plus a mean of only 0.4 minute). Evaluate the alternatives of two tellers and three tellers under this assumption.

     d. Suppose *you* were the manager of this bank. Use your computer simulation results as the basis for a managerial decision on how many tellers to provide. Justify your answer.

15.18.* Hugh's Repair Shop specializes in repairing German and Japanese cars. The shop has two mechanics. One mechanic works on only German cars and the other mechanic works on only Japanese cars. In either case, the time required to repair a car has an exponential distribution with a mean of 0.2 day. The shop's business has been steadily increasing, especially for German cars. Hugh projects that, by next year, German cars will arrive randomly to be repaired at a mean rate of four per day, so the time between arrivals will have an exponential distribution with a mean of 0.25 day. The mean arrival rate for Japanese cars is projected to be two per day, so the distribution of interarrival times will be exponential with a mean of 0.5 day.

For either kind of car, Hugh would like the average waiting time in the shop before the repair is completed to be no more than 0.5 day.

E*   a. Formulate a spreadsheet model to perform a computer simulation to estimate what the average waiting time until repair is completed will be next year for either kind of car.

E*   b. Perform this simulation for German cars over a period of 100 car arrivals.

E*   c. Repeat part *b* for Japanese cars.

Q*   d. Use the Queueing Simulator to do parts *b* and *c* with 10,000 car arrivals in each case.

Q*   e. Hugh is considering hiring a second mechanic who specializes in German cars so that two such cars can be repaired simultaneously. (Only one mechanic works on any one car.) Use the Queueing Simulator with 10,000 arrivals of German cars to evaluate this option.

Q*   f. Another option is to train the two current mechanics to work on either kind of car. This would increase the mean repair time by 10 percent, from 0.2 day to 0.22 day. Use the Queueing Simulator with 20,000 arrivals of cars of either kind to evaluate this option.

E*   g. Because both the interarrival-time and service-time distributions are exponential, the *M/M/*1 and *M/M/s* queueing models introduced in Sections 14.5 and 14.6 can be used to evaluate all the above options analytically. Use the template for the *M/M/s* queueing model (with $s = 1$ or 2) in the Excel file for Chapter 14 to determine W, the expected waiting time until repair is completed, for each of the cases considered in parts *b* through *f*. For each case, compare the estimate of W obtained by computer simulation with the analytical value. What does this say about the number of car arrivals that should be included in the computer simulation?

     h. Based on the above results, which option would you select if you were Hugh? Why?

15.19. Vistaprint produces monitors and printers for computers. In the past, only some of them were inspected on a sampling basis. However, the new plan is that they all will be inspected before they are released. Under this plan, the monitors and printers will be brought to the inspection station one at a time as they are completed. For monitors, the interarrival time will have a uniform distribution between 10 and 20 minutes. For printers, the interarrival time will be a constant 15 minutes.

The inspection station has two inspectors. One inspector works on only monitors and the other one only inspects computers. In either case, the inspection time has an exponential distribution with a mean of 10 minutes.

Before beginning the new plan, management wants an evaluation made of how long the monitors and printers will be held up waiting at the inspection station.

E*   a. Formulate a spreadsheet model to perform a computer simulation to estimate the average waiting times (both before beginning inspection and after completing inspection) for either the monitors or the printers.

E*   b. Perform this simulation for the monitors over a period of 100 arrivals.

E*   c. Repeat part *b* for the printers.

Q*   d. Use the Queueing Simulator to repeat parts *b* and *c* with 10,000 arrivals in each case.

Q*   e. Management is considering the option of providing new inspection equipment to the inspectors. This equipment would not change the mean time to perform an inspection but it would decrease the variability of the times. In particular, for either product, the inspection time would have an Erlang distribution with a mean of 10 minutes and shape parameter $k = 4$. Use the Queueing Simulator to repeat part *d* under this option. Compare the results with those obtained in part *d*.

Q* 15.20. Consider the case study introduced in Section 15.2. After observing the operation of the barber shop, Herr Cutter's nephew Fritz is concerned that his uncle's estimate that the time required to give a haircut has a uniform distribution between 15 and 25 minutes appears to be a poor approximation of the actual probability distribution of haircut times. Based on the data he has gathered, Fritz's best estimate is that the actual distribution is an Erlang distribution with a mean of 20 minutes and a shape parameter of $k = 8$.

    a. Repeat the simulation run that Fritz previously used to obtain Figure 15.15 (with a mean of 30 minutes for the interarrival-time distribution) except substitute this new distribution of haircut times.

    b. Repeat the simulation run that Fritz previously used to obtain Figure 15.17 (with a mean of 14.3 minutes for the interarrival-time distribution) except substitute this new distribution of haircut times.

15.21. For the Dupit Corp. case study introduced in Section 14.4, the management science team was able to apply a variety of queueing models by making the following simplifying approximation. Except for the approach suggested by the vice president for engineering, the team assumed that the total time required to repair a machine (including travel time to the machine site) has an exponential distribution with a mean of two hours (¼ workday). However, the team was somewhat uncomfortable in making this assumption because the total repair times are never extremely short, as allowed by the exponential distribution. There always is some travel time and then some setup time to start the actual repair, so the total time generally is at least 40 minutes (½₂ workday).

    A key advantage of computer simulation over mathematical models is that it is not necessary to make simplifying approximations like this one. For example, one of the options available in the Queueing Simulator is to use a *translated* exponential distribution, which has a certain *minimum* time and then the *additional* time has an exponential distribution with some mean. (Commercial packages for computer simulation have an even greater variety of options.)

    Use computer simulation to refine the results obtained by queueing models as given by the Excel templates in the figures indicated below. Use a translated exponential distribution for the repair times where the *minimum* time is ½₂ workday and the *additional* time has an exponential distribution with a mean of ⅙ workday (80 minutes). In each case, use a run size of 25,000 arrivals and compare the point estimate obtained for W_q (the key measure of performance for this case study) with the value of W_q obtained by the queueing model.

Q*   *a.* Figure 14.5.
Q*   *b.* Figure 14.6.
Q*   *c.* Figure 14.9.
Q*   *d.* Figure 14.10.
    e. What conclusion do you draw about how sensitive the results from a computer simulation of a queueing system can be to the assumption made about the probability distribution of service times?

R* 15.22. Reconsider Problem 7.12, which involves trying to find the probability that a project will be completed by the deadline. Assume now that the duration of each activity has a triangular distribution that is based on the three estimates in the manner depicted in Figure 15.24. Obtain a close estimate of the probability of meeting the deadline by using @RISK to perform 1,000 iterations of a computer simulation of the project on a spreadsheet. Generate the various kinds of outputs shown in Figure 15.26.

R* 15.23. Reconsider Problem 15.10. Now obtain a close estimate of the average cost of insurance coverage for the corporation's employees by using @RISK with a spreadsheet to perform 500 iterations of a computer simulation of an employee's health insurance experience. Also generate the frequency distribution of the cost of insurance coverage in both tabular and graphical form (@RISK's simulation statistics and output graph).

15.24. Consider the Heavy Duty Co. problem that was presented as Example 2 in Section 15.1. For each of the following three options, obtain an estimate of the expected cost per day by using @RISK to perform 1,000 iterations of a computer simulation of the problem on a spreadsheet. Also generate the simulation statistics and (when available) the output graph.

R*   *a.* The option of not replacing a motor until a breakdown occurs.

R*   *b.* The option of scheduling the replacement of a motor after four days (but replacing it sooner if a breakdown occurs).

R*   *c.* The option of scheduling the replacement of a motor after five days (but replacing it sooner if a breakdown occurs).

    d. An analytical result of $2,000 per day is available for the expected cost per day if a motor is replaced every three days. Comparing this option and the above three, which one appears to minimize the expected cost per day?

R*15.25. The Avery Co. factory has been having a maintenance problem with the control panel for one of its production processes. This control panel contains four identical electromechanical relays that have been the cause of the trouble. The problem is that the relays fail fairly frequently, thereby forcing the control panel (and the production process it controls) to be shut down while a replacement is made. The current practice is to replace the relays only when they fail. The average total cost of doing this has been $3.19 per hour. To attempt to reduce this cost, a proposal has been made to replace all four relays whenever any one of them fails to reduce the frequency with which the control panel must be shut down. Would this actually reduce the cost?

    The pertinent data are the following. For each relay, the operating time until failure has approximately a uniform distribution from 1,000 to 2,000 hours. The control panel must be shut down for one hour to replace one relay or for two hours to replace all four relays. The total cost associated with shutting down the control panel and replacing relays is $1,000 per hour plus $200 for each new relay.

Use computer simulation on a spreadsheet to evaluate the cost of the proposal and compare it to the current practice. In each case, use @RISK to perform 1,000 iterations (where the end of each iteration coincides with the end of a shutdown of the control panel) and generate the summary of results, the simulation statistics, and the output graph.

R*15.26. For one new product to be produced by the Aplus Company, bushings will need to be drilled into a metal block and cylindrical shafts inserted into the bushings. The shafts are required to have a radius of at least 1.0000 inch, but the radius should be as little larger than this as possible. With the proposed production process for producing the shafts, the probability distribution of the radius of a shaft has a triangular distribution with a minimum of 1.0000 inch, a most likely value of 1.0010 inches, and a maximum value of 1.0020 inches. With the proposed method of drilling the bushings, the probability distribution of the radius of a bushing has a normal distribution with a mean of 1.0020 inches and a standard deviation of 0.0010 inch. The clearance between a bushing and a shaft is the difference in their radii. Because they are selected at random, there occasionally is interference (i.e., negative clearance) between a bushing and a shaft to be mated.

Management is concerned about the disruption in the production of the new product that would be caused by this occasional interference. Perhaps the production processes for the shafts and bushings should be improved (at considerable cost) to lessen the chance of interference. To evaluate the need for such improvements, management has asked you to determine how frequently interference would occur with the currently proposed production processes.

Estimate the probability of interference by using @RISK to perform 500 iterations of a computer simulation on a spreadsheet. Also, generate the summary of results, simulation statistics, and output graph regarding the frequency distribution of the clearance (positive or negative).

15.27. Refer to the financial risk analysis example presented at the end of Section 15.6, including its results shown in Figure 15.28. Think-Big management is quite concerned about the risk profile for the proposal. Two statistics are causing particular concern. One is that there is nearly a 20 percent chance of losing money (a negative NPV). Second, there is a 10 percent chance of losing at least a full third ($6 million) as much as the mean gain ($18 million). Therefore, management is wondering whether it would be more prudent to go ahead with just one of the two projects. Thus, in addition to option 1 (the proposal), option 2 is to take 16.5 shares of the hotel project only (so no shares of the shopping center project) and option 3 is to take 13.1 shares of the shopping center option only (so no shares of the hotel project). Management wants to choose one of the three options. Risk profiles now are needed to evaluate the latter two.

R* a. Generate the same kinds of risk analysis outputs as in Figure 15.28 for option two after performing a computer simulation with 1,000 iterations for this option.

R* b. Repeat part *a* for option 3.

c. Suppose *you* were the CEO of the Think-Big Development Co. Use the results in Figure 15.28 for option 1 along with the corresponding results obtained for the other two options as the basis for a managerial decision on which of the three options to choose. Justify your answer.

R*15.28. Reconsider Problem 15.5 involving the game of craps. Now the objective is to estimate the probability of winning a play of this game. If the probability is greater than 0.5, you will want to go to Las Vegas to play the game numerous times until you eventually win a considerable amount of money. However, if the probability is less than 0.5, you will stay home.

You have decided to perform computer simulation on a spreadsheet to estimate this probability. Use @RISK to perform the number of iterations (plays of the game) indicated below *twice*.

a. 100 iterations.
b. 1,000 iterations.
c. 10,000 iterations.
d. The true probability is 0.493. What conclusion do you draw from the above simulation runs about the number of iterations that appears to be needed to give reasonable assurance of obtaining an estimate that is within 0.007 of the true probability?

CASE 15.1
PLANNING PLANERS

This was the first time that Carl Schilling had been summoned to meet with the bigwigs in the fancy executive offices upstairs. And he hopes it will be the last time. Carl doesn't like the pressure. He has had enough pressure just dealing with all the problems he has been encountering as the foreman of the planer department on the factory floor. What a nightmare this last month has been!

Fortunately, the meeting had gone better than Carl had feared. The bigwigs actually had been quite nice. They explained that they needed to get Carl's advice on how to deal with a problem that was affecting the entire factory. The origin of the problem is that the planer department has had a difficult time keeping up with its workload. Frequently there are a number of workpieces waiting for a free planer. This waiting has seriously disrupted the production schedule for subsequent operations, thereby greatly increasing the cost of in-process inventory as well as the cost of idle equipment and resulting lost production. They understood that this problem was not Carl's fault. However, they needed to get his ideas on what changes were needed in the planer department to relieve this bottleneck. Imagine that! All these bigwigs with graduate degrees from the fanciest business schools in the country asking advice from a poor working slob like him who had barely made it through high school. He could hardly wait to tell his wife that night.

The meeting had given Carl an opportunity to get two pet peeves off his chest. One peeve is that he has been telling his boss for months that he really needs another planer, but nothing ever gets done about this. His boss just keeps telling him that the planers he already has aren't being used 100 percent of the time, so how can adding even more capacity be justified? Doesn't his boss understand about the big backlogs that build up during busy times?

Then there is the other peeve—all those peaks and valleys of work coming to his department. At times, the work just pours in and a big backlog builds up. Then there might be a long pause when not much comes in so the planers stand idle part of the time. If only those departments that are feeding castings to his department could get their act together and even out the work flow, many of his backlog problems would disappear.

Carl was pleased that the bigwigs were nodding their heads in seeming agreement as he described these problems. They really appeared to understand. And they seemed very sincere in thanking him for his good advice. Maybe something is actually going to get done this time.

Here are the details of the situation that Carl and his "bigwigs" are addressing. The company has two planers for cutting flat smooth surfaces in large castings. The planers currently are being used for two purposes. One is to form the top surface of the *platen* for large hydraulic lifts. The other is to form the mating surface of the final drive *housing* for a large piece of earth-moving equipment. The time required to perform each type of job varies somewhat, depending largely upon the number of passes that must be made. In particular, for each platen or each housing, the time required by a planer has a translated exponential distribution, where the minimum time is 10 minutes and the additional time beyond 10 minutes has an exponential distribution with a mean of 10 minutes. (A distribution of this type is one of the options in the Queueing Simulator in this chapter's Excel file.)

Castings of both types arrive one at a time to the planer department. For the castings for forming platens, the arrivals occur randomly with a mean rate of two per hour. For the castings for forming housings, the arrivals again occur randomly with a mean rate of two per hour.

Based on Carl Schilling's advice, management has asked a management scientist (you) to analyze the following two proposals for relieving the bottleneck in the planer department:

Proposal 1: Obtain one additional planer. The total incremental cost (including capital recovery cost) is estimated to be $30 per hour. (This estimate takes into account the fact that, even with an additional planer, the total running time for all the planers will remain the same.)

Proposal 2: Eliminate the variability in the interarrival times of the castings, so that the castings would arrive regularly, one every 15 minutes, alternating between platen castings and housing castings. This would require making some changes in the preceding production processes, with an incremental cost of $60 per hour.

These proposals are not mutually exclusive, so any combination can be adopted.

It is estimated that the total cost associated with castings having to wait to be processed (including processing time) is $200 per hour for each platen casting and $100 per hour for each housing casting, provided the waits are not excessive. To avoid excessive waits for either kind of casting, all the castings are processed as soon as possible on a first-come, first-served basis.

Management's objective is to minimize the expected total cost per hour.

Use computer simulation to evaluate and compare all the alternatives, including the status quo and the various combinations of proposals. Then make your recommendation to management.

Are there any other alternatives you would recommend considering?

CASE 15.2
PRICING UNDER PRESSURE

Elise Sullivan moved to New York City in September to begin her first job as an analyst working in the Client Services Division of FirstBank, a large investment bank providing brokerage services to clients across the United States. The moment she arrived in the Big Apple after receiving her undergraduate business degree, she hit the ground running—or, more appropriately, working. She spent her first six weeks in training, where she met new FirstBank analysts like herself and learned the basics of FirstBank's approach to accounting, cash flow analysis, customer service, and federal regulations.

After completing training, Elise moved into her bullpen on the 40th floor of the Manhattan FirstBank building to begin work. Her first few assignments have allowed her to learn the ropes by placing her under the direction of senior staff members who delegate specific tasks to her.

Today, she has an opportunity to distinguish herself in her career, however. Her boss, Michael Steadman, has given her an as-

signment that is under her complete direction and control. A very eccentric, wealthy client and avid investor by the name of Emery Bowlander is interested in purchasing a European call option that provides him with the right to purchase shares of Fellare stock for $44.00 on the first of February—12 weeks from today. Fellare is an aerospace manufacturing company operating in France, and Mr. Bowlander has a strong feeling that the European Space Agency will award Fellare with a contract to build a portion of the International Space Station some time in January. In the event that the European Space Agency awards the contract to Fellare, Mr. Bowlander believes the stock will skyrocket, reflecting investor confidence in the capabilities and growth of the company. If Fellare does not win the contract, however, Mr. Bowlander believes the stock will continue its current slow downward trend. To guard against this latter outcome, Mr. Bowlander does not want to make an outright purchase of Fellare stock now.

Michael has asked Elise to price the option. He expects a figure before the stock market closes so that if Mr. Bowlander decides to purchase the option, the transaction can take place today.

Unfortunately, the investment science course Elise took to complete her undergraduate business degree did not cover options theory; it only covered valuation, risk, capital budgeting, and market efficiency. She remembers from her valuation studies that she should discount the value of the option on February 1 by the appropriate interest rate to obtain the value of the option today. Because she is discounting over a twelve-week period, the formula she should use to discount the option is (Value of the Option/(1 +Weekly Interest Rate)^{12}). As a starting point for her calculations, she decides to use an annual interest rate of 8 percent. But she now needs to decide how to calculate the value of the option on February 1.

a. Elise knows that on February 1, Mr. Bowlander will take one of two actions: either he will exercise the option and purchase shares of Fellare stock or he will not exercise the option. Mr. Bowlander will exercise the option if the price of Fellare stock on February 1 is above his exercise price of $44.00. In this case, he purchases Fellare stock for $44.00 and then immediately sells it for the market price on February 1. Under this scenario, the value of the option would be the difference between the stock price and the exercise price. Mr. Bowlander will not exercise the option if the price of Fellare stock is below his exercise price of $44.00. In this case, he does nothing, and the value of the option would be $0.

The value of the option is therefore determined by the value of Fellare stock on February 1. Elise knows that the value of the stock on February 1 is uncertain and is therefore represented by a probability distribution of values. Elise recalls from a management science course in college that she can use computer simulation to estimate the mean of this distribution of stock values. Before she builds the simulation model, however, she needs to know the price movement of the stock. Elise recalls from a probability and statistics course that the price of a stock can be modeled as following a random walk and either growing or decaying according to a lognormal distribution. Therefore, according to this model, the stock price at the end of the next week is the stock price at the end of the current week multiplied by a growth factor. This growth factor is expressed as the number *e* raised to a power that is equal to a normally distributed random variable. In other words:

$$s_n = e^N s_c$$

where

s_n = the stock price at the end of next week
s_c = the stock price at the end of the current week
N = a random variable that has a normal distribution

To begin her analysis, Elise looks in the newspaper to find that the Fellare stock price for the current week is $42.00. She decides to use this price to begin her 12-week analysis. Thus, the price of the stock at the end of the first week is this current price multiplied by the growth factor. She next estimates the mean and standard deviation of the normally distributed random variable used in the calculation of the growth factor. This random variable determines the degree of change (volatility) of the stock, so Elise decides to use the current annual interest rate and the historical annual volatility of the stock as a basis for estimating the mean and standard deviation.

The current annual interest rate is $r = 8$ percent, and the historical annual volatility of the aerospace stock is 30 percent. But Elise remembers that she is calculating the *weekly* change in stock—*not* the *annual* change. She therefore needs to calculate the weekly interest rate and weekly historical stock volatility to obtain estimates for the mean and standard deviation of the weekly growth factor. To obtain the weekly interest rate *w*, Elise must make the following calculation:

$$w = (1 + r)^{(1/52)} - 1$$

The historical weekly stock volatility equals the historical annual volatility divided by the square root of 52. She calculates the mean of the normally distributed random variable by subtracting one-half of the square of the weekly stock volatility from the weekly interest rate w. In other words:

$$\text{Mean} = w - 0.5(\text{Weekly Stock Volatility})^2$$

The standard deviation of the normally distributed random variable is simply equal to the weekly stock volatility.
Elise is now ready to build her simulation model.

1. Describe the components of the system, including how they are assumed to interrelate.
2. Define the state of the system.
3. Describe a method for randomly generating the simulated events that occur over time.
4. Describe a method for changing the state of the system when an event occurs.
5. Define a procedure for advancing the time on the simulation clock.
6. Build the simulation model to calculate the value of the option in today's dollars.

   b. Run three separate simulations to estimate the value of the cell option and hence the price of the option in today's dollars. For the first simulation, run 100 iterations of the simulation. For the second simulation, run 500 iterations of the simulation. For the third simulation, run 1000 iterations of the simulation. For each simulation, record the price of the option in today's dollars.

   c. Elise takes her calculations and recommended price to Michael. He is very impressed, but he chuckles and indicates that a simple, closed-form approach exists for calculating the value of an option: the Black-Scholes formula. Michael grabs an investment science book from the shelf above his desk and reveals the very powerful and very complicated Black-Scholes formula:

$$V = N[d_1]\, P - N[d_2]\, PV[K]$$

$$\text{where } d_1 = \frac{\ln[P/PV[K]]}{\sigma\sqrt{t}} + \frac{\sigma\sqrt{t}}{2}$$

$$d_2 = d_1 - \sigma\sqrt{t}$$

$N[x]$ = the Excel function NORMSDIST(x) where
$x = d_1$ or $x = d_2$

P = current price of the stock

K = exercise price

$\text{PV}[K]$ = present value of exercise price = $\dfrac{K}{(1 + w)^t}$

t = number of weeks to exercise date

σ = weekly volatility of stock.

Use the Black-Scholes formula to calculate the value of the call option and hence the price of the option. Compare this value to the value obtained in part *c*.

d. In the specific case of Fellare stock, do you think that a random walk as described above completely describes the price movement of the stock? Why or why not?

PARTIAL ANSWERS TO SELECTED PROBLEMS

Chapter 2

2.8. *d & e.*

	A	B	C	D	E	F
1		Resource Usage per Unit of Each Activity				
2		Activity				Resource
3	Resource	1	2	Totals		Available
4	Fraction of 1st	1	0	0.667	≤	1
5	Fraction of 2nd	0	1	0.667	≤	1
6	Money	5000	4000	6000.00	≤	6000
7	Work Hours	400	500	600	≤	600
8	Unit Profit	4500	4500	$6,000.00		
9	Solution	0.667	0.667			

2.13. *a.* If $x_2 = 0$, then $x_1 = 2$. If $x_1 = 0$, then $x_2 = 4$.
  c. slope $= -2$
  d. $x_2 = -2x_1 + 4$

2.16. *a.*

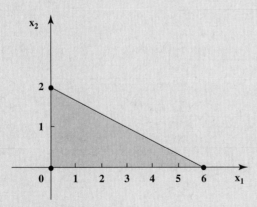

2.21. *b.*

	slope-intercept form	slope	x_2 intercept
Profit = 6	$x_2 = -\dfrac{2}{3}x_1 + 2$	$-\dfrac{2}{3}$	2
Profit = 12	$x_2 = -\dfrac{2}{3}x_1 + 4$	$-\dfrac{2}{3}$	4
Profit = 18	$x_2 = -\dfrac{2}{3}x_1 + 6$	$-\dfrac{2}{3}$	6

2.25. $x_2 = -\dfrac{8}{5}x_1 + 8$

2.29. *b & c.*

Resource Usage per Unit of Each Activity

Resource	Activity 1	Activity 2	Totals		Resource Available
1	0	1	5	≤	10
2	2	5	51	≤	60
3	1	1	18	≤	18
4	3	1	44	≤	44
Unit Profit	2	1	$31.00		
Solution	13	5			

2.40. *a.* Optimal Solution: $(x_1, x_2) = (2, 4)$ and $C = 110$.

b & c.

Activity

Benefit	1	2	Totals		Level
A	1	2	10	≥	10
B	2	−3	−8	≤	6
C	1	1	6	≥	6
Unit Cost	15	20	$110.00		
Solution	2	4			

Chapter 3

3.2. *a & c.*

Resource Usage per Unit of Each Activity

Resource	Activity 1	Activity 2	Totals		Resource Available
1	2	1	10	≤	10
2	3	3	20	≤	20
3	2	4	20	≤	20
Unit Profit	20	30	$166.67		
Solution	3.333	3.333			

3.5 *c.* The decisions to be made are how many of each product should be produced. The constraints on these decisions are the number of hours available on the milling machine, lathe, and grinder as well as the sales potential of product 3. The overall measure of performance is profit, which is to be maximized.

   d. milling machine: 9 (# units of 1) + 3 (# units of 2) + 5 (# units of 3) ≤ 500
   lathe: 5 (# units of 1) + 4 (# units of 2) ≤ 350
   grinder: 3 (# units of 1) + 2 (# units of 3) ≤ 150
   sales: (# units of 3) ≤ 20
   Nonnegativity: (# units of 1) ≥ 0, (# units of 2) ≥ 0, (# units of 3) ≥ 0

   Profit = $50 (# units of 1) + $20 (# units of 2) + $25 (# units of 3)

e & f.

	A	B	C	D	E	F	G
1		**Resource Usage per Unit of Each Activity**					**Resource**
2	**Resource**	**Product 1**	**Product 2**	**Product 3**	**Totals**		**Available**
3	**Milling Machine**	9	3	5	500	≤	500
4	**Lathe**	5	4	0	0	≤	350
5	**Grinder**	3	0	2	0	≤	150
6	**Sales Potential**	0	0	1	0	≤	20
7	**Unit Profit**	50	20	25	**$3,333.33**		
8	**Solution**	0	166.667	0			

3.10. *b & e.*

Nutritional Ingredient	Kilogram of			Totals		Minimum Level
	Corn	Tankage	Alfalfa			
Carbohydrates	90	20	40	200	≥	200
Proteins	30	80	60	180	≥	180
Vitamins	10	20	60	157	≥	150
Unit Cost	84	72	60	$242		
Solution	1	0	2			

f.

Minimize $Cost = 84C + 72T + 60A,$

subject to $90C + 20T + 40A \geq 200$

$30C + 80T + 60A \geq 180$

$10C + 20T + 60A \geq 150$

and $C \geq 0, T \geq 0, A \geq 0.$

3.15. *a.* This is a distribution-network problem because it deals with the distribution of goods through a distribution network at minimum cost.

c.

Requirement	Contribution Toward Required Amount per Unit Shipped Shipping Lane						Totals		Required Amount
	F1-C1	F1-C2	F1-C3	F2-C1	F2-C2	F2-C3			
F1 Amount	1	1	1	0	0	0	400	=	400
F2 Amount	0	0	0	1	1	1	500	=	500
C1 Amount	1	0	0	1	0	0	300	=	300
C2 Amount	0	1	0	0	1	0	200	=	200
C3 Amount	0	0	1	0	0	1	400	=	400
Unit Cost	600	800	700	400	200	400	$410,000		
Solution	300	0	100	0	200	300			

3.17. *c & d.*

Contribution Toward Required Amount per Unit

Year			*Investment*									*Remainder*			Totals		Required Amount
	A1	A2	A3	A4	B1	B2	B3	C2	D5	R1	R2	R3	R4	R5			
1	1	0	0	0	1	0	0	0	0	1	0	0	0	0	60000	=	60000
2	0	1	0	0	0	1	0	1	0	−1	1	0	0	0	0	=	0
3	−1.4	0	1	0	0	0	1	0	0	0	−1	1	0	0	0	=	0
4	0	−1.4	0	1	−1.7	0	0	0	0	0	0	−1	1	0	−1.33577E-12	=	0
5	0	0	−1.4	0	0	−1.7	0	0	1	0	0	0	−1	1	1.45519E-11	=	0
Unit Profit	0	0	0	1.4	0	0	1.7	1.9	1.3	0	0	0	0	1	$ 152,880		
Solution	60000	0	84000	0	0	0	0	0	117600	0	0	0	0	0			

3.20. *b.*

Resource Usage per Unit of Each Activity

Resource	1F	1C	1B	2F	2C	2B	3F	3C	3B	4F	4C	4B	Totals		Resource Available
Front Wt.	1	0	0	1	0	0	1	0	0	1	0	0	12	≤	12
Center Wt.	0	1	0	0	1	0	0	1	0	0	1	0	18	≤	18
Back Wt.	0	0	1	0	0	1	0	0	1	0	0	1	10	≤	10
Cargo 1 Wt.	1	1	1	0	0	0	0	0	0	0	0	0	15	≤	20
Cargo 2 Wt.	0	0	0	1	1	1	0	0	0	0	0	0	12	≤	16
Cargo 3 Wt.	0	0	0	0	0	0	1	1	1	0	0	0	0	≤	25
Cargo 4 Wt.	0	0	0	0	0	0	0	0	0	1	1	1	13	≤	13
Space Front	500	0	0	700	0	0	600	0	0	400	0	0	7000	≤	7000
Space Center	0	500	0	0	700	0	0	600	0	0	400	0	9000	≤	9000
Space Back	0	0	500	0	0	700	0	0	600	0	0	400	5000	≤	5000

Contribution Toward Required Amount

Requirement	1F	1C	1B	2F	2C	2B	3F	3C	3B	4F	4C	4B	Totals		Required Amount
%F = %C	0.0833	−0.0556	0	0.0833	−0.0556	0	0.0833	−0.0556	0	0.08333	−0.0556	0	0	=	0
%F = %B	0.0833	0	−0.1	0.0833	0	−0.1	0.0833	0	−0.1	0.0833	0	−0.1	0	=	0
Unit Profit	320	320	320	400	400	400	360	360	360	290	290	290	$13,330		
Solution	0	5	10	7.33333	4.167	0.000	0	0	0	4.66667	8.333	0.000			

Chapter 4

4.1. *d.*

Adjustable Cells

Cell	Name	Final Value	Reduced Cost	Objective Coefficient	Allowable Increase	Allowable Decrease
$B$6	Solution Produce Toys	2000	0	3	2	0.5
$C$6	Solution Produce Subassemblies	1000	0	−2.5	1	0.5

Constraints

Cell	Name	Final Value	Shadow Price	Constraint R.H. Side	Allowable Increase	Allowable Decrease
$D$3	Sub A Totals	3000	0.5	3000	1E + 30	1000
$D$4	Sub B Totals	1000	2	1000	500	1E + 30

Based on the allowable increase and decrease in the Excel sensitivity report,

Current value of P_T: 3.
Allowable increase in P_T: 2.   So, $P_T \leq 3 + 2 = 5$.
Allowable decrease in P_T: 0.5.   So, $P_T \geq 3 - 0.5 = 2.5$.
Range of optimality for P_T: $2.5 \leq P_T \leq 5$.

4.4. *f.*

Adjustable Cells

Cell	Name	Final Value	Reduced Cost	Objective Coefficient	Allowable Increase	Allowable Decrease
$B$15	Solution 6am Shift	48	0	170	1E + 30	10
$C$15	Solution 8am Shift	31	0	160	10	160
$D$15	Solution Noon Shift	39	0	175	5	175
$E$15	Solution 4pm Shift	43	0	180	1E + 30	5
$F$15	Solution 10pm Shift	15	0	195	1E + 30	195

Part a)
Optimal solution does not change (within allowable increase of $10).

Part b)
Optimal solution does change (outside of allowable decrease of $5).

Part c)
By the 100% rule for simultaneous changes in the objective function, the optimal solution may or may not change.

C_{8AM}: $160 → $165.   % of allowable increase $= 100\left(\dfrac{165 - 160}{10}\right) = 50\%$

C_{4PM}: $180 → $170.   % of allowable decrease $= 100\left(\dfrac{180 - 170}{5}\right) = \underline{200\%}$

Sum = 250%.

4.9. *a.*

Resource	Resource Usage per Unit of Each Activity		Totals		Resource Available
	Produce Toys	Produce Subassemblies			
Sub A	2	−1	3000	≤	3000
Sub B	1	−1	1000	≤	1000
Max. Demand	1	0	2000	≤	2500
Unit Profit	3	−2.5	$3,500.00		
Solution	2000	1000			

b. The shadow price for subassembly A is $0.50, which is the maximum premium that the company should be willing to pay.

4.13.

Constraints

Cell	Name	Final Value	Shadow Price	Constraint R.H.Side	Allowable Increase	Allowable Decrease
$E$4	Ad Budget Totals	4000	0.3	4000	250	1125
$E$5	Planning Budget Totals	1000	0.5	1000	450	50
$E$6	TV Spots Totals	5	5	5	1.667	5

a. The total number of expected exposure units could be increased by 0.3 for each additional $1000 added to the advertising budget.

b. This remains valid for increases of up to $250,000.

e. By the 100% rule for simultaneous changes in right-hand sides, the shadow prices are still valid.

$$C_A: \quad \$4000 \rightarrow \$4100. \quad \% \text{ of allowable increase} = 100\left(\frac{4100 - 4000}{250}\right) = 40\%$$

$$C_P: \quad \$1000 \rightarrow \$1100. \quad \% \text{ of allowable increase} = 100\left(\frac{1100 - 1000}{450}\right) = \underline{22\%}$$

$$\text{Sum} = 62\%.$$

Chapter 5

5.5

		Unit Cost ($) Destination		
		Today	Tomorrow	Supply
Source	Dick	3	2.7	5
	Harry	2.9	2.8	4
Demand		3	4	

		Daily Purchase Destination				
		Today	Tomorrow	Totals		Supply
Source	Dick	0	4	4	≤	5
	Harry	3	0	3	≤	4
Totals		3	4			
		=	=	Total Cost	=	$ 20
Demand		3	4			

5.18 *b & c.*

		Unit Cost ($) Task (Job)			
		1	2	3	Supply
Assignee	A	5	7	4	1
(Person)	B	3	6	5	1
	C	2	3	4	1
Demand		1	1	1	

		Assignments Task (Job)				
		1	2	3	Totals	Supply
Assignee	A	0	0	1	1	=	1
(Person)	B	1	0	0	1	=	1
	C	0	1	0	1	=	1
Totals		1	1	1		
		=	=	=	Total Cost	=	$ 10
Demand		1	1	1		

5.22. *a.* The problem fits into the format for an assignment problem with swimmers being assigned to strokes. The times of the swimmers replace the costs of a traditional problem.

Chapter 6

6.2. *a.*

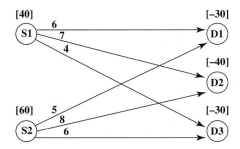

c.

From	To	Ship	Unit Cost
S1	D1	0	$6
S1	D2	10	$7
S1	D3	30	$4
S2	D1	30	$5
S2	D2	30	$8
S2	D3	0	$6
Total Cost =		$580	

Nodes	Net Flow		Supply/Demand
S1	40	=	40
S2	60	=	60
D1	−30	=	−30
D2	−40	=	−40
D3	−30	=	−30

6.5. *b & c.*

From	To	Ship		Capacity	Unit Cost
Stuttgart	Rotterdam	30	≤	50	$2,900
Stuttgart	Bordeaux	70	≤	70	$2,500
Stuttgart	Lisbon	30	≤	40	$3,200
Berlin	Rotterdam	0	≤	20	$2,400
Berlin	Hamburg	50	≤	60	$2,000
Rotterdam	New York	30	≤	60	$5,900
Bordeaux	New York	40	≤	40	$5,400
Bordeaux	New Orleans	30	≤	50	$6,800
Lisbon	New Orleans	30	≤	30	$6,100
Hamburg	New York	20	≤	30	$6,300
Hamburg	Boston	30	≤	40	$5,700
New Orleans	Los Angeles	60	≤	70	$3,100
New York	Los Angeles	60	≤	80	$4,200
New York	Seattle	30	≤	40	$4,000
Boston	Los Angeles	10	≤	10	$3,400
Boston	Seattle	20	≤	20	$3,000
Total Cost =	$2,187,000				

Nodes	Net Flow		Supply/Demand
Stuttgart	130	=	130
Berlin	50	=	50
Hamburg	0	=	0
Rotterdam	0	=	0
Bordeaux	0	=	0
Lisbon	0	=	0
Boston	0	=	0
New York	0	=	0
New Orleans	0	=	0
Los Angeles	−130	=	−130
Seattle	−50	=	−50

6.8.

From	To	Ship		Capacity
A	B	8	≤	9
A	C	7	≤	7
B	D	7	≤	7
B	E	1	≤	2
C	D	2	≤	4
C	E	5	≤	6
D	E	3	≤	3
D	F	6	≤	6
E	F	9	≤	9

Maximum Flow = 15

Nodes	Net Flow		Supply/Demand
A	15		
B	0	=	0
C	0	=	0
D	0	=	0
E	0	=	0
F	−15		

6.13. *a.*

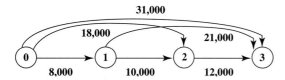

b.

From	To	On Route	Cost
Node 0	Node 1	1	$ 8,000
Node 0	Node 2	0	$18,000
Node 0	Node 3	0	$31,000
Node 1	Node 2	0	$10,000
Node 1	Node 3	1	$21,000
Node 2	Node 3	0	$12,000

Total Cost = $29,000

Nodes	Net Flow		Supply/Demand
0	1	=	1
1	0	=	0
2	0	=	0
3	−1	=	−1

6.16.

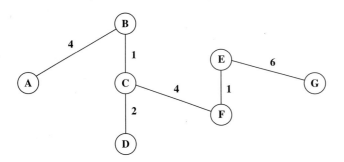

Chapter 7

7.2. *a.*

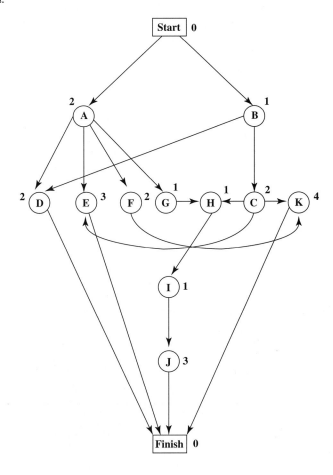

c. Critical Paths: Start → A → F → K → Finish
                      Start → A → G → H → I → J → Finish
                      Start → B → C → H → I → J → Finish

d. No, this will not shorten the length of the project because A is not on any of the critical paths.

7.5. *b.* Ken will be able to meet his deadline if no delays occur.

c. Critical Paths: Start → B → E → J → M → Finish
                      Start → C → G → L → N → Finish
    Focus attention on activities with 0 slack.

d. If activity I takes 2 extra weeks there will be no delay because its slack is 3.

7.8. Critical Path: Start → A → B → C → E → F → J → K → N → Finish

     Total duration = 26 weeks

7.10.

$\mu = 37$

$\sigma^2 = 9$

7.14. *a.*

Activity	μ	σ^2
A	12	0
B	23	16
C	15	1
D	27	9
E	18	4
F	6	4

    b. Start $\rightarrow$ A $\rightarrow$ C $\rightarrow$ E $\rightarrow$ F $\rightarrow$ Finish   Length = 51 days   *critical path

        Start $\rightarrow$ B $\rightarrow$ D $\rightarrow$ Finish   Length = 50 days

    d. $\dfrac{d - \mu_p}{\sqrt{\sigma_p^2}} = \dfrac{57 - 50}{\sqrt{25}} = 1.4 \Rightarrow P(T \le 57) = 0.9192$ (from the Normal table)

7.20. *a.* Critical Path: Start $\rightarrow$ A $\rightarrow$ C $\rightarrow$ E $\rightarrow$ Finish

        Total duration = 12 weeks

     b. *New Plan:*

Activity	Duration	Cost
A	3 weeks	$54,000
B	3 weeks	$65,000
C	3 weeks	$68,666
D	2 weeks	$41,500
E	2 weeks	$80,000

        $7834 is saved by this crashing schedule.

7.21.

Activity	Time Normal	Time Crash	Cost Normal	Cost Crash	Maximum Time Reduction	Crash Cost per Week Saved	Start Time	Time Reduction	Finish Time
A	5	3	$20	$30	2	$5	0	2	3
B	3	2	$10	$20	1	$10	0	1	2
C	4	2	$16	$24	2	$4	3	0	7
D	6	3	$25	$43	3	$6	3	0	9
E	5	4	$22	$30	1	$8	2	0	7
F	7	4	$30	$48	3	$6	2	0	9
G	9	5	$25	$45	4	$5	7	1	15
H	8	6	$30	$44	2	$7	9	2	15

Finish Time = 15
Total Cost = $217

7.24. *d.*

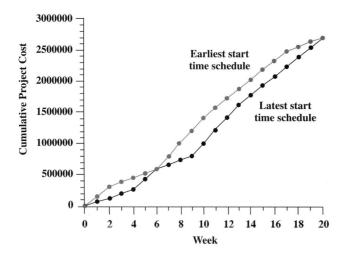

     e. The project manager should focus attention on activity D since it is not yet finished and is running over budget.

Chapter 8

8.3. *a.* Optimal solution: $(x_1, x_2) = (2, 3)$, $P = 13$.

    b. Optimal solution: $(x_1, x_2) = (2.6, 1.6)$, $P = 14.6$.

       None of the rounded solutions are optimal for the integer programming model. Two are not feasible and the other two have lower values of Profit.

8.5. *a.*

	Resource Usage per Unit of Each Activity					*Resource Available*
Resource	*Long-range*	*Medium-range*	*Short-range*	*Totals*		
Money	67	50	35	1,498	≤	1500
Pilots	1	1	1	30	≤	30
Maintenance	1.667	1.333	1	39.338	≤	40
Profit	$ 4.20	$ 3.00	$ 2.30	$95.60		
Solution	14	0	16			

8.8. *c & d.* Dorwyn should produce 1 door and 1 window.

8.14. *a.*

    Let S_1 = number of blocks of stock 1 to purchase

            S_2 = number of blocks of stock 2 to purchase.

    Minimize   Risk $= 4S_1^2 + 100S_2^2 + 5S_1S_2$,

    subject to $20S_1 + 30S_2 \leq 50$

                $5S_1 + 10S_2 \geq$ minimum acceptable expected return

    and $S_1 \geq 0, S_2 \geq 0$.

    d.

μ	σ	$\mu - \sigma$	$\mu - 3\sigma$
13	5.06	7.94	− 2.18
14	7.14	6.86	− 7.42
15	10.44	4.56	−16.32
16	14.12	1.88	−26.36

8.18. The coefficient for L7 is three times as large as the coefficient for K7.

8.20. *b.* Emax should produce 15 units of product 3. While this does increase the present level of employment by 25, it does not decrease earnings and does maximize profit over the life of the new product. Any product mix has some drawback in terms of these three factors, but this product mix is the most favorable one according to management's measure of performance.

Chapter 9

9.3. *b.*

	Yes-or-No Question										
Constraint	*Marketing by Eve*	*Marketing by Steven*	*Cooking by Eve*	*Cooking by Steven*	*Dishes by Eve*	*Dishes by Steven*	*Laundry by Eve*	*Laundry by Steven*	*Total*		*Right-Hand Side*
Eve's Chores	1	0	1	0	1	0	1	0	2	=	2
Steven's Chores	0	1	0	1	0	1	0	1	2	=	2
Marketing	1	1	0	0	0	0	0	0	1	=	1
Cooking	0	0	1	1	0	0	0	0	1	=	1
Dishwashing	0	0	0	0	1	1	0	0	1	=	1
Laundry	0	0	0	0	0	0	1	1	1	=	1
Time Needed	4.5	4.9	7.8	7.2	3.6	4.3	2.9	3.1	18.4 hours		
Solution	1	0	0	1	1	0	0	1			

9.7.

Constraint	Product 1	Product 2	Product 3	Product 4	Totals		Modified Right-Hand Side	Original Right-Hand Side
First	5	3	6	4	6,000	≤	6,000	6,000
Second	4	6	3	5	12,000	≤	105,999	6,000
Marginal revenue	$70	$60	$90	$80	$80,000			
Solution	0	2000	0	0				
	≤	≤	≤	≤				
	0	9999	0	0				
Set Up?	0	1	0	0	1	≤	2	
Start-up Cost	$50,000	$40,000	$70,000	$60,000				

Contingency Constraints:

Product 3:	0	≤	1	:Product 1 or 2
Product 4:	0	≤	1	:Product 1 or 2

Which Constraint (0 = First, 1 = Second):	0

9.11.

Constraint	Product 1	Product 2	Product 3	Total		Right-Hand Side
Milling	9	3	5	498	≤	500
Lathe	5	4	0	349	≤	350
Grinder	3	0	2	135	≤	150
Sales Potential	0	0	1	0	≤	20
Unit Profit	50	20	25	$2870		
Solution	45	31	0			
	≤	≤	≤			
	999	999	0			
Produce ?	1	1	0	2	≤	2

9.13.

	Yes-or-No? Arc Between Nodes										
Constraint	OA	OB	AC	AD	BC	BD	CT	DT	Total		Right-Hand Side
Stage 1	1	1	0	0	0	0	0	0	1	=	1
Stage 2	0	0	1	1	1	1	0	0	1	=	1
Stage 3	0	0	0	0	0	0	1	1	1	=	1
OA chosen	−1	0	1	1	0	0	0	0	0	≤	0
OB chosen	0	−1	0	0	1	1	0	0	0	≤	0
CT chosen	0	0	−1	0	−1	0	1	0	0	<	0
DT chosen	0	0	0	−1	0	−1	0	1	0	≤	0
Cost	3	6	6	5	4	3	3	2	10		
Solution	1	0	0	1	0	0	0	1			

The first three constraints are for mutually exclusive alternatives (at each stage, exactly one arc is used). The last four constraints are for contingent decisions (a route leaves a node only if a route enters the node).

Chapter 10

10.1. *a.*

	State of Nature	
Alternative	*Sell 10,000*	*Sell 100,000*
Build Computers	0	54
Sell Rights	15	15

  c. Choose to build computers (expected payoff is $27 million).

  e.

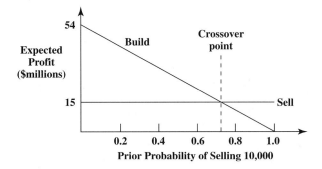

  f. They should build when $p \leq 0.722$, and sell when $p > 0.722$.

10.3. *c.* Warren should make the counter-cyclical investment.

10.5. *d.*

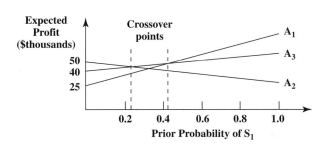

  A_2 and A_3 cross at approximately $p = 0.25$.
  A_1 and A_3 cross at approximately $p = 0.43$.

10.9. *a.* EVPI = EP (with perfect info) − EP (without more info) = 34.5 − 27 = $7.5 million.

  b. Since the market research will cost $1 million it might be worthwhile to perform it.

  d.

| **Data:** | | **P (Finding \| State)** | |
| | | **Finding** | |
State of Nature	*Prior Probability*	*Sell 10,000*	*Sell 100,000*
Sell 10,000	0.5	0.666666667	0.333333333
Sell 100,000	0.5	0.333333333	0.666666667

Posterior Probabilities:		P (State | Finding) State of Nature	
Finding	*P(Finding)*	*Sell 10,000*	*Sell 100,000*
Sell 10,000	0.5	0.666666667	0.333333333
Sell 100,000	0.5	0.333333333	0.666666667

10.11 *b.* EVPI = EP (with perfect info) − EP (without more info) = 53 − 35 = $18

   d. Betsy should consider spending up to $18 to obtain more information.

10.15. *a.*

	State of Nature		
Alternative	*Poor Risk*	*Average Risk*	*Good Risk*
Extend Credit	−15,000	10,000	20,000
Don't Extend Credit	0	0	0
Prior Probabilities	0.2	0.5	0.3

   c. EVPI = EP (with perfect info) − EP (without more info) = 11,000 − 8,000 = $3,000 This indicates that the credit-rating organization should not be used.

10.20. *a.* The optimal policy is to do no market research and build the computers.

10.23. *a.*

	State of Nature	
Alternative	*W*	*L*
Hold campaign	3	−2
Don't hold campaign	0	0
Prior Probabilities	0.6	0.4

   c. EVPI = EP (with perfect info) − EP (without more info) = 1.8 − 1 = $800,000

   d.

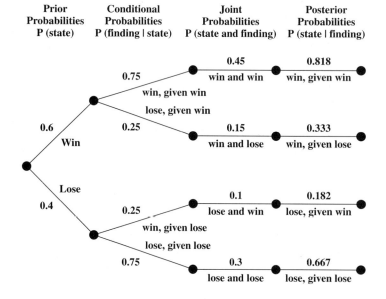

f & g. Leland University should hire William. If he predicts a winning season then they should hold the campaign. If he predicts a losing season then they should not hold the campaign.

10.27. *a.* Choose to introduce the new product (expected payoff is $12.5 million).

   b. EVPI = EP (with perfect info) − EP (without more info) = 20 − 12.5 = $7.5 million
   c. The optimal policy is not to test but to introduce the new product.
   e. Both charts indicate that the expected profit is sensitive to both parameters, but is somewhat more sensitive to changes in the profit if successful than to changes in the loss if unsuccessful.

10.31. *a.* Choose not to buy insurance (expected payoff is $249,840).

   b. U(insurance) = 499.82
   U(no insurance) = 499.8
   Optimal policy is to buy insurance.

10.33.   U(10) = 9

Chapter 11

11.1. *a.*

Data		
D =	676	(demand/year)
K =	$75	(setup cost)
h =	$600.00	(unit holding cost)
L =	3.5	(lead time in days)
WD =	365	(working days/year)

Decision		
Q =	5	(order quantity)

Results	
Reorder Point =	6.5
Annual Setup Cost =	$10,140
Annual Holding Cost =	$1,500
Total Variable Cost =	$11,640

d.

Data		
D =	676	(demand/year)
K =	$75	(setup cost)
h =	$600.00	(unit holding cost)
L =	3.5	(lead time in days)
WD =	365	(working days/year)

Decision		
Q =	13	(order quantity)

Results	
Reorder Point =	6.48
Annual Setup Cost =	$3,900
Annual Holding Cost =	$3,900
Total Variable Cost =	$7,800

The results are the same as those obtained in part *c.*

f. Number of orders per year = 52

$$ROP = 6.5 - \text{inventory level when each order is placed}$$

   g. The optimal policy reduces the total variable inventory cost by $3,840 per year, which is a 33% reduction.

11.6. *a.* h = $3 per month which is 15% of the acquisition cost.

   c. Reorder point is 10.
   d. ROP = 5 hammers which adds $20 to his TVC (5 hammers × $4 holding cost).

11.9. *c.*

Quantity	Basic EOQ Model	EOQ Model with Planned Shortages
Order quantity	244.95	316.23
Maximum shortage	0	126.49
Maximum inventory level	244.95	189.74
Reorder point	0	−126.49
Annual setup cost	$2,449.49	$1,897.37
Annual holding cost	$2,449.49	$1,138.42
Annual shortage cost	0	$758.95
Total variable cost	$4,898.98	$3,794.73

11.17. *a.*

Data

$D =$	6000	(demand/year)
$R =$	24,000	(production rate)
$K =$	$7,500	(unit setup cost)
$h =$	$120.00	(unit holding cost)

Results

Annual Setup Cost =	$45,000.00
Annual Holding Cost =	$45,000.00
Total Variable Cost =	$90,000.00

Decision

$Q =$	1,000	(production lot size)

  b. Production run duration = 0.5 months
   Time interval between production runs = 2 months
  c. Maximum inventory level = 750. This is less than the production lot size since monitors are being withdrawn from inventory while a production run is going on.

Chapter 12

12.3. *a.* Optimal service level = 0.667
   c. $Q^* = 500$
   d. The probability of running short is 33.3%
   e. Optimal service level = 0.833

12.6. *a.* This problem can be interpreted as an inventory problem with uncertain demand for a perishable product with euro-traveler's checks as the product. Once Stan gets back from his trip the checks are not good anymore so they are a perishable product. He can redeposit the amount into his savings account but will incur a fee of lost interest. Stan must decide how many checks to buy without knowing how many he will need.

$$C_{under} = \text{value of 1 day} - \text{cost of 1 day} - \text{cost of 1 check} = \$49$$
$$C_{over} = \text{cost of check} + \text{lost interest} = \$3$$

   b. Purchase 4 additional checks.
   c. Optimal service level = 0.94

   Buy 4 additional checks.

12.10. *a.* Q = 60
   b. R = 60
   d. Safety Stock = 10
   e. If demand during the delivery time exceeds 60 (the order quantity), then the reorder point will be hit again before the order arrives, triggering another order.

12.15. *b.* Ground Chuck: R = 145
   Chuck Wagon: R = 829
   c. Ground Chuck: Safety Stock = 45.
   Chuck Wagon: Safety Stock = 329.
   f. Ground Chuck: $39,378.71.
   Chuck Wagon: $41,958.61.

Jed should choose Ground Chuck as their supplier.

g. If Jed would like to use the beef within a month of receiving it, then Ground Chuck is the better choice. The order quantity with Ground Chuck is roughly one month's supply, whereas with Chuck Wagon the optimal order quantity is roughly three month's supply.

Chapter 13

13.1. a. Forecast = 39

b. Forecast = 26

c. Forecast = 36

d. It appears as if demand is rising so the average forecasting method seems inappropriate because it uses older, out of date data.

13.3. MAD = 15

13.8. Forecast = 2091

13.12. Forecast (0.1) = 2072

13.15. Forecast = 552

13.17. a. Since sales are relatively stable, the averaging method would be appropriate for forecasting future sales. This method uses a larger sample size than the last-value method, which should make it more accurate. Since the older data is still relevant, it should not be excluded, as would be the case in the moving-average method.

e. Considering the MAD values, the averaging method is the best one to use.

f. Unless there is reason to believe that sales will not continue to be relatively stable, the averaging method is likely to be the most accurate in the future as well. However, 12 data points generally are inadequate for drawing definitive conclusions.

13.24. Forecast for next production yield = 62%.

13.30. b. $y = 410 + 17.6x$

d. $y = 604$

e. $y = 762$

f. The average growth in sales per month is 17.6.

Chapter 14

14.3. a. True.

b. False.

c. True.

14.8. a. $L = 2$

b. $Lq = 0.375$

c. $W = 30$ minutes, $W_q = 5.625$ minutes.

d. $W - W_q = 24.375$ minutes

14.11. a. $P_0 + P_1 + P_2 + P_3 + P_4 = 0.96875$ or 97% of the time.

14.14. a. The customers are trucks to be loaded or unloaded and the servers are crews. The system currently has 1 server.

e. A one-person team should not be considered since that would lead to a utilization factor of $\rho = 1$ which does not enable the queueing system to reach a steady-state condition with a manageable load for the team.

f & g. Total cost = ($20)(# on crew) + ($30)(L_q)

TC(4 members) = (20)(4) + (30)(0.0833) = $82.50/hour
TC(3 members) = (20)(3) + (30)(0.167) = $65/hour
TC(2 members) = (20)(2) + (30)(0.5) = $55/hour

A crew of 2 people will minimize the expected total cost per hour.

14.17. L_q is unchanged and W_q is reduced by half.

14.21. a.

Data		
$\lambda =$	0.05	(mean arrival rate)
$1/\mu =$	15	(expected service time)
$\sigma =$	15	(standard deviation)
$s =$	1	(# servers)

Results	
$L =$	3
$L_q =$	2.25
$W =$	60
$W_q =$	45

b.

<table>
<tr><th colspan="3">Data</th><th colspan="2">Results</th></tr>
<tr><td>$\lambda =$</td><td>0.05</td><td>(mean arrival rate)</td><td>$L =$</td><td>2.96287563</td></tr>
<tr><td>$1/\mu =$</td><td>16</td><td>(expected service time)</td><td>$L_q =$</td><td>2.16287563</td></tr>
<tr><td>$\sigma =$</td><td>9.49</td><td>(standard deviation)</td><td></td><td></td></tr>
<tr><td>$s =$</td><td>1</td><td>(# servers)</td><td>$W =$</td><td>59.2575125</td></tr>
<tr><td></td><td></td><td></td><td>$W_q =$</td><td>43.2575125</td></tr>
</table>

    c. The new proposal shows that they will be slightly better off if they switch to the new queueing system.

    d. TC (status quo) = $85/hour

        TC (proposal) = $83/hour

14.23. *a & b.* Under the current policy an airplane loses 1 day of flying time as opposed to 3.25 days under the proposed policy.

          Under the current policy 1 airplane is losing flying time per day as opposed to 0.8125 airplane.

    c. The comparison in part *b* is the appropriate one for making the decision.

14.28. *a.* Combined expected wait time = 0.211

    c. An expected processing time of 3.43 minutes would cause the expected waiting times to be the same for the two procedures.

14.33. *a.* This system is an example of a nonpreemptive priority queueing system.

    c. $\dfrac{W_q \text{ for first–class passengers}}{W_q \text{ for coach–class passengers}} = \dfrac{0.033}{0.083} = 0.4$

    d. $\rho(12) = 7.2$ hours

Chapter 15

15.1. *b.* Let the numbers 0.0000 to 0.5999 correspond to strikes and the numbers 0.6000 to 0.9999 correspond to balls. The random observations for pitches are 0.7520 = ball, 0.4184 = strike, 0.4189 = strike, 0.5982 = strike, 0.9559 = ball, and 0.1403 = strike.

15.5. *a.* Here is a sample replication.

Summary of Results

Win? (1=Yes, 0=No)	0
Number of Tosses =	3

Simulated Tosses

Toss	Die 1	Die 2	Sum
1	4	2	6
2	3	2	5
3	6	1	7
4	5	2	7
5	4	4	8
6	1	4	5
7	2	6	8

Results

Win?	Lose?	Continue?
0	0	Yes
0	0	Yes
0	1	No
NA	NA	No
NA	NA	No
NA	NA	No
NA	NA	No

15.7. *b.* F(x) = 0.0965 when x = −5.18

       F(x) = 0.5692 when x = 18.46

       F(x) = 0.6658 when x = 23.29

    c. = −10 + 50*RAND()

15.9. *a.* Let the numbers 0.0000 to 0.3999 correspond to a minor repair and 0.4000 to 0.9999 correspond to a major repair.

       The average repair time is then (1.224 + 0.950 + 1.610) / 3 = 1.26 hours.

    c. The average repair time is 1.28 hours.

    e. The average repair time is 1.09 hours.

    f. The method of complementary random numbers in part *e* gave the closest estimate. It performs well because using complements helps counteract the more extreme random numbers (such as 0.9503).

15.12. *a.* $x = \sqrt{r}$

    d. = SQRT(RAND())

15.18. *a & b.*   Here is a sample simulation.

Mean Interarrival Time =	0.25 days
Mean Service Time =	0.2 days

Average Time in Line (Wq) =	0.68 days
Average Time in System (W) =	0.91 days

Customer Arrival	Interarrival Time	Time of Arrival	Time Service Begins	Service Time	Time Service Ends	Time in Line	Time in System
1	0.41	0.41	0.41	0.83	1.23	0.00	0.83
2	0.21	0.61	1.23	0.32	1.55	0.62	0.93
3	0.11	0.72	1.55	0.28	1.83	0.83	1.11
4	0.21	0.93	1.83	0.04	1.87	0.90	0.95
5	0.31	1.24	1.87	0.05	1.92	0.64	0.69
98	0.08	24.38	24.74	0.52	25.27	0.36	0.89
99	0.19	24.57	25.27	0.27	25.54	0.69	0.97
100	0.30	24.87	25.54	0.14	25.68	0.67	0.81

h. Answers will vary. The option of training the two current mechanics significantly decreases the waiting time for German cars, without a significant impact on the wait for Japanese cars, and does so without the added cost of a third mechanic. Adding a third mechanic lowers the average wait for German cars even more, but comes at an added cost for the third mechanic.

Chapter 16

16.16. *a.* Optimal Solution: $(x_1, x_2) = (0.667, 0.667)$ and Profit = $6,000.

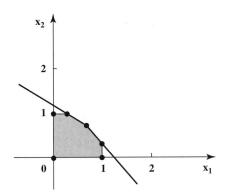

Note: corner points will be called A, B, C, D, E, and F going clockwise from (0,1).

b. Corner Point   A: F and B are adjacent
                               B: A and C are adjacent
                               C: B and D are adjacent
                               D: C and E are adjacent
                               E: D and F are adjacent
                               F: E and A are adjacent

16.20.

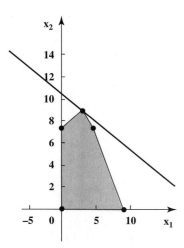

Corner Point	Profit = $10x_1 + 20x_2$	Next Step
(0, 0)	0	Check (0, 7.5) and (9, 0).
(0, 7.5)	150	Move to (0, 7.5).
(9, 0)	90	Check (3, 9).
(3, 9)	210	Move to (3, 9) Check (4.5, 7.5).
(4.5, 7.5)	195	Stop, (3, 9) is optimal.

INDEX